THE GIANT ALL-COLOUR DICTIONARY

THE GIANT ALL-COLOUR DICTIONARY

by **STUART A. COURTIS** and **GARNETTE WATTERS**

Illustrated by **BETH** and **JOE KRUSH**

HAMLYN

LONDON • NEW YORK • SYDNEY • TORONTO

Revised edition first published 1964
Fifteenth impression 1978
Published by
THE HAMLYN PUBLISHING GROUP LIMITED
London · New York · Sydney · Toronto
ASTRONAUT HOUSE · FELTHAM · MIDDLESEX · ENGLAND
ISBN 0 601 07300 2

Printed in Czechoslovakia
51006/14

THE WORLD

Western   Hemisphere

THE WORLD

Eastern *Hemisphere*

To Parents and Teachers

THIS book has been written to meet the long-felt need for a simple, attractive dictionary for children in the seven to eleven age group. Designed for the child to use by himself, it is easy to read and easy to understand. Every detail — size of print, page arrangement, definitions, pictures—has been planned with the single purpose of helping children to help themselves and to enjoy doing it.

Over 7,500 basic words plus their variants, such as plurals and comparative forms, are listed. Pronunciations and word division are simply indicated. Words are defined where possible in simpler terms, and just to make sure that they are fully understood, the meanings are demonstrated in clear, interesting sentences. The meanings are those that the children are most likely to encounter.

More than 2,000 pictures not only make the pages inviting but greatly expand the meaning of the words. They will stimulate the child's interest in using the book. Unlike most dictionaries, this book pictures objects almost always in their entirety, so that their real appearance and use will be completely clear.

Parents and teachers who introduce children to this book can do so with confidence that every effort has been made to make it as clear, understandable, and useful as possible. It is most important that the child be encouraged to use the book by himself: to make it his ever-handy companion in learning.

The teacher using this dictionary as supplementary material can help the child in developing self-direction and self-control, and, at the same time, set him free for functional reading on a wider and higher scale than he could possibly attain so long as he is dependent on her help alone. Similarly parents, by their interest and participation, can encourage their children to use the dictionary. Older children will be interested, too, in helping younger children.

All ages enjoy just thumbing through the dictionary, looking at pictures, reading definitions, and noticing various special features. Younger children enjoy recognising the contents of the pictures and naming them. They tend to imitate the behaviour of their older brothers and sisters and soon learn many words incidentally. The whole family, in fact, can have a good time with the book. Out of such enjoyable experiences come developments of understanding, power, and skill of lasting value.

This dictionary will be found suitable for use by readers at different stages of development. Slow learners in more advanced classes will find that it gives them just the help they need. Many adults in special English classes for foreigners can use it to great advantage.

It would be unreasonable to expect of this book either the simplicity essential for beginning readers or the complexity of an adult dictionary. Books for children must mature with the children. Other books provide fundamental dictionary experiences for beginners; the present volume is a step or two higher in complexity. The next steps are represented by junior dictionaries of broader scope and by school editions of standard dictionaries. Use of the whole series by the child, according to his growing capacities, should enable him, in due course, to use an adult dictionary with skill and understanding.

We confidently and joyously entrust to you the introduction of this book to the children, because we know you want to help them as much as we do ourselves.

THE AUTHORS

To the Boys and Girls Who Use This Book

The people who made this dictionary did their best to make it *easy to use, easy to read,* and *easy to understand.*

You will get more help and fun out of this book if you first notice just how it is made up.

The entry words, or words that are explained, are in alphabetical order — the same order as the letters in the alphabet. These words are printed in **heavy type** to help you find them quickly.

Here is a sample entry. Read all the parts of it so that you can see how to understand all the other entries in the book:

happy hap′-py *happier, happiest, happily.* 1. Pleased and glad.–The children are *happy* when they are playing.
2. Lucky; fortunate.–It was a *happy* chance that Bob found the money.

happy is the entry word.

hap′-py shows how the word is divided into syllables, to help you pronounce it and spell it. The accent mark (′) comes right after the syllable that should be 'accented', or said a little louder than the others. The hyphen (-) shows where the word can be divided at the end of a line, when you are writing it.

happier, happiest, happily are words that are related to the entry word. They are printed in slanting type called italics. Since you know what *happy* means, you will know what these related words mean.

The number 1 tells you that here is the first meaning of *happy:* 'Pleased and glad.' Then comes a sentence showing this meaning.

After the number 2, you find a second meaning for *happy.* Another sentence shows this second meaning.

Notice that the word *happy* is printed in italics everywhere in the definitions and sentences.

Sometimes it is very hard to *explain* what an entry word means. When this is so, you will not find any definition or explanation after the entry word. Instead, you will find one or more sentences. From these sentences you will be able to get the meaning of the entry word.

Pictures have been used whenever possible to tell you more about the meaning of a word. There are more than 2,000 of them — sometimes dozens of pictures for one word, like machines, trees, houses, or animals. The maps of the continents show countries, mountains, rivers, cities, and products.

The very best way to learn to use this book is to keep using it. Whenever, in reading or spelling, you meet a word you want to know more about, notice what its first letter is. Then hunt for it under that letter in your dictionary. The coloured index tabs will help to make this easy.

Aa

A, a *A's, a's.* 1. The first letter of the alphabet.
2. One or any.–We made *a* kite.–Can you lend me *a* pencil?
3. The 6th note of the c scale in music: c, d, e, f, g, *a*, b, c.

abandon a-ban'-don *abandons, abandoned, abandoning.* Leave for ever.–The birds *abandoned* their nest. They left it and never went back to it.

abbreviate ab-bre'-vi-ate *abbreviates, abbreviated, abbreviating.* Shorten. – We *abbreviate* the words United States of America by writing them U.S.A. Other words may be *abbreviated* by leaving out certain letters.–'Dr.' is the word 'doctor' *abbreviated.*

abbreviation ab-bre-vi-a'-tion *abbreviations.* A shortened form.–The *abbreviation* for the word 'foot' is 'ft.' 'Pt.' is the *abbreviation* for 'pint.'

abide a-bide' *abides, abode, abiding.* 1. Live up to; keep.–Bob always *abides* by the rules of the school: he obeys them.
2. Stand; endure.–Jack says he cannot *abide* being treated like a child.
3. Stay.–The traveller asked if he might *abide* with us overnight.

ability a-bil'-i-ty *abilities.* Skill, knowledge, power to do something.–Bob is a student of unusual *ability.*–I don't doubt your *ability* to solve the problem.

able a'-ble. 1. Having knowledge or power.–Jack is *able* to spell many words. He can spell them.–Bob is *able* to do his arithmetic without help.
2. Strong enough.–The baby is *able* to push the door open.–Grandmother was *able* to sit up today for the first time since her illness.
3. Capable, fine.–Bob is an *able* student. His work is better than most students' work.

aboard a-board'. On a boat, a bus, or a train. –When the guard calls, 'All *aboard*,' he wants all passengers to get on to the train.

about a-bout'. 1. Around; in all directions.– The dog looked *about* him.
2. Nearly, almost.–John's kite is *about* finished.

3. More or less; around.–Mary is *about* 10 years old.
4. Of.–Tell us the story *about* King Midas.
5. Around. – Flowers grow all *about* the house.
6. The other way.–The captain said, '*About*, face!' He meant, 'Face the opposite direction.'

above a-bove'. 1. Overhead.–The sun shines from *above*.
2. Higher than, over.–The picture on the wall is *above* the table.
3. Better than.–Bill thinks himself *above* the other boys.
4. More than.–That price is *above* what I wanted to pay.

abreast a-breast'. Side by side.–The children in the parade marched 8 *abreast*; 8 children marched side by side.

abroad a-broad'. 1. To many places, near and far. – The radio sends the news *abroad* quickly.
2. To another country.–Edward has gone *abroad* for the summer.

abrupt a-brupt' *abruptly, abruptness.* Sudden. –The dog ran down the street, but he came to an *abrupt* stop when he saw the cat.

absence ab'-sence. 1. Time spent away.–John returned to school after an *absence* of 3 days.
2. A lack.–These potatoes taste flat because of the *absence* of salt. They have no salt.

absent ab'-sent. Away; not present; not at a certain place.–John has never been *absent* from school.

absolutely ab'-so-lute-ly. All; every bit; entirely; completely.–The news of the accident was *absolutely* true.

A B C D E F G H I J K L M N O P Q R S T U V W X Y Z

absorb ab-sorb' *absorbs, absorbed, absorbing.*
1. Soak up.–The doctor used cotton-wool to *absorb* the blood in the cut.
2. Deep interest.–Mary is *absorbed* in the story. She is so interested that the is giving all her attention to it.

absurd ab-surd' *absurdly.* Foolish; not reasonable.–It is *absurd* to expect so small a child to read well.

abundance a-bun'-dance. A great amount, plenty.–There is an *abundance* of wheat in this country. We have more than is needed.

abundant a-bun'-dant. Plentiful.–Rubber trees are *abundant* in South America.

abuse a-buse' (rhymes with *news*) *abuses, abused, abusing.* 1. Take wrong advantage of; make the wrong use of.–The children do not *abuse* the privilege of a morning break.
2. Treat unkindly.–Do not *abuse* your dog, and he will be your friend.
3. Scold.–I heard the angry man *abuse* the boy.

abuse a-buse' (rhymes with *juice*). Bad or wrong treatment.–*Abuse* of people does not make friends for you.

accelerator ac-cel'-er-a-tor *accelerators.* Anything used to make something go faster.–If you step on the *accelerator* of a motor-car, it feeds more petrol to the motor, and makes the car go faster.

accent ac-cent' *accents, accented, accenting.* 1. Speak a word or part of a word with more force. We *accent* a syllable of a word when we make it sound louder than the other syllables. In this dictionary, the syllable you should *accent* in a word has a special mark (') after it.
2. Ac-cent'. Call to the attention.–We *accent* a certain part of a picture by making darker lines or brighter colours so that people will notice that part of the picture first.
3. A heavy tone or stress in speaking.–Put the *accent* on the first syllable in the word accent (ac'-cent).

accept ac-cept' *accepts, accepted, accepting.*
1. Take.–Bob will *accept* the gift offered him.
2. Say yes to.–Mary will *accept* the invitation to Bob's party.
3. Agree to the truth of.–Bob was absent from school. The teacher *accepted* the excuse from his father. She was satisfied with the excuse.

accident ac'-ci-dent *accidents.* 1. A happening that is not wanted or expected.–These are *accidents*: A man slipped and fell on the ice; a boy fell into the water; two motor-cars struck each other.

2. Chance.–It was just by *accident* that I found you at home.

accidental ac-ci-den'-tal *accidentally.* Just by chance; not intended.–When I bumped into Mother, it was *accidental*.

accommodate ac-com'-mo-date *accommodates, accommodated, accommodating.* 1. Make room for.–The teacher could *accommodate* only 20 children in her room.
2. Help; aid. – You will *accommodate* me very much by sewing for me.

accompany ac-com'-pa-ny *accompanies, accompanied, accompanying.* 1. Go with.–Our teacher will *accompany* us to the zoo.
2. Play music with (a soloist).–Mary will sing, and Mother will *accompany* her, at the piano.

accomplish ac-com'-plish *accomplishes, accomplished, accomplishing.* Do successfully, finish.–It is hard to *accomplish* your work when you are tired.

accord ac-cord' *accords, accorded, according.*
1. Agreement.–The boys were in *accord* as to who broke the window. All agreed that Jack did it.
2. *According to* means by or on the authority of.–*According to* the teacher's record, you were absent only 1 day.
3. *Of one's own accord* means by one's own decision, without being told or advised.–Jack opened the window *of his own accord*.

accordion ac-cor'-di-on *accordions.* A musical instrument consisting of bellows, metal reeds, and keys that look like piano keys. The *accordion* is played by pressing the keys down with the right hand, and moving the bellows

back and forth with the left hand. The left hand also presses down buttons called stops.

account ac-count′ *accounts, accounted, accounting.* 1. A record of money paid out and received.–Father has a bank *account.* The bank takes care of his money and keeps a record of the money he puts in and takes out.–Mother keeps an *account* of the money she spends for food. She writes down all the figures carefully.
2. An explanation; a telling.–When Mary returned from the zoo, she gave an *account* of what she had seen. She told all about it.
3. *Account for* means tell what happens to or becomes of.–One of the pencils was missing. Mary could not *account for* it.
4. *On account of* means because of.–Bob was absent from school *on account of* illness.

accuracy ac′-cu-ra-cy. Correctness; being without mistakes.–Bob was praised for his *accuracy* in arithmetic.

accurate ac′-cu-rate *accurately.* Correct; exact; right.–A banker must be *accurate* in counting money. He must not make mistakes.

accuse ac-cuse′ *accuses, accused, accusing.* Charge with doing wrong.–The man will *accuse* you of being lazy if you do not work harder.–The boy was *accused* of stealing, but he was not guilty.

accustom ac-cus′-tom *accustoms, accustomed, accustoming.* 1. Become used to.–It is hard for same people to *accustom* themselves to cold.
2. *Accustomed to* means used to; fitted for by practice or custom.–Mary is *accustomed to* sleeping in a cold room.

ace *aces.* 1. A playing card with only one pip on it.–To our surprise, Father showed 3 *aces.*
2. A person of the highest skill. – The opposing team had an  *ace* in the slips. He made 3 wonderful catches during the game.

ache *aches, ached, aching.* 1. A dull pain that lasts for some time.–John has a tooth*ache.*
2. Have a dull pain that lasts for some time. –John's tooth *ached.*

achieve a-chieve′ *achieves, achieved, achieving.* 1. Get done by trying.–I *achieved* my goal. I earned money for a bicycle.
2. Get; acquire.–The man *achieved* fame by his invention.

acid ac′-id *acids.* 1. Sour.–Vinegar has an *acid* taste.

2. A sour-tasting substance which causes a change in some metals. Lemons and green apples are sour because they have *acids* in them. When you cut a lemon or peel a sour apple with a steel knife, the *acid* in the fruit makes the knife become dark. *Acids* can be made so strong that they will eat holes in things.–Father spilt *acid* from the car battery on his shoe and it burned a hole in the shoe.

acknowledge ac-know′-ledge *acknowledges, acknowledged, acknowledging, acknowledgement.* 1. Express thanks for.–Bob sent Mary an invitation to a party. Mary *acknowledged* it at once.
2. Admit. – The burglar would not *acknowledge* the theft.

acorn a′-corn *acorns.* The seed of an oak tree.

acquaint ac-quaint′ *acquaints, acquainted, acquainting.* 1. Make familiar, make known to. –I will *acquaint* you with the work that is to be done.–The men are *acquainted* with aircraft building.
2. *Acquainted* means knowing or knowing about.–Bob and Jack are *acquainted.* They know each other.

acquaintance ac-quaint′-ance *acquaintances.* A person one knows personally.–Dr. Brown is an *acquaintance* of mine. I know him.

acquire ac-quire′ *acquires, acquired, acquiring.* Get for one's own.–Father would like to *acquire* the house on the corner.

acre a′-cre *acres.* One hundred and sixty (160) square rods or 43,560 square feet, used as a unit of measurement of land.–The farmer sold 3 *acres* of land.

acrobat ac′-ro-bat *acrobats, acrobatic.* A person who does stunts.–The *acrobat* we saw at the circus could walk a tight-rope and do stunts on a trapeze.

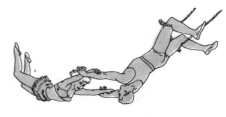

across a-cross′. From one side to the other.– The dog ran *across* the street.–There is a bridge *across* the river.–Mother sewed a hem *across* one end of the towel.

act *acts, acted, acting.* 1. A thing done.–Skating, eating, sleeping, and playing are *acts*.
2. A deed. – A Boy Scout does a kind *act* every day.
3. A main part of a play or other stage entertainment.–The children are giving a play during Christmas week. It has 2 *acts*.
4. Take a part in a play or other entertainment.–Mary *acted* in the school play.
5. Do; behave.–Mother told the children to *act* properly in school.

action ac'-tion *action.* 1. Doing or acting.–Through quick *action* on the part of the lifeguard, the boy was saved from drowning.
2. A thing done.–Mother told Bob that his *actions* were not those of a gentleman.

active ac'-tive *actively.* Busy; lively; moving a great deal.–Mr. Smith is very *active*. He is always doing something.–Some dogs are *active*. They are never still.

activity ac-tiv'-i-ty *activities.* 1. Motion; being busy or moving about.–There is not much *activity* in our playground after lunch.
2. Something being done. – Drawing pictures is an *activity*.

actor ac'-tor *actors.* A man who acts or takes part in a play or film.

actress ac'-tress *actresses.* A woman who acts or takes a part in a play or film.

actual ac'-tu-al. Real, true.–I have no *actual* proof that Bob took the biscuits, but I think he did.

actually ac'-tu-al-ly. Really, in truth. – Jack likes to pretend he is older than Bob, but *actually* Bob is older.

add *adds, added, adding.* 1. Put together.–We *add* 10 apples and 2 apples and get 12 apples.
2. *Add to* means put with.–Salt *added to* potatoes makes them taste better.–*Add* yellow paint *to* blue, and you will have green.

addition ad-di'-tion. 1. Adding or putting numbers together to find the sum or answer. 2 + 4 = 6 is *addition*.
2. Putting with. – The *addition* of salt to vegetables makes them taste better.

3. A part or thing added.–We have a new *addition* to our school, with 6 rooms in it.

additional ad-di'-tion-al. Extra, some more.–So many children came to the party that *additional* tables and chairs had to be used.

address ad-dress' *addresses, addressed, addressing.* 1. A speech, a talk.–Bob will give an *address* on safety at the meeting today.
2. Speak to, give a talk to.–Father stood up to *address* the men.
3. Number, street and place where one lives.–My *address* is 29 Parkfield Street, Seathorpe, Notts.
4. Write an *address* on.–Mary *addressed* the letter to her friend.

adenoids ad'-e-noids. Growths at the back of the nose and in the throat.–Bob had his tonsils and *adenoids* removed.

adhesive tape ad-he'-sive tape. A strip of cloth with a sticky substance on one side, used especially for fastening bandages. – Mother fastened the bandage to Mary's knee with *adhesive tape*.

adjourn ad-journ' *adjourns, adjourned, adjourning, adjournment.* Be dismissed; end (a meeting or gathering). – The club meeting *adjourned* because the chairman had to leave.

adjust ad-just' *adjusts, adjusted, adjusting, adjustment.* 1. Change to make right.–John will *adjust* the window blind so that the sun will not shine in your eyes.
2. Correct, make right.–The grocer will *adjust* your grocery bill if there is a mistake.

admiral ad'-mi-ral *admirals.* An officer in the navy ranking above captain.–The *admiral* ordered the ships into battle.

admire ad-mire' *admires, admired, admiring.* 1. Look up to with respect, wonder, and approval. – Most boys *admire* cricket heroes.
2. Like and enjoy.–The children *admired* the beautiful view from the mountain top.

admission ad-mis'-sion *admissions.* 1. The act of entering or getting in.–The boys voted for the *admission* of 4 more members into the club.
2. A price to be paid for getting in to see a film, game, etc.–*Admission* to the film show costs 20p.
3. A confession; telling the truth.–The boy's *admission* of having done wrong solved the mystery of the missing pencils.

admit ad-mit′ *admits, admitted, admitting.* I. Let in.–Children were not *admitted* to the theatre unless they were with a grown-up.
2. Confess, acknowledge.–Jack does not like to *admit* that he has made a mistake.

adobe a-do′-be. A kind of brick that is dried in the sun.–Some American Indians live in *adobe* houses.

adopt a-dopt′ *adopts, adopted, adopting, adoption.* I. Take and treat as one's own.–The family will *adopt* the baby whose parents were lost in the storm. They will take the baby into their home and treat it as their own child.
2. Accept as one's own. – Usually people who come to England from abroad *adopt* English customs. They follow English ways.

adorable a-dor′-a-ble. Very sweet and lovable. –We think that the baby is *adorable*.

adore a-dore′ *adores, adored, adoring.* Love and admire greatly.–Mary *adores* her piano teacher. She thinks her piano teacher is wonderful.

adult a-dult′ *adults.* I. A grown-up; a person who has grown to be a man or a woman.– Your parents are *adults*.
2. Grown-up.–Mary has very *adult* manners. She doesn't act childishly any more.

advance ad-vance′ *advances, advanced, advancing, advancement.* I. Go forward, go ahead.–The officer told the men to *advance*.
2. A forward movement. – The army's *advance* was 10 miles.
3. Give ahead of time.–Father will *advance* us part of next week's pocket money.
4. Raise.–They *advance* the theatre prices in the evening.

advantage ad-van′-tage *advantages.* I. A benefit; something good that makes a thing more wanted.–This book has an *advantage* over the other in that it is simple. It is better than the other because it is simpler.– It would be of *advantage* to Bob to go on the trip. It would be good for him.

2. An opportunity.–Mary has had more *advantages* than most children. She has had music and dancing lessons, and chances to travel abroad.

adventure ad-ven′-ture *adventures.* I. An exciting and daring thing to do. – Captain Scott's trip to the South Pole was a great *adventure*.
2. An exciting experience.–Riding in an aeroplane was an *adventure* for Bob.

advertise ad′-ver-tise *advertises, advertised, advertising.* Make something known to the public through the newspapers, hoardings, television, radio, etc.–Shops *advertise* things they have to sell.

advertisement ad-ver′-tise-ment *advertisements.* A notice to all the people.–If you do not find your dog, put an *advertisement* in the paper asking the person who finds him to bring him back.– Mother reads the classified *advertisements* every evening to see what is for sale.

advice ad-vice′ (rhymes with *ice*). Suggestions, ideas about what to do.–Mary had trouble with her arithmetic. Her teacher gave her some *advice*. She told Mary that she should learn her tables better.

advise ad-vise′ (rhymes with *size*) *advises, advised, advising.* I. Give advice or suggestions.–The dentist will *advise* you about what to do for your teeth.–The doctor *advised* Grandfather not to climb too many stairs. He told him it would be better if he didn't.
2. Tell. – A telegram *advised* us that our aunt would come to stay with us.

affair af-fair′ *affairs.* I. A matter of interest. –Father had many *affairs* to look after in the city.
2. A happening.–A wedding is an important *affair* in any family.

affect af-fect′ *affects, affected, affecting.* Change; make a difference in.–Because Bob studied at home, his absence from school did not *affect* his school marks.

affection af-fec′-tion. Love, tender feeling.– Mother has much *affection* for all her children.

A B C D E F G H I J K L M N O P Q R S T U V W X Y Z

affectionate af-fec'-tion-ate *affectionately*. Fond, loving.–Jack is very *affectionate*. He shows his fondness for his family and friends. – The children are *affectionate* towards Mother. They love her.

affirmative af-firm'-a-tive. Consenting or saying yes. – When Bob asked Mother if he might go camping, her answer was *affirmative*. She said yes.

afford af-ford' *affords, afforded, affording*. 1. Spare the money. – Jack spent so much money on sweets that he could not *afford* to go to the film show.
2. Spare, give up. – Mother had so much housework to do that she could not *afford* the time to go to the cinema.
3. Give.–Going to school *affords* you the opportunity to work and play with other boys and girls.

afraid a-fraid'. Scared, frightened. – Who's *afraid* of the big, bad wolf?

Africa Af'-ri-ca *African*. One of the 7 continents of the earth. *Africa* is nearer to Europe than to North America or South America. Much of *Africa* is very hot.

after aft'-er. 1. Behind.–Bob walked in the line *after* Jack.
2. Following.–The cat ran *after* the mouse. –Monday comes *after* Sunday.
3. Later than. – Father usually gets home *after* 6 o'clock.

afternoon aft-er-noon'. The time from noon until the sun goes down; the time between noon and evening.–Sally takes a nap in the *afternoon*.

afterwards aft'-er-wards. Later, following that time. – Mother came home at 6 o'clock and Father came soon *afterwards*.–We work first. We play *afterwards*.

again a-gain'. One more time, another time.– The bell rang once, then *again*. It rang a second time.–May I see the book *again*?

against a-gainst'. 1. On. – The ladder leaned *against* the house. The top end touched the house.–The branches hitting *against* the window panes frightened me.
2. Opposite.–John is standing for president *against* Bob. He is trying to win more votes than Bob.
3. Opposed to; not for, not in favour of.– Father is *against* Sally eating much sugar.

4. Next to.–In winter the tree branches look like fingers *against* the sky.–Grey looks nice *against* red.

age *ages, aged, aging*. 1. Number of years old. –What is your *age*? I am 8 years old. I am 8 years of *age*.
2. A time or period.–We are living in a machine *age*. Machines are used for a great many things these days.
3. A time in one's life–We learn to walk at an early *age*. We walk as babies.
4. Grow old.–Grandfather is *aging*.

agent a'-gent *agents*. A person or organization working for or selling things for someone else. – An *agent* came to the door selling brooms.–This company is the *agent* for a large timber company. – The ticket *agent* sells tickets for the railway company.

ago a-go'. Past; before now.–Father went to work some time *ago*; at least an hour *ago*.– Mary likes to read stories of long *ago*, when there were knights and people believed in magic.

agony ag'-o-ny. Great pain or suffering.–The child screamed as though he were in *agony*. He screamed as though he were suffering.

agree a-gree' *agrees, agreed, agreeing*. 1. Think the same; think alike.–The boys do not *agree* about whose turn it is to ride the bicycle. Jack says it is his turn, and Bill says it is his turn.
2. Consent. – Bob would not *agree* to the plan. He said no.
3. Match; equal the same.–The boys both added up the numbers but their answers did not *agree*. They got different answers.

agreeable a-gree'-a-ble *agreeably*. 1. Pleasant. –The actress is a very *agreeable* person to meet and talk to.–Snow White found that the apple had an *agreeable* taste.
2. Suitable, convenient; to one's liking.–If the hour is *agreeable* to you, we will start early in the morning.
3. Willing to accept or consent to.–If you are *agreeable* to our plan, meet us early.

agreement a-gree'-ment *agreements*. 1. An understanding, arrangement. – Bob and Mary have an *agreement* with each other that they will take turns caring for the baby. – The nations signed an *agreement* not to fight.
2. Equal to the same; fitting together.–The children's answers were in *agreement*. They all gave the solution as 225.

AFRICA

WHAT THE PICTURES MEAN

- vanilla
- dates (d) or oil (o)
- coffee
- wheat
- cacao

EUROPE

Mediterranean Sea

Algiers

Casablanca

MOROCCO

TUNISIA

Suez Canal

Cairo

Nile R.

ALGERIA

LIBYA

EGYPT

d

d

SPANISH SAHARA

Red Sea

MAURITANIA

MALI

NIGER

CHAD

SUDAN

TERRITORY OF AFARS & ISSAS

SENEGAL

Timbuktu

UPPER VOLTA

SOMALIA

GAMBIA

GUINEA

NIGERIA

ETHIOPIA

GUINEA BISSAU

SIERRA LEONE

IVORY COAST

GHANA

TOGO

BENIN

CAMEROUN

CENTRAL AFRICAN EMPIRE

L. Turkana

LIBERIA

EQ. GUINEA

GABON

CONGO

Zaire R.

o

UGANDA

KENYA

L. Victoria

Mombasa

ivory

ZAIRE

TANZANIA

ZANZIBAR

L. Tanganyika

cotton

ANGOLA

ZAMBIA

L. Malawi

MALAWI

Atlantic Ocean

Zambesi R.

MOZAMBIQUE

Indian Ocean

MALAGASY

fruit

RHODESIA

NAMIBIA (SOUTH WEST AFRICA)

BOTSWANA

Pretoria

Johannesburg

SWAZILAND

mining   coal   diamonds   gold

LESOTHO

REPUBLIC OF SOUTH AFRICA

Durban

Cape Town

sheep

jungle

desert

cattle

AGRICULTURE

reaper with sickle

medieval sower

medieval reaper

medieval harvester

modern hoe

medieval harrow

flail

scythe

horse-drawn hand plough

disc-harrow

tractor plough

grain drill and fertilizer spreader

spring-tooth harrow

automatic pick-up baler

spike-tooth harrow

manure spreader

combine-harvester

agricultural ag-ri-cul'-tur-al. Having to do with farming; farming.–The middle part of the U.S.A. is largely *agricultural*. Foods and farm animals are raised there.

agriculture ag'-ri-cul-ture. Farming, growing foods and farm animals.–The farmer's work is *agricultural*.–Much of the central part of the U.S.A. is given to *agriculture*.

ah! *Ah* shows a feeling of happiness, sorrow, victory, or the like.–*Ah*, now at last I can go to the circus!–*Ah*, there you are!–*Ah*, you found I was right after all.

ahead a-head'. 1. In front.–Bill could not get *ahead* of Jack in the line because the children behind wouldn't let him.
2. On.–The rain kept the carpenters from going *ahead* with their building. They could not continue.–The policeman told us that, if we drove straight *ahead*, we would come to the street we wanted.
3. Before.–The train arrived *ahead* of time.
4. Leading.–Bob's cricket team is *ahead* by 3 runs.

aid *aids, aided, aiding.* 1. Help.–Without your *aid*, I could not have done the work.
2. Give help to.–Thank you for *aiding* me with the work.

3. A helper or assistant.–The children take turns being their teacher's *aid*.
4. *First aid* means help for the sick or injured; quick treatment.–A good Boy Scout learns *first aid*.

ail *ails, ailed, ailing.* 1. Be wrong with.–I don't understand what *ails* Jack. I don't understand what's the matter with him.
2. Be ill.–Grandmother is *ailing* today.

aim *aims, aimed, aiming.* 1. Point.–The Boy Scout *aimed* the arrow at the target.
2. Pointing.–He missed, because his *aim* was bad.
3. Try.–We *aim* to do our best work.
4. A purpose, or thing one tries for.–Bob's *aim* is to be an engineer.

air *airs, aired, airing.* 1. A mixture of gases which is all about us, but which we cannot see. We breathe *air*. We put *air* into balloons, motor-car tyres, etc. Birds fly through the *air*.–Mother opened the windows to let some *air* in.
2. Get or put in fresh *air*.–Mother *airs* the beds before she makes them. She turns the covers back and lets the *air* in on them.–Jack will take his dog for an *airing*. He will take him outdoors to get some fresh *air*.

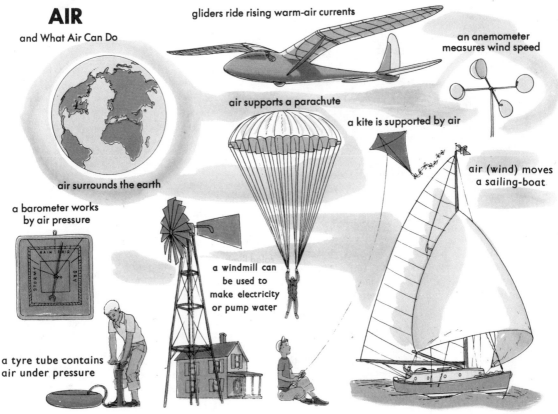

AIR
and What Air Can Do

gliders ride rising warm-air currents

an anemometer measures wind speed

air supports a parachute

a kite is supported by air

air surrounds the earth

air (wind) moves a sailing-boat

a barometer works by air pressure

a windmill can be used to make electricity or pump water

a tyre tube contains air under pressure

aircraft air'-craft. Any kind of aeroplane or flying-machine. Some *aircraft* are driven by a propeller which is turned by a motor. Other *aircraft*, called jet planes, are driven like skyrockets by a stream of hot gases from the engine. The air presses against the wings of an aeroplane and keeps the *aircraft* up. *Aircraft* are heavier than air and carry people, mail, and freight.

airport air'-port *airports*. A place where aeroplanes land and take off.–If you travel by aeroplane, you go to an *airport* to get in it.–Aeroplanes pick up oil and petrol at *airports*.

airship air'-ship *airships*. A long balloon with engines and propellers to make it go through the air; a dirigible. *Airships* are lighter than air.

airway air'-way *airways*. A route or path in the air which is followed by aircraft carrying passengers or freight. Many *airways* are marked at night by beacons, or guide lights, on the ground below.

aisle *aisles*. A path between rows of seats. – The children pick up the papers in the *aisle* to the right of their desks.–The usher at the theatre led us down the *aisle*.

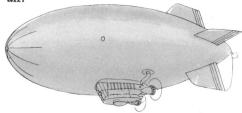

ajar a-jar'. Open a little way.–Mother left the door *ajar* so that the dog could get back into the house.

alabaster a-la-bas'-ter. A smooth, soft white stone used by sculptors and carvers of ornaments.–The museum attendant told us that many of the statues there were made of *alabaster*.

alacrity a-lac'-ri-ty. A cheerful and eager willingness to do something.–The teacher asked the children to clear the classroom so that they could rehearse their play, and they set to work with *alacrity*.

alarm a-larm' *alarms, alarmed, alarming*. 1. A warning signal.–As soon as he heard the stealthy footsteps outside, the watchman pressed the switch to give the *alarm*. – My *alarm*-clock wakes me up every morning at 7 o'clock. We heard the burglar-*alarm* ringing in the jewellery store.

2. A sudden fright.–Jack turned pale with *alarm* when he slipped and almost fell off the ladder.

3. Frighten; fill with dread. – Mother was *alarmed* because of the baby's cough, so she called the doctor.–We were sitting in the garden when Bob told us the *alarming* news about the earthquake.

alas a-las'. *Alas* is used to express feelings of sadness or pity.–'*Alas*, I cannot go to the ball,' said Cinderella.

album al'-bum *albums*. A book with empty pages to be written in or to have pictures, stamps, etc., pasted in. –The children pasted the pictures they took at the beach in the *album* – The actress signed her name in Mary's *album*.

alcohol al'-co-hol. A colourless liquid that looks like water. It is made chiefly by fermenting grains, such as corn, or from molasses or wood. Some drinks, such as whisky and beer, have *alcohol* in them. *Alcohol* is often used in medicines, and in making perfumes. Some kinds of *alcohol* are poisonous. One kind, if mixed with the water in the radiator of a motor-car, will keep the water from freezing in cold weather.

alder al'-der *alders*. A kind of shrub or tree.– The bark of the *alder* is used to dye and tan leather.

alert a-lert' *alertly, alertness*. Quick to notice or understand things. –Jack is very *alert* in class. He is wide awake, pays attention, and always knows what is going on. – Mother is always *alert* to hear baby's call.

AIRCRAFT

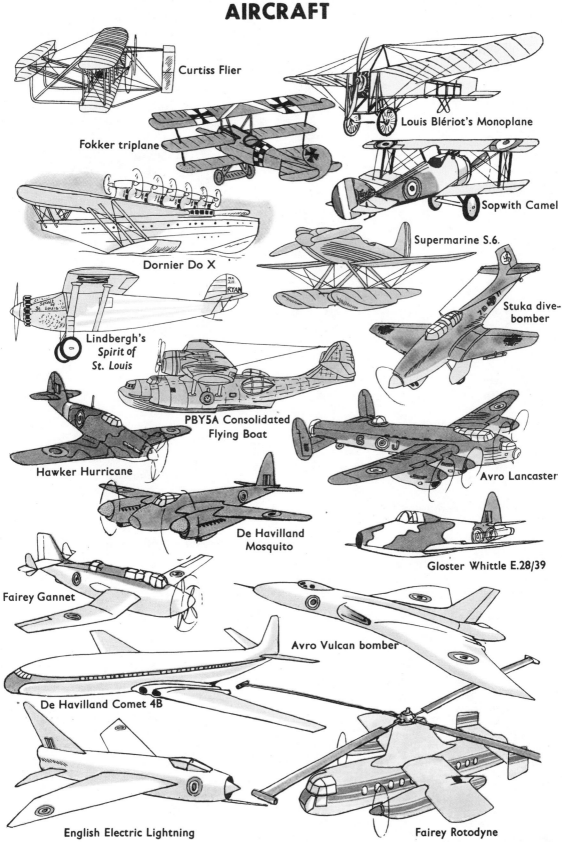

Curtiss Flier

Fokker triplane

Louis Blériot's Monoplane

Sopwith Camel

Dornier Do X

Supermarine S.6.

Lindbergh's *Spirit of St. Louis*

Stuka dive-bomber

Hawker Hurricane

PBY5A Consolidated Flying Boat

Avro Lancaster

De Havilland Mosquito

Gloster Whittle E.28/39

Fairey Gannet

Avro Vulcan bomber

De Havilland Comet 4B

English Electric Lightning

Fairey Rotodyne

A B C D E F G H I J K L M N O P Q R S T U V W X Y Z

algebra al'-ge-bra. A form of mathematics in which letters are used for numbers. $3a - 2b - 2c = 2$ is a problem in *algebra*.

alibi a'-li-bi (rhymes with *sky*) *alibis*. Being somewhere else at the time of a crime.–His *alibi* was that he was in Leeds on the night the robbery took place in London.

alien al'-ien *aliens*. A foreign person; one who lives in a country but is not a citizen of that country.–A Briton in France would be an *alien*.

alight a-light' *alights, alighted, alighting*. 1. Get off. – When the train stops, we will *alight*.
2. Land, come down and settle.–The aeroplane is about to *alight*.–The bee *alights* on the flower to get the sweet nectar.

alike a-like'. Very much the same; similar.–These dresses are so much *alike* that you can hardly tell them apart.–Bob and Mary look much *alike*. They both have blue eyes, light hair, and freckles.

alive a-live'. Living; not dead.–The cat that had fallen into the water was still *alive*. He was saved in time.

all. 1. Every bit of, the whole of.–We played ball *all* the time last summer.–Grandfather has lived in the country *all* his life up to now. He has never lived anywhere else.
2. Every one.–*All* the new puppies are black. –Uncle Jim brought gifts for *all* of us.

alley al'-ley *alleys*. 1. A narrow roadway. *Alleys* are built between or behind buildings for dust carts, delivery lorries, etc.–We put the rubbish in the *alley* so that it can be collected easily.

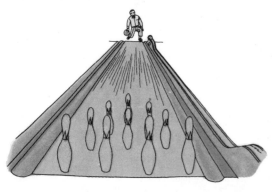

2. A smooth pathway made of boards. – Father bowls in a bowling *alley*.

alligator al'-li-ga-tor *alligators*. A large crawling animal with 4 short legs, large and strong jaws, and a long pointed tail. *Alligators* live in the warmer parts of North America, both in water and on land. The *alligator's* tough hide is sometimes made into leather for shoes, purses, etc.

allow al-low' *allows, allowed, allowing*. 1. Permit; let.–Mary's mother *allows* her to play the piano at any time. She lets Mary play without asking.
2. Give; let have.–Our teacher *allows* us 5 pages to write our test on.

allowance al-low'-ance *allowances*. A set amount given.–Some fathers give their children an *allowance* of money each week. They give them a certain amount to spend.

all right. 1. Correct.–John's answer was *all right*.
2. Satisfactory or agreeable.–If it is *all right* with you, we will meet at the school.
3. Yes; very well.–When Mary asked if she might go, Mother said, '*All right*.'

almanac al'-ma-nac *almanacs*. A yearly booklet that tells about the days, weeks, and months of the year, and about the moon, stars, weather, etc.

almost al'-most. Nearly. – Jack had *almost* enough money to go to the circus.

alone a-lone'. 1. By oneself; without others.–My Grandmother lives *alone*.
2. Only; by itself; without other things.–Sunshine *alone* will not make the plants grow. They also need water.

along a-long'. 1. Throughout the length of; beside.–The man walked *along* the street. –Bob walked *along* the wall. He walked beside the wall.
2. Onward.–The policeman told the driver of the car to go *along*.
3. With (one).–We are going to town, and Bob will go *along* too.

aloud a-loud'. With sound; out loud.–Speak *aloud*, do not whisper, if you want people to hear you.–Mother reads *aloud* to us on rainy days.

alphabet al'-pha-bet *alphabets*. A set of all the letters used in any language, arranged or put in a certain order.–In the English language, the *alphabet* is sometimes called the ABC, and has 26 letters.

Hebrew	א ₐ	ב ᵦ	ד ᴅ	ה ₕ	מ ᴍ	ס ₛ	ש ₛ	ל ʟ
Arabic	ب ᵦ	ح ₕ	س ₛ	ص ₛ	غ ᴿ	ف ꜰ	ل ʟ	ر ᴍ
Greek	Αα ₐ	Ββ ᵦ	Δδ ᴅ	Ωω ō	Ππ ᴘ	Σσ ₛ	Ττ ᴛ	Φφ ꜰ
Russian	А	Бб ᴘ	Г ɢᴋ	Дд ᴅ	Ж ꜱʜ	И ᴇʏ	Фф ꜰ	Кк ᴋ

development of letters from hieroglyphics   Chinese   Runic   Ogham

alphabetical al-pha-bet'-i-cal *alphabetically*. According to or in the order of the alphabet. –The children arranged their spelling words in *alphabetical* order, in the order in which the letters of the alphabet come. In an English dictionary, all the words starting with 'a' come first, those starting with 'b' come next, and so on.

already al-read'-y. By or before, this time.– We thought Father would be here *already*.

also al'-so. Too; in addition.–Bob is in the 5th form. Mary is in the 5th form *also*.

altar al'-tar *altars*. A raised table at the front of a church where sacred ceremonies are held.–The monk knelt at the *altar* to pray.

alter al'-ter *alters, altered, altering*. Change; make different; adjust.–Mother's dress did not fit well, so she *altered* it.

although al-though'. Even if; though.–*Although* I haven't a new hat, I shall go to church at Easter.

altitude al'-ti-tude *altitudes*. Height; distance from the earth or from the level of the oceans, called sea-level.–What is the *altitude* of this hill? How high is it?–Birds fly at different *altitudes*.

alto al'-to *altos*. 1. A part in music to be sung by women who have low voices.
2. A woman with a singing voice suitable to sing this part.

altogether al-to-geth'-er. Wholly; entirely.– The farmer's work was not *altogether* satisfactory. He was not entirely pleased with it.

aluminium a-lu-min'-i-um. A dull, silver-coloured metal that is very light. It is used for aeroplanes, cooking utensils, and many other things that must be strong but light.

always al'-ways. At all times.–*Always* think before you speak.

am *be, is, are, was, were, being, been*. One form of the word *be*, used only with I.–I *am* going to play ball.–I *am* in the top class at school.

amateur am'-a-teur or am-a-teur' *amateurs*. One who works or plays at some activity just for pleasure and not for pay.–The Eagles Club is an *amateur* football club. They play for fun but not for money.

amaze a-maze' *amazes, amazed, amazing, amazement*. Surprise.–Mary's ability to play the piano will *amaze* you.

amber am'-ber. 1. A hard, yellowish gum used in making beads and other articles of jewellery.
2. Yellowish.–The *amber* traffic light tells the driver to get ready to stop.

ambition am-bi'-tion. 1. An aim; a goal. – Mary's *ambition* is to become a great musician.
2. A great desire for success.–The reason Bob gets better marks than Bill is that he has more *ambition*.

ambitious am-bi'-tious *ambitiously*. Full of ambition; wanting success.–People who are *ambitious* are apt to be successful.

ambulance am'-bu-lance *ambulances*. A specially designed car for carrying sick and injured people.–Mary was taken to the hospital in an *ambulance*.

amen a'-men'. A word said at the end of a prayer, meaning 'So be it!'

America A-mer'-i-ca. *American, Americans*.
1. The continents of North *America* and South *America*. – The United States is in North *America*.
2. The name *America* can mean either North *America* or South *America*.
3. The United States is often called *America*; its citizens are known as *Americans*.

ammonia am-mo'-ni-a. A colourless gas with a sharp, strong odour. *Ammonia* is mixed with water and used for cleaning. *Ammonia* gas is often used in making ice.

ammunition am-mu-ni'-tion. Gunpowder, shells, bullets, etc., used in shooting guns and cannon.

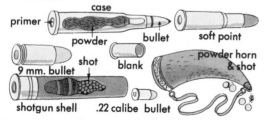

among a-mong'. 1. In the midst of.–There was a spy *among* the soldiers in the camp.
2. To each of. – Mother divided the cake *among* the children. She gave each child some.

amount a-mount' *amounts, amounted, amounting*. 1. Total; entire quantity.–Mother spent £2 for a hat and £1 for gloves. The *amount* of money she spent was £3.
2. A quantity.–Each year a large *amount* of sugar is made from sugar beets.
3. *Amount to* means come to, total, or become.–The money Mother spent *amounted to* £3. – A day without any housework *amounts to* a holiday for Mother.

ample am'-ple. Enough. – There was *ample* cake for all the guests at the birthday party.

amputate am'-pu-tate *amputates, amputated, amputating, amputation*. Cut off.–The doctor did not have to *amputate* the man's injured finger. It finally healed.

amuse a-muse' *amuses, amused, amusing*. Entertain; make laugh; please with humour.– Clowns *amuse* the children by doing tricks and funny stunts.

amusement a-muse'-ment *amusements*. 1. An entertaining thing; a sport or pastime.–Fishing, racing, and puppet shows are Jack's favourite *amusements*.
2. Entertainment; pleasure. – The clown does tricks for the *amusement* of the children.

an. (Used instead of 'a' when the following word begins with a vowel.) 1. One or any.– Grandfather is *an* old man.–Baby has *an* orange.
2. There are 4 lines to *an* inch on the paper. There are 4 lines in or for every inch.

analysis a-nal'-y-sis *analyses*. An examination made by separating into parts.–The farmer made an *analysis* of the soil to see if it contained the proper materials to make corn grow.

analyse an'-a-lyse *analyses, analysed, analysing*. 1. Separate a thing into parts to find out what it is made of.–In science class we *analysed* a bar of soap.
2. Examine each part of.–The teacher *analysed* the arithmetic problem by going over each part separately.

ancestor an'-ces-tor *ancestors*. A person who came before in a family line.–Your father, your mother, and your grandparents are your *ancestors*. Your grandparents' *ancestors* are also yours. They are your family of long ago.

anchor an'-chor *anchors, anchored, anchoring*.
1. A heavy metal object, usually with 2 points, used to hold boats in place in the water. One end of a rope or chain is fastened to the *anchor* and the other to the boat. When the *anchor*  is dropped into the water, it digs into the bottom and keeps the boat from moving about.
2. Fasten in place with an *anchor*.–Fishermen sometimes *anchor* their boats while they fish.
3. Fix or fasten.–The flag-pole was *anchored* to the roof with bolts.

THE AMERICAS

WHAT THE PICTURES MEAN

sheep		corn	
wheat		rubber	
cotton		rice	
pigs		fish	
tobacco		furs	
dairying		coffee	
fruit		pearls	
cacao		timber	
coconuts			

ALASKA

Hudson Bay

CANADA

Vancouver

Columbia R.

Winnipeg

Quebec

San Francisco

St. Lawrence R.

UNITED STATES

Chicago

Los Angeles

Colorado R.

Kansas City

Ohio R.

New York

Washington

Missouri R.

Mississippi R.

MEXICO

New Orleans

Rio Grande

Mexico City

CUBA

DOMINICAN REPUBLIC
PUERTO RICO

HAITI

BELIZE

JAMAICA

GUATEMALA

HONDURAS

WEST INDIES

EL SALVADOR

NICARAGUA

COSTA RICA

Atlantic

VENEZUELA

GUYANA

PANAMA

Orinoco R.

SURINAM

COLOMBIA

FRENCH GUIANA

ECUADOR

Ocean

PERU

Amazon R.

BRAZIL

BOLIVIA

PARAGUAY

Rio de Janeiro

Pacific Ocean

CHILE

Valparaiso

Buenos Aires

URUGUAY

ARGENTINA

shipping

farming

sugar

manufacturing

mining

cattle

oil

ancient an'-cient. 1. Of times long ago.–Mummies are relics of *ancient* Egypt.
2. Very old. – The custom of celebrating New Year is *ancient*.

and. 1. The word *and* is used to join words *and* groups of words.
2. Added to.–Four *and* four is eight.
3. *And* is used for the word *to* when used after *come, go,* and some other words.–Come *and* see my new hat.–Go *and* buy the toys.

angel an'-gel *angels*. 1. A winged messenger of God.
2. Sometimes people are called *angels* because of their goodness and loveliness.

anger an'-ger *angers, angered, angering.* 1. A fighting feeling; a feeling caused by receiving unfair treatment or by being kept from doing what one wishes to do.–John became angry when the bully tripped him.
2. Make angry.–His father's refusal to let him go to the game *angered* Jack.

angle an'-gle *angles*. A point where 2 lines meet, or the space between 2 lines meeting at a point.

right   obtuse   acute

angora an-gor'-a. A very soft woolly fabric made from the hair of Angora goats or rabbits.–This cardigan is made of *angora*.

angrily an'-gri-ly. In an angry or displeased manner.–Jack spoke *angrily* to his dog when it would not go home.

angry an'-gry *angrier, angriest.* 1. Feeling like fighting or doing injury; feeling anger.–When the boys tied Bob's hands behind him, he became *angry*.
2. Severe; dangerous. – The *angry* waves nearly wrecked the boat.
3. Red and sore.–The cut on Bob's arm looked *angry*.

animal an'-i-mal *animals*. Any living thing other than a plant. Most *animals* are able to move, and eat plants or other *animals*. A tiny spider is an *animal* and a great elephant is an *animal*, too.

ankle an'-kle *ankles*. The joint between the foot and the leg.–Mary sprained her *ankle* jumping off the fence.

anniversary an-ni-ver'-sa-ry *anniversaries*. A date of the year on which something happened in an earlier year.–September 12 is Mother's and Father's wedding *anniversary*. They were married many years ago on that date.–The *anniversary* of your birth is your birthday.

announce an-nounce' *announces, announced, announcing.* 1. Tell to everyone or to a large group of people; make a public notice of.–John will *announce* who the characters in the play will be.–When visitors call at the school, the teacher will *announce* their arrival to the class.
2. Make known to everyone by printing in a newspaper, telling by means of radio, etc.–The newspapers will *announce* the date of the first test match.

announcement an-nounce'-ment *announcements*. A notice to a large group of people.–The weather bureau sent out an *announcement* of what the weather would be the following day.–Jack made an *announcement* to the class this morning.–You can make an *announcement* by radio, in writing, or in person.

annoy an-noy' *annoys, annoyed, annoying, annoyance.* Bother; irritate; disturb. – Our neighbour's radio *annoys* Father.

annual an'-nu-al. 1. Once a year.–Boxing Day is an *annual* holiday in some countries.
2. Yearly.–The *annual* rent of our house is £300.

annually an'-nu-al-ly. 1. Once a year.–Our tax assessment comes *annually*.
2. Year after year.–Father has a two-week holiday *annually*.

another an-oth'-er. 1. One more.–Mary sang *another* song when the children asked her to.
2. A different.–Father put on *another* suit to go out.

answer an'-swer *answers*. 1. A reply. – The teacher asked a question and Jack gave the correct *answer*.–We wrote the *answers* to the test.
2. Go to see what is wanted or who is calling.–When the telephone rings, Mary *answers* it.–Will you *answer* the door-bell?
3. Serve.–If you hold this newspaper over your head, it will *answer* as an umbrella to keep off the rain.

ANIMALS

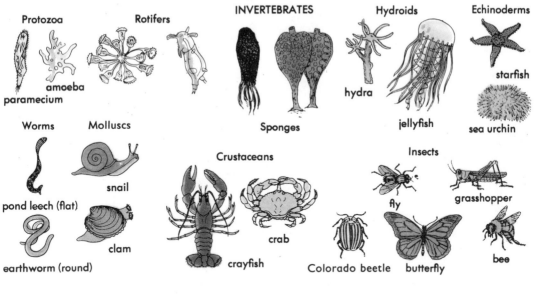

INVERTEBRATES

Protozoa — paramecium, amoeba

Rotifers

Hydroids — hydra

Echinoderms — starfish, sea urchin

Sponges

jellyfish

Worms — pond leech (flat), earthworm (round)

Molluscs — snail, clam

Crustaceans — crayfish, crab

Insects — fly, grasshopper, Colorado beetle, butterfly, bee

VERTEBRATES

Fish — shark, perch, eel, sea horse

Amphibian — frog

Reptiles — turtle, alligator, lizard, rattlesnake

Birds — hen, robin, duck, hawk, ostrich, penguin

bat, kangaroo

Mammals — whale, rabbit, man, horse, elephant, dog, cat

A
B
C
D
E
F
G
H
I
J
K
L
M
N
O
P
Q
R
S
T
U
V
W
X
Y
Z

ANTARCTIC AND ARCTIC REGIONS

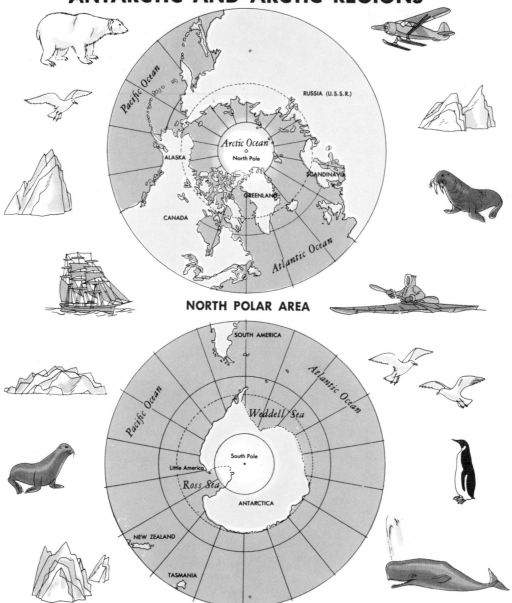

NORTH POLAR AREA

SOUTH POLAR AREA

ant *ants*. A small insect, with a body divided into sections like little beads. Some *ants* are black, some red. They live together in big 'colonies', and dig their homes, called *ant*-hills, in the ground. Some *ants* do a great deal of damage.

Antarctica Ant-arc′-ti-ca *Antarctic*. The name of a large continent on which the South Pole is located. No one lives in *Antarctica*, which is almost completely covered by ice. It is surrounded by the *Antarctic* Ocean.

antelope an′-te-lope *antelopes*. An animal similar to a deer.

anthem an′-them *anthems*. A song, especially a solemn or a sacred one.–The church choir sang an *anthem* at Easter.

antique an-tique′ *antiques*. I. Old; made a long time ago.–Some homes are furnished with *antique* furniture.
2. Something made long ago, and valuable because of its age.–Aunt Ella gives Mother *antiques*. Last year she gave us an *antique* desk made 200 years ago.

anvil an′-vil *anvils*. An iron block on which metal is pounded into shape. – A country blacksmith beats out metal horseshoes on an *anvil*.

anxious anx′-ious *anxiously*. I. Worried, nervous, concerned.–Mother is *anxious* about the baby's cough.
2. Eager, impatient.–Mary was *anxious* for Father to come home so that she could show him her new party dress.

any an′-y. I. No particular one.–Grandmother told me to take *any* flower I wanted from the garden.–I'd like to go at town with you *any* day you say.
2. Even one; a little.–I do not want *any* sweets.
3. Some.–Father asked us if we wanted *any* money to go shopping.

anybody an′-y-bod-y. Anyone, any person.– We did not hear *anybody* knock at the door.

anyhow an′-y-how. I. Anyway, in spite of something, nevertheless.–It looks like rain, but Father says we may go *anyhow*.
2. Besides, also.-Mary stayed at home because of her cold, but she wanted to stay at home and play *anyhow*.

anyone an′-y-one. Any person.–*Anyone* who wants to read may get a book from the table.

anything an′-y-thing. Something, one thing.– Have you had *anything* to eat?

anyway an′-y-way. Anyhow, no matter what happens.–It is cold out, but we will go *anyway*.

anywhere an′-y-where. In any place.–Sally lost her scarf and could not find it *anywhere*.

apart a-part′. I. Away, off, to one side.–The children who whispered sat *apart* from the others.
2. One from the other.–The twins look so much alike that only their mother can tell them *apart*.
3. To pieces.–The officer took his gun *apart* to clean it.

apartment a-part′-ment *apartments*. I. A room or group of rooms forming a home, rented or sometimes owned, within a larger building. –In the United States the word *apartments* is used for a block of flats.

2. One's own room or chamber.–The princess was kept prisoner in her own *apartments* in the castle tower till she was 21 years old.

ape *apes, aped, aping*. I. An animal that belongs to the monkey family. Unlike most monkeys, the *ape* does not have a tail. *Apes* are in many ways manlike.
2. Imitate, act like.– Mary likes to *ape* her mother.

apiece a-piece′. For each one.–Fifty pence *apiece* is too much to pay for kites.–If pears are 2p *apiece*, 5 pears will cost 10p.

apologize a-pol′-o-gize *apologizes, apologized, apologizing*. Admit making a mistake or doing wrong, and say that one is sorry.–Jack knew that he had been rude, and *apologized*.

apology a-pol′-o-gy *apologies*. Words saying that one has done wrong and is sorry.–The teacher accepted Jack's *apology* for interrupting her.

apostrophe a-pos′-tro-phe *apostrophes*. A mark or sign (') that looks like a comma, but is used above a word. I. The *apostrophe* takes the place of a letter or letters that are left out.–It's time to go. – We've only got an hour.
2. The *apostrophe* shows that someone owns something. – Bob's kite got away. – It was Bob's.
3. Sometimes an *apostrophe* is used in front of the 's' to make a word mean more than one.–There are 2 'e's' in the word fee.– Three 6's are 18.

apparatus ap-pa-ra′-tus *apparatuses*. The tools or things used in doing a piece of work.–A breakdown lorry has *apparatus* for hauling away cars.–A washing machine is an *apparatus* for doing the washing.

apparel ap-par′-el. One's clothes; dresses, suits, and other clothing.–Cinderella's rags turned to beautiful evening *apparel*.

appeal ap-peal′ *appeals, appealed, appealing*.
1. Attract, seem pleasant and inviting.–Travelling in the jungle does not *appeal* to Mother.–This picture *appeals* to me. I like the colours in it.
2. A request.–The children made an *appeal* to their teacher for more time to read.
3. Plead, ask.–After Father said no, Jack *appealed* to Mother.

appear ap-pear′ *appears, appeared, appearing*.
1. Come to be seen; show oneself.–The football team did not *appear* until it was time for the game.
2. Seem or look; give the impression.–The old man *appeared* to be a tramp, because he was poorly dressed.

appearance ap-pear′-ance *appearances*. 1. Showing of oneself.–Mother did not make an *appearance* until after the dishes were washed. She did not come in till then.
2. A public showing.–Shirley Temple made her first *appearance* in films when she was a very little girl.
3. The way one looks.–Indians used to use bright paint on their faces to improve their *appearance*.–From his *appearance*, the cat seemed asleep, but he was just pretending.–Mary's tired *appearance* worried Mother.

appetite ap′-pe-tite *appetites*. 1. A desire for food and drink.–Sometimes when people are ill they have no *appetite*.
2. A desire.–Bob's *appetite* for learning is never satisfied. He always wants to know more.

appetizing ap′-pe-tiz-ing. Delicious; good to eat; dainty and nice, so that you want to eat it.–Mother put cream cheese on the salad to make it *appetizing*.

applaud ap-plaud′ *applauds, applauded, applauding, applause*. Clap the hands to show that one approves, agrees, is enjoying a performance, speech, etc.–The children *applauded* Mary's playing of the piece called 'The Teddy Bears' Picnic'.

apple ap′-ple *apples*. A round fruit that grows on a tree and is red, yellow, or green. *Apples* are good to eat.–Green *apples* are used in making *apple* pie.

Jonathan

Winesap

Granny Smith

Delicious

apply ap-ply′ *applies, applied, applying, application*. 1. Put on.–Doctors *apply* iodine to cuts and sores.
2. Give close attention.–Good readers *apply* themselves to their reading.
3. Fit, suit, refer to.–Spelling rules do not *apply* to all words. They cannot be used to spell all words.–The teacher said her warning did not *apply* to the children who did their work on time.
4. Ask (for something).–Uncle Jim will *apply* for the job.

appoint ap-point′ *appoints, appointed, appointing*. Select, choose. – Mary's teacher *appointed* her to collect the books.

appointment ap-point′-ment *appointments*. 1. An agreement to be somewhere.–Bob has an *appointment* with the dentist this afternoon at three o'clock.
2. A naming or choosing of a person for an office or a job.–Bob is trying to get an *appointment* to the Flying Squad.

appreciate ap-pre′-ci-ate *appreciates, appreciated, appreciating*. 1. See the value or good of.–Bob *appreciates* the friendship of his class-mates.–I *appreciate* my good health.
2. Enjoy, get pleasure from.–Mary *appreciates* good music.

appreciation ap-pre-ci-a′-tion. 1. Thankfulness, gratitude.–The man expressed his *appreciation* for the help his neighbours had given him.
2. Enjoyment.–*Appreciation* of good music makes people's lives more fun.

approach ap-proach′ *approaches, approached, approaching*. 1. Come or go near to.–*Approach* Baby's cot quietly, in case she is asleep.–Christmas is fast *approaching*.
2. A passage-way; a means of reaching or getting to.–The *approach* to the house led through a rose-garden. The *approach* to the city is a bridge across the river or a tunnel under the river.–Jack's father suggested that the first *approach* towards getting a job would be to write a letter giving his qualifications.

appropriate ap-pro′-pri-ate *appropriately*. Something which is suitable for a particular time or person.–The children thought it would be *appropiate* to give a surprise party for their father on his birthday.–It would not be *appropriate* for Jill to go to the theatre while her mother is so ill.

approve ap-prove′ *approves, approved, approving, approval*. Like, be in favour of, think well of.–Father does not *approve* of our staying up late at night.–Father tasted the cake and *approved* it. He said it was good.– Mother *approves* of our new friends.

apricot a′-pri-cot *apricots*. An orange-coloured fruit of the peach family. *Apricots* are good to eat raw, stewed, dried, and in pies, jams, etc.

April A′-pril. The 4th month of the year.–30 days hath September, *April*, June, and November.

apron a′-pron *aprons*. An article of clothing worn over one's dress to keep it clean. – Mother wears an *apron* when she washes the dishes.

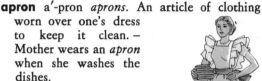

apt *aptly, aptness*. 1. Likely.–Mother is not *apt* to forget my birthday.–It is *apt* to rain here.
2. Promising.–Mary is an *apt* pupil at music. She learns quickly.

aquarium a-quar′-i-um *aquariums*. 1. A tank or bowl of water for keeping water animals and plants.–The teacher put the goldfish and water-weed in the *aquarium*.

2. A building in which water plants and animals are kept.–Our class visited the *aquarium*.

arbour ar′-bour *arbours*. 1. A shaded place.– The branches of the trees formed an *arbour*.

2. A trellis or wooden frame covered with vines or branches to make shade.–At the bottom of the garden there is an *arbour* where we can rest after playing tiring games.

arbutus ar-bu′-tus. An early spring flower, also called trailing *arbutus*, which crawls or trails along the ground. It is pink or white, and very fragrant.

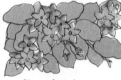

arc *arcs*. A curved line, or a line that is a part of a circle.

arch *arches, arched, arching.* 1. A structure curved like part of a circle. *Arches* are built of wood, stone, brick, or any other building material. Sometimes gates, doors and bridges have *arches* over them.
2. Shape like an *arch*; curve upwards.–The kitten *arches* her back when angry.

Arches

architect *ar'-chi-tect architects.* A person who designs buildings and sees that they are built according to his plans.

Arctic *Arc'-tic.* The most northern part of the world; the region near the North Pole. (See map on page 28.)

are *be, am, is, was, were, been, being.* One form of the word *be,* used with we, you, or they.–We *are* going.–They *are* coming.–You *are* here.

area *a'-re-a areas.* 1. An amount of space enclosed by boundaries. We have half an acre of land; the *area* of our land is half an acre. 2. A section or piece of land.–The *area* in front of the house was covered with long grass.

aren't. Are not.–We are going. They *aren't.*

argue *ar'-gue argues, argued, arguing.* Discuss thing disagreed upon; talk for and against something.–John and Mary often *argue* with each other about whether girls or boys are cleverer.

argument *ar'-gu-ment arguments.* 1. A dispute; a discussion of a thing disagreed upon.–The children had an *argument* about whose turn it was to wash the dishes. Mary said it was Ruth's turn. Ruth said it was Mary's turn.

2. A reason given for or against a question. –Bob offered a good *argument* in favour of holding the party on Saturday afternoon.

arise *a-rise' arises, arose, arisen, arising.* Come up.–If an argument *arises* over the works to be done, Mother will settle it.

arithmetic *a-rith'-me-tic.* The study of using numbers.–In *arithmetic* class, children learn how to work with numbers. They learn how to add, subtract, multiply, and divide.

Arizona *Ar-i-zo'-na.* A state in south-western U.S.A. *Arizona* is known for its healthy climate, its magnificent Grand Canyon National Park, and the Painted Desert. Cotton, lettuce, and fruits are grown on the fertile farmlands.

ark. The Bible tells us that Noah was saved from the great Flood in a large boat called the *ark.* He took his family and a pair of each kind of animal on the *ark* with him, and waited for the water to subside.

arm *arms, armed, arming.* 1. One of the 2 upper limbs of a person. Human beings have 4 limbs, or branches of the body. The 2 upper limbs are called *arms.* The 2 lower limbs are the legs.
2. A part at the side or end of a seat to support a person's *arms.*– Jack rests his *arms* on the *arms* of his chair. 3. Prepare for war, take up weapons.– A country *arms* to protect itself from its enemies.

armada *ar-ma'da armadas.* A fleet of warships taking its name from the *Great Armada* sent by King Philip II of Spain in 1588 to attack England.–The Spanish *Armada* was defeated by the English fleet under the command of Sir Francis Drake.

armadillo *ar-ma-dil'-lo armadillos.* A small burrowing animal living in South America.– The *armadillo* is related to the ant-eaters, and is protected by an armour-like covering of hard bony plates.

armchair arm'-chair *armchairs.* A chair with side pieces to support a person's arms.

armistice ar'-mi-stice. A temporary peace agreement. – The 2 countries which were at war made an *armistice* until they could make a final treaty. They stopped fighting for a time.

Armistice Day. November 11. In 1918, during the First World War, an armistice was signed on this date. November 11 has since been known as *Armistice Day,* in memory of the end of fighting.

armour ar'-mour *armoured.* 1. A suit of iron.– The knights of old wore *armour* to keep themselves from being hurt in battle. You can still see complete suits of *armour* in museums. 2. A sheet or covering of metal used for protection against bullets, explosives, etc. – A covering of strong metal *armour* protects the bank's money when it travels in an *armoured* car.

arms. Weapons used for fighting, especially in warfare. – During the war many factories were busy making *arms.*

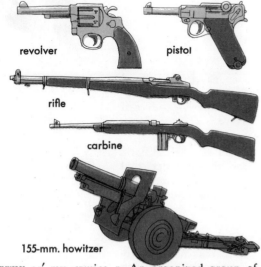

revolver

pistol

rifle

carbine

155-mm. howitzer

army ar'-my *armies.* 1. An organized group of men trained in the use of arms and the methods of war.

2. A great number.–An *army* of boys and girls took part in the sports events.

arose a-rose'. One form of the word *arise.*–An argument *arose* because the men disagreed.

around a-round'. 1. Along all sides.–The children ran *around* the school.
2. To another side of.–Jack walked *around* the corner.
3. About or near.–Mother told us not to play *around* the fire.
4. In a circle.–The dog ran *around* and *around.*
5. About.–I'll be there *around* nine o'clock.

arouse a-rouse' *arouses, aroused, arousing.* 1. Awaken. – At six o'clock, Mother tried to *arouse* Father.
2. Excite.–The circus *aroused* a lot of interest all over the town.

arrange ar-range' *arranges, arranged, arranging.* 1. Put in some order; place according to a plan. – Jack *arranged* the books on the shelves.–Mary *arranged* the silver on the table.
2. Make plans.–The chairman will *arrange* for the picnic.

arrangement ar-range'-ment *arrangements.* 1. A way or plan of putting things in a place.–The *arrangement* of the flowers in the bowl was pretty.
2. A plan.–Jack's *arrangements* for the party were pleasing to the rest of the class.

arrest ar-rest' *arrests, arrested, arresting.* 1. Seize and take to jail under the law.–Policemen have the power to *arrest* people who do not obey the laws.
2. Stop.–The flood was *arrested* when the rain stopped.

arrival ar-riv'-al. Coming.–Our *arrival* did not surprise Grandmother.–The *arrival* of spring was welcomed by all of us.

arrive ar-rive' *arrives, arrived, arriving.* Come; get to a place.–The train will *arrive* at 6.30 a.m.–If our friends *arrive* at the park first, they will wait for us.

arrow ar'-row *arrows.* 1. A pointed stick shot from a bow. – Indians used bows and *arrows* to shoot wild animals.

TO THE PARK

2. A sign which points in a certain direction. –You will find the park if you follow the *arrows.*

art *arts*. 1. Drawing, painting, or sculpture.– In our school, children go to the *art* class twice a week.
2. Pictures, sculpture, etc.–Mr Jones, the *art* teacher, produced some nice works of *art*.
3. A thing that requires much practice or skill. –Playing the piano is an *art*.

artery ar'-ter-y *arteries*. One of the tubes in the body that carry blood from the heart to other parts of the body.

article ar'-ti-cle *articles*. 1. An object; a separate part or piece.–Overcoats, hats and shoes are *articles* of clothing.
2. A written composition giving information. –The newspaper reporter wrote an *article* about safety.

artificial ar-ti-fi'-cial *artificially*. Not real; not found in nature; made as an imitation. – Some *artificial* flowers are made of paper.

artist art'-ist *artists*. 1. A person who paints or draws pictures.
2. A person who is very skilled in some special activity, such as music or writing, which requires original thinking and feeling.

as. 1. In the manner that.–Stand *as* you were standing when the picture was taken.
2. While.–Grandmother sings *as* she works.
3. When.–The fisherman arrived *as* the sun came up.
4. Because.–We must stay home, *as* it is raining.
5. For example, like.–Many trees, such *as* oaks, maples and elms, grow here.
6. Which.–Our team was better than the other, *as* the score proved.

ash *ashes*. A tree which belongs to the olive family. The wood of the *ash* is used in making furniture, and for many other things.

ashamed a-shamed'. Feeling guilt; unhappy because of failure or wrongdoing.–The small boy was *ashamed* because he had pulled the little girl's hair.

ashes ash'-es. The dusty material that remains after anything has been burned.–Grandfather emptied the *ashes* from his pipe.

ashore a-shore'. 1. To the shore; on to the land. –Sailors on the ship will go *ashore* when the ship arrives in port.
2. On land.–The sailors will stay *ashore* for several days.

Asia A'-sia *Asiatic*. The largest continent in the world. More people live in *Asia* than in any other continent. Some of the countries of *Asia* are India, Pakistan, Burma, China, Japan, Indonesia, Korea, and part of Russia.

aside a-side'. 1. To one side; apart.–The officers sat *aside* from the other men.
2. In safekeeping; away.–Mother puts *aside* some money for the rent each week.

ask *asks, asked, asking*. 1. Request. – Mary *asked* Mother for an apple.
2. Request an answer to.–The teacher *asked* many questions in class today.
3. Inquire.–Did you *ask* about the time of the party?– *Ask* if we may go.
4. Invite.–Ann *asked* Jack to come to her party.

asleep a-sleep'. 1. Sleeping; not awake.–The baby is *asleep*.
2. Numb.–Father's arm is *asleep* because he was lying on it and stopped the circulation of blood. He has no feeling in it.

asparagus as-par'-a-gus. A vegetable whose shoots or young stems are good to eat. If the shoots are not picked for eating, they grow to be large, fernlike plants with branches. Sometimes the branches are used in bouquets.

aspen as'-pen *aspens*. A kind of poplar tree. The leaves of the *aspen* shake or quiver if there is a breeze.

asphalt as'-phalt. A dark, tarlike substance that is mixed with other materials and used to pave roads.

aspirin as'-pir-in. A medicine that helps to relieve pain. – When Father had a headache, he took an *aspirin* tablet.

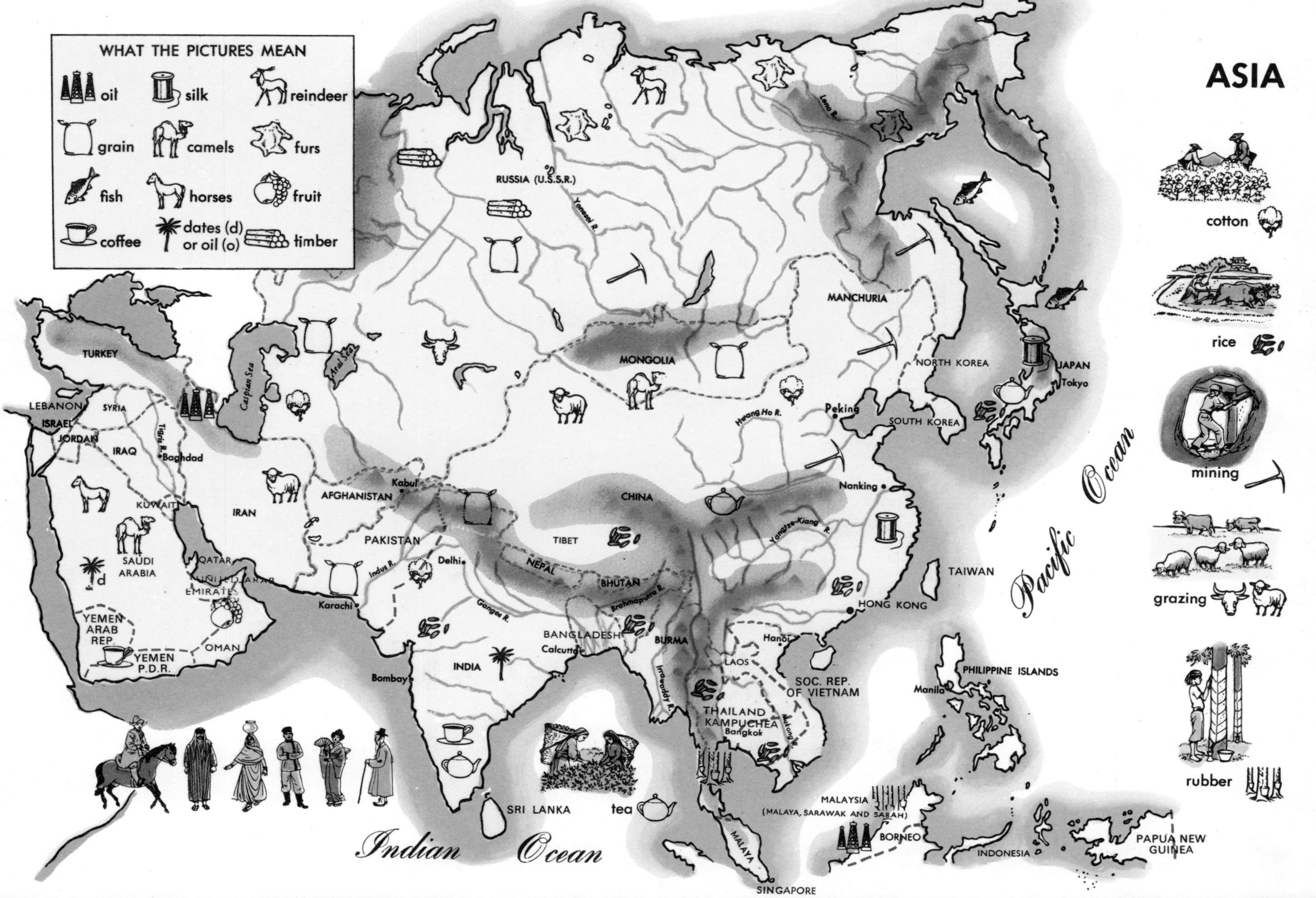

ASIA

cotton

rice

mining

grazing

rubber

WHAT THE PICTURES MEAN

oil   silk

grain   camels   reindeer

fish   horses   furs

coffee   dates (d)   fruit
or oil (o)   timber

Pacific Ocean

Indian Ocean

JAPAN
Tokyo

NORTH KOREA

SOUTH KOREA

MANCHURIA

Peking

Nanking

Hwang Ho R.

Yangtze R.

TAIWAN

HONG KONG

SOC. REP.
OF VIETNAM

Hanoi

LAOS

Mekong R.

THAILAND
Bangkok

KAMPUCHEA

BURMA

Irrawaddy R.

PHILIPPINE ISLANDS

Manila

MALAYSIA
(MALAYA, SARAWAK AND SABAH)

MALAYA

SINGAPORE

BORNEO

INDONESIA

PAPUA NEW
GUINEA

Lena R.

MONGOLIA

CHINA

Yenisei R.

RUSSIA (U.S.S.R.)

TIBET

NEPAL

BHUTAN

BANGLADESH
Calcutta

Brahmaputra R.

Ganges R.

INDIA

Delhi

Bombay

SRI LANKA

tea

Kabul

AFGHANISTAN

PAKISTAN

Indus R.

Karachi

Aral Sea

Caspian Sea

IRAN

QATAR

U. ARAB
EMIRATES

OMAN

Tigris R.

Baghdad

IRAQ

KUWAIT

SAUDI
ARABIA

YEMEN
ARAB
REP.

YEMEN
P.D.R.

TURKEY

SYRIA

LEBANON

ISRAEL

JORDAN

assemble as-sem'-ble *assembles, assembled, assembling.* 1. Come together.–The children *assemble* each morning for prayers.
2. Put together.–The girls *assembled* the parts of the jigsaw puzzle.

assembly as-sem'-bly *assemblies.* 1. A meeting. –All the classes went to the *assembly*.
2. Putting together. – The *assembly* of a motor-car is done by many men working on an *assembly* line.

assign as-sign' *assigns, assigned, assigning, assignment.* 1. Give out (work to be done).– Our teacher will *assign* us our tasks for the morning.
2. Appoint.–The training cadets have been *assigned* to their places of duty. They have been told where to work.

assist as-sist' *assists, assisted, assisting.* Help. –Mary will *assist* Mother in caring for the baby.

assistance as-sist'-ance. Help or aid. – The needy family was grateful for the *assistance* given by neighbours.

assistant as-sist'-ant *assistants.* A helper; a person who helps.–The headmaster's *assistant* helps him manage the school.

associate as-so'-ci-ate *associates, associated, associating, association.* 1. Be in company (with someone); be together.–Jack does not like to *associate* with Bill.
2. Think of in connection.–I *associate* strawberries with whipped cream.

aster as'-ter *asters.* A flower with a yellow centre. *Asters* bloom in late summer. They are of various colours.

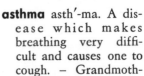

asthma asth'-ma. A disease which makes breathing very difficult and causes one to cough. – Grandmother's *asthma* is much better this winter.

astonish as-ton'-ish *astonishes, astonished, astonishing.* Amaze; fill with surprise.–When Jack looked up and saw his dog standing in the classroom doorway, he was *astonished*.

astonishing as-ton'-ish-ing. Amazing; surprising.–An *astonishing* thing happened today. Three little kittens were playing with a dog.

astray a-stray'. Away from home; wandering. –Our cat has gone *astray*. She is lost.

astronomer as-tron'-o-mer *astronomers.* A person who studies the sun, moon, stars, and other heavenly bodies.

astronomy as-tron'-o-my. The study of the sun, moon, stars, and other heavenly bodies.–The invention of the telescope made *astronomy* far easier.

asylum a-sy'-lum *asylums.* A place where people who are unable to take care of themselves, because of blindness or sickness of the mind, are cared for.

at. 1. *At* may indicate a place (where) or a time (when).–We met *at* the corner.–The sun came up *at* six o'clock.
2. In the direction of.–Bob threw a stone *at* the tree.

ate. One form of the word *eat*.–The horse *ate* his oats.

athlete ath'-lete *athletes.* A person who is skilful in some sport. – A football player is an *athlete*.

athletic ath-let'-ic. 1. Like an athlete; good at sports.–Some boys and girls are more *athletic* than others; they are better at sports.
2. Having to do with sports.–The school has a new *athletic* field.–Bob is organizing an *athletic* club.

athletics ath-let'-ics. Games and other sports that require action and strength.–Football and swimming are kinds of *athletics*.

atom at'-om *atoms, atomic.* The smallest bit or particle of which anything is made up.

atom bomb at'-om bomb *atom bombs*. The most powerful bomb ever used in warfare. A single *atom bomb* can blow up an entire city. When the *atom bomb* explodes, the atoms, or tiniest particles of the material it is made of, are broken up and changed. In this process, a tremendous amount of energy or force is released.

attach at-tach' *attaches, attached, attaching.* 1. Fasten; join.–When Tom *attaches* the string to his kite, it will be finished.
2. *Attached* to can mean fond of.–The old lady is very *attached to* her pretty cottage.

attachment at-tach-ment *attachments.* 1. Something to be attached to another object. –The vacuum cleaner has *attachments* to do different kinds of work.
2. Fondness; love.–Parents have a great *attachment* for their children.

attack at-tack' *attacks, attacked, attacking.*
1. Start a fight with.–The boxer *attacked* his opponent swiftly.
2. A use of force against a person or place.– The army started an *attack* on the city.
3. An occurrence or happening of a disease. –Mary had an *attack* of measles.

attempt at-tempt' *attempts, attempted, attempting.* 1. Try; make an effort.–Aviators seldom *attempt* to take off in thick fog.
2. A try.–Bob made an *attempt* to jump the fence.

attend at-tend' *attends, attended, attending,*
1. Be present at.–Father and Mother will *attend* the end-of-term concert.
2. Look after.–The manager of the hotel will *attend* to the dinner arrangements.
3. Go with; accompany.–Guide-dogs *attend* blind people. The dogs lead the blind people and help them find their way about.

attendance at-tend'-ance. 1. Being present.– Bob has a good record of *attendance* at school.
2. The number present.–The average class *attendance* is 30 pupils.

attention at-ten'-tion *attentions.* 1. Thought; notice.–When Jack called Father's *attention* to the smoke coming from the store, Father called the fire brigade.
2. A courtesy; a little thing done for someone.–Grandmother appreciates little *attentions*.
3. *Pay attention* means notice and think carefully about what is being said or done.– Children who *pay attention* learn quickly.

Golf   Swimming (diving)   Hockey   Rugger   Rowing   Ice skating

ATHLETICS   Javelin   Skiing   Tennis   Archery

Soccer   Sprinting   Cricket   Wrestling   Boxing

attic at'-tic *attics*. The space or room just under the roof of a house.–We have several old trunks in the *attic*.

attitude at'-ti-tude *attitudes*. One's thoughts and feelings about something; a way of looking at or dealing with.–What is your teacher's *attitude* towards the boy's laziness?

attorney at-tor'-ney *attorneys*. A lawyer; a person given legal or lawful right to act for another person.–The *Attorney*-General is the chief law-officer in the government.

attract at-tract' *attracts, attracted, attracting, attraction*. Draw, pull, get. – A horseshoe magnet *attracts* steel to itself.–Mary tried to *attract* attention by looking very sad.

auction auc'-tion *auctions, auctioned, auctioning, auctioneer*. A public sale at which people offer money for things which are finally sold to the person who will pay the most.

audible au'-di-ble *audibly*. Loud enough to be heard.–The child's voice is soft, yet *audible*.

audience au'-di-ence *audiences*. 1. A group of people watching or listening to a performance, as of a game, a cinema show, a play, etc.–Because of the rain, the *audience* at the concert was small.

2. A hearing, a chance to say what one has to say.–The mayor gave the man an *audience*.

auditorium au-di-to'-ri-um *auditoriums*. A room or space in a room for an audience, or a large group of people, to sit.–We hold our school entertainments in the *auditorium*.

auger au'-ger *augers*. A tool for making holes. –When Father built a swing for Sally, he used an *auger* to make two holes in the board for the ropes to go through.

August Au'-gust. The 8th month of the year. –*August* has 31 days.

aunt *aunts*. The sister of one's father or mother. The wives of your father's and your mother's brothers are your *aunts* by marriage.– Our *Aunt* Ann is Father's sister.

Australia Aus-tral'-ia *Australian, Australians*. The smallest continent in the world. *Australia* is an island continent located in the South Pacific. It consists of only one country, and is part of the British Commonwealth of Nations.

author au'-thor *authors*. A writer; one who makes up and writes articles, stories, poems, or books. – Robert Louis Stevenson was a famous *author*. – Who is your favourite *author*?

authority au-thor'-i-ty *authorities*. 1. The right to give orders, or to say that something shall be done.–The county council has the *authority* to close all the schools in case of bad weather.
2. A place, person or book from which information is taken.–A dictionary is a good *authority* on how to spell words.
3. The people in charge.–Jack reported to the *authorities* that he had seen some boys breaking windows at the school.

autobiography au-to-bi-og'-ra-phy *autobiographies*. A story of one person's life written by himself or herself.

autograph au'-to-graph *autographs*. The signature or name of a person in his own handwriting.–Mary's hobby is collecting *autographs* of actors and actresses and other famous people.

automatic au-to-mat'-ic *automatically*. 1. Working by itself.–Father bought an *automatic* pump to pump the water from the basement.
2. Done without thought and effort.–Breathing is *automatic*.

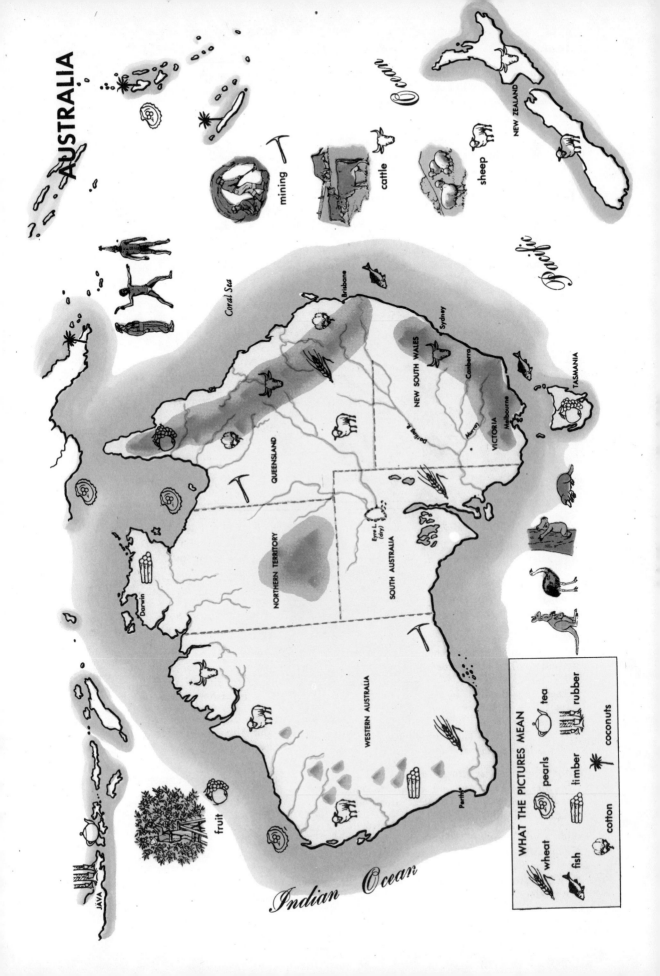

AUSTRALIA

Pacific Ocean

Indian Ocean

Coral Sea

mining

cattle

sheep

NEW ZEALAND

TASMANIA

QUEENSLAND

NEW SOUTH WALES

VICTORIA

Sydney

Brisbane

Canberra

Melbourne

Murray

Darling

NORTHERN TERRITORY

SOUTH AUSTRALIA

WESTERN AUSTRALIA

Eyre L. (dry)

Darwin

Perth

fruit

JAVA

WHAT THE PICTURES MEAN

wheat

fish

cotton

pearls

timber

tea

rubber

coconuts

automobile au'-to-mo-bile *automobiles*. A vehicle that moves unders its own power; a motor-car.–The United States produces more *automobiles* than any other country.

autumn au'-tumn. 1. The time of year between the hot weather of summer and the cold weather of winter.–Leaves fall from the trees in *autumn*.
2. One of the 4 seasons of the year, from September 21 to December 21. In *autumn* many crops are harvested. The other seasons are winter, spring, and summer.

avalanche av'-a-lanche *avalanches*. 1. A great quantity of snow, earth, etc., sliding down a mountain-side. – The *avalanche* buried the trees in the narrow valley.

2. A huge amount. – The film star received an *avalanche* of fan mail.

avenue av'-e-nue *avenues*. Roadway or drive, usually lined with trees.–The *avenue* leading to the stadium is shady in hot weather.

average av'-er-age *averages*. 1. On Monday Bob had a mark of 80 in spelling; on Tuesday he had 90. To find his *average* spelling grade for the 2 days, he added the 2 numbers together and divided by 2 (the number of days). $80 + 90 = 170$. $170 \div 2 = 85$, his *average* mark.
2. Usual; normal.–The attendance at school today is better than *average*.

aviator a'-vi-a-tor *aviators, aviation*. A man who flies an aeroplane; an aeroplane pilot.– *Aviators* must know a great deal about weather and mechanics.

avoid a-void' *avoids, avoided, avoiding*. 1. Keep away from.–Try to *avoid* bad company.
2. Keep from.–*Avoid* talking when others are talking.

await a-wait' *awaits, awaited, awaiting*. Wait for.–Mother will *await* me at the corner shop.

awake a-wake' *awakes, awoke, awaked, a-waking*. 1. Not asleep.–Baby is *awake*. She woke up.
2. Wake up.–It is hard for Bob to *awake* in the morning.

awaken a-wak'-en *awakens, awakened, awakening*. 1. Wake up.–It is hard for Bob to *awaken* in the morning.
2. Arouse.–It is easy for the scout leader to *awaken* the interest of the boys.

aware a-ware'. Conscious; knowing; noticing. –John was so interested in his reading that he was not *aware* of the time. He did not realize what time it was.

away a-way'. 1. To another place.–The family went *away* for the summer.–The dog ran *away*.
2. In or at another place. – The family is *away* now.
3. *Straight away* means at once.–When Mary cut herself, Mother put a bandage on the cut *straight away*.

awe. Fear and respect; wonder. – The girls watched the lightning with a feeling of *awe*.

awful aw'-ful *awfully*. 1. Dreadful.–An *awful* accident happened at the corner.
2. Fearful.–When the house caught fire, an *awful* feeling came over me. I was afraid.

awhile a-while'. For some time; for a while.– Father will be home *awhile* this evening.

awkward awk'-ward *awkwardly*. Clumsy. – The boy's large shoes made him *awkward*. He could not move gracefully.

awl *awls*. A pointed tool for punching holes. –Father used an *awl* to make the holes in the horse's harness.

awning awn'-ing *awnings*. A canvas cover to keep out the sun.–Father put up *awnings* at the windows.

awoke a-woke'. One form of the word *awake*. –When the baby *awoke*, she started to cry.

AUTOMOBILES

Daimler's first car, 1886

1907 Rolls Royce Silver Ghost

1912 Morris

Ford Model T coupé, 1923

coach

double-decker bus

motor scooter

pantechnicon

station waggon

land rover

tip-up lorry

fire engine

Triumph Herald

Morris Miniminor

Rolls Royce

Aston Martin

A
B
C
D
E
F
G
H
I
J
K
L
M
N
O
P
Q
R
S
T
U
V
W
X
Y
Z

axe or **ax** *axes*. A sharp-edged tool with a long handle.–The woodsman uses an *axe* to cut down trees and to chop wood.

axle ax'-le *axles*. A bar or rod to which wheels are fastened and on which they turn.

ay or **aye** (rhymes with *sky*). Yes.–If you vote *aye*, you vote yes or in favour of something.–The chairman said, 'all in favour of the motion to adjourn say *aye*.' – The sailor said, '*Ay, ay*, sir', when the captain gave him his orders.

azure az'-ure. Sky blue.–The colour of Mary's dress is *azure*.

B b

B, b *B's, b's*. The second letter of the alphabet.

baa. The cry of a sheep. – The farmer heard the *baa* of the lost sheep.

babe *babes*. A baby; an infant.–The *babe* in his mother's arms was fast asleep.

baboon ba-boon' *baboons*. A large kind of monkey with a dog-like muzzle.

baby ba'-by *babies*. 1. A very young child who is too young to walk or talk; an infant.–Our new *baby* must be fed every 4 hours.

bachelor bach'-e-lor *bachelors*. A man who has not been married.–Father's brother is still a *bachelor*. He has no wife.

back *backs, backed, backing*. 1. The part of anything that is opposite the front, as the *back* of the room, the *back* of a chair.
2. The side of the body opposite the chest.–Bob usually sleeps on his *back*.

3. Go, or make go, rear end first. – Father *backed* the car out of the garage.
4. Encourage; supply money for. – Father *backed* his brother in his shoe business.
5. In return.–My uncle will pay *back* the money Father let him have for his business.

backbone back'-bone' *backbones*. 1. The spine or main set of bones in the back of people and animals. The *backbone* is made up of many small bones.
2. Courage.–Jack has enough *backbone* to stand up for his rights. He will make sure he receives fair treatment.

background back'-ground *backgrounds*. 1. The part of a picture that seems to be behind all the main objects in the picture. – Mary painted a picture with a blue *background* to look like the sky.
2. *In the background* means in a place where one is not noticed much.–The little girl kept herself *in the background* at the party.

backward(s) back'-ward. 1. Opposite the front; towards the starting point. – The children looked *backwards* as they walked.
2. Slow in learning. – Ned is a *backward* pupil.
3. Shy. – Some girls are *backward* about playing with boys.
4. With the back first.–It is not safe to walk *backwards*.

bacon ba'-con. Meat from the sides of a pig, salted and smoked. – *Bacon* has stripes of lean and fat.–On Sunday morning, Mother cooks eggs and *bacon*.

bacteria bac-te′-ri-a. Plants that are so small they cannot be seen except through a microscope.–The doctor is trying to find the *bacteria* that cause the unusual disease.–Some kinds of *bacteria* are useful, like the *bacteria* in milk, used in making cheese.

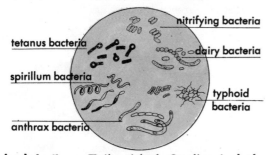

nitrifying bacteria
tetanus bacteria
dairy bacteria
spirillum bacteria
typhoid bacteria
anthrax bacteria

bad *badly*. 1. Evil, wicked.–Stealing is *bad*.–Some people are *bad*; they do evil things.
2. Unfortunate; not what is wanted.–It was too *bad* that the storm ruined the farmer's corn.
3. Severe.–Bob had a *bad* cold; but he is well now.
4. Rotten, spoiled.–This is a *bad* apple.

bade (pronounced *bad*). One form of the word *bid*.–Our guests *bade* us good-bye. They said good-bye.

badge *badges*. A sign or button that shows the wearer belongs to a certain group. – The traffic warden wore a *badge*.–Children in our class made paper *badges* which they wore to show to which class they belonged.

ARTISTS & WRITERS CONVENTION
Mr. Dodge
DELEGATE

badger badg′-er *badgers*. A grey animal that has long front claws, with which it digs holes in the ground to live in.

FLOUR

bag *bags*. 1. A sack; a deep container made of paper, cloth, or other soft material.–The grocer put the fruit in a paper *bag*.

2. A purse or hand*bag*. – Mother's *bag* is made of leather.
3. A suitcase or travelling *bag*.–The porter helped us with our *bags* at the train.

baggage bag′-gage. Trunks, suit-cases, hat boxes, etc.–On a long trip, you need several pieces of *baggage* to carry your clothes in.

bagpipe bag′-pipe *bagpipes*. A musical wind instrument, specially popular in Scotland. It has a leather windbag and pipes from which the music comes. One pipe plays the tune and the others make a soft sound which goes on at the same time.

bail *bails, bailed, bailing*. 1. Scoop or dip. – Sally watched Father *bail* the water out of the boat.
2. In cricket, the small piece of wood laid across the stumps.
3. Get someone out of jail by promising to pay a certain amount of money if the person under arrest fails to report to the court when he is sent for.
4. The money put up to get a prisoner released.–The gangster got out of jail on £300 *bail*.

bait *baits, baited, baiting*. 1. Food used to tempt fish when you want to catch them.–Worms and small insects are sometimes used for *bait* on the fishhook.
2. Anything used to lure an animal or person into being caught.
3. Put *bait* on.–Mother *baited* the mousetrap with a piece of bacon.

bake *bakes, baked, baking*. 1. Cook in an oven.–Mary will *bake* cakes today.–Grandmother *baked* a ham.
2. Dry and harden by heat.–Vases, bricks and tiles are *baked* in a kind of large oven called a kiln.

B C D E F G H I J K L M N O P Q R S T U V W X Y Z

B
C
D
E
F
G
H
I
J
K
L
M
N
O
P
Q
R
S
T
U
V
W
X
Y
Z

baker bak′-er *bakers*. A person who makes biscuits, Bread, pies, etc., to sell.—Jack went to the *baker's* to buy a coffee cake for tea-time.

bakery bak′-er-y *bakeries*. A shop where biscuits, bread and other baked goods are made and sold.—Jack likes to stand and look at the *bakery* counter.

baking bak′-ing *bakes, baked, baking*. 1. One form of the word *bake*.—Mother is *baking* a yellow birthday cake for Sally.
2. Things baked.—Jack asked Father whether he liked Mother's *baking* or Grandmother's *baking* better.

balance bal′-ance *balances, balanced, balancing*. 1. Keep weight, amount, force, etc., equal or the same on both sides of anything.—When the clown walked the tight-rope, he carried an umbrella to *balance* himself.—Mother made some pale yellow curtains to *balance* the dark colours in the living room.
2. It is hard to keep your *balance* on a bicycle when you ride very slowly.—Mary loses her *balance* when she walks in Mother's high-heeled shoes. She falls over.
3. The rest, or remainder; what is left. — Mother paid the grocer £2 on his bill today and will pay the *balance* tomorrow.

balcony bal′-co-ny *balconies*. A platform with a wall or railing around it, which sticks out from a building, or into a room or theatre.—The children sat in the *balcony* of the theatre.—There was a balcony outside our window in the hotel.

bald. 1. Without hair.—Father's head is growing *bald*. He is getting *bald*-headed.
2. Bare, or without trees or plants.—The mountain tops are *bald*. The rocks show pink above the point where the trees stop growing.

bale *bales, baled, baling*. A bundle of material pressed closely together. — Cotton and wool are made into *bales* to be shipped.

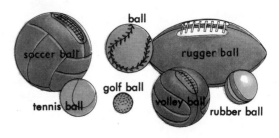

balk *balks, balked, balking*. Stop short and refuse to go on.—Mules are stubborn and often *balk*.—Jack *balked* at taking violin lessons.

ball *balls*. 1. Any round thing.—The kitten is a little *ball* of fur.—Jack bought a bag of lemon *balls*.—Grandmother winds her wool into a *ball*.—The earth is a *ball*.
2. A round object used in playing tennis, foot*ball*, cricket, basket*ball*, golf, etc. Rugger-*balls* are oval in shape.

ball

soccer ball

rugger ball

golf ball

tennis ball

volley ball

rubber ball

3. A game played with a *ball*, especially 'catch'.—Bob and Jack play *ball* every Saturday.
4. A dancing party.—Cinderella went to the *ball* in a handsome carriage.

ballast bal′-last. Something heavy, such as sand or rocks, to give balance. When a ship is not fully loaded with freight, *ballast* is put in it to keep it steady, or in position. *Ballast* is used in balloons, also.

balloon bal-loon′ *balloons*. A bag filled with heated air, or a gas lighter than air, so that it will rise into the air when set free. Some toy *balloons* have cold air in them, and do not rise.

ballot bal'-lot *ballots*. A voting ticket used in elections. On it you mark the names of the people you want to elect.

balm *balms*. An ointment or medicine that eases and soothes pain.–When Jack strained his back, Father rubbed it with *balm*.–Mary put *balm* on her sunburn.

balmy balm'-y *balmier, balmiest*. Mild, warm, soft, gentle.–A *balmy* breeze came in the window.–The weather is *balmy* in June.

balsam bal'-sam. 1. A sticky substance that comes from trees and is used in making balms, or soothing medicines.
2. A common flowering plant also known as the garden *balsam*.

balustrade bal'-us-trade *balustrades*. A row of balusters; short upright posts supporting a railing.–The terrace was separated from the garden by a *balustrade*.

bamboo bam-boo'. A stout, hollow grass that grows very thick and high. *Bamboo* grows in very hot places. The shoots of the *bamboo* are eaten as a vegetable in some countries.

bamboo   banana

banana ba-na'-na *bananas*. A long fruit with a heavy yellow or red skin. *Bananas* grow in large bunches on trees in warm climates. The part of the *banana* which you eat is soft and has a rich, creamy colour.

band *bands, banded, banding*. 1. A flat strip, or long, narrow piece. – Mother trimmed Mary's new dress with a *band* of black velvet.
2. A stripe or long, narrow marking.–A zebra is light-coloured, with black *bands* around his body.
3. A group.–While on our holiday, we saw a *band* of gypsies wandering through the country.
4. Gather in a group.–Gypsies *band* together to travel.
5. A group of musicians who play music together.–Instruments that you blow, or wind instruments, and drums, are generally played in *bands*.

bandage band'-age *bandages, bandaged, bandaging*. 1. A band or narrow strip of cloth.– When Bob cut his finger, the school nurse put a *bandage* round it to keep it clean.

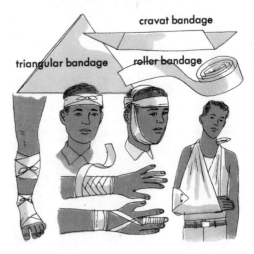

cravat bandage

triangular bandage   roller bandage

2. Put a *bandage* on.–Jack *bandaged* the puppy's hurt tail with his handkerchief.

bandit ban'-dit *bandits*. A robber, especially one in the woods or desert.–Long ago in the Wild West, many stage-coaches were held up by *bandits*.

B C D E F G H I J K L M N O P Q R S T U V W X Y Z

bang *bangs, banged, banging.* 1. A loud, sharp, sudden noise.–The car door blew shut with a *bang*.
2. Slam.–In the middle of the night someone *banged* the barn door.
3. An explosion.–When we heard the *bang* of a rifle, we knew someone was hunting near by.
4. Hit.–It is not polite to *bang* your plate with your cutlery.

banish ban'-ish *banishes, banished, banishing.* Force to leave one's home country or regular place.–The king *banished* the duke who had tried to betray him.–The teacher *banished* Bill from the classroom for squirting ink at Mary.

banister ban'-is-ter *banisters.* A hand railing along a flight of stairs. –Prevent accidents by taking hold of the *banister* when you go up or down stairs.

banjo ban'-jo *banjos.* A simple musical instrument with 5 to 9 strings, which is played with the fingers.

bank *banks.* 1. A long pile.–The children made a *bank* of sand along the beach.
2. The ground on the sides of a river, lake, stream, etc.–While fishing, Father slipped and fell off the *bank* into the water.
3. A business company which keeps people's money for them, lends money for a charge, etc. The *bank* makes money with the money which the people put in, or deposit.

4. A special container for putting money in to save.–Mary has a small china *bank* in the shape of a pig. She puts pennies in it.

banker bank'-er *bankers.* A man whose business or work is running a bank.

banner ban'-ner *banners.* A flag, pennant, or streamer, with pictures, writing, etc., on it.–The Boy Scouts carried many *banners* in the parade.–'The Star-Spangled *Banner*' is the national anthem of the United States.

banquet ban'-quet *banquets.* A feast, rich meal, or big dinner.–My uncle went to a *banquet* in honour of the mayor.

bantam ban'-tam *bantams.* A type of small domestic fowl.

banter ban'-ter *banters, bantered, bantering.*
1. Tease.–The children *bantered* the teacher.
2. Playful teasing. – Mother laughed at the children's *banter*.

baptize bap-tize' *baptizes, baptized, baptizing, baptism.* 1. Make a member of one of the Christian churches by sprinkling with or dipping into water, as a part of a religious service.
2. Give a name to a person at the time he is *baptized* or received into a church.

bar *bars, barred, barring.* 1. A long, solid piece of steel or wood.–Grandfather put a *bar* under the box to lift it.

2. A cake or piece (of something).–Mother bought 3 *bars* of soap.–Jack bought a chocolate *bar*.
3. A band or stripe.–There was a long *bar* of light across the sky at sunset.–The addition of a *bar* to the Victoria Cross shows that the wearer has won the medal twice.
4. A bank of sand at the mouth of a river.– A ship ran aground on the *bar*.
5. Anything that hinders or keeps back.–A tree across the road, keeping back the cars that wanted to pass, would be a *bar*.
6. An up-and-down line on a music staff to mark the measures, The double *bars* at the end of the music tell that the music has ended.
7. A place in a courtroom *barred* off by a railing, where prisoners stand.–The prisoner stood at the *bar*.
8. Forbid; keep out or away. – John was *barred* from the team because he was under weight.–A tree *barred* the way.

9. A long, high counter where drinks are served.–The boys gathered at the milk *bar*.

barb *barbs, barbed.* A short, sharp point.–The fence had *barbs* on the wire to keep the livestock in.–The arrows which the Indian hunter used had sharp *barbs* on them. –Grandmother's crochet hook has a *barb* on it.–Fishhooks are *barbed*.

barbarian bar-ba'-ri-an *barbarians.* A savage; a member of a tribe of people who are not civilized. *Barbarians* live mainly by hunting.

barbecue bar'-be-cue *barbecues, barbecued, barbecuing.* 1. A feast at which a cow, hog, or other animal is roasted whole.–The man held a great *barbecue* on his ranch.
2. Roast over an open fire.–Some restaurants and shops *barbecue* poultry and meat.

barber bar'-ber *barbers.* A person who cuts and shampoos hair, shaves men, and trims their beards or moustaches.

bard *bards.* A minstrel-poet in olden times, who composed and sang verses for special occasions, like the celebration of a victory.– In Wales, poets are still known as *bards*.– Shakespeare was called the *Bard of Avon*.

bare *bares, bared, baring.* 1. Uncovered.–When the coffin went by, the men stood with *bare* heads.
2. Without leaves.–In winter, the maple trees are *bare*.
3. Empty.–The cupboard was *bare*.

4. Uncover.–When the coffin went by, the men *bared* their heads.

barefoot bare'-foot. Without shoes, socks or stockings on.–Bob likes to go *barefoot* in hot weather.

bareheaded bare'-head'-ed. With the head bare; without a hat.

barely bare'-ly. Scarcely. – We had *barely* enough sugar to bake the cake.

bargain bar'-gain *bargains, bargained, bargaining.* 1. An agreement.–John and his father made a *bargain*. John said he would mow the lawn once a week, and his father said he would pay John 10p.
2. Something good bought for a low price.– Mother's dress was a *bargain*. She paid less for it than it was normally worth.
3. Argue about price. – The gypsy tried to *bargain* with the pedlar. She tried to make him lower his price.

barge *barges.* A large, flat-bottomed boat towed or pushed by another boat. – Coal and many other bulk products are shipped down rivers and canals, and also along coasts, on *barges*.

baritone bar'-i-tone *baritones.* 1. A part in music to be sung by a man whose voice is not as low as a bass and not as high as a tenor.
2. A singer with a voice suitable for this part.

bark *barks, barked, barking.* 1. The hard outside covering of a tree.

2. A sharp, loud sound made by a dog.
3. Make a short, sharp cry, as a dog.–Some dogs *bark* at all strangers.

B
C
D
E
F
G
H
I
J
K
L
M
N
O
P
Q
R
S
T
U
V
W
X
Y
Z

barley bar'-ley. The seed or grain of a grass-like plant.–Mother puts pearl *barley* in soup.–*Barley* is good to eat.

barn *barns*. A large building on a farm to keep farm animals and their feed in.

barn and barnyard

barnyard barn'-yard *barnyards*. A yard or space around a barn.–Sometimes the cows and horses come out of the barn into the *barnyard*.

barrel bar'-rel *barrels*. 1. A large container made of curved slats or staves that are held together with wooden or steel bands. A *barrel* is flat on the ends and a little larger in the middle than at the ends. – The farmer keeps oil in a large *barrel*.

2. The long metal tube of a gun, through which the bullet passes.–Father's shotgun has a long, shiny *barrel*.

barter bar'-ter *barters, bartered, bartering*. 1. Trading things without the use of money.–Before the use of money people exchanged what they had for what they needed by *bar-ter*.
2. Trade.–The farmer *bartered* his cow for a plough.

base *bases, based, basing*. The bottom part of anything, which holds up the rest of the structure.–The house stands on its *base* of stone. –The *base* of the lamp is made of brass.
2. One of the 4 stopping places for a runner in baseball or rounders.–The player reached third *base* before he was put out.
3. A place to which a ship, aeroplane, etc., returns for supplies, repairs, orders, etc.–The bomber returned to its *base* safely.
4. Build, set up (on something).–The man who *bases* his business on honesty and fairness is likely to succeed.

baseball base'-ball' *baseballs*. 1. An American

game played by 2 teams of 9 persons each, on a diamond-shaped field with 4 bases. – *Baseball* is played with a ball and bat.
2. The ball used in playing *baseball*.

basement base'-ment *basements*. The lowest part of a building; the part below the level of the ground.–Our washing-machine is in the *basement* of our new house.

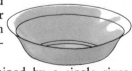

bashful bash'-ful *bashfully, bashfulness*. Shy or timid.–The baby is *bashful*. He doesn't like to be noticed.

basin ba'-sin *basins*. 1. A bowl, not very deep but wide at the top. – Mother washes the vegetables in a *basin*.–A bowl fixed to the wall or floor and equipped with water taps and a drain is called a wash-*basin*.
2. All the land drained by a single river.–The Mississippi River has a large river *basin*.

basket bas'-ket *baskets*. A container made of woven grasses, reeds, ropes, etc. – Grandmother keeps her thread in a sewing *basket*.

fruit basket

laundry basket

grass basket

wire basket

Indian basket

market basket

basketball bas'-ket-ball *basketballs*. 1. A game played with a large, round, leather-covered ball filled with air. At each end of the playing space is a bottomless basket placed high over the heads of the players. They try to throw the ball into the basket. The game is played indoors by 2 teams of 5 persons.
2. The ball used in playing *basketball*.

basketful bas'-ket-ful *basketfuls*. As much or as many as a basket will hold. – Grandfather brought us a *basketful* of apples.

bass (rhymes with *case*). 1. The lowest part in music. – Some men sing *bass*.
2. Very low in pitch; deep in sound. – My father has a *bass* voice.

bass (rhymes with *mass*). A kind of food fish found in fresh or salt water, which is much valued by sportsmen.

baste *bastes, basted, basting*. 1. Sew together by hand with long, loose stitches. – Before Mother stitched her dress on the sewing-machine, she *basted* it.
2. Drop melted fat over roasting meat. *Basting* a joint or a fowl keeps it from becoming dry and hard on the outside.

bat *bats, batted, batting*. 1. A strong wooden stick for hitting balls or other objects. – John hit the ball with the *bat*. – Cricket *bats* are made of willow because this wood is both strong and flexible. – The expression *to carry one's bat* means that an opening batsman plays through the entire innings without being got out.
2. Try to hit the ball in cricket or baseball. – It is Bob's turn to *bat*.
3. A short-furred animal that flies at night. *Bats* look like mice with wings. Some *bats* eat fruit; others live on insects.

bath *baths*. 1. A cleaning or washing of the body with water. – Every day Mother gives the baby a *bath*.
2. Water for a *bath*. – Mary helps Mother get the *bath* ready for Baby.
3. Give a *bath* to; wash. – Mother will *bath* the baby this afternoon.
4. Take a *bath*; wash the body. – Bob *baths* every day.

bathe *bathes, bathed, bathing*. Go into water for pleasure. – It is fun to *bathe* in a lake or in the ocean.

bathing hut bath'-ing hut *bathing huts*. A small building on the beach in which clothes can be changed for bathing. – During the summer holidays we hired a *bathing hut* for the season.

bathing suit

bathing suit bath'-ing suit *bathing suits*. A short, light garment worn for swimming. – Jane bought a new *bathing suit* for the summer.

bathroom bath'-room *bathrooms*. A room with a bath; more often, a room with bath or shower, wash basin, and lavatory.

baton ba'-ton *batons*. 1. A short stick carried by a high-ranking officer in the army.–The Field Marshal carries a *baton*.
2. A slender stick used by the conductor of an orchestra to beat time.–The conductor raised his *baton* and the concert began.

battalion bat-tal'-ion *battalions*. Part of an infantry regiment in the army. A *battalion* is made up of several companies and is usually about 1000 men. Is is commanded by a lieutenant-colonel.

batter bat'-ter *batters, battered, battering*. 1. A mixture of flour, eggs, milk, sugar, butter, etc.–Mother is beating the *batter*. When the *batter* is baked, it will be a cake.–Some *batters* make pancakes, waffles, etc.
2. Hit or pound on hard and often. – The waves *battered* the old dock to pieces.–The policemen *battered* at the door.

battery bat'-ter-y *batteries*. 1. A device that makes or stores electricity by chemical changes of the materials inside it.–A motor-car has a *battery* which makes the lights burn and helps start the motor.

2. A group of guns.–When the command was given, the *battery* opened fire.

battle bat'-tle *battles, battled, battling*. 1. A fight between 2 armed forces.–Our army won a big *battle*.

2. Fight.–Doctors *battle* against disease.
3. A contest. – The spelling bee was quite a *battle*.

battlefield bat'-tle-field *battlefields*. A place where a battle or fight between armies takes place.

battleship bat'-tle-ship *battleships*. A warship of the largest class, with powerful guns on it.–*Battleships*, rarely used today, carry thousands of men in the crew.

bawl *bawls, bawled, bawling*. 1. A loud cry.– We heard the boy's *bawl* for help when he became trapped by the tide.
2. Cry loudly.–The calf *bawled* when he was taken from the mother cow.

bay *bays, bayed, baying*. 1. A broad body of water partly surrounded by land.

2. Reddish-brown. – The farmer has a *bay* horse.
3. Bark or howl, as a dog.–The hunters could hear the *baying* of the hounds in the forest.

B C D E F G H I J K L M N O P Q R S T U V W X Y Z

bayonet bay'-o-net *bayonets*. A kind of short sword fastened to the barrel of a rifle.

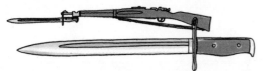

bay-window *bay-windows*. A window made of smaller windows which stand out from the wall of a building. A *bay-window* lets in more light.

bazaar ba-zaar' *bazaars*. 1. A sale of things donated to raise funds for a church, a charity, etc.–The church is having a Christmas *bazaar*.
2. A place where many kinds of things are sold.–At a *bazaar* Uncle Jim bought a beautiful oriental rug from the man who made it.

be *am, is, are, was, were, been, being*. You will *be* late unless you hurry.–John can *be* a good boy if he tries.–The word *be* has many forms.

beach *beaches, beached, beaching*. 1. A flat, sandy shore along an ocean, lake, or river.–When we go to the seaside we often play on the *beach* all day long.
2. Drag a boat on to the *beach*.–After the boys had rowed round the bay they *beached* their boat.

beachcomber beach'-comber *beachcombers*. A lazy, shiftless person who spends most of his time roaming around wharfs and beaches.–The *beachcomber* lived in a flimsy hut of sticks and leaves.

beacon bea'-con *beacons*. 1. A signal fire or light; a sign which marks a street-crossing. The coming of the Armada was signalled by a chain of *beacons*, lit on the top of each high hill.
2. A light along the shore to guide ships.–Ships at sea depend upon *beacons* to keep them from running on to the rocks at night.

bead *beads, beaded, beading*. 1. A round ball of wood, pressed paper, glass, metal, etc., with a hole through it for a string. *Beads* are usually brightly coloured. – Children like to string *beads* into necklaces.
3. Trim with *beads*.–The dressmaker will *bead* the front of the dress.
4. A drop.–Small *beads* of dew settled on the flowers during the night.

beagle bea'-gle *beagles*. A kind of dog used for hunting small game.–The *beagle* chased the rabbit.

beak *beaks*. The long, pointed part extending out from a bird's mouth. Birds eat with their *beaks*.

beam *beams, beamed, beaming*. 1. A ray or line (of light).–We saw the aeroplane in the searchlight's *beam*.

2. Shine.–The moon *beams* over the hill-top.
3. Smile.–Bob *beamed* as he read the good news.

4. A strong bar that supports a floor.–The carpenter fastened the floor of the house to long wooden *beams*.

B
C
D
E
F
G
H
I
J
K
L
M
N
O
P
Q
R
S
T
U
V
W
X
Y
Z

bean *beans.* A vegetable plant that grows seeds in pods. The seeds are good to eat, and so are the pods of some *beans,* when young and tender.

bear *bears, bore, borne, bearing.* 1. A large, hairy animal that has a very short tail and large, flat paws. There are several kinds: the polar *bear,* which is white; the black *bear;* and the grizzly *bear,* which is greyish or brownish, and sometimes very fierce.

2. Produce.–Apple trees *bear* apples. – Cherry trees *bear* cherries.

3 Carry.–Father *bears* the responsibility for supporting his family.

4. *Bear on* may mean to have to do with.– The facts which the witness gave did not *bear on* the case. They had nothing to do with it.

5. Press.–*Bear* down on the door knob and the door will open easily.

beard *beards.* 1. The hair that grows on a man's chin and face.– Great-grandfather had a long, grey *beard.*
2. The long, hair-like straws on the heads of grain. – Wheat, oats, and other grains have *beards.*

bearer *bear'-er bearers.* A carrier; one who holds or carries something. – Bob was the *bearer* of the torch in the midnight procession.–The bank paid the money to the *bearer* of the cheque.

bearing *bear'-ing bearings.* 1. One form of the word *bear.*–The fruit trees are not *bearing* much fruit this year.
2. A relation, something to do with (something else).–The statements which the witness made had no *bearing* on the case. They had nothing to do with it.
3. Way or direction.–The fireman lost his *bearings* in the thick smoke. He did not know where he was.

beast *beasts, beastly.* 1. A 4-footed animal.
2. An evil or very coarse person is sometimes called a *beast.*

beastly *beast'-ly.* Behaving in an unpleasant, disagreeable way.–Mother told Jack not to be *beastly* to his younger sister.

beat *beats, beaten, beating.* 1. Whip; hit; thrash.–The bad boy *beat* his dog. He hit the dog again and again.
2. Whip.–Mother *beat* the cake batter until it was smooth. She stirred it with a whipping motion.
3. Defeat.–Our cricket team can *beat* all the other teams in our school.
4. A throbbing sound.–The doctor listened to the *beat* of the baby's heart.–We heard the *beat* of the Indian's drums in the distance.
5. An accent or count in music.–In this piece of music there are 4 *beats* to the bar.
6. A route, or round of duties.–John met a policeman walking his *beat.*

beaten *beat'-en.* One form of the word *beat.*– The marks on the horse's back showed that it had been *beaten.*

beater *beat'-er beaters.* A person or tool that beats, especially a kitchen utensil for beating eggs, whipping cream, and mixing things.

beating *beat'-ing.* One form of the word *beat.* –Mr Jones gave his dog a *beating.*–Father is *beating* the rug to get the dust out of it.

beautiful *beau'-ti-ful beautifully.* 1. Lovely to look at, very pretty.–Mary has a *beautiful* hat.
2. Producing pleasant feelings.–Our teacher read a *beautiful* poem.–Birds have *beautiful* songs.–Music has *beautiful* sounds.

beautify *beau -ti-fy beautifies, beautified, beautifying.* Make beautiful.–You can *beautify* your appearance by keeping your hair combed nicely.–New curtains *beautify* the living-room.

beauty *beau'-ty beauties.* I. Loveliness; prettiness; a quality that produces pleasant feelings.–Grandmother's garden is a place of *beauty.*
2. A lovely or beautiful person or thing.– She was considered the *beauty* of her time.– Bob's new bicycle was a *beauty.*

beaver bea'-ver *beavers*. A brown-furred animal that lives in ponds and streams, and is about 2 feet long. It has a broad, flat tail. Its fur is used for coats and hats. *Beavers* cut down trees to build their homes and make dams.

became be-came'. One form of the word *become*.–The weather *became* cold during the night.

because be-cause'. For the reason that.–Mary could not go to the party, *because* she had to take care of the baby.

beckon beck'-on *beckons, beckoned, beckoning*. Signal.–The teacher *beckoned* to John by nodding her head.

become be-come' *becomes, became, becoming*. 1. Come to be.–If it *becomes* warmer tomorrow, we will have a picnic.
2. Look well on; suit.–Red hats do not *become* red-headed people.
3. *Become of* means happen to.–What has *become of* John's pet?

becoming be-com'-ing. 1. One form of the word *become*.–As it is *becoming* late, I must go.
2. Suitable; attractive.–Mary wears a very *becoming* hat. It is suitable for her.

bed *beds*. 1. A padded piece of furniture to lie or sleep on.
2. A small piece of ground planted with plants.–Grandmother has a pansy *bed*.

3. The bottom of a body of water. – The river's *bed* is sandy.
4. A sleeping place.–The farmer made a *bed* of straw for his cattle.

bedding bed'-ding. Blankets, bedspreads, quilts, sheets and other things used on beds.

bedroom bed'-room *bedrooms*. A room with beds for sleeping.

bedtime bed'-time. Time to retire or go to bed. –Mary's *bedtime* is nine o'clock.

bee *bees*. A small insect which has 4 gauzy wings. The front wings are larger than the back wings. *Bees* sting people only to protect themselves. *Bees*, like ants, live in colonies. Some *bees* make honey.

beech *beeches*. A tree with a light grey bark. The wood of the *beech* tree is very hard. The tree bears 3-cornered nuts that are good to eat. They are called *beech*nuts.

beef. The meat of a cow, steer, or bull. – For dinner Mother cooked roast *beef*.

beehive bee'-hive *beehives*. A box or small house built for bees to live in.–Some bees live and make honey in a *beehive*.

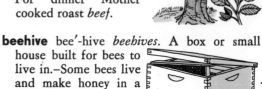

been. One form of the word *be*.–It has *been* a long time since I saw you.–We have *been* waiting 15 minutes for you.

beer. A fermented, bubbling drink which has malt and hops in it.

beet *beets*. A vegetable with a large red or white root. The root of the red *beet* (*beet*root) is cooked with the skin on, to keep the colour in. The leaves are sometimes cooked and eaten, too. Some sugar is made from sugar *beets*, which have white roots.

B
C D E F G H I J K L M N O P Q R S T U V W X Y Z

beetle bee'-tle *beetles*. An insect with 4 wings. One pair of wings forms a hard covering over the other 2 to protect them when the *beetle* is not flying. Some *beetles* cannot fly. Ladybirds are *beetles*.

before be-fore'. 1. Earlier than.–John arrived *before* Bob did.
2. At any time in the past.–We never played ball *before*.
3. In front of.–The guide dog walked *before* the blind man.

beforehand be-fore'-hand. Earlier or before the time.–When we had our party, Mother prepared the lunch *beforehand*.

beg *begs, begged, begging*. Ask; ask again and again.–The dog *begs* for food by barking.– Bob *begged* Mother for money to go to a show.

began be-gan'. One form of the word *begin*.– When Baby fell down, she *began* to cry.

beggar beg'-gar *beggars*. A person who begs or asks for money and other things; a very poor person who does not work for his own living.–In a large city you can see many *beggars*.

begin be-gin' *begins, began, begun, beginning*. Start.–If you *begin* your work now, you will be finished in time for supper.

beginner be-gin'ner *beginners*. A person trying to do something for the first time.–Mary has taken lessons at the piano for a long time, but Bob is just a *beginner*.–You were a *beginner* in school when you went for the first time.

beginning be-gin'-ning *beginnings*. The start or first part.–We arrived at the picture show just in time for the *beginning*. – John started the book at the *beginning*.

begonia be-go'-ni-a *begonias*. A plant with shiny leaves that are usually red or green. *Begonias* can have red, white, pink or yellow blossoms.

begun be-gun'. One form of the word *begin*.– The flowers have *begun* to bloom.

behave be-have' *behaves, behaved, behaving*.
1. Act; do.–Some children *behave* well, and some *behave* badly.
2. Act properly.– Mother said to Bob, 'Why don't you *behave*?'

behaviour be-hav'-iour. Actions; the way one acts.–Mary's *behaviour* is excellent; she is polite.

behind be-hind'. 1. At the back of.–The farmer put his plough *behind* the barn.
2. Late.–The milkman is *behind* with his milk delivery.

behold be-hold' *beholds, beheld, beholding*. Look at; see. – *Behold* the sun peeping through the clouds.

being be'-ing *beings*. 1. Existence.–When oil was found here, a town came into *being*. It began.
2. A human *being* is a man, woman, or child. –There were a thousand *beings* in the town.

belfry bel'-fry *belfries*. A tower or small room built for a bell, high up on a church roof or other building.

belief be-lief' *beliefs*. 1. Anything we believe as true.–Small children often have a *belief* in magic.
2. An opinion.–It was the teacher's *belief* that Jack would pass if he worked hard.
3. Faith or trust.–The men expressed their *belief* in their leader.

believe be-lieve' *believes, believed, believing*.
1. Have faith or trust (in).–We *believe* in our leader.
2. Think; hold the opinion.–I *believe* that the boy is honest.
3. Accept as true.–The teacher *believes* the excuse Bob gave for being late.

bell *bells.* I. A cup-like instrument, usually made of a mixture of tin and other metals, with a 'tongue' hanging inside. When the *bell* is shaken, the tongue strikes against the inside, making a musical tone. Some *bells* can be played upon to make tunes.

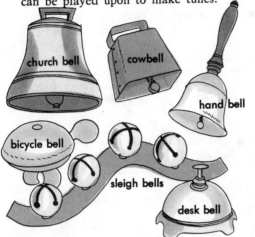

2. Any device for making a ringing sound.—The door-*bell* works by electricity.

bellow bel'-low *bellows, bellowed, bellowing.*
1. A loud roar or cry.—We heard the *bellow* of the animals at the zoo.
2. Make a loud roar.—Oxen *bellow.*

bellows bel'-lows. A device for making a strong gust of air. The bag-pipe and the accordion have *bellows* to help make musical sounds. *Bellows* take in air, then blow it out when squeezed. In olden times *bellows* were used to blow air into a fire to make it burn more quickly.

belly bel'-ly *bellies.* The lower front part of a person's body. The under-side of an animal's body is its *belly.*—Our kitten is black, with white chin and *belly* and white paws.

belong be-long' *belongs, belonged, belonging.*
1. Be owned by.—This pencil *belongs* to me. It is mine.
2. Be a member of.—Father *belongs* to the Men's Club.
3. Have as its right or proper place.—Jack's hat *belongs* in the cupboard.

belongings be-long'-ings. Things one owns; property.—We took all our *belongings* out of our desks when the term ended.—Mother sewed Jack's name on all his *belongings* when he went to camp.

beloved be-loved' or be-lov'-ed. 1. Loved.—Baby is the most *beloved* member of the family.
2. One who is loved.—Grandmother said to me. 'Good night, *beloved.*'

below be-low'. 1. Under, farther down than, lower than. – Hang this picture *below* the other one. Let the other hang above it.
2. To a lower deck on a ship.—When the third mate had stood his watch, he went *below.*

belt *belts.* 1. A band or narrow strip of leather, cloth, metal, etc., worn about the waist.

2. In machinery, a broad leather loop placed around 2 wheels that are some distance apart, to make the wheels turn together.

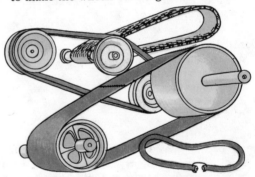

3. A broad area where a certain product is grown, or which has a particular climate, etc. –The farmer lives in the corn *belt,* a region where much corn is grown.

bench *benches.* 1. A long seat.—We sat on the *bench* in the park.

2. A long table to work on, sometimes with drawers for keeping tools in.—Father has a work*bench* in the garage.

bend *bends, bent, bending.* 1. A curve or turn. –The train goes slowly around the *bend* in the railway lines.
2. Curve or become crooked.—The nail may *bend* unless you hit it squarely on the head.
3. Stoop.—The gardener had to *bend* over to sow the seeds.

beneath be-neath'. Below, under, lower than. –The flowers were planted *beneath* the dining-room windows.–The small picture hangs *beneath* the larger one.

benefit ben'-e-fit *benefits, benefited, benefiting.*
1. Help, be good for.–The doctor said a long rest would *benefit* Mother.–The sunshine will *benefit* the children.
2. Be helped.–The farmers will *benefit* by the new road.–The children will *benefit* by the sunshine.
3. A show to raise money to help a particular group of people, etc.–The children gave a *benefit* for the orphanage.
4. Use, advantage.–The camp has the *benefit* of a lake near by.–The school children have the *benefit* of a new library.

bent. One form of the word *bend.*–The children *bent* the wire in the fence so that it touched the ground.–The wrecked car had two *bent* mudguards.

beret (pronounced be-ray) be-ret' *berets.* A soft, round cap. – Pictures of artists sometimes show them wearing *berets* and floppy bow ties.

berry ber'-ry *berries.* A small fruit with many seeds. There are many kinds of *berries*, such as rasp*berries*, straw*berries*, black*berries*, and goose*berries*. *Berries* usually grow on low bushes.

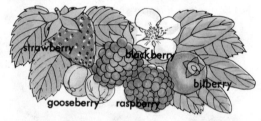

strawberry blackberry bilberry gooseberry raspberry

berth *berths.* A bunk or bed hung against a wall.–A person who travels at night on a ship or train may sleep in a *berth*. The upper *berth* is above the lower one. One needs a ladder to get into the upper *berth*.

beside be-side'. At the side of; close to.–A spider sat *beside* Little Miss Muffet.

besides be-sides'. In addition to; other than; too.–*Besides* these problems, we must work out those on page 10.–We read pages 10 and 11 *besides* page 9.–We have a lot of rabbits *besides* the ones in this pen.

best. One form of the word *good.* 1. Better than any other.–Mary is the *best* writer in the class.–The first apple Bob ate was good, the second was better, and the third was *best* of all.
2. *Get the best of* means to defeat.–Bob will *get the best of* him at wrestling.

bet *bets, bet, betting.* 1. An agreement to pay or give something to someone else, if he turns out to be right about a thing and you are wrong.–The children made a *bet* about the game.
2. Make or offer to make such an agreement. –Mary *bet* £1 that John's team would win; Bob *bet* £1 that it would lose. John's team won, so Bob paid Mary.

betray be-tray' *betrays, betrayed, betraying.*
1. Be false to; give away (a person, secret, etc.). – Bob would never *betray* a secret.
2. Show what was being hidden; indicate.–Father's smile *betrayed* that he was joking.

better bet'-ter. One form of the word *good.*–The first book I read was good, but the second was *better*. It was more interesting.–The medicine made Mother feel *better*.

between be-tween'. 1. There are 6 hours *between* noon and six o'clock.
2. Separating. – The fence *between* the 2 gardens was made of wire. – There are 10 houses *between* John's house and ours.
3. Father divided the money *between* the 2 boys. He gave each of them a share.
4. Joining.–There is good friendship *between* us.

beverage bev'-er-age *beverages.* Something to drink.–*Beverages* are usually listed separately on a menu.

beware be-ware'. Be careful.–*Beware* of fire or you may be burned. Keep away from fire. –*Beware* of fast-moving traffic along the main road.

beyond be-yond'. 1. On the other side of; farther than.–We stopped at a farm-house a mile *beyond* the city.–The baby tried to get the cup, but it was *beyond* her reach.– *Beyond* the mountains the sun is still shining.
2. Later than.–Do not stay *beyond* 4 o'clock.

bib *bibs*. A napkin fastened about a child's neck. – Mother put a *bib* on the baby so that she would not soil her dress at supper.

Bible Bi'-ble *Bibles*. The book of sacred writings of the Christian and Jewish religions. The *Bible* is divided into 2 parts; the Old Testament, used by Christians and Jews; and the New Testament, used by Christians only.

bicycle bi'-cy-cle *bicycles*. A vehicle with 2 wheels, handle-bars to guide it with, a seat, and 2 pedals to make it go.

girl's bicycle

boy's bicycle

bid *bids, bade, bid, bidden, bidding.* 1. Tell.– Always *bid* your mother good-bye before you start for school.
2. Order or command.–I *bid* you to obey the law.
3. Offer to pay. John *bid* 20p for the cricket bat.
4. The amount of money offered. My *bid* for the ball was 5p.
5. Invite.–John *bade* us come to the party.

big *bigger, biggest.* Large; great in size.–Our dog caught a *big* rat.–Once Baby was small; now she is *big*.

bill *bills*. 1. The beak or hard pointed mouth of a bird.– Birds use their *bills* to pick up food.

2. A written notice or statement telling how much is owed.–The milkman left Mother a *bill* for £1.
3. A suggestion for a law.–The new *bill* was presented to Parliament, and became law.

billet bil'-let *billets, billeted, billeting.* 1. Arrange for soldiers or other groups of people to live privately with other people for a certain length of time. – During the war many children from big towns were *billeted* with families in the country.
2. A temporary home or headquarters used in a time of emergency.–The soldier's *billet* was in the home of the village constable.

billiards bill'-iards. A game for 2 people played on a smooth, oblong, cloth-covered table, which has rubber cushions along the sides. 3 ivory billiard-balls are used, and the players try to knock the balls into the 6 pockets with long sticks called cues.–After dinner we all went into the *billiard*-room to play *billiards*.

billion bil'-lion *billions*. The number represented by 1 followed by 12 noughts. There are a million millions in a *billion*.
1,000 is one thousand.
1,000,000 is one million.
1,000,000,000,000 is one *billion*.

billow bil'-low *billows*. 1. A large, smooth wave of water.–We sat by the ocean and watched the *billows* rise and fall.

2. A wave.–*Billows* of smoke rose from the big fire.

bin *bins*. A large box or crib.–The farmer keeps his grain in a *bin*.–We keep coal in a coal *bin*.

bind *binds, bound, binding.* 1. Tie. – Father will *bind* the papers into a bundle before giving them to the Red Cross.
2. Sew a narrow piece of cloth over the edge of.–Mother will *bind* the sleeves of Mary's dress.
3. Put the pages of a book together and into a cover.–The leaves of Bob's book have come apart, so Father will have to *bind* it.
4. Put a bandage on.–The school nurse will *bind* your sore finger for you.
5. Pledge to do something.–We shall *bind* ourselves to give money to charity each month.

binding bind'-ing *bindings*. 1. A book cover. –The *binding* of Bob's book is blue.
2. A strip of cloth to cover the raw edge of material. – The *binding* on Mary's sleeve is red.

biography bi-og'-ra-phy *biographies*. A story of one person's life written by another person.–John is reading Abraham Lincoln's *biography*.

B
C
D
E
F
G
H
I
J
K
L
M
N
O
P
Q
R
S
T
U
V
W
X
Y
Z

biplane bi′-plane *biplanes*. An aeroplane with a lower and an upper wing on each side.

birch *birches*. A kind of tree with smooth, peeling bark. *Birch* wood is used in making furniture, and for woodwork in houses. Red Indians used *birch*-bark for canoes.

bird *birds*. A feathered animal with wings. Most *birds* can fly. Sparrows and robins are *birds*; so are chickens and ducks.

birth *births*. 1. Being born; beginning to live.–My parents came to England before my *birth*. 2. Beginning of anything. – When a new country is formed, we speak of its *birth*.

birthday birth′-day *birthdays*. The day on which a person is born, or yearly celebration of this day.–March 31 is Father's *birthday*. On March 31 each year we give Father *birthday* presents.

biscuit bis′-cuit *biscuits*. A thin, crisp, dry bread or cake made of flour and milk or eggs. *Biscuits* are either sweetened or unsweetened, and may be mixed with currants or coated with chocolate. –Mother baked ginger *biscuits* for our tea.

bishop bish′-op *bishops*. 1. A clergyman of high rank. A *bishop* is head of a number of churches in a district. 2. One of the pieces in the game of chess, the upper part being shaped like a *bishop's* mitre.

bison bi′-son. A wild ox; in America, the buffalo.

bit *bits*. 1. A small piece or amount. – The mouse ate a *bit* of the cheese in the trap.

2. A piece of metal which forms part of a horse's bridle and goes through his mouth.

3. A tool used for making round holes. A *bit* fits into a tool called a brace, by which the *bit* is turned.–Father made a hole in the board with his brace and *bit*.

bite *bites, bit, bitten, biting*. 1. Chop with the teeth; take into the mouth by cutting off with the teeth.–Animals have sharp teeth with which to *bite* their food. 2. An amount of something taken into the mouth at one time.–Bob took a big *bite* out of his apple. 3. Sting.–Mosquitoes *bite*. 4. A sore spot made by the sting an insect. –Mother had a mosquito *bite* on her arm.

bitten bit′-ten. One form of the word *bite*.–Do not put your hands into the animals' cages at the zoo, or you may be *bitten*.

bitter bit′-ter *bitterly*. 1. Sharp and unpleasant to the taste.–Some medicines are *bitter*. 2. Cold and raw.–We could not go skating because of the *bitter* wind. 3. Disappointed and angry.–Bob was *bitter* about not getting in the team.

black *blacker, blackest*. 1. The darkest colour or hue; the opposite of white.–Coal is *black*. 2. Dark; without light.–When the door of the cupboard blew shut, it was very *black* inside.

blackberry black′-ber-ry *blackberries*. A purplish-black berry that has many seeds. *Blackberries* grow on *blackberry* bushes. – Father's favourite pie is *blackberry* pie.

blackbird black′-bird *blackbirds*. A kind of bird that is all or nearly all black. The *blackbird* is one of the thrush family, and has a cheerful, melodious song.

blackboard black′-board *blackboards*. A

smooth, black board that you can write on with chalk.

BIRDS

robin

chaffinch

wren

humming-bird

bulfinch

goldfinch

green wood-pecker

grey wagtail

song thrush

golden oriole

jay

great tit

bittern

pheasant

pigeon

crow

hoopoe

partridge

blackbird

swallow

mallard

gull

kingfisher

toucan

sandpiper

puffin

swan

penguin

barn owl

macaw

cormorant

turkey

tern

peacock

flamingo

sparrowhawk

kookaburra

pelican

eagle

stork

ostrich

B
C
D
E
F
G
H
I
J
K
L
M
N
O
P
Q
R
S
T
U
V
W
X
Y
Z

B
C
D
E
F
G
H
I
J
K
L
M
N
O
P
Q
R
S
T
U
V
W
X
Y
Z

blacksmith black'-smith *blacksmiths*. A person who shapes iron or other metal into different things. A *blacksmith* makes horseshoes and fits them to horses' feet.

blade *blades*. 1. A flat, thin part of an instrument used for cutting; any flat part.–The *blade* of the knife was so blunt that we could not cut the meat.–The *blade* of the oar is pushed through the water to make the rowing-boat move. The propeller *blade* cut the air as it whirled.

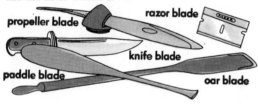

propeller blade   razor blade
knife blade
paddle blade   oar blade

2. A long, flat leaf.–The horse ate every *blade* of grass that Sally gave him.

blame *blames, blamed, blaming*. 1. Believe that (someone) is at fault; accuse.–The man did not *blame* us for the accident.
2. Guilt, responsibility.–Bill broke the window, and then tried to put the *blame* on Jack. He tried to make people think Jack had broken it.
3. *To blame* means at fault, responsible for. –Mary was not *to blame* for Baby's fall. She didn't make him fall. She tried to stop him, but couldn't.

blank *blanks*. 1. An empty space.–The children filled in the *blanks* on the cards with their names and addresses.
2. Empty; containing nothing.–The stamp album we gave Father had *blank* pages to which the stamps could be attached.
3. Looking shocked or without expression. –After the accident the man gave us a *blank* look.
4. Empty of ideas, having forgotten.–Bill could not answer the arithmetic problem; he said his mind suddenly went *blank*.

blanket blan'-ket *blankets*. 1. A woven cover.– In summer Mother puts a cotton *blanket* on our bed, but in the winter she puts on a woollen *blanket*.

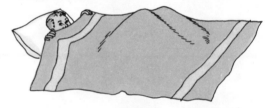

2. A covering. – During the sand-storm, a *blanket* of dust settled on the floors.

blast *blasts, blasted, blasting*. 1. A great rush (of wind).–The door was thrown open by a *blast* of wind.
2. A sound made by blowing.–We could hear the *blast* of horns across the lake.
3. Blow up.–The men building the new road had to *blast* the rocks with dynamite.
4. An explosion. – While we watched the burning building, we heard a loud *blast*.

blaze *blazes, blazed, blazing*. 1. Bright flames. –The Boy Scouts sat around the *blaze* of the camp-fire.

2. Burn brightly.–Before we arrived at the camp, we could see the camp-fire *blazing*.
3. A sparkling, a flashing.–The diamonds in the jeweller's window made a *blaze* of colours.

blazer bla'-zer *blazers*. A flannel jacket, usually of one or several colours, with a badge or crest, worn by a member of a school or club. –Our school uniform consists of a *blazer* and cap, coloured dark blue with red borders.

bleach *bleaches, bleached, bleaching*. Make white.–Mother hangs the clothes in the sun to *bleach* them.

bleak *bleaker, bleakest, bleakly*. 1. Dreary, wind-swept and bare of vegetation.–In the middle of winter, the moors are particularly *bleak*.
2. A small fish found in European rivers. The fish is silvery in appearance, and its scales are used by artificial-pearl makers.

blear *blears, bleared, blearing*. Dim or blur with water or vapour.–Fine spray on the car's windscreen *bleared* the driver's vision.

bleat *bleats, bleated, bleating.* 1. A high, thin cry.–We could hear the *bleat* of the lost sheep.
2. Make a *bleating* cry.–Sheep and lambs *bleat* when they are hungry.

bled. One form of the word *bleed.*–When Mary cut her finger, it *bled.*

bleed *bleeds, bled, bleeding.* Give out or flow blood. – Mother let her cut finger *bleed* for a few minutes before she bandaged it, so that the dirt would be washed out of the cut.

blend *blends, blended, blending.* 1. Mix pleasantly, harmonize. – The children's voices *blend* well. They mix so that you hear all the voices as one.–Will this green hat *blend* with your green dress? Will the 2 greens look well together?
2. Flow together.–The colours in the sky in the picture *blend* together. They shade into each other gradually so that you can hardly tell where the different colours meet.

bless *blesses, blessed* or *blest, blessing.* 1. Bring good to; watch over; look upon with favour.–God *bless* our parents. God guard and preserve them.–Mary has been *blessed* with great talent for music.
2. Make holy; make fit for a holy purpose.–The priest *blessed* the palms which the people received on Palm Sunday.
3. Praise, thank.–*Blessed* be God.

blessing *bless'-ing blessings.* 1. A prayer before a meal.–Grandfather says a *blessing* before every meal.
2. A prayer or wish that good may come to someone or something.–'*Blessings* on thee, little man.'
3. A good or desirable thing.–What a *blessing* that you were not hurt in the accident!

blew. One form of the word *blow.*–The wind *blew* so hard that it uprooted an old tree.–Sally *blew* her whistle twice.

blind *blinds, blinded, blinding.* 1. Without eyesight, unable to see. – The *blind* men could not see the elephant.
2. People who are *blind.* – Guide dogs lead the *blind.*
3. Make unable to see.–If you look at the bright sun too long, it will *blind* you. You will be unable to see for a while.

4. *Blind to* means refusing to take notice of. –Grandmother is *blind to* Jack's faults.
5. A shutter. – The white house has green *blinds.*
6. A wood or metal window shade.–Father put up the Venetian *blinds* after Mother washed the windows.
7. Having no way out. –A dead-end street, or a street that does not go through, is a *blind* street.

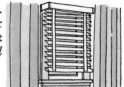

blindfold blind'-fold *blindfolds, blindfolded, blindfolding.* 1. Cover the eyes of. – In the game of 'pin the tail on the donkey', the children are *blindfolded* before it is their turn to try.

2. A cover for the eyes.–The children use a cloth for a *blindfold.*

blindness blind'-ness. Absence of sight; inability to see. – The operation cured the woman's *blindness.* It made her able to see again.

blink *blinks, blinked, blinking.* 1. Wink quickly; open and shut the eyes quickly and without always realizing it. – Sunshine through the windscreen made the driver *blink.*
2. Shine shakily; shine on and off.–We saw the many lights of the city *blinking* through the dark.

bliss *blissful, blissfully.* Perfect happiness.–It is *blissful* to dive into cool water on a very hot day.

blister blis'-ter *blisters, blistered, blistering.*
1. A place where the skin is raised, with water underneath. – Where Mary burned her arm, there is a large *blister.* – Jack has *blisters* on his hands from rowing the boat so long.
2. Make a *blister* on.–Father *blistered* his hand while hoeing in the garden.
3. A spot covered with a thin skin of something, and filled with air inside.–After the painter varnished the floor, a large *blister* formed on the wood.

blizzard bliz'-zard *blizzards.* A cold, windy snowstorm. – The hunter was caught in a *blizzard.*

block *blocks, blocked, blocking.* 1. A piece of stone, wood, ice, etc., in the form of a cube or with squared edges.–The court-house is built of big *blocks* of granite.

2. A toy made of small pieces of wood or plastic.–*Blocks* are also called bricks.

3. Be in the way of; close up.–A tree fell across the road and *blocked* the traffic.

4. Put into shape.–Mother had her felt hat cleaned and *blocked*.

5. A large building or group of buildings on one site, with no space in between.–Father works in a new office *block*.–We have lived in this *block* of flats for 5 years.

6. Stop a ball with a straight bat in cricket, without trying to score a run. – The new batsman *blocked* the first 2 balls; then he was clean bowled.

blond or **blonde** *blonds* or *blondes.* 1. A person whose hair, eyes and skin are very light-coloured.

2. Fair in colouring.–Sally is *blonde*; Jack is dark.

blood. A liquid in the veins and arteries that carries nourishment through the body and carries away waste. *Blood* is pumped to all parts of the body by the heart. *Blood* is red when it is exposed to the air.–When Mother cut her finger, *blood* came from the cut.

bloodhound blood'-hound *bloodhounds.* A large dog with a very keen sense of smell.–*Bloodhounds* can be used for tracking down criminals or people who are lost.

bloom *blooms, bloomed, blooming.* 1. Have flowers.–Violets *bloom* early in the springtime.

2. A blossom or flower.–The lily has a white *bloom*.

blossom blos'-som *blossoms, blossomed, blossoming.* 1. Bloom; produce flowers.–Lilacs *blossom* in the spring.

2. A flower.–The bride wore orange *blossom*.

blot *blots, blotted, blotting.* 1. A spot.–Mary got a *blot* of ink on her homework when her pen leaked.

2. Soak, absorb.–When she spilled the ink, she used blotting-paper to *blot* it up.

blotting-paper blot'-ting-paper. A soft, fuzzy paper for soaking up ink, water, etc.–We used *blotting-paper* to soak up the spilled ink.

blouse *blouses.* 1. A loose garment.–Some girls and women wear skirts and *blouses*, instead of full-length dresses.

blow *blows, blew, blowing, blown.* 1. A hit.–The boxer struck hard *blows*.

2. A shock, misfortune, or terrible happening.–It was a great *blow* to the rich man when he lost his money.

3. Drive or force air, breath, or wind.–I heard the wind *blow* through the trees last night.–The referee *blows* his whistle for the game to stop.–Father *blows* up Sally's balloons for her.

4. Carry by *blowing.*–The wind *blows* the seeds of many plants far and wide, so that they grow in different places.

5. *Blow up* means cause to explode.–The soldiers wil *blow up* the bridge with dynamite so that the enemy cannot cross it.

6. *Blow over* means to pass away or come to an end.–We have all been ill, but we hope our troubles will *blow over* before long.

blubber blub'-ber *blubbers, blubbered, blubbering.* 1. Weep and sob noisily. – Grandfather told Jack to stop *blubbering*.

2. The fat of whales, walruses, and other sea animals.–Some oil is made from *blubber*.

blue. 1. The colour of the sky.–The colours of the Union Jack are red, white, and *blue*.

2. Sad.–Mother felt *blue* the day she heard the bad news.

blueberry blue'-ber-ry *blueberries.* American berry, similar to the European bilberry.

bluebell blue'-bell *bluebells*. A blue wild flower with a long stalk. It grows in the spring. –Last week-end we all went into the woods to pick bunches of *bluebells*.

bluebottle blue'-bot-tle *bluebottles*. A large buzzing fly with a bluish body, also called the blow-fly.–We covered the food in the larder to keep the *bluebottles* off.

blue tit blue tits. A small bird with a bright blue crown, which has very energetic and acrobatic habits. – In the cold weather we always put out scraps of fat on a line for the hungry *blue tits*.

bluff *bluffs, bluffed, bluffing*. 1. Frighten off by pretending to have the advantage. – Bob *bluffed* the new boy who wanted to play marbles by pretending that he was a champion player.
2. A high, steep bank or cliff.–From the boat we saw the *bluff* along the shore.

blunder blun'-der *blunders, blundered, blundering*. 1. Make a bad mistake.
2. A bad mistake.–Bob made a *blunder* in English. He said. 'Ain't it the truth?' for 'Isn't it the truth?'

blunt *blunts, blunted, blunting*. 1. Dull. – Grandfather's knife is *blunt*. It does not have a sharp edge.
2. Make dull.–Bob *blunted* his knife by trying to cut a stone with it.
3. Likely to speak frankly, to say just what one thinks.–The officer was very *blunt*. He called the man a thief.

blush *blushes, blushed, blushing*. 1. Turn red in the face from shame or embarrassment.– Every time Mother spoke of Bob's mistake, he *blushed*.–Children who are bashful or shy *blush* easily.
2. A turning red from shame or from embarrassment.–The *blush* on Mary's cheeks made her more beautiful.

bluster blus'-ter *blusters, blustered, blustering*. 1. Blow noisily. – We heard the wind *blustering* in the trees.
2. Talk noisily, with threats.–When Jack is angry, he *blusters* about 'getting even'.

boar *boars*. A male wild or domestic pig.

board *boards, boarded, boarding*. 1. A long piece of wood.–Father ordered *boards* from a timber yard with which to repair the porch.

2. A stiff, flat piece of material for some special purpose.–We play draughts on a draught *board*.–The man puts his paper on a drawing *board* when he draws.

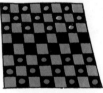 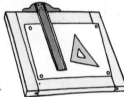

draught board   drawing board

3. Meals for which one pays.–Mrs Jones will give the workers *board* and lodgings.
4. Live at another's house, paying for one's meals and room.–Mr Smith *boards* at Mrs Jones's house.
5. Go on to or into a ship, train, etc.–The sailors *boarded* their ship.
6. *On board* means on or in a ship, train, etc. –The sailors went *on board* the ship.
7. A group of persons chosen to take care of business matters for an organization.–The water *board* is a group of men in charge of the water supply for a certain area.

boast *boasts, boasted, boasting*. Brag or talk too much about oneself and what one can do. – The boy who *boasted* all the time couldn't find anyone to play with him.

boastful boast'-ful *boastfully*. Bragging or boasting often.

BOATS

raft

bark canoe

basket boat

outrigger canoe

kayak

sea sledge

outboard-motor boat

rowing-boat

canal barge

motor-boat

galley

Viking ship

Chinese junk

centreboard sailing-boat

caravel

clipper

paddle steamer

tanker

destroyer

ocean liner

tug-boat

aircraft carrier

cargo ship

battleship

B C D E F G H I J K L M N O P Q R S T U V W X Y Z

boat *boats.* A vessel for travelling on water, *Boats* moved by oars are called rowing-*boats*. *Boats* moved by the wind blowing on sails are called sailing-*boats*. Some are moved by steam power and carry many people. They are steam*boats*. Small *boats* are often carried on big ships.

bob *bobs, bobbed, bobbing.* 1. Cut (hair) short.—The barber will *bob* Mary's hair so that her head will be cool in the summer.
2. Move up and down.—The floating bottle *bobbed* on the waves.
3. A float on a fishing line which *bobs* when a fish bites on the bait.

bobbin bob'-bin *bobbins.* A spool or reel.—Grandmother had to wind the *bobbin* with thread before she could sew on the sewing-machine. – Wire, thread, yarn and string are often wound on *bobbins*.

bobby bob'-by *bobbies.* A familiar word for a policeman, from the name of Sir Robert Peel, founder of the London police force.—We are good friends with the *bobby* on the corner.

bobsleigh bob'-sleigh *bobsleighs.* A sleigh with 2 pairs of runners.—At the winter sports we watched an exciting *bobsleigh* contest.

bodice bod'-ice *bodices.* The upper part of a woman's dress.—Mother pinned an artificial rose to her *bodice*.

bodily bod'-i-ly. In one lot, entire.—The bungalow was moved *bodily* to another site.

body bod'-y *bodies.* 1. All of a person or animal other than the mind.—Keep your *body* healthy and your mind will work better.
2. All of a person except his head, arms, and legs; the trunk or torso.
3. A dead person or animal.
4. A large mass or quantity of people or matter.—The sun is a heavenly *body*.

bodyguard bod'-y-guard *bodyguards.* A man who goes about with a person to protect him from harm.—Important statesmen have *bodyguards* to keep them safe.

bog *bogs.* A marsh; a swampy place.—Cranberries grow in the spongy ground of *bogs*.

boggy bog'-gy. Swampy. – Low land near a river is often *boggy*.

boil *boils, boiled, boiling.* 1. Bubble and give off steam or vapour.—Water will *boil* if heated enough. If water *boils* long enough, it will all become steam and disappear into the air.
2. Cook in boiling liquid. – Bob likes eggs fried; Mary likes *boiled* eggs best.
3. A hard, swollen, sore place with pus in it.—The *boil* on my arm has nearly gone.

boiler boil'-er *boilers.* 1. A large metal pan or container for boiling things in. – Mother boils the clothes in a wash *boiler*.
2. A tank in which water is heated to make steam. – In factories water is heated in *boilers,* to make steam to run the machines.

boisterous bois'-ter-ous. Loud, noisy, and rough.—The children were so *boisterous* in their play that they woke the baby.

bold *bolder, boldest, boldly.* 1. Willing to face danger; not afraid.—The knights of old were very *bold*. They were brave and daring.
2. Rough or rude. – Children are not well liked if they are *bold* and cheeky to adults.
3. Bright; clearly seen.—The tree in the picture is very *bold*. It stands out strongly.

bolt *bolts, bolted, bolting.* 1. A sliding bar, as on a door.—Mr. Smith fastened the door with a bolt.

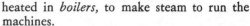

2. A metal rod with a head at one end and screw threads along its length so that a nut can be screwed on to it.— Many parts of a motor-car are held together with *bolts*.
3. Fasten with a *bolt*.—Father *bolted* the door before going to bed.—The top of the desk was *bolted* to the frame. It was fastened with *bolts* and nuts.
4. A roll (of cloth).—The dressmaker used a whole *bolt* of cloth to make the costumes.
5. A stroke of lightning.—We saw a *bolt* of lightning. It was followed by thunder.
6. Suddenly rush forward.—The horse *bolted* and threw its rider from the saddle.

B
C
D
E
F
G
H
I
J
K
L
M
N
O
P
Q
R
S
T
U
V
W
X
Y
Z

bomb *bombs, bombed, bombing.* 1. A container of material that explodes or blows up when it hits something after being dropped. or when a clock in it sets it off.–Aeroplanes drop *bombs* to destroy buildings in time of war.–The spies hid a *bomb* in the railway station, and an hour later the station blew up.

2. Drop *bombs* on.–The aeroplanes *bombed* the city.

bond *bonds.* 1. A written or printed statement given by the government or a business firm in return for a loan of money. The *bond* promises to pay back the money at a certain time with interest.
2. A tie. – The secret was a *bond* between them.

bone *bones, bony.* One of the hard, stiff pieces that make up the skeleton, or framework, of the body.–Dogs like to gnaw the meat from *bones.*

bonfire bon'-fire *bonfires.* A big outdoor fire. –Father made a *bonfire* in the garden and burned up the rubbish.

bonnet bon'-net *bonnets.* A close-fitting hat with a brim round the front. *Bonnets* are worn nowadays by babies and little girls.

bonus bo'-nus *bonuses.* A gift of money in addition to the amount earned.–Each Christmas Father gets a *bonus* from his employer.

boo *boos, booed, booing.* 1. Sally shouted '*Boo!*' at Father to frighten him.
2. Show that one is not pleased with something by yelling *boo!*–When the footballer committed a foul, the people *booed* him.

book *books.* Sheets of paper or pages, printed or blank, fastened together within a cover. –The children made *books* to draw pictures in by sewing sheets of paper together and putting a cover around them.–This dictionary is a *book.*

bookcase book'-case *bookcases.* A cupboard or case or shelves for putting books in. Some *bookcases* are open in the front and some have glass doors.

booklet book'-let *booklets.* A thin paper-covered book. – The children made *booklets* of poems for their mothers.

boom *booms, boomed, booming.* 1. A deep, loud, hollow sound.–The children heard the *boom* of the cannon.
2. Do much business; become rich.–Towns near the new oil fields are *booming.* They are busy and prosperous.
3. A time when much money is made.–There is a *boom* in the oil fields.

boost *boosts, boosted, boosting.* 1. A lift up.– Father gave Mary a *boost* to help her on to the horse.
2. Give a lift to.–Bob *boosted* Jack over the fence. He gave him a little push.
3. A rise, an increase.–There was a *boost* in the price of oil. The price went up.
4. Raise.–A war *boosts* prices because things are hard to get.

boot *boots.* A covering for the foot and leg. *Boots* are made of rubber or leather. Some *boots* cover the legs to the knees. Rubber *boots* often reach to the hips.

riding boot   hip boot

booth *booths.* 1. A cabinet or tiny room for telephoning, voting, etc. –Father went into a *booth* to phone Mother.
2. A covered stand or stall.–My sister sold sweets in a *booth* at the fair.

border bor'-der *borders, bordered, bordering.* 1. An outer edge; a margin.–The teacher told us to draw a 1-inch *border* all round our picture to make a frame.– Wild flowers grow at the *border* of the woods.–Our big rug in the hall has a dark blue *border.*

2. Be next (to).–Our farm *borders* on Mr Smith's farm on the south. Mr Smith's farm starts where ours ends on the south.

3. A legal boundary.–The travellers crossed the *border* into the neighbouring country.

bore *bores, bored, boring.* 1. Pierce, drill. – The carpenter can *bore* holes in a board with his brace and bit.

2. Weary, tire, make one lose interest.– People who talk too much about themselves *bore* others.–The long, dull story was *boring* to the children.

3. A person or thing that is not interesting.– Mary finds her arithmetic a *bore*.–Edward can be quite a *bore*.

borne. One form of the word *bear*.–Jack has *borne* abuse from Bill as long as he can; he can stand it no longer.

borrow bor'-row *borrows, borrowed, borrowing.* Take or use for a time, and then give back to the owner.–May I *borrow* your red pencil? Will you lend it to me?–I *borrowed* Father's hammer to make a kite.

boss *bosses, bossed, bossing.* 1. A person who directs others in their work.–My boss at the office is strict but fair.

2. Tell what to do; order about.–Most people do not like to be *bossed*.

both 1. The two. – When Mother asked Jack if he wanted an apple or an orange, he said *both*.

2. Some exercise is good for *both* weak and strong.–*Both* grey and green look pretty with yellow.

bother both'-er *bothers, bothered, bothering.* 1. Trouble, thing that annoys.–Mother thinks darning socks is quite a *bother*.

2. Take the trouble.–I didn't *bother* to look for the paper.

3. Trouble, annoy.–The noise *bothers* Mother.

bottle bot'-tle *bottles, bottled, bottling.* 1. A glass container with a narrow neck.–Many medicines are put up in *bottles*.

2. Put into *bottles*. – The farmer sends his milk in large cans to the city to be *bottled*.

bottom *bot -tom bottoms.* 1. The lowest part. –The olives at the *bottom* of the bottle are hard to reach.

2. Lowest.–The book you are looking for is on the *bottom* shelf.

3. Under part.–The *bottoms* or soles of my feet are sore from walking barefoot.

4. The ground beneath a body of water.– The lake was so clear that we saw pebbles on the *bottom*.

bough (rhymes with *how*) *boughs.* A branch. –The *boughs* of the trees swing back and forth in the wind.

bought. One form of the word *buy*.–Father has *bought* this house; we own it now.

bounce *bounces, bounced, bouncing.* 1. Hit something and spring back.–The rubber ball *bounced* up and down on the floor when it was dropped.–The car *bounced* into the air when it went over the rut.

2. Make *bounce*.–Sally *bounces* her ball.

3. Jump, spring, bound.–Jack *bounces* out of bed on Saturdays.

bound *bounds, bounded, bounding.* 1. Headed, going in the direction of.–Uncle Jim is *bound* for Birmingham.

2. Be next to; surround; mark the end of.– The Atlantic Ocean *bounds* North America on the east. It is on the eastern edge of North America.–A picket fence *bounds* our yard. It goes all round it.

3. Leap. – We saw a rabbit go *bounding* across the road. – When the bell rang, the children *bounded* from their seats and rushed from the room.

4. One form of the word *bind*.–Grandma's Bible is *bound* in real leather.

boundary bound'-a-ry *boundaries.*–The edge, end or line where something stops or meets something else. The line where a city or a town stops is called the *boundary* line. States and countries have *boundaries*, too. Sometimes lakes and mountains form the dividing line. The Cheviot Hills form part of the *boundary* between Scotland and England.

bouquet bou-quet' *bouquets.* A bunch of flowers.–Mary brought her mother a *bouquet* of daisies.

bow (rhymes with *so*) *bows*. 1. A kind of knot with 2 open loops. – Mary wore a blue *bow* of ribbon on her hair. –We tie our shoelaces in a *bow*.

2. A weapon used for shooting arrows. It is a curved, easily bent stick with a string fastened to each end.–Indians used *bows* and arrows to hunt animals with.

3. A slender stick with coarse hairs fastened to it, used to draw across the strings of a violin or other stringed instrument to make music.

bow (rhymes with *how*) *bows, bowed, bowing*. 1. Bend down, incline, stoop.–The children *bow* their heads when they say their prayers. 2. Bend the body or head forward as a greeting, to express thanks, etc. – The people clapped their hands when Mary sang. She came back to the stage and *bowed*.–Father lifts his hat and *bows* a little when he meets the teacher in the street. 3. The front part of a boat.–The girls sat in the *bow* of the boat. The boys sat in the stern.

bowels bow'-els. 1. A long, coiled tube in the body, also called the intestines. Food passes from the stomach into the *bowels*. The *bowels* send food into the blood stream to nourish other parts of the body. The waste parts of food pass out of the body through the end of the *bowels*. 2. Deep, inside part. – Precious metals lie buried in the *bowels* of the earth.

bowl *bowls, bowled, bowling*. 1. A deep, round dish. – We eat soup from a *bowl*.–Mother mixes cakes in a mixing *bowl*. 2. As much as a *bowl* will hold. – Goldilocks ate the Baby Bear's *bowl* of porridge all up. 3. Play the game of *bowling* by rolling large balls down a smooth wooden alley to knock down large wooden pins. *Bowls* is another game, played by rolling 'woods' on a green.

box *boxes, boxed, boxing*. 1. A cardboard, wood or metal container made to hold things. – We put the Christmas gifts in *boxes*. – We bought a *box* of soap powder. 2. As much as a *box* holds.–We used a *box* of soap powder. 3. A private section in a theatre balcony.–Mary went to the show and sat in a *box*. 4. Fight with the fists according to certain rules.–In *boxing* contests padded gloves are usually worn.

boxer box'-er *boxers*. One who boxes; a prizefighter.–Joe Louis was a great *boxer*.

boy *boys*. A male child.–*Boys* grow to be men. –Mary is a girl. Bob is a *boy*.

boyish boy'-ish *boyishly, boyishness*. Like a boy, or male child.–Sometimes grown men say and do *boyish* things. They act like boys.

brace *braces, braced, bracing*. 1. Something used to hold up a thing or give it support.–The table leg was loose, so Grandfather put a *brace* on it.–Men and boys wear *braces* to keep their trousers up. – Mary wears a *brace* on her teeth to straighten them. 2 A tool used with a bit to make a hole. The *brace* is the holder for the bit.

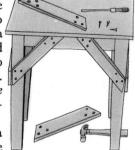

3. Strengthen, support. – Bob *braced* the table.

bracelet brace'-let *bracelets*. A band worn about the wrist as an ornament. *Bracelets* are made of gold, silver, beads, etc.

bracket brack'-et *brackets*. 1. An L-shaped piece of metal or wood used to hold up or support one end of something, such as a shelf. – Father fastened the *brackets* on the wall and then screwed the shelf to them.
2. One of 2 marks [ ] used to set apart certain words or numbers in print.

brag *brags, bragged, bragging*. Boast; talk much about one's ability, possessions, or doings. –Boys and girls who *brag* are not usually liked.–Edward *brags* about his new boat.

braid *braids, braided, braiding*. 1. Divide into 3 or more parts and weave into one large strand or thread. – Mary's hair is long enough to braid.
2. A *braided* lock.–Sometimes Mary wears her hair in 2 *braids*.
3. *Braided* bands used for trimming. – Military uniforms are often trimmed with *braid*.

brain *brains*. The large, greyish mass of nerves inside the skull, or head, of persons and animals. The *brain* contains nerve cells that control movements of our bodies and our thinking.

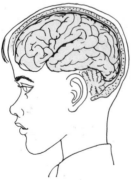

brake *brakes*. A device used to slow down or stop bicycles, cars, etc.–Mother stepped on the *brake* when she saw the traffic light turn red.

bramble bram'-ble *brambles*. A shrub with thorns on it.–Grandfather planted *brambles* along the back fence.

bran. The outer covering of grains. When wheat is made into flour, it is cracked open and sifted. The fine powdered part is the flour, and the remaining hull, or husk, is the *bran*.

branch *branches*. 1. A limb or stem of a tree. The trunk of the tree is the main part that grows up from the ground. The roots are joined to the bottom of the trunk, and the *branches* are joined to the upper part. Leaves grow on the *branches*.

2. One of the small rivers that flow into a large river.
3. One office or agency of a large organization.–The library at the corner is a *branch* of the central library.

brand *brands, branded, branding*. 1. Mark with a hot iron. – Cattle are often *branded* so that their owners will be able to tell them apart from other cattle. *Branding* is done with a *branding* iron.
2. The mark or symbol which is *branded* on.
3. A particular kind or make. – Uncle Jim always smokes this *brand* of tobacco.

brass. A yellowish metal made by putting copper, zinc and other metals together. *Brass* is used to make dishes, candlesticks, bells, musical instruments, etc.

brave *braves, braved, braving, braver, bravest*.
1. Ready to face danger; not afraid.–A good soldier is *brave*.
2. Face, defy.–The hunters *braved* the storm. They went out into it.

bravely brave'-ly. Without fear, with courage. –The animal trainer walked *bravely* into the lions' cage.

bravery brav'-er-y. Courage; being unafraid.– The officer was given a medal for his *bravery*.

bray *brays, brayed, braying*. 1. A loud, harsh cry. – One night at the farm we heard the *bray* of a donkey.
2. Make a loud, harsh cry.–Donkeys *bray*.

bread. 1. A food made of wheat flour, bran, rye flour, cornmeal, etc., and baked in loaves in an oven.
2. Food.–'Give us this day our daily *bread*' means give us this day our daily food.
3. Put a coating of crumbs on.–Mother has *breaded* the veal for our dinner. She dipped it in egg and *bread*crumbs and then fried it in deep fat.

B
C
D
E
F
G
H
I
J
K
L
M
N
O
P
Q
R
S
T
U
V
W
X
Y
Z

breadth. Width or distance across.–The length of the board is 4 feet and the *breadth* is 8 inches.

break *breaks, broke, broken, breaking.* 1. Crack. –Jack did not *break* the bone in his arm when he fell on it.
2. Smash, separate into pieces.–Dishes *break* easily if they are dropped.–Jerry dropped the dish and *broke* it.
3. Disobey, not keep (rules).–The children did not mean to *break* the rules of the school.
4. Force one's way.–The rabbit *breaks* out of its pen nearly every day.
5. Tell gently.–The teacher *broke* the bad news to the children.
6. Change, give up.–Bad habits are hard to *break.*
7. Appear, come out.–A rash has *broken* out all over Mary's face.
8. Plough.–Farmers *break* the ground before planting the seeds.
9. Quickly come forth, appear, or develop. –The storm *broke* suddenly.–Uncle Jim enlisted when the war *broke* out.

breakfast break'-fast *breakfasts.* The first meal of the day. It breaks the long fast, or time without food, of the night.–Fruit, cereal, egg, toast, and milk, make a good *breakfast.*

breast *breasts.* Chest, or upper part of the front of the body.–He stood with his hands upon his *breast.*–Some people like the *breast* of a chicken best.

breath *breaths.* 1. Air taken into and let out of the lungs.–Baby blew her *breath* against the window-pane to make a smear.
2. A stir, a movement of air.–It was so warm that there was not a *breath* of air.

breathe *breathes, breathed, breathing.* Take air into the lungs and let it out again.–Jack ran so fast that it was hard for him to *breathe.*

breathless breath'-less *breathlessly, breathlessness.* Unable to breathe; panting; out of breath.–The race left the boys *breathless.*–Mary was *breathless* with excitement at the concert.

breeches breech'-es. 1. Short trousers that fit tight over the knees.–In the eighteenth century men wore *breeches.*
2. A *breeches* buoy is a canvas seat on a rope and pulley, used to save people from sinking ships.

breed *breeds, bred, breeding.* 1. A certain kind of family.–On this ranch they keep a fine *breed* of horses.–Jersey cows are a *breed* of cows.
2. Raise.–The farmer *breeds* horses.
3. Produce young.–Sheep *breed* in the spring.

breeze *breezes, breezy.* A gentle or light wind. –The *breeze* stirred the leaves.

brew *brews, brewed, brewing.* 1. Make (beer, etc.).–Beer is *brewed* from hops and malt.
2. Form, start, or be about to break out.– Mother can always tell when the children are *brewing* mischief. – The black clouds showed that a storm was *brewing.*

briar or **brier** bri'-ar, bri'-er *briars, briers.* A plant that has thorns or sharp points along its stem. – Blackberries and wild roses are called *briars.*

bribe *bribes, bribed, bribing.* 1. Money or gifts given to a person to get him to do something dishonest or something he does not want to do.–Jack gave Bob an apple as a *bribe,* so that Bob would help him steal the chalk.
2. Give a *bribe* to.–The criminals tried to *bribe* the police to let them go free.

brick *bricks.* 1. A block of clay or mud that has been baked to make it hard. – Some houses are made of *bricks.*
2. Something shaped like the *bricks* used for houses is often called a *brick,* as a *brick* of ice cream, a *brick* of tea, etc.
3. Wooden building toys are called *bricks.*

bride *brides.* A woman who is about to be married, is being married, or has just been married. – My sister received many gifts when she was a *bride.*

bridal brid'-al. Of or for a bride.–My sister received many *bridal* gifts when she got married. She threw her *bridal* bouquet to the guests.

bridegroom bride'-groom *bridegrooms*. A man who is about to be married, is being married, or has just been married. – The *bridegroom* arrived at the church before the bride.

bridesmaid brides'-maid *bridesmaids*. A young woman who attends a bride and walks down the aisle with her at the wedding.

bridge *bridges*. 1. Something built over a river or low ground for people or vehicles to cross on.–The cars crossed the river on the *bridge*.

2. A platform on a ship where the officers stand watch and run the ship.–The captain stood on the *bridge* and gave quick orders.
3. A game played with playing cards. *Bridge* is played by 4 players.–Mother and Father like to play *bridge* with the neighbours.
4. A wooden piece on a stringed instrument, over which the strings are stretched.–While Jack was tuning his violin, the *bridge* fell over.

bridle bri'-dle *bridles*. The part of a horse's harness that fits on the horse's head. When you pull the reins which are fastened to the *bridle*, the horse slows down or turns.

brief *briefly*. Short.–Bob wrote his father a *brief* note.

BRIDGES

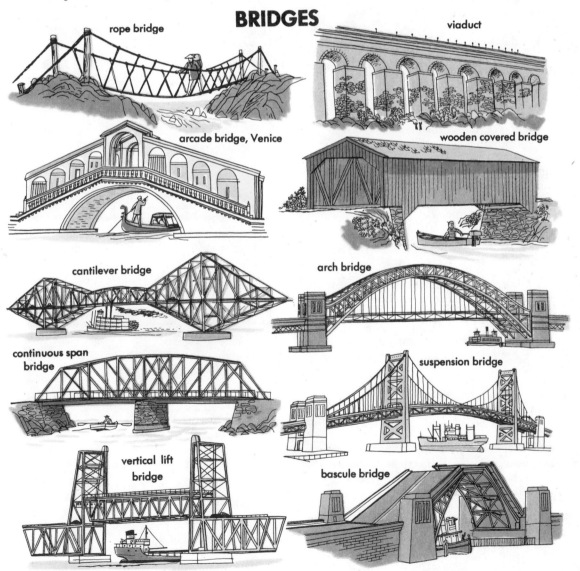

rope bridge

viaduct

arcade bridge, Venice

wooden covered bridge

cantilever bridge

arch bridge

continuous span bridge

suspension bridge

vertical lift bridge

bascule bridge

B C D E F G H I J K L M N O P Q R S T U V W X Y Z

B
C
D
E
F
G
H
I
J
K
L
M
N
O
P
Q
R
S
T
U
V
W
X
Y
Z

brier bri'-er *briers*. Another way of spelling the word *briar*, meaning a plant with thorns.

bright *brighter, brightest, brightly, brighten, brightness*. 1. Shining.–A *bright* light shone through the window.
2. Giving much light.–Sometimes the moon is very *bright*. It gives much light.
3. (Of a colour) clear; not mixed with duller shades.–Mary has a *bright* blue dress.
4. Clever.–Ned is the *brightest* boy in school.

brilliant bril'-liant *brilliantly*. 1. Very bright; sparkling and shining.–Diamonds are brilliant.
2. Very clever.–The child is *brilliant*. He can do many things well.

brim *brims*. 1. The part of a hat that sticks out from the bottom of the crown. – The *brim* on Father's hat is curled up at the edges.
2. The top edge.–The milk in the glass came up to the *brim*.

brine *briny*. Water with much salt in it. – Mother put the cucumbers in *brine* to get them ready to make into pickles.

bring *brings, brought, bringing*. 1. Cause to come with oneself; carry, lead, or accompany. –I will *bring* Jack to the party. I will see that he comes with me.–*Bring* your coat along. It may rain.
2. Cause.–The heavy rain *brought* floods in the valley.

brisk *briskly*. Quick and lively.–We went for a *brisk* walk in the cold morning air.

bristle bris'-tle *bristles*. One of the stiff hairs in brushes or in the coats of certain animals. Some brushes are made from the *bristles* of a hog.

broad *broader, broadest*. Wide; of large surface from side to side.–The board is long and *broad*.–The *broad* river flows slowly.

broadcast broad'-cast *broadcasts, broadcasting*. Send out in all directions, as in sowing seeds; send out over the radio.–The news was *broadcast* over the radio.

broil *broils, broiled, broiling*. Cook on an open fire or under a grill.–We went on a picnic and *broiled* beefsteak.

broke. One form of the word *break*.–The glass *broke* when it fell from the shelf.

broken bro'-ken. One form of the word *break*. –The windscreen of the car was *broken* into pieces by a flying stone.

bronco bron'-co *broncos*. A small, somewhat wild horse used in western North America. –Bob liked the Western film that showed cowboys riding *broncos*.

bronze. A yellowish metal made by melting copper and tin together. *Bronze* is made into dishes, jewellery, statues, etc.

brood *broods, brooded, brooding*. 1. A group of birds hatched out at one time.–There were 12 chickens in the *brood*.

2. A mother's children are her *brood*.
3. Think sadly and silently; mope. – Jack *broods* over the loss of his dog.

brook *brooks*. A small stream of water.–We fish in the *brook*.

broom *brooms*. A stiff brush with a long handle. The brush part of a *broom* is sometimes made of straws. *Brooms* are used to sweep rugs, floors, etc.

broomstick broom'-stick *broomsticks*. The handle of a broom. Superstitious people used to say that witches could fly on *broomsticks*.

broth. The water in which meat or fish has been boiled.–We ate biscuits and chicken *broth* for lunch.

brother broth´-er *brothers.* A boy or man born of the same parents as another child or person. If 2 boys or men have the same mother and father, they are *brothers.*–Bob is Mary's *brother.* Bob and Mary have the same father and mother.

brother-in-law *brothers-in-law.* The husband of one's sister, or the brother of one's husband or wife.

brought. One form of the word *bring.*–Today I *brought* my lunch to school.

brow *brows.* 1. Eyebrow; the short hairs above the eyes. – The girl's eye-*brows* were darker than her hair.
2. Forehead. – The fireman was so hot that his *brow* was covered with drops of sweat.

brown. A darkish colour; the colour of moist earth or of chocolate.–Some people have blue eyes, others have *brown* eyes.

brownie brown´-ie *brownies.* 1. An elf or fairy that does helpful things for people.–The children enjoyed the story about the *brownies.*
2. A junior member of the Girl Guides.–Now Jill is 8 she has joined the *Brownies.*

bruin bru´-in. A name given to the brown bear in children's stories and fairy tales.

bruise *bruises, bruised, bruising.* 1. An injury to flesh caused by a blow, bump, etc., that does not break the skin.–Mary has a black-and-blue *bruise* on her arm. She got it by falling on the pavement.
2. Cause a *bruise* by injuring.–Mary *bruised* her arm when she fell.

brunette bru-nette´ *brunettes.* The opposite of blonde.

brush *brushes, brushed, brushing.* 1. A tool with stiff hairs or bristles for scrubbing, etc. *Brushes* are made of stiff hairs, straw, wire, etc., set in some material such as wood, metal, or hard rubber.

2. Clean or rub with a *brush.*–We *brush* our teeth with a tooth*brush.*–We *brush* our hair.
3. Rub against; touch.–A dog *brushed* my hand as he passed by.

brute *brutes.* 1. A beast.–Animals are *brutes.* They cannot think or feel in the way people do.
2. A cruel, unkind person.–Mary called Bill a *brute* when he twisted her arm.

bubble bub´-ble *bubbles, bubbled, bubbling.*
1. A little ball of air or other gas formed in a liquid, or with a thin film of liquid around it.–Ginger ale is full of little *bubbles.*–Children like to blow soap *bubbles* and let them float through the air.
2. Form *bubbles.* – When you make toffee, the heat makes the toffee *bubble* while it is cooking.–The water at the bottom of a waterfall *bubbles.*

buck *bucks, bucked, bucking.* 1. A father or male deer. A *buck* has horns. The female deer does not have them.

2. Jump up and down violently (said of a horse, steer, etc.)–The wild horse *bucked* to throw the cowboy off.
3. The males of goats, rabbits, and many other animals, are called *bucks,* too.

bucket buck´-et *buck-ets.* An open container of wood or metal with a handle; a pail.–We put water, coal, and many other things, in *buckets.*

B
C
D
E
F
G
H
I
J
K
L
M
N
O
P
Q
R
S
T
U
V
W
X
Y
Z

B
C
D
E
F
G
H
I
J
K
L
M
N
O
P
Q
R
S
T
U
V
W
X
Y
Z

buckle buck'-le *buckles, buckled, buckling.*
1. A kind of fastening for belts, straps, etc.–

Mary's belt fastens with a brass *buckle.*
2. Fasten with a *buckle.* –The milkman *buckled* the horse's harness.
3. Bend or crumple up because of a heavy weight or strain.–Torrents of flood water surged against the bridge until its supports *buckled.*

bud *buds, budded, budding.* 1. A blossom or leaf of a plant before it unfolds.
2. Form *buds.* – The trees are beginning to *bud.*

buffalo buf'-fa-lo *buffaloes.* A kind of wild ox. *Buffaloes* look something like the bulls you see on farms. They are also called bison.

buffer buf'-fer *buffers.* A pair of short rods working on springs, fixed to the front of railway engines and carriages, and at mainline stations. They lessen the shock when the train stops.–Because the brakes were not working properly, the train hit the *buffers* too hard.

buffet buf'-fet *buffets, buffeted, buffeting.* 1. Strike or knock against.–The swimmer was *buffeted* by the waves.
2. A blow.–The boxer gave his opponent a *buffet* on the cheek.
3. (pronounced *boofay*) A refreshment room at a railway station.–Before the train left we had some sandwiches in the *buffet.*

buffoon buf'-foon *buffoons.* A clown or jester, or somebody who acts in a comical way.–When Alan dressed up in Mother's clothes, she laughed and called him a *buffoon.*

buggy bug'-gy *buggies.* A small, light carriage drawn by a horse.–Most people ride in cars today, but some people still ride in *buggies.*

bugle bu'-gle *bugles.* A kind of small brass horn with a coiled tube.–The bugler in the army blows the *bugle* to tell the soldiers it is time to come to meals, go to bed, get up, etc.

bugler bu'-gler *buglers.* A person who blows a bugle.

build *builds, built, building.* Construct; make; put together.–Beavers *build* dams.–Bricklayers *build* walls. – Grandfather *built* a chicken-house.

builder build'-er *builders.* A person who makes or designs buildings, bridges, etc.–The *builder* of our house said it would last 100 years.

building build'-ing *buildings.* A structure that provides shelter and protection. Houses, shops, garages, etc., are *buildings.*

bulb *bulbs.* 1. A thick root, often round, of certain plants. Some plants grow from seeds, and some grow from *bulbs.* Onions are *bulbs.* Lilies and irises grow from *bulbs.*
2. A thin glass globe or cylinder containing thin wires which light up when electricity passes through; a light *bulb.*–Father put a new *bulb* in the lamp.

onion bulb

light bulb

bulge *bulges, bulged, bulging.* 1. Swell out.–Mother's handbag was so full that it *bulged.*
2. A place that *bulges;* a swelling.–Mother told Bob that his pocket would have a *bulge* if he put his cricket-ball in it.

bull *bulls.* A male or he animal, especially one of the ox kind. A cow is a female or she animal; a *bull* is a male or he animal of the same kind. The male elephant is a *bull* elephant.

bulldog bull'-dog *bulldogs.* A strong, smooth-haired, courageous dog with a large head.

BUILDINGS

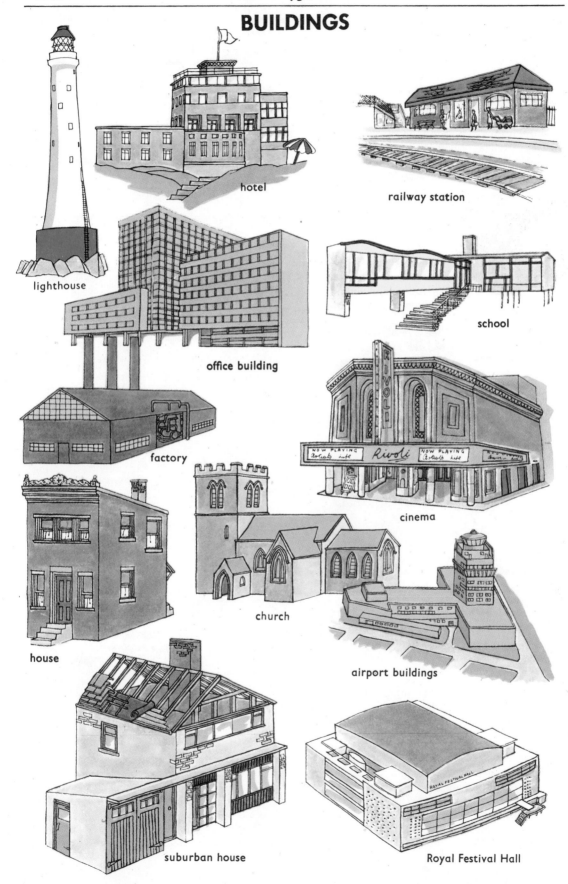

lighthouse

hotel

railway station

office building

school

factory

cinema

house

church

airport buildings

suburban house

Royal Festival Hall

bullet bul'-let *bullets*. A piece of lead with a rounded point that is shot from a gun.–The *bullet* from Edward's gun hit the target.

bulletin bul'-le-tin *bulletins*. A notice, announcement, or printed booklet of information.–Newspapers print news *bulletins,* or short articles telling the latest news.–The radio stations sent out news *bulletins* about the hurricane.–Father received a *bulletin* on farming from the Ministry of Agriculture. It told how to plant seeds.

bull-frog bull'-frog *bull-frogs*. An American frog which makes a deep croaking noise.

bumble-bee bum'-ble-bee *bumble-bees*. A large kind of bee. Its back has yellow and black stripes across it. *Bumble-bees* buzz loudly when they fly.

bump *bumps, bumped, bumping, bumpy*. 1. A swollen place.–Baby fell and made a *bump* on her head.
2. A raised place; a hump.–The road was full of *bumps* after the rain.
3. Hit or strike.–Father stopped the car so that he would not *bump* the car ahead.

bumper bump'-er *bumpers*. A heavy bar to protect a vehicle if it bumps into something. –The *bumper* on the front of a car protects it when it bumps against another car.

bun *buns*. A kind of sweetened roll or cake. –When Mother makes bread, she usually makes a batch of *buns* for us.

bunch *bunches*. A number of things held together; a cluster or group.–We took a *bunch* of flowers to our teacher.–Grapes grow in *bunches*.

bundle bun'-dle *bundles, bundled, bundling*. 1. A package or bunch bound up together.– Mother gave a *bundle* of newspapers to the Red Cross. They were tied together.
2. Wrap; bind together.–We are going to *bundle* up these old shoes and give them away.

bungalow bun'-ga-low *bungalows*. A small, 1-storey house.

bunk *bunks*. A plain, narrow bed, usually fixed to a wall or floor.–The twins sleep in *bunks,* one above the other.

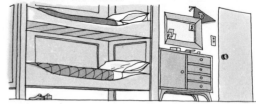

bunny bun'-ny *bunnies*. A pet name for a rabbit.–Jack is fond of his *bunny*.

bunting bun'-ting *buntings*. 1. A group of small birds related to the finches, including the corn-*bunting,* the reed-*bunting* and the yellow-hammer.
2. A brightly-coloured cloth used to make flags and banners for festive occasions.

buoy (pronounced *boy*) *buoys*. 1. A floating marker.–*Buoys* are anchored in the river to guide the ships.
2. A floating object used to keep a person up in the water.–The sailors clung to life-*buoys* to keep from sinking.

bur or **burr** *burs* or *burrs*. A thorny part of a plant. Seeds of some plants and trees are held in a case, or cover, that has prickles or thorns all over the outside. This thorny cover is a *bur*.– Some thorny *burs* cling to your clothing if you touch them.

burden bur'-den *burdens*. 1. A load.–The old man was carrying a heavy *burden* on his back.
2. A task that must be done.–Mother carries the *burden* of caring for the children.
3. The amount a ship can carry.–The ship's *burden* is 2,500 tons.

bureau bu'-reau *bureaus*. 1. A. writing-desk or table with drawers. – Father keeps his documents in the locked drawer of his *bureau*.
2. A branch or department, as of a government, for managing or studying a particular thing.–Farmers were warned by the Weather *Bureau* that there would be a frost.

burglar bur'-glar *burglars*. A person who breaks into a house, shop, etc., to steal.–The *burglar* was caught by the police as he was climbing out of the bedroom window.

burial bur'-i-al *burials*. Laying of the dead into the grave.–The *burial* took place in Shadyrest Cemetery.

burn *burns, burned* or *burnt, burning*. 1. Be on fire; make flames.–The coal in the furnace is *burning*.
2. Hurt by fire.–Children who play with fire may be *burned*.
3. Be destroyed by fire.–The house *burned* to the ground.
4. Cause to *burn*; set on fire.–The children *burned* the leaves in the garden.
5. A sore made by something very hot.– Mother had a small *burn* on her arm from the iron.
6. To sting, as if from something hot.–Iodine *burns* when you put it on a cut.

burrow bur'-row *burrows, burrowed, burrowing*. 1. Dig into the ground; dig a hole to live in.–Rabbits, badgers and moles *burrow*.
2. A nest or home made in the ground by a *burrowing* animal.

burst *bursts, bursting*. 1. Break open.–Mary blew so much air into the balloon that it *burst*.
2. Break into many pieces.–The fireworks *burst* while they were in the air.
3. Rush suddenly.–John *burst* into the room, and told of the fire.

bury bur'-y *buries, buried, burying*. 1. Put into the ground and cover up.–Dogs *bury* bones. –When people or animals die, their bodies are sometimes *buried*.
2. Cover completely.–Jack's cricket gear was *buried* under his clothes in the trunk.

bus *buses*. A large public vehicle with many seats. Some *buses* take people from one part of a town to another, and others serve small towns and villages in the country. Some *buses* have 2 decks, or floors, with seats on each deck. The points at which passengers get on and off are called *bus*-stops.–Father travels to work every day on a *bus*.

busby bus'-by *busbies*. A tall fur hat with a small bag hanging down on the right side, worn by certain regiments when in full dress uniform.–In the British Army, the Royal Horse Artillery wear *busbies*.

bush *bushes*. A low plant that has many branches or stems near, or coming from, the ground. Shrubs are *bushes*. Roses and berries grow on *bushes*.

bushel bush'-el *bushels*. A measure of certain dry things such as grain. We may buy tomatoes and potatoes either by the pound or by the *bushel*. A *bushel* is equal to 32 dry quarts, or 4 pecks.

bushy bush'-y. 1. Thick with fur or hair.–The squirrel has a *bushy* tail.
2. Overgrown with bushes.–The path is *bushy*.

busily bus'-i-ly. In a busy manner. – Father worked *busily* all day long.

business busi'ness *businesses*. 1. The work a man does to earn a living.–Painting houses is a painter's *business*.
2. A group of people organized to earn a living.–Father is in the shoe *business*. The company he works for sells shoes.
3. An amount of buying and selling. – The second-hand motor-car dealers do a big *business*. They buy and sell many used motorcars.

bustle bus'-tle *bustles, bustled, bustling*. Move hurriedly, excitedly, and noisily.–The children *bustle* about doing their work.

busy bus'-y *busier, busiest, busily*. 1. Active; at work.–Mother will be *busy* until her work is done.
2. Alive with activity or work.–The art room is a *busy* place.–Yesterday was a *busy* day.

B
C
D
E
F
G
H
I
J
K
L
M
N
O
P
Q
R
S
T
U
V
W
X
Y
Z

but. 1. Except.–All the boys *but* one are here. 2. However, yet.–The boys may play ball now, *but* they must work later.–They are tired *but* happy. 3. Only.–John has *but* 1 pencil.

butcher butch′-er *butchers.* A man who runs a meat shop or cuts up meat to sell for food.

butter but′-ter *butters, buttered, buttering.* 1. The solid yellow fat that comes from cream when it is churned or beaten.–We eat *butter* on bread. 2. Certain *butter*-like substances used for manufacturing, like cocoa-*butter,* made from cocoa beans; or for spreading, like peanut-*butter,* made from ground-up peanuts. 3. Put or spread *butter* on. – Mother *buttered* Baby's bread.

buttercup but′-ter-cup *buttercups.* A small, bright yellow flower with large leaves.

butterfly but′-ter-fly *butterflies.* An insect that has 4 beautifully-coloured wings. *Butterflies* fly in the daytime.

buttermilk but′-ter-milk. The milk (sometimes sour) that is left when the butterfat is taken out of cream.

button but′-ton *buttons, buttoned, buttoning.* 1. A piece of glass, pearl, brass, etc., used as a fastener or decoration on clothing, cloth covers, etc.–Mother sewed the green *buttons* on to Sally's dress with green thread.

2. Fasten with *buttons.*–Baby cannot *button* her dress. 3. A small, round device which is pressed to make something work.–John pressed a *button* and the bell rang.

buttonhole but′-ton-hole *buttonholes.* A hole in clothing, etc., through which a button goes. The *buttonholes* on Father's coat are too small for the buttons to go through.

buy *buys, bought, buying.* Get (anything) by paying money for it.–Father went to the shop to *buy* some oranges.

buyer buy′-er *buyers.* 1. A person who *buys* things. 2. A person who chooses and *buys* goods to be sold in a shop.–Mrs. Jones is the dress *buyer* for the big shop in town.

buzz *buzzes, buzzed, buzzing.* 1. A humming or murmuring noise. – Before the show started, we could hear the *buzz* of people talking softly. 2. Make a *buzz.*–Bees and other insects *buzz.*

buzzard buz′-zard *buzzards.* 1. A large bird that lives by eating small animals such as mice, frogs, etc. It is related to the hawk. 2. In America, the turkey *buzzard* (or turkey vulture) feeds on dead animals.

by. 1. Close to; near.–John sits *by* Jack. 2. Through the use of; with; through the effort or activity of.–4 divided *by* 2 is 2. –The window was broken *by* the ball.–We are going to Brighton *by* train. 3. Along.–They travelled *by* this route. 4. Not later than.–We will be there *by* 7 o'clock. 5. Past.–In times gone *by,* farmers cut hay with scythes.–We went right *by* the house.

bygone by′-gone. Belonging to the past, in olden times.–In *bygone* days men of fashion wore wigs.

by-pass by′-pass *by-passes.* A new road built off a main road so as to avoid a large town and to keep traffic moving.–By taking the *by-pass* we got home much earlier.

bystander by′-stand-er *bystanders.* A spectator. –Many *bystanders* saw the accident.

C c

C, c *C's, c's.* The third letter of the alphabet.

cab *cabs.* 1. A motor-car which is rented or hired with its driver; a taxi-*cab.*–Father took a *cab* to work while his car was being repaired.
2. A closed carriage drawn by a horse.–When Grandfather was young, he rode in a *cab.* Now he rides in a motor-car.
3. The space in a locomotive which shelters the driver.–The driver leaned out of his *cab* while the passengers boarded the train.

cabaret (pronounced *cabaray*) cab'-a-ret *cabarets.* An entertainment in a night-club.

cabbage cab'-bage *cabbages.* A vegetable somewhat similar to a lettuce. As the cabbage grows, it develops a big head or heart. *Cabbage* is white, green, or red. Sauerkraut is made of *cabbage.*

cabin cab'-in *cabins.* 1. A small house built of rough timbers or logs.–Robinson Crusoe lived in a *cabin.*
2. A room on a ship.–Most *cabins* on steamships are very small.
3. The part of an aeroplane where passengers sit.

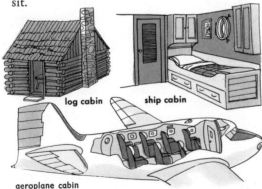

log cabin   ship cabin

aeroplane cabin

cabinet cab'-i-net *cabinets.* 1. A set of shelves or a chest of drawers.–We keep medicines in the bathroom *cabinet.* –Father keeps papers in a filing *cabinet.*
2. A group of men who conduct a nation's government.

cable ca'-ble *cables, cabled, cabling.* 1. A heavy metal rope or chain. Many wires wound together make a wire rope or *cable.*–The ship was held to the dock with large *cables.*
2. A way of sending telegraph messages to other countries through a *cable* laid under the ocean.
3. A message sent by *cable.*
4. Send a message by *cable.*–While in France, Edward *cabled* his father for more money.

cablegram ca'-ble-gram *cablegrams.* A message sent by a cable.–Uncle Frank sent Father a *cablegram* from Africa.

cacao (pronounced *ca-cow*) ca-cao' A tropical tree from whose seeds cocoa and chocolate are manufactured. The raw *cacao* beans are brown and shaped rather like almonds.

cache *caches.* A secret store-house or hiding-place.–When we went exploring, we left our food in a *cache* inside a cave.

cackle cack'-le *cackles, cackled, cackling.* 1. Make a high, cracked, chattering sound.–We heard the hens in the barn *cackling.*–The old witch *cackled* with glee when she saw Hansel and Gretel.
2. A high, cracked, chattering sound.–Have you ever heard the *cackle* of a hen?

cactus cac'-tus *cactuses* or *cacti.* A plant that has prickles, or thorns, instead of leaves. The *cactus* needs very little water, and can live in very hot places. Some *cactuses* grow into funny shapes. Many grow in the desert. Some kinds are small enough to grow indoors in flower pots.

caddie, caddy cad'-dy *caddies.* 1. A boy or man who carries a golfer's clubs.–Tom sometimes works as a *caddie* at week-ends.
2. A small box for holding tea.–Mother poured the tea from the packet into the *caddy.*

C D E F G H I J K L M N O P Q R S T U V W X Y Z

cadet ca-det′ *cadets*. A student at a military or naval school; member of a junior force.

café ca-fé *cafés*. A restaurant.–After the show we stopped at a *café* to get a bite to eat.

cafeteria caf-e-te′-ri-a *cafeterias*. A kind of restaurant in which you serve yourself from a long counter of food. There are no waiters or waitresses to take your order at your table.

cage *cages*. A room or space with one or more sides made of wire or bars.–Animals at the zoo are kept in *cages*. –Birds that are kept indoors live in *cages*.

cake *cakes, caked, caking*. 1. A food made of a batter of flour, eggs, butter, sugar, flavouring, and other things, and then baked in an oven. – Mother baked a birthday *cake* for me. Then she iced the *cake* and put seven candles on it.

2. Anything moulded or cut into a small rounded or squared shape.–Meat, salmon, mashed potatoes, and many other foods, can be patted or formed into *cakes* and fried like pan*cakes*.–Mother bought 3 *cakes* of soap.– We saw a big *cake* of ice in the river.
3. Become hard or solid.–The paint will *cake* on your brushes if you do not clean them after painting with them.

calendar cal′-en-dar *calendars*. A chart which shows the months of the year, the weeks, the days of the month, and the number of each day in each month. – Sometimes Christmas is on Monday, sometimes Tuesday, and so forth. The *calendar* shows us what day it will fall on this year.–Father has a desk *calendar*.

calf *calves*. 1. The young of a cow. The babies of some other animals, such as the elephant and the hippopotamus, are also called *calves*.
2. The thick, muscular part of the back of the leg that is just below the knee.

calico cal′-i-co. A cotton cloth, usually plain white and unprinted.–Mary made her doll a dress of *calico*.

California Cal-i-for′-nia. A state on the west coast of the United States, noted for its fine climate and its beauty. Fine fruit groves and large farms produce several crops each year. Many motion pictures are made in *California*.

call *calls, called, calling*. 1. Shout, cry out.– Bob *called* me from the window as I passed.
2. Cry out someone's name.–Mother *called* Bob.
3. Send for, ask to come.–We *called* Father to dinner. We asked him to come.
4. Name.–I know a man *called* Don Smith. –Jack *calls* his dog Spot.
5. A cry, a voice.–We heard the robin's *call*.
6. A shout.–We heard a loud *call* for help from out in the water.
7. A visit.–Mary paid us a short *call*.
8. *Call on* means make a visit to.–The minister *calls* on Grandmother.
9. *Call on* means ask the help of, turn to.– We can always *call on* Father when we are in difficulty.

caller call′-er *callers*. A visitor. – Mother is cleaning the house because we are expecting a *caller*.

callous cal′-lous *callously*. 1. Having a callus.– Jack had a *callous* area on his thumb.
2. Heartless, without pity.–The *callous* general ordered the mules to be killed.

callus cal′-lus *calluses*. A spot on which the skin has become hard and thick.–The farmer had a *callus* on the palm of his hand where the handle of his hoe had kept rubbing.

calm *calms, calmed, calming, calmly, calmness*. 1. Quiet, peaceful.–The lake was so *calm* that it looked like glass.–It was a *calm* summer day, without any wind.
2. Not excited.–Bob is always *calm*, whatever happens; Jack gets upset easily.
3. Make quiet.–Father tried to *calm* Baby by giving her his watch to play with.
4. Peace and quiet.–Grandmother enjoys the *calm* of the country.

calves. Two or more baby cows. – Grandmother's cow had one calf last spring, but twin *calves* this year.

came. One form of the word *come.*–The children *came* to school at nine o'clock.

camel cam′-el *camels*. A large, somewhat hairy animal that has either 1 or 2 humps on its back. *Camels* are used to carry loads across dry, sandy deserts. They can go without drinking water for many days.

camera cam′-er-a *cameras*. A machine for taking photographs of things by exposing a special film or plate to light.–When we go on our holiday, we take our *camera* so that we can take pictures.

studio camera

miniature camera

press camera

bellows camera

camouflage cam′-ou-flage *camouflages, camouflaged, camouflaging*. 1. Change the appearance of a thing so that it will not be seen or recognized easily.–The soldiers *camouflaged* the tops of the buildings by painting them to look like trees.

2. Something used to make a thing hard to see or recognize. – The soldier's covering of leaves was a good *camouflage*. It made him look like a part of the woods.

camp *camps, camped, camping*. 1. A place where people live in tents or simple buildings placed close together, in the country.– The boys are going to the Boy Scout *camp*. –Some soldiers live in *camps*.

2. Live outdoors, especially in a tent, for a time.–We *camped* for the night by a little brook.

campaign cam-paign′ *campaigns, campaigned, campaigning*. 1. A drive or plan to get money, or to get something done.–Once a year we have a Red Cross *campaign*.–The general is planning the army's *campaign*. He is working out where they are going to move, and how they will do it.
2. Work for a special purpose according to a plan or system.–Father is going to *campaign* for Mr Jones to be elected chairman. He will try to get people to vote for Mr Jones.

camper camp′-er *campers*. A person who lives for a time outdoors in a tent, rough building, sleeping bag, etc., and lives very simply. One who goes to a camp is also a *camper*.

camphor cam′-phor. A gum that comes from the *camphor* tree. *Camphor* is used in medicines. It has a strong, sharp odour.–Mother uses balls of *camphor* in cupboards and drawers to keep moths away.

can *cans, canned, canning*. 1. Know how to, have the ability to.–Jack *can* skate.–Sally *can* draw very well for her age.
2. Be able to, have the strength to.–Father *can* push the car.–*Can* you lift this?
3. A container, usually made of tin or other metal.–Vegetables, soups, fruit, and many other foods, may be bought in *cans*.–The boys tossed pebbles into a tin *can*.
4. Put in *cans* or jars and seal tightly.–The factory *cans* all kinds of fruits, vegetables, fish, meat and preserves.

C

D E F G H I J K L M N O P Q R S T U V W X Y Z

canal ca-nal′ *canals*. A waterway that looks like a river, but has been dug by man. *Canals* are deep enough for boats to sail on them. A *canal* makes it possible for boats to travel from one body of water to another.

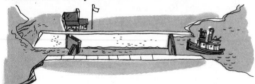

canary ca-nar′-y *canaries*. A yellowish song-bird. Many people keep *canaries* as pets in wire cages in their homes.

cancel can′-cel *cancels, cancelled, cancelling*. 1. Withdraw; call off; decide that something that was to happen shall not take place.– Mother ordered a new coat, and then *cancelled* the order when she decided to use her old coat instead. She told the shop not to send her the coat.–Because of rain, the cricket match was *cancelled*.
2. Mark out; draw lines through.–When Mary wrote the word badly, she *cancelled* it. She crossed it out.–The post office *cancels* postage stamps on letters. It makes marks across them with a rubber stamp to show that they have been used.

cancer can′-cer *cancers*. A kind of growing sore on or inside the body.–*Cancer* causes many deaths.

candidate can′-di-date *candidates*. A person who is being considered for a certain position; a person who is standing for office.–Mr Jones is a *candidate* for mayor. He is standing for mayor.

candle can′-dle *candles*. A stick of wax with a wick, or string, running through it. When the wick is lighted, it slowly burns up the wax to give light.–We burn *candles* at Christmas time, on birthday cakes, in church, etc.

candlestick can′-dle-stick *candlesticks*. A holder for a candle. We put candles in *candlesticks*. *Candlesticks* are made of glass, brass, wood, silver, and many other things.

candy can′-dy *candies, candied, candying*. 1. A sweet food made by boiling down sugar or syrup until it is thick enough to be shaped into pieces.–*Candy* is flavoured and often covered with chocolate or other coating. In the United States, toffees and other sweets are called *candy*.

2. To preserve by boiling in sugar or syrup until a coating is formed.–Father bought Mary a box of *candied* fruit.–Mother had crystallized or *candied* fruits as a present.

cane *canes*. 1. A walking stick.–The old man walks with a *cane* to lean on, because he is lame.
2. Rattan, or parts of a palm tree that have been cut into narrow strips. – The chair seat is woven with *cane*.
3. A large, grass-like plant.– Sugar is made from sugar beets and from sugar *cane*.
4. A name often given to the hollow stem of the bamboo, a giant grass plant.
5. A slender rod used in some schools for punishing pupils.–The boy received six strokes of the *cane* for stealing the stamps.

cannon can′-non *cannons*. A big gun. Some *cannons* are mounted on wheels so that they can be moved easily.–The soldiers fired the *cannon* at the fort.

cannot can′-not. Is not able to.–Because of her cold, Mary *cannot* go to school today.

canoe ca-noe′ *canoes*. A light, narrow boat that is pointed at both ends. A *canoe* is pushed swiftly through the water by paddles worked by hand.

canon can′-on *canons*. 1. A church decree; a clergyman belonging to a cathedral.–The *canon* conducted the service this morning.
2. A piece of music in which the tune is repeated in turn by different groups of voices or instruments.–The children sang 'Frère Jacques' in *canon*.

canopy can′-o-py *canopies*. A covering or shelter.–The queen sat under a *canopy*.

canteen can-teen′ *canteens*. 1. A store at an army camp.–The soldiers buy sweets, cigarettes, foods, soft drinks, and other things at the *canteen*.
2. A bottle-shaped, metal container.–Soldiers carry *canteens* filled with water.

canvas can'-vas *canvases*. A strong, coarsely woven cotton cloth. – The paper-hanger spread a *canvas* over the rug to protect it. – The cloth used for tents, and sails on boats, is *canvas*. – Pictures painted with oil paints are often painted on *canvas*.

canvass can'-vass *canvasses, canvassed, canvassing*. Go from door to door; inquire about, discuss, or ask for support, everywhere – particularly in the sense of persuading people to vote for somebody. – When Jack Robinson stood for Parliament, he and his helpers *canvassed* the town for votes.

canyon can'-yon *canyons*. A deep, narrow valley with very steep sides. Sometimes there is a stream at the bottom of a *canyon*.

cap *caps, capped, capping*. 1. A small hat that fits the head closely. Some *caps* have peaks, or small brims, in front to shade the eyes. – Soldiers, sailors, nurses, cooks, etc., wear special *caps* made for them.
2. The covering for the top of almost anything, as a bottle *cap*, a *cap* on the radiator of a car, a fruit-jar *cap*, etc.
3. Small pieces of paper with a little explosive powder between them. – On Guy Fawkes night we had some *caps* for our toy guns. They popped when we pulled the trigger.
4. Put a *cap* or cover on. – Mother *capped* the fruit jars.

capable ca'-pa-ble. *capably*. Able; knowing enough and having strength enough to do a thing well; qualified; good at doing something. – Jack is *capable* of doing better work than he has done lately. – Mother does not worry about leaving Baby with Mary, because Mary is so *capable*.

capacity ca-pac'-i-ty. Amount or number that can be contained or held. – The bottle has a *capacity* of 1 quart. – The church has a seating *capacity* of 800.

cape *capes*. 1. An outer garment, or cloak, without sleeves. It hangs down from the shoulders over the arms and body. Some *capes* are long and some short.
2. A narrow piece of land that extends or stretches out into the sea. A *cape* is surrounded on 3 sides by the ocean, like the *Cape* of Good Hope.

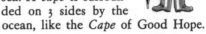

caper ca'-per *capers, capered, capering*. 1. Jump and spring about in a lively way. – The horse was *capering* about in the field.
2. Playful leaping and jumping. – We watched the *capers* of the lambs.

capital cap'-i-tal *capitals*. 1. *Capital* letters and small letters are used in writing and printing. You begin your name or start a sentence with a *capital* letter.
2. The *capital* of a state or country is the city where the government meets regularly. – London is the *capital* of England. – The *capital* of the whole United States is Washington, D.C.
3. Money or property. – Mr Jones did not have enough *capital* to start the new business, so he borrowed some from a bank.
4. *Capital punishment* means a death penalty for certain crimes. – In some countries, *capital punishment* is used for people who have killed someone intentionally.

capitulate ca-pit'-u-late *capitulates, capitulated, capitulating*. Give in or surrender. – After a powerful bombardment by air, land and sea, the enemy *capitulated*.

capricious ca-pri'-cious *capriciously*. Behaving in a fanciful manner, without any apparent reason. – When Alan upset all the ink-pots the teacher punished him for his *capricious* behaviour.

Capricorn Cap'-ri-corn. An imaginary line running 23½ degrees south of the equator and parellel to it. All the countries lying between the equator and this line are in the tropic of *Capricorn*. The similar region north of the equator is called the tropic of Cancer.

C D E F G H I J K L M N O P Q R S T U V W X Y Z

C
D
E
F
G
H
I
J
K
L
M
N
O
P
Q
R
S
T
U
V
W
X
Y
Z

capsize cap-size′ *capsizes, capsized, capsizing.* Upset, turn over.–The canoe *capsized* in the water when one of the boys stood up.

captain cap′-tain *captains.* 1. A leader.–The football *captain* was hurt.
2. An army officer ranking next above first lieutenant.
3. A naval officer ranking next above commander.
4. Anyone who commands a ship.–The *captain* of the ship gave the sailors their orders.

captive cap′-tive *captives.* A prisoner.–The *captives* in the prison camp had to wear chains.

captivity cap-tiv′-i-ty. Condition of being held prisoner.–Lions in the zoo are in *captivity.* –People in prisons are in *captivity.* They are kept in prison against their wishes.

capture cap′-ture *captures, captured, capturing.* 1. Take alive, or seize.–The enemy *captured* 50 men. They took 50 prisoners.
2. Catching, or being caught. – After their *capture,* the men were sent to a far-away city.

car *cars.* 1. An automobile.–Mother drove the *car* into town to meet Father.

2. Sometimes used to describe certain carriages on a train, for example dining-*car,* sleeping-*car,* etc. Public vehicles running on rails with an overhead cable are called tram-*cars.*

caracal ca′-ra-cal *caracals.* A kind of lynx with reddish fur and black ear-tips.–We saw a *caracal* in the lion-house at the zoo.

carafe ca-rafe′ *carafes.* A glass bottle used on the table.–Father asked the waiter to bring a fresh *carafe* of water.

caramel car′-a-mel *caramels.* 1. A fairly soft, sticky toffee made with brown sugar, butter, milk, etc.–Most children like *caramels.*
2. Flavoured with sugar, browned by burning it a little.–We made *caramel* pudding.

carat car′-at. A unit of weight for certain precious stones, such as diamonds; also a measure used to gauge the purity of gold.– Father bought mother a beautiful 18-*carat* gold watch for her birthday.

caravan car′-a-van *caravans.* 1. A group of people travelling together through wilderness or desert country.–There were many camels in the *caravan* that set out across the desert.

2. A wagon in which people travel and live. –Gypsies often live in *caravans.*

card *cards.* A piece of heavy paper or cardboard, blank or printed.–The teacher gave us our report *cards* today.–Uncle Jim sent us a post*card* from New York.– The tickets used by the railway are little green *cards.*– We play bridge and other *card* games with a pack of playing *cards.*

cardboard card′board. Heavy, stiff substance akin to paper.–Posters, boxes, book-covers, and many other things, can be made of *cardboard.*

cardigan car′-di-gan *cardigans.* A knitted woollen jacket with or without sleeves, worn over a shirt or blouse.–Mother told Jack to wear his *cardigan* as it was cold.

cardinal car′-di-nal *cardinals.* One of the high officials of the Roman Catholic Church.

care *cares, cared, caring.* 1. Love.–Parents *care* for their children.
2. Look after.–Mary will *care* for the baby.
3. Be interested in.–Grandfather *cares* greatly about the education of the boys.–Jack does not *care* for his violin lessons.
4. Attention, thought, and effort.–The children did their work with *care.*
5. Charge.–Mother will take *care* of the garden while Father is away.

career ca-reer′ *careers.* A way of life or method of earning a living.–Jack wants to take up medicine as a *career* when he grows up.

careful care'-ful *carefully, carefulness.* Using thought and effort; paying attention, watchful.–Bob is a *careful* worker.–Mary is *careful* of Baby.

careless care'-less *carelessly.* Not interested; thoughtless; not trying or paying attention. –Bill's poor writing shows that he is *careless.*–Do not be *careless* when crossing the street or you may be hurt.

carelessness care'-less-ness. Not thinking, bothering, or paying attention; not taking trouble.–*Carelessness* causes many mistakes.

caretaker care'-tak-er *caretakers.* A person who is hired to look after a building or other property.–The man who keeps watch at the museum at night is a *caretaker.*

cargo car'-go *cargoes* or *cargos.* A load of anything carried by a ship or plane.–The ship was loaded with a heavy *cargo.*

carnation car-na'-tion *carnations.* A kind of large, red, white, or pink flower which has a very spicy, pleasing odour.

carnival car'-ni-val *carnivals.* A time for merry-making and being gay.–The school is having a *carnival* next Monday evening. – At *carnival* time in many southern European cities the people put on masks and sing and dance in the streets.

carol car'-ol *carols, carolled, carolling.* 1. A song of joy, especially a Christmas hymn.–The choir sings *carols* at Christmas time.
2. Sing happily.–Children were *carolling* on the porch.–Birds *carol* in the spring.

carpenter car'-pen-ter *carpenters.* A person who builds things from wood.–Father hired a *carpenter* to lay a new floor.

carpet car'-pet *carpets, carpeted, carpeting.*
1. Thick woollen material covering floors.– We put a *carpet* on the living-room floor.
2. Cover smoothly, as with a *carpet.*–The field is *carpeted* with grass and fallen leaves.

carriage car'-riage *carriages.* 1. A wheeled vehicle drawn by horses and usually used to carry people.–Motor-cars have now taken the place of *carriages.*

2. Posture; way of holding the body.–The man's *carriage* showed that he was a soldier.

carrot car'-rot *carrots.* A vegetable with an orange root that is good to eat. *Carrots* grow in the ground as beetroots do.–Some farmers grow *carrots* to feed to their cattle.

carry car'-ry *carries, carried, carrying.* 1. Take from place to place. – Omnibuses *carry* many passengers each day. They take the passengers from one place to another. – The wind *carries* leaves through the air.
2. Have for sale; keep on hand.–Department stores *carry* many kinds of goods.
3. Pass by vote.–The suggestion to have a picnic was *carried.*

cart *carts, carted, carting.* 1. A 2-wheeled wagon used for carrying people or heavy loads.–The fruit vendor sells fruit from a *cart.*–A *cart* may be pushed by a person or drawn by a horse, donkey, or other animal.

2. Haul or carry in a *cart.*–The rag-and-bone-man *carted* away the old newspapers. He put them in his *cart* and carried them away.

carton car'-ton *cartons*. A stiff paper or pasteboard box.–The farmer sells eggs in *cartons*.

cartoon car-toon' *cartoons*. A funny or clever

drawing of people or happenings.–The children's comic has coloured *cartoons* in it.

cartridge car'-tridge *cartridges*. A case or shell that holds an explosive. – *Cartridges* are used in guns.

carve *carves, carved, carving*. 1. Cut into shape. –The statue was *carved* from stone. Many animal ornaments are carved out of wood.
2. Cut into pieces.–Mother *carved* the meat in the kitchen.
3. Cut a design on.–John got into trouble for *carving* his initials on the table.

carver carv'-er *carvers*. A person who cuts or carves things.–The wood-*carver* made little figures of people from wood.

case *cases*. 1. A box or carton.–Father bought a *case* of canned tomatoes.
2. A covering or holder.–Jack's new knife came in a leather *case*.
3. A condition or instance.–In *case* of accident, call the police.–Baby had a slight *case* of measles.
4. A matter to be settled by law.–The farmer who was cheated took the *case* to court.

cash *cashes, cashed, cashing*. 1. Money; money on hand.–Bob didn't have enough *cash* to pay for the bicycle. He had enough money in his bank account but not enough with him.
2. Exchange for money.–The workman took his cheque to the bank to have it *cashed*.

cashier cash-ier' *cashiers*. A person who handles or is responsible for handling money, or cash.–A *cashier* at the bank takes care of the money.–A *cashier* in a shop handles the money, gives change, etc.

casing cas'-ing *casings*. A frame.–The window *casing* needs to be painted.

cask *casks*. A barrel.–The grocer bought a *cask* of vinegar.

casket cas'-ket *caskets*. A small box for jewellery, letters or other valuable, possessions, often richly decorated. – The children gave their teacher a silver *casket*.

casserole cas'-se-role *casseroles*. A covered dish in which food can be baked and from which food can be served at the table; sometimes applied to the food served in this way. – Mother cooked a chicken *casserole* for dinner.

cast *casts, casting*. 1. Throw.–The fisherman *cast* the fish-hook and bait into the water.
2. Form in a mould.–Many parts of a motor-car are *cast* from metal. The metal is melted, poured into moulds of different shapes, and allowed to harden.
3. The actors in a play or film.–The *cast* for the school play has been chosen.
4. To *cast* a vote or ballot means to vote.– Father *cast* his vote for Mr Jones for M.P.

castanets cas-ta-nets'. Wooden or ivory clappers held in the hands and clapped together to the rhythm of music. – The dancer kept time with *castanets*.

caster or **castor** cast'-er *casters*. A small roller or wheel on the leg of a table, bed, etc.–The *casters* on the table legs allow the table to be moved easily.
2. A holder for salt, pepper or sugar.–Grandmother has a silver *caster* on her dining-room table.

castle cas'-tle *castles*. 1. A large building of olden times, used as a fort and dwelling place. *Castles* had towers, high walls, and moats or water-ways about them to hold off enemies.

2. A very large and grand house.–Princes and noblemen live in *castles*.

castor oil cas'-tor oil. An oil made from the seeds of the *castor-oil* plant. *Castor oil* is taken as medicine to bring about a movement of the bowels.

casualty cas'-u-al-ty *casualties*. 1. An accident. –The explosion was a serious *casualty*.
2. In war, a soldier killed, wounded, or taken ill.–There are often more *casualties* from disease than from battle.

cat cats. 1. A small, furred animal kept as a pet.–*Cats* are tame. They catch mice and rats.

lion

leopard

domestic cat

tiger

2. Any of the family of animals including pet *cats* and wild *cats*, such as the lion, tiger, and leopard.

catalogue cat'-a-logue *catalogues, catalogued, cataloguing*. 1. A book that describes and illustrates things and tells how much they cost.
2. An orderly list.–The teacher made a *catalogue* of the names of all the boys and girls in the school.
3. Make an orderly list of.–The librarian *catalogues* the books in the library.

catapult cat'-a-pult *catapults*. 1. An ancient engine of war which hurled stones and spears.
2. A forked stick with elastic, used by boys to shoot small stones and pellets.–The boy broke a window with his *catapult*.

cataract cat'-a-ract *cataracts*. A waterfall dropping down from a great height.–We watched the *cataract* plunging down over the precipice into the valley below.

catarrh ca-tarrh'. An inflammation of the nose, causing severe sneezing and coughing.–Last winter father suffered so badly from *catarrh* that he had to visit a doctor.

catch *catches, caught, catching*. 1. Get or take and hold on to; seize and hold.–I saw the ball player *catch* the ball. He got it while it was still in the air.–Fishermen *catch* fish.–Traps are used to *catch* some animals.
2. Come up to.–John started to run, and Bob could not *catch* him.
3. Discover, find out, surprise.–Just as Mary was getting a biscuit from the tin, Mother *caught* her.
4. Get; receive. – Bob was careful not to *catch* a cold.
5. *Catch fire* means to start burning.–Do not play with fire. Your clothes may *catch fire*.
6. *Catch up with* means to get to the same place as.–Mary finished so many problems at home that it was hard for the class to *catch up with* her.–We started for the park first, and the others could not *catch up with* us.
7. Become tangled with. – The dog's leash *caught* on a bush.
8. A fastener.–The *catch* on the screen holds it in place.

cater ca'-ter *caters, catered, catering*. Provide what is required.–This magazine *caters* for people who like art.–A person who supplies food for a party is a *caterer*.

caterpillar cat'-er-pil-lar *caterpillars*. 1. An insect, such as the moth, in its worm-like stage. – Moths and butterflies go through several stages before they are full-grown. One stage is the *caterpillar* form.

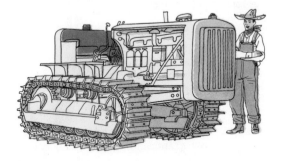

2. A tractor that runs on 2 flat metal belts. – Heavy loads can be pulled over rough ground by *caterpillar* tractors.

catfish cat'-fish. A fish that has a flat head with long feelers that look like a cat's whiskers.

C D E F G H I J K L M N O P Q R S T U V W X Y Z

cathedral ca-the′-dral *cathedrals*. The main church in a bishop's district, or diocese. A *cathedral* contains the bishop's throne.

Catholic Cath′-o-lic *Catholics*. 1. A person who belongs to the *Catholic* Church.
2. The *Catholic* Church, sometimes called the Roman *Catholic* Church, is a religious group led by the Pope in Rome.

catkin cat′-kin *catkins*. The fluffy flower of the willow and birch trees.

catmint cat′-mint. A plant something like mint. Cats are fond of *catmint*. It has a pleasing odour.

cat-o′-nine-tails. A whip with 9 knotted lashes, once used in the British army and navy as a form of punishment.

cat's-tail cats′-tail *cat's-tails*. A plant that grows in wet, marshy places. Usually called a bulrush. In the Bible it is known as papyrus, the plant from which paper was made.

cattle cat′-tle. Cows, bulls, and steers.–Some farmers grow grain, and others breed *cattle*.

caught. One form of the word *catch*. – Bob *caught* the apple as it fell from the tree.

cauliflower cau′-li-flow-er *cauliflowers*. A cabbage-like vegetable that is good to eat. It grows in a head made up of solid white flowers with leaves around them.

cause *causes, caused, causing*. 1. Bring about; make happen.–A lighted match thrown into the grass *caused* the fire.–Wind *causes* the yacht to sail.
2. That which makes something happen. – Sickness was the *cause* of Mary's absence from school.
3. A thing which people believe in.–Soldiers fight for the *cause* of freedom.

caution cau′-tion *cautions, cautioned, cautioning*. 1. Warn.–The policeman *cautioned* the driver to stay in line.
2. Care; watchfulness.–Cross the street with *caution*. Take no chances.

cautious cau′-tious *cautiously*. Careful.–Children should be *cautious* in crossing streets.

cavalry cav′-al-ry. Soldiers who ride horses.–The *cavalry* led the parade.

cave *caves, caved, caving*. 1. A hollow space in the earth.–The men went down into the *cave*.

2. *Cave in* means fall in.–The rains made the tunnel *cave in*.

cavity cav′-i-ty *cavities*. A hole or hollow space. –The dentist filled a *cavity* in Mother's tooth.

caw *caws, cawed, cawing*. 1. The cry of a crow.
2. Make the cry of a crow.–Crows *caw*.

cease *ceases, ceased, ceasing*. Stop; finish.– Father told John to *cease* shouting.–We shall go when the rain *ceases*.

cedar ce′-dar *cedars.* A tree with flat, web-like leaves that stay green all the winter. The wood is very durable and so is used on the outside of houses, and for making sheds, etc. The wood of the *cedar* tree has a pleasing odour.

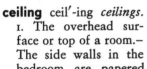

ceiling ceil′-ing *ceilings.*
1. The overhead surface or top of a room.– The side walls in the bedroom are papered, but the *ceiling* is painted.
2. The highest distance an aeroplane can go without losing sight of the ground. The height of the *ceiling* depends on the amount of clouds and haze in the sky.–The aviator reported a low *ceiling.* The clouds were low, and he could not go above them and still see the ground.
3. The highest an aeroplane can go.–The *ceiling* of this plane is 30,000 feet.

celebrate cel′-e-brate *celebrates, celebrated, celebrating.* 1. Take notice of and do honour to; observe by doing special things.–We expect to *celebrate* Father's birthday by having a party. – We *celebrate* Easter every year.
2. To perform with ceremony.–The marriage was *celebrated* in church.

celebration cel-e-bra′-tion *celebrations.* Special activities in honour of some event or holiday.–We went to the *celebration* in honour of the men who climbed Mount Everest.

celery cel′-er-y. A vegetable that grows in stalks which are cut apart and eaten raw, often in salads. It can be cooked or used in soups, also.

cell *cells.* 1. A small room in a jail.–The robber was put into a *cell.*

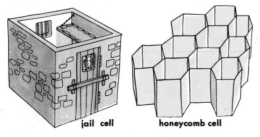

jail cell   honeycomb cell

2. One of a number of small spaces or parts. –A honeycomb is made up of small *cells.*

3. One of the tiny parts of living matter of which all living things are made. Your body is made up of *cells.* The *cells* in different parts of the body are somewhat different from one another.

cellar cel′-lar *cellars.* The space under a building below the ground. – The boiler in our house is in the *cellar.*

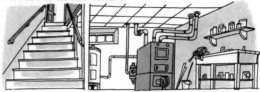

cello (pronounced *chello*) cel′-lo *cellos* or *celli.* Short for violoncello. A musical instrument like a large violin, deep in tone. It is stood on the floor between the knees to be played. It has 4 strings.

celluloid cel′-lu-loid. A plastic material used as a substitute for ivory, tortoise-shell, etc. It can be moulded into any shape and is used for making many useful and decorative objects. Combs, buttons, collars, toys and dolls are sometimes made of *celluloid.*

cement ce-ment′ *cements, cemented, cementing.* 1. A powder made by burning clay with a kind of rock known as limestone. *Cement,* when mixed with water and sand, dries hard. It is used in making pavements, roads, floors, etc., and for holding bricks and stones together in walls and buildings.
2. Any material, such as glue, that holds things together.–Mother used a china *cement* to mend the broken vase.
3. Stick.–She *cemented* the pieces together.

cemetery cem′-e-ter-y *cemeteries.* A place where the dead are buried, but not a churchyard.–The soldier was buried in a military *cemetery.*

census cen′-sus *censuses.* A count of the people living in a certain place. The *census* tells how many people there are, how old they are, etc.

cent *cents.* A small piece of money used in Canada and the United States; a penny. A *cent* is made of copper, tin, and zinc. Five *cents* make a nickel. Ten *cents* make a dime. One hundred *cents* make a dollar. One *cent* is usually written 1C.

C
D
E
F
G
H
I
J
K
L
M
N
O
P
Q
R
S
T
U
V
W
X
Y
Z

centipede cen'-ti-pede *centipedes.* An animal with a body made up of many sections or joints. At each joint is a pair of legs. *Centipedes* can run very fast. The name *centipede* means 'hundred feet,' but it does not really have that many.

central cen'-tral. 1. Middle.–The town hall is in the *central* part of town. It is not on the edge.
2. Leading, chief. – The acrobats were the *central* interest at the circus.

centre cen'-tre *centres, centred, centring.* 1. The middle point.–The *centre* of a circle is the point that is the same distance from all points on the edge of the circle.–In Blind Man's Buff the blindfolded person stands in the *centre* of the circle.
2. A main point or place.–At the zoo, the monkey cage is usually the *centre* of interest.
3. Put in the *centre.*–The teacher told us to *centre* our drawings on the page. She wanted us to leave an equal amount of space on all sides of our drawing.

century cen'-tu-ry *centuries.* One hundred years. –Few people live for a *century.* – From 1850 to 1950 is one *century.*

cereal ce'-re-al *cereals.* 1. Food such as rice, oatmeal, ground wheat, corn, and other things made from grain.–For breakfast many people eat some kind of *cereal.*
2. Any of the grasses that produce the grain from which *cereals* are made.

ceremony cer'-e-mo-ny *ceremonies.* A series of solemn, formal actions which people perform in a regular way on important occasions. There are church *ceremonies,* civic *ceremonies,* wedding *ceremonies,* patriotic *ceremonies,* royal *ceremonies,* etc.

certain cer'-tain. 1. Positive; sure; knowing without any doubt.–Bob was not *certain* he could go until he asked Father.–I am *certain* the sky is blue.–The weather report said that rain was *certain.*
2. Some; special; particular.–*Certain* fish live in salt water and *certain* others live in fresh water.–There is a *certain* book I want, but I can't find it.

certainly cer'-tain-ly. For certain; surely.–Father will *certainly* be here by 6 o'clock.–Will you excuse me? *Certainly.*

certificate cer-tif'-i-cate *certificates.* A written statement saying that something has taken place or is true.–When Father and Mother were married, the vicar gave them a marriage *certificate.*

chain *chains, chained, chaining.* 1. A number of links or rings fastened toegther. – The man's watch *chain* is made of gold. – Children like to make *chains* of daisies and dandelions.
2. An unbroken line of things.–Several mountains joined together are called a mountain *chain.*
3. Fasten with a *chain.*–Jack *chained* his dog to a stake so he could not run away.

chair *chairs.* A seat with legs and a back. We sit in a *chair.* Some *chairs* have rockers and are called rocking-*chairs.* A *chair* with arms is an arm*chair.*

chairman chair'-man *chairmen.* A person who is in charge of a meeting, committee, campaign, etc.–Jack will be the *chairman* at the club meeting. He will call the meeting to order and call on people to speak.

chalk *chalks, chalked, chalking, chalky.* 1. A stick of powdery white material made from limestone or other soft stone.–We write on the blackboard with *chalk.*
2. Mark with *chalk.*–It is thoughtless to *chalk* on people's fences.

challenge chal'-lenge *challenges, challenged, challenging.* 1. Dare, invite to enter a contest, etc.–The small boy *challenged* the big boy to fight.
2. A dare.–Tom accepted the *challenge.*

chamber cham'-ber *chambers.* 1. A bedroom; a private room.–Sleeping Beauty was found in a *chamber* at the top of the palace.
2. *Chambers* means an apartment or group of rooms in which people live or work.
3. A room or auditorium where a body of lawmakers meets; or the body of lawmakers itself.–The House of Lords is the upper *chamber* of Parliament.
4. A committee or department, as a *chamber* of commerce.
5. The part of a gun that holds the bullets or powder.

chamois (pronounced *shamwah*) cham'-ois. A mountain antelope like a large goat. The skin of a *chamois* is made into a soft leather, also called *chamois* (pronounced *shammy*). – Father cleans the car window with *chamois* leather.

champion cham'-pi-on *champions*. The winner, or the person or group which time after time comes out first, or ahead of all the others in a contest of any kind.–Surrey have been *champions* in the county cricket *champion*ship many times.

chance *chances, chanced, chancing.* 1. Luck, an accident, or an unexpected happening.– Our team won by *chance*. It wasn't really better than the other team.–Mary met her teacher by *chance*. It was a *chance* meeting. It was not planned.
2. An opportunity.–Jack has a *chance* to pass the test if he studies at home.–Grandfather did not have the *chance* to get an education when he was young.
3. Happen by *chance*. – We *chanced* to hear the radio programme. We happened to turn on the radio just when the programme was on.

chandelier chan-de-lier' *chandeliers*. A hanging light fixture with several sockets for bulbs or candles.–The *chandelier* hangs from the ceiling over the table. It has several bulbs fastened to it.

change *changes, changed, changing.* 1. Make or become different. – Mother *changed* her old dress by shortening the skirt and putting on a new collar. She made it look like a new dress.–The weather *changed*. The rain stopped and the sun shone brightly.
2. Substitute or put in place of; exchange or trade. – When Mother was caught in the rain, she had to *change* her clothes. She put on dry clothes in place of the wet ones. –The twins like to *change* seats with each other to confuse the teacher.
3. Money due in return because more has been given than the price of what was bought.–Mary spent 25p on groceries, and gave the grocer £1. The grocer gave her 75p *change*.
4. Small pieces of money.–We did not have the *change* to pay the paper-boy.

changeable change'-a-ble *changeably, change-ableness*. Able or likely to change or become different; turning from one thing to something else. – The colours in diamonds are *changeable*. The colours change from one colour to another when you turn diamonds in the light.–Mary is very *changeable*. She likes a thing one day and does not like it at all the next.

channel chan'-nel *channels*. 1. A narrow body of water that joins 2 larger bodies of water.

2. The deeper part of a river or harbour.–A ship passed through the *channel*.

chap *chaps, chapped, chapping.* 1. Make rough and broken (of skin).–When my hands are *chapped* from the cold, I put cold cream on them.
2. A man or boy; a fellow.–Jack is a good *chap*.

chapter chap'-ter *chapters*. 1. A part or section of a book. *Chapters* usually have numbers or titles to tell what each *chapter* is about.
2. An assembly of monks.–There is a *chapter* of Cistercian monks outside the town.

character char'-ac-ter *characters*. 1. A person in a play, book, etc.–Tom Sawyer is a *character* in a book.
2. One's nature, or the way a person really is, inside his mind. The ways you think, feel, and act make up your *character*.–If you do good things and have good thoughts and feelings towards others, you are a person of good *character*.
3. Strength of mind; honesty, sincerity, courage, and other good qualities taken together. –Father is a man of *character*.–Bob has too much *character* to blame someone else for something he himself did.
4. A person who is noticeable because of odd behaviour.–The old woman who goes round feeding the cats at night is quite a *character* in town.
5. A letter or sign.–The *characters* used in writing Chinese are different from those used in English.

C
D
E
F
G
H
I
J
K
L
M
N
O
P
Q
R
S
T
U
V
W
X
Y
Z

charcoal char'-coal. A black, coal-like material made by partly burning wood in ovens with little air.–Crayons are sometimes made of *charcoal* and many artists do *charcoal* drawings.

charge *charges, charged, charging.* 1. Ask a price for. – Bob *charges* 20p an hour for mowing lawns.
2. Accuse.–The officer *charged* the man with driving at 60 miles an hour.
3. Something one is accused of.–The witness said that the *charge* against the man was not true. He had not done the thing he was accused of.
4. Put on a bill to be paid later.–When Mary bought the groceries, she had them *charged*, since she did not have any money with her. – When Mother buys clothes, she *charges* them to Father's account.
5. Rush at, attack.–The angry bull *charged* the farmer.
6. Load, fill.–The soldiers *charged* the gun with shot.
7. Responsibility. – The teacher told Mary to take *charge* of the class while she was out of the room.

charity char'-i-ty *charities.* 1. Help given to poor, sick, and helpless people.–Each year Father gives something to *charity*. – Hospitals and homes for the needy and the helpless, who can afford to pay little or nothing, are *charities*.
2. Kindness, willingness to overlook faults.–The teacher treats small children with *charity*.

charm *charms, charmed, charming.* 1. Attraction.–The story of Huckleberry Finn holds much *charm* for boys. They like it.
2. Delight; please.–I was *charmed* with the book when I read it.
3. A quality which gives pleasure.–Mary's sweetness and politeness to everyone are her greatest *charm*.
4. A small object like a locket.–Father wears  a gold watch *charm*.– Long ago people wore *charms* because they thought *charms* would keep them from harm.
5. Bewitch, make obedient and helpless.–The man says that he *charms* snakes. He says he can make them do as he wishes.

charming charm'-ing *charmingly.* Pleasant, sweet, delightful, attractive. – Grandmother is a *charming* person.–The story of Cinderella is *charming*.

chart *charts, charted, charting.* 1. A list or diagram made to show certain information at a glance.–The children made a *chart* on a large sheet of paper to show what books they had read, when they had read them, etc.–The master drew a *chart* which showed how the parts of the government worked together.

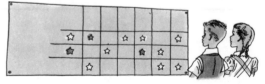

2. A map which shows where different important points are. – Sailors are guided in their sailing by *charts*.
3. Record on a *chart*.–Jack *charted* his marks in all his subjects.
4. Make a map of.–Captain Scott *charted* the country which he visited.

chase *chases, chased, chasing.* 1. Run after and try to catch.–Dogs like to *chase* cats.
2. Drive away.–The old man *chased* the boys from the orchard.

chat *chats, chatted, chatting.* 1. Talk in a friendly way about this and that.–Mary likes to *chat* with her friends before school begins.
2. A friendly talk about little things.–Mother had a *chat* with her neighbour.

chatter chat'-ter *chatters, chattered, chattering.* 1. Light, quick noises or voices. – We heard the *chatter* of the birds in the trees. They sounded as if they were talking to one another.
2. Talk fast or make quick little noises.–Mother asked the children to stop their *chattering* while she was on the telephone.–The room is so cold that my teeth *chatter*. They hit together, making a *chattering* sound.

chauffeur chauf'-feur *chauffeurs.* A person who drives a motor-car for pay.–Father asked the *chauffeur* to have the car ready at 2 o'clock to take us to the station.

cheap *cheaper, cheapest.* 1. Costing only a little money.–Bob bought a *cheap* knife.
2. Poor in quality.–This material is *cheap*. It is not good material.

cheat *cheats, cheated, cheating.* 1. Be unfair or dishonest; get something for oneself by a trick or dishonest act.–During the test the teacher left the room, since she knew she could trust the children not to *cheat*. She knew they would not look at each other's papers or look in their books.

2. A person who is unfair and dishonest.–The man is not a *cheat*. He will not sell his goods for more than they are worth.

check *checks, checked, checking.* 1. A position in the game of chess when the king is directly attacked by an opponent's piece.–Father moved his queen and put me in check.
2. Compare.–The teacher told us to *check* our words with those in the spelling book.
3. Be the same as. – Jack's spelling words *check* with mine.
4. The mark (V) meaning something is correct, or calling special attention to something. – Jack put a check after each word that he had spelt correctly.
5. Hinder or interrupt an action or a plan.–The accident caused a traffic jam and *checked* our progress. We were held up for an hour.

6. A sudden stoppage or setback. – Bob's illness put a *check* to our plans to go camping for the week-end.
7. One of the small squares in a pattern of squares.–Grandmother's tablecloth is made of green and white *checked* cloth.
8. Stop. – Grandfather *checked* the runaway horses by pulling on the reins.

checkmate check'-mate. The end of a game of chess, when the king is prevented from moving freely in any direction because of the position of the opponent's pieces.–Father moved his knight alongside his queen and it was *checkmate*. He had won the game.

Cheddar Ched'-dar. A village in Somerset and also the name of the cheese made in the district.–Mother sent me to the grocer for a pound of best *Cheddar* cheese.

cheek *cheeks.* The side of the face below the eyes and at the side of the mouth.–Baby has round, rosy *cheeks*.

cheep *cheeps, cheeped, cheeping.* 1. Peep or chirp.–We could hear the *cheeping* of the little chicks.
2. A small, chirping cry.–The bird's *cheep* meant that it was hungry.

cheer *cheers, cheered, cheering.* 1. A shout of joy or approval.–When Jack scored a goal, a *cheer* rose from the crowd.

2. Raise the spirits of.–The letters and flowers *cheered* the sick boy.
3. Shout encouragement and approval.–The crowd *cheered* the team when it came on to the field.

cheerful cheer'-ful *cheerfully, cheerfulness, cheerily.* 1. Happy, in good spirits.–A sunny day makes us *cheerful*.
2. Bright, pleasant.–Mary has a *cheerful* smile.–This is a *cheerful* morning.

cheerio cheer-i-o'. A friendly informal way of saying good-bye. – After the game I said *cheerio* to the other boys and went home.

cheery cheer'-y *cheerier, cheeriest.* Lively, gay, cheerful –The Boy Scouts were in a *cheery* mood as they sang songs round the camp-fire.

cheese *cheeses.* A food made by separating the solid or thick part of milk from the watery part and pressing it into a solid cake or loaf.

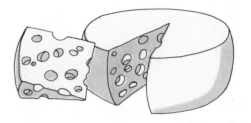

–Cream *cheese*, cottage *cheese*, Swiss *cheese*, Cheddar *cheese*, and many others are good to eat in sandwiches and salads.

cheese-cloth. Thin cotton cloth that is loosely woven. – Grandmother strained the juice through a piece of *cheese-cloth*.

cheetah chee'-tah *cheetahs.* A spotted member of the cat tribe, sometimes called the hunting leopard. The *cheetah* is a tremendously fast runner and has a comparatively gentle nature.

chemist chem'-ist *chemists.* 1. A student of chemistry.–Uncle Jim is a *chemist* and works in a big laboratory.
2. A seller of drugs, medicines and toilet articles.–Mother sent me to the *chemist* to buy some aspirin.

cheque (pronounced *check*) *cheques.* A written order which can be exchanged for money at the Bank. – The employees were paid by *cheque*.

cherish cher'-ish *cherishes, cherished, cherishing.* 1. Preserve or care for tenderly.–Sally *cherishes* her pet kitten.
2. Mary *cherishes* the hope that she will be an actress some day.

C
D E F G H I J K L M N O P Q R S T U V W X Y Z

cherry cher'-ry *cherries*. A small, round, smooth red or white fruit that grows on *cherry* trees. Some *cherries* are *sweet* and some are sour. They have long stems and a very hard stone.

chess. A game for 2 players on a board divided into 64 black and white squares. *Chess* pieces are called kings, queens, castles, bishops, knights and pawns.

chest *chests*. 1. A large box with a cover or with drawers in it.–Father keeps his tools in a tool *chest*. – A bureau is a *chest* of drawers.

2. The upper front part of the body.–Jack won a medal in the race. He wore it on his *chest*.

chestnut chest'-nut *chestnuts*. 1. Some *chestnuts* are good to eat, but the ones that are called 'conkers' are not edible. Both have green prickly covers. The tree on which *chestnuts* grow is the *chestnut* tree. The wood of the tree is sometimes used for furniture and in building houses.
2. Reddish brown. – The farmer has a *chestnut*-coloured horse.

chew *chews, chewed, chewing*. Cut or grind into tiny bits with the teeth.–*Chew* your food well before you swallow it.

chick *chicks*. A little chicken.–The farmer has 20 *chicks*.–Little birds are *chicks*, too.

chicken chick'-en *chickens*. A kind of large fowl or bird kept for its meat and eggs. The

meat of a *chicken* is good to eat. Hens and roosters are *chickens*. Hens lay eggs.

chicken pox. A sickness which causes a person to break out with red itchy spots.–When children have *chicken pox,* they should stay at home, so that they will not give the disease to others.

chief *chiefs*. 1. A leader.–Pontiac was an Indian *chief*.
2. Head; person in charge.–The *Chief* Constable is in charge of all the policemen in the city or county.
2. Most important. –The *chief* thing in Mother's life is her family.

chiefly chief'-ly. Mainly.–We came *chiefly* to see the new baby.

chiffonier chif-fo-nier' *chiffoniers*. A tall chest of drawers.–Mother keeps the towels in the *chiffonier*.

child *children*. A person who has not yet grown up.–A baby is a *child*.–A young boy or a young girl is a *child*.

children chil'-dren. More than one child.–Many *children* play in the park.

chill *chills, chilled, chilling*. 1. Make cool or colder.–We put melon on ice to *chill* it.
2. A shivering feeling of cold.–People who have a fever often have *chills*.
3. Coldness.–The north wind has a *chill* in it that makes one shiver.

chilly chill'-y. Cool or slightly cold.–Mary was *chilly,* so she put on her sweater.

chime *chimes, chimed, chiming*. 1. One of a number of bells or metal tubes that are in tune with each other so that tunes can be played on them.–We heard the *chimes* in the church tower.

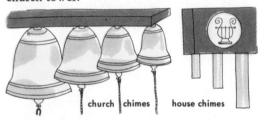

church chimes   house chimes

2. Music of *chimes*.–The *chimes* came to us across the fields.
3. Make ringing musical sounds. – Our clock *chimes* every 15 minutes.

chimney chim′-ney *chimneys*. 1. A long tube to draw smoke from a fire and to make a draught on the fire so that it will burn better. A *chimney* is often made of bricks or stone, and runs up through the roof of a building. It is hollow in the middle to let air, gas, and smoke pass through from the furnace, stove, or fireplace.

2. A glass tube on a paraffin lamp to provide a draught for the flame.

chimpanzee chim-pan-zee′ *chimpanzees*. A large brown ape with large ears and teeth, and paws something like a man's hands. A *chimpanzee* has no tail.

chin *chins*. The lowest part of the face.–When you chew or talk, your *chin* moves up and down.

china chi -na. 1. A white material made of baked clay and used for making dishes.

2. Dishes made of *china*.–Mary put the *china* on the table.

chintz. A very smooth cotton cloth printed with gay, bright figures or flowers.–Mother made curtains of *chintz*.

chip *chips, chipped, chipping*. 1. Break off small parts of.–Be careful not to *chip* the dishes.

2. A small piece broken or chopped off.–We gathered *chips* of wood to start the fire.

3. A thin strip of wood used for making baskets, etc.–A *chip* basket is called a punnet.

4. A thin slice of fried potato.–We had fish and *chips* for lunch.

chipmunk chip′-munk *chipmunks*. A small American squirrel with black and white stripes on its back.

chirp *chirps, chirped, chirping*. Make light, quick singing sounds.–Birds and insects *chirp*.

chisel chis′-el *chisels, chiselled, chiselling*. 1. A cutting tool with a long, flat blade that has a sharp edge at the end. – The carpenter uses a *chisel* to cut oft small pieces of wood. – The mason uses a *chisel* to carve or cut stone.

2. Cut with a *chisel*.–Father *chiselled* off the edge of the shelf so that it would fit into place.

chocolate choc′-o-late. 1. A food made by grinding the seeds or beans of the cacao tree.

2. A drink made by mixing *chocolate*, milk, and sugar.–We drink hot *chocolate* in winter.

3. A sweetmeat made of chocolate, often in bar form.– *Chocolates* are often filled with a sweet cream.

4. Dark brown.–The handbag was a *chocolate* colour.

choice *choices*. 1. A selection; something chosen.–The black hat with the white feather was my first *choice*.

2. A chance to choose.–We were so late that we did not have a *choice* of food. We ate just what was left.

3. Finest or best.–The butcher showed Mother his *choice* steaks.

choir *choirs*. 1. A number of singers who sing hymns or songs together.–The *choir* will sing Christmas carols tonight.

2. Part of the church where the church singers sit.–The *choir* in our church was painted.

choke *chokes, choked, choking*. 1. Have a blocking or checking of the breathing.–Food got into the boy's throat and he *choked*.– Father's collar was so tight that it almost *choked* him.

2. Clog; fill up.–Weeds *choked* the garden.– The river was *choked* with logs, and boats could not get through.

3. A device that regulates the amount of air in the mixture of petrol and air on which a petrol engine runs.

choose *chooses, chose, choosing.* 1. Select, pick out.–It is hard to *choose* a purse when there are so many to *choose* from.
2. See fit; decide.–The teacher *chose* to go to the hospital. She decided to go.

chop *chops, chopped, chopping.* 1. Cut by striking with a sharp tool.–The woodman will *chop* down the tree with an axe.
2. Cut into small pieces.–Mary *chopped* cabbage for salad.
3. A cut of meat with a rib in it.–We ate pork *chops* for dinner.–Lamb *chops* and veal *chops* also are good to eat.

chopsticks chop′-sticks. A pair of long sticks used by the Chinese to eat with. We lift food to our mouths with spoons or forks. The Chinese use *chopsticks.*

chord *chords.* In music, 3 or more musical notes sounded together to make a pleasing tone.

chore *chores.* A small odd job such as washing the dishes, sweeping the floor, etc.–On a farm the boy's *chores* include milking cows, feeding horses, and bringing in firewood.

chorus cho′-rus *choruses.* 1. A choir; a large group of singers.–The *chorus* sang over the radio.
2. A part of a song repeated after each verse.–The girls sang the verses or stanzas of the songs and the boys sang the *chorus.*
3. A song sung by a *chorus.*

chose. One form of the word *choose.*–The hat Mother *chose* was black and white.

chosen cho′-sen. One form of the word *choose.*–Bob was *chosen* to give the gift to the teacher.

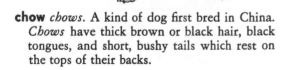

chow *chows.* A kind of dog first bred in China. *Chows* have thick brown or black hair, black tongues, and short, bushy tails which rest on the tops of their backs.

chowder chow′-der. A soup or stew made from clams or fish, with vegetables and seasoning.

Christ. Jesus; the founder of the Christian religion, worshipped by Christians as the Saviour and Son of God.

christen chris′-ten *christens, christened, christening.* Baptize; give a name to a person when he is baptized into the Christian church.

Christian Chris′-tian *Christians.* 1. A person who believes in and follows the teachings of Christ.
2. A *Christian name* is the first or given name.–Frank Smith is the boy's name. Frank is his *Christian name,* and Smith is his family name.
3. Having to do with Christ's teachings; doing as Christ taught.–It is not *Christian* to lie and steal.

Christianity Chris-ti-an′-i-ty. The religion and teachings of Christ.

Christmas Christ′-mas. The 25th day of December; the celebration of the birth of Christ.

chromium chro′-mi-um. A bright, shiny metal that does not tarnish.–Many motor-car parts are coated with *chromium.*

chrysanthemum chrys-an-′the-mum *chrysanthemums.* A late autumn flower of many colours. The very smallest blossoms are about the size of a 5 pence piece, the largest about the size of a tea-plate.

chubby chub′-by. Round and fat.–Sally's Teddy bear is *chubby.*

chuckle chuck′-le *chuckles, chuckled, chuckling.* 1. Laugh quietly.–Father *chuckled* at the funny way the puppies played together.
2. A low laugh.–We heard Father's *chuckle* as he watched the puppies play.

chug *chugs, chugged, chugging.* 1. The sound of an engine.–We heard the *chug* of the boat going up the river.
2. Make a sound like that of an engine.–The boat *chugged* up the river.

chum *chums.* A close friend.–Mary and Ruth have been *chums* for a long time.

chummy chum'-my *chummier, chummiest.* Friendly. – The boys were very *chummy.* They were together a great deal.

chunk *chunks.* A large lump.–Jack put a *chunk* of coal on the fire.

church *churches.* 1. A building where Christians gather to worship.–On Sundays we go to *church.*
2. An organization of Christians for worship and Christian activities. – The Methodist *Church* built a playground in the neighbourhood.

churn *churns, churned, churning.* 1. A machine or a vessel in which cream is stirred very rapidly to separate the butter from the milk.– The farmer makes butter in a *churn.*
2. Whip or shake cream rapidly in a *churn* to make butter. – Mary helped Grandmother to *churn* the butter.

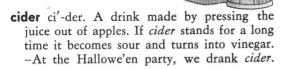

cider ci'-der. A drink made by pressing the juice out of apples. If *cider* stands for a long time it becomes sour and turns into vinegar. –At the Hallowe'en party, we drank *cider.*

cigar ci-gar' *cigars.* Tobacco leaves rolled tightly into a large solid roll.–Father smoked a *cigar* after dinner.

cigarette cig-a-rette' *cigarettes.* A small roll of finely cut tobacco rolled up in a thin piece of paper.–Some people smoke cigars or pipes; some smoke *cigarettes.*

cinder cin'-der *cinders.* A hard piece of partly burned coal, wood, etc. If coal or wood is completely burned, it leaves a powder called ashes.–Some *cinders* have many little holes in them. They look like hard sponges.

cinnamon cin'-na-mon. 1. A kind of tree that has an inner bark used as a spice for flavouring. This spice also is called *cinnamon.*
2. Flavoured with *cinnamon.*–Mother uses *cinnamon* in cakes and biscuits.
3. Reddish brown.–Some bears have a *cinnamon* colour.–Mother has a *cinnamon* suit.

cipher ci'-pher *ciphers.* 1. The figure 'o'. The *cipher* is also called a nought.
2. A secret alphabet or code of writing. The spy sent messages in cipher.

circle cir'-cle *circles, circled, circling.* 1. A ring that is perfectly round. Every point on a *circle* is the same distance away from the centre as any other point.
2. Move in a ring or *circle.*– The aeroplane *circled* round the field before it landed
3. A group of people who meet to do things together; a club.–Mother's sewing *circle* meets on Thursday afternoons.–We do not move in the same *circle* as the Smith family. We do not know the same people or do the same things.

circular cir'-cu-lar *circulars.* 1. Round; shaped like a circle.–Logs are cut with a *circular* saw.
2. An advertisement or handbill of which many copies are printed and given out.–We found a *circular* under our door telling us where to store fur coats in the summer.

circulate cir'-cu-late *circulates, circulated, circulating.* 1. Spread around.–With the radio nowadays, it doesn't take long for news to *circulate.*–We opened the door to let the air *circulate* freely in the room.
2. Send round, put out, give out publicly.– The neighbours *circulated* a paper asking people to vote for Mr. Jones.

circumference cir-cum'-fer-ence *circumferences.* The distance around a thing, especially a circle.–Mother measured the *circumference* of Mary's waist by putting a tape measure round it.

circumstance cir'-cum-stance *circumstances.* A state or condition.–We are sometimes excused for lateness, depending on the *circumstances,* depending on why we are late.–The policeman asked the witness to describe the *circumstances* of the accident, to tell how it happened.–The poor family is in reduced *circumstances.* They have much less money than they once had.

C
D
E
F
G
H
I
J
K
L
M
N
O
P
Q
R
S
T
U
V
W
X
Y
Z

C
D
E
F
G
H
I
J
K
L
M
N
O
P
Q
R
S
T
U
V
W
X
Y
Z

circus cir'-cus *circuses*. A show in which clowns, horses, other animals, acrobats, and tumblers perform. *Circuses* travel from town to town, and usually hold their shows in tents. Some *circuses* are shown in buildings.

cistern cis'-tern *cisterns*. A large tank, or cement-lined hole in the ground, for holding rain water.–Grandfather has a *cistern* in his attic.

citizen cit'-i-zen *citizens*. A person who belongs to a particular country, city, etc. You are a *citizen* of the country in which you were born. If you were born in one country and want to become a *citizen* of another country, you must take out *citizen*ship papers, pass certain tests, and pledge that you want to be a *citizen* of that country more than of any other. The government of a country gives its *citizens* protection and certain rights, and expects them to be good *citizens* in return.

citizenship cit'-i-zen-ship. The condition of belonging to a country, city, or other place, and having the rights and duties of a citizen. To become a citizen of a new country, one must give up *citizenship* in any other country.

city cit'-y *cities*. A large town; a place where many people live close together.–The people of a *city* elect a council and officers to take care of the *city's* affairs.–New York, Paris, and London are large *cities*.

civilian ci-vil'-ian *civilians*. A person who is not in the army, the navy, or the air force.

civilization civ-i-li-za'-tion *civilizations*. 1. The standard of government, education, science, art, etc., that a nation or people has. – British *civilization* is famous for its science and inventions.
2. A nation or region at a certain period.–Mummies are relics of an earlier *civilization*. –In school we talked about the early Indian *civilization*.

civilize civ'-i-lize *civilizes, civilized, civilizing*. Educate and train a person so that he can live peacefully with other people and enjoy the many good things of civilization.

clad. Dressed, clothed.–The beggar was *clad* in ragged clothes.

claim *claims, claimed, claiming*. 1. Say or make known that one owns something. – Jack *claimed* the ball which Joe found. He said it was his.
2. Say, declare as true.–Jack *claims* that he is a faster runner than Bob.
3. Take up (time, attention, etc.).–Arithmetic is hard for Mary; it *claims* most of her time.
4. A right.–The miner had no *claim* to the land; he just took it.

clamber clam'-ber *clambers, clambered, clambering*. Climb clumsily or with difficulty, catching hold with hands and feet.–The boys *clambered* up the steep cliff-face.–Baby tries to *clamber* up the side of her play-pen but always falls down.

clamp *clamps, clamped, clamping.* 1. A device for holding things tightly together.–We put a *clamp* on the boards after we had glued them together.

2. Fasten together with *clamps.* –We *clamped* the boards together after we had glued them.

clang *clangs, clanged, clanging.* 1. A loud ringing noise, like that of a bell or pieces of metal hitting together.–As we passed the blacksmith's shop, we heard the *clang* of his hammer.
2. Ring harshly.–The blacksmith's hammer *clanged* on the anvil.

clank *clanks, clanked, clanking.* 1. A dull, short ringing sound.–We heard the *clank* as the bumper of the car struck the stone wall.
2. Make a *clank.*–The runaway dog had a heavy, broken chain *clanking* behind him.

clap *claps, clapped, clapping.* 1. Hit the palms of the hands together; applaud.–The children *clapped* when the concert was over.
2. Slap, strike in a friendly way.–Grandfather *clapped* Bob on the shoulder.
3. A loud noise or crash.–The loud *clap* of thunder frightened us.

clarinet clar-i-net' *clarinets.* A musical instrument made of wood. It is played by blowing into one end through a mouthpiece while the keys are worked by the fingers. The mouthpiece has a thin strip of cane, called a reed, fastened to it.

clash *clashes, clashed, clashing.* 1. A harsh, flat ringing sound.– When the cars came together, we heard a loud *clash.*–The cymbals in the band make a *clash.*
2. Make a *clash.*–The saucepan *clashed* when it hit the floor.
3. An argument or disagreement.–Every time the boys see each other they have a little *clash.*
4. Fail to harmonize or go well together.– The colours of the girl's skirt and coat *clashed.*

clasp *clasps, clasped, clasping.* 1. A fastener.– The *clasp* on the belt broke.
2. Fasten. – Mary *clasped* the belt with a new *clasp.*
3. Hold tightly.–Father *clasped* Baby in his arms. – The children formed a circle and *clasped* hands.

clasp-knife clasp'-knife *clasp-knives.* A large knife with one or more blades which fold or shut into the handle.

class *classes, classed, classing.* 1. A group.– The teacher divided the children into *classes,* which she will teach separately.
2. A group of things somewhat alike.–The farmer sorted the potatoes into *classes* or grades. He put each potato with others like it in size, quality, etc.
3. A large number of people who live somewhat alike or who make their living in much the same way.–Farmers are sometimes called a *class.*
4. A gathering of students for studying a certain thing.–The children study art in art *class.*
5. Put into a *class* or group.–These books are *classed* with the better ones.

classmate class'-mate *classmates.* A person in the same class at school with one.–Three of Bob's *classmates* were absent yesterday.

classroom class'-room *classrooms.* A schoolroom; room where students are taught. – Music is taught in a different *classroom* from the *classroom* where we study art.

clatter clat'-ter *clatters, clattered, clattering.* 1. A confused crashing or rattling noise.– The *clatter* of pans in the kitchen awakened the baby.
2. Make a confused rattling noise.–The cups *clattered* to the floor.

claw *claws, clawed, clawing.* 1. One of the sharp nails on the paws of certain animals.–Cats have sharp *claws.*
2. Scratch and tear with *claws.* –The cat *clawed* Mary's stocking.
3. One of the pincers of a crab or lobster.

clay. A kind of earth that can be moulded easily. –Indians made dishes of *clay.* Tile, bricks, pottery, and dishes are made of certain kinds of *clay.* After they are shaped and dried, they are baked hard.

C
D
E
F
G
H
I
J
K
L
M
N
O
P
Q
R
S
T
U
V
W
X
Y
Z

clean *cleaner, cleanest, cleans, cleaned, cleaning.* 1. Free from dirt; not soiled.–Mother told Bob to be sure his hands were *clean* before dinner.
2. Exactly right; accurate; well done.–The ball player made a *clean* hit.
3. Remove dirt from; make *clean.* – Mary *cleaned* the kitchen.

cleaner clean'-er *cleaners.* 1. A person hired to clean anything.–The window *cleaner* calls on us regularly once a month.–Father sent his suit to the *cleaners.*

cleanly clean'-ly. In a clean manner.–John does his school work *cleanly.*

clear *clearer, clearest, clearly, clears, cleared, clearing.* 1. Free from anything that holds back light; not cloudy, misty, or muddy.– When the sun shines and there are no clouds, the sky is *clear.*–The river was muddy, but the lake was *clear.*
2. Easily understood. – The problem was *clear.*
3. Plain and easily seen or heard.–The boy's voice was *clear.* Everyone in the audience could hear and understand him.
4. Remove things from.–Mary *cleared* the dining-room table for Mother.–The woodsmen *cleared* the land. They removed the trees and brush.
5. Without touching. – The jumper passed *clear* over the bar.
6. Pass *clear* of.–The jumper *cleared* the bar by 4 inches. He went over it without coming nearer to it than 4 inches.

cleaver cleav'-er *cleavers.* A heavy, sharp hand tool used by butchers for chopping meat.

clergyman cler'-gy-man *clergymen.* A person officially named or chosen to hold religious services.–Priests and ministers are *clergymen.*

clerk (pronounced *clark*) *clerks.* 1. A person who types letters, puts away papers, and takes care of other work in an office.–My sister is a *clerk* in an insurance office.– A city or county *clerk* is an officer in the city government who takes care of records for the city or county. The word is also applied to certain officials in the British Government, such as *Clerk* of the House of Lords and *Clerk* of the House of Commons.

clever clev -er *cleverly, cleverness.* 1. Skilful and quick.–That man is a *clever* artist. He can draw quickly and well.
2. Smart.–Bob's dog does many *clever* tricks.

click *clicks, clicked, clicking.* 1. Make a sharp, short, hard noise.–The horses' hoofs *clicked* on the cobbles.–The lock *clicked* as the key turned.
2. A sharp, short, hard noise.–We heard the *click* as the pistol was cocked.

climate cli'-mate *climates.* The average weather conditions in an area. – Mary described the *climate* of Cornwall. She said it was very warm in summer, and not too cold in winter, and that there was plenty of rain.

climb *climbs, climbed, climbing, climber.* 1. Go up.–Firemen often *climb* high ladders to put out fires.
2. Go up and down.–Monkeys *climb* trees.– Baby *climbs* the stairs when no one is looking.
3. Grow along.–The grape-vine *climbed* up the tree. It grew up along the tree trunk.

cling *clings, clung, clinging.* Hold fast to something firm.–Some snow *clings* to your shoes.

clinic clin'-ic *clinics.* A place where diseases are studied and medical help is given.–Doctors learn how to treat diseases at a *clinic,* and patients are cared for.

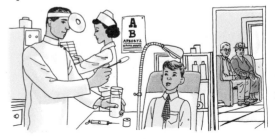

clink *clinks, clinked, clinking.* 1. A short, sharp, ringing noise. – We knew that Bob had money, because we heard the *clink* it made in his pocket.
2. Make a short, sharp, ringing noise.–The coin *clinked* when it dropped to the pavement.

clip *clips, clipped, clipping.* 1. Cut; cut off.– Do not *clip* the grass too short.–In warm weather Father *clips* the dog's hair.
2. Rate of speed.–The car was going at a fast *clip.*
3. A wire fastener.–The teacher put a *clip* on the papers to hold them together.
4. An ornament that clasps on. –The only ornament the dress had was a large gold *clip.*

clippers clip'-pers. A pair or set of scissors-like blades used for cutting hair, grass, etc., very short.—The gardener trimmed the hedges with *clippers*.—The barber trims Bob's hair with *clippers*.

cloak *cloaks*. A loose outer garment. Some *cloaks* have sleeves, like coats, and some are without sleeves, like capes.

clock *clocks*. An instrument that shows the passage of time. *Clocks* tell the time of day. Some *clocks* run by electricity and some have to be wound. A watch can be worn or carried, but a *clock* must stand on a level place to keep good time.

grandfather clock

wall clock

cuckoo clock

time clock

electric clock

mantel clock

travelling clock

alarm clock

clog *clogs, clogged, clogging*. 1. Block; stop up. —People are not allowed to *clog* the aisles in a theatre.—Mother called in the plumber to clean the *clogged* drain.
2. A shoe with wooden soles.— The children wore *clogs* for the dance.

close (rhymes with *dose*) *closer, closest*. 1. Near (a place).—Bob sits *close* to Mary.
2. Near (in time).—It is getting *close* to the end of term.
3. Very dear.—Bob and Joe are *close* friends.
4. Almost even. – The score of the football game was *close*. It was 3 to 2.
5. Stuffy; stifling.—The room was so *close* that we opened the window to let in fresh air.

close (rhymes with *those*) *closes, closed, closing*. 1. Shut.—If it is cold, *close* the window.
2. Come to an end.—School will *close* in July.
3. End.—The *close* of school is not far off.

closely close'-ly. 1. Tightly.—The prisoner was *closely* guarded.
2. Very near. – The dog followed *closely* behind.

closet clos'-et *closets, closeted, closeting*. 1. Shut oneself away in private.—The Prime Minister was *closeted* with his advisers for some hours.
2. A small private room or apartment.– A lavatory is sometimes described as **a** water-*closet*.

cloth *cloths*. 1. Material made of threads of cotton, wool, silk, etc., woven together. Clothes, table-*cloths*, and sheets are made of *cloth*.

2. A piece of *cloth*.—We wash up with a dish-*cloth*.—We use a table-*cloth* on the dining table.

clothe *clothes, clothed, clothing*. 1. Dress.– The tramp was *clothed* in torn clothes.
2. Cover.—The fields were *clothed* with ice and snow.

CLOTHES

Ancient Egyptian

Roman

Ancient Greek

14th Century European

Medieval Armour

16th Century European

Quakers

Victorian lady and gentleman

1920's young man and woman

Japanese

Chinese

Indian

C
D
E
F
G
H
I
J
K
L
M
N
O
P
Q
R
S
T
U
V
W
X
Y
Z

clothes. 1. Articles of dress; garments, things worn to cover the body.—We buy our *clothes* at a large clothing store.

2. Bed-*clothes* are coverings used on a bed.—In winter we use more bed-*clothes* than in summer.

clothing cloth'-ing. Clothes; things worn to cover the body.—We wear heavier *clothing* in winter than in summer.

cloud *clouds, clouded, clouding.* 1. A large grey or white mass of tiny drops of water floating in the sky.

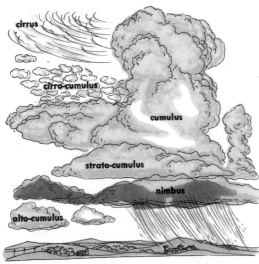

2. A large, floating mass of smoke, dust, steam, etc., in the air.—A *cloud* of smoke rose from the fire.—We drove down the gravel road, and a *cloud* of dust rose behind us.

3. Become sad or gloomy.—His face *clouded* when he heard that he had failed the exam.

cloudy cloud'-y *cloudier, cloudiest.* 1. Filled or covered with clouds.—Before the storm, the skies became very *cloudy*.

2. Muddy; not clear.—The water in the river became *cloudy* when we waded in it.

clove *cloves.* The dried bud of a *clove* tree. *Cloves* are ground, or used whole for flavouring puddings, cakes, etc.—*Cloves* are a spice, like pepper and cinnamon.

clover clo'-ver *clovers.* A small plant with leaves usually made up of 3 smaller leaves or leaflets. Dried *clover* blossoms and leaves are used as food for horses and cattle. *Clover* blossoms are red, yellow, or white. It is supposed to be good luck to find a 4-leafed *clover*.

clown *clowns.* A man with a painted face who wears a costume of many bright colours and does funny tricks at the circus. — Children laugh at the *clowns*.

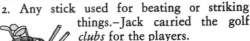

club *clubs, clubbed, clubbing.* 1. A heavy wooden stick for use as a weapon.—The criminal carried a *club*.

2. Any stick used for beating or striking things.—Jack carried the golf *clubs* for the players.

3. Hit with a heavy *club*.—The policeman *clubbed* the mad dog that was biting people.

4. A group of people who have joined together for pleasure and recreation.—We belong to a writing *club*. We have meetings at which we plan writing stories.

cluck *clucks, clucked, clucking.* 1. The sound a hen makes.—The old hen calls her little chicks by saying, '*Cluck, cluck*.'

2. Make the sound of a hen. — The hen *clucked* to the baby chicks.

clue *clues.* Anything that helps to solve a difficult problem or mystery.—A pair of glasses lost by the robber was the *clue* that helped to solve the mystery of the robbery.

clump *clumps, clumped, clumping.* 1. Close group or grove.—A thick *clump* of trees stands on the hill.

2. Walk heavily and noisily.—The tired soldier *clumped* along the road.

clumsy clum'-sy *clumsier, clumsiest.* 1. Awkward, not graceful.—Jack is a *clumsy* boy. His feet seem to get in his way, and he doesn't seem to know what to do with his hands. He is always falling over something, or knocking something down by accident.

2. Poorly done or made.—Older boys often think that the model aeroplanes their younger brothers make are *clumsy*.

C D E F G H I J K L M N O P Q R S T U V W X Y Z

clung. One form of the word *cling.*–The man in the water *clung* to the overturned boat.

cluster clus'-ter *clusters, clustered, clustering.*
1. A bunch or group.–Grapes, blackcurrants and redcurrants grow in *clusters.*–Mother arranged a *cluster* of autumn leaves on the mantelpiece.
2. Gather; form into a group.–The children *cluster* round Father when he comes home.

clutch *clutches, clutched, clutching.* 1. Grasp or hold tightly.–The old woman *clutched* the Boy Scout's arm as they crossed the icy street.
2. A tight grasp or hold.–The witch got Hansel and Gretel into her *clutches*, but they escaped.–Father kept a tight *clutch* on Sally's hand when he took her to the station.
3. A device that joins two parts of a machine so that it will run, or which throws the parts out of gear, or apart, when you do not want the machine to run.–To stop the car, push with your right foot on the brake, and with your left foot on the *clutch* pedal.

coach *coaches, coached, coaching.* 1. A closed carriage drawn by horses. – The fairy god-mother changed the pumpkin into a golden *coach.*

2. A railway carriage.–The train had six coaches and an engine.

3. A teacher or instructor.–The football *coach* trains the boys to play football.
4. Teach or help to learn.–Jack *coaches* Mary in arithmetic, and she helps him with his music.

coal *coals.* 1. A fuel that is sold in small, black chunks. It is burned to give heat and power. –*Coal* is a mineral that comes from mines in the earth.
2. A piece of wood or *coal* that is red-hot.–We cooked our steak over the hot *coals* of the camp fire.

coarse *coarser, coarsest.* 1. Not fine, not in small pieces.–The cook chopped the cabbage into *coarse* pieces for the salad.–Drip coffee is ground fine, not *coarse.*
2. Poor, rough.–The poor family ate *coarse* food. They could not afford better foods.
3. Having rough manners and rude ways.–Mary says that Jack is *coarse* when he teases her or takes big mouthfuls at the table.

coast *coasts, coasted, coasting.* 1. Seashore, the land along the water.–A boat was anchored just off the *coast.*–We went to the *coast* for our summer holiday.
2. Slide, move along with no effort.–Children *coast* downhill on their sledges.–Boys *coast* downhill on their bicycles.

coat *coats, coated, coating.* 1. A garment with sleeves that is worn over other clothing.–In winter I wear my heavy *coat.*
2. A covering. – The painter gave the house two *coats* of paint in order to preserve the woodwork.
3. Cover. – The sick boy's tongue is *coated* with a white film.

coax *coaxes, coaxed, coaxing.* Persuade, get to say yes.–Bob tried to *coax* Mother to let him go swimming. He said it was a warm day, and he would be very careful.

cob *cobs.* 1. A large kind of hazelnut, a *cob*nut.
2. A stocky riding-horse.
3. A *corncob.* Corn grows on a *cob.*–Some pipes are carved out of *cobs.*

cobweb cob'-web *cobwebs*. A network of very fine threads spun by a spider. Flies and insects get caught and tangled up in *cobwebs*; and the spider eats them. *Cobwebs* are often spun in high corners of rooms.

cock *cocks, cocked, cocking*. 1. A rooster. The hen is the female bird, and the *cock* is the male bird. The males of many kinds of birds are called *cocks*.
2. Turn up.–The man *cocked* his hat on one side.–Jack's dog Spot *cocks* his head when he hears Jack coming.

cocker spaniel cock'-er span'-iel *cocker spaniels*. A small hunting dog. *Cocker spaniels* have long curly hair, short tails, long floppy ears, and shaggy paws.

cockroach cock'-roach *cockroaches*. A brown or black beetle-like insect that infests kitchens, ships, etc., and other places where there is food. *Cockroaches* run very fast and travel at night. – Mother gets rid of *cockroaches* by spreading a poison powder around.

cocoa co'-coa. Ground or powdered chocolate. Children drink hot *cocoa*. It is made from powdered chocolate, sugar, and hot milk.

coconut co'-co-nut *coconuts*. The large, hardshelled, brown fruit of the coco palm tree. The *coconut* has an outer shell, or husk, which is very hard to break. Inside is a layer of white nutmeat that is good to eat. The centre of the *coconut* is filled with a clear liquid, called milk, that is good to drink. The white meat of the *coconut* is often shredded and used on cakes, in puddings, pies, and sweets.

cocoon co-coon' *cocoons*. The silky case or covering made by a caterpillar to live in while it is changing into a butterfly or moth.

cod or **codfish** cod'-fish. A kind of fish that lives in cold, deep, salt water. Many people eat *cod*. The oil from the liver of the *codfish* is used as a medicine.

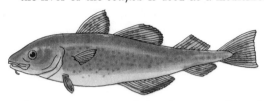

code *codes*. 1. Any set of signals, group of words or letters, etc., used for sending messages.– The Boy Scouts' *code* for sending messages is a set of flag-waving signals.–Jack and Bob write notes to each other in *code*.
2. A rule, law, or standard by which people live.–A Boy Scout must have a high *code* of honour.

coffee cof'-fee. A drink made from the dried, roasted seeds of the *coffee* plant. Many people drink *coffee*. The seeds of the *coffee* plant also are called *coffee*.

coffin cof'-fin *coffins*. A long box in which the body of a dead person is placed for burial.–The body of the old man who was drowned was buried in a grey *coffin*.

cog *cogs*. One of a row of little points or teeth which stick out from a part on a machine. A *cog*wheel is not smooth on the edge; it has *cogs* that fit into the *cogs* of other wheels to make them turn.

coil *coils, coiled, coiling*. 1. A ring or spiral made by winding something round and round.–After the gardener finished sprinkling the garden, he wound the hose into a *coil*.–*Coils* of wire are used in many electrical devices.

2. Wind round and round. – The monkey *coiled* his tail around the branch and swung on it.
3. Wound into a *coil*.–The springs on the bed are *coil* springs.

Ancient Chinese

Ancient Roman

Ceylon five-cent piece

English five pence piece

COINS

Mexican silver peso

Ancient Greek

Ancient Punic

Indian silver rupee

Spanish twenty-five centimos piece

coin *coins, coined, coining.* 1. A piece of metal money; a penny, halfpenny, etc. – Jack put some *coins* into his savings bank.–*Coins* are stamped to tell how much money they are worth, in what year they were made, etc.
2. Shape and stamp a piece of metal to make money.–The government *coins* money.
3. Make up.–He *coined* a new phrase to describe his first flight in Space.

coincide co-in-cide *coincides, coincided, coinciding.* 1. Happen at the same time.–My birthday *coincides* with Christmas Day.
2. Agree. – My opinion regarding the school holiday *coincides* with yours.

coincidence co-in'-ci-dence *coincidences.* Something which happens at the same time as something else without any obvious connection.–It is a *coincidence* that the circus is in town on Jack's birthday.

coke. A fuel used in refining metals. *Coke* is made by heating soft coal until some of the gases in the coal have passed off. Coke is also used in domestic boilers.

cold *colds, colder, coldest, coldly.* 1. Not warm. –In summer the weather is warm. In winter it is *cold.*–We put milk in the refrigerator to keep it *cold.*–Ice cream is *cold.*
2. A very common sickness that causes coughing and sneezing, a running nose, and sometimes a sore throat and fever.–If you have a *cold,* stay at home so that you will not spread it to other people.
3. Not friendly, interested, or cordial. – The man seems *cold* to strangers because he is shy.

collapse col-lapse' *collapses, collapsed, collapsing.* Break down, fall in.–When Baby sat in the doll's pram, it *collapsed.*–The burning roof *collapsed.*

collar col'-lar *collars, collared, collaring.* 1. A band of any kind which is worn around the neck.–Horses and dogs wear leather *collars.* –Men wear linen or cotton *collars* on their shirts.–Women wear *collars* of lace, silk, cotton, and other materials. – Some coats have fur *collars.*

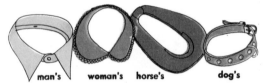
man's   woman's   horse's   dog's

2 A ring.–The plumber put a metal *collar* on the two pipes where they came together.
3. Catch or seize by the back of the *collar.*– The policeman *collared* the thief.

collate col-late' *collates, collated, collating.* Put or bring together for examination and comparison.–The professor had to *collate* a large amount of material before he was ready to write his book.

colleague col'-league *colleagues.* Someone who works closely with you.–Mr Smith is one of Father's *colleagues* at work; they do the same job in the same place.

collect col-lect' *collects, collected, collecting.* 1. Take up, call for. – The milkman *collects* money for the milk on Saturdays. – The teacher *collects* our homework in the morning.
2. Gather together and keep, as a hobby.– Jack *collects* stamps. He saves them.
3. Gather together in a group, pile up. – A large crowd *collected* to see the big military parade.–Leaves *collect* on the pavements in the autumn.

collection col-lec'-tion *collections.* 1. A group of things selected and kept, as a hobby, or to be shown. – Father has a *collection* of old pieces of money.

2. A sum of money made up by many contributions, or by many people each giving something.–The children took up a *collection* to buy flowers for their sick teacher. They each gave something to get enough money together.

college col'-lege *colleges*. A place of study higher up or more advanced than a secondary school. Many boys and girls go to *college*. Some of the older universities contain a number of colleges.

collie col'-lie *collies*. A large dog with a long, bushy tail and heavy, shaggy hair. *Collies* are sheep dogs.–Many children have *collie* dogs for pets.

collision col-li'-sion *collisions*. The coming together of things with great force.–The two boys riding bicycles had a *collision*.

colonel (pronounced *kernel*) colo'-nel *colonels*. An officer in the Army. – A *colonel* is in command of a regiment.

colonial co-lo'-ni-al. Having to do with colonies. –When the first British people came to America, they formed 13 colonies. The Americans refer to this as the *colonial* period.

colonnade col-on-nade' *colonnades*. A series of columns placed at regular intervals.–In the ruined temple we saw 2 walls and a *colonnade* of pillars.

colony col'-o-ny *colonies*. 1. A group of people who go from their own country to a new one, and live together in a settlement or town.– A *colony* of French people live in the southern part of our city.
2. A group of certain insects, animals, plants, etc., that live together, as a *colony* of bees, a *colony* of ants, etc.

colour col'-our *colours, coloured, colouring*. 1. Blue is the *colour* of the sky.–Green is the *colour* of the grass.–Yellow is the *colour* of the sun.–Red and green are the *colours* used at Christmas time.
2. Put *colour* on.–The children *colour* eggs for Easter. They paint or dye them.
3. *The colours* means the flag.–The soldiers marched up the street with *colours* flying.

COLOURS

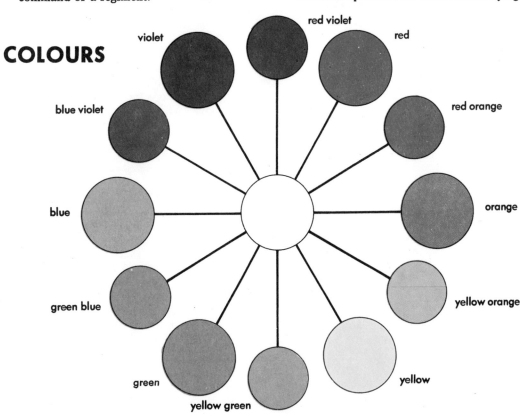

colour-blind *colour-blindness.* Not able to tell certain colours apart, particularly red and green.–People who are *colour-blind* have to be extra careful when driving.

colouring col'-our-ing *colourings.* 1. The way a picture is coloured.–The *colouring* in Ann's painting is delightful. It is much better than the actual design.
2. The colour of the face, particularly the hair and the eyes.–Alan's *colouring* is fair; he has light-coloured hair and blue eyes. Bob's *colouring* is dark; he has brown hair and eyes.
3. Something used to give colour.–Saffron and cochineal are *colouring* matters used in cooking.

colourless col'-our-less. 1. Without any colour. –The boy was so frightened that his face was *colourless.*–The water that we drink is *colourless.*
2. Dull; the same all the time.–Cinderella's life was *colourless* until she went to the ball. – The bashful boy told the story in a *colourless* voice, without emphasizing anything.

colt *colts.* A baby horse.–Grandfather's mare has a *colt.*–*Colts* have very long, wobbly legs.

columbine col'-um-bine *columbines.* A flower that grows both wild and in gardens. *Columbines* grown in gardens are many different colours.

column col'-umn *columns.* 1. A tall, up-and-down support, usually thin, used in buildings. – The veranda roof is held up by white *columns.*
2. A long, straight up-and-down line or row. – In arithmetic class we added several *columns* of figures. –The pages in this dictionary are divided into *columns.* – A *column* of smoke came from the chimney.

3. A long single row or line.–The boys marched in a *column* across the football field.
4. A special part of a newspaper written regularly by one person.–The household *column* in the newspaper tells how to cook and keep house.

comb *combs, combed, combing.* 1. A long piece of metal, rubber, or other material with close-set teeth used to straighten out hair or wool. –Coarse *combs* are used to untangle sheep wool before it is spun into threads.

2. Straighten and untangle by running a *comb* through.–Mother *combed* Baby's hair.

3. A crest; a ridge that sticks up.–Roosters have red *combs* on their heads.
4. A wax framework which bees make to store honey in.–Pieces of honey*comb* are often packed with honey that comes in jars.
5. Look all over; search thoroughly.–Mother *combed* the house in search of her thimble.

combination com-bi-na'-tion *combinations.* Several things put together or combined.– Mother's dress is a *combination* of pieces of cloth.–The *combination* of celery, cabbage, pineapple, and salad dressing makes a tasty salad.

combine com-bine' *combines, combined, combining.* Mix or put together.–If you *combine* blue plain and yellow paint, you will have green paint.

come *comes, came, coming.* 1. Move towards.– The horse will *come* to the fence if you hold out your hand.
2. Attend; arrive and stay.–My teacher is *coming* to my party. She *came* last year too.
3. Happen or take place.–Christmas *comes* once a year.
4. Reach.–Mother's short jacket *comes* down to her waist.
5. *Come about* means happen.–How did the accident *come about*?
6. *Come along* means hurry.–If you don't *come along* now you will be late for school.

comedian co-me'-di-an *comedians.* A funny person whose job is to entertain other people. –The *comedian* in the variety show told funny jokes and stories.

comedy com'-e-dy *comedies*. A funny play or film.–There was a *comedy* before the feature picture.

comet com'-et *comets*. A bright heavenly body that has a tail of light.–*Comets* move about the sun.

comfort com'-fort *comforts, comforted, comforting*. 1. Cheer up; make peaceful or happy. –The policeman tried to *comfort* the lost child and make him forget his fears.
2. Something which cheers.–The hunter's dog was a great *comfort* to him. The dog made life happier for him.
3. State of ease; freedom from trouble or worry.–The family lives in great *comfort*. They have plenty of money, food, clothes, etc.

comfortable com'-fort-a-ble *comfortably*. 1. Giving rest and peace for the body.–The new bed is *comfortable* to sleep in.
2. Free from trouble, pain, etc.; contented.– The family is *comfortable* in its new house.

comforter com'-fort-er *comforters*. 1. One who cheers and makes comfortable. – The old woman is a great *comforter* of the sick and poor. She brings them cheer and makes them happier.

comic com'-ic *comics*. 1. Funny.–The clown was a *comic* sight, balancing the little dog on his head.
2. *Comics* are funny pictures or cartoons.– Andrew's weekly paper has coloured *comics* in it.

comical com'-i-cal *comically*. Funny. – The comedian told many *comical* stories. They made us laugh.

comma com'-ma *commas*. A punctuation mark (,) used in sentences to help you read and understand them properly.

command com-mand' *commands, commanded, commanding*. 1. An order; a direction.–The soldiers obeyed the captain's *commands*.
2. Charge; control.–The captain is in *command* of the ship. Everyone there must obey him.
3. Order; tell to do.–The captain *commanded* the soldiers to halt.

commander com-mand'-er *commanders*. 1. A person who has charge of or control over people.–The captain was the *commander* of the company of soldiers.
2. An officer in the navy ranking just below captain.

commence com-mence' *commences, commenced, commencing*. Begin. – The teacher told us to *commence* writing.

commerce com'-merce. Buying and selling of goods.–There is much *commerce* between England and the United States.

committee com-mit'-tee *committees*. A group of people named to do certain things for a larger group.–The *committee* on decorations chose the decorations for the party.

common com'-mon *commonly*. 1. Frequent; usual.–Winds are *common* near the seashore.
2. Ordinary; seen often. – Dandelions are *common* weeds.
3. *In common* means shared.–Jack and Bob have many things *in common*. There are many things in which they share an interest.
4. Shared.–Grandfather gave Joe, Jack, and John a pony. The pony is the *common* property of all the boys.

communicate com-mu'-ni-cate *communicates, communicated, communicating*. Send a message or exchange messages or information with.–When Father gets to Manchester, he will *communicate* with us. He will telephone or write to us, or send us a telegram.

communication com-mu-ni-ca'-tion *communications*. 1. News, information, or message sent. – We do not know whether the *communication* came by letter, telephone, or telegram.
2. A way or means of sending messages.– During the storm there was no *communication* between the cities.

community com-mu'-ni-ty *communities*. A group of people who live together in a town or settlement.–Enough money was given by the *community* to build a large playground.

companion com-pan'-ion *companions*. 1. One who goes about with another.–The crippled woman has a travelling *companion*.–The old man and his dog are faithful *companions*. They go about together all the time.
2. A friend; a comrade.–The men were *companions* at school. They enjoyed each other's company.

C
D
E
F
G
H
I
J
K
L
M
N
O
P
Q
R
S
T
U
V
W
X
Y
Z

company com'-pa-ny *companies*. 1. Guests; people who are visiting.–We have *company* for dinner tonight.
2. In the army, a unit of soldiers commanded by a captain.
3. A business firm or organization into which people put money in order to make profit.–A new *company* has just been formed in our town to sell building materials.
4. Companionship; being with or together.–Bob enjoys Jack's *company*.

compare com-pare' *compares, compared, comparing*. Examine to see how things are different or alike.–The boys *compared* their knives. They looked at the knives to see how they were alike and how they were different.

compass com'-pass *compasses*. 1. An instrument with a needle or pointer which points to the north. *Compasses* are used to tell directions, especially at sea and in the air. The needle of a *compass* is a magnet.

direction compass

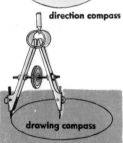
drawing compass

2. A device, like the one in the picture, used for making circles and for measuring distances. It is sometimes called a pair of *compasses*, because it has two points.

compel com-pel' *compels, compelled, compelling*. Force.–The deep snow *compels* us to stay at home today.–The law *compelled* the man to send his children to school.

compete com-pete' *competes, competed, competing*. Try to outdo or win over another; engage or take part in a contest.–Mary and Bob will *compete* in the spelling bee.–The brothers *competed* in the race.

competition com-pe-ti'-tion *competitions*. A contest.–One boy from our school is in the swimming *competition* for the city championship.

complain com-plain' *complains, complained, complaining*. 1. Find fault. – Father never *complains* about the food we eat. He thinks it is all right.
2. Talk about one's troubles.–The poor old man never *complains*.

complaint com-plaint' *complaints*. 1. A statement accusing one of wrongdoing; a statement that something is not right.–The *complaint* said that the man was driving on the wrong side of the street.–The woman made a *complaint* to the shop that the dress she bought had a hole in it.
2. A trouble; a thing to complain about.–The boy's *complaint* was that his stomach hurt.

complete com-plete' *completes, completed, completing*. 1. Finish.–It will take a long time to *complete* the building of the house. –My work is *completed*.
2. Whole; full; entire.–John has a *complete* set of tools for building model aeroplanes.
3. Perfect; thorough.–Our play was a *complete* success. Everyone liked it.

completely com-plete'-ly. Entirely; altogether. –Mary's work is *completely* done.–The boy was *completely* happy. There was nothing troubling him.

complicate com'-pli-cate *complicates, complicated, complicating*. Make difficult.–Heavy rains *complicated* the work of the farmer.– Too many big words *complicate* the reading of the story.

compliment com'-pli-ment *compliments, complimented, complimenting*. 1. A statement of praise.–The teacher gave Mary a *compliment* about her neatly written paper. She said nice things about it.
2. Praise.–The coach *complimented* Bob on his good innings in the match.

compose com-pose' *composes, composed, composing*. 1. Make up; put together; create.– Some people *compose* music; others *compose* poems.
2. Make by putting different things together. –Hot chocolate is *composed* of hot milk, chocolate, and sugar.
3. Make calm; control.–The actress was very *composed*. She was not excited.

composer com-pos'-er *composers*. A person who writes or makes up music, or poems, stories, etc.

composition com-po-si'-tion *compositions*. 1. Something made up and written down.– Poems, stories, music, and books are *compositions*.
2. A mixture.–Concrete is a *composition* of sand, cement, and water.–Bread is a *composition* of flour, salt, and yeast.

comrade com'-rade *comrades.* A friend; a companion.–The young men were *comrades* in the army. They spent much time together.

conceal con-ceal' *conceals, concealed, concealing.* Hide.–The robber *concealed* his gun under his coat.

conceit con-ceit'. Too high an opinion or judgment of oneself.–The boy's *conceit* caused people to dislike him. He thought too highly of himself.

conceited con-ceit'-ed. Vain; too proud.–The woman is very *conceited.* She thinks that she is better than anyone else.

concern con-cern' *concerns, concerned, concerning.* 1. Worry; serious consideration.–Bob showed much *concern* when he saw the size of the football players in the other team.
2. Be worried or anxious.–When Bob was late, Mother was *concerned* about him.
3. A business company.–A new *concern* has opened a shop around the corner.
4. Have an effect on.–The rail strike *concerned* all of us. It mattered to all of us.
5. Have to do with; be about.–The telephone message *concerned* Father only.

concert con'-cert *concerts.* 1. Musical programme.–Three symphonies were played at last night's *concert.*
2. *In concert* means together; at the same time.–The children sing and say poems *in concert.*

conch *conchs.* A spiral-shaped shell. – We found a large *conch* on the seashore.

conclude con-clude' *concludes, concluded, concluding.* 1. Decide after thinking. – The city officials *concluded* that a new playground was needed.
2. End.–The programme is *concluded.*

conclusion con-clu'-sion *conclusions.* 1. An end.–The story running in the paper came to a *conclusion* in today's issue.
2. What one decides after thinking.–What *conclusion* did you reach? What did you decide?

condition con-di'-tion *conditions, conditioned, conditioning.* 1. State of health. – Grandfather's *condition* is good.
2. State of repair.–The old house is in poor *condition.* It needs painting and repairing.

3. Something needed to make something else possible.–One of the *conditions* of your own happiness is to make others happy.
4. *On condition that* means if or provided.–The farmer will give Bob a dog *on condition that* Bob gets good marks in his report.
5. Make ready; put in good repair.–I had my car *conditioned* for the trip.

conduct con'-duct. Behaviour; way of acting.–The boy's *conduct* is very good.

conduct con-duct' *conducts, conducted, conducting.* 1. *Conduct oneself* means behave.–The boys *conduct themselves* well.
2. Guide; go along with.–The man will *conduct* us through the cave.
3. Direct; take charge of. – The chairman *conducts* our club meetings.
4. Direct or lead musicians in playing or singing.–Our music teacher will *conduct* at the concert.

conductor con-duc'-tor *conductors.* 1. A leader of a band, orchestra, or chorus.–Mr. Miller is the *conductor* of the school band.
2. A person who takes fares and looks after passengers on a public vehicle. – We bought our tickets from the *conductor* on the bus. Trams and trolley-buses have *conductors.*
3. Something through which electricity or heat will pass.–Copper wire is a *conductor* of electricity.–An aluminium pan is a good *conductor* of heat. It allows the heat to pass from the stove to the contents of the pan.

cone *cones.* 1. A long or tall figure that is round at one end and pointed at the other.

pine cone   ice cream cone   geometric cone

2. A crisp, *cone*-shaped, hollow cake to be filled with ice cream. – Children like ice-cream *cones.*
3. The seed pod of an evergreen tree.–The pine tree has *cones.*

confess con-fess' *confesses, confessed, confessing.* 1. Admit or own up that one has done wrong.–Jack *confessed* that he broke the window.
2. Tell, say, or make known something one did not want to tell.–I must *confess* I do not like arithmetic.

confession con-fes'-sion *confessions*. 1. A statement saying that one has done wrong.–The guilty man signed a *confession*.–Priests hear *confessions* of people who want to tell of something wrong they have done.
2. An acknowledgment or admission of something one did not want to tell.–At the boy's *confession* that he had not had breakfast, Mother gave him some cereal and toast.

confide con-fide' *confides, confided, confiding*. Tell private things to someone, with faith that they will be kept secret.–Mary *confides* in Mother.–Jack *confided* his plan to Bob.

confidence con'-fi-dence. 1. A feeling of faith in oneself.–Mary spoke with *confidence*. She was sure she was right.
2. Trust.–Mother has *confidence* in Bob's honesty.
3. Secrecy; an agreement not to tell.–Mary told Ruth her secret in *confidence*.

confident con'-fi-dent. Sure; having no doubts. –I am *confident* that my new dress will come today. – Bob is *confident* in himself. He is sure he can do what he sets out to do.

confidential con-fi-den'-tial *confidentially*. Secret; private; not to be made public.–What Mary told Mother is *confidential*. It is a secret between them.

confuse con-fuse' *confuses, confused, confusing*. 1. Mix up one's thinking.–So many things happened at once this morning that Mother got *confused*. She didn't know what she was doing.–Father gets *confused* when he goes shopping.
2. Mistake one for another.–The doctor told us not to *confuse* the two medicines, because they looked alike.–The teacher often gets the twins *confused*.

confusion con-fu'-sion. A mixed-up condition; disorder.–If your mind is in *confusion*, you may say and do things you do not mean.–Bob's desk was in *confusion*. There were papers, pencils, inky handkerchiefs, marbles, and many other things all mixed up together in it.

congratulate con-grat'-u-late *congratulates, congratulated, congratulating*. Give someone one's good wishes or praise for something he has done well or something nice that has happened to him.–The teacher *congratulated* Jack on winning the race.

congratulations con-grat'-u-la'-tions. Good wishes or praise given to a person for something he has done well or because something nice has happened.–The children gave the teacher their *congratulations* when they heard that he was engaged to be married.

congregation con-gre-ga'-tion *congregations*. The people attending a church service.– The minister spoke to a large *congregation* on Remembrance Sunday.

congress con'-gress *congresses*. 1. (Always spelled with a capital 'c.') A group of persons elected by the people of every state to make the laws for the United States.–*Congress* meets in the Capitol building in Washington, D.C. *Congress* is divided into two parts, or bodies. One is the Senate, and the other the House of Representatives.
2. A large meeting or gathering of people to make plans, laws, etc.

conjuror con'-ju-ror *conjurors*. A person who practises magic.–Everybody enjoyed the performance of the *conjuror* at the party. He did card tricks and made a rabbit appear out of a hat.

conkers con'-kers. A boy's game usually played with horse-chestnuts threaded on to string. You have to break the one belonging to your opponent by hitting it with your own.

connect con-nect' *connects, connected, connecting*. 1. Join, unite, put together. – We watched the men *connect* the trailer to the car.–The girls *connected* the pieces of rope to make a skipping rope.
2. I *connect* the word 'bed' with sleep and the word 'bread' with eat. I think of them as being used with or related to each other.
3. Be engaged in business.–Father is *connected* with a radio repair company.

connexion or **connection** con-nex'-ion *connexions*. 1. A place where things are joined together.–The hose leaks right at the *connexion* with the nozzle.
2. A relation; a going with or belonging together.–I am thinking of something in *connexion* with a finger. It would be ring, thimble, glove, or hand.–Although both our names are Smith, there is no *connexion* between our families. We are not related.
3. Business doings or relations.–Father has no *connexion* with the flower shop. He does not have anything to do with it.

conquer con'-quer *conquers, conquered, conquering.* 1. Overcome or get rid of.–At last Jack has *conquered* his bad habit of being late.

2. Defeat; overcome; win over.–The smaller army can *conquer* the larger one if it gets more aircraft.

consent con-sent' *consents, consented, consenting.* 1. Agree; give permission, allow.–Grandfather would not *consent* to my riding the frisky pony.–Mother *consented* to my going out tonight.

2. Permission.–Mother has given me her *consent* to go out. She said that I might go.

consider con-sid'-er *considers, considered, considering.* 1. Think about.–We will *consider* going to Brighton for our holiday.

2. Remember; keep in mind; take account of. –The child looks fine, when you *consider* her long illness.–Jack says Mary plays ball well *considering* she is only a girl.

3. Regard, think of as.–The coach *considers* Bob a good footballer.

considerable con-sid'-er-a-ble *considerably.* Quite a little; much.–We have had *considerable* snow this winter.

consist con-sist' *consists, consisted, consisting.* Be made up.–An hour *consists* of 60 minutes.–Syrup *consists* of sugar and water.– The programme *consisted* of songs and piano music.

consonant con'-so-nant *consonants.* Any letter of the alphabet except a, e, i, o, and u.

constable con'-sta-ble *constables.* A policeman. –The *constable* took the lost child to its home.

constellation con-stel-la'-tion *constellations.* A group of stars that, as seen from the earth, seemed to ancient people to form pictures in the sky. The Plough; also called Ursa Major, or the Great Bear, is easy to recognize. The *constellations* appear in different parts of the sky at different times of the year.

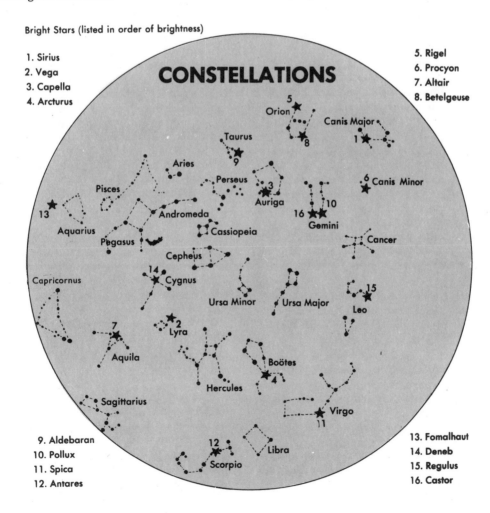

Bright Stars (listed in order of brightness)

1. Sirius
2. Vega
3. Capella
4. Arcturus
5. Rigel
6. Procyon
7. Altair
8. Betelgeuse
9. Aldebaran
10. Pollux
11. Spica
12. Antares
13. Fomalhaut
14. Deneb
15. Regulus
16. Castor

CONSTELLATIONS

C
D
E
F
G
H
I
J
K
L
M
N
O
P
Q
R
S
T
U
V
W
X
Y
Z

constitution con-sti-tu′-tion *constitutions.* 1. The physical make-up of a person or animal.–The sick boy has a poor *constitution.* His body is weak.

2. The most important rules of a group.–The *Constitution* of a country is a group of rules which guides it in its lawmaking and public affairs and grants civil rights.–Clubs often have *constitutions.*

construct con-struct′ *constructs, constructed, constructing.* Build, make. – The children *constructed* a house of blocks. – The men *constructed* a bridge.

construction con-struc′-tion. 1. The act of building.–The *construction* of the bridge took a year.

2. A way of building.–The *construction* of that building is unusual; it is built of glass and concrete.

consult con-sult′ *consults, consulted, consulting.* 1. Get advice from.–Bob *consulted* the coach about putting on a new bowler.

2. Consider together. – The boys *consulted* over the weather map before leaving for the picnic.

consume con-sume′ *consumes, consumed, consuming.* 1. Eat and drink, use up.–Pigs *consume* much food and water.

2. Destroy. – Fire *consumed* the building.

contact con′-tact *contacts, contacted, contacting.* 1. Touch.–The *contact* of the sick boy's cold hand made Bob shiver.–Father has been out of *contact* with his cousins for many years.

2. Connexion. – The light went on when Father brought the wires into *contact.*

3. Get in touch with (used informally).–We tried to *contact* you by telephone, but no one answered.

contagious con-ta′-gious. Catching. – Measles, chicken-pox, and some other diseases are *contagious.* They can be spread to other people by touch.

contain con-tain′ *contains, contained, containing.* 1. Hold; have in it.–This bottle *contains* one pint. – The old trunk *contained* many wonderful things.

2. Consist of; be made up of.–One pound *contains* 100 pence. Six *contains* three 2's.

3. Hold back; control one's feelings.–Mary was so excited that she could scarcely *contain* herself.

container con-tain′-er *containers.* A box, barrel, carton, can, jug, or anything else for holding something.–Milk is often sold in cardboard *containers.*–A dust-bin is a rubbish *container.*

content con-tent′ *contents, contented, contenting.* 1. Satisfied; pleased; at peace.–Jack was *content* with the mark he got on his spelling paper.

2. Satisfy.–I was sorry not to see you today, but I will be *content* if I see you next week. –Watching the men *contented* the child.

contents con′-tents. What something written says; what a thing holds or has in it.–Mother did not tell us the *contents* of Grandfather's letter, so we were very curious to know what he said.–Sally stuck her thumb into the jar to find out its *contents.*

contest con′-test *contests.* A game in which people try to win.–We have running *contests,* long-jumping *contests,* music *contests,* drawing *contests,* etc. – Today our class had a spelling bee or *contest,* and our team won.

continent con′-ti-nent *continents.* One of the 7 largest pieces of land on the earth. The world is divided into *continents,* and then into countries. Each *continent* may contain many countries. North America, South America, Europe, Asia, Africa, Antarctica, and Australia are the names of the *continents.*

You will find maps of the continents on the following pages; Africa, page 17; North and South America, page 25; Antarctica, page 28; Asia, page 35; Australia, page 39; Europe, page 163.

continue con-tin′-ue *continue, continued, continuing.* 1. Keep on with.–We *continued* our work without stopping until we were finished.

2. Not stop; proceed; go on.–They will *continue* travelling until they have gone all around the world.

3. Take up where something is left off and go on with it.–Mary told the first part of the story, and Jack *continued* it. He told what happened next.

contract con′-tract *contracts.* An agreement, usually written, between 2 or more people.– The *contract* said that the builder would build our house for £3,000.

contract con-tract′ *contracts, contracted, contracting, contraction.* 1. Agree in a *contract.*–

Father *contracted* to pay £20 a month on the mortgage.

2. Get smaller.–Most metals *contract* when they get cooler.

3. Make smaller.–In speaking, we often *contract* 'cannot' to 'can't'.

contrary con'-tra-ry. 1. Opposite; against; not agreeing with.–Driving on the right side of the street is *contrary* to law in Great Britain. We are supposed to drive on the left-hand side.–It is not a very clear morning; on the *contrary*, it looks like rain.

2. Stubborn; not agreeable.–Dickie is *contrary* (pronounced contrar'i). He never does what someone else wants him to do. He does only what he wants to do.

contrast con'-trast *contrasts*. Difference.–The *contrast* between night and day is that night is dark and day is light.–There is a great *contrast* between Jack's writing and Bob's. Jack's is large and heavy, and Bob's is small and light.

contribute con-trib'-ute *contributes, contributed, contributing, contribution*. 1. Give money.–Jack will *contribute* towards the new slide for the playground.

2. Give help, information, etc.–The farmer *contributed* a day's work to a sick neighbour. –The teacher asked Bill if he had anything to *contribute* to the discussion about birds.

3. Have a part in; be partly responsible for.– Too little sleep *contributes* to one's being tired. It helps to make one tired.

control con-trol' *controls, controlled, controlling*. 1. The power to manage.–The driver lost *control* over his motor-car, and it went into the ditch.

2. Direction; management; care.–The fire chief has many men under his *control*. He tells them what to do.–The children are not under the teacher's *control* during the summer holiday.

3. Keep back; check. – Jack *controlled* his tears when the ball hit him.

4. A device that guides or makes a machine do certain things.–The pilot knows how to handle the aeroplane's *controls*.

convenient con-ven'-ient *conveniently* 1. Handy; arranged so that it is easy to get around or do things.–Our kitchen is very *convenient*.–The hammer is in a *convenient* place.–It is *convenient* to have a telephone.

2. Suitable; to one's liking and comfort.–If it is *convenient* for you, I will come at seven.

convent con'-vent *convents*. A building or a number of buildings where nuns live. A nun devotes or gives all her life to her religion.

convention con-ven'-tion *conventions*. A meeting of many people of an organization for a special purpose.–The doctors are holding a *convention* in the city next week.–At a *convention* people talk about problems that they are all interested in.

conversation con-ver-sa'-tion *conversations*. A talk between two or more people.–Jack and Mary had a long *conversation* about the play.

convict con-vict' *convicts, convicted, convicting*, Find or prove guilty in court.–The driver was *convicted* of driving too fast.

convict con'-vict *convicts*. Person who has been proved guilty in court of a crime and sent to prison.–The *convict* was freed for good behaviour.

coo *coos, cooed, cooing*. 1. Make a soft, low sound.–Pigeons *coo*.

2. Soft, low sound.–We heard the *coo* of the pigeon.

cook *cooks, cooked, cooking*. 1. Prepare food to eat by using heat.
– We *cook* food. We broil, boil, fry, bake, or roast food over a fire or in an oven.

2. A person who prepares food. – The *cook* at the restaurant wears a tall white cap.

cooker cook'-er *cookers*. A stove for cooking food.–We could not decide whether to buy a gas or an electric *cooker*.

cool *cools, cooled, cooling, cooler, coolest*, 1. Without much heat; slightly cold.–Food that stands too long after being taken from the stove becomes *cool*.–We turn on an electric fan to keep us *cool* in the summer.–We wear light clothes to keep us *cool*.

2. Calm; not excited.–When the fire alarm sounded, the children were very *cool*.

3. Unfriendly.–The new boy is *cool* towards us.

4. Make *cool*; remove heat from.–The room was *cooled* by air conditioning.–We *cooled* the melon in the refrigerator.

coop *coops*. A small, cage-like pen.–Grandmother keeps her chickens in *coops*.

co-operate co-op′-er-ate *co-operates, co-operated, co-operating*. Work together.–The children in our school *co-operate* well.

copper cop′-per. 1. A reddish-brown metal. Most electric wire is made of *copper*. *Copper* does not rust. It is used in making vases and many other ornamental things.
2. Reddish-brown.–A sorrel horse is of a *copper* colour.

copy cop′-y *copies, copied, copying*. 1. Anything that is made exactly like something else.–My dress is a *copy* of one I saw in the shop window.–The picture is a *copy* of one painted by a great artist.
2. One of a number of books just alike.–Mary got a *copy* of 'Little Women' from the library.
3. Set down or make just exactly like something else.–The teacher wrote a poem on the blackboard for us to *copy*.

coral cor′-al. 1. A hard, shell-like substance formed in the sea from the skeletons of very small sea animals. It is red, white, or pink, and is used in jewellery, beads, etc.
2. Made of *coral*.–Mother bought a *coral* necklace.

cord *cords*. 1. A heavy string or thin rope.–We tied up the package with *cord*. – Bob put a new *cord* on his kite.
2. A string-like structure in the body. – *Cords* join the muscles to the bones.

3. A pile of wood 8 feet long, 4 feet wide, and 4 feet high.

core *cores*. The seedy centre part of apples, pears, and some other fruit.–We do not eat the *core*.

cork *corks, corked, corking*. 1. The bark of a cork oak tree. *Cork* is light and stretchy, but it does not soak up water. Because it floats, it is used for life-belts.

2. A piece of *cork* shaped to fit the opening of a bottle.
3. Put the *cork* or stopper in.–Father *corked* the bottle.

corn. 1. The seed of any cereal.–Birds eat *corn*.
2. In Great Britain, *corn* may be wheat, barley, oats or rye.
3. In the United States, *corn* is always maize, or Indian *corn*. The kernels, or seed of corn, grow on a cob. Corn is sometimes canned and described as sweet*corn*.
4. A pepper seed is a pepper*corn*.

corner cor′-ner *corners, cornered, cornering*.
1. A point where 2 straight surfaces, such as walls, meet.–A cupboard stands in the *corner*.
2. Where streets come together.–Bob met me at the street *corner*.–There is a grocer's shop on the *corner*.
3. A secret place.–The children hid the peanuts for the hunt in every *corner* of the house.
4. Force into a position where one cannot get out.–The dogs *cornered* the fox.

cornet cor′-net *cornets*. A musical instrument something like a trumpet, made of bent brass tubes.

corn-flour. A fine starchy flour made from various kinds of grain. *Corn-flour* is used to thicken gravy, soups, puddings, etc.

corporal cor′-po-ral *corporals*. A soldier in the army ranking below sergeant and above private.

corps (pronounced *core*). A number of people who have been trained to do certain things as a group under a leader.–An army *corps* is a division of an army.–Government representatives in a foreign capital are known collectively as the diplomatic *corps*.

corpse *corpses*. The body of a dead person.

corral cor-ral′ *corrals, corralled, corralling.*
1. A pen; a space with a fence around it.–
Cattle and horses are kept in a *corral.*–Wagons placed close together are used sometimes
to form a *corral.*

2. Place in a *corral* or pen.–The cowboy
corralled the ponies.

correct cor-rect′ *corrects, corrected, correcting.* 1. Right; true.–Your answer is *correct.*
–Is this the *correct* way to play the game?
2. Proper; well-mannered. – It is *correct* to
thank people for their gifts to you.
3. Make right; go over to see that all is right.
–I *corrected* your arithmetic problem, which
was wrong.–The teacher *corrected* our spelling tests and gave them back to us so that
we could see our mistakes.

correction cor-rec′-tion *corrections.* A change
that is made to make right something which
is wrong – The only *correction* made on
my paper was that an *ie* was changed to an
ei to make the word 'receive' right.

correspond cor-re-spond′ *corresponds, corresponded, corresponding.* 1. Write letters to
one another.–Grandmother and I *correspond*
when she is not with us.
2. Be in harmony; go together well.–The
colours of the rugs, curtains, and cushions all
correspond nicely.
3. Be like; fill the same purpose as.–The
wings of an aeroplane *correspond* to the
wings of a bird.

corset cor′-set *corsets.* A tight-fitting undergarment worn around the waist and hips to
support and give shape to the body. *Corsets*
are sometimes called foundations. *Corsets*
are worn for support by some women, and
sometimes, after certain sicknesses, by men.

cost *costs, costing.* 1. Amount paid for, or
amount for which something is selling.–The
cost of our new chair was £15.
2. Be priced at, be worth; be selling for.–
Mother asked the assistant how much the
hat *cost.* She said it *cost* £3.
3. Loss or sacrifice.–The hero saved the baby
at the *cost* of his own life.

costume cos′-tume *costumes, costumed, costuming.* 1. Dress or clothes worn to act parts,
or to make believe that one is a different person or a person of a different time or place.–
The art teacher and the sewing teacher made
the *costumes* for the school play. My *costume* represented Old Mother Hubbard.

2. Woman's clothing.–A coat and skirt of
the same material is called a *costume.*

cot *cots.* A low, narrow bed.–Most babies sleep
in *cots.*

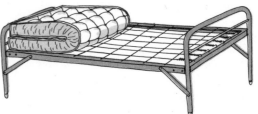

cottage cot′-tage *cottages.* A small, simple
house.–In the summer we go to our *cottage*
at the lake.

cotton cot′-ton *cottons.* A fluffy white substance that grows round the seeds of the
cotton plant. It is spun into threads, from
which *cotton* cloth is made. *Cotton* is also

cleaned and used to fill cushions and quilts,
and for dressing cuts, burns, and other
wounds.

couch *couches.* A lounge, sofa, or upholstered seat for several people.–When we have company, I sleep on the living-room *couch,* and give the company my bed.

cough *coughs, coughed, coughing.* 1. To force air from the lungs through the throat, making a sudden rough noise. A cold or a little tickling in the throat often causes people to *cough.*–One should cover the mouth with a handkerchief when *coughing.*
2. A sound made by *coughing,* or a sickness causing one to *cough* often.–Mary has a bad *cough,* so she stayed at home today.

could. One form of the word *can.*–Baby *could* walk when she was a year old.–Bob *could* make a kite if only he had some paste.

couldn't *could'-n't.* Could not; was not able to. –Baby *couldn't* talk when she was a year old, but she can now.

council *coun'-cil councils.* A group of people chosen to make rules and take care of other matters for a larger group of people.–The city *council* meets once a week.–A student *council* is a group of students who meet to discuss the problems of the school and try to solve them.

count *counts, counted, counting.* 1. To number.–The children *counted* the bricks in the box. They found out how many there were. –When you are angry, *count* 10 before you speak. Say the numbers 1, 2, 3, 4, 5, 6, 7, 8, 9, 10 in order.
2. Put down, record.–The batsman did not put his bat in the crease, so one of the runs could not be *counted.*
3. Adding up.–The *count* of the scores showed the girls were ahead.
4. Think, consider. – When the boat upset, the girl *counted* herself lucky to be able to swim.
5. Rely or depend.–If there is work to be done, you can *count* upon Bob to help.
6. Be valuable or worth while.–Every good deed you do *counts,* even little things.

counter *count'-er counters.* In a shop, a long cabinet or table behind which the assistant stands when serving the customer.–The man put the money for the goods on the *counter.*

counterfeit *coun'-ter-feit counterfeits, counterfeited, counterfeiting.* 1. Imitation; fake.– The men were put in jail for making *counterfeit* money.
2. Make an imitation, especially of money.– The men who *counterfeited* the five-pound notes are now in prison.

country *coun'-try countries.* 1. Land. – The *country* near the lake is sometimes covered with water.
2. A nation; one's native land, land where one was born.–England is a *country* with a pleasant, mild climate.
3. Land where people do not live close together, as they do in cities and towns.–We live in town, but Grandfather lives in the *country.*–We go to the *country* for the summer.

county *coun'-ty counties.* A section or division of a country. There are over 60 counties in England and Wales. The city of London also forms a *county.*–The people elect officers to take care of the business in their *county.*

coupé (pronounced *coopay*) *cou-pé' coupés.* A closed motor-car with only one seat, which has room for 2 or 3 people.

couple *cou-'ple couples, coupled, coupling.* 1. Two of anything.–Mother bought a *couple* of vases for the mantelpiece, one for each end.
2. A boy and girl, or man and woman.–That *couple* won the dancing contest.
3. A husband and wife.–The old *couple* like to play cards on the veranda after supper.– Father and Mother are a very happy *couple.*
4. Join to, put together, or connect.–The caravan was *coupled* to the motor-car for the trip.

coupon cou'-pon *coupons*. 1. A ticket or printed card showing that the holder of it is due to receive something. – For each pound of tea we buy, the grocer gives us a *coupon* which says that we are entitled to a free tin to put tea in.

2. A printed form to be filled in and posted to order something.–Father cut out and sent in the *coupon* ordering the new books.

courage cour'-age *courageous, courageously*. Bravery. – The people showed much *courage* when the lion got out of the cage. They did not show their fear and become excited.

course *courses*. 1. A route, a way.–The aeroplane got off its *course*. It no longer went in the right direction.
2. A movement forward; path.–The river leaves sand and mud in its *course*.
3. Regular happening. – To take things in their *course* means to take care of things one at a time as they come, without looking ahead to things that haven't happened yet.–We go to school in the morning as a matter of *course*. –The doctor said that the sickness would have to run its *course*.
4. Grounds.–Father plays golf on the Red Run golf *course*.
5. A series of classes or lessons.–Mother is taking an evening *course* in cooking at the night school.
6. A part of a meal which is served at one time.–Soup or grapefruit is often served for the first *course*; meat, vegetables, and salad for the next, and a sweet or savoury for the last *course*.
7. *Of course* means certainly, surely.–*Of course* we are going to the pictures; we always go.

court *courts, courted, courting*. 1. A hard, level place marked off for a game. – Tennis is played on a tennis *court*.

2. A yard, or the space between or nearly shut in by the walls of buildings.–Most *courts* are paved with concrete or stone.–Children who live in blocks of flats often play in the *court*.

3. To pay much attention to a woman with the wish of winning her for a wife.–The prince *courted* Cinderella.
4. Invite; try to bring on.–Children who cross the road without looking *court* accidents. They risk accidents.–Jack felt it would be *courting* trouble to ask Bill if he had seen his ball.
5. A place where matters are settled according to law. The judges who have charge of the trials are also known as the *court*.–The burglar was taken into *court* to be tried for robbing the petrol station.–The highest *court* in England is the House of Lords. In the United States, it is the Supreme *Court*.
6. The place where the king or any other ruler lives, and the people who attend him. –Cinderella went to the ball at *court*.
7. Attentions. – The soldier who wanted a higher position paid *court* to the king. He tried to please the king, to get the king to like him.
8. A reigning monarch together with his or her councillors and household officials.–In the fourteenth century, the English *court* resided at Westminster. Today the Royal Family lives in Buckingham Palace.

court-card *court-cards*. A picture-card in a pack of playing-cards.–There are 12 *court-cards* in every pack, namely the king, queen and knave of spades, hearts, diamonds and clubs.

courteous cour'-te-ous *courteously, courteousness*. Polite, kind, and thoughtful. – People always like Mary at once because she is so *courteous*.

courtesy cour'-te-sy *courtesies*. 1. Politeness; good manners; respect for other people's feelings.–The shop assistant is well liked because of his *courtesy*.
2. A special attention; a kindness.–Grandmother thanked the minister for his many *courtesies*, such as sending the flowers when she was ill.

C
D
E
F
G
H
I
J
K
L
M
N
O
P
Q
R
S
T
U
V
W
X
Y
Z

court-house court'-house *court-houses*. A building where trials of law are held.

courtier court'-ier *courtiers*. Someone in attendance at a court or palace.–Cinderella's beauty was admired by the prince, his guests and all his *courtiers*.

court-martial *courts-martial*. A special court which tries offences committed by members of the armed forces.–The officer was accused by the *court-martial* of cowardice.

courtyard court'-yard *courtyards*. A large yard, often paved, with buildings or walls all round, or nearly all round it. – Children who live in blocks of flats often play in the *courtyard*.

cousin cous'-in *cousins*. The children of one's aunts or uncles.–My father's sister and his brother both have children. These children are my *cousins*.–My mother's brother and her sister also have children. These children are my *cousins*, too.

cover cov'-er *covers, covered, covering*. 1. Put over the top or outside of.–To *cover* potatoes with water means to put water over them.–To *cover* the bed with a quilt means to spread a quilt over the bed.–To *cover* a book means to fit paper or other material over the outside of the book.
2. A lid or top.–Put a *cover* on the pot when you cook potatoes. –The box has no *cover*.
3. A wrapper or jacket on the outside of a book or magazine. –Books sometimes have leather *covers*, sometimes cloth *covers*, and sometimes *covers* of hard cardboard.
4. A blanket or spread for a bed. –Sally kicked her *covers* off because she was too hot.
5. Travel over, get through. – You cannot *cover* as much ground in an hour with a horse and cart as you can *cover* with a motor-car.–The teacher said we had another lesson to *cover*.
6. Include, take in.–Mary's diary *covers* the years 1959–1961. She kept her diary during those 3 years.–Jack's composition on what he wants to be when he grows up *covered* many fields.

covering cov'-er-ing *coverings*. Anything used to cover something.–Fruit drops have paper *coverings*.–Quilts and blankets are bed *coverings*.–A hat is a *covering* for the head.

cow *cows*. 1. A large farm animal kept to give milk.–Grandfather milks the *cows* each evening.

2. Mother elephants, seals, and many other animal mothers are known as *cows*.

coward cow'-ard *cowards*. A person who is afraid or who cannot face danger.–The biggest boy in our school is a *coward*. He is afraid of anyone who really wants to fight.

cowboy cow'-boy *cowboys*. A man who rides horses and looks after cows and other cattle on a cattle ranch.

cowshed cow'-shed *cowsheds*. A building in which cows live and where they are milked.

cowslip cow'-slip *cowslips*. 1. A wild plant of the primrose family that grows in pastures. It has fragrant yellow flowers in spring.
2. In the United States, the marsh marigold is called a *cowslip*.

coy *coyly*. Shy, and retiring.–Ann became *coy* when the mayor spoke to her.

coyote (pronounced *koy-oh-ty*) coy-o'-te *coyotes*. A kind of small wolf found on the plains of the western United States.

crab *crabs*. 1. A sea animal that has a hard shell on its back. *Crabs* have a pair of pincers with which they grab or hold on to things. Many *crabs* are good to eat.
2. To catch a *crab*. When rowing, if the oarsman misses the water altogether, or gets his oar too deep, he is said to 'catch a *crab*'.

crab-apple crab'-ap-ple *crab-apples*. A kind of small, sour apple. *Crab-apples* make very good jam or jelly.

crack *cracks, cracked, cracking*. 1. A quick, sharp, snapping or popping sound. – The horses were away at the first *crack* of the whip.
2. Snap.–The lion tamer *cracked* his whip to make the lions behave.

3. Break open. – Squirrels *crack* nuts with their teeth.

4. A thin, long opening or split.–We could see a light through the *crack* in the wall.

5. Split without separating into parts.–The old plate was *cracked,* but it was still in one piece.

6. Break down suddenly.–The speaker was shouting so loudly that his voice *cracked.*

7. Excellent, first-class.–Stanley Matthews is a *crack* football player.

crackle crack'-le *crackles, crackled, crackling.*
1. A sharp, cracking sound.–We heard the *crackle* of the fire.
2. Make a sharp, cracking sound.–Dry leaves *crackle* when you walk in them.

cradle cra'-dle *cradles.* A small baby's bed with sides and on rockers.–Mother rocks the baby to sleep in the *cradle.*

craft *crafts.* 1. A boat.–Many *craft* were in the boat race.
2. Any kind of skilled work done with the hands.–Boys may learn *crafts* at school. They may learn how to make and do many things with their hands.
3. Trickery.–The man got the horse by *craft.*

cramp *cramps.* A sudden, painful tightening of the muscles.–A *cramp* in the leg of the runner caused him to lose the race.

cranberry cran'-ber-ry *cranberries.* A kind of dark red berry that grows on low bushes in damp places. – We make *cranberry* sauce, jelly, and preserves to eat with turkey, chicken, and other meats.

crane *cranes, craned, craning.* 1. A large wading bird.–We saw a *crane* making a nest in the rushes in the water.

2. A machine for lifting heavy loads.–The workmen used a *crane* to lift very heavy things from the ship.

3. Stretch out (the neck). – Because a tall man sat in front of us, Bob had to *crane* his neck to see the film.

crank *cranks, cranked, cranking.* 1. A bar or handle used to turn or rotate something. – The old motor-car had to be started with a *crank.* –The organ grinder turns a *crank* to make music.
2. Make a thing go with a *crank.*–The organ grinder *cranks* his organ to make music.
3. A very queer person, especially one who imagines that many people are scheming against him.–The old man is a *crank.* He thinks everyone dislikes him.

crash *crashes, crashed, crashing.* 1. The loud breaking or banging noise of something falling down or striking something.–When the waiter dropped his tray of dishes, there was a loud *crash.*
2. Fall down noisily.–The pans *crashed* to the floor.
3. Break (through).–The ball hit the window and *crashed* through it.
4. Be wrecked suddenly. – The aeroplane *crashed* after taking off.
5. A sudden wrecking.–Both drivers were hurt in the *crash* of their cars.

crate *crates, crated, crating.* 1. A box or frame made of wooden slats. –The oranges and the apples were packed into *crates.*
2. Pack in a box or frame.–Our furniture was *crated* before we moved.

crater cra'-ter *craters* The hole or opening in the top of a volcano. – Hot melted rock flows from the *crater* of the volcano.

C
D
E
F
G
H
I
J
K
L
M
N
O
P
Q
R
S
T
U
V
W
X
Y
Z

crawl *crawls, crawled, crawling.* 1. Pull or draw the body along the ground.–Caterpillars and worms *crawl.*
2. Move about on the hands and knees.–Babies *crawl* before they learn to walk.
3. Move very slowly. – The traffic was so heavy that the cars *crawled* along the road.
4. *Crawling* may mean to be covered with *crawling* things. – The window-pane was *crawling* with insects.

crayon cray'-on *crayons.* A stick of coloured wax, chalk or charcoal.–We coloured pictures with *crayons.*

crazy cra'-zy *crazier, craziest. Insane;* sick in mind.–A *crazy* person often has no control over the things he says and does.

creak *creaks, creaked, creaking.* 1. Squeaking sound.–The door opened with a sharp *creak.*
2. Make a squeaking sound.–Father wanted to surprise us, but we heard the floor *creak* as he came near.

cream *creams, creamed, creaming.* 1. A thick, yellowish fat found in milk.–We let the milk stand and the *cream* rose to the top.–Butter is made from *cream.*
2. A light yellowish colour.–Mother wore a *cream*-coloured hat.
3. Any soft, thick, wet substance that suggests the *cream* in milk. – Father uses shaving *cream* for shaving.–Mother uses cold *cream* to keep her hands soft.
4. Make a smooth, pasty mixture by pressing together.–Mother *creams* butter, sugar, and milk to make icing for a cake.
5. The best part.–Bob always gets the *cream* of everything.

crease *creases, creased, creasing.* 1. A fold or ridge made by folding or pressing.–The legs of men's trousers have *creases* in the front and back.–Pressing the *creases* with a hot iron makes them last a long time.
2. Make a fold or wrinkle in.–The children *crease* their papers in the middle for a spelling test.
3. In cricket, the white lines near the wickets fixing the positions of the batsmen and the bowlers.–The batsman stepped out of his *crease* and was stumped.

4. Wrinkle.–Do not lie down while wearing your new dress or you may get *creases* in it.

create cre-ate' *creates, created, creating, creation.* 1. Cause.–We *created* much excitement when we dressed like ghosts.
2. Make; design; make up out of one's own mind.–Mary *created* a picture. She did not copy it; she made it up.

creature crea'-ture *creatures.* An animal or person.–All *creatures* require food to keep them alive.

credit cred'-it *credits, credited, crediting.* 1. A reputation for paying bills. – Our *credit* is good at the corner shop. We can get groceries and pay for them later. They know we will pay.
2. Buy *on credit* means to pay for something some time after it is purchased.
3. Acknowledgment.–When Father paid £5 on our grocery bill, the cashier gave him *credit.* He marked down in the book that Father had paid £5.
4. Reward; favourable regard.–Jack got *credit* for writing the school song, even though several children helped him.
5. Amount in one's favour.–Mother had £15 in the savings account. After she took out £10, she still had a £5 *credit* with the bank.
6. A person or thing that improves a reputation.–Bob is a *credit* to the cricket team. He helps to give it a good name or reputation.
7. Believe; put trust in.–The teacher *credits* the stories of the children. She believes them.

creek *creeks.* A small stream of water. – The boys went swimming in the *creek.*

creep *creeps, creeper, crept, creeping.* 1. Move very softly and quietly.–As soon as the boys heard the farmer's footsteps, they decided to *creep* away.
2. Crawl or move along close to the ground. –The boys had to *creep* to get under the fence.
3. Grow along the ground and take roots at many places.–Some vines are *creeping* plants.
4. Feel shivery.–The howling of dogs at night makes Mary *creep.*
5. Move along very slowly.–Traffic was so heavy that our car could only *creep.*

crêpe (pronounced *crape*). 1. A thin, crinkly cloth of silk, cotton, etc.–Grandmother has a new dress of black *crêpe*.
2. *Crêpe* paper is a soft, crinkly paper.–We decorated the table for the party with *crêpe* paper.

crept. One form of the word *creep*.–We *crept* up the stairs to surprise the other boys and girls.

crest *crests*. 1. A topknot or tuft of feathers on a bird's head.–*Crested* tits have black and white *crests* on their heads.
2. A top ridge.–As we rode along we saw the *crest* of the mountains.

3. The top edge (of a wave).–The boat rode over the *crest* of the wave coming in to the beach.
4. A plume or bunch of feathers on a hat.–In medieval times knights used to wear *crests* on their helmets.

crew *crews*. 1. The group of persons who run a train, aeroplane, or ship.–The *crew* has gone ashore for the evening.
2. A group of persons who do certain work together.–The city has a *crew* of workmen cleaning the park.

crib *cribs*. 1. A small bed with high sides.–The baby sleeps in a *crib*.

2. A manger or deep box for feed.–Horses eat from *cribs*.

cricket crick'-et *crickets*. 1. An outdoor summer game played between two teams of eleven players with bats, balls and wickets. The team which scores more runs wins the game. Men who play *cricket* either for amusement or for a living are called *cricketers*, and the game, which may last from one to five days, is called a *cricket* match. A *cricket* match between the best elevens of two countries is called a Test Match.

2. A black or brown jumping insect something like a grasshopper. *Crickets* make a chirping sound. They hide under large stones and logs.

cried. One form of the word *cry*.
1. The little girl *cried* when she burned her hand.
2. The pedlar *cried*, 'Apples for sale.'

cries. One form of the word *cry*. 1. Baby *cries* when she wants someone to hold her.
2. The paper-boy *cries*, 'Morning paper?'

crime *crimes*. An evil or bad act that is against the law.–The prisoner was guilty of many *crimes*.–People are punished for *crimes*.

criminal crim'-i-nal *criminals*. A person who does evil and unlawful things.–The *criminal* was sent to prison for stealing.

crimson crim'-son. A bright red.–Mary's new dress is *crimson*. – The angry man's face turned almost *crimson*.

cripple crip'-ple *cripples, crippled, crippling*. 1. A lame person; a person unable to use his body, legs, or arms properly.–A person without a leg or an arm is a *cripple*.–The *cripple* learned to do everything for himself without the help of others.
2. Make lame or disabled.–The sailor was *crippled* by a fall from the mast of his ship. –The taxes were *crippling*. They made it financially difficult to carry on business.

crisp. 1. Brittle; not soft; easily broken.–Good biscuits are *crisp*.
2. Fresh; refreshing.–A walk in the *crisp* morning air will make you feel wide awake.

critical crit'-i-cal *critically*. 1. Likely to find fault.–The teacher is *critical* of our work. She is quick to find fault with it.
2. Serious; dangerous.–The sick woman is in a *critical* condition.

criticism crit'-i-cism *criticisms*. A statement about the good or bad points or qualities of something.–Jack was very pleased with the teacher's *criticism* of his composition.

criticize crit'-i-cize *criticizes, criticized, criticizing*. 1. Find fault with.–Father does not *criticize* the work we do.
2. Point out the good and bad parts of something.–The teacher will *criticize* our compositions.

C
D
E
F
G
H
I
J
K
L
M
N
O
P
Q
R
S
T
U
V
W
X
Y
Z

croak *croaks, croaked, croaking.* 1. Make a low, hoarse, throaty noise.–Frogs *croak.*
2. A sound like that of a frog.–The *croak* of the bullfrog kept us awake.

crochet (pronounced *krochay*) cro-chet' *cro-chets, crocheted, crocheting.* 1. Do a kind of fancy hand work. – You *crochet* by making a series of loops, and then pulling the thread through the first loops with a hook to make more loops.
2. Lacework.–Mary's blue dress has a white *crochet* collar that Mother *crocheted.*

crock *crocks.* 1. A jar or pot made of clay and baked until hard.–Grand-mother puts milk in a *crock.*–
2. A broken-down person or thing. Our car is an old *crock.*·

crocodile croc'-o-dile *crocodiles.* A large, four-legged, flesh-eating animal that looks like an alligator but has a narrower, longer head.– *Crocodiles* have scaly skins. They live in warm waters and in marshes.

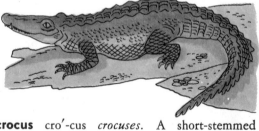

crocus cro'-cus *crocuses.* A short-stemmed early-spring flower, usually yellow, purple or white. The *crocus* belongs to the iris family. The flowers stick out of the ground like little spikes. The *crocus* grows from a corm.

crook *crooks, crooked, crooking.*
1. A bend or curve.–We saw a lady on horse-back coming around the *crook* in the road.
2. To bend or arch.–Mary *crooks* her little finger when she butters biscuits. She curls her little finger up.
3. A person who gets money by dishonest tricks.–The *crook* tried to sell Father a stolen car.

crooked crook'-ed *crookedly.* 1. Not straight. –This road is *crooked.* It has many curves and twists.
2. Not honest.–The man had made much of his money in *crooked* dealings, in which other people were cheated.

crop, *crops, cropped, cropping.* 1. A field of food plants.–The farmer plants his *crops* in the spring.
2. A harvest of anything; fruit or vegetables which are picked or reaped. – The cherry *crop* is large this year.–The cotton *crop* is poor.
3. Bite off.–The hungry rabbits *crop* the lettuce in the garden.
4. A chicken's *crop* is one of its stomachs, in which food is digested.
5. Cut off closely.–In summer some men *crop* their hair.
6. A thick growth.–Jack has a *crop* of bright red hair.
7. A whip with a loop on the whipping end of it.–The hunter carries a *crop.*

croquet (pronounced *krokay*) cro-quet. A game played by setting wire arches in smooth ground and hitting wooden balls through them with a long-handled wooden hammer or mallet.

cross *crosses, crossed, crossing.* 1. A mark (+) made by putting one line directly across another.
2. Anything in the shape of a *cross.*–A *cross* is the sign of the Christian religion.
3. Put one across another.–The children *crossed* their fingers.
4. Go from one side to another. –Bé careful when you *cross* the road.
5. A mixture.–This dog is a *cross* between a cocker and a chow. Its mother was a cocker and its father was a chow.
6. Go against, or disagree with.–Bob never *crosses* Jack.
7. Ill-tempered.–When I am tired, I get *cross.* Nothing suits me, and I get angry easily.

cross-eyed cross'-eyed. Having eyes which turn in towards the nose, so that one cannot look straight ahead with both eyes at the same time.

crossing cross'-ing *crossings.* 1. A place where streets cross or where a railway crosses a street.–We had to wait at the level-*crossing* until the train had gone by.
2. A place where a street is crossed by people. –Policemen stand at the *crossings* to help the children go across the street.

crouch *crouches, crouched, crouching.* Bend down with the back and knees; squat.–The escaped prisoner *crouched* on the bridge until the train had passed.

crow *crows, crowed, crowing.* 1. A large, black bird. – *Crows* eat the farmer's corn.
2. Call or cry.–We heard the cock *crow* early in the morning.
3. A call or cry.–The cock's *crow* woke us early in the morning.
4. Cry out gleefully.–Baby *crowed* with delight when Father held her on his head.
5. Boast or brag.–Edward likes to *crow* over all the things he has done and can do.

crowd *crowds, crowded, crowding.* 1. A large group of people.–A *crowd* gathered along the street to see the parade.
2. Pack, cram.–Do not *crowd* the eggs into the basket. Do not press them together.
3. Push and shove.–Do not *crowd* in the line, but wait your turn.

crown *crowns, crowned, crowning.* 1. A fancy circlet or band worn on the heads of kings and queens. *Crowns* usually have many jewels in them.
2. A wreath for the head.–The children made *crowns* of daisies.
3. Reward.–The man's efforts were *crowned* with success.
4. The centre part of a hat, which sticks up. –Sally stepped on Father's hat and squashed the *crown*.
5. Put a *crown* on; make king or queen.–The mayor *crowned* the girl who was voted most beautiful.

crude *crudely, crudeness.* 1. Impure; raw, not prepared for use. – *Crude* sugar must be treated or refined before it is used.
2. Rough or unfinished.–Robinson Crusoe lived in a *crude* cabin.
3. Not in good taste, not pleasing to others.– Bill's manners are *crude*.

cruel *cru'-el cruelly.* Taking pleasure in hurting others or in seeing them hurt; without kindness or pity.–Father became angry when he saw the *cruel* man beating the horse.

cruelty *cru'-el-ty.* Heartless treatment; lack of mercy.–The man was arrested for his *cruelty* to the horse.

cruise *cruises, cruised, cruising.* 1. A trip or journey in a boat.–Father and Mother went on a *cruise* for their holiday.
2. Travel from place to place on the water.– Father and Mother *cruised* round the coasts of the Mediterranean, calling at various ports.

cruiser *cruis'-er cruisers.* 1. A large, fast war-

ship, next in size to a battleship.–The navy has many *cruisers*.

crumb *crumbs, crumbed, crumbing.* 1. A small bit of bread.–Sally threw the *crumbs* to the birds.
2. Roll in breadcrumbs.–The cook *crumbed* the fish before frying it.
3. A very small amount.–We tried to find out the date of the cricket match but could not get a *crumb* of information.

crumble *crum'-ble crumbles, crumbled, crumbling.* Break into small crumbs or very tiny pieces. – Baby *crumbled* the biscuit in her hands.

crumple *crum'-ple crumples, crumpled, crumpling.* Wrinkle or curl up; crush. – Andrew *crumpled* his spelling paper in his hand and threw it into the waste-paper basket.

crunch *crunches, crunched, crunching.* Chew noisily with the teeth.–It is really almost impossible to eat celery without making a *crunching* noise.

crush *crushes, crushed, crushing.* 1. Break up by pressure.–The stones were *crushed* into small pieces by the stone-crusher.
2. Wrinkle; wad up.–Mary tried not to *crush* her new hair ribbon when she put on her hat.–The man's hat was *crushed* when the car ran over it.
3. Defeat completely; overcome.–The army was *crushed* by the enemy.
4. A closely packed crowd of people.–Bob and Bill went to the game together, but were separated in the *crush* of people going through the gates.

C
D
E
F
G
H
I
J
K
L
M
N
O
P
Q
R
S
T
U
V
W
X
Y
Z

crust *crusts, crusted, crusting.* 1. The pastry shell of a pie.–The *crust* of the pie burned but the filling was all right.
2. The hard outer covering of bread.–The *crust* of bread is good to eat.
3. A thin, hard coat or covering.–There was a *crust* of ice on the snow.
4. Cover with a hard film.–The syrup was *crusted* with sugar.

crutch *crutches.* A long prop which fits under the arm and is moved by the arm and hand to help one walk when one's leg is lame.

cry *cries, cried, crying.*
1. A loud call or shout. –We heard the *cry* of the boy who fell into the water.
2. A call.–We heard the cry of an owl.
3. Shed tears and make a noise showing pain or sorrow; weep; sob. – Most children *cry* when they are hurt.
4. Shout; call in a loud voice.–The workman on the roof *cried,* 'Look out below!' when he dropped his hammer.

crystal *crys'-tal crystals.* 1. A clear, shiny mineral.–The water is as clear as *crystal.*
2. A small piece of quartz used in place of a valve in simple radio receivers.
3. Clear, shiny glass.–Mother has some new *crystal* goblets. They are made of glass that is very clear and perfectly polished.

cub *cubs.* A young baby bear, wolf, lion, etc.– The lion *cubs* looked like large kittens.

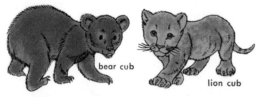
bear cub
lion cub

cube *cubes.* A solid figure that has 6 square sides which are all the same size.–Baby's blocks are *cubes.*

cuckoo *cuck'-oo cuckoos.* A migrant bird with a well-known call. Some *cuckoos* do not build their own nests, but lay their eggs in the nests of other birds. Other *cuckoos* build their own nests.

cucumber *cu'-cum-ber cucumbers.* A long, green vegetable that grows on a vine close to the ground. The outer skin is green and the inner part, which has many seeds in it, is white. *Cucumbers* are often eaten raw in salads, as pickles, or sometimes dipped in egg and flour and fried.

cud *cuds.* A lump of food brought back from the first stomach of a cow (or other animal with 2 stomachs) into the mouth for chewing again.

cuddle *cud'-dle cuddles, cuddled, cuddling.*
1. Hold closely and affectionately.–Mother *cuddles* the baby. She holds it closely.
2. *Cuddle up to* means wriggle close to.– The kittens *cuddle up to* their mother.

cue *cues.* 1. A long, braided tail of hair hanging down behind.–John took the part of a Chinese man in the play and wore a long *cue.* (Usually spelt *queue.*)

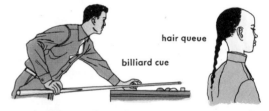
hair queue
billiard cue

2. A long stick with a soft tip used in the game of billiards or snooker.
3. A word or action in a play which serves as a signal to an actor.–The actor went on to the stage when he heard his *cue.*
4. A signal.–Bob got ready for the race when he got his *cue* from the coach.

cuff *cuffs, cuffed, cuffing.* 1. A band round the lower part of a long sleeve. – The *cuffs* of Father's old shirt were badly worn.
2. In the United States, the word *cuff* is used for the part of a man's trouser leg that is turned up at the bottom.
3. Strike with the open hand.–Grandfather *cuffed the dog when it jumped up.*

cultivate *cul'-ti-vate cultivates, cultivated, cultivating.* 1. Plant and tend a crop.–Farmers *cultivate* their crops. They help them grow. They plough the ground, make the ground rich, plant seeds, hoe out the weeds, and harvest the crops.
2. Try to improve. – Arthur *cultivates* his manners.

cunning cun'-ning *cunningly*. 1. Sly; tricky.–The fox is *cunning*.–Bob used *cunning* to persuade his mother to let him stay away from school. He pretended to be ill.

cup *cups, cupped, cupping*. 1. A small open vessel with a handle.–We drink from a *cup*. 2. A fancy-shaped vessel given as a prize.–Father won a silver *cup* for his high score in bowling.

drinking cup

prize cup

3. A portion or lot.–When the whole family visited Grandfather he said his *cup* of happiness was full.
4. Anything shaped like a *cup* is often called a *cup*.–Some machines have small *cups* into which oil should be put.
5. Form a *cup*like shape from.–The man *cupped* his hands and lifted water from the brook.
6. A *cup*ful.–Have a *cup* of coffee.

cupboard cup'-board *cupboards*. A cabinet or closet with shelves and drawers in it.–We keep dishes, food, table-linen, and silver in the *cupboard*.

cupid cu'-pid *cupids*. 1. (Written with a capital 'c') The god of love in the stories of the Romans.
2. A picture of a baby with wings, representing love.–Mary put a *cupid* on Jack's valentine.

curb *curbs, curbed, curbing* (Also spelt kerb). 1. A low stone walk along the outer edge of a street. – We stood on the *curb* and waited for the bus.

2. Control; check.–The city tried to *curb* the waste of water.–John tried to *curb* his anger.
3. The part of a horse's bridle that passes under the lower jaw. A *curb* is used to control the horse, to get him to do what is wanted.

curd *curds*. The thick part of sour milk. When sour milk is heated, the *curd* separates from the watery part and is made into cottage cheese.

curdle cur'-dle *curdles, curdled, curdling*. (Of milk) become sour and separate into curds and a liquid called whey.–The milk *curdled* when it was left out of the refrigerator.

cure *cures, cured, curing*. 1. Make well or healthy again.–The doctor said he could *cure* the sick woman.
2. Something that makes one well.–Medicine is a *cure* for some sicknesses.–Rest is a *cure* for some sicknesses.
3. Treat so as to preserve.–Farmers *cure* meats. They dry, salt, and smoke meats to keep them from spoiling.

curfew cur'-few *curfews*. The ringing of a bell or other signal in the evening telling people to get off the streets or to put out fires or lights.–The *curfew* at 9 o'clock warned the children to get off the streets.

curiosity cu-ri-os'-i-ty *curiosities*. 1. A desire to learn.–John has a great *curiosity* about butterflies.
2. A strange object that is not often seen.–The traveller brought back many *curiosities*.

curious cu'-ri-ous *curiously*. 1. Eager to learn.–Jack is *curious* about keeping chickens, ducks, and geese.
2. Odd.–We found several *curious* shells on the beach. They were different from the others.

curl *curls, curled, curling*. 1. A coiled or rolled bunch of hair.–Mary has long *curls*.
2. Roll into *curls*.–The hairdresser curled Mother's hair.
3. Anything coiled in a spiral shape.–The boys twisted the wire round and round to make a *curl*.

4. Wind.–Some plants *curl* round trees and bushes.

curly curl'-y *curlier, curliest*. Curled up; rolled into curls.–Baby's hair is *curly*.

currant cur'-rant *currants*. 1. A small, sweet berry that grows in clusters, or bunches, on bushes. *Currants* are black, white or red. *Currant* jelly is made from *currants*.
2. A small, black raisin without seeds. – Grandmother put *currants* into the cakes.

current cur'-rent *currents*. 1. Something flowing in a steady stream. When we say a *current* of air, a *current* of water, or a *current* of electricity, we mean a flowing or moving of air, water, or electricity.

2. A fast stream of water moving through a slower stream. – The boy could not swim through the *current* in the middle of the river.

3. In use at present.–Mother reads the *current* magazines, the ones that have just been printed.

curse *curses, cursed, cursing*. 1. Swear; use profane language.–Boys who *curse* at animals and people are not well liked.

2. Request that God make some harm or evil come to (a person.) – The man *cursed* his enemy.

3. Something that causes evil. – The boy's laziness is a *curse* to him.

curtain cur'-tain *curtains*. 1. A cloth covering for a window or door.–Mother hung *curtains* at the front window.

window curtain   stage curtain

2. A heavy cloth covering to hide a stage from the audience.–The *curtain* on the stage of the theatre opened and the play started.

curve *curves, curved, curving*. 1. A line that changes its direction little by little and regularly throughout its length.

2. Bend in a *curve*.–The road ahead *curved* round the lake.

3. Something which changes direction little by little; a bend.–The motor-car went round the *curve* in the road.

cushion cush'-ion *cushions, cushioned, cushioning*. 1. A pad or pillow to sit on, or to lean or rest against. – The *cushions* on the couch are filled with feathers.

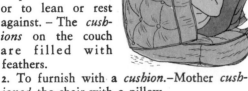

2. To furnish with a *cushion*.–Mother *cushioned* the chair with a pillow.

custard cus'-tard *custards*. A mixture of eggs, sugar, flavouring, and milk that is baked or steamed.–*Custard* pie is filled with *custard*.

custom cus'-tom *customs*. 1. Something usually done.

2. Something that has been done regularly so long that nearly everyone does it.–Greeting friends by shaking hands is an old *custom*.– It is Father's *custom* to shave each morning before breakfast.

customary cus'-tom-ar-y. Usual; commonly done.–It is *customary* for men to take off their hats in the house.

customer cus'-tom-er *customers*. One who is buying; one who often buys at a certain place.–The assistant waited on the *customer*. –Mother is a *customer* at Mr Smith's shop. She usually buys her groceries there.

cut *cuts, cutting*. 1. Separate into pieces, or make a *cut* in, with a knife or other sharp edge.–Father *cut* the meat into small pieces. –The woodmen *cut* down trees with axes.– Bob *cut* his finger with his knife.

2. Clip; *cut* off; make shorter.–John *cuts* the grass with a lawn-mower.

3. A way or route that goes across.–The boys took a short *cut* to the river.

4. Hurt keenly. – The teacher's words *cut* John's feelings.

5. A gash or place made by something sharp. –Bob fell on the glass and got a *cut* on his hand.

6. Make less or smaller.–Bob's pocket-money was *cut* from 25p to 20p.

cutlery cut'-le-ry. Steel implements used in the household.–Scissors, knives, forks and spoons are all articles of *cutlery*.

cutlet cut'-let *cutlets*. A piece of meat cooked by being fried, grilled, or rolled in egg and bread-crumbs and cooked in deep fat.–Veal *cutlets* are tasty.

cutter cut'-ter *cutters*. 1. A sleigh drawn by a horse.–People who live where there is much snow ride in a *cutter*.

2. A machine or tool for cutting.–We cut the vegetables into fancy shapes with a new vegetable *cutter*.

3. A kind of sailing-boat with one pole for sails.—The young man has a *cutter* to sail on the lake.

cutting cut'-ting *cuttings*. 1. Something cut out. —We saved the newspaper *cuttings* about the cricket match.
2. Sharp; hurting.—*Cutting* words are words that hurt one's feelings.
3. A part of a plant cut off for planting.—This bush grew from a *cutting*.

cycle cy'-cle *cycles, cycled, cycling*. 1. A length of time during which regular events occur.— The *cycle* of the seasons is one of nature's miracles.
2. Ride a bicycle.—Alan *cycles* to and from school every day.

3. A short word for bicycle.—Bob got a new *cycle* for his birthday.
4. A group of poems or stories.—Homer's 'Odyssey' is a famous *cycle* of poems.

cyclone cy'-clone *cyclones*. A very strong, fierce wind-storm.—A *cyclone* uprooted the trees.

cygnet cyg'-net *cygnets*. A young swan.—6 *cygnets* were swimming on the lake.

cylinder cyl'-in-der *cylinders*. A long, round body that is hollow or solid.—A roller is a *cylinder*.—A motor-car engine has hollow *cylinders* in it into which solid *cylinders* called pistons fit. The pistons work up and down in the *cylinders* to make the car run.

cymbal cym'-bal *cymbals*. A pair of *cymbals* is a pair of metal musical instruments shaped something like dinner plates. They are played by being struck together.

D d

D, d *D's, d's* The fourth letter of the alphabet.

dab *dabs, dabbed, dabbing*. 1. A small amount of something soft and wet.—Mary dropped a *dab* of cake batter on the floor.
2. Pat; touch lightly.—The kitten *dabbed* at Sally's face with its paw.

dad *dads*. A father is often called *Dad* by his children.

daddy dad'-dy *daddies*. Some fathers are called *Daddy* by their children.—Sally calls her father *Daddy*.

daffodil daf'-fo-dil *daffodils*. A yellow flower that blooms early in spring. The stems and leaves of the *daffodil* are long and slender.

dagger dag'-ger *daggers*. A short, pointed knife used as a weapon for stabbing.—The man was stabbed with a *dagger*.

dahlia dahl'-ia *dahlias*. A brightly coloured flower that blooms in the middle of summer. *Dahlias* grow from tubers that grow like sweet potatoes. The plants grow tall and bushy, and have many flowers.

daily dai'-ly. Every day.—The paper-boy brings the paper *daily*.—Anything that takes place every day is a *daily* happening.

dainty dain'-ty *dainties, daintily, daintiness*.
1. Pleasing, delicate, and pretty.—Mary's new dress is very *dainty*. It is of thin cloth with a tiny pattern of flowers.
2. A fancy food.—At the party we had ice cream, pastries, and many other *dainties*.
3. Having careful, particular little ways and tastes.—Mary has *dainty* manners.

D
E
F
G
H
I
J
K
L
M
N
O
P
Q
R
S
T
U
V
W
X
Y
Z

DAMS

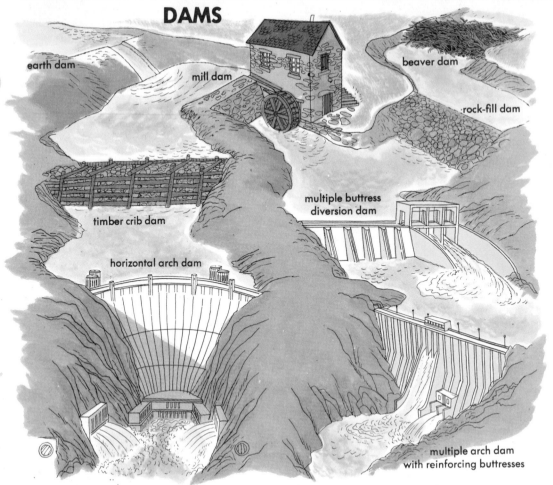

earth dam

mill dam

beaver dam

rock-fill dam

timber crib dam

multiple buttress
diversion dam

horizontal arch dam

multiple arch dam
with reinforcing buttresses

---

dairy dair'-y *dairies*. 1. A place where butter, cheese, and other milk products are made.– Grandfather takes his milk and cream to the *dairy* to sell.

2. A shop where milk, butter, cheese, and other milk products are sold. – Uncle Jim runs a *dairy*.

daisy dai'-sy *daisies*. A flower, often growing wild, with white petals and yellow centres. Garden *daisies* are pink, yellow, or white, and larger than wild ones.

dam *dams, dammed, damming*. 1. A wall built across a river or stream to hold the water back. – Father built a *dam* in the brook to make a swimming pool.

2. Put a *dam* or wall across.–They *dammed* the river to hold back the water.

damage dam'-age *damages, damaged, damaging*. 1. Harm; destruction. – The heavy frost did much *damage* to the farmer's crops.

2. Hurt, injure.–Forest fires *damage* trees.

3. *Damages* means money paid to make up for harm done to someone or someone's property – The man who was to blame for the accident had to pay the *damages* on the car.

damp *dampness*. A little wet.–The cellar is too *damp* for us to play in.–The air that blows in from the sea is *damp*.

dampen damp'-en *dampens, dampened, dampening*. Wet slightly; make damp. – Our clothes were a little *dampened* when we were caught in a sudden shower.

damper damp'-er *dampers*. A metal plate in a smoke pipe or chimney which can be turned to increase or reduce the draught for the fire.– Father turns the *damper* in the stovepipe to make the fire burn faster or slower.

dance *dances, danced, dancing*. 1. Take steps in time to music.–After school we are going to *dance* in a ring on the lawn.

2. A series of steps in time to a piece of music. –Mary did a little *dance* for the class.
3. A party for *dancing*.–Father and Mother went to a *dance*.
4. Jump about in a playful way.–The lambs *danced* in the field.
5. Music to *dance* by. – The band played a *dance*.

dancer danc'-er *dancers*. 1. A person who dances. – The older girls are good *dancers*.
2. A person whose work is dancing in public to entertain people.

dandelion dan'-de-li-on *dandelions*. A weed that bears thick, round, yellow flowers. – Children like to gather *dandelions* in the spring. They make chains of the hollow stems.

dandy dan'-dy *dandies*. 1. A man who dresses in fancy clothes.–Bob is a *dandy*. He pays a great deal of attention to the way he looks.
2. Very smart or fancy (used informally).– John bought himself a *dandy* new waistcoat.

danger dan'-ger *dangers*. 1. A chance or possibility that something bad or harmful will happen.–When floods come in the spring, there is great *danger*. People may be injured or lose their homes.
2. A thing that is a risk, or not safe.–A motor-car with poor brakes, a driver who is careless, a sharp turn in the road, are all *dangers*. They may cause bad accidents.

dangerous dan'-ger-ous *dangerously*. Not safe; likely to cause harm.–It is *dangerous* to play with matches. One may get burned.

dangle dan'-gle *dangles, dangled, dangling*. Hang so as to swing back and forth.–A long chain *dangled* from the back of the lorry.

dare *dares, dared, daring*. 1. A challenge to do something.–Bob would not take John's *dare* to jump off the porch roof.
2. Challenge.–John *dared* Bob to jump off the roof. He challenged him to see if he would really do it.
3. Have courage enough; be brave enough.– Only the animal trainer *dared* to go into the lion's den.

dark darker, darkest. 1. Without light.–Night is *dark*. – When it is completely *dark*, one cannot see.
2. More like black than like white.–Grandmother wore a *dark* dress.
3. Deep in shade; not pale.–The living-room walls are painted *dark* yellow, not a light yellow.

darkness dark'-ness. Lack of light.–The sun went down, and *darkness* came.–People cannot see well in *darkness*.

darling dar'-ling *darlings*. 1. Someone who is dearly loved.–Our baby is a *darling*.
2. Greatly loved. – Jack is Grandmother's *darling* boy.

darn *darns, darned, darning*. 1. Make stitches back and forth to close a hole.–Mary *darned* the toe of her stocking.
2. A mended place.–One *darn* in Bob's sock was very large.

dart *darts, darted, darting*. 1. A small arrow thrown by hand, not shot from a bow.–We had fun throwing *darts* at the *dart*-board.
2. Run suddenly and fast. – When Father opened the door, the dog *darted* into the house.

dash *dashes, dashed, dashing*. 1. Run fast.– The horse *dashed* across the bridge.
2. Splash; throw.–The teacher *dashed* water into the face of the boy who had fainted.
3. A speck; a tiny bit.–Grandmother put a *dash* of sherry into the trifle.
4. Shatter; ruin.–A shower of rain *dashed* our hopes for a picnic.
5. A mark (–) longer than a hyphen, used in writing and printing. A *dash* is sometimes used to set off one part of a sentence from another.

date *dates, dated, dating.* 1. The exact time: day, month, and year.–The *date* for the wedding has been set for September 12 of this year.

2. Write the month, day, and year on.–When we write letters we *date* them at the top of the first page.

3. Time.–Carriages were used at an earlier *date* than motor-cars.

4. A small brown fruit that grows on a *date* palm tree. It has a long seed, or pit, through the middle. *Dates* are very sweet.

daughter daugh'-ter *daughters.* Mary is a girl. She is the *daughter* of her mother and father. Bob is a boy. He is a son of his mother and father.

daughter-in-law *daughters-in-law.* The wife of a person's son.–Grandmother is Father's mother. Mother is Grandmother's *daughter-in-law.*

dawdle daw'-dle *dawdles, dawdled, dawdling.* Loiter, spend a long time doing something. –Jim had written only 3 lines of his composition at the end of half an hour. The teacher told him to hurry up and not to *dawdle.*

dawn *dawns, dawned, dawning.* 1. The time of day when it begins to get light.–Farmers get up at *dawn.*

2. Grow light.–The morning *dawned* cool and clear.

3. *Dawn on one* means come to one's mind.– It didn't *dawn on me* till after I got up that it was Saturday and there would be no school.

day *days.* 1. The time from morning till night. It is dark at night and light during the *day.* The time between the rising and the setting of the sun is *day.*

2. Sometimes night and *day* together are called a *day.*–There are 24 hours in a *day.*

3. One's lifetime, or the time in which one is living.–In our *day,* aeroplanes have become quite common.–In our great-grandmother's *day,* people usually travelled by train.

daybreak day'-break. Dawn; the time when it first gets light.–We arose at *daybreak.*

daydream day'-dream *daydreams, daydreamed, daydreaming.* 1. Dreamily imagine pleasant things.–Mary is apt to *daydream* about being an actress while doing her arithmetic.

2. Something one thinks about when *daydreaming.*

daylight day'-light. 1. Light that comes from the sun; the light of daytime.–We turn on electric lights after the *daylight* goes.

2. Dawn, when the darkness of night goes and the light of day comes.–The farmer gets up at *daylight.*

daytime day'-time. The time when it is light, or day.–We sleep at night and work during the *daytime.*

daze *dazes, dazed, dazing.* 1. Confuse; put in a condition of not knowing what to feel or what to do.–The driver of the car was *dazed* by the sight of the lorry coming towards him. He couldn't think clearly.

2. Stun; make senseless.–The boy was *dazed* for a moment by the blow on his head. He didn't know what had happened.

3. A confused condition; a state of not realizing what is going on around one.–The boy walked around in a *daze* after being hit by the cricket ball.

dazzle daz'-zle *dazzles, dazzled, dazzling.* Make blind or confused by a sudden great brightness. – Coming from a dark room into a brightly lighted room, one is often *dazzled.*

dead. 1. Not living.–The dog that was hit by the car is not *dead*; he is still alive.–The rosebush is *dead* from lack of water.

2. People no longer living.–We put flowers on the graves of our *dead.*

3. Complete.–Father's car ran out of petrol and came to a *dead* stop.

4. Quiet and dull.–The town is very *dead* on Sundays.

deaf *deafness.* Having poor hearing.–The old lady is *deaf.* She cannot hear well.–Some people are so *deaf* they cannot hear at all.

deafen *deafens, deafened, deafening.* Make deaf.–The noise *deafened* Jim for a minute. He could not hear.

deal *deals, dealt, dealing.* 1. Amount.—Mother spends a great *deal* of her time taking care of the baby.
2. Hand out; give to each of several others.—Bob likes to *deal* the cards when we play. —Mother *dealt* out the biscuits to the children.
3. *Deal with* means concern or be about.—This book *deals with* the life of William Shakespeare.
4. *Deal with* means treat. — The boy *deals* roughly *with* those who abuse his dog.
5. Trade.—A grocery shop *deals* in groceries. —A clothing shop *deals* in clothes.—We usually *deal* at the corner grocery shop
6. Strike.—Bill *dealt* Jack a sudden blow.
7. A bargain.—Jack asked Father if he could make a *deal* with him to mow the lawn for 2/- an hour.
8. An opportunity; an arrangement offering a chance.—The teacher said she wanted to give the children a fair *deal* on the test.

dealer *deal'-er dealers.* 1. A trader; one who buys and sells.—Mr. Smith is a motor-car *dealer*; he buys and sells cars.
2. One who deals or gives out the cards to the players in a card game.

dealt. One form of the word *deal.*—We have *dealt* with this milkman for many years. We have bought from him.—Father *dealt* the cards to each player.

dear. 1. Loved.—We have a *dear* baby at our house. She is loved by everyone.
2. A pet name.—Mother often calls us '*Dear.*'
3. Expensive.—John wanted to buy a football, but it was too *dear.* It cost too much.
4. When we write a letter, we put '*Dear*' before the person's name, as a polite way of beginning the letter.—Mary started her letter, '*Dear* Grandfather.'
5. '*Oh, dear!*' is an exclamation some people use when they mean, 'How sad!' or, 'What a pity!'

dearly *dear'-ly.* 1. Greatly. — Bob loves his mother *dearly.* He is very fond of her.
2. At a high cost.—Success comes *dearly.* One has to work very hard for it.

death *deaths.* The end of life.—After the *death* of Joe's dog, his father promised to get him another. — Accidents cause many *deaths.* Many people meet with *death* through accidents.

debate de-bate' *debates, debated, debating.*
1. An argument carried on as a contest before an audience.—Our school *debating* team won the *debate* on the question: 'Should the Government Own the Railways?'
2. Any discussion for and against something.—Father took part in a *debate* over the new town water system at the meeting last night.
3. Argue for or against something.—We *debated* having a picnic on the last day of school.

debt *debts.* 1. Something which is owed.—The men paid all their *debts* before going out of business.
2. State of owing something.—The sick man is very much in *debt.* He owes many people money.

debtor debt'-or *debtors.* A person who is in debt; one who owes someone something.

decay de-cay' *decay, decayed, decaying.* 1. Rot; go bad.—If an apple starts to *decay*, take it from the basket, or the others will *decay* also.
2. A slow rotting.—Tooth *decay* can often be prevented by eating the right foods.

deceit de-ceit'. Untruthfulness; hiding the truth by a trick or lie.—It was *deceit* on Bill's part to sell the broken bicycle by pretending it was new.

deceive de-ceive' *deceives, deceived, deceiving.* Make someone believe something which is not true.—Bill tried to *deceive* his mother. He tried to make her believe that he was at Jack's when he was really at the pictures.

December De-cem'-ber. The 12th month of the year.—Christmas comes in *December.*

decent de'-cent *decently.* 1. Fair; reasonable; good enough.—Uncle Jim gets a *decent* salary now.
2. Proper; respectable; modest.—The language the angry man used wasn't *decent.*—Grandmother thinks some modern clothes are not *decent.*

decide de-cide' *decides, decided, deciding.* 1. Make up one's mind.—Grandfather couldn't *decide* which horse to buy, because he liked them both.—The policeman *decided* to let the man go.
2. Settle; judge.—Father will *decide* the argument as soon as he gets home.

decimal dec′-i-mal *decimals.* You can write the fractions that tell tenths, hundredths, and thousandths, as *decimals.* The fraction 1/10 is written 0.1 when written as a *decimal.* The fraction 2/100 is written 0.02 when written as a *decimal.* The dot is called a *decimal* point.

decision de-ci′-sion *decisions.* 1. What has been decided; final opinion.–The race was so close that we had to wait for the judge's *decision* to find out who had won.–I have come to the *decision* that it is better to wait for Father than to go ahead.
2. A strong, determined way of thinking or acting, without changing one's mind back and forth.–'We shall certainly go, no matter what happens,' said Father, in a tone of *decision.*

deck *decks, decked, decking.* 1. The floor of a boat.–The boat we were on had 3 *decks.* Some of us were on the second *deck,* and some were on the third.

2. A pack (of playing cards).–Mother bought a new *deck* of cards.
3. Dress; array.–The children *decked* themselves out in Mother's clothes and played house.

declaration dec-la-ra′-tion *declarations.* A forceful announcement or statement. – The mayor made the *declaration* that he would definitely open the new playground next week.

declare de-clare′ *declares, declared, declaring.* Say or announce positively. – When Jack came home from playing football, Mother *declared* that she had never seen such a dirty boy. – Jack and Bill have *declared* peace. They have made it known that they will not fight any more.

decline de-cline′ *declines, declined, declining.* 1. Refuse; say that one cannot accept something.–Because Mary would be out of town on Joe's birthday, she *declined* the invitation to his party.
2. Become less. – Attendance at school *declined* during the bad weather.

3. A slow fall or sinking.–A *decline* in the man's health caused him to give up his job.
4. Slant downwards.–The roof of the house *declines* at a steep angle.

decorate dec′-o-rate *decorates, decorated, decorating.* 1. Put things on to make gay and pretty; trim. – The children *decorate* the Christmas tree every year.
2. Paint and otherwise dress up a room or other place.–Mother had the living-room *decorated* in blue and white.
3. Give a medal to.–The soldier was *decorated* for bravery.

decoration dec-o-ra′-tion *decorations.* 1. The act of making pretty, or *decorating.*–The *decoration* of the living-room cost £30.
2. Trimmings and other things used to make something gay and pretty.
3. A medal.–The soldier was very proud of his *decoration.*

decorator dec′-o-ra-tor *decorators.* A person who paints something or plans how to make it gay or pretty.–We had the *decorator* in last week to paint the dining-room.–Mother had an interior *decorator* to plan the colours of the living-room.

decrease de-crease′ *decreases, decreased, decreasing.* 1. Make or become less. – The policeman told the driver to *decrease* his speed. He told him not to drive so fast.
2. (de′-crease.) A reduction or cut; a lessening.–A *decrease* in the man's salary brought suffering to his family.

dedicate ded′-i-cate *dedicates, dedicated, dedicating, dedication.* 1. The writer *dedicated* his new book of stories to all the little children in the land. He wrote it in their honour. He said in the book that it was for them.
2. Give or devote; spend for one thing. – Sometimes a doctor *dedicates* his life to the study of certain diseases. He gives his whole life to this study.

deed *deeds.* 1. Act.–A good Boy Scout does one good *deed* each day.–Joe carried an old lady's bundles for her. Bob helped a lame man across the street. These were good *deeds.*
2. A written, legal statement of property sold. –The man who sold us our house gave us a *deed.* The *deed* said in legal language that he had sold us the house.

deep *deeper, deepest, deeply.* 1. Going far down.–We dug a *deep* hole in the ground. 2. In distance from front to back.–Our house stands on a site 50 feet wide and 200 feet *deep*. 3. Hard to reach, grasp, or understand; beyond the touch of something.–Father's jokes are often too *deep* for me. They are impossible for me to understand.–Mary was lost in *deep* thought. 4. Very dark.–Mary's new hat is a *deep* blue.

deer. A swift, pretty animal that lives in the woods and can run very fast. Full-grown *deer* are about as large as ponies. The male, or stag, has horns. *Deer*, like cattle, chew the cud: that is, they bring back into the mouth a part of their food and chew it again.

defeat de-feat' *defeats, defeated, defeating.* 1. Win a victory over; beat. – Our school played cricket against another school and *defeated* them. We won.–A small army can *defeat* a larger one if it has better weapons. 2. State of being beaten; failure.–After its *defeat*, the army retreated.

defect de'-fect *defects.* A flaw; something wrong with a thing.–We bought the plates for very little because they had *defects* in them. They were not perfect.

defence de-fence' *defences.* 1. A protection.– The army was not large enough for the *defence* of the town. – The farmer's *defence* against the sun was a big straw hat. 2. Something said or done in support of a person or thing that is blamed.–Bob spoke in Jack's *defence* when Jack was accused of breaking the window.

defend de-fend' *defends, defended, defending, defender.* 1. Protect.–The older boy *defends* the younger boy against bullies. 2. Stand up for; fight on behalf of.–Father *defended* the mayor's speech.

definition def-i-ni'-tion *definitions.* An explanation; a statement of what something means. –The teacher wrote a *definition* of the word 'inhabit' on the blackboard. She wrote, 'Inhabit means to live in.' 'To live in' is the *definition* of 'inhabit.'–This dictionary has many *definitions* in it.

defy de-fy' *defies, defied, defying.* 1. Dare.–I *defy* you to tell Mother about the window I broke. I say that you are afraid to tell her. –The boy *defied* us to follow him into the empty house. He did not want us to follow him, but he dared us to. 2. Act opposite to, act against; disobey, ignore, or pay no attention to.–The speeding driver was *defying* the law. 3. Be too much for. – Sometimes Mary's actions *defy* explanation. It is no use trying to explain them. They do not seem to make sense.

degree de-gree' *degrees.* 1. A short extent or distance; a small amount at a time.–Mr. Martin's success came by *degrees.* At first he sold fruit from a barrow. Then he worked as an assistant in a greengrocer's shop. Next he was able to buy a shop of his own.–There is a *degree* of improvement in the sick man's condition today. He is a little better than he was yesterday.

2. Class or rank; standing.–Bob is a student whose work is of a high *degree* of excellence. –Dan's job is one that demands a certain *degree* of skill.

3. A title which shows that one has finished certain work or certain courses satisfactorily. –*Degrees* are awarded at the end of university courses. Dick has gained his Bachelor of Arts *degree.* He studied for 4 years at the university and passed the final examination this summer.

4. A unit of measure.–Circles are measured at their centres by *degrees.* There are 360 *degrees* in any circle, no matter how big it may be.–Heat is measured by *degrees* on a thermometer. Thirty-two *degrees* can be written like this: 32°.

deity de'-i-ty *deities.* 1. A god.–The Greeks and Romans worshipped many *deities.* 2. (Spelt with a capital 'd'.) God; the Supreme Being.

dejected de-jec'-ted *dejectedly.* Unhappy, depressed.–Tom was *dejected* when he failed the spelling test.

D
E
F
G
H
I
J
K
L
M
N
O
P
Q
R
S
T
U
V
W
X
Y
Z

delay de-lay′ *delays, delayed, delaying.* 1. Waiting or putting something off. – When Father was ill, we called in a doctor without *delay.* We called him at once.
2. Hold up; cause to be stopped for a while. –Rain *delayed* the cricket match one hour.
3. Slow up; cause to be late.–The heavy rain washed away the bridge, and we were *delayed* getting home.
4. Stop; waste time.–Mother told Bob not to *delay* on his way to school.

delegate del′-e-gate *delegates, delegated, delegating.* 1. A representative; someone to act for other people.–The member countries sent *delegates* to the United Nations meeting.
2. Give out (responsibility); pass over to another to do.–Mother *delegated* part of the work to Mary.

delicate del′-i-cate *delicately.* 1. Easily damaged; not strong.–The girl is a very *delicate* child.–Orchids are *delicate* flowers.
2. Fine, not coarse.–The threads in the lace shawl were *delicate.*
3. Pleasingly mild or light.–Mother made a *delicately* flavoured pudding. It was pleasing to taste.
4. Soft; light.–Mary's new dress is a *delicate* blue.–The flower had a *delicate* fragrance.

delicious de-li′-cious *deliciously.* 1. Very tasty; very good to eat.–This is a *delicious* apple. It tastes very good.
2. Highly pleasing.–The roses have a *delicious* fragrance.

delight de-light′ *delights, delighted, delighting.* 1. Something that pleases.–The old man's cats were his greatest *delight.*
2. Make happy; please.–Mickey Mouse *delights* the boys and girls.

delightful de-light′-ful *delightfully.* Giving pleasure.–Aunt Emma's visit to our house was *delightful.* It gave happiness and pleasure to everyone.

deliver de-liv′-er *delivers, delivered, delivering.* 1. Bring and give.–The paper-boy *delivers* papers. He takes them to people's houses and leaves them there.
2. Set free.–The boy *delivered* the bird from the cage. He let the bird out.

delivery de-liv′-er-y *deliveries.* 1. Bringing and giving.–The *delivery* of the package caused excitement among the children.

2. A round of delivering.–We have 2 *deliveries* of letters each day. The postman makes two trips a day to leave letters.

delta del′-ta *deltas.* The earth that is left piled up by a river where it flows into the ocean. A *delta* is usually shaped like a triangle.

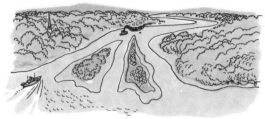

demand de-mand′ *demands, demanded, demanding.* 1. Insist; ask with the power to force obedience.–The policeman *demanded* that we tell him whether the dog had a licence. He had a right to know.
2. A desire to have.–There is a great *demand* for petrol.

democracy de-moc′-ra-cy *democracies.* A nation in which the people freely elect those who govern and make the laws, and in which the law gives everyone the same rights and privileges.–Great Britain is a *democracy.*

democrat dem′-o-crat *democrats, democratic.* A person who believes that the government of a country should be run by and for the people; one who believes in democracy.

demon de′-mon *demons.* An evil spirit.–The story was about fairies and *demons.*

den *dens.* 1. A small room furnished for a man. –Father goes to his *den* when he wants to study, read, or be alone.
2. The place where a wild animal lives.–The lion lives in a *den.*

3. The place where criminals meet and make plans.–The thieves met at their *den* to plan the robbery.

dense *denser, densest, densely, density.* 1. Thickly set; close; heavy. – The forest is *dense.*–During the fire the smoke was so *dense* we could hardly see.
2. Not very smart.–The boy is *dense* about arithmetic.

dent *dents, dented, denting.* 1. A hollow place bent in, as by a blow.–Baby hit the tin dish with a spoon and made a *dent* in it.
2. Make a hollow in.–She did not mean to *dent* the dish.

dentist den'-tist *dentist.* A doctor who repairs and cares for teeth.–You should visit your *dentist* at least twice a year.

deny de-ny' *denies, denied, denying.* Claim (a statement) is untrue.–Bob said that Joe was telling a lie. Joe *denied* it.

depart de-part' *departs, departed, departing.*
1. Go away; leave.–The famous man made a speech of farewell before he *departed*.
2. Change.–We *departed* from our usual programme. We did not do the usual things.

department de-part'-ment *departments.* A part or division that has certain work to do.–The housing *department* is a division of the council for building houses.–We buy shoes in the shoe *department* of a store.

departure de-par'-ture *departures.* A going away. – When school is over, the children make their *departure*. They leave.

depend de-pend' *depends, depended, depending.* 1. Be unable to do without; need; be under the care or control of. – Little babies *depend* on their mothers.
2. Put trust in.–The teacher *depends* on the children to keep the room in order.
3. Be the result of.–Success *depends* on hard work and good sense.

dependent de-pend'-ent *dependents.* 1. Having need for help or support.–Baby is *dependent* on Mother.
2. Resulting from.–Whether John passes or not is *dependent* on whether he makes up the work he missed.
3. A person who depends on another for support.–Bob and Mary are Father's *dependents*. He takes care of them.

deportment de-port'-ment. Behaviour; the way one acts.–Bob's *deportment* is very good.

depose de-pose' *deposes, deposed, deposing.* Remove from a high position.–The king's laws were so unpopular that the people rose in rebellion and *deposed* him.

deposit de-pos'-it *deposits, deposited, depositing.* 1. Put away to keep safe.–We *deposit* money in a bank.
2. Place; lay.–The wind carried the leaves to the fence corner and *deposited* them there.
3. Money placed in a bank account.–Father made a *deposit* in the bank today.
4. A part payment offered to show that one wishes to complete a purchase.–Mother chose a coat and paid a *deposit* on it so that the shop would keep it for her.

depot de'-pot *depots.* A room or building in which things are stored.–Milk is stored in a milk *depot*.–The army's supplies are stored in a supply *depot*.

depress de-press' *depresses, depressed, depressing.* Sadden; put into low spirits.–The sad story *depressed* me. I felt unhappy about things after reading it.

depression de-pres'-sion *depressions.* 1. Extreme sadness or gloom. – The doctor said that Grandmother was suffering from *depression*.
2. A dip or hollow.–Some birds lay their eggs in a small *depression* in the ground.

deprive de-prive' *deprives, deprived, depriving.* Take away, remove.–Mother told Jane she was naughty to *deprive* the baby of his sweets. She should not have taken them.

depth *depths.* How far down something goes, or how far it is from the top to the bottom. –The *depth* of the box is 12 inches. It is 12 inches deep, or 12 inches from the top to the bottom.–The *depth* of the water here is 12 feet.

deputy dep'-u-ty *deputies.* A substitute or assistant picked to do work for someone else.–When the director goes abroad, he appoints a *deputy* in his place.

descend de-scend' *descends, descended, descending.* 1. Go or come down. – Baby can climb the stairs easily, but she cannot *descend*. – Doh, ti, la, soh, fa, mi, re, doh is a *descending* scale in music.
2. Be handed down.–The jewels *descended* from my grandmother to my mother, and finally to me.

D
E
F
G
H
I
J
K
L
M
N
O
P
Q
R
S
T
U
V
W
X
Y
Z

descent de-scent′ *descents*. A coming down.–The mountain was so steep that the men couldn't make the *descent* without holding on to ropes.

describe de-scribe′ *describes, described, describing*. Give a picture of something in words.–I will *describe* something and you guess what it is. I will tell you its size, shape, colour, etc.

description de-scrip′-tion *descriptions*. 1. An account or telling about something. – We wrote a *description* of our trip to the zoo. We told the whole story of it.
2. A telling of how something looks.–'The Union Jack is red, white and blue' is part of a *description* of the flag.

desert de-sert′ *deserts, deserted, deserting*. Go away from and leave uncared for.–The man *deserted* his family. He left them.

desert des′-ert *deserts*. A large, sandy place where there is very little water and very few trees or plants.–Camels are often used to travel in the *desert*.

deserve de-serve′ *deserves, deserved, deserving*. Ought to have; be worthy of.–That kind woman *deserves* a better home.–A person who steals *deserves* to be punished.

design de-sign′ *designs, designed, designing, designer*. 1. Think up a plan of how something is to be made, and put the plan on paper.–An engineer *designs* bridges. Some people *design* dresses, some *design* tools, and some *design* motor-cars.

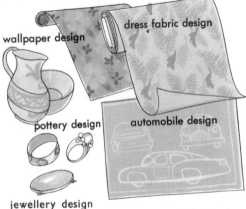

wallpaper design

dress fabric design

pottery design

automobile design

jewellery design

2. A pattern.–The cloth for Mother's dress has a *design* of flowers on it.

desirable de-sir′-a-ble. Worth having, worth wanting.–Good teeth are highly *desirable*.

desire de-sire′ *desires, desired, desiring*. 1. Wish for.–Some people *desire* money; others *desire* happiness.
2. The thing one wishes for. – Happiness is my *desire*.
3. A wish or longing (for something).–Bob has a great *desire* for ice cream.

desk *desks*. A piece of furniture like a table, sometimes with drawers at the sides.–There are 40 *desks* in our classroom. The children sit at their *desks* to write

despair de-spair′ *despairs, despaired, despairing*. 1. Lose hope, or give up.–The woman *despaired* of ever finding her lost money.
2. A feeling that all hope is gone.–Jack was in *despair* when he could not find his dog.

desperate des′-per-ate *desperately, desperation*. 1. Very dangerous.–The boy is *desperately* ill. There is little hope of recovery.
2. Not caring what one does any more, because one is frightened, unhappy, or without hope.–The robber was *desperate* enough to kill anyone who tried to catch him.

despise de-spise′ *despises, despised, despising*. Look down on, dislike, think badly of.–Jack is very honest and *despises* people who cheat.

despite de-spite′. In spite of.–*Despite* his firm promises, Bill was late again today.

dessert des-sert′ *desserts*. The part of a meal eaten after the main part; the last course. *Dessert* is usually something sweet, such as fruit or sweetmeats.

destiny des′-ti-ny *destinies*. Fate; the way something is sure to end, or turn out.–It was the sailor's *destiny* to reach home again after all his hardships.

destroy de-stroy′ *destroys, destroyed, destroying*. Ruin or put an end to suddenly.–Fire *destroyed* the old woodshed.–Saw-flies *destroy* flowers and vegetables. – The sudden rain *destroyed* our hope of playing cricket.

destruction de-struc′-tion. Wrecking; great damage; a violent end. – The forest fire brought *destruction* to many fine old trees.

D E F G H I J K L M N O P Q R S T U V W X Y Z

detail de′-tail *details*. A small part of anything. –Sending invitations, ordering the refreshments, and decorating the table are some of the *details* of giving a party. – Tell me the *details* of your trip to Canada.

detain de-tain′ *detains, detained, detaining*. Keep, or make to wait.–The teacher will not *detain* you after school if you work hard.

detective de-tec′-tive *detectives*. A policeman or a person who tries to find out about crimes and people without their knowing that he is trying to do so. – Many famous *detectives* worked on the murder case.

determine de-ter′-mine *determines, determined, determining, determination*. 1. Firmly decide.–John is *determined* to become a doctor.
2. Decide upon. – Father *determined* the amount of pocket money we should receive. –The weather will *determine* whether we go skating or not.

detour (pronounced *ditour)* de′-tour *detours, detoured, detouring*. 1. A roundabout road or route.–We had to make a *detour* when driving to Grandmother's, because the main road was closed.

develop de-vel′-op *develops, developed, developing*. 1. Grow.–Boys *develop* into men.
2. Build, slowly make or create.–Mary *developed* her love for music by listening to it every day.–Jack *developed* a story around how he got his dog, Spot.
3. In photography, to treat a film or print with chemicals so as to make the picture visible, to *develop* it.

development de-vel′-op-ment *developments*. 1. Growth.–Baby's *development* in the past few months has been fast. She has learned to talk and walk.
2. New happening or result.–The doctor told us to call him if there were any *developments* after taking the medicine.

device de-vice′ *devices*. A piece of machinery or a tool needed for certain work.–An egg-beater is a *device* for beating eggs.

devil dev′-il *devils*. 1. An evil spirit that is supposed to try to get people to do bad things; Satan.
2. A cruel or wicked person is sometimes called a *devil*.

devote de-vote′ *devotes, devoted, devoting*. Give completely.–Mary *devotes* much time to playing the piano.–The doctor *devoted* his whole life to the study of cancer.

devotion de-vo′-tion *devotions*. Great love.–Father's *devotion* to his family is one reason why he stays at home every evening.–The man's *devotion* to his music made him a great musician.

devour de-vour′ *devours, devoured, devouring*. 1. Eat the way an animal eats. – Children *devour* their food when they are very hungry.
2. Consume or destroy. – The fire *devoured* the whole forest.

dew *dewy*. Tiny drops of water which form on cold things. – At night *dew* gathers on the grass, plants, and trees.

diagram di′-a-gram *diagrams*. A drawing or drawn plan of a building, piece of machinery, or anything else made after a pattern. A *diagram* is like a map, not like a picture.–Bob drew a *diagram* of the classroom. He drew squares to show where each seat is, where the teacher's desk is, and where the windows are.

dial di′al *dials*. A round plate that has numbers or letters at equal distances apart round the edge. – We turn the *dial* of a radio to get another station.–Some telephones have *dials*. You call the number you want by turning the *dial*.–The face of a watch is a *dial*.

diameter di-am′-e-ter *diameters*. The distance from one side of a circle to the opposite side, measured through the centre.

D
E
F
G
H
I
J
K
L
M
N
O
P
Q
R
S
T
U
V
W
X
Y
Z

diamond di'-a-mond *diamonds*. 1. A bright, sparkling, clear, precious stone used in rings, pins, and other jewellery.
2. A figure drawn in this shape:
3. *Diamonds* are one of the 4 suits in a pack of playing cards.

diary di'-a-ry *diaries*. A written record of the things one does each day. – Mary keeps a *diary*.

dice *dices, diced, dicing*. 1. Cut into small pieces.–The cook *diced* the chicken to make salad.
2. Cubes, with different numbers of dots on their sides, which are tossed in playing games of chance. Just one of these cubes is called a *die*.

dictate dic'-tate *dictates, dictated, dictating*. 1. Tell what to do, and firmly see that it is done.–Father never *dictates* to Jack how he shall spend his allowance.
2. Tell another what to write, word for word. –The business manager will *dictate* a letter to the clerk.

dictator dic-ta'-tor *dictators*. A ruler who has absolute power in a country.–After the rebellion the *dictator* seized power. He was not elected by the people, and ruled without a proper government. He established a *dictator*ship.

diction dic'-tion. The way a person speaks or writes. His choice of words and phrases with which he expresses himself.

dictionary dic'-tion-a-ry *dictionaries*. A book of words and their meanings. The words in a *dictionary* are put in alphabetical order to help you find them easily.

did. One form of the word *do*.–I shall do my spelling this afternoon. I *did* my arithmetic this morning.

didn't did'-n't. Did not.–Mother called Bob, but he *didn't* hear her.

die *dies, died, dying*. Stop living.–Plants *die* without water.–The hurt dog will not *die* if we care for him properly.

diet di'-et *diets*. The food we eat regularly.–After I was ill, the doctor put me on a special *diet*. I had to eat foods chosen specially for me.

differ dif'-fer *differs, differed, differing*. 1. Be not alike.–The dresses *differ* only in colour. One is red and one is pink.
2. Disagree.–Mary and Jack find something to *differ* about every day.

difference dif'-fer-ence *differences*. A way or amount in which things vary, or are not the same.–The only *difference* between the 2 dresses is that one is red and one is pink.– The *difference* between £5 and £1 is £4.

different dif'-fer-ent *differently*. 1. Not the same.–A pen is *different* from a pencil.
2. Separate.–Mary has been absent 2 *different* times. She was absent yesterday, and she was absent another time last week.

difficult dif'-fi-cult. 1. Hard, not easy.–It is *difficult* to run uphill.
2. Hard to handle or manage.–Baby can be very *difficult* when she is teething.

difficulty dif'-fi-cul-ty *dificulties*. 1. A hard time, trouble; cause of trouble.–The man had much *difficulty* starting his car. – The main *difficulty* in this problem is understanding the big words.
2. A dispute.–The boys settled their *difficulties* by themselves.

dig *digs, digging, dug*. 1. Make a hole, especially in the ground.–Dogs like to *dig* with their front paws to bury bones.–People *dig* with shovels.
2. Make or get by *digging*.–Grandfather *dug* a well to get drinking water.–The fisherman *dug* bait before going fishing.
3. The rider *dug* his spurs into the horse to make it go faster.

digest di-gest' *digests, digested, digesting*. Turn (food) in the stomach into a liquid so that the body can use it.–Foods will *digest* more easily if you chew them well.

digestion di-ges'-tion *digestions*. The turning of food in the stomach into a liquid so that the body can use it.–If we eat when we are too tired or upset, it may hurt our *digestion*.

dignify dig'-ni-fy *dignifies, dignified, dignifying, dignity*. Make stately, grand, or worthy of respect and admiration.–The woman was very *dignified* in her manner. She acted as if she had much self-respect and pride.

dike *dikes*. A high wall to keep back the water from the sea or from a river.–Many *dikes* are needed along the coast of Holland.

diligent dil´-i-gent *diligently*. Active and busy about one's work.–Bob is a *diligent* student. He studies hard.

dim *dims, dimmed, dimming, dimly, dimness*. 1. Not bright and clear; faint, weak, or pale.– The lights in the town were *dim*. – The old man's sight is growing *dim*.
2. Make less bright. – Sometimes when we drive at night, Father *dims* the light on the dashboard.
3. Grow less bright.–As the light *dimmed* the houses on the opposite shore grew hazy and the air became more chilly.

dimension di-men´-sion *dimensions*. Length, width, or depth.–Father took the *dimensions* for a new cupboard door. He measured to see how long, how wide, and how thick it should be.

diminish di-min´-ish *diminishes, diminished, diminishing*. Become smaller or less.–The balloon *diminished* in size as the boy let the air out of it.–During the winter our supply of coal *diminishes* each day.

dimple dim´-ple *dimples*. A little hollow place in the flesh.–Baby has a *dimple* in each cheek.

din. A loud noise or disturbance.–The children make a great *din* when they play 'Musical Chairs.'

dine *dines, dined, dining*. Eat dinner.–We *dine* at 6 o'clock every evening.

dinghy din´-ghy *dinghies*. A small rowing-boat, often carried on board a warship.–The captain ordered the crew to lower the *dinghy* when he spotted the shipwrecked sailor.

dingy din´-gy. 1. Shabby, ill-dressed.–The poor girl wore a *dingy* brown dress.
2. Dark and dismal.–The old man lived in a *dingy* basement.

dining-room di´-ning-room *dining-rooms*. A room in which meals are eaten, especially dinner.–All the guests went into the *dining-room* and mother served soup.

dinner din´-ner *dinners*. 1. The biggest or main meal.–Father cannot come home at noon, so we have *dinner* at night.
2. A banquet.–We went to a *dinner* in honour of the explorer.

dip *dips, dipped, dipping*. 1. Put into a liquid and lift out.–Grandmother used a cup to *dip* the soup from the saucepan.–The artist *dips* his brush into the paint.–The rower *dips* the oars of the boat into the water.
2. A bathe.–We went for a *dip* in the lake.
3. Lower for a moment. – The sailor *dipped* the flag.
4. A low place or hollow.–We slowed down when we came to the *dip* in the pavement.

diphtheria diph-the´-ri-a. A dangerous disease of the throat. *Diphtheria* is catching; one person can get it from another.

diploma di-plo´-ma *diplomas*. A document awarded by a college or university to a person who has successfully completed his studies. – When Bob got his degree the university awarded him a *diploma*.

diplomat dip´-lo-mat *diplomats*. A person who negotiates with foreign governments.–The *diplomats* discussed a peace treaty.

dipper dip´-per *dippers*. 1. A ladle or deep, cup-shaped spoon.–We dip gravy from a bowl with a *dipper*.
2. A kind of bird which lives in or near water. The *dipper* gets its name from the way it bobs and dips its head, and sometimes builds its nest underneath a waterfall.

direct di-rect´ *directs, directed, directing*. 1. Guide; point out (the way).–The policemen will *direct* people about the city during the festival.
2. Address; put the address on.–The letter was not *directed* right, and was returned.
3. Give; turn.–The teacher asked the children to *direct* their attention to the map.
4. Order; instruct.–The officer *directed* his men to surround the burning building.
5. Straight; not roundabout. – Grandfather told Bob to take the *direct* road to the store. –When the teacher questioned me, I gave her a *direct* answer.

direction di-rec′tion *directions*. 1. Way; a point towards which one can face. North, south, east, and west are the main *directions*. – The stranger was going in the *direction* of the station.–A compass tells us the *directions*.

2. Management or leadership.–The store is under the *direction* of a very able man.
3. Order or instruction.–The officer gives his men *directions,* and they obey them.

director di-rec′-tor *directors*. A person who manages a business, leads an orchestra or band, or tells other people what to do.

directory di-rec′-to-ry *directories*. A book that has the names and addresses of people who live in a city or town.–A telephone *directory* has the names, addresses, and telephone numbers of people who have telephones.

dirt. 1. Earth; soil.–We put some *dirt* into the flower pot.
2. Anything that is not clean.–Mary swept the *dirt* from the porch.

dirt-track dirt′-track *dirt-tracks*. A course, usually made of cinders, used for motor-cycle racing. The sport is called *dirt-track* racing or speedway racing.

dirty dirt′-y *dirtier, dirtiest*. Not clean, soiled. –The child's hands were *dirty* after he made mud pies.

disable dis-a′-ble *disables, disabled, disabling*. Make unfit, injure or cripple.–The man was *disabled* during the war. He lost his right arm.–We collect money for disabled people.

disagree dis-a-gree′ *disagrees, disagreed, disagreeing, disagreement*. 1. Think differently. –Jack *disagrees* with his father about how much money a boy 10 years old needs.
2. Be different from, be not the same or alike. –What you say now *disagrees* with what you said yesterday.
3. Quarrel. – The boys *disagreed* over the game.
4. Make sick. – Cold milk *disagrees* with Baby. It upsets her stomach.

disagreeable dis-a-gree′-a-ble. 1. Cross, easily made angry; not friendly.–Sick children are often *disagreeable*.
2. Not pleasant.–The taste and odour of some foods are *disagreeable* to some people.

disappear dis-ap-pear′ *disappears, disappeared, disappearing, disappearance*. 1. Go out of sight.–We watched the aeroplane until it *disappeared*.
2. Vanish; go away.–Snow *disappears* in the springtime. It goes away.

disappoint dis-ap-point′ *disappoints, disappointed, disappointing*. 1. Make unhappy by failing to satisfy a wish or something expected. – If Grandmother doesn't come, it will *disappoint* the children. – Mother was *disappointed* with her new dress. It was not what she expected or hoped for.
2. Fail; let down.–John promised to stop for Bob. Bob told John not to *disappoint* him by failing to keep his promise.

disappointment dis-ap-point′-ment *disappointments*. 1. Something that causes an unhappy feeling because it does not turn out as it was expected to.–It was a *disappointment* to us that Grandmother couldn't come.
2. The feeling one has when a thing that was expected to happen does not happen.–Mary's *disappointment* over not receiving the letter did not last long.

disaster dis-as′-ter *disasters*. Anything that happens suddenly to bring great pain, sorrow, or suffering to people. Fires, storms, accidents, etc., are *disasters*.

discharge dis-charge′ *discharges, discharged, discharging*. 1. Dismiss from work; let go.– When the work was done, the men were *discharged*.
2. Give off.–The boil on the man's arm *discharged* pus.
3. Shoot off or fire.–The man *discharged* the cannon as a salute.
4. Unload.–The ship *discharged* its cargo.
5. Pay.–Father always *discharges* his debts.
6. Perform or do.–Bob *discharged* his duties with care.

discipline dis′-ci-pline *disciplines, disciplined, disciplining*. 1. Force to obey; punish.–The teacher *disciplined* the boys for throwing chalk at each other.
2. Control of behaviour. – *Discipline* in the army is strict. A soldier must do as he is told.

discontent dis-con-tent′ *discontented*. A feeling of not being satisfied.–Bob feels no *discontent* with his new job. He is satisfied.

discontinue dis-con-tin′-ue *discontinues, discontinued, discontinuing*. Stop.–Mother told the paper-boy to *discontinue* bringing the newspaper while we were away.

discourage dis-cour′-age *discourages, discouraged, discouraging.* 1. Cause to lose hope.–The old woman was *discouraged* over her poor health.
2. Cause to give up a desire.–We tried to *discourage* John from going swimming when it was so cold.

discover dis-cov′-er *discovers, discovered, discovering.* Find; learn of.–Columbus *discovered* America. He found it for the first time. – Mother *discovered* that her new stove cooked things fast.

discovery dis-cov′-er-y *discoveries.* 1. A finding.–The *discovery* of America was made by Columbus.
2. Something found or learned.–The scientist's *discovery* was a cure for a certain fever.

discuss dis-cuss′ *discusses, discussed, discussing.* Talk about; speak for and against.–Father will *discuss* the plans for the party tonight.

discussion dis-cus′-sion *discussions.* A serious talk.–John and Bob had a *discussion* about cricket.–At the meeting there was *discussion* about the men who were standing for election.

disease dis-ease′ *diseases.* A sickness or illness. –Mumps, chicken-pox, and measles are some common *diseases.*

disgrace dis-grace′ *disgraces, disgraced, disgracing, disgraceful.* 1. A shameful thing.–The boy's behaviour in stealing the money was a *disgrace.* He lost the respect of his friends.
2. Bring shame to.–The man *disgraced* his family by stealing.

disguise dis-guise′ *disguises, disguised, disguising.* 1. Make up to look like some other person or thing; change something to keep it from being recognized.–Mary went to the Hallowe'en party *disguised* as a ghost.–When Bob rang up Mother on the telephone, he *disguised* his voice. He talked like a woman, and tried to make Mother think he was a woman.
2. Things used to change appearance.–The boy's *disguise* was so good that his mother did not recognize him.

disgust dis-gust′ *disgusts, disgusted, disgusting.* 1. A feeling of deep dislike.–The man's *disgust* for certain foods was caused by his illness.
2. Give a feeling of strong dislike.–Bill's behaviour at the party *disgusted* Bob.

dish *dishes, dished, dishing.* 1. A container in which food is served; a saucer, plate, etc.– The children broke so many *dishes* in washing them that Mother decided to wash them herself.

2. A combination of foods.–A woman on the wireless told how to prepare a new *dish.*
3. A *dish* filled with something.–Mother set the *dish* of tomatoes on the table.
4. Serve; put in *dishes.*–Mary helped Mother *dish* the food.

dishonest dis-hon′-est *dishonesty, dishonestly.* Not honest, not fair. – The *dishonest* boy cheated in his spelling test. It was a *dishonest* thing to do.

dishonour dis-hon′our *dishonours, dishonoured, dishonouring, dishonourable.* 1. Shame.–The man brought *dishonour* to his position when he broke the law.
2. Disgrace; ruin the honour of.–Bob would not *dishonour* his school by cheating in the contest.

dislike dis-like′ *dislikes, disliked, disliking.* 1. Have an unpleasant feeling towards.–I *dislike* people who are not honest.
2. A feeling of not liking.–Mother has a *dislike* of rats.

dismal dis′-mal *dismally.* Gloomy; unpleasant. –We had *dismal* weather all week.

dismiss dis-miss′ *dismisses, dismissed, dismissing.* 1. Let go; send away.–It is almost time to *dismiss* the music class.
2. Put out of one's mind; forget about.–When Father and Bob finished their argument, Father said they would *dismiss* the subject.
3. Discharge; fire, let go.–The motor-car factory *dismissed* 50 men.

disobey dis-o-bey′ *disobeys, disobeyed, disobeying, disobedient.* Refuse to follow orders as to what to do or not to do.–Do not *disobey* the traffic policeman, or you may have an accident.

disorder dis-or′-der. Confusion, lack of order. –The classroom was in *disorder* after the play period.

display dis-play' *displays, displayed, display-ing.* 1. A showing to the public.–We saw a *display* of toys in the shop window.

dispose dis-pose' *disposes, disposed, dispos-ing.* 1. *Dispose of* means do away with.–Father *disposed of* the ashes by filling up the hole in the drive with them.
2. *Be disposed* means feel willing.–The teacher *was disposed* to read us a story.

disposition dis-po-si'-tion *dispositions.* The way one feels and acts towards others. – Mother has a pleasant *disposition.* She is pleasant and friendly towards people.

dispute dis-pute' *disputes, disputed, disputing.* 1. Argument; disagreement.–The girls had a *dispute* over the way to do the arithmetic.
2. Argue against. – Bob would not *dispute* Father's word.

disrupt dis-rupt' *disrupts, disrupted, disrupt-ing.* Break up.–We hope the rain will not *disrupt* our plans to go fishing.

dissolve dis-solve' *dissolves, dissolved, dissolv-ing.* Break up and disappear when put into a liquid.–Salt will *dissolve* in water.

distance dis'-tance *distances.* 1. Space meas-ured in a line.–The *distance* between our house and the school is half a mile.
2. A faraway place or position.–We saw the aeroplane in the *distance.*

distant dis'-tant *distantly.* 1. Far off.–Canada is a *distant* country.
2. Shy; not very friendly.–The new boy is *distant* because he does not know us.

distinct dis-tinct' *distinctly.* 1. Not alike or the same.–The colour green is *distinct* from both yellow and blue.
2. Plain; clear.–Mary's speech is *distinct.*

distinction dis-tinc'-tion *distinctions.* 1. Dif-ference.–Mary could not understand the *dis-tinction* between plus and minus.
2. Worth; excellence.–Our vicar is a man of *distinction.*

distinguish dis-tin'-guish *distinguishes, distin-guished, distinguishing.* 1. Notice the differ-ence.–Some people cannot *distinguish* one colour from another.
2. Recognize; see. – Grandmother's writing was so faint that we could hardly *distinguish* the words.
3. *Distinguished* means famous, well-known. –The man is a very *distinguished* writer.

distort dis-tort' *distorts, distorted, distorting, distortion.* Change the shape.–The ripples in the lake *distorted* the reflection of our faces.–The judge accused the witness of *distorting* the facts about the accident.

distract dis-tract' *distracts, distracted, distract-ing, distraction.* Draw attention away.–The radio *distracted* Mary from her homework.

distraught dis-traught'. Confused and anxious. –The woman was quite *distraught* when she discovered her dog was missing. She was unable to talk clearly and had to be taken home.

distress dis-tress' *distresses, distressed, dis-tressing.* 1. Pain and suffering.–The man's injury caused him much *distress.*
2. Trouble.–The whole family was *distressed* over the accident.
3. Unhappiness and trouble.–The burning of the barn brought *distress* to the farmer.
4. Danger; need of help.–The pilot gave a signal saying that his aeroplane was in *dis-tress.*

distribute dis-trib'-ute *distributes, distributed, distributing, distribution.* 1. Hand out; de-liver.–The teacher *distributed* the books.
2. Spread about.–Bob didn't *distribute* the butter evenly over his bread.

district dis'trict *districts.* Section; a division or part of a country.–We live in a farming *district.*

disturb dis-turb' *disturbs, disturbed, disturb-ing, disturbance.* 1. Upset; bother; cause to worry.–Mother is resting. Do not *disturb* her.–The news of the accident *disturbed* Father.
2. Cause to get out of order.–The wind *dis-turbed* the papers on the teacher's desk.

ditch *ditches.* A long, narrow hole in the ground. – The work-men dug a *ditch* at the side of the road to carry the water away.

dive *dives, dived* or *dove, diving.* 1. Plunge or throw oneself head first.–The children *dive* into the water from the diving-board.
2. Come down nose first.–We saw the aero-plane *dive.*
3. A plunge into water.–Joe made a beauti-ful *dive* from the high board.

divide di-vide′ *divides, divided, dividing.* 1. Separate into parts, portions, or shares.–Father *divided* the ice cream and gave each of us some.
2. Separate or form a boundary between.–The fence *divides* the gardens.
3. Do an arithmetic problem in division.–If you *divide* 10 by 2 the answer is 5.
4. Separate into parts. – *Divide* your test paper by folding it down the middle.

dividend div′-i-dend *dividends.* 1. When you divide one number by another, the number being divided is the *dividend.*–When you divide 10 by 2, 10 is the *dividend.*
2. A share of profits in a business paid to a person who owns stock.

divine di-vine′. Of God; holy.–To Christians, Jesus Christ is *divine.*

divisible di-vis′-i-ble. Able to be divided evenly. –30 is *divisible* by 5. 30 ÷ 5 = 6.

division di-vi′-sion *divisions.* 1. Dividing one number by another, or seeing how many times one number goes into another.
2. A portion or part.–The *division* of the money given to the children was fair to all.
3. A part or section of the army or navy under a single command.

divisor di-vi′-sor *divisors.* In a problem in division, the number that you divide by is the *divisor.*–If you divide 10 by 2, 2 is the *divisor.*

divorce di-vorce′ *divorces, divorced, divorcing.* 1. An ending of a marriage by law.–The judge granted the married couple a *divorce.* He made them free of each other. They are no longer legally married.
2. Bring a marriage to an end by getting a *divorce.*–The woman *divorced* her husband.

dizzy diz′-zy *dizzier, dizziest.* Having the feeling that one is whirling round.–Turning round fast may make you *dizzy.*

do *does, did, doing.* 1. Act; carry out a plan.–Try to *do* your best every day.–The children *do* their arithmetic in the morning and their spelling in the afternoon.–Baby tries to *do* everything that we *do.*
2. Be satisfactory.–The teacher said my pencil would *do* if I didn't have a pen.
3. *Do* is sometimes used to begin questions. –*Do* you have my book?
4. *Do* may take the place of other words so that we need not say them twice.–'He writes as well as I *do*' means 'He writes as well as I write.'

dock *docks.* A wharf; a platform that is built along the shore, or which runs out into the water so that boats can come along the sides of it to load and unload.

doctor doc′-tor *doctors, doctored, doctoring.* 1. A person who knows about illnesses and how to treat them. Physicians and surgeons are *doctors.* A *doctor* must be specially qualified to treat sick people.

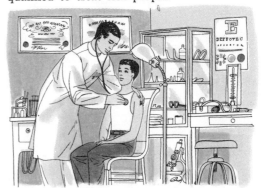

2. Treat.–The school nurse *doctors* the children for small injuries and illnesses.
3. The highest title or degree, awarded to students who finish certain required work in a college or university, or to those the university wishes to honour. – Jack's uncle has completed his studies for the degree of *doctor* of philosophy.

dodge *dodges, dodged, dodging.* Turn or move aside quickly to avoid something.–When the ball came through the window, the teacher had to *dodge* to keep from being hit.

doe *does.* The female or she animal of some animals, such as the deer. – The female deer, or *doe* does not have antlers or horns.

does. One form of the word *do.* – I do my work; he *does* his.

doesn't does′-n't. Does not.–John *doesn't* like to be ill.

dog *dogs*. A 4-legged animal kept as a pet or for work. Some *dogs* are as small as cats; others are very much larger. Some *dogs* are used to tend sheep; others are used to hunt animals; and some are kept as pets.

dachshund · English bulldog · collie · cocker spaniel · Great Dane · French poodle · Pomeranian

doings do'-ings. Things done, deeds, behaviour. –We heard all about his *doings*.

doll *dolls*. A toy that looks like a person– Children play with *dolls* and pretend they are people.

dollar dol'-lar *dollars*. A unit of money used in the United States and Canada, equal to 100 cents. It can be written $1. Some *dollars* are made of silver and some of paper.

dome *domes*. A circular roof that is shaped like the one in the picture. Some churches and important buildings have *domes*.

domestic do-mes'-tic. 1. Having to do with the home or family.–Cooking, sewing, and cleaning are *domestic* tasks.
2. Belonging to the home; tame.–Animals, such as cats and dogs, that live about the home are *domestic* animals.–Farm animals are *domestic* animals.
3. Of one's own country. – Things that are made in one's country are *domestic* products.

domino dom'-i-no *dominoes*. One of the small brick-shaped pieces used in playing the game of *dominoes*.

done. 1. Finished, completed, ended. – My arithmetic is all *done*.
2. Completely cooked.–We can't have dinner yet because the potatoes aren't *done*.
3. One form of the word *do*.–I would have *done* my work earlier if I had known you were coming.

donkey don'-key *donkeys*. 1. An animal that is something like a horse. *Donkeys* are strong work animals. They are often stubborn.

2. A very stupid person is sometimes called a *donkey*.

don't. Do not.–You do your work quietly. I *don't*. I like to talk while I work.

doom *dooms, doomed, dooming*. 1. Fate, usually a bad fate.–The ship met her *doom* on the rocky island coast. She broke in two.
2. Mark for a certain fate.–Those trees are *doomed* to destruction by the forest fire.

door *doors*. 1. Doorway; the opening you go through into a house, or from room to room. – Mary ran to Father as soon as he came through the *door*.
2. The wooden or metal covering in a doorway which is opened or closed.–We heard a knock on the *door*.

doorway door'-way *doorways*. The opening leading into a room or house.–We go into the house through a *doorway*.

dose *doses.* A certain amount of medicine taken at one time.–The doctor told Mother to cut down on the *dose* when she felt better.

dot *dots, dotted, dotting.* 1. A very small round mark.–The *dots* on Mary's green dress are white.

2. Put a *dot* or *dots* on.–Be sure to *dot* your i's and cross your t's.

double dou'-ble *doubles, doubled, doubling.* 1. Having two instead of one. – The word 'doll' has a *double* l in it. It has two l's that come together and sound like one.
2. Make twice as big or much.–John got 40 in spelling yesterday. Today he *doubled* that mark. He got 80 today.
3. Twice as much or many. – The farmer's hens laid 10 eggs yesterday and *double* that many today. They laid 20 today.
4. Fold in two.–Mary *doubled* the napkins neatly as Mother ironed them.

doubt *doubts, doubted, doubting.* 1. Be unsure about; not be able to believe. – I *doubt* if Father will be home so early.
2. A question in the mind as to whether something is true or not.–I have my *doubts* whether Bill has a new pony.

doubtful doubt'-ful *doubtfully, doubtfulness.* Not sure, not certain. – We are *doubtful* whether Tom will pass or not.

doubtless doubt'-less. Surely, no doubt.–You will *doubtless* be able to tell me how to get to the station.

dough. A soft mass of flour, salt, fat, water, and other things, which is to be baked into bread, pastry, etc.–Mary rolled the *dough* for the pie-crust.

doughnut dough'-nut *doughnuts.* A cake made of sweet bread dough and cooked in deep fat. Some *doughnuts* have a hole in the middle and are round.

dove *doves.* A kind of pigeon. Some *doves* are tame and live in barns or near houses.

down. 1. From a higher place to a lower place.–When we go from the top step to the bottom step of the stairs, we go *down*.

2. From a time long past to a time not so long past, or the present. – These jewels were handed *down* from my great-great-grandmother to us.
3. The soft feathers on ducks, chickens, and geese.–Mary has a *down* pillow.

downfall down'fall. A cause of shame or disgrace. – Cheating in the examination was Paul's *downfall*.

downhill down'hill'. Down the slope of a hill.– The boys cycled *downhill*.

downpour down'-pour. A heavy fall of water, especially rain.–We forgot to take our raincoats and were caught in a heavy *downpour* on the way home.

downright down'-right. 1. Straightforward. – Dick is *downright*. He says what he means.
2. Absolute.–John told Bob he was talking *downright* nonsense.

downstairs down'-stairs'. 1. To the lower floor of the house.–We come *downstairs* when we smell breakfast cooking.
2. On the lower floor of the house.–The kitchen, living-room, and dining-room are *downstairs*.

downward down'-ward. From a higher place to a lower place.–The soap bubbles floated *downward* from the window.

downy down'-y *downier, downiest.* Fuzzy; covered with tiny fine hairs. – Little ducks are *downy*. They have soft feathers.–Peaches are *downy*.–Baby's hair is *downy*.

doze *dozes, dozed, dozing.* 1. Sleep lightly.– The old woman sits in her chair and *dozes*.
2. A little nap.–I took a *doze* after school.

dozen doz'-en *dozens.* Twelve. – I bought a *dozen* eggs.

drab *drabness.* 1. Dull in colour.–Grandfather's old overcoat is *drab*.
2. Dull, not exciting.–Cinderella lived a *drab* life until she went to the ball.

draft *drafts, drafted, drafting.* 1. A sketch or early plan.–The builder made a *draft* of the plans for the new house.–The writer made a *draft* of his new story.
2. Draw carefully.–The builder *drafted* the house plans.
3. Call (a person) into service whether he wants to go or not.–Many men were *drafted* into the Army and Navy in World War II.

drag *drags, dragged, dragging.* 1. Pull along behind one.–The boy *dragged* his sweater on the ground.–The older boy *dragged* the little fellow along by the hand.
2. Go so slowly as to seem endless.–The rainy afternoon *dragged.*

dragon drag′-on *dragons.* A terrible beast, told about in stories and poems of long ago, that was said to have wings and scales on its long, snake-like body.

dragon-fly d r a g′-o n-f l y *dragon-flies.* An insect with a long, slim body and 4 wings that you can see through.

drain *drains, drained, draining.* 1. Pour the water off.–Mother *drains* the potatoes after they have boiled long enough.
2. A pipe, ditch, or gutter for carrying away water.–The ditch is a *drain* for the field.–The gutters carry rainwater from the roof through a down-pipe to a drain.

3. Use up.–The man's strength was *drained* from working both day and night.
4. Something that uses up, or draws upon, continuously. – There was so much sickness in the man's family that it was a *drain* on his money.
5. Let water drip off.–Mary took the dishes from the hot water and put them into a wire basket to *drain.*

drake *drakes.* A male duck.

drama dra′-ma *dramas, dramatic, dramatically.* 1. A play acted on the stage.–We are going to the theatre to see a *drama.*
2. Any very exciting event which is like a play on a stage.–To Mary, all life is one big *drama.*

dramatize dram′-a-tize *dramatizes, dramatized, dramatizing.* Make a play of. – The children will *dramatize* the story of Little Red Riding Hood, and Mary will act the part of Red Riding Hood.

drank. One form of the word *drink.* – Baby *drank* up all her milk.

drape *drapes, draped, draping.* Wrap or fasten so as to hang in soft folds.–The dressmaker .*draped* the cloth round Mother to plan the dress.–We *drape* windows with curtains.

draught (pronounced *draft*) *draughts.* 1. A strong current of air.–Do not sit in a *draught* or you may catch a cold.
2. A dose of medicine.–The chemist made mother a *draught* to take twice a day.
3. The game of *draughts* is played with 24 round, black and white pieces on the same board as chess. The object of the game is to capture your opponent's pieces.

draw *draws, drew, drawn, drawing.* 1. Make a likeness of something by making lines with a pen, pencil, or other writing tool.–Children *draw* pictures with coloured crayons.
2. Pull, attract, bring out.–The children *draw* their carts after them.–We expect our football match to *draw* many people to the field.–The man *drew* a knife from his pocket.
3. Come.–The motor-car *drew* up by our side. –Dinner time is *drawing* near.
4. A tie.–Neither team won the game. It was a *draw.*
5. Take in.–Mary *drew* a long breath of relief when her work was done.

drawer draw′-er *drawers.* 1. A box-like part that slides in and out of cupboards, cabinets, desks, tables, etc. We keep papers, silver, linen, and other things in the *drawers* of bureaux and chests.
2. *Drawers* are a piece of underwear to cover the legs and hips.–Grandma wore *drawers.*

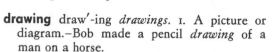

drawing draw′-ing *drawings.* 1. A picture or diagram.–Bob made a pencil *drawing* of a man on a horse.
2. The art of making pictures or diagrams with lines.–In the *drawing* class Mary made a picture of a daffodil in a vase.

drawn. One form of the word *draw.*–Mary had *drawn* a daffodil in a vase.

dread *dreads, dreaded, dreading.* 1. Be very much afraid of, look forward to with fear.– I *dread* crossing the lake in that leaky canoe.
2. Fear of something which may happen in the future.–Mary went towards the big dog with *dread* in her heart.

dreadful dread′-ful *dreadfully.* Terrible. – A *dreadful* accident happened on the corner.

dream *dreams, dreamed, dreaming, dreamer.*
1. The thoughts, feelings, and pictures that pass through your mind while you are asleep, or a happening you imagine while awake.–Mary has *dreams* of being an actress.
2. Have a *dream.* – Last night I *dreamed* I kept a pet bear in the dining-room.

dreary drear′-y *drearier, dreariest.* Dark, gloomy.–It was a *dreary* winter's day.

dredge *dredges, dredged, dredging.* 1. A machine used for digging, deepening, and cleaning out ditches or channels.

2. Clean out or deepen a river, channel, etc.–The men *dredged* the river with a *dredger.*

drench *drenches, drenched, drenching.* Soak through, make as wet as can be.–We were caught in the rain and our clothes were *drenched.*

dress *dresses, dressed, dressing.* 1. A woman's or girl's outer garment or clothes.–In winter Mary wears a heavy *dress.*

2. Clothe, put clothes on.–Baby cannot *dress* herself yet.
3. Put bandages and ointments on.–Doctors *dress* boils, burns, sores, and other wounds.
4. Make ready to cook.–The butcher *dresses* ducks, geese, chickens, and other fowl.
5. Trim, decorate. – Window-dressers *dress* windows.
6. To come into correct place in line. Soldier's '*dress* by the right' when they line up on the right-hand man.

dresser dress′-er *dressers.*
1. A kitchen sideboard with shelves for dishes.
2. A person who trims or decorates certain things.–Mary has gone to the hair*dresser* so that her hair is pretty for the dance.–Mr Smith is a window-*dresser.* He arranges the displays in shop windows.

dressmaker dress′-mak-er *dressmakers.* A person who earns money by designing and sewing clothes for women and children.–Mother ordered an evening dress from her *dressmaker.*

drew. One form of the word *draw.*–Sally *drew* a picture of Father carrying a green umbrella.

dried. One form of the word *dry.*–Mary *dried* the dishes for Mother.

drier dri′-er *driers.* 1. A device to take the water out of wet clothes.–Some washing machines have *driers* on them.
2. Anything that helps to make a thing dry. –Turpentine mixed with paint serves as a *drier.* It thins the paint and makes it dry faster.

drift *drifts, drifted, drifting.* 1. Float without being steered or guided.–A boat was *drifting* about on the river.
2. Blow and pile up together. – The leaves *drifted* into a corner of the yard.
3. A pile made of something, such as snow, blowing together. – Sally jumped into the snow*drift* and got all covered up.

drill *drills, drilled, drilling.* 1. A machine or tool for making holes.–Bob bored a hole through the board with a *drill.*
2. Bore a hole with a *drill.*–The workmen *drilled* the metal to put a bolt through.
3. Do a thing over and over again; practise.–Mary *drilled* at her piano exercise till she could play it perfectly.
4. Practice.–We have arithmetic *drill* every morning in class.
5. Go through exercises, or marching, in a body or group. – We watched the soldiers *drill* in the field.
6. Training in bodily exercises, in a group.– We watched the soldiers out on *drill.*

drink *drinks, drank, drunk, drinking.* 1. Put (liquid) into the mouth and swallow it.– Baby *drinks* milk.
2. A liquid food.–Ginger ale, cocoa, tea, water, and coffee are *drinks. Drinks* can be swallowed without chewing.
3. *Drink* alcoholic liquor.–The unhappy man *drinks* too much.
4. Alcoholic liquor.–The man went into the public house to buy himself a *drink.*

D
E
F
G
H
I
J
K
L
M
N
O
P
Q
R
S
T
U
V
W
X
Y
Z

D

E F G H I J K L M N O P Q R S T U V W X Y Z

drip *drips, dripped, dripping.* 1. Fall drop by drop. – The rain *dripped* from the roses in the garden.
2. So wet that water drops off. – The dog came running out of the river *dripping* wet.
3. A leak. – Father stopped the *drip* in the bath tap by putting in a new washer.

drive *drives, drove, driven, driving.* 1. A ride. –We went for a *drive* into the country in our motor-car.
2. A roadway.–Father parked the car in the *drive* at the side of the house.–David lives at 1 Lakeside *Drive*.
3. Direct, guide, or force to go.–Bob *drives* the cows to pasture for Grandfather when we are at the farm.–Jack has to *drive* himself to get up on time in the morning.
4. A campaign to raise money for a particular purpose. – We contributed £2 to the Red Cross *drive*.
5. Steer car and make it go. – Father is teaching Mother to *drive*.

driven driv'-en. One form of the word *drive*.– We had *driven* only a few miles when we ran out of petrol.

driver driv'-er *drivers.* A person who drives horses, lorries, cars, etc. – The taxi *driver* called to take Mother to the station.

drizzle driz'-zle *drizzles, drizzled, drizzling.* 1. Rain in fine drops.–It was *drizzling* when we went to school.
2. A mist-like rain.–The *drizzle* turned into a heavy downpour.

droll *drolly.* Funny, *amusing.* – Jack makes us laugh at school by pulling faces. He is a very *droll* fellow.

dromedary dro'-me-dar-y *dromedaries.* A camel with one hump. The *dromedary* carries passengers and goods in North Africa and South-West Asia.

drone *drones, droned, droning.* 1. A continuous low humming sound.–We heard the *drone* of the class across the hall reciting the lesson.
2. Make a *droning* or humming sound. – A bee *droned* around Grandmother's hollyhocks.
3. A male bee. *Drones* do no work. They gather no honey. They do not sting.

droop *droops, drooped, drooping.* Bend over, as if tired; wilt and bend over. – Flowers *droop* when they need water.

drop *drops, dropped, dropping.* 1. A small amount of a liquid that forms a tiny round globe or ball when it falls. – A *drop* of rain fell on my nose. – The doctor told me to take ten *drops* of medicine in a glass of water.
2. To fall or let fall.–The pilot *dropped* 500 feet before his parachute opened. – Do not *drop* the dish.
3. Stop, end, forget all about.–The teacher told the boys to *drop* their argument.
4. Lower or be let down. – The curtain *dropped* at the end of the play.
5. Leave out. – *Drop* the 'e' in the word 'make' and add 'ing' to spell 'making.'
6. A fall.–Bob hurt his ankle in his *drop* from the high wall.
7. A distance fallen; distance straight down. –The *drop* from the wall was a full 12 feet.

drove *droves.* 1. One form of the word *drive*.– We *drove* to John's house in our car.
2. A crowd of people, a swarm of insects, or a number of animals, moving along together. –People went to the football match in *droves*. –A *drove* of animals rushed out of the burning barn.

drown *drowns, drowned, drowning.* 1. Die from having the head kept under water so that the breathing is stopped; cause to die in this way.–Jack saved the black kitten from *drowning*.–Bob *drowned* the rat he caught in his trap.
2. Make enough sound to keep another sound from being heard.–The radio was turned on so loud that it completely *drowned* the ring of the doorbell.

drowsy drow'-sy *drowsier, drowsiest.* 1. Sleepy. –After supper the baby became *drowsy* and had to be put to bed.
2. Making one want to sleep. – On warm, *drowsy* days, the teacher lets us read stories in the afternoon.

drug *drugs, drugged, drugging.* 1. A medicine, or one of the things mixed together to make medicines. – Mother puts labels on all the *drugs* in the medicine cabinet.
2. A substance that dulls a person in body or mind. – The doctor gave Mother a *drug* to make her sleep after her operation.
3. Give a *drug* to, *especially* one that causes sleep. – The police said the man had been *drugged* before he was robbed.

druggist drug'-gist *druggists*. A person who sells medicines, or who mixes drugs to make medicines. Druggist is used in some places as another name for chemist.

drum *drums. drummed, drumming.* 1. A hollow musical instrument that is played by beating upon the flat ends with *drum*sticks or with the hands. The sides of a *drum* are usually made of wood or metal. The ends are made of skins or other material stretched tightly across them.

2. Anything shaped like a *drum.* – Oil for motor-cars sometimes comes in oil *drums*.
3. Beat. – Baby likes to *drum* on her high chair with her spoon.
4. Get together.–We *drummed* up a lot of people to see our show.
5. Teach. – The teacher tries to *drum* the lessons into Bill's head.

drummer drum'-mer *drummers*. A person who beats a drum. – Jack is the *drummer* in the school band.

drumstick drum'-stick *drumsticks*. 1. One of the short sticks with which a drum is beaten to produce sound.
2. The leg of a fowl.– When we have roast chicken for dinner, I ask for the *drumstick*.

drunk. 1. One form of the word *drink*.–Baby has *drunk* up her milk and wants more.
2. Having lost control of the body and mind through drinking too much alcoholic liquor. –The man who drove into the tree was *drunk*.

drunkard drunk'-ard *drunkards*. A person who makes a habit of drinking too much alcoholic liquor.–He was a *drunkard*.

dry *dries, dried, drying.* 1. Not wet; without any moisture. – The heat of the sun makes the ground *dry*.
2. Take the wetness from. – Mary *dries* the dishes for Mother every day. – Mother *dries* apples and apricots, and puts them away for the winter.
3. Lose moisture or wetness.–The leaves have *dried* up.
4. Thirsty. – The farmer's horses were very *dry* after ploughing the field.
5. Quiet and matter-of-fact.–John has a *dry* sense of humour. He is funny without making any effort.

duck *ducks, ducked, ducking.* 1. A flat-billed bird that swims. *Ducks'* feet are webbed. Oil on their feathers helps to keep them on top of the water. Some *ducks* are tame and some are wild. – Grandfather breeds *ducks* to sell and eat.

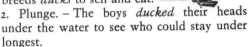

2. Plunge. – The boys *ducked* their heads under the water to see who could stay under longest.
3. Dodge down quickly.–When the ball came towards me, I *ducked* so it would not hit me.

due *dues.* 1. Expected to come, or to be done or paid.–Our gas bill is *due*.–The postman is *due* at any minute.
2. Just, fair, rightful.–The boys got their *due* reward for returning the money they found.
3. Money one pays for a membership. – To-day Father paid his union dues.
4. Directly. – If you go *due* south, you will find the house you are looking for.

duel du'-el *duels, duelled, duelling.* 1. A fight between two people who agree on the time, place, and weapons they will use. Each person has a witness to the fight, who is called a second. – In olden times, quarrels were sometimes settled by *duels*.
2. Fight a *duel*.–Mary often wishes she lived in the days of *duelling*.

duet du-et' *duets*. A song written for or sung by two people.–*Duets* are also written for piano, violin, saxophone, or other musical insttuments.

dug. One form of the word *dig*.–The dog *dug* a hole in the ground with his front paws.

duke *dukes*. A high-ranking nobleman. – The king called in the *dukes* of the kingdom to advise him.

dull *duller, dullest, dully, dullness.* 1. Blunt; not sharp. – The knife is *dull;* it should be sharpened.
2. Stupid. – Some people are *dull.* They do not understand things easily.
3. Not bright or colourful.–The beggar's coat was a *dull* colour.
4. Dim; not bright or cheerful. – Yesterday was a *dull* day. It wasn't clear and bright.
5. Not interesting. – The conversation was *dull.*

dumb *dumbly, dumbness.* 1. Not able to speak. –There are special schools for persons who are *dumb.* Animals are called *dumb* because they cannot talk.
2. A slang word meaning stupid; not clever.– There isn't a *dumb* person in this class.

dummy dum'-my *dummies.* 1. A very stupid person.–The boys called Mary a *dummy* because she didn't know the rules of football.
2. A sham object. A tailor's *dummy* looks like a person. A baby's *dummy* is a rubber object shaped like a nipple.
3. In some card games, a player who turns his cards face up and does not play the hand.–When we played bridge, I was the *dummy* 4 times. I put my cards face up on the table and my partner played them.

dump *dumps, dumped, dumping.* 1. Unload or empty a wagon, lorry, etc., by tilting the load so that it will slide off; to drop off in a heap. –The lorry-driver *dumped* the sand into the road.
2. A place set aside for throwing away rubbish or other things no longer wanted.–Old cans, boxes, and other rubbish are taken to the *dump.*

dumpling dump'-ling *dumplings.* A small ball of dough cooked in broth or enclosing an apple.

dunce *dunces.* A person who learns very slowly.

dune *dunes.* A hill or ridge of sand that the

wind has piled up.–There are *dunes* along the seacoast.

dungeon dun'-geon *dungeons.* A dark, underground cell or room. – Prisoners used to be put into *dungeons.*

duplicate du'-pli-cate *duplicates.* A copy; something just like an original.–If you like this picture, I will make a *duplicate* of it.

duplicate du'-pli-cate' *duplicates, duplicated, duplicating.* Copy; make a copy of. – The teacher *duplicated* the tests so that each child might have his own copy.

durable du'-ra-ble. Long-lasting; not easily worn away.–This has been a *durable* pair of shoes. They have lasted a long time.–Aluminium is more *durable* than tin.

during dur'-ing. While (something) is going on.–*During* the football game it started to rain.–*During* the winter we wear heavy coats.

dusk. 1. The time of evening just before dark. –The men went fishing at *dusk.*
2. Gloom and darkness.–The old woman sat in the *dusk* of her room.

dust *dusts, dusted, dusting.* 1. Dirt or another substance in very fine, dry particles; a powder.–The speeding car left a cloud of *dust* behind it. – The white *dust* on the kitchen floor is some flour that Sally spilled.
2. Wipe the *dust* from.–Mary *dusts* the furniture. She wipes off the tiny pieces of dirt.
3. Spread with a powdery stuff. – Mother *dusts* the pan with flour before putting the cake mixture into it.

dusty dust'-y *dustier, dustiest.* Full of or covered with dust or fine dirt.–The furniture is *dusty.*–The air is *dusty.*

duty du'-ty *duties.* 1. A task or work that one must do.–Mother's main *duties* are cooking, keeping the house, and taking care of the children.
2. Something one must do because it is right. –It is our *duty* to be honest.
3. A tax that must be paid on things brought from one country to another. – Mother had to pay *duty* on the necklace she brought from Canada.

dwarf *dwarfs.* 1. A person, plant, or animal that is very much smaller than others of its own kind or family.
2. In fairy tales a *dwarf* is often a small, ugly person who is strong and wicked.

dwell *dwells, dwelt, dwelling.* 1. Live; make one's home.–We *dwell* in houses.
2. *Dwell on* means think hard about; talk about. – The boys *dwelt on* the subject of football a long time. They talked and thought about football.

dweller dwell'-er *dwellers.* One who lives in a certain place. – A person who dwells or lives in a city is a city *dweller*.–A bird that nests in the swamp is a swamp *dweller*.

dwelling dwell'-ing *dwelling* . Place to live; house.–We live in a two-storey *dwelling*.–Their *dwelling* is a caravan-trailer.

dwelt. One form of the word *dwell*.–The princess *dwelt* in a foreign land for many years.

dye *dyes, dyed, dyeing.* 1. Change the colour of something by putting colouring into it.–Mary's dress was faded, so Mother *dyed* it red.
2. A colouring substance.–Mother dipped the dress in red *dye*.

dying dy'-ing. One form of the word *die*.–When they pulled the cat out of the water, they thought it was *dying*, but it lived.

dynamite dy'-na-mite. A chemical that explodes with great force.–*Dynamite* is used by workmen to blow up rocks.

E e

E, e *E's, e's.* The fifth letter of the alphabet.

each. If you speak of every person or thing in a group as separate from the others, you say *each* person or thing. – *Each* child has a Christmas gift.–*Each* gift was wrapped in a separate package.

eager ea'-ger *eagerly.* Wanting; having great desire.–We are *eager* to go to the farm. We are excited about going; we want to go very much.

eagerness ea'-ger-ness. Very great desire.–The boy had a great *eagerness* to learn about animals.

eagle ea'-gle *eagles.* A large bird that eats other birds and animals.–The bald *eagle* is the symbol of the United States.

ear *ears.* 1. The part of the body which hears sounds.–Man's *ears* are on each side of his head.–Some dogs' *ears* stand up, and some lie down.

2. The ability to recognize by hearing. – Bob has an *ear* for bird calls. He knows the call of each bird.
3. The bunch of grain on plants, such as wheat, oats, corn, etc.–Mother cooked several *ears* of Indian corn.

early ear'-ly *earlier, earliest.* 1. Before the set or usual time.–Some children come to school *early*; others come late.
2. In the *early* or first part. – The paper-boy comes *early* in the evening.
3. Soon to come. – Father is expecting an *early* telephone call.
4. One of the first.–One player was hurt during an *early* game. He was hurt in one of the first games of the season.

earn *earns, earned, earning.* 1. Receive as pay. –Father *earns* £20 a week.
2. Be entitled to.–Father *earns* every bit of the £20. He works hard and well enough to deserve £20 a week.

E F G H I J K L M N O P Q R S T U V W X Y Z

E
F
G
H
I
J
K
L
M
N
O
P
Q
R
S
T
U
V
W
X
Y
Z

earnest ear'-nest *earnestly.* 1. Sincere; conscientious. – The workman is an *earnest* worker. He is sincere, and he tries to do what he is supposed to do.
2. *In earnest* means serious or seriously. – Grandfather was *in earnest* when he told us not to climb the apple tree. He meant what he said.

earnings earn'-ings. Pay; wages or salary. – Father's *earings* are £20 a week.

earth. 1. The world we live on. The *earth* is called a planet because it circles about the sun. The *earth* is shaped like a ball, a little flattened at the top and bottom.
2. Ground; soil. – Plants grow in the *earth.*

earthen earth'-en. Made of clay or baked earth. –*Earthen* jugs, pitchers, and jars are those that are made of clay, baked until it is hard.

earthquake earth'-quake *earthquakes.* A shaking of a part of the earth's surface. Sudden changes inside the earth cause a shaking and sometimes an opening in the earth's surface.

earth-worm earth'-worm *earth-worms.* A long, crawling worm that lives in the ground. *Earth-worms* crawl about in the ground making little tunnels which keep the soil loose.– Fishermen often use *earth-worms* for bait.

ease eases, eased, easing. 1. Freedom from effort or difficulty.–Bob skates with *ease.*
2. Make comfortable; lessen (pain). – The nurse tried to *ease* the old man's pains.

easier eas'-i-er. One form of the word *easy.*– The second problem is *easier* than the first one.

easily eas'-i-ly. With ease; with no trouble.– He won the race *easily.*

east. 1. The direction towards the sunrise.–*East* is one of the four directions, as shown in the picture. The directions help us to find places. –We go *east* from England to get to Russia.

2. (Spelt with a capital 'e'.) The region of a country lying towards the *east.* – Norwich is in the *East* of England.
3. (Spelt with a capital 'e'.) The countries of China, Japan, India, etc.–the Far *East.*

Easter East'-er. The Sunday each year on which Christian peoples celebrate the rising of Christ from the grave. The date of *Easter* varies. But *Easter* always comes between March 22 and April 25.

eastern east'-ern. Lying to the east.–Norfolk, Suffolk and Essex are some *eastern* counties. They are in the *eastern* part of England.

eastward east'-ward. Towards the east; the direction in which the sun rises.–The car turned *eastward.*

easy eas'-y *easier, easiest.* Not hard or difficult. –Jack's work is *easy.*–The old farmer lives an *easy* life. He is comfortable; he has no cares or worries; he has enough money to buy what he needs.–The teacher is an *easy* person to get on with.

eat eats, ate, eaten, eating. 1. Take as food.– Cows *eat* grass. – People *eat* vegetables, fruits, and meats.
2. Take meals–We expect to *eat* at the café while Mother is away.
3. Dissolve.–Acids *eat* metals. They dissolve metals and make holes in them.

eaves. The part of a roof that sticks out beyond the walls.–Metal gutters are often fastened under the *eaves* to catch and carry away rain when it falls on the roof. Otherwise, water drips from the *eaves* on to the ground.

echo ech'-o *echoes, echoed, echoing.* 1. Sound that is reflected from a hard surface.–The children called out towards the hillside and heard the *echo* of their own voices.
2. Repeat; say again.–Little children *echo* the things they hear older people say.

eclipse e-clipse' *eclipses, eclipsed, eclipsing.* When the moon passes between the earth and the sun, it cuts off the sunlight in some places. This is an *eclipse* of the sun.

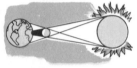

economy e-con'-o-my *economies.* Saving.–To practise *economy* means to save, to waste nothing, to use what one has without spending money for new things that are not really necessary.

edge *edges, edged, edging.* 1. The outside part of something where it ends; the top or bottom or one side.–The cup fell off the *edge* of the table.–The children put a line near the *edge* of the paper.–Father stood on the *edge* of the river fishing.
2. The sharp side of a blade.–The *edge* of the knife is very sharp.
3. Put a border round; decorate the *edges* of. –Mother's handkerchief was *edged* in green.
4. Move sideways little by little.–The doctor *edged* through the crowd to get to the man who had been hurt.

edition e-di'-tion *editions.* Number of copies of a book or other publication printed at one time.–Many *editions* of 'Oliver Twist' have been printed.

editor ed'-i-tor *editors, editorial, editorials.* A person in charge of publishing books, newspapers, or magazines. The *editor* decides what should be printed in the book or paper, corrects mistakes, and decides how the material should be arranged or placed. A newspaper *editor* sometimes writes articles called *editorials*, giving his opinions about the news.

educate ed'-u-cate *educates, educated, educating.* Teach; train.–Teachers try to *educate* children in reading, writing, arithmetic, and other subjects.

education ed-u-ca'-tion. 1. Teaching; training. –We go to school to receive *education*.
2. Things learned.–What you know or learn through reading, through going to school, through experience, or through training, is your *education*.

eel *eels.* A long, slippery, snake-like fish.–Some kinds of *eels* are good to eat.

effect ef-fect' *effects, effected, effecting.* 1. A result.–The *effect* of too much reading is tired eyes.
2. Force; being in action.–The new rule does not come into *effect* until Monday. It will not be followed until Monday.
3. Cause. – The doctor said the medicine would *effect* a cure.

effective ef-fec'-tive *effectively.* Bringing about the result wanted.–Sometimes children are spanked to make them behave. With some children spanking is not *effective*. It doesn't make them behave.

efficient ef-fi'-cient *efficiently, efficiency.* Getting the best results with the least effort.– The workman is very *efficient*. He is able, and does his work well. He gets results.

effort ef'-fort *efforts.* Spending energy; trying hard.–Bob's success in arithmetic was brought about by *effort*.–The fighter's success is due to his *effort* to win.

egg *eggs.* The first stage from which birds and some other creatures grow. Hens, ducks, geese, and other birds lay *eggs*. *Eggs* have shells. The centres of *eggs* are yellow and the part between the centre and shell is whitish. –Hen's *eggs* are good to eat. – Snakes, fish, and turtles also lay *eggs*.

eggplant egg'-plant *eggplants.* A plant whose large, purple and smooth - skinned fruit is cooked and eaten as a vege-table.

eight. The number (8) coming after 7 and before 9. – We have two thumbs and *eight* other fingers.

eighteen eigh-teen'. The number (18) coming after 17 and before 19.–Eight and ten make *eighteen*.

eighth *eighths.* 1. One of 8 equal parts. If you cut anything into 8 parts all the same size, each part is called one *eighth*. One *eighth* is written 1/8.
2. Coming in order as number 8 in a series. –August is the *eighth* month of the year.

eighty eight'-y. The number (80) coming after 79 and before 81.–Eight tens make *eighty*.

either ei'-ther. 1. One or the other of 2.–Mary brought Mother 2 pans. Mother said *either* pan was large enough for the cake.
2. Each one of two.–On *either* side of the street was a pavement. There was a pavement on both sides of the street.
3. John can't swim and Bob can't *either*.

elastic e-las'-tic. 1. Able to be stretched out and then go back to its usual length or size.– A rubber band is *elastic*; it stretches to go round a large package and becomes small again when taken off the package.
2. A kind of ribbon containing rubber threads which allow it to stretch and snap back.– Mother put *elastic* in the tops of Bob's socks to make them stay up.

E
F
G
H
I
J
K
L
M
N
O
P
Q
R
S
T
U
V
W
X
Y
Z

elbow el'-bow *elbows, elbowed, elbowing.* 1. The joint or place where the upper and lower parts of the arm come together. – Do not put your *elbows* on the table when you eat.
2. A curved metal band used to join pipes where they turn. Plumbers use *elbows*.
3. Push with the *elbows*.–Bob *elbowed* his way through the crowd to get to the shop.

elder eld'-er *elders.* 1. The older one of 2.– Jack is the *elder* of the 2 children.
2. A person who is older.–Bob is always respectful to his *elders*.
3. A church officer.–The *elders* of the church met last night.

elderly eld'-er-ly. Somewhat old.–An *elderly* gentleman knocked at the door.

eldest eld'-est. 1. Oldest of more than 2.–John is the *eldest* child in the large family.
2. The oldest person.–John is the *eldest* of the children.

elect e-lect' *elects, elected, electing.* Choose by a vote.–We are going to *elect* a person to be chairman of the club.

election e-lec'-tion *elections.* 1. A choosing or being chosen by vote.–After his *election,* the M.P. thanked those who had voted for him.
2. The time for voting.–Our city *elections* are held in November.

electric e-lec'-tric. Operated by or having to do with electricity.–*Electric* irons are heated by electricity.–*Electric* clocks are run by electricity.

electrical e-lec'-tri-cal. Electric; having to do with or operated by electricity.–Joe is studying to be an *electrical* engineer. He will learn to design and make *electric* things.

electrician e-lec-tri'-cian *electricians.* A person who repairs and installs electric tools and machines, wiring, etc.–Father sent for the *electrician* to come and put a new plug in the dining-room.

electricity e-lec-tric'-i-ty. A kind of force that can be sent through wires to give light, heat, or power. *Electricity* for our use is made by machines called generators or dynamos. *Electricity* is also found in nature. Lightning is a charge of *electricity* shooting through the air.

element el'-e-ment *elements.* 1. One of the simplest parts of anything.–Addition is an *element* of arithmetic.
2. One of the 100 or more substances which combine to make up all the material in the world.–Salt is a substance made up of two *elements* called sodium and chloride.

elephant el'-e-phant *elephants.* A large animal found in Africa and Asia.–An *elephant* has a thick grey skin, large ears, small eyes, 2 ivory tusks, and a long trunk which he uses to pick up food and water.

elevate el'-e-vate *elevates, elevated, elevating.*
1. Raise up; put at a higher place.–The car was *elevated* on the rack to be greased.
2. Build some distance from the ground.– Some cities have *elevated* railways.
3. Promote or raise in rank or position.–My uncle has been *elevated* to the peerage. He has been made an earl.

elevator el'-e-va-tor *elevators.* 1. A cage or room that is lifted and lowered to take people and supplies from floor to floor.–*Elevators* are also called lifts.
2. A tall building where grain is stored till it is to be shipped.–The farmer took his wheat to the grain *elevator*.

eleven e-lev'en. 1. The number (11) coming after 10 and before 12.–There are *eleven* men in a football team.
2. A football or cricket team.–Bob is captain of the *eleven*.

eleventh e-lev'-enth *elevenths.* 1. One of 11 equal parts.–If you cut anything into 11 parts of the same size, each part is called one *eleventh*.–One *eleventh* is written 1/11.
2. Coming as number 11 in a series.–John is playing in his *eleventh* football game. He has played in 10 games before this.

E
F
G
H
I
J
K
L
M
N
O
P
Q
R
S
T
U
V
W
X
Y
Z

elf *elves.* In fairy tales, a mischievous little dwarf or fairy.

elk *elks.* A large ani-mal, much like the moose, that has large flat antlers. It is found mostly in northern climates.

elm *elms.* A large shady tree. The branches of the *elm* spread out at the top like an um-brella.

else. 1. Other thing. – What *else* do you have in your pocket?
2. Other way. – How *else* can we solve the problem?
3. If not; otherwise.– Be good, or *else* you will be punished.

elsewhere *else'-where.* At or to another place. –The teacher told Bob and Jack to finish their conversation *elsewhere.*–The boys went *else-where* to play.

elves. More than one elf.–*Elves* are mischiev-ous little dwarfs or fairies.

embarrass em-bar'-rass *embarrasses, embar-rassed, embarrassing, embarrassment.* Make shy, uneasy, or ashamed.–Mary was *embar-rassed* when the teacher asked her to sing for the whole school.–It will *embarrass* Tom if the teacher asks if he has done his lesson.

ember em'-ber *embers.* A small piece of wood or fuel that is burning or glowing.–The boys sat by the dying fire and watched the *embers.*

emblem em'-blem *emblems.* 1. Sign; that which stands for something.–The *emblem* of the United States is an eagle.

2. A symbol.–The lily is an *emblem* of purity. It stands for purity.

embrace em-brace' *embraces, embraced, em-bracing.* 1. Hold in the arms to show love.– Mother *embraces* the baby.
2. A holding in the arms.–Father held Baby in a warm *embrace.*

embroider em-broi'-der *embroiders, embroi-dered, embroidering.* Decorate with fancy stitches made with a needle and fancy threads.–Mother *embroidered* a towel for Grandmother.

embroidery em-broi-'der-y. A kind of fancy decoration made with needle and thread.– Molly has the letter M *embroidered* on her handkerchiefs.

emerald em'-er-ald *emeralds.* 1. A valuable, bright green jewel.–The stone in Judy's ring is an *emerald.*
2. Bright green.–The costume Ann wore in the play was *em-erald* silk.

emerge e-merge' *emerges, emerged, emerging.*
1. Come out. – A deer *emerged* from the woods.
2. Come into view.–The sun *emerged* from behind a cloud.

emigrant em'-i-grant *emigrants.* A person who goes from his own country to live in another country. – *Emigrants* from many countries have settled in the United States.

emigrate em'-i-grate *emigrates, emigrated, emigrating.* Go from one's own country to live in another.–Some English people *emi-grate* to Canada and Australia.

emotion e-mo'-tion *emotions.* A feeling such as anger, joy, love, fear, hate, etc.–Mary is a person of strong *emotions.* She feels things deeply.

emperor em'-per-or *emperors.* The ruler or head of the government in an empire.

emphasis em'-pha-sis. 1. To force, stress, ac-cent.–To put *emphasis* on a syllable of a word, you make it stand out by saying it a little more loudly than the other syllables. You accent it.
2. Force, stress, accent.–The schoolteacher put *emphasis* on learning the multiplication tables. She told the children how important it is to learn them.

emphasize em'-pha-size *emphasizes, empha-sized, emphasizing.* To give emphasis to; to stress as important.–The teacher *empha-sized* the need for hard work.

empire em'-pire *empires.* A group of countries or states ruled by one government or one person.–Augustus was the first ruler of the Roman *Empire,* which at one time extended from Western Europe to Central Asia.

E F G H I J K L M N O P Q R S T U V W X Y Z

employ em-ploy′ *employs, employed, employing.* 1. Hire and pay for working.–Motor-car factories *employ* many men.
2. Use.–*Employ* the skills you have learned in playing this game.

employee em-ploy-ee′ *employees.* A person who works for pay for some other person or company.–The teacher is an *employee* of the Local Education Authority.

employer em-ploy′-er *employers.* A person who hires others to work for him.–The man who hired Father, who gave him a job and pays him for working, is his *employer.*

empty emp′-ty *empties, emptied, emptying.* 1. Having nothing in it.–The box is *empty.* It has nothing in it.
2. Take everything out of.–I will *empty* the basket for you.

enable en-a′-ble *enables, enabled, enabling.* Make (a person, animal, or thing) able to do something.–The boy's ability to swim *enabled* him to get to shore safely.

enamel en-am′-el *enamels, enamelled, enamelling.* 1. A hard, shiny paint or other coating.–Some of Mother's pots and pans are *enamel*-ware.–Father painted the walls of the room with green paint and the woodwork with white *enamel.*
2. Paint with *enamel.*–Father *enamelled* the woodwork in white.
3. The hard outer covering of the teeth.

enchant en-chant′ *enchants, enchanted, enchanting.* 1. Fill with delight and wonder.–The clowns at the circus *enchant* the children.
2. Cast a spell on by a magic charm.–The white deer was a princess whom a jealous fairy had *enchanted.*

encircle en-cir′-cle *encircles, encircled, encircling.* Surround; make a ring round.–The house was *encircled* by large maple trees.–The May Queen's head was *encircled* with a diadem of flowers.

enclose en-close′ *encloses, enclosed, enclosing, enclosure.* 1. Put inside something.–Bob wrote Grandfather a letter, and Mother *enclosed* it in the envelope with hers.
2. Close up; shut in by surrounding with walls, a fence, etc. – Father *enclosed* the veranda with glass windows and roof to make a conservatory.

encounter en-coun′-ter *encounters, encountered, encountering.* 1. Meet, come up against.–The men *encountered* trouble in digging the ditch. They struck rocks, and had much rain.
2. A coming up against something; a meeting.–The farmer had an *encounter* with the bees while trying to get the honeycombs.

encourage en-cour′-age *encourages, encouraged, encouraging.* 1. Give hope to, cheer, make eager to go on.–The doctor *encouraged* the sick man by telling him that he would be well in a few days.
2. Speak in favour of something.–The owner of the factory *encouraged* the men to seek homes near it.

encyclopedia en-cy-clo-pe′-dia *encyclopedias.* A book or a set of books that tells many facts about many things. To help you find things easily, the subjects in an *encyclopedia* are put in alphabetical order just like the words in a dictionary.–Bob looked up tropical fish in the *encyclopedia* to give the class a report about them.

end *ends, ended, ending.* 1. Finish.–The game has *ended.*
2. The last part.–At the *end* of the story, Red Riding Hood's grandmother jumps out of the wolf's stomach, safe and sound.
3. The tip, edge, or side of a thing, where it stops or starts.–In my pencil, one *end* has lead in it and the other has a rubber on it.– A little table stands at the *end* of the sofa.

endeavour en-deav′-our *endeavours, endeavoured, endeavouring.* 1. Try, make an effort.–John will *endeavour* to get his story written today.
2. An undertaking, an effort.–Building a bridge is a big *endeavour.* It is a big thing to try to do.

ending end′-ing *endings.* 1. The last part.–Alice likes stories that have sad *endings.*
2. One form of the word *end.*–The day is *ending.*

endless end′-less. 1. Going on for ever; never coming to a finish or a stop.–The lesson was so long that it seemed *endless.*
2. A circle is *endless* because it has no ends; it meets itself everywhere.

endurance en-dur′-ance. 1. Ability to stand something.–The explorers showed amazing *endurance.* In spite of great hardships, they reached the North Pole. They suffered from hunger and cold, but still went on.
2. Quality of wearing well.–Cheap shoes do not have the *endurance* of better shoes.

endure en-dure′ *endures, endured, enduring.* Undergo, stand.–The men travelling through the forest *endured* many hardships.

enemy en′-e-my *enemies.* Someone or something that works against one or fights one.–Laziness is the boy's greatest *enemy.* It keeps him from doing many things he could do.–Lions and tigers are great *enemies* of other jungle animals. They kill and eat other animals.

energy en′-er-gy *energies.* A strong desire to do things; the strength to do things.–The children have so much *energy* that it keeps their teacher busy planning work for them.

enforce en-force′ *enforces, enforced, enforcing, enforcement.* See that a programme, law, etc., is carried out or kept.–The police *enforce* the laws of the city. They see that the laws are obeyed.

engage en-gage′ *engages, engaged, engaging.* 1. Hire.–During the harvest season, Grandfather *engages* more men to work for him. 2. Be doing, be in the act of, be busy at.–Sally was *engaged* in feeding the goldfish when Mother called her. 3. Promise to marry.–Mother was *engaged* to Father for a year before they were married.

engagement en-gage′-ment *engagements.* 1. An appointment. – Mother has an *engagement* with Ann's teacher. She has agreed to meet her at a certain time and place. 2. A promise to be married.–The girl told us of her *engagement* to the soldier. 3. A battle.–The armies met in a fierce *engagement.*

engine en′-gine *engines.* 1. A machine that makes power which will make other machinery work.–Our car has a petrol *engine.* 2. A locomotive.–An *engine* can pull a long train of coaches.

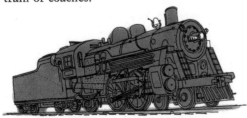

engineer en-gi-neer′ *engineers, engineered, engineering.* 1. A man who takes care of engines and makes them go.–Uncle Jim is a railway *engineer.*

2. A man who designs and builds bridges, railways, tunnels, and the like. 3. Manage, take charge of.–Bob likes to *engineer* all our school affairs.

engrave en-grave′ *engraves, engraved, engraving.* Carve markings on or into.–The boys *engraved* their names on the tree so that they could come back and find them there in 10 years' time.

enjoy en-joy′ *enjoys, enjoyed, enjoying.* 1. Find pleasure in, like.–We *enjoy* swimming, singing, and playing games. 2. Have the benefit or use of.–The old couple *enjoy* a steady income.

enjoyable en-joy′-a-ble. Happy, pleasant, delightful.–We had a very *enjoyable* time at the party.

enjoyment en-joy′ment. Pleasure, joy, happiness.–Father gets much *enjoyment* from inventing things.

enlarge en-large′ *enlarges, enlarged, enlarging.* Make bigger.–Mother ordered the picture of Father to be *enlarged,* so that she could frame it.–Father is going to have the house *enlarged* so that he can have a workroom.

enlist en-list′ *enlists, enlisted, enlisting.* 1. Join, enrol.–Bob *enlisted* in the army. 2. Get the help of.–We *enlisted* the teacher's help in preparing our play.

enormous e-nor′-mous *enormously.* Very big; much bigger than usual.–A man who weighs 300 pounds is *enormous.* – Elephants are *enormous.*

enough e-nough′. As many or as much as needed. – Will 12 apples be *enough?* – Bob didn't run fast *enough,* so he lost the race.

enrage en-rage′ *enrages, enraged, enraging.* Make angry.–The boys *enraged* the lion by throwing sticks at him.

enrol en-rol′ *enrols, enrolled, enrolling.* 1. Become a member.–Bob has *enrolled* in a Sunday school class. 2. Record on a list of membership.–Our teacher will *enrol* you in our class. She will write your name in a list or roll with the names of the rest of the class.

ensign en′-sign *ensigns.* A banner or flag.–The White *Ensign* is the flag of the Royal Navy.

entangle en-tan'-gle *entangles, entangled, entangling.* 1. Wind or mix up in.–The kitten became *entangled* in Grandmother's ball of wool.

2. Include; make mixed up in.–The boys tried to *entangle* Bob in the trouble they had on the football field.

enter en'-ter *enters, entered, entering.* 1. Go or come into. – The children *entered* the classroom.

2. Record.–The teacher will *enter* your name in her register.

3. Become a member of.–My sister will *enter* grammar school this autumn.

entertain en-ter-tain' *entertains, entertained, entertaining.* 1. Amuse in any way.–The children gave a play to *entertain* their parents.

2. Have as a guest. – We *entertained* the Smiths for dinner.

3. Have guests.–The Browns are *entertaining* tonight.

entertainment en-ter-tain'-ment *entertainments.* Anything that pleases, interests, or makes fun.–Reading books, watching animals at the zoo, listening to the radio, going to the cinema, and talking to interesting people are kinds of *entertainment.*

enthusiasm en-thu'-si-asm *enthusiasms.* Excited interest.–Bob has great *enthusiasm* for football.

enthusiastic en-thu-si-as'-tic. Full of eager interest; much pleased.–Bob is very *enthusiastic* about his new bicycle.

entire en-tire'. Whole; complete.–The hungry man ate an *entire* pie.–We expect to paper the *entire* house.

entirely en-tire'-ly. Wholly; fully; completely. –The driver was *entirely* to blame for the accident. He and no one else was to blame.

entitle en-ti'-tle *entitles, entitled, entitling.* Give the right or privilege.–The children are *entitled* to take books from the library.

entrance en'-trance *entrances.* 1. Door; place through which people pass to and from a building or house. – The teacher walked out of the front *entrance* of the school.

2. A coming in; an entering. – The clown's *entrance* into the ring made the children laugh.

3. A beginning; becoming a member of.–The man's *entrance* into the army surprised his family.

entry en'-try *entries.* 1. A passage or hall through which people pass when entering or leaving a building.

2. A coming in; entering.–The musician's *entry* was a signal for all to be quiet.

envelop en-vel'-op *envelops, enveloped, enveloping.* Wrap.–The man was enveloped in rugs to keep him warm.

envelope en'-vel-ope *envelopes.* A paper cover or holder used to put letters in when you send them through the post.

envious en'-vi-ous. Wanting what another has. –Bob gets better marks in school than Bill does. Bill is *envious* of Bob. He wishes he could get marks as good as Bob's.–People with little money are often *envious* of those with much money.

envy en'-vy *envies, envied, envying.* 1. Want what another has.–All the girls in the class *envy* Mary's dresses. They wish they had dresses like Mary's.–Bill *envies* John his new skates.

2. Something which people *envy.*–Our new car is the *envy* of everyone in our street. Everyone wishes it were his.

3. The feeling of unhappiness or dislike caused by wanting something another has.– *Envy* sometimes makes people do things that are wrong.

epidemic ep-i-dem'-ic *epidemics.* Fast spreading of a disease to many people.–The schools will close if the *epidemic* of measles continues.

equal e'-qual *equals, equalled, equalling.* 1. Of the same size, amount, worth, etc.–100 pence are *equal* to £1.–Two pints are *equal* to 1 quart.– Our team is equal to its opponents.

2. Strong enough.–Father was so tired that he was not *equal* to riding very far.

equator e-qua'-tor *equators.* An imaginary circle around the earth half way between the North Pole, or point farthest north on the earth, and the South Pole, or point farthest south on the earth.–It is hot near the *equator.*

equip e-quip′ *equips, equipped, equipping.*
Provide; furnish; fit out.–We must *equip* our
workshop with new tools.

equipment e-quip′-ment. The things with
which anything is fitted out or furnished;
things needed for certain uses.–The *equipment* of a factory includes machines and tools.

erase e-rase′ *erases, erased, erasing.* Rub out.
–It is easier to *erase* pencil marks than ink.

eraser e-ras′-er *erasers.* Anything used to rub
out a mark, usually a spongy piece of rubber.
–Many pencils have *erasers* on the ends.

ere. Before.–*Ere* is used in old-fashioned verse
and stories:

> *Ere* day was done,
> The fight was won.

erect e-rect′ *erects, erected, erecting.* 1. Build;
set up.–The workmen will *erect* a house at
the corner.–It took the men hours to *erect*
the fallen telegraph pole.
2. Straight, upright.–Soldiers stand *erect*.

err *errs, erred, erring.* Make a mistake.–Jack
erred in believing that there would be no
school on Friday. There was school on that
day.

errand er′-rand *errands.* 1. A trip or journey
taken to deliver a message or to do whatever
you are sent to do.–Mary likes to run *errands*
for the teacher during the arithmetic class.
2. A thing one goes to do.–Jack's *errand* was
to buy a newspaper for Father.

error er′-ror *errors.* A mistake.–John made one
error in spelling; he made a mistake in spelling one word.

escape es-cape′ *escapes, escaped, escaping.* 1.
Get away from something; get out of; run
away.–The man *escaped* from the burning
building by climbing down a rope.
2. Avoid, not fall into.–All the children had
the measles except Mary. She *escaped* having them.
3. Getting away, or the
means used in getting
away.–A fire *escape* is
an iron staircase on the
outside of a building.–
Sailors can *escape* from
a submerged submarine
by means of an *escape*-hatch.–The prisoner
made his *escape* through a tunnel he had dug
underneath the prison wall.

Eskimo Es′-ki-mo *Eskimos.* One of a people
who live in the northern part of North
America. They are not very tall, and have a
yellowish skin and straight black hair. Most
of them live by hunting and fishing.

especial es-pe′-cial. Particular, outstanding,
main. – Have you any *especial* reason for
wanting to stay at home?

especially es-pe′-cial-ly. 1. Very, exceptionally.
–Bob is *especially* good at spelling and arithmetic.
2. Particularly.–I *especially* like walnuts.

essential es-sen′-tial *essentially.* Necessary,
needed.–Knowing the multiplication table is
essential in solving many arithmetic problems.–Wings are *essential* to aeroplanes.

establish es-tab′-lish *establishes, established,
establishing.* 1. Set up, organize.–This church
was *established* in 1890.
2. Settle.–Mr. Jones is well *established* in his
new business. He is doing well.

establishment es-tab′-lish-ment *establish-
ments.* A church, school, shop, house, or business organization set up for some purpose.

estate es-tate′ *estates.* 1. A large piece of land
with several buildings, used as a dwelling
place.–That rich man has a large *estate* in
the country.
2. One's entire property.–The old woman
left her *estate* to a children's home.

estimate es′-ti-mate *estimates, estimated, esti-
mating.* 1. Judge, guess at from what one can
see.–It is hard to *estimate* the age of some
people.–Bob *estimated* the height of the soldier to be 6 feet.
2. Judgement, rough guess.–The agent gave
us an *estimate* of how much our house would
sell for. After he looked at it, he told us how
much he thought it would sell for.

E
F
G
H
I
J
K
L
M
N
O
P
Q
R
S
T
U
V
W
X
Y
Z

E
F
G
H
I
J
K
L
M
N
O
P
Q
R
S
T
U
V
W
X
Y
Z

etc. The way *et cetera* is usually written. *Etc.* means 'and so on,' 'and so forth', 'and others of like kind.'–Pigs, cows, horses, sheep, *etc.*, are all animals. There are many others.

eternal e-ter′-nal *eternally*. Lasting for ever.– God is *eternal*.–Mary said she was tired of the *eternal* rain. It didn't seem to her as if the rain would ever stop.

ether e′-ther. A drug used to make persons un- conscious. Doctors often use *ether* before an operation, so that the patient will feel no pain.

etiquette et′-i-quette. Manners that are ex- pected of polite people.–It is good *etiquette* to thank people for gifts.–It is *etiquette* for boys and men to take off their hats when they go into a house.

Europe Eu′-rope *European, Europeans*. A con- tinent that has more people than any other except Asia. The Americas were largely set- tled by *Europeans*. *Europe* is divided from Asia by the Ural Mountains in Russia.

evade e-vade′ *evades, evaded, evading*. Dodge, avoid slyly.–The robber tried to *evade* the police by having his hair dyed and growing a moustache.

evaporate e-vap′-o-rate *evaporates, evapo- rated, evaporating, evaporation*. Turn into vapour or steam.–If you boil water, it will *evaporate*. When the kettle boils dry, all the water has *evaporated*.

eve *eves*. 1. Evening.–It was a bitter winter's *eve*.
2. The day or evening before a special holi- day –December 25 is Christmas Day. De- cember 24 is Christmas *Eve*.

even e′-ven *evens, evened, evening*. 1. Level.– Mother used an *even* cupful of flour in the cake.
2. Flat.–The ground is *even* along the river. It is not hilly or rough.
3. Regular.–The horse runs at an *even* pace. He runs at just about the same pace all the time.
4. The numbers 2, 4, 6, 8, 10, 12, 14, *etc.*, are *even* numbers because they can be divided by 2 without any being left over.
5. Make equal or the same.–Bob's boundary *evened* the score.–The dressmaker will *even* the hem of Mother's dress.
6. Yet, still.–Mary spells well but Bob spells better than Mary, and John spells *even* better than Bob.

evening eve′-ning *evenings*. The end of the day or the beginning of the night.–The sun goes down in the *evening*, and then darkness comes.

event e-vent′ *events*. 1. Anything that happens. A cricket match, a party, a snowstorm, and an accident are all *events*.
2. An item in a sports programme. – The next *event* is the 100 yards hurdles.

eventually e-ven′-tu-al-ly. Finally, at last.– *Eventually* Mary did learn how to play dom- inoes.

ever ev′-er. 1. At any time.–Have you *ever* seen a bear?
2. Always.–That boy is *ever* ready to help.

evergreen ev′-er-green *evergreens*. A tree or plant that has green leaves all the year round. –Pine trees and cedars are *evergreens*.

spruce   fir   pine   cedar   cypress   balsam fir

every ev′-er-y. Each.–*Every* person in the class had a chance to talk.

everybody ev′-er-y-bod-y. Every person. – *Everybody* voted for Bob.

everyday ev′-er-y-day′. Happening or being used every day; not special.–My blue dress is my *everyday* dress.–Singing is an *every- day* event in our class.

everyone ev′-er-y-one. Each person.–Mary in- vited *everyone* in our class to her party.

everything ev′-er-y-thing. All the things, each thing.–The house and *everything* in it burned down.

everywhere ev′-er-y-where. In every place, in all places.–The sun shines *everywhere*.

EUROPE

Aral Sea

Caspian Sea

sheep

cattle

Black Sea

Stalingrad

RUSSIA (U.S.S.R.)

Volga R.

Moscow

TURKEY

Ankara

Istanbul

Dnieper R.

BULGARIA

Leningrad

FINLAND

Helsinki

CRETE

RUMANIA

Stockholm

Warsaw

POLAND

Budapest

HUNGARY

YUGOSLAVIA

GREECE

ALBANIA

Oslo

SWEDEN

Copenhagen

Berlin

Vienna

AUSTRIA

Rome

ITALY

SICILY

NORWAY

DENMARK

GERMANY

CZECHOSLOVAKIA

SARDINIA

Amsterdam

Rhine R.

LUXEMBOURG

Berne

SWITZERLAND

CORSICA

Mediterranean Sea

NETHERLANDS

Antwerp

BELGIUM

Paris

Marseilles

Rhone

Ocean

London

ENGLAND

FRANCE

Barcelona

SCOTLAND

Glasgow

WALES

N. IRELAND

Dublin

EIRE

SPAIN

Gibraltar

Atlantic

ICELAND

PORTUGAL

Lisbon

dairy farming

fish

timber

manufacturing

mining

E
F
G
H
I
J
K
L
M
N
O
P
Q
R
S
T
U
V
W
X
Y
Z

evidence ev′-i-dence *evidences, evidenced, evidencing.* 1. A clue to what has happened or to what is so.–The witness gave all the *evidence* he could about the accident. He told what he knew.
2. Signs, proof.–There were *evidences* of jam on the boy's face.
3. Show plainly.–The poor old man's clothes *evidenced* that he had had many hardships.
4. *In evidence* means showing very plainly. –The bad effects of the war were much *in evidence* everywhere.

evil e′-vil. 1. Bad, harmful, wrong.–An *evil* person is one who has bad thoughts, does things that are wrong, and hurts others.
2. Wrongdoing, wickedness.–Selfishness has always been an *evil* of human nature.

ewe *ewes.* A female or mother sheep.

exact ex-act′ *exactly.* Just correct; right. – Mary bought the groceries and gave the shopkeeper the *exact* money.

exaggerate ex-ag′-ger-ate *exaggerates, exaggerated, exaggerating.* Add to; make bigger, worse, greater, or more.–Some children *exaggerate* the stories they tell.–Bill *exaggerated* the size of the fish that got away.

examination ex-am-i-na′-tion *examinations.* 1. A test.–Mary passed her spelling *examination.*
2. An inspection; a careful looking over.–The dentist made an *examination* of each child's teeth.

examine ex-am′-ine *examines, examined, examining.* 1. Look at carefully; inspect. – The teacher *examined* the children's hands to see if they were clean.
2. Question.–The judge will *examine* the witness.

example ex-am′-ple *examples.* 1. A problem.–John could not work the second *example* in the arithmetic lesson.
2. A model.–Bob's drawing was put on the board as an *example* of the work the class was doing.

exceed ex-ceed′ *exceeds, exceeded, exceeding.* Be greater than; go more than. – Motor-car drivers should not *exceed* the speed limit. They should not go faster than the law allows.

exceedingly ex-ceed′-ing-ly. Very. – It is *exceedingly* warm today.

excel ex-cel′ *excels, excelled, excelling.* Do better than.–Bob *excels* the others in his class in reading. He is better at reading than all the others.

excellent ex′-cel-lent *excellently, excellence.* Very good.–The teacher said that the children did *excellent* work.

except ex-cept′. But. – John solved all the problems *except* the third one.

exception ex-cep′-tion *exceptions.* One left out; a different one.–The men work every day of the week except Sunday. Sunday is the *exception.*

exchange ex-change′ *exchanges, exchanged, exchanging.* 1. Give back for another one.– Mary's shoes were too small, and she had to *exchange* them. She took them back to the shop and got a larger size.
2. Trade; give back and forth.–The children *exchanged* spelling papers.
3. The central telephone office.–Mother called the telephone *exchange* to report that our neighbour's phone was out of order.

excite ex-cite′ *excites, excited, exciting.* Awaken or stir up the feelings of (a person, etc.).– The children were *excited* when the fire-bell rang.–The doctor told the boys that they shouldn't *excite* the sick boy. He said they should not arouse him.

excitement ex-cite′-ment. Stirred-up or active feeling.–The fire engine caused much *excitement.*–In our *excitement* to get away, we forgot to lock the door.

exclaim ex-claim′ *exclaims, exclaimed, exclaiming.* Cry out; speak excitedly. – When the children saw the Christmas tree, they *exclaimed* with wonder.

excursion ex-cur′-sion *excursions.* A special trip taken by a group, usually for fun.–Our class is going to go on an *excursion* to the lake on the last day of school.–Last week we went on an *excursion* to the dairy to learn about making butter.

excuse ex-cuse′ (pronounced *ex-kyooss*) *excuses.* A reason or explanation of why one has done something wrong. – If you are absent from school, you must have an *excuse.*

excuse ex-cuse′ (pronounced *ex-kyooz*) *excuses, excused, excusing.* 1. Dismiss; let go.–The teacher will *excuse* us from school at 2 o'clock so that we can go to the game.
2. Pardon; forgive. – The teacher *excused* Jack's bad manners because he was sick.

executive ex-ec′-u-tive *executives.* 1. Having to do with running or managing something.–Father has an *executive* position at the factory.
2. A manager; one who gives orders.–Father is an *executive* in the factory.

exercise ex′-er-cise *exercises, exercised, exercising.* 1. Use, apply.–The teacher told Jack to *exercise* more care in writing his lesson.
2. Do a thing again and again so as to make stronger and more skilful.–Mary plays the scales on the piano to *exercise* her fingers.
3. Activity that builds strength or skill.–After Billy's broken arm had healed, he had to do several *exercises* to make the muscles strong again.
4. A group of written problems.–Jack could not finish the French *exercise* set for homework.

exhale ex-hale′ *exhales, exhaled, exhaling.* Breathe out.–When you breathe air into your lungs, you inhale; when you breathe out air, you *exhale.*

exhaust ex-haust′ *exhausts, exhausted, exhausting.* 1. Tire; wear out.–The boys were *exhausted* after the race.
2. Use up.–When the Boy Scouts had *exhausted* all their matches, they started their fire by rubbing two sticks together.
3. Blow out; give out.–The fumes from burnt petrol are *exhausted* from a motor through the *exhaust* pipe.
4. Fumes from burnt petrol and oil.–The *exhaust* from the car quickly filled the garage.

exhibit ex-hib′-it *exhibits, exhibited, exhibiting.* 1. A showing.–Each year our class has an *exhibit* in the art display.

2. Show; display.–This year Mary *exhibited* a basket she had made.

exhibition ex-hi-bi′-tion *exhibitions.* A showing. – We had an *exhibition* of model aeroplanes at the school.

exile ex′ile *exiles, exiled, exiling.* 1. Send away as punishment.–The traitor was *exiled* from the country for life.
2. A person who is sent away.–The *exile* was lonely in the strange land.
3. State of being *exiled.*–The traitor was sent into *exile* for life.

exist ex-ist′ *exists, existed, existing.* 1. Live; keep alive.–The lost sailors *existed* for days without food or water.
2. Be; have reality.–Ghosts do not *exist.* They are not real.
3. Remain.–This cave has *existed* for as long as Grandfather can remember.

existence ex-ist′-ence *existences.* 1. Being; state of being real.–Some people believe in the *existence* of fairies.
2. Life; way of living. – The old lady led a peaceful *existence.*

exit ex′-it *exits.* 1. A way or door that takes one out of a building.–We left the cinema by the side *exit.*
2. Going out, especially leaving a stage after an appearance in a play. – There was great applause as Mary made her *exit* from the stage.

expand ex-pand′ *expands, expanded, expanding, expansion.* 1. Grow larger; spread out.–Yeast makes bread dough *expand.*
2. Make larger.–The shopkeeper will *expand* his business.

expect ex-pect′ *expects, expected, expecting.* 1. Look for.–We *expect* a letter from Mother every day.
2. Feel sure. – We *expect* that it will rain today.

expectation ex-pec-ta′-tion *expectations.* 1. Something expected. – Getting a watch for Christmas was Mary's one *expectation.*
2. Excitement of expecting.–Mary was full of *expectation.*

expedition ex-pe-di′-tion *expeditions.* 1. A trip for discovery or exploration.–Captain Scott went on two Antarctic *expeditions.*
2. A group of people travelling together.–The museum sent an *expedition* to the unknown jungle.

E
F
G
H
I
J
K
L
M
N
O
P
Q
R
S
T
U
V
W
X
Y
Z

E F G H I J K L M N O P Q R S T U V W X Y Z

expel ex-pel′ *expels, expelled, expelling.* Put out; force or drive out. – When a bullet is *expelled* from a gun, it is going so fast that you cannot see it.–Jack was *expelled* from school because he would not obey the rules.

expense ex-pense′ *expenses.* Cost; amount spent.–The *expense* of buying a home did not keep us from buying one.

expensive ex-pen′-sive *expensively.* High-priced.–Mother wanted the dress, but it was too *expensive.* It cost too much.

experience ex-pe′-ri-ence *experiences, experienced, experiencing.* 1. Anything that happens to one.–Going to the circus was a new *experience* to Sally.
2. Practice.–Father has had much *experience* driving cars.
3. Live through, have.–We have *experienced* many happy times together.–The wounded man *experienced* much pain.

experiment ex-per′-i-ment *experiments, experimented, experimenting.* 1. Try out; do something to see what will happen.–Bob *experimented* with a wider wing on his model aeroplane.
2. A trial or testing to see what will happen. Bob made an *experiment* with a wider wing on his model aeroplane.

expert ex′-pert *experts.* 1. A person who does something very well.–Father is an *expert* at driving a car.
2. Highly skilled.–Father is an *expert* driver.

expire ex-pire′ *expires, expired, expiring.* Become worthless; lose force; die.–The wireless licence *expires* on January 1. After January 1 it will be no good.

explain ex-plain′ *explains, explained, explaining.* 1. Tell about; make clear.–The teacher will *explain* the problem. She will try to make us understand it.
2. Tell the meaning of.–Bob *explained* the word.
3. Teach, tell.–Mother will *explain* to you how to make a reef knot.

explanation ex-pla-na′-tion *explanations.* Act of explaining, of telling what something means or shows.–Bob's absence needed no *explanation.* Mother knew he was playing cricket because his ball and bat were missing from the back porch.–Father's *explanation* of the word made its meaning clear to us.

explode ex-plode′ *explodes, exploded, exploding.* Blow up.–The lighted firework *exploded* with a bang.–The boy blew so much air into the balloon that it *exploded.*

explore ex-plore′ *explores, explored, exploring.* 1. Travel through newly found land or land that is little known.–Captain Scott *explored* the region of the South Pole.
2. Examine to find something new, or out of curiosity.–The boys thoroughly *explored* the rambling old manor house.

explorer ex-plor′-er *explorers.* A person who travels to find something new.–The *explorers* travelled through deep jungle.

explosion ex-plo′-sion *explosions.* A blowing up.–We heard the *explosion* of the dynamite among the rocks.

export ex′-port *exports, exported, exporting.* 1. Something sent out of one country to be sold in another.–Motor-cars are one of our most important *exports.*
2. Send out of the country to sell.–We *export* many motor-cars.

expose ex-pose′ *exposes, exposed, exposing.* 1. Lay open, leave uncovered.–Wet clothes will soon dry if they are *exposed* to the sun and wind.–The film was *exposed* to light. The house was in an *exposed* place.
2. Bring into contact with.–John was *exposed* to scarlet fever, but he did not get it.

express ex-press′ *expresses, expressed, expressing.* 1. Say, tell, or reveal in words, movements, etc.–It is hard for some people to *express* themselves, to say what they want to say.–Baby *expresses* her wants through motions of her hands or by crying.
2. A way of sending things.–Parcels can be sent from town to town by parcel post or by *express.*
3. A fast train. – The *express* does not stop between London and Edinburgh.

expression ex-pres′-sion *expressions*. 1. Way of speaking, telling, reading, etc.–Mary reads with *expression*. She makes the meaning clear by putting force on the right words.
2. A saying, or a particular way of saying something.–'We learn to do by doing' is an old *expression*.–'That's nothing' is an *expression* Jack uses when somebody praises him for something he has done.
3. The look on a person's face.–The old man said nothing, but his *expression* was sad.

extend ex-tend′ *extends, extended, extending*.
1. Hold out.–The blind man *extended* his cup for pennies.
2. Spread out, go as far as.–Grandfather's farm *extends* to the corner.
3. Make longer.–The city will *extend* the bus route several miles out.
4. Offer.– We *extended* our best wishes to our teacher on her birthday.

exterior ex-te′-ri-or *exteriors*. Outside. – The man painted the *exterior* of his house.

external ex-ter′-nal *externally*. Relating to the outside of a thing.–This medicine is for *external* use only. It should be rubbed on, not swallowed.

extinguish ex-tin′-guish *extinguishes, extinguished, extinguishing*. Put out (a light or fire).–At night we *extinguish* the light before going to bed.–The Boy Scouts *extinguished* the camp fire.

extra ex′-tra. In addition, more than needed.–There are a few *extra* pencils in the box.–Mary received *extra* spending money for Christmas shopping. She had more money than she usually has.

extract ex-tract′ *extracts, extracted, extracting*. Pull out, draw out.–The dentist will *extract* your tooth.–Mother *extracted* the juice from the oranges.

extract ex′-tract *extracts*. A flavouring taken from fruits, vegetables, etc.–I like lemon and vanilla *extracts* in puddings.

extraordinary ex-tra-or′-di-nar-y *extraordinarily*. Uncommon, unusual, surprising. – A flower that is twice as big as flowers of its kind usually are is of *extraordinary* size.

extravagant ex-trav′-a-gant *extravagantly*. Spending carelessly; wasteful.–Mrs Jones is very *extravagant*. She spends more money than she should and buys useless things.

extreme ex-treme′ *extremes*. 1. Farthest.–Bob lives at the *extreme* end of the street.
2. Belonging to either of the opposite ends of something; being at the limit.–I do not enjoy *extreme* weather. I do not like it when it is too cold or too hot.–The young woman wears *extreme* clothes. They are not in good taste, because they are too noticeable.

extremely ex-treme′-ly. Very; at or to the extreme.–It is *extremely* warm today.

eye *eyes, eyed, eyeing*. 1. The part of any person or animal with which he sees.–We see with our *eyes*.

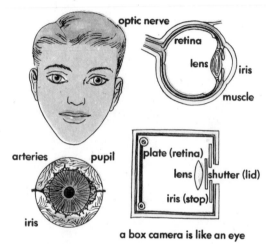

a box camera is like an eye

2. Watch.–The cat *eyed* the mouse closely.
3. A look-out; watch.–Mother asked Mary to keep an *eye* on the cake in the oven while she went to the shops. She wanted Mary to look at it once in a while.
4. A little loop or hole through which thread, a hook, etc., may be passed.–Grandmother couldn't get the thread through the *eye* of the needle.

eyeball eye-ball *eyeballs*. The part of the eye that is ball-shaped, over which the eyelids close.

eyebrow eye′-brow *eyebrows*. The bony arch above the eye, or the hairs that grow on this arch.

eyelash eye′-lash *eyelashes*. One of the long hairs that grow on the edge of the eyelids. *Eyelashes* help to protect the eyeball.

eyelid eye′-lid *eyelids*. The part of the eye that opens and closes. You have upper and lower *eyelids*. When you are asleep, your *eyelids* are closed.

eyesight eye′-sight. The ability to see.–Most children have good *eyesight*. They see well.

E F G H I J K L M N O P Q R S T U V W X Y Z

F f

F, f *F's f's*. The sixth letter of the alphabet.

fa. The 4th tone of the scale in music. Doh, re, mi, *fa*, soh, la, ti, doh.

fable fa'-ble *fables*. A short story written to teach a lesson. Animals usually do the talking in *fables*. The story of 'The Fox and the Grapes' is a *fable*.

fabric fab'-ric *fabrics*. Cloth. – Blankets are often made of a woollen *fabric*.–Some towels are made of a cotton *fabric*, and some of a linen *fabric*.

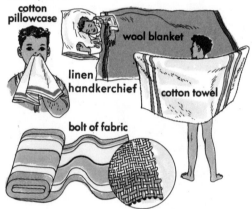

cotton pillowcase

wool blanket

linen handkerchief

cotton towel

bolt of fabric

face *faces, faced, facing*. 1. The front side of your head. Your chin, cheeks, nose, mouth, eyes, and forehead form your *face*.
2. The front, or the most important side, of anything.–The *face* of a watch is the side which shows the time. –The *face* of a building is the front of the building.
3. Expression of the *face*.–The clowns made funny *faces* at the children.
4. Look towards.–The house *faces* the north. The front of the house is towards the north. –The teacher asked the children to *face* the front of the room.

fact *facts*. A thing that is true.–The man told all the *facts* of the accident. He told exactly just how each thing happened.–It is a *fact* that Christmas comes on December 25.

factory fac'-to-ry *factories*. A building where things are made, usually by machines.–Motor-cars are made in *factories*.

fade *fades, faded, fading*. 1. Become less bright, less strong, grow fainter. – Sunlight often makes bright colours *fade*. – As they drove away, the dog's cries *faded*.
2. Wither and die.–Flowers *fade*.

fail *fails, failed, failing*. 1. Not succeed.–Unless you study hard, you are likely to *fail*.
2. Leave, not support or help.–The brave man's courage *failed* him when he met the tiger.
3. Get weak, grow worse. – The sick man seemed to be *failing*, and then he suddenly improved.
4. Disappoint.–The paper-boy *failed* us. He did not bring the newspaper.

failure fail'-ure *failures*. 1. An event, a happening, or an effort that is not a success.–The party was a *failure* because nobody came.– After one *failure* to solve the problem, Bob tried again.
2. A person who does not succeed in life.– The old tramp was a *failure*.

faint *faints, fainted, fainting*. 1. Fall suddenly into unconsciousness because of sickness, shock, or other disturbance to the body.– Hunger caused the old man to *faint*.
2. As if about to *faint*.–The heavy air in the bedroom made me feel *faint*.
3. Weak; not clear or strong in sound, looks, taste, etc.–The knock on the door was *faint*. –The writing on the board was *faint*.

fair *fairs, fairer, fairest, fairness.* 1. Honest.–
The boy is always *fair* in playing games. He
does not cheat.

2. Light.–Some people have *fair* skin and
hair, and some have dark.

3. Not very bad and not very good, but just
in between.–Bob got a good mark in arithmetic, but his mark in spelling was just *fair*.

4. Clear, sunny.–This is a *fair* day. The sky
is clear.

5. Beautiful.–Cinderella was far *fairer* than
her step-sisters.

6. A festive gathering, usually at a regular
time and place during the summer, at which
people enjoy themselves on merry-go-rounds
and swings, and at sideshows such as coconut
shies and shooting galleries. These *fairs* are
often run by gypsies.

7. At a trade *fair,* buyers and sellers of
particular goods gather to do trade.

fairly *fair'-ly.* 1. Quite.–Bob gets *fairly* good
marks in history. They are not too good and
not too bad.

2. According to the proper rules; honestly.–
The children play *fairly*.

fairy *fair'-y fairies.* A small, pretty, imaginary
man or woman who, in stories, uses magic to
bring happiness or unhappiness to people.
Fairies are not real people.

faith *faiths.* 1. Trust, belief, confidence.–John
has *faith* in his new friend. He believes in
him.

2. A religion or belief.–People of many *faiths*
live in Great Britain.

faithful *faith'-ful faithfulness, faithfully.* 1.
Loyal.–The man is Father's *faithful* friend.
He can be trusted.

2. Honest.–The witness was *faithful* in describing everything he had seen.

falcon *fal'-con falcons.* A kind of hawk which
can be trained to hunt
other birds.

fall *falls, fell, falling,
fallen.* 1. Drop, sink,
come down. – Apples
fall from the trees
when they are ripe.

2. Become less, go
down. – The number
of people who are hurt in accidents is *falling*.
–The temperature has *fallen* since morning.

3. Go down suddenly, so that the body is on
the ground.–The man *fell* over the hose.

4. Come or arrive.–Easter Day always *falls*
on Sunday.

5. *Fall asleep* means go to sleep.

6. Be captured.–The city *fell* to the enemy.

7. A coming down, a sinking, a drop.–The
fall of the picture startled us all.–Some people's feet have *fallen* arches. They are flat;
the whole bottom of the foot touches the
ground.

8. In the United States, another word for
autumn.–We pick apples in the *fall*.

9. A place where water *falls* over rocks from
a higher place to a lower place.–We paddled
slowly up the river towards the *falls*.

false *falsely.* 1. Not true.–It is *false* to say that
snow is green.

2. Not loyal.–A friend who is *false* is one
who is likely to fail you.

3. Make-believe; not real.–The doll's wig is
made of *false* hair.

falsehood *false'-hood falsehoods.* A lie; something that is false or not true.

fame. Wide reputation; state of being widely
known and respected.–Captain Cook had
great *fame*.

familiar *fa-mil'-iar familiarly.* 1. Well known.
–The song 'Annie Laurie' is *familiar* to
everyone in Scotland.

2. Acquainted.–Bob is *familiar* with many
books. He knows all about them.

3. Bold; forward.–Some people are far too
familiar with strangers.

F G H I J K L M N O P Q R S T U V W X Y Z

family fam'-i-ly *families*. 1. A father, a mother, and their children.
2. Children of a father and mother.–The children are called Father's and Mother's *family*.
3. A group of people related to each other.–Your whole *family* is all of your relatives: father, mother, aunts, uncles, cousins, grandparents, sisters, brothers, etc.
4. The people who live together in one house.
5. A group of plants or animals that are related.–The cat and the tiger both belong to the cat *family*.

famine fam'-ine *famines*. 1. A great shortage of food.–When there is a *famine*, people sometimes starve to death.
2. A shortage.–We had a petrol *famine*. We could not get enough petrol.

famous fa'-mous *famously*. Well known and respected.–Benjamin Disraeli was a very *famous* man.

fan *fans, fanned, fanning*. 1. Anything used to stir up the air.–In hot weather we keep the electric *fan* on all day.
2. Stir up the air, or blow air on, with a *fan*. –Mother *fanned* Baby to keep him cool.
3. A person who is fond of some public entertainment.–Bob is a football *fan*. He is much interested in football. –Film-stars have many *fans* who admire them and from whom they receive *fan*-mail.

fancy fan'-cy *fancies, fancied, fancying*. 1. Imagine; picture to yourself. – Just *fancy* Grandmother skating on roller skates.
2. Like.–I *fancy* having my hair short.
3. Ornate, not plain.–I wear a plain dress for school and a *fancy* one on Sunday.
4. Something imagined. – A round-the-world cruise is just an idle *fancy*.

far *farther, farthest*. 1. A long distance away.–It is not *far* to school from my house.
2. More distant.–We hung the picture on the *far* side of the room.
3. Very much.–It is *far* better to be safe than to be sorry.

fare *fares*. 1. Money charged for riding.–We paid our *fare* to the conductor when we got on the bus.
2. A paying passenger.–The taxi driver had several *fares* this morning.

farewell fare-well' *farewells*. 1. Good-bye.–The soldier said *farewell* to his mother.
2. The act of going away.–Bob did not look forward to his *farewell* to the school.

farm *farms, farmed, farming*. 1. A piece of land where plants and animals are grown for food. –Grandfather grows grain and keeps cattle on his *farm*.
2. Grow crops and keep animals on a *farm*. – Grandfather likes to *farm*.

farmer farm'-er *farmers*. A person who lives on a farm and makes his living from it.

farmhouse farm'-house *farmhouses*. A house in which people live on a farm.

farmyard farm'-yard *farmyards*. The yard or space around the barns and other farm buildings on a farm.

far-off *far -off*. At a great distance.–China is a *far-off* country.

farther far'-ther. One form of the word *far*.– Bob walked 4 miles and Bill walked 7 miles. Bill walked *farther* than Bob.

farthest far'-thest. One form of the word *far*.– Bob walked 4 miles, Bill walked 7, and Jack walked 8. Jack walked the *farthest*.

fascinate fas'-ci-nate *fascinates, fascinated, fascinating, fascination*. Hold the attention of.–The beautiful music *fascinates* Mother. It greatly interests her and completely holds her attention.

fashion fash'-ion *fashions, fashioned, fashioning*. 1. Shape; form; make.–Mary tried to *fashion* a bowl from clay.
2. A style.–It is the *fashion* to wear long hair.

fashionable fash'-ion-a-ble *fashionably*. In style; in fashion.–It is *fashionable* to wear the hair in curls.

fast *fasts, fasted, fasting, faster, fastest*. 1. Quickly; swiftly; at high speed. – The car goes *fast*.
2. Ahead.–Our clock was 10 minutes *fast*. It showed 10 minutes later than the correct time.
3. Quick.–We made a *fast* trip to the coast.
4. Firmly set.–If the colours in your dress are *fast*, they will not run when washed.
5. Firmly; tightly.–The climber held *fast* to the rope and was pulled to safely.
6. Deeply; completely.–Little Boy Blue was under the haycock *fast* asleep.
7. Go without food.–The man *fasted* for a week.
8. A period of time passed without food.– The man's *fast* was a week long.

FARM

F
G
H
I
J
K
L
M
N
O
P
Q
R
S
T
U
V
W
X
Y
Z

fasten fas'-ten *fastens, fastened, fastening, fastener*. 1. Lock or latch; make tight.–I will *fasten* the door.
2. Tie.–I will *fasten* your shoes.
3. Attach. – I will *fasten* a label to the package.

fat *fatter, fattest*. 1. Having much flesh on the body.–Some children are thin; others are *fat*.
2. An oily substance, especially in meat.– The *fat* in meat looks white. In chickens it is yellow.–Milk has *fat* in it; when separated from the rest of the milk, this *fat* is butter.
3. Full.–The rich man had a *fat* wallet.

fatal fa'-tal *fatally*. 1. Causing death.–The accident was not *fatal* to the dog. It did not kill him.
2. Causing ruin.–The frost was *fatal* to the fruit. It ruined it.

father fa'-ther *fathers, fathered, fathering*. 1. The man parent.–Your mother and *father* are your parents.
2. God is called *Father*.
3. A priest in a church is called *Father*.
4. Care for as a *father*.–Uncle James has *fathered* the boys for many years.

Father Christmas Fa'-ther Christ'-mas. The bringer of gifts to children at Christmas, also known as Santa Claus and Saint Nicholas.– *Father Christmas* has a white beard and a red cloak trimmed with fur.

father-in-law fa'-ther-in-law *fathers-in-law*. The father of one's wife or husband.–When a man marries, his wife's father becomes his *father-in-law*. When a woman marries, her husband's father becomes her *father-in-law*.

fault *faults, faulty, faultless*. 1. Something wrong.–Bob's greatest *fault* is talking too much.
2. *At fault* means to blame.–The man driving the small car was *at fault* in the accident.
3. A mistake.–It was Jack's *fault* that the bicycle was left out in the rain.

favour fa'-vour *favours, favoured, favouring*. 1. Oblige, show kindness to.–Will you *favour* us with your company?–The teacher *favoured* us with a story.
2. Approve, prefer. – The children *favoured* having the party after school.
3. Show extra kindness and attention to.– Mary thought Grandfather *favoured* Bob. She thought he paid more attention to Bob than to her.

4. A ribbon or rosette.–The election candidates wore *favours* in their buttonholes.
5. A kindness, a kind act.–Our neighbours do us many *favours*.
6. Liking; pleasure.–The king looked upon the soldiers with *favour*.

favourable fa'-vour-a-ble *favourably*. Agreeable; desirable; good.–If the weather turns out to be *favourable*, we will go to the park tomorrow.–When Bob asked Father for extra money, Father's answer was not *favourable*. He said no.

favourite fa'-vour-ite *favourites*. 1. Best liked.– Blue is a *favourite* colour of many people.
2. The one best liked.–Bob is the *favourite* of his father.

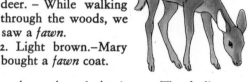

fawn *fawns*. 1. A young deer. – While walking through the woods, we saw a *fawn*.
2. Light brown.–Mary bought a *fawn* coat.

fear *fears, feared, fearing*. 1. The feeling you have when you are scared or afraid.
2. Be frightened of.–Girls *fear* mice.

fearful fear'-ful *fearfully*. 1. Dreadful; frightening. – A *fearful* animal came out of the woods.
2. Afraid; frightened.–I am *fearful* of windstorms.

fearless fear'less *fearlessly*. Not afraid of anything.–The soldiers were *fearless*.

feast *feasts, feasted, feasting*. 1. A rich meal; a big dinner.–On Christmas Day we have a *feast*.

2. *Feast on* means to get pleasure or delight from seeing, hearing, doing, or eating something.–Mary *feasted on* the music at the concert.–We *feast on* turkey at Christmas.
3. Eat a lot; eat a big or elaborate meal.–The men *feasted*.

feat *feats*. A great thing to do; a deed or act which takes skill or courage. – Swimming across the swift stream is a difficult *feat*.

feather feath'-er *feathers*. One of the light parts of the covering of a bird. *Feathers* are soft and light. They are used in pillows.

feathery feath'-er-y. Light and fluffy like feathers.–Thistledown is *feathery*.

feature fea'-ture *features, featured, featuring*.
1. Any one part of your face, such as your chin, your nose, etc.
2. A point or quality.–The teacher said there were many good *features* in Bob's drawings.
3. A part.–The main *features* of the programme were a play and a song.
4. Present as most important.–The shop is *featuring* raincoats in its sale today.

February Feb'-ru-a-ry. The 2nd month of the year.–Saint Valentine's Day is on *February* 14th.

fed. One form of the word *feed*.–The mother robin *fed* the baby robins with worms.

federal fed'-er-al. National; concerning a union of states.–The states of the United States are united under one government called the *Federal* Government.

fee *fees*. Money paid for something done for you, or for the right to do something.–Doctors, lawyers, dentists, etc., charge a *fee* for their work.–The library charges a *fee* of 2p a week for the use of a book.

feeble fee'-ble *feebler, feeblest, feebly*. Weak –The old woman is too *feeble* to walk far.

feed *feeds, fed, feeding*. 1. Give food to.– Mother will *feed* the baby his breakfast. She will place the food in his mouth.
2. Supply.–The car would not start because the petrol *feed* was blocked.
3. Food for farm animals. – Grandfather bought a bag of chicken *feed*.

feel *feels, felt, feeling*. 1. Notice by touching, handling, or being touched. – When you touch things, they may *feel* soft or hard, smooth or rough, warm or cold.
2. Have a condition of mind.–We *feel* happy, sad, angry, afraid, etc.
3. Believe.–Bob *feels* that his team will win.
4. Hunt by touching.–Mary *felt* in her desk to find her pencil.

feeler feel'-er *feelers*. One of a pair of long, stiff, hair-like arms that an insect uses to feel with. – A rabbit has *feelers* too. They are his whiskers.

feeling feel'-ing *feelings*. 1. A sensation.–When the ball hit me on the head, I had a dizzy *feeling*.
2. An emotion or sense of pleasure, anger, etc. –The child had a *feeling* of happiness when he got home.
3. The boys hurt the girl's *feelings* when they told her she was ugly.

feet. More than one foot. – A centipede has many *feet*.–Three *feet* make 1 yard or 36 inches.

fell. One form of the word *fall*.–Jack *fell* down. His body went to the ground.

fellow fel'-low *fellows*. 1. A word often used for a man or boy, or sometimes an animal.– Four of the *fellows* came to see Jack when he was ill.–One of the fish Bob caught was really a big *fellow*.
2. Belonging to the same group. – A *fellow* student came home with Dick.

felt. 1. One form of the word *feel*.–We *felt* the sand blowing in our faces.
2. A kind of stiff, smooth cloth made of pressed wool, hair, and fur.–Father wears a *felt* hat.

female fe'-male *females*. A woman, girl, or she animal.–Men and boys are males; women and girls are *females*.–Hens and cows are *female* animals.

feminine fem'-i-nine. Belonging to or relating to women.–High-heeled shoes and dresses are *feminine* belongings. They are worn by women.

fence *fences, fenced, fencing*. 1. A wall or barrier put up to keep things apart, or to keep people or animals in or out. *Fences* are usually made of wooden rails or of wire.

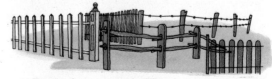

2. Put a *fence* round.–The farmer *fenced* in his pasture to keep his cattle from getting out.

F
G H I J K L M N O P Q R S T U V W X Y Z

F
G
H
I
J
K
L
M
N
O
P
Q
R
S
T
U
V
W
X
Y
Z

fender fend'-er *fenders*. A metal guard set in front of the fireplace.–When we went out we put the *fender* in place to prevent coal falling on to the carpet.

fennel fen'-nel. A tall, fragrant, yellow-flowered herb, used in sauces.–Mother grows *fennel* in the kitchen garden.

fern *ferns*. A kind of leafy plant that does not have flowers. Some *ferns* grow best in shady places.

ferry fer'-ry *ferries, ferried, ferrying*. 1. A boat that carries people and vehicles across a lake or river.

2. Carry on a *ferry* or other boat. – Father *ferried* the family to the island in a punt.

fertile fer'-tile. 1. Rich; productive.–The land on Grandfather's farm is very *fertile*. It produces good crops.
2. Able to produce.–A *fertile* seed is one that is able to grow into a plant that will bear fruits, seeds, etc.

fertilize fer'-ti-lize *fertilizes, fertilized, fertilizing*. Make (soil) richer by adding something to it.–If the land is not rich enough to make things grow, it must be *fertilized*.

fertilizer fer'-ti-liz-er *fertilizers*. Anything put on the ground to make it rich so that crops will grow.–Manure is a *fertilizer*.

festival fes'-ti-val *festivals*. A time for merry-making, celebrating, and feasting. – Christmas is a *festival*. It is the time for celebrating the birth of Christ.

fetch *fetches, fetched, fetching*. Get and bring back.–Jack and Jill went up the hill to *fetch* a pail of water.

fever fe'-ver *fevers*. 1. Unusual warmth or high temperature of the body caused by illness. Normal body temperature is about 98.4°. A body temperature higher than that is called a *fever*.
2. An excited condition.–The children were in a *fever* over the circus.

feverish fe'-ver-ish *feverishly*. 1. Having a fever; running a high temperature.–Baby is *feverish*. She has a fever.
2. Nervously excited.–The cattle were *feverish* during the storm.

few *fewer, fewest*. Not many; a small number. We ate only a *few* nuts. We didn't eat many.

fibre fi'-bre *fibres*. A thread-like or hair-like part of wool, cotton, or similar material.– Several *fibres* are twisted or spun into yarn or thread.

fiction fic'-tion. A writing about imaginary happenings; a story or stories.–Mary likes to read *fiction*.

fiddle fid'-dle *fiddles, fiddled, fiddling*. 1. A violin. – Father plays the *fiddle* in the orchestra.
2. Play on the violin.– Father *fiddles* while the children dance.

fiddler fid'-dler, *fiddlers*. A violinist; one who plays the fiddle or violin.

fidget fidg'-et *fidgets, fidgeted, fidgeting*. Squirm and move nervously. – The teacher told the children not to *fidget* so much.

fidgety fidg'-et-y. Restless; nervous. – When Bob has to stay in the house, he becomes *fidgety*.

field *fields*. 1. A piece of open land.–This is a grassy field where cows feed.–The farmer plants grain in large *fields*.
2. A special piece of ground marked off for a game.–The football team ran out on to the field.

fierce *fiercely*. Savage; wild; untamed; cruel. –Tigers are *fierce*. – The man had a *fierce* temper.

fife *fifes.* A small, flute-like musical instrument that makes a shrill, whistling sound. – We listened to the *fife* and drums.

fifteen fif-teen' *fifteens.* The number (15) coming after 14 and before 16. – Ten and five make *fifteen.*

fifteenth fif-teenth' *fifteenths.* 1. One of 15 equal parts.–If you divide anything into 15 parts all the same size, each part is one *fifteenth.* It may be written 1/15.
2. Coming as number 15 in a series. – My name was *fifteenth* on the list.

fifth *fifths.* 1. One of 5 equal parts.–If you divide anything into 5 parts, all the same size, each part is one *fifth.* It may be written 1/5.
2. Coming as number 5 in a series.–May is the *fifth* month of the year.

fiftieth fif'-ti-eth *fiftieths.* 1. One of 50 equal parts.–If you divide anything into 50 equal parts, each part is called one-*fiftieth.* It is also written 1/50.
2. Coming as number 50 in a series.–Today is Aunt Ellen's *fiftieth* birthday. She is fifty years old.

fifty fif'-ty *fifties.* The number (50) coming after 49 and before 51.–*Fifty* is 5 times 10.

fig *figs.* A small pear-shaped fruit that grows in some warm countries. It has many tiny, round seeds in it. – *Figs* may be eaten fresh or dried. They may also be stewed like prunes.

fight *fights, fought fighting.* 1. Try to win over someone or something by hurting or weakening him.–Dogs *fight* over bones.–Some children *fight* with one another.–Armies *fight* with guns, tanks, aeroplanes, bombs, and other weapons.
2. A struggle against someone or something. –Give money to help the *fight* against disease.

fighter fight'-er *fighters.* Someone or something which fights or is used in fighting. – Two *fighters* will have a boxing contest to see who is the champion.–A *fighter* plane is a small, fast aeroplane built for attacking bombers and other planes.

figure fig'-ure *figures, figured, figuring.* 1. A sign that stands for a number.–1, 2, 3, 4, 5, 6, 7, 8, 9, 0 are *figures.*
2. Find out something by working with numbers.–Bob tried to *figure* out the cost of his new ball, bat, and gloves. He wrote down how much each cost, and added the numbers.
3. *Figure out* means understand. – Bob couldn't *figure* out how he was going to pay for the things he wanted with the money he had.
4. A shape or form.–A circle, a square, and a triangle are *figures.*–We saw the *figure* of a black cat sitting on the back fence. – The *figures* on my dress are small moons and stars.
5. Mark with a design.–The cloth is *figured* with small leaves.
6. A person or character.–The clown is an important *figure* in the circus.
7. Play a part; enter into; be included.–Getting Mary on his side *figured* largely in Jack's plans for winning the game.

filbert fil'-bert *filberts.* A nut that belongs to the hazelnut family. –*Filberts* are good to eat.

file *files, filed, filing.* 1. A cabinet or a system for keeping papers in a certain order so that they can be found easily.–The clerk put the letters in the *file.*

2. Put in a *file.*–Mother *files* her bills according to the date.
3. A line or row.–Our teacher told us to walk in single *file.*
4. Walk in line.–The children *filed* out of the school building during the fire drill. They marched out in a row, one behind the other.
5. A long piece of steel with ridges across it.– Mother smoothed off her broken finger-nail with a *file.*
6. Make smooth or smaller by rubbing with a *file.*–Mother *files* her finger-nails before she polishes them.

fill *fills, filled, filling.* 1. Put as much into something as it will hold. – Mother will *fill* the jug with milk.
2. Take up all the room or time.–Smoke *filled* the air.–Tears *filled* Baby's eyes.–The doctor said his time was *filled* with appointments.
3. Give what is called for; serve.–The grocer will *fill* your order. He will get all the things you want for you.
4. Take or occupy.–Jack went to see about a job as paper-boy, but it had been *filled*.
5. Become full.–The boat had a hole in it, and it soon *filled* with water.
6. All that can be held or desired.–For once Bob had his *fill* of ice cream.

filling fill'-ing *fillings.* Material used to fill a space.–The dentist put a *filling* in the hole in my tooth.–Mother put lemon *filling* between the layers of the cake.

film *films, filmed, filming.* 1. A thin coating or layer.–It was cold enough last night to form a *film* of ice on the water.
2. A material which is sensitive to light and is used for taking photographs.–We have a roll of *film* for our camera.
3. A motion picture.–We saw a *film* last night.
4. Make (a moving picture).–It takes a long time to *film* a motion picture.

filthy filth'-y *filthier, filthiest.* Very dirty.–The man had not washed his hands for a long time, and they were *filthy*.

fin *fins.* One of the little flaps which a fish moves in swimming. Birds have wings to help them move about. Fish have *fins* to help them paddle and steer through the water.

final fi'-nal. Last, closing.–This is the *final* game of the championship.–The teacher said a few *final* words and then told us to go home.

finally fi'-nal-ly. At last. – *Finally* I have my work done.

finance fi'-nance *finances, financed, financing.* Pay for.–I can go to the show if Mother will *finance* me. I can go if she will give me the money for it.–Father will *finance* Bob's college education. He will pay for it.

financial fi-nan'-cial *financially.* Relating to money.–Edward reads the *financial* section of the newspaper, the part which tells about money matters.

finch *finches.* A kind of small song-bird. – A bull *finch* can do much damage in a garden.

find *finds, found, finding.* 1. Come upon; discover where a thing is.–Did you ever *find* a 4-leaf clover?–Mary lost her ring in the grass and it took a long time to *find* it.
2. See; discover; learn.–I *find* that you have been absent twice, according to the records. –Did you *find* anything of interest in that book?
3. Reach a decision.–After studying the case, the judge *found* the accused man innocent.
4. Something *found*.–The Roman coins dug up in the field were an important *find*.

fine *fines, fined, fining, finer, finest.* 1. Money paid as a punishment.–The policeman gave the man a summons for driving too fast. The man had to pay a *fine*.
2. Make (someone) pay money as a punishment.–The judge *fined* the man £5.
3. Beautiful, good, excellent.–Mother has a *fine* new dress.–Mary is a *fine* musician.
4. Not coarse.–Sugar is *fine*, but salt is *finer*. Salt is in smaller grains.
5. Narrow.–My fountain pen has a *fine* point. It makes a thin line.
6. Clear and sunny.–If the day is *fine*, we shall go sailing tomorrow.

finger fin'-ger *fingers, fingered, fingering.* 1. We have *fingers* on each hand. The thumb is shorter and thicker than the other *fingers*. We pick things up, turn pages, tie knots, point things out, write, and do many other things with the *fingers*.
2. Touch or handle lightly.–The grocer does not like you to *finger* the fruit.
3. Anything that is like a *finger* on the hand. –Mary couldn't get her *fingers* into the *fingers* of her glove.

finish fin'-ish *finishes, finished, finishing.* 1. Complete; become complete; come to the end of. –Mother expects to *finish* reading the book today.–The story running in the newspaper *finished* today.
2. An end. – One horse dropped out of the race before the *finish*.
3. A surface.–Father sanded the rough board so that it had a smooth, even *finish*.
4. Give a certain kind of surface to.–Bob made a letter box and *finished* it with varnish.

fir *firs.* A tree belonging to the pine tree family. *Firs* have cones on them.

fire *fires, fired, firing.* 1. Something burning.– The Boy Scouts made a *fire.* They touched a burning match to the paper to make it burn. –I smell *fire.*–We saw the *fire*-engine at the big *fire* in the main street.

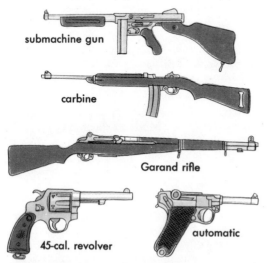

2. Shoot. – The soldiers *fired* at the enemy. They aimed and discharged their guns.
3. Made to go from a job.–The man who did poor work was *fired.*

fire-arms *fire'-arms.* Guns, revolvers, and the like.–Soldiers use *fire-arms* and other weapons to destroy the enemy.

submachine gun

carbine

Garand rifle

45-cal. revolver

automatic

fire-engine *fire'-en-gine fire-engines.* A vehicle used to carry firemen to a fire. It is equipped with ladders and hoses through which water is pumped with great force.–When the alarm rang, the *fire-engine* rushed to the fire.

fire escape *fire es-cape' fire escapes.* An outside stairway or ladder used for escape when there is a fire in the building.–The men left the burning building by the *fire escape.*

fire-fly *fire'-fly fire-flies.* A small insect whose body has a flashing yellowish light.–We sat on the terrace late in the evening and watched the *fire-flies* flitting about in the garden.

fire-irons *fire'-i-rons.* The implements used for tending the fire.–The poker, the shovel and the tongs are all *fire-irons,* and we keep them on the hearth.

firelight *fire'-light.* Light given off by a fire.– The Boy Scouts sat in the *firelight* and told stories.

fireman *fire'-man firemen.* 1. A man whose duty it is to put out fires.–The *firemen* arrived on their engine at the burning bank.
2. A man on a railway engine who takes care of the fire; a man whose job it is to take care of any fire.

fireplace *fire'-place fireplaces.* An open place built of stone or brick for a fire. – The children hung their stockings in front of the *fireplace.* – We keep the fire-irons beside the *fireplace.*

fireproof *fire'-proof fireproofs, fireproofed, fireproofing.* 1. Made so as not to catch fire, or not to catch fire easily.–Many buildings built today are *fireproof.*
2. Make *fireproof.*–Our house is *fireproofed.* It will not burn easily.

fireside *fire'-side firesides.* The part of the room round the fireplace.–On winter evenings we all like to gather round the *fireside* to read.

F
G
H
I
J
K
L
M
N
O
P
Q
R
S
T
U
V
W
X
Y
Z

fireworks fire'-works. Rockets, squibs and other things that make coloured lights and loud noises when they explode.–On Guy Fawkes night we went to see the *fireworks*.

firm *firms, firmly, firmer, firmest*. 1. Solid, not shaking or moving.–Father set the flag-pole in cement to make it stand *firm*.
2. Solid, not liquid.–Mother put the jelly in the refrigerator to make it *firm*.
3. Strong, steady, not changing back and forth; decided.–Father spoke in a *firm* voice when he said no.–Jack *firmly* believes that Spot is the smartest and most beautiful dog in the world.
4. A business company.–There is a new *firm* opening up for business in that building.

first. 1. Coming as number 1; before or in front of others.–The *first* day of the week is Sunday. It comes before all the rest.–The *first* person in the row collects the pencils. The person who sits in the seat ahead of all the others in the row collects the pencils.
2. *At first* means in the beginning.–*At first* Father had only a few men working for him; now he has many.
3. Before doing something else; rather.–'I'd die *first*,' Mary said when I asked her not to tell my secret to anyone.

fish *fishes, fished, fishing*. 1. A cold-blooded animal that lives in water and gets oxygen from the water it passes through its gills. Some *fish* are covered with scales. Some *fish* are good to eat.
2. Try to catch *fish*.–I like to *fish*.

fisherman fish'-er-man *fishermen*. A man who catches fish for a living; or, sometimes, a man who fishes just for fun.

fish-hook fish'-hook *fish-hooks*. A hook used to catch fish. Notice the little barb on the hook. The fish gets caught on it and cannot get away.

fist *fists*. The hand closed tightly into a ball. You make a *fist* by bending your fingers inward as hard as they will go.

fit *fits, fitted, fitting*. 1. Right, proper, suitable. –This book is not *fit* for this class. The stories are for smaller children.–Mary says her coat is not *fit* to be seen in the street.
2. Be the right size for.–Jack's shoes were too small. They did not *fit*.
3. Arrange or make in a particular way.–Bob tried to *fit* the parts of the puzzle together. He tried to make them go together right.
4. A kind of violent sickness that comes on very suddenly. Dogs sometimes have *fits*.
5. A short spell.–The baby had a *fit* of crying in the middle of the night.

five. The number (5) between 4 and 6.–I wear size *five* shoes.–You have *five* toes on each foot.

fix *fixes, fixed, fixing*. 1. Set firmly.–Father *fixed* the flag-pole in cement.–Mary wrote the history dates down to *fix* them in her mind.
2. Set. decide upon. – I will buy your dog when you *fix* a price for him.
3. Direct towards.–Bob's attention was *fixed* on the aeroplane.
4. Keep from changing–When Mother dyed the old curtains, she put vinegar in the dye to *fix* it, so that it would not fade.
5. Trouble, or a difficult position.
    'Now the clock is striking six.
    I am in an awful *fix*.'
6. Arrange, or put something a certain way. –Mary *fixed* up Mother's birthday present with little white bows.
7. Make right again.–Father *fixed* the flat tyre. He mended it and put it into working order again.

fixture fix'-ture *fixtures*. Anything that is put in place to be left there for a long time.–A bath, a basin, a lavatory seat and towel-rail are bathroom *fixtures*. – Classroom *fixtures* are desks, blackboards, cupboards, etc.

fizz *fizzes, fizzed, fizzing*. Bubble up, make a hissing sound.–When we put soda-water into the orange squash, it made it *fizz*.

FISH

FRESH WATER FISH

brown trout

bream

pike

carp

barbel

catfish

gudgeon

chub

eel

salmon

perch

sturgeon

SALT WATER FISH

bluefin tuna

shark

barracuda

swordfish

codfish

flounder

mackerel

grey mullet

sea bass

tarpon

halibut

plaice

herring

marlin

haddock

pollack

flying fish

shark sucker

skate

F
G
H
I
J
K
L
M
N
O
P
Q
R
S
T
U
V
W
X
Y
Z

flag *flags, flagged, flagging.* 1. A square of cloth that has stripes, figures, or other designs to show which country, group, or other organization it is the symbol of. Some *flags* are used for signals. – The *flag* of Great Britain is sometimes called the Union Jack.–Boy Scouts wave *flags* to send messages.
2. To give a signal to by waving a *flag.*–The watchman *flagged* down the train. He waved a *flag* to signal it to stop.

flake *flakes, flaked, flaking.* 1. A very small, thin piece of anything. – Each little piece of snow is a *flake.*–Soap shavings are *flakes.*
2. Break off in thin, flat pieces.–The bark on the tree *flaked* off.

flame *flames, flamed, flaming.* 1. A blaze; the coloured part of fire.–We smelt smoke, but we could not tell where the fire was until we saw the *flame* rise above the roof.–When you light the gas on the stove, it makes a *flame.*
2. Make *flames* or grow bright like *flame.*–Colour *flamed* in the boy's face at the praise.

flamingo fla-min'-go *flamingos* or *flamingoes.* A large water bird with a very long neck and legs. Its feathers are pinkish, and its flat bill hooks downwards.

flank *flanks, flanked, flanking.* 1. The side of the body between the ribs and the hip-bone. –He patted the horse on the *flank.*
2. Be on either side.– The general was *flanked* by members of his staff.

flannel flan'-nel *flannels.* A soft woollen cloth. –Father wears a grey *flannel* suit.

flap *flaps, flapped, flapping.* 1. Wave up and down.–Birds *flap* their wings when they fly. –The clothes hanging on the clothes-line *flap* in the wind.
2. A part that folds over. – The *flap* on Bob's pocket buttons to the pocket.–To seal an envelope, moisten the *flap* and press it down.

flash *flashes, flashed, flashing.* 1. A light that comes on suddenly and lasts a very short time.–Lightning appears in *flashes.*
2. A short time.–We will be back in a *flash.* –The accident happened in just a *flash.*
3. Shine quickly. – The boys *flashed* light from the sun into the room with a mirror.– The taxi driver *flashed* his torch on the house numbers.
4. Dart, dash.–A cat *flashed* across the road.
5. A quick, sudden feeling.–Jack recognized his lost dog with a *flash* of joy.

flashlight flash'-light *flashlights.* 1. A small electric light that has a battery in it to make it light up.–Bob carries a *flashlight* when camping out overnight.

2. A light used to take pictures indoors or at night.–The newspaper reporters used *flashlights* to take pictures of the wedding.

flask *flasks.* A bottle that has a small neck or opening. – Soldiers carry water in a *flask*, or canteen.

flat *flats, flatter, flattest, flatly.* 1. Level, even. –The land is *flat.*
2. Spread out.–It spoils a new book to open it out, face down, *flat* on the table.
3. Low.–Pansies look better in a *flat* bowl than they do in a high vase.
4. In music, a little lower than or below the true tone.–One violin sounds *flat.*
5. E *flat* in music is a semitone lower than E. *Flats* in music are shown by the sign ♭.
6. An apartment.–We live in the lower *flat*, or the rooms on the lower floor of the house.
7. Lemonade that has lost its fizz is *flat.*

flatten flat'-ten *flattens, flattened, flattening.* To *flatten* means to make flat.–Ironing *flattens* the clothes.–The wind *flattened* the corn in the field.

flatter flat'-ter *flatters, flattered, flattering.* 1. Praise more than is deserved.–Sometimes Grandfather *flatters* me.
2. Make to seem nicer than is really the case. –This picture doesn't *flatter* Mary. It doesn't make her look prettier than she really is.

flavour fla'-vour *flavours, flavoured, flavouring.* 1. Taste.–I like the *flavour* of this cake.
2. Season, add something to give a certain taste.–Grandmother *flavoured* the icing with lemon.

FLAGS

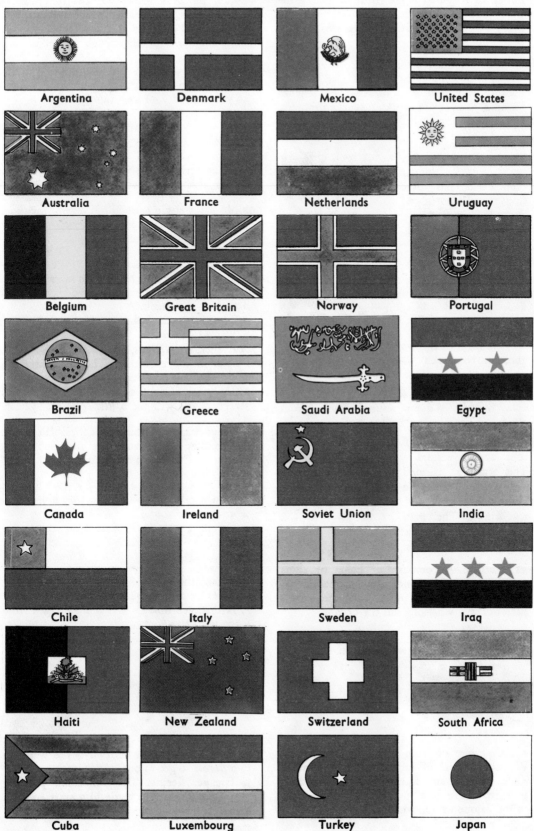

Argentina	Denmark	Mexico	United States
Australia	France	Netherlands	Uruguay
Belgium	Great Britain	Norway	Portugal
Brazil	Greece	Saudi Arabia	Egypt
Canada	Ireland	Soviet Union	India
Chile	Italy	Sweden	Iraq
Haiti	New Zealand	Switzerland	South Africa
Cuba	Luxembourg	Turkey	Japan

F
G
H
I
J
K
L
M
N
O
P
Q
R
S
T
U
V
W
X
Y
Z

flavouring fla'-vour-ing *flavourings.* Anything added to foods to make them taste like the thing added. – Onions, spices, vanilla, and many other strong-tasting foods are *flavourings.*

flaw *flaws.* A mar, error, fault, or something wrong. – Mother did not buy the pitcher, because it had a *flaw* in it. – The teacher found a *flaw* in our working of the problem. She found a mistake.

flax *flaxen.* 1. The thread-like stems of the *flax* plant, a tall, slender plant that has blue flowers. – Linen thread is made from *flax.*
2. *Flaxen* means pale yellowish.–The girl has flaxen hair.

flea *fleas.* A small insect that jumps. *Fleas* suck the blood of some furry animals and of people.–Our dog has *fleas.*

fled. One form of the word *flee.*–The man *fled* through the open window. He got away quickly.

flee *flees, fled, fleeing.* Run away, escape, get away quickly.–We saw animals *fleeing* from the forest fire.

fleece *fleeces, fleeced, fleecing.* 1. The woolly coat of an animal. – The farmer clipped the *fleece* from the sheep's back.
2. Swindle.–The man was *fleeced* of his money by the gamblers.

fleet *fleets.* 1. A company of boats or ships moving together or under one commander.– We watched the *fleet* move down the river.– *Fleets* of many nations sail the oceans.

2. Any group or team of moving vehicles.– We saw a *fleet* of lorries on the highway. There were many lorries moving together.
3. Swift.–An animal or person who is *fleet* of foot is one who moves fast.

flesh. 1. The part of your body that covers the bones. *Flesh* is meat. We eat the *flesh* of cows, lambs, and certain other animals.
2. The parts of fruits and vegetables that you eat.–The *flesh* of the peach is yellow and juicy.
3. Kindred, a relative.–A person who is one of your own *flesh* is a person who is related to you, one of your own family.

fleshy flesh'-y. Plump. – Father is growing *fleshy.*

flew. One form of the word *fly.*–The bird *flew* to her nest with a worm for her babies.

flexible flex'-i-ble. Bending easily without breaking.–The wire was so *flexible* that Bob could roll it into a ball.

flick *flicks, flicked, flicking.* 1. Strike lightly.– The rider *flicked* his horse with his whip.
2. A light blow.–The boxer gave his opponent a *flick* on the cheek.
3. Remove.–Jack *flicked* the insect off his coat.

flicker flick'-er *flickers, flickered, flickering.* 1. Flutter or move quickly.–The fire *flickered* a few times and then went out.
2. A quick, trembling movement.–The boy stared at me without a *flicker* of an eyelash.

flier fli'-er *fliers.* Anything that flies.–Birds and insects that have wings are *fliers.*–Aviators are *fliers.* They fly in aeroplanes.

flies. 1. One form of the word *fly.*–Bob flies his kite on windy days.–The bird *flies* home with worms for its young.
2. Small, 2-winged insects.–*Flies* carry diseases.

flight *flights.* 1. Movement through the air.– Bob shot the arrow but we could not see it in *flight* because it went too fast.
2. A distance flown.–It is a long *flight* from Canada to England.
3. A flock of birds.–A *flight* of geese just passed over our town.

4. A set of steps, or stairway.–We went up two *flights* to get to our classroom.
5. Escape, fleeing.–The policeman put the burglar to *flight.* He made him start running away.

flimsy flim'-sy *flimsier, flimsiest.* Soft, thin, and not very strong.–The cloth of Mary's dress is *flimsy.*–Tissue paper is *flimsy.* It tears easily.

flinch *flinches, flinched, flinching.* Draw back a little in fear of being hurt.–When the man started to hit the horse, it *flinched.*

fling *flings, fling, flinging.* 1. Throw or hurl from the hand.–Jack *flings* stones into the pond.
2. A Scottish dance.–Scottish people dance the Highland *fling.*
3. A time given up to complete enjoyment of oneself without any duties.–The boys are having their *fling* now during their holiday.

flint *flints.* A very hard stone also known as 'quartz.' – The Boy Scouts lit a fire with a spark made by rubbing *flint* against a piece of steel.

flip *flips, flipped, flipping.* 1. Toss.–The boys *flipped* a penny to see who would mow the lawn. Bob put a penny on his thumb and snapped it into the air.
2. A throw.–On the first *flip* the coin landed tails up.

flipper flip'-per *flippers.* A fin of fish or seal; also the foreleg of a turtle. *Flippers* are like paddles. They help water animals to swim.

flit *flits, flitted, flitting.* Dart, fly, move skimmingly.–Mary *flitted* across the hall in her long party dress.–A butterfly *flitted* through the window.

float *floats, floated, floating.* 1. Stay at the top of the water.–Some soaps *float.* They do not sink.–Uncle Bill can *float.*

2. Drift.–The toy balloon *floated* through the air.
3. Anything that stays on top of the water or other liquid, such as a raft. The fisherman uses a cork *float,* or bob, on his fishing-line to keep it from going into the water beyond where the *float* is fastened. The *float* goes up and down when a fish is biting.
4. A decorated platform which is drawn by a car, or a horse.–One society had several *floats* in the parade.

flock *flocks, flocked, flocking.* 1. A group.–We speak of a crowd of people, a herd of cattle, and a *flock* of sheep, chickens, other birds, etc.

2. Gather, come in groups.–A big crowd of people *flocked* to hear the speaker.

flog *flogs, flogged, flogging.* Whip, beat.–It is not kind to *flog* a horse.

flood *floods, flooded, flooding.* 1. Flow over, cover with water.–A river sometimes rises and flows over its banks. It *floods* the land on either side.–The long, heavy rains *flooded* the countryside.

2. Too much water.–We had a great *flood* after the heavy rain.
3. Fill to overflowing.–When Mary was ill, her room was *flooded* with flowers.
4. Anything that comes in great numbers or quantities, such as a *flood* of callers, a *flood* of sunlight, a *flood* of angry words, a *flood* of birthday greetings, *floods* of tears, etc.

floor *floors, floored, flooring.* 1. The ceiling is the top of the room; the *floor* is the bottom.–The table stands on the *floor.*–I dropped my hat on the *floor* of the car.
2. A storey or level of a building.–We live on the first *floor* of the house.
3. Make a *floor.* – We *floored* the garage with bricks.
4. Cause to fall to the *floor.* –One fighter *floored* the other.
5. Confound or nonplus.–Bob was *floored* by the question. He could not answer it.

flop *flops, flopped, flopping.* 1. Drop down.–Father was so tired after the race that he *flopped* on to the bed without undressing. He threw himself heavily on to the bed.
2. Toss heavily, or throw the body from side to side.–The fish *flopped* about in the net.

F G H I J K L M N O P Q R S T U V W X Y Z

Florida Flor'-i-da. A flat peninsular state on

the south-eastern coast of the United States, popular as a resort. Citrus fruits and vegetables are grown all the year round. *Florida* ships sugar, fruit, tobacco, timber, and fertilizer to other parts of the world.

florist flo'-rist *florists*. A person who sells and sometimes also grows flowers.–The *florist* on the corner understands all about flowers and how to take care of them.

floss. 1. A soft silk thread that is not twisted. –Mother is embroidering my woollen dress with a silk *floss*.
2. The silky threads on the ears of corn, the fluffy part of dandelion seeds, and other silky parts of plants.

flounder floun'-der *flounders, floundered, floundering*. 1. Flop about helplessly.–Jack *floundered* about in the water after he fell in.
2. Be awkward or helpless; hesitate.–When the teacher asked Bob a question, he *floundered*.
3. A *flounder* is a fish, about a foot long, used for food.

flour. A powdery substance made from a ground grain, such as wheat, rye, or barley. –Bread is made from *flour*.

flow *flows, flowed, flowing*. 1. Run; pour; go along as a liquid. – Water *flows* from the spring. Electricity *flows* along wires.
2. Move like a stream of water.–Many people are *flowing* into the grounds to see the circus.

3. Be loose or hanging.–Arabs wear *flowing* robes.
4. A stream.–There is a big *flow* of oil coming from the oil well.

flower flow'-er *flowers, flowered, flowering*.
1. The blossom of any plant.–*Flowers* are of many colours and shapes. The seeds of a plant are produced in the *flowers*.
2. Produce *flowers*.–The plant does not *flower* until late in the autumn.

flown. One form of the word *fly*.–The flier has *flown* many miles in his aeroplane.

fluff *fluffs, fluffed, fluffing*. 1. Make puffy and soft. – Grandmother *fluffs* up the pillows when she makes the bed. She shakes them so that they become fluffier.
2. Any soft, light substance.–Soft feathers, bits of cotton, wool, etc., are *fluff*.

fluffy fluff'-y *fluffier, fluffiest*. Soft and downy.– Baby's hair is *fluffy*.

fluid flu'-id *fluids*. 1. A liquid or gas.–Water and air are *fluids*.
2. Able to flow.–Water is *fluid*, but ice is not *fluid*. It will not flow.

flung. One form of the word *fling*.–Jack *flung* his coat into the cupboard.

flush *flushes, flushed, flushing*. 1. Flood; pour over.–Father *flushed* the steps with water to get the dust off.
2. Blush; turn red.–The girl's cheeks *flushed* when the teacher called on her to recite.
3. Even; level.–The milk is *flush* with the top of the glass.
4. Well provided.–Bob is *flush* with money today.

flute *flutes*. A musical instrument made of a tube closed at one end and with holes in the side. The holes are covered with the fingers and with keys to make the different notes of the scale. The sound is made by blowing across a hole in the side at the closed end.

flutter flut'-ter *flutters, fluttered, fluttering*.
1. Move rapidly back and forth.–The clothes *flutter on the clothes-line*.
2. Hurry excitedly. – Mary *fluttered* about, getting ready for school.
3. A state of excitement.–The crowd was in a *flutter*.

fly *flies, flew, flown, flying.* 1. Move through the air.–Birds and insects *fly* by moving their wings.–You can *fly* in an aeroplane.

2. Wave freely in the air.–The clothes on the clothes-line *fly* in the wind.–The flag is *flying* over the palace.

3. Move quickly.–When Mary saw her mother she *flew* into her arms.–Aunt Jane said she had to *fly* or she would miss her train.

4. A kind of insect with two wings. *Flies* spread diseases.

5. A fishing bait made to look like an insect.–The fisherman used a *fly* to catch the trout.

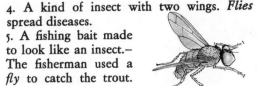

flyer fly'-er *flyers.* One way of spelling the word *flier,* meaning a person or thing that flies.

FLOWERS

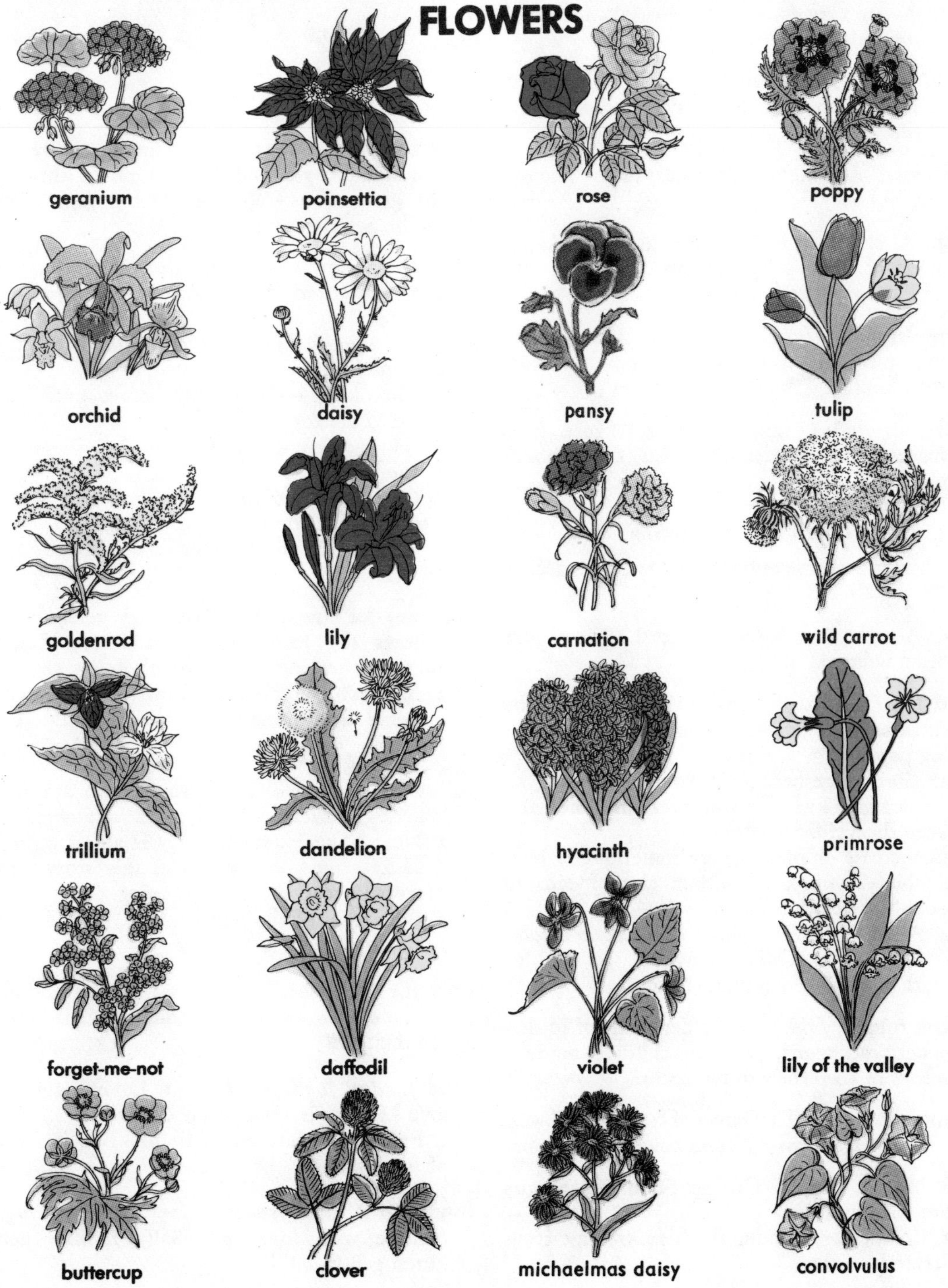

geranium

poinsettia

rose

poppy

orchid

daisy

pansy

tulip

goldenrod

lily

carnation

wild carrot

trillium

dandelion

hyacinth

primrose

forget-me-not

daffodil

violet

lily of the valley

buttercup

clover

michaelmas daisy

convolvulus

F
G
H
I
J
K
L
M
N
O
P
Q
R
S
T
U
V
W
X
Y
Z

foam *foams, foamed, foaming.* 1. A liquid filled with bubbles. – The whitish bubbles that bubble up when you open ginger ale, cider, beer, or some other drinks are *foam* on top of the liquid.
2. Make many tiny bubbles.–Many drinks *foam.*–The sea *foams* during storms.

foamy foam'-y *foamier, foamiest.* Filled with bubbles.–Hair shampoos are *foamy.* Bubble baths are very *foamy.*–Some drinks are much *foamier* than others.

fodder fod' der. Dried feed such as hay corn, etc., for farm animals.–Horses and cattle eat *fodder.*

foe *foes.* An enemy.–Bob has many friends, but no *foes.*

fog. A cloud lying near the ground. *Fog* is made of tiny drops of water floating in the air close together.

foggy fog'-gy *foggier, foggiest.* Heavy with fog; misty.–It is often *foggy* near lakes in the morning.

foil *foils, foiled, foiling.* 1. Upset; keep from success.–The policeman *foiled* the robber's plans. He kept the robber from carrying out his plans.
2. A light sword used for fencing.

3. A very thin sheet of metal.–Sweets are often wrapped in tin*foil.*

fold *folds,* folded, folding. 1. Bend so that the surfaces lie together.–Do not *fold* your spelling papers.
2. Clasp together.–*Fold* your arms and sit up straight. Put one arm over the other and keep them close together.
3. A crease or place where something is bent double.–To make a *fold* in cloth means to double the cloth back on itself.
4. A pen for sheep.–Sheep are kept in a *fold:*
5. Wrap round.–The traveller *folded* his scarf more tightly around his neck.

folder fold'-er *folders.* A holder made of folded paper, cardboard, etc.–The children made a *folder* to keep their drawings in.

foliage fo'-li-age. The leaves of trees and plants. –The *foliage* turns different colours in autumn.

folk *folks.* 1. People.–Our next-door neighbours are friendly *folks.*
2. Relations.–Grandmother's *folks* came from Ireland.

folk dance *folk dances.* 1. A dance made up by the common people and handed down through the generations.

2. The music for a *folk dance.*

folk song *folk songs.* A song made up by the common people and handed down through the generations.–We learned the *folk songs* of the Scottish people.

follow fol'-low *follows, followed, following.*
1. Come after, in order. – Page 10 *follows* page 9.
2. Go along behind.–Bob's dog *followed* him to school.
3. Go along. – *Follow* this street until you come to the corner.
4. Do according to.–*Follow* the directions at the top of the page.
5. Give attention to.–*Follow* me now while I tell you the story.
6. Be the result of. – Success *follows* hard work.

follower fol'-low-er *followers.* 1. A person who follows the leadership of another. – Little John was one of Robin Hood's *followers.*
2. A person who acts according to some teaching.–He is a *follower* of the Christian religion.

following fol'-low-ing. 1. People who are followers.–The leader has a large *following.*
2. Next.–The *following* story is about a dog.
3. Next after.–Bob will read this story and Mary will read the one *following.*
4. One form of the word *follow.*–The dog is *following* me.

folly fol'-ly *follies.* Foolishness; unwise action. –People who do unwise things usually pay for their *folly.*

fond *fonder, fondest, fondly.* 1. Loving; full of love.–Father is *fond* of his children.
2. Filled with interest or liking.–Bob is *fond* of football.

fondle fon'-dle *fondles, fondled, fondling.* Handle with love; pet.–Sally *fondles* her kitten gently.

FOOD

eggs
Poultry
Wheat
flour
cereal
bread
roast chicken
strawberry jam
steak
cocoa
Strawberries
Cocoa bean
Dairy Products
chocolate
cheese
Apple
cider
cow and milker
butter
cider press
apple pie
milk

grapefruit
rolls
biscuits
apple
milk
lettuce-and-ham sandwich
pudding
roll
milk
salad
coffee
lamb chop
baked potato
soup
bacon and eggs
Lunch
peas
Breakfast
Dinner

fondness fond'-ness. Liking; love.–Mary has a great *fondness* for music.

food *foods*. Something to eat.–Vegetables, meats, fruits, nuts, etc., are *foods*.–The restaurant served good *food*.

fool *fools, fooled, fooling*. 1. A person who is very unwise.–The man is a *fool*. He does things that are not sensible.

2. A clown; a person who amuses and entertains people by acting funnily.

3. To trick.–We *fooled* Bob on the first of April. We tricked him into believing there was no school on that day.

foolish fool'-ish *foolishly*. 1. Not wise; not sensible.–It is *foolish* to stay in swimming too long.

foolishness fool'-ish-ness. 1. Silly behaviour.–The teacher told the children to stop their *foolishness*.

2. Action that is not wise.–The boy's *foolishness* got him into trouble.

F G H I J K L M N O P Q R S T U V W X Y Z

foot *feet, foots, footed, footing.* 1. The part of the body on which a person or animal stands and walks.–We have 5 toes on each *foot.* – Dogs have 4 *feet.*

2. The bottom; the lowest part. –Bob stood at the *foot* of the stairs and called to his mother upstairs.

3. A measurement of length.– Twelve inches equal 1 *foot.*– There are 3 *feet* in a yard.

4. Pay; be responsible for.–We are going to the show and Father will *foot* the bill.

football foot'-ball *footballs.* 1. A game played between 2 teams of 11 men with a round leather-covered ball. The object is to kick the ball through the opponents' goal, the team scoring the greater number of goals winning the game. This game is called Association *football* or soccer.

2. A game played between 2 teams of 15 men with an oval-shaped leather-covered ball. The object is to run with and touch the ball down over the opponents' line (a try), or to kick it over the crossbar of their goal. The team scoring more points wins the game. This game is called Rugby *football* or rugger.

3. The ball used in either soccer or rugger is called a *football.*

footnote foot'-note *footnotes.* A note at the bottom of a page. It gives additional information.–Bob read the *footnote.* The *footnote* told where to get the directions for making a kite which was described on that same page.

footpath foot'-path *footpaths.* A path or narrow way for people walking.–The children walked on the *footpath.*

footprint foot'-print *footprints.* The track or mark made by a foot.–We saw the man's *footprints* in the snow.

footstep foot'-step *footsteps.* The sound or noise made by one's feet when walking or stepping along.–We heard a man's *footsteps* in the hall.

footstool foot'-stool *footstools.* A low stool for the feet. – Father sat with his feet on the *footstool* and smoked his pipe.

for 1. Mother left *for* Bristol today.

2. I will give you my knife in exchange *for* your book.

3. We all voted *for* Mary.

4. Here is a gift *for* you.

5. Since you worked so hard, you may have an hour *for* rest.

6. We looked *for* Father's hat.

7. Mary has a great fondness *for* music.

8. A mark of 7 out of 10 is good *for* her; that is as well as she can do.

9. Milk is good *for* you; it makes you strong.

10. Father rode on the train *for* a whole day. –Baby slept *for* hours.

11. Will you do something *for* me?

12. I know that she has the book, *for* I saw it.

forbade for-bade'. One form of the word *forbid.* – The policeman *forbade* the man to drive up the one-way street.

forbid for-bid' *forbids, forbade, forbidden, forbidding.* Refuse to allow.–I *forbid* you to leave town today.–Father *forbids* us to play in the street.

force *forces, forced, forcing.* 1. Strength.–The water runs with much *force.*

2. A thing that causes a change in motion.– A ball that is thrown into the air is pulled to earth by the *force* of gravity.

3. A body of men formed for a certain purpose.–The police *force* also marched in the parade.

4. Make, compel.–The officer *forced* the thief to surrender.

5. Make something go or move by strength.– We *forced* the top off the box to get the balls and bats.

fore. 1. Forward or front.–A horse has 2 *fore* feet.

2. The golf player calls '*fore*' when he wishes to warn people that they are in danger of being hit by a ball.

forearm fore'-arm *forearms.* The part of the arm below the elbow and above the hand.– Mary wore a bracelet on her *forearm.*

forecast fore'cast *forecasts, forecast, forecasting.* 1. Tell ahead of time; predict. – The weather bureau *forecasts* the weather. It tells us in advance what kind of weather we are going to have.

2. A telling of what will happen; a prediction. –I heard the weather *forecast* on the radio today.

forefather fore'-fa-ther *forefathers*. A person from whom one is descended; ancestor. – Your father, mother, and your grandparents are some of your *forefathers*.

forefinger fore'-fin-ger *forefingers*. The finger next to the thumb.

forehead fore'-head *foreheads*. The part of the face between the eyes and hair.–Bob wears his cap pulled down over his *forehead*.

foreign for'-eign. Of a country other than one's own.–The priest speaks several *foreign* languages. He speaks the languages of several countries besides his own.

foreigner for'-eign-er *foreigner*. A person in a country where he is not a citizen.–An Englishman is a *foreigner* when he is in France.

foreman fore'-man *foremen*. In charge of a certain number of workers; a supervisor.–Bob's uncle is a *foreman* in the factory. He is in charge of many workmen.

foremost fore'-most. Main; chief; most important.–The *foremost* reason we did not go was that it was raining.

forenoon fore'-noon *forenoons*. The morning, the part of the day before noon.

foresee fore-see' *foresees, foresaw, foreseen, foreseeing*. Know ahead of time.–Bob *foresaw* that his team would lose, but he played his best all the same.

foresight fore'-sight. 1. Concern or thought for the time to come. – Young men who have *foresight* save money to live on when they are old.
2. Ability to tell what will happen.–Many people do not have *foresight*. They cannot tell what is probably going to happen.

forest for'-est *forests*. Woods; land that is thickly covered with trees. – Wild animals live in the *forest*.

forester for'-est-er *foresters*. A man who takes care of a forest or woods.

foretell fore-tell' *foretells, foretold, foretelling*. Forecast; tell ahead of time. – Grandfather said he could not *foretell* what the weather would be tomorrow.

forethought fore'-thought. Thinking or planning ahead of time.–The boy's *forethought* kept the train from being wrecked. When he saw that the bridge was broken, he ran back and waved a flag to stop the train. He thought what to do to prevent an accident.

foretold fore-told'. One form of the word *foretell*. – The wise man *foretold* many of the things that have since happened.

for ever for ev'-er. For all time to come.–The snow will not last *for ever*.

forfeit for'-feit *forfeits, forfeited, forfeiting*. Give up.–In this game you have to *forfeit* something every time you do not guess the right answer.

forgave for-gave'. One form of the word *forgive*.–The gardener *forgave* the hurrying boy for running across the newly planted lawn.

forge *forges, forged, forging*. 1. Soften with heat and hammer into shape. – A blacksmith *forges* horseshoes. He shapes hot iron to fit the horse's hoofs.
2. The fireplace in which a blacksmith heats metal.
3. Sign (another's name) unlawfully. – The man *forged* Mr Smith's signature on a cheque.
4. Move with great difficulty, but steadily. – The army *forged* ahead.

forger forg'-er *forgers*. A person who signs someone else's name to cheques or papers, or who makes false things and pretends they are real.

forgery for'-ger-y *forgeries*. 1. The signing of another person's name to cheques or other papers; the imitation of someone else's writing or painting for the purpose of cheating.
2. The making of anything that is false and pretending that it is real.

F G H I J K L M N O P Q R S T U V W X Y Z

F
G
H
I
J
K
L
M
N
O
P
Q
R
S
T
U
V
W
X
Y
Z

forget for-get′ *forgets, forgot, forgotten, forgetting.* 1. Not think of something which one was supposed to think of at a certain time.—Do not *forget* to wear your slippers. Remember to wear them.
2. Be unable to think of a particular thing one is trying to think of.—I *forget* who it was that found my book.

forgetful for-get′-ful *forgetfully, forgetfulness.* Apt to let things go out of one's mind.—Grandmother is *forgetful* sometimes. She doesn't remember things.

forget-me-not for-get′-me-not *forget-me-nots.* A small, blue flower that grows on low plants. *Forget-me-nots* stand for friendship.

forgive for-give′ *forgives, forgave, forgiven, forgiving.* Excuse, pardon.—I will *forgive* you for not coming if you will promise to come another time.

forgiven for-giv′-en. One form of the word *forgive.*—The boys were *forgiven* for their unkind acts when they promised to be kinder.

forgiveness for-give′-ness. Pardon, forgetting a wrong done to one.—Cinderella's step-sisters begged her *forgiveness* for all their unkindness to her.

forgot for-got′. One form of the word *forget.*—Bob *forgot* to close the gate and the dog ran away.

forgotten for-got′-ten. One form of the word *forget.*—I have *forgotten* how much the dress cost. It has gone from my mind.

fork *forks, forked, forking.* 1. A table utensil with several long points, for picking up solid food. We eat meat, vegetables and salad with a *fork.*
2. Take up with a *fork.*—The farmer *forked* the hay on to the wagon. He lifted it on to the wagon with a tool called a pitch*fork.*
3. A place where something splits out into 2 or more directions.—We came to a *fork* in the road, and didn't know which turn to take.

forlorn for-lorn′. Lonely, pitiful, left all alone and uncared for.—The empty house looked *forlorn.*—The old woman looked *forlorn* sitting by the low fire with her cat.

form *forms, formed, forming.* 1. Shape.—What is the *form* of your new scarf – square or 3-cornered?
2. Make, take the shape of. – We *formed* a circle round the player who stood in the middle.—Cream *forms* butter when beaten or churned.
3. Come or bring into shape; develop, grow.—Buds are *forming* on the trees.—John has *formed* the habit of brushing his teeth twice a day.
4. Shape, condition.—The fighter is in *form* for the championship fight.
5. A kind.—Sand is a *form* of earth.
6. Rules of polite society. – The party was carried out according to *form.*—It is good *form* to thank people for gifts.
7. A way of presenting something, or arranging it.—I have heard the story told in the *form* of a poem.

formal for′-mal *formally.* 1. Stiff; not warm, friendly, and easy.—The big room seemed very *formal* when we went in. We were afraid to make ourselves comfortable in it.
2. According to form, or the rules of polite society.—The party was *formal.* It was all carefully planned, and the guests wore evening dress.

former for′-mer. Having happened or been in the past.—Miss Smith is a *former* teacher of mine. She was once my teacher, but she isn't now.—In *former* years means in time gone by.

formerly for′-mer-ly. In the past. – *Formerly* Mr Jones was a policeman; now he is a business man.

forsake for-sake′ *forsakes, forsook, forsaken, forsaking.* Leave, go away from.—Bob would not *forsake* his duty for pleasure.

forsaken for-sak′-en. 1. One form of the word *forsake.*—The people have *forsaken* the town. They have left it.
2. Lonely, left all alone.—The old house looks *forsaken.* It looks as if no one lives there.

fort *forts.* A place with strong walls, furnished with guns to repel attacks. – The soldiers guarded the *fort.*

forth. Forward.–Mother rocked the baby back and *forth*.–Bill stepped *forth* from behind the bush and called to Jack.

fortieth for'-ti-eth *fortieths*. 1. Coming as number forty (40) in a series.–This is Uncle Jim's *fortieth* birthday. Last year he celebrated his thirty-ninth birthday. Next year he will be forty-one.
2. One of forty equal parts.–If a piece of farmland is divided into forty equal parts, each piece will take up one-*fortieth* of the farm. In figures it is written 1/40.

fortnight fort'-night *fortnights*. Two weeks, or 14 days.

fortress for'-tress *fortresses*. A fort, building, or place that can be defended against an enemy.–A *fortress* was built along the river.

fortunate for'-tu-nate *fortunately*. Lucky. – Bob was *fortunate* to find the book he had lost.

fortune for'-tune *fortunes*. 1. Money, property, wealth.–The rich man left his *fortune* to the college he had gone to. – Father says Mr Brown is worth a *fortune*; he says Mr Brown is rich.–The youngest son made his clothes into a bundle and went out into the world to seek his *fortune*.
2. Luck.–It was my good *fortune* to find Mary at home when I called.
3. What is going to happen to one in the future.–The gypsy told us our *fortunes* by reading our palms.

forty for'-ty *forties*. The number (40) coming after 39 and before 41. Four tens make *forty*. –Father will be *forty* on his next birthday. He is thirty-nine now.

forward for'-ward *forwards, forwarded, forwarding*. 1. Towards the front. – The teacher told Mary to come *forward* and show her drawing to the class.
2. Send on.–If a letter comes for you after you have gone, we will *forward* it.
3. Bold, anxious to be noticed.–Some children are very *forward*, and others are shy.

fossil fos'-sil *fossils*. 1. The hardened form a living thing sometimes takes if preserved long after death, usually in sand or mud which becomes stone. It keeps its shape, and you can tell what it was like when it was living.

2. The print of a living thing in sand or mud hardened into rock is also called a *fossil*.

foster fos'-ter. A *foster*-child is a child brought up and cared for by parents not really his own. These parents are his *foster*-parents.

fought. One form of the word *fight*.–The boys were fighting today. Yesterday they *fought*, too. They often fight.

foul *fouls, fouled, fouling*. 1. In games, a play that is not fair or honest or not allowed; a *foul* is against the rules of the game.–Bob tripped the other side's centre-forward. The referee said it was a *foul* and awarded a free kick.–In boxing it is a *foul* to hit below the belt.
2. Dirty, not pleasant, not clean and fresh.–The air in a room or cellar that has been closed a long time becomes *foul*.
3. Not fair.–The boat did not sail, because of *foul* weather. It was windy and stormy.
4. Make impure or filthy. – The river water was *fouled* by waste flowing into it.

found *founds, founded, founding*. 1. Start, or help to start.–Mr Smith *founded* this school 23 years ago.
2. One form of the word *find*. – Bob *found* his lost knife.

foundation foun-da'-tion *foundations*. A base, the part on which something stands. – The *foundations* of our house are made of concrete.

founder found'-er *founders*. A person who starts or helps to start something.–Mr Brown was the *founder* of our local sports club.

foundry found'-ry *foundries*. A building where melted iron, steel or other materials are moulded into different shapes and allowed to harden.

fountain foun'-tain *fountains*. A place where water is made to spurt upwards, as from a pipe. – Children at school drink from a drinking *fountain*. – The men built a *fountain* in the park. The water piped into the *fountain* is thrown high up into the air and then drops back.

F
G
H
I
J
K
L
M
N
O
P
Q
R
S
T
U
V
W
X
Y
Z

fountain pen *fountain pens.* A writing pen in which there is a small bag filled with ink. As you write, the bag lets ink down to the point of the pen.–Mary fills her *fountain pen* before she goes to school.

four. The number (4) coming after 3 and before 5.–You have a thumb and *four* fingers on each hand.

fourscore *four'-score'.* Eighty, or four times twenty.–*Fourscore* years are eighty years.

fourteen *four'-teen'.* The number (14) coming after 13 and before 15.–Four and ten make *fourteen.*

fourteenth *four'-teenth' fourteenths.* 1. Coming as number fourteen (14) in a series.–To-day is my *fourteenth* birthday. I am fourteen years old.
2. One of fourteen equal parts.–If a cake is divided into fourteen equal parts, each part is one *fourteenth.* In figures it is written 1/14.

fourth *fourths.* 1. Coming as number four (4) in a series.–This is Baby's *fourth* birthday. It is the next birthday after her third.
2. One of four equal parts.–Father ate a *fourth* of the pie. He ate one of the four equal parts into which it was cut. In figures it is written 1/4.

fowl *fowls.* A bird or chicken.–Birds that are eaten, such as geese, ducks, and pigeons, are *fowl.*

turkey   duck   chicken   goose

fox *foxes.* An animal that belongs to the dog family. *Foxes* are sly. Their fur is used for coats, collars, and trimming. Some *fox* skins

are red, the colour of red hair, and some are dark with bits of silver.

foxhound *fox'-hound foxhounds.* A dog trained to hunt foxes.–The hunt has a fine pack of *foxhounds* at present.

fox terrier *fox terriers.* A kind of dog. Some *fox terriers* have smooth hair, and others have rough or wiry hair.

fraction *frac'tion fractions.* A part of anything. All of anything is a whole. A part of it is a *fraction* of it.–A slice of an apple is just a *fraction* of an apple.–Mary gives a small *fraction* of her time to her arithmetic.–*Fractions* are written in figures like this: 1/2, 1/5, 2/3, 1/6.

fracture *frac'-ture fractures, fractured, fracturing.* 1. Break, crack.–An old woman fell on the ice and *fractured* a bone in one of her legs.
2. A break or a crack.–She is suffering from a *fracture* of the leg.

fragile *frag'-ile.* Delicate, not strong and sturdy. –Window panes, dishes and mirrors are *fragile.* They break easily.

fragment *frag'-ment fragments.* A small part or broken-off piece of anything.–A *fragment* of stone fell from the top of the wall.–When Mother dropped the teapot on the floor, it broke into small *fragments.*

fragrance *fra'-grance.* A pleasant smell or odour. – The *fragrance* of the lilacs came through the open window.

fragrant *fra'-grant.* Smelling sweet, like perfume. – Lilacs and lilies of the valley are *fragrant.*

frail 1. Apt to become ill easily; not able to stand much discomfort or hardship, not strong.–Old people often become *frail.* They lose their strength and become weaker.
2. Easily broken.–Fine china is *frail.*

frame *frames, framed, framing.* 1. The skeleton, or part of anything that gives it shape and around which it is built.–Grandfather built a *frame* for the grapes to grow over.– The *frame* of a house makes the shape of the house. The *frame* is made of strong timbers. The *frame* usually does not show from the outside, but is covered by the walls.–The skeleton, made up of all the bones of the body, is a person's *frame.*

2. A border.–The *frame* on the mirror is round.
3. Put in a *frame.*–Mother *framed* the mirror herself. She put the *frame* on it herself.
4. Form, make.–The boys are *framing* some plans for starting a club.
5. *Frame of mind* means mood.–If Mother is in a good *frame of mind,* she will let us make toffee.

frank *frankly.* Honest and direct in talking.– Father is very *frank* in talking to people. He says just what he thinks.

frankness frank'-ness. Directness and honesty in saying what one thinks.–Father believes in *frankness* when talking to us.

frantic fran'-tic *frantically.* Excited, wild with upset feelings.–The lost child was *frantic.*– The sick man was *frantic* with pain.

fraternal fra-ter'-nal *fraternally.* Brotherly.– John and Jack, being brothers, have warm *fraternal* feelings towards each other.–The members of the club sent *fraternal* greetings to their colleagues abroad.

fraud *frauds.* 1. Cheating.–The man's *fraud* in selling rotten apples was discovered.
2. A person who cheats or deceives others.– That man selling furs is a *fraud.* He is not honest. He makes believe that poor furs are good ones.
3. Something which deceives or cheats people.–The fancy basket of fruit turned out to be a *fraud.* There was very little fruit in it.

fray *frays, frayed, fraying.* 1. Wear out into separate threads.–Grandfather's coat collar is *frayed.* It is worn and ravelled out where it has rubbed against his neck.

2. A loud quarrel or fight.–When Bob saw the big boys hitting the little ones, he entered the *fray.*

freak *freaks.* An extremely unusual thing or happening.–A rabbit with 3 ears would be a *freak.* It would be odd, strange, not like others.

freckle freck'-le *freckles, freckled, freckling.*
1. A tan spot on the skin.–Jack has red hair, and *freckles* all over his nose.–The sun makes *freckles* come out on one's face, arms, or body.
2. Break out with *freckles.*–Some people tan in the sun, but do not *freckle.*

free *frees, freed, freeing, freer, freest.* 1. Costing nothing.–Come to the show. It is *free.*
2. Turn loose, set at liberty.–Bob will *free* the mouse from the box. He will let it loose to go where it wants to go.
3. At liberty.–The prisoner is *free* from jail now.–You are *free* to go where you want and say what you want; no one will hold you back or keep you from saying what you want.

freedom free'-dom *freedoms.* Liberty; right to believe and act as one pleases.–Bob gave the mouse his *freedom.* He set him loose; he let him go.–We enjoy our *freedom.*

freeze *freezes, froze, frozen, freezing.* 1. Turn to ice.–Water will *freeze* when it gets cold enough.
2. Make so cold that it becomes solid.–One way to preserve foods is to *freeze* them. Many kinds of meat, fish, vegetables, fruits and juices are *frozen* and remain fit to eat for a long time.

freight. 1. Goods sent from one place to another, usually by water –A passenger liner often carries *freight.* Raw materials, machinery and finished goods are different kinds of *freight.*
2. The cost of shipping goods.–The business man paid the freight on the goods he had ordered. He paid the shipping charges.

freighter freight'-er *freighters.* A boat carrying freight or goods.–We saw a big *freighter* going down the river.

frenzy fren'-zy *frenzies*. Fury, a fit of rage or great excitement.–The driver was in a *frenzy* because someone ran into his car. He was excited and angry.

frequent (fré'-quent for 1st. meaning, fre-quent' for 2nd). 1. Coming often, or close together in time.–Mother has *frequent* headaches. She has them often.
2. Go often or habitually to –Bob *frequents* Mary's house. He spends a lot of time there.

frequently fre'-quent-ly. Often –Bill *frequently* stays after school.

fresh *fresher, freshest, freshly*. 1 Newly acquired, gathered, made, drawn, etc.–I drank a glass of *fresh* water from the spring.–These beets are *fresh* from the garden.–These cakes are *fresh* from the oven.
2. Rested and well.–A good night's rest will make you feel *fresh*.
3. Not salty.–The water in the ocean is salty. The water in lakes and rivers is usually *fresh*.

freshman fresh'-man *freshmen*. A student in his first year at university. – This is my brother's first year at college. He is a *freshman*. He is one of a group of *freshmen*.

fret *frets, fretted, fretting*. 1. Become disturbed and restless.–When Father is late we all *fret* about him. We worry and get uneasy.
2. Complain, get cross.–When Mary has to get up early in the morning, she *frets*.

fretful fret'-ful *fretfully*. Restless, nervous, and irritable.–Children become *fretful* when they are tired.

friction fric'-tion. If you rub smooth boards together, they slide back and forth easily. If you rub rough boards together, they do not slide so easily because the roughness makes the rubbing hard. This action against the rubbing, or the thing that makes it hard to slide the rough boards against each other, is called *friction*. *Friction* causes heat.–Sliding down a slide on the playground causes *friction*.–Rubbing a match on a matchbox causes *friction*. The heat made by the *friction* causes the match to light.–*Friction* between the tyres on a car and the roadway keeps the car from skidding.
2. Quarrelling, trouble.–There is *friction* between the neighbours. They annoy each other and do not get on well together.

Friday Fri'-day *Fridays*. The day after Thursday. *Friday* is the sixth day of the week.

fried. One form of the word *fry*. *Fried* foods are foods that are cooked in fat in a pan on top of the stove.

friend *friends*. 1. A person who likes another person and associates with him.–Mary and Ruth are close *friends*. They know each other very well. They are fond of each other.
2. A person who believes in a group, organization, idea, etc., and gives it help.–The man is a *friend* of the poor. He helps them.

friendless friend'-less. Without friends, all alone.–The poor boy found himself *friendless* in the strange city.

friendly *friendly, friendlier, friendliest*. Like a friend; warm in manner; ready to be nice to others. The girl is *friendly* towards me. She is like a friend. She acts as if she wants to help me and know me well.

friendship friend'-ship. The feeling of knowing and liking which friends have between them. –Bob and John are friends. Their *friendship* started when they were in kindergarten.

fright. 1. Fear.–The fire at the zoo caused *fright* among the animals. They were frightened.
2. A grotesque-looking person. Mary said she looked a *fright* in her old dress.

frighten fright'-en *frightens, frightened, frightening*. Scare.–When the telephone rang suddenly, it *frightened* me.

frightful fright'-ful *frightfully*. Horrible, terrible, awful.–We saw a *frightful* accident.

frigid frig'-id. Very cold.–At the North Pole, the air is *frigid*.

frill *frills*. A fancy ruffle. –Mother wears a *frill* on the front of ·her dress.

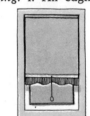

fringe *fringes, fringed, fringing*. 1. An edging made of heavy cord twisted and tied together, or just of loosehanging long threads. –Our window blinds have a *fringe* across the bottom.
2. Make a *fringe* on.– The edge of a piece of linen is sometimes ravelled back to make a *fringe*. – Mother *fringed* the napkins.

F
G
H
I
J
K
L
M
N
O
P
Q
R
S
T
U
V
W
X
Y
Z

3. Hair at the front of the head that is cut short and allowed to fall over the forehead. —Mary wears her hair in a *fringe*.

frisk *frisks, frisked, frisking.* Romp and play happily.—We watched the baby lambs *frisk* about in the field. They ran and played.

frisky frisk′-y. Playful.—Sally's kitten is *frisky*.

fritter frit′-ter *fritters, frittered, frittering.* 1. A piece of fried batter with apple, bananas, pineapple, or other foods in it.
2. Waste here and there, use up in silly ways. —Mary *frittered* away her whole morning trying to curl her hair.

fro. From. – The wind blew the branches to and *fro*, backwards and forwards.

frock. *frocks.* Dress. – Mary had a new *frock* for Easter.

frog *frogs.* 1. A small animal that lives in or near the water. *Frogs* have no tails and their feet are webbed like duck's feet to help them swim. Tadpoles grow to be *frogs*.
2. A fastener made of fancy braid and buttons.—The suits worn by the boys in the band are fastened with *frogs*.

frolic frol′-ic *frolics, frolicked, frolicking.* 1. Romp and frisk. – The little lambs *frolic* about the field.
2. A party, a time set aside for fun.—We are having a school *frolic*.

from. 1. The opposite of to. – I have a letter *from* Rose. She sent it to me.—It is miles *from* here to the park.—The boys took the nuts *from* the basket.—Five minutes *from* now we will be on our way home.—Sally knows her letters *from* a to z.—Some flowers grow *from* seeds, and some grow *from* bulbs.
2. By, according to.—We can not tell *from* the description who the man is.
3. *From* is used to show a difference.—It is not hard to tell blue *from* yellow.

front *fronts.* 1. The side opposite the back, or the side facing forwards.—The *front* of the house faces the street.—The radiator of a motor-car is at the *front*.

2. *In front of* means ahead of, before.—Bob sits *in front of* Jack. He sits in the seat just ahead of Jack's.

frost *frosts, frosted, frosting.* 1. Frozen dew.— We saw *frost* on the grass this morning.
2. Destroy by *frost*.—The fruit was *frosted* on the trees.
3. Frozen moisture.—There was *frost* on the window-pane. We could not see through it.

4. Cover with rime or *frost*, or with something that looks like *frost*, such as icing-sugar.—The windows are *frosted* this morning.—Mother will *frost* Mary's birthday cake with a vanilla *frosting*. She will put vanilla icing on it.
5. Give a roughened surface to.—There is *frosted* glass in our bathroom window.—This electric-light bulb is made of *frosted* glass. It is not clear glass. The *frosting* diffuses the light and makes it softer.

frostbite frost′-bite frostbitten. 1. Injure by freezing.—Because the mountaineer had lain exposed to the ice and snow all night, his feet were so numbed with cold that they were *frostbitten*.
2. The injury that comes from the freezing of the flesh.—The mountaineer had bad *frostbite*.

frosty frost′y *frostier, frostiest.* 1. Cold enough for frost.—It is *frosty* today. It is cold.
2. Covered with frost.—The windows are so *frosty* that we can't see out.
3. Cold; unfriendly.—We got home late and received a *frosty* welcome.

froth *frothy.* Foam; liquid filled with tiny bubbles.—The bubbles that rise on ginger beer and other drinks make *froth*.

frown *frowns, frowned, frowning.* 1. Wrinkle up the forehead.—When the sun shines in my eyes, I *frown*.
2. Wrinkle up the forehead to show that one is angry or not pleased.—Father *frowned* at the man's cruelty to his dog.
3. A scowl; a wrinkling of the brow.—The man's *frown* showed he was not pleased.

F
G
H
I
J
K
L
M
N
O
P
Q
R
S
T
U
V
W
X
Y
Z

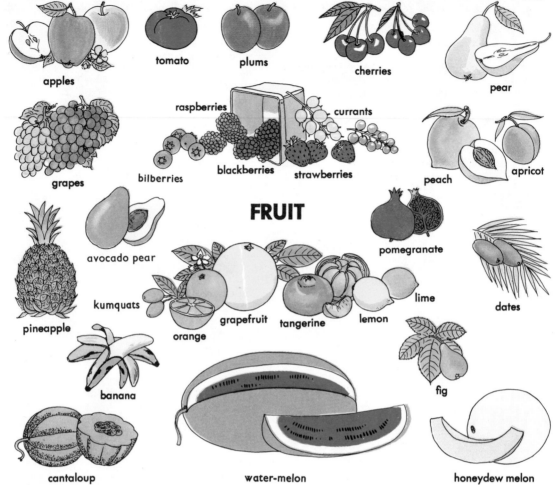

apples

tomato

plums

cherries

pear

raspberries

currants

grapes

bilberries

blackberries

strawberries

peach

apricot

FRUIT

avocado pear

pomegranate

pineapple

kumquats

grapefruit

tangerine

lemon

lime

dates

orange

banana

fig

cantaloup

water-melon

honeydew melon

froze. One form of the word *freeze.*–The pipes in the roof *froze* during the cold weather.

frozen fro'-zen. One form of the word *freeze.*– We could not skate on the lake, because the water was not *frozen*.

fruit *fruits.* The edible seed vessel of certain plants. *Fruits* are often good to eat. *Fruits* grow on bushes, trees, and vines.–Berries, apples, dates, oranges, grapes, and peaches are *fruits*.

fruitful fruit'-ful. 1. Bearing fruit.–That bush has been *fruitful*. It has had many berries on it.
2. Having results.–At last a *fruitful* plan has been made. The plan brings· about good results.

fruitless fruit'-less. 1. Bearing no fruit.–This apple tree has been *fruitless* for years. It has had no apples.
2. Useless; not effective.–The boys tried hard to win the game, but their effort was *fruitless*. They lost.

fry *fries, fried, frying.* Cook in grease.–We *fry* potatoes when we cook them in a little butter‚ or fat in a skillet or pan on top of the stove.

fudge. A soft sweetmeat made with sugar, milk, butter, chocolate, and flavouring.–On Sunday evenings Mother lets us make *fudge*.

fuel fu'-el *fuels.* Something used for burning. –Coal, oil, wood, coke, or any other material that is burned to keep houses warm, to run machines, or for other useful fires is *fuel*.

fugitive fu'-gi-tive *fugitives.* A person escaping or running away.–The man who robbed the bank is a *fugitive*. He is trying to escape being captured.

fulfil ful-fil' *fulfils, fulfilled, fulfilling.* 1. Keep; carry out.–Mary always *fulfils* her promises.
2. Satisfy.–Bob can *fulfil* the wishes of the boys and girls by winning the race.
3. Do to satisfaction.–The soldier *fulfilled* his duties. He did satisfactorily the things that he was supposed to do.

full. 1. Able to hold no more.–The jug is *full* of milk.–We ate until we were *full*.
2. Complete; entire.–We had a *full* week's holiday.
3. Well filled out, plump.–Aunt Jane has a *full* figure. She is plump.

fully ful'-ly. Completely; wholly.–Father *fully* understands the directions for making the model aeroplane.

fumble fum'-ble *fumbles, fumbled, fumbling*.
1. Feel clumsily.–Bob *fumbled* in his pocket for his pencil.
2. Handle awkwardly.–The wicket-keeper *fumbled* the ball. He did not stop it cleanly.

fume *fumes, fumed, fuming*. 1. Strong-smelling smoke or vapour.–We smelt the *fumes* from Grandfather's pipe.–You can smell the *fumes* from petrol or ether.
2. Show anger or irritation.–The shop assistant was so rude that Father *fumed* with rage.

fun. 1. Happy play; pleasure.–We had *fun* at the circus.
2. Entertainment; amusement. – The clowns added to the *fun* for the children.
3. *Make fun of* means to ridicule or tease.–The boys *made fun of* the boy riding the girl's bicycle.

function func'-tion *functions, functioned, functioning*. 1. Use; work.–It is the *function* of a watch to keep time.
2. To work; operate; run.–Bob's watch *functions* perfectly.

fund *funds*. 1. A supply of anything, especially of money.–Father and Mother have a £25 Christmas *fund*. They have put away £25 for Christmas.–Bob has a *fund* of good ideas for giving parties.
2. *Funds* means money.–College students often write home for *funds*.

funeral fu'-ner-al *funerals*. The service with which a person is buried.–After a person dies, friends gather at his home or a church or the cemetery and a funeral service is held at which prayers are offered for the dead.

fungus fun'-gus *fungi*. A plant that grows without light. A *fungus* does not have a green colour like most plants. – Toadstools, mushrooms, and moulds are *fungi*.

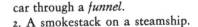

mushroom

bracket fungus

coral fungus

funnel fun'-nel *funnels*. 1. A cone-shaped container, open at the top and having a spout or tube at the bottom. It is used for pouring things into a narrow opening, such as the top of a bottle. – The man at the petrol station may put oil in the car through a *funnel*.
2. A smokestack on a steamship.

funny fun'-ny *funnier, funniest*. 1. Causing laughter; humorous.–A *funny* story is one that makes you laugh, or amuses you.
2. Strange; odd; curious.–It is *funny* that I have not heard from Father.

fur *furs*. 1. The hairy covering of some animals. –Beavers, cats, rabbits, and many other animals are covered with *fur*.
2. The pelt or skin of an animal which has *fur*.–*Furs* of animals are used for coats.

furious fu'-ri-ous *furiously*. 1. Very angry.– Grandfather was *furious* when he discovered that he had been cheated.
2. Fierce and strong.–There is a *furious* wind blowing over the lake.

furlough fur'-lough *furloughs*. A short holiday or leave of absence.–The soldier came home for a 10-day *furlough*.

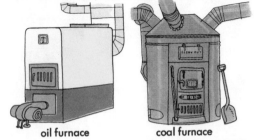

oil furnace   coal furnace

furnace fur'-nace *furnaces*. A structure built to hold a fire.–A *furnace* in a house has pipes running to the rooms to carry steam, hot water, or hot air to heat the house.–In foundries, fires are made in large *furnaces* to heat and melt metal.

F
G
H
I
J
K
L
M
N
O
P
Q
R
S
T
U
V
W
X
Y
Z

F

G
H
I
J
K
L
M
N
O
P
Q
R
S
T
U
V
W
X
Y
Z

furnish fur'-nish *furnishes, furnished, furnishing*. 1. Supply or provide.–Our school does not *furnish* pencils for the children.–The police asked people to *furnish* information about the accident they had witnessed.
2. Provide with furniture.–Mother *furnished* the living-room with new furniture.

furnishings fur'-nish-ings. Furniture; all the things needed to fit out a room.–Our new *furnishings* are mostly in blue.–Curtains and chair-covers are soft *furnishings*.

furniture fur'-ni-ture. Chairs, tables, beds, etc. used in a house, an office, etc.–Our *furniture* was bought at a *furniture* shop.

furrier fur'-ri-er *furriers*. A person who makes or sells fur coats and other things made of fur.

furrow fur'-row *furrows, furrowed, furrowing*.
1. A little ditch or groove made in the earth by a plough.

2. A wrinkle.–The old man had deep *furrows* in his forehead.
3. Make *furrows* in.–The man's forehead was *furrowed* from frowning in the sun.

furry fur'-ry. Soft like fur; covered with fur.– The kitten is very *furry*.

further fur'ther *furthers, furthered, furthering*. 1. More.–We had *further* surprises when Grandfather came.
2. Help forward.–Our plans were *furthered* by a gift of money.
3. A greater distance; farther.–The door is *further* down the hall than the window.

furthest fur'-thest. Lying at the greatest distance.–The *furthest* of the 3 runners is Bob.

fury fu'-ry. 1. Mad anger.–The lions at the zoo were in a *fury*. They were very angry.
2. Fierceness.–The *fury* of the storm was gone before it reached the town.

fuse (pronounced *fuze*) *fuses*. 1. The string which burns down to set off an explosive. – The men lighted the *fuse* on the stick of dynamite and then ran to safety.
2. In a system of electric wiring, a piece of metal which melts if too much current goes through the wires, making the wires too hot. When the *fuse* melts, it cuts off the electricity.

fuss *fusses, fussed, fussing*. 1. Fret; worry.– Grandfather *fusses* over little troubles.
2. An unnecessary worry or bother. – He makes a *fuss* over little troubles.

fussy fuss'-y *fussier, fussiest*. Too particular; apt to fret. – Some people are *fussy* about what they eat.

future fu'-ture. The time that is to come.–In the *future* aeroplanes will be used more than they have been in the past.

fuzz. Soft down or hair.–The little duck is covered with *fuzz*.–Peaches are covered with *fuzz*.

fuzzy fuzz'-y *fuzzier, fuzziest*. Covered with fuzz; soft as fuzz.–A *fuzzy* little kitten came to the door. It was covered with soft fuzz or fur.

FURNITURE

Elizabethan four poster and oak chest

Day-bed, English 17th Century

bureau cabinet

kitchen dresser

dining-room table

modern bench and cupboard

Sheraton table

ancient Egyptian stool

modern coffee table

Roman stone chair

Renaissance chair

Louis XV chair

modern chair

G g

G, g *G's, g's.* The seventh letter of the alphabet.

gable ga'-ble *gables.* An end of a pointed roof. –The house in the picture has 2 *gables.*

gaiety gai'-e-ty. Happy fun; jolliness.–There was much *gaiety* at the children's birthday party.

gaily gai'-ly. Merrily; happily.–On May Day the children danced *gaily* round the Maypole.

gain *gains, gained, gaining.* 1. Get ahead.– Our clock *gains.* It runs too fast.
2. Have or get more.–If you buy a pencil for 5 pence and then sell it for 7 pence, you *gain* 2 pence.
3. Move forward. – The crack sprinter *gained* 8 yards on his rivals.
4. Get; win.–The team expects to *gain* the championship this year.
5. Earn.–The pilot *gained* fame by flying round the world.
6. Improve in health. – Grandfather has *gained* so much this week that he can soon go home from the hospital.
7. To *gain weight* means to get heavier.
8. To reach.–At last the swimmer *gained* the shore.

gait *gaits.* A walk; a manner of walking.–The dancer has a smooth, graceful *gait.*

gale *gales.* 1. A strong wind.–A *gale* drove the ship far out to sea.
2. A roar; a loud burst.–*Gales* of laughter were heard through the windows.

gallant (gal-lant' for 1st meaning, gal'-lant for 2nd) *gallantly.* 1. Polite to ladies; courteous.–Uncle Jim is very *gallant.* He pays every courtesy to ladies.
2. Noble; brave; fine.–The soldier is *gallant.* He is brave and loyal.

gallery gal'-ler-y *galleries.* 1. A building or room for displaying works of art.–Pictures and statues are shown in the art *gallery.*

2. The highest floor of seats in a theatre.– We had to sit in the *gallery* at the cinema.

gallon gal'-lon *gallons.* A measurement of liquids. – Four quarts make 1 *gallon.*

gallop gal'-lop *gallops, galloped, galloping.* 1. The fastest gait of a horse.–When a horse *gallops,* all 4 feet are off the ground at once each time he takes a step.
2. Run at a *gallop.*–The horse *galloped* down the street.

galoshes ga-losh'-es. A pair of overshoes to protect the feet in bad weather.–The path through the fields was so muddy that Mother made us put on our *galoshes.*

gamble gam'-ble *gambles, gambled, gambling.*
1. Play games for money.–Father does not *gamble.*
2. A great risk.–Buying land along the marsh is a *gamble.* The land may become worthless.

gambler gam'-bler *gamblers.* A person who plays games for money, or who bets on things regularly.–The *gambler* lost £25 on the race.

game *games.* 1. A kind of playing that is done according to rules. – Football, dominoes, draughts and hide-and-seek are *games.*
2. An outfit or set of equipment for playing a *game.*–You can get many *games* at a toy shop.
3. Wild. – Game birds are birds that are hunted for fun or for food.
4. Wild animals that are hunted. There is less *game* in this country than there once was.

gander gan'-der *ganders.* A male or he-goose.– Grandfather showed us several fine *ganders* when we visited him on his farm.

gang *gangs.* 1. A group of workmen.–A *gang* is repairing the street.
2. A group of criminals.–The rival *gangs* had a battle with guns.

gang-plank gang'-plank *gang-planks*. A walkway from a ship to the shore. – The sailors walked across the *gang-plank* to the dock. –When all the people have left or gone on to the boat, the *gang-plank* is taken up.

gangster gang'-ster *gangsters*. A person who belongs to a criminal gang.–*Gangsters* do bad things. They steal, and even kill people.

gape *gapes, gaped, gaping*. 1. Yawn; open wide; open the mouth wide.–The sleepy boy *gaped*.–There was a *gaping* hole in the ground.
2. Stare with open mouth.–We *gaped* at the huge elephant.

garage ga'-rage *garages*. 1. A building to keep cars in. Some *garages* are built behind houses; others join the houses.–At night we keep our car in the *garage*.
2. A shop where cars are stored or repaired. –When Father's car needs to be repaired he takes it to a *garage*.

garb *garbs, garbed, garbing*. 1. Style of dress or costume.–He was wearing the *garb* of a clergyman.–Many of the visiting dignitaries wore native *garb*.
2. Clothe or dress.–The men at the funeral were *garbed* in black.

garden gar'-den *gardens, gardener, gardening*. 1. A piece of ground where flowers or vegetables are grown.–Bob has a vegetable *garden* and Mary has a flower *garden*.

2. Make a *garden*; care for a *garden*.–They had never *gardened* before.

gardener gar'-den-er *gardeners*. A person who takes care of gardens.–The council has a *gardener* to care for the flowers in the park.

gargle gar'-gle *gargles, gargled, gargling*. 1. Bathe the throat by holding liquid in the back of the mouth and breathing through the liquid.–When Mother's throat was sore, the doctor told her to *gargle* with salt water.
2. A liquid for bathing the throat.–Salt water is a good *gargle*.

garland gar'-land *garlands, garlanded, garlanding*. 1. A wreath.–On May Day we crowned the May queen with a *garland of daisies*.
2. Decorate with wreaths.–At Christmas time some people *garland* the front doors of their homes.

garlic gar'-lic. A plant something like an onion. It is used in soups and other foods for flavouring.

garment gar'-ment *garments*. A piece of clothing.–Coats, dresses, suits, etc., are *garments*.

garret gar'-ret *garrets*. An attic; the part of a house under a peaked roof. *Garrets* are not usually plastered or finished.

garter gar'-ter *garters*. A band, made partly of rubber, for holding up the stockings.

gas *gases, gassed, gassing*. 1. Any substance that is not solid like a rock, or liquid like water. *Gas* has no shape or form.–Air is a *gas*.–When Father has petrol put into the car, you smell the fumes from the petrol. These fumes are a *gas*. You cannot see it but you can smell it.
2. Poison with *gas*.–Bob's grandfather was *gassed* in the first World War, but he recovered.
3. *Gas* made from coal or oil is used for heating, lighting, cooking, etc.–Grandmother has a *gas*-fire in her room.–We have a *gas*-cooker in the kitchen.
4. In America gas is short for gasoline or petrol.–Step on the *gas* means go faster.

gash *gashes, gashed, gashing*. 1. A long, deep cut.–Bob fell and cut a *gash* in his leg.
2. Make a long, deep cut.–A sharp rock *gashed* Bob's knee.

gasp *gasps, gasped, gasping.* 1. Pant; breathe fast and heavily.–The boys *gasped* after running across the field.
2. Draw in a sudden breath.–The boy *gasped* when he was pushed into the cold water.

gate *gates.* The part of a fence or wall that opens and closes like a door. – Someone left the *gate* open and the dog ran out of the yard.

gather gath′-er *gathers, gathered, gathering.*
1. Pick up and put together; collect.–We *gather* violets in the spring.
2. Come together.–A large crowd of people *gathered* on the corner to watch the parade.
3. Sew in folds; a tiny fold made in sewing.–The sleeves of Mary's dress are *gathered* at the top. They are sewn into *gathers.*
4. Understand.–From what you say, I *gather* that you had a very good time.

gauze. A very thin cloth. *Gauze* is so thin that you can see through it. It is often used to cover sores or injuries.

gave. One form of the word *give.*–Grandfather *gave* Bob a rabbit to take home.

gawky gaw′-ky *gawkily.* Awkward, clumsy.–The new boy is very shy and *gawky.*

gay *gayer, gayest.* 1. Jolly; merry.–We had a *gay* time at the party. We had lots of fun.
2. Bright and cheerful.–Mary's new dress is very *gay.* It has bright colours in it.

gaze *gazes, gazed, gazing.* 1. Look long and steadily.–The little girl *gazed* at the doll in the window.
2. A steady look.–The boy's *gaze* rested upon the new bicycle.

gazelle ga-zelle′ *gazelles.* A small antelope that runs very fast.–A *gazelle* is something like a deer.

gear *gears.* 1. A set of equipment, clothing, or the like.–The sailor took all his *gear* aboard the ship in a canvas bag.–Grandfather keeps all the *gear* for the carriage in the barn.

2. A wheel with cogs or teeth on the edge to fit into the teeth on another similar wheel. – Motor-cars have *gears.*
3. *In gear* means with the teeth of the *gears* fitted together so that one turns the other.–When Father put the car *in gear,* the motor began turning the wheels.

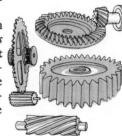

geese. More than one goose. *Geese* are large birds with long necks.

gelatine gel′-a-tine. A jelly-like substance from which glue is made. *Gelatine* is also used in making desserts to eat. *Gelatine* is made from the hoofs and bones of animals.

gem *gems.* 1. A precious stone. Rubies, diamonds and emeralds are *gems.*
2. A particularly valuable or outstanding thing.–The *gem* of all the pictures is the one of the old man smoking his pipe. It is the most beautiful and the best.

general gen′-er-al *generals.* 1. One of the highest officers in the army. He has charge of many men.–The Duke of Wellington was a famous *general.*
2. Happening or existing everywhere.–The rain was quite *general.* It rained everywhere, not just in one place.
3. Whole, entire, not special; covering everything or everybody.–The exhibition is open to the *general* public. It is open to all people who wish to go.–Bob is going to take a *general* course at university. He is not going to specialize in any single subject.
4. Rough, not clear.–Mother doesn't know exactly how the sweater should be made, but she has a *general* idea.

generally gen′-er-al-ly. Usually, most of the time. – *Generally* Mary gets better marks than Jack.

generous gen′-er-ous *generously, generosity.*
1. Willing and glad to share things with others.–Jack is very *generous.* He gives some of his biscuits to the other boys at lunch, and lends them his bicycle.
2. Large.–We had *generous* servings of ice-cream at the party.
3. Good, kind; not bearing hard feelings towards others.–It is *generous* of you to overlook my mistake.

genial ge′-ni-al *genially.* Warm and pleasant; hearty.–Grandfather has a *genial* manner. .

G
H
I
J
K
L
M
N
O
P
Q
R
S
T
U
V
W
X
Y
Z

genius gen'-ius *geniuses*. 1. A person who has a very unusual mind. A great musician, a great inventor, or a great poet is a *genius*.
2. A special ability that very few people have. –Grandmother believes that Mary has a *genius* for playing the piano

gentian gen'-tian *gentians*. A plant that has blue flowers. *Gentians* often grow in the mountains.

gentle gen'-tle. Soft, soothing, mild, not sharp or sudden.–A *gentle* breeze is blowing from the lake.–The old man is very *gentle* in manner.–If the sides of a hill slant gradually, little by little, we say the hill has a *gentle* slope.

gentleman gen'-tle-man *gentlemen*. A man who acts honourably, considerately, and politely to others.–Mr Jones is a *gentleman*. He is a courteous, well-bred man.

gently gen'-tly. In a careful, soft, or tender way. –The boys handled the kitten *gently*.–The snow falls *gently* on the roof.–We told him the sad news *gently*.

genuine gen'-u-ine *genuinely*. 1. Real, not imitation.–This coat is *genuine* mink.
2. True, honest, sincere.–Bob's friendship is *genuine*.

geography ge-og'-ra-phy *geographies*. The study of the earth and life upon it. In *geography* lessons we study the earth and its people, its animals, its mountains and valleys, its rivers, oceans, and other waters, its climate, and its products.

geology ge-o'-lo-gy. The study of the earth, particularly the shape and structure of its crust. Geologists can tell much about the history of the earth and about people and animals of bygone times by examining layers or strata of rock.

geometry ge-o'-me-try. A form of mathematics dealing with points, lines, surfaces and solids. In *geometry* we learn about triangles, cubes, spheres and other figures in space.

georgette geor-gette'. A thin silk crêpe cloth that you can partly see through.–Mother has a new *georgette* dancing dress.

geranium ge-ra'-ni-um *geraniums*. A flowering plant. Some *geraniums* are wild, and some are grown and cared for by people. The flowers are red, white, or salmon colour. They are often planted in window boxes.

germ *germs*. A tiny plant or animal, so small that it can be seen only with a microscope. *Germs* cause diseases. – Mother sterilizes Baby's bottle by putting it in boiling water to kill the *germs*.

gesture ges'-ture *gestures*. 1. A motion with the head, hand, or body.–Baby cannot talk, but she often makes *gestures* to tell what she wants. – Sometimes *gestures* are used with words to give extra force to what one means.
2. Something done to express a feeling to others, especially a pleasant feeling.–Mowing the old man's lawn was a nice *gesture* on Jack's part.

get *gets, got, getting*. 1. Receive, take.–I *get* a new pair of shoes about every 6 months. –Go and *get* your book and we'll read.– Did you *get* a letter today?–Bob *gets* his pocket-money from Father.
2. Earn.–I *get* 5op a week for mowing lawns.
3. Arrive, reach.–When we *get* home, I shall change my shoes.
4. Become, grow.–We *get* cold when the window is open wide.–Baby is *getting* big.
5. To *get* something done means to do or finish something. – When we *get* the dishes washed, we can play.
6. To *get* something done can mean to have it done by someone else. – Mother went to *get* the car mended.
7. Persuade – We could not *get* Mother to read to us till we had done our homework.

geyser gey'-ser *geysers* A hot spring which from time to time throws out mud, water or steam in the form of a fountain.

ghost *ghosts, ghostly.* The spirit of a dead person. The *ghost* is thought by some people to return in the form of the living person after the real person is dead.–On Hallowe'en the children dressed up in sheets and pretended to be *ghosts.*

giant gi'-ant *giants.* 1. A very large, strong man. 2. Anything that is larger than other things of its kind.–A *giant* ear of corn is one that is very, very large.–A *giant* crop of corn is an unusually large crop.

giblet gib'-let *giblets.* The heart, liver, or gizzard of a chicken or any other fowl.–Mother cooks the *giblets* of the turkey and cuts them up in the gravy.

gift *gifts, gifted.* 1. A present.–Mary received a new dress as a birthday *gift* from Mother. 2. A talent.–Sally has a great *gift* for music. It is natural for her to learn music easily and to perform it well. She is very *gifted.*

gigantic gi-gan'-tic. Very large.–The fisherman caught a *gigantic* fish. It was nearly as big as he was.

giggle gig'-gle *giggles, giggled, giggling.* 1. Laugh in a silly, jerky way.–Some children *giggle* at anything. 2. A tittering laugh.–We heard a *giggle* coming from the corner of the room.

gild *gilds, gilded, gilding.* Put a thin coating of gold over.–Mother's good dinner plates are *gilded* round the edges.

gilt. 1. Gold-painted.–The picture has a *gilt* frame. 2. A thin outer coating of gold.–The *gilt* on the frame is becoming tarnished.

gin *gins.* 1. A kind of alcoholic liquor.–*Gin* is sometimes mixed with other liquids to make a cocktail. 2. A cotton *gin* is a machine for taking the seeds out of cotton. 3. A *gin* is also a snare for catching game.

ginger gin'-ger. 1. The dried, ground roots of the *ginger* plant.–Mother puts *ginger* into the cakes. 2. A spice made from the root of the *ginger,* often used in medicines and in different soft drinks, like *ginger* ale.

gingerbread gin'-ger-bread. A kind of cake flavoured with ginger.

giraffe gi-raffe' *giraffes.* A very tall, yellowish, spotted animal. It has very long front legs and a long neck. *Giraffes* can eat leaves from tall trees. When they eat from the ground, they either get down as a person does when he kneels, or spread their front feet far apart. *Giraffes* come from Africa. You can see them in zoos and circuses here.

girl *girls.* A young woman; a female child, usually called a little *girl.*–Aunt Alice is a woman. Mary is a little *girl.*

give *gives, gave, given, giving.* 1. I will *give* you some flowers. I will make you a present of them. I will hand them to you and you may keep them.–Boy Scouts *give* first aid to those who need it.–Mother *gives* her children much attention. She pays lots of attention to them.–We will come if Mother *gives* her consent, if she says we may. 2. Produce, make. – Cows *give* milk. – Fire *gives* heat. 3. Feed.–Grandfather *gives* his horse hay. 4. Have, arrange.–The children are *giving* a party. 5. Cause, make for.–Our car *gives* us lots of trouble.–Reading *gives* pleasure. 6. Yield; move as a result of force.–Father tried to move the big rock, but it wouldn't *give* an inch. 7. *Give up* means stop trying.–Mary did not guess the answer, but she would not *give up.*

given giv'-en. 1. One form of the word *give.*–We have *given* our magazines to the hospital. 2. Already arranged or understood. – The boys arrived at the *given* time. They arrived at the time that had been set or named.

gizzard giz'-zard *gizzards.* A second stomach which birds have. In the *gizzard,* food is ground up very small.

G

H I J K L M N O P Q R S T U V W X Y Z

glacier gla'-cier *glaciers*. A whole river of ice that moves slowly down a mountain-side. The snow on the mountain packs down tightly and freezes to form the ice.

glad *gladder, gladdest, gladly*. Happy, pleased. –We are *glad* Mother is home.

glade *glades*. An open space in the woods where there are no trees. – The children picked daisies in the *glade*.

gladiolus gla-di-o'-lus or gla-di'-o-lus *gladioli* or *gladioluses*. A flower of various colours that grows on a long stem. The buds near the bottom of the stem blossom first, then the others. *Gladioli* grow from bulbs.

gladness glad'-ness. Joy, happiness.–Christmas is a time of *gladness*.

glance *glances, glanced, glancing*. 1. Look quickly.–We just *glanced* at the picture. We looked at it for just a moment.
2. A short look.–Bill shot a *glance* at the teacher to see if she was watching him.
3. Bounce off in a slanting direction.–The stones hit the wall and *glanced* off.

gland *glands*. An organ of a person's body. *Glands* do work in one's body just as the heart and lungs do. Saliva, the liquid in the mouth which helps digest the food, is made by *glands*.

glare *glares, glared, glaring*. 1. Stare angrily.– The boy *glared* at me.
2. Angry look or stare.–The angry farmer gave Bob such a *glare* that he ran away.
3. Strong, blinding light.–Jack moved his seat away from the *glare* of the sun.
4. Shine blindingly.–The light *glares* on my paper.

glass *glasses*. 1. A hard material that you can see through. Window-panes, mirrors, and many other things are made of *glass*.

2. A drinking container made of *glass*; the amount of a liquid that a *glass* will hold.– Mary drank a *glass* of milk.
3. *Glasses*, or spectacles, are round pieces of *glass*, ground to different thicknesses and fastened to a frame. People having something wrong with their eyes can see better when wearing *glasses*.

glassful glass'-ful *glassfuls*. As much as can be put into a glass. –Mary drank a *glassful* of milk.

glaze *glazes, glazed, glazing*. 1. Cover with a glassy sheet of something.–The windscreen on the car is *glazed* with ice.
2. A smooth, shiny finish.–The vase has a nice *glaze*.–Varnish is a *glaze*.

gleam *gleams, gleamed, gleaming*. 1. A beam or flash.–A *gleam* of light comes from the light-house.
2. Shine.–A light *gleams* in the window.

glee *gleeful, gleefully*. Joy, happiness, delight. –The children shouted with *glee* when the clown appeared.

glide *glides, glided, gliding*. Move smoothly and silently.–The dancers *glide* along the polished floor.

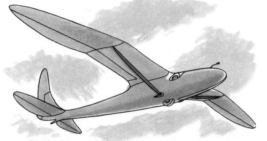

glider glid'-er *gliders*. An aeroplane that has no motor. A *glider* is kept up and carried along by the air or wind.

glimpse *glimpses, glimpsed, glimpsing.* 1. A short look.–Mother let us have a *glimpse* of Father's birthday cake before she put it out of sight.
2. Get a quick look at. To *glimpse* a thing means to peep at it.–We *glimpsed* the Queen as she drove by.

glisten glis′-ten *glistens, glistened, glistening.* Flash at quick intervals.–Diamonds *glisten* when held under a light.

glitter glit′-ter *glitters, glittered, glittering.* Sparkle brightly.–The snow *glitters* in the sunlight.

globe *globes, global.* 1. A ball; any solid object that is round. –
The earth is a *globe.*
2. A map of the world made on a ball or sphere. – Mary found China on the *globe.*

gloom. 1. Sadness; hopeless feeling.–A feeling of *gloom* came over the old man.
2. Darkness.–*Gloom* was everywhere about us as we entered the cave.

gloomy gloom′-y. 1. Dark and dreary.–Before the rain came, the sky was very *gloomy.*
2. Not hopeful; sad.–Aunt Ellen is *gloomy* about the future. She believes all the worst things will probably happen.

glorious glo′-ri-ous *gloriously.* 1. Brilliant and shining.–It is a *glorious* day. The sun is shining and it is very bright.
2. Excellent, fine in every way.–We had a *glorious* time at the party.

glory glo′-ry. 1. The praise and honour given a person for doing some great thing. – The soldier won great *glory.*
2. Brightness, great show, splendour. – The king arrived in all his *glory.*
3. Take delight and great pride. – Grandmother *glories* in Jack's good work at school.

gloss. A bright finish.–The maid put a *gloss* on the furniture by using furniture polish.

glossy gloss′-y *glossier, glossiest.* Shiny.–The waxed furniture is *glossy.* – The kitten has *glossy* fur.

glove *gloves.* We wear *gloves* on our hands to keep them warm. *Gloves* have a place for each finger and the thumb.

glow *glows, glowed, glowing.* 1. The light and colour made by something burning or fiery.–We sat by the dying fire and watched the *glow* of the coals.
2. Shine with heat.–The fire *glows.*
3. Brighten.–The child's face *glowed* when he saw Father Christmas. His face shone with eagerness and excitement.
4. A warm shine.–A *glow* came into his eyes.

glue *glues, glued, gluing.* 1. A sticky substance made from gelatine. Gelatine is made by boiling the bones and other waste parts of animals.–Bob used *glue* to fasten the parts of his aeroplane together.
2. Stick on with *glue.*–Father *glued* the rocker to the chair.

glum *glummer, glummest, glumly.* Quiet, gloomy, and sad.–Jack is *glum* because he did not get a good mark in arithmetic.

glutton glut′-ton *gluttons.* A person who eats too much and too fast. *Gluttons* seem to be afraid that they will not get their share.

glycerine or **glycerin** glyc′-er-in. A clear, thick, sweet liquid made from fats and oils. It is used in making medicines and explosives.

gnash *gnashes, gnashed, gnashing.* Hit (the teeth) fiercely together, making a sound. – The dragon *gnashed* his teeth when he saw the knight approaching with drawn sword.

gnat *gnats.* A small insect that has 2 wings and long feelers.

gnaw *gnaws, gnawed, gnawing.* Chew at.–Dogs like to *gnaw* the meat from bones. They bite or pick it off little by little with their teeth.

go *goes, gone, going.* 1. Move from one place to another.–We come to school in the morning. We *go* home from school in the evening.
2. Work, move.–What makes the engine *go*?
3. Leave.–The children were here, but they have *gone.*
4. Disappear.–Baby's milk is all *gone.* None is left.
5. Belong.–Your hat *goes* in the cupboard.
6. Attend regularly.–Do you *go* to school?

goal *goals.* 1. The posts and crossbar in soccer rugger, hockey, etc. In soccer, to kick the ball into the net behind the *goel* is to score a *goal.* The *goal* is defended by a *goal*keeper.
2. The thing one wants most.–The man's *goal* is to be a good citizen.

G
H
I
J
K
L
M
N
O
P
Q
R
S
T
U
V
W
X
Y
Z

goat *goats.* An animal about the size of a sheep, with horns and a beard. *Goats'* milk is good to drink.

gobble gob'-ble *gobbles, gobbled, gobbling.* I. Eat fast, taking too much at a time.–Bob was in such a hurry to get out to play that he *gobbled* his lunch.
2. Make a turkey's gurgling sort of cry. The turkeys gobbled.
3. The sound a turkey makes. – Turkeys seem to say '*Gobble, gobble, gobble.*'

gobbler gob'-bler *gobblers.* A male or he-turkey.

goblet gob'-let *goblets.* A drinking glass. A *goblet* has a long stem and a flat base.

goblin gob'-lin *goblins.* A little elf. *Goblins* are written about in fairy tales.

God. The maker and ruler of all things.

god *gods.* A male spirit that is worshipped. Some primitive people believe that there are many *gods.*

goddess god'-dess *goddesses.* A woman god; any female spirit that is worshipped.

goes. One form of the word *go.*–Father *goes* to work in the morning.–The train *goes.*–The clock *goes.*

going go'-ing. One form of the word *go.*–Never get off the train while it is *going.*–The watch is *going.*

gold. I. A precious yellow metal. *Gold* comes from mines. It is used in making watches, rings, chains, and other jewellery. Some coins are made of *gold.*
2. A deep, rich yellow colour.–Mother has a *gold* dress.
3. Much money.–The miser counted his *gold* every night by the light of a candle.

golden gold'-en. Made of gold; of the yellow colour of gold.–Baby has *golden* curls.–The king had *golden* plates.

golden-rod gold'-en-rod. A plant that blossoms in late summer. Its golden-yellow flowers grow on tall stems that have leaves all along them.

golden wedding gol'-den wed'-ding *golden weddings.* The fiftieth anniversary of a marriage. – Bob's grandfather and grandmother will celebrate their *golden wedding* next year. They will have been married fifty years.

goldfish gold'-fish. A small, gold-coloured fish.– The children feed the *goldfish* in the fish bowl each day.

golf. A game played on a large outdoor area called a *golf* course. *Golf* is played with a small, hard-rubber ball, which is hit with a club.

golfer gol'-fer *golfers.* A person who plays golf. –Father is a good *golfer.* He plays well.

golliwog gol'-li-wog *golliwogs.* A doll with a black face, staring eyes and fuzzy hair.–Mary gave Baby a *golliwog* for her birthday.

gondola gon'-do-la *gondolas.* A small boat, with a high point at each end, used on the canals in Venice.

gone. One form of the word *go.*–Bob put his hat in the hall but now it is *gone.*–The family has *gone* away for the summer.

gong *gongs.* A round curved piece of metal which rings when struck.–A *gong* is often sounded as an alarm.

good *better, best.* 1. Well-behaved. – Some children are bad; others are *good.*
2. Desirable; excellent; fine.–Some boys do poor work, but Bob's work is *good.*–This is my *good* hat.
3. Useful. – The broken chair cannot be mended. It is not *good* for anything.
4. Pleasant.–This is a *good* day.
5. Kind.–It was *good* of you to call.
6. Very.–Father has a *good* many customers.
7. Giving satisfaction.–This is a *good* book.
8. Benefit.–We gave the money for the *good* of all the family.

good-bye good-bye′ *good-byes.* A customary thing to say when parting. It is a wish of good fortune for those who are leaving.–We said *good-bye* to all our friends.

good-natured good-na′-tured *good-naturedly.* Pleasant; easy to get on with. – Grandmother is *good-natured*; she doesn't care how much noise we make.

goodness good′-ness. 1. Honesty and kindness. –The old woman is known and liked for her *goodness.*
2. An expression of surprise.–*Goodness,* how he can run!

goods. 1. Household property.–Tables, chairs, and other furniture are *goods.*
2. Things sold or for sale.–The department store sells many kinds of *goods.*

goodwill good′-will. Kindly feelings. – We show *goodwill* to our neighbours.

goose *geese.* A large bird, much like a duck except that its neck is longer. *Geese* are good to eat.

gooseberry goose′-ber-ry *gooseberries.* A berry, usually slightly hairy, that grows on a prickly bush. *Gooseberries* are good to eat when ripe. They are used in jams, pies, etc.

goose-flesh goose′-flesh. A rough pimply condition of the skin, lasting a short while, caused by sudden fright or cold.–The wailing of the dog at midnight gave me *goose-flesh.*

gore *gores, gored, goring.* 1. Blood.–The leg of the injured man was covered with *gore.*
2. Pierce or stab.–The bull-fighter was *gored* by the bull.

gorge *gorges, gorged, gorging.* 1. A narrow valley or passage-way. – We passed through a *gorge* between the mountains.

2. Eat too much.–It is not polite to *gorge.*

gorgeous gor′-geous *gorgeously.* Splendidly coloured; beautiful and magnificent. – The leaves on the trees in autumn are *gorgeous.*

gorilla go-ril′-la *gorillas.* A huge, man-like ape.

gossip gos′-sip *gossips, gossiped, gossiping.* 1. Talk about others' private affairs.–She was disliked because she *gossiped.*
2. One who talks about others' private affairs.

gouge *gouges, gouged, gouging.* 1. Kind of chisel used by carpenters and surgeons.
2. To cut or force out, as with such a chisel.

goulash gou′-lash. A stew of meat and vegetables.–Mother makes a wonderful *goulash.*

gourd *gourds.* A fruit that has a hard rind and grows on a vine.– *Gourds* are of many shapes and colours.

govern gov′-ern *governs, governed, governing.* Manage; control; rule.–Bob had great difficulty in *governing* his temper.–Laws *govern* the people of our country.

G
H
I
J
K
L
M
N
O
P
Q
R
S
T
U
V
W
X
Y
Z

government gov'-ern-ment *governments*. 1. The group of **persons** elected or appointed to govern or **rule** a country. – The *government* runs the health service.

2. The way a country is controlled or managed.–The *government* of Great Britain is a democracy.

governor gov'-er-nor *governors*. 1. A man at the head of the government of a state or territory.

2. A device that controls speed.–Our new car has a *governor* on the engine. The *governor* keeps it from going too fast.

gown *gowns*. 1. A dress, – Mother has a new party *gown*.

2. A long, loose garment. – The students wore caps and *gowns* when they received their degrees.

grab *grabs, grabbed, grabbing*. Snatch; take hold of suddenly.–Bob *grabbed* his coat from the chair and hurried away to school.

grace *graces, graced, gracing*. 1. Beautiful, easy movement.–Mary dances with *grace*.

2. Bob got in Mother's good *graces* by helping to wash the dishes.

3. A prayer of thanks for food.–Father said *grace* when the family sat down at the table.

graceful grace'-ful *gracefully*. 1. Beautiful and easy in movement.–The dancers are *graceful*.

2. Beautiful in form.–The vase has a *graceful* shape.

gracious gra'-cious *graciously*. Kind and pleasant. – Grandmother is very *gracious* to her guests.

grade *grades, graded, grading*. 1. Rank.–The major is a *grade* higher than the captain.

2. Quality.–Mother buys the best *grade* of meats.

3. Arrange, sort.–Classroom tests help the teachers to *grade* their pupils.

4. Smooth.–The men are *grading* the road.

5. A slope.–The hill has quite a *grade* to it.

gradual grad'-u-al. Happening or occurring little by little, or slowly and continuously.– The hill has a *gradual* slope.

gradually grad'-u-al-ly. A little at a time.–The snow fell *gradually*.–We did our work *gradually*.

graduate grad'-u-ate *graduates, graduated, graduating*. 1. Take a college or university degree.–Bob *graduated* this summer and is now taking a holiday.

2. A person who has taken a university degree.–Father is a university *graduate*.

3. Mark off in order to measure.–Thermometers and other instruments are *graduated*.

graduation grad'-u-a'-tion *graduations*. 1. Taking a degree at college or university.–After his *graduation* Bob went on holiday.

2. A line or mark to record measures.–Scientists use tubes and glasses with *graduations* to measure liquids.

grain *grains*. 1. The edible seeds of certain plants. Wheat, maize, barley and oats are *grains*.

wheat   maize   barley   oats

2. A plant that bears an edible seed, such as wheat or rye.

3. A tiny piece.–Father got a *grain* of sand in his eye.

4. The fibres of wood. – The *grain* in pine boards is easy to see.

5. The teacher would not give Sally even a *grain* of encouragement.

grammar gram'-mar. The study of how to use words together correctly.–In *grammar* lessons the children learn how to write and speak correctly.

granary gran'-a-ry *granaries*. A building for storing grain. – Farmers often keep their grain in a building called a *granary*.

grand *grander, grandest, grandly*. Large and splendid.–The rich man lives in a *grand* house.

grandchild grand'-child *grandchildren*. A child of one's son or daughter.

granddaughter grand'-daugh-ter *granddaughters*. A daughter of one's son or daughter.

G
H
I
J
K
L
M
N
O
P
Q
R
S
T
U
V
W
X
Y
Z

grandfather grand'-fa-ther *grandfathers*. The father of one's parent.–My father's father and my mother's father are my *grandfathers*.

grandma grand'-ma *grandmas*. A grandmother.

grandmother grand'-moth-er *grandmothers*. The mother of one's parent. – My father's mother and my mother's mother are my *grandmothers*.

grandpa grand'-pa *grandpas*. A grandfather.

grandparents grand'-par-ents. The parents of one's father and mother.–Your grandfathers and grandmothers are your *grandparents*.

grandson grand'-son *grandsons*. The son of one's son or daughter.

grandstand *grandstands*. The main stand or place with seats where people sit during games or other events.–We sat in the *grandstand* at the football game.

granite gran'-ite. A very hard, grey rock.– Many monuments and buildings are made of *granite*.

grant *grants, granted, granting*. 1. Allow; give. –The fairy *granted* the prince his wish.
2. Admit; agree.–I *grant* that I was mistaken.

grape *grapes*. A fruit that grows in bunches on *grape*-vines. *Grapes* are green, red, or purple. They are good to eat. Wine is made from grapes.

grapefruit grape'-fruit *grapefruits*. A large, often sour fruit like a large yellow orange.
–*Grapefruit* is good to eat for breakfast.

grape-vine grape'-vine *grape-vines*. A vine on which grapes grow.

graph *graphs*. A *graph* is a set of lines or blocks that shows how 2 or more changing things are related.

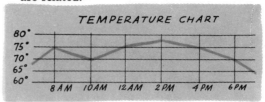

grasp *grasps, grasped, grasping*. 1. Take hold firmly.–The man *grasped* the side of the boat and held on tightly.
2. A hold or clasp.–The man's tight *grasp* on my arm made it hurt.
3. Understand, learn.–Bob *grasps* arithmetic quickly.

grass *grasses*. 1. Long, narrow, green leaves or blades that grow close together.
– The lawn is covered with green *grass*.–Cows eat *grass*.– Bob mows the *grass*.
2. The plants that bear grains, such as rye, wheat, and oats. Plants having long, slender stalks, such as the bamboo and sugar cane, are also *grasses*.

grasshopper grass'-hop-per *grasshoppers*. A kind of insect that jumps or hops long distances. *Grasshoppers* eat plants. Sometimes they eat up the farmers' crops.

grassy grass'-y *grassier, grassiest*. Covered with grass. – The field is *grassy*.

grate *grates, grated, grating*. 1. A container or a framework made of iron bars.–The core in a boiler rests on a *grate*, through which the ashes fall.
2. Rub against a rough piece of metal to cut into small bits.–Mother *grates* cheese, horse-radish, coconut, and the like.
3. Make a harsh sound.–Rough, dry things *grate* when they are rubbed together. – A piece of metal dragged along the pavement *grates* on the concrete.

grateful grate'-ful *gratefully*. Thankful, appreciative, glad of something.–We are *grateful* for our homes and for enough to eat.

gratitude grat'-i-tude. Appreciation, thankfulness; gladness for something given to or done for one.–Bob expressed his *gratitude* for the gifts.

grave *graves.* 1. A hole in the ground for burying a person or animal that is dead. – The boys dug a *grave* for their dog that died.
2. Thoughtful, serious.–The old woman had a *grave* look on her face. She was thinking about something important.

gravel grav'-el *gravels.* Stone broken into small pieces; pebbles.–We drove off the main road and down a side road covered with *gravel.*

gravestone grave'-stone *gravestones.* A stone tablet or marker put over a grave. The name of the person buried in the grave and the dates of his birth and his death are engraved on the *gravestone.*

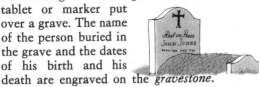

graveyard grave'yard *graveyards.* A cemetery; a large area where the dead are buried.

gravity grav'-i-ty. 1. An unseen force that draws all things towards the centre of the earth. When you throw a ball into the air, *gravity* brings it to earth again.
2. An unseen force that draws things together. –*Gravity* keeps the earth from getting further from the sun.–*Gravity* keeps the moon close to the earth.
3. Seriousness.–The *gravity* of war is known to all.

gravy gra'-vy. The fat and juice that cook out of meats and fowls. Sometimes flour or other thickening and milk or water are added to this juice to make a thick *gravy.*

graze *grazes, grazed, grazing.* 1. Eat grass from the ground where it grows.–The cows *graze* in the pasture.
2. Brush or barely touch in passing.–The flying ball just *grazed* my head. It just touched my head lightly as it went by me.
3. Rub the skin from.–Baby fell on the gravel path and *grazed* her knee.

grease *greases, greased, greasing.* 1. An oil or fat. Butter, lard, and olive oil are *greases.*

2. Put *grease* on.–Father *greased* his car. He put *grease* on the parts that rub together.

greasy greas'-y *greasier, greasiest.* 1. Covered with grease. – The workman's hands are *greasy.*
2. Having too much fat or oil in it.–The fried potatoes were too *greasy.*–Father likes his bacon crisp, not *greasy.*

great *greater, greatest, greatly.* 1. Much more than usual. – Bob takes *great* care of his younger sister.
2. Important, outstanding, famous and honoured.–Thomas Edison was a *great* inventor.
3. Very big, huge.–Elephants are *great,* heavy animals.

greatness great'-ness. Importance, fame, being better and finer than many others.–Nelson's *greatness* is known to everyone. – Can you tell what accounts for the *greatness* of this painting?

greed. Desire to have everything for oneself, or more than one needs.–The man had few friends because of his *greed* for money.

greedy greed'-y *greedier, greediest, greedily.*
1. Wanting to eat more than one's share, and as fast as possible, as if it were going to disappear.–The hungry man eats as if he were *greedy.*
2. Wanting too much for oneself.–The miser is *greedy.* All he thinks about is how to get more money for himself.

green *greener, greenest, greenish.* 1. The colour of grass.–Most leaves are *green* in the summer. They turn yellow, red, and brown in autumn.
2. Not ripe–We could not eat the melon, because it was still *green.*
3. New, not experienced.–Bob is *green* at playing tennis. He doesn't know much about it.

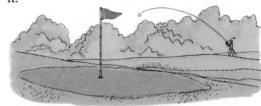

4. A smooth piece of ground covered with very short grass.–The man playing golf hit the ball on to the *green.*
5. (In the plural form *greens*) *green* vegetables, especially cabbage. – Meat, potatoes and *greens* make a very good meal.

greenhouse green'-house *greenhouses*. A house made of glass in which are grown delicate plants. Some *greenhouses* are warmed by hot pipes, others only by the sun.–Father grows tomatoes in his *greenhouse*.

greet *greets, greeted, greeting.* Welcome or speak to someone on seeing him. We *greet* people when we meet them by saying 'Good morning,' 'Hello,' or 'Good evening,' or by shaking hands.

greeting greet'-ing *greetings.* 1. A welcome.– We give Father a warm *greeting* when he comes home at night.
2. A message of good wishes.–Grandmother sent me a birthday *greeting*.–The stationer sells *greeting* cards, cards wishing people happiness on special days.

grew. One form of the word *grow*.–The plant *grew* fast in the rich earth.

grey. A colour that is a mixture of black and white.–Some rabbits are *grey*. – Grandmother's hair is *grey*.

griddle-cake grid'-dle-cake *griddle-cakes.* A pancake that is cooked on a griddle on top of the stove.

grief. Sorrow, sadness.–Much *grief* has come to the family. They have had all kinds of bad fortune.

grieve *grieves, grieved, grieving.* 1. Make unhappy and troubled.–Mother was grieved by Bob's thoughtlessness.
2. Feel sad. – Do not *grieve* over the lost money.

grill *grills, grilled, grilling.* 1. Broil, cook by a direct flame.–We *grill* meat by holding it right over a fire to cook it.
2. A dining-room which serves mostly *grilled* foods.–We ate in the *grill-room* at the hotel.
3. Question for a long time without stopping. –The police *grilled* the suspected man for hours.

grim *grimly, grimness.* 1. Solemn and stern.– Father was *grim* when Jack confessed that he had lost the ten pounds.
2. Very unpleasant and depressing.–The accident was a *grim* sight.

grime. Dirt rubbed or ground into a thing.– Bob's hands were covered with *grime* after playing ball.

grin *grins, grinned, grinning.* 1. Smile broadly, showing the teeth.–The man *grins* because he is so happy.
2. A big smile. – A *grin* spread over Jack's face when he saw the ice-cream.

grind *grinds, ground, grinding.* 1. Crush or cut very fine.–The grocer *grinds* the coffee. He puts it into a mill which cuts it into tiny pieces.
2. Rub against a rough stone.–Father sharpens knives by *grinding* them.
3. Make or work by turning a handle.–The organ grinder *grinds* out music by turning a handle on the organ.
4. Rub together and make a grating sound.– Baby sometimes *grinds* her teeth.

grindstone grind'-stone *grindstones.* A flat, rough stone turned by a motor or by hand to sharpen tools, knives, etc.

grip *grips, gripped, gripping.* 1. Take hold of and hold tightly. – The frightened child *gripped* his father's hand.
2. A tight grasp.–Sally keeps a *grip* on Father's hair when he carries her on his shoulder.
3. Power, control.–The country lay in the *grip* of the severest winter ever known.

grisly gris'-ly. Terrible to look at.–The giant was a *grisly* sight as he strode across the fields.

gristle (pronounced *grissel*) gris'-tle. A hard, white, stretchy substance found in meat. People do not eat the *gristle*. They cannot chew it.

grit *grits, gritted, gritting, gritty.* 1. Very small particles of sand.–The wind blew some *grit* into my eyes.
2. Courage.–The batsman showed plenty of *grit* in facing the fast bowler.
3. Press together firmly.–Jack *gritted* his teeth when he twisted his ankle.

G
H
I
J
K
L
M
N
O
P
Q
R
S
T
U
V
W
X
Y
Z

grizzled griz′-zled. Somewhat grey.–The elderly man has thick, *grizzled* hair.

grizzly griz′-zly *grizzlies*. A big, fierce, brown bear. There are many *grizzlies* in the Rocky Mountains of Canada.

groan *groans, groaned, groaning.* 1. Moan; make a low sound of pain or suffering.–The sick woman *groans* at times.
2. A low sound of pain or suffering.–The wounded man sank down with a *groan*.

grocer gro′-cer *grocers*. A man in charge of a grocer's shop.

grocery gro′-cer-y *groceries*. 1. The trade of a grocer. The *grocery* business consists of buying and selling food.

2. *Groceries* are foods bought at a *grocery*.–Butter, coffee, biscuits, and a jar of peanut butter are *groceries*.

groom *grooms, groomed, grooming.* 1. A man who cares for horses.–Grandfather employs a *groom* at his stable.
2. Care for (a horse).–The *groom grooms* the horses every day. He feeds them and brushes them.
3. *Groomed* means dressed and cleaned up.–Bob always looks well-*groomed*.
4. A bride*groom*; a man who has just been or is about to be married.

groove *grooves*. A hollow trough cut in a surface.–There is a *groove* on your desk to lay your pencils in.–Father put *grooves* in the draining-boards so that the water would run down them into the sink.

grope *gropes, groped, groping.* Feel around in the dark with the hands.–Father *groped* in the cupboard for his hat.

gross. 1. Large and fat.–The man was so *gross* that he waddled.
2. Twelve dozen, 144.–The teacher bought a *gross* of pencils.
3. Total.–The arithmetic problem asked us to find the *gross* profit the man made. This was the profit before any expenses were taken out.
4. Obviously wrong or clumsy.–The teacher said that the accident was caused by Dick's *gross* carelessness.

grotesque (pronounced *grotesk*) gro-tesque′. Fantastic; ridiculous.–The children laughed at the *grotesque* appearance of the clown, with his white face, red nose and baggy trousers.

grotto grot′-to *grottoes* or *grottos*. A picturesque cave.–When we were on holiday we went to see the famous *grotto* in the mountains. It was decorated all over with shells.

ground *grounds, grounded, grounding.* 1. The soil; the surface of the earth.–We plant seeds in the *ground*.
2. Land set aside for a particular purpose.–We play in the play*ground*.
3. Private land.–The *grounds* around the rich man's house have been planted with trees and shrubs.
4. On a level with the *ground*.–We live on the *ground* floor.
5. A reason; evidence. – The man had no *grounds* for accusing Jack of stealing the bicycle.
6. All the aeroplanes were *grounded*. They could not fly because of bad weather.
7. The small, hard, dark brown grains left in the pot after the coffee has been poured.–Mary emptied the *grounds* from the coffee pot.
8. One form of the word *grind*.–The flour was *ground* at the mill.

ground floor *ground floors*. The floor of a house on a level with the ground. – The drawing-room, dining-room and the kitchen of our house are all on the *ground floor*.

groundless ground′-less. Without any reason.–When Mother said she was worried about Baby's illness, the doctor told her that her fears were *groundless*.

G H I J K L M N O P Q R S T U V W X Y Z

group *groups, grouped, grouping.* 1. A number of persons or things all of one kind, put together.–Children form *groups* of 3 and 4 to play.–Several pictures hung together on the wall make a *group.*
2. A small crowd or collection.–A *group* of people stood at the corner.
3. Put into *groups.*–The teacher *grouped* the children according to age.
4. Form a *group.* – The children were all *grouped* around the teacher.

grouse. A game bird that looks something like a chicken. – There are many kinds of *grouse.* Hunters hunt them as sport or for food.

grove *groves.* A group of trees.–We can see a beautiful *grove* at the bottom of the hill.

grow *grows, grew, grown, growing.* 1. Get bigger.–Children *grow.*–Plants *grow.*–The city has *grown* since we moved here.
2. Become.–The sky *grew* black during the storm.–Alice has *grown* thinner.
3. Cultivate.–We *grow* vegetables and flowers in our garden.

growl *growls, growled, growling.* 1. Make a deep, throaty, frightening sound. – Dogs *growl* when they are angry.
2. A deep, throaty, fierce sound.–We heard the *growl* of the watchdog.
3. Talk grumpily; complain and grumble.– Jack is *growling* about having to wash up.

grown. 1. One form of the word *grow.*–Baby has *grown* a great deal this year. She has become much bigger.
2. Full-*grown* means finished getting bigger. –These plants are full-*grown.* They are as large as they will ever be.

grown-up *grown'-up grown-ups.* 1. No longer growing; no longer a child. – Father and Mother are *grown-ups.* They are adults.
2. An adult; a man or woman.–Mary is very anxious to become a *grown-up,* so that she can do just as she pleases.

growth. 1. The amount a person, a plant, an animal, or anything will grow, has grown, etc.–Bob's *growth* has been rapid. He has grown very fast during the past year.
2. Crop, or amount grown.–The sailor had a thick *growth* of whiskers.

grub *grubs.* An insect in its early, short, thick, wormlike form. When the *grub* has gone through several stages of growth, it becomes a beetle or some other insect.

grudge *grudges, grudged, grudging.* 1. Not liking to give something one has to give.–The employer *grudged* the man the money he earned. He paid him, but he didn't want to pay him.
2. Hard feeling; dislike because of a special reason.–The prisoner said the policeman had a *grudge* against him. He believed the policeman was holding something against him, and had always wanted to get back at him for it.

gruel *gru'-el.* A thick, liquid food frequently fed to sick people and to babies. *Gruel* is made by boiling meal or oatmeal in milk or water.

gruff *gruffly.* Rough, harsh, deep in sound.– Grandfather sometimes talks in a *gruff* voice when he is trying hard not to laugh.

grumble *grum'-ble grumbles, grumbled, grumbling.* Find fault or complain in a low voice. –Some children *grumble* about everything they have to do.

grumpy *grump'-y grumpier, grumpiest.* Gross and gruff, not satisfied, bad-tempered.–Baby gets *grumpy* when she is sleepy.

grunt *grunts, grunted, grunting.* 1. Make a deep, quick noise in the throat.–Dogs bark, cocks crow, but pigs *grunt.*
2. A deep, quick noise made in the throat.– We heard the *grunts* of the pigs when Grandfather was feeding them.

guarantee *guar-an-tee' guarantees, guaranteed, guaranteeing.* 1. Promise that something will be satisfactory.–The jeweller *guaranteed* that the watch would run for a year. He would replace or mend it if it didn't.
2. Promise to do something.–Grandfather borrowed some money from the bank. Father *guaranteed* to repay it if Grandfather did not.
3. A promise to make good if something or someone does not bring satisfaction. – The jeweller gave us a *guarantee* on the watch.

G
H
I
J
K
L
M
N
O
P
Q
R
S
T
U
V
W
X
Y
Z

guard *guards, guarded, guarding.* 1. Watch over; protect. – The dog *guarded* the baby while Mother went into the shop.–Soldiers *guarded* the storehouse.

2. A person or group that defends or protects things, or that prevents things from happening: as, a coast*guard*, a *guard* on a passenger train, a *guard* in a jail, or a life*guard* at the beach.

3. Be careful.–The teacher told us to *guard* against catching cold. She wanted us to take care of ourselves so that we would not catch cold.

4. *On guard* means ready to defend against danger or harm at any moment.

guardian *guard'-i-an guardians.* One who has the care of someone or something.–Fathers and mothers are the *guardians* of their children. They take care of them.–The orphan's uncle is her *guardian.* He is the person who was named by law to care for her till she is old enough to look after herself.

guess *guesses, guessed, guessing.* 1. Say what something is, or decide about something, without knowing much about it and on the chance of being right.–Bob described an object and we *guessed* what it was. We told what we thought or believed it to be without seeing the object or having him name it.

2. Think or suppose.–I can only *guess* that Jack took the money without thinking. I can't believe that he meant to steal it.–Can you *guess* why I don't want to go out?

3. A chance or turn to *guess.*–In this game each person has 3 *guesses.*

guest *guests.* 1. A visitor, a person invited.– Mother is expecting *guests* for dinner.–Bob invited many *guests* to his party.

2. A person living at a hotel or other place with rooms for hire.–When staying in the city, Father was a *guest* at a small hotel.

guide *guides, guided, guiding.* 1. One who shows the way, as through a wilderness, through a museum, etc.–When our parents came to visit the school, Bob was a *guide.* He showed them the way to the different rooms.

2. Show the way, lead.–We will go through the woods if you will *guide* us.

guilt. Having done wrong; deserving blame for a crime or bad act.–Jack had a feeling of *guilt* after taking the cover of the old man's dustbin for a shield.

guilty *guilt'-y* 1. At fault or to blame for a crime or wrong done.–The jury found the man *guilty.* It decided that the man had done wrong and should be punished.

2. Ashamed, conscious of guilt.–Bob said he felt *guilty* for telling a lie, and asked to be forgiven.

guinea hen *guin'-ea hen guinea hens.* A fowl often seen on farms. *Guinea hens* are purplish-grey with white spots. They can fly quite high and roost high up in trees. They are very noisy when excited.

guinea pig *guin'-ea pig guinea pigs.* A tiny animal that looks a little like a rat. *Guinea pigs* are used by scientists in experiments to study diseases and see how medicines act.

guitar *gui-tar' guitars.* A musical instrument with strings. The strings are plucked with the fingers to make music.

gulf *gulfs.* A large bay that extends far into the land.–The *Gulf* of California is a part of the Pacific Ocean. The *Gulf* of Mexico is a part of the Atlantic Ocean.

gull *gulls.* A large, web-footed sea bird. *Gulls* are grey or white. *Gulls* often follow a boat and eat bits of food thrown from it. They eat fish also.

gully *gul'-ly gullies.* Small ditch.–It rained so hard that the water running down the hillside cut a *gully.*

gulp *gulps, gulped, gulping.* 1. Swallow hard and loudly.–Bob was in such a hurry to play ball that he *gulped* his food. He filled his mouth very full and swallowed his food without chewing it.

2. A loud, hard swallow.–The thirsty boy drank the cool water in *gulps.*

gum *gums, gummed, gumming, gummy.* 1. A sticky juice that comes out of some trees. It hardens when exposed to air.
2. Make sticky with *gum* or anything else that is sticky.–Postage stamps are *gummed* on the back for sticking them on envelopes.
3. Chewing *gum*, which is made from *gums* and flavourings.
4. The fleshy part of one's mouth that covers the roots of one's teeth. Our teeth are partly covered by the *gums*.

gun *guns.* A weapon used for shooting bullets, shells, rockets, and the like. Cannons and rifles are *guns*.

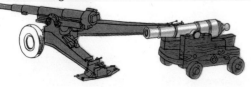

gunner gun´-ner *gunners.* One who fires a gun.–My brother is a *gunner* on a bombing plane. He fires guns.

gunpowder gun´-pow-der. A powder that explodes when struck or lighted.

gurgle gur´-gle *gurgles, gurgled, gurgling.* 1. Make a bubbling sound.–Baby *gurgles* when she is pleased and interested in something.
2. A bubbling sound.–If you blow through a straw into water, you hear a *gurgle*.

gush *gushes, gushed, gushing.* 1. Rush out suddenly.–When the water-pipe burst, water *gushed* out.
2. A sudden outpouring.–Water poured out in one big *gush*.

gust *gusts, gusty.* A sudden rush or blast of air or wind.–There was a big *gust* of wind, and the boat turned over.–A *gust* of wind whirled the dust round in a circle.

gutter gut´-ter *gutters.* 1. A shallow trough of metal, wood or stone fastened below the eaves to carry away rainwater from the roof.–In the autumn, fallen leaves may block the *gutters*.
2. A ditch or trough along the side of a road to carry away water.

gymnasium gym-na´-si-um *gymnasiums.* A building or room in which people exercise and try to build up their bodies. Badminton, boxing, indoor tennis, etc., take place in *gymnasiums*.

gypsy or **gipsy** gyp´-sy *gypsies.* A member of a tribe of people who wander about the country, They make their living telling fortunes, mending pots, and doing odd jobs. *Gypsies* probably came originally from India, a country in Asia.

H h

H, h *H's, h's.* The eighth letter of the alphabet.

ha. An exclamation of joy or surprise.–*Ha!* We won.

haberdasher ha´-ber-dash-er *haberdashers.* A seller of ribbons, tapes, handkerchiefs and small articles of dress in a shop or department store. Mother buys all her ribbons at the *haberdasher's.*–A *haberdasher* sells haberdashery of every sort.

habit hab´-it *habits.* A custom; the usual thing to do; a regular practice.–The children formed the *habit* of brushing their teeth twice a day.

habitat hab´-i-tat *habitats.* The place where an animal or person usually lives or where a plant is usually found.–A deer's *habitat* is the forest.

hack *hacks, hacked, hacking.* 1. Cut or chop roughly.–Father *hacked* the board in two with the blunt hatchet.
2. Cough dryly.–Bob had a cold and *hacked* continually in class. He had a *hacking* cough.

H

I
J
K
L
M
N
O
P
Q
R
S
T
U
V
W
X
Y
Z

had. One form of the word *have.*–If I *had* a pet, I would take care of it.–Yesterday I *had* £1.

haddock had′-dock. A large fish caught in the ocean for food.

hadn't. Had not.–I *hadn't* been home long before it started to rain.

hail *hails, hailed, hailing.* 1. Frozen raindrops. –The *hail* beat loudly on the tin roof.
2. Have a fall of *hail.*–It *hailed* when we had the big thunderstorm.
3. A shower of anything solid. – When the strong wind blew, there was a *hail* of acorns from the tree.
4. Call to.–Father *hailed* the taxi driver.
5. A call.–We heard the *hail* of the man on the boat.
6. Greet.–The class *hailed* the cricket captain when he came to the window.
7. Salute.–*Hail* to the king!
8. Come; be.–I *hail* from the South.

hailstone hail′-stone *hailstones.* A frozen raindrop; a small piece of hard ice that sometimes falls during a thunderstorm.

hair *hairs.* 1. The strands or a single one of the strands that grow on the head.–Mary's *hair* covers her ears.

2. *Hair* often grows on parts of the body other than the head, and many animals are covered with *hair.*

hairy hair′-y. Covered with hair.–The man's arms are *hairy.*

half *halves.* 1. One of 2 equal parts. If you divide anything into 2 parts the same size, each part is one *half.*–One *half* is written 1/2.
2. The glass is *half* full of milk. It can hold twice as much as it has in it now.

half brother half broth′-er *half brothers.* A brother by one parent only.–John and Tom have the same mother, but their fathers are different persons. John and Tom are *half brothers.*

half sister half sis′-ter *half sisters.* A sister by one parent only.–Jane and Ruth have the same mother, but their fathers are different persons. Jane and Ruth are *half sisters.*

halfway half′-way′ 1. Half of the distance.– Mary's belt will go only *halfway* round Mother's waist.
2. As far as the middle.–Bob has read *halfway* through the book.

hall *halls.* 1. A small room or passage-way at the entrance of a building or connecting different rooms in a building.– We walk through a *hall* to our room.
2. A large room where meetings are held. – The lecture was given in the school *hall.*

Hallowe'en Hal-low-e'en′. The night of the last day of October.–Children celebrate *Hallowe'en* by dressing up in funny costumes.

halt *halts, halted, halting.* 1. Come to a stop.– The officer ordered the men to *halt.*
2. Bring to a stop.–The officer *halted* the men.
3. A full stop.–The car came to a *halt.*

halter hal′-ter *halters.* A strap or rope used to lead a horse.–I led the horse by the *halter.*

halves. More than one half.–A whole apple divided into 2 equal parts is in 2 *halves.*

ham *hams.* The upper part of a pig's back leg, either fresh or salted and smoked.–*Ham* is good to eat with eggs.

hammer ham′-mer *hammers, hammered, hammering.* 1. A tool for pounding, or for driving nails. The head is metal and the handle is usually of wood. A *hammer* with a wooden head is a mallet.
2. Pound with a *hammer.*– Mother has a *hammered* metal bowl. It is made of metal *hammered* into shape with a *hammer*

hammock ham′-mock *hammocks.* A swinging couch hung by ropes at each end.–Sailors on some ships sleep in *hammocks.*

hamper ham'-per *hampers, hampered, hampering.* 1. A large basket with a cover.–Mother keeps the soiled clothes in a *hamper*.

2. Make difficult.–Bad weather *hampers* aeroplane travel.

hand *hands, handed, handing.* 1. The part of the body at the end of the arm, used for grasping and holding. We have 2 *hands*. Fingers are a part of the *hand*.

2. Give with the *hand*.–Bob *hands* out the papers to each one in the class.

3. A worker.–Grandfather has several hired *hands* on the farm.

4. One of the pointers on the face of a clock. –The *hands* of the clock show the time.

5. A unit of measure equal to 4 inches.–The horse is 10 *hands* high. He is 40 inches high.

6. Side.–On the one *hand,* Bob did not want to go to school; on the other *hand* he knew he should go.

7. *In hand* means under control.–The firemen had the fire *in hand* by the time we arrived.

handbag hand'-bag *handbags.* A bag small enough to carry in the hand. – Mother carries her money in her *handbag*.

handcuff hand'-cuff *handcuffs, handcuffed, handcuffing.* 1. One of a pair of metal bracelets fastened together with a chain. They are locked about the wrists of prisoners to keep them from running away.

2. Put *handcuffs* on.–The policeman *handcuffed* the 2 prisoners.

handful hand'ful *handfuls.* 1. As much as can be held in the hand.–Grandmother threw a *handful* of crumbs to the birds.

2. Very few.–There was just a *handful* of people at church this morning.

handicap hand'-i-cap *handicaps, handicapped, handicapping.* 1. Anything that hinders one. –A sore thumb is a *handicap* to a person when he tries to write.

2. Hinder.–A person is *handicapped* in writing if he cannot use his thumb.

3. An official advantage or disadvantage in a contest.–Bob had a *handicap* of 5 yards in the race with Bill. He started 5 yards behind Bill.

handkerchief hand'-ker-chief *handkerchiefs.* A small square of cloth used for wiping the face or the nose.

handle han'-dle *handles, handled, handling.* 1. A part of an object by which it is held.– Cups, buckets, and tools have *handles*.– Father turned the *handle* of the car door.

2. Hold and feel with the hands. – The greengrocer asked us not to *handle* the fruit.

3. Manage.–Father is a good foreman. He knows how to *handle* the men who work for him.

4. Buy and sell.–Our grocer *handles* only the very best foods.

handsome hand'-some. 1. Very good-looking. –John is *handsome* in his new Scout's uniform.

2. Generous and large; large and fine. – The man offered a *handsome* amount of money for the house.

handwriting hand'-writ-ing. Writing done with a pen, pencil, etc., held in the hand.– Mary's *handwriting* is easy to read.

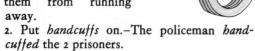

handy hand'-y. 1. Skilful.–Father is *handy* with the hammer and saw. He uses them easily and well.

2. Convenient.–Mother keeps the salt in a *handy* place.

hang *hangs, hung, hanging.* 1. Fasten at one or more points and let fall loosely.–Mother *hangs* the clothes on the clothes-line to dry.– Children *hang* their stockings on the mantelpiece at Christmas.

2. Droop.–The hot sun made the flowers *hang* down.

3. Decorate with *hanging* things.–The room was *hung* with Christmas bells and holly.

4. A knack.–Mary doesn't get the *hang* of knitting. She can't seem to do it.

hang *bangs, banged* or *hung, hanging*. 1. Kill by *banging* with a rope round the neck.–The murderer was *banged*.

2. Die by *banging* with a rope round the neck.–The murderer was told he would *hang* for his crime.

hangar hang′-ar *hangars*. A building or shed to keep aircraft in.

haphazard hap-haz′-ard *haphazardly*. Aimless.–The child does his work in a *haphazard* way.

happen hap′-pen *happens, happened, happening*. 1. Take place.–An accident *happened* just as we reached the corner.

2. Do something or occur by chance.–I *happened* to hear the music as I was passing by.

3. Go wrong.–Something has *happened* to Father's car. It will not run.

happening hap′-pen-ing *happenings*. An event; a thing that happens.–If an aeroplane landed on Grandfather's farm, it would be an unusual *happening*.

happiness hap′-pi-ness. Joy and gladness.– The children brought *happiness* to their parents.

happy hap′-py *happier, happiest, happily*. 1. Pleased and glad.–The children are *happy* when they are playing,

2. Lucky; fortunate.–It was a *happy* chance that Bob found the money.

happy-go-lucky. Carefree; without worries.– Mary is a *happy-go-lucky* person. Nothing worries her.

harbour har′-bour *harbours*. A sheltered body of water where ships and boats may go for safety from storms and waves; a port.

hard *harder, hardest*. 1. Solid, not soft; not easy to bend or dent.–Stones are *hard*.–A *hard* object does not give or change shape when you touch it.

2. Firm; not liquid.–Gelatine becomes *hard* when chilled.

3. Difficult; not simple. – Some arithmetic problems are *harder* than others.

4. Determined.–Bob is a *hard* worker. He works steadily and does his best.

5. With all or most of one's strength or skill. –Bob tries *hard* to get good marks.

6. Rough. – The hunters had a *hard* trip through the woods.

7. Full of trouble and suffering.–Times are *hard* when many men are out of work.

8. Strict and severe.–The man was a *hard* master. He treated those under him without mercy.–Father thought the punishment was *hard*.

9. Containing minerals.–*Hard* water does not make soapsuds easily.

10. The boxer gave his opponent such a *hard* punch that he knocked him down.

harden hard′-en *hardens, hardened, hardening*. Make or become hard.–Mother put the ice-cream in the frezzer to *harden*.–The sun *hardened* the clay.

hardly hard′-ly. 1. Scarcely; only just; barely. –We had *hardly* enough cake for everyone. –It is *hardly* 10 o'clock.

2. Not likely.–Since Bob has to work, he will *hardly* be able to attend the party.

hardship hard′-ship *hardships*. Something that is difficult to stand or endure.–Hunger is a *hardship*.

hardware hard′-ware. Articles made of metal, such as nails, wire, and tools.–We buy *hardware* at an ironmonger's shop.

hardy har′-dy. Strong and healthy. – Some plants are *hardy*. They are not easily destroyed.

hare *bares*. A grey or brown animal very much like a rabbit, but larger.–A *hare* can run very fast.

harm *harms, harmed, harming.* 1. Hurt.–The dog will not *harm* you.
2. Injury or damage.–Mother tries to keep the baby safe from *harm*.

harmful harm'-ful *harmfully.* Damaging; causing harm.–Freezing weather is *harmful* to plants.–Some snakes are *harmful*.

harmless harm'-less *harmlessly.* Not dangerous.–Most snakes are *harmless*.

harmonica har-mon'-i-ca *harmonicas.* A small, flat musical instrument played by blowing out and drawing in air through a row of holes. It is sometimes called a mouth-organ.

harmonize har'-mo-nize *harmonizes, harmonized, harmonizing.* Look or sound well together.–The colours of Mother's dress and hat *harmonize*.–The musical notes C and E *harmonize* well.

harmony har-mo-ny. 1. Peace and friendship. –If children live in *harmony* at home, they are apt to get on well together in school, too.
2. A beautiful combination of colour or sound. –There is *harmony* in the colours of the rainbow. The colours look well together.–Beautiful *harmony* can be created by the sounding of more than one musical note at a time.

harness har'-ness *harnesses, harnessed, harnessing.* 1. The set of straps with which a horse is hitched to a wagon, plough, etc.–

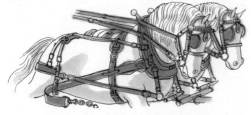

Grandfather put the *harness* on the horse.
2. Put a *harness* on.–The farmer *harnessed* the horse and hitched it to the wagon.
3. Control natural forces for human purposes. –The giant dam was built to *harness* the flow of the river in order to generate power.

harp *harps.* A large, stringed, musical instrument that stands on the floor and is played with the fingers of both hands.

harpoon har-poon' *harpoons, harpooned, harpooning.* 1. A spear with barbs that stick

backwards from the point.–Harpoons are used for catching whales and large fish.
2. Pierce with a *harpoon*.–The man stood up in the boat and *harpooned* the large fish.

harpsichord harp'-si-chord *harpsichords.* A musical instrument with a keyboard like that of a piano. Its music sounds like that of a harp.

harsh *harsher, harshest, harshly.* 1. Rough; grating or coarse. – The man's voice was *harsh*.–The stone felt *harsh* to the touch.
2. Severe.–The officer was *harsh* with his men. He treated them without mercy.

harvest har'-vest *harvests, harvested, harvesting.* 1. Gather.–The farmer *harvests* his grain, fruit, and other crops.
2. Crop.–There was a large *harvest* of potatoes this year.
3. The time of gathering crops.–*Harvest* is in the autumn or late summer.

harvester har'-vest-er *harvesters.* A person or a machine that gathers grain and other crops.

has. One form of the word *have.*–Mother *has* a new hat.

hash. A food made by chopping and cooking meat, onions, potatoes, and other foods together.

hasn't. Has not.–Father *hasn't* come home yet.

haste. A great hurry. – Grandmother left in *haste* when she read the letter from home.

hasten has'-ten *hastens, hastened, hastening.* Hurry.–Our teacher told us to *hasten* home.

hastily hast'-i-ly. 1. Quickly and a little carelessly.–Bob wrote his paper *hastily* and then went home.
2. Quickly; before thinking.–Do not speak *hastily*.

H
I
J
K
L
M
N
O
P
Q
R
S
T
U
V
W
X
Y
Z

hasty hast'-y. 1. Quickly made.–Mother cooked a *hasty* lunch.

2. Quick; without pausing to think.–Bob's *hasty* actions brought him sorrow afterwards.

hat *hats*. A garment to cover the head. *Hats* are made of felt, straw, and other materials.

hatch *hatches, hatched, hatching*. 1. The hen is patiently sitting on her eggs. She is *hatching* her chicks.–The mother robin sits on eggs in the nest until they *hatch*, until the baby robins come out of the shell.

2. An opening in the deck of a ship.–The sailor came up through the *hatch*.

hatchet hatch'-et *hatchets*. A small chopping tool with a short handle. You can pound with one end of the head of a *hatchet* and chop with the other.

hate *hates, hated, hating*. 1. Dislike very much. –Bill *hates* working.

2. Bitter dislike.–Our dog has great *hate* for cats.

hatred ha'-tred. A feeling of hating or great dislike.–There is *hatred* between these men. They hate each other.

haul *hauls, hauled, hauling*. 1. Pull. – The dog *hauled* the sledge over the snow.

2. Carry from place to place in a vehicle.–The man *hauls* sand for a living.

3. Amount gathered.–The boy had a big *haul* of chestnuts today.

4. A pull.–We helped the fishermen give the rope a strong *haul*.

haunch *haunches*. The upper part of an animal's hind legs.–Animals sit on their *haunches*.

haunt *haunts, haunted, haunting*. 1. Visit often.–The boys *haunt* the old shack in the woods.

2. A place one spends much time in.–The old shack is the favourite *haunt* of the boys.

3. *Haunt* is used in connection with ghosts. –This is a *haunted* house. Ghosts *haunt* it.

have *has, had, having*. 1. Own; possess; keep with one.–I *have* a ball.–I *have* a book in my desk.–The shop *has* balloons for sale.

2. Must.–People *have* to eat to keep alive.

3. Make.–Mother will *have* dinner ready soon.

4. Meet.–We do not expect to *have* trouble.

5. Be ill with.–Father *has* a cold.

6. Take.–Will you *have* an apple?

7. Hold.–We will *have* a contest.

8. *Have* is used with other verbs.–They *have* gone.–He *has* gone.

hawk *hawks*. A large, strong bird that lives by eating other birds and animals. *Hawks* have strong, hooked bills.

hawthorn haw'-thorn *hawthorns*. A kind of bush or tree that has red berries and long thorns on it.

hay. Grass dried for use as food.–In winter the farmer feeds his cattle on *hay*.

haycock hay'-cock *haycocks*. A small stack or pile of hay.–Little Boy Blue was under the *haycock*, fast asleep.

hay fever hay fe'-ver. Sneezing, watering of the eyes, and other discomfort caused by breathing the fine pollen of certain plants. –Mary gets *hay fever* in the country in August every year.

haystack hay'-stack *haystacks*. A pile of hay. –The farmer has a large *haystack* in the farmyard.

hazard haz-ard *hazards*. 1. A danger or risk. –Papers placed near a furnace are a fire *hazard*. They are in danger of catching fire.

2. Something in the way that obstructs.– Golf courses have *hazards* to make the game harder.

haze *hazy*. Mist or smoke in the air which makes it difficult for one to see.–We could not see the hill because of the *haze*.

he. A word used instead of the name of a boy, a man, or a male animal. *He* is a pronoun. –Father came home. *He* was tired.

head *heads, headed, heading.* 1. The upper part of the body, containing the ears, eyes, nose, and mouth. – Hair grows on the *head.* – Your face is part of your *head.*
2. The top part; anything like the *head* in shape or position.– Mother bought a *head* of lettuce.–The carpenter hit the nail on the *head* with the *head* of the hammer.–We sleep with our *heads* at the *head* of the bed.
3. Front.–The clown was at the *head* of the circus parade.
4. A leader; a manager.–The *head*master is the *head* of our school.
5. Lead; be ahead of.–Our school *heads* all schools in the scholarship results.
6. The place where a boil or other infection opens.–The boil on Mary's arm came to a *head.*
7. Ability to understand.–Father has a good *head* for mechanics. It is not hard for him to learn about machinery.
8. Self-control.–All the children kept their *heads* during the fire drill.
9. Grandfather sold 5 *head* of cattle last week.
10. Go towards.–The hunters *headed* north.

headache head'-ache *headaches.* An ache or pain in the head.

headlight head'-light *headlights.* A light at the front of a vehicle such as a motor-car, a bicycle, or in some countries a locomotive.

headline head'-line *headlines.* A few words in large print over an article in a newspaper. They tell what the article is about.

heal *heals, healed, healing.* Make or get well. –The sore on Mother's arm has *healed* now. –There's nothing wrong with him that fresh air and good food won't *heal.*

health. The condition of one's body.–If you are well, you are in good *health.* If you are ill, you are in poor *health.*

healthful health'-ful. Good for the health.– The climate in Switzerland is *healthful.*

healthy health'-y *healthier, healthiest.* In good condition; not ill.–Bob is a *healthy* boy. He is hardly ever ill.

heap *heaps, heaped, heaping.* 1. Pile. – After Father cut the grass, the children *heaped* it into a large pile.
2. A pile or stack.–We saw a *heap* of gravel by the roadside.

hear *hears, heard, hearing.* Notice (a sound) with the ears.–We see with our eyes, and *hear* with our ears.–Did you *hear* the radio programme?

hearing hear'-ing. 1. The ability to notice sounds with the ears.–Grandfather's *hearing* is not as good as it was when he was younger.
2. A chance to say what one has to say and be heard.–The boy asked the teacher to give him a *hearing* before punishing him.
3. The distance one can hear a sound.–The boys were talking within our *hearing.*

hearse *hearses.* A car or carriage used to carry a dead person to the cemetery.

heart *hearts.* 1. The organ of the body that pumps the blood to all parts of the body.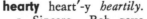
2. Anything shaped somewhat like the *heart.*–Some valentine cards have *hearts* on them.
3. Feelings.–The man has a kind *heart.* He has a kind feeling towards people and animals.
4. Courage.–Grandfather didn't have the *heart* to tell Bob that he had to go home.
5. The middle part of anything.–The shop is in the *heart* of the town.–The boys like the *heart* of the lettuce.
6. The most important part.–The motor is the *heart* of a motor-car.
7. *By heart* means from memory.–The children learned the poem *by heart.*

hearth *hearths.* The floor of a fireplace or the bricks or stone in front of it.–We sat by the *hearth* and told stories.

hearty heart'-y *heartily.*
1. Sincere. – Bob gave Jack *hearty* wishes for a happy birthday.
2. Big and cheerful. – Father has a *hearty* laugh.
3. Strong and cheerful.–The old woman is quite *hearty.*
4. Big and satisfying.–We ate a *hearty* meal at Christmas.

H
I
J
K
L
M
N
O
P
Q
R
S
T
U
V
W
X
Y
Z

heat *heats, heated, heating.* 1. Warmth; the opposite of cold. *Heat* is a form of energy. It can be felt but not seen. The sun gives off *heat.*
2. Make warm or hot.–Electricity *heats* the electric iron.

heater heat'-er *heaters.* Something used to make a room, car, etc., warm. Furnaces are *heaters.* Some cars have *heaters.*

heaven heav'-en *heavens.* 1. The space above the earth; the sky. – Aeroplanes fly in the *heavens.*
2. A place where there is perfect happiness and peace for ever.–Many people believe that they will go to *heaven* when they die.
3. A state of great happiness. – Mary is in *heaven* when she is dancing with Jack.

heavenly heav'-en-ly. 1. Being in the sky.–The moon and stars are *heavenly* bodies.
2. Sacred; having to do with God's heaven.– Angels are *heavenly* messengers.
3. Beautiful and delightful.–The garden is *heavenly* in the evening.

heavily heav'-i-ly. In a heavy fashion.–The man sat down *heavily.* He sat down as if burdened with a great weight.

heavy heav'-y *heavier, heaviest,* 1. Weighing much; not easy to move or lift.–Lead is *heavy*; it weighs a lot for its size.
2. Very large or great.–There was a *heavy* snowfall last night.–Traffic was so *heavy* that we had to drive slowly. There were many cars and other vehicles.
3. Bulky; weighty; thick.–Father wears a *heavy* overcoat when it is cold.
4. Unhappy; sad.–The old man has a *heavy* heart. He is weighed down with troubles.

he'd. A short way of writing the words 'he had' or 'he would'.–He said *he'd* done it.

hedge *hedges, hedged, hedging.* 1. A row of bushes or shrubs used as a fence.–We have a *hedge* round our garden.

2. Surround.–The policemen *hedged* the man in to prevent him escaping.
3. Avoid giving a frank or plain answer.– Bill tried to *hedge* when the teacher asked him about the broken window.

hedgehog hedge'-hog *hedgehogs.* A small four-footed animal covered in sharp spines. *Hedgehogs* roll themselves into a ball when attacked. They feed on insects and slugs, usually at night.

heed *heeds, heeded, heeding, heedless, heedful.* 1. Pay attention to.–The boy did not *heed* the directions given him, so he became lost.
2. Attention, notice, thought.–Bill paid no *heed* to his mother's call.

heel *heels.* 1. The rounded part at the back of your foot just below your ankle.
2. The part of your stocking or other footwear that fits over the *heel.*–Bob's shoe rubbed a hole in the *heel* of his sock.
3. The leather or rubber part fastened to the bottom of your shoe just below your *heel.*– Mother wears shoes with high *heels,* and Mary wears shoes with low *heels.*

hefty hef'-ty. Large and strong.–Jack is a *hefty* fellow.

heifer heif'-er *heifers.* A young cow that has not had a calf.

height *heights.* 1. How high anything is from the ground or from a given place.–Bob's *height* is 4 feet 6 inches. He is that tall.–The *height* of that mountain is 12,500 feet.
2. Peak, topmost point.–The writer was at the *height* of his career when he was 48 years old. He was doing better work then than at any other time in his life.
3. A mountain, cliff, or other very high place. –The eagle flew to its nest on a stony *height.*

heir *heirs.* The person who has a right to another's property and money when that person dies.

heiress heir'-ess *heiresses.* A woman who has a right to another's property and money when that person dies–particularly a woman who has inherited or will inherit a large amount of money.

heirloom heir'-loom *heirlooms.* Something valuable that has been handed down from person to person for many years, in one family. –Mother's locket is an *heirloom.* It once belonged to her great-grandmother, then to her grandmother, then to her own mother. Now it is hers.

held. One form of the word *hold.*–Bob *held* the ball. He caught it and kept it.

hell *hells.* The place where evil persons are supposed to go to be punished after they die.

he'll. A short form for *he will* or *he shall.*–*He'll* go to school tomorrow.–*He'll* return at once.

hello hel-lo'. A friendly greeting.–Mary said *hello* to her teacher.

helm *helms.* The wheel or handle used to steer a boat.

helmet hel'-met *helmets.* A covering worn to protect the head.–Racing drivers, soldiers, and deep-sea divers wear *helmets.* – The motor-cyclist's *helmet* protected him from injury.–Knights wore *helmets* in battle.

help *helps, helped, helping.* 1. Do something to make a person's work or efforts easier; give aid to.–Mary *helped* Mother get dinner by laying the table.–Bob *helped* Father get his work done by mowing the lawn.–Sleep and rest *helped* Mother's headache.
2. An aid; something or someone that *helps.* –Jack was a *help* to Father in painting the house.
3. Avoid; keep oneself from doing something, or prevent something from happening.–Bob could not *help* being late, because the bus was late.
4. *Help to* means give or serve. – Mother *helped* us *to* some potatoes.

helper help'-er *helpers.* A person who does things for another. – Mary is our teacher's *helper.* She hands out pencils for the teacher.

helpful help'-ful *helpfully.* Useful. – Bob is *helpful* about the farm. He does things to help.

helping help'-ing *helpings.* A serving. – Jack had a second *helping* of ice-cream.

helpless help'-less *helplessly, helplessness.* 1. Not able to do anything for oneself.–Illness made the old man *helpless.*
2. Not able (to do something).–The firemen, with their small hose, were *helpless* in the face of the great fire.

helter-skelter hel'-ter-skel'-ter *helter-skelters.*
1. A tall tower at a fair, down which people slide on mats.
2. In disordered haste. – When the thunderstorm broke, the crowds on the beach ran *helter-skelter* in all directions.

hem *hems, hemmed, hemming.* 1. A folded edge on a dress, sleeve, coat, etc. A *hem* is made by folding back the material and sewing it along the edge. – Mary's new dress was too long, so Mother put a wider *hem* on the bottom of the skirt to shorten it.

2. Make a *hem* in. – Mother *hemmed* the dress.

hemisphere hem'-i-sphere *hemispheres.* Half of a ball or globe. A sphere is a ball or globe. A *hemisphere* is half of one. The earth can be divided into Northern and Southern *Hemispheres,* or into Eastern and Western *Hemispheres.*

hemlock hem'-lock *hemlocks.* A small plant with divided leaves and small white flowers, yielding a poisonous juice.

hemp. A plant that has a very tough stem. The fibres or thread-like parts of the *hemp* are made into rope or coarse cloth called burlap. Some large bags for grain, potatoes, etc., are made from this coarse cloth.

hempen hemp'-en. Anything made of hemp or resembling hemp.–Hundreds of years ago, peasants wore *hempen* jackets and trousers.

hemstitch hem'-stitch *hemstitches, hemstitched, hemstitching.* 1. A fancy stitch often used in hemming towels and other linens.
2. Make such a fancy stitch.– Mother *hemstitched* Mary's dress.

hen *hens.* A female chicken. Female birds and other female fowls are called *hens,* too. *Hens* lay eggs.

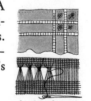

her. 1. *Her* stands for the name of a woman or a girl, or any female animal.–The cat hid, and Mother could not find *her.* – A woman knocked at the door, and Mother let *her* in.
2. Belonging to a girl or woman or female animal.–Mary brought *her* doll. It belonged to *her,* to Mary.–Mother lost *her* purse.

H
I J K L M N O P Q R S T U V W X Y Z

herb *herbs*. 1. A plant that has no wood in its stem and dies down to the roots when the season is over.

2. A plant whose leaves or stems are used for medicines or for seasoning foods.—Mint is a *herb*. It is used to flavour tea, sweets, meat, etc.

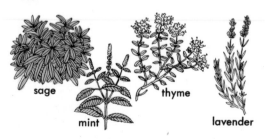

sage   thyme   mint   lavender

herd *herds*. 1. A large number of cattle or other animals that are all together.—A few cows would not be a *herd*. Twenty-five cows would be a *herd*.

2. Drive together in a group.—The shepherd *herds* his sheep. He keeps them together while they move from place to place.

herdsman *herds'-man herdsmen*. A man who takes care of a herd of cattle or other animals.

here. 1. In or at this place.—Who sits *here*?
2. To this place.—Send the boy *here*.
3. Present.—The children said '*Here*' when the teacher called their names.

hereafter here-af'-ter. From now on; in the future.—You were nearly hurt; *hereafter*, be more careful.

here's. Here is.—*Here's* your coat.

hermit her'-mit *hermits*. A person who goes to a lonely place and lives alone. *Hermits* live simply.

hero he'-ro *heroes*. 1. A man or boy who has done a very brave thing. — The man who saved the drowning boy was a *hero*.
2. The man or boy who takes the leading or most important part in a book or play.—Tom Sawyer is the *hero* of a book by Mark Twain.

heroic he-ro'-ic. Brave.—The man who saved the drowning boy was heroic.

heroine her'-o-ine *heroines*. 1. A woman or girl who does very brave thing.
2. The woman or girl who is the leading or most important character in a book or play.

heroism her'-o-ism. Courage and brave deeds; saving or helping others without thinking of one's own safety.—The man who saved the drowning boy showed great *heroism*.

heron her'-on *herons*. A wading bird that lives in marshes or near the water. It has very long legs and a long, pointed bill.

herring her'-ring *herrings*. A small fish caught in great numbers for food.

hers. Belonging to a woman or a girl or a female animal.—Grandmother gave Mary a cat. It belongs to Mary now. It is *hers*.

herself her-self'. 1. Sally dressed *herself* this morning. She put on her own clothes.
2. *Herself* is used to make a statement stronger.—Mary made the cake *herself*; nobody helped her.—Mother *herself* sometimes puts salt instead of sugar in the cocoa. Even Mother does that.

he's. He is.—Grandfather is getting old. *He's* 68 years old today.

hesitate hes'-i-tate *hesitates, hesitated, hesitating*. 1. Wait, as if not sure how to go on. — The boy *hesitates* when he speaks. He speaks slowly, with little pauses between his words.
2. Feel doubt about doing something.—I *hesitate* to do his work for him. I'm not sure that I should.

hesitation hes-i-ta'-tion. A slight pause or stop, as a *hesitation* in one's speech or actions.

hey. A word or cry often used to show that a person is pleased or surprised, or to call one's attention to something.—*Hey!* Bring back my umbrella!

hibernate hi'-ber-nate *hibernates, hibernated, hibernating*. Spend the winter sleeping.—Bears *hibernate*. They eat a lot and store up fat, and then go into caves and sleep until spring.

hiccup hic′-cup *hiccups, hiccupped, hiccupping.*
1. A jerky gulp made when the muscles that control our breathing do not work properly.
2. Make a *hiccup.* – Sally *hiccupped* after drinking her milk too fast.

hide *hides, hid, hidden, hiding.* 1. Put or go out of sight, or where it is hard to be found.–We have to *hide* sharp things from Baby.–Jack *hid* behind the tree.
2. Keep secret.–Bob tried to *hide* his mistake.
3. Keep from being seen.–The clouds *hid* the sun.–The sun was *hidden* by the clouds.
4. The skin, especially of an animal.–Bags, belts, etc., are made of animals' *hides.*–Father has a cow*hide* belt.

hide-and-seek. A children's game in which some hide and the others try to find them.– Since it was a fine afternoon we played *hide-and-seek* in the garden.

hideous hi′-de-ous *hideously.* Dreadful, horrible.–The dragon in the pantomime was a *hideous* sight.–The man was convicted for a *hideous* crime.

high *higher, highest, highly.* 1. Tall, far above the ground.–Bob stands 4 feet 6 inches *high.* –The aeroplane flies *high.*
2. First, excellent.–He is a man of *high* standing in the town. He is *highly* respected.
3. Costly, dear.–We pay a *high* rent. We pay more rent than is usually paid, or than should be paid, for a house like ours.
4. In music a *high* note is one that is far up the scale.–On the piano, the keys at the right end give out *high* notes.–Most women have *higher* voices than men. They can sing *higher* notes.

highland high′land *highlands.* High or hilly country.

highness high′-ness. 'Your *Highness,*' 'Her *Highness,*' and 'His *Highness*' are titles of honour given to princes and princesses, and the term used when speaking to or about such royal people.

high-spirited high′-spir′-it-ed. Lively and full of fun. – David is *high-spirited.* He is always playing tricks and laughing.

high street *high streets.* The main street of a town.–We do most of our shopping in the *high street.*

highway high′-way *highways.* 1. A main road.– Motor-cars travel on *highways.*
2. A route by land or sea.–The Atlantic Ocean is one of the busiest *highways* of commerce.
3. A direct course.–Hard work is one of the *highways* to success.

highwayman high′-way-man *highwaymen.* A man, usually on a horse, who used to hold up travellers on foot or in stage-coaches, and rob them.–Dick Turpin was a famous *highwayman.*

hike *hikes, hiked, hiking.* 1. A long walk.–We went for a *hike* through the woods.
2. Take a long walk.–We *hike* every Sunday.

hill *hills.* Land that is higher than the land around it.–Jack and Jill went up the *hill.*

hill-side hill′-side *hill-sides.* The side of a hill.– Sally slid down the *hill-side* where the mud was smooth and slippery.

hill-top hill′-top *hill-tops.* The top of a hill.

hilly hill′-y *hillier, hilliest.* With many hills.– This country is *hilly.* The land goes up and down.

hilt *hilts.* The handle of a sword, dagger, or other weapon with a blade.

him. A boy, man, or male animal. –Father wanted a new tie, so Bob gave *him* one. – Jack looked for his dog, but could not find *him.*

himself him-self′. 1. *Himself* is used to make a statement stronger. – The Mayor *himself* visited our class today.
2. Sometimes *himself* is used instead of the word him.–Jack seated *himself* at his desk to draw a plan of his new boat.

hind. Back.–The *hind* legs of a dog are the legs at the back.–Rabbits have very long *hind* legs, which help them take big jumps.

hinder hin′-der *hinders, hindered, hindering.* Prevent, or make difficult for.–The rain *hinders* the farmer's ploughing. Rain makes it hard for him to plough.–Lack of coal *hindered* us. Because we had no coal, we were kept from making a fire.

hindrance hin′-drance *hindrances.* Anything that gets in one's way or keeps one from doing a thing.–Music on the radio is a *hindrance* when one wants to read or play the piano.

H
I
J
K
L
M
N
O
P
Q
R
S
T
U
V
W
X
Y
Z

hinge *hinges.* A jointed metal piece used on a door, a cover to a box or trunk, etc., to allow it to swing back and forth or move up and down.

hint *hints, hinted, hinting.* 1. Suggest something in a roundabout way.–Mary told Father that her old coat would not hold together much longer. She was *hinting* that she wanted a new one.
2. A suggestion. – Bob gave Mary a *hint* about how to spell a word. He said, ' "i" before "e." '

hip *hips.* A part of the human body. The *hips* are on both sides, just below the waist-line.– The teacher told us to put our hands on our *hips* to do the deep-breathing exercise.

hippopotamus hip-po-pot'-a-mus *hippopotamuses.* A big animal with popping eyes and an ugly face, that lives near and in the rivers in Africa. It eats water-plants. The *hippopotamus* has skin that looks like heavy leather.

hire *hires, hired, hiring.* 1. Rent, or borrow for money.–For £3, Father *hired* a trailer to move some furniture to the cottage.
2. Buy the work of; pay a person for work done for one.–Many men were *hired* at the factory. They were given jobs and will be paid for working there.

his. Belonging to a boy, man, or male animal. –Bob has a new football; it is *his.*–Jack's dog, Spot, came home with *his* tail between *his* legs.

hiss *hisses, hissed, hissing.* 1. Make a sound like sss.–Steam coming from the radiator makes a *hissing* sound.–Geese make a *hissing* sound.
2. A *hissing* sound.–We could tell by the *hiss* of the kettle that the water was boiling.

history his'-to-ry *histories, historic, historical.* The story or step-by-step record of everything known about what people have done since the beginning of the world, and what has happened to them. Boys and girls study *history* in school.
2. A story or account of the past.–Father asked the man to tell his *history,* to tell about his life.

hit *hits, hitting.* 1. Strike; give a blow; come up against with force.–A motor-car *hit* the tree. –The bad boy *hit* the baby.–Baby rolled the ball and it *hit* Father's shoe.
2. Bring sudden trouble on.–The family was hard *hit* when their home was burned.
3. A blow.–The fighter landed a good *hit* on the jaw.
4. A great success.–The play which has been running for years is a great *hit.*
5. In cricket, to strike the ball with the bat.– John *hit* 3 boundaries in a row.–The new bowler was *hit* for 6.
6. *Hit upon* means suddenly find something or a way of getting something done. – The boys *hit upon* a way to solve the problem.

hitch *hitches, hitched, hitching.* 1. Tie or fasten, as with a harness.–Grandfather *hitched* his horses to the plough.
2. Move jerkily.–Bob *hitched* up his socks.
3. Something that prevents or gets in the way.–The rain put a *hitch* in our plans to go to the football match.
4. A knot that can be undone easily.–The boys in the boat took a *hitch* round the post with a rope.

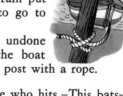

hitter hit'-ter *hitters.* One who hits.–This batsman is a hard *hitter.*

hive *hives.* 1. A box or a small house in which bees live. The queen bee is put into the *hive,* and all the other bees follow.
2. A great number of bees all together in one box or bee*hive.*
3. A place where many people work busily together.–The kitchen is a regular *hive* just before dinner.

hoard *hoards, hoarded, hoarding.* 1. Store away or save up things secretly. – Some people *hoard* food, some *hoard* money.–Some animals *hoard* food for the winter.
2. A store or secret supply.–We found the squirrel's *hoard* of nuts.

hoarse *hoarsely, hoarseness.* 1. Deep and rough in sound.–When you have a cold, your voice may be *hoarse.*
2. Having a *hoarse* voice.–Bob shouted at the football match until he was *hoarse.*

hoax *hoaxes, hoaxed, hoaxing.* 1. Deceive, play a practical joke.–Bill *hoaxed* his sister by pretending to put salt into her cereal.
2. A trick.–The children played a *hoax* on the teacher by putting an imitation ink-blot on his desk.

hobble hob'-ble *hobbles, hobbled, hobbling.*
1. Limp or walk as though crippled.–The man hurt his leg and *hobbled* around for a week afterward.
2. A limping walk.–The man's *hobble* kept him from walking fast.
3. Tie the legs together.–The cowboys *hobbled* their horses for the night.

hobby hob'-by *hobbies.* Something a person likes to do that is not his everyday work.–Mary's *hobby* is collecting queer buttons.–Bob's *hobby* is making model aircraft.

hobgoblin hob-gob'-lin *hobgoblins.* An ugly mischievous imp in fairy stories.

hobnail hob'-nail *hobnails.* A nail with a large head used to protect the soles of heavy boots.–The shoemaker drove *hobnails* into the farmer's boots.–Grandfather wears *hobnailed* boots.

hockey hock'ey. A game played on ice or on a field by 2 teams of 6 or 11 players each. Each player has a *hockey* stick. He uses it to hit a disk or a ball into a net or goal.

hoe *hoes, hoed, hoeing.* 1. A garden tool with a long handle and a broad blade.–The farmer uses a *hoe* to weed his garden, dig potatoes, and loosen the soil about the plants.
2. Dig with a *hoe.*–Bob helps *hoe* the garden.

hog *hogs.* 1. A pig, particularly a large pig.

2. A person who is greedy, selfish and dirty is sometimes called a *hog.*

hoist *hoists, hoisted, hoisting.* 1. Raise or lift up.–The Boy Scouts *hoisted* the flag to the top of the flagpole.
2. A device for lifting.–The mechanic put the car on a *hoist* and raised it off the ground.

hold *holds, held, holding.* 1. Get something into one's hands and keep it there.–I will *hold* your book while you put on your coat.
2. Be able to have inside; contain.–This bottle *holds* 1 pint of milk. You can put 1 pint of milk in it and it will be full.
3. Fasten.–A nail *holds* the boards together. –Glue *holds* the papers together.–Buttons *hold* the sides of my coat together.
4. A grasp.–Do not lift the baby until you have a good *hold* on her.
5. Have.–The dramatic society will *hold* a meeting today.
6. Own, have.–Grandfather *holds* some land in the country.
7. Keep.–The lost property office will *hold* your umbrella until you call for it.
8. The part of a ship where cargo is carried. –The barrels were stacked in the *hold.*

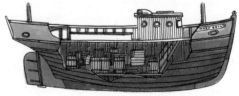

holder hold'-er *holders.* A person or a thing that holds something.–Candlesticks are *holders* for candles.–Pot *holders* are used to lift hot pots and pans.

hole *holes.* 1. An opening.–A *hole* in your shoe is a place where leather has worn away and left an open space.
2. A hollow space in anything.–The boys dug a *hole* where they believed the pirate treasure was buried.

holiday hol'-i-day *holidays*. 1. A day when we play and do the things we want to do, or a special day in memory of a certain event.– Christmas Day, Boxing Day, Easter and Whitsun are *holidays* in England. They are days we all celebrate.

2. A vacation.–We go to Grandmother's for our Christmas *holiday*.–Bill decided to take a *holiday* from school and pick apples.

hollow hol'-low *hollows, hollowed, hollowing*. 1. Not solid; empty in the middle.–A brick is solid. A stove-pipe is *hollow*; it has a hole running through the centre. – Balloons are *hollow*.

2. A hole.–The squirrel popped into a *hollow* in the tree.

3. Empty-sounding.–Bob put his head down to the top of the barrel and called out. His voice sounded *hollow*, like an echo.

4. Dig out the inside of.–Jack *hollowed* out the log to make a canoe.

5. A little valley.–We picked violets in the *hollow*.

holly hol'-ly *hollies*. An evergreen tree or bush that has shiny, prickly leaves and bright red berries on it.–The chil-dren hung wreaths of *holly* on the walls at Christmas time.

hollyhock hol'-ly-hock *hollyhocks*. A tall flower which comes in many colours. *Hollyhocks* grow all along a long stem. The plant has large, fuzzy leaves.

holster hol'-ster *holsters*. A leather holder for a pistol, worn on a belt over the shoulder or round the waist. The *holster* is shaped somewhat like a pistol.–The cowboy car-ries his gun in his *holster*.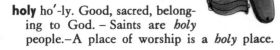

holy ho'-ly. Good, sacred, belong-ing to God. – Saints are *holy* people.–A place of worship is a *holy* place.

home *homes*. 1. The place one comes from.– My *home* was in Paris. It is the place where I was born.

2. The place where one lives.–My *home* is at 37 High Street, in Newtown.

3. A building run for people who need spe-cial care of some kind.–The blind man lives in a *home* for the blind.

4. The *home* place or the goal in many games. –The rounders player reached *home* safely. –The children made the tree stump *home* in their game of hide-and-seek.–Robin Hood shot the arrow *home*.

homeless home'less. Having no place to live. –After the old woman's house burned down, she was *homeless*.

homely home'-ly. 1. Home-like.–The hotel had a *homely* atmosphere.

2. Plain and simple.–Hash is a *homely* dish.

home-made home'-made'. Made in the home.– Did you buy this cake at the bakery, or is it *home-made*?

homesick home'-sick. Lonely for home, missing home very badly.–After Bob had been away from home a week, he became *homesick*.

homeward home'-ward. Towards home, in the direction of home.–Bob turned *homeward* when it began to get dark.

hone *bones, boned, boning*. 1. A fine stone for sharpening knives, tools, and razors.–Father sharpened the knife on a *hone*.

2. Sharpen on a fine stone.–Father *honed* the knife.

honest hon'-est (pronounced *onnest*) *honestly*. Just, fair; telling the truth; not cheating.– Abraham Lincoln was an *honest* man. He was truthful; he didn't cheat or steal. He was fair with all people.

honesty hon'-es-ty. Fairness and truthfulness in all one says and does.–*Honesty* pays.

honey. 1. A sweet, sticky, syrup-like, yellow liquid made by bees. They make it from a sweet liquid called nectar, which they gather from flowers.

2. The sweet liquid which bees gather from flowers; nectar.

3. A pet name. – Mother calls Baby '*honey*.'

honey-bee hon'-ey-bee *honey-bees*. The kind of bee that gathers nectar and makes honey.

honeycomb hon'-ey-comb *honeycombs*. A great number of little hollow boxes or compartments of wax fastened together. *Honeycombs* are made by bees. Bees store honey in the *honeycomb*.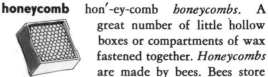

honeydew hon'-ey-dew. 1. A sweet, sticky substance often found on leaves and stems of plants.
2. A sweet melon with a very smooth white or greenish skin.

honeymoon hon'-ey-moon *honeymoons, honeymooned, honeymooning.* 1. A holiday taken by a couple after their marriage.
2. Go on a *honeymoon* trip.–The couple expect to *honeymoon* in the mountains.

honeysuckle hon'-ey-suck-le *honeysuckles.* A climbing vine that has sweet-smelling blossoms on it.

honk *honks, honked, honking.* 1. The cry that a wild goose makes.
2. Any sound like the wild goose's cry.–We heard the *honk* of the horn on the motor-car.
3. Make a *honking* sound.–Father will *honk* the horn when he is ready to go.

honour hon'-our (pronounced *onner*) *honours, honoured, honouring.* 1. High character and reputation, or name.–'He was a man of *honour*' means that he was honest, fair, and upright, and deserved to be thought well of.
2. Show respect for.–The men removed their hats to *honour* the dead man.
3. A credit, something to be proud of.–Mary is an *honour* to her class.
4. 'Your *Honour*' and 'his *Honour*' are titles given certain officials such as a judge.
5. *Do honour to* means show respect and admiration for.

honourable hon'-our-a-ble *honourably.* 1. Worthy of honour, of respect, of being thought well of.–Mr Gladstone was an *honourable* man. He was an able Prime Minister.
2. A title of courtesy.–A judge is spoken of as the *Honourable* Mr Justice Smith.

hood *hoods.* 1. A covering for the head. It comes over the ears and is fastened under the chin. Some *hoods* are attached to a coat or cloak.–Little Red Riding Hood's *hood* was fastened to her cape.
2. The folding roof of a motor-car.–Father put up the *hood* when the rain started to make the seats of the car wet.
3. Any covering that is like a *hood*.

hoof *hoofs* or *hooves.* A covering of horn on the feet of horses, cattle, pigs, and some other animals. *Hoofs* protect their feet as shoes protect ours.

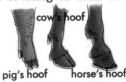
cow's hoof
pig's hoof   horse's hoof

hook *hooks, hooked, hooking.* 1. A piece of metal that is curved or turned back at one end so that it will catch or hold things. – A fish-*hook* is used to catch fish.–*Hooks* and eyes, or metal loops, are often used in place of buttons to fasten a dress.–Coats are hung on clothes *hooks*.
2. Fasten or catch on a *hook*.–The fisherman *hooked* a fish.–Mary *hooked* the door to keep it closed.

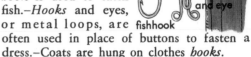
clothes hook
hook and eye
fishhook

hooked. 1. Curved at the end like a hook.–The handle on Grandfather's cane is *hooked*.
2. Done with a hook.–*Hooked* rugs are made by pulling narrow strips of cloth or wool through a coarse cloth with a hook. The rug is smooth on one side and has loops on the other.

hoop *hoops.* 1. A circle or band of wire, metal, or wood. – *Hoops* are used round wooden buckets, barrels, kegs, etc., to hold them together.–*Hoops* are used as toys, too.
2. A wire or wooden frame used by women in olden times to make their skirts stand out round them.

hoot *hoots, hooted, hooting.* 1. The call or cry of an owl.
2. Give the call of an owl.
3. Make fun of, mock.–The crowd *hooted* at the speaker. They called out to him scornfully to show that they did not like the things he said.–Jack *hooted* at Mary's fear of the circus animals.

hop *hops, hopped, hopping.* 1. Move by leaps or jumps.–The frog *hops*.–Birds *hop*. They spring along with both feet off the ground at once.–Children like to *hop* on one foot while they hold up the other foot.
2. A jump.–The rabbit took a *hop* and disappeared into his hole.

hope *hopes, hoped, hoping.* 1. Want something to happen.–We *hope* Father will be well soon.

2. Expect. – Mother *hopes* to be home by noon.

3. A desire or wish that something will happen.–Our one *hope* is that Father will be well soon.

hopeful hope'-ful *hopefully.* Believing that a thing will work out right; thinking a good thing will happen.–The doctor is very *hopeful* about the sick baby. He feels sure that the baby will get well soon.

hopeless hope'-less *hopelessly.* 1. Without much chance of turning out right.–Building a fire with wet wood is almost *hopeless.*– The boys made a *hopeless* attempt to move the big rock.

2. Thinking things will surely turn out badly.–Bill feels *hopeless* about passing the test. He is sure he will not pass.

hopscotch hop'-scotch. A game in which children hop from square to square and try not to touch the lines between the squares.

horizon ho-ri'-zon *horizons.* The line where the sky seems to meet the earth or the sea.–The sun seems to come up in the morning from behind the *horizon* and to sink below the *horizon* at night.–Jack saw a boat on the *horizon.*

horizontal hor-i-zon'-tal *horizontally.* A line that runs straight up and down is a vertical line. A line that runs straight across is a *horizontal* line. – A telegraph pole stands in a vertical position, and the pieces of wood across the top are in a *horizontal* position.–The lines across your writing paper are *horizontal* lines.

horn *horns.* 1. A hard, bone-like thing that grows on the heads of cattle, goats, sheep, deer, and some other animals. Animals' *horns* were often scraped and made into drinking  *horns,* powder *horns,* and other containers.

2. A musical instrument played by being blown through.

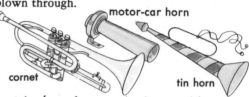

motor-car horn

cornet

tin horn

hornet hor'-net *hornets.* An insect with a severe sting. *Hornets* are something like wasps, but are bigger and have a worse sting.

horrible hor'-ri-ble *horribly.* Terrible, frightful. – We saw a *horrible* fire that burned many homes. –We saw a *horrible* accident at the corner.

horrid hor'-rid. Dreadful or terrible.–Dragons in fairy stories were *horrid* beasts that breathed fire.

horrify hor'-ri-fy *horrifies, horrified, horrifying.* Frighten and shock.–The road accident *horrified* us.

horror hor'-ror *horrors.* A feeling of fear, shock, or great disgust.–I have a *horror* of fire. I am very much afraid of it.–Mother has a *horror* of mice.

horse *horses.* 1. A large, hoofed animal used for working or for riding. – The farmer uses horses to pull heavy loads.–Bob rides on the *horse's* back.

hunter

race horse

cowboy's horse

draught Percheron

2. A kind of frame supported by legs.–The carpenter puts boards across sawing-*horses* to saw them.–Clothes are often put on a clothes-*horse,* towels on a towel-*horse.*

horseback horse'-back. On the back of a horse. –Bob likes to ride on *horseback*. He is a good *horseback* rider.

horse chestnut horse' chest'-nut *horse chestnuts*. A tree that has large leaves, clusters of large, white and pinkish, bell-shaped flowers, and big brown nuts in prickly cases. The nuts are also called *horse chestnuts* or, quite often, 'conkers'.

horse-fly horse'-fly *horse-flies*. A large fly that bites cattle and horses.

horsehair horse'-hair *horsehairs*. The hairs from a horse's mane or tail. These hairs are sometimes woven into cloth called haircloth.

horseman horse'-man *horsemen*. A man who rides, trains, or takes care of horses.–Bob is a fine *horseman*.

horse-radish horse'-rad'-ish *horse-radishes*. A plant with a large root that is ground to make a relish which is eaten with meats and other foods. It tastes hot, like mustard.

horseshoe horse'-shoe *horseshoes*. A curved piece of metal nailed to the hard hoof of a horse to protect it.–The blacksmith put *horseshoes* on the horse's feet.

horsewoman horse'-wom-an *horsewomen*. A woman who rides horseback.–Mary is a good *horsewoman*.

hose. 1. Stockings. – Mary has new *hose*. 2. A long tube, usually of rubber, through which liquid can flow. –Bob used the *hose* to sprinkle the lawn. 3. Tights; long, close-fitting breeches or leggings. – The brownie in the play wore *hose*.

hosiery ho'-sier-y. Stockings.–The shop sells *hosiery*.

hospitable hos'-pi-ta-ble *hospitably*. Friendly towards company, enjoying entertaining people.–Grandmother is very *hospitable*. She loves to have guests.

hospital hos'-pi-tal *hospitals*. A place where sick and injured people are cared for.–When Father was very ill, the doctor sent him to the *hospital*.

hospitality hos-pi-tal'-i-ty. Warm welcome and friendly entertainment.–We were shown much *hospitality* when we visited the country. Everyone was kind and friendly towards us.

host *hosts*. 1. A man or boy who entertains a guest.–Bob was a fine *host* at his birthday party. He made everyone feel at home so they had a good time. 2. A man who keeps an inn. 3. A great many.–Father has a *host* of friends.

hostage hos'-tage *hostages*. A person who is held by an enemy as a guarantee that a promise or an agreement will be carried out. When the promise is kept, he is returned. Soldiers are often taken as *hostages*.

hostel hos'-tel *hostels*. A house where people can stay the night.–When we went hiking in the mountains we stayed at a different *hostel* each night.

hostess host'-ess *hostesses*. 1. A girl or woman who entertains guests.–The Smiths are giving a party tonight. Mr Smith is the host and Mrs Smith the *hostess*.–Jane is an air-*hostess*. She looks after the passengers in the aeroplane.

hostile hos'-tile. Not friendly; like an enemy.–Jack told Sally they might meet *hostile* Indians on their walk in the woods.

hot *hotter, hottest, hotly*. 1. Very warm.–Ice and snow are cold. Fire is *hot*.–Things get *hot* when put over a fire. 2. Sharp, burning, biting to the taste.–Pepper, horse-radish, and mustard are *hot*. 3. Fiery, quick, excitable.–The boy has a *hot* temper. He becomes angry easily.

hotel ho-tel' *hotels*. A large building where travellers can eat and spend the night.–We stayed at a large *hotel* when we went to Eastbourne.

hothouse hot'-house *hothouses*. A building whose roof (and usually sides) are of glass. The glass lets sunlight in. Plants and flowers are grown in *hothouses*. In winter, a *hothouse* is heated to keep the plants warm.

hotpot hot'-pot *hotpots*. Meat cooked in a pot with potatoes.–One of our favourite dishes is Lancashire *hotpot*.

H

I J K L M N O P Q R S T U V W X Y Z

HOUSES

modern house

African hut

Indian cliff dwellings

H

igloo

log cabin

pioneer sod hut

medieval chateau

thatched cottage

Indian adobe house

lake dwelling

Arab tent

Alpine chalet

mansion

Chinese houseboat

East Indian grass-roofed house

half-timbered house

Laplander's hut

Roman house

I J K L M N O P Q R S T U V W X Y Z

hound *hounds.* A kind of hunting dog.–Grandfather uses a *hound* when he goes hunting.

hour *hours.* 1. Time is measured by weeks, days, *hours,* minutes, and seconds. There are 60 minutes in an *hour* and 24 *hours* in a day.
2. The time for a certain thing.–Children study during school *hours.*–Father's working *hours* are from 9 to 5.
3. The time.–I shall call for you at an early *hour.*–The clock struck the *hour* of 12.

hourly hour'-ly. Happening once every hour, or every 60 minutes.–Our clock strikes *hourly.*–Buses stop at our corner *hourly.*

house (rhymes with *mouse*) *houses.* 1. A building in which people live.–Our *house* is made of bricks.
2. Any building or shelter used for a special purpose.–A theatre is often called a play*house.*–We keep chickens in a hen*house.*
3. Audience.–We had a full *house* for the Christmas play. All the seats were taken.
4. A group of *lawmakers.*–In Great Britain, Parliament consists of the *House* of Commons, the members of which are elected, and the *House* of Lords, whose members are peers of the realm.

house (rhymes with *cows*) *houses, housed, housing.* Provide room for.–Grandmother can *house* many people in her home. She has enough room.

household house'-hold *households.* 1. All the people who live together in one house.–There are 7 people in our *household.*
2. Having to do with home and family.–*Household* furnishings are the things it takes to furnish a home.–*Household* duties are the duties one has in keeping house.

housekeeper house'-keep-er *housekeepers.* The person who keeps or takes care of a house.–Mother is a good *housekeeper.* She keeps our home neat and clean, and cooks good meals for us.

housekeeping house'-keep-ing. Caring for the home or the house.–*Housekeeping* keeps Mother busy.

housewife house'-wife *housewives.* A woman who takes care of the house, buys the food and clothing, and cooks the food.–Mother is a *housewife.* She is the manager of our house.

hover hov'-er *hovers, hovered, hovering.* 1. Stay near a place in the air.–Helicopters *hovered* over the ship.–Hawks *hovered* over the hen-house.
2. Hang about or loiter.–Mary *hovers* near Mother when she is making a cake.

how. 1. In what way.–*How* did you make the cake?–Tell me *how* you came. Did you walk or ride?
2. What amount.–*How* old are you?–*How* far is it to school?–*How* much toffee have you?
3. In what condition.–*How* are you today? What is the state of your health?
4. Why, for what reason.–*How* is it that we do not have school today?

however how-ev'-er. 1. Nevertheless.–The sky looks clear; *however,* I shall take an umbrella just in case it should rain.
2. In any kind of way.–You may do the work *however* you want to. You may do it in whatever way you want.

howl *howls, howled, howling.* 1. Give a long, deep cry; make a wailing noise.–Dogs sometimes *howl* when they hear bells ringing.–The winter wind *howled* around the house.
2. A long, deep cry or wail.–We heard the *howl* of the hungry dog.–Grandfather told of hearing the *howl* of wolves.–There was a long *howl* when our team lost.

hub *hubs.* The centre part of a wheel, where it fits over the axle.
2. A centre of activity.–Sheffield, the great steel city, is a *hub* of industry.

hubbub hub'-bub *hubbubs.* A confused noise.–There was a terrible *hubbub* from the crowd when the referee disallowed the goal.

huddle hud'-dle *huddles, huddled, huddling.*
1. Crowd close together.–The little chickens *huddle* under the hen's wings to get warm.
2. A number of things crowded together.–From the air, the little village was just a *huddle* of roofs.
3. Push in a heap.–When the fire broke out, the attendants *huddled* the audience out quickly.–Jack's clothes were all *huddled* together in his drawer.

hue *hues.* A colour, or shade of a colour.–Dark red, light red, and pink are all *hues* of red.

huff. A spell of anger.–The boy is in a *huff* because he was not asked to the party.

H I J K L M N O P Q R S T U V W X Y Z

H

I J K L M N O P Q R S T U V W X Y Z

hug *hugs, hugged, hugging.* 1. Hold tightly in the arms.–Mother *hugs* the baby lovingly.
2. A tight hold with the arms.–Mother gave Bob a sudden *hug*.
3. Keep close to.–The old man *hugs* the high buildings to keep out of the wind.

huge *hugely.* Very large.–An elephant is a *huge* animal.

hull *hulls, hulled, hulling.* 1. The covering of a seed.–The long green pods that peas grow in are *hulls*.
2. Remove or take the *hull* from.–Mother is *hulling* peas.
3. The body of a boat or ship.– Ships are made with steel or wood *hulls*.

hum *hums, hummed, humming.* 1. Sing with the lips closed.–The boys will sing the words of the song, and the girls will *hum*.
2. The sound of the voice when the lips are closed; or any similar sound.–Keep your lips closed and say the letter 'm'. The sound you make is a *hum*.
3. Make a *hum*.–Hundreds of bees *hummed* about the hive.

human hu'-man. Of or like people.–All men, women and children are *human* beings.– Talking is a *human* ability.

humane hu-mane'. Kind and sympathetic.– The old man is very *humane*; he wouldn't hurt anyone or anything.

humble hum'ble *humbly.* 1. Feeling no pride; modest.–A person who is not proud, who does not think highly of himself, is *humble*.
2. Not grand; simple and poor.–The poor man loved his *humble* home.
3. Unimportant; lowly. – The man has a *humble* job.

humming-bird hum'-ming-bird *humming-birds.* A tiny, bright-coloured bird that flutters its wings so fast when flying that they make a humming sound. A *humming-bird* has a long bill with which it sucks honey from flowers. It can fly backwards.

humorous hu'-mor-ous *humorously.* 1. Funny. –Bob's jokes are always *humorous*.
2. Loving fun and laughter.–Bob is *humorous*.

humour hu'-mour *humours, humoured, humouring.* 1. Something that makes one laugh.–The comedian amused us with his *humour*.
2. A person's disposition or mood; the way one feels.–Father was in a bad *humour* because he was late for work. He was angry and ill-tempered.
3. Agree with, give in to (someone's wishes) in every way.–Mother *humours* Sally when she is ill. She lets Sally have her way.

hump *humps.* A lump; a raised place.–Camels have *humps* on their backs.–The house stood on a *hump* of land. It stood on a small hill.

hunch *hunches, hunched, hunching.* 1. A feeling one has about something for no particular reason.–I have a *hunch* that our team will win.
2. Bend.–The boy *hunched* over in his seat, and the teacher told him to sit up.

hunchback hunch'-back *hunchbacks.* A person with a curved spine which makes a hump on his back.

hundred hun'-dred *hundreds.* The number (100) coming after 99 and before 101. One *hundred* is ten tens.

hundredth hun'-dredth *hundredths.* 1. One of 100 equal parts.–If anything is divided into 100 parts all the same size, each part is a *hundredth*.–One-*hundredth* may be written 1/100 or 0.01.
2. Coming as number 100 in a series.–We have had 99 days of school. Today is the *hundredth* day, or the day after the 99th.

hung. One form of the word *hang*.–The children *hung* up their stockings last Christmas.

hunger hun'-ger *hungers, hungered, hungering.* 1. The feeling of needing or wanting food.– Bob's *hunger* made him eat too fast.
2. *Hunger for* means want.–People *hunger for* peace.

hungry hun'-gry *hungrier, hungriest, hungrily.* 1. Wanting food.–The baby is *hungry*. She wants something to eat.
2. *Hungry for* means wanting.–The child is *hungry for* a playmate.

hunt *hunts, hunted, hunting.* 1. Go out to find and catch or shoot a person or animal.—The hunter *hunts* rabbits and kills them for food.
2. A trip made to catch or kill a person or animal.—The men have gone on a deer *hunt* today.—They have gone to find and kill deer. —The policemen went out on a *hunt* for the escaped murderer.
3. Look (for); try to find.—Grandmother lost her thimble, and we had to *hunt* for it.

hunter hunt′-er *hunters.* A person who hunts and kills animals for food or sport.

hurl *hurls, hurled, hurling.* Throw hard.—The angry boys *hurled* stones at the dog who bit them.

hurrah hur-rah′. A cheer, or cry of joy or success.—*Hurrah* for the winner!

hurricane hur′-ri-cane *hurricanes.* A very strong wind-storm. In a *hurricane* the wind blows at 75 miles or more an hour.—The *hurricane* blew down trees and houses.

hurry hur′-ry *hurries, hurried, hurrying, hurriedly.* 1. Act or move quickly.—Father had to *hurry* to get to work on time.
2. Send or take quickly.—We *hurried* the injured boy to the doctor.
3. Do hastily and carelessly.—The teacher told Bob not to *hurry* his work.
4. Quick action, or an intention to act quickly. —Mother is in a *hurry* to go.

hurt *hurts, hurting.* 1. Cause pain or suffering to.—The dog's bite *hurt* the boy.
2. Harm or damage.—The frost did not *hurt* the fruit.
3. Something that causes pain.—Wounds, such as cuts, burns, bruises, etc., are *hurts.*
4. Have a pain.—John's head *hurts.* He has a pain in his head.

husband hus′-band *husbands.* A married man; the man a woman is married to.—Father is Mother's *husband.*

hush *hushes.* 1. Be quiet; stop making noise.— *Hush!* You will wake the baby.
2. A silence; a stillness.—A *hush* came over the crowd as the mayor rose to speak.

husk *husks, husked, husking.* 1. The dry outer covering of some seeds and fruits.
2. Remove the *husks* from.— The farmer *husks* his corn.

husky husk′-y *huskies, huskier, huskiest.* 1. An Eskimo dog that is used for pulling sledges in the Far North.

2. Big and strong.—The fighter is *husky.*
3. Hoarse; low and rasping.—Bob yelled so much that his voice became *husky.*

hustle hus′-tle *hustles, hustled, hustling.* 1. Rush; move, send, or take quickly.—We *hustled* the injured boy to the doctor.
2. Push roughly.—Bob *hustled* through the crowd to get to his seat.
3. Hurry; move quickly.—Mother told us to *hustle* to school.

hut *huts.* A small, roughly-made house.—The hunters lived in the woods in a small *hut.*

hyacinth hy′-a-cinth *hyacinths.* A flowering plant that grows from a bulb and blossoms in the spring. — *Hyacinths* are blue, pink, white or yellow and have a pleasant smell.

hydrant hy′-drant *hydrants.* A large water pipe with a valve to control the flow of water.— Fire engines usually get water to fight fires from *hydrants.*—When the *hydrant* is open, water spurts into the street.

hyena hy-e′-na *hyenas.* A large wild animal

something like a dog.—The *hyena* eats the flesh of other animals.

H

I
J
K
L
M
N
O
P
Q
R
S
T
U
V
W
X
Y
Z

hygiene hy'-giene. The science of health. In school, we study *hygiene*. We learn how important cleanliness is to health.

hymn *hymns*. A song of praise.–We sing *hymns* in praise of God.

hyphen hy'-phen *hyphens*. A small mark (-) used to connect two words that are used as one word or to break a word at the end of a line.–Good-bye is written with a *hyphen*. –A *hyphen* is about half as long as a dash.

hypnotize hyp'-no-tize *hypnotizes, hypnotized, hypnotizing*. Put (a person) into a state something like sleep, in which he has little control over what he says, and will usually answer any questions. Hypnotism is used by doctors on patients who are mentally ill.

hypocrite hyp'-o-crite *hypocrites*. A person who pretends to be something that he is not, or who says things he doesn't really think or feel.–When the bully said he was sorry he had hit the little boy, he was a *hypocrite*.

I i

I, i *I's, i's*. The ninth letter of the alphabet.

I. A word used to mean oneself. – When you speak about yourself, you say *I*. – *I* like to read. Don't you?–Jack and *I* went skating yesterday.

ice *ices, iced, icing*. 1. Frozen water. – *Ice* is hard and keeps foods cold.
2. A kind of flavoured frozen dessert.–Mother likes orange *ice*.
3. Cover with *icing*–The baker *iced* the cake. He put chocolate *icing* on it.
4. Make cold with *ice*.–Mother likes *iced* tea.

iceberg ice'-berg *icebergs*. A very large piece of ice that floats in the sea. Most of an *iceberg* is below the surface of the water.

ice-cream. A frozen dessert made of cream, milk, eggs, sugar, and flavouring.

icicle i-ci-cle *icicles*. A long, slender piece of ice that is formed by the freezing of drip-. ping water.

icing ic'-ing. A sweet covering put on cakes. *Icing* may be made of sugar and water, or of sugar, egg-white and flavouring. Butter may also be used.

icy i'-cy *icier, iciest*. 1. Covered with ice.–The street is *icy*.
2. Cold; unfriendly.–The man gave us an *icy* look.
3. Cold as ice.–The *icy* wind came from the lake.

I'd. I had; I would; I should.–*I'd* have come if *I'd* known you wanted me to.

idea i-dea' *ideas*. 1. Understanding, knowledge. –The teacher can form an *idea* of the children's ability from their work.–I have no *idea* how to bake a cake.
2. A plan.–Bob's *idea* is to dig up the patch near the fence and make a flower-garden.
3. A feeling.–I had an *idea* that Jack would not come today.
4. Opinion.–You should not try to force your *ideas* on other people.–Father says Uncle Jim's *ideas* are crazy.

ideal i-de'-al *ideals*. 1. A model; something thought of as perfect.–David Livingstone is Bob's *ideal*. Bob would like to be like Livingstone.
2. Exactly right.–This is an *ideal* spot from which to see the races.–This is an *ideal* day for a picnic.

idealist i-de'-a-list *idealists*. A person who believes in and works for an ideal state of affairs.–Father says that people who believe that all nations can live together in peace are *idealists*. They are not realists.

ideally i-de'-al-ly. Perfectly.–Mary is *ideally* suited to the part of Cinderella in the play. She is pretty and charming.–*Ideally* all nations should live together in peace.

identical i-den'-ti-cal. Exactly alike.–The writing on the two papers is *identical,* so they must have been written by the same person.

identify i-den'-ti-fy *identifies, identified, identifying.* 1. Make known to be a certain person or thing.–The policeman told the man to *identify* himself, to tell who he was.
2. Recognize; know as a certain one.–You may have the dog if you can *identify* it among the others.

idiot id'-i-ot *idiots.* A very weak-minded person who cannot take care of himself.–An *idiot* cannot learn to read.

idle i'-dle. 1. Doing nothing; not busy.–While the machines were being repaired, the men were *idle.*
2. Lazy.–The idle man would rather go hungry than work.
3. Useless.–It is *idle* to cry over things that have already happened.
4. *Idle away* means to waste.–Bob *idled away* his time during school, so he had to study after school.
5. Run slowly.–Father let the motor of the car *idle.*

idleness i'-dle-ness. 1. Condition of being without anything to do.–*Idleness* often leads boys into mischief.
2. Laziness.–The man lives a life of *idleness.*

idly i'-dly. 1. Doing nothing.–Mary sat *idly* in the rocking chair.
2. Slowly; without interest or enthusiasm. –Bob *idly* turned the pages of the magazine, looking at the pictures.

idol i'-dol *idols.* 1. An image of a god.–In many countries, people worship *idols.*

Buddhist idol   Peruvian idol

Hindu idol

2. A person who is very much admired.–The racing driver is an *idol* of many boys.

if. 1. Whether.–I do not know *if* the train has gone.
2. Though.–Even *if* it rains, we shall play football.

igloo ig'-loo *igloos.* An Eskimo's house. It is sometimes made of snow and ice blocks.

ignite ig-nite' *ignites, ignited, igniting.* 1. Set fire to.–Bob *ignited* the waste paper in the alley with a match.
2. Catch fire; begin to burn.–Dry paper *ignites* more easily than wet paper.

ignorance ig'-no-rance. Not having knowledge (of); not knowing about.–Our *ignorance* of the lesson was due to having been absent.

ignorant ig'-no-rant. Without knowledge.–An *ignorant* person is one who doesn't know much.

ignore ig-nore' *ignores, ignored, ignoring.* Not to notice or pay attention to.–The cricketer *ignored* the boos of the crowd. He paid no attention to them.

ill. 1. Having something wrong with the body; sick.–Baby has measles. She is *ill.*
2. Bad; evil; harmful.–If you do *ill* deeds, you must expect to be punished.
3. Badly; poorly.–A job *ill* done may be better not done at all.

I'll. I will or I shall.–*I'll* go to town tomorrow if I finish my work in time.

illegal il-le'gal *illegally.* Against the law.–Driving on the wrong side of the road is *illegal.*

illegible il-leg'-i-ble. Not able to be read.–The boy's writing is *illegible.*

I
J
K
L
M
N
O
P
Q
R
S
T
U
V
W
X
Y
Z

illiterate il-lit′-e-rate *illiterates, illiteracy*. Unable to read or write.–There are millions of *illiterate* people all over the world. They are people who have had little or no schooling.

illness ill′-ness *illnesses*. Sickness; poor health. –Grandmother's *illness* kept her at home on Christmas day.

illuminate il-lu′-mi-nate *illuminates, illuminated, illuminating, illlumination*. I. Light up; make bright with lights.–When we came nearer to the church, we could see that it was *illuminated*.
2. Decorate with fancy letters. – The invitations to the golden wedding anniversary were *illuminated* with golden letters.

illusion il-lu′-sion *illusions*. Something which seems real or true but which is not.–The travellers in the desert thought they saw an oasis but it was just an optical *illusion*.

illustrate il′-lus-trate *illustrates, illustrated, illustrating*. I. Show.–The handicraft teacher will *illustrate* how to make a box. She will make each step clear to us by doing it herself.
2. Decorate or make clear with pictures.– The book was *illustrated* with drawings.

illustration il-lus-tra′-tion *illustrations*. I. A picture that helps to explain.–Children like story-books with *illustrations* of the important happenings.
2. An explanation.–The teacher gave an *illustration* of how to make a paper box.

I'm. I am.–*I'm* ten years old today.

image im′-age *images*. I. A likeness.–A photograph of you is an *image* of you because it looks like you.
2. A picture in the mind.–The boy had an *image* of the aeroplane he was going to build.
3. A statue; an idol.–In olden times, some people worshipped *images*.

imaginary im-ag′-i-nar-y. Existing only in the mind; not real.–Baby has an *imaginary* playmate. The playmate isn't real.

imagination im-ag-i-na′-tion *imaginations*. The power to picture things in the mind.–Some children have great *imagination*. They picture many things that they have never seen.

imagine im-ag′-ine *imagines, imagined, imagining*. Picture in the mind.–Bob *imagines* that he is a football star.

imitate im′-i-tate *imitates, imitated, imitating*.
I. Act like.–The children tried to *imitate* their teacher.
2. Make something just like something else. –Bob can *imitate* bird calls. He can make the sound of a bird call by whistling.

imitation im-i-ta′-tion *imitations*. I. A copying. –Bob gave an *imitation* of the song of a canary.
2. Something made to look like something else.–This is not a real diamond, but an *imitation* of one. It is made of glass and cut to look like a diamond.
3. Not original or real; copied.–This jewel is an *imitation* diamond.

immediate im-me′-di-ate. I. Coming at once. –We received an *immediate* answer to our letter.
2. Close; near.–My father and mother are my most *immediate* living relatives.

immediately im-me′-di-ate-ly. At once.–The fire engine came *immediately* after getting our call.–Mary sang a song *immediately* after the dance.

immense im-mense′ *immensely*. Very large; huge.–The rich man has an *immense* amount of money.

immigrant im′-mi-grant *immigrants*. A person from a foreign land coming into a country to live there.–If you should go to live in Canada, you would be an *immigrant* there.

immigrate im′-mi-grate *immigrates, immigrated, immigrating, immigration*. Come from a foreign land into a country to live there.–Many people *immigrate* into Great Britain.

immune im-mune′. Protected against infection. –After being vaccinated, a person is *immune* against smallpox for a number of years. He cannot get smallpox.

imp *imps, impish*. I. A mischievous child.– The boy is a little *imp*. He loves to tease and play jokes.
2. In fairy stories, a small mischief-making fairy.

impatient im-pa′-tient *impatiently*. Cross; anxious and uneasy; unable to wait quietly.– Mother sometimes becomes *impatient* when we are late getting ready for breakfast.

imperfect im-per′-fect *imperfectly*. Not perfect; having flaws, faults, or mistakes.–John's spelling paper was *imperfect*. He had made two mistakes.

I
J
K
L
M
N
O
P
Q
R
S
T
U
V
W
X
Y
Z

implement im'-ple-ment *implements.* A tool; something used for a certain job.–A harrow is a farm *implement.*

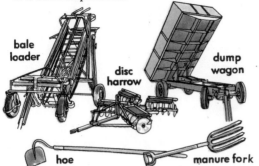

bale loader

disc harrow

dump wagon

hoe   manure fork

impolite im-po-lite' *impolitely.* Not polite; not courteous.–It is *impolite* to talk when someone else is talking.

import im'-port *imports, imported, importing.*
1. Something brought into one country from another.–Foods, clothing, and other articles bought into our country are *imports.*
2. (Im-port'.) Bring into a country.–England *imports* coffee from South America.

importance im-por'-tance. To say that something is of *importance* means that it matters very much. The *importance* of a thing is the reason why it matters.–It is *importance* to spell correctly. – The *importance* of being careful with fire is that you may be burned if you are not careful.

important im-por'-tant. 1. Mattering a great deal; having great meaning or value.–Good habits and manners are *important.* They mean much to people.
2. Having much power and influence.–The headmaster is an *important* person in our town.

impossible im-pos'-si-ble *impossibility.* Not possible; not able to happen or be done.–It is *impossible* for me to sing well when I have a cold.

impress im-press' *impresses, impressed, impressing.* 1. Mark; stamp; press on or in.–The rabbit *impressed* his footprints in the snow.
2. Strongly fix in the mind.–Mary repeated the poem so many times that it was *impressed* upon her mind. She knew it well.
3. Have an effect on someone's mind.–He *impressed* me as a good worker. It seemed to me that he was a good worker.

impression im-pres'-sion *impressions.* 1. A print; a mark pressed in.–The rabbit left the *impression* of its feet in the snow.

2. An effect on someone's thoughts.–Mary wanted to make a good *impression* on her new teacher. She wanted the teacher to think well of her.
3. An idea; a belief.–It is my *impression* that Bob is at his Grandmother's. He may not be.

improve im-prove' *improves, improved, improving.* 1. Make better.–You can *improve* your piano playing by practising.
2. Get better.–Grandmother is *improving* each day. Her health is getting better.
3. Make good use of.–The children *improve* their spare time by reading.

improvement im-prove'-ment *improvements.*
1. Anything that makes a thing better.–Grandmother has made many *improvements* in her kitchen; she has a new stove, a new sink, and a new light.
2. A making or getting better.–Bob's handwriting shows much *improvement.* It is much better than it was.

impudent im'-pu-dent *impudently, impudence.* Forward; saucy; not polite; bold.–The *impudent* boy threw a snowball at the teacher.

impure im-pure'. Not pure, clean, or refined.–Do not drink *impure* water. It may make you ill.

in. 1. Bob has his hand *in* his pocket.
2. There are 30 days *in* June.
3. Uncle Jim is *in* training for the sports.
4. The dog lived *in* fear of the cat.
5. The old lady came *into* the house.
6. The doctor isn't *in.* He is not *in* his office.
7. The door closed and we were locked *in.*
8. A car turned *in* at the driveway.
9. I'll be there *in* a minute.

incense. 1. (in'-cense). A substance that has a sweet smell when burned.–In some churches *incense* is burned during the service.
2. (in-cense'). Enrage, make angry.–I was *incensed* by the man's stupidity.

inch *inches, inched, inching.* 1. A measurement of length.–Twelve *inches* make a foot.–We measure ribbon by the yard, the foot, and the *inch.*

2. *Inch by inch* means slowly.–We are getting to the top of the hill *inch by inch.*
3. Move very slowly.–We *inched* along the icy path.

I

J K L M N O P Q R S T U V W X Y Z

incident in'ci-dent *incidents, incidental*. A happening; something that happens. – John lost his balance and fell into the brook. Mary thought the *incident* was very funny.

incline in-cline' *inclines, inclined, inclining*. 1. Bow; bend over.–Grandfather sat with his head *inclined* forward.
2. Have a tendency.–Father was not *inclined* to believe the man. It seemed that Father would not believe him.

incline in'-cline *inclines*. A slope or slant.–The car went slowly up the *incline*.

include in-clude' *includes, included, including*. 1. Contain; cover.–The price of my piano lessons *includes* the teacher's pay, books, and the use of the piano.
2. Take count of.–There are 5 people here, *including* Mary.

incognito in-cog'-ni-to. Under another name. –The general did not wish to be recognized so he travelled *incognito* as Mr White.

income in'-come *incomes*. The money that one gets for work, for rent, or for interest.– Father's *income* is £1,000 a year.

income-tax. A tax whereby a part of one's earnings goes to the government.

incorrect in-cor-rect' *incorrectly*. Wrong; in error; not correct or right.–It is *incorrect* to say, 'I seen the boy yesterday.'

increase in-crease' *increases, increased, increasing*. Make or become greater in size, number, speed, amount, etc.–Father's pay was *increased* to £20 per week.–You can *increase* your speed in writing if you practise enough.

increase in'-crease *increases*. The amount or degree by which something is made or becomes larger.–Father got an *increase* of £2 per week in his pay.

incubator in'cu-ba-tor *incubators*. 1. A device for hatching eggs without having a hen sit on them. Eggs are placed in the *incubator*, which is kept at just the right temperature to make the eggs hatch.

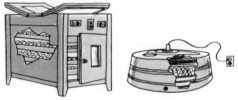

2. A special kind of box that very tiny babies are sometimes kept in when they are first born. It keeps them warm all the time.

indeed in-deed'. Really; in truth.–*Indeed*, I will not be 10 years old until my next birthday.–Yes, *indeed*. I should very much like to come.

indent in-dent' *indents, indented, indenting*. 1. Notch; put a notch or hole in.–The edge of a saw is *indented*.
2. Set in from a line or margin.–We *indent* the first line of each paragraph in a story. We start it further in from the left margin than the other lines.

independence in-de-pend'-ence. Freedom from control or help from others.–John will get his *independence* from his family when he is 21 years old.–The United States won its *independence* from England long ago.

independent in-de-pend'-ent *independently*. 1. Free from control or help from others.–A person who can do things for himself without help from others is *independent*.
2. Having no help from others; having enough money to care for oneself.–Grandfather is *independent* now; he doesn't have to work any more.

index in'-dex *indexes*. 1. A list that names in alphabetical order the things that are written about in a book and tells the pages on which they may be found.–The *index* comes at the end of a book.
2. The *index* finger is the one next to the thumb.

indicate in'-di-cate *indicates, indicated, indicating.* 1. Show, point out.–The hands on the clock *indicate* the time.–The police dog *indicated* the way for the officer to follow. 2. Make known.–Smoke in the room *indicated* to us that there was a fire. 3. Be a sign of; show that something will happen.–Dark clouds *indicate* a storm.

indication in-di-ca'-tion *indications.* 1. Act of indicating, or of being indicated.–The *indication* of rain made us cancel the picnic. 2. Something that indicates.–Fever is an *indication* of illness. It shows that one is ill.

indifferent in-dif'-fe-rent *indifferently, indifference.* Not interested, not caring.–Jack's father explained why he should make an effort to work harder, but Jack seemed quite *indifferent.*

indigestion in-di-ges'-tion. A condition in the stomach that occurs when food is not being digested properly. When the stomach digests food, it changes it so that the body can use it. When one has *indigestion,* the stomach is not changing the food properly for use.

indignant in-dig'-nant *indignantly.* Angry at a wrong done.–Bob was *indignant* because he was treated meanly and unfairly.

indignation in-dig-na'-tion. Anger at, or strong disagreement with, something that has been done; strong belief that something is wrong. –The unjust law aroused the *indignation* of the citizens.

indigo in'-di-go. 1. A deep, violet-blue colour. 2. A plant from which a blue dye or a blue colouring is made.

indirect in-di-rect' *indirectly.* 1. In a roundabout way.–The road was blocked by a tree, so we had to take an *indirect* route. 2. Not intended.–An *indirect* result of Bob's passing the exam was that he became a friendlier person.

indistinct in-dis-tinct' *indistinctly.* Not clear; not easily understood, seen, or heard.–The voices on the radio were *indistinct.*–The fog on the lake made the boat *indistinct.*–The teacher had explained the problem, but Bob remembered it *indistinctly.* He wasn't sure of it any more.

individual in-di-vid'-u-al *individuals.* 1. One person, one thing, or one animal.–Mary is a happy *individual.* 2. For one only.–A bicycle is an *individual* means of travelling. It is for one person only.

3. Personal; all one's own.–Each child has an *individual* way of writing. It is different from every other child's way.

individually in-di-vid'-u-al-ly. One at a time, each by himself.–Each child sang *individually,* and then they all sang together.

indivisible in-di-vis'-i-ble. Not able to be divided or separated into parts.–The friends are *indivisible.* They are always together.

indoors in-doors, *Inside* the house, school, or other building.–It is cold outdoors and warm *indoors.*

induce in-duce' *induces, induced, inducing.* 1. Persuade, get (someone) to do something. –Bob tried to *induce* John to go skating. He tried to get him to go. 2. Bring on; cause.–Too little sleep *induces* a tired feeling. It causes a tired feeling.

industrial in-dus'-tri-al. Having to do with manufacturing; relating to factories and the making of things to be sold.–Sheffield is an *industrial* city. It has many industries, with many men working there.

industrious in-dus'-tri-ous *industriously.* Hardworking.–Bob is very *industrious.* He is always hard at work.

industry in-dus'-try *industries.* 1. A kind of manufacturing.–The motor-car *industry* is the business of making motor-cars.–The woollen *industry* is the business of making woollen yarns, blankets, etc. 2. All businesses taken together.–European *industry* has grown since the war. 3. Hard work.–*Industry* will bring one good marks in school.

inexpensive in-ex-pen'-sive *inexpensively.* Cheap; not costing much. – Mary's cotton frocks are *inexpensive.* They cost little.

infant in'-fant *infants.* 1. A baby, especially a very young baby.

2. Having to do with babies.–Mother likes to make *infant* clothing. She likes to make clothes for babies. 3. Started only a short time ago.–Our chess club is an *infant* club.

I
J
K
L
M
N
O
P
Q
R
S
T
U
V
W
X
Y
Z

infantry in'-fan-try. The branch of an army that fights on foot; the soldiers in this branch. –The hill was defended by a regiment of *infantry*.

infect in-fect' *infects, infected, infecting.* Make ill or diseased by spreading or adding to the germs that cause disease.–If you have a cold, sneeze into your handkerchief, so that you will not *infect* others.–A cut may become *infected* if not properly cleaned and cared for.

infection in-fec'-tion *infections.* 1. The causing of a disease by the spread of germs.–The *infection* of the cut in Sally's finger happened very quickly.
2. A sick or bad condition of any part of the body caused by the presence of egrms.–The *infection* in the cut was hard to cure.
3. A disease which is spread from person to person. – Colds, measles, chicken-pox, and many other diseases are *infections*.

infer in-fer' *infers, inferred, inferring, inference.* Come to a conclusion.–From his staggering I *inferred* that the man was drunk.

inferior in-fe'-ri-or. Poorer; not as good as others.–The cloth Mary bought was of *inferior* quality. It wasn't the best.

infernal in-fer'-nal *infernally.* 1. Connected with hell.–In Milton's 'Paradise Lost' we read how Satan was flung into the *infernal* regions.
2. Outrageous.–When William spilt paint on the carpet, Mother called him an *infernal* nuisance.

infest in-fest' *infests, infested, infesting.* Attack in numbers.–Locusts *infest* many parts of Asia and Africa, ruining crops.

inflame in-flame' *inflames, inflamed, inflaming, inflammation.* 1. Arouse, or fill with angry feelings.–The murder of their neighbour *inflamed* the townspeople.
2. To cause to burn or become red and tender.–Bob's arm was *inflamed* where he was stung by nettles.

inflate in-flate' *inflates, inflated, inflating, inflation.* 1. Put air into.–Father stopped at a petrol station to *inflate* the spare tyre.–*Inflating* the tyre made it swell or puff up.
2. Swell out.–Bob *inflated* his chest when he marched in the parade.

inflict in-flict' *inflicts, inflicted, inflicting.* Bring something cruel or very unpleasant (upon someone). – Jack loves animals too much ever to *inflict* pain on one.

influence in'-flu-ence *influences, influenced, influencing.* 1. Use one's power upon someone ot get him to do something.–Father tried to *influence* the man to do better. He tried to make him want to do better.
2. Power, persuasion, or ability to cause. something to happen.–Mother's presence has a soothing *influence* on the children. Just by being near she makes them feel quiet and peaceful.

influenza in-flu-en'-za. A very infectious disease. One has a cold, a fever, and aches all through the body when one has *influenza*.– If you have *influenza*, stay at home, for you may spread the germs to others.

inform in-form' *informs, informed, informing.* Tell; give notice or information to.–I phoned to *inform* you that Bob is better.–We *informed* the neighbours that we had found their dog.

information in-for-ma'-tion. What is told; facts; news; what one knows or can find out. –The newspaper has much *information* in it. –I shall give you all the *information* about the accident.–Grandfather wants some *information* about a stamp in his collection. He wants to find out all about it.

inhabit in-hab'-it *inhabits, inhabited, inhabiting.* Live in.–Mary wild animals *inhabit* the woods.–Eskimos *inhabit* the northern countries.–Many people *inhabit* the city.

inhabitant in-hab'-it-ant *inhabitants.* A dweller; one who lives in a certain place.–Deer are *inhabitants* of the woods. They live there. –Most of the *inhabitants* of this town are miners.

inhale in-hale' *inhales, inhaled, inhaling.* Take into the lungs.–We *inhale* air when we breathe in. We exhale air when we breathe out.

inherit in-her'-it *inherits, inherited, inheriting.*
1. Have at birth from one's ancestors.–Mary *inherits* her curly hair from her mother. Her mother has curly hair.
2. Get money or property rightfully from someone after that person is dead.–Father *inherited* a house and land from his brother who died.

inheritance in-her'-it-ance *inheritances.* Something that you rightfully receive from someone who has died.–Mother's *inheritance* from her aunt was a diamond ring.

inhuman in-hu'-man. Cruel; having no pity or kind feeling at all.–The man is *inhuman*. He is as cruel as a beast.

initial in-i'-tial *initials, initialled, initialling.* 1. The first or beginning.–Bob is going to the *initial* meeting of his football club. It is their first meeting.
2. The letter which a word or, usually, a name begins with.– Mary's handkerchief has her first *initial* on it. It has an M on it.
3. Put *initials* on.–Mother had Father's Bible *initialled*. She had his *initials* put on it.
4. Sign by writing one's *initials* on.–John Smith *initialled* his note J. S.

injure in'-jure *injures, injured, injuring.* 1. Harm; damage.–Frost will *injure* the fruit. –The boy was *injured* in the accident.
2. To *injure* a person is to do wrong to him.– Bob felt *injured* at being left behind.

injurious in-ju'-ri-ous *injuriously.* Harmful.– It is *injurious* to iron silk with a very hot iron. It damages the silk.

injury in'-ju-ry *injuries.* 1. A hurt.–The motor-race ended without an *injury* to any of the cars or drivers.
2. An act which is unfair or unkind to another.–To tell a lie about a person is to do him an *injury*.

ink *inks, inked, inking.* 1. A liquid used with a pen for writing.–*Ink* is red, blue, black, green, purple, etc.
2. Cover with *ink*, or mark with *ink*.–Jack *inked* the pencil lines on his plan of the boat.

ink-well ink'-well *ink-wells.* A container for ink. –Bob filled the *ink-wells* in the desks with ink.

inland in'-land. In or towards the inner part of a country.–The explorers came to the island by boat and travelled *inland* on horseback.

inmate in'-mate *inmates.* 1. A person who lives in the same house with others.–The students are *inmates* of the boarding-house across the street.

2. A person who is put in a prison, a home for old people, a hospital, or other big institution.–The *inmates* of the prison were frightened when fire broke out.

inn *inns.* A house where travellers stop to eat and rest for the night.–The travellers stopped at an *inn* in the mountains.

inner in'-ner. Inside; further away from the outside.–Father always carries his wallet in an *inner* pocket, not an outside pocket.

innings in'-nings. In cricket, the time a batsman is at the wicket is called his *innings*. The time a whole team is batting is the team's *innings*. Both teams have 2 *innings* and the team scoring the greater number of runs wins the match.

innocent in'-no-cent *innocently.* 1. Not guilty. The man was *innocent* of the crime. He had not committed it or had anything to do with it.
2. Pure; knowing nothing wrong. – Little babies are *innocent*.
3. Harmless.–Playing ball is *innocent* sport.

inquire or **enquire** in-quire' *inquires, inquired, inquiring.* Ask about; find out about.–Mother sent me to *inquire* about the accident.

inquiry or **enquiry** in-quir'-y *inquiries.* 1. A question.–We received many *inquiries* about the house we had to sell.
2. An investigation; a looking into. – The police are making an *inquiry* about the cause of the accident.

insane in-sane' *insanely.* 1. Sick in mind; mad. People who are *insane* are cared for in special hospitals.
2. Foolish and silly.–The ten-year-old boy had the *insane* idea of running away to join the army.

I
J
K
L
M
N
O
P
Q
R
S
T
U
V
W
X
Y
Z

INSECTS

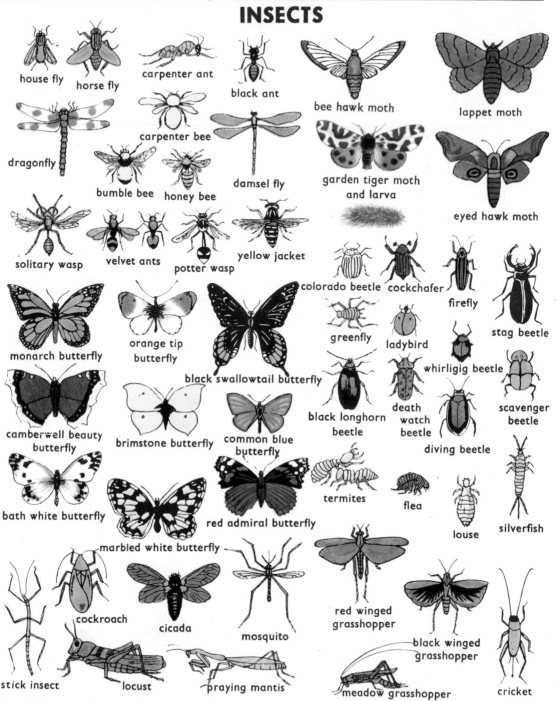

house fly   horse fly

carpenter ant

black ant

bee hawk moth

lappet moth

dragonfly

carpenter bee

honey bee

damsel fly

bumble bee

garden tiger moth
and larva

eyed hawk moth

solitary wasp   velvet ants   potter wasp

yellow jacket

colorado beetle   cockchafer

firefly

greenfly   ladybird

stag beetle

whirligig beetle

monarch butterfly

orange tip
butterfly

black swallowtail butterfly

black longhorn
beetle

death
watch
beetle

scavenger
beetle

camberwell beauty
butterfly

brimstone butterfly

common blue
butterfly

diving beetle

bath white butterfly

red admiral butterfly

termites

flea

louse

silverfish

marbled white butterfly

cockroach

cicada

mosquito

red winged
grasshopper

black winged
grasshopper

stick insect   locust   praying mantis

meadow grasshopper

cricket

insect in'-sect *insects*. A tiny animal with 6 jointed legs and, in most cases, wings. *Insects'* bodies have 3 parts or sections.–Ants and bees are *insects*.

insert in-sert' *inserts, inserted, inserting*. Put in.–Mary spelled the word 'sweet' with one 'e', and later *inserted* another 'e' to correct it.–Mother *inserted* a piece of cloth in the back of Bob's coat to make it bigger.

inside in-side' *insides*. 1. The side that is in, not out.–The *inside* of Bob's coat is lined with fur.–The *inside* of the cupboard is painted red, the outside white.

2. To or on the *inside* of.–Mother put her money *inside* her purse.–We went *inside* to eat.

3. Privately known; secret.–Bill told Jack he had *inside* information about the arithmetic test.

I
J
K
L
M
N
O
P
Q
R
S
T
U
V
W
X
Y
Z

insight in´-sight. Knowledge, familiarity.–The teacher gained an *insight* into Jack's character by talking to his parents. He got to know him better that way.

insignia in-sig´-ni-a. Badges or special emblems worn by soldiers or other people to show their rank or branch of service, or to show that they have done something outstanding.

insignificant in-sig-nif´-i-cant *insignificantly*. 1. Unimportant.–The teacher advised Jack not to waste so much time on *insignificant* details in his history essay. The important thing was to stick to the subject.
2. Seeming weak or trivial.–Father said that his new assistant at the shop was a very *insignificant* person. He was not a good worker and did not seem to try.

insincere in-sin-cere´ *insincerely, insincerity*. Not straightforward and honest.–Father thinks that Mr Brown, the candidate for Parliament, is *insincere*. Father believes that he does not mean what he says and will not do anything if he is elected.

insipid in-sip´-id *insipidly*. 1. Without taste. –This lemonade is *insipid*; it has too much water in it.
2. Dull, uninteresting.–Our new neighbour is an *insipid* person. She has nothing to talk about and does not seem interested in anything.

insist in-sist´ *insists, insisted, insisting*. Make a point of wanting a thing done and seeing that it is done.–Mother *insists* that we wear our overshoes when it rains. She tells us to wear them, and she doesn't change her mind about it.

insistent in-sis´-tent. Being quite definite about something.–When Father was ill, the doctor was *insistent* that he should stay in bed at least 4 days. He refused to let him get up earlier.

insolence in´-so-lence. Rudeness.–The teacher told Jack that she would not put up with his *insolence* and that if he answered back again he would be punished.

insolent in´-so-lent *insolently*. Cheeky or insulting.–When Jack answered back in class the teacher told him not to be so *insolent*. She said she would report him for *insolent* behaviour.

inspect in-spect´ *inspects, inspected, inspecting*. Look closely and carefully at, to be sure it is as it should be. – Mother *inspects* our hands each morning to see if they are clean.–Father *inspects* tools at the factory. He examines them to see if they are in good condition.

inspection in-spec´-tion *inspections*. A close looking over, to be sure that things are as they should be.–The soldiers lined up for morning *inspection*.–The *inspection* of aircraft before they fly is very important.

inspector in-spec´-tor *inspectors*. A person who looks over or examines things to see that they are as they should be.–Father is an *inspector* of tools in a tool factory. He looks at the tools to see if they are all right.

inspiration in-spi-ra´-tion *inspirations*. 1. A deep and strong desire to do something. especially something new and different.– Sally had an *inspiration* to write a poem.
2. A good influence.–Mary's music teacher is her *inspiration*. She makes Mary want to play well.

inspire in-spire´ *inspires, inspired, inspiring*. –Fill with good and uplifted feelings, and a desire to do fine things.–Grandmother found the minister's sermon *inspiring*. – Mother hopes the concert will *inspire* Jack to become a violinist.

install in-stall´ *installs, installed, installing, installation*. 1. Set up or fix in place.–We had a new oil burner *installed* in our home.
2. Put formally into office.–The officers in our club will be *installed* tonight.

instalment in-stal´-ment *instalments*. One of several parts of something that goes on over a period of time.–Mary is reading the second *instalment* of the magazine story.–Our car cost £1200. We paid for it in *instalments* of £50 a month.

instance in-stance *instances*. An example. –Helping the old man across the road was an *instance* of Bob's generous nature.–Mother always helps a neighbour; for *instance*, if she is ill, Mother will do her shopping.

instant in´-stant *instants*. 1. Happening at once. –The poison for rats brings *instant* death. The rats die at once after eating it.
2. A moment.–Come here this *instant*!–I shall be ready in an *instant*.

I J K L M N O P Q R S T U V W X Y Z

instantly in'-stant-ly. At once; without any delay.–Come here *instantly*!

instead in-stead'. In place (of).–Some people use margarine *instead* of butter.–Bob came *instead* of Mary.

instep in'-step *insteps*. The upper part of your foot between the toes and the ankle.–The *instep* of your shoe is the part that covers your *instep*.

instinct in'-stinct *instincts*. 1. A feeling or way of acting that one is born with, that guides or determines one's actions, and is not taught. –Mother's *instinct* is to love and protect her children.–Squirrels bury nuts by *instinct*. 2. A talent that one is born with.–Mary has an *instinct* for music.

institution in-sti-tu'-tion *institutions*. 1. An organization or society of any kind. There are *institutions* of learning, *institutions* for the diseased, *institutions* for orphans, etc. 2. A custom.–Father thinks an after-dinner nap is a good *institution*. 3. Setting up or founding.–The children have benefited by the *institution* of a school library.

instruct in-struct' *instructs, instructed, instructing*. 1. Teach.–Our teacher *instructs* us in reading. 2. Give an order to; direct.–Father *instructed* the men to dig the ditch wider.

instruction in-struc'-tion *instructions*. 1. Teaching.–The teacher gives free *instruction* in knitting. 2. Direction.–Mother read the *instructions* for making the sweater.

instructor in-struc'-tor *instructors*. One who teaches or instructs.–Miss King is our *instructor* in arithmetic.

instrument in'-stru-ment *instruments*. 1. A tool; something used to work with.–Dentists use many special *instruments*.–A screwdriver is an *instrument* for putting in screws. 2. A musical *instrument*. – Violins, violas, pianos, and cellos are musical *instruments*.

insulate in'-su-late *insulates, insulated, insulating, insulation*. Protect against loss of heat or transfer of electricity.–Many homes are *insulated*. A material is placed inside the walls to keep the heat in.–Electric wires are *insulated* to prevent injury to people and damage to buildings. They are wrapped with tape, rubber, or other covering.

insult in-sult' *insults, insulted, insulting*. Treat with great scorn and rudeness.–The angry boy *insulted* the other children. He said rude things to them.

insult in'-sult *insults*. A very rude act or remark, meant to offend.–The children did not like the boy's *insults*.

insurance in-sur'-ance. An amount of money paid to protect against loss in case of accident, fire, theft, death, damage by storm, or whatever misfortune the *insurance* is to cover. A person agrees to pay an *insurance* company a certain amount of money at regular times, and the company agrees to pay him a certain amount if anything happens which the *insurance* is arranged to cover. The amount you pay to the company is called the *insurance* or the premium. The amount you receive from the company is called *insurance* or indemnity.–We pay £10 a year for fire *insurance*. When our garage burned, the *insurance* company paid us *insurance* of £200.

insure in-sure' *insures, insured, insuring*. Protect by insurance; arrange to pay an insurance company a certain amount of money so that, if harm comes to someone or something, the insurance company will pay back a larger amount of money.–Mother has her fur coat *insured*.–Our garage was *insured* for £200.

intelligence in-tel'-li-gence. Ability to learn or understand things.–The bright boy has much *intelligence*.

intelligent in-tel'-li-gent *intelligently*. Able to understand and learn.–It was *intelligent* of Spot to learn how to open the door with his paw.

intend in-tend' *intends, intended, intending*. 1. Plan; mean.–Bob *intends* to go to Grandmother's on Saturday if it doesn't rain. 2. Do a thing purposely; mean to do a thing. –Mary did not *intend* to hurt your feelings.

intense in-tense' *intensely*. 1. Very great; deep; very strong.–The injured man suffered *intense* pain.–The soldiers in the North felt the *intense* cold. 2. Very earnest and emotional.–Bob is a very intense person. He is very serious and feels deeply about things.

intent in-tent'. Deeply interested; giving strict attention.–Mary was so *intent* on her practising that she did not hear Jack come up behind her.

intention in-ten'-tion *intentions, intentional, intentionally*. A purpose.–Bob accidentally broke a glass. It was not his *intention* to break it.

interest in'-ter-est *interests, interested, interesting*. 1. Get the attention of.–The story of David Copperfield *interests* most boys. They want to know all about it.
2. A desire to know about a thing.–The class took a great *interest* in their teacher's getting married.–Mary has no *interest* in arithmetic. She would just as soon never hear about it.
3. Advantage; benefit.–It is in your *interest* to listen when your teacher explains a problem.
4. A share; a part.–Father owns an *interest* in Grandfather's farm.
5. Money paid for the use of money.–Father paid £5 per year *interest* on £100 which he borrowed from the bank.

interesting in'-ter-est-ing. Holding one's thought and attention.–Bob is reading an *interesting* story. It makes him anxious to know what will happen next.

interfere in-ter-fere' *interferes, interfered, interfering*. 1. Try to do another person's work or handle his affairs when he wants to take care of them himself; meddle.–Mother never *interferes* with other people's business. She does not try to help unless people need help and want it.
2. Prevent by coming at the same time, being in the same place, etc.–The deep snow *interfered* with our plans to go ice skating.

interior in-te'-ri-or *interiors*. The inside, the inner part.–The *interior* of a country is the part near the middle, the part away from the border or coastline. – The *interior* of our house is cool, even on a hot day.

internal in-ter'-nal *internally*. Inside, having to do with the insides.–When it says on a medicine bottle 'Not to be taken *internally*,' it means one should not swallow it.

interpret in-ter'-pret *interprets, interpreted, interpreting*. 1. Give the meaning of; explain.–Bob tried to *interpret* the sentence for the class. He tried to tell what it meant.
2. Translate; put into a different language.–What the man said in French had to be *interpreted* into English so that we could understand it.
3. Show the meaning of something for others. –A musician *interprets* music. He tries to bring out for his hearers the feeling or meaning the composer wanted brought out.

interrupt in-ter-rupt' *interrupts, interrupted, interrupting*. Do something that suddenly stops or hinders what is being done or happening; break in on.–While I was talking on the telephone, someone else who wanted to use the phone *interrupted* me. – It is not polite to *interrupt* someone who is talking. –A rainstorm *interrupted* the picnic.

interruption in-ter-rup'-tion *interruptions*. A sudden breaking in on or stopping; a remark or happening which breaks into something already going on.–There was an *interruption* in the cricket match during the storm.

interval in'-ter-val *intervals*. 1. A space in between, or a length of time in between.
2. In music, the distance between two notes in the scale.

intestine in-tes'-tine *intestines*. The bowels; the tube-like organs of the body which help to change the food one eats so that the body can use it. The *intestines* also pass out the waste which cannot be used by the body.

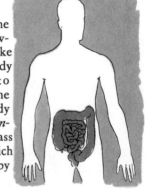

intimate in'-ti-mate *intimately*. Very close and familiar. – Ruth is Mary's *intimate* friend. They know each other very well.

into in'-to. 1. Towards and in; to the inside of.–The children went *into* the house when it began to rain.
2. *Into* describes a change from one kind of thing to another.–Churning changes cream *into* butter.–Spring passed *into* summer.

intoxicate in-tox'-i-cate *intoxicates, intoxicated, intoxicating, intoxication*. Make drunk; poison with alcohol.–Drinking too much whisky will *intoxicate* one.

introduce in-tro-duce' *introduces, introduced, introducing*. 1. Present; bring one person to another so that they will get to know one another.–Bob *introduced* his mother to the new teacher.
2. Bring in. –The new witness *introduced* more facts about the accident. – Fireworks were first *introduced* into the western world from China.
3. Bring to notice.–The dancers are *introducing* a new kind of dance.

I J K L M N O P Q R S T U V W X Y Z

introduction in-tro-duc'-tion *introductions*. 1. The act of making things known to people, or of making people known to each other.– Before the *introduction* of electric light, people used lamps, candles, or gas lights. 2. The beginning or first part.–The *introduction* to the book told about the writer.

invade in-vade' *invades, invaded, invading, invasion*. 1. Go in by force and take over.– The enemy *invaded* the country.
2. Interfere with; meddle with.–Do not *invade* the rights of others.

invalid in'-va-lid *invalids*. A sick person; one who needs to be cared for.–The old man was a helpless *invalid* after he lost the use of his legs.

invent in-vent' *invents, invented, inventing*. 1. Plan and make something that has never been made before. – Alexander Bell *invented* the telephone.

2. Imagine; make up in the mind.–Writers *invent* stories.

invention in-ven'-tion *inventions*. 1. Something planned and made for the first time, by skill and imagination.–The tractor is a wonderful *invention* for the farmer.
2. Inventing; thinking up and making.–The *invention* of radio has taken many years.– That story is Bob's own *invention*.

inventor in-ven'-tor *inventors*. A person who thinks up and makes new things.–Thomas Edison, who invented the electric light, was an *inventor*.

invest in-vest' *invests, invested, investing*. Use money to buy something that will help make more money.–If you *invest* £75 in Government securities, it will earn you £25 in ten years. You will get £100 for it.

INVENTIONS

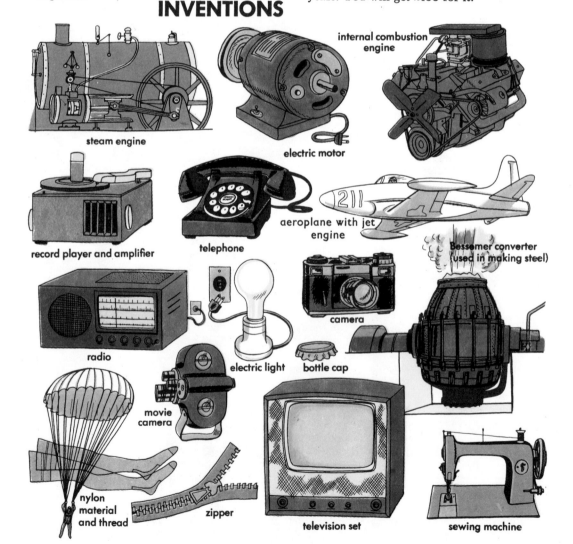

steam engine

electric motor

internal combustion engine

record player and amplifier

telephone

aeroplane with jet engine

radio

electric light

bottle cap

camera

Bessemer converter (used in making steel)

nylon material and thread

movie camera

zipper

television set

sewing machine

investigate in-ves′-ti-gate *investigates, investigated, investigating, investigation.* Look into; examine; find out about.–Father *investigated* the noise in the attic to find out what made it.

invincible in-vin′-ci-ble. Unable to be defeated or conquered.–The huge fleet was so powerful that it seemed *invincible.* – The chess champion is *invincible*; no other player can beat him.

invisible in-vis′-i-ble *invisibly.* Not able to be seen.–The fog made the boat *invisible.*

invitation in-vi-ta′-tion *invitations.* The polite asking of someone to attend a party, pay a visit, or do something.–'Will you come to the dance with me?' is an *invitation* to the dance.

invite in-vite′ *invites, invited, inviting.* 1. Ask someone to come to a party, to visit, etc.; politely ask someone to do something.–Bob will *invite* his teacher to the party.
2. Call for; give cause for.–Jack's bad behaviour *invited* punishment from his father.
3. Tempt.–On hot summer days the swimming pool is very *inviting.*

involve in-volve′ *involves, involved, involving.* 1. Include.–Three cars were *involved* in the accident.
2. Require.–Learning to play the piano *involves* many hours of practice.
4. Complicate; mix up.–The puzzle is very *involved.*

iodine i′-o-dine. A kind of dark brown medicine used on cuts and sores to kill disease germs.

irate i-rate′. Extremely angry. – When John broke the living-room window with the cricket ball Father was *irate.* He was so furious that he stopped John's pocket-money for 2 weeks.

iris i′-ris *irises.* 1. A flower with long, flat, pointed leaves that grows from a bulb. *Irises* may be blue, yellow, white, purple, or some other colour. *Irises* are sometimes called flags.
2. The circle of colour round the pupil of the eye.–A blue-eyed person has blue *irises.*

iron i′-ron *irons, ironed, ironing.* 1. A hard metal from which steel is made.
2. Press with a flat-*iron.*–Mother *irons* the clothes.

3. A flat-*iron*; a device for pressing cloth.–Mother *irons* the clothes with an *iron.*
4. Strong; tough. – The airman has *iron* nerves: he can stand almost anything.

irregular ir-reg′-u-lar. 1. Not even or straight. –The coastline along the lake is *irregular.*
2. Not in the usual or proper order or way.–Father usually comes home at 6 o'clock, but tonight he came at 7. This was *irregular.*

irrigate ir′-ri-gate *irrigates, irrigated, irrigating, irrigation.* Water land by a system of ditches or pipes.–In dry parts of the country, farmers *irrigate* the land.

irritate ir′-ri-tate *irritates, irritated, irritating, irritation.* 1. Make nervous or angry.–Noise *irritates* Grandmother.
2. Cause to be sore.–Harsh soap *irritates* the baby's skin.

is. one form of the word *be.*–Father is home. –Winter *is* coming.–The rose *is* red.

island is′-land *islands.* 1. A piece of land that has water all round it. –Ireland is an *island* near England.
2. Anything like an *island.* – The policeman stands on an *island* and guides the traffic.

isle *isles.* An island; land with water all around it.

isn't. Is not.–It *isn't* time to go yet.

issue is′-sue *issues, issued, issuing.* 1. Pass or give out.–The teacher will *issue* books to us.
2. A single printing.–This is the third *issue* of the newspaper today.
3. Result.–A fight often *issues* from angry words.
4. A point on which people have different opinions.–Taxes are an *issue* in the elections.

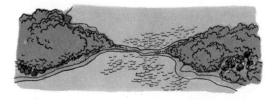

isthmus isth′-mus *isthmuses.* A narrow strip of land that connects two larger pieces of land. –The *Isthmus* of Panama connects South and Central America.

I J K L M N O P Q R S T U V W X Y Z

it. 1. A word used in speaking about a place, an animal, or a thing.–The snow fell fast. *It* covered the fields.–The cow is in the garden. *It* may eat all the grass.–The city is large. *It* has many beautiful parks.

2. *It* is used to tell about the weather or the general condition of any place.–*It* is raining. –*It* is hot in here.

3. *It* is time to go to bed.–*It* is not nice to do that.

itch *itches, itched, itching.* 1. Have a prickly feeling of the skin which makes one want to scratch or rub the place.–My mosquito bite *itches.*

2. A disease that makes spots break out on the body.–The old beggar had the *itch.*

item i´-tem *items.* 1. A separate article or thing in a list or group.–Apples, bread, and sugar are *items* on Mother's shopping list.

2. A bit of news.–Father read in the newspaper a short *item* about the fires.

its. A word used to show that something belongs to or is a part of a thing or animal.– The bird sings. *Its* song is beautiful.–The flower is beautiful. *Its* fragance is sweet.

it's. It is.–*It's* raining.

itself it-self´. 1. A word used to refer to a thing or animal. – The cat licks *itself* with its tongue.–The road curves round and crosses *itself.*

2. A word used to emphasize the word it refers to. – The box *itself* weighs a pound without anything in it.

I've. I have.–*I've* travelled all over the British Isles.

ivory i´vo-ry. The substance of which the tusks of the elephant and the walrus are made. *Ivory* is very hard and has a whitish colour. – Piano keys are often made of *ivory.*

ivy i´vy *ivies.* A climbing plant with green leaves and inconspicuous flowers.

J j

J, j *J's, j's.* The tenth letter of the alphabet.

jab *jabs, jabbed, jabbing.* 1. Stick into; punch; stab.–Someone *jabbed* me in the back with a pencil.

2. A poke, punch, or stab.–Someone gave me a sharp *jab* in the back.

jack *jacks, jacked, jacking.* 1. A cranking device used for lifting heavy things.–Father put the *jack* under the bumper to raise the car.

2. Lift with a *jack.*–It is not hard to *jack* up a heavy car with a *jack.*

3. A nickname for John. – *Jack's* real name is John.

4. In bowls, the *jack* is the small ball which the players aim at.

5. A playing card with the picture of a young man on it.–The *jacks* in a pack of cards are also called knaves.

jackal jack´-al *jackals.* A wild, doglike animal that eats other animals.

jacket jack´-et *jackets.* 1. A short coat.–Mary wears a long coat, but Ruth wears a *jacket.*

2. Any outside covering. – When we have baked potatoes, Father eats the *jacket.*

jack-knife jack´-knife *jack-knives.* 1. A large folding knife. – Bob carries a *jack-knife* in his pocket.

2. A forward dive during which the diver touches his feet with his hands and then straightens out before entering the water.

J
K
L
M
N
O
P
Q
R
S
T
U
V
W
X
Y
Z

jack-o'-lantern jack'-o'-lan-tern *jack-o'-lan-terns*. A hollowed-out pumpkin with a face cut into it and a light inside. – On Hallowe'en the children make *jack-o'-lan-terns*.

jack-rabbit *jack-rabbits*. A long-legged, long-eared prairie hare, found in America.

jackstraws jack'straws. A game of picking up small sticks one at a time from a jumbled pile without disturbing the rest of the sticks in the pile.

jade *jades*. 1. A kind of green stone used in making jewellery.–Mary has a necklace of *jade*. 2. The colour of *jade*.–Mother has a *jade* dress.

jagged jag'-ged. Having points sticking out; having rough edges.–Bob scraped his leg on a *jagged* stone.–Mary got a *jagged* tear in her stocking when she walked through the bushes.

jaguar jag'-uar *jaguars*. A large, fierce, spotted animal of the cat family. A *jaguar* is something like a leopard.

jail or **gaol** *jails* or *gaols*. A place where prisoners are kept for their crimes, or until their trials for those crimes.–The burglar was put in *jail* until the time for his trial.

jailer or **gaoler** jail'-er *jailers* or *gaolers*. The man who has charge of a jail.

jam *jams, jammed, jamming*. 1. A sweet made by cooking fruit and sugar together until the mixture thickens. It is then poured into jars, where it cools and becomes thick enough to spread on bread, scones, muffins, etc. 2. Crowd into.–A large crowd *jammed* the football stadium. 3. Crush.–Bob *jammed* his finger in the door. It got caught and bruised in the door. 4. A crowded condition.–The accident caused a traffic *jam*.

jangle jan'-gle, *jangles, jangled, jangling*. Make a loud clanging sound. – The bells *jangled* unpleasantly. They were out of tune.

January Jan'-u-ar-y. The first month of the year.–New Year's Day is *January* 1st

jar *jars, jarred, jarring*. 1. A small container with a wide opening.–Mother bottles fruit in glass *jars*. 2. Shake.–The thunder *jarred* the whole house.

jaw *jaws*. The lower part of the face. Your *jaw* is hinged so that you can open your mouth.

jay *jays*. A noisy and brilliantly coloured bird belonging to the crow family.

jazz. A popular style of music, played by *jazz* bands, particularly to accompany dancing.

jealous jeal'-ous *jealously, jealousy*. Feeling unhappy and angry towards someone who has something which you believe you should have.–Mary is *jealous* of Baby. She feels that Baby gets all the love and attention that was once given to her.–Dick is *jealous* of Bob, because Bob got a higher mark in spelling.

jeer *jeers, jeered, jeering*. 1. Make fun of.–The bad boys *jeered* at the boy who made the mistake. 2. A mocking remark.–The *jeers* ot the boys made him uncomfortable.

jelly jel'-ly *jellies, jellied, jellying*. 1. A food made by boiling sugar and fruit juice together. It becomes solid and clear when cool. –Mother makes grape *jelly* by boiling grape-juice and sugar together. The *jelly* will stand up in shape when taken from the glass. 2. Any *jelly*like substance. 3. Turn to *jelly*.–In warm weather we sometimes have *jellied* soup for dinner.

jerk *jerks, jerked, jerking, jerky*. 1. Move quickly.–The baby *jerked* her hand away from the hot stove. 2. Cause to *jerk*.–The car stopped quickly and *jerked* our heads. 3. A sudden, short movement. – The train stopped with a *jerk*.

jest *jests, jested, jesting*. 1. A joke; fun.–The class laughed at the teacher's *jest*. 2. Make a joke.–The clown *jests* about his big feet.

Jesus Je'-sus. The founder of the Christian religion. You can read about *Jesus* in the Bible.

J
K
L
M
N
O
P
Q
R
S
T
U
V
W
X
Y
Z

JEWELS

diamond   star sapphire   ruby   tourmaline   cat's eye   pearls   jade

garnet   emerald   pearl earrings   amber

brooch with garnet cluster   diamond ring   jewelled wrist watch   prehistoric Indian turquoise beads

jet *jets.* 1. A shiny black substance.–Grandmother has *jet* buttons on her dress.
2. A gush of liquid or gas.–Sally ran under the *jet* of water from the hose.
3. *Jet-black* means completely, solidly black.
4. A *jet* plane is an aeroplane that is propelled or driven by a *jet* of hot gases.

jewel jew'-el *jewels.* Diamonds, pearls, rubies, and other precious stones.–The rich woman wears many *jewels.*

jeweller jew'-el-ler *jewellers.* A person who makes jewellery; one who sells jewels.

jewellery jew'-el-ler-y. Brooches, rings, and other ornaments set with precious or pretty stones.

jig *jigs.* A kind of lively dance.

jingle jin'-gle *jingles, jingled, jingling.* 1. A tinkling sound.–We heard the *jingle* of the bells.
2. Make something ring or tinkle.–Bob *jingled* his pennies in his pocket.
3. A rhyme.–Our teacher reads *jingles* to us. 'Jack and Jill went up the hill' is a *jingle.*

job *jobs.* 1. Regular work.–My brother has a *job* as an office boy. He is paid to help in an office.
2. Piece of work.–Repairing the street is a big *job.*

jockey jock'-ey *jockeys.* A person paid to ride a horse in a horse race. *Jockeys* usually do not weigh very much.

jog *jogs, jogged, jogging.* 1. Nudge or push.–Someone *jogged* me in the ribs with his elbow.
2. Arouse, awaken.–The teacher *jogged* our memory about the work that was not done. She reminded us that it was not done.
3. Go forward with a bobbing movement.–The milkman's horse *jogs* along.

join *joins, joined, joining.* 1. Fix together, clasp, fasten together.–The children *joined* hands for the game.–Father *joined* the two ends of the rope by tying them together.
2. Become a member of.–Bob *joined* the Boy Scouts. He became one of them.
3. Unite with, come in among.–Won't you *join* us in a game of marbles?
4. Meet or touch.–Canada *joins* the United States on Canada's southern border.

joint *joints, jointed, jointing, jointly.* 1. The place where two or more things meet, or where they are fastened together. – The *joints* in your body are the places where the bones join or fasten together. The elbow and knee are *joints.*–The *joints* in a water pipe are the places where two pipes meet.
2. Shared, taken part in by more than one.–Doing things together is *joint* action.–Owning things together is *joint* ownership.
3. Cut or split into pieces at the *joints.*–Grandmother *jointed* the chicken to make soup of it.

joke *jokes, joked, joking.* 1. Something funny which makes us laugh; a funny story or a funny happening.–Bob told us a good *joke.*
2. A trick.–The boys played a *joke* on Father on April Fool's day.
3. Tease, have fun.–The children *joke* with the policeman on the corner.

joker jok'-er *jokers.* 1. A person who tells jokes, plays tricks, and teases people.
2. An extra playing card used in some card games.

jolly jol'-ly *jollier, jolliest.* Happy and gay.– Jack is a *jolly* fellow. He laughs and plays and has fun.

jolt *jolts, jolted, jolting.* 1. Jerk; bounce roughly. –The car with a flat tyre *jolted* along.
2. Jerk.–The train stopped with a sudden *jolt.*

jonquil jon'-quil *jonquils.* An early spring flower. *Jonquils* are white and yellow, have a pleasant odour, and grow from bulbs.

jostle jos'-tle *jostles, jostled, jostling.* Push, crowd, shove.–Bill *jostled* his way through the crowd.

journal jour'-nal *journals, journalist.* 1. A daily record of everything that happens. – The children in the nature-study class kept a *journal.* They wrote down what time the sun rose, what kinds of flowers and insects they saw, and what bird calls they heard.
2. A daily newspaper; any newspaper or magazine.

journalist jour'-nal-ist *journalists.* A person who writes for newspapers or magazines; an editor of a newspaper or magazine.

journey jour'-ney *journeys, journeyed, journeying.* 1. A trip.–It is a long *journey* across the country.
2. Travel.–The men *journeyed* far to see the king.

jovial jo'-vi-al *jovially.* Jolly, merry, and happy. –Grandfather is a *jovial* person. He is always joking.

joy *joys.* 1. Happiness, great gladness. – Baby brings much *joy* to the family.
2. Something which brings happiness. – Grandmother's visit was a *joy* to the whole family.

joyful joy'-ful *joyfully.* Happy and gay; glad. –The children are *joyful* on Christmas Day.

joyous joy'-ous *joyously, joyousness.* Happy, joyful.–There was a *joyous* crowd of people at the party.

jubilee ju'-bi-lee *jubilees.* A time of rejoicing and gaiety. A *jubilee* is sometimes set to celebrate some particular event or anniversary.–A Diamond Jubilee was held in 1897 to celebrate the sixtieth year of Queen Victoria's reign.

judge *judges, judged, judging.* 1. Decide about the quality of a thing.–The teacher will *judge* your handwriting. She will say whether it is good.
2. A person who examines anything and decides how good or bad it is.–Let the teacher be the *judge* of the drawings.
3. A person who is elected or appointed to hear all the facts about crimes or other law cases. He then decides what should be done to settle the case, or what punishment should be given.

judgement judge-ment *judgements.* 1. Ability or intelligence about deciding what to do.– Mary showed good *judgement* in calling the doctor straight away.
2. Opinion; final decision.–The teacher gave her *judgement* of the plans for the party. She liked them.
3. A court's decision.–The judge will pronounce his *judgement* when all the witnesses have been heard.

jug *jugs.* A heavy pitcher or container for holding water or other liquids. – Mother puts vinegar in a *jug.*

juggle jug'-gle *juggles, juggled, juggling.* Do tricks which require much practice. – Bob can *juggle* 5 balls at once. He can keep them in the air without letting them drop to the floor.

juggler jug'-gler *jugglers.* A person who amuses people by doing tricks, such as keeping 5 or 6 balls moving in the air without dropping them.

juice *juices*. The watery or liquid part of fruits, vegetables, or meat.–We drink tomato *juice* and orange *juice*.–Grandmother poured the *juice* off the roast beef to make gravy.

juicy juic′-y *juicier, juiciest*. Containing or having much juice; not dry.–The orange was so *juicy* that it squirted when Mary squeezed it. –A good melon is *juicy*.

July Ju-ly′. The 7th month of the year.–*July* has 31 days.

jumble jum′-ble *jumbles, jumbled, jumbling*. 1. Mix up.–The things in Mother's sewing basket were *jumbled* up. 2. A mess; confused heap.–The things were not in proper order. They were in a *jumble*.

jump *jumps, jumped, jumping*. 1. Leap; raise or throw oneself through the air without using the hands to help.–The cow *jumped* over the moon.–Frogs *jump*.–The boy *jumped* off the roof of the barn. 2. Jerk suddenly.–Father *jumped* when Sally said 'Bob!' 3. A leap or start.–Mother gave a great *jump* when she saw the mouse.

jumper jum′-per *jumpers*. 1. Someone or something that jumps.–Bob is a high-*jumper*. He can jump higher than Bill.–Mary's pony is a good *jumper*.–A flea is a *jumper*. 2. A loose upper garment.–Nancy has knitted herself a *jumper* in blue wool. 3. The spindle, inside a tap, on which the washer is fitted is called the *jumper*.

junction junc′-tion *junctions*. 1. The place where railway lines meet and unite.–We met at the railway *junction*. 2. The meeting place of highways, rivers, etc. –Turn left at the *junction* of the roads.

June. The 6th month.–*June* has 30 days.

jungle jun′-gle *jungles*. Land, mostly in hot countries, which is covered with trees, vines, and bushes growing so close together that it is hard to get through them. It rains often in a *jungle*. Lions, tigers, and other wild animals live in the *jungles*.

junior jun′-ior *juniors*. 1. A person younger than another.–Bill is Bob's *junior* by several years. He is several years younger. 2. A lower position.– Uncle Dick is *junior* to the managing director at the office.

juniper ju′-ni-per *junipers*. An evergreen tree or shrub of the pine family. It has blue berries.

junk *junks*. 1. A Chinese sailing boat.

2. Old iron, cans, paper, broken furniture, and other things that are considered useless. –The empty garden was full of *junk*.

jury ju′-ry *juries*. A group of people who listen to cases in court and then decide whether the person on trial is innocent or guilty.

just *justly*. 1. Fair.–The bad boy received *just* punishment. 2. Barely.–These shoes *just* fit. They are very nearly too small. 3. Very recently.–I cannot eat anything; I have *just* had dinner. 4. By only a moment.–You *just* missed Mary; she left a few minutes ago.

justice jus′-tice *justices*. 1. Fairness, honesty; what is right.–Bob said that there was no *justice* in the way he was treated. 2. A judge.–In England, the senior judge is called the Lord Chief *Justice*.

justify jus′-ti-fy *justifies, justified, justifying*. Give or be a reason for being fair or right.– Bill could not *justify* his behaviour. He could not prove that he was right.–The heavy rain *justifies* your coming late. It is a fair reason for your coming late.

jut *juts, jutted, jutting*. Stick out or stand out. –Jack tore his sweater on a sharp rock that *jutted* out of the wall.

jute. A plant from which we get a heavy fibre or thread which is also celled *jute*. Ropes, burlap bags, and coarse cloth are made from *jute*.

K k

K, k *K's, k's.* The 11th letter of the alphabet.

kale or **kail.** A kind of cabbage with curly leaves. *Kale* may be used as a vegetable or as an ingredient in soup, especially in Scotland.

kaleidoscope ka-lei'-do-scope *kaleidoscopes.* 1. A tube containing differently shaped pieces of coloured glass and reflectors. Seen through an eye-piece at the top, the pieces fall into pretty patterns, and as the tube is turned the pieces fall into different positions and the patterns are changed.–Alan gave Mary a *kaleidoscope* for her birthday.
2. A changing pattern or scene.–The sun and shifting cloud turned the sea into a *kaleidoscope* of light and shade.

kangaroo kan-ga-roo' *kangaroos.* A large animal that lives in Australia. It has short front legs, very strong back legs, and a long, thick tail. The *kangaroo* leaps something like a rabbit. He can go very fast. The mother carries her baby *kangaroo* in a pouch or pocket on the under-side of her body.

kapok ka'-pok. A soft fibre obtained from the seeds of the cotton tree. *Kapok* is used for stuffing cushions and filling life-belts.

kayak kay'-ak *kayaks.* A small boat, pointed at both ends, and covered over the top except for a hole or cockpit in the middle for people to sit in.

The Eskimos were the first to make *kayaks,* using seal skins stretched over a frame made from walrus or whale bone.

keel *keels.* A long piece of wood or metal that goes along the bottom of a ship or boat from end to end.

keen *keenly, keenness.* 1. Sharp.–Father uses a *keen* razor blade when he shaves.
2. Sharp and biting. – Vinegar has a *keen* taste.
3. Quick, bright.–Bob has a *keen* mind.
4. Interested, anxious to do a thing. –The children are *keen* about reading. They are eager to read.

keep *keeps, kept, keeping.* 1. To have for one's own as long as one wants. – Grandmother gave me a basket to *keep.*
2. Take care of regularly. – Mother *keeps* house.–Bill *keeps* rabbits.
3. One's room and meals, or board.–The man who lives at our house pays for his *keep.*
4. Hold for a time.–I will *keep* your key until you come home.–Bob could not *keep* a straight face when he told the joke.
5. Stay.–*Keep* to the right side of the street.
6. Continue, not stop.–*Keep* trying; go on trying.
7. Celebrate, observe, show respect for.–We *keep* Christmas by going to church.

keeper keep'-er *keepers.* A person who keeps or takes care of persons or things.–A *keeper* at a zoo takes care of the animals.

keeping keep'-ing. 1. Care.–Mother left the children in the neighbour's *keeping* while she went to the shops.
2. One form of the word *keep.*–Grandmother believes in the *keeping* of the Sabbath.
3. Harmony; going well with.–Brown is not in *keeping* with a green and yellow colour scheme.

keepsake keep'-sake *keepsakes.* Something to keep and remember someone by. – Grandmother gave Mary her locket and chain as a *keepsake.*

K
L
M
N
O
P
Q
R
S
T
U
V
W
X
Y
Z

keg *kegs.* A small barrel holding up to 10 **gallons.** – Grandfather sent us a *keg* of vinegar.

kennel ken'-nel *kennels.* 1. A dog's house. – Spot sleeps in a *kennel.*
2. A place where dogs are bred, or fed and taken care of for a small amount of money. – When we go away from home, we leave Spot at the *kennels* in the village.

kept. One form of the word *keep.* – We have always *kept* our fruit in the basement.

kerb *kerbs.* A low stone or cement edge to a pavement in a street. – The children stood on the *kerb* and looked in both directions before crossing. – The blind man tapped his way along the *kerb.*

kerchief ker'-chief *kerchiefs.* A square piece of cloth, lace or silk used by women as a head-covering instead of a hat. – Mother puts a *kerchief* on her head when we go driving to keep her hair from flying about.

kernel ker'-nel *kernels.* 1. The body of the seed within the husk of a cereal. – A grain of wheat, or of Indian corn, is a kernel.
2. The part of a nut which one eats. – Bob broke the shell to get at the *kernel.*

kerosene ker'-o-sene. A kind of oil burned in lamps and in stoves for cooking or heating. *Kerosene* is usually called paraffin.

ketchup ketch'-up. Catsup; a sauce made from tomatoes, vinegar, sugar, spices, and other things. – *Ketchup* tastes good on cold meat.

kettle ket'-tle *kettles.* A covered metal cooking pot. – Tea *kettles* have spouts. – We heat water in a *kettle.*

key *keys.* 1. A piece of metal cut or shaped to fit a lock. We lock and unlock doors with *keys.*
2. An answer; the way to solve a problem. –

The *key* to the puzzle will be given in to-morrow's paper.
3. A list of answers. – The teacher gave us a *key* so that we could mark our own papers.
4. Any part one presses or strikes to make something work. – A piano has black and white *keys* that one strikes to make notes of music. – Some horns have *keys.* – Typewriters and adding machines have *keys.*
5. In music, the note which is '*doh*' in a particular piece of music. – A song in which the note C is 'doh' is written in the *key* of C.

keyboard key'-board *keyboards.* A row or rows of keys on a piano, typewriter, etc.

keyhole key'-hole *keyholes.* The hole in a lock into which the key is put. – Bob turned the key in the *keyhole* to lock the door.

kick *kicks, kicked, kicking.* 1. Hit or strike with the foot or feet. – Bob *kicks* the football a long way. – The cow *kicked* Grandfather while he was milking her.
2. Jerk the feet. – Baby *kicks* when she lies on her back. – In swimming we *kick* with the feet and paddle with the hands.

kid *kids.* 1. A baby *goat.*
2. Thin, soft leather made from the skin of a baby goat. – Mother wears *kid* gloves.
3. In slang, a child.

kidnap kid'-nap *kidnaps, kidnapped, kidnapping, kidnapper.* Steal a child or a person. – The *kidnapper* took the rich man's baby from the pram. – Robert Louis Stevenson wrote a famous book called *Kidnapped.*

kidney kid'-ney *kidneys.* An organ of the body. The heart pumps blood to all parts of the body. The work of the *kidneys* is to separate waste and water from the blood. This waste passes from the body as urine.

kill *kills, killed, killing.* 1. Cause to die; injure so as to cause death. – Grandfather *killed* a big rat. – Father was afraid the frost would *kill* the flowers.
2. Game that has been *killed.* – The hunter's *kill* was two rabbits and a squirrel.

killer kill'-er *killers*. A person or an animal that kills or puts to death other persons or animals.–The hawk is a *killer*. It kills mice.

kiln *kilns*. An oven or furnace for hardening and baking bricks, tiles, pottery, etc.

kilt *kilts*. A short, pleated skirt that comes to the knees. – The men in the Scottish Highlands wear *kilts*.

kimono ki-mo'-no *kimonos*. A loose gown originally worn by both men and women in Japan. A *kimono* usually has wide, flowing sleeves, and a wide sash.

kin. The people related to a person.–Your aunts, uncles, brothers, sisters, mother, father, and other relations are your *kin*.

kind *kinds*. 1. Good to others.–When Mother was ill, our neighbours were very *kind* to us. They helped us with our work.
2. A sort or type.–What *kind* of dog does Jack have? Is it a spaniel, a terrier, or a collie? –What *kind* of dress did you get? Is it a party dress or a school dress?

kindergarten kin'-der-gar-ten *kindergartens*. A school for very young children. Children learn to work and play and get used to each other in *kindergarten*.

kindle kin'-dle *kindles, kindled, kindling*. 1. Set fire to.–The fire in the stove had gone out, so Father *kindled* it again.
2. Catch fire.–The dry grass *kindled* from a lighted cigarette that was thrown there.
3. *Kindling* is small wood for lighting fires.

kindly kind'-ly *kindliness*. Friendly; sympathetic; in a kind or pleasant way.–The girl spoke *kindly* to the lost little boy.

kindred kin'-dred. One's relations; the people who are related to a person.–Your father, grandfather, mother, sisters and brothers are some of your *kindred*.

king *kings*. A ruler. A country ruled by a king or queen is called a monarchy. A country which does not have a *king* but whose government is directed by a president is called a republic.

kingdom king'-dom *kingdoms*. 1. A country that is ruled by a king or queen.
2. In nature, things are divided into 3 groups: an animal group, a vegetable group, and a mineral group. Each group is called a *kingdom*; for example, the animal *kingdom*.– Man is a member of the animal *kingdom*.

kingfisher king'-fish-er *kingfishers*. A brilliantly coloured bird with a long beak, generally found near water. *Kingfishers* eat fish and make their nests at the end of long tunnels burrowed in the river-bank.

kink *kinks, kinky*. 1. A twist, curl, or tangle.– when the kitten played with the ball of wool, the wool became full of *kinks*.
2. A stiffness.–Father had a *kink* in his neck and could not turn his head.

kiss *kisses, kissed, kissing*. 1. Touch with the lips to show love.–Mother *kissed* the baby.
2. A touch of the lips.–She gave her a *kiss*.
3. Touch gently.–The light breeze *kissed* the waves.

kit *kits*. A set of instruments, tools, or equipment of any kind, sometimes fitted into a case.–Father has a *kit* of tools.

kitchen kitch'-en *kitchens*. A room where food is prepared and cooked.

kite *kites*. 1. A frame of wooden sticks with a string stretched round the edges, covered with paper, and with a long string tied to the middle. A long tail of cloth is added for balance. *Kites* are made to be flown in the air.

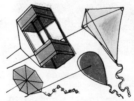

2. A bird of the hawk family.

K
L
M
N
O
P
Q
R
S
T
U
V
W
X
Y
Z

kitten kit'-ten *kittens*. A baby cat.–*Kittens* are blind when they are born but soon become frisky and playful.

knack *knacks*. A natural ability.–Some children have a *knack* for painting pictures. They learn quickly how to paint.

knapsack knap'-sack *knapsacks*. A leather or canvas bag or case for carrying clothes, food, etc., as on a hike. It is carried strapped to the back.–Boy Scouts and soldiers carry *knapsacks*.

knave *knaves*. A man who is tricky, not honest; a rascal.–'The *Knave* of Hearts, he stole the tarts, and took them clean away.'

knead *kneads, kneaded, kneading*. Work over or mix with the hands.–Grandmother *kneads* the bread dough with her hands.

knee *knees*. A joint in the leg. It joins the upper and lower parts of the leg.

knee-cap knee'-cap *knee-caps*. A flat, oval bone which protects the front of the knee joint.

kneel *kneels, knelt, kneeled, kneeling*. Get down on the knees.–Bob trained his pony to *kneel* down.

knell. The sound or ringing of a bell used to tell that someone has died.

knelt. One form of the word *kneel*.–We *knelt* and prayed.

knew. One form of the word *know*.–John *knew* how to drive the car when he was 16.

knife *knives*. 1. A sharp blade of steel, silver, glass, or other hard substance that is fastened to a handle. It is used for cutting.–We peel fruit with a *knife*.

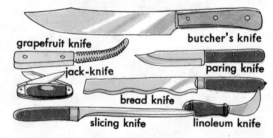

grapefruit knife
butcher's knife
jack-knife
paring knife
bread knife
slicing knife
linoleum knife

2. A cutting blade like that used on a farm tool, a lawnmower, etc.

knight *knights, knighted, knighting, knightly*.
1. In times long ago, a man who was taught all about fighting and weapons, the arms of war, and was given a high military rank. A *knight* promised to be brave, courteous, and faithful.
2. Nowadays, in England, a man is given the title of *knight* because of some service to his country.
3. Make a *knight*.–The king *knighted* Robin Hood.

knit *knits, knitted, knitting*. 1. Make locked loop stitches on two or more long needles. – Mother *knits* sweaters for the children.
2. Draw close and grow together.–Broken bones, *knit*, or heal.

knives. More than one knife.–Mother has many *knives* and forks.

knob *knobs, knobby*. 1. A handle to turn.–Someone turned the *knob*, and the door opened.
2. A little lump or raised place. –There was a little *knob* on the side of the tree where a branch had once been.

knock *knocks, knocked, knocking*. 1. Hit or give something a hard blow.–One fighter tried to *knock* the other one down. He tried to hit him so he would fall.–When Baby is angry, she *knocks* her head against her high chair.
2. Tap; rap with the knuckles.–If there is no doorbell, just *knock*.
3. A blow or rap.–I heard a *knock* at the door.

knocker knock'-er *knockers*. A metal tongue or ring fastened to a door with hinges so that you can swing it to make a knocking sound.

knock-kneed. Having legs which turn in at the knees. Sometimes the knees touch when a *knock-kneed* person walks.

knoll *knolls*. A small, round hill.–Grass grows on the *knoll*.

knot *knots, knotted, knotting, knotty*. 1. A looping or tying of threads, ropes, ribbons, or other cords together.
2. A bow.–Sally wears a *knot* or ribbon on her hair.
3. A hard part in wood formed at the place where a branch has grown out from the tree.
4. A measure of the speed of a boat.–One *knot* is a little over 6,080 feet per hour.

K
L
M
N
O
P
Q
R
S
T
U
V
W
X
Y
Z

KNOTS

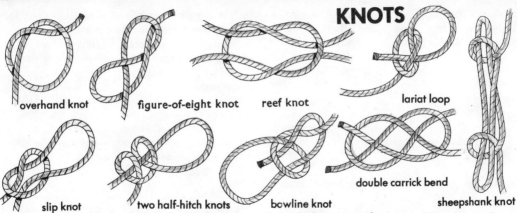

overhand knot figure-of-eight knot reef knot lariat loop

slip knot two half-hitch knots bowline knot double carrick bend sheepshank knot

5. A group.–A little *knot* of people were gathered at the corner.
6. A tangle.–The kitten played with the ball of wool and got it into a *knot*.

knot-hole knot'-hole *knot-holes*. A hole in a board where a knot has fallen out.

know *knows, knew, known, knowing*. 1. Understand, be able.–Tom *knows* how to swim.
2. Be acquainted or familiar with (a person, place, language, etc.).–Do you *know* Mary? –Bob *knows* Somerset well; he has lived there a long time.–How well do you *know* French?
3. Have information.–Do you *know* when the train will be here?

knowledge knowl'-edge. 1. The things that we know; all that we have learned.–Jack has much *knowledge* of boats.
2. The knowing of something.–Mary made a cake without Mother's *knowledge*, without her knowing about it.

known. O₁e form of the word *know*.–I have *known* ever since I was in the second form that the world is round.

knuckle knuck'-le *knuckles*. 1. One of the joints of your hands. – Your fingers join your hand at the *knuckles*.
2. The knee or ankle joint of an animal.–Mother boiled a beef *knuckle* to make soup.

L l

L, l *L's,* l's. The 12th letter of the alphabet.

la. The 6th tone of a musical scale.–Doh, re, mi, fa, soh, *la*, ti, doh.

label la'-bel *labels, labelled, labelling*. 1. A tag or small piece of paper, cardboard, cloth, etc., fastened to a garment, bottle, or something else, to tell something about it.–The doctor

put a *label* on the medicine bottle. It read 'Take one teaspoonful after meals.' – The *label* on my scarf says '100% wool.'

2. Put *labels* on.–Mother will *label* the gifts. She will put a tag on each to tell whom it is for.

laboratory la-bo'-ra-to-ry *laboratories*. A room or building where experiments are tried out. A scientist uses a *laboratory* to experiment in, to try to find out more about things.

labour la'-bour *labours, laboured, labouring*. 1. Work.–The farmer *labours* in the fields.
2. Workers.–*Labour* is hard to get on a farm.
3. Work done or to be done.–Building roads is hard *labour*.

labourer la'-bour-er *labourers*. A worker.–The man is a *labourer* in a factory.–A man who can do heavy work which does not need special training is a *labourer*.

L M N O P Q R S T U V W X Y Z

lace *laces, laced, lacing, lacy.* 1. A cord for tying the parts of a thing together.–Our shoes are held together with *shoelaces*.
2. Fasten with *laces*.–Baby cannot *lace* her shoes.–Bob uses a leather *lace* to *lace* up his football.

3. An openwork trimming used on dresses, towels, tablecloths, etc.

lack *lacks, lacked, lacking.* 1. Be without, have none.–We cannot go to the show, because we *lack* the money.
2. Absence, not being or happening.–*Lack* of rain caused the plants to dry up.

lacquer lac'quer *lacquers, lacquered, lacquering.* 1. A kind of varnish that dries quickly. *Lacquer* comes from the Japanese varnish tree.
2. Put *lacquer* on.–Bob *lacquered* the table he had made.

lad *lads.* A boy.–Jack is a small *lad*.

ladder lad'-der *ladders.* A set of wood or metal steps made by fastening round or flat pieces, called rungs, to two long side pieces. *Ladders* are used to climb on. – The painter uses a *ladder* to climb up when he paints a house.

ladies la'-dies. More than one lady.–The speaker said, 'Good evening, *ladies* and gentlemen.'

ladle la'-dle *ladles, ladled, ladling.* 1. A deep, cuplike spoon with a long handle.–Mother served the soup with a *ladle*.

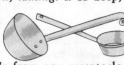

2. Transfer with a *ladle* from one receptacle to another.–Mother *ladled* the soup.

lady la'-dy *ladies.* 1. A well-bred woman; a woman with fine manners.
2. The woman who is the head of a household.–Mother is the *lady* of the house.
3. In England, a peeress or the wife of a peer or knight may be called lady.

ladybird la'-dy-bird *ladybirds.* A reddish-brown beetle. It has black spots on its smooth, rounded back.

lady's-slipper la'-dy's-slip'-per *lady's-slippers.* A yellow, pink, or white flower belonging to the orchid family, shaped rather like a slipper. *Lady's-slippers* grow wild in the woods.

lag *lags, lagged, lagging.* 1. Fall behind, or get behind. – The wounded soldier *lagged* behind the others.
2. Cover with heat-insulating material.– Father *lagged* the cold pipes.

laid. One form of the word *lay*.–Bob *laid* the book on the table.–The hens have *laid* eggs every day for a week.

lain. One form of the word *lie*.–The tired dog has *lain* on the rug all morning. He likes to lie there.

lair *lairs.* A den.–Lions and other wild beasts rest and sleep in their *lairs*.

lake *lakes.* A large body of water with land all around it.

lamb *lambs.* A baby sheep. The flesh or meat of a *lamb* is good to eat. – We eat *lamb* chops often.

lame *lamely, lameness.*
1. Crippled; not able to walk without limping or showing that the legs have been injured.–The boy who was hurt by the motorcar will be *lame* for a time.
2. Weak.–A *lame* excuse is one that is poor or not easy to believe.

lamp *lamps.* A device for making light.–A paraffin *lamp* makes light by burning paraffin.–An electric *lamp* makes light by heating a tiny wire white hot.

lance *lances, lanced, lancing, lancer.* 1. Open with a sharp instrument.–The doctor *lanced* the boil on the boy's arm.
2. A sharp instrument used by a doctor to open an infection.
3. A spear.–Soldiers who carried *lances* were called *lancers*.

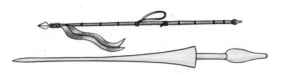

land *lands, landed, landing.* 1. The solid part of the earth; ground.–About one-third of the earth's surface is *land*; two-thirds is covered with water.
2. Ground; soil.–Most of the *land* on the farm is good for growing crops.
3. A country or territory.–We learn about many *lands* in geography lessons.
4. Come to the *land* from air or water.–The sailors *landed* safely at the dock.–The aeroplane *landed* on Grandfather's farm.
5. Arrive.–We *landed* in the city after dark.
6. Catch (a fish or sea animal).–The fisherman *landed* a big fish.

landing *land'-ing landings.* 1. A coming to the ground.–The aeroplane made a safe *landing*.
2. A place for boats to land. – The fisherman brought his boat to the *landing*.
3. A platform part of the way up a flight of stairs. – The baby fell down the stairs as far as the *landing*.

landlady *land'-la-dy landladies.* 1. A woman who lets rooms, houses, or property to others.
2. A woman who keeps a house in which people rent rooms.

landlord *land'-lord landlords.* 1. A man who lets rooms, houses, or property to other people.
2. A man who keeps a hotel or other place where people pay to live and eat.

landmark *land'-mark landmarks.* 1. Any object that can be easily seen and is used as a guide in travelling.–The tall chimney is a *landmark* that shows you are entering the town.
2. A happening that marks off or distinguishes a period of history.–The invention of the aeroplane is a *landmark* in the history of travel.

landscape *land'-scape landscapes, landscaped, landscaping.* 1. A view of land.–We stood on a high hill and admired the *landscape* below.
2. A picture of a view. – The *landscape* showed a river winding through the valley.

landslide *land'-slide land-slides.* A portion of land falling down from the side of a hill or cliff.

lane *lanes.* 1. A path or narrow road between fences or hedges.
2. A route; a set course. – Ships follow certain *lanes* in going across the ocean.
3. A section of a road marked off by lines on the surface.–We drive in the correct *lane* on the highway.

language *lan'-guage languages.* 1. Speech; spoken or written words.–We exchange ideas by means of *language*.
2. The set of words used by a large group of people in talking and writing.–In Spain, the people speak the Spanish *language*.
3. Any means of communication.–Sign *language* is communication by making motions with the hands and body.

lanky *lanky.* Tall and thin.–The man was long and *lanky*.

lantern *lan'-tern lanterns.* A case with glass sides used for carrying or holding a light. A *lantern* has an arched handle to carry it by.– The farmer carried the *lantern* out to the barn at night.

lap *laps, lapped, lapping.* 1. A flap.–The *lap* on a jacket is the part that folds over to button.
2. The front part of the body from the waist to the knees when a person is sitting down. –The baby likes to sit on mother's *lap*.
3. Fold; wrap. – Mother *lapped* a blanket round the baby.
4. One turn round a racecourse.–Bob's car won the first *lap* of the race.
5. Lick; take with the tongue. – The dog *lapped* up the milk we put in the feeding pan.
6. Slap gently. – The waves *lapped* against the side of the boat.

lapel *la-pel' lapels.* The front parts of a coat that fold back. –Father often wears a flower in the buttonhole of his *lapel*.

larch *larches.* A kind of pine tree with very hard wood.

lard. The melted-down and refined fat of pigs. *Lard* is used in cooking.

large *larger, largest,* 1. Big; of great size.—Cats are small. Elephants are *large.*
2. *At large* means free, not held under control.—The lion that escaped is still *at large.*

largely large'-ly. Mostly; chiefly.—The flowers in this garden are *largely* those that come up from seeds.

lariat lar'-i-at *lariats.* A lasso; a rope with a sliding loop.—The cowboy ropes cattle with his *lariat.*

lark *larks.* 1. A song-bird, also known as the sky-*lark.* It is a plain-coloured bird, but has a vigorous and beautiful song.—Many poets have written in praise of the *lark.*
2. A good time or a joke is sometimes called a *lark.*

larkspur lark'-spur *larkspurs.* A slender plant that has blue, pink, white, or purplish blossoms along the top of the stem.

larva lar'-va *larvae.* An insect in its first, worm-like stage as it comes from the egg.—Caterpillars are *larvae.*

lash *lashes, lashed, lashing.* 1. A whip, or the flexible part of a whip.
2. Whip; beat.—The waves *lashed* the shore.
3. Beat with a *lash* or whip.—The angry man *lashed* his horse.
4. One of the little hairs along the edges of the eyelids.

lass *lasses.* A girl.—Betty is a tiny *lass.*

lasso las'-so *lassos* or *lassoes, lassoed, lassoing.*
1. A long rope with a slip loop at one end.—The cowboy ropes cattle with his *lasso.*

2. Catch with a *lasso.* – Bob would like to *lasso* horses.

last *lasts, lasted, lasting.* 1. Final; coming at the end.—Sunday is the first day of the week. Saturday is the *last* day of the week.
2. Keep on; continue. – The storm will not *last* long.
3. Hold out. – Our supply of water-must *last* until we reach home.
4. A mould shaped like a foot.—The cobbler puts shoes on a *last* to mend them.

lastly last'-ly. Finally; at the end.—Firstly, it is too far away; secondly, we haven't time; and *lastly,* I don't want to go.

latch *latches, latched, latching.* 1. A fastener used to hold a door or gate closed. – 'Lift the *latch* and come in!'
2. Lock; fasten with a *latch.*—Grandfather *latched* the barn door after the horse was stolen.

late *later, latest* or *last.* 1. After the proper or expected time.—Bob was *late* for school.
2. Near the end.—Mary came home *late* in the week.
3. Recent; that has just happened.—The *late* news came over the radio.
4. *Late* is used in speaking of a person who has died recently. – The *late* King George VI was the father of Queen Elizabeth II.

lately late'-ly. Not long ago; recently.—I have not seen Jim *lately.* He must be away.

lath *laths, lathed, lathing.* 1. A thin, narrow, rough strip of wood. – The carpenter nails *laths* on to the walls. Plaster sticks to *laths.*
2. Put *laths* on.—It does not take long to *lath* a wall.

lathe *lathes.* A machine to which a piece of wood or metal is fastened to be turned for shaping.—Father made Bob a rounders bat on his *lathe.*

lather lath'-er *lathers, lathered, lathering.* 1. Foam, such as soapsuds, or the sweat of an animal.—Father puts *lather* on his face before shaving.
2. Cover with foam. – The racehorse was *lathered* when he finished the race.

latter lat'-ter. 1. Coming later; the second of two.–Bob read 'Tom Sawyer' and 'Little Women.' The former was written by Mark Twain, the *latter* by Louisa Alcott.
2. Later; towards the end. – Mother will be home the *latter* part of the week.

lattice lat'-tice *lattices*. A framework made of crossed pieces.–Mother trained the rose bushes to climb the *lattice*.

laugh *laughs, laughed, laughing.*
1. Make sounds of merriment with the voice.–A funny joke makes you *laugh*.
2. The sound of *laughing*.–Mary gave a short *laugh* when she heard the story.

laughter laugh'-ter. The sounds made by laughing. – We heard *laughter* in the next room.

launch *launches, launched, launching.* 1. Set (a ship) afloat.–The ship was named when it was *launched*.
2. Start.–The council is going to *launch* a drive to clean up the streets.
3. A motor-boat that is used to carry people and supplies between a ship and the shore.

launder laun'-der *launders, laundered, laundering.* Wash.–On Monday, Mother *launders* our clothes.

laundress laun'-dress *laundresses*. A woman who washes and irons clothes.–Our neighbour employs a *laundress*.

laundry laun'-dry *laundries*. 1. A room where clothes are washed. – The *laundry* is in the basement in our house.

2. A building where clothes and linens are washed for many people.
3. Clothes to be washed.–Our *laundry* is kept in a large hamper.

laundry-man laun'-dry-man *laundry-man*. A man who works for a laundry.–The *laundry-man* came to pick up our laundry.

laurel lau'rel *laurels*. 1. An evergreen shrub or bush that has smooth, stiff leaves. Some *laurels* have pink blossoms.
2. An honour or recognized success. *Laurel* leaves were once used to make wreaths to crown heroes and great poets.–Bob won his *laurels* in athletics.

lava la'-va. Melted rock that comes out of a volcano.–Volcanoes throw out hot *lava* when they erupt.

lavatory lav'-a-to-ry *lavatories*. 1. A water-closet.
2. A room used for washing oneself.

lavender lav'-en-der. 1. A plant with small narrow leaves and small, pale purple flowers which are sweet-smelling. – Dried *lavender* is often used to make drawers or cabinets smell sweet.

2. A light purple colour. – Grandmother has a *lavender* dress.

law *laws*. One of a set of rules made to control people's actions or behaviour. The *laws* protect us from those who wish to do harm.

lawful law'-ful *lawfully*. According to the laws; allowed by law. – It is not *lawful* to keep a dog without having a dog-licence.

lawn *lawns*. 1. A grass-covered plot of ground, usually part of a garden.–Bob mowed the *lawn* in front of his house.

2. A thin cotton or linen cloth.–Mary has a dress of *lawn*.

lawyer law'-yer *lawyers*. A person trained and licensed to handle all matters having to do with the laws. – Father asked a *lawyer* to draw up the lease for the house. The *lawyer* wrote the lease so that it would be right according to the law.

L
M
N
O
P
Q
R
S
T
U
V
W
X
Y
Z

lax *laxly*. 1. Loose.–The rope became *lax* when the knot was loosened.
2. Careless.–Do not become *lax* about your homework.

laxative lax'-a-tive *laxatives*. A medicine to make the bowels move.–Never take a *laxative* unless you are told to.

lay *lays, laid, laying*. 1. Place or put in a flat position.–*Lay* your gloves in the drawer.
2. Produce and give out (eggs).–Hens *lay* eggs.
3. Hold down.–Oil on the road will *lay* the dust.
4. Put or place (used in many ways).–We always *lay* the dinner-table for Mother.–The carpenter came to *lay* the floor.

lay. One form of the word *lie*.–Yesterday, Baby *lay* in her crib all day.

layer lay'-er *layers*. 1. A thickness; one flat piece next to others. – The road has two *layers* of cement on it.– The cake has two *layers* with icing in between.
2. One who lays something.– A brick*layer* lays bricks.–That hen is a good *layer*. She lays many eggs.

lazy la'-zy *lazier, laziest, laziness*. 1. Not willing to work.–The *lazy* boy will fail in school, because he doesn't do his work.
2. Slow-moving; weary-acting. – The boy walked down the street in a *lazy* way.

lb. The abbrevation or short way of writing the word *pound*.–Fifteen pounds can be written 15 *lb*.

lead (pronounced *leed*) *leads, led, leading*. 1. Guide; show the way.–I will *lead* you to the place where the road turns off.
2. Have the highest record; be first.–The captain *leads* the team in runs scored.
3. Direct.–Our teacher *leads* the singing each morning.
4. Tend or help to bring about.–Paying attention in class *leads* to good marks.
5. Amount ahead; place ahead. – Our team has a *lead* of two games.–The brown horse took the *lead* in the race.

lead (pronounced *led*). 1. A heavy, bluish-grey metal. *Lead* is used to make some water pipes, bullets, and many things that need to be heavy or must not rust.
2. The name commonly given to graphite, when used in pencils.–The *lead* in this pencil is too hard.

leader lead'-er *leaders*. A person who leads, goes ahead, directs, or guides others, or shows how to do things.–The band *leader* directs the band.

leaf *leaves*. 1. One of the flat, usually green parts that grow on trees, plants, and bushes.

horse chestnut ivy holly begonia tulip tree

willow poplar elm beech acacia

maple lily of the valley water lily oak

2. A printed sheet.–One *leaf* of the book was torn out.
3. A board used to make a table larger.– When we have guests for dinner, Mother puts an extra *leaf* in the table.

leaflet leaf'-let *leaflets*. 1. A small, young leaf. –In early spring the *leaflets* on the trees are bright and green.
2. A single or folded page of printed matter –Father received a *leaflet* on gardening.

leafy leaf'-y *leafier, leafiest*. Having leaves; of the material of a leaf.–The trees are very *leafy* this year.–Spinach is a green, *leafy* vegetable.

league *leagues*. A union of nations, peoples, teams, etc., joined together by a set of rules for a particular purpose.–All the teams in the 4 divisions of the Football *League* compete for the Cup.

leak *leaks, leaked, leaking*. 1. An accidental crack or hole that lets a gas, liquid, powder, etc., in or out of something.–Father found a *leak* in the water-pipe.
2. Come out through a small opening.–The water was *leaking* through the *leak* in the pipe.
3. The spreading of secret information.–The news of the party *leaked* out.

leaky leak′-y *leakier, leakiest.* Having leaks.–The boat is *leaky.* It has cracks in it which let the water in.

lean *leans, leaned, leaning, leaner, leanest.* 1. Not fat; thin.–The dog that had not had enough to eat was *lean* and hungry.
2. The red part of meat that is made up of muscle. – Jack Sprat would eat no fat, his wife would eat no *lean.*
3. Poor; producing very little wealth. – The farmer had a *lean* year last year; he had a poor harvest.
4. Rest against slantingly.–The ladder *leans* against the wall.
5. Be at an angle; slant.–The tree *leaned* with the wind.
6. Bend.–Mother *leaned* over to pick up the baby's toys.
7. Depend; rely. – Boys *lean* upon their parents for support until they can take care of themselves.

leap *leaps, leaped, leaping.* 1. Jump. – The horse *leaped* over the fence.
2. A jump; a springing up.–The horse made a big *leap.*

leap-frog leap′-frog. A game in which one person leaps over others bent over in a row.

leap year *leap years.* The year in every four that has 366 days. In *leap year,* February has 29 days instead of 28.

learn *learns, learned, learning.* Come to know. –In school we *learn* to read, write, and do arithmetic.

lease *leases, leased, leasing.* 1. A written agreement to occupy a property for a stated time for a stated amount of rent.
2. Rent under a written agreement.–We *lease* the house from the local council.

leash *leashes.* A leather strap or chain with which hounds are held.–The man kept the greyhound firmly on the *leash.*–To strain at the *leash* means to want to be free in order to do something.

least. 1. Smallest in amount or size.–Mary has a pound, Bob has a five pence piece, and Baby has a penny, the *least* of all.–Move the picture the *least* bit to the right.
2. *At least* means not less than.–One should have *at least* 8 hours of sleep a night.
3. *At least* means in any case, anyhow.–If you won't stay for supper, *at least* come in and say hello.

leather leath′-er *leathers.* 1. The prepared hide or skin of certain animals. The hair is removed and the hide is soaked in a special liquid to make *leather* of it.–Shoes, suitcases, and many other things are made of *leather.*
2. Made of *leather.*–Bob has a new *leather* belt.

leave *leaves, left, leaving.* 1. Go away.–The teacher had to *leave* before the lesson was over.
2. Allow to stay.–Do not *leave* your hat on the table. – *Leave* your bundles here while you shop.
3. Let go till later.–I shall *leave* practising the piano until after the party.
4. Permission.–The teacher gave us *leave* to play ball.
5. Permission to be away; time away from duty.–The soldiers had a short *leave.*

leaves. More than one *leaf.* – The *leaves* are falling.

lecture lec′-ture *lectures, lectured, lecturing, lecturer.* 1. A speech; a talk about a definite subject.–The teacher will give a *lecture* on cowboys at the meeting tonight.
2. Give a talk or *lecture.* – The teacher will *lecture* tonight.
3. Scold.–Mother *lectures* me every time I forget to wash my hands before eating.

led. One form of the word *lead.*–Bob *led* the horse to the barn.

ledge *ledges.* 1. A narrow shelf.–Mother put the plates on the *ledge* around the dining room.

2. A narrow, shelf-like formation of rock.– The eagle had a nest on the *ledge* high up on the cliff.

leer *leers, leered, leering.* 1. A mean, evil, sideways look.–The man had a *leer* on his face.
2. Look evilly.–The man *leered* at us.

left. 1. At or towards the side of the body that points north when you face the rising sun.– Mary writes with her *left* hand. Most people write with their right hands.
2. One form of the word *leave.*–Father *left* early this morning.

left-hand *left-handed.* On the left side. *Left-handed* people are those who do things more easily with their left than with their right hands.

L M N O P Q R S T U V W X Y Z

leg *legs.* 1. The lower limbs of the human body. Your feet are at the lower end of your *legs,* and your body is at the upper end. We walk and run by means of our *legs.*

2. Cows, cats, dogs, and horses have 4 feet and 4 *legs.*

3. A long, slim part of a piece of furniture, on which it stands. Most tables and chairs have 4 *legs.*

legal le′-gal *legally.* Lawful; right according to the rules of the country.–In Great Britain it is *legal* to drive on the left-hand side of the road.

legend leg′-end *legends.* A story of the past, which may not be true, but was once thought to be so.–The adventures of Robin Hood are *legends.*

legging leg′-ging *leggings.* Long, heavy coverings for the legs. Children wear *leggings* in the winter.

legible leg′-i-ble *legibly.* Readable, or easily read.–Mother's writing is *legible.*

legislator leg′-is-la-tor *legislators, legislation.* One of a group of people who make the laws of the country or of a city. Members of Parliament who are elected by the people are law-makers, or *legislators.*

legislature leg′-is-la-ture *legislatures.* A group of people who are elected to make laws.

leisure lei′-sure *leisurely.* The free time you have after your work is done, to read or do other things you want to do.

lemon lem′-on *lemons.* 1. A sour, juicy fruit that has a pale yellow skin. The juice of *lemons* is used in drinks, in pies, for flavouring, and for many other purposes.

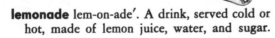

2. A light yellow, the colour of the fruit.

lemonade lem-on-ade′. A drink, served cold or hot, made of lemon juice, water, and sugar.

lend *lends, lent, lending.* 1. Let someone else use a thing belonging to one.–Will you *lend* me your pencil?
2. Give.–Boy Scouts *lend* help to old people.

length *lengths.* How long a thing is, how long a thing lasts.–The *length* of the boat is 36 feet.–The *length* of the show depends on how many reels of film are shown.

lengthen length′-en *lengthens, lengthened, lengthening.* Make longer. – Mother had to *lengthen* Mary's dress.

lengthy length′-y. Long.–Bob gave a *lengthy* talk on snakes.

lens *lenses.* A specially shaped piece of glass used in glasses, cameras, field–glasses, and the like. *Lenses* are usually so made as to make things look larger.

lent. A 40-day period just before Easter, set aside for fasting and for worship. Many Christian people keep *Lent.*

lent. One form of the word *lend.*–I *lent* you my book yesterday.

leopard leop′-ard *leopards.* A large animal of the cat family. It has a yellowish skin with black spots. *Leopards* are very fierce. *Leopards* come from Asia and Africa.

less. Not so much, smaller in amount. – We have *less* money today than we had last week, because we spent some.

lesson les′-son *lessons.* 1. Something learned or taught. – The teacher taught a *lesson* in geography.–Have you learned your *lessons*?
2. The amount to be learned at a time.–There were 10 words in the first spelling *lesson.*
3. A reading from the Bible in church.

lest. In order not to; so that (something) won't happen.–Don't run, *lest* you should fall.

let *lets, letting.* 1. Allow, permit.–*Let* me help you with your work.
2. Rent, hire.–We have trailers to *let.*

let's. Let us.–*Let's* have a picnic.

L
M
N
O
P
Q
R
S
T
U
V
W
X
Y
Z

letter let′-ter *letters.* 1. A symbol used for a sound.–There are 26 *letters* in the English alphabet. A, b, c, d, e, f, g are the first 7 *letters.*
2. A written message; a note.–We write *letters* to our friends and relations. We put our *letters* in envelopes and send them through the post.

lettering let′-ter-ing. Letters or words printed, painted, pasted, or drawn.–The *lettering* on the poster is very even.

lettuce let′-tuce. A leafy garden plant used in salads. Some *lettuce* grows in heads like cabbage, and some grows just as large leaves.

level lev′-el *levels, levelled, lev-elling.* 1. Flat and even everywhere.–The bowling green must be *level* so that the balls will roll smoothly.
2. Make smooth and flat.–Bob *levelled* the earth down with his rake.
3. The point to which a thing rises or reaches; height.–Jack comes to the *level* of Father's shoulder.
4. An instrument used for telling whether a table, floor, or any *level* surface is really flat.

lever le′-ver *levers.* A bar used to lift and move objects.

levity lev′-i-ty. Light-hearted, frivolous behaviour.–When the boys laughed at the lecturer, the headmaster rebuked them for their *levity.* He told them it was a serious subject.

levy le′-vy *levies, levied, levying.* 1. Raise money by special tax.–The government *levies* a tax on all car-owners.
2. A special tax or fine.

liable li′-a-ble. 1. Likely, apt.–You are *liable* to catch cold if you get your feet wet.–You are *liable* to have an accident unless you look both ways before crossing the street.
2. Responsible.–The sign read, 'We are not *liable* for lost hats and coats.'

liar li′-ar *liars.* A person who tells things he knows are not true but wants people to believe.

liberal lib′-er-al *liberally.* Generous, plentiful. –Father gave us *liberal* helpings of ice-cream.

liberate lib′-er-ate *liberates, liberated, liberating.* Set free.–Father *liberated* the lamb that was caught in the fence.

liberty lib′-er-ty *liberties.* Freedom.–A person who enjoys *liberty* is free to think or worship as he likes.

librarian li-bra′-ri-an *librarians.* A person who has charge of a library or a collection of books.

library li′-bra-ry *libraries.* A place where many books are kept; a room or building with many books, which can be borrowed.–We get books to read from a public *library.*

lice. More than one louse. *Lice* are small, flat, wingless insects which live on the heads and bodies of people and animals. Chickens and birds pick *lice* off their bodies with their bills.

licence li′-cence *licences.* A written order giving one the legal right to do something.– Father has a driving *licence.*–One must have a *licence* to fish, to hunt, to marry, and to do many other things.

license li′-cense *licenses, licensed, licensing.* Give a *licence* to. – Father is *licensed* to drive.

lick *licks, licked, licking.* 1. Rub or stroke with the tongue.–The dog *licked* the milk from his pan.–Cows *lick* large pieces of rock salt.
2. In talking, people sometimes say *lick* when they mean whip.–Bob would like to *lick* the bully at school.
3. A small amount.–Mother put a *lick* of sugar in the pudding.
4. To move like a lapping tongue. – Flames *licked* up the walls of the burning house.

licking lick′-ing *lickings.* 1. A rubbing with the tongue.–The cat gave his fur a thorough *licking.*
2. A beating.–Many of the boys would like to give the bully a *licking.*

L M N O P Q R S T U V W X Y Z

lid *lids.* 1. A cover or top.–She puts a *lid* on the saucepan when she cooks potatoes.
2. An eye*lid*, or the covering of one's eye.

lie *lies, lied, lying, lay, lain.*
1. Tell a thing that you know is not true.–Do not *lie*.
2. A statement that is not true.–*Lies* usually get the liars into trouble.
3. Stretch the body out flat.–When we sleep in bed we are *lying* down.
4. Rest; stay in the same flat position without moving.–The rug *lies* on the floor.
5. Be at; be located.–The city *lies* at the foot of the mountains.

lieutenant (pronounced *leftenant*) lieu-ten'-ant *lieutenants.* An officer in the army or navy, the former ranking below captain, the latter below *lieutenant*-commander.

life *lives.* 1. Living, growing, and producing more of the same kind. Plants, animals, and people have *life*. The earth and the rocks do not have *life*.
2. The period during which a person, animal, or plant is alive.–Grandfather has lived in this house all his *life*.
3. A person.–The guard saved many *lives*.
4. A way of living.–*Life* in Japan is different from *life* in England.
5. The story of a person during the time he was alive.–Bob read a *life* of Captain Cook.
6. Energy, vigour, and interest.–After a hard day's work, the boys couldn't put much *life* into their football.

lifeboat life'-boat *lifeboats.* A small boat carried on a ship to save the passengers if the ship sinks. *Lifeboats* are also kept on some beaches.

life-guard life'-guard *life-guards.* An expert swimmer who is paid to watch bathers in the water at a beach and help them in case of accident.

lifelong life'-long. Lasting a lifetime.–The boys swore a *lifelong* friendship.

lifetime life'-time. As long as one lives.–Pitt achieved much in his *lifetime*.

lift *lifts, lifted, lifting.* 1. Put up higher; go up higher; raise or rise.–Father *lifted* Baby into her high-chair. – The lorry-driver *lifted* the basket up to the lorry.
2. A free ride.–Bob asked the driver for a *lift*.
3. Something which raises things up. – A *lift* in a building carries people up and down.

ligament lig'-a-ment *ligaments.* A strong band of fibres or thread-like body tissues that holds the bones of the body together.

light *lights, lighted, lit, lighting.* 1. The opposite of dark.–At night it is dark; in the daytime it is *light*.–The sun gives *light*.
2. Anything that gives *light*. – The *lights* on the Christmas tree were in many colours.

3. Catch or cause to catch fire.–Matches *light* when they are struck.–Father *lit* his pipe.
4. Turn on the *lights* of.–A little girl *lighted* the Christmas tree.
5. Come down to the ground. – The crow *lighted* on the fence.
6. Pale.–Mother wore a dark blue dress and Mary wore a *light* blue dress.
7. Not heavy.–Father's basket was heavy, but Bob's was *light*.
8. Cheerful, gay.–The dentist was in a *light* mood today.

lighten light'-en *lightens, lightened, lightening.*
1. Lessen, make lighter.–Many people helping will *lighten* the work for each one.
2. Make or grow lighter.–Mix white with the paint to *lighten* the shade.
3. Become cheerful.–The sad boy's face *lightened* when he heard the good news.

lighter light'-er. 1. Not so dark.–It is *lighter* now that the moon has risen.
2. Not so heavy.–The bucket is *lighter* without the water in it.
3. A boat used for loading and unloading ships not brought to the wharf.

light-hearted light'-heart-ed *light-heartedly, light-heartedness.* Cheerful and gay.–Jack is always *light-hearted* on Saturday.

lighthouse light'-house *lighthouses.* A tower built in the sea or on the shore from which a bright light shines. Ships are guided by a light beaming from the *lighthouse.*

lightning light'-ning. Light caused in the sky by a flash of electricity. –We saw the *lightning* and then we heard the thunder.

lightning conductor light'-ning con'-duc-tor *lightning conductors.* A rod of metal to take lightning into the ground, thus preventing it from damaging the building.–The barn has *lightning conductors* on it.

like *likes, liked, liking.* 1. Much the same as.– Sally's dress is *like* mine.
2. Enjoy, be pleased by, get pleasure from. I *like* ice-cream.–I *like* to play football.
3. *The like* means other things which are much the same.–Mary enjoys biscuits, sweets, and *the like.*

likeable like'-a-ble. Pleasant and friendly, so that one is liked by everybody.–Mary is a very *likeable* person.

likely like'-ly *likelier, likeliest.* 1. Probable.–It isn't *likely* that the express train will stop at village stations.
2. Probably.–We will very *likely* have our house painted soon.

likeness like'-ness *likenesses.* 1. Sameness, being alike.–There was much *likeness* between the twins.
2. Guise, dress, shape.–Bob appeared in the play in the *likeness* of a sailor.
3. One's portrait or picture.–A *likeness* of Grandmother as a young girl hangs over the mantelpiece.

likewise like'-wise. 1. The same.–The man jumped into the water and the boy did *likewise.*
2. Also, too.–Jack must go to bed early, and Bob *likewise.*

liking lik'-ing. Enjoyment of, pleasure in.–The artist has a *liking* for painting landscapes.

lilac li'-lac *lilacs.* 1. A purple or white flower that grows in clusters on *lilac* bushes.
2. Pinkish-purple, the colour of the *lilac* flower.

lily lil'-y *lilies.* A plant that grows from a bulb. The flowers of the *lily* are cone-shaped on the under side.–The *lily* is regarded as standing for purity.

lily of the valley *lilies of the valley.* A flower that grows from a bulb. The fragrant white flowers are like little bells growing along a stem.

limb *limbs.* 1. An arm or leg.–The man broke no *limbs* in the accident.
2. Branch.–We had a swing tied to the *limb* of the tree.

lime *limes.* 1. A white powder made by heating *lime*stone, which is a certain kind of stone. *Lime* is used in whitewash. Farmers sometimes use *lime* on soil to make it less sour or acid.

2. A small, sour, light green, lemon-like fruit that grows on the *lime* tree.

limestone lime'-stone. A rock from which lime is made.

limit lim'-it *limits, limited, limiting.* 1. A boundary line; a line that shows where a thing ends; a stated amount or number.–We walked as far as the city *limits.*–At the sale there was a *limit* of two pairs of stockings to a customer.
2. Keep within a certain amount or number. –Mother *limits* herself to three cups of coffee a day.

L
M
N
O
P
Q
R
S
T
U
V
W
X
Y
Z

limited lim'-it-ed. Held within a certain number, a certain kind, or the like.–A *limited* number of people can enter the cinema.

limousine lim'-ou-sine *limousines*. A motorcar in which the chauffeur or driver sits in the open, with the back section for the passengers enclosed.

limp *limps, limped, limping, limply, limpness*. 1. Put more weight on one foot than on the other, in walking.–The crippled man *limps*.
2. A hobbling or lame step.–He walks with a *limp*.
3. Drooping; having lost stiffness.–The flowers have gone without water so long that they are *limp*.

line *lines, lined, lining*. 1. A slender rope, cord, or wire such as a telephone *line*, a fishing *line*, or a chalk *line* used for measuring and levelling by bricklayers.
2. A long straight or curved mark made by a pencil, a piece of chalk, a paint-brush, or the like.–Our writing paper has *lines* across it.

3. A row.–A long *line* of people were waiting to get tickets.
4. Make *lines* on.–The children *lined* their papers for spelling.
5. A *line* of writing or printing.–Read the first *line* of the story again.
6. Business.–My father's *line* is painting.
7. A system of transport.–The P. and O. is a famous shipping *line*.
8. Course.–The soldier died in *line* of duty.
9. Cover the sides or insides of.–The street was *lined* with people. People stood all along the edge of the street.–Mother *lined* Father's coat with grey silk.

linen lin'-en *linens*. 1. Cloth or thread made from flax or from hemp.
2. Table-cloths, towels, napkins, sheets, pillow-cases, and other household cloths.

liner lin'-er *liners*. 1. A large passenger steamship.–Mary wants to go to India some day on a big *liner*.

linesman lines'-man *linesmen*. A man who helps to judge either in football or tennis whether the ball is out of play.

linger lin'-ger *lingers, lingered, lingering*. Be slow, delay.–Mother told Bob not to *linger* on his way to school.

liniment lin'-i-ment *liniments*. A liquid medicine that is rubbed on.–Grandfather rubbed *liniment* on his sore wrist.

lining lin'-ing *linings*. An inside covering.–The tailor sewed the *lining* into Father's coat.– The *lining* in Mary's purse is blue.

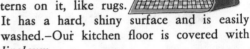

link *links, linked, linking*. 1. One of the rings that form a chain when joined together.–A chain is made of *links*.
2. Anything that joins other things together to make a complete thing.–Facts that join together to make a complete story are *links*.
3. Connect.–A noted criminal is *linked* with the bank robbery.

linoleum li-no'-le-um *linoleums*. A kind of hard floor covering. It has a rough cloth back, covered with a mixture of linseed oil and ground cork. *Linoleum* has different kinds of patterns on it, like rugs. It has a hard, shiny surface and is easily washed.–Our kitchen floor is covered with *linoleum*.

linseed lin'-seed. The seeds of flax. Oil made from *linseed* is used in some paint.

lintel lin'-tel *lintels*. A piece of stone or timber over a door or window. The *lintel* supports the weight of the structure immediately above.

lion li'-on *lions*. A large, yellowish, flesh-eating animal of the cat family. *Lions* live in rocky places in Africa and Asia.

lioness li'-on-ess *lionesses*. A female lion.

lip *lips*. 1. Either of the two edges of your mouth. Your *lips* move when you open your mouth to speak, sing, eat, etc. When you whistle, you pucker up your *lips*.–You smack your *lips* when you taste something good. 2. The part of a jug or other vessel that bends out so that liquids will pour out in a narrow stream.

liquid liq'-uid *liquids*. Not solid, and not a gas. –Water and milk are *liquids*. They flow easily.–Many medicines are *liquids*.

liquor liq'-uor *liquors*. 1. Wines, whisky, or other drinks that contain alcohol. 2. The juice or watery part of anything.

liquorice or **licorice**. A plant whose roots are used to make medicines and as a sweetmeat.

lisp *lisps, lisped, lisping*. 1. Say the 'th' sound for the sounds of s and z.–To say 'The thun will thet thoon' for 'The sun will set soon' is *lisping*. 2. A *lisping* sound.–She talks with a *lisp*.

list *lists, listed, listing*. 1. A row or column of words or numbers.–Our teacher wrote a *list* of spelling words on the blackboard. 2. Write in a row or column.–Mother *listed* the groceries she expected to buy.

listen lis'-ten *listens, listened, listening*. Try to hear, pay attention so that one hears.–The teacher told us to *listen* to what he had to say.–We *listen* to the radio, to birds singing, and to people talking.

listener lis'-ten-er *listeners*. A person who listens or tries to hear.–Bob is a good talker and also a good *listener*.

lit. One form of the word *light*.–During the storm, Father *lit* the candle.

literary lit'-er-ar-y. *Connected* with written works, such as poetry, novels, and stories.– Writing books is *literary* work.

literature lit'-er-a-ture. Poems, stories, and other writings.–In school, all the pupils study *literature*.

litter lit'-ter *litters, littered, littering*. 1. A mess; little bits scattered about.–The children cut out pictures and made a *litter* all over the floor. 2. Leave things scattered about.–Mother told us we could get lunch if we would not *litter* the kitchen. 3. The number born to one animal at one time.–Our dog had a *litter* of 4 puppies. 4. The hay or straw used for bedding for animals. 5. A stretcher or frame used to carry wounded or sick people.

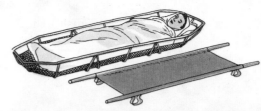

little lit'-tle *littler, littlest*. 1. Small.–Elephants are big, but ants are *little*. 2. A small amount of.–Mother takes a *little* sugar in her tea. 3. Slight.–Baby still has a *little* cold.

live (rhymes with *give*) *lives, lived, living*. 1. Have life; grow and produce others of the same kind.–Plants, animals, and people *live*. 2. Continue to *live*.–The man *lived* to be very old. 3. Get a *living*, or money to get food, clothing, and homes.–Men must work to *live*. 4. Dwell, have one's home.–We have *lived* in this house many years. We have made our home here. 5. Feed (on); be kept alive by.–Cattle *live* upon grass. 6. Go through life.–The old man *lives* in ease. 7. Act, behave.–The man *lives* as he believes. He does the things he believes in.

live (rhymes with *dive*). 1. Alive, not dead.– Only a few *live* trees were left after the fire. 2. Burning.–The Boy Scouts poured water on the *live* coals of the fire before they left the camp. 3. Carrying electricity.–After the storm, the people were warned that many *live* wires were down. 4. Actual, not pretended.–Bob is a real *live* paper-boy.

L
M
N
O
P
Q
R
S
T
U
V
W
X
Y
Z

lively live'-ly *livelier, liveliest.* 1. Active, full of life.–Mary's lamb is *lively.*
2. Gay.–The band played *lively* music.
3. Exciting.–We saw a *lively* film.

liver liv'-er *livers.* An organ of the body. Its work is to make bile (a yellowish, bitter liquid) which helps to change the food one eats so that the body can use it.–The *livers* of many animals are used as food.

live-stock live'-stock. Cattle, horses, pigs, and other farm animals. – The farmer sold his *live-stock.*

lizard liz'-ard *lizards.* A four-legged, snakelike animal. *Lizards* have long, scaly bodies and long tails, but short legs.

llama lla'-ma *llamas.* A large, long-haired animal used in South America to carry loads.

load *loads, loaded, loading.* 1. Anything that is carried.–The wagon is carrying a *load* of hay.
2. Put a *load* on.–The men *loaded* the lorry with stones.
3. The amount of current drawn from an electrical source at any given time.
4. Fill (a gun) with cartridges.–The officer *loaded* his pistol.

loaf *loaves, loafs, loafed, loafing.* 1. A large piece of bread baked in one piece. – Mother bought two *loaves* of bread and sliced them to make sandwiches.
2. Something baked in one piece shaped like a *loaf* of bread.–We had a meat *loaf* for dinner.
3. Spend time doing nothing.–If you *loaf* while the other children are working, you will have to work after school.

loam. A kind of rich earth made up of sand, clay, and decayed plants.

loan *loans, loaned, loaning.* 1. A lending; a giving for use for a time.–The farmer gave us the *loan* of his cart.
2. Something lent. – Father got a *loan* of money from the bank to start his business.
3. Lend.–The bank *loaned* Father £1,000.

loath. Not willing.–Bob was *loath* to tell a lie.

loathe *loathes, loathed, loathing.* Feel disgust or strong dislike for; despise.–Mother *loathes* people who are dishonest.

loaves. More than one loaf.–The baker bakes many *loaves* of bread each day.

lobby lob'-by *lobbies.* An outer hall or entrance room. – Men may smoke in the *lobby* of the museum, but not inside.

lobster lob'-ster *lobsters.* A large shellfish found in the sea. It has two large claws and four pairs of legs. *Lobsters* are good to eat.

local lo'-cal *locally.* 1. Having to do with one certain place.–*Local* laws are those that are made in a place and apply only to that place. –A *local* theatre is one near by.
2. A *local* train stops at all the stations.

locality lo-cal'-i-ty *localities.* A place; a certain area.–Bob lives in a different *locality* from Bill.

locate lo-cate' *locates, located, locating.* 1. Find; discover the position or location of.– Jack lost his knife and did not *locate* it for a week.–The enemy air force tried to *locate* our ships so that it could bomb them.
2. Put or stand in a place.–The post office is *located* in West Street. It is in West Street.

location lo-ca'-tion *locations.* 1. Place where something is or happens.–The *location* of the castle is on a high hill.
2. Act of locating.–The *location* of our ships by the enemy made our admiral change his battle plans.

lock *locks, locked, locking.* 1. A fastening for doors, drawers, etc., that cannot be opened without a key or a combination of turns. – Grandfather put a *lock* on the barn door.
2. Fasten with a *lock.* –We *lock* our doors at night.
3. Put in a *locked* place.–The farmer *locked* the horse in the barn. He put the horse in the barn and *locked* the door.

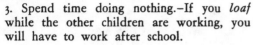

4. An enclosed section of a river or canal in which the water can be raised or lowered so that boats can pass through it to a different level.

5. Join.–The girls *locked* arms and walked down the street.

6. A curl; a few short strings of curly hair.–A *lock* hung down on the baby's forehead.

locker lock'-er *lockers*. A small cubicle or cupboard that can be locked. – The children hang their coats in *lockers*.

locket lock'-et *lockets*. A small case for holding pictures. – *Lockets* are worn on chains that fasten about the neck.

locomotive lo-co-mo'-tive *locomotives*. A railway-engine, or any engine that moves by its own power.

steam locomotive

electric locomotive

diesel locomotive

locust lo'-cust *locusts*. 1. A kind of grasshopper.–*Locusts* often destroy farmer's crops.

lodge *lodges, lodged, lodging*. 1. A house used during the hunting season.–Father went hunting and stayed at his friend's hunting *lodge* in the country.

2. A cottage at the gates of a country estate occupied by a gardener or other servant.

3. Porter's room at the entrance to a college or factory.–Father found a message for him at the porter's *lodge*.

4. A beaver's or otter's lair.–The beaver built its *lodge* on the river bank.

2. Live.–We *lodged* in a boarding-house for a week.

3. Land and become stuck.–A piece of steel *lodged* in my eye.

4. A men's club.–Father goes to the meeting of the *lodge* on Thursday nights.

lodging lodg'-ing *lodgings*. A room to live in for a while.–You can get *lodgings* at Mrs Jones's house.

loft *lofts*. 1. The part of a barn under the roof. –Pigeons made a nest in the barn *loft*.

2. An attic.–Grandmother has an interesting trunk in the *loft*.

log *logs, logged, logging*. 1. All or part of the trunk or a large branch of a tree after it has been cut down.–Robinson Crusoe lived in a cabin made of *logs*.

2. Cut down trees and make them into *logs*. –Some men in the northern woods live by *logging*.

3. A daily record of a ship's voyage.

4. An instrument to measure the speed of or distance travelled by a ship.

log-book log'-book *log-books*. A book in which the daily record of a ship's voyage is kept.

loiter loi'-ter *loiters, loitered, loitering*. Loaf; hang around doing nothing.–Do not *loiter* in the hall.

loll *lolls, lolled, lolling*. Lie lazily.–Sit up. Do not *loll* about in your seat.

lollipop lol'-li-pop *lollipops*. A kind of hard sweet on a stick, made in various flavours.

lone. 1. Alone; without company or contact with others.–A *lone* wolf is one that does not travel with the pack.

2. Single.–The man had a *lone* penny.

loneliness lone'-li-ness. The feeling you have when you are all alone and want to be with other people.

lonely lone'-ly *lonelier, loneliest*. 1. Having few people.–This is a *lonely* country.

2. Sad from being alone.–Mary felt *lonely* when the other children were in school.

lonesome lone'-some. 1. Lonely; sad from being alone.–The soldier was *lonesome* when he thought of home.

2. Having few people.–This is a *lonesome* country.

long *longs, longed, longing, longer, longest*. 1. Having great distance from one end to the other.–Bob's pencil is *longer* than Mary's.

2. In length; from end to end.–The ruler is one foot *long*.

3. Wish sadly.–The sick man *longs* to go home.

L
M
N
O
P
Q
R
S
T
U
V
W
X
Y
Z

longhand long'-hand. Writing by hand in the usual fashion. – We learn to write *long-hand* in school. *A Golden Book.*

longing long'-ing *longings*. A desire; a wish. –Bob had a *longing* to go to the camp.

look *looks, looked, looking*. 1. Notice by seeing; turn the eyes towards to see.–*Look* at the sunset.
2. Search.–Father is *looking* for his lost pen.
3. Appear; seem.–It *looks* as though we are late.
4. Appear to the sight.–The fresh snow *looks* beautiful on the hills.
5. Face.–Our cottage *looks* to the sea.
6. Appearance.–From the *look* of the cabin, no one lives in it.
7. A stare; the act of looking or watching.– The stranger gave us a long *look*.

looking-glass look'-ing-glass *looking-glasses*. A mirror; a glass that reflects an image.–Mother looks into a *looking-glass* when she does her hair.

look-out look'-out *look-outs* 1. A state of watchfulness.–A person watching for something to happen is on the *look-out*.
2. A place from which one watches.–The policeman's *look-out* is a high tower.
3. A watchman; a person watching.–The *look-out* saw the train coming.

loom *looms, loomed, looming*. 1. A machine for weaving threads into cloth. – Jane's great-grandmother made cloth for her family's clothes on her *loom*.
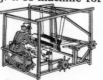
2. Appear slowly.–Out of the clouds *loomed* an aeroplane.–A ship *loomed* over the horizon.

loop *loops, looped, looping*. 1. A figure formed by something turned to cross itself. A pencil line, a rope, or a thread, when curved round so that it closes or crosses, forms a *loop*.
2. Enclose with a *loop*. – Bob *looped* the rope over the post.

loose *looser, loosest, loosely, looseness*. 1. Not firm or snug; not tight.–My shoe is *loose*.– The gravel on the road is *loose*.
2. Not fastened.–One end of the dog's leash is *loose*.
3. Free.–Bob's pony got *loose* and ran away.

loosen loos'-en *loosens, loosened, loosening*. Make loose or less tight.–The boy ate so much that he had to *loosen* his belt.

loot *loots, looted, looting*. 1. Rob.–The thieves *looted* the store.
2. Stolen goods.–They took their *loot* with them.

lope *lopes, loped, loping*. Run with long, easy steps.–See the horse *lope*.

lop-sided lop-sid'-ed. Crooked; uneven.–Mary's picture of the chair is *lop-sided*.

lord *lords*. 1. A ruler; a master.–The man is *lord* of all he owns.
2. In England, a man of noble birth.

Lord. God or Jesus Christ.

lose *loses, lost, losing*. 1. Accidentally drop or leave something where one cannot find it; fail to keep; allow to disappear by chance.– If you *lose* your pencil, you will have to use a pen.
2. Have taken away or destroyed. – The farmer *lost* his fruit because of the storm.
3. Be defeated in.–Unless everyone plays well, we may *lose* the game.
4. Waste.–We will *lose* no time in getting to school.
5. Wander from. – Hansel and Gretel *lost* their way.
6. *Be lost* means not be able to find one's way. – Hansel and Gretel were *lost* in the woods. They did not know where they were, or how to get home.

loser los'-er *losers*. 1. A defeated person or side. –We were the *losers* in the game.
2. One who has lost something.–Who is the *loser* of this pencil? Who lost it?

loss *losses*. 1. Destruction.–The storm caused great *loss* of property.
2. Failing to keep; a losing; end of having. –The *loss* of the dog caused Bob to be unhappy.
3. Defeat.–The *loss* of the game put our team in last place.

lost. One form of the word *lose*.–Mary *lost* her books yesterday.–We *lost* the game.

lot *lots*. 1. Much.–Our team has had a *lot* of luck recently.
2. Something used to make a decision by chance.–We drew *lots* to see who would go to the shops for Mother.
3. A collection.–This *lot* of coconuts came by train.

lotion lo'-tion *lotions.* A liquid used for healing skin troubles or for keeping the skin in good condition.–When we go on the beach we rub sun-*lotion* all over our bodies to prevent sunburn.–The doctor gave Mother a *lotion* for her hands.

lottery lot'-ter-y *lotteries.* A plan for giving out prizes by chance.–We had a *lottery* to raise money for the club. We sold many tickets, then drew a number which won a prize for the person whose ticket had that number on it.

lotto lot'-to. A game played with numbered counters and cards. The counters are drawn from a bag, and the first player to get one row or sometimes one card filled is the winner.–Ann gave me a box of picture-*lotto* for Christmas.

loud *louder, loudest, loudly, loudness.* 1. Of great sound; not soft or quiet. – The wind blew the door shut with a *loud* noise.
2. Showy; bright in colour.–Bob's new suit is *loud*.

loud-speaker loud-speak'-er *loud-speakers.* A machine or device which makes sounds louder so that they can be heard more easily.– We heard the speeches over the *loud-speaker*.

lounge *lounges, lounged, lounging.* 1. A room in which one can sit or lie around and feel comfortable.–After dinner we sat in the *lounge* and talked.–Mother has bought 2 armchairs and a sofa for the *lounge* in our new house.
2. Lie or sit lazily.–We *lounged* about until it was time to go out.

louse *lice.* A small, flat insect that lives on the bodies of animals, plants, or sometimes human beings.

lovable lov'-a-ble. Inviting love; attractive.– We have a *lovable* baby. She is easy to love.

love *loves, loved, loving.* 1. A feeling of deep liking; a pleasant feeling resulting from liking something or someone very much.– Mother has a great *love* for Baby.
2. Have this feeling for.–Mother *loves* the baby.
3. Like; enjoy.–I *love* reading. I get pleasure from it.

lovely love'-ly *lovelier, loveliest.* 1. Beautiful.– Mother has a *lovely* new hat.
2. Likable; winning. – Grandmother has a *lovely* way of explaining things to us.

low *lows, lowed, lowing, lowly, lower, lowest.*
1. Near the ground; of small height.–Trees are tall, but bushes are *low*.
2. Mean.–It was a *low* trick to hide the baby's toys.
3. Weak; in poor health.–The sick man is very *low*.
4. Small.–Mary bought a dress for a very *low* price.
5. Almost used up.–Our sugar supply is *low*.
6. Of deep pitch; towards the bottom of the scale.–The girls sang the high notes, and the boys sang the *low* notes.
7. Unimportant.–The man is in a *lowly* position.
8. Call softly; moo.–We heard the *lowing* of the cattle.

lower low'-er *lowers, lowered, lowering.* 1. Pull down.–Mother *lowered* the blinds to keep out the sun.
2. Make less; reduce. – Rents have been raised, not *lowered*.
3. Not as high; more low.–The water in the lake is *lower* than it was last year.

lowland low'-land *lowlands.* Land that is not as high as the land around it.

loyal loy'-al *loyally, loyalty.* Faithful; unchanging in devotion.–Mary is a *loyal* friend. You can always count on her.

lubricate lu'-bri-cate *lubricates, lubricated, lubricating, lubrication.* Put oil or grease on to make it work smoothly.–Father had our car *lubricated* so that it would run smoothly.

luck. Chance, especially good fortune.–It was just by *luck* that I found the money.–It was bad *luck* for the team when the centre-half sprained his ankle.

lucky luck'-y *luckier, luckiest, luckily.* Fortunate; having good luck. – The sailor was *lucky* to reach shore in the leaky boat.

lug *lugs, lugged, lugging.* Drag; carry with difficulty. – Bob's dog *lugged* a big boot into the living-room.

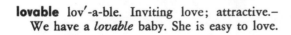

luggage lug'-gage. Trunks and bags.–Mother packed our *luggage*.

lukewarm luke'-warm'. 1. Of medium warmth; a little warm.–Baby drinks milk that is *lukewarm*; it is neither too cool nor too hot.
2. Having slight enthusiasm or interest.–Father was only *lukewarm* towards the plan.

lull *lulls, lulled, lulling.* 1. Quiet; soothe or hush to sleep.–Mother *lulled* the child to sleep.
2. A period of quiet or lack of activity.–After the crash, there was a *lull*. All was quiet and still.

lullaby lull'-a-by *lullabies*. A song sung softly to put a baby to sleep.

lumber lum'-ber. 1. Roughly prepared wood. At a *lumber*-camp (see below), trees are felled, and sent down-river to be sawn up.
2. Disused articles of furniture, etc.–There is a lot of *lumber* in the attic.

luminous lu'-min-ous. Bright and shining.– A certain kind of paint which shows up in the dark is called *luminous* paint.

lump *lumps, lumped, lumping.* 1. A mass or a bit of anything that has no particular shape. –A *lump* of earth fell off the lorry.
2. A hump; a swelling; a raised place; a bump.–Baby fell off the bed and got a *lump* on her head.
3. Put together into one. – The children *lumped* their savings together to buy a present for Mother.
4. Form *lumps*.–The gravy *lumped* because it was not stirred well.

lunatic lu'-na-tic *lunatics*. A mad or insane person; a person whose mind is sick.–*Lunatics* are sent to mental hospitals, where they are cared for properly.

lunch *lunches, lunched, lunching.* 1. A light meal.–We eat *lunch* at noon.
2. Eat *lunch*.–We *lunched* at the restaurant today.

luncheon lunch'-eon *luncheons*. A lunch; a light meal usually served around noon.–Mother invited some of her friends in for *luncheon*.

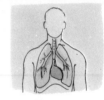

lung *lungs*. One of the pair of organs in the chest that take in fresh air for the body to use.

lure *lures, lured, luring.* 1. Tempt by offering bait.–The boys *lured* the rabbit into the barn by holding out a carrot.
2. An attraction.–The *lure* of the cinema drew Bob to town.
3. Something to tempt animals or fish.–Father has many *lures* in his fishing kit.

lurk *lurks, lurked, lurking.* Hide; wait unseen and unheard.–The boys *lurked* in the bushes, waiting to see the rabbit come out.

lustre lus'-tre. Brightness; shininess.–The maid polished the furniture to a high *lustre*.

luxury lux'-u-ry *luxuries*. 1. Rich comfort; condition of having much that is pleasant but not necessary to have.–The rich man lives in *luxury*.
2. Something which one has just for the pleasure of having it and not because it is needed.–Mother said a piano would be a *luxury* for our family, since no one could play it.

lye. A substance used in making soap and for cleaning. *Lye* is a deadly poison.

lying ly'-ing. 1. One form of the word *lie*, meaning to rest.–The boy is *lying* on the bed.
2. One form of the word *lie*, meaning to tell a deliberate falsehood.–*Lying* gets you into trouble.

lynx *lynxes*. A wild cat.–The hunter shot a *lynx*.

lyre *lyres*. A stringed musical instrument that was played by people long, long ago.

lyric lyr'-ic *lyrics*. 1. A short poem that expresses some strong feeling of the writer.
2. A poem written to be set to music. The words of songs are the *lyrics*.

M m

M, m *M's m's.* The 13th letter of the alphabet.

ma *mas.* Some children call their mothers *Ma.*

macaroni mac-a-ro′-ni. A food made of flour and water dried into long, slender tubes.– Have you ever eaten *macaroni* cooked with tomatoes and cheese?

machine ma-chine′ *machines.* A thing designed and built to do certain work more quickly and better than people could do it. Some *machines,* such as carpet sweepers, are simple and are worked by hand. Others, such as aircraft and printing presses, are large and run by burning fuel or by electricity.

MACHINES

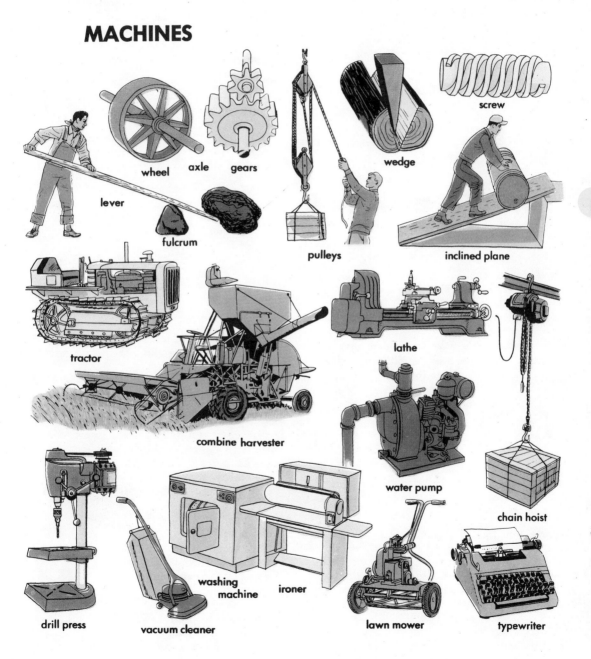

wheel   axle   gears

lever

fulcrum

pulleys

wedge

screw

inclined plane

tractor

combine harvester

lathe

water pump

chain hoist

drill press

vacuum cleaner

washing machine

ironer

lawn mower

typewriter

M
N
O
P
Q
R
S
T
U
V
W
X
Y
Z

machine gun ma-chine' gun *machine guns.* A gun that fires bullets rapidly and by itself as long as the trigger is pressed.

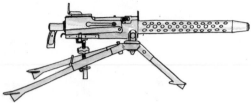

machinery ma-chin'-er-y. 1. A group of machines.–It takes *machinery* to make a motor-car.
2. The parts of a machine.–My watch has stopped; something must be wrong with the *machinery* (or mechanism).

machinist ma-chin'-ist *machinists.* Someone who makes or runs machines, or keeps them in working order.

mackerel mack'-er-el. A medium-sized ocean fish that is good to eat.

mad *madder, maddest, madly, madness.* 1. Crazy or insane.–The miser went *mad* when he lost his money.
2. Wild and foolish.–Mary has a *mad* desire to be a film actress.
3. Some people say *mad* when they mean angry.–Jack was *mad* at Bill for taking his bicycle without asking for it.
4. Some people say *mad* when they mean delighted with something.–Mary is *mad* about her new dress.
5. Having the disease of rabies or hydrophobia.–If one is bitten by a *mad* dog, one should go at once to the doctor.

madam mad'-am. A polite name for a woman. –The assistant said to Mother, 'May I help you, *madam*?'

made. One form of the word *make.*–Sally *made* a cake for Mother.

magazine mag-a-zine' *magazines.* 1. A paper-covered publication that comes out at regular times. Some *magazines* are published once a week, some once a month, etc.
2. A place for storing gunpowder and other war supplies.

3. The compartment or chamber of a gun which holds the cartridges.

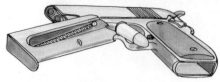

maggot mag'-got *maggots.* The worm-like first stage of development of some insects. Some *maggots* turn into flies.

magic mag'-ic *magical, magically.* 1. Things happening by mysterious powers.–In olden times people believed in *magic.*
2. Charmed, able to work *magic.*–The fairy godmother waved her *magic* wand, and the pumpkin turned into a coach.

magician ma-gi'-cian *magicians.* 1. A man who does tricks that mystify or puzzle people.–The *magician* pulled a rabbit out of Father's hat.
2. In olden times, a man believed to have magic powers.–The *magician* gave the king a sword which would cut through stone.

magnet mag'-net *magnets.* A piece of iron or stone that pulls or attracts iron or steel objects towards it.–We can pull pins out of a pin-cushion with a *magnet.*

magnificent mag-nif'-i-cent *magnificently.*
1. Grand and splendid.–The opera house is *magnificent.*
2. Beautiful and brilliant.–We watched the *magnificent* sunset.

magnify mag'-ni-fy *magnifies, magnified, magnifying.* 1. Cause to look larger.–Grandmother's glasses *magnify* things.
2. Exaggerate, make something sound bigger than it is.–Fishermen sometimes *magnify* the size of the fish they catch.

magnolia mag-no'-li-a *magnolias.* A tree with large white or yellowish-white flowers. Certain cultivated varieties have pink or purplish flowers before the leaves appear.

magpie mag´-pie *magpies*. A black-and-white bird known for its noisy chattering.

mahogany ma-hog´-a-ny. A tree found in hot countries. Its hard, reddish-brown wood is used for making furniture.–Mother has a *mahogany* table.

maid *maids*. 1. A girl or woman who does housework in someone else's house, for pay.
2. A young woman who is not married.

maiden maid´-en *maidens*. 1. A girl or young woman who is not married.
2. First (trip, voyage, etc.).–Father went on the ship's *maiden* voyage. It was the ship's first trip.

mail *mails, mailed, mailing*. 1. Letters, cards, packages, and other things sent through the post.–Sally received a great deal of *mail* on her birthday.
2. Drop into a pillar-box, or send through the post.–Bob went to the corner to *mail* the letter.

mail-bag mail´-bag *mail-bags*. A leather or canvas bag used for carrying mail.

mail-coach mail´-coach *mail-coaches*. 1. In olden times, a stage-coach used for carrying the mail.–The highwayman held up the *mail-coach* near York.
2. A carriage on a train used for carrying parcels and letters.–We stood on the platform and watched the *mail-coach* being loaded.

maim *maims, maimed, maiming*. Hurt badly so as to cripple.–If you play in the street, a car may strike you and *maim* you.

main *mains*. 1. Chief or most important.–We eat our *main* meal at noon.–We eat dinner at noon.–A high road running through all the largest towns in a district is called a *main* road.–A railway line serving such towns is called a *main* line.

2. Great strength.–The tug-o'-war team pulled with might and *main*.

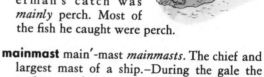

3. Ocean or sea.–The pirates went sailing over the bounding *main*.
4. A large pipe.–When the water *main* burst, water ran all over the street.–Gas for cooking often comes through gas *mains*.

main-deck main´-deck *main-decks*. The chief and upper deck of a ship.–As soon as the weather cleared up, the passengers came out on the *main-deck* of the liner.

mainland main´-land. A large body of land.– When we lived on the island for the summer, we had to row to the *mainland* to buy food.

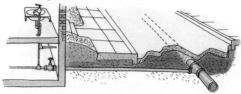

mainly main´-ly. Chiefly or mostly. – The fisherman's catch was *mainly* perch. Most of the fish he caught were perch.

mainmast main´-mast *mainmasts*. The chief and largest mast of a ship.–During the gale the *mainmast* of the yacht was snapped in half.

mainsail main´-sail *mainsails*. The chief sail of a ship.–The yacht's *mainsail* billowed in the fresh breeze.

maintain main-tain´ *maintains, maintained, maintaining*. 1. Keep; hold; have and support.–Grandfather *maintains* a large farm.
2. Insist; say strongly.–I *maintain* that this is the right way to solve the problem.

maize. 1. The kind of corn grown originally in America. It is also known as Indian corn. *Maize* is used as an article of food all over the world. It can be eaten on the cob and is also canned as sweetcorn. Cornflour also is made from *maize*.

majesty maj´-es-ty *majesties, majestic*. 1. Stateliness, dignity, and grandeur.–The music of the hymn had great *majesty*.
2. *Your Majesty* is a title used in speaking to kings and queens.
3. *His Majesty* and *Her Majesty* are titles used in speaking of kings and queens.

M
N
O
P
Q
R
S
T
U
V
W
X
Y
Z

major ma′-jor *majors*. 1. An army officer whose rank is just above that of captain.
2. Greater.–We spent the *major* part of our holidays at Grandmother's.
3. In music, the *major* scale begins and ends on 'doh.'

majority ma-jor′-i-ty *majorities*. 1. Greater number, most.–The *majority* of children in town go to our school.
2. More than half.–Bob received a *majority* of the votes for captain.
3. Bob won by a *majority* of five.–He received five more votes than anyone else.

make *makes, made, making*. 1. Build; construct; prepare.–Many boys like to *make* model aircraft.–Most girls would rather *make* sweets.
2. Cause.–Mary never *makes* trouble for her teacher.
3. Cause to become.–The boiler *makes* the house warm.
4. Be or become.–Bob will *make* a good captain.–Kind people *make* friends easily.
5. Be, or amount to.–Ten and five *make* fifteen.
6. Earn.–Jack *makes* £2 a week from his newspaper round.
7. Force or compel.–If Baby does not want to eat, Mother does not *make* her.
8. A kind or sort.–Father's new car is of a different *make* from the old one.
9. *Make believe* means pretend.–Mary likes to *make believe* she is an actress.
10. *Make any difference* means matter.–Does it *make any difference* to you where you go to school?

maker mak′-er *makers*. 1. A person who makes something.–The shop of the toy-*maker* was bright and sunny.
2. Something which makes something else.–On New Year's Eve, people sound horns, rattles, and other noise-*makers*.

male *males*. A man, boy, or he-animal. – A cock is a *male* chicken.

mallard mal′-lard *mallards*. A kind of wild duck.

mallet mal′-let *mallets*. A wooden hammer.–Jack used a *mallet* to shape the copper bowl.–We use *mallets* with long handles to hit the ball in croquet.

malt. Barley or other grain that has been soaked in water until it sprouts, or begins to grow. *Malt* is used in making some kinds of drinks.

mamma mam′-ma *mammas*. A child's word for mother.

mammal mam′-mal *mammals*. One of the order, or group, of animals that have warm blood and feed their young at the breast. Man is a *mammal*. Cats, dogs, bears, and whales are other examples of *mammals*. Fish, birds, and insects are some of the animals that are not *mammals*.

mammoth mam′-moth *mammoths*. 1. Huge; very, very large.–The *Queen Mary* is a *mammoth* ship.
2. Tremendous or very great.–It was a *mammoth* task to rebuild the burnt city.
3. A kind of hairy elephant with long tusks, that lived long ago.

man *men, mans, manned, manning*. 1. A full-grown male person.–Boys grow up to be *men*.
2. *Man* sometimes means the human race.– *Man* has invented many wonderful things.
3. Provide with *men*.–The ship was *manned* by a crew of 50.

manage man′ age *manages, managed, managing*. 1. Control, handle; do things with.–Jack *managed* the horse well at the show.
2. Run or carry on a business for someone.–Father *manages* a shoe shop.
3. Find a way; be able.–Mother *manages* to give us lunch and feed Baby at the same time.
4. Get along.–Jack will *manage* on the money he earned.

MAMMALS
EXISTING MAMMALS

dolphin

goat

whale

lion

sheep

giraffe

bison or buffalo

fox

wolf

mountain lion

kangaroo

squirrel

zebra

deer

llama

peccary

rabbit

bear

armadillo

elephant

monkey

camel

yak

seal

EXTINCT MAMMALS

eohippus

glyptodont

mammoth

megatherium

mastodon

M
N
O
P
Q
R
S
T
U
V
W
X
Y
Z

management man'-age-ment. 1. Direction, control; way of running a thing.–With careful *management*, you can make your money last all the week.

2. The managers; people in control.–Bob spoke to the *management* of the restaurant about the mistake in his bill.

manager man'-ag-er *managers*. A person in charge.–Father is the *manager* of the shoe shop.

mandolin man'-do-lin *mandolins*. A musical instrument with strings stretched over a soundbox. We play a *mandolin* by picking the strings with a flat pick.

mane *manes*. The long hair that grows on some animals' heads and necks.–My horse's *mane* streams in the wind when we gallop.

manful man'-ful *manfully*. Courageous and bold, like a man.–Jack made a *manful* effort to save the football team from defeat.–The sailors struggled *manfully* to get the ship safely back to port during the gale.

manganese man'-ga-nese. A black mineral used in the making of glass and in manufacturing iron and steel.

manger man'-ger *mangers*. An open box from which horses and cows eat.

mangle man'-gle *mangles, mangled, mangling*. 1. Crush and tear.–A good machinist would never catch his hand in a machine and *mangle* his fingers.
2. A machine with rollers that irons sheets, clothing, linen, etc.

manicure man'-i-cure *manicures, manicured, manicuring, manicurist*. 1. Clean, file, and polish the finger-nails. – Mother *manicures* her nails.
2. A cleaning, filing, and polishing of the finger-nails.–Sometimes she gives Mary a *manicure*.

mankind man-kind. All people; human beings. –All *mankind* desires peace.

manner man'-ner *manners*. 1. A way.–The children treat Baby in a gentle *manner*.
2. Kinds; sorts.–We study all *manner* of living things in our nature study class.
3. *Manners* means ways of doing things.– Sally has good *manners*. She is polite to her guests.–Bob has bad *manners*. He eats with his knife.

mansion man'-sion *mansions*. A large, beautiful house.–The rich family lives in a *mansion*. –The Lord Mayor of London lives in the *Mansion* House.

mantelpiece man'-tel-piece *mantelpieces*. A shelf above a fireplace.–We hung our stockings from the *mantelpiece*.

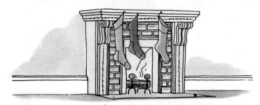

mantle man'-tle *mantles*. 1. A loose, sleeveless cloak, an enveloping robe. – King Arthur's knights wore *mantles*.
2. Something that envelops or covers. – A *mantle* of snow covered the ground on Christmas morning.
3. A fragile hood or tube fixed over a gas jet to give an even, bright light.–Mary broke the gas-*mantle* when she lit the gas without taking proper care.

manual man'-u-al *manuals*. 1. A book of easy directions.–Mary received a *manual* telling how to make the marionettes.
2. The keyboard of an organ.–A piano has one keyboard but an organ often has three or four *manuals*.
3. Done with the hands.–Hoeing the garden is *manual* work.

M
N
O
P
Q
R
S
T
U
V
W
X
Y
Z

manufacture man-u-fac'-ture *manufactures, manufactured, manufacturing*. 1. Make in factories in great numbers.–They *manufacture* many motor-cars in Birmingham.
2. Making in factories.–The *manufacture* of motor-cars is a big business.

manufacturer man-u-fac'-tur-er *manufacturers*. A person who owns a factory where goods are manufactured.–The *manufacturer* supplies Father with shoes for his shoe shop.

manure ma-nure'. Animal waste or compost. –The farmer spreads *manure* over his fields. *Manure* helps the crops grow.

manuscript man'-u-script *manuscripts*. A book or article written by hand or on a typewriter; a piece of writing not in published form.

many man'-y. 1. A great number of.–*Many* people go to football matches.
2. A large number.–Father is one of the *many* who listen to them on the radio.

map *maps, mapped, mapping*. 1. A drawing of all or a part of the earth. On a *map* the cities are often represented by dots, and the rivers by lines.

2. Make a *map* of.–Some parts of the world have never been *mapped*.
3. Plan.–Each day we *map* out our work.

maple ma'-ple *maples*. A large shady tree. *Maple* syrup and sugar are made from the sap of one kind of *maple* tree. Furniture is made from the light-coloured wood of another kind. –Father has a *maple* desk.

mar *mars, marred, marring*. Spoil, ruin.–The teacher asked us not to *mar* the tops of our desks by writing or scratching on them.

marble mar'-ble *marbles*. 1. A hard stone, often white, used for statues and big buildings.– Our library has marble pillars.
2. A small ball, usually of glass, with which you can play games. – Do you ever play *marbles*?

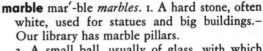

march *marches, marched, marching*. 1. Walk in time, taking steps of the same length.–Jack's uncle is a soldier. He taught the boys to *march*.
2. Music to *march* by.–The school band played a *march* in the parade.
3. Distance to *march*.–The soldiers in the parade had a long *march* to the reviewing stand.

March. The third month of the year. January, February, *March*. – Father's birthday is *March* 31.

mare *mares*. A female or she horse.

margarine mar'-ga-rine. A food made of fats and vegetable oils. – We sometimes use *margarine* in cakes instead of butter.

margin mar'-gin *margins*. A blank border round a printed or written page. – When Mary writes a composition, she leaves a *margin* on her paper.

marigold mar'-i-gold *marigolds*. A flower with many yellow or orange flower petals.

marine ma-rine' *marines*. 1. Of or belonging to the sea.–Fish are *marine* animals.–Ships and men engaged in trade are known as the mercantile *marine*.

mariner mar'-i-ner *mariners*. A seaman or sailor. – The *mariner* was glad to be on his ship again.

marionette mar-i-o-nette′ *marionettes*. A doll or little figure which moves by the pulling of strings fastened to its arms and legs.–Mary made the *marionette* dance across the stage.

mark *marks, marked, marking*. 1. A target or object aimed at.–The hunter's shot hit the *mark*.
2. A scar.–The deep cut on Father's thumb left a *mark*.
3. A sign or indication.–The city presented the retiring mayor with an inscribed book as a *mark* of gratitude.
4. A line, cross, or any written figure.–The children made chalk *marks* on the pavement.
5. Bob *marked* with a large stone the place where he found the strange flowers.
6. Put a tag or name on.–On Christmas Eve we wrap and *mark* the presents.
7. A grading.–Jack got a high *mark* in arithmetic, though his *mark* in spelling was bad.
8. Make a grading. – The teacher let us exchange our spelling papers and *mark* them.
9. *Mark my words* means 'You will see!'–*Mark my words*, Jack will be a great man some day.

market mar′-ket *markets, marketed, marketing*.
1. A place where goods are traded, bought, or sold.–Grandfather took the calves to *market* yesterday.
2. A demand.–There is a great *market* for sugar in this country because we drink much coffee.
3. Shop for food.–Mother *markets* on Saturday.
4. Sell.–Grandfather *markets* his cattle in the nearest town.

market-place mar′-ket-place *market-places*. An open square where a market is held.–When we reached the *market-place* it was already crowded with people and animals.

marksman marks′-man *marksmen*. A person expert in shooting or aiming at a target.–The major is the best *marksman* on the rifle-range. He always gets the highest score.

marmalade mar′-ma-lade. A kind of preserve eaten on bread. Orange *marmalade* is made of sugar, oranges, and orange peel.

maroon ma-roon′ *maroons, marooned, marooning*. 1. Dark red.–Mother has a *maroon* suit.
2. Put (a person) on a lonely island and leave him there.–The captain threatened to *maroon* the stowaway on an island.

marriage mar′-riage *marriages*. 1. The ceremony by which a man and a woman become husband and wife.–The bride wore white for her *marriage*.
2. Life together as husband and wife.–The *marriage* of Father and Mother is a very happy one.

marry mar′-ry *marries, married, marrying*.
1. Take as husband or wife.–Jean will *marry* John.
2. Become husband and wife. – They will *marry* in June.
3. Make husband and wife.–The Vicar will *marry* Jean and John.

marsh *marshes*. A swamp or lowland partly covered by water. – Bulrushes grow in the *marsh*.

marshal mar′-shal *marshals, marshalled, marshalling*.
1. A high officer of the court; a police officer; in some countries a high army officer.
2. An officer who makes arrangements for special events, such as parades.
3. Call together and place in order.–The general *marshalled* his forces for the attack.

marshmallow marsh′-mal′-low *marshmallows*. A kind of soft, white sweetmeat covered with powdered sugar. – *Marshmallows* are good toasted. Sometimes they are used as a decoration for cakes.

martin mar′-tin *martins*. A bird something like a swallow.

M
N
O
P
Q
R
S
T
U
V
W
X
Y
Z

martyr mar'-tyr *martyrs*. A person who dies or undergoes great hardship for something he believes in rather than give up his belief.– In the Middle Ages many *martyrs* were burnt because they refused to give up their religion. 2. Someone who suffers from something.– Father is a *martyr* to hay-fever in the summer. He gets it badly.

martyrdom mar'-tyr-dom. Suffering or death for one's beliefs.–The men and women who died in the Middle Ages were not forgotten; people remembered their *martyrdom*.

marvel mar'-vel *marvels, marvelled, marvelling*. 1. A wonder; a wonderful thing.–Electricity is one of the *marvels* of the world today. 2. Wonder. – We stopped to *marvel* at the beauty of the waterfall.

marvellous mar'-vel-lous *marvellously*. Amazing and wonderful.–The magician did some *marvellous* tricks.–The view from the top of the mountain was *marvellous*.

marzipan mar'-zi-pan. A thick paste made from ground almonds and sugar.–*Marzipan* is used as a filling for cakes and chocolates.

mascot mas'-cot *mascots*. Someone or something that is kept because it is supposed to bring good luck.–Bob's football team has a white mouse as a *mascot*.

masculine mas'-cu-line. 1. Strong and manly. –Jack's voice is very *masculine*. 2. Mannish; like a man's.–Jean likes to wear very *masculine* clothes.

mash *mashes, mashed, mashing*. 1. Crush or beat.–Mary likes to help Mother *mash* the potatoes. 2. A mixture containing boiled grain, meal, or bran used as a food for farm animals.

mask *masks, masked, masking*. 1. A covering to hide the face and disguise the person wearing it.–A false face is a *mask*.

2. Wear a *mask*.–Mary *masked* for the Hallowe'en party. 3. Hide by covering or concealing.–Jack tried to *mask* his feelings.

mason ma'-son *masons*. A person who works with stone or brick.–Father hired a *mason* to build a stone wall round our house.

masquerade mas-quer-ade' *masquerades, masqueraded, masquerading*. 1. A party at which people wear masks or disguises.

2. Pretend to be.–The rich miser *masquerades* as a poor man.

mass *masses, massed, massing*. 1. A lump or a large quantity of something. – Mashed potatoes make a *mass* of potatoes. 2. Greater number or majority.–The *mass* of people voted for a new park. 3. Put together or collect.–The flags were *massed* at the head of the parade. 4. (Spelled *Mass*) a service in the Roman Catholic church.

massacre mas'-sa-cre *massacres, massacred, massacring*. 1. A cruel killing of many people, 2. Kill without pity.–The savages *massacred* their prisoners.

massage mass'-age *massages, massaged, massaging*. 1. A treatment used to cure or improve certain ailments or illnesses by means of rubbing and kneading.–When Mother had rheumatism she was given *massage* every day for a fortnight. 2. To treat by rubbing and kneading.–Mother *massaged* Bob's stiff neck.

massif mas'-sif *massifs*. A large mass of mountains, sometimes a part of a mountain range.

massive mas'-sive *massively*. Large and heavy. –The new hotel is a *massive* building.–The elephant has a *massive* head and body.

M
N
O
P
Q
R
S
T
U
V
W
X
Y
Z

mast *masts*. A tall pole on a ship or boat, to which sails and ropes are fastened.

master mas'-ter *masters, mastered, mastering, mastery*. 1. A person who rules or controls. –In olden times, a king was the real *master* of his country. Everyone had to do as he said.
2. An expert; one who knows all about a certain subject.–Mary's music teacher is a *master* of his subject.
3. A title of respect for a boy.–Bob's father is called Mr Smith. Bob is sometimes called *Master* Bob Smith.
4. A male school-teacher.
5. Overcome or control.–Bob has learned to *master* his temper.
6. Thoroughly learn.–Sally has *mastered* the alphabet.

mastiff mas'-tiff *mastiffs*. A kind of large, powerful dog.–A *mastiff* makes a good watchdog.

mat *mats, matted, matting*. 1. A small rug.– Mother keeps a *mat* at the door for us to wipe our feet on.
2. A pad.–Small *mats* are placed under hot dishes to protect the table.
3. (Also spelt *matt*.) Dull, without lustre.–The doors and windows are painted with *mat* colours. They are not glossy and shining.
4. Tangle and stick together.–The puppy's fur was *matted* with mud.

match *matches, matched, matching*. 1. A little stick of wood or cardboard tipped with a material that makes a flame when the tip is scratched against a rough or chemically prepared surface.–Father lights his pipe with a *match*.

2. A contest. – Our team won the cricket *match* against the next village.

3. An equal; one as good as.–Jack is a good runner, but he is no *match* for Bob.
4. A well-suited pair. – Father and Mother are a good *match*.
5. Find or make something just like another. –Mother could not *match* the material of Mary's dress.
6. Be the same as, especially in colour.– Sally's hair ribbon *matches* her dress. They are both light blue.

mate *mates, mated, mating*. 1. One of a pair. –Bob cannot find the *mate* to his blue sock.
2. A husband or wife.
3. On a ship, an officer who ranks just below the captain.
4. Pair off in couples. – Birds *mate* in the spring.

material ma-te'-ri-al *materials*. 1. The substance from which something is made. – Cement is the *material* used to lay bricks.
2. Cloth.–Mary's dress is made of very fine *material*.

mathematics math-e-mat'-ics. The study of numbers and measurements. – Arithmetic is one kind of *mathematics*.

matinée (pronounced *matinay*) mat'-i-née *matinées*. An afternoon show.–The cinema in our street has a *matinée* for children.

matter mat'-ter *matters, mattered, mattering*.
1. Trouble.–What is the *matter* with Bob?
2. A topic; a question; a subject.–The meeting will be short, since we have only a few *matters* to talk about.
3. It is only a *matter* of one week before Mary will be well enough to go out.
4. The substance that things are made of.– The world of *matter* is the world of things.
5. Make a difference.–Does it *matter* to you if we cannot come?

mattress mat'-tress *mattresses*. A large, thick pad used to sleep on. Some *mattresses* have springs in them.

mature ma-ture' *matures, matured, maturing, maturity*. 1. Adult; grown-up.–Bob showed *mature* judgement in calling the doctor promptly.
2. Become adults or grow up.–We grow wiser as we *mature*.
3. Ripen.–Peaches *mature* in late summer.

M
N
O
P
Q
R
S
T
U
V
W
X
Y
Z

maul *mauls, mauled, mauling.* 1. Handle roughly.–If you *maul* your pets, they will suffer.
2. (Also spelt *mall*.) A heavy hammer. – The carpenter used a *maul* to pound the posts into the ground.

maximum max'-i-mum. 1. Most or greatest number of.–The *maximum* number of points that you can get in this test is 100.
2. Highest.–Thirty miles an hour is the *maximum* legal speed in the town.

may. 1. Be allowed or permitted.–*May* I have an apple?
2. Possibly will.–It *may* be too late for the matinée.
3. Let it be that. – *May* you have a merry Christmas! I hope you do!

May. The 5th month of the year.–April showers bring *May* flowers.

mayonnaise may-on-naise'. A thick salad dressing made of eggs, oil, vinegar, and spices.

mayor may'-or *mayors.* The head of local government.–The *Mayor* is elected during October each year.

me. A word used to refer to oneself. – When you speak of yourself, you use the words I and *me*.–Let *me* do the work.–Give it to *me*.

meadow mead'-ow *meadows.* A grassy field.– The children pick flowers in the *meadow*.

meadow-sweet mead'-ow-sweet. A plant commonly found in meadows and alongside rivers and streams. It has creamy-white, sweet-smelling flowers, which grow on long stems.

meagre mea'-gre *meagrely, meagreness.* 1. Barely enough.–Jack's wages are *meagre*; he can hardly pay for his lunches.
2. Thin and ill-looking.–The animals on this farm look extremely *meagre* and unhealthy because they are not receiving proper care.

meal *meals.* 1. An amount of food prepared to be eaten at one time.–We eat 3 *meals* a day.
2. Ground grain.–The miller ground the corn into *meal*.

mean *means, meant, meaning, meaner, meanest, meanly.* 1. Intend.–Bob didn't *mean* to hurt you.
2. Be intended to say or convey.–A dictionary tells you what words *mean*.–Strike *means* hit.–Bob didn't know what the word *meant*.
3. Spiteful and unkind.–Jack felt sorry for his *mean* remarks.
4. Selfish and stingy.–The man was too *mean* to pay for the work.
5. Poor.–The prince found Cinderella wearing *mean* clothing.

meaning mean'-ing *meanings.* A thought; idea intended.–I do not understand the *meaning* of your question. I do not know what you are asking me.

meantime mean'-time. The time during some named activity; at the same time. – Father walked to the store. In the *meantime*, Jack washed the car.

meanwhile mean'-while. Meantime; the time during some named activity. – Red Riding Hood walked on. *Meanwhile*, the wolf ran on to Grandmother's house.

measles mea'-sles. A disease or sickness which makes a person break out in red spots.

measure meas'-ure *measures, measured, measuring.* 1. Find the size, amount, etc., of something.–When we *measure* milk we find out how many pints or quarts of it there are.– Father *measured* the board and found that it was 15 feet long.
2. A degree or amount.–Mary has already met with some *measure* of success in singing.
3. In music, the notes and rests between two bars.

4. *Measure off* means mark to certain measurements or size.–The boys *measured off* the football field.
5. *Measure up* means come up to some standard. – Bob more than *measured up* to the teacher's opinion of him. He was as good as she thought he was.

measurement meas'-ure-ment *measurements.* 1. A finding out of the size or amount of anything. – The *measurement* of the board required the use of a ruler.
2. A size or dimension measured.–The boys took the *measurements* of the board. The *measurements* were 8 by 2 by 4 inches.

M
N
O
P
Q
R
S
T
U
V
W
X
Y
Z

M N O P Q R S T U V W X Y Z

meat *meats*. 1. Animal flesh (other than that of fish and fowl) that can be eaten.–We usually eat *meat* for dinner.
2. When a book or play gives one plenty to think about we sometimes say it is full of *meat*.

mechanic me-chan'-ic *mechanics*. A person who makes or repairs machinery.–A *mechanic* repaired Father's car.

mechanical me-chan'-i-cal *mechanically*. 1. Anything to do with machines or machinery. –Modern industry depends almost entirely on *mechanical* processes. Nearly everything is done by machinery.
2. Machine-like, or not needing much thought or originality.–Jack sorted the cards *mechanically*. It was a simple and repetitive job.

mechanism mech'-an-ism. The working parts of a machine.–When Father's watch broke, the watchmaker opened it up to look at the *mechanism*.–Bob fully understands the *mechanism* of his father's car.

mechanize mech'-an-ize *mechanizes, mechanized, mechanizing*. To make mechanical.–This is a *mechanized* age. We rely on machines for most of our daily needs.

medal med'-al *medals*. A badge given to someone as a reward for an outstanding act.–The soldier received a *medal* for bravery.

medallion me-dal'-lion *medallions*. A large oval or round disk with a picture or inscription engraved on it.

meddle med'-dle *meddles, meddled, meddling*. Interfere with someone else's doings; pry; snoop, ask curiously.–Do not *meddle* in your neighbour's affairs.

meddlesome med'-dle-some. Prying or interfering.–Mr Green is a *meddlesome* person. He is always trying to find out what we are doing.

medical med'-i-cal *medically*. Having to do with medicine and treating sickness.–Uncle Jim went to *medical* school to learn to be a doctor.

medicine med'-i-cine *medicines*. 1. Something taken to make one well.–*Medicines* may be pills, tablets, powders, or liquids.–The doctor gave Mother a bottle of *medicine*.
2. The study of how to treat sick people. – Jim studied *medicine* at medical school.

medium me'-di-um. In between.–The mother bear was the *medium*-sized bear. She was neither the largest nor the smallest bear in the zoo.

meet *meets, met, meeting*. 1. Come upon.–I did not expect to *meet* you here.
2. Come or get together.–We shall *meet* at my house.
3. Come together; join.–The roads *meet* at the top of the hill.
4. Welcome; greet.–We are going to the station to *meet* Father.
5. Be introduced to, get to know.–I would like to *meet* the new teacher.
6. Pay; make good.–Father always *meets* his bills.

meeting meet'-ing *meetings*. 1. A gathering together; an assembly.–We had a *meeting* of all the players this morning.
2. A coming together.–The *meeting* of the armies took place this morning.

melancholy mel'-an-chol-y. Sad.–Jack is never *melancholy*. He is always happy.

mellow mel'-low *mellows, mellowed, mellowing, mellowly*. 1. Soft and ripe. – *Mellow* pears hung on Grandfather's trees.
2. Softened by age and experience. – The red bricks have *mellowed* to a soft, warm colour. –Uncle Jim has *mellowed*. He is less fierce than he was.
3. Rich and soft.–We heard the *mellow* song of a bird.
4. Slightly intoxicated, genial. – Father was *mellow* after the party.

melody mel'-o-dy *melodies*. A tune.–The song has a beautiful *melody*.

melon mel'-on *melons*. A large juicy fruit that grows on a vine. *Melons* have a heavy rind.– Water-*melons* are red inside.

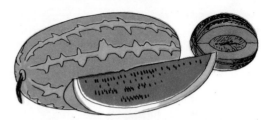

melt *melts, melted, melting*. 1. Become liquid. –When some hard or solid substances get warm, they *melt*.–Ice *melts* into water.
2. Dissolve.–Sugar *melts* in water.
3. Disappear little by little. – The clouds *melted* away.
4. Soften.–The old man's anger *melted* at the boy's unhappiness.

member mem'-ber *members, membership*. One who belongs to an organization or group.–Bob is a *member* of the Boy Scouts.

memorial me-mo'-ri-al *memorials*. 1. A building or monument to remind people of a great person or event of the past.–The city built a *memorial* to the soldiers who died in two world wars.

2. Anything recalling the past.–We still have an album of photographs as a *memorial* of the happy days we spent on the farm five years ago.

memorize mem'-o-rize *memorizes, memorized, memorizing*. Learn by heart; learn to repeat exactly. – In literature lessons we *memorize* poems.

memory mem'-o-ry *memories*. 1. The ability to bring to mind something that happened in the past. – Grandmother has a good *memory*. 2. Something remembered.–Jack has pleasant *memories* of the summers he has spent in the country.

men. More than one man.–Two *men* were in the car.

menagerie me-nag'-er-ie *menageries*. A place where wild animals are kept in cages so that people can see them.–At the circus we visited the *menagerie* to see the lions and tigers.

mend *mends, mended, mending*. 1. Repair; put in proper condition.–Mary tore a hole in her sweater and had to *mend* it. 2. A *mended* place. – The *mend* looks very neat. 3. Get better or improve.–Grandmother has been ill, but now she is *mending*.

mental men'-tal *mentally*. Of the mind; having to do with thinking. – Bill is physically stronger than Jack, but Jack has better *mental* powers. Jack thinks faster and more clearly.

mention men'-tion *mentions, mentioned, mentioning*. 1. Speak of. – *Mention* your special interests to your teacher. 2. A notice; a speaking of.–I saw a *mention* of you in the school magazine.

menu men'-u *menus*. A list of foods being served. – Mother looked at the *menu* in the restaurant and chose a cheese omelette.

merchandise mer'-chan-dise. Goods or articles for sale.–The shops have a large stock of *merchandise* before Christmas.

merchant mer'-chant *merchants*. 1. A person whose business is to buy and sell goods. 2. Engaged in carrying goods. – *Merchant* ships carry goods to different countries.

merchant navy mer'-chant na'-vy. All the ships of one country that carry goods and passengers to and from different countries.

merciless mer'-ci-less *mercilessly*. Heartless or pitiless.–The *merciless* king condemned his prisoners to death.

mercury mer'-cu-ry. A heavy silver-white liquid metal. It is used in some thermometers; it expands and rises in the tube as it gets warmer, and contracts and falls as it cools off.

mercy mer'-cy *mercies*. 1. Pity. – The gentle princess had *mercy* on the prisoner and set him free. 2. A kindness.–In our prayers we thank God for his *mercies*.

mere. Only; nothing more than. – It is *mere* foolishness to run into danger.

merely mere'-ly. 1. Only.–Bob *merely* wanted to be helpful. 2. Simply.–This is *merely* a suggestion; you may do as you wish.

merit mer'-it *merits, merited, meriting*. 1. A good quality.–Bob's essay has many merits and few faults. 2. Deserve. – Bob's work *merits* the highest praise.

mermaid mer'-maid *mermaids*. A sea maiden told about in fairy tales. *Mermaids* were supposed to have the form of a woman down to the waist and the form of a fish from the waist down.

M
N
O
P
Q
R
S
T
U
V
W
X
Y
Z

merrily mer'-ri-ly. Joyfully; gaily; cheerfully.– Sally laughed *merrily* to see the kitten play with the string.

merry mer'-ry. Happy, gay, and joyful. – A *merry* Christmas to you!

merry-go-round *merry-go-rounds*. A round platform with a ring of horses or other animals on which children can ride. Music plays as the *merry-go-round* turns.

mesh *meshes*. 1. One of the holes or open spaces in a net. – Small fish can get through the *meshes* in a fisherman's net.
2. Openwork or net. – Mary pinned a rose in the *meshes* of her lace costume.

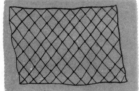

mess *messes, messed, messing, messy*. 1. An untidy condition.–The careless campers left the picnic grounds in a *mess*. They left papers all over the place.
2. Upset.–Try not to *mess* up your room after Mother has cleaned it.
3. Trouble.–If you do not do your work daily, you will be in a *mess* before the test.
4. A meal or meals, in the army or navy.– Soldiers eat together in a *mess* hall.

message mes'-sage *messages*. 1. Word, information.–*Messages* can be sent by radio, mail, phone, etc.–Bob sent his mother a *message* that he would be late for dinner.
2. A formal speech.–Did you hear the Prime Minister's *message* on the radio?

messenger mes'-sen-ger *messengers*. One who carries messages from one person to another. –The Post Office has many *messengers* to deliver telegrams.

met. One form of the word *meet*.–I *met* Mary on my way to the shops.

metal met'-al *metals*. A hard, shiny substance that comes from ore mined from the earth. Iron, gold, silver, and copper are *metals*.

meteor me'-te-or *meteors*. A shooting star.– Mary made a wish when she saw the *meteor* flash across the sky.

meter me'-ter *meters*. A machine which measures without help, all by itself. A gas *meter* tells the amount of gas you use. An electricity *meter* tells the amount of electricity you use.

method meth'-od
methods, methodical. 1. A way of doing something.–Mother has one *method* of making pastry and Grandmother has another *method*. 2. A system for doing something. – If you have a *method* for doing your homework, you get it done faster.

meticulous me-tic'-u-lous *meticulously*. Very careful and painstaking.–The police officer was very *meticulous* in taking details of the accident. He wanted to know exactly how, when and where it happened.

metre me'-tre *metres*. 1. Rhythm in poetry.– Shakespeare wrote in a *metre* called blank verse. Each line has 10 beats, 5 heavy and 5 light.
2. A unit of measurement in the metric system, equal to 39.37 inches.

metric met'-ric. The metric system is a system of weights and measures used in many parts of the world. It is based on decimals, that is on multiples of 10, 100, 1000, etc. Metres are used instead of feet, kilograms intead of pounds, etc.

metropolis me-trop'-o-lis *metropolises*. The largest, most important city of a state, area, or nation.–Paris is the *metropolis* of France.

mew *mews, mewed, mewing*. The noise made by a cat.–The kitten *mewed* when it wanted to be let in.

mews. A group of stables set round a yard, but nowadays also applied to a group of houses built round a yard with an entrance at one end only.–We have some friends with a delightful cottage in a *mews*.

microphone mi′-cro-phone *microphones*. An instrument that changes sound into electricity so that it can be sent out to your radio.–The radio announcer speaks into a *microphone* so that you can hear him.

microscope mi′-cro-scope *microscopes*. A strong magnifying instrument which makes things look many times larger than they really are. Things that cannot be seen at all with the eyes alone can be seen clearly through a *microscope*.

mid. Middle; half-way between the beginning and the end of anything.–In *mid*winter it is very cold.–*Mid*night is 12 o'clock at night.

midday mid′-day. Noon, or the middle of the day.–We eat lunch at *midday*.

middle mid′dle *middles*. 1. The part or point that is the same distance from each end or side.–The teacher told us to fold our papers evenly to make a crease down the *middle*.
2. The centre.–The child who is 'it' stands in the *middle* of the circle.
3. Medium.–The mother bear was the *middle*-sized bear.

midget midg′-et *midgets*. 1. A dwarf or very tiny person. – We saw the *midgets* at the circus.
2. Very small. – Jack drives a *midget* motorcar. It is much smaller than most cars.

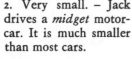

midnight mid′-night *midnights*. The middle of the night, or 12 o'clock at night. A new day begins at *midnight*.

midshipman mid′-ship-man *midshipmen*. A junior naval officer ranking between naval cadet and sub-lieutenant.

midst. Middle.–Mother was in the *midst* of her housework when the bell rang.

midsummer mid-sum′-mer. The middle of the summer.–Today it was as hot as *midsummer*.

midwinter mid-win′-ter. The middle of the winter.–In *midwinter* it is very cold.

might. 1. One form of the word *may*.–Jack *might* have won the race if he had not stumbled.–The teacher said that we *might* have a spelling bee if we wanted to.
2. Strength.–Jack tried with all his *might* to lift the huge stone.

mighty might′-y *mightier, mightiest, mightily*. Very strong.–An elephant is a *mighty* animal.

migrate mi-grate′ *migrates, migrated, migrating*. 1. Go to another place to live. – Many settlers *migrated* to California.
2. Travel to another place.–Birds *migrate* north in spring, and south in autumn. They fly from one part of the country to another part, or to warmer lands.

mileage mile′-age, also *milage*. The number of miles that have been travelled.–What is the *mileage* on Father's car?

mild *milder, mildest, mildly, mildness*. 1. Warm and gentle.–A *mild* wind blew in from the sea.
2. Not strong-tasting. – Father smokes *mild* cigars.
3. Kind and gentle.–Bob has a *mild* disposition.

mildew mil′-dew. A kind of mould, or fungus, that sometimes appears on things left in a damp place.

mile *miles*. A unit of measure equal to 5,280 feet. Long distances are measured by *miles*. –We live 35 *miles* from London.

military mil′-i-tar-y. Having to do with soldiers, war, and the army. *Military* training is training given to soldiers.

milk *milks, milked, milking*. 1. A white liquid food produced by animal mothers to feed their young. Most of the *milk* that we drink comes from cows.
2. Take *milk* from (an animal).–Grandfather *milks* the cows.
3. The white juice of a coconut.

milkman milk′-man *milkmen*. A man who sells or delivers milk.

milkweed milk′-weed *milkweeds.* A weed that has a sticky, white juice in it. *Milkweed* pods are filled with feathery seeds.

mill *mills, milled, milling.* 1. A machine for grinding coffee, corn, or other grains or seeds.
2. A building where grain is ground by a machine.–Grandfather takes his wheat to the *mill.*
3. A factory.–There are many steel *mills* in Pittsburgh.

coffee mill

old flour mill

steel mill

4. Grind.–The miller *mills* the grain.
5. Move about in a disorderly way. – The angry crowd *milled* about the jail.

miller mill′-er *millers.* A person who owns or works at a mill.–The *miller* grinds the grain.

million mil′-lion *millions.* One thousand thousands. 100 = one hundred, 1,000 = one thousand, 1,000,000 = one thousand thousands, or one *million.*

millionaire mil-lion-aire′ *millionaires.* A very rich person, one who has at least one million pounds, dollars, francs, etc.

mimic mim′-ic *mimics, mimicked, mimicking.*
1. One who can do things that others do, in exactly the same way.–Jack is a good *mimic.* He can imitate birds, animals, and different people. He can make his voice sound like theirs.
2. Imitate, particularly in fun.–Jack sometimes *mimics* his *friends.* He makes fun of them by doing things just as they do them.

mince *minces, minced, mincing.* 1. Chop up.– Mother *minced* the onion.
2. Walk with short, careful steps.–Pigeons *mince* along the pavement.

mincemeat mince′-meat. A mixture of dried fruits, spices, sugar, and fat. Mince-pies are filled with *mincemeat.*

mind *minds, minded, minding.* 1. The part of a person that thinks, feels, knows, and guides his actions. If you have a good *mind,* you are intelligent and can learn much.
2. Object.–I do not *mind* if you play the piano while I read. It does not bother me.
3. Take care of. – Mary has to *mind* Baby while Mother is out.
4. Pay attention to.–*Mind* the traffic lights when you cross the street.
5. *On one's mind* means in one's thoughts.– Mary forgot about her homework because she had the film *on her mind.*
6. *In two minds* means undecided.–Mother was *in two minds* about which hat to wear.

mine *mines, mined, mining.* 1. Belonging to me. –This hat is *mine,* not Jack's. I own it.
2. A large hole or tunnel dug into the earth, from which metals or minerals are taken. Coal comes from *mines.*

3. Take out or dig from a *mine.*–The men *mine* copper from the copper *mine.*
4. A bomb which blows up when it is touched or disturbed. *Mines* are placed under water to blow up enemy ships during war. Land *mines* are buried in the ground or hidden in buildings in time of war.

5. Lay or plant *mines* in warfare. – Submarines *mined* the harbour.

M
N
O
P
Q
R
S
T
U
V
W
X
Y
Z

miner min'-er *miners.* A man who works in a mine. *Miners* go underground to dig metals, coal, and other minerals.

mineral min'-er-al *minerals.* I. A substance, such as iron, salt, or gold, that is taken from the earth. Most *minerals* are solids.

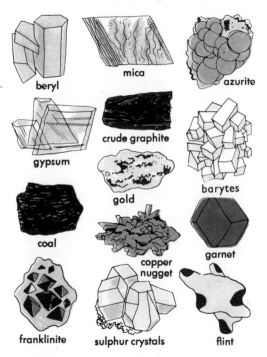

beryl   mica   azurite

gypsum   crude graphite

coal   gold   barytes

franklinite   copper nugget   sulphur crystals   garnet   flint

2. *Mineral* water is water with many *minerals* dissolved in it. It is good to drink.

mingle min'-gle *mingles, mingled, mingling.* Mix.—After the meeting, the Mayor *mingled* with the crowd.

miniature min'-i-a-ture *miniatures.* I. Tiny.—Father made a set of *miniature* furniture for Sally's doll's house.
2. A very small portrait, or other picture.—Inside Mary's locket is a *miniature* of Grandmother as a young girl.

minimum min'-i-mum. The least amount or the smallest number of anything.—The *minimum* age for entering school in our town is four and a half.

minister min'-is-ter *ministers, ministered, ministering.* I. A pastor, preacher, or clergyman. —Our *minister* lives next door to the church.

2. A person who goes to a foreign country to carry on business for his government.
3. In many countries, the head of a particular department of the government is called a *minister.*
4. Serve, look after, attend to.—We had a nurse to *minister* to Grandmother's needs while she was ill.

ministerial min-is-te'-ri-al. A person carrying out the duties of a minister, or a position occupied by a minister. – In the British government, the offices of Home Secretary and President of the Board of Trade are both important *ministerial* posts. – Holding services, preaching sermons and visiting the sick are among the *ministerial* duties of a clergyman.

ministry min'-is-try *ministries.* I. A government department.—There are many *ministries* attached to the government, such as the *Ministry* of Agriculture, the War *Ministry,* the *Ministry* of Transport, etc.
2. The office of a clergyman. – In the nineteenth century, most well-to-do families expected one of their sons to enter the *ministry.*

mink *minks.* A small furry animal that lives in and around the water. Coats made of the brown fur of *minks* are very valuable.

minnow min'-now *minnows.* A very small fish that lives in fresh water. *Minnows* are used for bait to catch larger fish.

minor mi'-nor *minors*. 1. Less important.–Our teacher knows even the *minor* details of Lord Nelson's life, such as what he ate for breakfast.
2. A person who is less than 21 years old is a *minor*.
3. In music, based on the *minor* scale. The major scale goes doh, re, mi, fa, so, la, ti, doh; the *minor* scale goes la, ti, doh, re, mi, fa, so, la. La is the first and the last note of the *minor* scale.

minstrel min'-strel *minstrels*. 1. A man who sings songs and tells jokes in a show called a *minstrel* show.
2. In olden times, a musician who travelled from place to place, playing and singing songs for people.

mint *mints, minted, minting*. 1. A pleasant-smelling plant. The juice of its leaves is used as flavouring. Pepper*mint* and spear*mint* are kinds of *mint* often used to flavour chewing-gum.
2. Make coins.–Many pennies are *minted in* London.
3. A place where coins are made.–Pennies, and all the other coins of the realm, are made at the *mint*.
4. Great amount (of money). – Uncle Joe made a *mint* of money from his business. It has made him rich.

minuet min'-u-et' *minuets*. A slow, dignified dance.–In the eighteenth century, ladies and gentlemen danced the *minuet*.–The music for a *minuet* is also called a *minuet*.

minus mi'-nus. 1. Less.–6 *minus* 2 leaves 4. 2 taken away from 6 leaves 4.–A *minus* sign is a dash used instead of the word *minus*. Example: 6 – 2 = 4.
2. Without. – After the sudden wind had passed, Father found that he was *minus* his hat. His hat was gone.

minute min'-ute *minutes*. 1. A measure of time which equals 60 seconds. Sixty *minutes* make one hour.–From 6 o'clock to 7 o'clock there are 60 *minutes*.
2. A very short time.–Dinner will be ready in a *minute*.
3. A record of what business took place.–Bob kept the *minutes* of the meeting. He wrote down everything that was done at the meeting.

minute mi-nute' *minutely, minuteness*. 1. Very small.–The doctor removed a *minute* splinter of steel from Father's finger.
2. Including every little fact about a thing.–Mary described the play to Sally in *minute* detail.

miracle mir'-a-cle *miracles*. 1. A wonderful thing that happens which cannot be explained by the laws of nature. If the water in a river suddenly turned and flowed uphill, it would be a *miracle*.
2. An extraordinary happening. – It was a *miracle* that no one was hurt in the wreck.

mire *mires, mired, miring*. Mud. – Father's car got stuck in the deep *mire*.

mirage (pronounced *mirarj*) mi-rage' *mirages*. An optical illusion caused by heat. *Mirages* are often seen in deserts, but may also be seen on a flat road in summer.–The men in the desert saw an oasis, but it turned out to be a *mirage*. It was not really there.

mirror mir'-ror *mirrors, mirrored, mirroring*. 1. A looking-glass; a glass in which you can see yourself.–Father looks into a *mirror* while he shaves.

2. Picture or reflect.–The dog crossing the bridge looked into the water and saw himself *mirrored* there, and thought it was another dog.

mirth *mirthful, mirthless*. Merry laughter and fun.–The clown caused much *mirth* at the circus.

miscellaneous mis-cel-la'ne-ous. Of many different kinds.–The teacher's desk is covered with *miscellaneous* things, such as marbles, flowers, books, pencils, and pea-shooters.

mischief mis'-chief. 1. Trouble or damage caused by someone.–Letting air out of car tyres for fun is *mischief*. It is harmful.
2. A person who annoys others by making jokes in talk or actions.–Sally is a little *mischief*.
3. A person who causes harm or trouble.

mischievous mis'-chie-vous *mischievously, mischievousness.* Apt to play pranks and tricks on people.–Bob is a *mischievous* person.

miser mi'-ser *misers.* A person who loves money and saves it just for the sake of having it.–King Midas was a *miser*.

miserable mis'-er-a-ble *miserably.* 1. Unhappy. –The wet, lost puppy looked so *miserable* that Mother said we might keep him.
2. Bad or unpleasant.–The weather was so *miserable* that we were glad to play indoors.

misery mis'-er-y *miseries.* 1. Suffering and un-happiness.–War causes terrible *misery*.
2. Wretched surroundings.–Many families live in *misery* in time of war.

misfortune mis-for'-tune *misfortunes.* 1. Bad luck.–I had the *misfortune* to lose my brace-let.
2. Unlucky happenings or accidents.–The story-book hero met with many *misfortunes* before he found the magic city.

miss *misses, missed, missing.* 1. Fail to do some-thing.–Bob *missed* the first ball. He failed to hit it.–I went to meet Father at the station, but I *missed* him. I didn't find him.
2. Fail to catch.–The traveller *missed* the boat. He was too late to get on the boat be-fore it sailed.
3. Lose.–Mary *missed* only one day of school all the year. She was absent only one day.
4. Feel lonely for.–We *miss* Mother when she goes away. We wish that she were with us.
5. Notice an absence, see that someone is gone.–Baby *misses* Mother at once when she leaves the room.

Miss *Misses.* A title given to a girl or woman who is not married.–My teacher's name is *Miss* Smith.

missile mis'-sile *missiles.* Something that can be thrown or shot.–A stone is a *missile* which can be shot from a catapult.–Modern sci-entists build guided *missiles* and rockets which can reach the moon.

missing miss'-ing. Gone, no longer in place.–Mary counted her books and found that one was *missing*. She had had six books. Now she has only five.

mission mis'-sion *missions.* 1. A special errand or job.–The government sent out a *mission* of experts to study farming conditions in other countries.

2. A settlement to help poor or uncivilized people.–Many *missions* were set up in Africa and Asia to educate the natives and convert them to Christianity.

missionary mis'-sion-a-ry *missionaries.* A person sent on a mission.–The *missionaries* taught the natives to read.

mis-spell mis-spell' *mis-spells, mis-spelt, mis-spelling.* Spell wrong.–Look up your words in the dictionary so that you will not *mis-spell* them.

mist *mists, misted, misting.* 1. Fog.–The air is sometimes filled with *mist* before sunrise. Very fine drops of water in the air make it look grey.
2. A fine rain.–A *mist* is falling.
3. Cloud.–The sky *misted* over.

mistake mis-take' *mistakes, mistook, mistaken, mistaking.* 1. An error.–Mary made one *mis-take* in the spelling test. She spelt one word the wrong way.
2. Mix up; confuse.–Our teacher often *mis-takes* one of the twins for the other. She often thinks Ted is Bill. She calls them by the wrong names.
3. A bad idea. – It is a *mistake* to start for school too late. It is the wrong thing to do.

mistaken mis-tak'-en *mistakenly.* Wrong.–Bob was *mistaken* about the score of the football match. He thought the score was 6 to 2. It was really 5 to 2.

Mister Mis'-ter. A title used before a man's name. It is usually written *Mr.*–Our post-man's name is *Mr* Brown.

mistletoe mis'-tle-toe. An evergreen plant that has white berries that look like wax. *Mistletoe* lives on or clings to trees. It does not grow from the ground. We hang *mistletoe* in the door-way at Christmas time. Anyone who stands under the *mistletoe* is kissed.

mistress mis'-tress *mistresses.* A woman who is in charge, as a *mistress* of a household.–A school-*mistress* is a school-teacher. She has charge of the class.

misty mist'-y *mistily, mistiness*. 1. Foggy. – It is a *misty* morning.
2. Covered with mist.–The windscreen of Father's car is *misty*.

mite *mites*. 1. Anything very small; a tiny amount.
2. A very small child.–Baby is just a *mite*.

mitre mi'-tre *mitres*. A tall linen head-dress worn by a bishop. A *mitre* is shaped at the back and front like a steep arch, and is divided by a deep cleft.

mitten mit'-ten *mittens*. A covering for the hand that has a part for the thumb by itself and another part for all the other fingers.

mix *mixes, mixed, mixing*. 1. Stir together.–We make hot chocolate by *mixing* hot milk and cocoa.
2. Join, mingle.–The stranger did not *mix* with the other people at the party. He wasn't friendly.
3. Confuse.–Sally gets *mixed* up when she tries to find east and west.

mixer mix'-er *mixers*. 1. A device that mixes things.–Mother has an electric *mixer* to beat the dough for her when she makes cakes.
2. A person who mixes. –Mary is a good *mixer*. She gets on well with any group of people.

mixture mix'-ture *mixtures*. Anything made by mixing or stirring several things together. Fudge is a *mixture* of sugar, chocolate, and milk.

moan *moans, moaned, moaning*. 1. A low, sad sound, a sound of pain.–The wounded soldier's *moans* stopped when the doctor had dressed his injury.
2. Make sad sounds.–In the winter the wind *moans* in the trees.
3. Complain.–The old man *moans* about everything.

moat *moats*. A large ditch dug round a castle,

a fort, or a town, to protect it from enemies.

mob *mobs, mobbed, mobbing*. 1. A crowd of people who are so excited that they will do things without thinking.
2. Gather angrily about.–The boys *mobbed* the umpire when he gave the batsman out.

moccasin moc'-ca-sin *moccasins*. A soft leather shoe or sandal.–American Indians wore *moccasins* sewn by hand from pieces of leather.

mock *mocks, mocked, mocking*. 1. Make fun of. –The actor *mocks* famous people by trying to do things the way they do them. He ridicules them by imitating them.
2. Make-believe.–A *mock* bull fight is not real.

mockery mock'-e-ry *mockeries*. 1. Scornful laughter.–Jack teased Jane all morning until she cried at his *mockery*.
2. A poor imitation.–The understudy's performance was a *mockery* of the fine acting of the star.

mode *modes*. 1. A way or manner.–People of different parts of the world have different *modes* of life. They have different customs and habits.
2. The way a thing is being done at a certain time; the fashion.–The *mode* of wearing the hair was quite different when Mother was a girl.

model mod'-el *models, modelled, modelling*.
1. Worth trying to be like.–Bob is a *model* student.
2. A small copy.–Bob makes *model* aircraft.
3. A pattern from which something is made. –*Models* for statues are often made of clay and then copied in stone.
4. Shape or make.–Mary *modelled* an ashtray for Father out of clay.
5. A style.–Jack's car is a recent *model*.
6. A person in a shop who wears clothes owned by the shop, to show them to customers.
7. A person who poses for an artist or photographer to have his picture made, often for advertisements.

moderate mod'-er-ate *moderately*. 1. Medium. –Jack's father gets a *moderate* salary. It is neither large nor small.
2. Not extreme; neither very much nor very little.–Mother likes *moderate* styles. She doesn't like clothes to be very noticeable.– Jack drank a *moderate* amount of milk. He drank enough, but not a lot.

modern mod'-ern. 1. Existing now; not known in earlier times; recently made or discovered. –Electric refrigerators, aircraft, and radios are *modern* inventions.
2. Having the ideas, the manners, and the habits that most people of today have.

modernize mod'-ern-ize *modernizes, modernized, modernizing*. Make or bring up to date. –The encyclopedia was first published 30 years ago. The editors have *modernized* it so as to include recent events.

modest mod'-est *modestly, modesty*. Not vain or conceited, not thinking too highly of oneself.–Bob is *modest*. He doesn't boast even when he does things well.

modicum mod'-i-cum. A very small amount.– Mother expects a *modicum* of comfort when she stays at a hotel. She just needs a bed, a wash-basin, a cupboard and a chest of drawers.

modify mod'-i-fy *modifies, modified, modifying*. 1. Describe or add to the meaning of.– One word sometimes *modifies* another. 'We live in a white house.' The word white *modifies* or describes the house spoken of.
2. Change.–Jack decided to *modify* the design of his model aeroplane. He decided to give it one set of wings instead of two.

modulate mod'-u-late *modulates, modulated, modulating*. In music, to change from one key to another.–This tune is delightful; it has a strong rhythm and is well *modulated*.

mohair mo'-hair. The fine hair of the Angora goat; the wool made from the hair or an imitation made of wool and cotton.–Mother has been given a lovely *mohair* shawl.

moist. Damp or slightly wet. – Grandmother keeps the soil round her ferns *moist*.

moisten (pronounced *moyssen*) mois'-ten *moistens, moistened, moistening.* Dampen; make slightly wet. – Mother *moistens* the clothes before she irons them.

moisture mois'-ture. Dampness or wetness.– The *moisture* in the cellar caused mildew to form on the things stored there.

molar mo'-lar *molars*. Any of the broad, flat teeth in the back of the mouth.

molasses mo-las'-ses. A thick, dark syrup that comes from sugar cane.–*Molasses* is sweet and slightly bitter.

mole *moles*. 1. A spot on the skin. Most *moles* are brown.
2. A little, soft, furry animal that lives under the ground and digs tunnels. *Moles* cannot see well.

molecule mol'-e-cule *molecules*. A very small particle of matter.

moment mo'-ment *moments*. A very short time. –My work will be done in a *moment*.

monarch mon'-arch *monarchs*. A ruler, such as a king or queen.

Monday Mon'-day *Mondays*. The second day of the week; the day after Sunday. – Our school week starts on *Monday*.

money mon'-ey. 1. Pieces of metal or printed paper notes of agreed value, issued by a government and used in buying and selling.–He saved his *money* so that he could buy a motor-car.
2. Wealth.–Uncle Joe is a very rich man; he has a great deal of *money*.

mongrel mon'-grel *mongrels*. A dog with parents of different breeds. – Jack's dog is a *mongrel*. He is part terrier and part bulldog.

monitor mon'-i-tor. *monitors*. Someone chosen to help and see that certain things are done.– The teacher told the *monitors* to pass out the books.

monk *monks*. A man who belongs to a religious group of men who live by themselves, usually in a building called a monastery.

monkey mon'-key *monkeys, monkeyed, monkeying*. 1. A tree-climbing animal with a long tail, and paws that look something like a man's hands. – The children watched the *monkeys* at the zoo.

2. Play or fool.–It is dangerous to *monkey* with fire.

monogram mon'-o-gram *monograms.* Initials put together to make a design. –Mother embroidered Tom's *monogram* on his handkerchief.

monoplane mon'-o-plane *monoplanes.* An aeroplane with only one set of wings.

monotone mon'-o-tone *monotones, monotonous.* An unchanging tone of voice. – The boy recited in a *monotone.* His tone of voice was always the same.

monotonous mo-not'-o-nous. Repetitive and boring.–Mary found the story *monotonous.* It was too long and unvaried.

monsoon mon-soon' *monsoons.* A wind blowing from the Indian Ocean twice a year, and the rainy season which it ushers in from June to September.–The mountaineers wanted to climb the mountain before the *monsoon* started.

monster mon'-ster *monsters.* 1. A very large or unusual animal.–A dog as big as a horse would be a *monster.*
2. A very cruel and dreadful animal or person.–The dragons in fairy tales are *monsters.* –Bluebeard was a *monster.*

monstrous mon'-strous *monstrously.* 1. Enormous, gigantic.–The whale is a mammal with a *monstrous* body.
2. Terribly or shockingly bad.–The judge said that the prisoner was accused of a *monstrous* crime.

month *months.* A measure of time.–Twelve *months* make a year.

monthly month'-ly *monthlies.* 1. Once each month.–We pay our rent *monthly.*
2. A publication put out once each month.– Some magazines are *monthlies.*

monument mon'-u-ment *monuments.* Something built or set aside to make people remember a great person or happening.–The citizens built a *monument* in honour of the victory.

mood *moods.* The way one feels in one's mind–happy, sad, merry, etc.–Baby is in a playful *mood.*

moon *moons.* The *moon* is a heavenly body nearer the earth than any of the stars or planets. It goes round the earth. The *moon* appears to shine because the sun is shining on it.

crescent moon quarter moon gibbous moon full moon

moonlight moon'-light. 1. Light from the moon. –Sometimes the *moonlight* shines in our bedroom window.
2. Bright with light from the moon.–We went swimming on a *moonlight* night.

moor *moors, moored, mooring.* 1. Fasten or tie (a boat).–Bob keeps his boat *moored* to the dock.
2. A stretch of waste land, often heather-covered, especially in England or Scotland.

moose. A large animal of the deer family, common to North America.

mop *mops, mopped, mopping.* 1. A sponge or bunch of pieces of wool tied together at one end and fastened to a handle to use for cleaning.
2. Wash with a *mop.*–Ann *mops* the hall floor twice a week.

moral mor'-al *morals.* 1. The lesson of a story or fable.–The *moral* of the story is: Don't ask for help unless you really need it.
2. An idea of right and wrong.–A person's *morals* are his beliefs as to what is right and what is wrong.
3. Concerned with right and wrong. – A *moral* person is a good person, one who lives by the standards of right and wrong set up by civilized people.

morale mo-rale'. The way people feel about the life they are leading.–If the *morale* of a school is high, it means that the pupils are interested, satisfied, and proud of their school.

more. 1. A larger amount or number.–Two pounds is *more* than one pound.–Bob ate *more* apples than I did. He ate three and I ate two.
2. To a greater extent or degree.–Bob writes *more* easily than Bill.

moreover more-o′-ver. Further; besides; in addition to what has been said.–Mary didn't wish to go to the show; *moreover*, she didn't have enough money.

morning morn′-ing *mornings*. The first half of the day.–*Morning* ends at 12 o'clock noon.

morning glory morn′-ing glo′-ry *morning glories*. A climbing vine with flowers of many colours that blossom in the morning.

morsel mor′-sel *morsels*. A tiny piece.–Not even a *morsel* of food was left.

mortal mor′-tal *mortals, mortally*. 1. Certain to die some day.–All men are *mortal*.
2. Causing death. – Sir Lancelot gave the dragon a *mortal* wound.
3. A human being. – *Mortals* cannot know everything.

mortar mor′-tar *mortars*. 1. A mixture of cement, lime, sand, and water.–Bricks used in building houses are held together with *mortar*.
2. A strong bowl in which to pound materials into a powder. –The chemist uses a *mortar*.

mortgage mort′-gage *mortgages*. A written agreement to give up one's property if money borrowed is not paid back when due.

mosquito mos-qui′-to *mosquitoes*. A small flying insect. The female *mosquito* bites.

moss *mosses*. A mass of tiny, green plants. *Moss* grows on trees, rocks, and the ground. It is soft and velvety.

mossy moss′-y *mossier, mossiest*. Covered with moss.–The ground under the trees is *mossy*.

most. 1. The greatest number or amount.–Bob solved the *most* problems. He solved more than anyone else in the class.
2. Almost all; more than half.–Baby drank *most* of her milk.

3. To the greatest extent or degree.–Bill runs quickly, Jack runs more quickly than Bill, and Bob runs *most* quickly of all.

mostly most′-ly. Almost all,, chiefly.–The stories in Sally's book are *mostly* fairy tales.

moth *moths*. An insect that looks something like a butterfly. The tiny worms from which some *moths* come eat holes in woollen things.

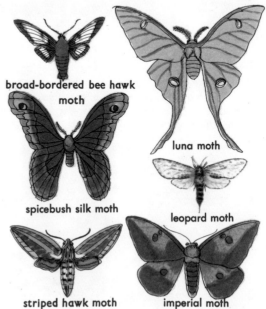

broad-bordered bee hawk moth

luna moth

spicebush silk moth

leopard moth

striped hawk moth

imperial moth

mother moth′-er *mothers, mothered, mothering*. 1. A woman who has a child or children. –Your parents are your *mother* and father.
2. Care for.–Mary likes to *mother* Baby.
3. Any female animal that has young.–The calf gets milk from its *mother*.

mother-in-law moth′-er-in-law *mothers-in-law*. The mother of one's husband or one's wife.– Grandmother is Father's mother. She is Mother's *mother-in-law*.

motherly moth′-er-ly. Like a mother; kind and sympathetic.–Our teacher is *motherly*.

motion mo′-tion *motions, motioned, motioning*.
1. Movement.–Every *motion* that the dancer made was beautiful.
2. Make a movement or signal to show what is meant.–Bob *motioned* to us with his hand to tell us to hurry.
3. A suggestion to be voted on.–Mary proposed a *motion* that we should have a party.
4. *In motion* means moving.–Never open the door of a car that is *in motion*.

motionless mo′-tion-less. Without moving.– The dog will fall down and lie *motionless* when Jack orders him to play dead.

M
N
O
P
Q
R
S
T
U
V
W
X
Y
Z

motion picture mo′-tion pic′-ture *motion pictures*. A film; a series of pictures that a appear to move when projected or shown rapidly, one after the other, on a screen.

motor mo′-tor *motors, motored, motoring*. 1. An engine; a machine that makes other machinery work.–Our washing machine is run by an electric *motor*.–A motor-car is run by a petrol *motor*.

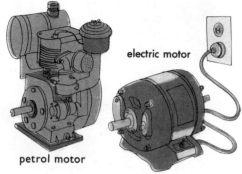

electric motor

petrol motor

2. Travel by motor-car.–We *motored* to Newcastle.

motor-boat mo′-tor-boat *motor-boats*. A boat run by a motor.

motor-cycle mo′-tor-cy-cle *motor-cycles*. A heavy bicycle run by a motor. – Mr Jones rides a *motor-cycle* and takes part in races.

motorist mo′-tor-ist *motorists*. A person travelling in a motor-car.–On Sundays, there are many *motorists* on the road.

motorway mo′-tor-way *motorways*. A main road or highway.–The traffic is very fast on the new *motorway*.

motto mot′-to *mottoes*. A short saying meant to guide one's actions.–Bob's *motto* is, 'If at first you don't succeed, try, try, again.'

mound *mounds*. A small round pile or hump.– Sally made a *mound* of sand in the sand pit.

mount *mounts, mounted, mounting*. 1. Climb up or upon.–Sally *mounted* the stairs to go to bed.–Bob *mounted* the horse and rode off. 2. A horse to ride.–Bob's *mount* was a beautiful black horse. 3. Go up or rise.–The temperature usually *mounts* at midday. 4. A mountain.–*Mount* Everest is the tallest mountain in the world.

mountain moun′-tain *mountains, mountainous*. A very high hill.–The *mountains* are capped with snow.

mounting mount′-ing *mountings*. Anything upon which something is set or fixed.–Bob's butterflies were pinned on a black velvet *mounting*.

mourn *mourns, mourned, mourning*. Grieve or sorrow for.–The people *mourned* the death of Queen Victoria.

mouse *mice*. A little animal, usually grey but sometimes brownish grey or even white, that lives in people's houses, in barns, or in the fields of woods.

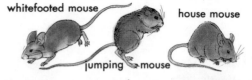

whitefooted mouse

house mouse

jumping mouse

moustache mous-tache′ *moustaches*. The hair that grows just above a man's mouth. Grandfather has a black *moustache*.

mouth *mouths*. 1. The opening in a person's face through which he eats, speaks, or makes sounds. –Your tongue and teeth are in your *mouth*.

2. The *mouth* of a cave is the opening where one enters.–The *mouth* of a river is the part where the river flows into the sea.

mouthful mouth'-ful *mouthfuls*. As much as the mouth will hold.–Jack could not answer the telephone, because he had a *mouthful* of cake.

movable mov'-a-ble. Able to be moved.–Most furniture is *movable*. It can be taken from place to place.

move *moves, moved, moving*. 1. Change the position of.–Father *moved* the sofa.
2. Change position.–When Jack's dog plays dead, he lies without *moving*.
3. Go; be in motion.–Sally's tortoise *moves* slowly.
4. Set in motion. – The water in the river *moves* the logs.
5. Go to live.–We expect to *move* to the city soon.
6. Cause strong feeling, such as sadness, happiness, etc.–The people were *moved* by the play. It made them sad.
7. Make a resolution or suggestion.–The city council *moved* to build a new playground.

movement move'-ment *movements*. 1. A moving or change from one place or position to another.–The *movements* that help most to make Baby strong are kicking and crawling. –When we go hiking we write home regularly to let our parents know our *movements*.
2. A united effort by many people to bring about a certain thing.–There is a *movement* in town for more playgrounds.
3. Part of a long musical composition.–Most symphonies have four *movements*.

moving staircase mov'-ing stair'-case *moving staircases*. A flight of steps on a moving belt to carry people up or down. It is also called an escalator.

mow *mows, mowed* or *mown, mowing*. Cut down.–Bob will *mow* the grass with the lawn-mower.

mower mow'-er *mowers*. A machine for cutting hay, grass, weeds, or the like.

Mr A short way to write *Mister*. *Mr* is used before a man's name as a title.–*Mr* Brown came to see us.

Mrs (pronounced *missiz*). A short way of writing *Mistress*. *Mrs* is used before the name of a married woman.–*Mrs* Brown is the wife of Mr Brown.

much *more, most*. 1. A great quantity or amount.–*Much* milk is sold each day.
2. *Too much* means more than is needed.– Some people talk *too much*.
3. *How much* means what amount. – *How much* pocket-money do you get?

mud. Wet, sticky earth.–Our car got stuck in the *mud*.

muddle mud'-dle *muddles, muddled, muddling*.
1. A mess. – Mary got her arithmetic in a *muddle*. She got it all confused and mixed up.
2. Confuse; mix up.–Jack got *muddled* trying to find his way home in the dark.

muddy mud'-dy *muddier, muddiest*. 1. Covered with mud.–The cat's feet were *muddy*.
2. Having mud in it.–The water from the old well was *muddy*.

muff *muffs, muffed, muffing*. 1. A soft tube made of fur or other warm material into which women put their hands to keep them warm.
2. Fail to catch.–The fielder *muffed* the ball and lost the game.
3. Do anything badly; miss an opportunity. –Bill *muffed* his chance to join the team by not coming to practise.

muffin muf'fin *muffins*. A light flat cake, toasted, buttered and eaten hot.

muffle muf'-fle *muffles, mufflled, muffling*. 1. Cover up to silence or make quieter.–Mother *muffled* the telephone so that it would not wake the baby if it rang.
2. Make low and stifled.–Jack's voice sounded *muffled* from beneath the bedclothes.
3. Wrap in warm coverings. – Mother was *muffled* up in a warm coat.

muffler muf'-fler *mufflers*. 1. A scarf. – Grandfather wears a *muffler* about his neck to keep it warm.

2. Something that deadens sounds.–A piano has a felt pad called a *muffler* between the hammers and the strings.

mug *mugs*. A tall drinking cup with a handle.

mulberry mul'-ber-ry *mulberries*. 1. A tree that has dark purple berries on it called *mulberries*.

2. A dark, reddish-blue colour.

mule *mules*. 1. An animal which is half horse and half donkey.—*Mules* are used as work animals.

2. A flat house slipper without any covering for the heel.
3. A spinning machine.

multiplicand mul-ti-pli-cand'. In arithmetic, the number that is multiplied or taken a certain number of times.—In 2 times 6 equals 12, 6 is the *multiplicand*.

multiplication mul-ti-pli-ca'-tion. A short way of adding.—6 times 2 or 2 taken 6 times equals 12. This is *multiplication*, or a short way of adding six 2's together.

multiplier mul'-ti-pli-er. In multiplication, the number by which one multiplies.—In 2 times 6 equals 12, 2 is the *multiplier*. It tells that 6 is taken 2 times.

multiply mul'-ti-ply *multiplies, multiplied, multiplying*. 1. Take a number a certain number of times in multiplication.—Two *multiplied* by 6 equals 12.
2. Increase in number.—Rabbits *multiply* fast. They have baby rabbits often and in large numbers.

multitude mul'-ti-tude *multitudes*. A very great number (of persons or things).—A *multitude* of people came to the last game of the year. Every seat in the stands was taken.

mum. Silent.—The captured spy kept *mum*. He did not tell anything.

mumble mum'-ble *mumbles, mumbled, mumbling*. Speak so that it is hard to be understood; speak with the mouth partly closed.—The toothless old man *mumbles*. He doesn't talk clearly.

mummy mum'-my *mummies*. The dead body of a person that has been preserved, or kept from decaying.—Many *mummies* are found in Egypt.

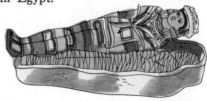

mumps. A disease which causes glands in the face and neck to swell.—Do not go to school if you have the *mumps*. Other children may get the *mumps* if you go near them.

munch *munches, munched, munching*. Chew.—Bob likes to *munch* an apple while he takes a walk.

municipal mu-nic'-i-pal. Having to do with the laws or affairs of a city or town.—The *municipal* buildings, the buildings in which city business is carried on, are in West Street.

munitions mu-ni'-tions. Guns, bombs, and other materials used in war. A *munitions* factory is a factory where war supplies are made.

murder mur'-der *murders, murdered, murdering*. 1. An unlawful killing of a person.
2. Kill unlawfully.—The gangster *murdered* the man who betrayed him.

murderer mur'-der-er *murderers*. One who kills unlawfully.—The *murderer* said that he had planned the killing of his victim beforehand.

murmur mur'-mur *murmurs, murmured, murmuring*. 1. A soft low sound; soft, low talking.—We could hear the *murmur* of the running brook outside the tent.
2. Talk too low to be understood.—Do not *murmur*; speak clearly.
3. Grumble and complain in an undertone.—The children *murmured* against the teacher for keeping them in.

muscle mus'-cle *muscles*. The cord-like tissues in the body of a person or animal that move the body and the parts of the body. Exercise makes the *muscles* strong.

M
N
O
P
Q
R
S
T
U
V
W
X
Y
Z

museum mu-se′-um *museums.* A building where interesting objects of art or science, such as paintings, machines, stuffed animals, etc., are arranged for public exhibition.–We saw a fossil at the Natural History *Museum.*

mush *mushy.* Anything that is soft and thick and wet. – Mother cooked the apples to a *mush* to make apple purée.

mushroom mush′-room *mushrooms, mushroomed, mushrooming.* 1. An edible fungus that grows in fields and is also cultivated for the market. *Mushrooms* grow very rapidly.– Bob got up early to go *mushrooming.*
2. Anything shaped like a *mushroom.*–Mother darns socks with a wooden *mushroom.*
3. Grow rapidly. A new town *mushroomed.*

music mu′-sic. 1. Pleasing sounds made by singing voices or musical instruments. – Pianos, violins, and many other instruments make *music.*
2. Written notes or signs which, when played or sung, make pleasing sounds.

3. Any sounds that are pleasing to listen to. –We camped where we could hear the *music* of the waterfall.

musical mu′-si-cal *musically.* 1. Having to do with music, or the art of putting pleasing sounds together.–Pianos, violins, organs, and harps are *musical* instruments. They make music when we play them.–Mary is receiving a *musical* education. She takes piano lessons and singing lessons.
2. Fond of music, or having a talent for music. –Mary is *musical.* She enjoys music. Learning music is easy for her.
3. Sweet and pleasant (of sounds).–The wind in the pine trees makes a *musical* sound.

musician mu-si′-cian *musicians.* A person who sings, or plays some musical instrument; also, one who earns his living by making music.

musket mus′-ket *muskets.* An old-fashioned gun, light enough to be fired from the shoulder.

musketeer mus′-ket-eer *musketeers.* A soldier armed with a musket.–Boys of many generations have enjoyed reading the famous novel by Dumas called 'The Three *Musketeers.*'

muslin mus′-lin. A fine, closely woven cotton cloth. Sheets and pillow cases are made of *muslin.* Thin *muslin* is often used for dresses.

mussel mus′-sel *mussels.* One of several kinds of molluscs found both in the sea and in fresh water. The sea variety can be eaten and is used as a bait for fish.–There is a famous Irish ballad called 'Cockles and *Mussels*'.

must. 1. Have to; be obliged or required to.– Most people *must* work in order to live.
2. Should.–We *must* hurry.
3. Surely or certainly is, am, or are. – Your mother *must* be happy over your good marks.
4. The unfermented juice of the grape.

mustard mus′-tard. A plant that has hard seeds which are ground and used for flavouring. Ground *mustard* seeds are mixed with water to make English *mustard,* or with vinegar to make French *mustard.*

muster mus′-ter *musters, mustered, mustering.* 1. Assemble or call together.–We had difficulty in *mustering* 11 fit boys for the cricket match.
2. An assembly or parade. – The *muster* of soldiers was incomplete. There were a number away sick.

mustn't. Must not.–You *mustn't* cross the street without first looking both ways.

musty mus′-ty *mustier, mustiest.* Mouldy; having an odour or taste like that of something rotting.–The old house which had been shut up smelled *musty.*

mute *mutes, mutely, muteness.* 1. Silent.–The witness remained *mute.* He didn't say a word.
2. A person who is not able to talk.

mutiny mu′-ti-ny *mutinies.* Rebelling against authority.–The captain's cruelty to the sailors caused a *mutiny.*

M
N
O
P
Q
R
S
T
U
V
W
X
Y
Z

mutter mut′-ter *mutters, muttered, muttering.* Speak in a low voice that cannot be understood.–As the angry boy went away, we heard him *muttering* to himself.

mutton mut′-ton. The flesh or meat of a sheep. –We had *mutton* broth for dinner.

muzzle muz′-zle *muzzles, muzzled, muzzling.*

1. The nose and jaws of an animal.

2. A covering made of straps for the nose and jaws.–Jack puts a *muzzle* on his dog to keep him from biting people.

3. Put a *muzzle* on.–He *muzzles* his dog before taking him for a walk.

4. End or mouth (of a gun). – The man looked into the *muzzle* of the gun without flinching.

my. Of or belonging to me. The word shows that something belongs to me. – This is *my* kitten. She belongs to me. I am her owner.

myrrh (pronounced *murr*). A gum used in perfumery and in some medicines.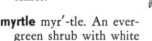

myrtle myr′-tle. An evergreen shrub with white or blue flowers. The berries and the oil made from the leaves are used in medicines.

myself my-self′. 1. My very self, me.–I can dress *myself*.–I have enough money to pay for *myself* at the cinema.

2. Even I.–I *myself* can solve this problem, though I am not good at arithmetic.

mysterious mys-te′-ri-ous *mysteriously.* Strange and not understood; hard to explain.–The loss of the teacher's glasses is very *mysterious*. It is very strange how they disappeared. –Mother saw a *mysterious* man watching our house. She did not know who he was or why he was there.

mystery mys′-ter-y *mysteries.* 1. A deep secret or problem.–What could have happened to the lost ball was a *mystery* to Bill.

2. A detective story; a tale of strange events which are explained in the end.–Father likes to read *mysteries*.

myth *myths.* A very old legend or story, often an attempt to explain natural events, like the weather, the seasons, etc.–Long ago people explained the rising and setting of the sun by a *myth* that the sun god, Apollo, drove his horses across the sky each day.

mythology my-thol′-o-gy *mythologies.* All the myths or stories of a race of people.–Greek *mythology* is all the myths of the Greeks.– Roman *mythology* is all the myths of the Romans.

N n

N, n *N's, n's.* The 14th letter of the alphabet.

nab *nabs, nabbed, nabbing.* Suddenly catch or seize.–The policeman *nabbed* the thief as he ran out of the door.

nag *nags, nagged, nagging.* 1. Continually scold and find fault with.–Some parents *nag* their children.

2. A horse, especially a worn-out one.–The old *nag* could hardly pull the wagon.

nail *nails, nailed, nailing.* 1. One of the hard scales on the ends of your fingers and toes. Finger*nails* protect the ends of your fingers and help you to pick up small things.

2. A slender, smooth piece of metal, pointed at one end and flat at the other.–*Nails* are hammered into boards to hold them together.

3. Fasten by hammering *nails* into.–Father *nailed* the top of the box on.

naked na′-ked *nakedly, nakedness.* Unclothed; bare.–Baby walked out into the living-room *naked*. She had nothing on.

name *names, named, naming.* 1. The word a person or a thing is known by.–The *name* of the thing you sleep in is a bed.–The *name* of the things you wear on your feet is shoes.– Spot is the *name* of Jack's dog.–Jack's *name* is Jack–Plymouth is the *name* of a city.

2. Give a *name* to.–Jack *named* his dog Spot.

3. A reputation.–The mayor made a good *name* for himself. He did good things for the people. People spoke well of him.–The dishonest boy made a bad *name* for himself. People spoke badly of him.

4. Mention or say. – The man told Jack to *name* the amount of money he wanted for his bicycle.

5. Choose or appoint.–The *class* named Mary for the part of Snow White.

6. Mention by *name*. – The school magazine *named* the cricket team.

namesake name'-sake *namesakes*. A person or thing named after another. John Smith, the butcher, is my *namesake*. Although we are not related, we both have the same nome – we are both John Smith.

nap *naps, napped, napping*. 1. A short sleep.– Baby takes a *nap* each afternoon.

2. Take a short *nap*.–Grandmother was *napping* in her rocking chair.

3. The short, woolly thread-ends that stand up like hairs on rugs and woollen cloth. – Baby likes to dig her toes into the soft *nap* on the rug.

napkin nap'-kin *napkins*. A square or oblong piece of cloth or paper which is used at the table to wipe your mouth and fingers while eating. You should keep your *napkin* on your lap while at the table.

narcissus nar-cis'-sus *narcissuses* or *narcissi*. A fragrant yellow and white flower that blossoms early in the spring. *Narcissuses* grow from bulbs instead of seeds.

narrow nar'-row *narrows, narrowed, narrowing*. 1. Not far across; not wide.–We went in single file down the *narrow* lane because it was not wide enough for two.

2. Close.–The child playing in the street had a *narrow* escape. He was nearly hit by a bus. –We are ahead in the game by a *narrow* margin. Our score is 18 and their score is 16.

3. Become less wide. – The mountain road *narrows* between the cliffs.

4. *Narrow-minded* means not able to see or understand things beyond the little that one already knows or believes. – The *narrow-minded* man would not listen to other people's ideas.

nasal na'-sal. Having to do with the nose. *Nasal* diseases are diseases of the nose. *Nasal* tones are tones that are made through the nose.

nasturtium nas-tur'-tium *nasturtiums*. A trailing plant with yellow or orange flowers and round, pungent leaves.

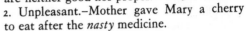

nasty nas'-ty *nastier, nastiest*. 1. So dirty that it displeases people. *Nasty* thoughts are evil thoughts, thoughts that are neither good nor proper.

2. Unpleasant.–Mother gave Mary a cherry to eat after the *nasty* medicine.

nation na'-tion *nations*. A country in which the people live under one government. The people of a *nation* usually speak a common language and have similar customs.–Sweden is a *nation*. The people speak the same language and live under one government.

national na'-tion-al *nationals, nationally*. 1. Anything that belongs to or is related to a nation.–The *national* anthem of Great Britain is 'God Save the Queen.' It is the country's song.

2. A citizen of a nation.–Jack's uncle, who lives in Canada, is a Canadian *national*.

nationality na-tion-al'-i-ty *nationalities*. Marie is French. Her *nationality* is French. She lives in France.–Of what *nationality* are you? To what nation do you belong?

native na'-tive *natives*. 1. A person is a *native* of the place in which he was born.–Bob is a *native* of Great Britain. He was born in Great Britain.–Jack is a *native* of Glasgow, Scotland. He was born there.

2. Having had one's beginning or origin in a certain place.–Plants and animals are *native* to the place in which they were first found.– The zebra is *native* to Africa.

3. A person living in an uncivilized place is sometimes spoken of as a *native*.

natural nat'-u-ral *naturally, naturalness*. 1. In the original state; not changed.–Mother has a table of *natural* wood. The wood has not been painted or changed in any way.

2. Coming as a matter of course, without teaching or training.–It is *natural* for Mary to sing. It is easy for her.

3. To be expected.–It is *natural* that Jack should want to do everything Bob can do.

naturalist nat'-u-ral-ist *naturalists*. A person who studies plants and animals.

naturalize nat'-u-ral-ize *naturalizes, naturalized, naturalizing.* Give a person from a foreign country the right of citizenship in another country after he has lived up to certain rules. – Jack's grandfather was *naturalized* in 1900. He was born in France, and became a British subject in 1900 after living here for several years.

naturally nat'-u-ral-ly. 1. By nature.–Tom is *naturally* good at arithmetic. Arithmetic has always been easy for him.
2. Without affecting or pretending anything. –Sally talks *naturally*. She doesn't try to copy or imitate anyone.
3. Of course.–It started to snow; so *naturally*, we wore our galoshes.

nature na'-ture. 1. The whole world that we live in.–We live our whole life in *nature*.
2. Those parts of the world that have not been changed by man, especially the outdoors and its animal life.–Bob is fond of *nature*. He likes the woods and fields, the wild animals, the moon, the stars, and the sky.
3. All the traits that make a person or thing do certain things or behave in a certain way. –It is the *nature* of fish to swim.
4. Disposition or temper.–Ned has a gentle *nature*.

naught. Nothing. – Bob's suggestion was all for *naught*; for Jack did not follow it.

naughty naugh'-ty *naughtier, naughtiest, naughtily, naughtiness.* Bad in little ways; mischievous.–Do not be *naughty*. Obey your mother.

nauseate nau'-se-ate *nauseates, nauseated, nauseating.* Make sick in the stomach.–Do not eat too much fudge. It may *nauseate* you.

naval na'-val. Having to do with the navy.– *Naval* officers serve in the navy.

navigate nav'-i-gate *navigates, navigated, navigating, navigation.* 1. Steer or manage a boat, ship, or aeroplane.–Jack *navigated* the canoe down the river very expertly.
2. Sail over.–The captain *navigates* the seas.
3. Use a compass and other instruments to tell where a ship or aeroplane is at a certain time.–Aeroplanes that fly across the ocean carry an officer whose duty is to *navigate*.

navigator nav'-i-ga-tor *navigators.* An officer on a ship or aeroplane who keeps track of where the craft is.

navy na'-vy *navies.* An armed force which defends a nation at sea. Warships and aircraft are a *navy's* chief weapons.

nay. No.–*Nay* is an old-fashioned word used in stories and poems.

near *nearer, nearest, nears, neared, nearing.*
1. Not far away from; close to. – Grandmother's house is *near* ours.
2. Not far off in time.–The opening of school is *near*. – It is too *near* dinner to have ice-cream.
3. Closely related.–Only *near* relations attended the wedding.
4. Get close to. – As we *neared* the station, the train came in.

nearly. Almost.–It is *nearly* three o'clock. It is a few minutes to three.

neat *neater, neatest, neatly.* 1. Clean and tidy. –Mother's cupboards are always *neat*.
2. Fond of order; orderly in personal habits. –Father is a *neat* person. He likes to keep all his things in place.

neatness neat'-ness. Being clean and orderly.

nebula neb'-u-la *nebulae.* In astronomy, a cloudlike cluster of distant stars.–One can see a *nebula* only through a powerful telescope.–Some *nebulae* can be seen in or near the Milky Way.

nebulous neb'-u-lous *nebulously.* 1. Anything like a nebula. – There are many *nebulous* patches near the Milky Way.
2. Vague and hazy.–Mr. Brown's ideas about foreign affairs are *nebulous*. They are not properly thought out.

necessary nec'-es-sar-y *necessarily.* Needed; required.–Sleep is *necessary* for good health.

necessity ne-ces'-si-ty *necessities.* A need; something we cannot do without.–Food and drink are *necessities* of life.

neck *necks.* 1. The part of the body that joins the head to the body.–Mother wears a string of pearls round her *neck*.
2. The part of a piece of clothing that fits round the *neck*.–The *neck* of Bob's shirt is too tight.
3. A narrow piece of land with water on both sides.

necklace neck'-lace *necklaces.* An ornament worn about the neck. – Gold and silver chains, and strings of pearls or beads, are *necklaces*.

N O P Q R S T U V W X Y Z

necktie neck'-tie *neckties*. A band of cloth worn about the neck and tied in front.–Father's *necktie* is new.

nectar nec'-tar *nectars*. 1. Any sweet, delicious drink.
2. A sweet juice that comes from flowers.–The bees take *nectar* from flowers and make honey of it.

need *needs, needed, needing*. 1. Must have.–We *need* milk for dinner.
2. Have to; be required. – Do you *need* to spend so much time on your work?
3. Ought to have.–Mary *needs* a new skirt.
4. Something required or *needed*.–The hermit's *needs* are few.
5. Poverty; lack of necessities.–Many families are in great *need*.

needle nee'-dle *needles*. 1. A slender piece of steel, pointed at one end, and with an eye or hole in the other end for thread to go through. A *needle* is used for sewing.
2. Anything like a sewing *needle* in shape or use.–A knitting *needle* is very long so that the material which has been knitted can be held on it.–Cleopatra's *Needle* is a needle-shaped monument in London.
3. An indicator or pointer. – The *needle* on a compass points north. – The *needle* on a speedometer shows how fast the car goes.

needless need'-less *needlessly*. Unnecessary.–*Needless* to say, Jack was happy to find his dog.

needn't. Need not.–You *needn't* wait for me if you are in a hurry.

needy need-y *needier, neediest*. Poor; in need of many things.–Every Christmas we take baskets of food to *needy* families.

negative neg'-a-tive *negatives, negatively*. 1. Saying or meaning no.–Mother's answer was *negative*. She said no.
2. An image, usually on a camera film, in which light areas are dark and dark ones are light.–I will have a print made from this *negative*.

neglect neg-lect' *neglects, neglected, neglecting, neglectful, neglectfully*. 1. Fail to take care of; pay no attention to.–If you *neglect* your dog, he will not keep happy and well.
2. Fail.–Do not *neglect* to brush your teeth twice a day.

3. Lack of care. – The ragged lawn shows *neglect*.

Negro Ne'-gro *Negroes*. A person of the black race, originally from Africa.

neigh *neighs, neighed, neighing*. 1. Make the sound that horses make.–I heard Grandfather's horses *neigh*.
2. The call or cry of a horse.–Have you ever heard the *neigh* of a horse?

neighbour neigh'-bour *neighbours*. A person who lives next door or near by.–Father is talking over the back fence with the *neighbours*.

neighbourhood neigh'-bour-hood *neighbourhoods*. 1. A part of a town or section.–In our *neighbourhood*, all the children play together.
2. Surrounding area.–We live in the *neighbourhood* of the school. The school is just round the corner.

neither nei'-ther. 1. Not one or the other; not either.–*Neither* Jack nor Mary heard Mother call. Jack didn't hear her and Mary didn't hear her.
2. And not; nor.–Jack didn't hear her; *neither* did Mary.

nephew neph'-ew *nephews*. A son of one's brother or sister. – Father's and Mother's *nephews* are our cousins.

nerve *nerves*. 1. One of the little thread-like bands that join the brain and the spinal cord with all the other parts of the body. The *nerves* control the actions of the body.
2. Courage.–The firemen had *nerve* to go into the burning house.

nervous nerv'-ous *nervously, nervousness*. 1. Restless; uneasy; upset.–Mother grew *nervous* as the time came for Mary to appear on the stage.
2. Having to do with the nerves.–Your brain, spinal cord, and nerves are your *nervous* system.

nest *nests, nested, nesting*. 1. The home of a bird, or of certain other creatures.–Birds build *nests* in which they lay eggs and rear their young. – We found the nest of a mouse in the cellar.

2. A cosy place to rest and sleep.–Our kitten has a *nest* in a basket.
3. Make a *nest*.–Robins *nest* in the spring.
4. A group of things that fit together.–Mother has a *nest* of tables in the living-room.

nestle nes'-tle *nestles, nestled, nestling.* 1. Snuggle. – The little kittens *nestled* against their mother.
2. Cuddle; hold close and tenderly. The policeman picked up the hurt dog and *nestled* it in his arms.

net *nets, netted, netting.* 1. A web made by tying pieces of cord, string, or other material across each other and together in such a way that meshes or holes of the same size are made. – Ed caught the fish in a *net.* – Mother wears a hair*net.*
2. An open-work cloth. – Mary's party dress is made of *net.*

fish net   butterfly net   hair net   tennis net

3. A trap. – The rabbit was caught in a *net.*
4. Catch in a *net.* – Bob is *netting* butterflies.
5. Amount remaining after necessary amounts are taken out. – The *net* profit on the apples was 20p. They cost Jim 50p a box and he sold them for 70p.

nettle net'-tle *nettles, nettled, nettling.* 1. A plant that has little hairlike stickers on it that sting when one touches them.
2. Irritate, provoke, anger. – Mary was *nettled* at Jack's mimicking her.

network net'-work *networks.* 1 A system of lines that cross or weave in and out. – A net is a *network.*
2. A criss-cross system of rivers, canals, railways, radio stations, etc. – England's *network* of water-ways has helped her industries to develop.

neutral neu'-tral *neutrals, neutrality.* 1. Not on either side in a fight or struggle. – A *neutral* country is one that does not take part in a war or a dispute.
2. A *neutral* country. – Switzerland was a *neutral* in the war.

3. Greyish. – Grandmother likes to wear *neutral* colours.
4. When the gears of a car are in *neutral,* the engine can run without turning the wheels.

neutrality neu-tral'-i-ty. The state of being neither on one side nor the other. – In a football match the referee has to preserve strict *neutrality.* He must not show special preference for either team. – Switzerland maintained her *neutrality* throughout the war.

never nev'-er. Not at any time. – Bob would *never* tell tales on anyone. – Mary has *never* been late.

nevertheless nev-er-the-less'. *However*; in spite of that. – Bob's hands were sore; *nevertheless,* he held on to the rope.

new *newer, newest, newly, newness.* 1. Not known or found before; not old. – Father has a *new* idea for making paper. – Our house is *new*; it is just built. – Mother has a *new* dress. She has just bought it.
2. Different. – Father has a *new* book-keeper. – The rain came down so hard that we decided to start a *new* game.
3. Fresh. – Jack had *new* hope when he heard that his lost dog had been seen.
4. Not usual for; never done before. – Working at night is *new* to Father.
5. The first of the *new* season. – *New* potatoes are good to eat with butter and parsley.
6. Many countries, states and towns named after older ones start with the word *New,* like *New* Zealand, *New* Guinea, *New* South Wales, *New* York, etc.

new-born new'-born. Just born. – All the relations called to see the *new-born* baby.

newcomer new'-com-er *newcomers.* Someone who has just come. – There is a *newcomer* in our class. He has just come into our class.

new-fangled new'-fan'-gled. Very new and modern, but otherwise not worth much. – Grandmother says she cannot stand the *new-fangled* dances which we like. She prefers waltzes and fox-trots.

newish new'-ish. Fairly new. – This is a *newish* dress. I bought it last summer and have only worn it once or twice.

new-laid new'-laid. Freshly laid. – When we were on the farm we collected the *new-laid* eggs every day.

newly new'-ly. Recently.–The *newly* married couple went to France for their honeymoon.

news. A report of something that has happened.–We read the newspaper to learn the *news,* to find out what has happened.–The *news* that you had moved was a surprise.

newsagent news'-a-gent *newsagents.* A person who sells papers and magazines. – Father orders all his daily papers and weekly magazines from the local *newsagent.*

newsboy news'-boy *newsboys.* A boy who sells newspapers in the street.

newspaper news'-pa-per *newspapers.* A large sheet or sheets of papers printed and sold regularly. It tells people what is happening in the world and what they can buy at the shops and gives other information and entertainment.

newsprint news'-print. The paper used for printing newspapers, usually made from wood-pulp.–During the war, *newsprint* was in very short supply and was rationed. The papers contained only a few pages.

news-reel news'reel *news-reels.* A film showing outstanding recent events.–The *news-reel* showed pictures of the earthquake.

newsy news'-y. Full of news or gossip.–When we were staying with Grandfather on the farm, we wrote *newsy* letters home. We told Mother everything we had been doing.

newt *newts.* A small water creature which lives on tadpoles, insect larvae, etc.–We saw several *newts* in the pond.

New Year. The beginning of another year. *New Year's Day* is on January 1st. – On *New Year's Eve* we sometimes have a party to see the old year out and to welcome in the new one.

New York. A state in the eastern United States, with beautiful lakes and forest-covered mountains, important for farming, manufacturing, production of granite, marble, and other building materials, for its colleges and the United States Military Academy. It is known also for New York City. One of the world's largest cities, this is one of the world's busiest ports

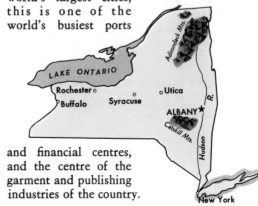

and financial centres, and the centre of the garment and publishing industries of the country.

next. 1. The one nearest. – Miss Jones is the teacher in the *next* room.
2. The one after this.–A, B, C, D, E, F. The letter C is the *next* letter after B.–*Next* time it will be Bob's turn to pass the books.
3. Directly after.–Mary will speak *next*. She will speak after the person now speaking finishes.

nice *nicer, nicest, nicely.* 1. Agreeable; pleasant.–This is a *nice* day.–Our neighbours are *nice* people.
2. Very careful and particular; neat.–Bob is a *nice* worker. He works carefully and neatly.

nick *nicks, nicked, nicking.* 1. A cut; a notch. –The thoughtless boy made *nicks* in his desk with his knife.–Mary dropped a knife on her plate and made a *nick* in it. She broke off a small piece of the china.
2. Make a small cut or notch in.–Bob *nicked* the table with his knife.

nickel nick'-el *nickels.* 1. A metal that looks something like silver.
2. An American coin worth 5 cents. It is a coin made of copper and covered with *nickel*.

nickname nick'-name *nicknames, nicknamed, nicknaming.* 1. A friendly name by which someone is called.–Bob's real name is Robert. Bob is his *nickname.*
2. Give another name to, besides the real name, just in fun.–Jack *nicknamed* everyone in the class. Jack's *nickname* is Skinny.

N O P Q R S T U V W X Y Z

N
O
P
Q
R
S
T
U
V
W
X
Y
Z

niece *nieces.* A daughter of one's brother or sister.—Father's and Mother's *nieces* are our cousins.

night *nights.* The time between evening and morning.—It is dark at *night,* and sometimes the moon shines.

nightdress night-dress *nightdresses.* A dress worn by some women and children at night when they sleep.

nightingale night'-in-gale *nightingales.* A European bird somewhat like a brown thrush. The father bird is known for his sweet singing, both night and day.

nightly night'-ly. Happening at night or every night.—The man makes *nightly* visits to the house. He goes there each night.

nightshirt night'-shirt *nightshirts.* A long shirt which some persons wear to sleep in.

nimble nim'-ble *nimbly, nimbleness.* 1. Quick and lively.—Jack be *nimble,* Jack be quick.—Grandfather is very *nimble* for a man of his age.
2. Keen; alert.—Tom has a *nimble* mind. He understands things quickly and answers quickly.

nine *nines.* 1. The number (9) after eight and before ten.—School starts at *nine* o'clock.—Cats are popularly believed to have *nine* lives.

nineteen nine'-teen. The number (19) coming after eighteen and before twenty. Nine and ten make *nineteen.*

nineteenth nine'-teenth *nineteenths.* 1. Each of 19 equal parts into which anything is divided.
2. Coming between number 18 and number 20.—The *nineteenth* page of a book is the page after page 18.

ninetieth nine'-ti-eth *ninetieths.* 1. One of 90 equal parts into which a thing is divided.
2. Coming between number 89 and number 91 of anything.—The old woman has just had her *ninetieth* birthday. Last year she had her eighty-ninth birthday.

ninety nine'-ty *nineties.* The number (90) coming just after 89 and before 91. *Ninety* is ten less than 100.

ninth *ninths.* 1. Each of 9 equal parts into which anything is divided.
2. The one coming after number 8 and before number 10 of anything.—Your *ninth* birthday is the one after the eighth.

nip *nips, nipped, nipping.* 1. A pinch or a bite. —The puppy gave Baby a *nip* when she pulled its tail.
2. Pinch.—The maid was in the garden hanging out the clothes. Along came a blackbird and *nipped* off her nose.
3. Injure the tip of.—The heavy frost *nipped* our flowers.

nipple nip'-ple *nipples.* 1. The small part of a mother's breast from which a baby draws or sucks milk.
2. The rubber top on a baby's bottle, through which the baby sucks milk.

nitrogen ni'-tro-gen. One of the gases in the air we breathe. The air is a mixture of gases which we cannot see.

no. 1. The opposite of yes.—When Mother asked the children if they wanted some more ice-cream, Sally said, 'Yes, I want some.' Mary said, '*No,* I cannot eat any more.'
2. Not any.—Mary wants *no* more ice-cream. She has had enough.

nobility no-bil'-i-ty. 1. Great or high character. —Captain Scott was a man of great *nobility.*
2. A special, privileged class of people.—Dukes and earls are people of the *nobility.*

noble no'-ble *nobles, nobler, noblest, nobly.*
1. Great and good.—Captain Scott was a *noble* man.
2. Like or relating to persons who hold the high position of duke, baron, count, etc., in certain countries.—Some people in England are of *noble* birth.
3. A person of the *noble* class, or nobility.— The prince invited many *nobles* to the tournament.

nobly no'-bly. Splendidly; as a noble person would.—The soldier served *nobly.* He served with honour.

nobody no'-bod-y *nobodies.* 1. No one; not even one person.—*Nobody* heard the bell ring. —*Nobody* was late today.
2. An unimportant person.—In a few years, the man who had begun as a mere *nobody* was a famous actor.

nod *nods, nodded, nodding.* 1. Say yes by bending or bowing the head forward and downward, or moving it up and down.–When Mary asked if she might go, Mother *nodded*.
2. A bend of the head.–Mother gave a *nod*.
3. Let the head fall forward as though one were going to sleep.–Grandmother sat in her chair and *nodded*.

noise *noises, noised, noising.* 1. Loud, harsh sounds.–We heard a *noise* in the basement. It was the *noise* made by a falling lawn-mower.
2. Tell everywhere.–It was *noised* abroad that the prince would marry the owner of the glass slipper.

noiseless *noise'-less noiselessly.* Without making a noise. – Bill's return home was *noiseless*; neither Mother nor Father heard him.–Baby's pram is *noiseless*; it has rubber wheels.

noisily *nois'-i-ly.* In a noisy way.–The children jumped *noisily* on the nursery floor. They made an awful din.

noisy *nois'-y noisier, noisiest, noisiness, noisily.* Making many noises or loud, mixed-up sounds; not quiet. – The teacher told the children that they were too *noisy*.–The old car is a *noisy* one.

nomad *no'-mad nomads.* A person who belongs to a tribe or group of people who have no homes. They go from place to place to find food and water for their cattle and sheep.

nominate *nom'-i-nate nominates, nominated, nominating.* Name a person to stand for an office.–Mary was *nominated* for club secretary.

nomination *nom-i-na'-tion nominations.* A suggestion of someone to stand for an office.–Mary accepted the *nomination* for the office of secretary. She was willing to be proposed for election to the office.

nominee *nom-i-nee' nominees.* A person named for office – Mary is the *nominee* for club secretary. .

non-combatant *non-com'-ba-tant non-combatants.* A person who does no fighting.–Uncle Dick was a *non-combatant* in the war; he was in the Pay Corps.–Civilians are also *non-combatants*.

non-commissioned *non-com-mis'-sioned.* In the armed forces, an officer without a commission.–Corporals and sergeants are *non-commissioned* officers.

nondescript *non'-des-cript.* Not easy to describe, of no particular kind.–This book is *nondescript*. It cannot be called a novel, or a biography, or a collection of essays.

none. 1. Not any.–*None* of the biscuits is left.
2. Not at all.–Sally is *none* the worse for having jumped into the snow.

nonsense *non'-sense.* Talk and actions that are foolish, or that mean nothing.–It is *nonsense* to say that the moon is made of green cheese.

noodle *noo'-dle noodles.* A food made of flour, eggs, water, and salt. *Noodles* are rolled very thin and cut into long strips. They are often cooked in beef or chicken broth.

nook *nooks.* 1. A small sheltered place.–We had a picnic in a shady *nook* near the river.
2. A little room open on one side to a larger room.–We have our breakfast in a *nook* off the kitchen.

noon *noons.* Twelve o'clock in the daytime; the middle of the day.– We come home for lunch at *noon*.

noose *nooses.* A loop in a rope with a slip knot tied in it. When you pull the end of the rope through the knot, the loop becomes smaller and tighter. – The cowboy caught the steer with a *noose*.

nor. Neither Jack *nor* Mary heard Mother call. Jack did not hear and Mary did not hear. They were too busy playing.

normal *nor'-mal normally.* 1. Average.–Jack's weight is *normal*. He weighs as much as most boys of his age.
2. Usual.–Grandmother has been in her *normal* health since she got well.

north. 1. A direction.–Turn your face towards the sun as it comes up in the morning. Raise your left hand. Your left hand is pointing *north*. Raise your right hand. It is pointing south.
2. Towards the *north*.–The birds fly *north* in the spring.
3. Blowing from the *north*.–The *north* wind doth blow and we shall have snow.
4. (Spelled *North*) the northern part of the country.–Winter is cold in the *North*.

N
O
P
Q
R
S
T
U
V
W
X
Y
Z

north-east north-east' *north-eastern*. 1. A direction halfway between north and east.

2. In a direction halfway between north and east.

3. The part that lies north and east from the middle of a country or region. – The country of Yorkshire is in the *north-east*.

northern north'-ern. The part lying on the north side, or farthest to the north. – The United States is in the *northern* part of the Western Hemisphere. It lies between the Equator and the North Pole.

northward north'-ward. Towards the north.– Birds fly *northward* in the spring.

north-west north-west' *north-western*. 1. A direction halfway between north and west.

2. In a direction halfway between north and west.

3. The part that lies north and west from the middle of a country or region. –Lancashire is in the *north-west*.

nose *noses, nosed, nosing*. 1. The part of the face or head of a person or animal that is just above the mouth. – You breathe and smell through your *nose*.

2. A sense of smell.–Jack's dog has a good *nose*. He can trace squirrels, rabbits, and other creatures by smelling their tracks or footprints.

3. The front tip, as the *nose* of an aeroplane.

4. Push with *nose* first.–The boat *nosed* into the harbour.

5. Search or pry.–Jack *nosed* around in the deserted house.

nostril nos'-tril *nostrils*. One of the two openings in the nose.–We breathe through the *nostrils*.

not. *Not* makes the word it goes with say just the opposite. – Baby is *not* awake. She is asleep. Asleep is the opposite of awake.

notable not'-a-ble *notably*. Worth seeing or noting, remarkable.–The visit of the President was a *notable* occasion.–My birthday is a *notable* date in my calendar.

notch *notches, notched, notching*. 1. A V-shaped cut.–Jack cut a *notch* in a stick with his penknife.

2. Make V-shaped cuts in.–Mother *notched* the seams of Mary's dress so that the cloth would not separate into threads.

note *notes, noted, noting*. 1. A short written message; a few written words.–Bob left a *note* telling his mother that he would be home late.

2. A few words to serve as a reminder.–Bob was afraid he would forget the appointment, so he made a *note* of it.

3. A short explanation, usually at the bottom of a page.–Mary didn't know what the word meant, so she read the *note* at the bottom of the page.

4. A musical tone.–The song ended on the *note* of C.

5. A sign used in written music to represent a *note*. – Father can play the piano, but he cannot read *notes*.

6. Well-known reputation. – Major Johnson is a man of *note* in our town.

7. Notice.–Jack *noted* that the footprints had been made by someone wearing plimsolls.

note-book note'-book *note-books*. A blank book of writing paper in which to write down things to be remembered or referred to.

noted not'-ed. Well known or famous.–Stanley Matthews is a *noted* footballer.

nothing noth'-ing. 1. Not a thing. – The old woman found *nothing* in the cupboard.

2. Nought (o). – 4 taken away from 4 leaves *nothing*.

notice no'-tice *notices, noticed, noticing*. 1. A warning.–The whistle blew to give *notice* that there was a fire.

2. An announcement, printed or spoken.– The *notice* said that the game was cancelled.

3. Attention.–The guide called to our *notice* the black bear standing on the rock.

4. See.–I *notice* that you have on a new dress.

5. A word in advance.–Father gave the shop where he works *notice* that he could not work there any longer

noticeable no'-tice-a-ble *noticeably*. Easy to see, hear, feel, smell, or the like.–The blue patch on Bob's grey shirt was quite *noticeable*. It could be seen easily.

notify no'-ti-fy *notifies, notified, notifying*. Give notice to; tell officially; let know.–The school board *notified* the headmaster that school would be closed a week before Christmas.

notion no'-tion *notions*. An idea, or what one thinks.–I have a *notion* that we can solve the problem this way.

nought *noughts*. Nothing; the figure (o).–One and two *noughts* is a hundred (100).

noun *nouns*. A word that names a person or thing. Mary, hunger, beef, sky, are all *nouns*. Verb, sentence, *noun*, are *nouns*.

nourish nour'-ish *nourishes, nourished, nourishing, nourishment*. Feed; give (a living thing) whatever it needs to keep alive and grow. – Sun, soil, and water *nourish* the plants. Food and drink *nourish* a person.

novel nov'-el *novels*. 1. A long story of book length.–A *novel* is not a story of true happenings.–Mother is reading a *novel*. 2. New and unusual.–Jack had a *novel* idea for saving money.

novelty nov'-el-ty *novelties*. 1. Anything new or unusual.–It was a *novelty* for Bob to stay up until midnight. 2. An unusual trinket, toy, game, etc.–The little shop sold stationery and *novelties*.

November No-vem'-ber. The eleventh month of the year.

now. 1. At this time; at the present time.–I shall leave *now* in order not to be late. 2. The present time.–Father should be home by *now*. 3. As it is.–You took too long to dress; *now* you will be late. 4. *Now that* means since, seeing that.–*Now that* it is raining, we cannot play outdoors.

nowhere no'-where. Not in any place at all.– There is *nowhere* Mary would rather be than at the cinema.

nozzle noz'-zle *nozzles*. A metal pipe or tip on the end of a hose or container for liquid to come through.

nude. Naked.–We are *nude* when we get into the bath.

nudge *nudges, nudged, nudging*. 1. Lightly touch.–Bob *nudged* Jack to let him know that it was his turn to spell. 2. A light push.–He gave him a little *nudge*.

nugget nug'-get *nuggets*. A lump.–The miner found a *nugget* of gold.

nuisance nui'-sance *nuisances*. A person, thing, animal, etc., that bothers others or makes trouble.–When Mary would not sit still at the table, Father said she was being a *nuisance*.

numb *numbs, numbed, numbing*. 1. Without feeling.–Mary sat on her foot so long that it became *numb*. 2. Make *numb*; stop feeling in.–The cold *numbed* the boy's fingers so that he could not write.

number num'-ber *numbers, numbered, numbering*. 1. How many.–The farmer counted his sheep to find out their *number*. 2. 1, 2, 3, 4, 5, 6, 7, 8, 9, 0 and any combination of these are *numbers*. 3. Some, a few.–A *number* of children were playing in the yard. 4. The bees swarmed in great *numbers*. There were very many of them. 5. An issue of a publication.–The last *number* of the Boy Scout magazine tells how to take care of the flag. 6. Count; give a *number* to.–The children *numbered* their spelling words. 7. Amount to.–The children in this class *number* twenty-five.

numeral nu'-mer-al *numerals*. A word or figure that stands for a number. 7, 85, two, and III are *numerals*.

numerous nu'-mer-ous. Large in number.–We received Christmas cards too *numerous* to count.

nun *nuns*. A woman who belongs to a religious organization of women who give their entire lives to religious work.

nurse *nurses, nursed, nursing*. 1. A trained person who works in a hospital or home taking care of the sick, of babies, or old people.

2. A *nurse*-maid; a woman who takes care of children and babies for someone else.
3. Take care of.–Bob *nursed* the sick puppy back to health.

N
O P Q R S T U V W X Y Z

nursery nurs'-er-y *nurseries.* 1. A room for small children.–The children are in the *nursery* playing with their toys.

2. A kindergarten or other place where many small children are cared for.–Mothers who work often leave their children at a *nursery* during the day.

3. A place where trees and plants are grown and sold for replanting.–Father bought our shrubs at a *nursery.*

nut *nuts.* 1. The fruit of certain trees. *Nuts* are covered with hard shells to protect the kernels that are inside. 2. A piece of metal that has a threaded hole through it which fits on a bolt.

nuthatch nut'-hatch *nuthatches.* A small bird which eats nuts and insects.

nutmeg nut'-meg *nutmegs.* The seed of the *nutmeg* tree, which grows in the East Indies. *Nutmeg* is ground and used as a flavouring.

nutshell nut'-shell *nutshells.* 1. The hard shell or covering of a nut. – Some *nutshells* are easier to crack than others. 2. A brief outline.–That's the story in a *nutshell.*

nymph *nymphs.* A beautiful goddess who was supposed, in olden times, to live in forests, mountains, or rivers. *Nymphs* were the goddesses of nature.

O o

O, o *O's, o's.* The 15th letter of the alphabet.

oak *oaks.* A kind of tree that has very hard wood and large, wide leaves. The seeds of the *oak* tree are called acorns. The wood is

used for furniture, buildings, and many other things.–We have *oak* floors in our house.

oar *oars.* A long wooden pole that is flat like a paddle at the end that goes in the water. We row a boat with *oars.*

oasis o-a'-sis *oases.* A place in the desert where there is water, and where a few plants grow.

–Travellers in the desert often stop at an *oasis.*

O
P
Q
R
S
T
U
V
W
X
Y
Z

oat *oats*. A kind of grass that produces seed, or grain, which is used for food. *Oat*meal is made from *oats*.

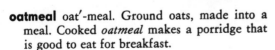

oath *oaths*. 1. A promise made by a person, with God as the witness, to tell the truth.
2. A swear word or curse.–The angry man used many *oaths*.

oatmeal oat'-meal. Ground oats, made into a meal. Cooked *oatmeal* makes a porridge that is good to eat for breakfast.

obedience o-be'-di-ence. Doing the things one is told to do.–Bob is teaching his dog *obedience*; he is teaching the dog to come when he is called.

obedient o-be'-di-ent *obediently*. Willing to do what one is told.–Jack's dog is *obedient*; he does what Jack tells him to do.

obey o-bey' *obeys, obeyed, obeying*. Do what one is told.–Always *obey* your mother. Do the things she tells you to do.

object ob'-ject *objects*. 1. A thing that one can see or feel.–Clocks, books, pins, dishes, and anything else you can touch are *objects*.
2. Purpose or aim.–The *object* of this book is to tell you what words mean and show you how to use them.

object ob-ject' *objects, objected, objecting*. Not approve; not want a thing done.–Mother *objects* to our going swimming alone.

objection ob-jec'-tion *objections*. A reason for not wanting something done, or for not liking something.–I should like to look at your book if you have no *objection*.–Mary's *objection* to taking cough medicine is that she does not like the taste of it.

obligation ob-li-ga'-tion *obligations*. 1. A duty, a responsibility.–Do not feel any *obligation* to accept my invitation if you do not wish to do so.
2. A debt.–Mother felt under an *obligation* to the neighbours for minding Baby. She wanted to do something for them in return.

oblige o-blige' *obliges, obliged, obliging*. 1. Do a favour.–'Will you lend me a pencil?' 'I should be glad to *oblige* you if I had an extra one.'
2. Force or compel.–Because of the snowstorm, we were *obliged* to stay at home.

oblong ob'-long *oblongs*. 1. Being longer than wide.–Most books are *oblong*.
2. Something that is longer than it is wide. –Our living room is an *oblong*.

oboe o'-boe *oboes*. A musical instrument that is played by blowing into it through two reeds that are held between the lips.

observation ob-ser-va'-tion *observations*. 1. Act of observing. – The teacher kept Jack under close *observation*. – Our *observation* of the moon was made with a telescope.
2. That which is observed. – The teacher's *observation* was that Jack had finished the test quickly.

observe ob-serve' *observes, observed, observing*. 1. See or notice.–The teacher *observed* that Jack had finished the test and told him to look it over.
2. Obey or follow.–Always *observe* the safety rules.
3. Celebrate.–We *observe* Christmas by having a tree and exchanging gifts.
4. Watch and study.–If you *observe* a drop of water under a microscope, you may see tiny bodies moving in it.

obstinate ob'-sti-nate *obstinately*. Stubborn; refusing to give in to others, or to do what others wish.–The donkey is *obstinate*. He won't go when we want him to.

obstruct ob-struct' *obstructs, obstructed, obstructing, obstruction*. Block. – A wrecked car *obstructed* the traffic. It made it difficult for the traffic to pass.

obtain ob-tain' *obtains, obtained, obtaining*. Get.–Bob went to the cupboard to *obtain* some coloured chalk.

occasion oc-ca'-sion *occasions*. 1. A time.–The form play was the *occasion* of Mother's first visit to our school.
2. A reason.–It was the first time she ever had *occasion* to come.
3. A special happening.–A play is always a great *occasion* for Mary.

occasional oc-ca'-sion-al *occasionally*. Happening once in a while.–We make an *occasional* visit to the country.

OCCUPATIONS

shopkeeper

policeman

secretary

reporter

chef

factory worker

cashier

sailor

sculptor

miner

soldier

farmer

surgeon

lift-man

dressmaker

train engineer

artist

judge

gardener

actor

pilot

woodsman

fisherman

postman

musician

O P Q R S T U V W X Y Z

occupation oc-cu-pa'-tion *occupations.* 1. Business or work.–Father's *occupation* is selling shoes.

2. What one is doing.–Mother was sweeping the floor, but she paused in her *occupation* to listen to us.

occupy oc'-cu-py *occupies, occupied, occupying.* 1. Take up (time or space).–Reading *occupies* most of my spare time.–This desk *occupies* too much space.

2. Live or be in.–A different family *occupies* the house next door now.

3. Take over; take possession of.–The army *occupied* the big hotel. The soldiers moved into it.

4. Make busy.–Father is *occupied* with his mail just now.

occur oc-cur' *occurs, occurred, occurring, occurrence.* 1. Take place or happen. – The monument marks the place where the battle *occurred.*

2. Come to one's mind.–It didn't *occur* to Mary that she could help Mother by dressing Baby. She didn't think of it.

3. Be found.–The word 'God' *occurs* often in the Bible.

ocean o'-cean *oceans.* The sea, or large body of salt water, that covers the greater part of the earth. The sea is divided into 5 large parts, known as *oceans.* – The Atlantic *Ocean* is east and the Pacific *Ocean* west of the United States.

o'clock. By the clock.–School starts at 9 *o'clock.*

octave oc'-tave *octaves.* In music, the space between one note and the eighth note up or down from it.–From C to C or from G to G

is an *octave.*–Mary's fingers are long enough now to reach an *octave* on the piano.

October Oc-to'-ber. The tenth month of the year. *October* has 31 days. Hallowe'en comes on *October* 31.

octopus oc'-to-pus *octopuses.* A sea animal that has eight arms. Along these arms are suckers, and these make it possible for the *octopus* to take hold of things.

oculist oc'-u-list *oculists.* A doctor who treats diseases or disorders of the eye.–Father went to the *oculist* to see if he should have new glasses.

odd *odder, oddest, oddly.* 1. Not able to be divided evenly by the number 2. – 4 is an even number. It can be divided by 2 with no fraction left over. 2 will go into 4 twice. 3 is an *odd* number. 2 will go into 3 once, with 1 left over.

2. Extra, not matching.–All Bob can ever find are *odd* socks. They do not go with any of the others.

3. Strange or queer.–It would seem *odd* if men wore dresses.

odour o'-dour *odours.* A smell or scent.–A daffodil has an *odour* like honey.

o'er. Over. *O'er* is used in poetry.–
  '*O'er* hills, *o'er* dells,
  Sweet evening bells.'

of. 1. About or dealing with.–This is the story *of* Snow White and the Seven Dwarfs.

2. From.–Bristol is west *of* London.

3. Made from.–The prince wore a coat *of* flame-coloured satin.

4. Who has; that has.–Bob is a boy *of* great ability.–This is a place *of* great beauty.

5. Out of.–Mary and Jack made a game *of* their homework.

6. About or because *of.*–We were glad *of* the warm weather for Easter.

7. In, belonging to. – The children *of* the neighbourhood are going on a picnic.

8. Among.–Some *of* us should help to clean up after the party.

9. Concerning, or about.–If you cannot speak well *of* other people, do not speak *of* them at all.

O
P
Q
R
S
T
U
V
W
X
Y
Z

off. 1. From.–Spot jumped *off* the bed when he saw Mother.

2. Away.–The pigeon flew *off* when Sally tried to pick him up.–My birthday is two days *off*.

3. Away from.–Grandmother lives *off* the main road.–Mary often gets *off* the question in giving her answer.

4. From one's body.–Bob took *off* his gloves. He removed them.

5. Father cleaned *off* a shelf in the cellar for his tools. He removed everything from it.

6. Free.–Father took the afternoon *off* to take us to the beach.

7. Not in place, not on as it should be.–The knob is *off* that door.

8. So that it is not working or running.–Turn the water *off*.

9. Not what it should be, not up to standard. –Our star bowler had an *off* day, and bowled badly.

offend of-fend' *offends, offended, offending, offence*. Displease or hurt the feelings of.– Do not *offend* other people by using bad language.

offer of'fer *offers, offered, offering*. 1. Volunteer or show that one is willing to give.– Mary *offered* her help in making the sandwiches.–Jack *offered* Bob a pound for the bat. He said he would give a pound for it.

2. An invitation or suggestion.–Mr Smith accepted Father's *offer* to drive into town with him.

office of'-fice *offices*. 1. A place in which a business or profession is carried on. – We went to the solicitor's *office* to get the deeds of the house.–Mother went to the *office* of the gas company to pay her gas bill.

2. A position of public or social duty.–The Inspector has held his *office* for three years.– Mary was elected to the *office* of club secretary.

officer of'-fi-cer *officers*. 1. A man in the army or navy who directs or tells other men what to do.–A captain is an *officer*.

2. A policeman.–The *officer* stopped the traffic while the children crossed the street.

3. A person who holds an office, or has charge of a certain job, in a business, a club, or an organization of any kind.–Mary is one of the *officers* of her club. She is the secretary.

official of-fi'-cial *officials, officially*. 1. Anyone holding an office or a public position.–The Foreign Secretary is a high government *official*.

2. By order; according to the rules; done by someone who has authority.–It is not *official* that there will be no school tomorrow; it is just talk.

offset off'set *offsets, offset, offsetting*. Something which balances or makes up for something else.–The weight of the other team was *offset* by our lightness and speed.

offside off'-side. In football, hockey, etc., to be in an unlawful position to score.–The centre-forward was *offside*; our goal was disallowed and the other team got a free kick.

offspring off'-spring. A child or children.–You are the *offspring* of your mother and father.

often (pronounced *offen*) of'-ten. Frequently –We *often* go to see Grandmother.

oh. 1. An exclamation, or a word that expresses a sudden feeling, such as surprise, interest, etc., or makes the words that follow it more emphatic.–*Oh!* It's you. I didn't hear you.– *Oh*, no! I wouldn't think of going alone.–*Oh*, how wonderful!

2. *Oh* used by itself may express understanding of a question.–'This is the way to solve the problem,' said Jack. '*Oh*,' said Mary.

oil *oils, oiled, oiling*. 1. Grease or fat that comes from plants, animals, or minerals. Some *oils* burn and are used instead of coal for fuel. Petrol is made from *oil*. *Oil* is used to lubricate machines. Castor *oil* is medicine. Olive *oil* is a food. *Oil* floats on top of water.

2. Rub *oil* on.–Mother *oiled* the furniture to make it shiny.

3. Put *oil* on or in.–Mather *oiled* the crank-case of the car.

oilcloth oil'-cloth. A heavy cloth that is covered with a shiny paint.–Mother put *oilcloth* on the cupboard shelves instead of paper.

O
P
Q
R
S
T
U
V
W
X
Y
Z

oil'-y *oilier, oiliest.* Greasy, or covered with oil.–Father's hands are *oily* from oiling the car.

ointment oint'-ment *ointments.* A salve or a liquid made of oils and medicines.–The doctor gave Mother an *ointment* to put on Baby's mosquito bites.

okapi o-ka'-pi *okapis.* An African animal, something like a giraffe, but with a short neck. The legs are marked black and white like a zebra's. The *okapi* is a very rare animal and not often seen in zoos.

old *older, oldest.* 1. Not young.–Grandfather is *old.* He has lived a long time.
2. Not new.–*Old* shoes are more comfortable for walking.
3. Of age.–Mary is eleven years *old.*
4. Having come down to us from times long past.–It is an *old* custom for a wife to wear a wedding ring.
5. Former.–Our *old* house stood on a high hill. The house we live in now is in a valley.

olden old'-en. Long past. – In *olden* times, people believed that the earth was flat.

old-fashioned old-fash'-ioned. 1. Doing and thinking as people did long ago. – Grandmother is *old-fashioned* in her dress.
2. Out of date or out of style.–Grandmother's velvet hat is *old-fashioned.*

old-time old'-time. Belonging to times gone by. –Morris dancing is an *old-time* form of dancing which is only performed today in England in a few places on special days.–Tossing the pancake on Shrove Tuesday is an *old-time* custom.

olive ol'-ive *olives.* The fruit of the *olive* tree. Ripe *olives* are a dark purplish brown colour. Unripe *olives* are a soft green colour. Both kinds are good to eat.

olive oil ol'-ive oil. An oil made from olives. It is used in salad dressings and in cooking.

omelette or **omelet** om'-e-lette *omelettes.* A mixture of eggs and milk or water, and seasoning, beaten and cooked in a frying pan. When it is done, it is folded over and served.

omit o-mit' *omits, omitted, omitting, omission.* Leave out, skip over.–Our teacher told us to *omit* the first page of problems and start on the second page.

on. 1. Resting above, held up by.–The book is *on* the table. The table holds up the book.
2. *On* is usually used with other words to tell where, when, how, and the like.–Where is the clock? The clock is *on* the shelf.–Grandfather is coming *on* Sunday.–When you go to school, be *on* time.–Grandmother went to sleep with her glasses *on.*–We left the lights *on.*–The Prime Minister spoke to us *on* the radio.–Keep *on* trying, and you will succeed at last.–The army marched *on* in spite of the snow.
3. So that it works or runs.–Turn *on* the light so that we can see.–Is the motor *on* or off?

once. 1. One time.–Mary has been in a boat only *once.*
2. At one time in the past.–The poor man *once* had much money.
3. After.–It is easy to multiply, *once* you learn your multiplication tables.
4. *At once* means right away.–Mother told us to come home *at once* when school was over.
5. *At once* also means at the same time.–All the horses in the race started *at once.*

one. 1. The number written as the figure 1.
2. A single.–I have *one* pound. Only *one* boy was late.–There are 7 days in the week. Monday is *one* day.
3. A person.–The *one* sitting in the front seat is Mary.
4. *One* is sometimes used instead of the name of a thing that has been mentioned before.–Mother looked at many hats, and then bought the *one* she had seen first.
5. Each person.–*One* must eat to keep alive.
6. The same.–The boats were all sailing in *one* direction.
7. United.–We are *one* in purpose.
8. Some. – Grandmother will be here *one* day this week.

oneself one-self'. One's own personal being. – It is selfish to think of *oneself* more than of others.

onion on'-ion *onions.* A bulb-like vegetable that grows in the ground.

O
P
Q
R
S
T
U
V
W
X
Y
Z

only on'-ly. 1. One; single.–Bob lost his *only* sweater.
2. Just; no more than.–It is *only* a little way to the shops.–The car holds *only* 3 people.
3. Merely.–It is *only* I.
4. Expect that.–I would go, *only* I have to study.

on to on'to. On.–The farmer pitched the hay *on to* the wagon.

onward on'-ward. Forward. – The soldiers marched *onward*.

ooze *oozes, oozed, oozing*. Leak slowly.–The blackberry juice *oozed* out of the crust of the pies.

opal o'-pal *opals*. A precious stone with a milky background. It is marked with colours that change in the light.

open o'-pen *opens, opened, opening*. 1. Not shut or closed.–Mother left the door *open* so that we could get in.
2. Take apart so as to expose or show the contents.–Father *opened* the package.
3. Spread out.–It must be raining outside, for people have their umbrellas *open*.–That flower will *open* soon.
4. Not covered.–A lifeboat is an *open* boat.
5. Not set; able to be changed.–A person with an *open* mind will listen to new ideas.
6. Begin business.–A new grocer's shop has *opened* at the corner.–This shop *opens* at 9 every morning.

opener o'-pen-er *openers*. Something used to open tins, jars, and bottles.–Mary opened the ginger ale with a bottle-*opener*.

opening o'-pen-ing *openings*. 1. A hole or open space.–We saw the sun through an *opening* in the clouds.
2. A position or job.–The shopkeeper said there was an *opening* for a delivery boy.
3. A chance.–Mary waited for an *opening* to ask if she might go to the pictures.
4. Beginning.–At the *opening* of the story, the king is in his castle.
5. First showing.–Father and Mother are going to the *opening* of the new play.

opera op'-er-a *operas*. A play in which the actors sing instead of speaking and are accompanied by an orchestra.

operate op'-er-ate *operates, operated, operating*. 1. Work or make run.–Can you *operate* a sewing machine?
2. Keep working or running.–Many factories *operate* night and day.
3. Cut into the body in order to remove or treat an injured or diseased part.–The doctor *operated* on Mary; he took out her appendix.

operation op-er-a'-tion *operations*. 1. The act of cutting into the body to remove or treat an injured or diseased part.–The doctor did an *operation* on the man's foot.
2. An act or process.–Mary was engaged in the *operation* of putting on her galoshes.
3. A movement.–The paper told about the military *operations* of our troops.
4. The way a thing works or acts.–Father likes the *operation* of his new car.

operator op'-er-a-tor *operators*. A person who operates or runs a machine. – A telephone *operator* works a switchboard.

opinion o-pin'-ion *opinions*. 1. A belief or way of thinking.–It is my *opinion* that you could solve the problem more quickly this way.
2. Mary likes people to have a good *opinion* of her. She likes them to think well of her.

opossum o-pos'-sum *opossums*. A small American animal that has greyish fur and a long skinny tail.

opportunity op-por-tu'-ni-ty *opportunities*. 1. A suitable time or chance. – There was no *opportunity* to ask the teacher about the party, because she was too busy.–We have an *opportunity* to ride to school every day.
2. The chance to better oneself.–Many people who migrated to America thought of it as the land of *opportunity*.

oppose op-pose' *opposes, opposed, opposing, opposition*. Be against; disagree with.–Mary *opposed* Bob's suggestion.

opposite op'-po-site *opposites*. 1. Something that is as different as possible from, or just the reverse of, something else.–Black and white are *opposites*. – Up is *opposite* to down.
2. Facing from two sides.–The teacher told the partners to stand *opposite* each other.

O
P
Q
R
S
T
U
V
W
X
Y
Z

optimist op′-ti-mist *optimists, optimistic, optimistically.* A person who always looks on the bright side of things, and believes that everything will end well.

or. 1. A word used to connect words *or* groups of words that offer a choice.–Will you have milk *or* hot chocolate?
2. *Or* is used to introduce words that explain something that was said before.–This is a mug, *or* cup, to drink from.

oral o′-ral *orally.* Spoken. – We had an *oral* spelling test. We spoke the words and spelt them out loud.

orange or′-ange *oranges.* 1. A reddish-yellow fruit which grows on the *orange* tree.

2. A bright colour that can be made by mixing red and yellow; the colour of an *orange*.

orchard or′-chard *orchards.* 1. A piece of ground where fruit trees are grown.–We like to play in Grandfather's *orchard*.

2. The fruit trees in an *orchard*.–Grandfather has a large apple *orchard*. He has many apple trees growing together.

orchestra or′-ches-tra *orchestras.* 1. A group of people who play musical instruments together.–Mary plays the violin in the school *orchestra*.

2. The space between the stage and the audience, occupied by the orchestra or band.

orchid (pronounced *orkid*) or′-chid, *orchids,* or *orchis, orchises.* A beautiful race of flowers. The exotic kind, usually called *orchids,* have brilliantly coloured flowers of fantastic shapes. The English wild kind, usually called *orchises,* have red or purple flowers.

ordeal or′-deal *ordeals.* A severe trial, a trying experience.–Jack found the climb an *ordeal*. It was very difficult, and he needed all his courage to accomplish it.

order or′-der *orders, ordered, ordering.* 1. The way in which things happen, or the way they follow one another.–The days of the week come in this *order*: Sunday, Monday, Tuesday, Wednesday, Thursday, Friday, Saturday.
2. *In order* means in a neat arrangement.–After the party, the children put the room *in order*. They put things in their right places.
3. Condition.–Jack found the bicycle in good *order*, so he bought it.
4. Social peace; lawful conduct.–Policemen keep *order*. They see that traffic rules and other laws are obeyed.
5. Attention.–The teacher called the class to *order*. She asked us to stop talking and get ready for our lesson.
6. An instruction or command.–The police received *orders* to arrest the suspects.
7. Direct, command.–The biggest boy in the class often *orders* the smaller boys around. He tells them what to do.
8. A request for goods one wants.–Father sent in an *order* for 60 pairs of shoes for the shop.
9. Give an *order* for goods.–Mother *ordered* the meat for dinner. She told the butcher to send it.
10. People must eat in *order* to live.

orderly or′-der-ly *orderlies.* 1. In order, neat.–Mother's dresser drawers are always *orderly*. Everything is in its place.
2. Well-behaved.–The crowd was quiet and *orderly*.
3. A soldier who waits on an officer of high rank.–The general's *orderly* brought him his coat.
4. A man in a hospital who keeps things clean and helps to wait on patients.–The *orderly* brought lunch to the patient.

ordinarily or′-di-nar-i-ly. Usually; as a rule.–*Ordinarily* we have a light lunch at midday and a hot dinner at night.

O
P
Q
R
S
T
U
V
W
X
Y
Z

ordinary or'-di-nar-y. 1. Usual or average.–In *ordinary* cases no one is excused from homework; but if you were ill, you have a special reason.
2. Not especially good or especially bad.–The food served at the hospital was just *ordinary*.

ore *ores*. Rock or earth that has iron, silver, copper, or other metals in it.

organ or'-gan *organs*. 1. A musical instrument played from a set of keyboards called a console. Most churches have pipe *organs*, in which the tones are made by air blowing into pipes of various sizes.

2. A part of the body which does certain work.–The heart is an *organ*. It pumps blood to all parts of the body.–The stomach, lungs, and liver are *organs*.

organ-grinder or'-gan-grind-er *organ-grinders*. A street musician who makes his living by playing tunes on a barrel-organ by turning a handle.–The *organ-grinder* let us play with his tame monkey.

organist or'-gan-ist *organists*. A person who plays an organ.–The church *organist* played for the wedding.

organization or-gan-i-za'-tion *organizations*. 1. A group of people who join together to work for a special purpose.–The Boy Scouts and the Red Cross are *organizations*.
2. Planning. – Thoughtful *organization* of your homework will help you to finish it more quickly.

organize or'-gan-ize *organizes, organized, organizing*. Form plans for; work out in advance; set up.–The boys will *organize* the football team on Saturday. They will decide in which position each will play.–*Organize* your work carefully.

organ-loft or'-gan-loft *organ-lofts*. The gallery of a church where the organ is built and where the organist sits.

Orient O'-ri-ent *Oriental*. The countries of eastern Asia, including the near-by islands. –China and Japan are parts of the *Orient*.

orifice or'-i-fice *orifices*. An opening.–A chimney is an orifice in the roof to let out the smoke.–The mouth is an *orifice* in the face.

origin or'-i-gin *origins*. The beginning: the thing from which something came.–The *origin* of the Italian language was Latin, the language of the ancient Romans.

original o-rig'-i-nal *originally*. 1. The first one, or the one from which the others were copied. –This copy of my story is the *original*, so it may have some mistakes in it.–The paintings in the museum are *originals*. They are not copies.
2. New.–Sally has many *original* ideas. She thinks of things that no one else has ever thought of.

originally o-rig'-i-nal-ly. At first.–This book was mine *originally*, but I gave it to Mary. I was the first owner of the book.

ornament or'-na-ment *ornaments, ornamented, ornamenting*. 1. A thing that makes other things more beautiful.–Rings, necklaces, brooches, earrings, and bracelets are *ornaments* which make one look prettier.–Candlesticks, vases, and the like are *ornaments* that make the house look prettier.
2. Decorate.–Sally *ornamented* Mary's homework with her crayons.

orphan or'-phan *orphans, orphaned, orphaning*. 1. A child whose parents are dead.
2. Leave an *orphan*.–The child was *orphaned* by the accident in which his parents were killed.

orphanage or'-phan-age *orphanages*. A home for orphans.–Some children whose parents are dead and who have no relations to live with live in *orphanages*.

ostrich os'-trich *ostriches*. A very large bird

with beautiful plumes, or large fluffy feathers. *Ostriches* do not fly, but they run fast.

other oth'-er *others.* 1. A different one; another. –I will read the book some *other* time; I am too busy now. I must read this *other* book first.–It was not this boy who threw the ball, but the *other.* It was not Jack, it was Bill.
2. More, besides this.–We have no *other* work, so we can go out and play.
3. Second.–Every *other* child standing in line was a boy. The children stood in this order: Mary, Bob, Ruth, Jack, Ellen, Harry.

otter ot'-ter *otters.* An animal that lives in and near the water. It feeds on fish. *Otters* are playful, and sometimes they build mud slides to coast down

ouch. A word used to show that a person is in pain, that something hurts him.–*Ouch!* I burned my finger.

ought. 1. Should.–You *ought* to get up earlier so that you can get to school on time. It is your duty to do so.
2. Be likely.–It *ought* to be warmer inside. It probably is warmer inside.

ounce *ounces.* 1. A unit of dry measure.–Milk is measured by the pint or quart. Meat, sugar, butter, and many other things are measured by the pound and the *ounce.* There are 16 *ounces* in a pound.
2. A tiny bit.–Bob hasn't an *ounce* of selfishness in him.

our. Belonging to us: *our* dog, *our* house, *our* toys. They all belong to us. We own them.

ours. Something belonging to us.–This dog is *ours.* He belongs to us. We own him.

ourselves our-selves'. We, or us, not somebody else.–When we *ourselves* heard the noise in the cellar, we believed the story.–The teacher told us to read the next question to *ourselves* and then tell her the answer.

out. 1. Outside.–Father let the dog *out.*
2. Not at home.–We are sorry that we were *out* when you came to see us.
3. Not burning or not lit.–The light in the hall is *out.*

4. No longer actively in the game.–If the ball hits the wicket the batsman is *out.*
5. No longer a secret.–The news of the wedding is *out.* It is known.
6. Aloud.–The parrot cried *out.*
7. Till finished.–Mother let Baby have her sleep *out.* She let her sleep until she woke up by herself.
8. To others.–The farmer lets *out* part of his farm. He rents it.
9. From the others.–The teacher told us to pick *out* the books we wanted to read.

outbreak out'-break *outbreaks.* Beginning or start of something violent, as war, a riot, etc. –Edward was in London at the *outbreak* of the war.

outburst out'-burst *outbursts.* A sudden bursting forth.–When the dog walked into the classroom, there was an *outburst* of laughter.

outcast out'-cast *outcasts.* A person from whom everyone has turned away.–The boy who had cheated found himself an *outcast.* People would not associate with him.

outcome out'-come *outcomes.* A result.–What was the *outcome* of the game? Who won?

outcry out'-cry *outcries.* A clamour or uproar.– There was an *outcry* when the referee blew his whistle for a foul.

outdoors out'-doors. Outside the house, out in the open air.–On clear days we play *outdoors.*

outer out'-er. Outside.–Mary took the *outer* wrapping off the package, but left the inner wrapping on till Christmas.

outfit out'-fit *outfits, outfitted, outfitting.* 1. Clothes.–Mary put on her Easter *outfit.*
2. Equipment or supplies.–The carpenter's *outfit* is a kit of tools and ladders which he uses in his work.
3. Equip or supply.–The Boy Scouts were *outfitted* for camping. They were given all the things they needed for living in it.

outgrow out-grow' *outgrows, outgrew, outgrown, outgrowing.* Grow too large or too old for.–Mother bought Mary a coat that was a little too large for her so that she would not *outgrow* it right away.–Bob gave away the story books he had *outgrown.*

outing out'-ing *outings.* A short outdoor pleasure trip.–On Sunday we are going for an *outing* up the river.

O
P
Q
R
S
T
U
V
W
X
Y
Z

outline out'-line *outlines, outlined, outlining.*
1. The line made by the outer edges of an object, showing its shape.–Bob drew the *outline* of a ship.

2. A plan.–Mary made an *outline* of the story she was to write.
3. Make an edge round.–Mary *outlined* the ship in red.
4. Make or tell about a plan.–The coach *outlined* the plan he wanted the team to follow.

out-of-doors. Outside the house or in the open air.–We play *out-of-doors* in summer more than we do in winter.

output out'-put *outputs.* The number made or produced.–The *output* of aeroplanes in the factory is 15 each week.

outside out-side . 1. The side that is out.–The house is plastered inside. It has bricks on the *outside.*–Mother's pocketbook is leather on the *outside* and cloth on the inside.
2. Farthest from the centre.–Jack was running in the *outside* lane of the track.
3. Outdoors.–Children like to play *outside.*
4. Near, but not in.–Bob waited for Jack *outside* the school.

outstanding out-stand'-ing. Best or most important.–Bob is the *outstanding* athlete in his class.

outwards out'-wards *outwardly, outward.* Away from the middle or towards the outside.–The girls in the circle stepped towards the middle, and the boys stepped *outwards,* so that it was a double circle.

outweigh out-weigh' *outweighs, outweighed, outweighing.* 1. Be greater than.–The importance of doing your homework *outweighs* the pleasure of going to the cinema.
2. Weigh more than.–The champion *outweighs* the challenger. He is heavier than the boxer who is challenging him.

outwit out-wit' *outwits, outwitted, outwitting.* Beat or defeat by clever tricks.–The opposing football team had bigger boys than Bob's team, so Bob's team had to *outwit* them in order to win.

oval o'-val. Shaped like an egg. – Mary has an *oval* face. – The picture of Grandmother as a bride hangs in an *oval* frame.

oven ov'-en *ovens.* 1. The closed part of a kitchen stove in which cake, bread, pies, etc., are baked and meat is roasted.

modern oven   primitive oven

2. A furnace or kiln.–Bricks are baked or hardened in an *oven.*

over o'-ver. 1. Above. – An awning was stretched *over* the speaker's platform.
2. Along or upon.–The wind blew the snow *over* Grandfather's fields.
3. Across the top of.–Mother ran the vacuum cleaner *over* the rug.
4. Across.–Bob tried to jump *over* the ditch.
5. During.–We stayed at home *over* the holidays.
6. Across.–Mary has gone *over* to Ruth's house.
7. Down from the top, on the outside.–Ann put so much milk in the jug that it ran *over.*
8. Upon or on top of.–Father put leaves *over* the flowers to keep them from freezing.
9. Ended.–The snowstorm should be *over* by night.
10. About.–Mother was laughing *over* the playfulness of the kitten.
11. More than.–*Over* three hundred children go to our school.
12. Down.–Spot knocked the lamp *over.*
13. The other side up.–Mother turned the tablecloth *over.*
14. More than was used.–We had several apples left *over.* There were several we didn't eat.
15. Again.–Mary did the problem twice *over* and got the same answer both times.
16. Upon.–A smile came *over* Baby's face when Mother came in.

overalls o'-ver-alls. Loose garment, often with a bib, worn to keep one clean while working or playing.

overboard o'-ver-board. Over the side of a ship into the water. –Mary threw some food *overboard* for the ducks.

overcoat o'-ver-coat *overcoats.* A heavy coat which is worn as an outer garment to keep one warm.

overcome o-ver-come′ *overcomes, overcame, overcoming.* 1. Get the better of someone or something; conquer. To be *overcome* means to become helpless, or be conquered.—Our team was *overcome* by the other side.—The swimmer was *overcome* by the waves, and had to be rescued by the lifeguard.
2. Make unconscious.—The rescue squad revived the fireman who was *overcome* by smoke.

overcrowd o-ver-crowd′ *overcrowds, overcrowded, overcrowding.* 1. Get too many people into at one time.—Do not *overcrowd* the hall.
2. Put too many things into.—The room is *overcrowded* with furniture.

overdo o-ver-do′ *overdoes, overdone, overdoing.* 1. Work too hard and become very tired.—Father told Mother not to *overdo* things.
2. Carry too far.—Mabel often *overdoes* her teasing.

overeat o-ver-eat′ *overeats, overate, overeaten, overeating.* Eat too much.—Do not *overeat,* or you may be sick.

overhaul o-ver-haul′ *overhauls, overhauled, overhauling.* Check the condition of and repair completely.—Father had his car *overhauled* before we took our trip.

overhead o-ver-head′. 1. Above.—The stars shine *overhead.*—The ceiling is *overhead.*
2. Raised.—Trolley-buses run from *overhead* wires. The wires are above the street.

overhear o-ver-hear′ *overhears, overheard, overhearing.* Hear something that one is not supposed to.—Mary *overheard* Mother telling Father about her birthday party.

overjoyed o-ver-joyed′. Delighted.—The children were *overjoyed* with their gifts.

overlap o-ver-lap′ *overlaps, overlapped, overlapping.* Lie partly over another.—A fish's scales *overlap.*—The petals of a pine cone *overlap.*—Slates on a house *overlap.*

overshoe o′-ver-shoe *overshoes.* A rubber shoe or a cloth shoe with a rubber sole which is worn over one's leather shoes to keep them dry.

overtake o-ver-take′ *overtakes, overtook, overtaken, overtaking.* 1. Catch up with.—Sally ran to *overtake* Mary, who was going out of the door.
2. Come upon.—Darkness *overtook* us, and we could not see where we were going.

overtime o′-ver-time. Past one's usual leaving or stopping time.—Father sometimes works *overtime.*

overturn o-ver-turn′ *overturns, overturned, overturning.* Upset.—Sally's kitten *overturned* Father's inkwell.

overweight o′-ver-weight. Weighing too much for a person of one's age and height.—Jim is *overweight.*

overwork o-ver-work′ *overworks, overworked, overworking.* Work too hard or too long.—The doctor told Grandfather not to *overwork.*

owe *owes, owed, owing.* Have to pay.—Jack bought the ball from Bob but still *owes* him for it.—If I borrow a penny from you, I *owe* you a penny.

owl *owls.* A large bird that has large eyes and sharp claws. *Owls* eat mice and other small animals. *Owls* fly mostly by night, and some make a hooting cry.

own *owns, owned, owning.* 1. Have.—I *own* a bicycle. It belongs to me.
2. One's *own* means one's property.—This bicycle is my *own.*

owner own′-er *owners.* The person to whom a thing belongs.—Father is the *owner* of the house.

ox *oxen.* A full-grown male animal of the cattle kind, adapted to use as a work animal for ploughing, pulling loads, and other heavy jobs.

oxen ox′-en. More than one *ox.*

oxygen ox′-y-gen. A gas which you cannot see, taste, or smell. Air has *oxygen* in it.—Animals must have *oxygen* to live.

oyster oys′-ter *oysters.* A kind of shellfish which lives in rough shells that open and close. *Oysters* are found along the sea-coast. They are used for food.

P p

P, p *P's p's.* The 16th letter of the alphabet.

pa. A name sometimes used instead of papa or father.

pace *paces, paced, pacing.* 1. A person's step; the way one walks.–Father walks with a rapid *pace*.
2. The length of a step.–A man's *pace* is about 2$\frac{1}{2}$ feet.
3. Measure by stepping along.–The boys *paced* off the distance for the cricket pitch.
4. The rate at which a thing is done.–The men are working at a fast *pace*.

pack *packs, packed, packing.* 1. Put away carefully.–Mother *packed* the china in a barrel.
2. Fill.–Father *packed* the suitcase.
3. A bundle of food, blankets, etc., carried by a hiker. – Jack set out on the hike with a *pack* on his back.

4. A set (of playing cards).–Father bought a new *pack* of cards.
5. A number of animals that travel together. –The hunter saw a *pack* of wolves.

package *pack'-age packages.* A bundle or parcel; something wrapped and tied or sealed.

pad *pads, padded, padding.* 1. A kind of cover or flat cushion with a soft filling.–Mother puts a *pad* under the tablecloth to protect the table.
2. Cover with a *pad* or *pads*.–Mother *padded* the kitchen chairs by fastening *pads* to the seats.

memo pad   chair pad

3. A small tablet of paper.–Mother keeps a *pad* on the door to write her grocery list on.
4. The little cushions on the bottoms of the paws of dogs, cats, and some other animals.

5. Walk softly.–The dog *padded* across Mother's clean kitchen floor.
6. A leg-guard in cricket, hockey, etc.

paddle *pad'-dle paddles, paddled, paddling.*
1. A stick, flattened at the end, which is pulled through the water to make a boat move.

2. Make move with a *paddle*.–Bob *paddled* the canoe across the lake.
3. Wade in the sea.–Baby loves to *paddle* when we go to the seaside.

padlock *pad'-lock padlocks.* A lock that can be put on and taken off.

page *pages, paged, paging.* 1. One side of a leaf of paper in a book.–This is *page* 326 in this book.
2. Call.–The *page* at the hotel was *paging* Mr Smith.
3. A boy who serves at a royal court.–The *page* found Cinderella's glass slipper on the stair.

pageant *pag'-eant pageants.* 1. A performance or entertainment in which a story is told in a series of scenes.–The village gave a *pageant* which showed scenes from English history.
2. Any colourful spectacle or show.–In the water *pageant* the swimmers held red balloons.

paid. One form of the word *pay*.–We *paid* the milkman. We gave him £1.

pail *pails.* 1. A bucket or large vessel with a handle over the top for carrying.
2. As much water as a *pail* will hold.–Jack and Jill went up the hill to fetch a *pail* of water.

pain *pains, pained, paining.* 1. The hurt which one feels when ill or injured. – Jack's sprained ankle gave him much *pain*.
2. Hurt.–Bob's finger still *pained* him a little after the splinter was removed.
3. A careful effort.–Mother takes great *pains* to please.

painful pain'-ful *painfully.* Causing or having pain.–Father said it was not *painful* to have his tooth pulled out.–Jack's ankle was very *painful* after he had twisted it.

paint *paints, painted, painting.* 1. A kind of colouring mixture that can be spread on a surface to colour and, sometimes, to protect it. *Paint* is liquid when it is put on, and dries hard.
2. Spread *paint* on; cover with *paint.*–Father *painted* the shutters blue.
3. Make (a picture) with *paint.*–Sally *painted* a picture of Mother.

painter paint'-er *painters.* 1. An artist; a person who paints pictures.

artist   house painter

2. A person who paints buildings and other things for a living.
3. A rope which is used for tying up a boat.–The boatman jumped ashore and tied the *painter* to a post on the pier, to stop his boat drifting away.

painting paint'-ing *paintings.* A picture.–We saw many *paintings* and drawings in the art museum.

pair *pairs, paired, pairing.* 1. Two things of a kind that go together, such as a *pair* of boots.
2. Anything such as scissors, pliers, trousers, etc., made of two parts joined together is called a *pair* of scissors, a *pair* of pliers, a *pair* of trousers, etc.
3. A married couple.–Father and Mother are a happy *pair*.
4. Group in twos.–The children *paired* off to play London Bridge.

palace pal'-ace *palaces.* A large, grand house in which kings and queens live.

pale *paler, palest.* 1. Very white, or colourless. –The frightened boy's face turned *pale*.
2. Light.–Mary's new dress is *pale* blue.

palm *palms.* 1. The inside of the hand between the wrist and the fingers.
2. A tree that grows in very warm regions. The leaves of the *palm* are long and flat, and grow in bunches near the top of the tree.– Dates grow on date *palms*, and coconuts on coconut *palms*.

pamphlet pam'-phlet *pamphlets.* A booklet; a thin little book with a paper cover.

pan *pans.* An open metal vessel used in cooking.–Mother cooks bacon in a frying *pan*.

pancake pan'-cake *pancakes.* A thin, flat cake made of batter and fried on a griddle or skillet.

pane *panes.* A sheet of glass.–The *panes* in the windows were covered with frost this morning.

panel pan'-el *panels.* 1. A piece of wood or other material set into doors or walls, with other pieces placed around to frame it like a picture.
2. A long strip of cloth in a garment. – Mary's new skirt has *panels* in the front and back.

panic pan'-ic *panics.* Wild behaviour caused by fear.–The fire caused a *panic* among the people. Everyone rushed for the door.

P
Q
R
S
T
U
V
W
X
Y
Z

pansy pan'-sy *pansies*. A flower with broad petals that grows on a low plant. *Pansies* are of many beautiful colours, with several colours combined in each flower.

pant *pants, panted, panting*. Breathe hard and quickly.–The dog came back *panting* after he chased the cat up the tree.

panther pan'-ther *panthers*. A leopard, puma or other kind of wildcat.–Jack likes to watch the black *panther* in the zoo.

pantry pan'-try *pantries*. A small room near the kitchen where food and dishes are kept.

pants. A short lower undergarment; drawers. –I wear *pants* and a vest.

papa pa'-pa *papas*. A child's word for father.

tracing paper
newspaper
writing paper
paper cup
paper book
preparing wood pulp
making paper by hand
modern paper-making machine

paper pa'-per *papers, papered, papering*. 1. A material made in thin sheets from crushed wood or rags.–The pages of this book are *paper*.

2. A news*paper*.–Father reads the *paper* every evening.

3. A composition.–Bob read his *paper* to the class.

4. A printed or written legal agreement.– Father bought a new house and got the *papers* saying it was his.

5. Put wall*paper* on.–*The paper*-hanger *papered* the dining-room walls.

parable par'-able *parables*. A short, fictitious story from which a moral is drawn.–The preacher took as his text the *parable* of the Good Samaritan.

parachute par'-a-chute *parachutes*. An umbrella-shaped device with which a person may float safely down from an aeroplane high in the air.

parade pa-rade' *parades, paraded, parading*. 1. An assembly of troops for inspection.– The *parade* was held on the parade-ground at 12 o'clock.

2. Assemble for review or other purpose.– The soldiers were told to *parade* at noon.

3. March through streets with display.–The battalion *paraded* through the city.

4. Public square or promenade. – Father's shop is on the *parade*.

5. Display or show off.–Bob *paraded* his knowledge. He showed off.

paradise par'-a-dise. 1. Heaven, where God and his angels dwell.–In Milton's poem 'Paradise Lost' God hurled Satan out of *Paradise* into Hell.

2. A wonderful, beautiful place.–The house, with its large garden and view of the sea, is a real *paradise* for children.

paraffin par'-af-fin. A tasteless, colourless substance used for making candles, and as fuel.– A paraffin heater warms my bedroom.

P
Q
R
S
T
U
V
W
X
Y
Z

paragraph par'-a-graph *paragraphs*. A group of sentences telling about one thing.–Mary's composition was made up of four *paragraphs*.

parallel par'-al-lel *parallels*. Being the same distance apart through-out.–The opposite sides of your desk are *parallel*.–Railway lines are *parallel*. They are the same distance apart along their entire length.

paralyse par'-a-lyse *paralyses, paralysed, paralysing*. 1. Make unable to move or feel.–The soldier's leg is *paralysed*. He can't move it.
2. Make inactive or helpless.–The traffic was *paralysed* by the snowstorm.

paralysis pa-ral'-y-sis. 1. Loss of the ability to move or feel in some part of the body.–The soldier has *paralysis* in one leg.
2. Condition of being unable to move or act. –*Paralysis* of traffic resulted from the snowstorm.

parasol par'-a-sol *parasols*. A fancy umbrella carried by women for protection from the sun.

parcel par'-cel *parcels*. A package or bundle. –We got a *parcel* in the post today.

parch *parches, parched, parching*. Make hot and dry. – The thirsty boy's mouth was *parched*.

parchment parch'-ment. The dried skin of goats, sheep, or other animals, treated so that it can be written on.

pardon par'-don *pardons, pardoned, pardoning*. 1. Excuse or forgive.–If you are really sorry, the teacher will *pardon* you.
2. Forgiveness.–Mary said, 'I beg your *pardon*,' when she interrupted Father.
3. Release from punishment.–The prisoner was *pardoned* because he was so young.

pare *pares, pared, paring*. Peel.–Mary helped Mother *pare* the potatoes.

parent par'-ent *parents*. A mother or father.– Either of your *parents* may sign your report card.

parenthesis pa-ren'-the-sis *parentheses*. 1. The phrase enclosed in *parentheses*.–(The first day of the week) is a *parenthesis*.

2. Either of two marks ( ) used to set off certain words from the rest of a sentence. *Parentheses* are sometimes put round words in a sentence to explain something that has been said just before.–Monday (the second day of the week) is a school day.

paring par'-ing *parings*. A peel or skin.–The potato *parings* were fed to the pigs.

park *parks, parked, parking*. 1. A place outdoors set aside for people to visit, to see the scenery, have picnics, play games, and enjoy themselves.

2. Put a motor-car in a certain place and leave it there.–It is unlawful to *park* too near a pedestrian crossing.
3. A space where cars may be *parked*.–When we went to the theatre we left the car in a car-*park*.

Parliament Par'-lia-ment *Parliaments*. An assembly of people who make laws and discuss a country's affairs.–In England, *Parliament* consists of the House of Commons and the House of Lords. The Houses of *Parliament* are at Westminster in London.

parrot par'-rot *parrots*. A kind of brilliantly coloured bird with a hooked bill. – *Parrots* can be taught to say the things they hear people say.

parsley pars'-ley. A plant that has fine curly leaves which are used to flavour foods and to decorate food dishes.

parsnip pars'-nip *parsnips*. A white vegetable shaped something like a carrot. *Parnips* grow in the ground.

P
Q
R
S
T
U
V
W
X
Y
Z

parson par'-son *parsons*. A minister or pastor of a church.–The *parson* came to visit Grandmother when she was sick.

parsonage par'-son-age *parsonages*. A minister's home provided by his church.–The *parsonage* is next door to the church.

part *parts, parted, parting*. 1. A piece or amount less than the whole.–Baby ate *part* of an orange.
2. A share.–Bob always does his *part* to keep the house neat.
3. Mary played the *part* of Snow White in the play.
4. A side.–The twins always take Jack's *part* in a quarrel.
5. Make separate, force apart.–Jack *parted* the fighting dogs.
6. Go away from one another; separate.–Bob and Jack *parted* when they reached the corner.
7. A section.–We live in a hilly *part* of the country.
8. Give up.–Little girls do not like to *part* with their dolls.
9. A dividing line.–The *parting* in Jack's hair is on the left.
10. A piece.–When Bob had put the clock together again, he had one *part* left over.
11. A voice.–There are several *parts* in this song. Mary sings the alto, or lower *part*.
12. Each of the equal pieces into which a thing can be divided.–A fifth *part* of a pie is one of 5 equal pieces the same size.

partial par'-tial *partially*. 1. Prejudiced; likely to favour one side.–The umpire seemed to be *partial* to our team.
2. Likely to prefer. – I have always been *partial* to the colour green.
3. Part.–Father made a *partial* payment on our car. He paid part of the amount owed.

particular par-tic'-u-lar *particularly*. 1. Very careful; fussy.–Mother is *particular* about the baby's food.
2. Special or outstanding.–There is one *particular* point I must warn you about.
3. Certain.–On this *particular* morning the sun shone warm and bright.

partition par-ti'-tion *partitions*. An inside wall that separates rooms or compartments.

partly part'-ly. In part.
–The house is *partly* finished.

partner part'-ner *partners*. 1. One of several persons who play on a side in a game.
2. One of several owners of one thing.–Two men are *partners* in owning the shop.
3. A person with whom one is paired for a dance, a game, etc.–Mary and Bob were *partners* in the last dance.

party par'-ty *parties*. 1. A group entertainment.–We had a *party* at school for our class.
2. A group of people who work together to try to elect certain persons to office.–The most important *parties* in Great Britain are the Conservative *Party*, the Labour *Party* and the Liberal *Party*.

pass *passes, passed, passing*. 1. Go by, or move past.–We saw the parade *pass* the school.
2. Hand.–The teacher asked us to *pass* our papers up.–*Pass* me the salt, please.
3. Be mistaken.–When Mary is dressed in Jack's clothes, she could *pass* for a boy.
4. Spend.–Bob *passed* the time reading.
5. A path or narrow road. – We walked through the mountain *pass*.

6, A written permit.–The children must have a *pass* to go through the halls.
7. A free ticket.–The owner of the cricket club gave Bob and Jack *passes* to the match.
8. Finish the work of a school course and succeed in an examination on it.–Everyone in our class *passed*.
9. Make or approve (a law). – The town council *passed* a law that forbids overnight parking in the streets.
10. Die.–The old man *passed* away.

passage pass'-age *passages*. 1. Movement or travel from one place to another.–The ship had a stormy *passage* to New York.
2. A tunnel, hall, or other place through which one can pass from place to place.– We walked through the *passage*.

3. Approval of a law, resolution, etc.–*Passage* of a law against overnight parking was urged by the mayor.

passage-way pas'-sage-way *passage-ways*. A hall or narrow path through which people can pass.

passenger pas'-sen-ger *passengers*. A person travelling on a plane, train, bus, boat, car, etc.

passport pass'-port *passports*. A special paper given to a citizen of one country which gives him the right to travel in other countries.

past. 1. Already gone by.–In *past* years we have always gone to Grandmother's for Christmas; this year she is visiting us.
2. Time gone by.–In the *past* we started for school at 8.30 in the morning; now we go at 9.00.
3. One's life up to now.–Grandfather told us stories of his *past*.

paste *pastes, pasted, pasting*. 1. A soft substance used for sticking things together.–Mary used *paste* to make the picture stick in her scrap-book.
2. Stick with *paste*.–She *pasted* the pictures in.

pasteboard paste'-board. A material made in stiff sheets by pasting paper together, or by pressing into sheets chopped-up paper mixed with a special paste.

pasteurize pas'-teur-ize *pasteurizes, pasteurized, pasteurizing*. Treat with heat to kill harmful germs.–We drink *pasteurized* milk.

pastime pas'-time *pastimes*. A game or pleasant activity.–Bob's favourite *pastime* is building model aircraft.

pastor pas'-tor *pastors*. A minister or a priest who has charge of a church.

pastry pas'-try *pastries*. 1. Food, such as pies or tarts, made of rich dough.
2. A piece of *pastry*.–The bakery window displayed many *pastries*.

pasture pas'-ture *pastures, pastured, pasturing*.

1. A grassy field where cattle feed. – Bob drove Grandfather's cow to the *pasture*.

2. Grass or other plants which cattle eat.–The *pasture* is very good this year.
3. Graze, or put out to graze.–The sheep are *pastured* on the hillside.

pat *pats, patted, patting*. 1. Touch or slap gently.–Sally likes to *pat* the dog.
2. A light touch or slap.–Sally gave the dog a *pat*.
3. A small cake or piece.–The waiter brought a *pat* of butter.

patch *patches, patched, patching*. 1. A piece of cloth sewn over a hole or tear in cloth.– Mother sewed a *patch* on Jack's old trousers.
2. Any piece of material, such as cloth or sheet metal, used to cover a hole, crack, in-

jury, or damage, etc.–The workman put a *patch* on the leaking metal roof.
3. A piece of land.–Grandfather has a small *patch* planted with onions.
4. Put a *patch* on.–Mother *patched* Jack's sleeve.
5. Fix up; make right.–Jack and Bill have *patched* up their troubles.

patent pat'-ent *patents, patented, patenting*.
1. A written paper from the government which gives an inventor, and no one else, the right to make and sell his invention for a certain number of years.
2. Receive a *patent* for.–Father *patented* his new shoe-repairing machine last month.

path *paths*. A narrow trail or track worn by animals or people walking, or made for animals or people to walk on.

patience pa'-tience. The ability to be calm or to stand discomfort or other annoyance without complaining.–We do not realize how much *patience* Mother has with us.

patient pa'-tient *patients, patiently*. 1. Calm, not bothered. – Our teacher is very *patient* with us when we ask questions. She does not become disturbed or irritated with us.
2. A person in the care of a doctor.–Our doctor has two other *patients* living in this road.

P
Q
R
S
T
U
V
W
X
Y
Z

patriot pa'-tri-ot *patriots*. A person who shows great love for his country.–Sir Francis Drake was a great English *patriot*.

patriotic pa-tri-ot'-ic *patriotically*. Showing great love for one's country.–Abraham Lincoln was *patriotic*. He worked for the good of the people of his country.

patrol pa-trol' *patrols, patrolled, patrolling*. 1. A guard or guards who go over a certain route again and again to watch and keep order. – Police *patrols* watch the highways. 2. Watch; go back and forth along and keep a watch over. – The soldiers *patrolled* the border of the country.

patter pat'-ter *patters, pattered, pattering*. 1. A gentle tapping. – We heard the *patter* of little feet upstairs. 2. Tap lightly.–The rain was *pattering* on the window-panes.

pattern pat'-tern *patterns, patterned, patterning*. 1. A form or guide to follow in cutting out or building something –Mother bought a *pattern* to make Mary a dress. 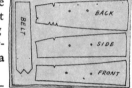 2. A design or figure.– The cloth for Mary's dress had a leaf *pattern*. 3. Model, copy.–Mother's hat is *patterned* after a more expensive one. 4. An ideal or an example.–Bob is a *pattern* for the other boys to follow.

patty pat'-ty *patties*. A cup-shaped shell made of dough and baked.

pauper pau'-per *paupers*. A very poor porson, –The man said that he could not pay his bills, because he was a *pauper*.

pause *pauses, paused, pausing*. 1. A short stop or wait.–Mary waited for a *pause* in the talk to ask if she might go to the cinema. 2. Stop for a moment. – Mother *paused* to think before she began the letter to the teacher.

pave *paves, paved, paving*. Cover with pavement. – The workmen are *paving* the worn road with concrete.

pavement pave'-ment *pavements*. The hard surface of concrete, asphalt, or other substance covering roads and walks.

pavilion pa-vil'-ion *pavilions*. A low building with open sides.–We watched the match from the cricket *pavilion*.

paw *paws, pawed, pawing*. 1. A foot of an animal that has claws.–The kitten batted the ball with her *paw*. 2. Scrape with the *paws* or feet.–The horse *pawed* the ground. 3. Handle roughly. – Do not *paw* the baby chicks.

pay *pays, paid, paying*. 1. Give money in exchange.–We *pay* for work done for us by others or for things which we buy. – Jack *paid* sixpence for the ice-cream. 2. Salary or wages.–Jack's *pay* from his paper round is £2 a week. 3. Offer; give.–Our teacher told us to *pay* attention to what she said. 4. Be worth while.–Honesty *pays*.

payment pay'-ment *payments*. An amount of money paid. – Father makes a *payment* on the new car every month.

pea *peas*. The small, round, green seed of the pea plant. It is eaten as a vegetable. *Peas* grow in pods on vines.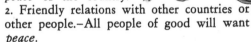

peace. 1. Quiet and calm; absence of any disturbance. – Grandmother enjoys the *peace* of the country. 2. Friendly relations with other countries or other people.–All people of good will want *peace*. 3. Not in war.–The country of Switzerland remained at *peace* during the war.

peaceful peace'-ful *peacefully*. Quiet and calm, undisturbed. – After the storm, it was *peaceful* in the wet garden.

peach *peaches*. 1. A round, juicy fruit with a fuzzy, reddish-yellow skin. In the middle of the *peach* is a rough stone or pit. *Peaches* grow on *peach* trees.  2. Yellowish-pink.–Mary has a pair of *peach*-coloured pyjamas.

P
Q
R
S
T
U
V
W
X
Y
Z

peacock pea'-cock *peacocks*. A bird with beautiful green feathers, spotted with other colours. The *peacock* spreads his very long tail feathers out like a fan.

peahen pea'-hen *peahens*. The female of the peacock.

peak *peaks*. 1. The very top point.–There is a weather vane on the *peak* of the schoolhouse. –The *peak* of the mountain is covered with snow.–Bob is at the *peak* of his form on the cricket field. He scored another century today.
2. The part of a cap which sticks out.–Jack pulled the *peak* of his cap further down to keep the sun out of his eyes.

peal *peals, pealed, pealing*. 1. A long, loud ringing.–We heard the *peal* of the church bells.
2. Ring.–The bells *pealed* clearly.

peanut pea'-nut *peanuts*. A thin, soft shell containing a nutlike seed that is good to eat. Usually there are two seeds in one shell. *Peanuts* grow in the ground.

pear *pears*. The juicy, sweet fruit of a *pear* tree. Some *pears* are yellow, some are green, and some are brown, when ripe. *Pears* have cores like apples.

pearl *pearls*. *Pearls* are formed in the shells of some oysters round a grain of sand that gets into the shell. They are bluish, pinkish, or creamy white, and are used in necklaces and other jewellery.

peasant peas'-ant *peasants*. In some countries, a person who works on the land.

pebble peb'-ble *pebbles*. A small, round stone. –Sally picked up *pebbles* on the beach.

pebbly peb'-bly. Covered with pebbles. – The beach was *pebbly*, not sandy.

peck *pecks, pecked, pecking*. 1. Nip with the beak.–The hen *pecked* Bob.
2. A measure of dry material, especially of vegetables. Four *pecks* make one bushel.

peckish peck'-ish. A slang word for hungry.– Mary came home from school and said she was feeling *peckish*, so Mother gave her some milk and biscuits.

peculiar pe-cul'-iar *peculiarly*. 1. Odd or strange.–Jack could tell that this was the boy they were looking for by his *peculiar* walk.
2. Belonging to one thing or one class of things.–Fathers are *peculiar* to birds. Only birds have feathers.

pedal ped'-al *pedals, pedalled, pedalling*. 1. A lever worked by the foot. – Father put his foot on the brake *pedal* to slow down the car.
2. Push *pedals* to move a vehicle.–Sally likes to *pedal* her tricycle across the driveway.

peddle ped'-dle *peddles, peddled, peddling*. Carry about and sell.–The old man *peddles* shoe-laces to make a living. He goes from house to house selling shoe-laces.

pedestal ped'-es-tal *pedestals*. A base for something to stand on. – The little bronze statue on Father's desk stands on a *pedestal*.

pedigree ped'-i-gree *pedigrees, pedigreed*. Ancestry; the record of a breed from a long time past up to the present.–Some of Grandfather's cattle have fine *pedigrees*.

pedlar ped'-lar *pedlars*. A person who goes along the streets or from house to house selling things.–The old *pedlar* had shoe-laces for sale.

peek *peeks, peeked, peeking*. 1. Peep; take a quick, sly look. – Mother told Mary not to *peek* while she opened the parcel.
2. A quick, sly look.–Mary took a *peek* at the parcel.

peel *peels, peeled, peeling*. 1. The outer skin or rind of some fruits and vegetables.– Banana *peel* is yellow or pink when ripe.
2. Take off the outer skin.–We *peel* bananas before we eat them.

P
Q
R
S
T
U
V
W
X
Y
Z

peep *peeps, peeped, peeping.* 1. A quick look. –Mother took a *peep* at the cake in the oven. 2. Look slyly.–The boys *peeped* through a hole in the fence to watch the game. 3. The cry of a bird or baby chicken.

peer *peers, peered, peering.* 1. Look intently at. –Mother *peered* at Sally's picture of Father. 2. A member of the British nobility. A duke is a peer; so is a baron.

peevish pee'-vish *peevishly, peevishness.* Cross; easily made angry.–Baby is sometimes a bit *peevish* when she is cutting teeth.

peg *pegs, pegged, pegging.* 1. A small, round piece of wood or metal that fits into a hole, goes into the ground, etc., to hold something. 2. Fasten with a *peg*.–The tent rope was *pegged* to the ground.

pelican pel'-i-can *pelicans.* A large water-bird. Beneath its bill is a big pouch in which food is stored.

pelt *pelts, pelted, pelting.* 1. The hide of an animal before it is made into leather. 2. Throw things at.– The boys *pelted* the target with pebbles.

pen *pens, penned, penning.* 1. A small enclosed space in which animals are kept.–The pig is in the pig*pen*.

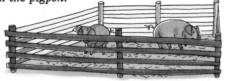

2. Shut in a *pen*.–The farmer *penned* his pigs. 3. A writing instrument used with ink.

4. Write.–Bob *penned* a letter to Mother. 5. Shut in, as if in a *pen*.–The boys caught the rabbit by coming from all sides and *penning* him in.

penalty pen'-al-ty *penalties.* A punishment.– The lawful *penalty* for stealing is being fined or going to jail.

pencil pen'-cil *pencils.* A small stick of wood that has a long thin stick of 'lead' or graphite through the middle, and sometimes a rubber at one end.–I write best with a *pencil*.

pendulum pen'-du-lum *pendulums.* A weight that is hung so that it can swing back and forth. – The grandfather clock has a brass *pendulum* that you can see through the glass door.

penguin pen'-guin *penguins.* A sea bird that can swim, but cannot fly. *Penguins* live near the South Pole, where it is very cold.

peninsula pen-in'-su-la *peninsulas.* A narrow strip of land that sticks far out into the water. –Italy is a *peninsula*.

penitent pen'-i-tent *penitence.* Ashamed and apologetic.–Jack was *penitent* as soon as he had broken the window.

penknife pen'-knife *penknives.* A small knife with folding blades that can be carried in the pocket.

penmanship pen'-man-ship. Handwriting; the skill of writing by hand.–Dick is very proud of his *penmanship*.

pennant pen'-nant *pennants.* A long, narrow flag, usually pointed at one end.

penniless pen'-ni-less. *Without* any money, very poor.–We gave the beggar a five pence piece because he said he was *penniless*.

penny pen'-ny *pennies* or *pence*. In Britain, a bronze coin, one-hundredth of a pound. In the United States a cent is sometimes called a penny.

penny-farthing pen'-ny-far'-thing *penny-farthings*. An old-fashioned bicycle with a very large front wheel and a very small back one. –Grandmother just remembers seeing *penny-farthings* when she was a girl.

pennyworth pen'-ny-worth *pennyworths*. Whatever can be bought for one penny. – After school we went into the sweet-shop and bought a *pennyworth* of bubble-gum.

pension pen'-sion *pensions*. A sum of money paid regularly to a person to support him when he is unable to work because of injury or old age.–Mr Wilson used to be a night watchman. Now he gets a *pension* from the firm of £10 a month.

peony pe'-o-ny *peonies*. A large red, pink, or white perennial flower that grows on a bush-like plant.

people peo'-ple *peoples*. 1. Human beings; men, women, boys, and girls. – Great crowds of *people* were at the circus.
2. A race; all the citizens of a country or a part of a country.–All the *peoples* of the earth want freedom.

pepper pep'-per *peppers, peppered, peppering*.
1. A plant whose small red or black berries or seeds have a hot, stinging taste. These seeds are called *pepper* when ground and used as a seasoning on foods.
2. A kind of green or red vegetable used in salads and as a seasoning.
3. Put *pepper* on.–Mother salted and *peppered* the potatoes.

peppermint pep'-per-mint. A herb or plant from which is made a pleasant-smelling oil, used for flavouring. – We hung *peppermint* drops on the Christmas trees.

per cent per-cent'. Per hundred; hundredths. – One *per cent* (1%) is one out of every hundred, or one-hundredth (written 1/100 or 0.01).

perch *perches, perched, perching*. 1. A stick or bar on which a bird sits.
2. A high seat of any kind. – From his *perch* on the fence, Jack could watch the cricket match.
3. Sit.–Saffy likes to *perch* on the fence.
4. A small fresh-water fish that is good to eat.

percolator per'-co-la-tor *percolators*. A kind of coffee pot in which water shoots up through a tube and drains back through the ground coffee.

perennial per-en'-ni-al *perennials*. A flowering plant that lives from year to year.–Peonies and irises are *perennials*. They bloom every year.

perfect per'-fect. Completely without faults. –Bob's arithmetic paper was *perfect*. He made no mistake on it.

perfect per-fect' *perfects, perfected, perfecting*. Remove all mistakes or faults from.–Bob and Jack are working to *perfect* their model aeroplane.

perfectly per'-fect-ly. Completely or entirely.– It is *perfectly* all right for you to go to the cinema if you finish your work first.

perforate per'-fo-rate *perforates, perforated, perforating*. Make small holes through something.–Sheets of postage stamps are *perforated* so that they can be torn apart easily.

perform per-form' *performs, performed, performing*. 1. Do.–The boys *performed* their work well.
2. Entertain an audience. – Actors *perform*.

performance per-form'-ance *performances*. 1. A show at a theatre.–There will be two *performances* of the play tonight.
2. An action or deed.–Jack's *performance* in the play was very good. He did well.

performer per-form'-er *performers*. A person who entertains by acting, playing an instrument, singing, dancing, or in any other way.

P
Q
R
S
T
U
V
W
X
Y
Z

perfume per'-fume *perfumes*. 1. A sweet-smelling liquid made from oils that are pressed from plants or obtained from certain animals. –Mother puts a drop of *perfume* behind her ears when she goes out.
2. A sweet odour.–We could smell the *perfume* of flowers in the garden.

perfume per-fume' *perfumes, perfumed, perfuming*. Make fragrant. – The flowers *perfumed* the air.

perhaps per-haps'. Maybe; possibly. – *Perhaps* Father will be home early today.

peril per'-il *perils, perilled, perilling*. 1. Danger. –The ship was in *peril* because of the storm.
2. Put in danger of being destroyed. – The storm *perilled* the ship.

period pe'-ri-od *periods*. 1. A dot (.) used in writing and printing. We put a *period* after every sentence, and after abbreviations to indicate that the full word is not being used.
2. A division of time.–We have reading during the first *period* at school.

periscope per'-i-scope *periscopes*. A curved tube which contains mirrors so arranged that one can look into the lower end of the tube and see what is in front of the upper end. *Periscopes* are used in submarines to see what is happening above the surface of the water.

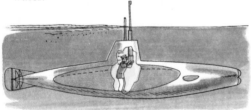

perish per'-ish *perishes, perished, perishing*. Die.–Some plants *perish* in the winter.

perishable per'-ish-a-ble. Liable to become rotten.–Milk and butter are *perishable*; they will spoil unless kept cold.

permanent per'-ma-nent *permanently*. Unchanging; long-lasting, never needing to be replaced.–The dentist put a *permanent* filling in Father's tooth after the temporary one had fallen out.–This is our *permanent* home. We have lived here a long time, and do not intend to move.

permission per-mis'-sion. Leave or consent.– The teacher gave Bob *permission* to go to the library. She said he might go.

permit per-mit' *permits, permitted, permitting*. Allow.–Will you *permit* me to use your pen?

permit per'-mit *permits*. A licence, or written permission.–Father has a *permit* to hunt.

persecute per'-se-cute *persecutes, persecuted, persecuting*. Harm often and unjustly; pick on.–The bad boys *persecuted* the stranger by throwing stones at him whenever they saw him.

persist per-sist' *persists, persisted, persisting, persistence*. Refuse to stop or change.–Jack *persists* in talking in class.

person per'-son *persons*. A human being.– Every *person* should be treated fairly.

personal per'-son-al. 1. Private.–Father takes care of his *personal* mail, and his secretary takes care of his business letters.
2. In person.–Jean made a *personal* request to the teacher. She spoke to the teacher herself.
3. Of the body.–One's *personal* appearance is the way one looks.

personality per-son-al'-i-ty *personalities*. The traits of a person all together; a person's ways and manners. – Mary has a charming *personality*. People like her.

personally per'-son-al-ly. 1. In person.–Mother called on our teacher *personally*.
2. In one's own interest.–*Personally*, I would rather have the picnic in the afternoon.

perspiration per-spi-ra'-tion. Sweat. – In hot weather, *perspiration* comes out of the skin in large quantities, and often forms large drops.

perspire per-spire' *perspires, perspired, perspiring*. Sweat.–When we *perspire*, drops of water come through the tiny openings of the skin.

persuade per-suade' *persuades, persuaded, persuading*. Convince by urging; get someone to believe or do something.–At first Father didn't want to go swimming, but we *persuaded* him to come with us.

persuasion per-sua'-sion. The act of persuading.–Bob is good at *persuasion*. He is good at getting people to do things willingly.

pest *pests*. 1. A nuisance; something or someone who makes trouble.–Bill is a *pest*; he annoys others.
2. Something that causes destruction.–Grasshoppers are *pests*. They destroy crops.

pet *pets, petted, petting.* 1. An animal kept to love and play with. – Bob's *pet* is a little puppy.
2. Someone who is specially favoured.–Jack called Mary a teacher's *pet*.
3. Pat or stroke lovingly.–Sally likes to *pet* her kitten.

petal pet'-al *petals.* The coloured leaf-like parts of a flower.–Rose *petals* fall off when the rose dies.

petition pe-ti'-tion *petitions, petitioned, petitioning.* 1. A formal request, usually written. –All the children signed a *petition* asking the school officials for a half-holiday on the day of the fair.
2. Formally request, usually in writing.–The children *petitioned* the school officials for a half-holiday.

petroleum pe-tro'-le-um. The crude oil found in the ground.–*Petroleum* is made into paraffin, petrol, oils, and a great many other products.

petty pet'-ty *pettier, pettiest.* Small, mean, or unimportant. – The story about the quarrel between the neighbours was just *petty* gossip.

petty officer pet'-ty of'fi-cer *petty officers.* A naval officer corresponding to a non-commissioned officer in the army.

petunia pe-tu'-ni-a *petunias.* A plant that has many pink, purple, or white blossoms.

pew *pews.* A bench or long seat with a high back, used in churches.

pewter pew'-ter. 1. A metal made from tin and lead. *Pewter* usually has more tin than lead in it. It was used many centuries ago for tableware and eating utensils.
2. Made of *pewter.*–Grandmother has many *pewter* pieces in her dining room.

phalanx pha'-lanx *phalanxes.* A group of people banded together for a common purpose.– When the procession drove by, a *phalanx* of policemen kept the crowd from bursting through into the roadway.

phantom phan'-tom *phantoms.* A ghost; a likeness of something which a person imagines is real.–In the darkness the dead tree looked like a *phantom.* It looked like an old woman.

pharmacist phar'-ma-cist *pharmacists.* Druggist. – The *pharmacist* mixes different drugs together to make medicines.

P
Q
R
S
T
U
V
W
X
Y
Z

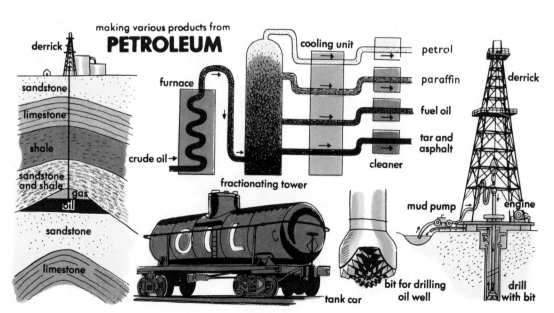

making various products from
PETROLEUM

derrick
sandstone
limestone
shale
sandstone and shale
gas
oil
sandstone
limestone

furnace
crude oil
fractionating tower

cooling unit
petrol
paraffin
fuel oil
tar and asphalt
cleaner

derrick

mud pump
engine

bit for drilling oil well

drill with bit

tank car

pharmacy phar'-ma-cy *pharmacies*. 1. A chemist's shop.–The doctor sends a prescription to a *pharmacy* to have medicine made according to his directions.
2. The preparation and dispensing of drugs and medicines. Druggists practise *pharmacy*.

pheasant pheas'-ant *pheasants*. A long-tailed game bird. Its feathers are brilliantly coloured. Men hunt *pheasants* for food.

phenomenal phe-nom'-e-nal *phenomenally*. Extraordinary, remarkable.–When John was ill, he was given a series of injections and made a *phenomenal* recovery within a few days.

philanthropy phi-lan'-thro-py *philanthropist*. Love and sympathy towards other people.–Giving money to deserving causes, and helping the sick and poor, are examples of *philanthropy*.

philately phi-lat'-e-ly *philatelist*. The collection of postage-stamps.–Bill has a collection of over 5,000 stamps. *Philately* is his favourite hobby.

philosopher phi-los'-o-pher *philosophic, philosophy*. A person who loves and seeks truth and wisdom.–Socrates was a famous Greek philosopher who tried to discover the true meaning of life.–The *philosopher's* subject is called *philosophy*.

phlox. A plant that has large clusters of flowers growing on a tall stem. *Phlox* is white, pink, or of mixed colours.

phone *phones, phoned, phoning*. A short word for tele*phone*.–We can talk on the *phone* to friends who are far away.–We can *phone* people who are far away.

photo pho'-to *photos*. A short word for *photograph*.–For Christmas I gave Grandmother a *photo* of myself holding my puppy.

photograph pho'-to-graph *photographs, photographed, photographing*. 1. A picture made with a camera.–Bob brought his camera to school to take a *photograph* of our class.–A *photograph* is produced by light striking a specially prepared film or plate.
2. Make a *photograph* of. – Bob *photographed* our class with his camera.

photographer pho-tog'-ra-pher *photographers*. A person who takes pictures with a camera. –The *photographer* came to our house to take pictures of Baby.

photography pho-tog'-ra-phy. The art, skill or business of making pictures with a camera.

phrase *phrases, phrased, phrasing*. 1. A group of words which go together. Sometimes a *phrase* is used like one word.–'The drawing class is fun.' 'The drawing class' is a *phrase*.
2. Divide into *phrases*.–In reading it helps you to get the meaning if you *phrase* correctly, or put the words into their right groups.

physic phys'-ic *physics*. A medicine that makes the bowels move.–Castor oil is a *physic*.

physical phys'-i-cal *physically*. 1. About or having to do with the body. – The doctor gave the children a *physical* examination. He examined their bodies.
2. About or having to do with things that one can see, feel, hear, taste, or smell. Natural things like mountains, wind, rivers, and sunlight are *physical*. Things that we can think about but can't observe, like justice or goodness, are not *physical*.

physician phy-si'-cian *physicians*. A doctor of medicine.–When Grandmother was ill, we called a *physician*.

pianist pi'-an-ist *pianists*. A person who plays the piano. – Mary is studying to be a *pianist*.

piano pi-an′-o *pianos*. A large musical instrument played by striking keys arranged in order in a keyboard. Striking a key makes a small wooden hammer hit a string, which gives out a musical note.

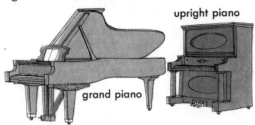

upright piano

grand piano

pianoforte pi-an′-o-forte *pianofortes*. The full name for a piano, from the Italian words piano (soft) and forte (loud).

picador pic′-a-dor *picadors*. A bull-fighter on horseback. The man who fights the bull on foot is called a matador.

piccolo pic′-co-lo *piccolos*. A small flute.–A *piccolo* is played by blowing into a hole on one side of it.

pick *picks, picked, picking*. 1. Choose or select. –Mother finally *picked* a green dress, after looking at several others.
2. A choice.–We arrived at the theatre early enough to have our *pick* of the seats.
3. Lift.–Mother *picked* up Baby to dress her.
4. Pluck, gather, or pull.–Sally likes to *pick* the flowers.–Mother *picked* the stalks off the strawberries.
5. Remove small pieces from.–It is not polite to *pick* one's teeth.–Grandmother gave Sally a chicken wing to *pick*.
6. A sharp, pointed tool fastened to a handle. –The roadman used a heavy *pick* to loosen the hard earth when he dug the ditch.– Mother used an ice *pick* to break ice for the lemonade.
7. Dig with a *pick*.–The men picked the earth away from the sewer.
8. Gather.–The sledge *picked* up speed as it coasted down the hill. It went faster and faster.
9. Learn without studying.–Mary *picked* up some French words from her music teacher.
10. Improve or recover.–The dry plant began to *pick* up after Grandmother watered it.
11. Start or cause.–Bill *picked* a fight with Jack. Bill started the fight.
12. Open without a key.–The burglar *picked* the lock with a hairpin.

pickaxe or **pickax** pick′-axe *pickaxes*. A pick, or long-handled tool, with a heavy head that has a point at one end and a blade at the other.–The workman used a *pickaxe* to break the hard earth.

picket pick′-et *pickets, picketed, picketing*. 1. A pointed stake.–Grandmother's garden has a white fence made of *pickets*.
2. A soldier on guard at a certain place; a sentry or sentinel.–When the attack started, the *pickets* gave the alarm.
3. A worker on strike who marches outside the place of work to keep other workers from going in to work or to keep customers from buying at the place.
4. March as a *picket* or surround with *pickets*. –The union men on strike were *picketing* the factory.

pickle pick′-le *pickles, pickled, pickling*. 1. A vegetable or fruit preserved in vinegar or salt water.–Most *pickles* are made from cucumbers.
2. Preserve in vinegar or salt water, usually with spices.–Mother *pickles* beets, peppers, and other vegetables.

pickpocket pick′-pock′et *pickpockets*. A person who robs another person's pockets.–The police captured a *pickpocket*.

picnic pic′-nic *picnics, picnicked, picnicking*. 1. An outdoor party with food.–The teacher and the children went for a *picnic*.
2. Take food on an outdoor party; go on a *picnic*.–We *picnicked* in the woods.

picture pic′-ture *pictures*. 1. A painting, drawing, or photograph of something.–A *picture* of a fishing village hangs on the wall.
2. See in the mind; imagine.–Mary said she could not *picture* Bob as a cowboy.

picture-book pic′-ture-book *picture-books*. A book for children consisting mainly of pictures.–We liked *picture-books* before we learnt to read.

picturesque pic′-tu-resque *picturesquely*. Pleasant to look at.–The village nestling among the trees was *picturesque*.

P
Q
R
S
T
U
V
W
X
Y
Z

pie *pies*. Meat, fruit or other food baked in or under pastry.–Mother baked a blackberry *pie*.

piece *pieces, pieced, piecing*. 1. A part, a bit, a scrap, a chunk, etc.–Mary gave Bob a *piece* of paper.–Please give me a *piece* of cake.
2. One thing of its kind.–A *piece* of poetry is a poem.–A *piece* of music is a song or other complete work of music.
3. An instance; an example. – Losing his money was a *piece* of bad luck for the boy.
4. Put together from small pieces.–Grandmother likes to *piece* quilts from small scraps of cloth.

pier *piers*. A dock; a landing place for boats and ships.

pierce *pierces, pierced, piercing*. 1. Go or thrust through or into.–The chimney *pierces* the roof.–The arrow *pierced* the tree.
2. Stab; make a hole in.–Mother *pierced* the apple with a knife.

pig *pigs*. 1. A hog, especially a young hog.–Pork is meat from *pigs*.

2. Name sometimes applied to a very greedy or dirty person.

pigeon pi'-geon *pigeons*. A large bird of the same kind as a dove.–Many *pigeons* live in the city park.

pigtail pig'-tail *pigtails*. A braid of hair that hangs down from the back of the head.–Jack teased Mary by pulling her *pigtails*.

pike *pikes*. 1. A long, freshwater fish with a pointed head.

2. A road with a toll gate, or gate where money is collected for use of the road. Many roads that once had toll gates are still called *pikes* or turn*pikes*.
3. A weapon with a long shaft and an iron or steel point which was once used by infantry. The soldiers who carried them were called *pike*men.

pilchard pil'-chard *pilchards*. A small sea fish belonging to the herring family.–*Pilchards* are good to eat on toast.

pile *piles, piled, piling*. 1. A number of things stacked or heaped up in one place.–The children put their books in a neat *pile*.
2. Stack; put in a *pile*.–The children *piled* their books together.
3. A pointed stake or beam of timber.–The workmen drove *piles* into the river-bed to support the bridge.
4. Cover with a heap or stack.–The floor beneath the Christmas tree was *piled* with gifts.

pilfer pil'-fer *pilfers, pilfered, pilfering*. Steal in small quantities.–The headmaster accused the boy of *pilfering* pencils and rulers from the desks of the other boys.

pilgrim pil'-grim *pilgrims*. 1. A wanderer; a traveller.
2. A person travelling to worship at a religious shrine.–Many *pilgrims* go to Rome each year.

pill *pills*. A medicine made into a small ball.–The doctor gave Father some *pills*. *Pills* are swallowed whole.

pillar pil'-lar *pillars*. A heavy post that supports a roof or ceiling.–The roof of the veranda is held up by *pillars*.

pillow pil'-low *pillows*. A bag filled with feathers, cotton, or some other soft material, used to rest one's head on when lying down.

pilot pi′-lot *pilots, piloted, piloting.* 1. A person who guides or steers a ship or aircraft.–The ship was met near the harbour and taken into port by a *pilot.*–The pilot landed skilfully at the airport.
2. Guide, steer.–The ship was *piloted* safely through the storm.

pimple pim′-ple *pimples.* A small, raised place on the skin which may be filled with pus.

pin *pins, pinned, pinning.* 1. A piece of metal or wood shaped so that it can be used to fasten things together. There are safety *pins,* straight *pins,* hair*pins,* and other kinds for different uses.

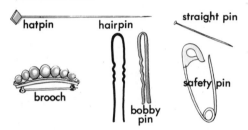

hatpin hairpin straight pin
brooch bobby pin safety pin

2. Hold fast.–The boy's leg was *pinned* by the falling tree trunk.
3. A peg.–The boys made a box and fastened it together with wooden *pins.*
4. Fasten with a *pin.*–The teacher *pinned* a flower on Mary's coat.
5. A wooden piece shaped something like a large bottle. The game of skittles is played with a bowling ball and nine*pins.*

pinafore pin′-a-fore *pinafores.* An apron made like a low-necked dress without sleeves.–The little girl wore a *pinafore* to keep her new dress clean.

pincers pin -cers. 1. A tool something like a pair of scissors, except that it clasps and holds things tightly instead of cutting them.

2. The claws of crabs, lobsters, and the like. The crab or lobster grabs and pinches with its *pincers.*

pinch *pinches, pinched, pinching.* 1. Squeeze between the fingers.–The old lady *pinched* Baby's cheek.

2. Catch and crush slightly.–Baby pushed the drawer shut and *pinched* her fingers in it. The drawer pressed against her fingers.
3. A tiny bit.–Mother put a *pinch* of soda into the sour milk, as much as she could take between the ends of her thumb and first finger.
4. Be very saving; spend very little money. To *pinch* one's pennies means to be stingy.

pine *pines.* An evergreen tree which has long needles for leaves, and cones for seeds. We use the wood of *pine* trees for building material. Turpentine is obtained from some sort of *pine.*

pineapple pine′-ap-ple *pineapples.* A large juicy fruit that has a rough outer skin, and stiff leaves with sharp points along the edges. *Pineapples* grow close to the ground, not on trees. They grow in hot countries.

pink *pinks, pinked, pinking.* 1. Light red.–Mary has a new *pink* dress.
2. A flower that smells and looks like a small carnation.–Grandmother has *pinks* in her garden.
3. Notch, cut in little notches along the edges.–The seams of Mary's dress were *pinked* so that they wouldn't fray off in threads.

pint *pints.* A unit of liquid measure. Milk is measured by the quart, by the *pint,* and by the half *pint.* It takes two *pints* to make a quart.

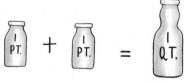

pioneer pi-o-neer′ *pioneers.* 1. A person who does something before anyone else does it; one who prepares the way so that others may follow.–Thomas Edison was a *pioneer* in the use of electricity. He started to use it for things it had never been used for before.
2. An early settler; a person who goes to a country or part of a country that has not been lived in before.–Many *pioneers* travelled to California in covered wagons.

P
Q
R
S
T
U
V
W
X
Y
Z

pipe *pipes, piped, piping.* 1. A smoking device with a small bowl and stem. The bowl is filled with tobacco, which is lit, and the smoker draws the smoke through the stem.

2. A metal tube through which water, gas, etc., can move or flow.–Water comes from the well through a *pipe*.

3. Move or convey by *pipes*.–The farmer *piped* water to his crops out in his fields.
4. A tube.–The music of the *pipe* organ comes out through *pipes*.

5. A musical instrument played by blowing into it.

pirate pi′-rate *pirates.* A robber on the seas. In olden times, *pirates* had their own ships, and used to stop and rob other ships.

pistil pis′-til *pistils.* One of the slender little stalks inside the cup of a flower. Insects or the wind bring yellow powder called pollen from other flowers to the *pistils.* With the help of this pollen, seeds develop down inside the *pistils.*

pistil

pistol pis′-tol *pistols.* A small hand gun. A revolver is one kind of *pistol.*

piston pis′-ton *pistons.* A round piece shaped like a solid cylinder, which fits inside a tube and is pushed up and down in it by some form of power. *Pistons* are used in different kinds of machinery. There is a *piston* in each cylinder of a motor-car engine.

pit *pits, pitted, pitting.* 1. A deep hole.–Miners go down into the *pit* to dig coal.
2. Any small hole on a surface.–Chicken pox may leave little *pits* on the skin.
3. Put holes in. – Chicken pox may *pit* the skin.
4. The back seats on the ground floor of a theatre.–We always sit in the *pit*.

pitch *pitches, pitched, pitching.* 1. Rock back and forth violently.–The ship *pitched* in the storm.
2. Throw, toss. – The boy *pitched* a stone through the garage window.
3. Put up; open out and erect.–The campers *pitched* their tent for the night.
4. A certain point.–Mary's excitement at the theatre reached its highest *pitch* just before the curtain went up.
5. A tone; the height or depth of a sound. –The singing teacher gives us the *pitch* with her tuning-fork.
6. A thick, black, tar-like substance used on the cracks in road pavements, to mend leaks in boats, etc.

pitcher pitch′-er *pitchers.* 1. A container used for pouring out liquids. The lip on a *pitcher* makes pouring easy.
2. The player in a baseball game who throws the ball to the batter, who tries to hit it.

pitchfork pitch′-fork *pitchforks.* A long-handled fork.–The farmer uses a *pitchfork* for lifting hay and putting it on to the wagon.

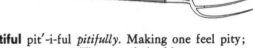

pitiful pit′-i-ful *pitifully.* Making one feel pity; sad; piteous.–The crippled old man was a *pitiful* sight.

pity pit′-y *pities, pitied, pitying.* 1. Feel sorry for or sympathize with someone who has trouble.–We *pity* people who are crippled or blind, or have other misfortunes.
2. A feeling of how sad someone else's trouble is.–The old man did not want *pity*; he wanted friends. He didn't want people to feel sorry for him.

P
Q
R
S
T
U
V
W
X
Y
Z

place *places, placed, placing.* 1. Where someone or something belongs, or usually is.– The children stood in their *places*. They stood where they usually stand. – Your home or house is your *place* of residence.–A building where people work is their *place* of business.
2. A city, town, country, or other region or location.–The teacher asked us to find several *places* on the map.
3. A part, a spot.–One *place* in the apple was rotten.
4. A position.–Our chess team is in first *place*. It has the highest score, the best record.
5. A seat.–The people on the aeroplane took their *places* and the aeroplane started.
6. Put.–Father *placed* the gifts under the Christmas tree.
7. A duty.–It is a father's *place* to care for his family.
8. A job; work.–Bob hopes to find a *place* in an architect's office.
9. Find a job for.–Uncle Jim is trying to *place* Bob with an architect.

placket *plack'-et plackets.* The opening in a skirt or dress that makes it easy to pull over the head. Some *plackets* close with zippers, others have fasteners.

plaid (pronounced *plad*). A pattern of stripes arranged to form checks or squares as they cross each other.–Mary has a *plaid* suit.

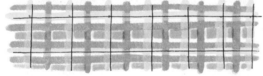

plain *plains, plainer, plainest, plainly.* 1. Clear; easy to understand, see, hear, etc. – The teacher made the directions very *plain*. – The light in the house was quite *plain* from the road.–The noise in the cellar was *plain* to us all.
2. Simple, ordinary.–Mary wore a *plain* dress, one without trimming.–We eat *plain* food. It isn't fancy or rich.–The people living in this town are very *plain* people. They are not rich or elegant.
3. Not good-looking.–That boy is *plain*, but honest and good.
4. Frank and honest.–After the fight in the playground, the teacher gave us a *plain* talk. She said just what she thought.
5. A stretch of flat, level country.–Herds of cattle feed on the *plains* of the West.

plait (pronounced *plat*) *plaits, plaited, plaiting.*
1. A braid.–This girl has *plaits* of hair.
2. Make into a braid.–The children *plaited* the straw to make baskets.

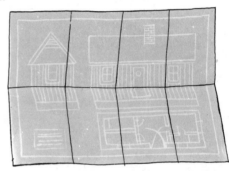

plan *plans, planned, planning.*
1. Work out in advance; think up a way of doing something. – The boys *plan* their work. Before they start their work, they decide how it should be done, which things should be done first, second, and so on, and what things will be needed, etc.
2. An idea worked out for what one is going to do.–We have made *plans* for Christmas. We know what we are going to do, where we are going, what gifts we shall buy, etc.
3. A drawing.–Father has the *plans* for our new home. The *plans* show just where and how large each room, window, door, etc., will be.

plane *planes, planed, planing.* 1. A tool with a sharp blade used to smooth wood and metal.–The door was too large, so the carpenter used a *plane* to shave

off a little of the wood to make the door fit the frame.
2. Make smooth with a *plane*.–Father *planed* the edge of the box.
3. Flat.–The top of a table is a *plane* surface.

4. An aero*plane* is often called a *plane*.

P
Q
R
S
T
U
V
W
X
Y
Z

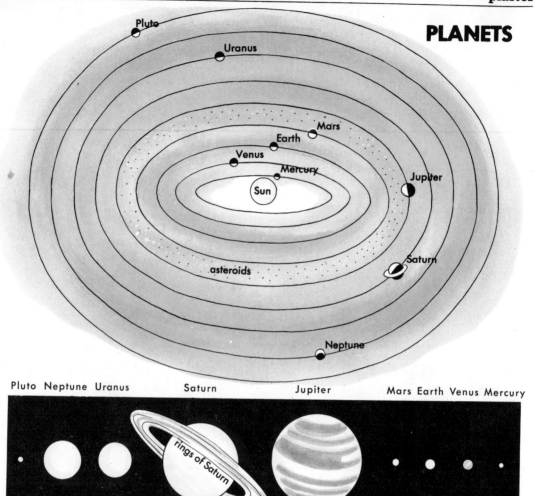

PLANETS

Pluto Neptune Uranus   Saturn   Jupiter   Mars Earth Venus Mercury

rings of Saturn

planet plan'-et *planets*. A heavenly body that moves round the sun.–The earth and Mars are two of the *planets*.

plank *planks*. A wide, flat board or piece of timber.–The bridge was made of *planks*.

plant *plants, planted, planting*. 1. A tree, shrub, grass, flower, vegetable, grain, or other living thing that grows in the earth, water, or air. Animals are not *plants*.
2. Put into the ground to grow.–If you *plant* flower seeds in the spring, you will have flowers in the summer.
3. Set firmly.–The dog *planted* himself in front of the stove. He put himself down in front of the stove and stayed there.
4. A factory with machinery and tools for making things.–Bill's father works in a car-assembly *plant*.

plantation plan-ta'-tion *plantations*. A large farm on which cotton, sugar, or other large

crops are grown and cared for by workers who live on the farm.–There are many *plantations* in the southern States of the U.S.A.

planter plant'-er *planters*. 1. A person or a machine that plants seeds.–The farmer plants corn with a corn *planter*, a machine that drops the seed corn.
2. A person who owns or runs a plantation.

plaster plas'-ter *plasters, plastered, plastering*.
1. A mixture of lime, sand, and water. The walls in houses are usually covered with *plaster*. *Plaster* is wet when put on the walls. When it dries, it becomes hard.
2. Put *plaster* on.–We saw a man *plastering* the walls of the new house.
3. A covering with some sort of medicine or preparation inside, used to ease pain.– Father put a *plaster* on his sore arm.
4. Cover thickly.–After the rain, our car was *plastered* with mud.

plate *plates, plated, plating.* 1. A flat dish that has slightly turned-up edges.–We eat from *plates*.

2. A thin, flat piece of metal.–The electrician covered the hole he had made in the wall with a small *plate*.

3. Any fairly thin, flat part or piece.

4. Cover with a thin coat of a substance different from that of which the article is made. –Mother has a silver-*plated* cup.

5. A piece of brass with a name engraved on it.–The doctor put up a *plate* outside his house.

plateau *pla'-teau plateaus.* A high, flat-topped stretch of land.

platform *plat'-form platforms.* A stage; a raised

floor.–Father made a small *platform* for the boys to give plays on.

platinum *plat'-i-num.* A metal that looks like silver, but is very much harder. *Platinum* is very rare and valuable, and is used in making jewellery.

platter *plat'-ter platters.* A long plate; a large, flat dish with the edges turned up a little. Meat, fish, and other main dishes are usually served from a *platter*. –A meat plate is called a *platter*.

play *plays, played, playing.* 1. Fun; doing things for fun.–Games are *play*.

2. Take part in a game or activity from which one gets fun.–Mary likes to *play* with her doll.–Bob likes to *play* football.

3. A story to be acted on a stage.–We acted the story of Cinderella as our class *play*.

4. Act a part in a *play*.–Mary *played* Cinderella.

5. Make music on a musical instrument. – Mary *plays* the piano.

6. Make believe.–The children *played* at cowboys and Indians.

7. Toy with, fool with, handle.–Baby likes to *play* with Father's watch.

player *play'-er players. One* who plays.–Jack Hobbs was a cricket *player*. He played cricket.–Stanley Matthews is a football *player*.–Mary is a good piano *player*.

PLANTS

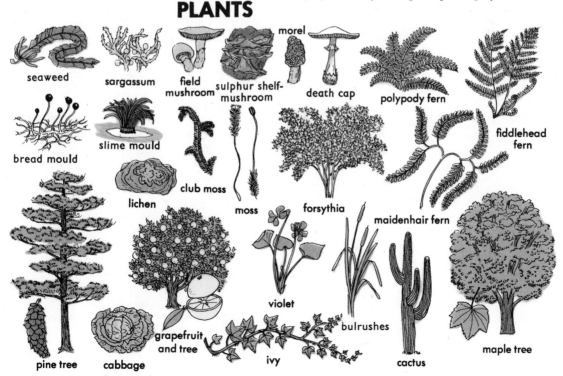

seaweed   sargassum   field mushroom   sulphur shelf-mushroom   morel   death cap   polypody fern

bread mould   slime mould   club moss   lichen   moss   forsythia   fiddlehead fern   maidenhair fern

pine tree   cabbage   grapefruit and tree   ivy   violet   bulrushes   cactus   maple tree

P
Q
R
S
T
U
V
W
X
Y
Z

playful play'ful *playfulness, playfully*. Full of fun.–Bob's dog is *playful*.

playground play'-ground *playgrounds*. A piece of ground set aside for games.–Children play in the *playground* next to the school.

playhouse play'-house *playhouses*. A theatre. –We saw the play at the new *playhouse*.

playing-field play'-ing-field *playing-fields*. An open space where games are played.

playmate play'-mate *playmates*. A child who plays with another. – Mary and Jane have been *playmates* since they were babies.

plaything play'-thing *playthings*. Something to play with; a toy.–The children sent many of their *playthings* to other children who had none.

pleasant pleas'-ant *pleasantly, pleasantness*. 1. Joyful, delightful.–We went for a *pleasant ride*. It gave us much pleasure.
2. Fair and bright.–Today is a *pleasant* day. The sun is shining, and it isn't too cold or too hot.
3. Friendly and agreeable.–Grandmother is a very *pleasant* person.

please *pleases, pleased, pleasing*. 1. Give enjoyment to.–The clowns at the circus *please* the children. They bring pleasure to the children.
2. Choose, wish.–The teacher told the children they might do as they *pleased* for a while. They might do anything they wanted to do.
3. Mary is very polite. When she asks for things, she says *please*. – *Please*, may I sit here?
4. Satisfy.–The grocer tries to *please* us when we buy food at his shop.

pleasure pleas'-ure *pleasures*. 1. Joy, delight.– It was a *pleasure* to receive so many letters from my friends.
2. Amusement. – The sick man's greatest *pleasure* is the books he has to read.

pleat *pleats, pleated, pleating*. 1. A pressed fold.–Mary has a new skirt with *pleats*.
2. Make *pleats* in. – Mother *pleated* the folds with a hot iron.

pledge *pledges, pledged, pledging*. 1. Promise, swear.–Alan *pledged* his word that he would do his homework before going out to the cinema. He promised to do his homework.
2. A promise; word of honour.–The boys gave a *pledge* to be kind to old people.

plentiful plen'-ti-ful *plentifully*. In great quantities.–Peaches are *plentiful* this year. There are many, all that people want.

plenty plen'-ty 1. Enough, all that is needed. –There isn't much paper, but we have *plenty* to finish the work.
2. A great deal; an abundance.–The farmer's crops were large because there was *plenty* of sunshine and rain.–We are fortunate to live in a land where there is peace and *plenty*.–In times of *plenty*, save for poorer days.

pliers pli-ers. A tool used to hold, turn, cut, or bend wire or other materials. – Father used the *pliers* to hold the bolt while he tightened the nut.

plight *plights*. A very difficult, sad, or unfortunate situation.–When Father lost the keys of his car, he was in a sorry *plight*.

plod *plods, plodded, plodding*. Walk with slow, heavy steps.–We heard the tired horse *plodding* along the road.

plot *plots, plotted, plotting*. 1. A small piece of ground; a site.–Father gave Mary a *plot* in the corner of the garden so that she might raise flowers. – Some land near the city has been divided up into *plots* for new houses.
2. A secret plan, usually a wicked one.–The soldiers made a *plot* to kill the general of their own army.
3. Plan to do something secretly.–The spies *plotted* to destroy the bridge.
4. A plan of action.–Stories and plays have *plots*. The *plot* is what happens in the story or play.–The book I have just read had a very exciting *plot* but I could not really believe in the characters.

P
Q
R
S
T
U
V
W
X
Y
Z

5. Map out.–The scouts *plotted* the route for their ramble.–The navigator *plots* the course of the aircraft.–The builders *plotted* the new playing-field.

plough (pronounced *plow*) *ploughs, ploughed, ploughing*. 1. A farm tool with a sharp blade, used to turn over the earth so that the farmer can plant or sow seeds. Ploughs are pulled by horses or oxen, or worked by tractors.

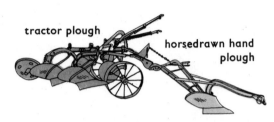

tractor plough

horsedrawn hand plough

2. Turn over the earth.–The farmer *ploughs* his fields early in the spring.
3. Make a path by pushing things aside.–We *ploughed* our way through the crowd.

pluck *plucks, plucked, plucking*. 1. Pick, pull off.–The boys *plucked* apples from the apple tree. – Grandfather killed a chicken and *plucked* its feathers.
2. Courage, bravery.– The firemen showed *pluck* in saving the child from the burning building.

plucky pluck'-y *pluckier, pluckiest, pluckily*. Brave, courageous.–It was *plucky* of Mary to take the part of the little girl whom the others were teasing.

plug *plugs, plugged, plugging*. 1. A piece of wood, metal, etc., pushed tightly into a hole to stop it up.
2. Stop up.–Father *plugged* the hole in the pipe with a rag.
3. An electrical connexion.–Mother put the *plug* into the socket so the vacuum cleaner would work.

plum *plums*. 1. The fruit of a plum tree. *Plums* are red, green, purple, or yellow. They are good to eat.
2. A raisin used for cooking, as in *plum* pudding.
3. The best. – Of all the prizes Jack's was the *plum*.

plumage plum'-age. A coat of feathers.–Our canary has yellow *plumage*.–A crow, however, has black *plumage*.

plumb *plumbs, plumbed, plumbing*. 1. A weight fastened to a cord.–The mason used a *plumb* to see if the wall was straight.–A *plumb* is also used to measure the depth of water in a lake.
2. Straight up and down.–The wall was out of *plumb*. It was leaning a little to one side.
3. Measure by a *plumb*, or measure the depth of.

plumber plumb'-er *plumbers*. A person whose work is fixing and putting in gas and water pipes, bathroom fixtures, kitchen sinks, etc.– A *plumber* put in our new hot-water heater.

plumbing plumb'-ing. 1. Fixing and putting in pipes, bathroom fixtures, kitchen sinks, etc.; what a plumber does.
2. A system of water pipes and drain pipes. –The *plumbing* in our house needs repair.

plume *plumes, plumed, plumy*. A fine, beautiful, and fluffy feather, like those used to trim hats.

plump *plumper, plumpest*. Rather fat, chubby.–Our baby is *plump*.

plunder plun'-der *plunders, plundered, plundering*. 1. Rob, especially in groups. – The enemy soldiers *plundered* the town. They stole everything they wanted from the people.
2. Stolen goods.–The *plunder* was taken back to our enemy's camp.

plunge *plunges, plunged, plunging*. 1. Dive.– The boys *plunged* into the water for a swim.
2. Push (into something). – Baby *plunged* her hand into the glass of milk.
3. Rush.–The children *plunged* out of the classroom when the bell rang.
4. A dive, a quick swim.–Bob took a *plunge* in the lake.

plural plu'-ral *plurals*. More than one. – The word 'baby' means one baby. The word 'babies' means more than one baby. 'Babies' is the *plural* form of the word 'baby'.

plus 1. Added to.–5 *plus* 2 equals 7. 5 with 2 added to it equals 7. The sign + stands for *plus*. It means to add.
2. And.–The doctor said that some sunshine *plus* a little rest would make Grandmother feel better.
3. Somewhat more, somewhat higher.–Mary had B minus in arithmetic, but Bob had B *plus* for his work.

P
Q
R
S
T
U
V
W
X
Y
Z

plush. A heavy cloth something like velvet, but softer.–The custions in Father's chair are covered with *plush*.

pneumonia pneu-mo'-ni-a. A disease that affects the lungs.

poach *poaches, poached, poaching, poacher.* Cook (eggs) by dropping without shell into boiling water.–The nurse gave Grandmother a *poached* egg.
2. Steal or take game or fish by illegal methods.–The *poacher* was caught *poaching* salmon by the gamekeeper.

pocket pock'-et *pockets, pocketed, pocketing.*
1. A bag sewn into or on to one's coat, dress, or other clothing. – Boys carry marbles in their *pockets*.–Men carry money and papers in their *pockets*.
2. Any small bag that is attached to something to hold small articles.–Father's golf bag has a *pocket* for golf balls.
3. Put into one's *pocket*.–The man *pocketed* the money.
4. A hole in the ground containing mineral.
5. To be carried in one's *pocket*, as a *pocket* knife, a *pocket* watch, etc.

pocket-book pock'-et-book *pocket-books.* 1. A small case, often of leather, used for carrying money in the pocket.

pocket-money pock'-et-mon-ey. A regular allowance of money given to children.

pod *pods.* The seed case of a plant. Peas and broad beans grow in *pods*.

poem po'-em *poems.* A rhythmic and usually rhymed piece of writing.

poet po'-et *poets.* A person who writes poetry.–Robert Louis Stevenson was a very famous children's *poet*. He wrote verses for children.

poetic po-et'-ic. 1. Of poetry. – A ballad is a *poetic* form. It is one kind of poetry.
2. Like poetry.–Grandmother found the minister's sermon on beauty very *poetic*.

poetry po'-et-ry. Writing which has a certain rhythm, often in lines that rhyme. *Poetry* is arranged in lines to show its rhythm.

point *points, pointed, pointing.* 1. A narrow tip, a sharp end.–The pin has a flat head at one end and a sharp *point* at the other.–The town was on a *point* of land reaching into the sea.

2. A use, a reason.–Jack sees no *point* in practising on his violin, because he expects to be a great football player.
3. The meaning or idea in something spoken or written.–Mother did not see the *point* of Father's joke.
4. A characteristic, or thing which makes something the way it is.–The good *points* in Bob's composition were the interesting story and the simple way it was written.
5. A place.–We stopped at different *points* along the road to buy food and petrol.
6. Show or indicate, as with the first finger.–Mary *pointed* out all the places of interest to Grandmother.
7. Aim.–The policeman *pointed* his gun at the robber.
8. A time or condition when a certain thing happens.–I was just on the *point* of leaving when you came.–If milk is brought to the boiling *point*, it is apt to curdle.

pointer point'-er *pointers.* 1. Anything which points.–The *pointer* on the speedometer stood at 60 m.p.h.
2. A sporting dog.–When the *pointer* scented the rabbit he stood absolutely still.

poise *poises, poised, poising.* 1. Bearing; manner of holding or conducting oneself.–Mary has fine *poise* for one so young. She is graceful and at ease.
2. Balance in a certain position.–The dancer *poised* on her toes.

poison poi'-son *poisons, poisoned, poisoning.*
1. A substance which injures the body. A drug which is a deadly *poison* is one which may cause death.
2. Give *poison* to.–Father *poisoned* the rats by putting rat *poison* in the cellar.

poisonous poi'-son-ous *poisonously.* Very dangerous to the body; containing something which poisons.–Some toadstools are *poisonous*. They may kill a person who eats them, or make that person violently ill.

poke *pokes, poked, poking.* 1. Stick, dig, push.–Baby *poked* her finger into the paint to see what it felt like.
2. A push, a dig.–Bob gave Bill a *poke* to let him know the teacher was watching him.

poker pok'-er *pokers.* 1. A long metal rod or stick for poking at or stirring up a fire.
2. A kind of card game usually played for money.

polar po'-lar. Having to do with the North or the South Pole; arctic or antarctic.–Captain Scott made two *polar* expeditions.

P
Q
R
S
T
U
V
W
X
Y
Z

polar bear po′-lar bear *polar bears*. A fierce, white-furred bear that lives in the far North, where it is very cold.

pole *poles*. 1. A long stick.–The keeper at the zoo used a *pole* to push the meat *into* the lion's cage.
2. Either end of the earth's axis, which is the imaginary line going down the centre of the earth and on which the earth turns; that is the North *Pole* or the South *Pole*.

North Pole

South Pole

police po-lice′ *polices, policed, policing*. 1. A group of men employed by the government, a company, etc., to keep law and order; the members of a *police* force.
2. Keep peace and order in.–The soldiers *policed* the captured city.

policeman po-lice′-man *policemen*. A member of the police force. *Policemen* help to keep order and protect us from people who break the laws.

police station po-lice′ sta′-tion *police stations*. The headquarters of a police force.–The policeman took the suspect to the *police station* and charged him with burglary.

policy pol′-i-cy *policies*. 1. A plan of action.–It is our *policy* to treat everyone the same. –There is a famous saying that honesty is the best *policy*.
2. An insurance *policy* is a written agreement that one has with an insurance company. If one makes certain regular payments to the company, the company will pay back a certain amount in case of certain misfortunes named in the *policy*.–Grandfather had an accident insurance *policy* for which he paid £10 a year. When he broke his leg, the insurance company paid him £8 a week for the month he could not work.

polish pol′-ish *polishes, polished, polishing*.
1. A substance that is rubbed on to something to make it bright and smooth.
2. Make shiny or smooth by rubbing.–We *polish* the furniture by rubbing it with furniture *polish*.

polite po-lite′ *politely*. Having good manners; courteous.–It is *polite* to thank a person who does anything for you.

politeness po-lite′-ness. Courtesy; a showing of good manners.–Mary is well liked for her *politeness*. She is always pleasant and thoughtful towards others.

political po-lit′-i-cal. Having to do with politics or government.–A *political* party is a group of people organized to elect certain people to public office and get certain laws passed.

politician pol-i-ti′-cian *politicians*. A member of Parliament or a person who spends much time in working for the success of a political party. Politics may be such a person's chief occupation.

politics pol′-i-tics. The business of governing a community, city, state, nation, etc. The business of getting people elected and appointed to public office is also *politics*.

pollen pol′-len. The dusty yellow material that is found in flowers. The flowers use it in making the seeds that will grow into new plants.

polls. A voting place.–At election time, Father and Mother go to the *polls* to vote.

pollute pol-lute′ *pollutes, polluted, polluting*. Make unclean; foul.–The boys *polluted* the well by throwing rubbish into it.

polo po′-lo. A game played by players on horseback. The players, using long mallets, try to

hit a small wooden ball through the opposing team's goal.

P
Q
R
S
T
U
V
W
X
Y
Z

pond *ponds.* A pool; a little lake.–Children like to sail their boats on the *pond.*

ponder pon'-der *ponders, pondered, pondering.* Think deeply.–Father *pondered* over the question for a long time.

ponderous pon'-der-ous *ponderously.* 1. Huge, massive.–The new hotel is an ugly and *ponderous* building.
2. Heavy and rather dull. This book is written in a very *ponderous* style. The words and sentences are long and it is very difficult to read.

pontoon pon-toon' *pontoons.* 1. A kind of float that looks like a flat-bottomed boat. *Pontoons* are used to hold up rafts or temporary docks, bridges, etc.
2. A floating raft or dock.

pony po'-ny *ponies.* A small horse, not more than 14 hands high.–Children like to ride the *ponies* at the seaside.

poodle poo'-dle *poodles.* A popular breed of curly-haired dog. The *poodle,* of which there are several different sizes, is intelligent and easy to train.

pool *pools, pooled, pooling.* 1. Any small body of still water.–The heavy rain of last night formed a large *pool* in the garden.

2. A large tank filled with water.–In summer we often go to the swimming *pool.*
3. A popular card game also called vingt-et-un or 21.
4. Put together in a common fund.–The children *pooled* their money to buy a gift for Mother.

poor *poorer, poorest, poorly.* 1. Having little property and money.–*Poor* people often cannot buy enough to eat.
2. Not good in quality.–*Poor* clothing will not last as long as good clothing.–John is a *poor* footballer. He does not play well.
3. Pitiable.–The *poor* dog was hungry.
4. People who have very little.–Every Christmas we give food to the *poor.*

pop *pops, popped, popping.* 1. A soft drink that fizzes when the bottle is opened.
2. A quick, loud, sharp noise.–The cork came out with a *pop.*
3. Make a quick, loud, sharp noise.–The cork *popped* as it was removed from the bottle.
4. Cause to burst suddenly.–Sally *popped* her balloon with a pin.
5. Burst.–Pop-corn *pops* when it is heated.

pop-corn pop'-corn. A kind of corn that bursts open when the kernels are heated. It is good to eat.

pope *popes.* The head of the Roman Catholic Church. When you use the word as a title or name, you spell *Pope* with a capital P.

pop-gun pop'-gun *pop-guns.* A small toy gun that shoots corks. – Boys like to play with *pop-guns.*

poplar pop'-lar *poplars.* A very tall, slim tree that has shiny, heart-shaped leaves which tremble in even the slightest breeze.

poppy pop'-py *poppies.* One of a large group of flowers of different colours, especially the red *poppy.* *Poppy* seeds are often sprinkled on the tops of bread and rolls.

popular pop'-u-lar *popularly, popularity.* Well-known and liked.–Bob is *popular* at school. He is liked by almost everyone.

population pop-u-la'-tion. The number of people living in a community, town, city, country, etc.–The *population* of this city is 10,000.

porcelain por'-ce-lain. A fine, glossy earthenware; china.–Our new plates are made of *porcelain.*

porch *porches*. A covered entrance to a house or other building.–When it is raining, Mother often puts Baby's pram out on the *porch* instead of in the garden.

porcupine por'-cu-pine *porcupines*. A small animal that has sharp quills or spines mixed in with its hair. These quills protect it.

pore *pores, pored, poring*. 1. One of many tiny holes in a surface.–There are *pores* in skin. 2. Study thoroughly.–Bob is *poring* over a book.

pork. The meat of a pig.

porous por'-ous. Full of tiny holes through which liquids can pass.–Most articles of clothing are *porous*. They let through water and are not waterproof.

porridge por'-ridge. A cereal, such as oatmeal or cream of wheat, boiled in milk or water.

port *ports*. 1. A harbour; a place where ships may load and unload.

2. To or on the left side of a ship.–The lookout saw a whale off the *port* bow.
3. A kind of wine.
4. A window in a ship–also called a *porthole*.

portable port'-a-ble. Able to be carried.–Mary has a *portable* typewriter. It is small, and fits into a case; it can be easily carried.

porter por'-ter *porters*. 1. A man paid for carrying baggage.–At the station, the *porter* took our baggage.
2. A man who cleans, moves furniture, etc., in a building.–The manager called the *porter* to clean up the spilt ink.

porthole port'-hole *portholes*. An opening in the side of a ship to let in light and air. *Portholes* are usually round.

portion por'-tion *portions, portioned, portioning*. A part or share. –Bob ate a small *portion* of the food.–My *portion* of the money was only £5.

portrait por'-trait *portraits*. A picture of a particular person. – The artist painted a *portrait* of Ann.

portray por-tray' *portrays, portrayed, portraying*. Picture by drawing, painting, acting, or describing in words.–Bob *portrayed* a prince in the play staged at his school.

pose *poses, posed, posing*. 1. A position in which a person stands, sits, or reclines.– Mary held a *pose* so that the class could paint her portrait.
2. Hold a position to be painted, sketched, or the like.–Mary *posed* for the art class.
3. Pretend to be.–The captain *posed* as a major. He pretended to be a major.

position po-si'-tion *positions*. 1. A particular place.–The boy stood in his *position* during the fire drill.
2. A certain posture or way of holding the body.–The cricketer got into *position* to bat.
3. A job.–Uncle Tom has a new *position* in the factory.
4. A rank.–General is one of the highest *positions* in the army.
5. A way of thinking.–Mother's *position* on the question is different from Father's. She disagrees.

positive pos'-i-tive *positively*. Very sure; certain.–I am *positive* that I heard the bell ring.

possess pos-sess' *possesses, possessed, possessing*. 1. Have; own.–This house is all that I *possess*.
2. Hold; occupy.–The enemy *possessed* the fort.

possession pos-ses'-sion *possessions*. 1. The papers are in my *possession*. I have them.
2. Ownership.–The house passed into our *possession* when the papers were signed.
3. Something owned.–Poor people do not have many *possessions*.

P
Q
R
S
T
U
V
W
X
Y
Z

possessive pos-ses′-sive *possessively*. Belonging to someone or something.–His, hers, ours, yours and theirs are called *possessive* pronouns.–Jack's aunt is a *possessive* person. She is very jealous of all the things she owns.

possibility pos-si-bil′-i-ty *possibilities*. Something that can happen or be done.–Getting 100% in the test is a *possibility*.

possible pos′-si-ble. Able to happen or be done. –It is *possible* to talk by telephone to a person thousands of miles away. Ten years ago few people thought it would be *possible* to send a rocket to the moon. Now it has been done.

possibly pos′-si-bly. 1. Perhaps; maybe.–*Possibly* Father will come on the next train. 2. Within the limits of what can happen or be done.–Bob cannot *possibly* get here in time for lunch.

post *posts, posted, posting*. 1. Put up so that people can see.–The names of the honours students were *posted* on the bulletin board. 2. Send through the mail.–Mary will *post* your letter on the way to school. 3. An upright rod or column of wood or metal set in the ground to hold something up.–Telegraph *posts* hold wires up. 4. A place where a person is supposed to be when on duty. –The sentry was found asleep at his *post*. 5. A kind of store in places where few people live, at which people may trade or buy things. –The trappers trade furs for food at the *post*.

postage post′-age. The charge for posting things.–Mary did not post the package, because she didn't have the *postage*. The *postage* on the package was 5op.

postal post′-al. Having to do with the mail.– *Postal* service is the delivering of mail.

postal order post′-al or′-der *postal orders*. A money order bought at a post office. It is payable to somebody else through another post office.–Bob bought a 75p *postal order* to pay for the tickets.

postcard *postcards*. A small card that may be sent through the mail.–It costs less to send a *postcard* than it does to send a letter.

poster post′-er *posters*. A sign.–A *poster* about the Red Cross was placed in the window of the shop.

posterity pos-ter′-ity. Future generations.–Real works of art will go down to *posterity*. They will be known and admired hundreds of years from now.

posthumous post′-hum-ous *posthumously*. After death.–The soldier's medal was *posthumous*. It was awarded after he died.

postman post′-man *postmen*. A man who delivers letters and parcels.–Mary took the letter from the *postman*.

postmark post′-mark *postmarks*. A mark put on a letter or parcel to tell the date and place where it was posted.

postmaster post′-master *postmasters*. A man in charge of a post office or a group of post offices.

postmistress post′-mis-tress *postmistresses*. A woman who has charge of a post office or a group of post offices.

post office post′ of′-fice *post offices*. A place where letters, parcels, etc., are posted, and received in the post to be sorted for delivery, and where postage stamps are sold.

postpone post-pone′ *postpones, postponed, postponing, postponement*. Put off; wait.– Do not *postpone* caring for your teeth.–Let's *postpone* the party until next week.

postscript post′-script *postscripts*. A short message written at the end of a letter after the writer's name has been signed. The letters P.S. stand for *postscript*.

posture pos′-ture *postures*. The position of the body; how the body is held.–Children learn good *posture* in their health lessons.

posy po′-sy *posies*. A bunch of flowers.–Baby picked a *posy* and brought it to Mother.

pot *pots, potted, potting*. 1. A round vessel used for cooking, serving foods, or other uses. –*Pots* are made of metal, glass, or pottery. 2. Put in a *pot*.–Mother has *potted* the plants she has in the house.

potato po-ta'-to *potatoes*. A vegetable whose fleshy root is one of the most important foods in many parts of the world.

pottery pot'-ter-y. 1. Dishes and other vessels made of clay and hardened by heat or baking.
2. The art or trade of making dishes and other vessels in that way.
3. A place where clay vessels are made.

potter's wheel — ancient Greek jug — Chinese vase — Roman wine jug — Chinese dish — California Indian jug — ancient Egyptian bottle — New Mexico Indian dish and jar

pouch *pouches*. A bag or sack.–The mother kangaroo carries her baby in a *pouch*.

poultry poul'-try. Birds, especially chickens, ducks, or turkeys, that are reared for food.

goose — turkey — cock — duck — chicken

pounce *pounces, pounced, pouncing*. Jump suddenly.–The cat *pounced* on the dog from above.

pound *pounds, pounded, pounding*. 1. A measurement of weight. There are 16 ounces in a *pound*.–Meat is measured in *pounds*.–I weigh 65 *pounds*. How heavy are you?
2. In Great Britain, a sum of money worth 100 pence.
3. Hit; strike; beat.–*Pound* on the door so that the deaf woman will hear you.
4. Beat heavily.–The waves *pounded* against the rocks.

5. A walled enclosure where straying cattle or sheep used to be sheltered until claimed.

pour *pours, poured, pouring*. 1. Make a liquid flow in a steady stream.–To *pour* from a jug, you tilt the jug until the liquid flows out.
2. Flow in a stream.–When you tilt the jug, the liquid *pours* out.

pout *pouts, pouted, pouting*. Push out the lips to show anger or disappointment. – Some children *pout* when they cannot get their own way.

poverty pov'-er-ty. 1. Condition of being poor; lack of money, food, clothing, etc.–People in the slums of great cities live in *poverty*.
2. Poor quality.–The *poverty* of the land made it impossible to grow anything on it.

powder pow'-der *powders, powdered, powdering*. 1. Anything that is in fine grains like dust.–Baking *powder* is a white, dust-like substance used in baking.
2. Grind or reduce to a *powder*.–Powdered sugar is ground very fine.
3. Dust or sprinkle with *powder*.–Mother *powders* Baby's skin after Baby's bath.

power pow'-er *powers*. 1. Strength or ability to do work; force.–It takes *power* to lift heavy things.–The motor of our car has a great deal of *power*.–Our country has *power* in international affairs.
2. Ability.–The doctor does all that is in his *power* for his patients.
3. The right.–The judge in the contest has the *power* to say who won and who lost.
4. A *power*ful nation.–It is vital for the great *powers* to live in peace.

powerful pow'-er-ful *powerfully*. Having great strength or force.–A machine which can lift heavy things is *powerful*.–A person who can make others obey is *powerful*.

powerless pow'-er-less. Helpless. – The men were *powerless* to prevent the large rock from falling.

practical prac'-ti-cal *practically*. 1. Useful.–Mary's new dress is very *practical*. She can wear it for many different occasions.–The man had many *practical* ideas.
2. Able to do many things well; good at making ideas work out.–Mother is a very *practical* person. She can understand and handle most situations.

P Q R S T U V W X Y Z

practice prac'-tice *practices*. 1. Something regularly or commonly done.–It is the *practice* to exchange gifts at Christmas time.
2. Doing something over and over again to perfect it.–Regular *practice* is the only way to learn to play a musical instrument.
3. The business of a professional person.– The doctor has a large *practice*. He has many patients.
4. Use.–The new plan was immediately put into *practice*.

practise prac'-tise *practises, practised, practising*. 1. Do regularly.–Mary *practises* the piano.
2. Work in a profession.–A doctor *practises* medicine.

prairie prai'-rie *prairies*. A plain where grass grows, but trees do not.–Cattle graze on the *prairie*.

praise *praises, praised, praising*. 1. Speak well of.–Our teacher *praises* our work in spelling.
2. A favourable comment; a statement that something is good.–Our work in spelling receives much *praise*.
3. *Praise* the Lord means worship the Lord.

prance *prances, pranced, prancing*. Move proudly with high steps.–Horses in the circus parade *prance*.

prank *pranks*. A trick. – The children play *pranks* on people on April 1st.

pray *prays, prayed, praying*. 1. Ask from God; speak to God.–Children *pray* to God to bless their loved ones.
2. Ask earnestly.–The princess said, 'Set me free, I *pray* you.'

prayer *prayers*. What one says when speaking to God.–The vicar said a *prayer*.

preach *preaches, preached, preaching*. 1. Make a speech or sermon about a religious subject. –In church the vicar *preaches*.
2. Speak earnestly about.–Mother *preaches* honesty to us every day.

preacher preach'-er *preachers*. A person who preaches in church.

precede pre-cede' *precedes, preceded, preceding*. Come before.–Monday *precedes* Tuesday.

preceding pre-ced'-ing. Coming before.–On the *preceding* day we had packed to go.

precious pre'-cious. Valuable.–*Precious* stones or jewels are very expensive.

precipice prec'-i-pice *precipices*. A high, steep cliff.

precise pre-cise' *precisely*. 1. Accurate and careful.–Mother is very *precise* about her work.
2. Exact. – Father speaks very *precise* English. He makes almost no mistakes.

predicate pred'-i-cate *predicates*. The part of a sentence that tells what the subject does or is.–The boys play ball. The words 'play ball' form the *predicate* of the sentence. They tell what the boys do.

predict pre-dict' *predicts, predicted, predicting, prediction*. Tell beforehand.–The farmer *predicted* that the grain would be ripe next month.

prefer pre-fer' *prefers, preferred, preferring*. Like better.–I *prefer* swimming to hockey.

prefix pre'-fix *prefixes*. Letters or syllables put before a word to make a new word.–In the word unfasten, un- is a *prefix*.

premium pre'-mi-um *premiums*. 1. A prize; a reward.–The farmer received a *premium* for growing the biggest pumpkin.
2. A payment for insurance. – Father pays monthly *premiums* on his insurance.

prepaid pre'-paid. Paid for beforehand.–The package came *prepaid*.

preparation prep-a-ra'-tion *preparations*. 1. A thing or things done to get ready.–The *preparations* for the picnic are almost finished.
2. Something mixed or prepared.–A *preparation* may be a medicine, a food, or anything that is prepared for some special use.

prepare pre-pare' *prepares, prepared, preparing*. 1. Get ready.–Mary *prepares* to go to school early.
2. Make ready. – Mother *prepares* Baby's breakfast.

P
Q
R
S
T
U
V
W
X
Y
Z

prescribe pre-scribe' *prescribes, prescribed, prescribing, prescription.* Order the use of; suggest as a cure, treatment, or procedure; advise.– The doctor *prescribed* a new medicine for the baby. He wrote out an order for us to take to the chemist.

presence pres'-ence. State or condition of being in a place or of being present. – The clown's *presence* at the circus meant fun for the children.

present pres'-ent *presents.* 1. On hand; here.– All the children in the class are *present* today. None is absent.
2. Existing or happening at this moment; now.–Mary isn't at home at the *present* time. She isn't at home now.
3. This time; the time in which we are living now; this moment.–In history lessons we study everything man has done from times long past right up to the *present*.

4. A gift.–Baby received a *present* on her birthday.

present pre-sent' *presents, presented, presenting.* 1. Introduce.–Mary *presented* her friend to the teacher.
2. Send in, give.–The dentist *presented* his bill for the work he had done.
3. When a soldier *presents* arms, he brings his gun up in front of him with the trigger away from his body and the barrel of the gun pointing upward.

presently pres'-ent-ly. Before long; soon.–Father will be home *presently*.

preserve pre-serve' *preserves, preserved, preserving.* 1. Keep from spoiling; save.–Mother bottles fruits to *preserve* them.
2. A kind of jelly with the whole fruit left in. –Strawberries and sugar boiled together make strawberry *preserves*.
3. Keep up, keep in good repair. – The old farm is well *preserved*.

preside pre-side' *presides, presided, presiding.* Have charge (of a meeting or group).–Bob will *preside* at the club meeting.

president pres'-i-dent *presidents.* 1. The head of a college, a society or an institution.
2. The head of the government in a republic, such as the *President* of the United States.

press *presses, pressed, pressing.* 1. Push.–*Press* the button and the lift will stop.
2. Hug.–Father *pressed* the lost child to him.
3. Urge, ask.–Because the money was due, Father *pressed* the man to pay it.
4. Push with all one's weight and force.– Bob *pressed* against the door, but it would not open.
5. A printing machine. – Newspapers are printed on big *presses*.
6. Any machine that works by squeezing or *pressing*.
7. Newspapers.–The story of the accident will be printed in the *press*.
8. Reporters. – The *press* turned out in full force for the society wedding.

pressure pres'-sure *pressures.* A pressing against or on; the pushing force of surrounding things.–The eggs were broken by the *pressure* of other groceries.

presume pre-sume' *presumes, presumed, presuming.* 1. Suppose.–I *presume* you asked your mother if you might go.
2. Dare.–The saucy boy *presumed* to ask his teacher to give the class a holiday.

pretend pre-tend' *pretends, pretended, pretending.* 1. Make believe.–The hedgehog *pretends* that he is dead to fool his enemies. – Mary *pretends* to be 13 years old, but really she is only 10.
2. Claim.–Bob doesn't *pretend* to be a good speller.

pretty pret'-ty *prettier, prettiest, prettily.* 1. Quite beautiful, pleasing to look at. – Baby is *pretty*.
2. Rather, fairly.–It is *pretty* cold today.

prevent pre-vent' *prevents, prevented, preventing.* 1. Stop.–The work of the fireman *prevented* the fire from spreading.
2. Keep from happening.–Bob's quick thinking *prevented* an accident.
3. Hinder, interfere.–Father will be home at six if nothing *prevents* him.

prevention pre-ven'-tion *preventions.* The act of keeping something from happening.–'An ounce of *prevention* is worth a pound of cure' means it is better to prevent a thing than to try to remedy it after it has happened.

previous pre'-vi-ous. Just before; earlier.–You will find a picture of a precipice on the *previous* page, on the page before this.

previously pre'-vi-ous-ly. At a time before; formerly. – *Previously* I attended a different school, in the town where we used to live.

P
Q
R
S
T
U
V
W
X
Y
Z

prey *preys, preyed, preying*. 1. Any animal that is caught by another animal for food. – Mice are the *prey* of hawks. Hawks catch and eat mice.

2. Use (another animal) for food. – Hawks *prey* upon mice.

3. *Prey upon* also means be a constant threat to in any way; feed on, gnaw. – The old woman's illness *preys upon* her mind; . it worries her and does her harm.

price *prices, priced, pricing*. 1. The amount of money a thing costs.–The *price* of my shoes was £2.–The jeweller displayed a pearl of great *price* in his shop window.

2. Set a *price* on.–The man *priced* the bicycle at £12. That was the amount he wanted for it.

priceless *price'-less*. So valuable that a price can hardly be set.–Many great and famous paintings are *priceless*.

prick *pricks, pricked, pricking*. 1. Make a little hole in with a pin, needle, etc.; stick.–Mother *pricked* her finger with a needle.

2. A little hole made by something sharp.– The *prick* hurt Mother's finger.

prickle *prick'-le prickles, prickled, prickling*. 1. A sharp point. – Blackberry bushes have many *prickles* on them.

2. Sting, smart.–Mary's hand *prickled* when she touched the nettle, a plant that has little stingers on it.

prickly *prick'-ly pricklier, prickliest*. Thorny, covered with little sharp points.–Thistles are *prickly*. They have hairlike points or thorns on them that prick you when you hold or touch them.

pride *prides, prided, priding*. 1. A feeling of happiness at being thought well of, or having something one has done, or owns, thought well of.–Mother takes *pride* in keeping our house neat and clean. She would be ashamed if it were not.

2. A thing one is proud of.–Grandfather's garden is his *pride* and joy.

3. Grandmother *prides* herself on her cakes. She thinks they are very good.

4. High opinion of oneself; respect for oneself. – Jack's *pride* wouldn't let him admit his fault.

priest *priests*. A minister or clergyman in a church. *Priests* help people with their religion just as teachers help the students with their schoolwork.

prim *primmer, primmest*. Correct and dignified in a stiff sort of way, as if one is always thinking about being very proper.–Mary is very *prim* when she goes visiting.

primary *pri'-ma-ry primarily*. 1. First in time or order.–The *primary* classes in school are the first classes above the kindergarten.

2. Main, most important.–The *primary* reason that Mother visited the school was to meet Mary's new teacher. – The *primary* colours are red, blue, and yellow. They form the basis for mixing other colours in painting.

primer *prim'-er primers*. A first book.–Children learn to read from a *primer*. After they can read the *primer*, they try the first reader.

primitive *prim'-i-tive*. Referring to, or like, people or things of the earliest times on the earth; crude and simple; ancient.–The cavemen were *primitive* people. They lived a rough and simple life.–*Primitive* dishes were made of clay.–When the boys go camping, they live in a *primitive* way.

primrose *prim'-rose primroses*. A woodland plant that has clusters of pale yellow flowers. –In the spring we often go into the woods to pick *primroses* and other wild flowers.

prince *princes*. 1. The son of a king, or the son of a king's son.

2. A nobleman of the highest rank, having royal blood.

princess *prin'-cess princesses*. The daughter of a king or of a king's son, or the wife of a prince.

principal *prin'-ci-pal principals, principally*. 1. Chief, main.–One of the *principal* reasons for going to school is to learn how to get along with other people.

2. The head of a college, as the *principal* of the Royal College of Art.

3. An amount of money which a person owns and puts into a business or a bank so that it will earn more money for him.

principle *prin'-ci-ple principles*. 1. One of the rules or beliefs by which people live.–Treating people as you would like to have them treat you is a good *principle*.

2. The idea on which something is based; a truth or fact which makes it possible to do many things.–Bob explained to the class the *principles* by which radio works.

PRINTING

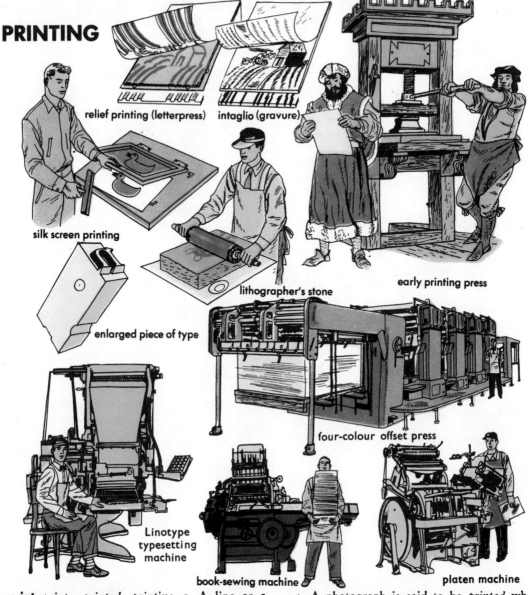

relief printing (letterpress)

intaglio (gravure)

silk screen printing

lithographer's stone

early printing press

enlarged piece of type

four-colour offset press

Linotype typesetting machine

book-sewing machine

platen machine

print *prints, printed, printing.* 1. A line or a mark made by pressing one thing against another, as foot*prints* in the sand, or finger*prints* on the furniture.—No two people have finger*prints* exactly alike.—Bob left a clear hand*print* in the sand.

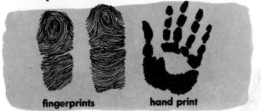

fingerprints

hand print

2. Mark by pressing.—*Printing* presses *print* books. They stamp the letters and pictures on to the pages in ink.—This book was *printed* on a very large press.

3. A photograph is said to be *printed* when it is put on paper so that you can see it. What you see is a photographic *print*.

4. Form letters the way they appear in books and newspapers, instead of the way they are made in handwriting.—Little children sometimes learn to *print* their names before they learn to write them.

MARY B. SMITH

5. Covered with a pattern or design.—Mother has a new *print* dress.

6. A copy made from the first one.—The picture is not the original, it is a *print*.

7. Words stamped on paper by a *printing* press.

printer print'-er *printers*. A person whose work is printing, or setting up type to be printed.

prison pris'-on *prisons*. A place where people are kept as prisoners to punish them for breaking the law.–The thieves were sent to *prison*.

prisoner pris'-on-er *prisoners*. A person or animal that is held captive or kept shut up against his wishes. – A robin shut up in a cage is a *prisoner*.–*Prisoners* kept in a penal settlement have to work.–Our army took many *prisoners*.

private pri'-vate *privates, privately*. 1. Not for everyone, but only for a certain person or persons.–Our teacher had a *private* talk with Mother. No one else was there to listen.
2. Secret.–What I have to tell you is *private*. It is between us alone.
3. Holding no public office, like that of mayor or inspector.–Father is a *private* citizen.
4. A soldier of the lowest rank.–My brother is a *private* in the army.

privilege priv'-i-lege *privileges*. The right to do a special thing.–Our teacher gave us the *privilege* of going home for our books. She let us go.

prize *prizes, prized, prizing*. 1. A gift won by doing something better, or by being luckier, than other people.–The teacher gave a pencil as a *prize* to the person who could name the greatest number of flowers.–Bob won a *prize* at the party when he drew the lucky number from the hat.
2. Fit to win a *prize*; most valuable.–This lily is Grandmother's *prize* flower.
3. Value highly.–We *prize* this picture. It is worth much to us.

probable prob'-a-ble. Likely; likely to happen. –Illness is the *probable* reason for Mary's absence from school.–Rain is *probable* today.

probably prob'-a-bly. It is likely that.–*Probably* Mary stayed at home because of illness.

probation pro-ba'-tion. A trial, or chance to show how well one can do.–The man went to work on *probation*. He was given a chance to show that he could do the work well.

problem prob'-lem *problems*. 1. Something to be worked out; a hard question to be answered.–This is a *problem*; If one apple costs twopence, how much will six apples cost?
2. Anything that is hard to understand or deal with.–A naughty child is sometimes a *problem*.

procedure pro-ce'-dure *procedures*. A way of doing things.–Bob follows this *procedure* in learning to spell: first he says the word, then he spells it to himself three times, then he writes it three times.

proceed pro-ceed' *proceeds, proceeded, proceeding*. 1. More forward.–The old man *proceeded* down the road. He went on.
2. Get along according to plans.–Bob and Father are *proceeding* with their modern aircraft.
3. Come forth.–The wedding party *proceeded* from the church.

proceeding pro-ceed'-ing *proceedings*. Action, activity, things said or done.–Mary gave a report of the *proceedings* at the meeting.

process pro'-cess *processes*. Plan or method.– What *process* is used in making jelly? What steps are taken in making it? What is done first, second, third, and so on?

procession pro-ces'-sion *processions*. The moving forward of persons or things in an orderly way.–A circus parade is a *procession*.–Children marching along in a line make a *procession*.

produce pro-duce' *produces, produced, producing*. 1. Show or exhibit something.–The children *produced* a play. They put it on for others to see.–Mary *produced* the pieces of glass as proof that the vase was broken.
2. Make or manufacture; create.–Factories in Birmingham *produce* hundreds of motorcars every week.
3. Grow or cause to grow. – Seeds *produce* plants.–Farmers *produce* crops.

P
Q
R
S
T
U
V
W
X
Y
Z

produce prod´-uce. Crops grown on a farm. –The farmer takes his *produce* to market.

producer pro-duc´-er *producers*. 1. A person who makes or grows things to sell.–Grandfather is a *producer* of corn.
2. A person who produces a moving picture or play.–Uncle Robert is a play *producer*. He tells the actors and actresses how to move and how to speak their lines.

product prod´-uct *products*. 1. A thing that is grown or made. –Cars are manufactured *products*.–Foods are *products* of the farms.
2. In a problem in multiplication, the answer you get by multiplying two or more numbers together. 2 × 9 = 18. Eighteen is the *product* of 2 and 9.

production pro-duc´-tion. 1. The act of producing or making something.–*Production* is better in well-lit factories. More goods are made in less time.
2. Anything produced or brought out, especially a book, play, etc.–The film we saw last night was a fine *production*.

profession pro-fes´-sion *professions, professional*. A kind of work or occupation for which people must have a special education. –The work of a doctor, dentist, clergyman, or teacher is a *profession*.

professor pro-fes´-sor *professors*. One of the higher-ranking teachers in a college or university.

profile pro -file *profiles*. An outline picture of anything; or, particularly, the picture of the side view of a person's face.

profit prof´-it *profits*. 1. A gain; money made.– Jack's profit from selling papers last week was £1. That was the amount of money he had left after all his expenses were paid.
2. Benefit, use, or good.–What *profit* is there in working till you are over-tired?

programme pro´-gramme *programmes*. A list of the things that are going to happen.–The teacher put our *programme* of classes on the blackboard.–A *programme* for a concert tells what is to be played and by whom.

progress prog´-ress. 1. Movement forward.– A snail makes slow *progress*.
2. Improvement; movement forward.–Have you made any *progress* in your work?

progress pro-gress´ *progresses, progressed, progressing*. Go forward, advance.–Some children *progress* more quickly in school than others.

progressive pro-gres´-sive *progressively, progressiveness*. Favouring improvements and movement forward.–A city that is *progressive* is one that makes improvements, carries out new ideas, and is quite modern.

prohibit pro-hib´-it *prohibits, prohibited, prohibiting*. Not allow by law; forbid.–The sign said 'Smoking *Prohibited*.'

prohibition pro-hi-bi´-tion *prohibitions*. 1. A law or rule forbidding something; not allowing a thing.–There is a *prohibition* against parking for more than an hour in this street.
2. A law against producing or selling alcoholic drinks.

project pro-ject´ *projects, projected, projecting*. 1. Point forward; stick out.–The porch roof *projects* a little to keep the rain from blowing into the porch.
2. Cast or throw upon a flat surface.–Father *projected* the shadow of his hand on to the wall in the shape of a donkey's head.

project proj´-ect *projects*. A plan or design for something that is to be done; an idea which is all worked out.–Building a house-boat is Father's favourite *project*.

projection pro-jec´-tion *projections*. A part that juts out.–Jack stood on the rocky *projection* and looked out over the valley.

projector pro-jec´-tor *projectors*. An apparatus

movie projector   slide projector

or machine used to throw still or moving pictures on to a screen.

prolong pro-long' *prolongs, prolonged, prolonging*. Make longer, increase in length.–The teacher said she would not *prolong* her talk, but would leave time for us to ask questions.

prominent prom'-i-nent. 1. Sticking out.–A long nose is a *prominent* nose.
2. Well-known; noted.–A group of *prominent* businessmen are trying to get the Council to build the playground.

promise prom'-ise *promises, promised, promising*. 1. A person's statement or word that he will surely do something.–Bob gave me his *promise* to be here at 9 o'clock.
2. Make a *promise*.–Bob *promised* to be here at 9 o'clock.
3. Seem likely.–This *promises* to be a hot summer.

promote pro-mote' *promotes, promoted, promoting*. 1. Raise in rank, position, grade, etc. –Bob was *promoted* from the second eleven to the first.
2. Help to happen successfully.–The boys are *promoting* the Red Cross appeal by giving a benefit football game.

promotion pro-mo'-tion *promotions*. 1. A raising in rank or grade.–Uncle Jim got a *promotion* from captain to major.
2. A furthering or helping towards success.–The *promotion* of Mary's career as a musician requires much practice.

prompt *prompts, prompted, prompting*. 1. On time.–Bob is always *prompt* at school.
2. Cause, lead.–The good weather *prompted* us to go outside.
3. Remind.–The teacher *prompted* Mary when she forgot her lines in the play.

pronoun pro'-noun *pronouns*. A word used instead of the name of something or someone. –The word 'you' is a *pronoun* used instead of your name.–The word 'he' is a *pronoun* used in speaking of men and boys.

pronounce pro-nounce' *pronounces, pronounced, pronouncing*. 1. Speak the sounds of. – The word 'quay' is *pronounced* just like the word 'key.'
2. The jury *pronounced* the man innocent. They declared him innocent.

pronunciation pro-nun-ci-a'-tion *pronunciations*. The sound of a spoken word; the act of speaking sounds.–The *pronunciation* of the *word* 'quay' is the same as the *pronunciation* of the word 'key.'

proof *proofs*. 1. That which shows the truth of something.–Bob offered *proof* that he had been in Paris. He showed a photograph of himself in front of the Eifel Tower.
2. Safe or protected (against something).– This coat is *proof* against water. Water will not come through it. It is water*proof*.

prop *props, propped, propping*. 1. A stick or the like that leans against something to hold the thing up.

2. Hold up or support with a *prop* or *props*. –The barn wall was *propped* up with long poles.

propeller pro-pel'-ler *propellers*. A device with curved blades that whirl around. *Propellers* are turned by engines and are used on boats and aircraft. The whirling blades push the water or air and thus make the boat or aircraft move.

proper prop'-er *properly*. 1. According to rule; correct.–It is *proper* to drive on the left-hand side of the road.
2. A *proper noun* is the name of a certain person, place, or thing. *Proper nouns* always begin with capital letters. –London, Mary, France are *proper nouns*.

property prop'-er-ty *properties*. That which is owned, especially land and buildings.–The *property* along the river has been worth more since the park was made. – The bicycle is Bob's *property*. It belongs to him.

prophecy proph'-e-cy *prophecies*. A prediction, a telling beforehand.–The old man's *prophecy* that there would be a war came true. There was a war.

prophesy (rhymes with *eye*) proph'-e-sy' *prophesies, prophesied, prophesying*. Predict, tell beforehand.–The old man *prophesied* that there would be a war.

prophet proph'-et *prophets*. 1. A person who predicts the future.–Bob was a good weather *prophet*. He said it would snow, and it did.
2. A person who preaches what he claims God has told him.–Jeremiah is one of the *prophets* in the Bible.

proportion pro-por'-tion *proportions.* 1. A part. –A great *proportion* of the earth's surface is under water.

2. The relation between parts.–A normal person's body grows in proper *proportions.* The size of each part is properly related to the size of the whole body.

proposal pro-pos'-al *proposals.* 1. A suggestion; something put forward to be done.–Bob's *proposal* to have a picnic was agreed to.

2. A request for marriage.–The young man's *proposal* was accepted by the young woman. She agreed to marry him.

propose pro-pose' *proposes, proposed, proposing.* 1. Suggest; put forward as a thing to do. –Bob *proposed* that the group have a picnic.

2. Ask to marry.–The young man *proposed* to the young woman.

proposition prop-o-si'-tion *propositions.* Something suggested or proposed.

proprietor pro-pri'-e-tor *proprietors.* The owner and manager of a business.–The *poprietor* of the shop gave us a box of chocolates.

prose. Ordinary writing (not in the form of poetry). *Prose does* not have the rhythm and rhyme of poetry.

prosecute pros'-e-cute *prosecutes, prosecuted, prosecuting.* Take to a law court; bring to trial.–The man was *prosecuted* for driving on the wrong side of the road. He was taken to court and tried.

prospect pros'-pect *prospects.* 1. Something looked forward to.–The *prospect* of getting a better job pleased Father.

2. A view.–The *prospect* from our front porch is very beautiful.

prosper pros'-per *prospers, prospered, prospering.* Do well, be successful.–Uncle Jim's new shop is *prospering.*

prosperity pros-per'-i-ty. Good fortune; wealthy condition.–A man who has a good job and all he needs for comfortable living has *prosperity.*

prosperous pros'-per-ous. Successful; well off. –The *prosperous* businessman gave a great deal of money to the playground fund.

protect pro-tect' *protects, protected, protecting.* Guard; keep from danger or harm.–Police *protect* us from criminals.

protection pro-tec'-tion. 1. Keeping from danger.–The job of the Police Force is the *protection* of people from criminals.

2. That which keeps from harm, or protects. –A raincoat is a *protection* against rain.

protest pro-test' *protests, protested, protesting.* Speak against; object. – The boy *protested* against his low mark. He was sure he had done better, and said so.

protest pro'-test *protests.* A statement objecting to something.–The boy made a *protest* against his mark.

Protestant Prot'-es-tant *Protestants.* A member of any Christian church or sect other than the Roman Catholic and Greek Orthodox Churches.

proud *prouder, proudest, proudly.* 1. Having a high regard for oneself or one's family, possessions, etc.–The boy was too *proud* to cheat.

2. Conceited; having too high an opinion of oneself.–The *proud* boy boasted a great deal.

3. Splendid.–The *proud* building towered over the other buildings.

prove *proves, proved, proving.* Establish the truth of something.–The photograph of Bob in front of the Eiffel Tower *proved* that he had been in Paris.

proverb prov'-erb *proverbs.* An old saying that gives advice.–'A stitch in time saves nine' is a *proverb.*

provide pro-vide' *provides, provided, providing.* 1. Supply.–I will *provide* the ice-cream if you will *provide* the cake.

2. Give as a condition. – The rules *provide* that no one over 12 years old may enter the contest.

3. Prepare (for a situation) beforehand, look out for in advance.–Father has *provided* for his old age with insurance.

province prov'-ince *provinces.* 1. A large division of a country.–Canada is divided into *provinces.*

2. A section of a country far from the main city.–People from the *provinces* attended the great fair in the capital.

P
Q
R
S
T
U
V
W
X
Y
Z

provision pro-vi´-sion *provisions*. 1. A given condition.–One of the *provisions* of the rules is that no one over 12 may enter the contest.
2. A preparing, a making ready ahead of time. –The town had made *provision* for a heavy snowfall, and the snow-ploughs started to work as soon as the storm began.
3. (Always plural.) A supply, usually of things to eat and drink. – The campers will not go hungry: they have plenty of *provisions*.

provoke pro-voke´ *provokes, provoked, provoking*. 1. Bring on, be the cause of.–Harsh words *provoke* anger.
2. Annoy, make angry.–Bob's bad behaviour *provoked* the teacher.

prow *prows*. The very front part of a ship or boat.–The *prow* of the ship cut through the water.

prowl *prowls, prowled, prowling*. 1. Rove or wander about looking for food.–The hungry dog *prowled* about the alley.
2. Sneak about. – The man *prowled* about looking for something to steal.

prudence pru´-dence. Wise carefulness.–Bob shows *prudence*. He is not reckless, but tackles things with care.

prudent pru´-dent *prudently*. Wisely careful. –No *prudent* person spends all his money as soon as he gets it.

prune *prunes, pruned, pruning*. 1. A kind of dried plum.
2. Cut off (parts of plants). – The farmer *prunes* the dead branches of his trees.

pry *pries, pried, prying*. 1. Try to find out about other people's affairs.–Nobody likes a person who is always *prying*.
2. Force with something used as a lever.–Mother *pried* the cover off the jam jar with a knife.

psalm *(sarm) psalms*. 1. A sacred song or poem.
2. (With a capital P.) One of the poems to be found in a part of the Bible known as the Book of *Psalms*.

public pub´-lic *publicly*. 1. The people as a whole.–The Government asked the *public* not to waste food.
2. Of or for all the people.–A *public* park is open to everyone.

publication pub-li-ca´-tion *publications*. 1. The act of telling or announcing something to the public, as in a newspaper or magazine.–This news is for *publication*.
2. A book, magazine, or paper printed to sell to the public.
3. The printing and sale to the public of a book, magazine, etc.

publicity pub-lic´-i-ty. The condition of being noticed by the people; public notice.–The airman received much *publicity* through the radio and newspapers. People heard much about him.

publish pub´-lish *publishes, published, publishing*. 1. Make known to the public.–The newspaper *published* the news of the accident on the day after it happened.
2. Make up and print books, magazines, etc., to sell to the public.

publisher pub´-lish-er *publishers*. A man or a company whose business is making up, printing, and selling books, magazines, etc.

pucker puck´er *puckers, puckered, puckering*. Draw together into wrinkles. – Baby *puckered* her lips to kiss Mother.

pudding pud´-ding *puddings*. A sweet, soft dessert, such as suet *pudding*, tapioca *pudding*, bread *pudding*, etc.

puddle pud´-dle *puddles*. A small pool of water.–Mary fell into a mud *puddle* and got her dress muddy.

puff *puffs, puffed, puffing*. 1. A little short, quick breath, as a *puff* of wind or steam.
2. Take in or let out little short breaths.–Father *puffed* at his pipe.–After the race, the boys *puffed* hard. –The locomotive *puffed* past the station.
3. A soft fluffy pad.–Mother puts on her face powder with a powder *puff*.
4. A hollow pastry shell filled with cream.– Most children like cream *puffs*.

pug *pugs.* A small, tan, short-haired dog that has snub nose and a curly tail.

pull *pulls, pulled, pulling.* 1. Use force to move or draw towards one; drag.—The horse *pulled* the cart up the hill.—Father *pulled* a penny from his pocket. – Bob *pulled* up the weeds from the garden.
2. A drawing towards.—The man gave a *pull* on the string and it broke.

pullet pul'-let *pullets.* A young hen.

pulley pul'-ley *pulleys.* A wheel with the rim hollowed out so that a rope or chain can run on it without slipping off. *Pulleys,* usually several together, are used to lift heavy objects.

Pullman Pull'-man *Pullmans.* A railway carriage with tables and comfortable seats. You pay an extra charge to travel by *Pullman.*

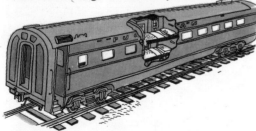

pulp *pulpy.* 1. The soft, juicy part of fruit.
2. Papers, wood, cloth, or anything else ground up very fine and mixed with enough water to make a paste.

pulpit pul'-pit *pulpits.* A platform in a church where the preacher stands to preach.

pulse *pulses, pulsed, pulsing.* 1. Beating of the heart.—The nurse listened to the boy's *pulse.*

2. Any regular beating or throbbing like that of the heart.—The boys heard the *pulse* of the motor in the steamship.
3. Beat regularly, as a heart.

puma pu'-ma *pumas.* A large American wild cat, also called a cougar.

pump *pumps, pumped, pumping.* 1. A machine for forcing liquid or gas through a pipe or hose from one place to another.—Bob *pumped* air into the tyres.
2. Fill with a *pump.*—Bob *pumped* up his bicycle tyres with air.
3. Move, as by a *pump.*—One's heart *pumps* blood to all parts of the body.
4. Force (a person) to tell secrets.—Mary had a secret, but the others could not *pump* her.
5. A kind of low shoe without laces.—Many girls wear *pumps* to dance in.

pump shoe
water pump
bilge pump
tyre pump

pumpkin pump'-kin *pumpkins.* A large yellow fruit that grows on a vine on the ground.

punch *punches, punched, punching.* 1. Hit; strike. – One boxer *punched* the other.
2. A blow.—One boxer gave the other a *punch* on the nose.
3. A drink made by mixing fruit juices and other liquids.
4. A tool used to make holes. – Mary made holes in the paper with a paper *punch.*
5. Knock or make a hole in with a *punch.*

punctuate punc'-tu-ate *punctuates, punctuated, punctuating.* Divide up with commas, full-stops, question marks, etc., to make for easier reading and understanding. – The teacher told us to *punctuate* our stories.

P
Q
R
S
T
U
V
W
X
Y
Z

punctuation punc-tu-a′-tion. Dividing up with marks such as the full-stop, comma, etc., to make for easier reading and understanding. –Mary made three mistakes in *punctuation*.

puncture punc′-ture *punctures, punctured, puncturing*. 1. A small hole pierced by something sharp.–We had a *puncture* in our front tyre.
2. Pierce. – Mary *punctured* the toy balloon with a pin.

punish pun′-ish *punishes, punished, punishing*. Bring pain or unpleasantness to a person for some wrong done.–Some parents *punish* their children by denying them treats.

punishment pun′-ish-ment *punishments*. The act of giving pain or taking away pleasure from one who has done wrong. – Spanking children is *punishment*.–Taking away a person's freedom is *punishment*.

punt *punts, punted, punting*. 1. Hold a football out, drop it, and kick it before it touches the ground.
2. A flat-bottomed boat, propelled by a pole. –The sport is called *punting*.

puny pu′-ny *punier, puniest*. Small and weak. –The baby is *puny*.

pup *pups*. Some baby animals, especially baby dogs, foxes, etc., are called *pups* or puppies.

pupa pu′-pa *pupae* (pronounced pew-pee). A chrysalis. The stage through which some insects pass between the larva and the fully grown form. The *pupa* of many insects is found in a cocoon.

pupil pu′-pil *pupils*. 1. A boy or girl who is in school or studying under a teacher. – There are 30 *pupils* in our class.
2. The dark centre of the eye.

puppet pup′-pet *puppets*. A doll moved by strings on a tiny stage, or by hand.

puppy pup′-py *puppies*. Some baby animals, especially baby dogs, foxes, etc., are called *puppies* or pups. – Father bought a new *puppy* for Sally.

purchase pur′-chase *purchases, purchased, purchasing*. 1. Buy.– Mother has gone to the shop to *purchase* a dress.
2. Anything bought.–Mother's *purchase* was a dress.

pure *purely*. 1. Clean and clear; not mixed with dirt or other unwanted things. – This water is *pure*.
2. Only; not including anything else. – The joke was played in *pure* fun, in fun only.

purify pu′-ri-fy *purifies, purified, purifying*. Make pure or clean.–The council *purifies* our drinking water.

purity pu′-ri-ty. Condition of being pure; pureness.–You may count on the *purity* of this water.

purple pur-ple. A dark, rich colour that can be made of red and blue mixed together.–Some kinds of violets are *purple*.

purpose pur′-pose *purposes*. 1. An aim.–What is your *purpose* in going to school?
2. Deliberate intention. – You dropped your handkerchief on *purpose*. You meant to drop it.

purposely pur′-pose-ly. Intentionally. – You dropped your handkerchief *purposely*.

purr *purrs, purred, purring*. 1. Make a low, humming sound.–The cat *purrs* when she is very comfortable.
2. A humming sound.–I heard the *purr* of the cat.

purse *purses, pursed, pursing*. 1. A small bag or pouch, usually of leather, used to carry money and other articles.
2. A sum of money put up as a prize in boxing, horse racing, etc. – The men fought for a *purse* of £1,000. The winner received the sum of £1,000.
3. Pucker up.–When Baby cries, she *purses* her lips.

pursue pur-sue′ *pursues, pursued, pursuing*. Chase.–The policeman *pursued* the speeding car.

pursuit pur-suit' *pursuits*. 1. A chase.–The policeman is in *pursuit* of the speeding car.
2. Occupation.–What is your father's *pursuit*?

pus. The yellowish-white matter that is found in boils and some other sores.

push *pushes, pushed, pushing*. 1. Use force to move something away from one.–The boys *pushed* the motor-car to start it.
2. Shove.–The policeman *pushed* through the crowd.
3. A shove.–We gave the man's car a *push* to see if we could start it.

pussy-willow puss'-y-wil'-low *pussy-willows*. The furry flower of a small willow tree. It blossoms early in the spring.

put *puts, putting*. 1. Place; set; lay. – *Put* the basket on the table. – *Put* the baby on the bed.
2. Cause to change in place, feeling, or condition. – The hostess *puts* her guests at ease.–The children *put* their desks in order.–Mother *put* the cat out.

putt *putts, putted, putting*. 1. In golf, to strike the ball with a special club called a *putter*

so that it rolls across the *putting*-green, and into the hole.
2. The stroke made in *putting* is a *putt*.

putty put'-ty. A thick paste that becomes hard after standing. It is made of a chalky powder and linseed oil.–Window-glass is held in the window-frame with *putty*.

puzzle puz'-zle *puzzles, puzzled, puzzling*. 1. A problem to be worked out for fun.–There is a crossword *puzzle* in the paper every day.
2. Confuse.–The teacher was *puzzled* over the girl's behaviour. The girl's behaviour *puzzled* the teacher. She didn't know what to think about it.

pyjamas pi-ja'-mas. A two-piece suit worn to sleep in at night.

pyramid pyr'-a-mid *pyramids*. 1. Any object that has a flat bottom and three or more sides forming triangles meeting at one top point.

2. In Egypt there are great *pyramid*-shaped monuments called the *pyramids*.

Q q

Q, q *Q's, q's*. The 17th letter of the alphabet. –In spelling English words, the letter *u* always follows *q*.

quack *quacks, quacked, quacking, quacker*.
1. The cry of a duck.–A sheep says 'Baa, baa.' A duck says '*Quack, quack.*'
2. Make the sound *quack*. – The duck *quacked* loudly when Bill chased it.
3. A person who fools others by pretending to know much about something of which he knows nothing.–The doctor who gave the sick old lady sugar pills was a *quack*.

quadrille qua-drille' *quadrilles*. 1. A square dance with 4 couples.–The couples form a square and follow the directions of a person who calls out the different kinds of steps.
2. Music to which a *quadrille* can be danced.

quadruple quad'-ru-ple *quadruples, quadrupled, quadrupling*. 1. Four times as much, or four times as many.
2. Made up of 4.–It is supposed to be good luck to find a *quadruple* or 4-leaved clover.
3. An amount 4 times as great as another.– Eight is the *quadruple* of 2.

quadruplet quad'-ru-plet *quadruplets*. One of four children born to one mother at the same time.–Mrs Jones had *quadruplets*.

quail *quails, quailed, quailing*. 1. A plump game bird something like a partridge.–Father hunts *quail*. 2. Shrink with fear and dread. –Jack *quailed* at the thought of swimming the icy creek.

quaint *quaintly, quaintness*. Odd, strange, or old-fashioned, but interesting and charming.–Grandmother has a *quaint* velvet jacket like those worn years ago.

quake *quakes, quaked, quaking*. Tremble; shake. – Mary *quaked* with excitement as the time drew near for her party.

Quaker Quak'-er *Quakers*. A member of the Society of Friends, a Christian religious group or sect.

qualify qual'-i-fy *qualifies, qualified, qualifying, qualification*. Be able or well suited.– Mary's teacher believes Mary is *qualified* to enter the musical contest.

quality qual'-i-ty *qualities*. 1. Grade or degree of excellence.–A good *quality* of shoe leather will wear better than a poor *quality*. 2. Jack's best *qualities* are honesty and truthfulness. 3. Merit or good value. – Mother looks for *quality* rather than for bargains when she shops.

quantity quan'-ti-ty *quantities*. 1. Amount.– Great Britain imports a large *quantity* of timber. 2. A large number. – Grandmother baked *quantities* of cakes for the holidays.

quarantine quar'-an-tine *quarantines, quarantined, quarantining*. 1. Keep away from others because of illness.–The children who had scarlet fever were *quarantined*. 2. A ship is in *quarantine* in the harbour. No one is allowed to leave until doctors make sure that the people on it have no disease which might be spread to others on land. 3. We were in *quarantine* when Mary had the measles. We were not allowed to leave the house, and no one except the doctor was allowed to come in.

quarrel quar'-rel *quarrels, quarrelled, quarrelling, quarrelsome*. 1. Dispute or disagreement.–Jack and Bill made friends again after their *quarrel*. 2. Disagree or argue angrily. – The boys *quarrelled* over the bicycle. 3. Find fault. – Jack is always *quarrelling* with the decisions of the umpire.

quarry quar'-ry *quarries, quarried, quarrying*. 1. A place in the ground from which stone is dug.–There are many marble *quarries* in Derbyshire.

2. Dig from a *quarry*.–Very beautiful marble is *quarried* in Derbyshire.

quart *quarts*. A unit for the measurement of liquids. – Milk and other liquids are measured by the space they fill. Two pints make a *quart*. Four *quarts* make a gallon.

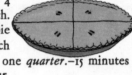

quarter quar'-ter *quarters, quartered, quartering*. 1. One of 4 equal parts; one fourth. –If you divide a pie into 4 equal parts, each part is one fourth or one *quarter*.–15 minutes is a *quarter* of an hour.

2. A place to live (always *quarters*).–The troops moved into new *quarters*. 3. Provide living space for.–After the flood, many families were *quartered* in hotels. 4. Divide into 4 equal parts.–Mother *quartered* the orange for Sally. 5. A section or region. – We visited the French *quarter* of the city.

6. Each of the 4 monthly phases of the moon. They are called; new moon, ıst *quarter*, full moon, and last, or 4th, *quarter*.

quarterly quar'-ter-ly *quarterlies*. 1. Happening or being done 4 times a year, or every 3 months. – Some people pay their household bills *quarterly*.
2. A magazine published 4 times a year.– Some magazines are *quarterlies.*

quartet quar-tet' *quartets*. 1. A group of 4 persons or 4 things.–4 persons who sing songs together, or who play musical instruments together, are a *quartet*.

2. A piece of music written for 4 voices or instruments.–The 4 boys sang a *quartet*.

quartz. A kind of mineral that is made up of very hard crystals. – *Quartz* is colourless, pink, yellow, brown, green, or purple.

quay (pronounced *kee*) *quays*. A wharf or landing place where boats can load and unload.–The merchant went down to the *quay* every day to watch for his ship.

queen *queens, queenly*. 1. A woman ruler, or the wife of a king.
2. A girl or woman who is chosen to be the most important one at some special event, or one who is very popular. – Mary was chosen *queen* of the May.
3. A fully developed female bee or ant. – The *queen* insect lays the eggs.
4. A playing card with the picture of a *queen* on it.

queer *queerer, queerest, queerly, queerness*. Peculiar or strange; odd.–The old man has developed many *queer* ways since he lost his son.–The empty house seemed very *queer* to Sally.

quench *quenches, quenched, quenching*. Extinguish or put out; put an end to.–Cool water will *quench* your thirst better than iced water.–The rain *quenched* the forest fire.

query que'-ry *queries, queried, querying*. 1. A question. – 'Where are you going?' is a *query*.
2. Ask a question.–'What is your name?' *queried* Sally.

question ques'-tion *questions, questioned, questioning, questioner*. 1. A sentence that asks something.–Sally asks many *questions*, because there are many things she wants to know.
2. Ask.–The teacher *questioned* us about the lost book.
3. Subject or problem.–At the meeting tonight, the staff will discuss the *question* of improving the playgrounds.
4. A doubt or uncertainty.–If there is any *question* of the safety of the ice, do not go skating.
5. Be uncertain of, or doubt.–No one can *question* Jack's honesty.

queue (pronounced *kyu*) *queues*. 1. A long plait of hair that hangs down the back.–In China men used to wear *queues*.
2. A waiting line, as at a shop counter or ticket office.–During World War II, people stood in *queues* for things that were hard to buy.

quick *quicker, quickest*. 1. Fast or rapid; swift.–The magician was so *quick* that we could not follow his movements.
2. Hasty or unthinking.–Jack's worst fault is his *quick* temper.
3. Deep and sensitive part.–Mary bit her nails to the *quick*.

quicken quick'-en *quickens, quickened, quickening*. 1. Hasten or move faster; hurry.–Jack *quickened* his steps as the rain began to fall.
2. Arouse or excite.–The man's story *quickened* Ed's interest in him.

quickly quick'-ly. Fast, hastily, with speed; rapidly.–We must pack *quickly* if we hope to catch the train.

quickness quick'-ness. Speed; swiftness.– Bob's *quickness* in the football match surprised the other team.

Q
R
S
T
U
V
W
X
Y
Z

quiet qui'-et *quieter, quietest, quiets, quieted, quieting, quietly.* 1. Silent and still: calm. –The garden was so *quiet* that we could hear the bees humming.
2. Motionless.–There was no breeze, and the leaves were *quiet*.
3. Restful and peaceful.–We spent a *quiet* day in the country.
4. Gentle, mild.–Mother has a *quiet* way.
5. Not bright or flashy.–Grandmother wore a *quiet* lavender dress.
6. Silence and soothe, or calm down.–The teacher *quieted* the excited boy.
7. Stillness and peace.–The *quiet* of the country is restful to Grandmother after a week in the city.

quietness qui'-et-ness. Stillness; calmness. – The *quietness* in the country is restful to Grandmother.

quill quills. 1. A large, stiff feather taken from the wing or tail of a goose, duck, or other fowl.
2. A pen made from a sharpened feather.– In the picture in our classroom, Columbus is drawing a map with a *quill*.
3. A stiff hair or spine.–Porcupines' bodies are covered with *quills*.

quilt *quilts, quilted, quilting.* 1. A stuffed or filled bed cover used for warmth.–Grandmother stuffs her patchwork *quilts* with cotton.

2. Make a *quilt*, 2 layers sewn together with something soft inside.–Mother is *quilting* a dressing-gown for Sally.

quintuplet quin-tu'-plet *quintuplets.* 1. Five things of a kind.
2. One of 5 animals or children born to the same mother at the same time.–It is very rare for *quintuplets* to be born.

quit *quits, quitted, quitting.* 1. Stop; halt.– The farmer *quits* work at 8.
2. Leave.–Bob *quitted* his summer job to go back to college.

quite. 1. Fully; entirely; completely. – The story is not *quite* finished.
2. Truly, really.–Mary's cold is *quite* bad.
3. More than a little.–Bob was *quite* disappointed by the results of the game.
4. Very much of.–You have *quite* a sun tan.

quiver quiv'-er *quivers, quivered, quivering.*
1. Tremble or shiver gently. – The leaves *quivered* in the breeze.
2. A case for carrying arrows. – Robin Hood wore a *quiver* over his shoulder.

quiz *quizzes, quizzed, quizzing.* 1. A test or examination.–Our teacher gave us a *quiz* in arithmetic.
2. Ask questions of.–It is not polite to *quiz* others about their private affairs.
3. Many *quiz* programmes may be seen on television.

quoit *quoits.* A ring of flattened metal that is used in playing the game of *quoits*. The game is played by throwing the metal *quoits* at a peg in the ground to see who can get the *quoit* on or nearest the peg.

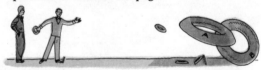

quotation quo-ta'-tion *quotations.* 1. The exact words spoken or written by one person when repeated by another person.–Bob said, 'I would like to go to the football game.' The words in *quotation* marks are a *quotation*. The marks ('. . .'), before the word I and after the word game are *quotation* marks. They show the beginning and the end of the *quotation*.–'The Lord is my shepherd; I shall not want' is a *quotation* from the Bible.

quote *quotes, quoted, quoting.* 1. Repeat exactly what someone else has said or written. –Father likes to *quote* things he has read.
2. Set the price of.–The farmer *quoted* £10 for his load of hay.
3. A quotation, the exact words spoken or written by one person and repeated by another.

quotient quo'-tient *quotients.* The answer or number which you get after working a problem in division. – 12 ÷ 3 = 4 (the *quotient*). 3)12

4 (*quotient*).

Q R S T U V W X Y Z

R r

R, r *R's, r's.* The 18th letter of the alphabet.

rabbi rab'-bi *rabbis.* A scholar and clergyman of the Jewish religion.

rabbit rab'-bit *rabbits.* A small, swift animal with soft fur, long ears, and a short, puffy tail. The *rabbit* belongs to the hare family. It has strong hind legs for jumping.

snowshoe rabbit   cottontail rabbit

jack rabbit   Belgian hare

rabies ra'-bi-es. A disease which makes dogs and other animals go mad.–If a person is bitten by a mad dog, he too may get *rabies.*

race *races, raced, racing.* 1. A contest of speed. –There are car *races,* foot *races,* horse *races,* etc.

2. Run in competition.–I will *race* you boys to the corner.
3. Run fast.–Father *raced* the motor of his car. He made it go fast while the car stood still.–The horse *raced* across the pasture.

children of different races

4. A large group of people who have the same skin colour and kind of hair, and other common traits.–Some Americans are of the white *race,* and some are of the black *race.*

5. The stream of water which turns a waterwheel.–The strong, fast current of water that turns a mill is a mill *race.*

racer rac'-er *racers.* A person, animal, or thing that races. A motor-car, a horse, a boat, or a person that takes part in a race is a *racer.*

rack *racks.* 1. A framework that is used as a holder, such as a toothbrush *rack,* a towel *rack,* a *rack* to drain plates on, a shoe *rack,* or a hat *rack.*
2. A box made of slats.–Grandfather puts the hay for the horses in a feed *rack.*
3. A device used long ago for torturing or hurting people by stretching their limbs.

racket rack'-et *rackets.* 1. A loud, confused noise.–The children made so much *racket* playing circuses that Mother didn't hear the bell ring.
2. Also spelt *racquet.* A bat with a long handle and a flat, oval frame laced tightly with strong cord.–Tennis and some other games are played by hitting a ball with a *racket.*
3. A dishonest scheme or plan for getting people's money.–Gambling is often a *racket.*

racoon or **raccoon** racoon' or raccoon' *racoons* or *raccoons.* A small fur-bearing American animal that lives in trees and moves about mostly at night.

radiant ra'-di-ant *radiantly.* Shining; bright; brilliant and joyous. – Sally has a *radiant* smile. Her whole face lights up with joy when she smiles.

radiator ra'-di-a-tor *radiators.* A heater made up of tubes or pipes through which hot water or steam passes. *Radiators* are used to heat houses.

radio ra′-di-o *radios, radioed, radioing.* 1. A way of sending sounds over a long distance by means of electrical waves, without connecting wires. One instrument, called the 'transmitter,' receives sounds and sends them out in the form of the waves. Another instrument, called the 'receiver,' receives the waves and changes them back into sound.
2. A *radio* transmitter.
3. A *radio* receiver.

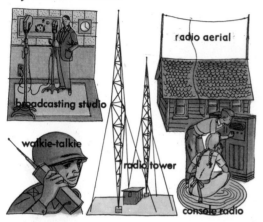

4. Send out by *radio.*–The ship *radioed* a message for help.
5. A message sent by *radio.*

radish rad′-ish *radishes.* A vegetable that grows in the ground like a carrot or a turnip. *Radishes* are round or long, red or white, and are eaten raw. Some *radishes* have a sharp taste.

raffle raf′-fle *raffles, raffled, raffling.* 1. A way of raising money by selling chances of a prize to many people. The prize is given to the holder of the winning ticket.
2. Sell by selling chances.–We *raffled* a quilt to get money for the society. We sold it by selling chances on it.

raft *rafts.* A platform of boards, logs, etc., fastened together, which will float on the water like a boat.

rafter raf′-ter *rafters.* One of the large crosswise beams or timbers that hold up the roof of a building.

rag *rags.* 1. A piece of used cloth.–Mother often uses *rags* for cleaning.
2. Old, torn clothing.–At midnight, Cinderella's ball gown turned to *rags.*

3. Remains of worn-out cloth.–Some kinds of paper are made from *rags.*

rage *rages, raged, raging.* 1. Wild anger.– Jack was in a *rage* over the theft of his bicycle.
2. Act wildly.–The wrongly accused prisoner *raged* like a mad person.
3. A fashion or fad.–Hair ribbons are all the *rage.* All the girls are wearing them.

ragged rag′-ged. 1. Torn in pieces.–After the football match, Jack's clothes were all *ragged.*
2. Dressed in *ragged* clothing.–The tramp was *ragged.*
3. Rough, or not regular.–The rocks along the cliff are sharp and *ragged.*

ragwort rag′-wort *ragworts.* A common weed with a yellow flower. The fine pollen from its blossoms gives some people hay fever.

raid *raids, raided, raiding, raider.* 1. A swift attack.–The enemy aircraft made a *raid* on the city.
2. Make an attack.–The aeroplanes *raided* the city.
3. Break into and seize property from.–The burglars *raided* the bank.
4. The policeman made a *raid* on the gambling club. They forced their way in and arrested the gamblers.

rail *rails.* 1. A slender bar of wood or metal. Tramcars and trains run on tracks made of metal *rails.*–Fences are sometimes made of wooden *rails.*
2. A bar in a railing.–Baby's crib has *rails* round the sides.

railing rail′-ing *railings.* An enclosure or fence made of rails.–Father put a *railing* round the veranda so that Baby would not fall off.

railway rail′-way *railways.* 1. A track for trains, made of steel rails fastened to wooden ties with spikes.
2. A system of train tracks, trains, stations, and the body of men in charge of them.– Uncle Jim works for the *railway.*

raiment rai′-ment. Dress, clothes.–The children in the Christmas play all wore white *raiment.*

R
S
T
U
V
W
X
Y
Z

RAILWAYS

Tom Thumb, 1829

Locomotion No 1, 1825

Rocket, 1829

G.W.R. North Star, 1837

American Civil war train

Gladstone, 1882

L.N.E.R. Mallard, 1935

water tower

coaling tower

semaphore signals

viaduct

tunnel

engine sheds

overhead electric train

breakdown crane

diesel shunting engine

station

siding

signal box

GTON

colour light signal

diesel electric locomotive

steam locomotive

tender

passenger coach

open wagon

tank wagon

cattle wagon

bogie well-wagon

brake van

underground tube train

R
S
T
U
V
W
X
Y
Z

rain *rains, rained, raining.* 1. Water which falls from clouds.–Drops of *rain* beat against my face.

2. A fall of *rain.*–We had a heavy *rain.*

3. Fall in drops from the clouds.–It *rained* today.

4. A shower of anything falling like *rain.*– A *rain* of stones came from the angry crowd.

5. Fall like *rain.*–Rice and bits of coloured paper *rained* on the bride and groom.

rainbow rain'-bow *rainbows.* A large arch or bow of colours which is often seen in the sky opposite the sun during a light rain. It is caused by the sun shining through raindrops.

raincoat rain'-coat *raincoats.* A waterproof coat to keep the rain off.–When it rains, Bob wears his *raincoat.*

 Japanese raincoat fisherman's raincoat

 fireman's raincoat

raindrop rain'-drop *raindrops.* One drop of water falling from the clouds.

rainfall rain'-fall *rainfalls.* 1. A shower of rain. –Today we had a heavy *rainfall.*

2. The total amount of rain that falls in a particular place during a month, year, etc.– The *rainfall* in Scotland is greater than the *rainfall* in England.

rainstorm rain'-storm *rainstorms.* A rainfall, sometimes with wind.–On our way home from school we were caught in a *rainstorm.*

rainy rain'-y *rainer, rainiest.* 1. Raining or having rainfall.–In some parts of the world there is a *rainy* season and a dry season.

2. A *rainy* day sometimes means a time of distress or misfortune.–Now you are earning more money you can put some aside for a *rainy* day.

raise *raises, raised, raising.* 1. Lift, bring, or put up.–The witness *raised* his right hand.

2. Pick up.–When Tom *raised* the stone, he found a frog under it.

3. Erect or build.–The city *raised* a monument in honour of its soldiers.

4. Get together or collect from different places.–The poor family could not *raise* enough money to pay the rent.

5. Bring up for attention.–Bob *raised* the question of buying more books for the school library.

6. Stir up.–The speaker's remarks *raised* excitement in the crowd.

raisin rai'-sin *raisins.* A special kind of grape that has been dried. – Grandmother puts *raisins* in cakes and in rice pudding.

rake *rakes, raked, raking.* 1. A gardening tool with a long handle and a cross rod with comb-like teeth in it.

2. Comb up (ground, leaves, etc.) with a *rake.*–Sally likes to *rake* the leaves in the yard. She likes to use the *rake.*

3. Search through thoroughly.–Mary *raked* through the contents of the old trunk trying to find a costume to wear.

rally ral'-ly *rallies, rallied, rallying.* 1. Start to improve or take a turn for the better.–The sick boy *rallied* after the doctor had cared for him.

2. A large, informal meeting of people to get them enthusiastic about something.–We held a *rally* to raise money for the pageant.

3. Gather for fresh effort. – The General *rallied* his troops after the defeat.

4. In tennis, etc., a series of strokes ending with the ball being hit out or into the net.

ram *rams, rammed, ramming.* 1. A male sheep. –Some *rams* have horns.

2. Strike or crash into. – A lorry behind us *rammed* our car when we stopped.

3. Crush or drive down firmly. – The dustman *rammed* the paper into the barrel.

ramble ram'-ble *rambles, rambled, rambling.* 1. Wander aimlessly. – We *rambled* about the woods all the afternoon.

2. A stroll or walk for pleasure.–The girls went for a *ramble* in the woods.

3. Talk first of one thing and then another.– The teacher told the children not to *ramble* when they made their two-minute speeches, but to keep to the point.

4. Grow in a wandering, untrained fashion.– Vines *rambled* over the porch.

ramp *ramps*. A slanting way joining two places, one of which is higher than the other.–We walked up the *ramp* in the stadium.

rampart ram'-part *ramparts*. A broad, high, protecting wall made of earth, sometimes with watch-towers on the top.–The soldiers climbed the cliffs unseen and drove the enemy off the *ramparts*.

ran. One form of the word *run*.–The child *ran* to his mother. .

ranch *ranches*. Large farm for raising cattle, sheep, or horses. – The cowboy lived on a *ranch*.

rancher ranch'-er *ranchers*. A man who works on, owns, or runs a ranch or big stock farm.

rang. One form of the word *ring*.–The teacher *rang* the bell.

range *ranges, ranged, ranging*. 1. Row or chain of mountains or hills.–The Rockies are the highest mountain *range* in North America.

2. Extend.–The prices of the books *ranged* from 20p to 50p.
3. A stove to cook on. –Mother has a new electric *range*.
4. Reach. – The gun's *range* is 1000 yards.– Bob was careful to stay out of *range* of the in-jured dog's teeth.

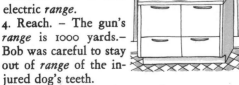

5. Unfenced land where cattle graze, or eat grass.
6. Wander or roam.–In the days of the early settlers, buffaloes *ranged* the prairies.

rank *ranks, ranked, ranking*. 1. A row.–The soldiers marched in *ranks* of 4, side by side.
2. Standing or class.–A sergeant's *rank* is above that of a corporal. He is in a higher class.
3. Have a certain standing.–A corporal *ranks* lower than a sergeant.
4. List in order.–The students were *ranked* according to their marks.
5. Strong and disagreeable in odour and taste. –Butter and other fats that stand a long time sometimes become *rank*.

ransack ran'-sack *ransacks, ransacked, ransack-ing*. Search thoroughly, turn things upside-down to find something.–Bob *ransacked* his room for his cricket bat.–The burglars *ran-sacked* the house for jewellery.

ransom ran'-som *ransoms*. 1. Money paid to free a person who has been kidnapped or captured.–The rich man paid a *ransom* of £10,000 to free his son from the kidnappers.
2. Pay *ransom* for. – The prince offered to *ransom* his men, who were prisoners of the enemy.

rap *raps, rapped, rapping*. 1. Tap, or hit lightly and quickly.–On Hallowe'en the children *rapped* on the neighbours' windows.
2. Light knock.–I heard a *rap* on my window.

rapid rap'-id *rapidly*. Fast or quick.–After the race, Bob could hear the *rapid* beating of his heart.–Travel by aeroplanes is more *rapid* than travel by train.

rapidly rap'-id-ly. Speedily, quickly, fast.– The train passed *rapidly*.–Jack can add fig-ures *rapidly*.

rapids rap'-ids. A place in a river where the water flows very fast over rocks and stores, but not over falls.–The boys went through the *rapids* in their canoe.

rapture rap'-ture *raptures*. Great joy and de-light.–The family's *rapture* at their daughter's return was great.

R
S
T
U
V
W
X
Y
Z

rare *rarer, rarest.* 1. Seldom to be found. – This piece of china is valuable because it is so *rare*. There are very few of its kind.– The birth of quintuplets is *rare*.
2. Cooked only a short time, so as to be still juicy and pink (of meat).–Mother likes her meat well done. Father likes it *rare*.

rarely *rare'-ly.* Seldom.–We *rarely* go swimming at night.

rascal *ras'-cal rascals.* 1. Mean, wicked, tricky person.–The *rascals* who sold land they did not own were arrested as they tried to leave town.
2. Mischievous or trouble-making child or young person.–Grandmother told us Father was a *rascal* when he was a little boy.

rash *rashes, rashly.* 1. A breaking out of red spots on the skin.–A *rash* may be a sign of measles.
2. Reckless.–It is *rash* to promise to do more than you are sure you can do.

raspberry *rasp'-ber-ry raspberries.* A small, seedy berry that grows on a raspberry bush. *Raspberries* are usually red, but may be black, purple, or yellow. – *Raspberry* jam has many little seeds in it.

rat *rats.* An animal that looks like a large mouse. – *Rats* gnaw with their sharp teeth. –*Rats* are pests, and may carry diseases.

rate *rates, rated, rating.* 1. The plane flew at the *rate* of 300 miles an hour. At that speed it could go 300 miles in 1 hour.–The *rate* of interest on the loan will be 6 per cent. You will have to pay £6 a year for each £100 you borrow.
2. A price.–The theatre *rates* are higher for the evening show than for the afternoon show.
3. Set a value on.–The estate agent *rated* the house at £3,000.
4. Rank or consider.–Bob is generally *rated* the best student in his class.
5. We stayed at a first-*rate* hotel.–It was one of the best.
6. At any *rate*, we reached home before the rain started.

rather *rath'-er.* 1. More gladly; with more willingness. –I'd *rather* travel by train than by bus; the bus makes me ill.

2. Somewhat. – Mother is *rather* worried about Baby's cold.
3. *Rather than* means instead of.–The road runs north-east, *rather than* directly north.
4. Instead.–The plant is not dead; *rather*, it is asleep.

ration *ra'-tion rations, rationed, rationing.*
1. Give out (a supply that is limited) in fair amounts to each person.–Sugar, coffee, meat, petrol, and other articles are *rationed* in some countries during wartime.
2. The amount of a certain article each person may have.–The doctor had an extra *ration* of petrol.
3. A certain amount of food allowed for each day.–The soldiers were given *rations* of chocolate for the march.

rational *ra'-tion-al rationally.* In a sensible, thoughtful manner.–Dick's behaviour is *rational*. He does not act madly.

rattle *rat'-tle rattles, rattled, rattling.* 1. Make the sound of something loose being shaken. –The wind makes the windows *rattle*.
2. The sound of something shaking. – We heard the *rattle* of the garden door during the storm.
3. A toy that makes a noise when shaken.– Baby likes to throw her *rattle* out of the pram.

rattlesnake *rat'-tle-snake rattlesnakes.* A poisonous American snake. Its tail has rattles, or loose rings, that make a rattling noise when the tail moves.

rave *raves, raved, raving.* 1. Talk insanely.– The sick man was *raving* with fever. He did not know what he was saying.
2. Talk with great excitement and enthusiasm.–Mary was *raving* about the hero of the film.

ravel *rav'-el ravels, ravelled, ravelling.* Separate or become separated into threads or yarn.– Mother hemmed the towel so that it would not *ravel*.

raven *ra'-ven ravens.* 1. A very shiny, black bird somewhat like the crow, but larger.
2. Black and shiny.– Snow White had pure white skin, red lips, and *raven* hair.

R
S
T
U
V
W
X
Y
Z

ravine ra-vine′ *ravines*. A deep, narrow hollow made by running water. – We stood on the cliff and looked down into a *ravine*.

raw. 1. Not cooked. – Cabbage can be eaten *raw*.

2. Not ready to use (of materials).–Cotton as it comes from the fields, iron ore as it comes from the mines, logs as they come from the woods are *raw* materials.

3. Cold and wet (of weather).–A *raw* March wind was blowing.

4. Not trained, or not experienced.–Many *raw* sailors become seasick.

5. Sore from having the skin scraped off.– The *raw* sore on Mary's knee was caused by her falling on the pavement.

ray *rays*. 1. Narrow beam, as of light.–A *ray* of light shone through the keyhole.

2. A faint sign (of hope).–Jack can always see a *ray* of hope when things look bad.

3. One of many lines extending from a centre in all directions.– Sally's picture of the sun was a big yellow circle with *rays* round it.

4. A kind of flat fish.

rayon ray′-on. A smooth, soft cloth woven of threads made from wood. *Rayon* looks something like silk.

raze *razes, razed, razing*. Destroy or tear down. –The workmen *razed* the old building. They tore it down level with the ground. – Fire *razed* the forest.

razor ra′-zor *razors*. A sharp-bladed tool used by men for shaving their beards. Some *razors* have folding blades, like large jack-knives; others are of a safety type in which the blade is partly covered.

safety razor   electric razor   cut-throat razor

reach *reaches, reached, reaching*. 1. Thrust or push out (one's hands or arms).–Baby *reached* to Mother to be taken out of her cot.

2. Get hold of and hand over. – Father *reached* the book for Mother.

3. A stretching of the arms.–Baby made a sudden *reach* for Father's hat.

4. Extend.–A branch of the tree *reached* to the window.

5. Get to or arrive at.–We *reached* school.

6. Impress or have influence on.–The teacher tried to *reach* Bill by appealing to his sense of fair play.

7. Range.–The bomber plane kept out of *reach* of the searchlight.

8. A long expanse, especially of water.–The steamboat pilot entered the long *reach* of rapids with caution.

read *reads, read, reading*. 1. Look at and get meaning from (something written or printed). –You are now *reading* this dictionary.–We may *read* by saying words aloud or by thinking of them silently. – We *read* music by singing or playing an instrument while looking at the notes.

2. Understand or get the meaning of.–When we understand a map, we can *read* it.–When we understand a speedometer on a car, we can *read* it.

3. Predict, or tell beforehand.–The weather man *reads* the weather. He tells beforehand what kind of weather we will have.

4. Show or indicate.–The gas meter *reads* 10 units of gas used.–The speedometer *reads* 25 miles per hour.

read (pronounced *red*). One form of the word *read*.–Have you *read* 'Robinson Crusoe'?

reader read′-er *readers*. 1. Person who reads. –Mary is quite a good *reader*. She understands books and stories that she reads.

2. A book used to teach reading.–Mary reads fluently from the *reader*.

readily read′-i-ly. Easily or quickly. – Mary can understand *readily* what she reads.

readiness read′-i-ness. 1. Condition of being ready or prepared.–Everything is in *readiness* for the picnic.

2. Willing promptness.–The man's *readiness* to work got a job for him.

reading read′-ing. The act of seeing and getting the meaning of something written or printed.–*Reading* is easy for Mary, so she reads many books.

ready read′-y (pronounced *reddy*). 1. Prepared. –When Father comes home, he likes to find his dinner *ready*.

2. Willing.–We are *ready* to take less money for the bicycle now that the tyres are worn out.

3. Quick.–Jack always has a *ready* answer in arithmetic class.

4. Right at hand, or to be had right away.– The hospital had a *ready* supply of bandages.

R
S
T
U
V
W
X
Y
Z

real re'-al. Actual and true; not false, imaginary, or artificial.–Sally likes fairy tales, but Mary likes stories about *real* people.–Mother has *real* roses on her dress.

reality re-al'-i-ty *realities*. What is; the truth; the way things actually are.–Mary and Jack like to tease each other, but in *reality* they are very fond of each other.

realize re'-al-ize *realizes, realized, realizing*. 1. Understand or know; be aware of.–Jack doesn't *realize* that his remarks sometimes hurt people's feelings.
2. Achieve, or make come true or happen.–Grandmother finally *realized* her wish when she moved back to the country.
3. Get as profit from the sale of something.–Bob *realized* £2 on the sale of his bicycle. He sold it for £2 more than he paid for it.

really re'-al-iy. Truly or actually. – If you *really* want something, you will work for it.–The sun does not *really* go round the earth. The earth goes round the sun.

reap *reaps, reaped, reaping*. 1. Cut and gather. –The farmer *reaps* his grain in the summer.
2. Obtain or get in return.–Give happiness to others and you will *reap* happiness.

reaper reap'-er *reapers*. A machine for cutting grain, or a person who cuts grain.

reappear re-ap-pear' *reappears, reappeared, reappearing*. Appear or show again; come to be seen again.–The sun went behind a cloud, and then it *reappeared*.

rear *rears, reared, rearing*. 1. Back; hind.–The front garden is in front of the house, and the back garden is at the *rear* of the house. The *rear* wheels of the car got stuck in the soft earth when we backed up.
2. Rise or raise.–The horse *reared* up on his hind legs.
3. Raise or bring up.–Grandmother *reared* three children.

rear-admiral rear-ad'-mi-ral *rear-admirals*. A high officer in the navy, ranking below vice-admiral.

rearrange re-ar-range' *rearranges, rearranged, rearranging*. Arrange again; put in different positions. – Mother likes to *rearrange* the furniture.

reason rea'-son *reasons, reasoned, reasoning*.
1. Cause of a happening; explanation.–Can you give a *reason* for believing that the earth is round?
2. Think out or solve. – Mary tried to *reason* out the problem in arithmetic.
3. Thought or good sense.–The angry man did not use *reason* when he hit the policeman.
4. Sanity or senses.–The old miser lost his *reason* when his money was stolen.
5. Argue, or point out the other side of a question.–It.is hard to *reason* with Jack when he is angry.
6. Power or ability to think.–You must use your *reason* to solve problems in arithmetic.

reasonable rea'-son-a-ble *reasonableness, reasonably*. 1. Fair and just. – Our teacher is *reasonable* in the amount of homework she assigns us. – Mary's wish for a new dress seems *reasonable*, since she has outgrown several of her others.
2. Logical, sensible.–The answer to the problem seems too large a figure to be *reasonable*.
3. Moderate. – In June the price of strawberries is *reasonable*. They are not expensive then.

rebel reb'-el *rebels, rebelled, rebelling*. Fight against lawful control.–Prisoners sometimes *rebel* and try to escape.

rebel reb'el *rebels*. A person who fights against lawful control. – The *rebels* tried to overthrow the government.

rebellion re-bel'-lion *rebellions*. A rising up of people against the government or other authorities.–The discontented citizens started a *rebellion*.

recall re-call' *recalls, recalled, recalling*. 1. Remember. – Bill couldn't *recall* which day he was absent.
2. Call back.–The messenger was *recalled*. He was told to come back.
3. Order to leave or give up office. – The ambassador was *recalled* from abroad by his government.

receipt re-ceipt' *receipts*. 1. A written statement which says that one has received something. – When the registered letter came, Mother signed a *receipt*.
2. Money received. – The *receipts* from the flower show will be used to buy library books.
3. Act of receiving.–I wrote to Grandmother on *receipt* of her letter.

R
S
T
U
V
W
X
Y
Z

4. An old form of recipe. A set of directions telling how a thing, especially a food dish, should be prepared. – This cake was made from an old *receipt*.

receive re-ceive' *receives, received, receiving.*
1. Get, or have given or brought to one; accept (something offered). – We *receive* an allowance from Father each week.–We *received* a letter every week from Jack while he was at camp.–Baby *received* a bad bump when she fell.
2. Greet or welcome.–Sally likes to *receive* Mother's guests. She greets them at the door and invites them in.
3. Hold.–We left a box on the table to *receive* the Christmas presents.
4. Have as an experience.–Mary is *receiving* a good musical education.

receiver re-ceiv'-er *receivers.* 1. A person who gets or accepts.–Bob gave Mother a present for her birthday. Bob was the giver of the present, and Mother was the *receiver*.
2. A thing that receives.– We talk on the telephone through the mouthpiece, and listen to or receive the message through the *receiver*.
3. A container, or something used to put things in.

recent re'-cent. Happening or made not long ago.–This is a *recent* book. It was written just lately.

recently re'-cent-ly. Lately, or a short while ago. – We are going to telephone Grandmother, since we have not heard from her *recently*.

reception re-cep'-tion *receptions.* 1. A party at which people are greeted by an honoured guest.–After the wedding, there was a *reception*. The bride and groom received many friends.
2. Way of receiving.–They gave me a friendly *reception*. They received me in a friendly way.
3. Condition of receiving.–The *reception* (of radio signals) on the radio is poor during a thunderstorm.

recess re-cess' or re'-cess *recesses.* 1. A short time during which work stops. – In some schools children have a *recess* in the morning and in the afternoon. Children play during *recess*.
2. A nook, or hollow space. – Mother put Uncle Jim's trunk in a *recess* in the bedroom wall.

recipe (pronounced *ressipy*) rec'-i-pe *recipes.* A set of directions telling how a thing, especially a food dish, should be prepared.– This cake was made from a new *recipe*.

recital re-cit'-al *recitals.* 1. A musical entertainment at which one or more persons play, sing, or dance.
2. An account or tale. – The soldier's *recital* of his travels was exciting to the children.

recitation rec-i-ta'-tion *recitations.* 1. The repeating aloud of what has been learned.– After learning the verses, the children were ready for the *recitation*.
2. The repeating of a *piece* to entertain an audience.–At the entertainment Mary gave a *recitation*. She repeated from memory a poem she had learned.–Mary's *recitation* was a long poem.

recite re-cite' *recites, recited, reciting.* Repeat or say aloud from memory.–The children can *recite* many poems.–A small boy *recited* all the rules of the game.

reckless reck'-less *recklessly, recklessness.* Heedless of danger, very rash.–Do not drive *recklessly*. Do not drive dangerously fast, or without due caution.

reckon reck'-on *reckons, reckoned, reckoning.*
1. Count up.–Jack is *reckoning* the weeks before school breaks up.
2. Judge or regard.–Mr Smith is *reckoned* the best man for the job. He is thought to be the best.

recline re-cline' *reclines, reclined, reclining.* Lean back.–I like to *recline* in an easy chair and read.

recognition rec-og-ni'-tion. 1. Being known or identified.–The books were burned beyond *recognition*.
2. Favourable attention.–The soldier received *recognition* for his bravery. He received many honours in *recognition* of his bravery.

recognize rec'-og-nize *recognizes, recognized, recognizing.* 1. Know; identify from familiarity. – Mother didn't *recognize* my voice over the telephone. She didn't know it was my voice.
2. Appreciate. – The teacher *recognized* the children's efforts to get their work done.
3. Admit.–Jack *recognized* that it was his duty to stay at home and help Mother.

recollect rec-ol-lect' *recollects, recollected, recollecting.* Remember.–Bob certainly doesn't *recollect* who borrowed the book.

R
S
T
U
V
W
X
Y
Z

recommend rec-om-mend′ *recommends, recommended, recommending.* 1. Show favour for. –We *recommend* Mary to act as leader of her group.
2. Suggest or advise. – The doctor *recommended* that Father stay in bed several days. He advised him to do so.

recommendation rec-om-men-da′-tion *recommendations.* A statement of praise for or advice about a person's work, behaviour, ability, or the like.–When Jack wanted to get a job in an office, he asked his teacher for a *recommendation.*

recompense rec′-om-pense *recompenses, recompensed, recompensing.* 1. A payment or reward (for doing something),–Jack's *recompense* for the work was some spending money.–Bob got a new book as a *recompense* for his sacrifice.
2. Repay or reward.–The man was *recompensed* many times for helping others by the happiness it gave him.

reconcile rec′-on-cile *reconciles, reconciled, reconciling.* 1. Make up a quarrel, dispute or disagreement.–Jack and Mary had a quarrel, but they were *reconciled* after Mary found Jack's ball for him.
2. Make content; satisfy.–Ted was *reconciled* to staying at home when he found that Bert was staying at home, too.

record re-cord′ *records, recorded, recording.* 1. Write down in a form that will last a long time.–The teacher will *record* the names of the children in her class. She will write them down in her book to use later.
2. Put in a form that can be saved.–We *record* music on wax disks or records so that it can be heard later on a record player.
3. Show or indicate.–A maximum and minimum thermometer *records* the highest and lowest temperatures over a certain period.

record rec′-ord *records.* 1. Something written to be kept.–Bob made a *record* of all the things that happened while the teacher was away.
2. A grooved disk that gives back sounds recorded on it.–Mary played a *record* on the record player.
3. The things known about a person or thing. –The football team's *record* is 5 matches lost and 10 won.
4. The best performance.–When a racer goes faster than any other has yet gone, it breaks a *record*, and sets a new *record*.

recover re-cov′-er *recovers, recovered, recovering.* 1. Get back again.–The lost dog was *recovered.*
2. Get well.–It will take a long time for the sick man to *recover.*

re-cover re′-cov′-er *re-covers, re-covered, re-covering.* Put a new cover on.–We had a chair *re-covered.* We had new cloth put over it.

rectangle rec′-tan-gle *rectangles.* A plane (flat) figure that has 4 sides and 4 perfectly square corners or angles.–A square is a *rectangle* with equal sides.

red *redder, reddest.* The colour of blood.–The colours of the Union Jack are *red,* white, and blue.

Red Cross. A worldwide organization whose purpose is to help people everywhere in times of disaster or misfortune. It cares for the sick and wounded in time of war. It gives help to those who need it during and after floods, fires, earthquakes, and other disasters. The sign of the *Red Cross* is a red cross on a white background.

redeem re-deem′ *redeems, redeemed, redeeming.* 1. Get back by paying an amount owed. –The man *redeemed* his watch at the pawnshop after he found a job.
2. Make good or fulfil.–Do not make a promise you are not sure you can *redeem.*
3. Make up for.–Bill's generosity does much to *redeem* his quick temper.

reduce re-duce′ *reduces, reduced, reducing,* 1. Make smaller or lower.–Letting some air out of a toy balloon *reduces* its size.–Charging less money for shoes *reduces* their price.
2. Change to a different form.–A fire soon *reduced* the box to ashes.
3. Bring. – Mary was *reduced* to tears by Jack's teasing.–The family was *reduced* to poverty.

reduction re-duc′-tion *reductions.* 1. Cutting down on something, making it less.–After a *reduction* was made in the price of the bicycle, Tim was able to buy it.
2. The amount which is taken off a thing.– The price of the bicycle was lowered from £15 to £12. The *reduction* was £3.

redundant re-dun′-dant *redundantly*. More than is necessary, repeating oneself.–Writing a letter to Grandfather would have been *redundant*. We had already sent a telegram and a present.

redwood red′-wood *redwoods*. A very large, tall tree that grows in California. Its wood is reddish. It belongs to the pine-tree family.

reed *reeds, reedy.* 1. A kind of tall grass that grows in marshy places. It has hollow, jointed stems.

2. A strip of wood, metal, or other material in the mouthpiece of some musical instruments that are played by blowing or forcing air through them or against them.–Clarinets have *reeds* in them.

reef *reefs.* A ridge of rocks or sand that comes to or nearly to the top of the water in the sea.–The shipwreck occurred when the ship struck a *reef*.

reel *reels, reeled, reeling.* 1. A big wide-edged wheel or spool that is set into a frame so that it will turn easily.–A fisherman winds his fishing line on a *reel* that is fastened to a rod.

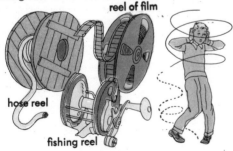

reel of film

hose reel

fishing reel

2. A length of something that is wound on a *reel*.–We saw the first *reel* of the film.–The men used a huge *reel* of wire.

3. Wind on a *reel*.–The fisherman *reeled* in his fishing line.

4. Recite or say quickly and easily.–Jack knows his multiplication tables so well that he can *reel* them off.

5. Whirl, or go round and round.–Bert was so sleepy that the room seemed to *reel*.

6. Sway, or move around dizzily.–The prize fighter *reeled* when hit on the head.

7. A very lively and gay folk dance.–At the fancy-dress ball the guests danced the eightsome *reel*.

re-enter re-en′-ter *re-enters, re-entered, re-entering.* Go back in. – Mary came out and found it was raining. So she *re-entered* the house to get her umbrella.

refer re-fer′ *refers, referred, referring.* 1. Turn to.–We *refer* to the table of contents in a book to find out on which page a story can be found.

2. Send or direct.–The teacher *referred* us to the library for other books on North and South America.

3. Speak about, or call attention to. – Our teacher often *refers* to the dangers of crossing the road without taking care.

referee ref-er-ee′ *referees, refereed, refereeing.* 1. A person who acts as a judge of plays made in games and sports such as basketball, football, prize fights, and the like.–The *referee* in a cricket match is called an umpire. –The *referee* in the basketball game blows a whistle every time the ball goes out of bounds.

2. Person who decides who is right and who is wrong.–The boys asked their father to act as *referee* of the argument.

3. Act as *referee*.–Bob *refereed* the soccer match on Saturday.

reference ref′-er-ence *references.* 1. A mention or calling of attention. – The doctor made *reference* to the importance of good teeth. He spoke about it.

2. A person able to describe one's ability or character.–Bob gave his teacher's name as a *reference* in applying for the job.

3. A statement describing one's abilities or character. – Bob got a *reference* from his teacher.

4. Supplying information.–A dictionary is a *reference* book.

refill re-fill′ *refills, refilled, refilling.* Fill again. –Mary's fountain pen ran dry, and she had to *refill* it.

refill re′-fill *refills.* Something to replace a filling that is used up. – Grandfather gave Tom a *refill* for his loose-leaf notebook. He gave him a packet of new sheets of paper to *refill* it.

R
S
T
U
V
W
X
Y
Z

refine re-fine' *refines, refined, refining, refinement*. 1. Make pure or fit for some special use. – Cotton, sugar, rubber, and other raw materials are *refined* before they are used. 2. Mother is *refined*. She is educated and kind, and has good manners.

reflect re-flect' *reflects, reflected, reflecting*. 1. Give back (light, heat, etc.) – A mirror *reflects* light. Polished metal *reflects* heat.– When you look into still water or into a mirror, your image, or likeness, is *reflected*.

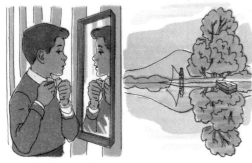

2. Cause blame.–Bad behaviour *reflects* on one's training. It brings back blame to one's home or school. It shows that one has had poor training or teaching. 3. Think over carefully.–One should *reflect* on the things one reads.

reflection re-flec'-tion *reflections*. 1. An image, light, or anything else reflected. – A dog looked into the water, saw his *reflection,* and thought it was another dog. – The children used a mirror to throw the *reflection* of the sun about the room. 2. Thinking, or a thought.–After *reflection,* Bob found the right answer to the teacher's question. 3. Cause of blame.–The boy's bad behaviour is a *reflection* upon the way he was brought up. It brings blame to those who taught him or brought him up.

reflector re-flec'-tor *reflectors*. That which reflects light, heat, or the like.–Car headlamps have *reflectors* to throw out the light in one direction.

refrain re-frain' *refrains, refrained, refraining*. 1. Keep oneself (from doing something).– Jack cannot *refrain* from laughing when Mary tries to act very grown-up. 2. Chorus.–The song had a merry *refrain.*

refresh re-fresh' *refreshes, refreshed, refreshing*. Make fresh again.–A swim in the lake *refreshes* one on a hot day.–Rain on a hot day *refreshes* the air.–Before the test Bob *refreshed* his memory by studying.

refreshment re-fresh'-ment *refreshments*. Food and drink.–Coffee and sandwiches were the *refreshments* served at the party.

refrigerator re-frig'-er-a-tor *refrigerators, refrigeration, refrigerated*. A box or room for keeping foods cold. Ice is used in some boxes. Others have in them freezing units which are run by electricity or gas.

refund re-fund' *refunds, refunded, refunding*. 1. Give back. – Mother returned the soiled dress to the shop and they *refunded* her money. 2. (re'fund) A sum paid back. – The shop gave Mother a *refund* on the soiled dress.

refuse (rhymes with *shoes*) re-fuse' *refuses, refused, refusing, refusal*. Decline, or say no. –Mary *refused* to go with us, because she didn't want to walk so far.–When the hungry man asked for a meal, Father couldn't *refuse.*

refuse (rhymes with *juice*) ref'-use. Rubbish, dregs, or other waste.–After the picnic, we put the *refuse* in a litter basket.

regain re-gain' *regains, regained, regaining*. Get back.–Father has *regained* his health.

regal re'-gal *regally*. 1. Of royalty; of a king or queen; royal.–The *regal* procession moved slowly through the church. 2. Splendid; good enough for a king. – The rich man lived in *regal* style.

regard re-gard' *regards, regarded, regarding*. 1. Thought to be, or considered.–Bob is *regarded* as the best player in the team. 2. Attention or heed.–The children paid no *regard* to what their Mother told them. 3. Think well of.–We *regard* the new vicar very highly. 4. Respect or consideration.–Jack usually has *regard* for the rights of other people. 5. Look at.–The judge *regarded* the prisoner sternly. 6. A look.–The judge fixed the prisoner with a steady, earnest *regard*. 7. (plural) Good wishes.–The teacher sent Mother her best *regards*. 8. *With regard to* means, about or concerning. –We received a letter *with regard to* the lost purse.

R
S
T
U
V
W
X
Y
Z

regarding *re-gard -ing.* About or concerning. –We received a letter *regarding* the lost purse.

regatta *re-gat'-ta regattas.* A meeting at which sailing or rowing races are held.–Jack rowed in the *regatta* at Henley.

regiment *reg'-i-ment regiments, regimented, regimenting.* 1. An organized group of soldiers usually commanded by a colonel.
2. Put (persons) under strict control.–The people did not want to be *regimented* by the government.

region *re'-gion regions.* 1. Section or part of a country.–Eskimos live in a cold *region*.
2. Part (of the body).–The ball hit Bob in the *region* of the stomach.

register *reg'-is-ter registers, registered, registering.* 1. A list of people's names kept for some particular purpose.–The school keeps a *register* of the names of its pupils.
2. Range.–The *register* of your voice is from the lowest note you can sing to the highest one you can sing.–Musical instruments have *registers*, too.
3. Have one's name recorded or put on a list. –On the first day of school, 40 children *registered*.
4. Show or indicate.–Speedometers *register* the speed at which a car is going.
5. Record.–Father received a *registered* letter. The postmaster had made a record to show that it had passed through the post office and had been delivered.–Mother's and Father's marriage was *registered* at the village church.
6. Express, show.–A good actor must be able to *register* joy, sorrow, fear, and many other feelings, emotions and reactions by the look on his face.

regret *re-gret' regrets, regretted, regretting.* 1. Feel sorry.–I *regret* that I lost my dog.
2. Sorrow.–It was with much *regret* that Bob parted with his bicycle.
3. (plural) A polite message saying that one is sorry one cannot accept an invitation. –Mary couldn't go to the party; so she sent her *regrets*.

regular *reg'-u-lar regulars, regularly.* 1. Even. –The shore round the lake is quite *regular*. –The car runs at a *regular* speed.–The teeth of the comb are *regular*. They are all the same in size and spacing.

2. Usual or customary.–The *regular* August Bank holiday comes on the first Monday in August. It comes on the same day again and again.–The *regular* place to keep a car is in a garage.
3. One who is not a substitute.–Bob is a *regular* in the team. He always plays.
4. Belonging at all times.–Uncle Dave is a *regular* soldier in the army.
5. Usually done in a certain way and in a certain order.–Father is a man of *regular* habits. He does the same things at about the same time and in about the same way every day.
6. Real or complete.–Jack and Mary make a *regular* game of their homework.

regulate *reg'-u-late regulates, regulated, regulating, regulation.* 1. Control.–The bathroom tap *regulates* the water that comes from it. –The thermostat *regulates* the oil burner in the house. It makes the oil burner run just often enough to keep the house at the desired temperature.
2. Adjust the speed of.–The jeweller *regulated* Father's *watch*. He made it keep good time

rehearse *re-hearse' rehearses, rehearsed, rehearsing, rehearsal.* Practise.–The actors *rehearsed* their parts for the play.

reign (pronounced *rain*) *reigns, reigned, reigning.* 1. Rule.–The king *reigned* over his people.
2. The length of time one ruler rules a country. – England was prosperous during the *reign* of Queen Elizabeth I.

rein *reins.* 1. A long strip of leather fastened to the part of a horse's bridle that goes through its mouth. A *rein* is used to guide the horse. Pull on the right *rein* and the horse will turn to the right.
2. Control.–During Mother's absence, Grandmother took over the *reins* of the household. She managed the house.

reindeer *rein'-deer.* A kind of deer with large horns or antlers. *Reindeer* live in the North where it is cold.

reinforce re-in-force′ *reinforces, reinforced, reinforcing.* Make stronger.–Mother *reinforced* the elbow of Bob's sweater by sewing an extra piece of cloth on it.–The invasion fleet was *reinforced* with more troops, ships, and planes.

reinforcement re-in-force′-ment *reinforcements.* Anything that strengthens something else.–An extra board on a fence, additional troops in the army, an extra piece of cloth on the elbow of a sleeve, are all called *reinforcements.*

reject re-ject′ *rejects, rejected, rejecting, rejection.* 1. Refuse to take.–The teacher *rejected* Bill's paper because it wasn't neat.
2. Throw away or discard.–Mother *rejected* all the buns that were burnt.
3. Refuse to consider.–The judges *rejected* the prisoner's plea for pardon.

rejoice re-joice′ *rejoices, rejoiced, rejoicing.* Feel glad, or feel joyful.–We will *rejoice* when Baby is well.

relate re-late′ *relates, related, relating.* 1. Tell. –Grandfather *related* the story of his first fishing trip.
2. Think of together.–Shoe is *related* to foot. Shoe reminds you or makes you think of foot.

related re-lat′-ed. Belonging to the same family.–Brothers are *related.* They belong to the same family.

relation re-la′-tion *relations.* 1. A telling.–The captain's *relation* of all the events during the storm at sea was thrilling.
2. Connexion.–The *relation* between bread and meat is that they are foods.
3. Members of a family.–Parents, sisters, and brothers are some of one's *relations.*

relative rel′-a-tive *relatives.* Person who is related to another, who belongs to the same family.–Father, mother, aunts, uncles, brothers, sisters, and the like are *relatives.* They belong to one family.

relax re-lax′ *relaxes, relaxed, relaxing.* 1. Become loose or less tense.–When you sleep, your muscles are *relaxed.*
2. Make less rigid or strict.–During hot weather, the rules in school are *relaxed.* We can do things that we can't do at other times.

relaxation re-lax-a′-tion. 1. The act of loosening the muscles.
2. Easing or making less rigid or strict.–*Relaxation* of the rules in school lasts just for the hot weather.

3. Recreation, play, or pleasant change from work.–For *relaxation* we swim and fish.

relay re′-lay *relays, relayed, relaying.* 1. A fresh replacement.–A *relay* of fire fighters marched towards the forest to relieve those who had been fighting the fire all night.

2. A race in which a runner carries something, runs a certain distance, and hands the thing he is carrying to another player, who takes up the race at that point. Several sets of runners take part in the race.
3. (re-lay′) Pass on from one to another.–The message was *relayed* to the general by radio, telephone, and messenger.

release re-lease′ *releases, released, releasing.* 1. Let go.–The woman *released* the child's hand, and he fell.–Bob took off the dog's collar and *released* him.
2. Freedom.–The prisoner was given his *release.*

reliable re-li′-a-ble *reliably, reliability.* Trustworthy or dependable. – Mary is *reliable* about getting her work in on time.

relic rel′-ic *relics.* Things left from times long past.–Arrow-heads and stone hammers are Stone Age *relics.*

relief re-lief′. 1. Help, comfort; easing or removing difficulty.–Medicine brings *relief* to the sick. It helps to make them well.–The Red Cross brings *relief* to wounded soldiers.
2. Freedom from a task.–The sailor kept a lookout until 6 o'clock and then got *relief.* Another man took his place.
3. A design that stands up higher than the surface from which it is cut.

R
S
T
U
V
W
X
Y
Z

relieve re-lieve' *relieves, relieved, relieving.*
1. Comfort, ease, or help.–Medicine will *relieve* pain.
2. Free from a task.–Mary washed the dishes to *relieve* her mother.–A new bowler *relieved* Bob. He freed Bob by taking his place as bowler.
3. Change the sameness of.–The whiteness of the table-cloth and dishes on the table was *relieved* by a blue bowl of yellow roses.

religion re-li'-gion *religions, religious, religiously.* A belief in or worship of God or gods. *Religion* is any faith or method of worship.

rely re-ly' *relies, relied, relying, reliance,* Trust or depend.–Mother can *rely* upon Bob to take good care of Sally.

remain re-main' *remains, remained, remaining.*
1. Stay.–The children came, but they could not *remain* for lunch.
2. Be left over.–Only 2 pencils *remained* in the box when we had each taken 1.
3. Stay the same.–Some metals *remain* bright all the time. They never tarnish.

remainder re-main'-der *remainders.* 1. The part that is left.–I ate part of the apple and Father ate the *remainder.*
2. A number found by subtracting.–If you take 4 apples from 6 apples, the *remainder* is 2.

remains re-mains'. 1. That which is left or not used.–The children ate the *remains* of the picnic when they got home.
2. A body after death.–The man's *remains* will be buried today.

remark re-mark' *remarks, remarked, remarking.* 1. A statement, or something said.–The teacher made a few *remarks* about the lesson.
2. Say or notice.–Sally *remarked* that Father was growing fat.

remarkable re-mark'-a-ble *remarkably.* Worth noticing, or wonderful.–The child's manners are *remarkable* for her age.

remedy rem'-e-dy *remedies, remedied, remedying.* 1. A relief or cure.–Medicine is a *remedy* for sickness.
2. Correct, or make right.–We will *remedy* the mistake at once. We will correct it.

remember re-mem'-ber *remembers, remembered, remembering.* 1. Recall, or bring back to mind.–Mother can *remember* things that happened when she was a little girl.
2. Keep in mind.–*Remember* that you are invited to come. Do not forget it.
3. Show that (someone) is thought of.–The children always *remember* Mother on her birthday. They show that they love her by giving her a gift.
4. Pass greetings on.–*Remember* me to all my friends. Mention my name and give them my regards, or best wishes.

remembrance re-mem'-brance *remembrances.* Gift, keepsake, or something to remember one by.–Mary gave me a little *remembrance* for my birthday.

remind re-mind' *reminds, reminded, reminding, reminder.* Cause to recall or remember. –*Remind* me to take an umbrella. – Mary sometimes *reminds* me of Mother.

remnant rem'-nant *remnants.* 1. A piece of cloth that is left over.–Mother made a doll's dress from a *remnant.*
2. Left-over.–We ate the *remnants* of Sunday's dinner for our supper.

remodel re-mod'-el *remodels remodelled, remodelling.* Change and improve.–Next spring we plan to *remodel* our house.–Mother has had her dress *remodelled.*

remorse re-morse' *remorseful, remorsefully.* Regret or sorrow for something one has done. –The child felt *remorse* for having stolen the pencils. He wished he had not done it.

remote re-mote' *remotely.* 1. Far-off.–The explorers had visited *remote* corners of the world.–To people in South America, Alaska is a *remote* country.
2. Long past, long ago.–In *remote* times people lived in caves.
3. Vague or slight.–Bob has a *remote* idea that he wants to be an engineer.

remove re-move' *removes, removed, removing, removal.* 1. Take off. – Mary *removed* her wellingtons before going into the house.
2. Take away.–*Remove* the broom from the doorway before someone trips over it.
3. Put out of.–Dishonest persons are often *removed* from their positions.
4. End.–This medicine will *remove* your pain.
5. Take out.–*Remove* the pencil from your mouth.

remover re-mov'-er *removers.* Anything that removes something, or takes it out, away, or off.–Certain fluids are good spot *removers.*

R
S
T
U
V
W
X
Y
Z

renew re-new′ *renews, renewed, renewing.*
1. Start again, continue.–I shall *renew* my subscription to the magazine. – Mary *renewed* her efforts after the teacher praised her work.
2. Make like new again.–Father *renewed* the finish on the chair by varnishing it.

renounce re-nounce′ *renounces, renounced, renouncing.* Refuse; deny.–Jack *renounced* responsibility for what his baby brother did. He said he would not be responsible.

renovate ren′-o-vate *renovates, renovated, renovating.* Clean, repair, or make like new again.–The old house will have to be *renovated* before the family moves in.

rent *rents, rented, renting.* 1. Money paid regularly for the use of a building or property.– Father pays the *rent* on the 1st of the month.
2. Use a building or property for which one makes regular payments.–We *rent* our house from an estate company.
3. Allow a building or property to be used in return for regular payment.–Last year we *rented* our summer cottage to the Browns.
4. A tear, or torn place.–Bob got a *rent* in his sleeve when he caught it on a nail.

reopen re-o′-pen *reopens, reopened, reopening.* Open again.–The theatre that closed this summer will *reopen* during the winter.

reorganize re-or′-gan-ize *reorganizes, reorganized, reorganizing, reorganization.* 1. Arrange differently, or according to a new plan. –Our headmaster *reorganized* the classes this term. He changed the hours, some of the subjects, and the method of teaching.
2. Form or get together again.–The football team will *reorganize* this autumn.

repaid re-paid′. One form of the word *repay.*– The money you lent me will be *repaid* by the first of the month.

repair re-pair′ *repairs, repaired, repairing.*
1. Mend, put back in working order.– The mechanic *repaired* the radio.
2. Necessary work on something; mending, replacement of parts.–What *repairs* will have to be made to the house before it can be lived in?
3. Condition.–If you keep your shoes in good *repair*, they will wear longer. Have them mended as soon as they need it.
4. Make right.–Jack tried to *repair* the damage his thoughtless words had done.

repay re-pay′ *repays, repaid, repaying.* Pay back.–I will *repay* the money you lent me as soon as I receive my wages.

repeat re-peat′ *repeats, repeated, repeating.*
1. Say again.–I did not quite understand. Please *repeat* what you said.
2. Do again.–Yesterday you burned your finger; be careful not to *repeat* the accident.
3. Say from memory.–Can you *repeat* the words of 'The Minstrel Boy'?

repeatedly re-peat′-ed-ly. Again and again. –Mother asks Jack *repeatedly* to take his boots off when he comes in.

repent re-pent′ *repents, repented, repenting.* Regret, or be sorry for.–If you do wrong, you are sure to *repent* it.

replace re-place′ *replaces, replaced, replacing.*
1. Put in place again.–*Replace* the dishes in the cupboard after you have dried them.
2. Substitute another for.–Mother *replaced* the broken mirror.
3. Follow, or fill the position of.–The bowler was *replaced* by a younger boy.

replenish re-plen′-ish *replenishes, replenished, replenishing.* Fill again with supplies.– –Mother *replenished* the cupboards. She stocked them up with food.

reply re-ply′ *replies, replied, replying.* 1. An answer.–It is wiser to make no *reply* to angry words.
2. Respond.–Grandmother always *replies* to our letters at once.

report re-port′ *reports, reported, reporting.*
1. A story or account.–The children gave a *report* of their visit to the zoo.
2. A statement.–Each term our teacher sends home a *report* that tells of our record in school. Jack had an 'A' in arithmetic on his *report*.
3. News or rumour.–We heard a *report* that school would start earlier this year.
4. A sound or explosive noise.–The *report* of the gun startled Sally.
5. Present oneself, or go in person.–The boys *reported* for football practice at 4 o'clock.
6. Tell, or give the information.–Mary *reported* that enough money had been collected by the class to buy 2 new books.

reporter re-port′-er *reporters.* A person whose job is to gather news to be printed in a newspaper.–*Reporters* hurried to the scene of the accident.

R
S
T
U
V
W
X
Y
Z

repose re-pose′ *reposes, reposed, reposing.*
1. Rest; relaxation.–Mother needs some *repose* every day, because she works so hard.
2. Be resting.–Baby *reposed* on Father's lap.

represent rep-re-sent′ *represents, represented, representing.* 1. Mean or show.–The picture Mary drew *represented* the story of Little Red Riding Hood.
2. Act the part of, or pretend to be.–Two boys *represented* soldiers in the play.–The spy *represented* himself to be a British citizen.
3. Stand for.–A red cross on a background of white *represents* the Red Cross.

representative rep-re-sent′-a-tive *representatives.* 1. Someone chosen by a group to speak and act for it.–The class chose Dick for their *representative.*

2. Typical.–These pictures are *representative* of the artist's work.

reprint re-print′ *reprints, reprinted, reprinting.*
1. Print again.–When all the copies of the book were sold, the publisher *reprinted* it. He printed more like it.
2. (re′-print). A second printing, not the first.–This picture is a *reprint.*

reproach re-proach′ *reproaches, reproached, reproaching.* 1. Put blame on.–The teacher *reproached* us for not having done our lesson.
2. Blame.–The *reproach* made us sorry.

reprove re-prove′ *reproves, reproved, reproving.* Scold.–Father *reproved* Mary for being late.

reptile rep′-tile *reptiles.* A cold-blooded, crawling animal.–Alligators, turtles, and snakes are *reptiles.*

REPTILES

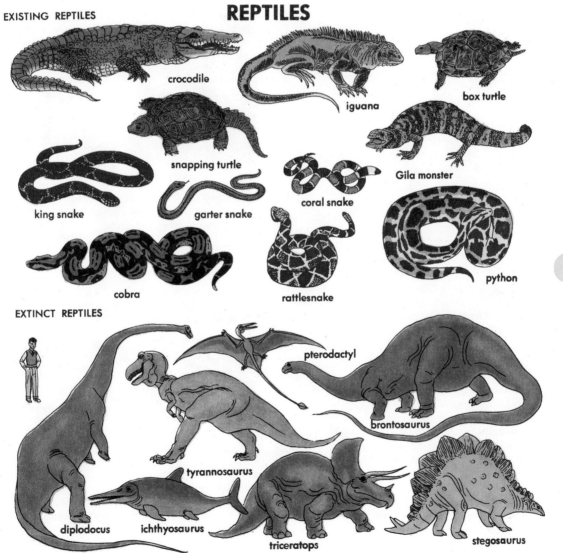

EXISTING REPTILES

crocodile
iguana
box turtle
snapping turtle
Gila monster
king snake
garter snake
coral snake
cobra
rattlesnake
python

EXTINCT REPTILES

pterodactyl
brontosaurus
tyrannosaurus
diplodocus
ichthyosaurus
triceratops
stegosaurus

R
S
T
U
V
W
X
Y
Z

republic re-pub'-lic *republics*. A nation in which the people elect or choose their rulers or representatives.–The United States is a *republic*.

repulse re-pulse' *repulses, repulsed, repulsing*.
1. Turn down or refuse.–The bitter old man *repulsed* all offers of friendship.
2. Beat or drive back.–It took many soldiers to *repulse* the enemy.
3. A holding off or beating back; a failure to make good an attack.–The *repulse* of the enemy was made possible by many ships and planes and men.

reputation rep-u-ta'-tion *reputations*. What people think and say about a person's behaviour, character, or work.–Our doctor has an excellent *reputation*.

request re-quest' *requests, requested, requesting*. 1. Ask.–The teacher *requested* us to work quietly.
2. A thing one asks for.–All Bob's *requests* were granted at Christmas.

require re-quire' *requires, required, requiring, requirement*. Have to have.–Baby *requires* much sleep.

rescue res'-cue *rescues, rescued, rescuing*.
1. Save or set free from danger.–The sailor *rescued* the man from the sinking ship.
2. Saving.–The *rescue* of the pilots lost at sea was difficult.

rescuer res'-cu-er *rescuers*. A person who rescues or saves someone from harm or danger.–The lost pilots thanked their *rescuers*. They thanked the men who had saved them from the sea.

resemblance re-sem'-blance *resemblances*. A like or similar appearance.–There is a strong *resemblance* between Mother and Ann. They look much alike.

resemble re-sem'-ble *resembles, resembled, resembling*. Look somewhat like.–Tigers *resemble* cats.

resent re-sent' *resents, resented, resenting*. Feel angry and hurt at.–Bob *resents* being called a coward.

resentful re-sent'-ful *resentfully*. Showing anger and ill feeling.–Bob is *resentful* because someone called him a coward.

reservation res-er-va'-tion *reservations*. 1. Anything that is held back for a special use or purpose. – Bob has a *reservation* for the train. A reserved seat is being held for him.
2. A restriction or limit.–The teacher recommended Bob without *reservations*.

reserve re-serve' *reserves, reserved, reserving*.
1. Set aside or hold.–Father said he would *reserve* a day to take us to the park.
2. Care not to be too friendly; restraint in speech or manner.–Mary answers the questions of strangers with *reserve*.

reservoir res'-er-voir *reservoirs*. A huge tank, pool, or lake where water is kept for use when needed.

reset re-set' *resets, resetting*. Place in a new setting, or set again.–The pearls were *reset* in a modern style.

reside re-side' *resides, resided, residing*. Live or have one's home.–Grandmother *resides* in the country.–We *reside* in town.

residence res'-i-dence *residences*. 1. A house or place where one lives.–Alan's *residence* is in Wycoff Street.

2. *Take up residence* means make one's home, go to live.–We have *taken up residence* on a farm.

resident res'-i-dent *residents*. Someone who lives or makes his home in a particular place. –The *residents* of the town built a new playground for the children.

R
S
T
U
V
W
X
Y
Z

resign re-sign' *resigns, resigned, resigning.*
1. Give up.–Father *resigned* his position for a better one.
2. Give way.–Mary has *resigned* herself to spending the day at home, since it is raining too hard to go out. She has given in to the fact that she must stay at home.

resignation res-ig-na'-tion *resignations.* 1. The act of giving up a job or position.–John's *resignation* from the committee made a new election necessary.
2. A statement that one is resigning.–John made his *resignation* in writing.
3. Quiet patience, or quiet giving in.–Father receives bad news with *resignation.* He doesn't complain.

resin res'-in. A sticky sap that flows from such trees as the pine.–*Resin* is used in varnish and in medicines.

resist re-sist' *resists, resisted, resisting.* 1. Fight or hold out against.–The thief did not *resist* the policeman who arrested him.–The child was not strong enough to *resist* the disease.

resistance re-sist'-ance *resistances.* 1. Opposing action or power.–The soldiers put up no *resistance* when they saw they were outnumbered.
2. Strength to fight off.–The child has little *resistance,* so she catches cold easily.

resolution res-o-lu'-tion *resolutions.* 1. A decision, or something one decides to do.–Mary made a New Year's *resolution* to do better work in school.
2. A statement that something should be done. – The Council passed a *resolution* that the parks of the city should be made larger and pleasanter for the people.

resolve re-solve' *resolves, resolved, resolving.* 1. Decide or determine.–Bob *resolved* to eat less chocolate.
2. Decide by a vote.–The class *resolved* that paper in the playground should be picked up by the children each afternoon.

resort re-sort' *resorts, resorted, resorting.* 1. A place to go, especially for recreation.–In summer many people go to *resorts* for fun.
2. Go frequently.–Many people *resort* to the parks in the summer.
3. Turn for help.–The old man *resorted* to begging in order to obtain food.
4. What a person gets help from.–Begging was the poor old man's last *resort.*

resource re-source' *resourceful, resources,* 1. A supply of anything to be used when needed.–The United States has great *resources* of cotton, metal, timber, and other natural products.
2. Ability to meet difficult situations.–Here is a job that will test your mental *resources.*

respect re-spect' *respects, respected, respecting.* 1. Admiration and honour.–The children have great *respect* for their teacher.
2. Show or feel admiration for.–The children *respect* their teacher.
3. The children show *respect* for their books. They take care of them.
4. A regard or way.–In what *respect* do you disagree with Mary? In what way do you disagree with her?

respectful re-spect'-ful *respectfully.* Showing that one thinks highly of a person or thing.–Jack disagreed with the teacher's idea in a *respectful* way. He told her very politely how he thought differently.–We should treat old people *respectfully.* We should be polite and helpful to them.

respite res'-pite *respites.* A time off for rest; a relief.–We had a short *respite* between classes.–We are having a *respite* from cold weather.

respond re-spond' *responds, responded, responding.* 1. Answer.–Sally did not *respond* to Mother's call, because she did not hear her.
2. Show effect, or react.–Some children *respond* to medicine more quickly than others. Medicine acts more quickly on some than on others.

response re-sponse' *responses.* An answer.–Father is waiting for a *response* to his letter.

responsibility re-spon-si-bil'-i-ty. *responsibilities.* Anything one is expected to do or attend to.–Mother's *responsibilities* are keeping the house clean, cooking, caring for the children, and helping us when we come to her.

responsible re-spon'-si-ble. 1. Reliable.–Bob is a *responsible* person. You can depend upon him.
2. Answerable or accountable.–The driver of the car was held *responsible* for the accident. He had to answer for it.

R
S
T
U
V
W
X
Y
Z

rest *rests, rested, resting.* 1. Relaxation; freedom from work or trouble. – Father must have *rest* so that he can work tomorrow.
2. Stillness, absence of motion. – The ball whizzed through the air and came to *rest* on the grass.
3. A pause, or sign showing a pause. – A *rest* in music is a slight pause, a short time when no note is sounded.
4. Be still or free from work or action. – Grandfather let his horses *rest* for a time so that they would not get too tired.
5. Get over being tired. – Stop and *rest* when you are out of breath.
6. Remain. – The kitten's eyes *rested* on the mouse. She kept looking at the mouse.
7. Something to lean on. – Many motor-cars have arm-*rests* on the doors.
8. Lie. – The broom *rests* against the wall. – The book *rests* upon the table.
9. *Rest with* means depend upon. – The prisoner's freedom *rests with* the court.
10. The remainder, or all that is left. – Mary ate all the ice-cream that she wanted, and Bob ate the *rest*.

restaurant res'-tau-rant *restaurants.* A public place where food is served. – We stopped at a *restaurant* and ordered dinner.

restful rest'-ful *restfully, restfulness.* 1. Giving relaxation and rest. – The man had a *restful* night. It freed him from being tired.
2. Peaceful or calm, quiet. – We found a *restful* place in the hills to stay. There we could become rested.

restless rest'-less *restlessly, restlessness.* 1. Not able to keep calm or quiet. – Children in school are often *restless* in warm weather.

2. Without rest or sleep. – Father had a *restless* night because of his bad sunburn.
3. Easily disturbed. – The old man is *restless.* Small disturbances bother him.

restore re-store' *restores, restored, restoring.* 1. Renew or repair. – Bald-headed men often want to *restore* their hair. They try to grow hair again. – When the patient's health is *restored,* he will leave the hospital.
2. Put back. – The boy *restored* the stolen pen because he had a guilty conscience.

restrain re-strain' *restrains, restrained, restraining, restraint.* Hold in check or keep back. – It was hard for the rider to *restrain* the nervous horse. – The children could not *restrain* their laughter when Mary wore Mother's hat.

result re-sult' *results, resulted, resulting.* 1. A thing which happens because of something else that has happened before. – Good marks in school are a *result* of hard work.
2. Cause. – Carelessness often *results* in accidents.
3. Happen because of something. – Accidents often *result* from carelessness.

retail re'-tail. Selling things in small amounts. – *Retail* shops sell goods to people who buy for their own use.

retain re-tain' *retains, retained, retaining.* 1. Hold or keep. – Some cloth does not *retain* its colour when hung in the sunshine.
2. Remember. – Some children *retain* what they learn longer than others.
3. Hire for a fee. – After the accident, Father *retained* a barrister to defend him in court.

retire re-tire' *retires, retired, retiring, retirement.* 1. Go to bed. – We *retire* at 8 o'clock.
2. Stop working for good. – Grandfather has *retired* because he is getting old.

retreat re-treat' *retreats, retreated, retreating.* 1. Move back or fall back when facing an enemy. – The enemy's ships were caught in a trap and could not *retreat*.
2. A moving or falling back. – The army made a quick *retreat*.

return re-turn' *returns, returned, returning.* 1. Give or send back. – *Return* your aunt's umbrella the first time you go to see her.
2. Put back. – *Return* the book to the shelf when you have finished it.
3. Pay back. – Lend me a pound, and I will *return* it soon.
4. Go back. – Mother had to *return* to the house for her key.

5. Come back.–Father will *return* after work.

6. Coming back.–We welcome the *return* of the swallows in the summer.

7. A report.–We sat up to hear the election *returns*.

8. A payment or something received in *return*.–Bob's *return* for hard study was an 'A' in arithmetic.–The *returns*, or amount of money made, from the puppet show were £8.

9. Used for coming back.–Father bought a *return* ticket to Bristol.

reveal re-veal' *reveals, revealed, revealing*.
1. Make known.–At last the truth was *revealed* to us.
2. Indicate, display, or show.–Mary's voice *revealed* her nervousness.

revenge re-venge' *revenges, revenged, revenging*. 1. Harm or injury done to another in return for harm or injury.–When the angry man hit the boy, the boy's *revenge* was to kick the man.
2. To harm or to hurt in return.–The boy *revenged* himself by kicking the man who hit him.

revenue rev'-e-nue *revenues*. Money coming in, or income. – The government's *revenue* comes from taxes.

reverence rev'-er-ence. Solemn respect and love.–We bow our heads in *reverence* for the soldiers who died.

Reverend Rev'-er-end. The title of a minister or vicar of a church.–The *Reverend* Frank Smith is the vicar of our church.

reverse re-verse' *reverses, reversed, reversing*.
1. The back.–Write on the *reverse* side of the paper so as not to waste it.
2. A misfortune. – During the war, many persons met with *reverses*. Their fortunes changed from good to bad.
3. The opposite or backward direction.–To back a car out of a garage, move it in *reverse*.
4. Turn or change to the opposite direction, position, and the like.–*Reverse* your glove to pull it off. Turn it inside out.–At first Father's answer was 'No,' but he *reversed* his decision. He changed it to 'Yes.'

review re-view *reviews, reviewed, reviewing*.
1. Go over again.–We did not know our lesson well, so we had to *review* it.–The judge *reviewed* the case. He examined carefully all the stories about the accident.
2. A going over again.–We have a *review* in spelling every week.

3. A report about a book, play, concert, etc.– The newspaper gave a *review* of the new book. It told what the story was about, and revealed its good and bad points.

4. Give a report of a book, play, concert, etc. –Our teacher asked us to *review* the book.

5. An inspection.–The officer made a *review* of the troops. He looked them over to see whether they were well trained.

6. Inspect.–He *reviewed* the troops.

revise re-vise' *revises, revised, revising, revision*. Correct, or change to improve.–After writing our stories, we had to *revise* them.

revolt re-volt' *revolts, revolted, revolting*.
1. Fight against a leader, the government, or those in lawful control.–The prisoners *revolted* against their guards.
2. Fighting against those in control.–All the prisoners joined the *revolt*.

revolution rev-o-lu'-tion *revolutions, revolutionary*. 1. The complete changing of the government or rulers by the people of a country. –In the American *Revolution*, the Americans freed themselves from England and became a separate country with a government they made themselves.
2. A sudden, complete change.–The use of the motor-car has made a great *revolution* in people's lives. They can do things they could never do before.
3. A complete turning round of something. –The children in the circle made 3 *revolutions* to the right.

revolve re-volve' *revolves, revolved, revolving*. Roll or go round.–A wheel, the hands on a clock, and a merry-go-round all *revolve*.

revolver re-volv'-er *revolvers*. A short, repeating gun which can be held in one hand and has a cylinder to hold the cartridges.

reward re-ward' *rewards, rewarded, rewarding*. 1. Recognize by giving a prize or payment.–The policeman's bravery was *rewarded* by promotion.
2. A payment or prize given for some special act.–The teacher gave a *reward* of £2 for the return of her lost ring.

rewrite re-write' *rewrites, rewrote, rewritten, rewriting*. Write again to make better.–Bob will *rewrite* his story.

rheumatism rheu'-ma-tism. A disease of a person's joints or muscles.–*Rheumatism* causes pain, stiffness, and swelling.

R
S
T
U
V
W
X
Y
Z

rhinoceros rhi-noc'-er-os *rhinoceroses*. A large 4-legged animal with a very thick, grey skin

and with 1 or 2 horns that stand up on its snout. *Rhinoceroses* live in Asia and Africa. They have poor eyesight but very acute hearing. They are bad tempered and rather unintelligent animals, and often charge without being provoked.

rhododendron r h o-do-d e n'-d r o n *rhododendrons*. A shrub or low tree with evergreen leaves, bearing large and beautiful flowers. They are white, pink, red or mauve and appear in the spring.

rhubarb rhu'-barb. A plant with very large, green leaves that grow on large stalks, or stems. The long, juicy stems are stewed and used for sauce, and as a filling for pies.

rhyme *rhymes, rhymed, rhyming*. 1. End with the same sound. – The words 'snow' and 'show' *rhyme*.
2. A verse or poem in which the lines *rhyme*. –This is a rhyme:
> 'Jack and Jill
> Went up the hill.'

rhythm rhythms. The regular beat of sound or movement. – It is easy to dance to music because of its *rhythm*. Our dance steps have the same regular beat as the music.

rib *ribs*. 1. One of a group of bones that fasten to the spine, or backbone, and curve round to the front of the body over the chest. *Ribs* form a 'box' to protect the lungs and the heart. People and many kinds of animals have *ribs*.

2. Anything like a person's *ribs* in shape or use.–The *ribs* of an umbrella are the thin metal 'spokes' or rods to which the cloth is fastened.

ribbon rib'-bon *ribbons*. A strip or narrow band of cloth.–Girls wear bows of *ribbon* on or in their hair.

rice. A grass whose seeds are used for food.– *Rice* grows in a warm climate.

rich *richer, richest, richly, richness*. 1. Wealthy, or having much money, land, or the like.– The *rich* family lives in a big house with beautiful grounds.
2. Able to produce much.–A *rich* soil is soil that has plenty of food to make plants grow.
3. Having plenty.–America is *rich* in copper ore. It has a great supply of it.
4. Expensive or valuable.–Things that cost much, and are of the best quality, are *rich*.– The queen wore a *rich* velvet gown.
5. Nourishing or satisfying to the appetite; having much sugar, butter, etc. – The cake Mother baked was too *rich*.–*Rich* soups are very nourishing.
6. Filled with deep, pleasing shades of colour, sound, etc.–Mother's party dress is of a *rich*, warm green colour.–The story of Robinson Crusoe is filled with *rich* description.

riches rich'-es. Money or valuable things.– *Riches* alone could not make King Midas happy.

richly rich'-ly. Expensively or elegantly. – The queen was *richly* dressed in velvet embroidered with emeralds.

rid *rids, rid, ridding*. 1. Free.–The Pied Piper *rid* the city of rats.
2. We got *rid* of our old car.

ridden rid'-den. One form of the word *ride*.– After we had *ridden* in the car for 2 days, Mother was very tired.

riddle rid'-dle *riddles, riddled, riddling*. 1. This is a *riddle*: The more you take from it, the bigger it grows. What is it? Answer: A hole.
2. Pierce many holes in.–The aeroplane was *riddled* with bullets when it crashed.

ride *rides, rode, ridden, riding.* 1. Sit on or in and be carried along.–Jack likes to *ride* on his pony.–We *ride* on a boat, on a train, and in a car.

2. A trip or journey.–Last night we went for a *ride* in the car.

rider rid'-er *riders.* A person who rides.–When we ride in the car, Father is the driver, and we are the *riders.*–The wild horse threw his *rider.*

ridge *ridges.* 1. A raised line or edge where two slanting surfaces meet. – The long top part of the roof on a house is a *ridge.*

2. Any narrow raised strip.–A heavy thread in a piece of cloth makes a *ridge.*

ridiculous ri-dic'-u-lous *ridiculously, ridiculousness.* Very silly.–Men would look *ridiculous* wearing women's clothes.

rifle ri'-fle *rifles, rifled, rifling.* 1. A firearm fired from the shoulder with a spirally grooved barrel. The groove or *rifling* spins the bullet so that it will go straight.

2. Search and rob.–The thief *rifled* the till. He took all the money from it.

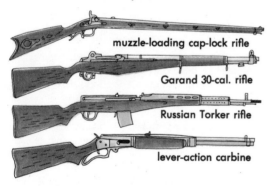

muzzle-loading cap-lock rifle

Garand 30-cal. rifle

Russian Torker rifle

lever-action carbine

right *rights, righted, righting.* 1. Good, proper, decent, or lawful.–*Right* is the opposite of wrong. Bad deeds are wrong. Good deeds are *right.*

2. On or towards the side opposite your left hand.–If you face south and raise your *right* hand, it will be pointing towards the west; your left hand will be to the east.

3. Correct.–This clock gives the *right* time.

4. True.–John says that you have a new book. Is that *right*?

5. Intended to show, or to be worn outwards. –There is a wrong and a *right* side to this table-cloth.

6. Satisfactory.–Bob's teeth are all *right* since he had them cleaned.

7. Directly.–Mary looked *right* at the book and yet didn't see it.

8. Straight–Go *right* ahead.–The theatre is *right* opposite our house.

9. A privilege; a lawful claim. – In a free country it is a person's *right* to go to the church he chooses.

10. To correct.–Mary *righted* the misunderstanding between herself and Mother.

11. Set in the proper position.–The upset boat must be *righted* before it can be used.

12. When 2 lines meet at an angle of 90°, they form a *right* angle.

righteous right'-eous *righteously, righteousness.* Acting properly; good.–That woman is a very *righteous* person. She does the things that are good and right.

right-hand right'-hand.' At or towards the hand that is on the right.–Put your book on the *right-hand* side of your desk.

right-handed right'-hand'-ed. 1. Mary is *right-handed.* She writes with and uses her right hand more easily and more often than her left hand.

2. For use by *right-handed* persons.–A pan with a lip on the left-hand side, so that it can be held in the right hand when something is poured from it, is a *right-handed* pan.

rightly right'-ly. 1. Exactly or correctly.–I cannot say *rightly* how far it is to the city.

2. Honestly or in fairness. – Mother cannot *rightly* give more to Jack than she gives to Mary.

rigid rig'-id *rigidly.* 1. Stiff and hard to bend. –Iron bars are *rigid.*

2. Unchanging, or allowing no exceptions; strict.–In some schools the rules are very *rigid.*

rill *rills.* A small brook or rivulet.–The boys went wading in the *rill.*

rim *rims.* A border or edge. – The *rims* on Mother's glasses are gold. –The *rim* of a tumbler is the top edge.

R
S
T
U
V
W
X
Y
Z

rime. Hoar-frost; the tiny needles of ice forming on the ground, on leaves, etc.–Early on cold winter mornings, the lawn is covered with *rime*.

rind *rinds*. The outer skin on oranges, melons, apples, cucumbers, bacon, etc. –We eat the fruit but throw away the *rind*.

ring *rings, rang, rung, ringing*. 1. A circle.–When Father smokes his pipe, he makes *rings* of smoke in the air.

diamond ring

smoke ring

2. A round band worn on the finger.–Mother wears a wedding *ring*.
3. Any round band.–The farmer put a *ring* in the pig's nose to keep him from rooting or digging up the ground with his nose.
4. A band or group.–A group of people who work together for bad purposes is a *ring*.–A *ring* of thieves stole the gold.
5. Sound of or like a bell.–We heard 3 short *rings* and knew it was Bob at the door.–Mary's *ringing* laugh could be heard from the garden.
6. Make a sound of or like a bell. – Mary dropped the cover of the saucepan, and we could hear it *ring*.
7. Make (a bell) sound.–*Ring* the door-bell, please.
8. Be filled (with sound).–The room *rings* with laughter when the teacher makes a mistake in his arithmetic.

ringlet *ring'-let ringlets*. Small, tight, curls.– After rain, Baby's hair curls in *ringlets* all over her head.

rink *rinks*. A floor or sheet of ice marked off or fenced in for ice hockey or skating.

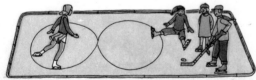

rinse *rinses, rinsed, rinsing*. 1. Pour water over, or dip in water, especially to wash away the soap.–Mary washed the dishes in soapsuds, and *rinsed* them with very hot water.– Clothes that have been washed in soapy water are *rinsed* by moving them in and out of clear water again and again.

riot *ri'-ot riots*. Noisy quarrelling and fighting by a large number of people, especially in a public place.

rip *rips, ripped, ripping*. 1. Tear, or pull apart by force.–Mother *ripped* off the bandage on her arm.–Mother *ripped* up Mary's old coat to make a coat for Baby. She cut or pulled out the threads from the seams.
2. A tear or opening, especially in a seam.– Bob had a *rip* in his coat sleeve, where the threads of the seam had come out.
3. Saw (wood) with the grain. – Father used a *rip*saw to *rip* the piece of timber. He cut it the long way.

ripe *riper, ripest*. Completely grown and ready to be picked for eating.–Mother told Bob to pick only the *ripe*, dark red cherries off the tree.

ripen *rip'-en ripens, ripened, ripening*. Become ripe or ready to eat.–Tomatoes *ripen* in the sun more quickly than they do in the shade.

ripple *rip'-ple ripples, rippled, rippling*. 1. A tiny wave.–There isn't a *ripple* on the lake to-day. – When the fish jumped up above the water, little *ripples* formed around it.

2. Make little waves. – The lake *rippled* in the breeze.

rise *rises, rose, risen, rising*. 1. Get up or stand up.–*Rise* before you speak in class.
2. Go or move up.–A balloon *rises* because it is lighter than air.
3. Increase.–The temperature sometimes *rises* during the daytime. The air grows warmer.
4. An increase.–The *rise* in the price of milk made it hard for the large family to buy milk for the children.
5. Slant upwards. – Where the bank *rises* sharply, we have made a rock garden.
6. Result (from) or be caused (by).–Mischief often *rises* from idleness.
7. A slope or slant.–The steep *rise* of the roof makes it difficult to climb.

risk *risks, risked, risking*. 1. Take the chance of. –Do not *risk* crossing the road in front of a moving car.
2. Put in danger of loss or harm.–The man *risked* his own life to save the child.
3. Chance or danger.–There is no *risk* of falling if you hold on to the ladder.

risky *risk'y riskily, riskiness*. Dangerous or full of chance.–It is *risky* to let yourself get too tired while swimming.

R
S
T
U
V
W
X
Y
Z

rite *rites.* A solemn act or special service usually carried out according to a set form or pattern. – Marriage *rites* in our church are carried out in the same way each time a man and a woman are married.

rival ri'-val *rivals, rivalled, rivalling.* 1. One of two or more persons who are trying to get something only one can have. – Mary and Ruth were *rivals* in the final spelling bee.
2. Be a *rival* to.–The girls *rivalled* each other in the spelling bee.

rivalry ri'-val-ry *rivalries.* Competition or contest between rivals.–There is great *rivalry* between Bob and Mary to see who will get the higher marks.

river riv'-er *rivers.* Large brook or stream.– Boats steam up and down the *river.* – Cars cross the *river* on bridges.

rivet riv'-et *rivets, riveted, riveting.* 1. A metal bolt with a rounded head and without threads. A *rivet* is put through matching holes in the pieces to be fastened together, and then the small end is flattened with an automatic hammer to make another head so that the *rivet* will not come out.
2. Fasten with one or more *rivets.*

rivulet riv'-u-let *rivulets.* A small stream or brook.–There is a *rivulet* at the bottom of the field near the village where the cows go to drink.

road *roads.* 1. An open way; a long, smoothed strip, often paved, on which people, cars, animals, and other things travel.–*Roads* lead from one place to another.
2. A way.–Kindness is a *road* to happiness.

road-hog *road-hogs.* A motorist who drives without any consideration for others.

roadside road'-side. 1. Land at the side of a road.–The *roadside* was covered with weeds of many kinds.

2. Located at the side of a road.–We buy vegetables at a *roadside* market, a market at the side of a road.

roam *roams, roamed, roaming.* Wander about. –On Sundays we like to *roam* through the woods.

roar *roars, roared, roaring.* 1. A loud, deep sound or noise.–We heard the *roar* of the guns.
2. Make a deep, loud sound. – The lions at the zoo *roar.*

roast *roasts, roasted, roasting.* 1. Bake or cook in an oven or over live coals on an open fire.–Mother *roasted* the beef in the oven.
2. A piece of meat to be *roasted* or cooked in the oven.–We ate the entire *roast* for dinner.

rob *robs, robbed, robbing.* 1. Steal from, or force one to hand over.–The bandits *robbed* the man of his pocket-book.

robber rob'-ber *robbers.* A person who robs or steals.–The highway *robbers* hid at the side of the road, waiting to hold up travellers who passed by.

robbery rob'-ber-y *robberies.* The act of robbing or stealing. – The bank *robbery* took place at night.

robe *robes, robed, robing.* 1. A long, loose gown worn over other clothing. –Men in certain offices, such as judges, priests, ministers, wear *robes* that show their positions.
2. Dress oneself in a *robe* or *robes.* – The judge was *robed* before entering a court.– All the peers and peeresses were *robed* in ceremonial dress in honour of the coronation.

robin rob'-in *robins.* A small and cheerful bird. It has a reddish breast and is sometimes called a redbreast. – *Robins* have a cheerful song and adopt a piece of land, such as a garden, as their territory. *Robins* are less timid than most wild birds.

robot ro'-bot *robots.* 1. A machine made to look like a man, that can walk around and do certain other things a man can do.
2. A person who acts like a machine.

R
S
T
U
V
W
X
Y
Z

rock *rocks, rocked, rocking.* 1. A large stone.–The boys threw *rocks* into the lake and watched them splash.
2. A large mass of stone.–The mountain is a huge *rock.*
3. Stone–The bottom of the artificial lake is solid *rock.*
4. Move to and fro and from side to side.–The boat *rocked* dangerously during the storm.–Sally *rocked* her doll to sleep in its cradle.

rocker rock'-er *rockers.* A curved piece of wood on which the legs of a piece of furniture are set.

rockery rock'-e-ry *rockeries.* A bed of earth and stones in which to grow rock-plants.

rocket rock'-et *rockets.* A kind of firework or other object that shoots up into the air. It is pushed ahead by gases formed inside it and blown out at the rear end.–*Rockets* are sometimes used as signals or weapons.

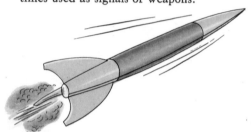

rocking chair rock'-ing chair *rocking chairs.* A chair on rockers. – Grandmother sits in her *rocking chair* and rocks Baby to sleep.

rocky rock'-y *rockier, rockiest.* Made up of rocks or covered with rocks. – The coast is very *rocky* here.

rod *rods.* 1. A straight, slender piece of wood or metal.–Some of the cages at the zoo are made of iron bars or *rods.*
2. A stick used to whip a person or an animal.
3. A pole for fishing.–Father has a new fishing *rod.*

4. A distance of 16½ feet.–Ribbon is measured by the yard. Land is measured by the foot and by the *rod.*

rode. One form of the word *ride.*–Yesterday I *rode* my bicycle.

rodent ro'-dent *rodents.* An animal, such as a rat or squirrel, that has long, sharp teeth which it uses to gnaw or bite things away little by little. – Rabbits and mice also are *rodents.*

rodeo ro-de'-o *or* ro'-de-o *rodeos.*–1. A cowboy show at which men rope cattle and ride bulls and wild horses.–Father went to a *rodeo* when he was in Texas.

2. In the west of the United States, a round-up, or a gathering together of many cattle by riding round them and driving them in.

rogue *rogues.* 1. A dishonest, tricky person; a rascal.–A *rogue* cheated Father by selling him worthless goods.
2. A mischief maker.–Sally is a little *rogue.* She likes to play tricks on people.

roll *rolls, rolled, rolling.* 1. Turn over and over and move ahead.–The bowling ball *rolled* down the alley.
2. Wind up, or turn over and over.–The children *rolled* a snowball.–Grandmother *rolled* the wool into a ball.–The children *rolled* up their papers and put a rubber band round them to take them home.
3. Push along on wheels or rollers. – Sally *rolled* the crippled old man's wheel-chair out on to the veranda.
4. Flatten out with a *rolling*-pin.–Mother *rolled* the dough a quarter of an inch thick, and Mary cut out the biscuits.
5. Swing from side to side.–During the storm the ship *rolled.*

R
S
T
U
V
W
X
Y
Z

6. Move continuously in a *rolling*, curved fashion.–The waves *rolled* in to shore.

7. A continuous rumbling sound.–The prisoners heard the *roll* of the drums and the tramping of feet.–We saw a flash of lightning and heard a *roll* of thunder.

8. Trill.–Some people *roll* their *r's* when they speak. They make their tongue vibrate against the roof of their mouth when they pronounce the letter *r*.

9. A list of names.–Mary checked the *roll* to see if all the children were in school.

10. Anything *rolled* up round something else, such as a *roll* of cloth, paper towels, wrapping paper, or the like.

11. Anything *rolled* about itself.–The children made a *roll* of the clay in art class.

12. A kind of bread *rolled* into buns or small pieces before it is baked. – We have freshly baked *rolls* for breakfast every Sunday.

roll-call *roll-calls*. A calling of names to see if anyone is absent.–After *roll-call*, the teacher read us a story.

roller roll'-er *rollers*. Anything that rolls or moves along by turning over and over.–Casters, or the small round wheels on the legs of beds, tables, and chairs, are *rollers*.–The wringer on the washing machine has two *rollers*.

roller-skate roll'-er-skate *roller-skates*. 1. A skate with rollers, or wheels, instead of a runner or blade.
2. Skate or glide on *roller-skates*.–Children should not *roller-skate* in the street.

rolling-pin roll'-ing-pin *rolling-pins*. A roller of wood or other material with a handle at each end. It is used to roll pie crust, to crush bread into crumbs, to roll dough, and the like.

Roman Ro'-man *Romans*. Connected with ancient Rome.–Augustus was the first *Roman* Emperor.

romance ro-mance' *romances*. A poem or a story about heroes, adventure, or love.–Many people call any love story a *romance*.

romp *romps, romped, romping*. 1. Play roughly and noisily.–Jack and his dog *romp* in the yard every day.
2. Rough-and-tumble play. – The boys have not had their *romp* yet today.

roof *roofs*. 1. The top covering of a building.–Our *roof* is made of green tiles.
2. The top of a car or a tent.

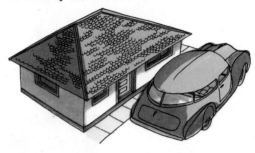

rook *rooks, rooked, rooking, rookery*. 1. A large black bird like a crow, with a hoarse cry. *Rooks* nest in colonies called *rookeries*.
2. Swindle.–Father said that he had been *rooked*. He had been charged too much.
3. In chess the castles are called *rooks*.

room *rooms*. 1. One of the inside divisions or parts of a building. *Rooms* are separated by walls and connected by doors.–We sleep in a bed*room*, and bath in the bath*room*.

2. Space.–There wasn't *room* for one more thing in Mother's handbag.

3. The whole company.–Jack kept the *room* in fits of laughter.

4. Opportunity or chance.–There is *room* for improvement in Mary's handwriting. It should be better.

roomful room'-ful. As much or as many as a room can hold.–When we arrived there was already a *roomful* of guests.

room-mate room'-mate *room-mates*. The person who shares one's room, or the person who lives in the same room with one.–When Jean went to college, Betty was her *room-mate*.

roomy room'-y *roomier, roomiest.* Having plenty of room or space.–This cupboard is *roomy* enough to hold all your clothes.

roost *roosts, roosted, roosting.* 1. A perch, bar, branch, or anything else on which birds sit, stand, or rest while they sleep.–The wooden stick across a bird-cage is a *roost.*
2. Sit on a *roost.*–The canary *roosts* on his swing to sleep.

root *roots, rooted, rooting.* 1. A part of a plant, bush, or tree that grows downward into the earth.–*Roots* hold the plants in place and feed them moisture and food from the soil.–We eat some *roots,* such as potatoes, beets, carrots, and turnips.
2. A part that is like the *root* of a plant.–Teeth have *roots* to hold them firmly in place.
3. Plant, set, or fix deeply.–The tree is well *rooted.*–It is hard to break a deeply *rooted* habit.
4. Dig, pull, or remove.–The dogs *rooted* the fox out from his hiding-place.–The farmer put rings in the pigs' noses so that they would not *root* up the earth.
5. A beginning or source.–The drinking of too much whisky was the *root* of the man's troubles.
6. Begin or start with.–Bill's dislike of school is *rooted* in his trouble in getting on with other people.

rope *ropes, roped, roping.* 1. A strong, heavy cord made by twisting together a number of smaller cords.
2. Any large twisted strand or braid. – The children made a *rope* of dandelions to wear round their necks.
3. Separate, tie off, or divide with a *rope.*–A part of the street was *roped* off so that the children could play in it.
4. Lasso or capture by throwing a *rope* round. – The cowboy *roped* the runaway horse.
5. Bind or tie with a *rope.* – The goat was *roped* to the stake.

rosary ro'-sa-ry *rosaries.* 1. A string of beads used to keep count in saying a number or series of prayers.
2. A group of prayers recited on a *rosary.*

rose *roses.* 1. A fragrant flower that grows on a bush. It has a prickly stem.– *Roses* are red, yellow, pink, or white.
2. A deep pinkish colour.–*Rose*-coloured curtains blend with the rug.
3. One form of the word *rise.*–The sun *rose* bright and hot.

rosin ros'-in. A gummy brownish substance made from turpentine. *Rosin* is used on a violin bow to keep it from slipping when one plays.

rosy ros'-y *rosier, rosiest.* 1. Deep pink or reddish.–Baby has *rosy* cheeks.
2. Cheerful, full of promise of good things.–The days ahead of us look *rosy.*

rot *rots, rotted, rotting.* 1. Decay, or become soft and spoiled. The potatoes remained in the wet ground so long that they *rotted.*
2. A disease of certain plants.

rotate ro-tate' *rotates, rotated, rotating, rotation.* 1. Turn round about a centre or axis, –The earth *rotates* on its axis.–The wheels of a moving cart *rotate.*
2. Arrange one after the other, take in turn.– The farmer *rotates* his crops. One year he plants barley in the field, the next year he plants wheat in that field, and so on.

rotten rot'-ten *rottener, rottenest.* 1. Decayed; soft and spoiled.–The tomatoes that were not kept in the refrigerator are *rotten.*
2. In bad condition, weak, not sound.–The boards in the steps are *rotten,* so be careful.
3. Dishonest or wicked.–The government was *rotten.*

rouge. 1. A pink or red powder or cream for colouring the skin.–Mother wears *rouge* on her cheeks.
2. Put *rouge* on.–Mother *rouges* her cheeks.

rough (pronounced *ruff*) *roughs, roughed, roughing, rougher, roughest, roughly, roughness.* 1. Uneven, irregular; not smooth or level.–Ploughed ground is *rough.*–Sand-paper is *rough.*
2. Stormy, not quiet or still.–The sailors found the sea *rough.*
3. Wild and active.–Boys seem to like *rough* play. Many are hurt in *rough* games.

R
S
T
U
V
W
X
Y
Z

4. Difficult, or filled with hard work.–Grandfather had a *rough* life when he was a boy.

5. *Rough it* means to live without the comforts of home life.

6. Unpolished; not finished.–Diamonds are polished when you buy them in rings, but they are *rough* when they come from the mines.

7. Tangled.–The dog's fur was *rough*.

8. Rumple or tangle.–Father *roughed* up the baby's hair.

9. Rude or ill-mannered.–The man met our offers of help with *rough* refusals.

10. Crude; not detailed or accurate.–Bob made a *rough* drawing of the model aeroplane he wants to build.

11. Make a *rough* outline, shape, or model of.–At first the children *roughed* out the vases they were making; then they made them smooth and true to form.

roughen (pronounced *ruffen*) rough'-en *roughens, roughened, roughening*. Make rough or coarse.–Cold weather *roughens* one's hands. Creams make them smooth again.

round *rounds, rounded, rounding, roundness*.
1. Shaped like a ball, a circle, a wheel, or a water pipe.–Anything *round* and smooth will roll.

2. A regular route.–A milkman goes his *rounds* each day.

3. A dance which moves in a circle.–The Maypole dance is a *round*.

4. A number of duties, sports, pleasures, or other happenings coming one after the other.–During our holiday we had a *round* of parties.

5. A part or period into which a fight or a game is divided.–The heavyweight champion knocked out his opponent in the third *round*.

6. Something which many people join in doing at the same time.–There was a *round* of boos when the left-half was tripped.

7. A song sung by a number of people beginning at different times.–Children think it is fun to sing *rounds*.

8. Go round.–The speeding car *rounded* the corner on 2 wheels.

9. Make or become circular.–Jack *rounded* the wheels of his model aeroplane.

10. *Round out* means complete. – Bob *rounded out* his story with one more paragraph.

roundabout round'-a-bout, *roundabouts*. 1. Not straight or direct.–Because the road was being repaired, we went a *roundabout* way to the farm.

2. A merry-go-round.–After we had tried the coconut-shy we had a ride on the *roundabout*.

3. A circular verge of grass, sometimes fenced in, round which traffic moves.–*Roundabouts* are useful in reducing the speed of traffic on long stretches of road.

rounders round'-ers. A game, similar in some ways to baseball, played between 2 sides of 10 players, with a bat and a soft ball. The batsman hits the ball as far as he can and then tries to run round 4 bases marked by posts. A complete circuit is called a *rounder*.

round-shouldered round'-shoul'-dered. Having shoulders that lean forward.–The tall, thin girl is *round-shouldered*. She does not stand up straight.

round-up round'-up *round-ups*. 1. Bringing cattle together.–The cowboys carried out the *round-up*. They brought together a large number of cattle by forming a circle round them and driving them into one herd.

2. Any gathering together of people by the efforts of others.–The police were praised for their *round-up* of gangsters in the town.

rouse *rouses, roused, rousing*. 1. Disturb, wake up, or excite.–You may *rouse* the sleeping baby if you make so much noise.

2. Stir up or make angry.–The people of the town were *roused* over the kidnapping.

rout (pronounced *rowt*) *routs, routed, routing*.
1. Force to run away.–The policeman *routed* the robbers. He made them flee.

2. A wild and confused flight of an army.–Our army's use of flame-throwers caused the *rout* of the enemy's troops.

R
S
T
U
V
W
X
Y
Z

route (pronounced *root*) *routes, routed, routing.*
1. A way of travel; a road or path.–What *route* did you take to the city?
2. Send along a way or road.–The policeman *routed* the cars round the washed-out bridge. He told them how to go by another way.

routine rou-tine′ *routines.* A regular plan or way of doing things that is followed every time.–Mother gets her work done early because she follows a *routine.*

rove *roves, roved, roving.* Roam or wander.–The children like to *rove* in the woods.

row (rhymes with *so*) *rows, rowed, rowing.*
1. A line.–We sat in the first *row* of seats.–The wind destroyed a *row* of trees.
2. Move (a boat) with oars.–Bob *rowed* the boat to the spot where we fished.

row (rhymes with *cow*) *rows.* Noisy fight or quarrel.–The boys had a *row* over the biggest piece of pie.

rowing-boat row′-ing-boat *rowing-boats.* A small boat moved by rowing.–The fishermen hired a *rowing-boat.*

royal roy′-al. Having to do with, or fit for, kings and queens.–The king and queen and their family live in the *royal* palace.–We were given a *royal* welcome.

royally roy′-al-ly. In a manner fit for a king or queen.–The king was welcomed *royally.* –Our hosts treated us *royally.*

royalty roy′-al-ty *royalties.* 1. Kings, queens, and members of their families.–The feast was prepared for *royalty.*
2. Money paid to an inventor, author, or composer, as his share of money made from the sale of his work.–Persons who write books often receive *royalties.*

rub *rubs, rubbed, rubbing.* 1. Press against or together, and move back and forth.–Father's hands were so cold that he had to *rub* them together to get them warm.
2. Clean or polish by *rubbing.*–The maid *rubbed* the pots and pans with a cloth and scouring powder.
3. Erase.–*Rub* out the pencil marks with an eraser.

rubber rub′-ber *rubbers.* 1. A stretchy material made from the thick sap or juice of many plants that grow in certain warm countries; something made of this material.–Erasers, tyres for cars, galoshes, water-hose, hot-water bottles, balls, and many other things are made of *rubber.*

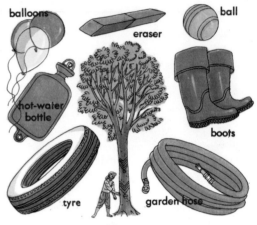

rubber tree

2. A contest decided by the winning of two games out of three, or the odd game when there has been a tie.

rubbish rub′-bish. Things to be thrown out; worthless things.–The children cleaned the basement and put the *rubbish* in the dustbin.

ruby ru′-by *rubies.* 1. A deep-red precious stone. –Grandmother has a ring set with a large *ruby.*
2. A deep red colour. – Snow White had coal-black hair, skin as white as snow, and *ruby* lips.

rudder rud′-der *rudders.* A flat piece of wood or metal on the back of a boat, used for steering.–Aeroplanes have *rudders,* too.

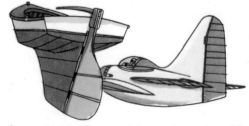

rude *ruder, rudest, rudely, rudeness.* 1. Not polite, not courteous.–The boy was *rude*; he talked while others were talking.
2. Rough.–The boys made a *rude* boat of some old boards and a log.

ruffian ruf′-fi-an *ruffians.* A cruel, rough person. –The *ruffians* seized the aged man and beat him.

R
S
T
U
V
W
X
Y
Z

ruffle ruf'fle *ruffles, ruffled, ruffling*. 1. A narrow piece of cloth or lace gathered at one edge and used as a trimming. – Mary's dress has *ruffles* round the hem and round the sleeves.

2. Gather or make tiny pleats in cloth. – Mother *ruffled* the curtain borders on the sewing machine.

3. Puff out, or cause to become rough or rear up.–The cock *ruffles* his feathers when you go near him.

4. Disturb or vex.–Jack's teasing *ruffled* Mary. It made her angry.

rug. *rugs.* 1. A large carpet or other floor covering.–Mother wants a new living-room *rug.–Rugs* are made of wool, cotton, rags, reeds, or grass.

2. A blanket.–Grandmother puts her *rug* over her lap when she rides in the car.

rugged rug'-ged *ruggedly, ruggedness.* 1. Uneven; rough.–The mountain country in Scotland is very *rugged*.

2. Rough and very simple.–Camping out is too *rugged* for Mother.

3. Strongly marked and irregular.–The man's features were *rugged*.

ruin ru'-in *ruins, ruined, ruining.* 1. Spoil or destroy.–The hail-storm *ruined* the fruit in the orchard.

2. Partly destroyed remains.–The country was in *ruins* after the storm. Buildings, trees, and other things were destroyed or damaged. –The *ruins* of some ancient buildings are still standing.

3. Useless or worthless condition.–The farmer's machines are in *ruin* from standing out in the weather.

4. Something which causes destruction or downfall. – Laziness and drink were the man's *ruin*, the things that made him worthless.

5. Downfall or destruction. – War brought *ruin* to the country.

rule *rules, ruled, ruling.* 1. A direction telling what may and what may not be done.–The children know the *rules* of the game.

2. A flat stick, marked with evenly spaced lines, used for measuring and drawing straight lines; a ruler.–Bob used a *rule* to measure the border on his paper and to guide his pencil in drawing the border.

3. Mark with straight lines.–We *ruled* the paper for 10 spelling words.

4. Usual custom.–Planting gardens in the spring is the *rule*.

5. Control or govern. – The king *rules* over his country.

6. Decide.–The children *ruled* that the *rules* of the game should be followed carefully.

ruler rul'-er *rulers.* 1. A person who governs or controls.–A king is a *ruler*.

2. A flat stick marked off in inches, half inches, and so on.–A *ruler* is used to measure with and to guide one's pencil in making lines.

ruling rul'-ing *rulings.* A judgement given by a judge or court.–It is the judge's *ruling* that the man be sent to prison.

rum. A drink containing alcohol and made from sugar cane. – *Rum* is sometimes used as a flavouring in cake.

rumble rum'-ble *rumbles, rumbled, rumbling.* 1. Make a low, heavy, rolling sound.–Father's old car *rumbled* as it went down the road. 2. A low, heavy, rolling sound.–During the night we heard the *rumble* of thunder.

rummage rum'-mage *rummages, rummaged, rummaging.* Look for something by moving things about carelessly. – Father *rummaged* through the tool chest for a few nails.

rumour ru'-mour *rumours, rumoured, rumouring.* 1. A report or story told as news without knowledge of whether it is true.–There is a *rumour* going about that teacher is getting married.

2. Tell or spread news without knowing if it is true.–It is *rumoured* that the king is sick.

rumple rum'-ple *rumples, rumpled, rumpling.* 1. Wrinkle.–The baby *rumpled* the bedspread when he played on the bed.

2. Disorder or tangle. – The wind *rumpled* Baby's curls.

R
S
T
U
V
W
X
Y
Z

run *runs, ran, running.* 1. Move so fast that all or both the legs are off the ground at the same time.–When Jack whistles for his dog, the dog doesn't walk, he *runs* to him.

2. Go or move.–The motor of the car *runs* fast and smoothly. If you leave the brake off, the car will *run* down the hill.

3. Flow.–Water *runs* from the tap when you turn it on.

4. Reach or stretch out.–Our garden *runs* from the house to the corner.

5. Operate or make go.–Mary can *run* the sewing-machine.

6. Thrust or push.–Do not *run* your finger into your eye.

7. A swift trip on foot.–Bob and his dog went for a *run* in the field.

8. A trip.–The engine-driver has made his last *run* on the train.

9. A place where a thread has pulled out of some material; a row of ravelled stitches.–Mother caught her stocking on a splinter and got a *run* in it.

10. A series of happenings.–The cricket team had a *run* of bad luck. They lost five matches one after the other.

11. A score in cricket.–The team needed 2 *runs* to win the game.

12. A sudden great demand.–When coffee was scarce, there was a *run* on the shops for it.

13. A spreading.–There is a *run* of measles in the school now.

14. Become. – The child's temperature *ran* higher every hour.

15. Average, be usually.–The fish in this lake *run* about 10 inches long.

runaway run'-a-way *runaways.* 1. A person or animal that runs away.–A fleeing robber is a *runaway.*

2. Running out of control. – A car moving without a driver is a *runaway* car.

rung *rungs.* 1. A round bar, usually of wood, used as a crosspiece on a ladder or between the legs of a chair, as a wheel spoke, and so on.–The painter stood on one of the top *rungs* of the ladder.

2. One form of the word *ring.*–The bell had already *rung* when we got to school.

runner run'-ner *runners.* 1. A smooth, narrow strip on which something slides.–Sledges, ice skates, and drawers in cabinets move on *runners.*

2. Small stems that stretch along the ground and form roots from which new plants grow. –Strawberry plants have *runners.*

3. A person who runs races, or carries messages.–A native *runner* stopped at the trading post with a message.–There were 5 *runners* in the 100-yard sprint.

runner-up run'-ner-up. In a race, an animal, a person or a team finishing in second place.

running run'-ning. One form of the word *run.*
1. Flowing.–We have *running* water in the bathroom.

2. Operating.–Mother attends to the *running* of the house.–Father attends to the *running* of the car; he drives it.

3. One after another, in a row.–It has rained now for 6 days *running.*

runt *runts.* A person or animal that doesn't grow to be as large as others of the same kind.–Our dog is just a *runt,* but he can run faster than most big dogs.

runway run'-way *runways.* 1. A track or roadway on which something runs, slides, or moves.–The new ship slid down the *runway* into the water.–Aircraft take off from *runways.*

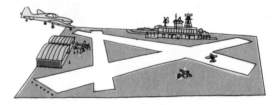

2. A path that is beaten down by animals in going to and from their feeding or drinking places.

rural ru'-ral *rurally.* Having to do with the country or living in the country.–*Rural* life is life in the country.

rush *rushes, rushed, rushing.* 1. Go fast or in a hurry.–The fire engine *rushed* to the burning building.–The water *rushed* over the rocks.

2. Hurry.–Do not *rush* through your meals.

3. Attack or charge. – The football players *rushed* their opponents' goal.

4. A time of great hurrying and crowding.–We came home on the underground during the evening *rush.*

5. A sudden movement.–A *rush* of wind blew the door open.

6. A hollow reed or stem that grows in marshy or wet places.–Indians made baskets of *rushes.*

R
S
T
U
V
W
X
Y
Z

Russia Rus'-sia *Russian*. The old name for the Union of Soviet Socialist Republics, usually written U.S.S.R., the largest country in Europe. The U.S.S.R. is made up of states something like states in the U.S.A. The largest of these states is now called *Russia*.

rust *rusts, rusted, rusting.* 1. A rough, orange-brown crust that forms on iron and steel.–Unpainted iron or steel tools left out in the air or in a wet place are soon covered with *rust*.
2. Become covered with *rust*.–Your bicycle will *rust* if you leave it out all night.
3. A plant disease that makes spots on leaves and stems.–The wheat crop was spoiled by *rust*.

rustic rus'-tic. Rural, or having to do with the country. – Grandfather lives in a *rustic* cottage.

rustle rus'-tle *rustles, rustled, rustling.* 1. A crackling noise.–We can hear the *rustle* of the leaves on the oak trees in winter.
2. Make a crackling or whispering sound.–Mother's taffeta dress *rustles* as she walks.

3. Steal (cattle or other livestock).–A band of thieves *rustled* cattle from the ranches.

rustler rus'-tler *rustlers*. A person who steals cattle or other livestock. – The *rustler* was caught by the cowboy.

rusty rust'-y *rustier, rustiest.* 1. Covered with rust.–The old saw is *rusty*.
2. Out of practice. – The musician is *rusty* because he hasn't practised.

rut *ruts, rutted.* 1. A groove or track such as one worn in the ground by the wheels of cars. –The *rut* in the road is filled with water.
2. Habit, or unchanging ways of doing things. –People who do the same work in the same way day after day may get into a *rut*.

ruthless ruth'-less *ruthlessly, ruthlessness.* Cruel and heartless; without pity or mercy.–The *ruthless* landlord put the poor family out in the street.

rye. A grain.–Farmers grow *rye*.–*Rye* is made into flour which is used in making *rye* bread.

S s

S, s *S's, s's.* The 19th letter of the alphabet.

Sabbath Sab'-bath. Day of rest and worship. –Sunday, the 1st day of the week, is the Christian *Sabbath*. – Saturday, the 7th day by the calendar, is the Jewish *Sabbath*.

sabre sa'-bre *sabres.* A sword with a heavy, curved blade. – Soldiers on horseback use *sabres*.

sack *sacks.* A large bag usually made of burlap or other coarse material.–*Sacks* are used for

burlap sack   string sack   paper sack   cotton sack

potatoes, onions, wheat, and the like.

sacred sa'-cred *sacredness.* Holy; worthy of worship and deep respect. Things having to do with God or religion are *sacred*.–We sing *sacred* songs in Sunday school.–The name of God is *sacred*.

sacrifice sac'-ri-fice *sacrifices, sacrificed, sacrificing.* 1. Give up.–Mother *sacrifices* many pleasures for her children. – Many soldiers have *sacrificed* their lives for our freedom.
2. Something offered to a god as a religious act. – Ancient Hebrews sometimes killed a lamb as a *sacrifice* to Jehovah.
3. A loss.–Bob sold his bicycle at a *sacrifice*.

sad *sadder, saddest, sadly, sadness.* 1. Having a feeling of sorrow or unhappiness.–Children are *sad* when they lose or break a toy, or when their pet dies.
2. Causing sorrow or unhappiness.–The train wreck was a *sad* accident.

sadden sad'-den *saddens, saddened, saddening.* Make unhappy.–The war *saddened* the people.

saddle sad'-dle *saddles, saddled, saddling.* 1. A seat, usually of leather, for a person riding on a horse, bicycle, tricycle, motor-cycle, or the like. – Tom sits up straight in the *saddle* on his new horse.

2. Put a *saddle on.*–The farmer *saddled* the pony for his little boy.
3. Have and not be able to get rid of.–The man was *saddled* with an old house which he could not use or sell.

sadness sad'-ness. Sorrow or grief.–Much *sadness* was caused by the death of the father of the family.

safe *safer, safest, safely, safeness.* 1. A steel cabinet, with a lock, for keeping valuable things.–The grocer keeps his money in a *safe.*
2. Free from danger.–It is *safer* to cross the street at a pedestrian crossing. – The lost child has turned up *safe* and sound at a neighbour's house.

safety safe'ty. 1. Freedom from danger.–The veranda has a railing round it so that the baby can play there in *safety.*
2. Giving or making sure of *safety.*–Father uses a *safety* razor.–Mother uses *safety*-pins in dressing baby.

sag *sags, sagged, sagging.* Droop or hang unevenly.–The curtain *sags* in the middle.–The tennis net is not stretched tight enough. It *sags.*

sage. A plant whose dried leaves are used as flavouring. – We put *sage* in stuffing to flavour it.

said. One form of the word *say.* –I *said,* 'It is a nice day.'

sail *sails, sailed, sailing.* 1. A large piece of heavy cloth raised over a boat so that the wind blows on it and moves the boat along.
2. A trip on a *sailing*-boat. We went for a *sail* with Bob.
3. Start a voyage. – The steamer *sailed* on Monday.
4. Move along (of a ship).–The ship *sailed* slowly down the river.

5. Soar or move smoothly and swiftly.–The arrow *sailed* right over the top of the target. –The aeroplane *sailed* over the city.
6. Direct and operate (a ship or boat).–The captain and sailors *sailed* the ship.

sailing-boat sail'-ing-boat *sailing-boats.* A boat moved by the wind blowing against its sails.–We went for a sail in Bob's new *sailing-boat.*

sailor sail'-or *sailors.* A man who sails, or works on, a boat or ship.–There were only 3 *sailors* in the crew of the small ship.

saint *saints.* A holy person worthy of worship.

Saint Bernard Saint Ber'-nard *Saint Bernards.* A very large, tan-and-white breed of dog.– *Saint Bernard* dogs are very intelligent.

sake *sakes.* Because of, on account of.–I hope Baby sleeps this afternoon, for Mother's *sake.* It will give Mother a chance to rest.–Soldiers gave their lives for the *sake* of freedom.

salad sal'-ad *salads.* Raw vegetables or fruits, usually served with oil and vinegar, or some other *salad* dressing.–We eat cabbage *salad,* potato *salad,* and fruit *salad.*–Eggs, chicken, meat, or fish mixed with vegetables and a *salad* dressing are *salads,* too.

salary sal'-a-ry *salaries.* Money paid to a person at regular times for work done.–Father receives his *salary* twice a month.

sale *sales.* 1. A selling of something, or an exchanging of something for money.–The *sale* of his bicycle gained Bob £5.
2. A selling at prices lower than usual.–The shop had a *sale* of shoes.
3. Goods sold.–The Christmas *sales* were very large.
4. A demand.–There is a large *sale* for used cars now.

salesman sales'-man *salesmen.* A man who is paid to sell things.–Father is a *salesman.* He sells cars.

saleswoman sales'-wom-an *saleswomen.* A woman who is paid to sell things.–The *saleswoman* sold me 2 books.

saliva sa-li'-va. The liquid that forms in the mouth and keeps it moist.–The sight of meat makes *saliva* run from the dog's mouth.

S
T
U
V
W
X
Y
Z

salmon salm'-on. 1. A kind of large fish whose pink flesh is good to eat.–*Salmon* is also sold in tins.
2. Yellowish pink.– Mary's hair ribbon is of a *salmon* colour.

saloon sa-loon' *saloons*. 1. A covered-in motor-car.–We have a *saloon*, but our neighbour has a sports car.
2. A bar in a public-house or hotel, usually called a *saloon* bar.
3. A large room in a private house or hotel.

salt *salts, salted, salting*. 1. A grainy white substance used to give flavour to foods and also to preserve them.–*Salt* is put on meats to keep them from spoiling, to preserve them. –The water in the ocean has *salt* in it.
2. Put *salt* on or in.–Mother *salts* the water in which she boils potatoes.
3. Preserve in *salt* or brine.–The butcher *salts* beef which we eat in sandwiches.
4. An old and experienced sailor.–A sailor is called a *salt* because he sails the *salt* water of the sea.–The old *salt* knew many good stories.

salt-cellar salt'-cel-lar *salt-cellars*. A small dish or other container to hold salt. –You lift the salt from a *salt-cellar* with a small spoon, or shake it through a top or cap with little holes in it.

salty salt'-y *saltier, saltiest*. Having much salt.– The vegetables were too *salty*.

salutation sal-u-ta'-tion *salutations*. 1. A greeting.–Shaking hands, raising the hat, saying good morning, and saluting are all *salutations*.
2. The beginning of a letter, which addresses the person to whom one is writing.–'Dear Mother' is a *salutation* used in writing to one's mother.

salute sa-lute' *salutes, saluted, saluting*. 1. A formal greeting between officers and men in the armed forces, exhanged by raising the right hand to the forehead.–A bow or hand-shake is also a *salute*.
2. To make a *salute*, or formal greeting.–The soldier *salutes* his officers. He shows respect and honour for the officers by raising his right hand to his head as if touching his hat.– Mary *saluted* the audience with a bow.
3. A ceremonial firing of guns.–A *salute* was fired on the Queen's Birthday.

salvage sal'-vage *salvages, salvaged, salvaging*.
1. Save from damage. – When the factory burned down, the men *salvaged* everything they could from it.
2. Things saved from damage.–Machines and other equipment were among the *salvage* from the burned factory.
3. Money paid for saving a ship and its cargo. –The men received £5,000 in *salvage* for *saving* the sinking ship.

salve. A kind of soft, creamy substance used as a medicine on sores, burns, and the like.– Mother rubbed *salve* on Bob's sore finger.

same *sameness*. 1. The very one; not another. –Mary wore the *same* dress for school that she wore on Sunday–not a different one.
2. Just like.–Sally's handbag is the *same* as Mary's.–It is the *same* colour and the *same* style. Both of them are red and close with zippers.

sample sam'-ple *samples, sampled, sampling*.
1. A small part that shows what the rest is like.–This is a *sample* of my handwriting.
2. One of a number of like things used to show what all the rest are like.–This book is a *sample* copy. There are many others just like it.
3. Try or test.–Won't you *sample* these new cakes to see if you like them?

sand. 1. A large number of tiny bits of stone, often found along the shores of oceans, lakes, and rivers.–Children like to play in the white *sand* on the beach.
2. Scrape, polish, or smooth with *sand* or *sand*-paper.–Father *sanded* the floor before varnishing it.

sandal san'-dal *sandals*. 1. A shoe that is just a sole with a strap or straps to fasten it on to the foot.–Children wear *sandals* in warm weather.

sandbag sand'-bag *sandbags*. A bag filled with sand. It is generally used as ballast for boats and for lining trenches.–The soldiers prevented the sides of the trench from crumbling by piling up *sandbags*.

sand-man sand'-man. An imaginary person told of in stories who is supposed to sprinkle sand in the eyes of children to make them sleepy.

S
T
U
V
W
X
Y
Z

sand-martin sand'-mar-tin *sand-martins*. A bird of the swallow family, related to the house-martin. The *sand-martin* is a very sociable bird and builds its nest in a hole bored in a sand-pit or a bank.

sandwich sand'-wich *sandwiches, sandwiched, sandwiching*. 1. Two or more slices of bread with cheese, eggs, lettuce, jam, or other food between them. – *Sandwiches* are good to take on picnics.
2. Squeeze (someone or something) between 2 other persons or things.– The little house was *sandwiched* in between two tall buildings.

sandy sand'-y *sandier, sandiest*. 1. Full of sand or covered with sand.–The beach is *sandy*.
2. Yellowish brown.–Jack has *sandy* hair and freckles.

sane *sanely, sanity*. Having good sense and a healthy mind. – The prisoner was found *sane*.

sang. One form of the word *sing*.–The children *sang* a group of folk-songs and ballads at the school concert.

sanguine san'-guine. Hopeful, optimistic.–The minister said he was *sanguine* of success. He thought the conference had a good chance of success.

sanitary san'-i-ta-ry. Clean and healthful.– Everything in the hospital is very *sanitary*. It is kept free from germs and all kinds of dirt.

sanitation san-i-ta'-tion. Anything to do with preserving the public health.–A pure water-supply and a proper drainage system are important matters for the city's *sanitation* department.

sap. A juice that flows through trees and other plants and helps them to live and grow.– The *sap* of some maple trees is made into maple sugar and maple syrup.

sapling sap'-ling *saplings*. A young, slender tree.

sapphire sap'-phire *sapphires*. 1. A very costly, hard, bright blue gem.–Mother has a ring set with a *sapphire*.
2. Bright blue.–The fairy has golden hair and *sapphire* eyes.

sardine sar-dine' *sardines*. A tiny fish tinned in oil, mustard, or tomato sauce. –*Sardines* are good to eat.

sash *sashes*. 1. A long, wide band of cloth or ribbon worn round the waist or hips or over the shoulder. – The dancer wore a red *sash*.
2. The movable part of a window.

satchel satch'-el *satchels*. A small bag with a strap which hangs over the shoulders.–We always carry our school-books in a *satchel*.

sateen sa-teen . A cotton cloth that is shiny on one side and made to look like satin.–Mary's costume for the play was made of *sateen*.

satellite sat'-el-lite *satellites*. 1. A small planet revolving round a larger one.–The moon is a *satellite* of the earth.
2. The name *satellite* is also given to a man-made metal object filled with scientific instruments, shot into space and sent into orbit round the earth or another planet.

satin sat'-in. A silk cloth that is shiny on one side.–Grandmother's new dress is made of grey *satin*.

satisfaction sat-is-fac'-tion. 1. A feeling of being satisfied or contented.–Father's new car gives him much *satisfaction*.
2. Something which causes a contented feeling.–Keeping up to date on one's school work is a *satisfaction*.

satisfactory sat-is-fac'-to-ry *satisfactorily*. Good enough or sufficient to satisfy or please.–Jack asked his teacher if his paper was *satisfactory*, and she said that it was all right.

satisfy sat'-is-fy *satisfies, satisfied, satisfying*.
1. Please.–Baby is perfectly *satisfied* with her old toys.
2. Make one feel sure, convince.–Mary *satisfied* Father that the clock was slow.
3. End (a need) by filling it.–Bob *satisfied* his thirst by having a drink of water.

saturate sat'-u-rate *saturates, saturated, saturating, saturation*. Soak or fill completely.– The blotter was *saturated* with spilt ink.

Saturday Sat'-ur-day *Saturdays*. The 7th day of the week.–We have no school on *Saturday*.

sauce *sauces*. 1. A liquid put over food to make it tastier.–Father likes tomato *sauce* on meat loaf.
2. A fruit purée.–Mother put lemon rind in the apple-*sauce* to make it taste better.

S
T
U
V
W
X
Y
Z

saucepan sauce'-pan *saucepans*. A metal pan with a handle, used for cooking.–Mary cooked the fudge in a *sauce-pan*.

saucer sau'-cer *saucers*. A dish used to set a cup in.–Do not leave your spoon in your cocoa cup after stirring the sugar; lay it in the *saucer*.

saucy sau'-cy *saucier, sauciest, saucily*. 1. Not courteous; rude.–I hope you are not *saucy* in school.–*Saucy* children are troublesome to their parents.
2. Lively, bold. – The *saucy* little sparrow chirped noisily.

sauerkraut sauer'-kraut. Chopped cabbage that is salted and allowed to stand for a long time. The salt preserves the cabbage and gives it a sharp taste.–*Sauerkraut* is good to eat with sausages.

sausage sau'-sage *sausages*. Meat prepared by mincing up and seasoning beef, pork, or other meat. Sometimes it is stuffed into a long, thin casing, like a tube. – *Sausages* are good to eat with mashed potatoes.

savage sav'-age *savages*. 1. A person who is not civilized; one who lives a wild, simple, rough life in ignorance and superstition.–The cave men of long ago were *savages*.
2. Wild or untamed.–Animals of the jungle are *savage* animals.
3. Cruel or vicious; bloodthirsty.–The *savage* king ordered all his prisoners to be put to death at once.

save *saves, saved, saving*. 1. Rescue or free from danger.–The fireman *saved* the child from the burning house.
2. Set aside; keep without using; keep for later use.–Father *saves* some money for us to buy a new car.
3. Lessen.–A washing machine *saves* work.
4. Prevent.–Minding one's own business *saves* trouble.
5. Treat with care, or protect.–*Save* your eyes by reading only in a good light.
6. Except. – The fisherman boxed up all his fishes *save* one.

saviour sav'-iour *saviours*. One who saves others.–Christians call Jesus their *Saviour*.

saw *saws, sawed, sawing*. 1. A tool for cutting wood, metal, and the like. – *Saws* are made of thin steel with sharp teeth along one edge for cutting. Some *saws* are run by electricity, some are used by hand.

2. Cut with a *saw*.–Bob *sawed* the sticks for his kite out of an old crate.
3. One form of the word *see*.–Mary *saw* the accident.
4. A proverb.–'A rolling stone gathers no moss' is an old *saw*.

sawdust saw'-dust. The tiny bits of wood made in sawing wood.–Sally found that the inside of her doll was *sawdust*.

sawmill saw'-mill *sawmills*. A mill or factory with machines for cutting logs into timber or planks.

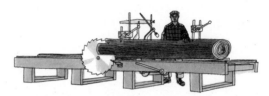

saxophone sax'-o-phone *saxophones*. A brass musical instrument with a reed mouthpiece.–The *saxophone is* played by blowing into the mouthpiece and pressing down on the keys.

say *says, said, saying*. Speak words, or write words.–We *say* 'Good morning' to our teacher when she comes into the room.–This book *says* that elephants live to be over 100 years old.

saying say'-ing *sayings*. A proverb, or wise words that have been handed down to us from the past. This is an old *saying*:
'Early to bed and early to rise
Makes a man healthy, wealthy, and wise.'

scab *scabs*. A thin crust that forms over a sore or wound.–The *scab* drops off when the sore is healed.

scabbard scab'-bard *scabbards*. A case to cover

the blade of a sword.–The knight drew his sword from the *scabbard*.

S
T
U
V
W
X
Y
Z

scaffolding scaf'-folding *scaffoldings*. A platform for men to stand on when they build or paint houses, or do other work in high places.–Some *scaffoldings* can be raised or lowered to the place where the workmen want to work.

scald *scalds, scalded, scalding*. 1. Burn with steam or hot water.–Baby *scalded* her finger when she tried to pick a carrot out of the hot soup.
2. Clean with boiling water.–*Scald* the baby's bottle before you fill it.
3. Heat until nearly boiling.–In making this pudding, you *scald* the milk and then add the sugar, eggs, and flavouring.

scale *scales, scaled, scaling*. 1. Small, thin, horny piece something like a finger-nail.–Some fish are almost covered with *scales*.
2. Scrape the *scales* off.–We *scale* fish before we cook them.

3. Small, thin flakes of skin. – Mary's back was covered with little *scales* from her sunburn.
4. A device for weighing things. – Bob stood on the *scales* while the nurse weighed him.
5. A regular series of marks on a stick, dial, etc., used for measuring.–A ruler is a *scale*. The little lines along the edge that mark off the inches, half inches, etc., form a *scale*.–Gas meters and electricity meters have *scales* which measure the amounts of gas or electricity used.
6. A series of notes in music arranged in the order of their pitch.–Mary had to practise *scales* when she took music lessons.
7. Small distance between places on a map or drawing compared with the real distance between the same places.–The map is drawn to *scale*. Each inch on the map stands for 50 miles of country.
8. Climb.–The men *scaled* the cliff. They climbed the side of the mountain by the use of ropes.

scallop scal'-lop *scallops, scalloped, scalloping*.
1. A shellfish that is good to eat. Notice the shape of its shell in the picture.
2. One of a series of curves, like the curves on a *scallop's* shell.–Mother embroidered *scallops* on the end of the towel.
3. Cut a pattern of repeated curves in.–She *scallops* the edge of many of Baby's dresses.
4. Bake in a special way with milk and crumbs.–I like *scalloped* potatoes.

scalp *scalps, scalped, scalping*. 1. The skin on one's head that is covered by the hair.
2. Cut off the *scalp* of.–Indians used to *scalp* people whom they killed.

scamp *scamps*. A worthless, good-for-nothing fellow.

scamper scam'-per *scampers, scampered, scampering*. Run hastily.–The pony *scampered* off when we went to saddle him.

scandal scan'-dal *scandals, scandalous, scandalously, scandalousness*. 1. Disgrace or shame caused by bad actions or deeds.–The boy's bad behaviour is a *scandal*.
2. Exciting and harmful gossip or talk about someone.–The discovery of bribery in the government department caused a great deal of *scandal*.

scant. Barely full; barely enough; not much.–Mother used a *scant* teaspoonful of baking powder in the cake.

scar *scars, scarred, scarring*. 1. A lasting mark left on the body after a sore, burn, or wound has healed.–The dog's bite left a *scar* on Jack's wrist.
2. Mark with *scars*.–Jack's wrist was *scarred* by the bite of the dog.
3. A mark or dent that spoils the look of something.–The table top has many *scars* from long use.

scarce *scarcer, scarcest*. Hard to get, not plentiful; rare.–Butter is often *scarce* in time of war. There isn't much butter to be had then. –Black pearls are *scarce*; they are not found often.

S
T
U
V
W
X
Y
Z

scarcely scarce'-ly. Hardly.—We had *scarcely* enough food to go round at the picnic. We had barely enough for everybody.

scarcity scar'-ci-ty. Not a big enough supply. —There is a *scarcity* of meat here. There isn't enough.

scare *scares, scared, scaring.* 1. Make afraid.— The noise *scared* the baby. It frightened her. 2. A fright.—We had a big *scare* when the house caught fire. We were afraid.

scarecrow scare'-crow *scarecrows.* 1. A figure dressed to look like a man, used to scare off crows and other birds. — The farmer put a *scarecrow* in the corn-field. 2. A person dressed so raggedly that he looks like a *scarecrow*.

scarf *scarves.* 1. A long woven or knitted strip of cloth worn around the neck and shoulders or over the head.—Mother knitted a *scarf* for a soldier. 2. A broad band of silk; a sash.—The official wore a crimson *scarf* around his waist.

scarlet scar'-let. A brilliant red.—Our school colours are *scarlet* and blue.

scatter scat'-ter *scatters, scattered, scattering.* 1. Toss or sprinkle in all directions.—The boys *scattered* corn for the squirrels. 2. Break up and go in different directions.— The crowd *scattered* when it started to rain. 3. Drive away in all directions.—The explosion *scattered* the people.

scene *scenes.* 1. Time and place of a story.— The *scene* of this play is summer-time in the mountains. 2. A painted screen or curtain serving as background for a play.—The *scene* is a beautiful mountain-top covered with pines. 3. A division of a play.—The first *scene* is the story of an old man. 4. A view, or thing to look at.—You can see beautiful *scenes* from the top of that hill.

5. An action which causes people to stare.— The man with the dog made a *scene* on the corner. He yelled at the dog and beat him, so that people stared.

scenery scen'-er-y. 1. Painted scenes for an entertainment on the stage.—The children painted their own *scenery* for their play.

2. Things to look at seen all together.—The *scenery* in the mountains is beautiful.

scent *scents, scented, scenting.* 1. Smell; notice or follow by smelling.—The dog *scented* a squirrel. 2. Give a fragrant odour to.—Roses *scented* the whole room. 3. An odour, fragrance, or smell.—The *scent* of fried bacon and coffee makes one hungry. 4. A trail, or a means of tracking down.—The police were thrown off the *scent* of the robber because he had exchanged cars.

sceptre scep'-tre *sceptres.* A long, fancy rod or staff carried by a ruler of a country as a sign of his power.

schedule (pronounced *shed-ule*) sched'-ule *schedules, scheduled, scheduling.* 1. A written or printed list or catalogue.—The firm issued a *schedule* of their products and prices. 2. Plan or arrange in a *schedule*.—The train was *scheduled* to arrive at 2 o'clock.

scheme *schemes, schemed, scheming, schemer.* 1. A secret plan or plot.—The criminals have a *scheme* to get out of jail. 2. A planned arrangement.—Mother has a nice colour *scheme* in her bedroom. She has used colours that look well together. 3. Plan secretly.—The criminals *schemed* to free their leader from prison.

scholar schol'-ar *scholars.* 1. A student or pupil. —We have 600 *scholars* in our school. 2. One who has studied thoroughly and learned a great deal.—Mr Smith is a *scholar* in history.

school *schools.* 1. A place for teaching and learning.—Children learn how to read in *school*.—A medical *school* is a place for teaching and learning about medicine. 2. The pupils who go to a *school*.—Our *school* will have a sports day on Saturday. 3. A large gathering (of fish) which swim together.—We saw a *school* of fish.

S
T
U
V
W
X
Y
Z

schoolboy school'-boy *schoolboys*. A boy who goes to school.–Uncle Jack often tells us amusing stories about when he was a *schoolboy*.

schoolfellow school'-fel-low *schoolfellows*. The boys and girls who go to the same school at the same time as you do.–Jack and John are *schoolfellows*. They are in the same class.

schoolgirl school'-girl *schoolgirls*. A girl who goes to school.–When Mother was a *schoolgirl*, the rules were much stricter than they are today.

schooling school'-ing. Education, the things taught in school.–The man who applied for the job admitted that he had not been given much *schooling*.–Father's *schooling* lasted until he was 16.

schoolmaster school'-mas-ter *schoolmasters*. A man schoolteacher.

schoolmate school'-mate *schoolmates*. A fellow pupil. – Your *schoolmates* are the children who go to school with you.

schoolmistress school'-mis-tress *schoolmistresses*. A woman schoolteacher.

schoolroom school'-room *schoolrooms*. A room in a school.–The *schoolroom* was decorated with drawings.

schoolteacher school'-teach-er *schoolteachers*. A person who teaches in a school.

schooner schoon'-er *schooners*. A sailing ship with two or more masts and sails.

science sci'-ence *sciences*. 1. A way of learning about things by a planned method of seeing how things work and act, and by experimenting and testing.

2. An orderly collection of all the known facts and laws about any one kind of thing. – Botany is the *science* of plants.–Zoology is the *science* of animal life.–Mathematics is the *science* of numbers and amounts.

scientific sci-en-tif'-ic *scientifically*. Having to do with science; like science.–John likes the *scientific* subjects in school best. He has a *scientific* mind.

scientist sci'-en-tist *scientist*. A person who is learned or skilled in some science.–Charles Darwin was a great *scientist*.

scissors scis'-sors. A cutting tool with 2 handles and 2 sharp blades fastened together so that the sharp blades move past each other when the handles are brought together. –Sally uses *scissors* to cut out her paper dolls.

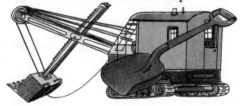

scoff *scoffs, scoffed, scoffing, scoffer*. Show doubt by making fun of.–When Columbus said the earth was round, people *scoffed* at him.

scold *scolds, scolded, scoldings*. Find fault with in an angry way.–The teacher *scolded* her class for being disorderly during the fire drill.

scoop *scoops, scooped, scooping*. 1. A tool like a shovel, but deeper.–The man who brought the coal shovelled it with a *scoop*.

2. A big bucket-like holder which *scoops* up sand, earth, etc.–The men used a steam shovel with a large *scoop* to lift the sand.
3. A small shovel-shaped ladle with a short handle.–The assistant puts sweets and peanuts into bags with a *scoop*.

4. Get news before others.–The reporter *scooped* his rivals in writing about the fire.
5. Pick up with a *scoop*.–Mother *scooped* up the spilled flour.
6. Hollow or dig out.–Faher *scooped* a hole in the ground to plant seeds.

scoot *scoots, scooted, scooting*. Dart quickly.–The child *scooted* across the street.

scorch *scorches, scorched, scorching.* 1. Burn slightly.–The iron was so hot that Mother *scorched* a towel while ironing it.
2. Make dry and withered.–The hot sun has *scorched* the grass.

score *scores, scored, scoring.* 1. Mark.–Alan *scored* the wood with his penknife.
2. The record of points made in a game.– The football *score* was 5 to 1.
3. Win points for the score.–Jack *scored* twice during the game.
4. Keep a record of points.–Bob was appointed to *score* the cricket match.
5. Twenty.–Four *score* years ago, Grandfather was born. Grandfather is 80.

scorn *scorns, scorned, scorning.* 1. Look down on or despise.–The children *scorned* the boy who copied from someone else in the examination.
2. Contempt; feeling of shame for.–The children looked with *scorn* at the child who copied.

scornful scorn'-ful *scornfully.* The children were *scornful* of the boy who copied.

scorpion scor'-pi-on *scorpions.* A small, backboneless animal with a long tail that has a poisonous sting in it.

Scotch, Scottish. Having to do with Scotland. –*Scotch* is whisky made in Scotland.– Angus is a Scot: he is *Scottish.* He lives in the *Scottish* Highlands, and he wears *Scottish* clothes; but he drinks *Scotch.*

Scotland Scot'-land. The country just north of England, on the same island.

scour *scours, scoured, scouring.* 1. Clean; scrub the grease and dirt off.–Mother *scours* the pots and pans with steel-wool soap pads.
2. Search.–The Boy Scouts *scoured* the shops for a tent.

scout *scouts, scouted, scouting.* 1. A member of an organization of boys, founded in 1908. Boy *Scouts* learn to be loyal, responsible citizens and are taught useful indoor and outdoor crafts. The *scout* movement has now spread to many countries all over the world. There is a similar movement for girls, known in Great Britain as the Girl Guides, and in some countries as Girl *Scouts.*

2. A person who goes out looking for news of the enemy, or for other information.–Daniel Boone was a famous Indian *scout.*
3. Examine, search.–The children *scouted* the town for Jack's lost dog.

scowl *scowls, scowled, scowling.* 1. Frown; look angry.–Baby *scowls* when she can't have her own way.
2. A frown; an angry look.–Bill read his report with a *scowl.*

scramble scram'-ble *scrambles, scrambled, scrambling.* 1. Push, struggle, or crowd.–The children *scrambled* for the pennies.
2. A hasty crowding and struggling.–There was a *scramble* for the pennies.
3. Climb, crawl, or walk on hands and knees. –The soldiers *scrambled* up the hillside.
4. Mix together.–Mother *scrambled* the eggs for breakfast.

scrap *scraps, scrapped, scrapping.* 1. A small bit; a small piece.–The children picked up the *scraps* of paper.
2. Bits of left-over food.–We fed the *scraps* to the chickens.
3. Discard, or throw away as useless.–Jack *scrapped* the work he had done wrong and started again.
4. Broken up, taken apart.–Cars are sometimes *scrapped* and the useful steel and parts used again.
5. Quarrel or fight (slang).–The children *scrapped* over who should be first.

scrapbook scrap'-book *scrapbooks.* A book with blank pages for pasting in different kinds of clippings.–Mary made a *scrapbook* for the sick children.

scrape *scrapes, scraped, scraping.* 1. Scratch things off.–A painter *scrapes* loose paint from the house before he puts on new paint.
2. Rub.–Baby *scraped* the skin off her knee when she fell on the pavement.
3. Drag.–The children *scraped* their feet on the pavement.
4. Get together with difficulty.–The girls *scraped* together enough money to buy their mother a gift.
5. A harsh, grating sound.–We heard the *scrape* of the wheels of the milk cart in the road.
6. Bill is always in a *scrape.* He is always in trouble because he has done something he should not have done.

S
T
U
V
W
X
Y
Z

scratch *scratches, scratched, scratching.* 1. Dig into with a sharp point.–The kitten *scratched* Sally when Sally tried to put her doll's dress on him.

2. Mark made by a *scratch.*–There was a red *scratch* on Sally's hand from the kitten's claws.

3. Make a mark by digging or *scratching* with anything sharp or rough. – The carpenter *scratched* a line on the board with a nail.

4. Cut slightly.–Mother *scratched* her finger on a pin.

5. Rub with the fingers.–When Mary's nose itches, she *scratches* it.

6. Mark out or draw a line through.–Bob *scratched* out one word in his story that was not spelt right, and re-wrote it.

7. Write poorly.–Father *scratches* his signature when he is in a hurry.

8. The sound made by *scratching*, scraping, or rubbing with something rough.–A *scratch* at the door reminded us that the dog wanted to come in.

scrawl *scrawls, scrawled, scrawling.* 1. Scribble, or write poorly.–The teacher told us not to *scrawl* when we did our arithmetic, but to write neatly.

2. Careless handwriting. – Father signs his name in a *scrawl* when he is in a hurry.

scrawny scraw′-ny. Thin; skinny.–A *scrawny* little kitten came up to Father to be petted.

scream *screams, screamed, screaming.* 1. Cry out loudly and sharply.–People *scream* when they are in pain, terror, or great grief.–The girl *screamed* when she saw the flames in the barn.

2. A loud, sharp outcry.–We ran to the window when we heard a *scream* in the street.

screech *screeches, screeched, screeching.* 1. Cry out or sound loudly in a shrill harsh way. – The children *screeched* when the clown fell down on his face.

2. A shrill, harsh cry or noise. – The car stopped with a *screech* of the brakes.

screech-owl *screech-owls.* A kind of owl that has a cry like a scream, instead of a hoot.

screen *screens, screened, screening.* 1. Anything used to hide, cover, or protect a thing, or for sifting.–A *screen* door or a window *screen* is a frame covered with a wire netting to keep out flies, mosquitoes, and other insects.–A frame covered with a coarse wire mesh used to sift coal, sand, and other materials is also a *screen.* – Another kind of *screen* is a frame, usually folding, used to cover a doorway, protect against draughts, set off part of a room, etc.–A smoke-*screen* is a lot of smoke made to hide from the enemy something that is going on, like the movements troops or ships.

2. Cover with a *screen.*–Father *screened* off the window to make the room warmer.

3. A white or silver curtain on which motion pictures are shown.–Mary squealed when her favourite actor appeared on the *screen.*

screw *screws, screwed, screwing.* 1. A nail with a ridge or 'thread' twisting around it from the point to the head, which has a groove into which the *screw*-driver fits. –*Screws* are twisted or turned into the wood instead of being hammered like a nail.

2. Fasten together with *screws.*–The sides of the box were *screwed* together.

3. Turn, twist.–Mother *screwed* the cover of the fruit jar down tight.

scribble scrib′-ble *scribbles, scribbled, scribbling.* Write poorly and carelessly. – Bob *scribbled* a hasty note to Mother.

script *scripts.* 1. Handwriting; also, a kind of printing that looks like handwriting.–German is often printed in *script.*

2. A copy of a play.–The actor forgot his part in the play and had to look at the *script.*

scripture scrip′-ture *scriptures.* Bible, or other sacred writing.–The minister read to us from the *Scriptures.*–The *scripture* of the Mohammedans is called the Koran.

scroll *scrolls.* 1. A roll of paper or other writing material.–In olden times much writing was done on *scrolls* of parchment. *Scrolls* were rolled at both ends. The reader rolled the parchment from one roll to the other instead of turning the pages as we do.

2. A design drawn to look like a partly rolled streamer of paper. – The first page of the book of fairy tales was decorated with *scrolls*.

scrub *scrubs, scrubbed, scrubbing.* 1. Clean by rubbing hard.–Mother *scrubbed* the table with soapy water and a brush.
2. Washing, or rubbing.–Jack gave his dog a good *scrub* after he had fallen in the puddle.

sculptor *sculp′-tor sculptors.* A person who carves or moulds statues or other figures of stone, wood, plaster, etc.

sculpture *sculp′-ture sculptures.* The art of carving or moulding statues and other fig-ures from stone, wood, or other materials. – Many pieces of *sculpture* can be seen in an art museum.

scum. A thin coating that forms on the top of liquids.–*Scum* often collects on shallow, still water.

scurry *scur′-ry scurries, scurried, scurrying.*
1. Hurry or scamper.–When the bell rang, the children *scurried* into the room.
2. Lively running or patter.–We heard the *scurry* of Sally's feet as she tried to catch the kitten.

scythe *scythes.* A farm tool used for cutting weeds, grain, and long grasses by hand.–A *scythe* has a long handle and a long, curved blade.

sea *seas.* 1. Large bodies of salt water smaller than oceans are called *seas*.–The island of Sicily is in the Mediterranean *Sea*.
2. The ocean; a very large body of salt water that covers more of the earth's surface than land does.–He sailed the seven *seas*.

3. A body of salt water that is rough from heavy waves.–The fishermen could not fish because of a high *sea*.

sea-coast *sea′-coast sea-coasts.* Land along the ocean or sea.–New York City is located on the eastern *sea-coast* of the United States; San Francisco is on the western *sea-coast*.

seafaring *sea′-far-ing.* Working, travelling, or living on the sea or ocean.–The old sailor misses his *seafaring* life.

seagull *sea′-gull seagulls.* A large, graceful sea bird with mostly white feathers. – *Seagulls* often follow ships and eat bits of food that are thrown from the ship. They eat fish, too.

sea horse *sea′-horse sea horses.* A fish with a head that looks like a horse's head, and a tail that curls up.

seal *seals, sealed, sealing.* 1. A sea animal that lives near the coast, especially in cold north-ern waters.

2. The fur of certain *seals*.–Coats and coat collars are often made of *seal*.
3. Close tightly.–Mother *sealed* the fruit jars with screw-caps.–Mary *sealed* Grandmother's letter.
4. A stamping device with a raised symbol or design used for stamping leters, official papers, and the like.–Olive has a *seal* with her initials on it to *seal* letters. She puts a little melted red wax on the envelope and then presses her *seal* against the wax. The *seal* presses her initials into the wax.

5. Mark with a *seal*.–The lawyer *sealed* the will.
6. Settle or make final.–The boys shook hands to *seal* the bargain.

seam *seams.* A fold or line where two pieces of material join.–The *seam* of Father's coat-sleeve is torn.

seaman *sea′-man seamen.* A sailor.

S
T
U
V
W
X
Y
Z

seaport sea -port *seaports*. A port or harbour where ships that sail the seas load and unload cargoes and passengers. – New York City is a *seaport*.

sear *sears, seared, searing*. 1. Burn the surface of.–The hot stove *seared* Father's finger.
2. Dry up, wither.–The bitter north wind *seared* the leaves.–The fields were *seared* during the hot summer.

search *searches, searched, searching*. 1. Look for, or try to find.–The children all *searched* for the lost purse.
2. Look through, or examine.–Bob *searched* the book for the picture of the dragon.
3. An effort made to find something.–After a long *search* for his keys, Father found them in his pocket.

searchlight search'-light *searchlights*. A very strong, turning light that can throw a powerful ray of light in any direction. – A *searchlight* can be seen for many miles.

seashore sea'-shore *seashores*. The land along the ocean or sea.–We often walk along the *seashore* to see if anything interesting has been washed up by the tide.

sea-sick sea'-sick. Sick in the stomach because of the rolling movement of a boat.–Even old sailors sometimes get *sea-sick* during bad storms at sea.

seaside sea'-side. Seashore, or the land along the sea or ocean.–Sally likes to cover Father up with sand when we go to the *seaside*.

season sea'-son *seasons*. 1. One of the 4 parts into which the year is divided.–Spring, summer, autumn, and winter are the 4 *seasons*.
2. A special time of the year in which a particular thing happens.–The planting *season* is the time of year for planting.
3. The time of year when something can be found, or is at its best.–Fresh strawberries taste best in *season*.
4. Flavour.–Mother *seasoned* the soup with onions and celery salt.
5. Treat or prepare for use.–Timber to be made into furniture should first be *seasoned*, or dried thoroughly.

seasoning sea'-son-ing *seasonings*. Flavouring; something added in a small quantity to improve the taste.–Salt, pepper, spices, onions, and the like are *seasonings*.

seat *seats, seated, seating*. 1. A place in which to sit, or thing to sit on.–The usher at the theatre took us to our *seats*.–Chairs, benches, stools, and the like are *seats*.

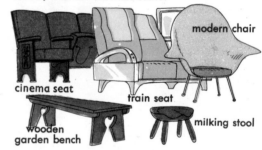

modern chair

cinema seat

train seat

wooden garden bench

milking stool

2. The part of anything that you sit on.–We have leather *seats* on our dining chairs.–Father wore a hole in the *seat* of his trousers.
3. A residence or headquarters.–Westminster, in London, is the *seat* of the British Government.–Chatsworth, in Derbyshire, has been the *seat* of the Dukes of Devonshire for over 250 years.
4. Show to a *seat* or place in a *seat*.–The usher *seated* us in the fourth row.
5. Have enough *seats* for.–This room *seats* 40 pupils.

seaweed sea'-weed' *seaweeds*. A kind of plant that grows in the sea. – Slippery strings of

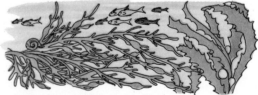

seaweed sometimes catch round your feet when you go swimming.

second sec′-ond *seconds, seconded, seconding.*
1. One of 60 equal parts into which a minute is divided.–If you count slowly to 60, it will take you about 1 minute, or 60 *seconds.*
2. Directly following the first.–Sunday is the first day of the week. Monday, the day following Sunday, is the *second* day of the week.
3. One next after the first–Jack won first prize, and Bob won *second.*
4. Like the first.–The cricketer wanted to be a *second* Jack Hobbs.
5. Below the first in rank or quality.–This cloth is *second* quality.
6. A person chosen to help a prize fighter or duellist.–The tired boxer's *second* kept urging him on.
7. Speak in agreement or support of.–At the meeting, Mary made a motion to start a club, and Ruth *seconded* it.

second-hand sec′-ond-hand′. Not new; used before.–We bought a *second-hand* piano.–This shop sells *second-hand* goods. It buys goods from people who have been using them, and resells them to others.

secret se′-cret *secrets, secretly.* 1. Hidden; not known. – The man disappeared through a *secret* door.
2. Something that people are kept from knowing.–What we have for Mother's birthday is a *secret.*

secretary sec′-re-ta-ry *secretaries.* 1. A person who writes letters, makes records, and takes care of many office duties for a person, a business, or a club.–Bob is the *secretary* of his club.
2. A kind of old-fashioned writing desk.

section sec′-tion *sections.* 1. A part of anything; one of the pieces into which a thing is divided or cut.–Grapefruit and oranges are divided inside into *sections* by thin walls, or membranes.–Our class is divided into two *sections.*
2. A region.–Miners live in the mining *sections* of the country.

secure se-cure′ *secures, secured, securing.* 1. Get or obtain.–We hope to *secure* enough money to buy the new books.
2. Tightly fastened.–The lock is not *secure.*
3. Free from danger or fear.–At last we are *secure* from fear of war.–The cat felt *secure* from the dog when she was up the tree.

security se-cur′-i-ty *securities.* 1. The feeling of being safe and protected.–Bolting the doors and windows at night gives us a feeling of *security.*
2. Something given as a guarantee of repayment.–Father handed over the deeds of the house as *security* for the loan from the bank.

sedate se-date′ *sedately.* Calm and unhurried.– Mary made a sedate entry on to the stage. She was not flustered or nervous.

sedative sed′-a-tive *sedatives.* Something which calms.–The doctor gave Mother a *sedative* when she was overworked. It had a *sedative* effect and calmed her down.

see *sees, saw, seen, seeing.* 1. Have the power of sight.–We hear with our ears, and *see* with our eyes.
2. Notice with the eyes.–Did you *see* the baby?
3. Make certain.–*See* that the door is locked before you go to bed.
4. Go with.–Mother will *see* you to the door.
5. Visit.–We went to *see* Grandpa last week.
6. Understand. – We *saw* how to do the problem after our teacher explained it.
7. Find out.–*See* if someone is at the door.
8. Experience or live through.–That poor family has *seen* better days.

seed *seeds, seeded, seeding.* 1. The part of a plant from which another plant will grow.–Fruits and vegetables have *seeds* in them.–The farmer plants vegetable *seeds* and flower *seeds.*

2. Sow *seeds* in.–Bob helped Grandmother *seed* her garden.
3. Take the *seeds* from. – Mother *seeds* grapes before making fruit salad.
4. Produce or have *seeds.*–Radishes and lettuce *seed* earlier in the summer than some other vegetables.

seedling seed′-ling *seedlings.* A young tree or plant that grows from a seed.

seedy seed′-y *seedier, seediest.* 1. Full of *seeds.* –Raspberries are *seedy.*
2. Shabby and much worn (slang).–The old man wore a rather *seedy*-looking old coat.

S
T
U
V
W
X
Y
Z

seek *seeks, sought, seeking.* 1. Look for, hunt, try to find.–We are *seeking* a house to live in.

2. Try.–The old man *seeks* to make happiness among his friends.

seem *seems, seemed, seeming.* Appear to be. –The old man seemed very unhappy.–The child *seemed* hungry.

seen. One form of the word *see.*– I have *seen* the film you are speaking of.

seep *seeps, seeped, seeping.* Leak slowly or ooze.–The milk *seeped* through the crack in the bottle.

seesaw see'-saw *seesaws.* 1. A game in which a person rides on each end of a heavy board that rests on something near the middle to balance it. First one end of the board goes up in the air and then the other.

2. Something balanced near the middle so that the ends go up and down, first one and then the other.

3. Teeter or rock like a board balanced in the middle.

seize *seizes, seized, seizing.* 1. Suddenly or violently take hold of; grab.–The angry man *seized* a stick and threw it at the dog that had attacked him.

2. Capture or take over. – The soldiers *seized* the enemy's guns.

seldom sel'-dom. Rarely, or not often.–We *seldom* see the boys, because they live too far away.

select se-lect' *selects, selected, selecting, selection.* 1. Choose or pick out.–Mary likes to *select* her own dresses.

2. Chosen as best.–These are *select* oranges. They are the largest, juiciest, and sweetest.

self *selves.* One's own being.–my*self* is I. Your*self* is you. *Self* is used with many words; as: *self*-control, meaning control of one's behaviour; *self*-discipline, meaning directing and guiding one's own work or actions.–Father him*self* sometimes makes mistakes in spelling.–You owe it to your*self* to do the best work you know how.

selfish self'-ish *selfishly, selfishness.* Too interested in oneself, without thought for others. –Bill is too *selfish* to help the class raise money to give the caretaker a present.

self-respect self-re-spect'. Concern with or interest in one's own decency, honesty, and goodness.–We have *self-respect* if we are not ashamed of our own actions.

sell *sells, sold, selling.* 1. Exchange for money. –The farmer *sells* chickens. He exchanges chickens for money.

2. Be exchanged.–Oranges *sell* at the corner shop for 10p a pound.

selves. A form of the word *self.* Him*self* refers to one *self*, or to one boy or man alone. Them*selves* means many persons.–Mary and Sally wanted to go to bathe all alone, all by them*selves.*

semi sem'-i. A prefix, or group of letters joined to the front of a word to change the meaning of that word in one of the following **ways:**

1. Partly, as in *semi*-skilled, meaning partly or somewhat skilled.

2. Half, as in *semi*circle, meaning one-half of a circle.

semicolon sem'-i-co-lon *semicolons.* A punctuation mark made by a dot with a comma under it (;). It stands between two main parts of a sentence.–The weather was very cold; the roads were frozen hard.

senate sen'-ate *senates.* 1. A group of persons elected to make the laws. Most states in the United States have *senates* to make the laws. Julius Caesar was murdered while he was addressing the *Senate* in Rome.

2. (Spelt with a capital S) One of two bodies of elected people making up the Congress of the United States, or one of the houses of a state legislature. The United States has a *Senate* and a House of Representatives to make laws for the country.

senator sen'-a-tor *senators, senatorial.* 1. A person elected or appointed to be a member of a senate.

2. (Spelt with a capital S). The title of a member of the U.S. Senate or of a state senate.–*Senator* Brown was re-elected.

send *sends, sent, sending.* Cause a person or thing to go or be taken from one place to another.–I will *send* your sweater to you.– Please *send* Bob home.

senior sen'-ior *seniors.* 1. An older person.–I am your *senior* by ten years. I am ten years older.
2. The older (of 2 people with the same name).–At school, Robert Smith is known as Smith *senior,* and his younger brother John as Smith junior.
3. Older or higher in rank or length of service.–Mr Miller is the *senior* member of the Miller and Black Timber Co.–The *senior* classes in school gave a play.–The British Navy is usually referred to as the *Senior Service.*

sensation sen-sa'-tion *sensations.* 1. A feeling. –Riding the merry-go-round gives Mary a dizzy *sensation.*–A burning match gives your fingers a *sensation* of heat.
2. Great excitement.–When the lion got loose, it caused a big *sensation.*

sense *senses, sensed, sensing.* 1. Feeling.–The boy who stole the marbles had a *sense* of guilt.
2. A quality of the body which makes us aware of things around us.–The five *senses* which a person has are: sight, hearing, smell, touch, and taste.
3. Judgement or intelligence. – The boy uses good *sense* in crossing the road. He knows when to cross it and when not to.
4. Meaning. – Mary couldn't get the *sense* of the sentence.
5. Idea or understanding. – The boy has a good *sense* of fairness in the games he plays.
6. Feel or be aware of.–The teacher *sensed* that the boy was not telling the truth.
7. Mind or sanity.–A person who behaves in a strange, unreasonable way is out of his *senses.*

sensible sen'-si-ble *sensibly.* Wise or intelligent. –A *sensible* person is one who uses good sense or judgement.

sensitive sen'-si-tive *sensitively, sensitiveness.*
1. Easily affected.–Mary's tooth is *sensitive* to heat. Hot tea makes it hurt.
2. Easily offended or hurt.–The lame boy was *sensitive* because the children would not play with him. His feelings were easily hurt.

sent. One form of the word *send.* – We *sent* flowers to the teacher who was ill.

sentence sen'-tence *sentences, sentenced, sentencing.* 1. A group of words that tells something or asks something. These are *sentences:* (*a*) Mary a new dress. (*b*) Where did she get the dress?
2. A decision made by a judge as to what a person's punishment shall be for doing something not lawful.
3. Pass official judgement on.–The judge *sentenced* the man to a year in prison.

sentry sen'-try *sentries.* A soldier who guards a place to keep away persons who have no right to be there. Many visitors watch the *sentries* changing guard at Buckingham Palace.

sepal se'-pal *sepals.* One of the leaf-like parts of a flower that are found on the outside at the base of the petals. The *sepals* cover and protect the bud until it is ready to blossom; then they spread, and the flower opens.

separate sep'-a-rate *separates, separated, separating.* 1. Divide or put in different groups. –The teacher told Mary to *separate* the blue and the red crayons.
2. Keep apart or divide.–The two towns are *separated* by a large river.–The children are *separated* during the summer. They are no longer together.
3. Not joined or connected.–We live in *separate houses.* They are in different places, and you cannot go from one to the other without going outside.
4. Alone; just one.–A *separate* plate costs more than it would if you were to buy it as part of the whole set.

separately sep'-a-rate-ly. One at a time.–We bought the plates *separately.*

separation sep-a-ra'-tion. A parting or division. – The war caused a *separation* of the family.

separator sep'-a-ra-tor *separators.* A machine to separate cream from milk.–The farmer uses a *separator* to separate the cream from the milk.

S
T
U
V
W
X
Y
Z

September Sep-tem'-ber. The 9th month of the year.–The school summer holidays end in *September*.

serene se-rene' *serenely*. 1. Fair and clear.– During the summer the skies are usually *serene*.
Placid and calm. – Mary looks *serenely* happy. She is not excited, but is very happy.

serf *serfs*. A person working for somebody else in miserable conditions.–Noblemen used to employ *serfs* to work for them.

serge. A woollen cloth with ridges that slant. –Father's new suit is made of blue *serge*.

sergeant ser'-geant *sergeants*. 1. A non-commissioned officer in the army or air force. His rank is next above that of corporal, but below that of lieutenant.
2. In the British police force, an officer higher in rank than a constable, and next below an inspector.

sergeant-major ser'-geant-ma'-jor *sergeant-majors*. A non-commissioned officer in the army of highest rank.

serial se'-ri-al *serials*. A story, film, or radio play presented in parts.–Mother is reading a *serial* in a magazine.–Children like to watch the *serials* on television.

series se'-ries *series*. A number of like happenings one after the other, like a *series* of cricket matches, a *series* of articles about the war, a *series* of lessons in cooking.–Mother listened to a *series* of radio talks on how to bottle fruits and vegetables.

serious se'-ri-ous *seriously, seriousness*. 1. Dangerous or harmful. – The boy's injuries did not prove to be *serious* when they were examined.
2. Thoughtful or earnest.–The old man's face grew *serious* as he began his story.–Bob is a *serious* student.
3. Important; worthy of concern.–To Mary, becoming a film actress is a *serious* problem.
4. Honest or in earnest. – Are you *serious* about leaving school?

sermon ser'-mon *sermons*. 1. A religious talk.– Bob went to church and listened to the vicar's *sermon*.
2. A very serious talk.–Father delivered a *sermon* to the children about getting their work done before they played.

serpent ser'-pent *serpents*. A snake.

serum se'-rum *serums*. 1. The liquid part of the blood. When blood thickens, the *serum* separates from the clot, or the part that gets somewhat hard.
2. Liquid taken from the blood of an animal that has had a certain disease. When this liquid is injected into a person, it may keep the person from having the disease.

servant serv'-ant *servants*. 1. A person employed by others to do personal or house work.– Many *servants* work for the rich man.
2. Persons whose lives are given to serving others. – Teachers are public *servants*. They serve their city and their country by teaching boys and girls.

serve *serves, served, serving*. 1. Work, help, or do good for.–A shop assistant *serves* the customers.–The mayor *serves* the people of the city.
2. Be used or useful.–Boy Scouts can make two stones *serve* as a fireplace.
3. Bring food to.–The waitress *served* us. She waited on us.
4. Supply or furnish.–The baker *serves* us with bread.
5. Spend or pass (time).–The sailor *served* three years in the navy.
6. Treat.–Having his pay period taken away *served* the boy right for being late.
7. We *served* a notice on the family to move. We sent them a written note asking them to move.
8. Put the ball in play in certain games.– It was Mary's turn to *serve* in the tennis match.

service serv'-ice *services, serviced, servicing*.
1. Help or aid.–May I be of *service* to you?
2. Repair.–A man *serviced* our electric iron. He put it in working order.
3. Use.–Our car is out of *service* now.
4. The work one does for another.–A nurse's *services* are needed when someone is very ill.
5. A religious meeting or ceremony. – We attend *services* every Sunday.
6. A set of silver dishes or tableware. – We have a tea-*service* for 8 people.

7. A serving. – The *service* at the restaurant is good. The food is served well and promptly.

8. A military organization, as the army, navy, etc.–Many men are in the *services* now.

9. Government work. – Postmen are Civil Servants. They are employed by the State and are members of the Civil *Service*.

session ses′-sion *sessions*. 1. A meeting of a court, law-making body, or conference.

2. A number of meetings, one after the other, by a court, conference, etc.–The conference's morning *session* is from 9 o'clock to noon.

3. A time when an organization is active.– The University has a summer *session* and a winter *session*.

set *sets, set, setting*. 1. Put or place.–Mary *set* the basket on the table.

2. Put in proper condition or position.–The doctor *set* the broken bone.–Mary *set* the table for Mother.–Father *set* the alarm for 5 o'clock. – The farmer *set* out the young plants in boxes.–The men *set* the stage for the next scene of the play.

3. Put (in to some condition). – The man trapped in the fire was *set* free by the fireman.–The boys *set* the old Christmas tree on fire.

4. Established or fixed.–The time is *set* for the match.–It is a *set* rule to get to school at 9 o'clock.

5. Get solid; take on a definite form.–Mother put the jelly in the refrigerator to *set*.

6. A group of articles used together. – Father has a *set* of tools. – Mother has a *set* of dishes.

7. Go down (of the sun, moon, or stars).– The sun rises in the east and *sets* in the west.

8. Start or begin.–We *set* out on our trip at sunrise.

setter set′-ter *setters*. A hunting dog that is trained to stand very still with his tail

straight out and his nose pointing towards the bird or other game which he smells.

settle set′-tle *settles, settled, settling*. 1. Get quiet and comfortably placed and prepared. –The teacher told the children to *settle* down and study their spelling.–Bob *settled* himself in the big armchair to read.

2. Make a permanent home, or go to live.– My uncle wants to *settle* in the country.

3. Sink to the bottom.–Sand in water *settles* if the water is allowed to stand.

4. Pay.–Father *settled* the bill at the grocer's.

5. Come to rest; stop.–The golf ball rolled and then *settled* on the green.

6. Put in order; arrange.–Mother wants to get her house *settled* before visitors come.

7. Decide upon; agree upon. – The day for the picnic has not been settled upon yet.

8. End.–The quarrel has not been *settled*.

settlement set′-tle-ment *settlements*. 1. An agreeable ending. – After the *settlement* of the quarrel, the boys shook hands.–The two countries arranged a peaceful *settlement* of their dispute.

2. A new community or village. – A small *settlement* of French people may be found near the river.

3. A payment.–The shop asked for a *settlement* of the bill.

4. A place or building in a community where help is given to the needy.

settler set′-tler *settlers*. One who makes his home in a new land.–The Pilgrim Fathers were among the early *settlers* in America.

seven sev′-en. The number (7) between 6 and 8.–There are *seven* days in a week.–Six and one make *seven*.

seventeen sev′-en-teen′. The number (17) between 16 and 18.–Ten added to seven makes *seventeen*.

seventeenth sev′-en-teenth′. 1. Following the sixteenth, or one more than the sixteenth of anything.–One's next birthday after the sixteenth is the *seventeenth* birthday.

2. One of 17 equal parts into which anything is divided.–If a watermelon were cut into 17 equal slices, each of these slices would be one *seventeenth* (1/17).

S
T
U
V
W
X
Y
Z

seventh sev'-enth. 1. Following the sixth, or one more than the sixth of anything.–Billy has had 6 birthdays. His next one will be his *seventh*.
2. One of 7 equal parts into which anything is divided.–If an apple tart is cut into 7 equal pieces, each piece will be one *seventh* (1/7) of the whole.

seventy sev'-en-ty. The number (70), which you get by taking 7 ten times.–Ruth can count by 10's: 10, 20, 30, 40, 50, 60, 70. *Seventy* is ten more than sixty.

several sev'-er-al. More than 2, but not many. –*Several* flowers are in bloom already.

severe se-vere' *severely, severeness*. 1. Sharp, intense, great.–Mother had a *severe* pain in her tooth.–The poor man was shivering from the *severe* cold.
2. Hard; difficult.–Bill's insulting words were a *severe* test of Bob's self-control.
3. Strict; harsh.–Father sometimes tries to be *severe* with the children when they have disobeyed.
4. Very plain; without any trimming.–The new evening dress Mother has is a *severe*, straight black gown.

sew (pronounced *so*) *sews, sewed, sewing*. Fasten cloth together by drawing a thread through the material with a needle; stitch. – Mother *sews* on the *sewing*-machine. Mary *sews* by hand.–Mother *sewed* up the tear in Father's sleeve.

sewer (pronounced *suer*) sew'-er *sewers*. A drain, usually underground, made of large pipes, to carry waste away from homes.– Bath-water is carried away by the *sewer*.

shabby shab'-by *shabbier, shabbiest*. 1. Worn and faded.–The poor old woman had on *shabby* clothes.
2. Mean; not generous.–The boy's feelings were hurt because of the *shabby* way the children treated him.

shack *shacks*. A small, poorly or roughly built house.–We went into the fisherman's *shack* when we were down at the shore.

shackle shack'-le *shackles, shackled, shackling*.
1. Tie with chains to prevent movement.–The prisoner was *shackled* to the wall.
2. A chain or chains, put on a prisoner.–The convict was in *shackles*.

shade *shades, shaded, shading*. 1. A shadow or partial darkness made by something blocking the light.–We ate our picnic lunch in the *shade* of the tree.

2. Something made to shut out light.–Window *shades* cover the windows of a house.– A lamp*shade* keeps the light out of your eyes.
3. A small degree.–Bob is just a *shade* taller than Bill.
4. A tone of a colour.–Mother s green dress is a lovely soft *shade*.–The sky has several different *shades* of blue.
5. Shield or partly cover.–Father *shaded* his eyes from the sun with his hands.
6. Make darker in some places than in others. –The artist *shaded* the drawing of the vase to make it look round.

shadow shad'-ow *shadows, shadowed, shadowing*. 1. A shaded spot made by a solid body which is blocking off a light.–The *shadow* cast by the tree is longer in the morning than at noon, when the sun is right above it.

2. A suggestion; slight bit.–There cannot be a *shadow* of a doubt of Jack's honesty.
3. Follow closely.–The burglar didn't know he was being *shadowed* by the detective.

shady shad'-y *shadier, shadiest*. Having plenty of shade; protected from direct light.–The lawn under the tree is quite *shady*.

shaft *shafts.* 1. A pole, long stick, handle, or the like.–The *shaft* of the spear was wooden,

but the point was steel.–A tall *shaft* on the building supported a radio aerial.

2. A long up-and-down tunnel or opening.–The miners went down a *shaft* to get into the mine – The lift runs up and down in a *shaft.*

shaggy shag'-gy *shaggier, shaggiest.* Covered with long, coarse, thick, woolly hair.–Jack likes *shaggy* dogs, and Mother likes smooth, sleek dogs.

shake *shakes, shook, shaken, shaking.* 1. Jerk, or move up and down or to and fro quickly. –We *shake* salt out of a salt-shaker.–We *shake* rugs to get the dust out of them.–The angry man *shook* his fist at us.
2. Clasp (hands).–The minister *shakes* hands with the people at the door after the service.
3. Tremble.–Mary *shook* with excitement.
4. Jerk, or quick movement up and down or to and fro. – After a few *shakes*, the salt-shaker was empty.

shall. 1. Is, am, or are going to.–We *shall* see the film tomorrow.
2. Expect or intend to.–I *shall* study my lessons before school.
3. Be required to.–He *shall* repay the money if it takes his last penny.

shallow shal'-low *shallower, shallowest.* Not deep.–Small children bathe where the water is *shallow.*

sham. Make-believe or pretended.–The boys had a *sham* battle.

shame *shames, shamed, shaming.* 1. An un-comfortable feeling caused by having done something wrong or foolish.–The boy who was caught cheating felt much *shame.*
2. Disgrace or loss of respect.–The boy's bad behaviour brought *shame* to the team.
3. A thing to be sorry about.–It is a *shame* that Mary couldn's go to the play.
4. Cause to feel *shame.*–We tried to *shame* the boy for not telling the truth. We tried to make him feel bad about it.

shampoo sham-poo' *shampoos, shampooed, shampooing.* 1. A hair-washing.–Mother went to the hair-dresser to get a *shampoo.*

2. Wash (hair). – Mary is *shampooing* her hair.
3. soap to wash the hair with.–Some *shampoo* is liquid and comes in bottles.

shamrock sham'-rock *shamrocks.* A 3-leaved plant that looks like a clover. It is the national emblem of Ireland.

shanty shan'-ty *shanties.* 1. A small rough house, or shack. – The fisher-man lives in a *shanty.*
2. A sailor's song.–We sang a sea-*shanty.*

shape *shapes, shaped, shaping.* 1. A form.–The *shape* of the ball is round.–The *shape* of the box is square.

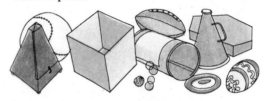

2. A figure.–We saw the *shape* of a black cat on the fence in the moonlight.
3. Order, readiness.–Mother has everything in *shape* for us to start for school.
4. Mould, form.–Mary *shaped* a little bear out of clay.

share *shares, shared, sharing.* 1. A part.–My *share* of the money is £5.–Bob always does his *share* of the work in the garden.
2. Divide, or allow use or enjoyment of by others; have part in.–Sally *shares* her toys with the other children.

shark *sharks.* A large fierce fish that lives on

other fish.–Some large *sharks* attack people swimming.

sharp *sharper, sharpest, sharply, sharpness.*
1. Keen; made for cutting or piercing.–The knife is *sharp*.–The kitten's claws are *sharp*.
2. Not rounded; having a point or angle.–Mary knocked herself on the *sharp* corner of the table in the dark.–We came to a *sharp* curve in the road.
3. Biting, keen.–Vinegar has a *sharp* taste.–A *sharp* wind almost froze our faces.
4. Harsh; angry.–The teacher's *sharp* words hurt the boy's feelings.
5. Piercing. – Bob had a *sharp* pain in his stomach.
6. Quick; keen; alert.–The boy has a *sharp* mind. He is quick to solve a problem, quick to learn, quick to see a joke. – Birds have *sharp* eyes. They see well.
7. A note in music that is half-step above or higher than a given note.–F *sharp* is the first black key above F on the piano. It is between F and G. It is marked ♯.
8. Promptly.–School starts at 9 o'clock *sharp*.

sharpen sharp'-en *sharpens, sharpened, sharpening.* Put a point on, or make an edge keener for cutting.–Mary *sharpened* her new pencil. –Father *sharpened* his razor.

shatter shat'-ter *shatters, shattered, shattering.*
1. Break into many small pieces.–When the picture fell to the floor, the glass *shattered*.
2. Destroy. – The heavy snowfall *shattered* Mary's hopes for a sunny weekend.

shave *shaves, shaved, shaven, shaving.* 1. Cut hair off with a razor.–Father *shaves* his face every morning.
2. A narrow escape.–The car almost hit the tree. It was a close *shave*.

shaving shav'-ing *shavings.* A thin slice or strip cut off with a knife or a carpenter's plane. – The *shavings* of wood curled up when cut off.

shawl *shawls.* A square or oblong piece of material worn over the head or shoulders.–Grandmother has a woollen *shawl* with fringe on the ends.

she. A word that stands for a girl, woman, or female animal.–Grandmother said *she* would come to see us.–The cow's name is Bessie. *She* is red and white.

sheaf *sheaves.* A bundle of flowers, grain, arrows, or the like.

shear *shears, sheared or shorn, shearing.* Cut off.–The farmer *shears* the sheep's wool with large scissors.

shears. Large scissors. – The farmer uses *shears* to cut the sheep's wool.

sheaves. More than one *sheaf*. – The farmer tied the grain into *sheaves* after it was cut.

shed *sheds, shed, shedding.* 1. A low, lightly built building.–The farmer keeps his tools in a *shed*.

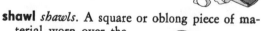

2. Let fall, pour out, drop. – The unhappy child *shed* tears.–This brush is *shedding* its bristles.
3. Give off or throw out.–The sun and moon *shed* light on the earth.

sheep. An animal from which we get wool for clothes, flesh (mutton) to eat, and *sheep*skin for leather.

sheer *sheerly, sheerness.* 1. Thin enough to see partly through.–Mary has a pair of *sheer* silk stockings.–The living-room curtains are *sheer*.
2. Complete.–Baby fell asleep in her highchair from *sheer* exhaustion.
3. Very steep; straight up and down, or almost so.–The north side of the mountain is a *sheer* cliff 3,000 feet high.

sheet *sheets.* 1. A piece of white cloth big enough to cover a bed and tuck in at the sides and ends.–We sleep between 2 *sheets*.
2. A broad, thin piece of anything. – The teacher gave each of us a *sheet* of paper.– The ground and pavements were covered with a *sheet* of ice.

shelf *shelves*. A board or flat piece of metal fastened horizontally and used to put things on.–The cupboard has two *shelves* upon which to put dishes.

shell *shells, shelled, shelling.* 1. A hard outside covering, as on nuts, vegetables, animals, and eggs. – Walnuts, peas, tortoises, lady-birds, oysters, and clams have *shells*.

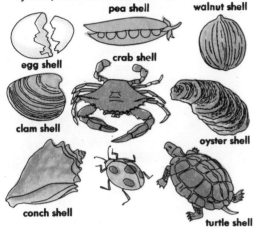

pea shell

walnut shell

egg shell

crab shell

clam shell

oyster shell

conch shell

turtle shell

2. Remove from a *shell*. – Mary *shelled* the peas. She took them out of the *shells* or pods.
3. The hull of a ship or boat, particularly a racing-boat.
4. A case holding gunpowder to be fired in a gun.
5. Fire *shells* at. – The soldiers *shelled* the enemy's lines until the enemy surrendered.
6. A framework.–Only the *shell* of the house is built so far.

she'll. A short way of writing 'she will.'–*She'll* be here by 3 o'clock.

shellac shel-lac'. A clear varnish-like liquid used in finishing woods, furniture. – Father put a coat of *shellac* on the bedroom floor.

shelter shel'-ter *shelters, sheltered, sheltering.* 1. A covering that shields or protects. – An umbrella is a *shelter* from the rain.–A roof is a *shelter* from weather.
2. Protection. – We found *shelter* from the storm in the old shed.
3. Protect or provide *shelter* for.–Grandfather didn't know he was *sheltering* thieves when he let the strangers sleep in the barn.

shelves *shelf*. More than one *shelf*.–We have 3 cupboard *shelves* to put dishes on.

shepherd shep'-herd *shepherds*. A man who takes care of sheep.

shepherdess shep'-herd-ess *shepherdesses*. A woman who takes care of sheep.

sherbet sher'-bet *sherbets*. An Eastern drink made of fruit juice, sugar and water cooled with snow. It is also a fizzy drink made of *sherbet*-powder, and flavoured.

sheriff sher'-iff *sheriffs*. In England, an official of the country or shire, appointed each year by the Crown.

she's. A short way of writing 'she is.'–*She's* 6 years old today.

shield *shields, shielded, shielding.* 1. Anything that protects or keeps one from harm. – The boy who stood in front of Baby to protect her from the flying stones was a *shield*.
2. A large plate of metal or wood carried on the arm to protect one in battle. – The knights of old carried *shields*.
3. Protect.–Father would not *shield* the thief from the policeman.

shift *shifts, shifted, shifting.* 1. Change position. –The boy *shifted* in his seat.
2. Exchange positions of.–Mary had her slippers on the wrong feet, so she *shifted* them.
3. A group of people who work during a certain time; also the period of time they work. –Father now works on the day *shift*. Next month Father will work on the night *shift*.
4. A change of position.–There are 2 *shifts* of position in the football teams.

shiftless shift'-less *shiftlessly, shiftlessness*. Lazy or good-for-nothing.–Because the girl was so *shiftless*, she was not promoted.

shilling shil'-ling *shillings*. A British silver coin, one-twentieth of a pound, now called a five pence piece.

shin *shins, shinned, shinning.* 1. The front part of the leg below the knee.–Bob skinned his *shin* when he fell off the box.
2. Bob can *shin* up a pole or tree. He pulls himself up by hugging the pole with his arms, then with his legs, while he reaches higher.

S
T
U
V
W
X
Y
Z

shine *shines, shined, shone, shining.* 1. Send or give out light.—The sun *shines.*

2. Polish or make bright.—Mary *shined* the knives and forks for Mother.

3. Look bright; reflect light.—Wax makes the furniture *shine.*

4. Be noticeably smart or bright.—Bob *shines* in arithmetic.

5. Clear or bright weather. – Rain or *shine,* the postman delivers the mail.

shingle shin'-gle *shingles, shingled, shingling.*

1. One of many thin pieces of wood, thicker at one end, that are used to cover roofs and sometimes outside walls. The thick end of one *shingle* laps over the thin end of another, to keep out water. *Shingles* made of fireproof materials are the same thickness from end to end.

2. Small round pebbles.—The beach was covered with *shingle.*

3. Put *shingles* on.—Grandfather *shingled* his barn.

4. Cut (hair) quite short.—During the summer, Mary has her hair *shingled.*

shiny shin'-y *shinier, shiniest.* Bright and glistening.—The tinsel on the Christmas tree is *shiny.*

ship *ships, shipped, shipping.* 1. A large vessel that sails on the seas. – In olden times, *ships* were moved by wind blowing on the sails.

2. A *ship's* company. A contented crew is a happy *ship.*

3. Send.—We shipped the package by mail.

4. Go as a member of a *ship's* crew.—The sailor has *shipped* on the same vessel for many years.

shipment ship'-ment *shipments.* Goods sent at one time to a certain place.—We expect a *shipment* of coal today.

shipwreck ship'-wreck *shipwrecks, shipwrecked.* Destruction or loss of a ship.—A big windstorm at sea caused the *shipwreck.*

shipyard ship'-yard *shipyards.* Place where ships are built or repaired.—A new keel was put on the old schooner at the *shipyard.*

shirk *shirks, shirked, shirking.* Fail to do one's duty.—A lazy person often *shirks.*

shirt *shirts.* Cloth garment worn on the upper part of the body by boys and men. – Mother told Bob to buy himself a new *shirt* for the party.

shiver shiv'-er *shivers, shivered, shivering, shivery.* Shake or quiver from cold, fright, or excitement. – The boy who didn't wear his overcoat *shivered.*

shoal *shoals.* A place where the water is shallow.—The wind blew the boats into the *shoal.*

shock *shocks, shocked, shocking.* 1. A sudden jar or blow.—The *shock* of the collision with the other car made Father speechless.

2. Something very upsetting or disturbing.—When the man's house burned, it was a great *shock* to him.

3. The feeling caused by electricity passing through a person. – When Bob touched the broken electric wire, he got a *shock.* – An electric *shock* can be very dangerous.

4. Upset, disturb, or offend.—The boy's dishonesty *shocked* the grocer.

5. Bundles of straw or grain.—The farmer put the wheat into *shocks.* After the wheat was cut, he stood about 12 bundles or sheeves on end together in a group or *shock,* so that the rain would run off them.

S T U V W X Y Z

shod. One form of the word *shoe.*–A black-smith *shod* the horses. He put shoes on them.

shoe *shoes, shod, shoeing.* 1. A covering for the feet.–Most *shoes* are made of leather.

2. A curved strip of iron nailed to the hoofs of a draught animal, such as a horse. It protects the hoofs just as a person's *shoe* protects his foot.
3. Provide with *shoes.*–The blacksmith *shoes* horses. He fastens horse*shoes* to their hoofs.

shoemaker shoe'-mak-er *shoemakers.* A person who makes or repairs shoes. – When Bob's shoes needed repair, he took them to a *shoe-maker.*

shone. One form of the word *shine.* – Mary rubbed the big red apple until it *shone.*

shoo *shoos, shooed, shooing.* 1. A sound made to scare away animals.–The farmer says *shoo* when he wants to chase the chickens away.
2. Scare away by shouting. – The farmer *shooed* the chickens from his garden.

shook. One form of the word *shake.*–The boys *shook* the apple tree to make the apples fall.

shoot *shoots, shot, shooting.* 1. Fire (a gun).– The hunter knew just when to *shoot.*
2. Hit with an arrow or bullet.–The hunter tried to *shoot* a squirrel.
3. Move very fast. – I saw the dog *shoot* through the door after the cat.
4. A small branch.–The bush has many new *shoots,* now that spring has come.
5. Send (a ball, arrow, or the like) swiftly and with force.–The footballer *shoots* the ball into the net.

shop *shops, shopped, shopping.* 1. A small store.–Mother went to the hat *shop* to buy a new hat.
2. A place where things are made.–Father works in a machine *shop.*

3. Look at and buy things in shops or stores. –We *shop* every Saturday for groceries.

shopkeeper shop'-keep-er *shopkeepers.* A person who runs a shop.–The *shopkeeper* showed us several pocket-books.

shore *shores.* Land along the edge of an ocean, lake, or stream.–After the storm, we found many beautiful shells swept up on the *shore.*

shorn. One form of the word *shear.*–All the farmer's sheep have been *shorn.*

short *shorter, shortest.* 1. Not long; little in height or length.–The pencil has been sharpened so many times that it is very *short.*–A man is tall, and a little boy is *short.*–The children went for a *short* walk.
2. Having less than the right or needed amount.–We ran *short* of sugar when Mother bottled the fruit. – My change from the grocer was sixpence *short.*
3. Suddenly.–Father put on the brakes and we stopped *short.*
4. So brief as to be almost rude.–Jack was rather *short* with Mary when she asked him the same question for a third time.
5. Crisp, rich, and crumbly (of baked goods). –Mother puts lard in the pastry to make it *short.*–*Short* pastry is tender and flaky.

shortbread short'-bread *shortbreads.* A hard crisp biscuit or cake made with flour, butter and sugar, mixed so that it is short when baked.

S
T
U
V
W
X
Y
Z

shorten short′-en *shortens, shortened, shorten-ing.* Make shorter, or less long.–The sleeves in Mary's new coat were too long, so Mother had to *shorten* them.

shortening short′-en-ing. Fat used in baking to make the dough crisp, rich, and crumbly.–Butter and lard are two kinds of *shortening.*

shorthand short′-hand. A system of writing words quickly by using little marks some-thing like the ones in the picture. The marks stand for sounds, or for whole words or groups of words.

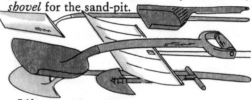

shortly short′-ly. 1. In a short time; very soon. –We are going home *shortly,* for it is getting late.
2. Very briefly, so as to be almost rude.– Bill answered us *shortly* when we asked him where he got the bicycle he was riding.

short-sighted short-sight′-ed *short-sightedness.* Unable to see far-away objects clearly.–Jill is rather *short-sighted.* She has to wear glasses to strengthen her eyes.

shot *shots.* 1. One form of the word *shoot.*–The hunter *shot* the rabbit with his gun.–The men *shot* at a circle on a post.
2. The tiny balls of lead used in cartridges for *shot*guns.
3. The noise made when a gun is fired.–The soldiers heard *shots* from the enemy's guns.
4. A marksman.–The men werent' very good *shots,* for no one hit the circle.
5. A throw, a strike or a try at doing some-thing.–When Father drove the golf ball a long way, he made a good *shot.*

should. 1. Ought to.–You *should* drink more milk for your health.
2. Expect to.–I told her that I *should* eat lunch before going to the park.
3. Would.–I *should* have been glad to help you if you had asked me, but you didn't.

shoulder shoul′-der *shoulders, shouldered, shoul-dering.* 1. The part of the body to which the arms of a person or the front legs of a 4-footed animal are joined. – The soldier carried his gun on his *shoulder.*
2. The part of a dress or coat that fits over a person's *shoulders.* – The *shoulder* seam on Bob's coat is ripped apart.
3. Take upon oneself.–The teacher was not

willing to *shoulder* the responsibility of tak-ing the children unless they had the consent of their parents.
4. Pick up and carry on one's *shoulder.*–Bob *shouldered* Sally and marched down the hall with her.

shout *shouts, shouted, shouting.* 1. Yell, or call out loudly.–The teacher told the children to talk softly, not to *shout.*
2. Yell or loud call.–We heard the *shout* of the paper-boy.

shove *shoves, shoved, shoving.* 1. Push.–The children *shoved* each other to get into the front row.
2. A push.–Bill gave Jack a *shove* and he fell off the diving-board.

shovel shov′-el *shovels, shovelled, shovelling.* 1. A tool used to lift and move snow, coal, earth, or the like.–Father uses a *shovel* to put coal into the boiler.–Baby has a toy *shovel* for the sand-pit.

2. Lift up with a *shovel* and put somewhere else.–The boys *shovelled* the snow from the paths.

show *shows, showed, showing.* 1. Allow to look; allow or cause to be seen.–I will *show* you my stamp collection.–Mother *showed* pleasure at the compliment.
2. Be visible.–Mother's slip was longer than her dress, so it *showed.*
3. Teach by doing.–Our teacher *showed* us how to make a kite. She taught us by letting us watch her do it first.
4. Point out to.–The assistant *showed* us where to buy stockings.
5. A display, or a place where things are taken to be looked at and admired.–We are going to a dog *show.* The finest dogs will get prizes.
6. An entertainment.–We went to the cartoon film *show.* We saw Donald Duck.

showcase show′-case *showcase.* A glass case where things are put so that they can be seen or looked at.– We saw the rings and watches in the *showcase* in the jew-eller's window.

shower show'-er *showers, showered, showering.*
1. A short rainstorm.– We had a *shower* this morning.
2. Anything that falls like a *shower* of rain.– A *shower* of paper came from the windows.
3. Drop, or rain down.–The children *showered* rice upon the bride and groom.–It *showered* this morning.
4. A bath in which water is *showered* down from above.–Bob takes a *shower* when he gets up in the morning.

shown. One form of the word *show.*–The books were *shown* to the children.

shrank. One form of the word *shrink.*–Mary's dress *shrank* when it was washed.

shred *shreds, shredded, shredding.* 1. Narrow strip or rag.–The old flag was burned because it was worn into *shreds.*
2. Cut into small strips.–Mother *shredded* the cabbage.
3. Bit.–Not one *shred* of food was left after the picnic.

shriek *shrieks, shrieked, shrieking.* 1. A scream; a loud piercing sound like one made by a whistle, or a person who is afraid, hurt, or angry.
2. Make this noise.–The train whistle *shrieked* as it passed.

shrill *shrills, shrilled, shrilling.* 1. High and piercing in tone.–Whistles and alarm bells make *shrill* sounds.
2. Make a *shrill* sound.–The birds *shrilled* loudly. They called out in high, sharp voices.

shrimp *shrimps.* 1. A kind of small shellfish.– The meat of *shrimps* is good to eat.
2. A little person (often used scornfully). – Jack's feelings were hurt when the big boys called him a *shrimp.*

shrine *shrines.* Any place or thing that is sacred or holy or held in reverence.–The *shrine* of St Thomas à Becket is in Canterbury Cathedral.–We knelt beside the *shrine* in the churchyard.

shrink *shrinks, shrank, shrunk, shrinking.* 1. Become or make smaller.–If Baby's stockings *shrink* when they are washed, she will not be able to wear them.
2. Draw back or away.–The horse is so afraid that it *shrinks* every time it sees a whip.

shrivel shriv'-el *shrivels, shrivelled, shrivelling.* Dry up; wrinkle; wither.–The old apples were *shrivelled.*

shrub *shrubs.* A bush or low tree with many stems that come from the ground instead of from a trunk, as those of most trees do.– *Shrubs* are used around houses and in gardens to make them beautiful.

shrubbery shrub'-ber-y. A group of low bushes or shrubs.

shrug *shrugs, shrugged, shrugging.* 1. A raising of the shoulders to show that one is not sure about something, or does not care, or does not like something.
2. Raise the shoulders in a *shrug.*–When the teacher asked Bill a question, he *shrugged* his shoulders.

shrunk. One form of the word *shrink.*–After Mother washed Mary's dress, she found that it had *shrunk.*

shrunken shrunk'-en. Dried up, withered.–The old man's face was *shrunken,* but his eyes were bright.

shudder shud'-der *shudders, shuddered, shuddering.* 1. A trembling or shaking caused by fear, horror, disgust, or the like.–Mother gave a *shudder* when Sally showed her the little mouse.
2. Tremble with fear, horror, or disgust.–The ghost story Jack told made us all *shudder.*

shuffle shuf'-fle *shuffles, shuffled, shuffling.* 1. Walk, barely lifting the feet.–The old man was so tired that he just *shuffled* along.
2. Mix up (cards).–Bob likes to *shuffle* the cards when we play card games.
3. A dragging movement of the feet.–The old man was so tired that he walked with a *shuffle.*
4. A mixing of cards.–Before Mary's deal she gave the cards a good *shuffle.*

S
T
U
V
W
X
Y
Z

shun *shuns, shunned, shunning.* Keep away from or avoid.–Father *shuns* driving during times when there is heavy traffic.

shut *shuts, shutting.* 1. Close.–Please *shut* the door when you leave.
2. Keep out.–The window-pane *shuts* out the rain.–Do not *shut* the new boy out of your games.
3. Imprison or close in.–Father *shut* the dog in the garage for the night.
4. Closed.–The shop seems to be *shut*, for there is no light inside.–Baby's eyes are *shut*; she must be asleep.
5. Close up.–We have *shut* up our country cottage for the winter.
6. Turn off.–Father forgot to *shut* off the water while he mended the tap, and flooded the kitchen.

shutter shut'-ter *shutters.* A cover for a window, usually on the outside. *Shutters* are generally made of many slats fastened across a frame, and swing on hinges.– –We live in a white house with green *shutters*.

shuttle shut'-tle *shuttles, shuttled, shuttling.* 1. A sliding thread holder that is used in weaving cloth. The *shuttle* holds the spool of thread that is thrown from side to side between the lengthwise threads.
2. On a sewing machine, the part into which the bobbin or spool that holds the lower thread is put.–The *shuttle* goes back and forth when you sew.

shuttle-cock shut'-tle-cock *shuttle-cocks.* A small piece of cork or plastic fitted with a ring of feathers, used in the game of battledore and *shuttlecock* and also in badminton.

shy *shies, shied, shying, shyer, shyest.* 1. Bashful, uneasy in front of people, especially strangers.–Baby is *shy*.
2. Easily frightened. – Birds are very *shy*. They fly away if you come too near them.
3. Jump to one side, jump away from.–The horse *shied* when he heard the whistle of the train.
4. Avoid, shrink away.–Mary is apt to *shy* away from difficult tasks.

shyness shy'-ness. Bashfulness.–The boy's *shyness* was caused by the fact that he was not used to playing with other children.

sick. 1. Not well; ill.–Grandmother is *sick* today. She has a bad cold.–When people have measles, or any other disease, they are *sick*.
2. People who are ill.–Many *sick* are cared for in hospitals.
3. *Sick* in the stomach.–Sally often gets *sick* from riding in the car.
4. Tired, bored.–Jack is *sick* of working on his model boat.
5. Miserable.–The girl is *sick* with longing to see her family.–Mother was *sick* with worry the night Jack was late coming home.

sickle sick'-le *sickles.* A farm tool with a sharp, curved blade set into a short handle; it is used for cutting grass.–The farmer cut the grass round the barn with a *sickle*.

sickness sick'-ness. Illness; bad health. –The man's *sickness* was caused by bad food.

side *sides, sided, siding.* 1. Edge; outline.–Father put rails round the *sides* of the veranda so that Baby could not fall off.

2. Not the front, back, top, or bottom, but one of the other two *sides*.–There are portholes in the *sides* of a ship.–The broken window is on the other *side* of the house.
3. A particular face or *side* of anything.–Print your name and age and the date on the other *side* of your picture.
4. A section or part.–Father has to drive to the other *side* of the town to get to work.
5. An opinion, position, or part in a game, argument, or fight.–Which *side* are you on in the discussion? Whom do you agree with?–Our *side* won the spelling bee.
6. Take the part of, stand up for.–Bob usually *sides* with Jack in a quarrel with the other boys; he is on Jack's *side*.

sideboard side'-board *sideboards.* A piece of furniture usually placed against a wall in a dining-room, used for holding plates, glasses and cutlery.–Mother keeps our best dinner service in the *sideboard*.

side-saddle side'-sad-dle. Riding sideways, not across the saddle.–Ladies in skirts ride horses *side-saddle*.

sideways side-ways. Towards the side, not towards the front or back.–Look *sideways* before crossing the street.

S
T
U
V
W
X
Y
Z

sieve *sieves.* A utensil used for separating finer from coarser particles. A mesh in the base of the *sieve* allows the finer particles to fall through but not the coarser.–Mother sifts flour through a *sieve* to get the lumps out of it.–Father shakes earth in a *sieve* to remove the stones and get fine soil for his seeds.

sift *sifts, sifted, sifting.* Strain, or put through a screened frame like a sieve, to separate smaller pieces from larger ones.–The workmen *sifted* the gravel.–Mother *sifts* the flour before baking.

sigh *sighs, sighed, sighing.* 1. Breathe out a deep, long breath to show that one is tired, sad, or glad that something has happened or is finished.–Mother *sighs* over the holes in Jack's sweaters.
2. A sound like sighing.–We heard the *sigh* of the wind as it blew through the treetops.

sight *sights, sighted, sighting.* 1. Power or ability to see.–People and animals have *sight.* They can see.–Father wears glasses when he reads to aid his *sight.*
2. Something to see.–The flower gardens are a beautiful *sight.*
3. Something seen.–The girl was very happy at the *sight* of her new doll.
4. Aim.–The man *sighted* on the target and then pulled the trigger on his gun.
5. A little piece of metal on the upper side of a gun barrel which helps in aiming at the target.
6. A glimpse; a short look at. – Mother caught *sight* of the children hiding in the barn.
7. The distance that one can see.–The aeroplane is now out of *sight.*
8. See.–We *sighted* the tall buildings long before we reached the city.

sign *signs, signed, signing.* 1. A mark or movement used to stand for or mean something.–A red cross on a white background is the *sign* of the Red Cross.–The *sign* for adding is + ; – is the *sign* for subtracting.–A nod of the head is a *sign* that one says 'yes.'
2. A board with lettering on it to advertise goods, name the owner of a shop or office, or tell anything else to people who see it.–Road *signs* say 'Slow,' '10 Miles to York,' etc.

3. A thing that tells that something exists, is about to happen, or has happened.–The first swallow is a *sign* that summer will soon be here.
4. Write one's name on.–I *signed* the letter.

signal sig'-nal *signals, signalled, signalling.* 1. A sign or indication to do something, or that something is about to happen, or has happened.–A green traffic light is the go *signal.*

–The caretaker gave the fire-drill *signal.* He rang the bell 5 times.
2. Tell by means of a *signal.*–The policeman *signalled* the driver to slow down.

signature sig'-na-ture *signatures.* 1. One's own name, written by oneself.–The teacher put her *signature* on Bob's excuse to go home when he felt ill.

signed by:
Hazel Jacobson

2. A sign written at the beginning of music to tell the time and the key in which the music is written.–The children looked at the *signature* before starting to sing the music.

significance sig-nif'-i-cance 1. A meaning.–The children did not know the *significance* of the bell ringing at 11 o'clock.–Do you know the *significance* of Easter?
2. Importance.–Father got a letter of great *significance* to his business.

significant sig-nif'-i-cant *significantly.* 1. Important.–The headmaster made a *significant* statement today. He said there would be no school tomorrow.
2. Carrying meaning; having meaning. – Father and Mother exchange many *significant* looks round Christmas time.

signify sig'-ni-fy *signifies, signified, signifying.* 1. Mean.–A red traffic light *signifies* danger. –This sign * next to a word usually *signifies* a note at the bottom of the page.
2. Make known; express.–If you are pleased with the music, *signify* it by clapping your hands.

S
T
U
V
W
X
Y
Z

signpost sign′ post *signposts*. A post with a sign or message fastened to it.– The sign on the *signpost* read, 'Berwick-upon-Tweed 25 miles.'

silence si′-lence *silences, silenced, silencing*. 1. A stillness, quietness, or absence of noise or sound.–The *silence* of the country is restful after the noise of the city.
2. Make quiet or make still.–Mother *silenced* Baby's crying by feeding her.

silent si′-lent *silently*. 1. Quiet; still; without sound.–The children were *silent* while their teacher read to them.–In *silent* reading we do not say the words out loud. We read to ourselves.
2. Not pronounced.–The 'e' in the word 'make' is *silent*. It is not pronounced.

silk *silken, silkiness*. 1. A kind of fine, shiny thread made by silkworms. These threads are woven into cloth which is called *silk*.
2. Made of *silk* thread or cloth. – Mother wears *silk* stockings.–Father wears *silk* ties.

silkworm silk′-worm *silkworms*. A caterpillar that makes a cocoon of silken threads from which silk is made.–*Silkworms* eat mulberry leaves.

silky silk′-y *silkier, silkiest*. Smooth, fine, soft, and shiny; like silk.–Baby's hair is *silky*.

sill *sills*. A ledge or shelf across the bottom of the frame of a window, door, or building.– Mary set the plants on the window-*sill,* where they would get the sun. – Today Mother scrubbed the door *sill*.–When the men pulled down the house, they found that the *sills* were rotten.

silly sil′-ly *sillier, silliest*. Foolish, giddy.–The children were playing a *silly* game. It didn't make much sense but it was a lot of fun.

silo si′-lo *silos*. A tall, round, tower-like building made of wood, stone, cement, or brick. Sometimes a *silo* is a large hole in the ground.–The farmer puts green food or grain in a *silo* to keep it for his cows. Air cannot get to the grain in a *silo* and so it does not spoil.

silver sil′-ver. 1. A kind of soft, whitish, valuable metal.–Some knives, forks, and spoons are made of *silver*.–*Silver* shines when it is polished.–Dishes, vases, money, and jewellery are often made of *silver*.
2. Made of *silver*.–I have a *silver* spoon.
3. Bright, pale grey, shining like *silver*.– Grandfather has *silver* hair.

silverware sil′-ver-ware. Knives, forks, spoons, and other tableware made out of silver.– Mary put the *silverware* on the table for Mother.

similar sim′-i-lar *similarly*. Very much alike; about the same.–Mary did not buy the dress, because it was so *similar* to the one she had.

simple sim′-ple *simpler, simplest*. 1. Easy to understand.–This dictionary is very *simple*.
2. Plain; not fancy; not trimmed much.– Mary's new dress is quite *simple*.
3. Sincere; not deceitful.–Grandmother is a very *simple* person. She is good and sincere. She doesn't try to fool you in any way.
4. Weak-minded; stupid.–The clown pretended to be *simple*.

simpleton sim′-ple-ton *simpletons*. A very stupid or weak-minded person.–Simple Simon in the nursery rhyme is a *simpleton*.

simplicity sim-plic′-i-ty. Plainness; quality of being simple, or of being not complicated.– The *simplicity* of the arithmetic problems made Jack smile. He thought they were too easy.

simply sim′-ply. 1. Plainly.–The woman was dressed *simply*.
2. Just.–It is easy to find our house; you *simply* turn left at the next corner.

sin *sins, sinned, sinning*. A wrong-doing; a bad act or deed.–It is a *sin* to kill, steal, or do any other evil thing.

since. 1. From that time until now.–Grandmother came on Sunday, and it has rained ever *since*.
2. At some time between that time and now. –Yesterday Father said he could not go, but *since* then he has changed his mind.
3. Before now; ago.–The postman has passed our house long *since*.

4. Ever after.–Bob has felt much better *since* he got over his cold.

5. Because; seeing that.–*Since* it is your birthday, you may stay up an hour later.

sincere sin-cere' *sincerely*. Honest; not deceitful.–Grandmother is a very *sincere* person. She doesn't try to fool you in any way.

sinew sin'-ew *sinews, sinewy*. A cord which fastens muscles to bones.–Bob strained the *sinews* in his ankle when he slipped.

sinful sin'-ful *sinfully, sinfulness*. Evil; wicked. –The man is *sinful*. He does evil, wicked deeds.

sing *sings, sang, sung, singing*. 1. Make music with the voice.–The teacher plays the piano when the children *sing*.–Sometimes they hum and sometimes they *sing* the words.

2. Make a humming or whistling sound.– When the kettle makes a humming sound. we say that it *sings*.–Birds *sing*, too.

singe *singes, singed, singeing*. Burn slightly.– When Mother got her fur coat too near the fire, she *singed* the fur.

singer sing'-er *singers*. A person who makes music with the voice.

single sin'-gle *singly, singles, singled, singling*. 1. One.–A *single* cake was left on the plate. 2. Made for one only; having one.–We have a *single* garage. It holds one car only. 3. Not married.–The woman is *single*. 4. A hit in cricket which allows the batsman to get one run.–Jack's *single* brought the team's score up to 100. 5. Pick.–The policeman *singled* out one car that was speeding and arrested the driver.

singular sin'-gu-lar *singularly*. 1. Only one.– The word 'boy' is *singular*; it means only one boy. If we mean more than one boy, we say 'boys.' 2. Strange; queer.–It is very *singular* that the cat was able to get into the house when all the doors were closed.

sink *sinks, sank, sinking*. 1. A basin with a pipe to drain off whatever is poured in. – Mary poured the water out of the glass into the kitchen *sink*. 2. Go down. – Boats sometimes *sink* to the bottom of the sea. 3. Fall slowly.–The old man was so weak that he *sank* to the floor.

sinker sink'-er *sinkers*. A small piece of lead put on the end of a fishing line to pull the hook deep into the water.

sinner sin'-ner *sinners*. A person who does bad or wrong things.

sip *sips, sipped, sipping*. 1. Drink slowly in small amounts.–Do not drink iced water too fast. *Sip* it. 2. A small drink; swallow.–Take a *sip* of this lemonade.

sir. A title of honour or respect used in speaking to older men or officers of the army or navy. –Bob said to the policeman, 'Will you help me, *Sir*?'–Mary started her business letter with the words 'Dear *Sir*.'

siren si'-ren *sirens*. A kind of whistle which makes a loud noise by whirling round.– The ship blew a loud blast on the *siren* before sailing.–The factory *siren* sounds at lunchtime.

sirloin sir'-loin *sirloins*. The upper part of a loin of beef.–Mother bought a *sirloin* of beef for Sunday dinner.

sister sis'-ter *sisters*. 1. A girl or woman born of the same parents as another person.–Mary is Bob's *sister*. Mary and Bob have the same father and mother. 2. A nun in the Catholic Church. 3. A senior nurse in a hospital.

sister-in-law sis'-ter-in-law *sisters-in-law*. The sister of one's wife or husband, or the wife of one's brother.–Your mother's sister is your father's *sister-in-law*.–Your father's sister is your mother's *sister-in-law*.–The wife of your mother's brother is your mother's *sister-in-law*.–The wife of your father's brother is your father's *sister-in-law*.

sit *sits, sat, sitting*. 1. Rest on the backs of the thighs or upper part of the legs. Bob *sits* in a big chair. 2. Remain, stand, lie, perch, etc.–Chickens *sit* on a roost at night.

site *sites*. A location; place to put a building or other structure.–A new post office will be built on this *site*.

situated sit'-u-at-ed. Located or placed.–An old house is *situated* on top of the hill.

S
T
U
V
W
X
Y
Z

situation sit-u-a′-tion *situations*. Set of conditions. – When Mother returned home, she found a bad *situation*; the meat had burned, Baby was sick, and the dog had chewed up a pillow.

six. The number (6) after five and before seven.

sixpence six′-pence. A British silver coin, one-fortieth of a pound, now used as a 2½ pence piece.

sixteen six′-teen′. The number (16) after fifteen and before seventeen.–Six added to ten equals *sixteen*.

sixteenth six′-teenth′. 1. One of 16 equal parts. –If a meal is divided into 16 equal parts, each part is called one-*sixteenth*.
2. Coming after fifteen and before seventeen in a series.–The *sixteenth* soldier in the line was out of step.

sixth. 1. One of 6 equal parts.–If a pie is divided into 6 equal parts, each part is called one-*sixth*.

2. Coming after five and before seven in a series.–June is the *sixth* month of the year.

sixtieth six′-ti-eth. 1. One of 60 equal parts.– One part of anything divided into 60 equal parts is called one-*sixtieth*.
2. Coming after fifty-nine and before sixty-one in a series.–Grandmother celebrated her *sixtieth* birthday yesterday.

sixty six′-ty. The number (60) after 59 and before 61.–*Sixty* eggs are five dozen eggs.

size *sizes*. *Size* is the bigness or smallness of a thing. It is the amount of room or space a thing takes up.–The *size* of an elephant is large compared with the *size* of a dog.–I wear *size* 5 shoes and *size* 6 gloves.

skate *skates, skated, skating*. 1. A short runner attached to each shoe for gliding over ice.
2. Glide on *skates* or roller *skates*.–Bob likes to *skate* on the pond in the winter.

3. A roller *skate*; a platform with 4 wheels attached to the shoe for rolling over any smooth surface.

skater skat′-er *skaters*. A person who skates.– Bob is a good *skater*.

skein (pronounced *skayn*). An amount of wool put up in long loops. –Mary helped to wind a *skein* of wool into a ball.

skeleton skel′-e-ton *skeletons*. 1. A bony framework. – This picture shows the *skeleton* of a person's body.
2. A framework of any kind.–The *skeleton* of a house is of wood.

skeleton key skel′-e-ton key *skeleton keys*. A key which opens many different locks.

sketch *sketches, sketched, sketching*. 1. Draw a rough picture or outline of.–Bob *sketched* the aeroplane.
2. A rough drawing.–He showed the *sketch* of the plane to Father.
3. A short play or story.–The children gave some little *sketches* about school life.

ski (pronounced *skee* or *she*) *skis, skied, skiing*. 1. One of 2 long wooden runners that are fastened to the boots for gliding over snow.

2. Glide on *skis*.–It is fun to *ski*.

skid *skids, skidded, skidding*. 1. Slip or slide.– Do not put on the brakes too quickly when driving on icy roads, or your car may *skid*.
2. A beam or plank on which something is held in position. – The boat was placed on *skids* for repairing.

skilful skil′-ful *skilfully*. Expert, having much ability. – A *skilful* workman knows much about his work and does it well.

skill *skills*. Ability to do a certain thing well as a result of practice.–Bob shows much *skill* at football.

skillet skil'-let *skillets*. A heavy, shallow, metal pan with a long handle. – A *skillet* is used for frying foods.

skim *skims, skimmed, skimming*. 1. Take off from the top. – Mary helped Grandmother *skim* the cream from the milk.
2. The milk that is left after the cream is *skimmed* off is skimmed milk.
3. Move lightly over.–The speedboat just *skimmed* the water.–The skaters *skimmed* smoothly over the ice.
4. Read hurriedly and not thoroughly.–Bob *skimmed* through the story just to get an idea of what it was about.

skimp *skimps, skimped, skimping, skimpy*. 1. Save carefully. – Mother has to *skimp* to make her money last all the week.
2. Provide or use too little of. – Bob told Mother not to *skimp* the icing on the cake.

skin *skins, skinned, skinning*. 1. The outer covering of the body of a person, animal, vegetable, or fruit.–If you cut through the *skin* on your hand, it will bleed.–Bob cut off the *skin*, or peel, of the orange.

2. Rub off the *skin* of.–Mary *skinned* her arm when she ran into the stone wall.
3. Take the *skin* from.–The butcher *skinned* the rabbit so that it could be cooked.

skinny skin-'-ny. Thin; lean; not fat.–The hungry cat is *skinny*.

skip *skips, skipped, skipping*. 1. Jump or move with little hopping steps.–Children like to *skip* over a rope.–The girls *skipped* to the music.
2. Pass over.–Bob was so anxious to finish the book that he *skipped* some pages. He didn't read them.

skipper skip'-per *skippers*. A commander of a boat or ship.–Bob stood on the bridge with the *skipper*.

skirt *skirts, skirted, skirting*. 1. The part of a dress that hangs from the waist down. – Mary wears a sweater and *skirt*.
2. Pass along the outer edge of.–We *skirted* the city to avoid the heavy traffic.

skull *skulls*. The bones of the head that form a case for the brain. – The man's *skull* was fractured in the accident.

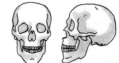

skunk *skunks*. A small American animal with black fur with white stripes down the back, and a bushy tail. *Skunks* protect themselves by giving off a very unpleasant odour when they are frightened or hurt.

sky *skies*. The air high above us.–On clear days, the *sky* looks blue.–Birds fly high in the *sky*.–The *sky* is often called heaven, or the heavens.

sky-rocket sky'-rock-et *sky-rockets*. A firework on a stick that shoots high into the sky and then explodes.–On Guy Fawkes night, we shot off many *sky-rockets*.

sky-scraper sky'-scrap-er *sky-scrapers*. A very tall building.–New York is a city with many *sky-scrapers*.

slack. 1. Loose. – The rope-walker said the rope was too *slack* to walk on; it was not tight.
2. Quiet, not active.– Father has enough work to do in winter, but in summer his work is *slack*.
3. Careless. – We were *slack* about getting our arithmetic papers in on time.
4. Looseness, or loose part. – When the dog ran, he took up the *slack* in the rope.
5. trousers (always plural). Men and women often wear *slacks* for sport, and also casual dress.

slacken slack'-en *slackens, slackened, slackening.* 1. Slow down.–Much work must still be done, so do not *slacken* now.–When one is tired, one's energy *slackens*.
2. Become loose.–When it rains, the clothes-line tightens. When it is dry, it *slackens*.

slain *slay, slays, slew, slaying.* Killed roughly and suddenly.–The bear was *slain* by the hunter.–Many men were *slain* in the battle.

slam *slams, slammed, slamming.* 1. Shut with a bang or with much force.–Do not *slam* the door.
2. A noise made by *slamming.* – We knew Jack had come home, for we heard the *slam* of the front door.

slang. Made-up words and expressions that are used chiefly in talk.–The sleepy man said, 'It's time to hit the hay.' He meant it was time to go to bed.–'Step on it!' is *slang* for 'Hurry!'

slant *slants, slanted, slanting.* 1. Slope.–Most roofs *slant*.–The flagpole stands straight up, but the roof *slants* downwards from the top.
2. A leaning to one side.–Mother writes without any *slant* to her letters. She writes straight up and down.

slap *slaps, slapped, slapping.* 1. Hit with the open hand. – When the dog got on to the chair, Mother *slapped* him gently to teach him not to do it.
2. A blow with the open hand.–Mother gave the dog a *slap*.

slash *slashes, slashed, slashing.* 1. A long cut or slit.–The Boy Scouts' tent had a *slash* in one side, and the rain came in.
2. To cut. – Someone *slashed* the tent accidentally with a knife.

slat *slats.* A thin, narrow bar of wood or metal. – Grandfather nailed some *slats* across the chicken coop to keep the chickens in.–Bed-springs are sometimes held up by *slats*.

slate *slates.* 1. A smooth blue-grey rock that splits into thin layers. – Our blackboard is made of *slate*.
2. A framed square of *slate*. – When Father went to school, the children used *slates* to write on.
3. Bluish-grey.– Mother has a *slate*-coloured suit.

slaughter slaugh'-ter *slaughters, slaughtered, slaughtering.* 1. Kill, butcher. – The farmer *slaughtered* a lamb today.
2. Killing or butchering.–The farmer led the lamb to the *slaughter*.

slave *slaves.* 1. A person who is owned by another person and can be sold by that person. –A *slave* had to work without pay.–There are no *slaves* in America any more.
2. Work as hard as a *slave* does.–The mother *slaves* for her children.

slavery slav'-ery. 1. Condition of a slave.–The captives of the ancient army were sold into *slavery*.
2. The owning of slaves.–*Slavery* was abolished in America during the Civil War.

slavish sla'-vish *slavishly.* Obedient, like a slave.–One should not be a *slavish* follower of fashion.

slay *slays, slew, slain, slaying.* Kill with force. –The stained-glass window shows St George *slaying* the dragon.

slayer slay'-er *slayers.* A person who kills another. – The police are tracking down the *slayer*.

sledge *sledges, sledged, sledging.* 1. A low platform on runners that slides easily over snow.–Children like to coast on a *sledge*.
2. Ride on a *sledge*.–We went *sledging* after the snowfall.

sledge-hammer sledge'-hammer *sledge-hammers.* A heavy hammer for driving in posts, large nails, etc.

sleek *sleekly, sleekness.* Smooth and glossy.– The kitten's fur is *sleek*.

sleep *sleeps, slept, sleeping.* 1. To slumber, rest the mind and body.–When we *sleep* at night, we close our eyes.
2. Slumber or rest.–Father had only 4 hours' *sleep* last night because he got to bed so late.

sleeper sleep'-er *sleepers*. 1. A person sleeping. –Mother was never a late *sleeper*.
2. A railway carriage that has berths, or beds, for sleeping. –Father made the long railway trip in a *sleeper*.
3. A wooden support for a rail.

sleepless sleep'-less *sleeplessly, sleeplessness*. Restless; wakeful; without sleep. –It was so hot that Mother had a *sleepless* night.

sleepy sleep'-y *sleepier, sleepiest*. Drowsy; ready to go to sleep. –When Baby is *sleepy*, Mother puts her to bed.

sleet *sleety*. Rain that freezes into tiny pieces of ice as it falls. –*Sleet* covered the streets and made them very slippery. –*Sleet* rattled on the window-panes.

sleeve *sleeves*. The part of a coat, dress, or other garment that covers the arm.

sleeveless sleeve'-less. Without sleeves; ending at the shoulder of the garment. –Men's waist-coats are *sleeveless*.

sleigh (pronounced *slay*) *sleighs*. A large sledge. *Sleighs* are large sledges pulled by horses.

slender slen'-der *slenderness*. Thin, slim. –Aunt is *slender*, but Uncle is stout.

slept. One form of the word *sleep*. –Baby *slept* soundly all night.

slice *slices, sliced, slicing*. 1. A thin, flat piece. –Mother cut the watermelon into *slices*.
2. Cut into thin, flat pieces. –Mary *sliced* the bread for Mother.

slick *slicker, slickest, slickness, slickly*. Smart and skilful. –Bill is very *slick* with his hands.

slide *slides, slid, sliding*. 1. Anything on which something can move smoothly and easily. – The picture shows a *slide* for the children to go down.
2. Move smoothly and easily. –Children like to *slide* down a hill on their sledges.

3. A thin piece of glass on which there is a picture, which may be thrown on a screen by a projector. –Our teacher showed us some *slides* of animals at the zoo.

4. A small sheet of glass to put something on to look at through a microscope.

slight *slights, slighted, slighting*. 1. Slim; slender. –Grandmother is *slight*. She isn't stout.
2. Little; small; not great. – Mother has a *slight* cold. –There will be a *slight* charge for the work.
3. Neglect or give too little attention to.– Do not *slight* your work, or you may not pass.
4. Neglect, or treat rudely. –Bob felt *slighted*, because he was not asked to play.

slightly slight'-ly. Somewhat; a little. – It is *slightly* after 8 o'clock.

slim *slimmer, slimmest*. 1. Thin; slight; slender. –Mary has a *slim* waist. She does not measure much round her waist.
2. Small; slight. –We have a *slim* chance of winning the game if Bob does not play.

slime. Soft, slippery mud, or any other damp, soft, slippery substance. –Snails and snakes leave a trail of wet, shiny, sticky matter called *slime*.

sling *slings, slung, slinging*. 1. A device for throwing stones or other small objects. It is made of 2 cords joined by a piece of leather or cloth which holds the stone while the cords are whirled round in the air. –A catapult is a kind of sling, where the stone is shot by the force of rubber bands.
2. A piece of cloth looped about the neck.– When Jack broke his arm, he carried it in a *sling*.
3. Hang.–When Jack goes on a hike, he *slings* his knapsack over his shoulder.
4. A chain or heavy rope used to lift heavy things.–Boats are unloaded with *slings*.

slip *slips, slipped, slipping.* 1. Slide; move quickly and smoothly.–The boy's shoes *slip* on easily.–Mother *slipped* into her dress.

2. Slide accidentally and fall. – The man *slipped* and fell on the icy street.–The dish *slipped* through my fingers and fell.

3. To cause to move quickly and easily.– Bob *slipped* the toffee into his pocket.

4. A mistake.–Do not make a *slip* of the tongue and tell Mother about her present.

5. Pass quickly.–The day at the farm *slipped* by before we knew it.

6. A cutting; little branches cut from other plants.–These plants grew from *slips*.

7. A woman's undergarment.–Mother wears a *slip* under her dress.

8. To move around quietly.–He *slipped* in and out without being seen.

slip-knot slip′-knot *slip-knots.* A knot made so that if you pull the cord, the knot will slide along the cord.

slipper slip′-per *slippers.* A light shoe that slips on to the foot easily.–Mother has silver evening *slippers*.

slippery slip′-per-y. Easy to slide or slip on; too smooth to get a firm hold on.–A waxed floor and an icy street are *slippery*.–Fish are *slippery*.

slit *slits, slitting.* 1. A straight cut, tear, or opening.–A ray of light streamed through the *slit* in the barn door.

2. Cut a long line in. – The doctor *slit* the soldier's coat so that he could dress his wounds.

sliver sliv′-er *slivers.* A long, thin piece of wood or metal that has been cut off or broken off a larger piece; a splinter.–Father got a *sliver* in his thumb while cutting wood.

slobber slob′-ber *slobbers, slobbered, slobbering.* Let saliva or liquid flow from the mouth. –Hounds *slobber* at the sight of food.

slogan slo′-gan *slogans.* A word, a group of words, or a saying used as a motto. – 'We work to win' is the *slogan* of our class.

sloop *sloops.* A sailing-boat with 1 mast and at least 1 mainsail and jib.

slop *slops, slopped, slopping.* 1. Spill, splash.– Do not *slop* the water out of the pail on the clean floor.

2. Dirty water and liquid food scraps.–The farmer feeds *slop* to the pigs.

3. Any spilt liquid. – Wipe the *slop* off the floor before it makes a stain.

4. Thin and tasteless food.–The prisoners said the food was *slop*.

slope *slopes, sloped, sloping.* 1. Slant.–The hill *slopes* downward to the river.

2. Slanting land.–The children climbed the *slope* to the top of the hill.

sloppy slop′-py *sloppier, sloppiest.* 1. Wet, slushy. – Melting snow makes the ground *sloppy*.

2. Careless, not neat.–Jack reads in a *sloppy* way. He goes too fast and does not make sure of the words first. –Mother does not like us to look *sloppy* at dinner.

slot *slots.* A short, narrow opening. – Mary put the penny through the *slot* in her piggy bank.

sloth *sloths.* A hairy animal that lives in South America. It eats leaves and fruits, lives in trees and hangs upside down.

slouch *slouches, slouched, slouching.* Move, walk, or sit in a lazy, drooping way.–Do not *slouch* at your desk or you will spoil your posture.

slow *slows, slowed, slowing, slowly, slowness.* 1. Not fast or quick.–Bob is rather *slow* in doing his work. He takes a lot of time.– Father took a *slow* train. It didn't travel fast.

2. Behind time.–Bob was late because the clock was 15 minutes *slow*. The clock said 8.15 when it was really 8.30.

3. Go slower.–Always *slow* down when you come to a corner on your bicycle.

4. Dull; not bright.–A *slow* person does not learn easily or quickly.

slug *slugs, slugged, slugging.* 1. A slow-moving animal something like a snail, but without a shell. – Mary found some *slugs* in the garden.

2. A metal bullet. – The boy had a pocket full of *slugs* for his gun.

3. Hit hard.–The man was *slugged* by the robber and left lying unconscious.

S
T
U
V
W
X
Y
Z

slum *slums.* A very dirty and crowded part of a city, where poor people live.

slumber slum′-ber *slumbers, slumbered, slumbering.* Sleep.–Father didn't want us to disturb his *slumber.*

slump *slumps, slumped, slumping.* 1. Fall or sink down suddenly.–The boy *slumped* over when the ball hit him.
2. A falling off.–There was a *slump* in trade last month.

slush *slushy.* Partly melted snow. – We wore galoshes because of the *slush.*

sly *slyer, slyest, slyly.* Cunning or wily, doing things secretly.–The burglar was *sly.* He waited until we were watching television before climbing in. On the *sly* means in secret, without publicity.

smack *smacks, smacked, smacking.* 1. Open and close (the lips) noisily. – In some countries it is considered polite to *smack* the lips when eating to show that one likes the food.
2. A blow.–Grandfather gave his horse a *smack.*
3. To slap.–He *smacked* the naughty child's hand.
4. A kind of fishing boat.

small *smaller, smallest.* 1. Little.–A *small* child went up to the policeman and asked him for sixpence.
2. Mean and petty.–It was *small* of the man to argue over the coin the boy found.

smallpox small′-pox. A catching disease that causes fever and a severe rash on the body. –Do not go near a person with *smallpox* or you may get it. – People are vaccinated to prevent *smallpox.*

smart *smarts, smarted, smarting, smarter, smartest, smartly, smartness.* 1. Stylish and in good taste.–Mary's Easter outfit is very *smart.*
2. Quick and clever.–Jack is a *smart* fellow. He learns many things easily.
3. Sting or pain sharply.–When the nurse put medicine on the sore, it started to *smart.*

smash *smashes, smashed, smashing.* 1. Break into many pieces.–When Mary dropped the plate, it *smashed.*
2. Break with force. – The convict *smashed* through the hedge. He did not try to find a way over or round, but rushed straight through it.
3. Crash or fall heavily and noisily. – The aeroplane *smashed* into the house.

smear *smears, smeared, smearing.* 1. Spread or rub over.–Mary *smeared* her hands and face with cold cream.
2. A spot left by something rubbed on. – Mother had a big *smear* on her new apron.

smell *smells, smelled, smelling.* 1. Get odours of things through the nose.–We *smell* bacon when it is cooking.
2. Give off an odour. – Roses *smell* sweet. The room *smells* of tobacco smoke.
3. An odour. – The *smell* of tobacco smoke came from the room.

smile *smiles, smiled, smiling.* 1. A look of amusement, happiness, etc.–The new puppy brought a *smile* to the boy's face.
2. Look amused or happy by turning the mouth up at the corners.

smith *smiths.* A person who makes things out of metal.–A gold*smith* shapes things out of gold. – A black*smith* shapes horseshoes and other things out of iron.

smithy smith′-y *smithies.* The workshop in which a person makes things from iron or other metals.–A blacksmith's shop is a *smithy.*

smock *smocks.* A loose gown worn over one's other clothes to keep them clean.

smoke *smokes, smoked, smoking.* 1. The cloud of tiny particles or vapour that rises from anything burning.– *Smoke* poured out of the big chimney.
2. Breathe in and out the smoke from burning tobacco.–Father *smokes* a pipe.
3. Give off *smoke.*–The stove *smokes.*
4. Cure (meat) or prepare by exposing to *smoke.*–Grandfather *smokes* meat. He hangs it in a small room over a small fire that fills the room with *smoke.*–*Smoked* meat keeps for a long time without spoiling.

smoke-stack smoke´-stack *smoke-stacks*. A tall chimney to let out smoke from a furnace.–Smoke poured out of the factory *smoke-stack* when the fire was started.

smoky smok´-y *smokier, smokiest*.
1. Full of smoke.–The room is *smoky*.–Places where there are factories are often *smoky*.
2. Covered or darkened by smoke that has settled. – The windows are *smoky*.

smooth *smooths, smoothed, smoothing, smoother, smoothest, smoothly, smoothness*. 1. Level; even; without bumps or roughness.–A pane of glass is *smooth*.–The lake was not *smooth*, because the wind made ripples in it.
2. Free from lumps.–Mother stirred the gravy to make it *smooth*.
3. Make *smooth*; remove bumps, wrinkles, etc.–Mary *smoothed* the wrinkles out of the table-cloth.–The board was rough; so Father planed and sand-papered it to *smooth* it.
4. Make peaceful or calm.–Bob and Mary quarrelled this morning but now they have *smoothed* over their troubles.
5. Evenly moving; in a level course.–We had a *smooth* ride in the boat. It was not jerky and bumpy.

smother smoth´-er *smothers, smothered, smothering*. 1. Die from lack of air.–Do not cover the baby's head too closely or she may *smother*.
2. Kill or extinguish by cutting off air from.–Father *smothered* the fire by covering it with earth.–In the play the man, crazed by jealousy, *smothered* his wife with a pillow.

smoulder smoul´-der *smoulders, smouldered, smouldering*. Give off smoke but no flame.–The camp fire *smouldered* long after we went to bed.

smudge *smudges, smudged, smudging*. 1. A dirty mark or spot.–When Mary rubbed the soot on her cheek, it made a *smudge*.
2. Smear; make a dirty mark on.–Baby's face was *smudged* with jelly.

smug *smugness, smugly*. Self-satisfied.–Bob had a *smug* smile on his face.

smuggle smug´-gle *smuggles, smuggled, smuggling*. 1. Take anything in or out of a country secretly when it is against the law to do so.
2. Take in or out secretly.–The boy tried to *smuggle* his dog into his bedroom.

smuggler smug´-gler *smugglers*. A person who takes things into or out of a country when it is against the law to do so.–The River Police arrested the *smugglers*.

snag *snags, snagged, snagging*. 1. A projecting jagged point such as a stump of broken branch.–Bob tore his coat on a *snag*.
2. Unexpected trouble.–Mother couldn't finish Mary's dress on time, because she struck a *snag*.
3. Catch on something rough or sharp.–Mother *snagged* her stocking. It caught on something rough, which made a small hole in it.

snail *snails*. A slow-moving animal that lives in water and on land. –*Snails* have a coiled shell into which they crawl for protection.

snake *snakes*. A long crawling animal without legs.–Some *snakes* live in the ground, some in the water. They eat insects, small animals, and the like. – Some *snakes* have poisonous bites.

snap *snaps, snapped, snapping*. 1. Make a sudden biting motion; snatch with the teeth.–The dog will not *snap* at you if you do not tease him.–The hungry dog *snapped* up the bone and ran away.
2. Take a quick photograph of.–Bob snapped Mary as she was licking her ice-cream.
3. A quick, sharp noise.–The stick broke with a *snap*.
4. Break suddenly.–The ice made the telephone wire *snap*.
5. A fastener which clicks when squeezed together.–Some of Mary's dresses have buttons on them and some have *snap*-fasteners.
6. A crisp, thin biscuit.–Mother makes ginger *snaps*.

snapdragon snap´-drag-on *snapdragons*. A garden flower with blossoms shaped like dragons' heads growing along the sides of the stem.

snapshot snap´-shot *snapshots*. A photograph taken quickly without much preparation. – Father took a *snapshot* of Baby.

snare *snares, snared, snaring.* 1. A trap or noose designed to catch birds and small animals. – The trapper caught the rabbit with a *snare*.
2. Catch with a trap or noose.–The trapper *snares* animals to sell their skins.

snarl *snarls, snarled, snarling.* 1. Growl or curl the lip up fiercely.–The little dog *snarled* at the big dog.
2. A growl or curling of the lip. – The lion looked at the children with a *snarl*.
3. Tangle. – The kitten *snarled* up Grandmother's wool by rolling in it.
4. A tangle.–Father could not comb the *snarls* out of Sally's hair.

snatch *snatches, snatched, snatching.* 1. Grab or catch hold of.–A thief tried to *snatch* Mother's purse in the shop.–The drowning boy *snatched* at the rope thrown to him.
2. A bit or small part. – Father just read *snatches* of the book.

sneak *sneaks, sneaked, sneaking.* 1. Go slyly.– After killing the chicken, the dog *sneaked* into the barn.
2. A sly, mean person–The *sneak* told the master about the boys who had played a trick on him.

sneer *sneers, sneered, sneering.* 1. Show by the look on one's face that one looks down on a person.–Bill *sneers* at Bob for trying so hard in school.
2. A mocking or scornful look or remark.– Bob tries to pay no attention to Bill's *sneers*.

sneeze *sneezes, sneezed, sneezing.* Force air out through the nose so hard that it causes a sharp, sudden noise.–A tickling in the nose often causes one to *sneeze*.

sniff *sniffs, sniffed, sniffing.* 1. Take little short breaths through the nose. – When a dog smells a rabbit, he *sniffs*.
2. Breath; smell.–Take a *sniff* of this perfume.

snigger *snigg'-er sniggers, sniggered, sniggering.* 1. A slight giggle.–The teacher heard a *snigger* at the back of the room.
2. To giggle slightly.–Jack *sniggered* when Mary came in wearing Mother's dress.

snip *snips, snipped, snipping.* 1. Quickly cut off.–The barber *snipped* Baby's hair.
2. Quick cut.–With one *snip* Sally cut off the kitten's whiskers.

3. A scrap, a small cutting.–Mother took a *snip* of cloth to the shop to get more like it.

snipe *snipes, sniped, sniping.* 1. A long-billed bird that lives in marshes.
2. To shoot from a place where one cannot be seen.

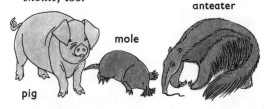

sniper *snip'-er snipers.* A fighter who shoots from a place where he cannot be seen by the enemy.

snoop *snoops, snooped, snooping.* Try to find out about other people's business; pry into things.–Jack likes to *snoop* around in the kitchen.

snore *snores, snored, snoring.* Breathe with a harsh, rough noise while sleeping.–Father *snores* when he lies on his back.

snort *snorts, snorted, snorting.* 1. Force air through the nose so that it makes a sudden noise.–Horses *snort*.
2. A *snorting* noise.– Jack gave a *snort* when Mary said that she was going to be the greatest actress in the world.

snout *snouts.* A long nose that sticks out.–A pig's *snout* is his nose. Other animals have *snouts*, too.

anteater

mole

pig

snow *snows, snowed, snowing.* 1. Small, white, star-shaped flakes of frozen water that fall from the sky in winter.–When *snow* melts, it is water.
2. Drop down *snow*.–Do you think it will *snow* in time for Christmas?

snowball *snow'-ball snowballs.* 1. A ball made of snow pressed together. – Sally likes to throw *snowballs* at Father.
2. A kind of white flower that grows on a bush also called the guelder rose.

snowbound *snow'-bound.* Surrounded by the snow so that one cannot get out.–Grandfather could not go to the city, because he was *snowbound*.

snowdrift *snow'-drift snowdrifts.* A snowbank; a large pile of snow.–The wind blew the snow into *snowdrifts*.

S
T
U
V
W
X
Y
Z

snowflake snow'-flake *snowflakes*. One of the small, lacy pieces in which snow falls to the earth.–Mother showed Sally how to catch *snowflakes* on a piece of black velvet.

snow-man snow'-man *snow-men*. A figure of a man made of snow. –The children put Father's pipe in the *snow-man's* mouth.

snow-plough snow'-plough *snow-ploughs*. A machine used to push the snow from streets, roads, railways, and other places.

snowshoe snow'-shoe *snowshoes*. A frame that looks something like a tennis racquet. *Snow-shoes* are tied to the feet and worn when travelling by foot over deep snow to keep one from sinking into the snow.

snowstorm snow'-storm *snowstorms*. A storm during which much snow falls; a blizzard.–We were caught in a heavy *snowstorm*.

snowy snow'-y *snowier, snowiest*. 1. Having much snow.–This is a *snowy* part of the country. Much snow falls here.
2. Covered with snow.–The pavements are too *snowy* to walk on without wellingtons.
3. White as snow. – Mother's washing is *snowy* white.

snub snubs, snubbed, snubbing. 1. Slight; treat coldly.–The boy felt *snubbed* because he wasn't invited.
2. A slight.–Mary usually tries to ignore Jack's *snubs*.
3. Short and turned up.–Baby has a *snub* nose.

snuffle snuf'fle *snuffles, snuffled, snuffling*. 1. To sniff; breathe with a thick, heavy sound. –Walking in the cold often makes one *snuffle*.
2. A cold in the head.–Mary had the *snuffles* after getting her feet wet.

snug snugger, snuggest, snugly. 1. Close-fitting. Mary's new dress fits her *snugly*.
2. Cosy, warm, and comfortable.–The library is *snug* when there is a fire in the fireplace.

snuggle snug'-gle *snuggles, snuggled, snuggling*. Lie close; cuddle.–The kitten *snuggled* up close to Sally.

so. 1. As. – Bob's story was not *so* good as Mary's.
2. To such a degree or amount.–Do not eat *so* much.–It is *so* beautiful out, that I should like to take a walk.
3. Very.–It is *so* hot today!
4. Therefore.–I was ill, *so* I could not go.
5. Likewise.–Jack was talking, and *so* was Bob. Bob was talking, too.
6. More or less.–Mary was an hour or *so* late.
7. In order.–We eat *so* that we will grow.– Father works *so* as to earn money.
8. Referring to something said before.– If Father says *so*, it is true.

soak soaks, soaked, soaking. 1. Wet through and through.–When Bob waded into the water, he *soaked* his shoes and socks.–Water *soaked* through the thin soles of Mary's shoes.
2. Suck, absorb.–A blotter *soaks* up ink.

soap soaps, soaped, soaping. 1. A material which makes suds in water. It is used to wash dishes, clothes, and other things, and to bath with.–*Soap* is made in cake form, in liquid form, and in flakes and powders.
2. Rub *soap* on.–Mother *soaps* the collars of Father's shirts to get them clean.

soap-suds soap'-suds. The foam caused by mixing soap and water.

soapy soap'-y *soapier, soapiest*. Covered with, or full of, soap or soap-suds.–Mary's hands were *soapy*.–The dish-water is *soapy*.

soar soars, soared, soaring. Fly upward; fly high.–Some eagles *soar* above mountains.

sob sobs, sobbed, sobbing. Cry with short, jerky, loud breaths.–We heard the little child *sobbing* pitifully when he lost his tricycle.

sober so'-ber *soberly, sobers, sobered, sobering*. 1. Quiet; earnest.–Bob is a very *sober* boy. He takes things seriously.

S
T
U
V
W
X
Y
Z

2. Not drunk, not having had too much alcohol to drink.–The driver was *sober* when the accident happened.

3. Stop laughing; become quiet.–The children *sobered* down after their mother scolded them.

soccer soc'-cer. A game played with a round football that is kicked or hit with any part of the body except the hands or arms.

social so'-cial *socially*. 1. Fond of the company of others.–Mary is a very *social* person. She likes to talk and have fun.

2. Having to do with people.–*Social* study is the study of people and how they live together.–Geography and history are *social* studies.

3. A friendly party.–We had an evening *social* at our club.

society so-ci'-e-ty *societies*. 1. Company.–Bob enjoys Jack's *society*. He likes being with Jack.

2. All people, living and working together; the way human beings live together.–Scientists do work of great value to *society*,

3. A club or group of people who work together for some purpose.–We have formed a *society* to help others.

4. The rich, fashionable group of people in a community.

sock *socks*. Short-legged stocking. – Mother wears long stockings. The children wear *socks*.

socket sock'-et *sockets*. A hollow part into which something fits.– Father made a *socket* to hold the flag-pole.– The light did not work because the bulb was not fixed tightly into the *socket*. – The bolt fitted into the *socket* in the door-frame.

sod *sods*. A piece of turf; grassy top-soil that is held together by the roots of the grass. –Jack kicked a *sod* out of the lawn.

soda so'-da *sodas*. 1. A white powder used in cooking.–Baking *soda* is usually used in making cakes that have sour milk in them.

2. *Soda* water, water that fizzes. – Father brought home a case of *soda* for the party.

3. A drink made with ice-cream, syrup, and *soda* water.–Jack likes chocolate ice-cream *sodas*.

sofa so'-fa *sofas*. An upholstered couch that usually has a back and arms.

soft *softer, softest, softly*. 1. Not hard.–The pillow is *soft*.

2. Quiet, gentle, and mild.–A *soft* breeze blew through the trees.–Mother spoke *softly*.

3. The letter 'c' in the word 'cat' is hard. It has a throaty sound. The 'c' in 'cell' is *soft*. It is pronounced like an 's.'–The letter 'g' in 'game' is hard. The 'g' in 'giraffe' is *soft*. It is pronounced like a 'j'.

soft water. Water that is more or less free from minerals that make it hard to form soap-suds. –Rain water is *soft water*.–It doesn't take much soap to make suds in *soft water*.–*Soft water* feels smooth to the hands.

soggy sog'-gy *soggier, soggiest*. Soaked, wet through. – The bottom crust of the blackberry pie is *soggy*.

soil *soils, soiled, soiling*. 1. Ground; earth; dirt. –The *soil* in our garden is black and rich.

2. Make dirty.–Baby *soiled* her clean dress making mud pies.–Her dress was *soiled*.

solar so'-lar. To do with the sun.–The earth is part of the *solar* system; it revolves round the sun.–A *solar* eclipse occurs when the moon is mid-way between the sun and the earth. A total *solar* eclipse is not often seen.

sold. One form of the word *sell*.–Father bought a new house, but now he has *sold* it.

soldier sol'-dier *soldiers*. A man serving in an army.–*Soldiers* fight the enemy in time of war.

S
T
U
V
W
X
Y
Z

sole *soles.* 1. Bottom of a shoe.—The *soles* of Bob's shoes were worn out.—He had new *soles* put on.—Most *soles* are of leather.

2. Bottom of the foot.—Father walked so far that the *soles* of his feet were sore.
3. A kind of fish that is good to eat.

solemn sol'-emn *solemnly.* 1. Earnest, sober, serious.—Bob has *solemn* blue eyes; Jack has twinkling blue eyes that are full of fun.
2. Happening or done in a serious and formal way.—The coronation of a monarch is a *solemn* event.

solid sol'-id *solids.* 1. The same all the way through.—A stove pipe or drain pipe is hollow. A cricket bat is *solid.*
2. The same all over.—Mary's new dress is a *solid* blue.
3. Firm and strong.—The parts of a table must be glued together to make it *solid.*—The house has a *solid* foundation.
4. Firm and hard.—Water is liquid. When it freezes, it becomes *solid.*

solo so'-lo *solos.* 1. A piece of music to be played or sung by one person at a time.
2. Without companions.—The aeroplane pilot made a *solo* flight. He flew all alone.
3. A card game, one form of the game of whist.

soloist so'-lo-ist *soloists.* A person who sings or plays a piece of music alone.

solve *solves, solved, solving.* Find the answer to.—Mary tried to *solve* the arithmetic problem.—The police tried to *solve* the mystery.

sombrero som-bre'-ro *sombreros.* A high-crowned hat with a broad brim worn by men in Spain, Mexico, and some other parts of America.

some. 1. A number of.—*Some* sailors came to town.
2. Any amount of.—Put *some* sugar on Baby's oatmeal.
3. Any number of.—*Some* apples are red.

somebody some'-bod-y. 1. Some person, not named or not known.—The mother bear said, 'Somebody has been eating my porridge.'

2. A person of importance.—Father always says to Bob, 'Be *somebody*, Bob.'

somehow some'-how. By some means, in one way or another.—Father will manage to get to work *somehow* while the car is being repaired.

someone some'-one. Some person.—*Someone* I do not know is talking to Father.

somersault som'-er-sault *somersaults.* A head-over-heels turn. — Some children can turn a *somersault* backwards.

something some'-thing. 1. A thing not named or not known.—Bob bought *something* for Mother's birthday.
2. An action not named or not known.—*Something* must be done to kill the rats.

sometimes some'-times. Now and then; once in a while.—Baby cries *sometimes.*

somewhat some'-what. A little.—It is *somewhat* warmer today.

somewhere some'-where. A place not known or named.—Mother has gone *somewhere.*—The ball is *somewhere* in the cellar.

somnolent som'-no-lent. Sleepy. 1. The warmth of the room made Father *somnolent.*

son *sons.* A boy or man as related to his father and mother. A boy is his father's *son.* Your father is your grandfather's *son.*

sonata so-na'-ta *sonatas.* A rather long piece of music to be played by 1 or 2 instruments. A *sonata* is divided into parts called movements.

song *songs.* A short piece of music with words to be sung.—'Ten Green Bottles' is the name of a popular *song.*—Short poems are set to music. Then they are *songs.*

son-in-law son'-in-law *sons-in-law.* The husband of a person's daughter.—Sister's husband is the *son-in-law* of Father and Mother.

sonnet son'-net *sonnets.* A poem of 14 lines.

soon *sooner, soonest.* 1. Before long; at a time not far away.—Dinner will be ready *soon.*
2. When; at the time.—As *soon* as the bell rings, the children are quiet.
3. Rather.—I would *sooner* sleep than eat.

soot. A black dust formed when something burns.—*Soot* from the sitting-room fire collects on the window sill.

soothe *soothes, soothed, soothing.* 1. Relieve; remove pain from. – This ointment will *soothe* the burn.
2. Calm; comfort; quiet.–Mother tried to *soothe* the lost child.

sop *sops, sopped, sopping.* Soak. – Baby *sops* her bread in milk.–Mary was *sopping* wet.

soppy sop'-py. Soft or foolish.–Mother told Mary not to look so *soppy*.

soprano so-pra'-no *sopranos.* 1. A woman or girl who has a high singing voice, one who can sing high notes.
2. The highest kind of voice.–Mother sings *soprano*, but Father sings bass.
3. The highest part in a piece of music written for more than 1 voice.–Mother sang the *soprano* part in the quartet.

sore *sores.* 1. Painful.–Bob's cut is *sore*.
2. A painful spot where the skin is broken or bruised.–The *sore* on Bob's hand hurts.

sorrow sor'-row *sorrows.* 1. Grief; sadness; unhappiness.–Much *sorrow* was caused by the accident.
2. Trouble; something which makes one feel sad.–The old king had many *sorrows*.

sorrowful sor'-row-ful *sorrowfully.* Sad; full of sadness.–It was a *sorrowful* day when the fishing boat went down.

sorry sor'-ry *sorrier, sorriest.* 1. Filled with sadness or sorrow.–I am *sorry* that you are ill.
2. Politely regretful.–I am *sorry* I was standing in your light.

sort *sorts, sorted, sorting.* 1. Separate things and put like things together in groups.–Bob helped the teacher *sort* the children's papers.
2. Kind or type.–What *sort* of books do you like to read?

soul *souls.* 1. A person.–Not a *soul* heard the bell.
2. Deep feeling; strong spirit.–Mary puts her heart and *soul* into her piano playing.
3. The part of a person concerned with his thinking and feeling.–Most people believe that the *soul* is not part of the body and that the *soul* can never die.

sound *sounds, sounded, sounding.* 1. A noise. –The room was so quiet you could not hear a *sound*.
2. Make a noise.–The squeaking door *sounds* like the squeak of a mouse.
3. Cause to *sound* or make a noise.–*Sound* the fire alarm!

4. Seem, appear.–The news *sounds* bad to me.
5. Stable, healthy.–The boy is *sound* in body and mind.

soundly sound'-ly. 1. Thoroughly; as much as needed.–The old woman who lived in a shoe whipped her children *soundly*.
2. Deeply.–Baby sleeps *soundly*.

soup *soups.* A liquid food made by boiling meat or vegetables in water or milk, with seasonings.–I like creamed tomato *soup*.

soup-plate *soup-plates.* A plate with a deep centre in which soup is served.–There are 6 *soup-plates* in our new dinner service.

sour *sours, soured, souring.* 1. Not sweet.– Sugar is sweet. Lemons are *sour*.
2. Spoiled; gone bad.–The soup has turned *sour*. It has mould on the top.
3. Become *sour*, spoil.–Do not leave the milk out of the refrigerator, or it may *sour*.
4. Cross, bad-tempered.–When we waved to the man he just gave us a *sour* look.

source *sources.* The place from which anything comes; the starting place.–Farms are the *source* of most of our food.–The *source* of the river is a spring high up in the mountains.

sourly sour'-ly. Crossly, in a bad-tempered way. –The man looked at us *sourly* when we asked him whether there was anything wrong with his car.

souse *souses, soused, sousing.* 1. A drenching. –John got a real *souse* when he fell into the pond.
2. Soak, drench with water.–We got thoroughly *soused* in the thunderstorm.
3. Dip into a salt pickle.–Many people like *soused* herring. It is a highly salted herring.

south. 1. One of the 4 main directions. *South* is opposite north. The sun rises in the east.–Turn your face to the east. Your left hand is to the north, and your right hand to the *south*.
2. Towards the *south*.–We live *south* of High Street.–The birds fly *south* in the summer.
3. The southern part of a country.–Father's family lived in the *South*.

south-east south-east'. The direction halfway between south and east.

S
T
U
V
W
X
Y
Z

southern south'-ern. Of the south, towards the south.–We live in the *southern* part of town. –Father's family was *Southern*. They lived in the South.

south-west south-west'. The direction halfway between south and west.

souvenir sou-ve-nir' *souvenirs*. A keepsake; something to bring back memories. – Uncle Ned brought Mary a *souvenir* of Brussels. It was a scarf with pictures of buildings on it.

sovereign sov'-er-eign *sovereigns*. The highest ruler of a country, such as a king, queen, or emperor.

sow (pronounced like *how*) *sows*. A fully grown mother pig. – Grandfather's *sow* has a litter of little pigs.

sow (pronounced like *grow*) *sows, sowed* or *sown, sowing*. Plant by scattering seeds, scatter.–The farmer *sows* the grain in the spring.

soya-bean soy'-a-bean *soya-beans*. A kind of bean used for food, and for making flour, oil, and many other things.

space *spaces, spaced, spacing*. 1. Room, or a place.–There is *space* in the refrigerator for one more dish. 2. A blank; an empty place; a distance.–We wrote one word on the typewriter, then skipped a *space* and wrote another.–The teacher asked us to leave a *space* at the bottom of the page.–Telegraph poles have short *spaces* between them. 3. Sky; nothingness.–Aeroplanes fly in *space*. –The horse and rider plunged off the cliff into *space*. 4. To place with certain distances between.– Jack *spaced* the paragraphs in his composition to make it look longer.

spade *spades, spaded, spading*. 1. A gardening tool with a shorter handle and a flatter blade than a shovel. –We use a *spade* to dig up earth. 2. Dig up.–Father *spaded* the earth to look for some angleworms.

spaghetti spa-ghet'-ti. A food made of flour and water. It is something like macaroni, but finer and in solid sticks, while macaroni is hollow.

span *spans, spanned, spanning*. 1. Extend or stretch across.–The bridge *spans* the river. 2. The distance from the tip of the little finger to the tip of the thumb on a grown person's hand when the hand is stretched out. It is about 9 inches. 3. To measure by one's stretched-out hand. 4. The distance between one support or foundation and the next on a bridge, arch, etc.

bridge span   span of horses

5. In some countries 2 horses, mules or oxen driven together are called a *span*. 6. A period of time.–Father and Mother lived in the city for the *span* of 3 years.–The old man's *span* on earth is nearly over.

spangle span'-gle *spangles*. 1. Piece of sparkling melt. – Mother sewed *spangles* on Mary's angel costume. 2. Any little thing that glitters and sparkles.

spaniel span'-iel *spaniels*. A medium-sized dog with long, wavy hair, and long ears that hang down. Originally used as gun-dogs, *spaniels* make good pets.

spank *spanks, spanked, spanking*. Hit with the open hand.–Mother told Baby to be good or she would *spank* her.

spar *spars, sparred, sparring*. 1. Box with the fists.–The boxers are learning to *spar*. 2. A mast, or a wooden pole that holds or helps to hold a sail on to a mast. 3. Principal support of the wing of an aeroplane.

spare *spares, spared, sparing*. 1. Extra.–We have a spare tyre for our car. We keep it to use only when one of the others is being repaired. 2. Free.–We read stories during our *spare* time.

3. Lend, give up, get along without.–Since Mother was sewing, she could not *spare* her thimble.–I can *spare* a pot or two of jam; I have plenty.

4. Have mercy on, not punish or hurt.–The hunter *spared* the deer. He did not shoot the deer, even though he could have.

spark *sparks*. A little piece or bit of fire.–The Boy Scouts watched the *sparks* from the camp-fire to see that they did not start another fire.

2. A little flash of fire.–When Mother pulled the flex out of the electric iron, Mary saw *sparks*.

sparkle spar'-kle *sparkles, sparkled, sparkling*.
1. Glitter, flash, or throw off little glints of light.–Mother's diamond ring *sparkles*.
2. A little bit of fire, a gleam.
3. Twinkle or dance.–Sally's eyes *sparkle* when she is planning something new.

sparking-plug *sparking-plugs*. A plug used in the cylinders of motor-cars to make electrical sparks which will explode the petrol vapour. These explosions, which take place one after the other, make the motor run.

sparrow spar'-row *sparrows*. A small grey or  brownish bird. There are many different kinds of *sparrows*, the house-*sparrow* being the most common.

spat *spats*. 1. An outer covering for the ankle, made of cloth and worn over the shoe. *Spat* is short for spatterdash.
2. The spawn of shell-fish, particularly oysters.

spatter spat'-ter *spatters, spattered, spattering*. 1. To splash or sprinkle with water, grease, mud, or any other wet substance.–The rain *spattered* the clean car.
2. Fall in drops on.–Grease from the frying-pan *spattered* the stove.
3. A spot.–Mary got a *spatter* of grease on her dress.
4. A noise made by the fall of little drops.–We heard the *spatter* of rain on the roof.

speak *speaks, spoke, spoken, speaking*. 1. Talk.
–Bob was so surprised that he couldn't *speak*.
–We always *speak* English.
2. Give a talk or speech.–The Prime Minister will *speak* on the radio tonight.

3. Tell about.–The policeman *spoke* of the accident.
4. Talk to one another.–Mary and Jack are not *speaking*.

spear *spears, speared, spearing*. 1. A weapon with a sharp tip and a long, straight handle.–Guards stood outside the king's palace holding their *spears*.

2. Put a *spear* through, or pierce.–It is against the law to *spear* certain kinds of fish.–Father *speared* a piece of potato on his fork.

special spe'-cial. 1. Particular.–Making model aircraft is Jack's *special* hobby.–This is a *special* soap. It is good for Baby's skin.
2. Unusual, extra nice.–Father thinks that strawberry flan is a very *special* dessert.–Mother wears her blue lace dress for *special* occasions.

specialist spe'-cial-ist *specialists*. A person who makes a study or a business of some particular subject or line of work.–When Baby had an earache, Mother took her to an ear *specialist*. She took Baby to a doctor who had studied all about and treated things wrong with the ear.–A lawyer is a *specialist* in law.

speciality spe'-cial-i-ty *specialities*. Something one does unusually well.–Making model aircraft is Jack's *speciality*.–Coconut cream pie is Mother's *speciality*.

specially spe'-cial-ly. Unusually; particularly.–Mary was *specially* hungry after going horseback riding.–This dress is *specially* well made.

species spe'-cies *species*. A group of plants or animals that are very much alike.–Tiger lilies are one *species* of the lily family.

specific spe-cif'-ic *specifically*. Particular; exact.–If you have no *specific* reason for staying at home, why not come with us?–When Mother told the doctor Baby didn't seem well, he asked her to be more *specific*. He asked Mother to tell him exactly what seemed to be the trouble.

specimen spec'-i-men *specimens*. A sample.–Our teacher asked each of us for a *specimen* of our drawing to hang up for parents' day.–Bob collects moths. He took one of his *specimens* to school.

S
T
U
V
W
X
Y
Z

speck *speckes, specked.* 1. A small spot. – Father's glasses are usually covered with *specks*.
2. A small bit.–Sally took out a black *speck* that had fallen into her milk.

speckle speck'le *speckles, speckled, speckling.* Marked with spots or specks.–Robins' eggs are blue-green, *speckled* with brown spots.

spectacles spec'-ta-cles *spectacles.* Eyeglasses. Grandmother now wears *spectacles* to help her to see better.

spectator spec-ta'-tor *spectators.* Someone who watches or looks on.–Jack told Mother he did not take part in the fight, but was just a *spectator*.

sped. One form of the word *speed.*–The dog *sped* home when he heard Jack whistle.

speech *speeches.* 1. The ability to speak.– People have *speech*. They are able to speak or talk. Animals do not have *speech*.
2. A talk; what one says to a group of people who have come to listen.–The mayor made a *speech* at the dinner.
3. Way of talking.–The drunken driver's *speech* was slurred. He could not speak clearly or pronounce his words properly.

speechless speech'-less *speechlessly, speechlessness.* Not able to talk. – Mother was *speechless* with surprise.

speed *speeds, sped, speeded, speeding.* 1. Swiftness; quickness.–Mary dressed with all possible *speed*.
2. Move very fast.–The train came *speeding* down the line.
3. Hurry; move faster.–The teacher asked us to try to *speed* up our work.
4. Rate of motion or movement.–The *speed* limit is 30 miles an hour. That is as fast as one may drive.–The *speed* of this train is 90 miles an hour.
5. Go faster than is allowed.–Mother had a summons for *speeding*.

speedily speed'-i-ly. Quickly.–Do not try to do your homework too *speedily*, or you may not do it right.

speedometer speed-om'-e-ter *speedometers.* An instrument for measuring speed. *Speedometers* on cars usually also have a meter that records the distance the car has travelled.

speedway speed'-way *speedways.* A track or road built for fast driving.–Car races are run on *speedways*.

speedy speed'-y *speedier, speediest.* Fast, quick, hasty.–The doctor made a *speedy* trip to the hospital.

spell *spells, spelt, spelling.* 1. Speak or write the letters of words in the right order.–C A T *spells* cat.
2. A period; a length of time.–We went to the lake during the hot *spell*.
3. A charm; an enchantment.–The fairy cast a *spell* over the princess.

speller spell'-er *spellers.* 1. A person who spells. –Mary is a good *speller*.
2. A spelling book; book with words in it to learn to spell.–Our form has a new *speller*.

spelling bee spell'-ing bee *spelling bees.* A spelling contest; contest to see who can spell the best.–Our team won the *spelling bee*.

spend *spends, spent, spending.* 1. Pay out.– Do not *spend* your money just because you have it.–Mother *spent* £2 for a new hat.
2. Pass (time). – Bob *spends* his holidays making model aeroplanes.

sphere *spheres.* A ball or globe.–Every part of the outside of a *sphere* is the same distance from the centre. –The earth is a *sphere*.

spice *spices.* A sharp-tasting seasoning made from dried leaves, seeds, or bark of certain plants.–Cloves, allspice, cinnamon, and nutmeg are *spices*.–Mother puts many *spices* in her gingerbread.

spicy spic'-y *spicier, spiciest.* 1. Flavoured with spice.–Gingerbread is *spicy*.
2. Having the sharp odour or taste of spice.– Carnations have a *spicy* smell.

spider spi'-der *spiders.* 1. A small animal with 8 long legs. *Spiders* are not insects, for they have 8 legs and no wings; insects have 6 legs, and usually have wings. – *Spiders* spin webs to catch insects for food. They are very useful to gardeners.

spike *spikes, spiked, spiking.* 1. A long, strong, thick nail.–The men put *spikes* in the railway sleepers to hold the rails in place.
2. A sharp, pointed piece of metal.–Runners and other athletes wear shoes with *spikes* sticking out of the soles.
3. Cut or pierce with *spikes.*–Bob was *spiked* in the leg by another runner.
4. A pointed cluster on a plant.–This is a *spike* of grain. The picture next to it is a *spike* of flowers.

spill *spills, spilled, spilling.* 1. Let a liquid run out over the edge of its container, or let loose material like sand or sugar fall or scatter about.–Baby often *spills her milk.*
2. Let fall.–The sledge ran into a tree and *spilled* the children into the snow.
3. A fall.–We had a big *spill* when our sledge hit the tree.

spin *spins, spun, spinning.* 1. Whirl or make whirl.–Bob *spins* his top.–The top *spins.*
2. Draw out and twist wool, silk, or cotton into threads.–Long ago women *spun* their own thread and yarn on *spinning* wheels.
3. Make of thread-like strands.–Spiders *spin* webs to catch insects in for food.
4. Feel dizzy.–My head is *spinning.* It feels as though it were going round and round.

spinach spin'-ach. A green vegetable whose leaves are good to eat.

spindle spin'-dle *spindles.* A long rod that goes round and roud. It is used to wind thread when spinning.

spindly spin'-dly. Weak and slender. – The doctor said Jane was too *spindly* and gave her a tonic.–This plant is *spindly.*

spine *spines.* 1. The backbone.– A person's *spine* is made up of many bones fitted together.
2. A thorn, pricker, or sharp point.–A porcupine's quills are *spines.*

spinning wheel spin'-ning wheel *spinning wheels.* A machine to spin and wind thread or yarn. It has a large wheel turned by hand or by a foot pedal.

spiral spi'-ral *spirals.* Something shaped like a coil.–A corkscrew or a coiled bedspring is a *spiral.*

spire *spires.* The pointed part of a steeple.– We saw the church *spire* from a distance.

spirit spir'-it *spirits.* 1. Soul or mind; the unseen part of a person concerned with thinking and feeling.
2. A ghost, elf, fairy, or other imaginary being.
3. Way of feeling; nature.–When Father went to work he was in good *spirits.* He was happy.

spirited spir'-it-ed. Lively; vigorous.–Grandfather has a *spirited* horse. It is full of energy and courage.

spit *spits, spat, spitting.* 1. The saliva or liquid that forms in one's mouth.
2. Throw out saliva or anything from the mouth.–*Spitting* may spread disease.–Baby *spits* out food she doesn't like.

spite. 1. An unfriendly feeling.–The man let his dog run in the garden out of *spite* for the person who owned the garden.
2. Show unfriendly feelings or a dislike for someone.–The boy didn't want the book but he took it to *spite* the other boys.
4. *In spite of* means notwithstanding; nevertheless.–John went to school *in spite of* the pain in his leg.

spiteful spite'-ful *spitefully, spitefulness.* Full of unfriendly feelings.–The child is very *spiteful.* He wants to hurt people, annoy them, make them angry.

splash *splashes, splashed, splashing.* 1. Throw; dash; scatter (liquid) about.–A passing car *splashed* muddy water on Mary's clothes.
2. A noise made by the *splashing* of water.– When Bob dived into the water, we heard a big *splash.*
3. A spot made by something *splashed.*– When Father paints, he gets *splashes* of paint on his shirt.

splatter splat'-ter *splatters, splattered, splattering.* Splash; scatter (liquid). – Do not *splatter* ink on your paper.

splendid splen'-did *splendidly.* Brilliant; excellent; glorious. – The soldiers fought a *splendid* fight.

S
T
U
V
W
X
Y
Z

splice *splices, spliced, splicing.* 1. Join together –Mother *spliced* the 2 pieces of wool to make 1 long piece. She twisted the 2 ends together instead of making a knot.
2. Place where 2 pieces are joined by *splicing.* –The *splice* she made in the wool could hardly be seen.
3. In a cricket bat, the part of the handle that is let into the blade.

splint *splints.* A thin strip of wood or other material.–The doctor put a *splint* on the boy's broken finger.

splinter splin′-ter *splinters, splintered, splintering.* 1. A sliver of wood, metal, etc.–The nurse took a *splinter* from the child's foot.
2. Break, sliver, or split into long, thin pieces. –The box fell from the lorry and *splintered.*

split *splits, split, splitting.* 1. Break or pull apart, especially along the grain.–Bob *split* the stick from end to end to make kite sticks.
2. Divide.–The boys *split* the reward.
3. A crack; a long break.–There is a big *split* in the tree.

splutter splut′-ter *splutters, spluttered, spluttering.* 1. Make a spitting or sputtering noise. –Sausages *splutter* when frying.
2. Talk fast and not clearly.–The child *spluttered* when he described the carnival.

spoil *spoils, spoilt* or *spoiled, spoiling.* 1. Ruin, or damage.–The hail *spoilt* the lettuce.
2. Become unfit to eat.–Some foods will *spoil* if not kept cold. They may become sour or mouldy, or may decay.

spoke *spokes.* 1. One form of the word *speak.* –Mary *spoke* to the teacher about the lesson.–At dinner, the Mayor *spoke* on the subject of improving the town.
2. One of the bars leading from the axle of a wheel to the rim.–The wheels of the cart turned so fast that it was hard to tell one *spoke* from another.

spoken spo′-ken. One form of the word *speak.* –I have *spoken* to her on the telephone, but not face to face.

spokesman spokes′-man *spokesmen.* A person chosen to speak for a group.–At the meeting the students elected Bob as their *spokesman* to present their idea to the tutor.

sponge *sponges, sponged, sponging.* 1. A kind of animal that lives in the sea. – We use its cleaned and dried skeleton as a *sponge.*–A *sponge* soaks up much water. – We use a *sponge* to wash things.

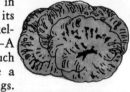

2. Rub with a *sponge.* – Mother *sponged* Father's suit with a damp *sponge.*
3. Let someone else pay one's way or do one's work.–It is better to work for yourself than to *sponge* on someone else.

sponge-cake sponge′-cake *sponge-cakes.* A light, sweet cake made of eggs, milk, sugar and flour.–Mother put a layer of apricot jam in the *sponge-cake.*

spook *spooks.* A ghost (said in fun).–On Hallowe'en the children dress up in sheets, and pretend they are *spooks.*

spooky spook′-y. Ghostly; scary. – The dark, empty house was *spooky.* It made you think of ghosts.

spool *spools.* A short, round piece of wood or metal with a hole through it from end to end. Thread, cord, and films are often wound on *spools.*

spoon *spoons.* A small tool with a bowl and handle for lifting liquids or soft foods.– Baby eats with a *spoon.*

spoonful spoon′-ful *spoonfuls.* As much as a spoon will hold.–The doctor gave me a *spoonful* of medicine.

spore *spores.* A cell from which some new plants grow. – Ferns and other flowerless plants have *spores.*

sport *sports.* 1. Fun, play, or amusement.–It is good *sport* to go fishing.
2. Any particular kind of game, particularly an active game.–Hockey, cricket, football, skiing, and basketball are *sports.*
3. One who takes troubles well, or is a good loser.–Bob was a good *sport* about missing the game.

sportsman sports′-man *sportsmen.* 1. A man who takes part in outdoor games or sports, such as fishing and hunting.
2. One who plays or acts fairly in sports or games.

S
T
U
V
W
X
Y
Z

sportsmanship sports'-man-ship. Fair play; ability to follow rules or to accept conditions cheerfully.

spot *spots, spotted, spotting.* 1. A mark, stain, speck or pimple.–It is hard to get ink *spots* out of clothes.
2. Stain, or get a *spot* on.–Mother put a bib on Baby so that Baby would not *spot* her clean dress.
3. One of a pattern of dots or round markings.–A giraffe has *spots*.
4. A place.–We have found a pretty *spot* to put up our tent.

spotless spot'-less *spotlessly, spotlessness.* Having no marks.–Mother's dresses are always *spotless*.

spotlight spot'-light *spotlights.* 1. A circle of strong light thrown on something. – The singer stood in the *spotlight* so that everyone could see her easily.

2. The lamp that makes a *spotlight*.

spotted spot'-ted. 1. Stained, marked with spots.–Baby's bib is *spotted* with egg.
2. Covered with spots or marks not of the same colour as the rest.–Sally's tortoise has a *spotted* shell. His shell is yellow with black spots.

spotty spot'-ty *spottier, spottiest.* Spotted, marked with pimples or spots.–The boy's face was spotty with chicken-pox.

spout *spouts, spouted, spouting.* 1. A tube or pipe through which water or other liquids may run or be poured.–Tea-pots and coffee-pots have *spouts*.–Tea pours through the *spout*.
2. Pour; gush.–Water *spouts* from the fountain.

sprain *sprains, sprained, spraining.* Injure by twisting or overstretching the muscles or ligaments. Bob *sprained* his ankle while playing football.

sprang. One form of the word *spring*.–The cat *sprang* at the mouse.

sprawl *sprawls, sprawled, sprawling.* Lie with the arms and legs stretched out.–The tired boys *sprawled* on the grass.

spray *sprays, sprayed, spraying.* 1. A branch of a plant with its flowers and leaves.–Mary put a *spray* of apple blossoms in the teacher's vase.
2. An instrument used to pump out liquid in a *spray*.–Mother puts on her perfume with a *spray*.
3. Sprinkle.–The good farmer *sprays* potato plants with a liquid to kill insects.
4. Fine drops of water.–The wind blew a *spray* from the sprinkler into our faces.

sprayer spray'-er *sprayers.* An instrument for spraying liquids.–The farmer uses a *sprayer* on his apple trees.

spread *spreads, spreading.* 1. Lay smoothly.–Mother *spread* jam on the toast. – Mary *spread* her dress on the ironing board to press it.
2. Get farther apart.–The captain told the boys on the leg side to *spread* out so that someone would catch the ball.
3. Stretch out, unfold.–The bird *spread* its wings and flew away.
4. Scatter; distribute; reach over a wide area.–News of the accident soon *spread* far and wide.–Scarlet fever *spreads* fast.
5. A cover for a bed.–Grandmother made a patchwork *spread* with a pattern of stars.

spring *springs, sprang* or *sprung, springing.*
1. Jump, leap.–Have you ever seen a cat *spring* at a mouse or a bird?
2. A leap.–With one *spring*, Jack was out of bed.
3. Come up quickly, shoot up.–Mushrooms *spring* up overnight.
3. Ability to stretch and then go back to the usual size.–A rubber band has *spring*.
4. A coil or strip of metal that gives under pressure and then jumps back to its original shape.–These are *springs* for a chair or bed. Push them down and then let go, and they will *spring* back to their usual size.
5. The season of the year which lasts from March 21 to June 21.–The 4 seasons of the year are *spring*, summer, autumn, and winter. – The farmer plants his seeds in the *spring*.
6. A bubbling stream of water coming out of the ground.–The Boy Scouts found a *spring* in the woods.

spring-board spring'-board *spring-boards.* A diving board; a springy board from which a swimmer dives or jumps.

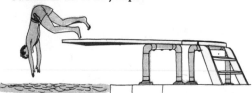

springtime spring'-time. The spring of the year.–In the *springtime*, the farmer plants seeds.

springy spring'-y *springier, springiest.* Able to be pressed down or together and then go back to its usual shape and size when the pressure is gone.–The mattress on Mother's bed is soft and *springy*.

sprinkle sprin'-kle *sprinkles, sprinkled, sprinkling.* 1. Scatter drops or small bits.–Mother *sprinkled* the clothes with warm water.
2. Spray, put liquid on by *sprinkling*.–Father *sprinkled* the garden.
3. Rain a little.–It started to *sprinkle*, so we came into the house.
4. A light rainfall.–We had a *sprinkle* this morning, but the sun is shining now.
5. A very small amount.–Mother put just a *sprinkle* of pepper in the soup.

sprinkler sprink'-ler *sprinklers.* 1. A device fastened to a hose, for spraying.–Father uses a *sprinkler* to water the lawn.

2. A water cart with tanks from which water is sprayed on the roadway.–Men sprinkle the city streets with *sprinklers* to keep down the dust.

sprint *sprints, sprinted, sprinting.* 1. A fast, short race. – The boys had quite a *sprint* across the playground.
2. Run fast.–Jack *sprinted* up the path when he smelt the dinner cooking.

sprite *sprites.* Fairy or elf.–The water *sprites* are supposed to have long, pale green hair.

sprout *sprouts, sprouted, sprouting.* 1. Start to grow.–Beans *sprout* very soon after they are planted.
2. A shoot, a tiny new stalk from a seed or another plant. – Mother started this plant from a *sprout*.

spruce *spruces, spruced, sprucing.* 1. An evergreen tree. – *Spruce* trees have cones.
2. Neat, smart, trim.–Father looks very *spruce* in his new suit.
3. Get neat and clean. – The boys had to *spruce* up before dinner.

sprung. One form of the word *spring.* – Jack looked behind the bush out of which the little rabbit had *sprung*.

spry *spryer, spryest.* Quick, lively, full of life. –Grandfather is *spry* for his age.

spur *spurs, spurred, spurring.* 1. A pointed device fastened to a horseman's heels to help him make his horse go by pricking it.
2. Anything that forces, urges, or drives one to do a thing.–The man's hunger was a *spur* that drove him to work.
3. Any point that sticks out like a horseman's *spur*.–The cock dug his *spurs* into Grandfather's hand when he was caught.
4. Prick a horse's sides with *spurs*.–The cowboy *spurred* his horse.
5. Urge; drive; force. – The man's hunger *spurred* him to work hard in order to get enough food.

spurn *spurns, spurned, spurning.* 1. Drive away with the foot; kick in scorn. – The man *spurned* the barking dog.
2. Refuse scornfully. – Father *spurned* the man's offer.

spurt, *spurts, spurted, spurting.* Squirt or gush. –Water *spurted* out of the hole in the hose.

sputter sput'-ter *sputters, sputtered, sputtering.* 1. Make a spitting, hissing sound. –Hot chips *sputter* when frying.
2. Talk fast and in a way that cannot be understood.–Baby sometimes *sputters*.

spy *spies, spied, spying.* 1. See; find with the eyes.–When Mary found the thimble, she cried, 'I *spy* it.'
2. A person who secretly watches another person to find out something.–In time of war, a *spy* tries to get information about the enemy. He tries to find out the enemy's plans and positions.
3. Watch secretly; act as a *spy*.–The policeman *spied* on the robbers.

S
T
U
V
W
X
Y
Z

squad *squads*. A small group of as many people as are required for some activity.–A *squad* of workers cleaned up the park.–The gymnastic *squad* gave a display of exercises in the gymnasium.

squadron squad'-ron *squadrons*. A fighting unit of aircraft, warships, or cavalry.–A *squadron* of aircraft flew over the city.

squall *squalls, squalled, squalling*. 1. A sudden, strong, whirling rush of wind, usually with rain.
2. A loud squawk or cry.–The duck let out a *squall* when the dog chased it.
3. Cry out loudly.–The baby was squalling because it was hungry.

squander squan'-der *squanders, squandered, squandering*. Waste; spend unwisely.–The man did not *squander* his money. He saved it.

square *squares, squared, squaring*. 1. A flat shape with 4 sides of the same length and 4 corners all alike.–A chessboard is divided into *squares*.

geometric square

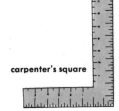
carpenter's square

2. Having 4 equal sides.–The top of our card table is *square*.
3. A carpenter's tool for measuring corners to make sure that they are perfectly *square*, that they are like the corners of the figure in the picture.
4. A place or space in a city with streets on all four sides.–A large fountain stands in the middle of the town *square*.
5. Make the 4 sides even, and the 4 corners alike.–The children *squared* a paper.
6. Honest and fair.–Grandfather says that it pays to be *square* with everyone.
7. Settle; make right.–Bob *squared* his debt with Father.

squash *squashes, squashed, squashing*. 1. Mash or crush.–Sally stepped on the tomato and *squashed* it.
2. A fruit drink.–The children drank lemon *squash* at the party.
3. The game of *squash*-rackets, for 2 people, played in a walled court, with a long racket and a small rubber ball.

squat *squats, squatted, squatting*. 1. Sit on one's heels.–Grandfather *squatted* down to weed the garden.
2. Short and thick.–One vase is tall and slender, the other is *squat*.

squeak *squeaks, squeaked, squeaking*. 1. Make a sharp, shrill sound.–A door with hinges that need oiling often *squeaks*.
2. A short, shrill noise.–The *squeaks* of the barn door kept Grandmother awake.

squeaky squeak'-y *squeakier, squeakiest*. Making a shrill noise.–Bob's shoes are *squeaky*.

squeal *squeals, squealed, squealing*. Make a sharp, shrill noise.–Little pigs *squeal*.

squeeze *squeezes, squeezed, squeezing*. Press hard. – Mother *squeezed* Baby. – You make orange juice by *squeezing* the juice out of oranges. - Mary *squeezed* her way through the crowd to see the procession.

squeezer squeez'-er *squeezers*. A device used for pressing the juice out of oranges, lemons, and the like.–Mother uses a *squeezer* to make lemonade.

squint *squints, squinted, squinting*. 1. Look with eyes partly shut.–The sun was so bright that I had to *squint* to see at all.
2. When a person's eyes turn in different directions, he is said to have a *squint*. Jim was given glasses because of his *squint*.

squirm *squirms, squirmed, squirming*. Wriggle, twist, and turn this way and that.–Do not *squirm* at the dinner table.

squirrel squir'-rel *squirrels*. A small red, black, or grey animal with a long bushy tail.–*Squirrels* can run fast and climb trees. – *Squirrels* put away nuts to eat in winter.

stab *stabs, stabbed, stabbing*. 1. Pierce with a pointed weapon.–The policeman *stabbed* the mad dog with a knife.
2. A jab or thrust.–The robber made a *stab* at the policeman with a knife.
3. A wound made by something pointed.–The child had a small *stab* in his hand from the point of the pen.

stable sta'-ble *stables*. A barn or building in which horses or cattle are kept.–The farmer has 3 *stables*.

stack *stacks, stacked, stacking.* 1. A large pile. –Little Boy Blue was under the hay*stack* fast asleep. – Mary carried a big *stack* of plates out to the dining-room.

2. Arrange in a pile.–Mother *stacked* the dinner dishes in the sink.

3. A chimney (usually of a factory or other large building, or of an engine). – Smoke from the furnace goes out through the smoke-*stack*.

stadium sta'-di-um *stadiums.* An outdoor field with many rows of seats built around it.– Football matches and athletic meetings are often held in *stadiums*.

staff *staffs* or *staves.* 1. A pole, stick, or rod.– Little Bo-Peep carried a *staff* to guide the sheep.–The Boy Scouts raised the flag on the flag-*staff*. Scoutmasters carry *staffs*.

2. The 4 spaces and 5 lines on which the notes are put in written music. Here are 2 *staves*:–

3. A group, especially of workers.–A hospital has a *staff* of doctors. A school has a *staff* of teachers.–A *staff* of officers in the army plans when and where to fight, and what to do.

stag *stags.* A male deer that is fully grown.– *Stags* have horns. Female deer have no horns.

stage *stages, staged, staging.* 1. A raised platform or floor for public performances.–The children went on the *stage* to sing.

2. A scaffold.–Painters stand on a *stage* when they are painting high buildings.

3. The theatre; acting.–Mary wants to go on the *stage*. She wants to be an actress.

4. Arrange, bring about, put on (a *stage*).– The boys *staged* a boxing match. They made all the arrangements for having it in public.

stage-coach stage'-coach *stage-coaches.* A coach or carriage that travelled in olden times to and from certain places at certain times and carried passengers and mail.–Buses are used instead of *stage-coaches* nowadays.

stagger stag'-ger *staggers, staggered, staggering.* Walk unsteadily, or sway back and forth or from side to side.–The sick man *staggered* down the pavement.

stagnant stag'-nant. Water that has stood still in a pool is *stagnant*.–Mosquitoes breed in *stagnant* water.

stain *stains, stained, staining.* 1. A soiled spot. –Do not spill blackberry juice on your dress or it will make a *stain*.

2. Make a spot. – The juice will *stain* your dress.

3. Colour, or put a finish on.–Father *stained* the unpainted table.

4. A colouring or finish.–He used a maple *stain* for the table.

stainless stain'-less. Impossible to tarnish or spot. – These knives are made of *stainless* steel. Food will not stain them.

stair *stairs.* A step. – We go down a flight of *stairs* to get to the basement.–We go up the *stairs* to get to the second floor.

S
T
U
V
W
X
Y
Z

stairway stair'-way *stairways*. A set of steps.– The *stairway* leading to the second floor has a rail at the side.

stake *stakes, staked, staking*. 1. A pointed stick or rod pounded into the ground.–The goat was tied to a *stake*.
2. Mark off with *stakes*.–Bob *staked* out his garden. He drove in sticks round it to show where his garden ended.
3. An issue, a thing to be won or lost.–The soldier's life was at *stake*.

stale *staler, stalest*. 1. Not new or fresh.–This cake is *stale*.
2. Overtrained.–Bob played football badly because he was *stale*. He had played too much.

stalk *stalks, stalked, stalking*. 1. The main stem of a plant. – Mary broke the *stalk* of a lily.–Bob ate a *stalk* of celery.
2. Try to get near an animal or person without letting that animal or person know it. – The hunter *stalked* the deer in the woods.
3. Walk slowly and proudly.–The cat *stalked* through the door.

stall *stalls, stalled, stalling*. 1. A space in a barn or stable for one horse or one cow.–The horse stands in his *stall* and eats hay from a rack.
2. A booth, or small enclosed counter. – The girls had a *stall* from which to sell sweets at the fair.
3. Stop when you don't want it to.–Our motor *stalled* and we couldn't get it started.

stamen sta'-men *stamens*. The part in the middle of a flower on which the fine, yellowish powder called pollen is found. Insects take pollen from the *stamens* and carry it to other flowers.

stammer stam'mer *stammers, stammered, stammering*. To stutter or to say a sound again and again when trying to speak. – The boy said, 'Th-th-th-this is m-m-my b-b-book.' Children sometimes *stammer* when excited.

stamp *stamps, stamped, stamping*. 1. A small printed piece of paper sold by the Post Office. It is glued to letters and parcels to show that one has paid for sending them.–Before posting letters or parcels, you must put *stamps* on them.

Penny black

Mauritius blue

Cape of Good Hope triangular

2. Put a *stamp* on.–Remember to *stamp* the letter before posting it.
3. Beat the ground with the foot; pound or crush with the foot. – The hungry pony *stamped* noisily.–Some little children believe that if you *stamp* on an ant, it will rain.
4. A mark, signature, or the like pressed upon anything.–The secretary put the firm's *stamp* on the application form.
5. Mark with a *stamp*.–The secretary *stamped* the application form.
6. A block (usually rubber) with a name, picture, or the like on it. When wet with ink and pressed on paper, it prints the paper.
7. *Stamp out* means get rid of.–The police did much to *stamp out* crime in the city.

stand *stands, stood, standing.* 1. Rest on one's feet with the body upright.–We lie down to sleep; we sit down to eat our meals; we *stand* up to sing 'God Save the Queen.'

2. Rise, get to one's feet.–Our teacher makes us *stand* up, face the windows, and stretch our arms every hour.

3. Set up on end.–*Stand* the broom there.

4. Rest upright.–The candlestick *stands* on the sideboard.

5. Bear or endure.–Mother cannot *stand* hearing Baby cry.

6. Hold good; remain.–Mother's promise still *stands*.

7. A position.–The policeman took his *stand* at the corner to help the little children cross the road.–What *stand* do you take on this subject? What do you think about it?

8. Take or have a position.–Where do you *stand* in your class?

9. An outdoor counter where things are sold. –We bought a pound of big red cherries at the fruit *stand*.

10. A small table; a base that something *stands* on.–Mother put the lamp on the bedside *stand*.

bedside stand   fruit stand

standard *stand'-ard standards.* 1. A banner or flag.–The man who carries our flag is our *standard* bearer. He carries the *standard*.

2. Any post, pole, or the like that stands up straight to support or hold up something.–A flag-pole is a *standard*.

3. Something by which things can be judged, measured, or compared; something set up as a rule or model.–Bob's mark in the arithmetic test was not up to his usual high *standard*. He can do better.

4. Accepted as being correct and in general use.–We use *standard* weights and measures so that there can be no argument in buying and selling.–Professor Brown has written a *standard* book on history, which is used in most schools.

standing *stand'-ing standings.* 1. Still; at rest.– Mother left the water *standing* in the washing machine. – The box is *standing* on the table.

2. Upright.–*Standing* trees are those that have not been cut down.

3. A period of time.–Mary is my friend of long *standing*.

4. Permanent.–The *standing* army is one that a country has all the time, not just during time of war.

5. A position; a rank.–Mr Jones is a lawyer of good *standing*. He is well thought of. He has a good name and position.

stanza *stan'-za stanzas.* A group of lines of a poem, especially of a poem set to music. In a song, the tune is sung once for each *stanza*. –We learned one *stanza* of 'God Save the Queen.'

staple *sta'-ple staples, stapled, stapling.* 1. A U-shaped piece of metal with the ends pointed.– The farmer fastened the wire fence to the posts with *staples*.

2. A piece of wire that bends over at each end to fasten papers together.–The teacher fastened the pages together with *staples*.

3. Fasten with *staples*.–She *stapled* the booklet.–She put the *staples* in place.

4. Most important; chief.–The *staple* articles in a grocer's shop are sugar, coffee, tea, etc.

5. Most important products raised.–Coffee and rubber are the *staples* of parts of South America.

star *stars, starred, starring.* 1. A 5- or 6-pointed figure.–The teacher puts *stars* on our spelling papers if the words are spelt right.

2. The small bright lights in the sky at night. They are like our earth and sun, but are very far away.

3. A leading actor or performer. – Mickey Mouse was the *star* of the cartoon we saw.

4. A person who can do something exceptionally well.–Jack Hobbs was a cricket *star*.

5. Be the chief performer. – Mickey Mouse *starred* in the cartoon.

6. Put a *star* on.–The teacher *starred* the good spelling papers.

starch *starches, starched, starching.* 1. A white substance that has no taste or odour, found in certain plants.–Potatoes, macaroni, rice, and many other foods contain *starch*.

2. A white powder used to stiffen clothes.– Mother puts *starch* in Father's collars.

3. Stiffen with *starch*.–Starch is mixed with water and used to *starch* shirts and other clothes before they are ironed.

S
T
U
V
W
X
Y
Z

stare *stares, stared, staring.* 1. Look straight and steadily with eyes wide open.–The hungry girl *stared* at the food on the table.
2. A steady look with wide-open eyes.–The boy's *stare* frightened the baby.

starfish star'-fish. A star-shaped animal that lives in the sea.

starlight star'-light. Light coming from the stars. –The *starlight* helped us find our way through the woods.

starling star'-ling *starlings.* A brownish-black bird whose feathers look greenish and purplish in the sunlight.

starry star'-ry. 1. Bright and shiny like stars.– Baby's eyes are *starry*.
2. Lighted by stars.–The sky is *starry* tonight.

start *starts, started, starting.* 1. Begin; set out. –I *start* for school at 8 o'clock.–I *start* working on time.–Bob turned on the radio and the music *started*.
2. Set in motion.–Father *started* the car.
3. A sudden, startled movement. – A loud crash of thunder made me awake with a *start*.
4. A setting out; beginning. – The whistle blew and Bob was off to a good *start* in the race.
5. Place where something is begun.–All the runners lined up at the *start*.–It is 3 miles from the *start* to the finish.

starter start'-er *starters.* 1. A person who tells others when to start or begin doing something.–The person who blows a whistle for a race or a game to begin is a *starter*.
2. A person or horse who begins in a race. –There were 15 *starters* in the race.
3. A mechanical device to set something in motion.–Father pulled the *starter* in the car to start the motor.

startle star'-tle *startles, startled, startling.* Shock; surprise; frighten for a moment.–The ringing of the door-bell *startled* Mother.

starvation star-va'-tion. Being without food.– The farmer's pigs died of *starvation*.

starve *starves, starved, starving.* Be without food; die of hunger.–If you do not eat, you will *starve*.

state *states, stated, stating.* 1. A group of people who work and live under one government, or the territory in which these people live and work.–The United States is made up of 50 *states*.
2. Say something by writing or speaking.– The doctor *stated* that Baby had the measles.
3. A condition.–Mary was in an excited *state* on the night of the form play.

stated stat'-ed. Fixed or definite; set.–Most clubs meet at *stated* times and places. Our club meets on Monday evenings at 8 in the gymnasium.

statement state'-ment *statements.* 1. A report; formal account, written or spoken.–The man who saw the accident made a *statement* to the police.
2. A listing showing how much money you owe or how much is due to you.–According to my bank *statement*, I have £22.50 in the bank.

stateroom state'-room *staterooms.* A private sleeping room on a ship.–We slept in a *stateroom* on the big steamship.

static stat'-ic. 1. A crackling noise heard on a radio and caused by electricity in the air.– We could not hear the music, because there was so much *static*.
2. Standing still. – The water in a river is never *static*; it is always moving.

station sta'-tion *stations, stationed, stationing.* 1. A regular stopping place for trains or buses. –A railway *station* is a building in which people wait for trains.

2. An appointed place of duty.–The policemen stood at their *stations* to help the little children cross the roads.
3. Locate for duty.–My brother is *stationed* at an army camp near by.

stationary sta'-tion-ar-y. 1. Not moving; staying in one place.–The car was moving but it is now *stationary*. It has stopped moving.
2. Not changing in size or number.–The size of our class has been *stationary* all the year.

stationery sta'-tion-er-y. Writing materials, such as paper and envelopes.–Mother keeps her *stationery* in the desk.

S
T
U
V
W
X
Y
Z

statue stat'-ue *statues*.  A carved or moulded figure of a person or animal. *Statues* are made of stone, clay, metal, wood, etc.–There is a *statue* of Abraham Lincoln in Washington.

stay *stays, stayed, staying.* 1. Remain; live; reside; be (in one place).–You go and I will *stay* here.–Bob has gone to Grandmother's to *stay* for the summer.
2. A time of *staying* in a place.–We had an enjoyable *stay* at the farm.

steadily stead'-i-ly. Constantly; regularly.–Mary goes to school *steadily*.–The rain fell *steadily*.

steady stead'-y 1. Regular; always the same; not jerky.–Grandmother's writing is *steady*.–Father drives the car at a *steady* speed.
2. Firm, not shaky or wavering.–The man's step is *steady*. He doesn't totter or shake when he walks.–The big tree is *steady*.

steak (pronounced *stake*) *steaks*. A slice of meat, usually beef, to be fried or grilled.–Mother ordered a 2-pound *steak* for dinner.

steal *steals, stole, stolen, stealing.* 1. Take something that belongs to another person.–The Bible tells one not to *steal*.–The boy *stole* the book from Mary.
2. Move quietly and secretly.–Bob *stole* into his room to sleep.

steam *steams, steamed, steaming.* 1. Water turned into gas or vapour by heat. When water boils, it throws out moisture into the air. This moisture is *steam*. You cannot see *steam*. When *steam* is turning back to water, it forms a white cloud of tiny drops, also called *steam*.–Some homes are heated by *steam*.–Some engines are run by the power of *steam*.
2. Treat or cook with *steam*.–Mother *steams* bread to freshen it. She puts hard bread into a pan with holes in it, sets it over a saucepan of boiling water, and covers it up. Foods can be cooked in this way, too.
3. Give off *steam*.–The water in the kettle is *steaming*.

steamboat steam'-boat *steamboats*. A boat which goes by steam power.

steam engine steam' en'-gine *steam engines*. An engine which goes by steam power. – Many railway engines are *steam engines*.

steamer steam'-er *steamers*. 1. A ship, boat, or engine that is moved by steam.
2. A kind of pan with holes in it for steaming food.–Mother cooked the pudding in a *steamer*.

steamship steam'-ship *steamships*. A ship which goes by steam power.

steel. Iron that has been heated and mixed with carbon and other substances to make it harder and stronger. *Steel* is used to make many things that get hard use and must be very strong.–The bodies of cars are made of *steel*.

steep *steeper, steepest, steeps, steeped, steeping.* 1. Slanting sharply.–The boys climbed the *steep* hill.
2. Soak.–Tea is better if it is *steeped* in boiling water.

steeple stee'-ple *steeples*. The pointed top of a church. The spire is the pointed part at the top of a *steeple*; the *steeple* is the pointed tower on the church roof.

steer *steers, steered, steering.* 1. Direct; guide; cause to go in the direction desired.–Ronald *steered* his bicycle through the crowded street.–We turn the *steering* wheel on a motor-car to *steer* the car.
2. The young male of beef cattle.–*Steers* are killed to provide meat.

stem *stems*. 1. The main stalk of a plant.–Flowers and leaves are joined to the main *stem* by smaller *stems*.
2. The tube of a smoking pipe through which smoke is drawn into the mouth.
3. A slender support like the *stem* of a plant.–The glass has a *stem* at the bottom.

S T U V W X Y Z

stench. A bad smell.–The *stench* of that stagnant water is unpleasant.

stencil sten'-cil *stencils*. 1. A sheet of paper or metal with designs or letters cut through it. When you lay out a *stencil* on paper and brush ink across the *stencil,* the designs or letters will show on the paper.

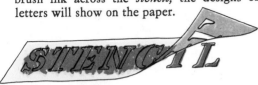

2. A design or letters made with a *stencil.*–Mother made a *stencil* round the wall in the kitchen.

stenographer ste-nog'-ra-pher *stenographers.* A person who can write down spoken words as fast as they are said by a special way of writing called shorthand.

step *steps, stepped, stepping.* 1. Move by placing one foot in a new forward position while the other foot remains where it was, as in walking.–Father *stepped* out of the house.
2. The placing of one foot forward.–Jack took 6 *steps* to get to the blackboard.–The distance which one can put one foot forward is also a *step.*
3. A regular movement of the feet in dancing. –Mary tried to teach Jack the new dance *step.*
4. A foot*step* is the sound of feet when walking or running.
5. One footboard of a stairway or ladder.– The first *step* of our hall stairs is covered with a rubber mat.
6. An act; a thing to do.–The first *step* in building a house is to dig the foundations.

stepfather step'-fa-ther *stepfathers.* The husband of one's mother, but not one's real father.–After Bill's father died, his mother married another man. This man is Bill's *stepfather.*

step-ladder step'-lad-der *step-ladders.* A ladder with 2 parts hinged together so that it will stand up by itself. A *step-ladder* has flat steps instead of rungs to stand on.

stepmother step'-moth-er *stepmothers.* The wife of one's father, but not one's real mother.–After Cinderella's mother died her father married another woman. This woman was Cinderella's *stepmother.*

stern *sternly.* 1. Strict. – The captain is very *stern.* He expects his men to obey exactly all his orders and all the rules of the ship.
2. Harsh; angry.–Jack called his dog away from the smaller dog in a *stern* voice.
3. The back part of a boat.

stew *stews, stewed, stewing.* 1. Cook by boiling slowly.–The cook *stewed* the prunes.
2. A dish of vegetables and meat boiled together slowly.–Lamb *stew* is Father's favourite dish.

steward stew'-ard *stewards.* 1. An officer on a ship in charge of food and sleeping quarters for passengers and crew.
2. A man on a ship who takes care of rooms, waits at table, etc., under the direction of a chief *steward.*
3. An official who manages a household or an estate.

stewardess stew'-ard-ess *stewardesses.* 1. A woman steward.
2. A woman on a plane or ship who sees to the comfort of the passengers and feeds them.

stick *sticks, stuck, sticking.* 1. A long, slender piece of wood.–The boys cut *sticks* to make a kite.
2. Something shaped like a *stick* of wood, as a *stick* of rock, a *stick* of chewing-gum, *sticks* of dynamite.–A cane is a walking-*stick.*
3. Fasten together with glue or paste.–*Stick* these 2 pieces of paper together.
4. Hold fast.–The dish *stuck* to the table.– Chewing gum *sticks* to one's shoes.
5. Prick; pierce.–Be careful or you will *stick* your finger with the pin.
6. Put or thrust.–The cat *stuck* its nose into the milk.
7. *Stick to* sometimes means to keep at.– *Stick to* your work until it is done.

sticky stick'-y *stickier, stickiest.* Causing things to stick together; gluey.–Mud is sometimes *sticky.*–Paste is *sticky.*–Toffee is *sticky.*

stiff *stiffer, stiffest.* 1. Not easily bent or moved. –Cardboard is *stiff*; paper is easy to fold. –The boy's sore arm is *stiff* now, but it will loosen up as he uses it.
2. Thick; solid; firm.–Gelatine becomes *stiff* when it cools.

stiffen stiff'-en *stiffens, stiffened, stiffening.* Make or become stiff or firm.–Mother uses starch to *stiffen* the collars and cuffs on Father's shirts.–The pudding *stiffens* when it cools.

S
T
U
V
W
X
Y
Z

stile *stiles.* 1. A step or steps used in going over a fence or a wall.–The old woman's pig would not go over the *stile.*

2. A turn*stile;* a kind of gate which allows only one person to pass through at a time.

still. 1. Not moving.–Stand *still.* Do not move.
2. Quiet; silent.–Be *still.* Do not make a sound.
3. Nevertheless; and yet. – Ruth says her tables again and again; *still,* she doesn't seem to know them.
4. Even.–Bob can write well when he writes fast; he can write *still* better when he writes slowly.
5. Yet.–At noon the fire was *still* burning. It had not gone out.
6. A device used in purifying water and in making whisky and other spirits.–You can make fresh water out of salt water with a *still.*

stillness still′-ness. Quietness; calm.–The *stillness* of the night is restful. – This lake is known for its *stillness.* The water is never ruffled.

stilt *stilts.* One of a pair of long poles with places for the feet to stand on some distance up from the ground.– *Stilts* make one look tall.

sting *stings, stung, stinging.* 1. Bite (of an insect).–Bees and other insects *sting.*
2. The injury made by the bite of an insect.
3. The part of a bee, insect, or animal used for *stinging.*
4. Cause a sharp, burning pain.–Salt or vinegar *stings* if it gets into a cut on your finger.
5. A sharp, burning pain.–The *sting* of the salt in Jack's eyes made him come out of the water.

stingy stin′-gy *stingier, stingiest.* Not generous; unwilling to spend or give away money or other things. – The *stingy* man would not spend money on anyone but himself.

stink *stinks, stank* or *stunk, stunk, stinking.*
1. A bad smell; foul odour.–A leak in the gas pipe caused a *stink* in the house.
2. Give off bad odour.–Garbage, if allowed to stand a long time, *stinks.*

stir *stirs, stirred, stirring.* 1. Move or mix, as with a spoon.–Mother *stirs* the custard when it is cooking to keep it from burning.
2. Move a little.–The wind made the leaves *stir.*
3. Arouse; excite.–The man *stirs* up trouble wherever he goes.
4. Excitement.–The accident in the factory caused a *stir.*

stirrup stir′-rup *stirrups.* One of a pair of footrests or supports for the feet of a person riding on a horse. *Stirrups* are fastened to the saddle and hang down on each side.

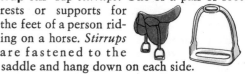

stitch *stitches, stitched, stitching.* 1. A single passage of thread through the cloth in sewing.
2. In embroidering, crocheting, or knitting, *stitches* are made by twisting the thread round the needles in certain ways.
3. Sew; make *stitches.*–Mother *stitched* the hem in Mary's dress.
4. A sharp, sudden pain.–Grandmother got a *stitch* in her back when she bent over to pick up her glove.

stock *stocks, stocked, stocking.* 1. Keep on the premises to sell. – The grocer's shop *stocks* butter, sugar and eggs.
2. A supply of things to sell.–After the Christmas rush, the shops had only a small *stock* left.

stocking stock′-ing *stockings.* One of a pair of coverings for the feet and lower legs.–Mary wears woollen *stockings* in the winter.

stoke *stokes, stoked, stoking.* Tend, put fuel in (a furnace, boiler, etc.). – Father *stokes* the furnace. He stirs up the fire and puts coal on when it is needed.

stoker stok′-er *stokers.* A person or a machine that takes care of a furnace by putting coal into it. A *stoker* in a factory or on a ship takes care of the fires which heat the boilers.

stole. One form of the word *steal.*–The hungry man *stole* food.

stolen sto′-len. One form of the word *steal.*– The jewellery was *stolen.*

S
T
U
V
W
X
Y
Z

stomach stom'-ach *stomachs*. The pouch inside the body into which food goes when swallowed. The *stomach* helps to digest the food so that our bodies can use it.

stone *stones, stoned, stoning*. 1. A piece of rock. –The house was built of large *stones*.
2. A rock; a hard mineral material found in the earth.–The house was built of *stone*.
3. A gem.–Rubies, opals, and diamonds are precious *stones* used in jewellery.
4. A large seed in a fruit, such as the peach and plum.–Mother took the *stones* out of the peaches before preserving them.
5. Throw *stones* at.–The bad boys *stoned* the cat.
6. Take the seeds out of.–Mary helped to *stone* the cherries before preserving them.
7. Made of rock.–Grandfather built a *stone* wall.

stony ston'-y *stonier, stoniest*. Covered with rocks or stones.–The ground was too *stony* to walk on with bare feet.

stood. One form of the word *stand*.–The boy *stood* by his chair until it was time to sit down.

stool *stools*. 1. A seat without a back.–Mother sits on a kitchen *stool* to mix the cake.
2. A low bench for resting the feet.–Father put his feet up on the foot*stool*.

stoop *stoops, stooped, stooping*. 1. Bend down. –Can you *stoop* and touch the floor with your fingers without bending your knees?
2. Let the shoulders and head lean forward. –That girl does not stand straight; she *stoops*.
3. A slumping posture.–She has a *stoop*.
4. Be low and mean.–Do not *stoop* to stealing. Do not be so low as to steal.

stop *stops, stopped, stopping*. 1. Halt; come to a standstill.–*Stop*, look, and listen before you cross the street.
2. Cease.–The bell *stopped* ringing.
3. Close or stuff up.–The boy *stopped* the leak in the dike by putting his thumb into the hole.
4. Block; prevent from moving.–A big, fat man with packages *stopped* the turnstile.
5. Cause to cease or come to an end.–Mother *stopped* the baby's crying by giving her a sweet.–Father *stopped* the water from running by turning off the tap.
6. Prevent.–Father caught Baby just in time to *stop* her from falling.
7. A halt, a standstill.–Bring the car to a *stop* at a red light.

stopper stop'-per *stoppers*. A piece of cork, rubber, or glass used to close a bottle or other container.–Mary put the *stopper* in the vinegar bottle.–The perfume bottle has a fancy glass *stopper*.

stop-watch stop'-watch *stop-watches*. A watch divided into fractions of a second, with a hand which can be stopped immediately by pressing a button. A *stop-watch* is used mainly for timing races.

storage stor'-age. 1. A place where things may be stored or kept for safekeeping.–We have some furniture in *storage*.
2. The amount paid for storing a thing.–The woman paid £2 *storage* on her fur coat.

store *stores, stored, storing*. 1. A shop, or place where things are sold.–Bob went to the hardware *store* to buy a saucepan.
2. Keep in a special place for later use.–We *store* potatoes, onions, and canned goods in the cellar.–Mother *stores* the rugs during the summer.
3. A supply.–We have quite a *store* of preserved fruit on the cellar shelves.

storehouse store'-house *storehouses*. A building for storing goods.–The crates of machinery were piled high in the *storehouse*.–A well-informed person is sometimes called a *storehouse* of information.

stork *storks*. A wading bird with long legs, a long neck, and a long bill.

storm *storms, stormed, storming*. 1. Any strong natural disturbance in the air. Sometimes there is the falling of much rain, snow, sleet, or hail, and a strong wind blowing during a *storm*.– Thunder and lightning often come with a rain*storm*. – The children made snowmen after the snow-*storm*.
2. Rush into by force and numbers.–The winners of the match *stormed* the schoolroom.–The soldiers *stormed* the city.
3. An explosion or outburst of any kind.– Mary burst into a *storm* of tears.
4. Scold and rage.–Jack came *storming* into the room asking who had taken his bicycle.

stormy storm'-y *stormier, stormiest*. 1. Filled with storms.–We have had a very *stormy* month.
2. Violent; angry.–Bill and Jack had a *stormy* argument.

S
T
U
V
W
X
Y
Z

story sto′-ry *stories*. 1. A report of things that have happened, or of imaginary happenings made up by someone.–Sally likes the *story* of Black Beauty.
2. A falsehood; a lie.–If you do something wrong, do not tell a *story* about it; tell the truth.
3. (Usually spelt *storey*). A floor, or a level of a building.–We live in a 2-*story* house. It has 2 floors, on 2 different levels. The kitchen, dining-room, and living-room are on the ground floor, the bedrooms on the second *story*.

stout *stoutly, stoutness*. 1. Heavily built; fat; thick.–Jack Sprat was thin and his wife was *stout*.–The tramp carried a *stout* stick to defend himself against dogs.
2. Sturdy; strong.–The boy set out to seek his fortune with a *stout* heart.

stove *stoves*. A box built of iron, brick, or some other material that does not burn, in which a fire can be made for cooking or heating.–Our *stove* is an electric *stove*.–Grandmother

has a gas *stove*.–In some *stoves*, coal or wood is burned.–Houses used to be heated by *stoves*, but **now** *stoves* are used mostly for cooking.

straddle strad′-dle *straddles, straddled, straddling*. To spread the legs far apart; to sit on something with one leg on either side. – Bob *straddled* the horse to ride it.–The boy is *straddling* a stool.

straight. 1. Not crooked; without turns, curves, or bends.–The road goes *straight* for 5 miles, and then it turns.–A ruler helps one to draw a *straight* line.
2. Right; in order.–Our teacher asked us if we had all our lessons *straight*.–Mother told Mary to put the sofa cushions *straight*.
3. Directly.–Go *straight* to school. Go now and go the shortest way.
4. Honest.–That man is *straight*. You can trust him.

straighten straight′-en *straightens, straightened, straightening*. 1. Make straight.–The carpenter *straightened* the crooked nail before he hammered it in.
2. Tidy; make neat.–The teacher told us to *straighten* up our desks.

strain *strains, strained, straining*. 1. Stretch, pull too tight.–The clothes-line was *strained* by the wet clothes hanging on it.
2. Sprain, injure by pulling a muscle or ligament.–Father lifted a heavy rock in the garden and *strained* his back.
3. Injury caused by pulling a muscle or ligament.–The *strain* kept Father from working.
4. Press through a sieve or strainer to remove little pieces. – Mother *strained* the orange juice to get out the seeds and pulp.
5. Pressure; weight; tension.–The *strain* on the telephone wires caused by the falling tree made them break.–Mother was under a great *strain* when Father and Baby were ill.
6. Try as hard as possible.–Jack *strained* to lift the table.

strainer strain′-er *strainers*. A kitchen tool with a fine screen or wire net used for straining things; a pan with small holes at the bottom; a sieve.–Tomatoes, fruits, and soups are often strained or pressed through a *strainer* to take out seeds and other small pieces.

strait *straits*. A comparatively narrow, natural channel of water that joins 2 larger bodies of water.–The *Straits* of Gibraltar connect the Atlantic Ocean and Mediterranean Sea.

strand *strands, stranded, stranding*. 1. Placed in a helpless position.–The lost boy was *stranded* in the strange town without money.
2. Run aground (applied to vessels).–A ship was *stranded* on the big rocks.
3. One of the many fine threads twisted together to make heavier threads, ropes, yarns, and so forth.
4. A string.–Mother wore a *strand* of pearls with her black dress.–Grandmother brushed a *strand* of hair off Mary's forehead.

strange *stranger, strangest*. 1. Not known, seen, or heard of before; new and not familiar.–The man's face was *strange* to Bob.–This part of the city is *strange* to me.
2. Queer; not natural; odd. – Mother felt *strange* after eating the fish. – Mary looks *strange* in a baby's bonnet; she's a big girl now.
3. Shy.–The new boy felt *strange* among so many boys he didn't know.

S
T
U
V
W
X
Y
Z

stranger stran'-ger *strangers*. A person whom one has never known, seen, or heard of before.–Mother opened the door and found a *stranger* standing in the porch.–This boy is a *stranger* in our school.

strangle stran'-gle *strangles, strangled, strangling*. 1. Kill or die by choking.–The hero in the play *strangled* the villain. He killed him by holding him tightly by the neck so that he could no longer breathe.–Do not fasten your puppy's collar too tight, or he may *strangle*. 2. Choke; cut off the breath.–The scared woman gave a strangled cry.

strap *straps, strapped, strapping*. 1. A narrow strip of leather or other material that can be bent easily.–Father put a *strap* round the suitcase.–*Straps* of metal are used on boxes to make them stronger. 2. Fasten with a *strap*.–Bob *strapped* the basket on to his bicycle. 3. Whip with a *strap*.–The very angry man *strapped* the boy with his belt.

straw *straws*. 1. A dry stem of wheat, rye, oats, or other grain after the grain has been threshed or taken off.–*Straw* is used as bedding for cattle, to make hats and paper, to 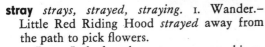 pack china, bricks, or other breakable things, and for other purposes. 2. A thin tube of paper.–Bob sips his ice-cream soda through a *straw*.

strawberry straw'-ber-ry *strawberries*. A red berry that grows on creeping vines, close to the ground.

stray *strays, strayed, straying*. 1. Wander.–Little Red Riding Hood *strayed* away from the path to pick flowers. 2. Lost.–Jack found a *stray* puppy shivering with the cold.

streak *streaks, streaked, streaking*. 1. A long line or stripe.–Father got a *streak* of paint on the window-pane. 2. Mark with long lines or stripes.–The petal was red, *streaked* with yellow. There were long yellow lines on the red petal.

stream *streams, streamed, streaming*. 1. A flow of water or other liquid, or gas.–A *stream* of water came from the tap. 2. A river or brook.–We went to the *stream* to fish.

3. Run or flow.–When the ball hit Bob's nose, blood *streamed* down his face. 4. Wave or blow.–The children marched in the parade with flags and banners *streaming*. 5. Move steadily in large numbers.–People *streamed* out of the theatre after the play. 6. A steady line of people or things.–A *stream* of people poured out of the theatre.

streamer stream'-er *streamers*. A long narrow flag, ribbon, or anything that will wave.–The children carried *streamers* in the parade.

stream-line stream'-line *stream-lines, stream-lined, stream-lining*. To shape so that surrounding air, water, or gas will pass to the sides without being blocked off, and not check speed of movement. – Aeroplanes must be *stream-lined* to fly well.

street *streets*. 1. An open way in a town or city on which people travel.–Motor-cars, bicycles, and people walking filled the narrow *streets*. 2. The people living in the *street*.–When Miss Jones was married, the whole *street* turned out to wish her good luck.

strength. The quality of being strong. – The workman had great *strength*. He could lift big rocks.–Grandmother didn't have much *strength* after her illness.

strengthen strength'-en *strengthens, strengthened, strengthening*. Make strong; give strength to. – The men *strengthened* the bridge by putting more timbers under it.

strenuous stren'-u-ous *strenuously*. Very vigorous and energetic.–Rowing is a *strenuous* sport. It requires great strength and fitness. –Bill is making the most *strenuous* efforts to pass the examination.

stress *stresses, stressed, stressing*. 1. In our school, much *stress* was put on spelling. Much attention was given to learning to spell. 2. Accent or emphasize.–In some music we *stress* the first note of each measure.–In saying the word 'kitten' we *stress* the first syllable. 3. A strain; a force.–The rafters in the building are under constant *stress*.

S
T
U
V
W
X
Y
Z

strefch *stretches, stretched, stretching.* 1. Extend; reach out.–The children *stretched* their arms high over their heads.–The cat always *stretches* when she wakes up.

2. Spread apart.–Bob had to *stretch* his fingers to play the piano.

3. Reach.–Baby *stretched* out her hand for the glass of milk.

4. Make or get larger under strain.–Mary *stretched* the rubber band to get it round her book.

5. Extend or reach. – Our garden *stretches* from the house to the back fence.

stretcher stretch'-er *stretchers.* 1. A person or thing that stretches or makes larger.–Father's shoes were stretched on a shoe *stretcher*.

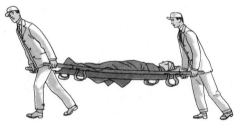

2. A carrier for injured or sick people, made of 2 poles with heavy cloth fastened between them. A *stretcher* is carried by 2 men, one at each end.–The injured boy was carried to the ambulance on a *stretcher*.

strew *strews, strewed, strewn, strewing.* Scatter. – Do not *strew* your toys all over the house.–When Mary dropped the bag, beans were *strewn* all over the floor.

strict *strictly.* 1. Demanding obedience to rules. –The headmaster is very *strict*. He makes all the children obey the rules carefully.

2. Exact; just right.–Bob made the measurements for the model aeroplane with *strict* accuracy.

stride *strides, strode, striding.* 1. A long step.–Bob measured the football field with 100 *strides*.

2. Walk with long steps.–The teacher *strode* to the back of the room to open the window.

strike *strikes, struck, striking.* 1. Hit; come or bring into sharp contact with.–The boy tried to *strike* me.–The car skidded and *struck* a pole.

2. Light (a match). – Be careful when you *strike* matches.–Do not *strike* matches on the furniture.

3. Sound by hitting a bell or gong.–Mary heard the clock *strike* 2.

4. Come suddenly to (one's mind).–An idea of how to make a model plane *struck* Bob today.

5. Stop work as a group to get higher pay or better working conditions.–The men at the factory have *struck*; they left work yesterday and said they would not go back till they were promised more money.

6. A stopping of work as a group to get more money or better working conditions.–There is a *strike* at the factory now.

7. Find; come upon.–The miners *struck* gold while digging.–Bob and Mary have *struck* a plan for saving money.

8. Lower, take down. – When the boat returned to harbour, the crew *struck* sails.

9. *Strike out* sometimes means to mark out. –Mary spelt the word wrong and corrected it by *striking out* the wrong letter.

10. *Strike out* may mean to start.–The Boy Scouts *struck* out through the woods.

11. Settle or agree on terms.–The two boys *struck* a bargain not to fight each other.

12. Cause to be overcome with pity, horror, etc.–When the thunderstorm broke, the dog was *struck* with terror.–The man's condition *struck* us with pity.

string *strings, strung, stringing.* 1. A cord; light rope; a heavy thread or anything used for tying, binding, etc.–Bob's kite *string* broke and his kite blew away.

2. Ornaments on a *string*.–Mary has a *string* of beads.

3. A fine, strong cord or wire used on violins, pianos, and some other musical instrument to make the notes.

4. A tough thread-like part of a plant.–Beans in the shell or pod have *strings* along the sides of the shell.

5. Remove *strings* from.–Mother *strings* beans before she cooks them.

6. A row.–A *string* of stockings was hung near the Christmas tree.

7. Put on a *string*.–Children like to *string* beads to wear when they 'dress up.'

8. Put *strings* on.–The violinist could not play until he had *strung* his violin.

9. A series.–The children bombarded the teacher with a *string* of questions.–Uncle Jack kept the whole family amused with a *string* of funny stories.

10. *String out* means to stretch out like a *string*.–The parade was *strung out* from the river to the park.

11. To *string up* something means to hang it up by a *string* or rope.–The butcher *strung up* a leg of beef.

S
T
U
V
W
X
Y
Z

string bean *string beans*. The French or kidney bean. Along each side of the pod or shell is a stringy part that is pulled off before cooking.

strip *strips, stripped, stripping*. 1. A long narrow piece.—Mary cut off a *strip* of paper to write her spelling words on.
2. Undress.—Mother *stripped* Baby to give her a bath.—The doctor asked the boys to *strip* before he examined them.
3. Peel off, or cut off in *strips*.—The hunter *stripped* the skin from the rabbit.
4. Make bare or empty.—The hungry children *stripped* the cupboard of all the food.

stripe *stripes, striped, striping*. 1. A broad line; a long, narrow band or strip. Mother has bought a new dress with blue and white *stripes*. – Zebras are marked all over with black and white *stripes*.
2. Cover or mark with *stripes*. – The boys *striped* the pole with paint so it could be used for a Maypole on May Day.

striped. Marked with stripes.—We saw a *striped* snake in the woods. It had stripes of yellow and black along its body.

stroke *strokes, stroked, stroking*. 1. Rub gently and caressingly. – Mother *stroked* Baby's head.
2. A blow.—Bob chopped the piece of wood in two with one *stroke* of the axe.
3. A kind of sudden illness which often makes a person helpless.—The old man had a *stroke* last night.
4. A complete movement made over and over again in a certain activity, like skating, tennis, or rowing.—Tom rowed with long, even *strokes*.
5. A sound caused by striking.—Father Christmas came at the *stroke* of 12 by the clock.

stroll *strolls, strolled, strolling*. 1. A slow walk for pleasure.—The girls have gone for a *stroll* through the woods.
2. Walk slowly for pleasure.—They *strolled* about for an hour.

strong *stronger, strongest*. 1. Not weak; having strength or force.—Boxers are *strong*.
2. Forceful.—A *strong* wind is blowing the ships about.
3. Large and able; sufficient.—Great Britain has a *strong* navy. It has many men and ships, and much equipment.
4. Sharp, keen, powerful.—This cheese has a *strong* taste.—The smell filled the man with *strong* disgust.

5. Concentrated.—Father likes *strong* coffee, but Mother likes it with more water in it.
6. Tough; not easily broken.—The kite string is *strong*.—The old chair is *stronger* than it looks. It will hold your weight.

strop *strops, stropped, stropping*. 1. A leather strap on which razors are sharpened.
2. Sharpen on a *strop*. –Father always *strops* his razor before he uses it.

struck. One form of the word *strike*.—The man *struck* the dog.

structure struc'-ture *structures*. 1. Anything built, as a factory or bridge.—We saw many large *structures* as we came nearer the city.
2. The way in which anything is formed or shaped.—The *structure* of Mary's face is like that of Mother's.

struggle strug'-gle *struggles, struggled, struggling*. 1. Work very hard: fight against difficulties.—The poor man had to *struggle* to feed his children.—The lion *struggled* to get out of his cage.
2. A strong effort or fight.—The men put up a great *struggle* to keep the fire from spreading. It was hard work.

strung. One form of the word *string*. – We *strung* tinsel on the Christmas tree.

stub *stubs, stubbed, stubbing*. 1. Short, dull piece left after the main part is gone.—Mary has used the pencil down to a *stub*.—Father threw the *stub* of his cigar away.
2. A tree-stump.—There were only *stubs* where the trees had been cut down.
3. Bump (one's toe).—Don't *stub* your toe against the low step.
4. A part of a ticket which is torn off when used.—Keep the *stub* of your ticket to show to the inspector when he comes round.

stubborn stub'-born *stubbornly, stubbornness*. Refusing to give in to others or to change one's mind; obstinate.—Father told Jack he was solving the problem in the wrong way, but Jack was *stubborn*. Jack insisted that he could do it his own way.

stubby stub'-by *stubbier, stubbiest*. Short and thick.—Baby's toes are *stubby*.—Jack's dog has a *stubby* tail.

stuck. One form of the word *stick*.—Bob *stuck* the stamp on the envelope.

S
T
U
V
W
X
Y
Z

student stu'-dent *students*. A person who studies; a pupil.—There are 500 *students* in our school.—People who study law are *students* of law.—The vicar of our church is a *student* of the Bible.

studio stu'-di-o *studios*. 1. A room where a painter, musician, or other artist works.

2. A place from which radio and television programmes are broadcast.
3. A place where films are made.

study stud'-y *studies, studied, studying*. 1. To try to learn or understand by reading, thinking, or practising.
2. A particular subject about which one tries to learn.—Geography, English, and History are some of Bob's *studies*.
3. A room used for reading, *studying*, or writing.—The writer went into his *study* to work on his new book.
4. Try to figure out.—Bob *studied* the puzzle. He tried to think out a way to solve it.
5. Look at carefully. — Sally picked up the snail and *studied* it closely.

stuff *stuffs, stuffed, stuffing*. 1. The material that things are made of.—Cotton is the best *stuff* for children's clothes. — The teacher thinks Bob has the *stuff* in him to be a great engineer.
2. Material or objects of any kind.—If there were less *stuff* in this room, it would look prettier.
3. Fill.—The doll is *stuffed* with cotton.

stuffing stuff'-ing *stuffings*. 1. A material used for filling a thing.—Cotton and sawdust are *stuffings* used for dolls.
2. A dressing usually made of breadcrumbs mixed with seasonings and stuffed into chicken, turkey, or other meat or food.—When we have turkey, we always have chestnut *stuffing*.

stumble stum'-ble *stumbles, stumbled, stumbling*. 1. Trip by catching the foot. — Mary *stumbled* on the garden hose and fell.

2. Walk unsteadily, walk shakily.—Baby is learning to walk and often *stumbles*.
3. Make a mistake.—Mary *stumbled* in spelling the long word.

stump *stumps*. 1. The short part left in the ground after a tree or plant has been cut down.—The squirrel sat on a tree *stump* and ate a nut.

2. The part of anything that is left when the main part is gone. The part of a leg, arm, finger, and so forth that is left when a part has been removed.

stumpy stump'-y *stumpier, stumpiest*. Short and thick like a stump.—A *stumpy* little man came waddling down the street.—Jack's dog likes to thump his *stumpy* tail on the floor to show that he is pleased.

stun *stuns, stunned, stunning*. 1. Make senseless or unconscious. — A blow on the head *stunned* the boy. For a time he knew nothing.
2. Shock, surprise.—We were *stunned* at the news of the accident.

stung. One form of the word *sting*. – A bee *stung* Grandmother.

stunt *stunts, stunted, stunting*. 1. An unusual trick, something that is hard to do.—Acrobats and clowns amuse people by doing *stunts*.
2. Check or stop (growth).—Too little exercise, fresh air and nourishing food may *stunt* one's growth.

stupid stu'-pid *stupidity, stupidly*. Dull; not bright or clever.—Because the child is too shy to talk much, he sometimes seems *stupid*.—The things the man said were *stupid*.

sturdy stur'-dy *sturdier, sturdiest*. 1. Strong; well-made.—This is not a very *sturdy* chair to sit on; it may not hold you.
2. Robust, hardy.—Mary is not so sturdy as Sally; Mary gets ill more easily.

sturgeon stur'-geon *sturgeons*. A kind of fish that is good to eat. Caviare comes from *sturgeon*.

stutter stut'-ter *stutters, stuttered, stuttering*. Stammer, or repeat a sound again and again when trying to speak.—'N-n-n-no,' the boy *stuttered*.

sty *sties*. 1. A pen built for pigs. Mother said the house was as dirty as a *sty*.

2. (sometimes spelt *stye*). A red, swollen sore on the edge of the eyelid.

style *styles*. 1. A fashion.–It is the *style* for women to wear flowers in their hair.–High-button shoes are not in *style*.
2. A way of doing something. – There are different *styles* of handwriting.

stylish styl'-ish *stylishly, stylishness*. Fashionable.–*Stylish* clothes are the kind that well-dressed people are wearing.–The clothes worn 100 years ago are not *stylish* now.

subject sub'-ject *subjects*. 1. The person or thing about which one is talking, writing, thinking, studying, etc.–The *subject* that Mary and Bob were talking about was the party for Tuesday.–The *subject* of Mary's story was 'Life as a Film Star.' – My favourite *subject* is arithmetic.
2. Apt to have.–Father is *subject* to colds in the head.
3. Depending upon or resting on.–I accept your invitation, *subject* to Mother's consent. I shall come if Mother will let me.
4. A citizen of a kingdom.–I am a British *subject*, a *subject* of the British Queen.

subject sub-ject' *subjects, subjected, subjecting*. Force to endure or submit.–The explorers were *subjected* to great hardships. – The king's armies *subjected* all the small surrounding countries to his rule.

submarine sub'-ma-rine *submarines*. A boat that can run under water.

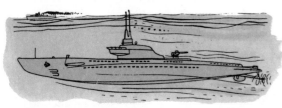

submit sub-mit' *submits, submitted, submitting*.
1. Give in or surrender.–The boy *submitted* to having his tooth pulled.
2. Hand in or offer.–Mary *submitted* a report to her teacher.

subscribe sub-scribe' *subscribes, subscribed, subscribing*. 1. Agree to take and pay for.–Mother has *subscribed* to the daily paper and a monthly magazine.
2. Make a written promise to give a certain amount.–We *subscribed* £2 to the Red Cross.

subscriber sub-scrib'-er *subscribers*. A person who promises to take and pay for something, such as a magazine or newspaper.–The magazine is advertising for new *subscribers*.

subscription sub-scrip'-tion *subscriptions*. 1. Agreement to take something and pay for it. –Mother has renewed her *subscription* to the paper for another year.
2. An amount promised.–Our *subscription* to the Red Cross has been paid.

subside sub-side' *subsides, subsided, subsiding*. Become less.–The wind *subsided* in the evening.

substitute sub'-sti-tute *substitutes, substituted, substituting, substitution*. 1. A person or thing serving in place of another. – The doctor could not come, so he sent a *substitute*. He sent another doctor. – Father didn't have a saw, so he used a knife as a *substitute*.
2. Provide in place of. – They didn't have any chocolate ice-cream, so they *substituted* vanilla.–Bill was not at all satisfied with his English composition. He kept on rubbing words out and *substituting* others.

subtract sub-tract' *subtracts, subtracted, subtracting*. Take away.–One *subtracted* from 4 leaves 3.

subtraction sub-trac'-tion. Taking one number from another.–1 taken from 4 leaves 3 is an example of *subtraction*.

suburb sub'-urb *suburbs*. A section or small community on the edge of a town or city.–We could not get a house in the town, so we live in a *suburb*.

suburban sub-urb'-an. Belonging to the suburbs or outlying parts.–There are many new factories in the *suburban* districts of the town.

subversive sub-ver'-sive *subversively*. Destructive, likely to overthrow something.–Spying is a subversive activity. Its aim is to help in bringing about the defeat of the enemy or suspected enemy.

subway sub'-way *subways*. An underground tunnel to take people from one place to another without crossing a street.

S
T
U
V
W
X
Y
Z

succeed suc-ceed′ *succeeds, succeeded, succeeding.* 1. Come after.–Miss Jones was our first teacher; then Miss Smith *succeeded* her.
2. Win a desired goal; finish a thing satisfactorily.–'If at first you don't *succeed*, try, try, try again.'

success suc-cess′ *successes.* 1. Getting what one wants; carrying out what one wants to do satisfactorily.–Bob had *success* in making his kite.
2. Fame; fortune.–The man won *success* by working very hard.
3. A person on thing that succeeds or turns out well.–The singer was a great *success*. She was famous, because she sang well.–The fire drill was a *success*.

successful suc-cess′-ful *successfully.* 1. Having success.–That lawyer is *successful*. He succeeds in what he tries to do. He earns a good living, and people respect him.
2. Rich and famous. – The man became a *successful* actor because of his talent and hard work.

succession suc-ces′-sion. The happening or coming of one thing right after another.–In the circus parade, the elephants walked in *succession*. They followed one another without anything between them.

such. 1. So bad, so good, so big, so much, and so forth.–Baby is *such* a mischief!–The boy is *such* an eater!
2. Of a certain kind. – Bob had *such* vegetables as corn, peas, and cabbage in his garden.–Mary reads *such* stories as 'The Three Bears' and 'Cinderella' to Sally.

suck *sucks, sucked, sucking.* 1. Draw into the mouth by working the lips and tongue.–The baby *sucks* milk from a feeding-bottle.–We eat ice-cream sodas by *sucking* the liquid through a straw.
2. Soak or draw up.–Plants *suck* water from the ground.
3. Dissolve in the mouth.–Children *suck* lollipops.

sucker suck′-er *suckers.* 1. A pad or disk which enables certain creatures or objects to stick firmly to a surface.–An octopus has *suckers* on its arms.–Jack's darts have rubber *suckers* instead of points.
2. The little shoots or stems that come up from the roots of trees and bushes.–We cut down the *suckers* from the bush so that the main bush will be stronger.
3. A kind of fish.

sudden sud′-den *suddenly.* 1. Unexpected.–A *sudden* clap of thunder made us jump.
2. Quick; rapid.–Father made a *sudden* trip to the country.
3. *All of a sudden* means *suddenly* or unexpectedly.–*All of a sudden* the door opened.

suds. Water with enough soap in it to make bubbles.–Mother washed the clothes in *suds*.

sue *sues, sued, suing.* Take action against someone through the courts.–The man would not pay for the damage he had done, so Father had to *sue* him. Father started action against him in court to get him to do the right thing.

suet su′-et. Hard fat taken from the meat of cattle and sheep.–*Suet* is used for cooking and for making candles.

suffer suf′-fer *suffers, suffered, suffering.* 1. Feel great pain.–Grandmother *suffered* when she broke her arm.
2. Endure; undergo.–The poor man has *suffered* many hardships during the cold winter.
3. Be harmed or hurt.–The farmer's crops have *suffered* because we have had no rain.

suffering suf′-fer-ing. Hardship; pain; unhappiness.–We know of the *suffering* the family has had.

sufficient suf-fi′-cient *sufficiently.* Enough; as much as is needed.–We have *sufficient* coal for the winter.

sugar sug′-ar *sugars, sugared, sugaring.* 1. A sweet substance made from *sugar* beets or *sugar* cane.–We put *sugar* in coffee, on fruit, and on cereals to make them sweet.
2. Make sweet by adding some *sugar*.–Father *sugared* the cereal for Baby. He sprinkled *sugar* on it.
3. We talk of *sugaring the pill* when we combine bad news with something more comforting.

sugar beet sug′-ar beet *sugar beets.* A large, white kind of beet used in making sugar.

sugar cane sug′-ar cane. A plant with tall, hollow stalks that are used in making sugar. It usually grows where it is warm.

S
T
U
V
W
X
Y
Z

sugary sug'-a-ry. 1. Covered with or tasting of sugar.–The grapefruit was not *sugary* enough. It was too sour.
2. In an over-sweet or flattering way.–The assistant spoke in a *sugary* tone to persuade Mother to buy the hat.

suggest sug-gest' *suggests, suggested, suggesting.* 1. Bring up or mention as a possible and desirable thing to do.–The teacher *suggested* that we read the story before going home.– Bob *suggested* that we work first and then play.
2. Bring something to someone's mind or attention.–If I say 'cloud' to you, what does it *suggest*? It *suggests* rain.
3. Hint or imply.–The lawyer *suggested* that the witness was not speaking the truth.

suggestion sug-ges'-tion *suggestions.* A thought or idea that someone has and suggests or offers to someone else.–Mary gave us a *suggestion* as to how we might save paper.

suicide su'-i-cide *suicides.* 1. Killing of oneself. –The man's death was not an accident; it was *suicide*. He killed himself purposely.
2. A person who kills himself.–The man was a *suicide*.

suit suits, *suited, suiting.* 1. A set of clothing worn together, as a coat, waistcoat, and trousers.–Father's winter *suit* is brown.
2. Satisfy or please.– A picnic on the last day of the holiday *suited* the children very well. They liked it.
3. Go well with; match.–A yellow dress *suits* a person with brown hair and brown eyes.
4. In a pack of playing cards, all those cards that have spots of the same shape.–Hearts, clubs, spades, and diamonds are the 4 *suits*.

suitable suit'-a-ble. Proper; fit.–Men's straw hats are not *suitable* for winter weather.– Overalls are *suitable* for farm work.

suit-case suit'-case *suit-cases.* A flat travelling bag. – Mother packed our clothes in a *suit-case* when we went to Grandmother's.

suitor suit'-or *suitors.* A man who wants to marry a certain woman.–The woman's *suitor* called on her every night last week.

sulk *sulks, sulked, sulking.* Show bad humour by keeping quietly to oneself.–The girl *sulks* when she does not get her own way.

sulky sulk'-y *sulkier, sulkiest, sulkies.* 1. Cross; bad-tempered.–Mother said that no one likes a *sulky* person.
2. A small, 2-wheeled carriage drawn by a horse and seating 1 person.

sullen sul'-len *sullenly.* 1. Quietly angry.–Baby is *sullen* when she can't have her own way.
2. Dull; gloomy.–The *sullen* day made everyone feel sad.

sulphur sul'-phur. A yellowish substance that burns easily and gives off a strong odour that makes it hard for one to breathe.–The heads of some matches have *sulphur* in them.

sultan sul'-tan *sultans.* A ruler in certain countries of the Far East.

sultry sul'-try *sultrier, sultriest.* Hot and damp. –A *sultry* day is one that is hot and moist, with very little breeze.

sum *sums, summed, summing.* 1. The number made by adding numbers.–The *sum* of 4 and 2 is 6.
2. Arithmetic problems.–Bob sometimes has trouble doing his *sums*.
3. An amount of money.–Mary has a small *sum* for pocket-money each week.
4. *Sum up* means to tell in a few words.– The teacher asked us to *sum up* what we had learned during the day.

sumac or **sumach** su -mac. A bush that has large, reddish blossoms and, later, red berries on it. The berries are not good to eat. –The leaves of *sumac* are bright red in the autumn.

summary sum'-ma-ry *summaries.* A short report.–Mary gave us all a *summary* of what happened at the meeting.

summer sum'-mer *summers.* One of the 4 seasons. – The seasons of the year are spring, *summer*, autumn, and winter.–In our part of the world, *summer* is the hottest season.

summit sum'-mit *summits.* The top; the highest point.–It is a hard climb to the *summit* of the hill.

summon sum'-mon *summons, summoned, summoning.* Call or send for.–The teacher *summoned* the boy to her desk.

S
T
U
V
W
X
Y
Z

sun *suns, sunned, sunning.* I. The brightest body we can see in the sky; it gives us light and heat.–The earth goes round the *sun* once in a year.–The stars shine at night. The *sun* shines during the day.
2. Heat and light of the *sun.*–The *sun* makes the plants grow.–The living-room faces the east, so it gets the morning *sun.*
3. Expose to the light of the *sun.*–Father sat on the sand and *sunned* himself.

sunbeam sun'-beam *sunbeams.* A ray of sunlight.–A *sunbeam* danced on the wall.

sun-bonnet sun'-bon-net *sun-bonnets.* A bonnet with a broad brim.–A *sun-bonnet* is worn to keep the sun off the face and the neck.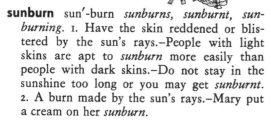

sunburn sun'-burn *sunburns, sunburnt, sunburning.* I. Have the skin reddened or blistered by the sun's rays.–People with light skins are apt to *sunburn* more easily than people with dark skins.–Do not stay in the sunshine too long or you may get *sunburnt.*
2. A burn made by the sun's rays.–Mary put a cream on her *sunburn.*

Sunday Sun'-day *Sundays.* The first day of the week.–*Sunday* is the Christian Sabbath, or day of rest.

sundial sun'-di-al *sundials.* An instrument for telling time by the sun's shadow. The sun makes a shadow that points towards numbers on the dial. The numbers on which the shadows fall tell what time it is.

sundown sun'-down. The time when the sun goes down out of sight; sunset.–The wind stopped blowing at *sundown.*

sundry sun'-dry. Several, various.–We have *sundry* matters to discuss.

sunflower sun'-flow-er *sunflowers.* A tall plant that has large, yellow flowers with large, brown centres which are full of seeds–Birds eat *sunflower* seeds.

sung. One form of the word *sing.* –We sing the song 'John Peel' in school. We have *sung* it every day this week.

sunk. One form of the word *sink.* –The boat that had *sunk* was lifted up and taken away.

sunlight sun'-light. Light of the sun.–We sat in the *sunlight* to get warm.

sunny sun'-ny *sunnier, sunniest.* I. Filled with sunshine.–This is a *sunny* day.
2. Bright; pleasant.–Sally has a *sunny* smile.

sunrise sun'-rise *sunrises.* I. The time of day when the sun comes up.–Grandfather gets up at *sunrise.*
2. Dawn; light in the sky when the sun comes up.–We watched the *sunrise* from the mountain top.

sunset sun'-set *sunsets.* I. The going down of the sun.–Take down the flag just before *sunset.*
2. The changing light and colour in the sky when the sun goes down.–We watched the *sunset* over the lake.

sunshine sun'-shine. Light from the sun.–The *sunshine* came through the window.

superintendent su-per-in-tend'-ent *superintendents.* I. A person who has charge of a place or people.–The *superintendent* of a block of flats sees that the building is kept clean and in good condition.
2. In the British police force, a *superintendent* is an officer above the rank of inspector.

superior su-pe'-ri-or *superiors.* I. Higher in position.–A major is *superior* to a captain.– –The headmaster is *superior* to the other members of the staff.
2. A person higher in position than another. –The headmaster is our teacher's *superior.*
3. Better.–Our armies have *superior* weapons.–Bill thinks he is *superior.* He acts as though he were better than the other boys.

superstition su-per-sti'-tion *superstitions.* I. A false belief or fear.–It is an old *superstition* that it is good luck a black cat to cross a path ahead of you.–Educated people today know that *superstitions* are not true.
2. The habit of believing in mysterious powers or forces which do not really exist.--*Superstition* makes people think it is unlucky to walk under a ladder.–Science tries to fight *superstition.*

superstitious su-per-sti'-tious *superstitiously.* Believing in and fearful of unknown powers. –*Superstitious* people think it is bad luck for 13 people to sit at a table.

supper sup'-per *suppers.* The last meal of the day.–Some people have dinner at midday. In the evening they have *supper,* a lighter meal.

supply sup-ply' *supplies, supplied, supplying.* 1. Give, produce, provide.–The farmers *supply* food for the people of the city.–City people *supply* clothing machines, and other things to the farmer. 2. An amount or quantity on hand. – The stores have a *supply* of shoes for the winter season.–Father has our *supply* of coal in the coal bunker. 3. Add or furnish.–Mary got all the words in the puzzle but one. Bob *supplied* that one.

support sup-port' *supports, supported, supporting.* 1. Hold up, keep (a thing) from falling.–A clothes-prop *supports* a clothes-line.–Posts *support* the roof of the veranda. 2. Furnish a home, food, and clothing for, or everything necessary for living.–The father *supports* his children. 3. Help in getting food, clothing, and the things necessary for living; getting a living. –Old people sometimes have no means of *support.* 4. Help, encourage.–The sick man felt *supported* by the good wishes of his neighbours. –Mother said she would *support* Jack's plan to go camping. 5. Be in favour of, uphold.–Father *supports* Mr Jones in the election. 6. Anything that holds something up.–A clothes-prop is a *support* because it *supports* the clothes-line.

suppose sup-pose' *supposes, supposed, supposing.* 1. Believe; guess.–I *suppose* Jack will come to the party. 2. Imagine.–Just *suppose* you were on a desert island. What would you do? 3. The children are *supposed* to be in bed.

supreme su-preme' *supremely.* 1. Greatest.– This news is of *supreme* importance to us. 2. Highest in position or power. – In the United States the *Supreme* Court is the highest court.

sure sureness. 1. Certain, positive.–Mary is *sure* that she heard Mother call us. 2. Dependable. – This is a *sure* recipe for chocolate cake. It will not fail. 3. Confident. – Jack is *sure* of making the hat-trick. He is certain he will.

surely sure'-ly. Certainly. – *Surely* that was Father we saw; I am sure that it was.

surf *surfs.* Waves of the sea hitting or washing against the shore.–We stood on the rocks and watched the *surf.*

surface sur'-face *surfaces.* 1. A side, the outside.–The *surface* of a brick is rough. 2. A top, or flat upper part.–The *surface* of the table needs to be painted.–A stick was floating on the *surface* of the water.

surge *surges, surged, surging.* 1. Roll up and fall.–During the storm, the waves *surged* over the rocks on the coast. 2. A sudden great wave.–A *surge* of the water carried the tiny boat to shore.

surgeon sur'-geon *surgeons.* A doctor who operates on people.–A *surgeon* operated on Mary. He took out her tonsils.

surplus sur'-plus. Extra amount.–We had a *surplus* of money this week. We had some left over.

surprise sur-prise' *surprises, surprised, surprising.* 1. Something not expected.–Father had a *surprise* in his pocket for Sally. 2. Not expected.–We are planning a *surprise* party for Mother. She doesn't know about it or expect it. 3. A feeling caused by something that was not expected.–A look of *surprise* came over Bob's face when he saw his new bicycle. 4. Come upon suddenly and unexpectedly.– The policeman *surprised* the robbers in their headquarters. 5. Amaze, take unaware.–Mother was *surprised* to see us.

S
T
U
V
W
X
Y
Z

surrender sur-ren′-der *surrenders, surrendered, surrendering*. 1. Give up.–The enemy held the town for a long time, but at last they had to *surrender* it.–The robbers *surrendered* to the police.
2. A giving up.–The *surrender* of the enemy came when their supplies ran out.
3. Give in to something.–Jack realized that his dog had disappeared, so he *surrendered* to despair.

surround sur-round′ *surrounds, surrounded, surrounding*. 1. Enclose.–A fence *surrounds* the garden. It goes all the way round the garden to keep the chickens from getting in.
2. Close in upon on all sides.–When Robin Hood found himself *surrounded,* he blew his horn for his Merry Men to come to his aid.
3. A border or piece of material used as a floor-covering.–There is a linoleum *surround* in the nursery. Linoleum surrounds the carpet.

surroundings sur-round′-ings. Things or conditions all about one.–The children have always lived in pleasant *surroundings*. They have had a pretty home in nice country, with pleasant neighbours.

survey sur-vey′ *surveys, surveyed, surveying*. 1. Look over, examine.–The teacher *surveyed* the room to see that everything was neat and orderly.
2. Measure carefully to get the size, shape, and position of an area and to determine where the boundaries are.–The men are *surveying* the field next to our house.

survey sur′-vey *surveys*. A study, examination, comparison.–The teachers made a *survey* of the parents' opinion of the progress of their children. They tried to find out what the parents thought.

surveyor sur-vey′-or *surveyors*. A person who uses surveying instruments to measure land for size, shape, and position.

survive sur-vive′ *survives, survived, surviving*. – 1. Remain alive after; live through. – All the families *survived* the flood.
2. Live longer than.–The mother *survived* all 3 of her children.
3. Last through.–The old flag has survived 3 wars. We still have it.

survivor sur-vi′-vor *survivors*. A person who is still alive.–The ship was sunk, and 2 sailors were the only *survivors*. All the others were drowned.

suspect sus-pect′ *suspects, suspected, suspecting*. 1. Guess, imagine.–I *suspect* that you have had enough to eat.
2. Think or believe guilty without being able to prove it.–The teacher *suspected* the boy of taking the fountain pen.
3. Doubt.–Father *suspected* the man's motives.

suspect sus′-pect *suspects*. A person thought guilty of something.–The policeman arrested one *suspect* for the murder.

suspend sus-pend′ *suspends, suspended, suspending*. 1. Hang.–The swing was *suspended* from a broad branch of the tree.
2. Stop, put off.–Work on the road was *suspended* because of the rain.
3. Not allowed to attend or perform one's work.–Bill was *suspended* from the team for his rough play.

suspenders sus-pend′-ers. A device used for holding up a sock or stocking.–Father bought himself a new pair of *suspenders* at the outfitters' shop.

suspension bridge sus-pen′-sion bridge *suspension bridges*. A bridge hung from cables. –The engineers built a *suspension* bridge across the river.

suspicion sus-pi′-cion *suspicions*. What one feels when one suspects something.–Bob had a grave *suspicion* that it was Jim who broke the plate. He suspected it, but could not prove it.

suspicious sus-pi′-cious *suspiciously, suspiciousness*. 1. Thinking someone has done wrong, or that something is wrong, without real proof.–The policeman is *suspicious* of the man standing in front of the bank.
2. Causing one to doubt or suspect.–The boy's sneaky habits are *suspicious*. They make people think he is not to be trusted.

S
T
U
V
W
X
Y
Z

swagger swag'-ger *swaggers, swaggered, swaggering.* Strut; walk in a bold, swinging way.–The boy *swaggered* into the classroom and sat in the front seat.

swallow swal'-low *swallows, swallowed, swallowing.* 1. Take into the stomach through the throat.–Do you want some water to help you to *swallow* the pill?
2. As much as one can *swallow* at a time.– The thirsty boy asked for a *swallow* of water.
3. Believe too easily.–The boy *swallows* everything anyone tells him.
4. A small bird that flies swiftly and smoothly.– Some *swallows* build their nests in barns.

swam. One form of the word *swim.*–Ducks swim in the pond. One duck *swam* all the way across the pond.

swamp *swamps, swamped, swamping.* 1. Soft, wet, marshy land.–We gathered bulrushes in the *swamp.*

2. Fill with water and sink.–The boat was *swamped* by a big wave.
3. Mother said she was *swamped* with work. She had too much to do.

swampy swamp'-y *swampier, swampiest.* Soft and marshy (of land).–The land around the lake is *swampy.*

swan *swans.* A big water bird with short legs and a long neck.–The graceful *swans* swim in the pond at the park.

swarm *swarms, swarmed, swarming.* 1. A large group, a crowd. A *swarm* of bees is a group that leaves the beehive and flies away together to form a new colony somewhere else. –*Swarms* of people rushed to the fire.
2. Gather into a big group.–Bees are *swarming* in the flower garden.
3. Be crowded or full.–The barn is *swarming* with flies.

swarthy swarth'-y *swarthier, swarthiest.* Dark in colour.–People who are outdoors much of the time in the hot sun are apt to have a *swarthy* skin.

swathe *swathes, swathed, swathing.* Wrap up in bandages or clothes.–The wounded man's head was *swathed* .in bandages.–Father *swathes* himself in scarves to go out in the snow.

sway *sways, swayed, swaying.* Move or swing slowly back and forth or from side to side.– After being hit on the head, the boy *swayed* unsteadily.–The trees *swayed* in the wind.

swear *swears, swore, sworn, swearing.* 1. Make a statement asking God or some sacred being to witness the truth of what you say.–The witness in court *swore* to tell the truth.
2. Vow or promise.–When Bob joined the Boy Scouts, he had to *swear* to obey certain rules.
3. Curse; use sacred names without reverence.

sweat *sweats, sweated, sweating.* 1. Perspire; give off moisture through the skin. We *sweat* when we run or exercise and become warm.
2. Perspiration; moisture which comes through the skin.–*Sweat* ran from the man's forehead.
3. Moisture; droplets of water.–*Sweat* formed on the cold glasses of water.
4. Collect moisture.–Cold water pipes *sweat* when it is very warm. Drops of water form on the pipes. They become wet.
5. Join two metal surfaces by applying heat.– The plumber *sweated* a new pipe to the old.

sweater sweat'-er *sweaters.* A knitted wool garment worn on the upper body. –Mary is knitting a *sweater* for Bob.–The teacher asked the children to take off their sweaters in the schoolroom so that they would not get too warm.

sweep *sweeps, swept, sweeping.* 1. Brush with a broom.–Mary likes to *sweep* the path.
2. Push or carry along or away.–The rushing water *swept* away everything in its path.
3. A cleaning with a broom. Mother said that a daily *sweep* was all that the floor needed.
4. Pass over lightly.–The teacher *sweeps* her hand over her desk each morning to see if there is dust on it.
5. Pass over or through rapidly.–Fire *swept* the forest. It passed quickly through.
6. A chimney-*sweeper.* The *sweep* comes regularly once a year to *sweep* our chimney.

S
T
U
V
W
X
Y
Z

sweet *sweeter, sweetest, sweetly.* 1. Of the pleasant taste of sugar.–Sugar is *sweet.* Vinegar is sour.
2. Pleasing.–Roses have a *sweet* smell.
3. Fresh.–Baby likes *sweet* milk, milk that isn't sour or spoiled.
4. Not salted.–*Sweet* butter has no salt.
5. Soft and pleasing.–Mary has a *sweet* voice. –The sounds of the violin were *sweet.*
6. Lovable; good and pleasant. – Baby is *sweet.*

sweeten sweet'-en *sweetens, sweetened, sweetening.* Make sweet by adding sugar or syrup. –*Sweeten* the cherries while they are still cooking.

sweetheart sweet'-heart *sweethearts.* 1. A loved one.–Baby is Mother's *sweetheart.*
2. A lover.–Aunt Ruth has a *sweetheart.*

sweet potato sweet po-ta'-to *sweet potatoes.* A kind of large yellow root that is somewhat sweet. *Sweet potatoes* grow in warm countries and are eaten boiled or baked.

sweet-william sweet-wil'-liam *sweet-williams.* A kind of flower of many colours that grows in flat clusters. *Sweet-william* belongs to the family of pinks.

swell *swells, swelled, swollen, swelling.* Become larger in size, amount, force, or sound. –The mosquito bite made Mary's hand *swell.* –A balloon *swells* when the air is blown into it.–The river *swells* when the snow melts.– Music *swells* when it becomes louder and louder.

swelling swell'-ing *swellings.* A swollen place; a place that is puffed up.–The *swelling* on Father's finger has gone down.

swelter swel'-ter *swelters, sweltered, sweltering.* Suffer from the heat.–People in the city often *swelter* in the summer.

swept. One form of the word *sweep.*–Mary *swept* the front room.

swift *swifter, swiftest, swiftness.* 1. Very fast. –The racehorse is *swift.*
2. Prompt; quick.–Mother had a *swift* reply to her letter.
3. A bird with long pointed wings, capable of flying very fast.–The *swift* has sooty-black wings.

swiftly swift'-ly. Very fast; quickly.–The dog ran *swiftly* through the gate.

swill *swills, swilled, swilling.* 1. Waste food mixed with water; slop.–The farmer feeds his pigs *swill.*
2. Gulp or swallow greedily.–The pigs *swill* their food.

swim *swims, swam, swum, swimming.* 1. Move through the water by moving the arms and legs, or fins and tail.–A fish *swims* by moving its fins and tail.–A duck *swims* with its feet.

2. Cross by *swimming.*–The boys could not *swim* the river.
3. Glide smoothly.–The balloon went *swimming* through the air.
4. Float about.–Rings of butter *swim* on the soup. They float. They stay on the top.
5. Be covered. – Mary's favourite dessert is strawberries *swimming* in cream.
6. A period of *swimming.*–The boys went for a *swim* in the lake.
7. Be dizzy.–My head is *swimming* from excitement.

swimmer swim'-mer *swimmers.* An animal or person who swims.

swindle swin'-dle *swindles, swindled, swindling.* Cheat or get something dishonestly.– The dishonest salesman tried to *swindle* Father by selling him a car that was no good.

swindler swin'-dler *swindlers.* A person who gets things by dishonesty or cheating.– Father had the *swindler* arrested for trying to sell him a car that was no good.

swine. 1. A hog or hogs.
2. A person whose habits are coarse and sloppy. – The man's rudeness led people to call him a *swine.*

swing *swings, swung, swinging.* 1. A seat hung

so that it can move back and forth.–Father hung the *swing* from a tree branch.

S
T
U
V
W
X
Y
Z

2. Move back and forth in a *swing*.–Children like to *swing*.

3. Move or cause to move in a circle or part of a circle.–A golfer *swings* the golf club to hit the ball.–Can you stand on one foot and *swing* the other?

swish *swishes, swished, swishing*. 1. Move with a whistling or rushing noise.–The lion-tamer's whip *swished* through the air.

2. A whispering sound.–We heard the *swish* of the water against the boat.

switch *switches, switched, switching*. 1. A whip, or a small branch of a tree used for whipping.

2. Whip.–The man *switched* the dog with a *switch*.

3. Swing back and forth or up and down like a whip.–A cow *switches* her tail to drive the flies off.

4. Change over; transfer. – The engine *switched* from one line to another.–Bob *switched* coats with Jack.

5. On a railway, a mechanical device that moves part of a rail so that a train can move from one line to another.

6. A device for turning off and on.–Electric lights are turned on by a *switch*.

7. Turn (on or off) with a *switch*.–*Switch* the light on so that you can see to read.

swollen swol'-len. One form of the word *swell*. –Mary's face was *swollen* with mumps.

swoop *swoops, swooped, swooping*. Move swiftly and smoothly down.–The aeroplane *swooped* down upon the enemy and then got away.

swop or **swap** *swops, swopped, swopping*. Exchange.–The girls *swop* books with the other girls after they have read them.

sword *swords*. A weapon that has a long blade sharpened on one or both edges.

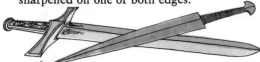

swore. One form of the word *swear*. – Billy *swore* when he burned his finger.

sworn. One form of the word *swear*. – Billy should not have *sworn*.

swung. One form of the word *swing*.–The monkey *swung* by his tail from a branch.

sycamore syc'-a-more *sycamores*. A tree of the maple family with broad leaves.

syllable syl'-la-ble *syllables*. 1. A part of a word that is pronounced separately. We say the word 'sweeping' in 2 parts; sweep-ing. Each part is a *syllable*. The words 'boat' and 'school' have but 1 *syllable*.

2. A very small portion of speech.–The teacher asked John to explain the arithmetic problem, but he did not utter a *syllable*. He did not even say a single word.

symbol sym'-bol *symbols*. 1. A thing that stands for something else.–A white flag is a *symbol* of surrender.–The lion is the *symbol* of Great Britain.

2. A mark which has a definite meaning.–In arithmetic we use + as a *symbol* for addition.

sympathetic sym-pa-thet'-ic. Sharing the feelings of others, and feeling kindly towards them.–Mother is *sympathetic* towards the sick woman. She seems to know how the woman feels, and feels sorry for her.

sympathize sym'-pa-thize *sympathizes, sympathized, sympathizing*. Feel sympathy for; share the feelings of.–When Bob is ill, he wants you to *sympathize* with him. He wants you to show that you understand how he feels.

sympathy sym'-pa-thy *sympathies*. 1. A kind feeling that one person has for another. A person shows *sympathy* for another person when he feels that person's sorrows and troubles.

2. Agreement. – Father is in *sympathy* with our plans for the holiday.

3. A state of understanding and sharing ideas and feelings about things.–If music makes both Bob and Mary feel happy at the same time, they are in *sympathy* with each other.

symphony sym'-pho-ny *symphonies*. A long piece of music in 3 or 4 parts written for all the instruments of an orchestra.

symptom symp'-tom *symptoms*. A sign; an indication.–The doctor did not find any *symptoms* of measles when he examined Baby; he found no red spots.

synonym syn'-o-nym *synonyms*. One of 2 or more words that mean the same or nearly the same thing.–'Small' and 'little' are *synonyms*. –'Big' and 'large' are *synonyms*.

S
T
U
V
W
X
Y
Z

syrup or **sirup** syr'-up *syrups*. A thick, sticky, sweet liquid containing much sugar and sometimes fruits and other flavouring. – Mary wanted chocolate *syrup* on her ice-cream and Bob asked for pineapple *syrup*. – Bob and Mary always eat lots of golden *syrup* with their pudding.

system sys'-tem *systems*. 1. An orderly plan or method.–Mother has a *system* for doing her housework.
2. A whole body.–The doctor said that Bob's *system* was unusually strong.
3. A group of related objects.–The sun and the planets make up the solar *system*.

T t

T, t *T's, t's*. The 20th letter of the alphabet.

table ta'-ble *tables*. 1. A piece of furniture with a flat top resting on legs.–We put lamps on *tables* in the living-room.

2. A list of things, or information given in a very short form.–We looked in the *table* of contents at the front of the book to find out what stories were in the book.–In arithmetic we learn the multiplication *table*:

$$2 \times 1 = 2$$
$$2 \times 2 = 4$$
$$2 \times 3 = 6$$

table-cloth ta'-ble-cloth *table-cloths*. A cloth spread on a dining-table before the plates and food are put on.–Mary put the *table-cloth* and napkins on the table for supper.

table-spoon ta'-ble-spoon *table-spoons*. A large spoon.–Mother serves the vegetables with a *table-spoon*.

tablet tab'-let *tablets*. 1. A pad.–A writing *tablet* has many sheets of paper fastened together at the top.
2. A sheet or thin piece of metal, stone, or wood with something written on it. – The schoolchildren put up a *tablet* in the main hall in honour of the first headmaster of the school.
3. A small, flat pill.–The *tablets* which the doctor gave Father were hard to swallow.

tack *tacks, tacked, tacking*. 1. A short nail with a large flat or rounded head.– The children used brass *tacks* to fasten their drawings to the wall.
2. To fasten with *tacks*.–The sign was *tacked* on to the garage.

3. Sew loosely and temporarily. – Mother *tacked* the hem of Mary's dress. She put in loose stitches until she could sew it the right way.
4. Change direction in a sailing boat so that the wind blows on the other side.–The boat *tacked* up the river. It went from side to side.

tackle tack'-le *tackles, tackled, tackling*. 1. Things used for doing a job.–Fishing *tackle* is the equipment used by a fisherman in fishing.
2. Ropes specially arranged for lifting heavy loads.
3. Grab; try to stop. – One football player *tackled* the other.
4. The act of *tackling* in football, etc.–The referee said Bob's was a fair *tackle*.
5. Try to do; undertake.–Father will *tackle* any work that has to be done.

tact *tactful, tactfully*. A person who has *tact* knows how to do and say things without annoying people and hurting their feelings.

tadpole tad'-pole *tadpoles*. The young of a frog or toad. *Tadpoles* have tails which disappear before they become full-grown frogs or toads.

taffeta taf'-fe-ta. A stiff silk cloth. – Grandmother has a brown *taffeta* dress that makes a rustling or whispering sound when she walks.

tag *tags, tagged, tagging*. 1. A small piece of cardboard fastened to anything to tell the name or give directions, price, etc.–The assistant told us we could find the price of the skates by looking at the *tag*.–The children tied Christmas *tags* to their gifts to tell who was to get each gift and whom it was from.

T
U
V
W
X
Y
Z

2. Fasten a *tag* to.–After they were *tagged* the gifts were put under the Christmas tree.

3. Follow close behind.–Jack's dog always *tags* after him.

4. A game in which one player, who is 'it,' chases the others until he touches one of them.

5. To touch in the game of *tag*.–Mary *tagged* Ruth, and then Ruth was 'it.'

tail *tails*. 1. A part which grows at the back or rear end of many animals.–Cows switch their *tails* to keep the flies away.

2. The last or back part of anything; as, the *tail* of a kite, the *tail* of an aeroplane, the *tail* of a person's coat or shirt. A light at the back of a car is sometimes called a *tail* light.

tailor tai'-lor *tailors*. A man who makes or alters clothes.–Mother took her suit to the *tailor* to have it shortened.

take *takes, took, taken, taking*. 1. Hold, clasp, grasp.–The children *take* each other's hands when playing 'The Farmer in the Dell.'

2. Accept.–Grandfather said that he would not *take* the money from Bob for the pony.

3. Choose, select, pick for yourself. – *Take* the book you want.–*Take* that seat.

4. Carry, bring. – We *take* our lunch to school.

5. Receive; get; win.–Mary will surely *take* the prize for the best story.–The girls won the first game, but the boys *took* the second.

6. Capture. – The police *took* the bandits at their hide-out.

7. Use up, need. – Bread *takes* an hour to bake. It needs to be baked an hour.

8. Rent or buy.–The boys will *take* the boat for the day.

9. Remove.–Mother *took* the dishes off the table.

10. Accompany; escort.–I will *take* you to school. I will go with you. – Father *takes* Mother out to dinner on Thursdays.

11. Go on.–Father *took* the train to town.– We *took* a ride.

talcum tal'-cum. A kind of smooth, white powder used on the face or body to soothe the skin.

tale *tales*. 1. A story.–Sally told Grandmother an exciting *tale* about the bear she fought.

2. A bad report about someone, told to get him into trouble.–Mary likes to carry *tales* to Mother about Jack.

talent tal'-ent *talents*. A natural ability to do a thing easily.–Mary has *talent* for music.

talented tal'-ent-ed. Having a special natural ability.–Mary is *talented* in music. She learns music easily and quickly.

talk *talks, talked, talking*. 1. Speak; put ideas or thoughts into spoken words.–We *talk* to our friends about things we're interested in.

2. A discussion.–Let's have a *talk* about your problems.

3. A speech; a lecture.–The policeman gave a *talk* on safety.

4. A rumour.–There is *talk* of school closing early.

talkative talk'-a-tive. Likely to talk much.– Some children are *talkative*. They talk a great deal. `

talker talk'-er *talkers*. Speaker; person talking. –The boy is a good *talker*.

tall *taller, tallest*. 1. Long or high from head to foot.–One boy is short; the other is *tall*.–A person who stands 7 feet high is very *tall*.

2. High.–A skyscraper is a *tall* building.

3. Exaggerated, difficult to believe.–When Bob told us he had seen a two-headed lion at the zoo, Mother said it was a *tall* story.

tallboy tall'-boy *tallboys*. A tall chest of drawers, often in two parts.–Father keeps his shirts and underwear in the *tallboy* in his bedroom.

tallow tal'-low. The fat of cows, sheep, and some other animals. *Tallow* is used in making soap and candles.

tally tal'-ly *tallies, tallied, tallying*. 1. A score or count.–During the game, Mary kept the *tally*.

2. An identifying mark or label. When the merchandise was packed, a *tally* was put on each crate, showing the number, the weight, the contents, etc.

3. Match or agree.–Bob's figures *tally* with Mary's; Bob and Mary both think the answer is 369.

4. Make a count; keep score.–Bob and Mary *tallied* the votes for club secretary.

talon tal'-on *talons*. 1. A claw of a bird that kills other birds or animals for food.–Hawks have long, sharp, *talons*.

2. Sharp, grasping fingers.–The miser's long *talons* reached for the gold.

T
U
V
W
X
Y
Z

tambourine tam-bou-rine′ *tambourines*. A very small drum with only one head and with flat pieces of metal fastened loosely to the rim. It is played by tapping it with the fingers and shaking it to make the metal pieces jingle.

tame *tames, tamed, taming*. 1. Make gentle and obedient; accustom to people. – Some animals, such as horses, that were once wild have been *tamed* so that people can use them.
2. Not wild; accustomed to people. – The squirrels in the park are *tame*.
3. Not exciting; dull.–Mary said the book was so *tame* that she did not finish it.

tam-o′-shanter tam-o-shan′-ter *tam-o′-shanters*. A flat, round cap with the top larger than the headband. Some *tam-o′-shanters* are crocheted from wool and others are made from felt.

tamper tam′-per *tampers, tampered, tampering*. Meddle with something; try to repair something without knowing how. – Father never *tampers* with the clock. He has it repaired by someone who knows how.

tan *tans, tanned, tanning*. 1. A light brown colour.–Mother's gloves are *tan*.
2. Turn to a brownish colour from exposure to the sun.–The children played outdoors so much that their faces became *tanned*.
3. Make (hides) into leather.–The hides and skins of certain animals are *tanned*.

tang *tangs*. 1. A strong, distinctive taste or smell.–As we neared the coast we breathed the *tang* of the sea.
2. A distinctive quality.–Shakespeare's plays have the *tang* of genius.

tangerine tan-ge-rine′ *tangerines*. A kind of small, sweet orange which peels easily.

tangle tan′-gle *tangles, tangled, tangling*. 1. Knot and twist together.–Bob's kite-string is so *tangled* that it can hardly be straightened.
2. A twisted knot.–Mary got a *tangle* in her thread and had to break it.

tank *tanks*. 1. A large container for liquid.– We have a cold-water *tank* in the attic.
2. A heavily armoured war machine mounted with guns. A *tank* can travel over rough ground and crush everything before it.

tap *taps, tapped, tapping*. 1. Strike or hit lightly.–*Tap* on the window twice if you can go.
2. A light knock.–We heard but one *tap* on the window.
3. A device with a valve to control the flow of a liquid.–We turned on the *tap* to get a drink of water.
4. Make a hole to let the liquid out.–The men *tapped* the rubber trees so that the liquid rubber would flow out.
5. Open up and make available.–A newspaper has to *tap* all possible sources of information.

tape *tapes, taped, taping*. 1. A long, narrow strip of cloth, paper, steel, etc.
2. A narrow strip of paper or cloth with glue on one side.–The teacher mends books with *tape*.–The nurse put *tape* over the cut.
3. Put a *tape* on; bind with *tape*.–The doctor *taped* the boy's foot so that he could walk.

tape-line tape′-line *tape-lines*. A strip of steel or cloth marked off into inches for measuring. It is also called a tape measure.

taper ta′-per *tapers, tapered, tapering*. 1. A long, thin candle.
2. Become smaller towards one end.–The end of a pencil that is sharpened *tapers* towards the point.

tapestry tap′-es-try *tapestries*. A piece of cloth with figures or pictures woven into it. *Tapestries* are hung on the walls just as painted or printed pictures are.

tapioca tap-i-o′-ca. A kind of starchy food made from the roots of a tropical plant. It is used to make puddings.

T U V W X Y Z

tapir ta'-pir *tapirs*. A pig-like animal with a short, flexible nose. The *tapir* is a native of Central and South America, and the East Indies.

tar *tars, tarred, tarring*. 1. A thick, sticky, black substance made from coal.–*Tar* is used on roads, and to waterproof roofs, etc.
2. Put *tar* on.–The men *tarred* the road.
3. A sailor.–The old *tar* likes to tell the children sea stories.

tarantula ta-ran'-tu-la *tarantulas*. A large spider whose bite is poisonous.

tardiness tar'-di-ness. Slowness. – The workmen's *tardiness* prevented the repairs from being finished by the week-end.

tardy tar'-dy *tardier, tardiest, tardily, tardiness*. Slow, behindhand.–The teacher told Jack off for being *tardy* with his homework.

target tar'-get *targets*. Anything used to shoot or aim at.–The boys put a tin can on the post for a *target*; they tried to hit the can with the stones they were throwing.

tarnish tar'-nish *tarnishes, tarnished, tarnishing*. 1. Lose brightness; turn dark on the surface.–Silver *tarnishes* when left out in the air.
2. Cause to turn dark.–Gas will *tarnish* silver. It will make it lose its brightness.

tarpaulin tar-pau'-lin *tarpaulins*. A large sheet of waterproof canvas. – When it rains, the groundsman at the cricket ground puts a *tarpaulin* over the wicket.

tarry tar'-ry *tarries, tarried, tarrying*. Stop; waste time; wait.–Do not *tarry* by the way.

tart *tarts*. 1. A small crust of pastry filled with fruit, jelly, or jam, and baked.–Grandmother makes *tarts* from pastry that is left over from making pies.
2. Sour; biting or sharp to the taste.–Grapes that are not quite ripe are *tart*.

task *tasks*. A piece of work.–If a *task* is once begun, never leave it till it's done.–Bob's weekly *task* is cutting the grass.

tassel tas'-sel *tassels*. 1. An ornament made of a number of cords fastened together at one end and loose at the other. A *tassel* hangs down.–Mary's hat has a *tassel* on the side.
2. The silky threads on an ear of corn.

taste *tastes, tasted, tasting*. 1. Test the flavour of food or drink by putting a little into the mouth.–Mary *tasted* the soup and said it was too salty.
2. The sensation or feeling one gets when food or drink is in the mouth.–The *taste* of sugar is sweet; the *taste* of vinegar is sour. Sea water *tastes* salty; some medicine *tastes* bitter.
3. Judgement and understanding of beauty, or of what is good or proper.–Mary has good *taste* in clothes.

tatter tat'-ter *tatters*. A torn or ragged piece or strip of cloth, paper, etc.–The wind blew the banner into *tatters*.

tattered tat'-tered. Ragged and torn. – The tramp's clothes were *tattered*.

tattoo tat-too' *tattooes, tattoed, tattooing*. 1. Mark the skin with colours which will not come off. – The sailor had a picture of a crown *tattooed* on his arm.
2. A design or picture *tattooed* on the skin.
3. A large-scale military display.

taught. One form of the word *teach*.–Mother *taught* Mary how to sew.

taut *tauter, tautest, tautly, tautness*. Tightly stretched.–The clothes-line was so *taut* that it broke in two.

tavern tav'-ern *taverns*. A public-house, an inn. A place where beer, wine, and other alcoholic drinks are served and drunk.

tax *taxes, taxed, taxing*. 1. Money that must be paid by a person or company to help with the cost of government. Firemen and policemen are paid from rates and *taxes* collected by a city. The Army and Navy are partly paid for by *taxes* collected from the *tax*payers by the government.
2. Require a *tax* from.–A person's wages are *taxed* according to the amount of money he earns.

taxation tax'-a-tion. The system of raising money by imposing taxes.–*Taxation* according to what one earns is a fair and effective way for a government to raise money for the needs of the country. Income-tax is only one of several kinds of *taxation*.

taxi or **taxicab** tax'-i-cab *taxis, taxicabs*. A motor-car, driven by a regular driver, that can be hired to carry passengers.–Most *taxis* have a meter to show how long the journey is and how much one must pay.

T
U
V
W
X
Y
Z

tea *teas.* 1. A drink made by pouring boiling water over the dried leaves of the *tea* plant. –Mother drinks *tea.*
2. The dried leaves of the *tea* plant.
3. A late afternoon party where *tea* and other refreshments are served.–Mother is going to a *tea* at the church house.

teach *teaches, taught, teaching.* 1. Instruct; show how; help one to learn.–Miss Jones will *teach* you how to sew.–Father *teaches* the boys to play football.–Our teacher *teaches* us reading, arithmetic, and spelling.
2. Give lessons in.–Mr. Smith *teaches* painting.

teacher *teach'-er teachers.* A person who instructs others, or helps others to learn something.–Mary takes singing lessons from a private *teacher.*

teaching *teach'-ing teachings.* 1. Father is *teaching* Bob to skate.
2. Instruction; the work of teachers. – Our teacher finds *teaching* very pleasant work.
3. A thing taught or preached.–The *teachings* in the Bible are good rules to live by.

team *teams, teamed, teaming.* 1. A number of people who work, play, or act together.–One *team* plays against another *team.*
2. Two or more horses or other animals harnessed to 1 carriage or machine.
3. Join or work together for something.–Two dancers *teamed* up in 1 act of the show.

tea-pot *tea'-pot tea-pots.* A container something like a kettle, made of metal or china, for making and pouring out tea.–Grandmother has a pretty china *tea-pot.*

tear (rhymes with *there*) *tears, tore, torn, tearing.* 1. Pull apart, rip.–Baby likes to *tear* up newspapers. – Father *tore* his sleeve on the saw.
2. A rough, jagged cut. – Father hit his arm against the saw and made a long *tear* in his sleeve. His sleeve was *torn.*
3. Pull hard, pull hard on.–The angry artist *tore* down the pictures.–The miser *tore* his hair when his gold was stolen.
4. Run wildly, rush.–Bob *tore* across the field to get his kite.

tear (rhymes with *here*) *tears.* A drop of salt water that comes out of one's eyes.–Big *tears* fell on Baby's cheeks when she cried.

tease *teases, teased, teasing.* 1. Make fun of. –Mary *teases* Father about getting fat.
2. Beg.–Baby *teases* Mother for lollipops.
3. A person who *teases.*–Jack is a great *tease.* He likes to make fun of people.

teaspoon *tea'-spoon teaspoons.* A small spoon. – We use a *teaspoon* to eat ice-cream, pudding, melon, and other soft foods.

teaspoonful *tea'-spoon-ful teaspoonfuls.* As much as a *teaspoon* will hold. – The doctor told Father to take a *teaspoonful* of cough medicine every 3 hours.

teeter *tee'-ter teeters, teetered, teetering.* Go up and down or from side to side; seesaw.– Mother screamed when she saw Sally *teetering* on the window-sill.

teeth. More than 1 tooth. The sharp, white, bony points that grow in 2 rows in the mouths of people and many animals. – We chew our food with our *teeth.*–A rake has *teeth.*–To escape by the *skin of one's teeth* is to have a narrow escape.

rake teeth

human teeth

telegram *tel'-e-gram telegrams.* Written message sent over wires by electricity.–Father's *telegram* read 'Home Saturday night in time for supper. Love Father.'–We sent a greetings *telegram* to Grandfather on his seventieth birthday.

telegraph *tel'-e-graph telegraphs, telegraphed, telegraphing.* 1. A device or way by which written messages are sent over wires by electricity.–Father sent Mother a message by *telegraph* when he was away.
2. Send a written message over wires by electricity.–Father *telegraphed* Mother.

telephone *tel'-e-phone telephones, telephoned, telephoning.* 1. A device which carries the sound of voices, music, etc., over wires by electricity.–Sally talked to Father on the *telephone.*

2. Talk to someone or call someone on the *telephone.*–Mother *telephoned* Father to ask him when he would be home.

telescope tel'-e-scope *telescopes.* An instrument which, when looked through, makes far-away objects look larger, clearer, and closer to you. – *Telescopes* are used to study the stars. – We looked at the moon through a *telescope* and saw the mountains on it.

television tel'-e-vi-sion. A method of sending pictures of people or objects in motion by radio. The moving pictures appear on a screen which is part of the receiving set.– Father sat at his new *television* set, watching and hearing the Test Match being played in Leeds.

tell *tells, told, telling.* 1. Say or speak about something.–I will *tell* you about my trip.–I will *tell* you a story.
2. Show.–The speedometer on the car *tells* how fast you are going.
3. Order, command.–Father *told* the man to leave.
4. Let know.–*Tell* me how far it is to school.

temper tem'-per *tempers.* 1. One's behaviour or way of acting.–Mother has an even *temper.* She is calm and is not easily disturbed or made angry.
2. An angry mood.–Jack flies into *tempers* quickly, and feels sorry afterwards.

temperate tem'-per-ate. Mild; not extreme or excessive.–We live in a *temperate* climate, where the weather is not usually very hot or very cold.–Father is a man of *temperate* eating habits; he likes to eat, but doesn't eat too much.

temperature tem'-per-a-ture *temperatures.* Heat as measured in degrees; hotness or coolness. Temperature is measured by a thermometer. –Mother set the oven control for a *temperature* of 400 degrees (400°).–Water boils when its *temperature* is about 212° Fahrenheit. – When the temperature is zero (0°) Fahrenheit, it is very cold.

tempest tem'-pest *tempests.* A very bad, windy storm.– *tempest* kept the ships from sailing.

temple tem'-ple *temples.* A sacred building used for religious worship.

temporary tem'-po-ra-ry *temporarily.* Not permanent; lasting for a little while only.–Jack will take a *temporary* job during his summer holiday.

tempt *tempts, tempted, tempting.* 1. Lead someone to want to do wrong or evil.–The money which the man left out on his desk *tempted* the hungry boy to steal.
2. Make one want something; attract.–The cold pool *tempted* the thirsty soldier. It made him long for water.

temptation temp-ta'-tion *temptations.* A thing that leads one to want to do something though he tries not to do it.–An open box of chocolates on the table is a *temptation* to eat.

ten *tens.* The number (10) after nine and before eleven.

tenant ten'-ant *tenants.* Someone who pays rent for the use of land or any kind of building.–Grandfather has *tenants* on his farm.– We are *tenants.* We pay rent for our house.

tend *tends, tended, tending.* 1. Look after.– Mary *tends* the baby when Mother is away. –Bob *tends* the front lawn in the summer.
2. Be usually.–Bill *tends* to be lazy; he usually is lazy.

tender ten'-der *tenderly, tenderness.* 1. Soft, easily cut or broken. – Some meat is tough, but this piece is *tender.*
2. Not strong; delicate; easily harmed.–Baby has *tender* skin.
3. Kind; easily moved; sympathetic.–Grandmother has a *tender* heart. She shares other people's sorrows and troubles.
4. Sore.–Baby has a *tender* spot on her head where she bumped it.

T
U
V
W
X
Y
Z

tendon ten'-don *tendons*. A strong cord that fastens a muscle to a bone. – The football player pulled one of the *tendons* in his leg and had to leave the game.

tendril tend'-ril *tendrils*. A slender thread-like attachment in certain plants which stretches out and coils round other plants and objects. –The *tendrils* of sweet peas help to support the plant and aid its growth.

tenement ten'-e-ment *tenements*. A flat or rented rooms in a house.–The family lived in a small *tenement*.

tennis ten'-nis. A game played by hitting a ball back and forth over a net with a kind of bat called a *tennis* racquet.

tenor ten'-or *tenors*. The highest singing voice that grown men have.–Some men have bass voices and some have *tenor* voices.–Father sings *tenor*.

tenpins ten'-pins. A game of bowling. Each player tries to knock over 10 wooden pins by rolling a large ball down an alley at them.

tense *tensely, tenseness*. Strained; stretched tightly; taut.–The wires were so *tense* that they snapped.–Excitement may cause one to have *tense* nerves.

tent *tents*. A movable shelter, usually made of a heavy cotton cloth called canvas; it is held up by poles and fastened to the ground by pegs.–Boy Scouts, soldiers, and campers often sleep in *tents*.

tenth *tenths*. 1. Following the ninth. – The teacher told every *tenth* child to stand up.
2. One of 10 equal parts.–Ten is a *tenth* of a hundred.

tepee te'-pee *tepees*. A wigwam; a pointed tent. – The Indians of America and Canada used to live in *tepees*.

term *terms, termed*. 1. A set length of time.– In our school the first *term* is from the 8th of September until the 20th of December.
2. A word or expression.–We must know the meaning of certain *terms* in order to understand arithmetic. Plus, minus, add, subtract, etc., are *terms* used in arithmetic.
3. A condition; a thing agreed to.–Bill did not live up to the *terms* of the bargain.

terrace ter'-race *terraces*. A flat piece of ground that is raised like a platform or a broad step.

terrible ter'-ri-ble. Causing great fear or awe.– A *terrible* accident happened in the theatre.

terribly ter'-ri-bly. Awfully; dreadfully.–I was *terribly* frightened when the fire started.

terrier ter'-ri-er *terriers*. A small, short-haired dog. *Terriers* were once used for hunting small animals that live in the ground.

terrific ter-rif'-ic *terrifically*. Terrible; awful; dreadful. – A *terrific* fire broke out in the factory.

terrify ter'-ri-fy *terrifies, terrified, terrifying*. Frighten very much. – The baby is *terrified* by dogs.

territory ter'-ri-to-ry *territories*. A large stretch of land; a part of a country.–Some *territory* in North America is covered with forests.

terror ter'-ror *terrors*. 1. Great fear. – *Terror* came over the crowd when the lion got loose.
2. A thing that causes great fear.–The escaped lion was a *terror*.

terse *terser, tersest, terseness, tersely*. Short and to the point.–The policeman made a *terse* statement about the accident.

test *tests, tested, testing*. 1. A trial or examination which shows how much a person knows about a thing.–Our teacher gave us a spelling *test*.
2. Examine by trial.–The teacher *tested* our spelling ability by giving us a *test*.

T
U
V
W
X
Y
Z

testify tes'-ti-fy *testifies, testified, testifying.* Make a solemn statement; tell what one knows to be true.–Bob *testified* that he saw the man steal the money.

Texas Tex'-as. The largest state in the United States and the greatest farming state, located in the south central part of the U.S. It produces cotton, grain, rice, petroleum, and much meat. *Texas* claims the largest cattle ranch in the world.

text-book text'-book *text-books.* A school-book; a book that one studies from in school.–Our school is using a new *text-book* for geography.

textile tex'-tile *textiles.* 1. A woven cloth.–Some *textiles* are woven from wool.
2. Having to do with weaving.–The big *textile* plant weaves many kinds of *textiles.*

than. The word *than* is used in comparing things.–Baby is smaller *than* Mary.–My pencil is longer *than* yours.–I would rather sleep *than* eat.

thank *thanks, thanked, thanking.* Tell that one is grateful; show gratitude.–Bob *thanked* his grandmother for the gift by saying 'Thank you.'

thankful thank'-ful *thankfully, thankfulness.* Grateful; appreciative. – Mother is *thankful* for so many friends. She is glad to have friends and shows it by her actions.

thankless thank'-less. 1. Ungrateful. – Mother rebuked Mary for being *thankless* when she received the present.
2. Bringing no thanks.–Shelling peas is a *thankless* task, but it has to be done.

thanks. An expression of gratitude or thankfulness.–We offer *thanks* to God when we go to church.–Bob said to the man, 'Thanks for the ride.'

that. 1. We use the word *that* in speaking of or pointing to a person or thing *that* is not here. –*That* tree is a maple; this one is an oak.
2. Who.–He is the boy *that* sells papers.
3. Whom.–The boy *that* you saw was Jack.
4. Which. – The book *that* I lost has been found.
5. *That* is used to connect 2 parts of a sentence and show how they are related.–Mary knew *that* Sally would be late.–Baby ate so much *that* she was sick.
6. So.–No child should eat *that* much.

thatch *thatches, thatched, thatching.* 1. Grass or straw used as roofing.
2. Cover (a roof) with straw in overlapping layers.–This house has a *thatched* roof.

that's. That is.–*That's* the best book I know.

thaw *thaws, thawed, thawing.* 1. Melt; become soft.–If the ice *thaws*, we cannot go skating.
2. A time when snow and frost melt.–We had an early *thaw* in February.

the. *The* is used in speaking of some particular person or thing.–*The* dog with Bob is black. –I read *the* book you gave me.

theatre the'-a-tre *theatres.* 1. A large building where something is presented for many people to see or hear.–The children saw a play in the new *theatre.*

2. A place of action; a place where great things happen.–Europe and the Pacific areas were *theatres* of war in World War II.

thee. *Thee* is an old way of saying you, meaning one person only. It is used in the Bible, in prayer, and in some poetry.–'Blessings on *thee*, little man, barefoot boy with cheeks of tan.'

theft *thefts.* Stealing; robbery.–The paper-boy reported to the police the *theft* of his money.

T
U
V
W
X
Y
Z

their *theirs*. Belonging to them.–Bob and Jack could see *their* house from the top of the hill.

theirs. Something belonging to them. – This bicycle is yours and that one is *theirs*.

them. The things or animals or people already mentioned or spoken of.–The boys took the dog with *them*. *'Them'* refers to the boys.– Grandmother had 3 spotted kittens, but she gave *them* away.

themselves them-selves′. The children *themselves* prepared the dinner. Nobody helped them. – The boys *themselves* admitted they had done wrong. Even the boys admitted it.– Mother told the children to dress *themselves*. Each child was to dress himself or herself.

then. 1. At that time.–If you want me to come to your house at 3 o'clock, I will be there *then*.
2. Soon or immediately afterwards.–We arrived home, and *then* it started to rain.
3. Next.–First came the band and *then* the horses.
4. Therefore, because of that. – If you play this morning, *then* you must study this afternoon.

there. 1. In that place.–Put the basket *there*.
2. At the place.–Stop *there* for lunch.
3. To that place.–The circus is in town. We were just going *there* when it started to rain.
4. Used to point out or call attention to.– *There* is Father now!–*There* is the trouble.
5. *There* are 10 more days until Christmas.– It *there* room for one more in your car?
6. Used to soothe or comfort.–Mother kissed the bump on Baby's head and said, *'There, there!* Now it doesn't hurt any more.'

thereafter there-af′-ter. After that, afterwards. – The child burnt his hand playing with matches, and *thereafter* he was always afraid of matches.

therefore there′-fore. For that reason; because of that.–Mary had a bad cold, and *therefore* could not go to school.

there's. There is.–*There's* a circus in town this month.

thermometer ther-mom′-e-ter *thermometers*. An instrument for measuring one's temperature, or for telling how cold or hot it is.–Mother took Baby's temperature with a *thermometer* when Baby was ill. – We have a *thermometer* in the kitchen to tell us if the room is warm enough or too warm.

thermos flask ther′-mos flask *thermos flasks*. Trade name of a bottle so made that it will keep cold things cold and hot things hot for hours.–Father carries a *thermos flask* of hot soup with his lunch. –The boys took a *thermos flask* of cold milk on their hike.

thermostat ther′-mo-stat *thermostats*. An instrument that makes a heating or air-conditioning unit work just enough to keep a building from getting too warm or too cold.–If you set your *thermostat* for 70°, the temperature in your house will stay near 70°.

these. Used when we point out or speak of more than one person or thing that is nearer to us than some others are. – *These* are the children who live next door.–*These* yellow daisies are from my garden.

they. Used in speaking about persons or things or animals already named.–The boys work hard so that *they* will get good marks.

they'll. They will. – The girls said they would come early, so *they'll* be here soon.

they're. They are.–The boys are usually early, but today *they're* late.

they've. They have.–We expect the children, but *they've* been delayed by the rain.

thick *thickly, thicker, thickest*. 1. Not thin, not slender; plump.–One book is thin, the other is *thick*. The *thick* one is wider from cover to cover.
2. Close together, crowded together.–The plants in the garden are too *thick* to have room to grow.–The weeds are *thick* in the garden.
3. Partly solid; not completely liquid.–Water is thin. Gravy is *thick*.
4. Foggy; heavy; clouded.–The air was *thick* with smoke. You could hardly see through it.
5. Husky, deep, or hoarse.–When Father had a cold, his voice was *thick*.

thicken thick′-en *thickens, thickened, thickening*. 1. Make thick or more solid.–Mother *thickens* the pudding with corn-flour.
2. Become thicker.–The ice on the windscreen *thickened* as we drove.

thicket thick′-et *thickets*. A thick growth of underbrush and bushes.–We had to cut our way through the *thicket* with our knives.

T U V W X Y Z

thickness thick'-ness *thicknesses.* 1. Distance from top side to bottom side.–What is the *thickness* of this board? I have measured its length and width, but how thick is it?
2. A layer.–The nurse put 6 *thicknesses* of bandage on the boy's sore arm.

thief *thieves.* A robber; a person who steals.–The policeman caught the *thief* as he left the shop with the stolen watches.

thieves. More than one thief; robbers.–The *thieves* were soon caught.

thigh *thighs.* The part of one's leg between the knee and the hip.

thimble thim'-ble *thimbles.* A cap usually worn on the middle finger when sewing, to push the needle through the cloth, and to protect the finger. *Thimbles* are made of metal or other hard materials.

thin *thins, thinned, thinning, thinly, thinner, thinnest.* 1. Slender; not thick.–One book is thick, the other *thin.* The *thin* book has less distance from cover to cover.–Mother likes bread cut in *thin* slices.
2. Lean; having little flesh or fat.–Mother is *thin,* but Father is stout.
3. Scattered; far apart.–The grass is still *thin* in April. The blades are not close together.
4. (Of a liquid) easily poured.–We use *thin* cream for coffee, and double cream for whipping.
5. Not strong or deep. – The little old lady has a *thin* voice.
6. Make thinner.–Father *thinned* the carrots in the garden. He pulled out some to give the others more room to grow. – Mother *thinned* the gravy with hot water.

thine. An old form of the word *yours.*–The sword was *thine,* not mine.

thing *things.* Any object, idea, or matter.–Furniture, clothes, and other objects are *things.*–There are marbles, pencils, paper, crayons, and many other *things* on teacher's desk.–He talked of every*thing* except the *thing* on his mind.–Interrupting a person is not a polite *thing* to do.

think *thinks, thought, thinking.* 1. Use one's mind.–To solve a problem, to learn to spell, or to study anything, one must *think.*
2. Believe.–I *think* it pays to be honest.
3. Get an idea.–Can you *think* of anything to do now that it is raining?

third *thirds.* 1. Following the second.–Mary was first, Jack second, and Bob *third* in the row.
2. One of 3 equal parts of anything.–If an apple is cut into 3 equal parts, each part is one *third* of the apple.

thirst. 1. A dry feeling in the throat and mouth caused by the need of liquid.–The soldiers lost in the desert nearly died of *thirst.*
2. A great desire.–A scholar has a *thirst* for learning about things.

thirsty thirst'-y *thirstier, thirstiest, thirstily.* Feeling thirst; needing water. – Baby is *thirsty.* She wants a drink.

thirteen thir'-teen'. The number (13) coming after 12 and before 14. Ten plus three (10 + 3) equals *thirteen.*

thirteenth thir'-teenth' *thirteenths.* 1. Coming after 12 and before 14 in a series.–Jack was the *thirteenth* person in the line. There were 12 people before him.
2. One of 13 equal parts.–If a thing is divided into 13 equal parts, each part is called one *thirteenth.*

thirty thir'-ty. The number (30) coming after 29 and before 31.–Three times ten (3 × 10) equals *thirty.*

this. The one at hand or the one just mentioned. The word *this* is used to speak of or to point out a person or thing that is present, very near, or has just been spoken of.–*This* boy here is Bob's cousin; that boy over there is *this* boy's friend.–*This* is my book.

thistle this'-tle *thistles.* A prickly plant that has purple flowers.

thorn *thorns.* A prickle; a sharp point on a rose-bush or some other plant.

thorny thorn'-y *thornier, thorniest.* Covered with thorns.–A plant that has thorns or prickles on it is *thorny.*

thorough thor'-ough *thoroughly, thoroughness.* 1. Doing all that should be done.–The girl is very thorough with her work. She does it all very carefully.
2. Done completely.–That girl did a *thorough* job.

T
U
V
W
X
Y
Z

those. Used in speaking of or pointing out more than one person or thing farther away than some others. – *Those* apples are the best. These are not so good. *Those* apples over there are better than the ones here.

though. 1. Even if.–We will come to the party even *though* we are late.
2. In spite of the fact that.–Bob was on time, *though* he got up late.
3. However.–You may have spoken to me; I didn't hear you, *though*.
4. *As though* means as if.–Mother spoke *as though* she expected to go.

thought *thoughts.* 1. An idea; anything one thinks about.–A penny for your *thoughts.*– The man has some good *thoughts* about building aircraft.
2. Thinking; working of the mind.–Father said he would give the problem some *thought*.
3. One form of the word *think.*–We *thought* of you on your birthday.

thoughtful thought'-ful *thoughtfully, thoughtfulness.* 1. Busy thinking; in the habit of thinking.–George is *thoughtful* about going to college next month. He is always a *thoughtful* boy.
2. Careful of the welfare or the feelings of others.–Mother said it was *thoughtful* of Mary to send the card to Grandmother.

thoughtless thought'-less *thoughtlessly, thoughtlessness.* 1. Careless.–A *thoughtless* person is always making mistakes.
2. Not careful of the welfare or the feelings of others.–The *thoughtless* boy played the piano when his father was trying to sleep.

thousand thou'-sand *thousands.* A number (1,000) ten times as big as 100. Ten one hundreds make a *thousand*.

thrash *thrashes, thrashed, thrashing.* 1. Separate grain from its stalk by beating; thresh. –The farmer *thrashes* his grain.
2. Beat; whip.–The angry man *thrashed* his dog for running away.

thread *threads, threaded, threading.* 1. A fine string made by twisting strands of silk, cotton, etc. – This is a spool of *thread*. – We use *thread* for sewing.
2. Put *thread* through (a needle).–Mother *threads* her needle before she starts to sew.

threat *threats.* A promise to do harm.–Peter was not frightened by the *threat* of the bully to hit him.–The *threat* of rain made us go into the house.

threaten threat'-en *threatens, threatened, threatening.* 1. Promise to do harm to.–The bully *threatened* to hit Peter.
2. Give notice of, warn of.–The wind *threatens* a storm. It warns that a storm may come.

three. The number (3) coming after 2 and before 4. Two plus one (2 + 1) equals *three*.

thresh *threshes, threshed, threshing.* Separate grain from its stalk by beating; thrash.–The farmer *threshes* his grain. He separates the grain from the straw with a machine.–In olden times, grain was *threshed* by beating it with a jointed stick called a flail.

threshold thresh'-old *thresholds.* The piece of wood or stone at the bottom of a door-way.–Baby sat on the *threshold* and watched for Father.

threw. One form of the word *throw.*–Bob *threw* the ball to Jack after Bill had *thrown* it to him.

thrice. Three times.–The old woman told the prince to knock *thrice* on the door.

thrift. Avoiding waste; habit of saving.–*Thrift* is a good habit to form.

thrifty thrift'-y *thriftier, thriftiest, thriftily, thriftiness.* Saving; careful in spending.– Grandfather is *thrifty*. He doesn't waste anything.

thrill *thrills, thrilled, thrilling.* 1. A shivery or excited feeling.–The sight of the horses gave Jack a *thrill*.
2. Cause to feel excited. – The boy was *thrilled* when he heard the music. He had a tingling, excited feeling.

thrive *thrives, throve, thrived, thriven, thriving.* 1. Grow strong and be healthy.–The plants will not *thrive* unless you water them.
2. Be successful; grow or improve; get along well.–Father's new business is *thriving*.

T
U
V
W
X
Y
Z

throat *throats.* 1. Front part of the neck.– Mother puts cream on her *throat* to keep it from wrinkling.

2. The tube inside the neck.–When one swallows food, it passes through the *throat*.

throb *throbs, throbbed, throbbing.* Beat fast or hard; pound. – The boy's heart *throbbed* after he ran the race.

throne *thrones.* 1. A chair used by a king, queen, or other ruler.

2. The office or rank of king.–The boy prince came to the *throne* during the war. He became king.

throng *throngs, thronged, thronging.* 1. A crowd.–A *throng* gathered for the game.
2. Crowd.–People *thronged* the stadium as soon as it was opened.

through. 1. In one side and out of the other.– The train went *through* the tunnel.–Grandmother put the thread *through* the eye of the needle.–The children looked *through* the microscope.
2. Along; from one end to the other; in.–We walk *through* the hall to go from one class to another. – The wind blew *through* the house.
3. Among; in the midst of.–We walked *through* the tall sunflowers.–Bob stands by Jack *through* thick and thin.
4. During; throughout; from beginning to end.–Baby cried all *through* the night.
5. Express; non-stop.–We took the *through* train.
6. Because of; from.–Father became ill *through* over-eating.

throw *throws, threw, thrown, throwing.* 1. Hurl, fling, cast.–The fielder *throws* the ball at the wicket.–*Throw* your waste paper into the basket.–The car stopped suddenly and we were *thrown* from our seats.
2. Act of throwing.–Bob's fine *throw* from the boundary won the game.

thrush *thrushes.* One of a group of songbirds known for their sweet singing. The song-*thrush* is the most famous.

thrust *thrusts, thrusting.* 1. Push hard; shove.– The boy *thrust* his way through the crowd.–

The workman *thrust* his shovel deep into the sand.
2. Hard push.–With *thrusts* of her elbow, the girl made her way through the crowd.
3. Stab, pierce.–The hunter *thrust* the wildcat through with a knife.
4. Stab.–One *thrust* killed the wildcat.

thud *thuds, thudded, thudding.* 1. Dull, bumping sound.–We heard the *thud* as the man fell to the floor.
2. Make a dull, bumping sound.–The book *thudded* on to the floor.

thumb *thumbs, thumbed, thumbing.* 1. The short, thick finger set apart from the other fingers.
2. A place for the *thumb*.– Mittens have *thumbs* but not separate fingers.
3. Turn (pages of) with the *thumb*.–Mary *thumbed* through the book looking for pictures.

thump *thumps, thumped, thumping.* 1. Hit with a heavy sound.–Bob *thumped* the table with his fist in his excitement.
2. A heavy sound.–When Father heard the *thump*, he thought Baby had fallen out of bed.

thunder thun'-der *thunders, thundered, thundering.* 1. The loud rumbling or cracking sound that often follows a flash of lightning. –The dog hides under the bed when he hears *thunder*,
2. A noise like *thunder*.–We heard the *thunder* of the enemy's guns.
3. Make the noise of *thunder*.–It *thundered* during the storm.
4. Speak very loudly.–'Where have you been?' Father *thundered*.

thunder-cloud thun'-der-cloud *thunder-clouds.* The heavy grey cloud from which thunder and lightning are produced.

thunderstorm thun'-der-storm *thunderstorms.* A storm with thunder and lightning.–We ran to get home before the *thunderstorm*.

Thursday Thurs'-day *Thursdays.* The 5th day of the week.–Sunday, Monday, Tuesday, Wednesday, *Thursday*.

thus. 1. In this way.–If you do the work *thus*, you will be finished sooner.
2. Therefore.–He started early; *thus* he was on time.
3. So; this.–You may go *thus* far, and no farther.

thy. Your (used of one person only). *Thy* is used in the Bible, in praying, and in old poems.–Love *thy* neighbour; do good to them that hate thee.

thyself thy-self' An old form of the word yourself.

tick *ticks, ticked, ticking.* 1. Make light, quick sounds over and over again, like *tick*-tock, *tick*-tock, *tick*-tock.–The clock *ticks*.
2. Ticking sound.–We heard the *tick* of the watch.
3. A small spider or insect that sucks the blood of animals and people.

ticket tick'-et *tickets.* 1. A printed card or paper which shows that one has paid to ride on a train, go into a cinema or theatre, see a football match, etc.
2. A tag.–There are *tickets* showing the prices on the different pieces of jewellery.

tickle tick'-le *tickles, tickled, tickling.* 1. Touch lightly, causing a tingling feeling.–Bob *tickled* Mother's neck with a feather.
2. Amuse; delight.–Mickey Mouse *tickles* the children.
3. A ticklish feeling.–Father had a *tickle* in his throat which made him cough.

ticklish tick'lish *ticklishness.* 1. Sensitive to being tickled.–Sally's feet are *ticklish*.
2. Difficult to do and handle right; requiring tact or great care.–It will be a *ticklish* job to get Mother's consent to have a party.–Pasting tiny pictures in a scrapbook is *ticklish* work.

tide *tides.* 1. The rising and the falling of the ocean. When the *tide* is low, the water is not so deep at the shore line. When the *tide* is

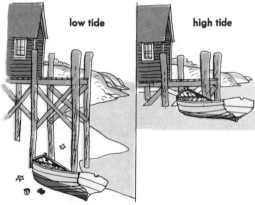

low tide   high tide

high, the water is deeper and higher up on the shore line. The *tide* is caused by the pulling power or attraction of the moon and the sun, which varies according to their positions relative to the Earth.

2. A current, or movement of water.–The row-boat was carried out to sea by the *tide*.
3. *Tide over* means to help out, carry over, –Grandmother gave us a pint of milk to *tide* us *over* until the milkman came.

tidy ti'-dy *tidies, tidied, tidying, tidier, tidiest, tidiness.* 1. Make neat, put in order.–Mary helps Mother *tidy* up the house on Saturday mornings.
2. Neat and in order.–Bob has a *tidy* desk.
3. Considerable.–Bill has saved up a *tidy* amount of money.

tie *ties, tied, tying.* 1. Fasten, bind, make a knot or bow of.–Baby is too little to *tie* her shoe-laces.–The children *tied* up their Christmas gifts with red ribbon.–The organ grinder *tied* the monkey to the barrel-organ.
2. A necktie; a strip of cloth extending round the neck under the collar and knotted in front.–Father likes to wear a red *tie*.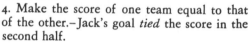
3. An equal score.–The football match ended in a *tie*; the score was 1 to 1.
4. Make the score of one team equal to that of the other.–Jack's goal *tied* the score in the second half.
5. A bond.–Bob is bound to Dick by *ties* of friendship.

tier *tiers.* One of several rows placed one above the other; a layer.–We sat in the top *tier* of seats at the circus.–The wedding cake had 3 *tiers*.

tiger ti'-ger *tigers.* A large wild animal of the cat family with yellow fur striped with black. *Tigers* eat the flesh of other animals. At the zoo, the *tigers* are kept in strong cages.

tight *tighter, tightest, tightly, tightness.* 1. Close-fitting; too close-fitting.–Baby's feet have grown so much that her shoes are too *tight*.–Screw the nozzle on *tight* if you don't want the hose to leak.
2. Stretched taut.–The clothes-line is *tight*.
3. Firm; hard; difficult to undo.–Baby pulled her shoe-lace into a *tight* knot.
4. Put close together.–The apples were packed *tight* in the box.
5. A thing that is air*tight* will not let air in.–Anything water*tight* will not let water in.

T U V W X Y Z

tighten tight'-en *tightens, tightened, tightening*. Make firmer, tighter, or more close-fitting.–The workmen *tightened* the rope. They pulled it hard and tied it securely so that it did not sag.–Mother *tightened* the top on the jar. She turned it to close it more tightly.

tights. A close-fitting garment worn by acrobats, dancers, and other performers. *Tights* fit smoothly over the skin.

tigress ti'-gress *tigresses*. A female *tiger*.–The *tigress* defends her cubs fiercely.

tile *tiles*. Baked clay or stone in thin pieces, used for roofs, floors, walls in bathrooms, and many other things.

till *tills, tilled, tilling*. 1. Until; up to the time when.–Wait *till* Father gets home.
2. Plough; turn (earth) to prepare for planting. – The farmer *tills* the ground.
3. A money drawer.– The grocer put the money in the *till*.

tilt *tilts, tilted, tilting*.
1. Slant; tip; lean to one side.–The telegraph pole is not straight up and down. It *tilts*.
2. Tip; set at an angle.–Do not *tilt* your chair back or you may fall.

timber tim'-ber *timbers*. 1. Wood used for building.–In some parts of the world, most of the houses are made of *timber*.

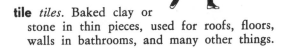

2. A strong, thick piece of wood.–Large *timbers* were used in building the bridge.
3. Woods or forest where trees grow.–The *timber* burned down.

time *times, timed, timing*. 1. A measured period that something lasts; duration. – Minutes, hours, days, weeks, months, and years are all measures of *time*. They answer the question 'How long?'
2. A part of a measured period.–Morning is a *time* of day.–Spring is a *time* of the year.
3. A definite point or moment (of or in *time*). Noon is the *time* for lunch.

4. In music, *time* means the regular beat.–A waltz is in $^3/_4$ *time*. It has 3 beats in each bar.
5. Measure the duration or length of.–The teacher *timed* our test. She watched the clock and told us when to start and when to stop.
6. Multiplied by.–6 *times* 2 equals 12. (6 × 2 = 12.)
7. An occasion; a repeated happening.–We heard the whistle 3 *times*.

timepiece time'-piece *timepieces*. A clock or watch.–We tell time by a *timepiece*.

time-table time'-ta'-ble *time-tables*. A list showing when trains, buses, etc., come to or go from the stations.

timid tim'-id *timidly, timidity*. Shy; bashful; afraid of people and things.–Baby is *timid*.

tin *tins*. A light, soft metal used in making pans, kettles, cans, etc.

tinder tin'-der. Anything such as paper or soft, dry wood that catches fire easily.

tine *tines*. One of the slender, pointed finger-like pieces on a fork.

tingle tin'-gle *tingles, tingled, tingling*. 1. A stinging or prickly feeling caused by excitement, fear, etc.
2. Have a prickly feeling.–The sound of the fire engine makes Bill *tingle* with excitement.

tinker tink'-er *tinkers, tinkered, tinkering*. 1. A person who mends pots and pans.
2. Try to repair or improve.–Bob *tinkers* with his bicycle. He tries to make it run better.

tinkle tin'-kle *tinkles, tinkled, tinkling*. 1. A soft, ringing sound.–We heard the *tinkle* of the cowbell.
2. Make or cause something to make ringing sounds.–The boy *tinkled* his knife and fork by hitting them together. The fork *tinkled* when struck by the knife.

tinsel tin'-sel. 1. Long strings of glistening threads made of bright metal. – The children trimmed the Christmas tree with *tinsel*.
2. A sparkling cloth with shiny metal threads woven into it.

tint *tints, tinted, tinting.* 1. A light or pale colour. –Pink, light blue, and pale green are *tints.* –When the sun sets, the clouds have many reddish *tints.*
2. Colour lightly; put light colours on.–Mary likes to *tint* pictures.

tiny ti′-ny *tinier, tiniest.* Very small, as a *tiny* shell, a *tiny* flower.–Baby's hand looks *tiny* next to Mother's.

tip *tips, tipped, tipping.* 1. An end.–The seal balanced the ball on the *tip* of his nose.
2. A small piece put on the end of something, as the cap on the end of a cane or umbrella.
3. Put a *tip* on.–Grandfather *tipped* his cane with a rubber cap.
4. Tilt; slant.–Baby *tipped* her glass of milk so far that it fell over.
5. Raise or lift (a hat).–Gentlemen *tip* their hats when they meet a lady.
6. Give money for service or for some favour done.–Father *tipped* the boy who brought the message.
7. Money given for service or for some favour done.–He gave the boy a *tip.*

tiptoe tip′-toe *tiptoes, tiptoed, tiptoeing.* 1. The ends of the feet, the toes.–Mary walked on *tiptoe* because Baby was asleep.
2. Walk on the toes.–Mary *tiptoed* across the room.

tire *tires, tired, tiring.* 1. Become tired or weary.–Do not work too fast or you will soon *tire.*
2. (Also spelt *tyre*). An outer rim of rubber that fits on to the rim of a wheel.
3. Any rim on which a wheel rolls.–The wheels of wagons have iron bands for *tyres.*

tireless tire′-less *tirelessly, tirelessness.* Not becoming weary or tired.–A *tireless* person is one who never seems to be weary.–The *tireless* boy worked harder than a man.

tissue tis′-sue *tissues.* 1. A section of living matter which works in a particular way. Your body is made of *tissues.*
2. *Tissue* paper.

tissue paper tis′-sue pa′-per. Very thin, soft paper.–The children wrapped their gifts in *tissue* paper.

title ti′-tle *titles, titled, titling.* 1. The name of a book, story, song, picture, etc.–The *title* of the song is 'John Peel.'
2. Name; give a *title* to.–Jack *titled* his picture 'Rabbit in a Snowstorm.'
3. A special name used before a person's name to show his position or occupation, as Dr Smith, Mrs Jones, King Harold, etc.
4. Legal ownership, or papers showing such ownership.–Father paid for the car and has the *title* to it.

to. 1. Give it *to* me. It is mine.
2. I want *to* go. Children like *to* play.
3. Bob walked *to* the woods.
4 Our class won the game 4 *to* 3.
5. Baby can count *to* 5.
6. Send the letter *to* Grandmother.
7. The girls danced *to* lively music.
8. Mother rocked the baby *to* sleep.
9. He plays *to* win. He plays in such a way as or in order *to* win.
10. Bob tied the dog *to* the post.

toad *toads.* A frog-like animal. It can live in the water, but usually lives on land.

toadstool toad′-stool *toadstools.* An umbrella-shaped fungus. *Toadstools* are found in many colours. Some toadstools are poisonous.

toast *toasts, toasted, toasting.* 1. A piece of bread dried and browned by heat.–We eat *toast* for breakfast.
2. Make brown by heating. – Children like to *toast* marshmallows.
3. Warm. – Grandmother sat by the stove and *toasted* her feet.

toaster toast′-er *toasters.* A device for toasting bread, for browning it by heat.

tobacco to-bac'-co *tobaccos*. A plant with large leaves which are dried for smoking or chewing. Cigarettes and cigars are made of *tobacco*, as is snuff.

toboggan to-bog'-gan *toboggans*. 1. A flat sledge that has no runners.–The children like to slide downhill on a *toboggan*.

2. Slide on a *toboggan*.–We will *toboggan* down the long hill after school.

today to-day'. 1. On this day.–It is hot *today*.
2. This day.–*Today* is Monday.
3. Nowadays; at the present time.–Many women work in factories *today*.

toe *toes*. 1. One of the parts at the end of the foot. We have 5 *toes* on each foot. Some animals have no *toes*.
2. The end of the shoe, stocking, boot, etc., that covers the *toes*.–Mary had a hole in the *toe* of her stocking.

toffee tof'-fee *toffees*. A sticky sweetmeat made with sugar, butter, flavouring, etc.

together to-geth'-er. 1. With one another; in a group.–The children play well *together*.–We sat *together* in one seat.
2. In one group or pile.–We put our money *together*.
3. Into one unit, one large piece made of smaller pieces.–The men put the parts *together* to make the motor-car.

toil *toils, toiled, toiling, toilsome*. 1. Work very hard.–The farmer *toils* in the fields.
2. Any hard work.–Grandfather doesn't mind the *toil* of ploughing the land.

toilet toi'-let *toilets*. 1. A name sometimes used for a lavatory.
2. *Make one's toilet* means to bath, dress, comb one's hair, etc.

token to'-ken *tokens*. 1. A sign.–A white flag is a *token* of surrender.
2. A keepsake; a souvenir.–When Ruth moved away, she gave Ann a ring as a *token*.

told. One form of the word *tell*.–Mother *told* us a story yesterday.

toll *tolls, tolled, tolling*. 1. Ring or sound slowly or evenly.–The church bells *toll* for a funeral. –The old clock *tolled* the hour.
2. Money paid for the right to use something. –We paid a ten pence *toll* to cross the bridge.

tomahawk tom'-a-hawk *tomahawks*. A hatchet or axe used by the Indians in North America. – The Indian hurled his *tomahawk* at his enemy.

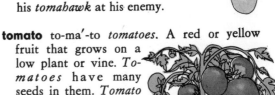

tomato to-ma'-to *tomatoes*. A red or yellow fruit that grows on a low plant or vine. *Tomatoes* have many seeds in them. *Tomato* juice is good to drink.

tomb *tombs*. A grave; a place where the bodies of the dead are kept.–*Tombs* are often built of marble or other hard stone.

tomboy tom'-boy *tomboys*. A girl who romps wildly and plays boys' games.

tomcat tom'-cat *tomcats*. A male cat.–*Tomcats* are often bigger and wilder than female cats.

tomorrow to-mor'-row *tomorrows*. The day following today.–Today is Monday. *Tomorrow* will be Tuesday.

tom-tom tom'-tom *tom-toms*. A kind of drum used by primitive peoples. It is beaten by the hands.

ton *tons*. A unit or measure of weight.–We measure hay, steel, coal, etc., by the *ton*. In Great Britain 2,240 pounds make 1 *ton*. In The United States and Canada 2,000 pounds make 1 *ton*.

tone *tones*. 1. A sound, a note.–The shrill *tone* of the whistle frightened us.–The sweet *tones* of the organ echoed in the empty church.
2. A voice.–Mother's soft *tones* soothe Baby. –Jack spoke in an angry *tone*.
3. A shade.–The picture has many *tones* of blue.

tongs. Scissors-like tools used for lifting and holding, as ice *tongs*, sugar *tongs*, curling-*tongs*. – Mother used sugar *tongs* to pick up sugar cubes and drop them into her cup.

T
U
V
W
X
Y
Z

tongue *tongues.* 1. The flexible and movable organ in the mouth with which one tastes. We use our *tongues* also in speaking.
2. A language.–The Frenchman spoke in his native *tongue.* He spoke French.
3. A thing shaped or used like a *tongue.*–The *tongue* of a shoe is the leather piece under the laces of the shoe. – The *tongue* of a wagon is the long pole at the front.

tonic ton′-ic *tonics.* A medicine or treatment to make one strong and give one an appetite.– The doctor gave Grandmother a *tonic.*–Sunshine and fresh air are a *tonic.*

tonight to-night′. 1. The night following this day.–We are going to a show *tonight.*
2. This night, the night we are in.–The children seem happy *tonight.*

tonsil ton′-sil *tonsils.* One of 2 small organs on the sides of the throat at the back of the mouth.

too. 1. Also.–We have a dog, and a kitten, *too.* –I should like to go, *too.*
2. More than enough; more than is good. –Mother gave the children *too* much candy to eat.
3. Very.–The boy was only *too* glad to come to the party.

took. One form of the word *take.*–I *took* my doll to school with me yesterday.

tool *tools.* Anything used for some kind of work, such as a hammer, a saw, a broom, a ruler.–A carpenter's *tools* are used for building.–Guns and other weapons are *tools* of war.

toot *toots, tooted, tooting.* 1. A sound made by blowing.–We heard the *toot* of the boat's whistle.
2. Sound or blow. – Baby likes to *toot* the motor-car horn.

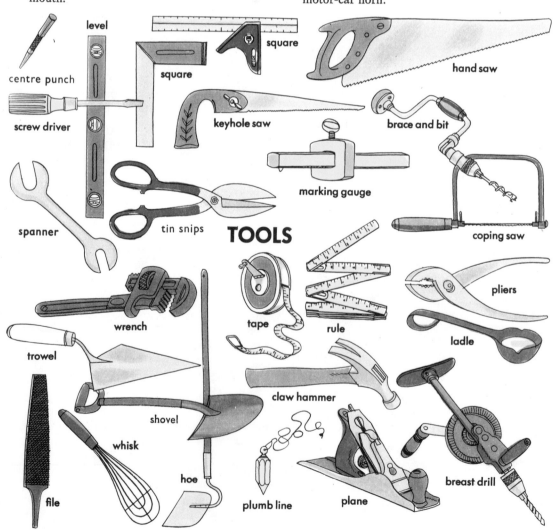

level, square, square, hand saw, centre punch, screw driver, keyhole saw, brace and bit, marking gauge, spanner, tin snips, **TOOLS**, coping saw, wrench, tape, rule, pliers, trowel, ladle, file, whisk, shovel, hoe, plumb line, claw hammer, plane, breast drill

T
U
V
W
X
Y
Z

tooth *teeth*. 1. One of the sharp, white, bony, pointed parts in the mouth with which we chew.–Baby opened her mouth to show her new *tooth*. She now has 6 *teeth*.
2. One of the points on a rake, a comb, etc.

toothache tooth'-ache *toothaches*. A pain in a tooth.–When food gets into a cavity or hole in a tooth, one may get *toothache*.

toothbrush tooth'-brush *toothbrushes*. A brush for cleaning the teeth. –Bob uses his *toothbrush* twice a day.

toothpick tooth'-pick *toothpicks*. A small, pointed piece of wood used for removing food from between the teeth.–It is not polite in Britain to use a *toothpick* at the table.

top *tops, topped, topping*. 1. Highest point or part.–We walked up to the *top* of the hill.– The weather vane on *top* of Grandfather's barn pointed east.
2. The upper edge or side.–The snow came up to the *tops* of our shoes.–Mother wiped the table *top*.
3. The head.–Bob is usually at the *top* of his class.

4. A leafy part that grows above the ground on vegetables such as carrots and beets. – Beet *tops* are good to eat.
5. Cover.–Mother *topped* the birthday cake with pink icing.
6. A round toy made with a pointed tip, on which it can be spun.

topic top'-ic *topics*. A subject one is talking about, thinking about, or writing about.– The *topic* we were discussing was the Test Match. Mary didn't like cricket and tried to change the *topic* of conversation.

topple top'-ple *topples, toppled, toppling*. Fall forward, tumble.–The tower of bricks *toppled* over because it was too heavy at the top.

topsy-turvy top'-sy-tur'-vy. Upset, upside down. –The nursery was *topsy-turvy* after the party. Nothing was in order.

torch *torches*. 1. A light made of something that burns easily, and can be carried in the hand, like a stick of wood.– The man carried a *torch*.
2. A flashlight.

tore. One form of the word *tear*.–Yesterday Mother *tore* up 2 old sheets for bandages.

torment tor'-ment *torments*. Suffering; torture, –The boy's feeling of guilt filled him with *torment*.

torment tor-ment' *torments, tormented, tormenting*. 1. Tease, annoy.–The dog *torments* the cat. He chases her, steals her food, and jumps at her.
2. Give pain to.–The sore throat *tormented* the boy all night.

torn. One form of the word *tear*. – The poor old woman's dress was tattered and *torn*.

tornado tor-na'-do *tornadoes*. A strong, whirling windstorm that often destroys trees and buildings.

torpedo tor-pe'-do *torpedoes*. 1. A large metal shell filled with material that explodes when it hits something. It has a propeller and machinery to drive it forward under water. *Torpedoes* are used to blow up ships.

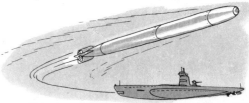

2. Destroy or blow up with *torpedoes*.–The aeroplane *torpedoed* the enemy cruiser.

torpor tor'-por. An inability to feel or move.– The workmen were reduced to *torpor* by the intense heat of the sun.

torrent tor'-rent *torrents*. A rushing stream of water.–The boat was caught in the *torrent* and carried down the river.–It was raining in *torrents*.

torrid tor'-rid. Very hot.–The jungles of Africa lie in the *Torrid* Zone.

tortoise tor'-toise *tortoises*. A four-footed reptile with a horny shell. It lives on land.

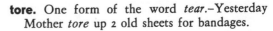

torture tor'-ture *tortures, tortured, torturing, torturer*. 1. Great pain. – The victims of the fire suffered *torture* from their burns.
2. Cause (a person or animal) to suffer greatly.–The bad boy *tortured* the girl by twisting her wrist.–The jailer *tortured* the prisoners by not giving them water.

T
U
V
W
X
Y
Z

toss *tosses, tossed, tossing.* 1. Throw lightly with an upward movement.–Jack *tossed* the ball to Bob.

2. Cause to move up and down, and to and fro.–The wind *tossed* the kites in the sky.

3. Roll back and forth.–The heat made Baby *toss* in her crib.

4. Throw back proudly.–Mary *tossed* her head as she went past Jack.

tot *tots.* A wee, tiny child.–Baby is still just a *tot*.

total to'-tal *totals, totalled, totalling.* 1. Whole, complete.–The teacher said Bob could buy the ball if 10p was the *total* cost.

2. Entire amount.–Bob said that 10p would be more than the *total*.–If you add 4 + 5 + 2, the *total* is 11.

3. Complete, absolute.–There was *total* silence in the room when our teacher came in.

4. Add.–*Total* 4 + 5 + 2, and you get 11.

5. Amount to, add up to.–Our expenses for our holiday *totalled* £30 apiece.

totem pole to'-tem pole *totem poles.* A pole built by primitive people, with animals or other figures carved or painted on it. The figure was the chosen token or symbol of the family or tribe.

totter tot'-ter *totters, tottered, tottering.* 1. Walk with trembling steps.–An old man with a cane *tottered* down the street.

2. Shake as if about to fall.–A person who has been ill a long time often *totters* when he tries to walk.

touch *touches, touched, touching.* 1. Feel something by placing the fingers or any other part of the body against it.–The blind man *touched* the elephant's ears.

2. Be or come together or in contact with.–Put the books on the table so that they *touch* each other.

3. Reach.–Mother's housecoat *touches* the floor.

4. Strike lightly.–Bob just *touched* the ball. He hit it lightly.

5. Lay hands on.–Do not *touch* the kitten.

6. Cause a feeling of kindness, sadness, or pity.–My parents were greatly *touched* by the stranger's story of his troubles.

7. One of the senses of the body.–*Touch* makes us able to learn about things by feeling or *touching* them.

8. A slight or mild trace.–Bob put a *touch* of salt on his egg.

9. A stroke of a brush or pencil.–The painter gave the picture a few *touches* and it was done.

10. *Touch up* means to make small improvements in.–The picture needs *touching up*.

11. *In touch* means in communication.–Father keeps *in touch* with us by letters and telephone.

12. Do or take something in the least way.–Baby has not *touched* her pudding; she has not tasted it.–Mary has not *touched* the piano for weeks; she has done no practising.

tough *tougher, toughest.* 1. Not easily chewed or cut.–Some meat is tender, some is *tough*.

2. Able to stand much use or strain without breaking.–The ropes used to tie a ship to the dock must be *tough*.

3. Not pleasant; difficult.–This has been a *tough* winter for the poor family whose home was burned.

4. Sturdy and lasting.–Some plants are *tough*; others die with the first frost.

5. Stubborn and hard to manage.–The prisoner got *tough* when taken from his cell.

6. Rough and lawless.–The family moved from a *tough* part of the town to a better part.

tour *tours, toured, touring.* 1. Travel about for pleasure.–We *toured* on the Continent during our holiday.

2. A journey for pleasure.–We cannot take a *tour* this year.

tourist tour'-ist *tourists.* One who travels for pleasure. – Many *tourists* stop to see the Tower of London.

tournament tour'-na-ment *tournaments.* 1. In olden times, a contest in which mounted knights tilted at each other and engaged in similar tests of skill and strength.

2. A sports contest.–There were 36 entrants for the tennis *tournament*.–Jack has put his name down for the school chess *tournament*.

tow *tows, towed, towing.* 1. Pull or draw along by a connecting rope, chain, or cable.–The bus had a broken axle and had to be *towed* by a breakdown lorry.

2. Something *towed*.–The bus being pulled was the *tow*.

3. A rope or chain used to *tow*.

4. *In tow* usually means being pulled.–While the bus was *in tow*, the *tow* rope broke.

toward or **towards** to-ward' or to-wards'. 1. In the direction of.–The dog ran *towards* the garage.

2. Near; close to.–It is getting *towards* the time to quit work.

3. For the purpose of, to help buy.–Mary gave some money *towards* the sick boy's flowers.–Bob has saved £2 *towards* a new bicycle.

4. To.–The boy's behaviour *towards* his classmates was not what it should be.

towel tow'-el *towels*. A piece of cloth or paper used for wiping or drying.

tower tow'-er *towers, towered, towering*. 1. A tall, slender part of a building, or a tall, slim building that stands alone.–The church bell is in the *tower*.

2. Be much taller or higher.–The tall girl *towers* above the rest of the class.–The chimney *towers* above the rest of the building.

town *towns*. 1. A place where many people live near each other.–Grandmother lives in the country. We live in a *town*.

2. The people living in a *town*.–The whole *town* went to see the circus.

toy *toys, toyed, toying*. 1. A thing for children to play with.–There were many *toys* under the Christmas tree.

2. Play (with); amuse oneself (with).–Baby *toys* with her toes.

trace *traces, traced, tracing*. 1. Draw an outline of; sketch.–The man *traced* a plan of the playground.

2. Copy by drawing over the lines of.–Mary *traced* the picture by placing tissue paper over it and marking the lines of the picture on the tissue.

3. Follow.–The hunter *traced* the rabbit by its footprints or tracks in the snow.

4. A sign; a mark; an indication.–He saw *traces* of deer in the woods.

5. A small bit.–The dog licked the plate so clean that not a *trace* of food was left.

track *tracks, tracked, tracking*. 1. A mark left by the passing of something, as bicycle *tracks*, wagon *tracks*, rabbit *tracks*. – Judy left a *track* in the snow as she walked.

2. A road or path.–The hunters followed the narrow *track* to their cabin.

3. A roadway or path, usually circular, built for racing.–The racers roared round the *track*.

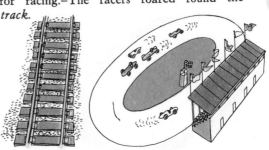

4. A line of steel rails.–Trains run on *tracks*.

5. Trace; follow.–The dog *tracked* the rabbit to the old log.–The policeman *tracked* the burglar to his hide-out.

T
U
V
W
X
Y
Z

tractor trac'-tor *tractors*. A heavy machine with a motor used for pulling a plough or some other machine.–Many farmers use *tractors* instead of horses.

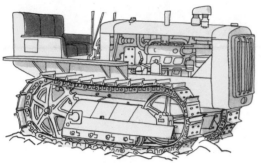

trade *trades, traded, trading*. 1. The work one does to make a living.–Father's *trade* is tool-making.
2. Exchange.–Mary *traded* books with Ruth. –Bob *traded* his knife for a ball.
3. An exchange.–Bob thought it was a good *trade*.
4. Do business.–We *trade* at the corner shop.

trade-mark trade'-mark *trade-marks*. A mark, picture, or printed stamp put on goods by a manufacturer so that one can tell his goods from those made by someone else.

trader trad'-er *traders*. A person who buys, sells, or exchanges goods.–That man is a horse *trader*.

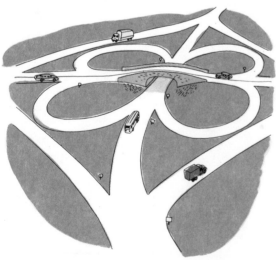

traffic traf'-fic. 1. Movement of people or of cars, lorries, or other vehicles.–*Traffic* is very heavy on Sundays. Many cars are on the road.

2. Having to do with movement of people or vehicles.–There are many *traffic* accidents on holidays.

tragedy trag'-e-dy *tragedies*. 1. A play that has a sad ending.
2. A sad happening.–The death of the fireman in the burning house was a *tragedy*.

trail *trails, trailed, trailing*. 1. To drag something along behind.–The runaway horse ran home *trailing* the broken rope.
2. Follow.–The dog *trailed* Jack to the woods.
3. Track, trace, follow the tracks of.–We *trailed* the rabbit to the hollow log.
4. A path worn through the woods.–An old Indian *trail* led to the brook.
5. Straggle.–Ivy *trailed* over the walls of the old house.

trailer trail'-er *trailers*. 1. A kind of caravan, drawn by a motor-car.–We rented a *trailer* to live in during our holiday.

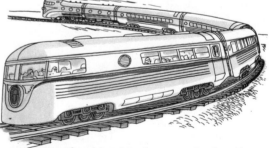

2. Any wheeled vehicle, such as the body of a truck, designed to be pulled by another vehicle with a motor.
3. A plant that crawls along the ground.–Nasturtiums are *trailers*.

train *trains, trained, training*. 1. A line of coaches joined together and pulled by an engine.

2. A part of a skirt that drags on the floor behind the wearer.–The bride's dress had a long *train*.
3. Bring up; teach.–The children's good manners showed that they were well *trained* at home.–Jack tried to *train* his dog to jump through a hoop.

4. Practise; prepare.–Soldiers *train* for service. They make themselves fir and ready by exercising and drilling, by eating properly, by getting enough rest.

5. Coax or fix in a certain way, till it becomes natural.–Grandmother *trained* the rambler roses over the fence.

6. Aim, point.–The sailors *trained* the ship's guns on the pirate vessel.

training train'-ing. Study and practice.–It takes *training* to learn to be a carpenter or a mechanic.–The prize-fighter went to bed at 9 o'clock while he was in *training*.

traitor trai'-tor *traitors*. A person who is not true to his country; one who helps the enemies of his country.

tramp *tramps, tramped, tramping*. 1. Walk; march.–The children *tramped* through the halls.–Soldiers *tramp* miles each day.

2. Walk (on) heavily.–The cows *tramped* on the new plants in the garden.

3. A walk; a hike.–Bob and Father went for a long *tramp*.

4. A homeless man who goes from place to place.–A *tramp* came to the farm for food and water.

5. A steamship that goes from one port to another, picking up what freight it can.

trample tram'-ple *tramples, trampled, trampling*. 1. Step on and crush.–The cows got into the corn-field and *trampled* the corn.

2. Walk very heavily.–The children *trampled* all round the room.

transfer trans'-fer *transfers*. A picture or design which can be transferred in reverse from one surface to another.–Dick stuck *transfers* of animals into his scrapbook.

transfer trans-fer' *transfers, transferred, transferring*. 1. Move, put in a different place.–Mr Jones was *transferred* to a different department.

2. Alter.–Dogs are loyal animals and do not often *transfer* their affection from one owner to another.

3. Copy, trace, or reproduce.–Mary used tracing paper to *transfer* the picture in the book to her notebook.

transform trans-form' *transforms, transformed, transforming*. Change from one thing to another.–Cream is *transformed* into butter by churning.–The fairy godmother *transformed* the pumpkin into a splendid coach.

transfusion trans-fu'-sion *transfusions*. The transfer of blood from a vein of one person into a vein of another person.–The injured man, who had lost much blood, was given a blood *transfusion*.

translate trans-late' *translates, translated, translating, translation*. Change into a different language.–Father *translated* the German letter into English.

transmitter trans-mit'-ter *transmitters*. An instrument by which messages are sent by telephone, telegraph, radio, etc.

transom tran'-som *transoms*. A bar across a door or window. –A *transom*-window is a small window over a door.

transparent trans-par'-ent. Able to be seen through. – Window glass is *transparent*.– The water in the pool was so *transparent* that we could see the pebbles on the bottom.

transplant trans-plant' *transplants, transplanted, transplanting*. Move; plant again somewhere else.–We planted tomato seeds in a box in the house. When the plants were large enough, we *transplanted* them into the garden.

transport trans-port' *transports, transported, transporting*. Carry or take from place to place.–Coal is *transported* from mines to towns or factories.

transport trans'-port *transports*. 1. A ship that carries passengers, troops or goods from one place to another.

2. An aeroplane that carries people and things from one place to another.

T U V W X Y Z

transportation trans-por-ta′-tion. 1. The carrying of goods or passengers from one place to another.–*Transportation* is important to business.
2. A way of getting from one place to another.–The only *transportation* out to our house is the bus.

trap *traps, trapped, trapping.* 1. A device to catch animals.–Father caught a rat in a *trap.*

2. Catch in a *trap.*–The hunter *trapped* the fox.
3. A U-shaped part of a drainpipe that allows water to pass out but keeps sewer gas from coming back through it. It *traps* the harmful gas.

trap-door *trap-doors.* A door in a floor or ceiling or on a roof. –
The man found a *trap-door* in the floor.

trapeze tra-peze′ *trapezes.* A swing high above the ground.–The acrobats performed on a *trapeze.*

trapper trap′-per *trappers.* A person who traps wild animals to sell their furs.

trash *trashy.* Rubbish; broken and used-up things.–The barrel in the yard is filled with *trash.*

travel trav′-el *travels, travelled, travelling.* Go from place to place.–Mary wants to *travel* round the world when she grows up.–*Travel* broadens the mind.

traveller trav′-el-ler *travellers.* A person who is journeying from one place to another.–A *traveller* on the road stopped us to ask the way.–*Travellers* by plane travel fastest.

tray *trays.* A large, flat piece of metal, wood, or other material with a shallow rim round the edge. Food, dishes, glasses, and so on, are often carried on a *tray.* –Mary served Mother her breakfast in bed on a *tray.*

tread *treads, trod, trodden* or *trod, treading.*
1. To step; to walk; to step on.–Do not *tread* on my toes.–The cows sometimes *tread* on the little chickens.
2. Trample; beat down.–The animals at the circus *tread* the grass with their feet.
3. Walking; steps.–We heard the heavy *tread* of marching feet.
4. The part of a rubber tyre that touches the ground.
5. The part of a stair step that one puts one's foot on. If the *treads* are narrow, it makes the stairs steep.

treason trea′-son. Being untrue to one's country, secretly helping the enemies of one's country.–The rich man was found guilty of *treason.* He had sold supplies to the enemy.

treasure treas′-ure *treasures, treasured, treasuring.* 1. Money, jewels, or any things of value that have been collected or saved up. –The boys were digging in the cave for *treasure.*
2. Value dearly.–Mother *treasures* the old picture of Grandmother and Grandfather.

treasurer treas′-ur-er *treasurers.* A person chosen or elected to take care of money that is taken in and paid out.–As club *treasurer,* Mary collects the dues and writes down how much the club spends.

treasury treas′-ur-y *treasuries.* A place where money is received or paid out.

treat *treats, treated, treating.* 1. Act towards.–Bob *treats* his friends well.
2. Take care of; give medical attention to.–The doctor *treated* Father for a strained back.
3. Pay for a pleasure for someone.–Mary lost the bet, so she had to *treat* Bob to an ice-cream.
4. An unusual pleasure.–It was a *treat* to get a chance to swim in the ocean.

treatment treat′-ment *treatments.* 1. A cure or remedy; care. – The doctor is giving Father heat *treatments* for his sprained back.
2. A way of acting towards, or dealing with.–Grandfather's *treatment* of his animals is always gentle and thoughtful. – Jack felt he had received unfair *treatment* from his teacher.

treaty trea′-ty *treaties.* A written agreement among countries.–The nations that were at war have signed a peace *treaty.*

T
U
V
W
X
Y
Z

TRANSPORTATION

aeroplane

motor-car

tramcar

caravan

jeep

lorry

train

underground train

outrigger canoe

ocean liner

sailing boat

stagecoach

motorcycle

submarine

llama

raft

umiak

horse

wheelbarrow

camel

dogcart

sleigh

sedan chair

elephant

T
U
V
W
X
Y
Z

walnut

coconut

orange

banana

yellow pine

rubber

TREES

willow

red spruce

eucalyptus

cypress

banyan

apple

cork

cacao

redwood

maple

cedar

acacia

larch

magnolia

elm

oak

birch

poplar

T
U
V
W
X
Y
Z

tree *trees.* A very large, woody, leafy plant with a stem called a trunk. Some *trees* have fruit or nuts on them. Wood for building houses and furniture comes from the trunks and branches of *trees.*

tremble trem'-ble *trembles, trembled, trembling.* 1. To shake slightly from a strong feeling such as fright, cold, nervousness, or the like.–Jack *trembled* with eagerness as he unwrapped his present.
2. Shake slightly.–The wind made the leaves *tremble.*
3. Shaking.–We could feel the *tremble* of the house after the explosion.

tremendous tre-men'-dous *tremendously.* Very great.–The fire caused a *tremendous* loss for the owners of the building.

trench *trenches.* 1. A ditch. – The farmer dug a *trench* at the side of the barn to drain the water off.
2. A ditch with a bank of earth in front to provide protection. – Soldiers dig *trenches* to shoot from.

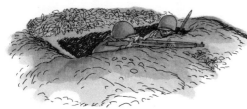

trespass tres'-pass *trespasses, trespassed, trespassing.* Go on to the property or land of someone else without their saying that you may do so.–Hunters sometimes *trespass* on the farmer's land.

tress *tresses.* A lock of hair.–Rapunzel let her long golden *tresses* down from the tower window.

trestle tres'-tle *trestles.* A strong framework that holds something up. – The bridge was built on *trestles.*

trial tri'-al *trials.* 1. A test. – Father took the new car out for a *trial*; he wanted to see how it would run.

2. A hearing before a judge in court.–The thief was given a *trial* and found guilty.

triangle tri'-an-gle *triangles.* 1. A flat figure or shape with 3 sides and 3 corners.
2. A musical instrument made of a steel rod, shaped like a *triangle,* and played with a small steel rod.

tribe *tribes.* A group of people of the same race or kind, who have the same beliefs or customs, and who live together under the same leaders.–American Indians once lived in *tribes.*

tribute trib'-ute *tributes.* Thanks; respect; praise. – On Remembrance Sunday we pay *tribute* to the soldiers who gave their lives for their country.

trick *tricks, tricked, tricking.* 1. A clever act, stunt, or movement which amuses people.– The magician's best *trick* was pulling rabbits out of a hat that seemed to be empty.
2. A joke; a prank. – Bill played a *trick* on Mother by filling the salt shaker with sugar.
3. Cheat; deceive.–The dishonest boy tried to *trick* Bob into exchanging his bicycle for a knife.

trickle trick'-le *trickles, trickled, trickling.* 1. Run in a fine stream; fall in drops.–It was so hot that perspiration *trickled* down the man's forehead.–Water *trickled* from the leak in the water-pipe.
2. A thin stream. – A *trickle* of water leaked from the pipe.

tricky trick'-y *trickier, trickiest.* 1. Likely to deceive, crafty. – Father said the slow bowler was *tricky*. It was difficult to tell which way the ball would break.
2. Full of snags and pitfalls.–Hardly anybody could find the right answer to such a *tricky* problem. It required great skill.

tricycle tri'-cy-cle *tricycles.* A small, 3-wheeled vehicle that is run by pedals and steered by handlebars.

tried. 1. One form of the word *try.*–I *try* each day to do a kind deed. Yesterday I *tried* hard.
2. Proved, sure.–Joe is Jack's *tried* and true friend.

trifle tri′-fle *trifles*. 1. A little thing that is not important.–Don't fret over *trifles*.

2. A very small amount of money. – We bought this knife for a *trifle;* it cost only fifty pence.

3. A sweet made of sponge-cake soaked in sherry or liqueur, jam and custard, etc.

trigger trig′-ger *triggers*. The small, movable piece on the underside of a gun that is pulled back to fire the gun.

trill *trills, trilled, trilling*. 1. Sing or play an instrument with a shaking or vibrating sound. –The soprano *trilled* the final note of her song.–Birds *trill* merrily.

2. A shake.–The oboist played a *trill*.

3. A bird's warble.–We heard the merry *trill* of the thrush.

trim *trims, trimmed, trimming*. 1. Make neat and orderly by cutting some away. – Bob *trims* the rose bushes.–Mother *trims* her finger-nails.

2. Decorate; add decoration to. – Mother *trimmed* the birthday cake with pink flowers.

3. Condition.–Our football team is in good *trim* for the game.

4. Neat and orderly. – The room is *trim*. Everything is in place.

trimming trim′-ming *trimmings*. Something added as decoration.–Buttons, lace, and ribbons are dress *trimmings*.

trinket trin′-ket *trinkets*. A small or cheap toy or piece of jewellery.–The children bought some *trinkets* at the fair.

trio tri′-o *trios*. 1. group of 3 persons or things. –A *trio* of girls sang the song.

2. Music for 3 people to sing or play.–The *trio* was played by a violin, a 'cello, and a piano.

trip *trips, tripped, tripping*. 1. A journey.–We are going for a *trip* in her car soon.

2. Step lightly and quickly. – The children *tripped* along after the Pied Piper.

3. Catch one's foot; stumble.–Grandfather *tripped* on the edge of the rug and almost fell.

4. Cause to stumble.–The boy put his foot in the gangway and *tripped* the girl.

triple tri′-ple *triples, tripled, tripling*. 1. Of 3 parts.–The fork is *triple*-pronged.

2. Three times as great.–Jack's income from his paper round is *triple* what it was when he started. He used to make £1 a week; now he makes £3.

3. Make 3 times as great.–Jack *tripled* his income from his paper round.–The population of the country has more than *tripled* in the last fifty years.

triplet trip′-let *triplets*. 1. A group of 3 things that are alike or related; a trio.

2. One of three children born at one birth to the same mother.

triumph tri′-umph *triumphs, triumphed, triumphing*. 1. A victory; a success.–After their team's *triumph* in the Cup Final, thousands of supporters welcomed it home with cheering and music.

2. Be victorious; win.–Our cricket team should *triumph* this afternoon.

trodden trod′-den. One form of the word *tread*. –The path had been *trodden* by the cows until it was packed hard.

trolley trol′-ley *trolleys*. 1. A low truck or cart, usually pushed by hand.–The porter put our luggage on the *trolley* and wheeled it to the train.

2. A table on wheels with two or more tiers, used in homes, hospitals, restaurants, etc.–We asked the waiter to show us the cakes on the *trolley*.

3. The wheel that runs along an electric wire and carries electricity to a tram or *trolley*-bus. – The *trolley* came off the wire and the bus stopped.

4. A bus running from electric overhead wires, usually called a *trolley*-bus.

trombone trom′-bone *trombones*. A musical instrument made of a bent brass tube, with a section which slides in and out to make different notes.

troop *troops, trooped, trooping*. 1. A group of soldiers, or other united group.–A Boy Scout *troop* is camping at the lake.–A *troop* of soldiers marched through the city.

2. Soldiers. – The general said there were 10,000 *troops* in his army; there were 10,000 men.

3. March together. – The children following the Pied Piper *trooped* into the side of the hill.

trophy tro´-phy *trophies*. Something given as a sign of victory; something won. – The winner of the race won a silver cup as a *trophy*.

trot *trots, trotted, trotting*. 1. Run slowly. – The dog *trots* along after its master.
2. A gait of a horse in which a front foot and the opposite hind foot move together.
3. Move at a *trot*. – The cowboy's horse *trotted* slowly along the fence.

trouble trou´-ble *troubles, troubled, troubling*.
1. To worry. – Baby's illness *troubles* Mother.
2. A worry; a concern; a disturbance. – The girl's mischievous pranks at school make *trouble* for her family.
3. A nuisance; additional work. – We will stay for lunch, if it isn't too much *trouble* for you.
4. A difficulty; something that causes worry, unhappiness, unpleasantness, and so on; misfortune. – That family has had many *troubles*.

troublesome trou´-ble-some. Causing trouble, difficulty, disturbance, and so on. – Sometimes the boy is *troublesome*.

trough *troughs*. 1. A narrow box or holder for animal food. – Horses, cattle, and pigs eat and drink from *troughs*.

2. A gutter or drain. – *Troughs* carry water from the roofs of buildings into drain-pipes.

trousers trou´-sers. The lower part of a man's or boy's clothing, which covers the legs and waist.

trousseau (pronounced *troo´-so*) trous´-seau *trousseaux* or *trousseaus*. A set of clothes for a bride. – The bride's *trousseau* was given to her by her mother.

trout. 1. A kind of fish that is found in fresh water, and used for food. It tastes a little like salmon but has a rather more delicate flavour.

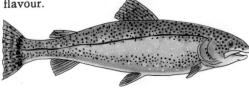

trowel trow´-el *trowels*. 1. A hand tool with a broad, flat blade used to smooth plaster, cement, and the like. – A bricklayer uses a *trowel* for putting mortar between bricks.
2. A small digging tool. – Mother uses a garden *trowel* for digging up plants.

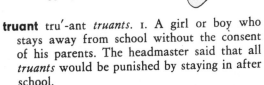

truant tru´-ant *truants*. 1. A girl or boy who stays away from school without the consent of his parents. The headmaster said that all *truants* would be punished by staying in after school.
2. Absent without permission. – Bob was *truant* from school once when he went fishing.

truce *truces*. A pause or short stop in fighting. – The 2 armies called for a *truce*. During the *truce* the leaders talked about peace.

truck *trucks, trucked, trucking*. 1. An open railway-wagon used for carrying coal and other heavy goods.
2. A small platform on wheels pushed by hand. – The porter loaded our luggage on to a *truck*.
3. Transport or carry on a *truck*. – The coal was *trucked* by rail to London.
4. Worthless rubbish. – Bob's room was littered with *truck*.
5. A group of wheels that holds up one end of a railway coach.

truculent truc´-u-lent *truculence, truculently*. Fierce and defiant. – When the teacher rebuked him for rudeness Jack was *truculent*. He slammed his desk-lid.

trudge *trudges, trudged, trudging*. 1. Walk wearily but steadily. – The soldiers *trudged* up the steep hill in full kit.
2. A long tiring walk. – We were exhausted after the long *trudge* up the hill to Grandfather's farm.

T
U
V
W
X
Y
Z

true. 1. Correct; real: – This is *true*: the sun shines here in the daytime. This is false: the sun shines here at night.–Mary likes imaginary stories, but Bob likes *true* stories.
2. Sincere; faithful.–Sally is a *true* friend to the postman.
3. Rightful; actual; real.–The teacher asked us who the *true* owner of the ball was.

truly tru'-ly. 1. Sincerely; faithfully.–The letter ended, 'Very *truly* yours.'
2. Really.–I am *truly* coming to see you.

trumpet trump'-et *trumpets*. A musical instrument sounded by blowing.–The *trumpet* is a wind instrument.

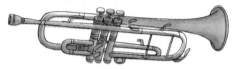

trumpeter trump'-et-er *trumpeters*. One who plays or blows a trumpet.–Jack is the *trumpeter* in the school band.

trunk *trunks*. 1. The main stem of a tree.–The owl lived in the hollow *trunk* of an old oak.
2. The body of a person or animal, without the legs, arms, or head.
3, The snout of an elephant.–The elephant can pour water over his head with his *trunk*.

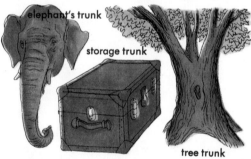

elephant's trunk

storage trunk

tree trunk

4. A large covered chest for storing or moving clothing or other belongings securely.–When travelling a long way, we send our clothes in a *trunk*.

trunks. Short, tight pants.–Men wear *trunks* when they swim.

trust *trusts, trusted, trusting*. 1. Have faith in; believe in; depend upon. – Children *trust* their parents.–The teacher knew she could *trust* Jack to bring back the book.–We did not have enough money with us to pay for the groceries, but the shopkeeper *trusted* us.

2. Hope; expect.–I *trust* you will be coming home soon.
3. Faith.–The children have complete *trust* in what their teacher tells them.
4. A duty; something one promises to do.–Bob lived up to his *trust* to take care of the garden while Father was away.

trustworthy trust'-wor-thy *trustworthily, trustworthiness*. Dependable; true to one's word or duty.–The teacher found the boy to be *trustworthy*.

trusty trust'-y *trustier, trustiest*. 1. Dependable; not failing.–Robin Hood bent his *trusty* bow and shot the arrow through the deer's heart. –The rich man left a large bequest to his *trusty* servant.

truth *truths*. What is true or real, exactly what happened.–Mother taught us to tell the *truth*. –It would not be telling the *truth* to say that the children are perfect.

truthful truth'-ful *truthfully, truthfulness*. Honest, telling what really is so.–It pays to be *truthful*. – In the story George Washington was *truthful* about what happened to the cherry tree.

try *tries, tried, trying*. 1. Attempt; make an effort.–At first Bob could not solve the puzzle. He *tried* again and finally worked it out.
2. Use or test; give a trial to.–If you cannot work out the problem this way, *try* another way.–*Try* one of these sweets.
3. A test or trial.–Mother is giving the new soap a *try* today.
4. Give a court hearing to, before a judge.– The man was *tried* for stealing.

tub *tubs*. 1. A large, open vessel that holds water in which to wash clothes or bath. – Bob takes showers, but Jack baths in the bathtub.

2. A low, wooden, barrel-like vessel.–The grocer had a *tub* half full of butter.

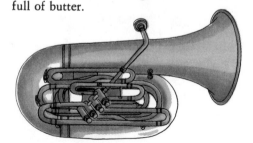

tuba tu'-ba *tubas*. A large, low-toned horn.

tube *tubes.* 1. A pipe, a long, hollow piece of rubber, metal, or glass.
2. Any hollow stem.– We drink milk and lemonade through paper *tubes* called straws.
3. A round container of thin metal with a top that screws on.–Medicines, shaving creams, and toothpaste often come in *tubes.*
4. An underground railway. – Father travels to work on the *tube.*

tuberculosis tu-ber-cu-lo′-sis. A disease, usually of the lungs. When a person has *tuberculosis,* he is often sent to a sanatorium or hospital for treatment and rest.

tuck *tucks, tucked, tucking.* 1. Place, fit, or squeeze in neatly. – Mother *tucked* Baby's curls into her bonnet.–Mary *tucked* the blankets in.
2. A stitched fold.–Father's shirt-sleeves were too long, so Mother put a *tuck* in them.

Tudor Tu′-dor. Of the period in English history from Henry VII to Elizabeth I (1485–1603). The monarchs belonged to the House of *Tudor.*

Tuesday Tues′-day. The 3rd day of the week.– Sunday, Monday, *Tuesday.*

tuft *tufts, tufted.* 1. A group of threads, hair, feathers, or anything of the kind, fastened together at one end and loose at the other.– The cockatoo has a *tuft* of feathers on his head.
2. A bunch of wool. – The bedspread was white with blue *tufts.*

tug *tugs, tugged, tugging.* 1. A small boat that can pull or tow other boats, even those much larger than the *tug* is.
2. Pull hard. – The boys *tugged* at the wagon to get it out of the mud.
3. A hard pull.–Father gave just one *tug* and out it came.

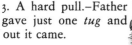

tulip tu′-lip *tulips.* A bright-coloured, cup-shaped flower that grows from a bulb. The bulbs are put into the ground in autumn. The flowers blossom in the spring. Many *tulips* grow in Holland.

tumble tum′-ble *tumbles, tumbled, tumbling.*
1. Fall.–Baby *tumbled* out of bed.
2. Roll or toss.–The apples *tumbled* about in the basket when Bob ran.
3. Turn handsprings, somersaults, and the like.–Of all the circus acts, Bob liked the *tumbling* best.

tumbler tum′-bler *tumblers.* 1. A person who can turn somersaults, handsprings, and the like; an acrobat.
2. A drinking glass.–Mary dropped a water *tumbler* and broke it.

tuna tu′-na. A large fish that is good to eat. The meat of *tuna* fish is tinned and sold in shops.

tune *tunes, tuned, tuning.* 1. A melody. – I know the *tune* of 'Greensleeves.'
2. A piece of music, song.–Play a *tune* for us.
3. Bring to the proper pitch or note.–Mary *tuned* her violin. – Mother had the piano *tuned.*

tunnel tun′-nel *tunnels, tunnelled, tunnelling.* A passageway made underground. – Trains and motor-cars go through a *tunnel* to get through a mountain or under a river.

turban tur′-ban *turbans.* 1. A cap with a scarf wound round it. – The man is wearing a *turban.*

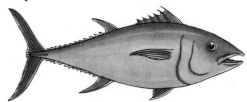

2. A scarf wound round the head. – The woman is wearing a *turban.*
3. A kind of small, close-fitting hat without a brim, resembling a wound scarf.

T
U
V
W
X
Y
Z

tureen tu-reen′ *tureens*. A large, covered dish. –Mother served the soup from a *tureen*.

turf. Grass with its tangled roots.–Men playing golf often dig up *turf* with their clubs.

Turk *Turks*. A person whose native country is Turkey, a country in Asia.

turkey tur′-key *turkeys*. 1. A kind of large bird with wrinkled, red skin on its head and neck. Some *turkeys* are wild, some are tame. 2. The meat of a *turkey*.–We eat *turkey* on Christmas Day.

turn *turns, turned, turning*. 1. Change direction, go a different way.–We were driving west. Then we *turned* a corner and drove south.–Bob *turned* when I called to him. 2. Move in a circle.–The hands of the clock *turn*.–A top *turns*. 3. A chance, opportunity, time. – We took *turns* driving.–The children formed a queue, and each waited his *turn* to get a drink. 4. Change, become.–Ice *turns* to water when it gets warm. 5. Transform, change.–The witch *turned* the little girl into a toad in the fairy story. – Caterpillars *turn* into butterflies. 6. Upset.–The sight of a mouse *turns* Mary's stomach. She feels quite sick. 7. A deed, an act.–If you will help me now, I will do you a good *turn* another day. 8. A sudden change.–Bill's behaviour takes a *turn* for the better just before Christmas. 9. A complete circular movement.–If you give the clock key too many *turns* when winding it, it will break.–Father unlocks his safe with 2 *turns* to the right, and 3 to the left.

turnip tur′-nip *turnips*. A kind of plant with a root that can be eaten, or the root of that plant.–*Turnips* are cooked as table vegetables, or eaten raw.

turnstile turn′-stile *turnstiles*. A turning gate with crossed bars at the top. Some *turnstiles* register the number of persons passing through. –When going from the ticket office to the train, we passed through a *turnstile*.–As soon as we pay our money, the attendant lets us through the *turnstile*.

turpentine tur′-pen-tine. An oily substance that comes from trees that have cones.–Father thinned the paint with *turpentine*.–*Turpentine* is sometimes used in medicine.

turquoise tur′-quoise *turquoises*. 1. A greenish-blue stone.–Mary's new ring is set with a *turquoise*. 2. Greenish blue.–Mother has a *turquoise* silk dress.

turtle tur′-tle *turtles*. An animal with a hard shell over its back. *Turtles* are tortoises that live in water.

tusk *tusks*. A long, pointed tooth.–Elephants have a *tusk* on each side of the head.– Seals and some other animals also have *tusks*.

tussle tus′-sle *tussles, tussled, tussling*. 1. A scuffle, a struggle.–The hunter had a *tussle* with a bear. 2. Wrestle.–The boys *tussled* until they were tired out.

tutor tu′-tor *tutors, tutored, tutoring*. 1. A teacher who gives private lessons.–The sick boy could not go to school, so he had a *tutor* at home. 2. Teach privately.–Father *tutored* the boy in arithmetic.

tweed. A kind of woollen cloth with rough threads woven into it.–Father's suit is made of *tweed*.

twelfth *twelfths*. 1. Following the eleventh.– Jack was the tenth person in the row, Mary the eleventh, and Bob the *twelfth*. 2. One of 12 equal parts of anything.

T
U
V
W
X
Y
Z

twelve. The number (12) between 11 and 13. –Ten and two make *twelve.*–*Twelve* eggs make a dozen eggs.

twentieth twen'-ti-eth *twentieths.* 1. Following the nineteenth.–Today is the nineteenth day of the month. Tomorrow is the *twentieth.*
2. One of twenty equal parts of anything.

twenty twen'-ty *twenties.* The number (20 between 19 and 21.–5, 10, 15, 20.–Ten and ten make *twenty.*

twice. Two times.–The teacher told us *twice* how to spell the word, but I cannot remember.

twig *twigs.* A tiny branch of a tree.–The sparrow sat on a *twig* of the apple tree.

twilight twi'-light *twilights.* Dusk; the half light just after the sun sets in the evening, or just before it rises in the morning.

twin *twins.* 1. One of 2 children or animals born to the same mother at the same birth. *Twins* often look alike.

2. One of 2 things that are just alike or nearly alike.–The aeroplane has *twin* engines.

twine *twines, twined, twining.* 1. Heavy cord or string.–We put *twine* round the package before we posted it.
2. Twist and wind.–The ivy *twines* round the fence.

twinge *twinges.* A sharp, sudden pain.–Jack felt a *twinge* in his leg when he fell down.

twinkle twin'-kle *twinkles, twinkled, twinkling.* Sparkle.–Baby's eyes *twinkle* when she sees something good to eat.–The reflection of the stars *twinkled* in the lake.

twinkling twin'-kling. A very short time.–Mother called Mary and Mary was there in a *twinkling.*

twirl *twirls, twirled, twirling.* Spin; whirl; go or make go round and round.–Bob *twirls* his key-ring when he is thinking.

twist *twists, twisted, twisting.* 1. Wind.–The girl stood *twisting* her handkerchief round in her hands.–The woman *twisted* the wool together.

2. Move restlessly.–The children *twist* and turn in their seats when they are too tired to sit still.
3. Bend round; bend out of shape. – The rim of Bob's bicycle was *twisted* where it hit the kerb.
4. A special thread made by *twisting* 2 strands of thread together.–Mother mended the buttonholes in Bob's old coat with *twist.*

twitch *twitches, twitched, twitching.* 1. Jerk or move suddenly. – The muscles in one's eyes often *twitch.*
2. A sudden, jerky movement.–I felt a *twitch* in my hand.

twitter twit'-ter *twitters, twittered, twittering.*
1. Chirp; make small shrill sounds. – Birds twitter.
2. A chirping; small shrill sounds.–We heard the *twitter* of the birds in the trees.

two. The number (2) coming after 1 and before 3.–We have *two* eyes and *two* ears.

tying ty'-ing. One form of the word *tie.*–Baby can't *tie* her shoe-laces, so Mary is *tying* them for her.

type *types, typed, typing.* 1. Write on a typewriter.–Mother can *type.*
2. A kind; sort.–Children like books of different *types.* Fairy stories are the *type* that Mary likes.
3. Metal blocks with letters on them, used in printing.–Books and papers are printed with *type.*

typewrite type'-write *typewrites, typewrote, typewritten, typewriting.* Write with a typewriter. – Mother *typewrites* Father's letters for him.

typewriter type'-writ-er *typewriters.* A machine which prints letters and figures by an arrangement of keys which are struck by hand.

typhoid ty'-phoid. An infectious fever caused by a germ usually found in impure water.

typhoon ty-phoon' *typhoons.* A very strong or severe whirling windstorm. – The ship was blown ashore by the *typhoon.*

typist typ'-ist *typists.* A person whose work is writing on a typewriter. – There are many *typists* in the office where Father works.

T
U
V
W
X
Y
Z

U u

U, u *U's, u's.* The 21st letter of the alphabet.

ugly ug'-ly *uglier, ugliest, ugliness.* 1. Not at all pretty, not pleasing to see.–A witch's face is usually *ugly.*
2. Unpleasant; threatening.–The sky looks *ugly.* It looks as if a storm is coming.
3. Very severe and causing ruin.–A very *ugly* accident happened at the corner.

ukulele u-ku-le'-le *ukuleles.* A small musical instrument with 4 strings, played by picking the strings.

umbrella um-brel'-la *umbrellas.* A collapsible frame with a cloth covering that is used to keep off the rain or sun.

umpire um'-pire *umpires, umpired, umpiring.*
1. A person who decides who is right and who is wrong in games like cricket.–The *umpire* gave the batsman out l.b.w.
2. Make decisions as an *umpire.*–The headmaster *umpired* the cricket match.

un- The letters *un* are often put before a word to make it mean the opposite or reverse.–To cover means to put a lid on. *Un*cover means to take the lid off.–The letters *un* also mean 'not' when put in front of words; *un*happy means not happy.

unable un-a'-ble. Not able; not strong or capable enough. – Mary has been ill, so she is *unable* to go to school yet.

unabridged un-a-bridged'. A book or other artistic work which is not shortened, but given in full.–Alan read an *unabridged* version of 'David Copperfield' but Bob read a shortened version.

unaware un-a-ware'. Not aware; without knowledge.–We were *unaware* of your illness. We didn't know that you were ill.

unbuckle un-buck'-le *unbuckles, unbuckled, unbuckling.* Undo a buckle; loosen a buckle. –*Unbuckle* your belt.

unbutton un-but'-ton *unbuttons, unbuttoned, unbuttoning.* Loosen or undo the buttons of; remove buttons from their buttonholes.

uncertain un-cer'-tain. Not certain; not sure. –I am *uncertain* about going to the party.

unchanged un-changed'. Not changed; remaining the same.–The time for the party is *unchanged.*

uncle un'-cle *uncles.* The brother of either one's mother or father, or the husband of one's aunt. – Father's brother is David's *uncle.* – *Uncle* Joe is the husband of Mother's sister.

unclean un-clean'. 1. Filthy; dirty.
2. Impure; evil.–Boy Scouts are taught to avoid *unclean* thoughts.

uncomfortable un-com'-fort-a-ble. Not comfortable; causing or feeling discomfort.–This chair is *uncomfortable.* Bob is *uncomfortable* when he sits in it.

unconscious un-con'-scious. Not conscious, not aware of things about one. – The man was *unconscious* after the accident.

uncover un-cov'-er *uncovers, uncovered, uncovering.* 1. Take the cover off. – *Uncover* the butter dish.
2. Make known, find out.–A big secret was *uncovered.*
3. Take off the hat.–The men *uncovered* when the funeral went by.

under un'-der. The opposite of on or over; beneath; below. – Put your hands on your desk and your feet *under* it.–Miners go *under* the earth to work.

underbrush un'-der-brush. Shrubs, small trees, bushes that grow under the larger trees.– The rabbit ran into the *underbrush.*

underclothes un'-der-clothes. Clothes worn next to the body, under other clothes.–In winter children wear woollen *underclothes*; in summer they wear cotton *underclothes.*

underfoot un-der-foot′. Under one's feet; on the ground.–It is often wet and slushy *underfoot* in the winter.

undergraduate un-der-grad′-u-ate *undergraduates*. A student at university who has not yet taken a degree.–David is an *undergraduate* at Oxford.

underground un′-der-ground. 1. Under the ground or under the surface of the earth.–Miners work *underground*.
2. An *underground* railway.–The quickest way to get into town is by *underground*.

undergrowth un′-der-growth. Small trees, bushes and shrubs, growing under larger trees in a wood.–We lost our ball in the *undergrowth*.

underline un′-der-line *underlines, underlined, underlining*. Put a line under.–*Underline* the title of the book that you enjoyed most.

underneath un-der-neath′. Under, below, beneath.–We found a small snail *underneath* the log.

underrate un-der-rate′ *underrates, underrated, underrating*. Put too low a value on something or someone.–We *underrated* Jack's ability in swimming.–Never *underrate* your opponents.

undershirt un′-der-shirt *undershirts*. A shirt worn next to the skin under one's outside clothing.

understand un-der-stand′ *understands, understood, understanding*. 1. Get the meaning of. –Mary *understands* the directions for making the box. She knows what they mean.
2. Know the meaning of.–Father *understands* French.
3. Have heard, have learned that.–I *understand* that you have a new car.

understanding un-der-stand′-ing *understandings*. 1. An agreement.–Bob and his father have an *understanding* about the work.
2. The ability to know what things mean.–How Mother can do so many things at once is beyond my *understanding*.

understood un-der-stood′. One form of the word *understand*.–I *understand* the problem now that Mary has explained it to me. Mary *understood* it before I did.

undertake un-der-take′ *undertakes, undertook, undertaken, undertaking*. Try to do, agree to do. – Mother has so much work to do as it is that she will not *undertake* any more. – Bob *undertook* to find the missing books.

undertaker un′-der-tak-er *undertakers*. A person whose business is getting dead persons ready to be buried and taking charge of funerals.

underwear un′-der-wear. Underclothing, clothing worn under one's outer clothes. – *Underwear* keeps one warm.

undid un-did′. One form of the word *undo*.– Father *undid* the knot in Baby's shoe-lace.

undo un-do′ *undoes, undid, undone, undoing*. Loosen, unfasten.–Baby pulled her shoe-lace into a knot, and Grandmother tried to *undo* it.

undone un-done′. 1. Not accomplished, not finished. – The work was still *undone* at 6 o'clock.
2. One form of the word *undo*.–Jack found that Baby had *undone* the knot.

undress un-dress′ *undresses, undressed, undressing*. Take off the clothes.–Mother has to *undress* Baby and bath her before we have dinner.–*Undress* quickly and go to bed, for it is late.

uneasy un-eas′-y *uneasily*. Restless, nervous. –The dog is *uneasy* when his master is away.

unemployed un-em-ployed′. Out of work, without a job.–When times are hard, many people are *unemployed*.

uneven un-e′-ven *unevenly, unevenness*. 1. Not straight and flat, not level.–The table rocks because the floor is *uneven*.
2. Not the same size.–The stakes in the fence are *uneven*.
3. Odd (of numbers).–The houses are numbered so that the even numbers are on one side of the street and the *uneven* numbers (numbers ending in 1, 3, 5, 7, 9) are on the other side. – An *uneven* number cannot be divided evenly by 2.

unexpected un-ex-pect′-ed *unexpectedly, unexpectedness*. Not looked for, not waited for. –I received an *unexpected* gift from Uncle Jim.

unfair un-fair′ *unfairly, unfairness*. Not just.– Jack felt it was *unfair* of the teacher to expect him to know the answer to the question when none of the others did.

unfaithful un-faith′-ful *unfaithfully, unfaithfulness*. Not true.–Do not be *unfaithful* to your old friends. Do not desert them.

U
V
W
X
Y
Z

unfamiliar un-fa-mil'-iar. Not known; not seen before.–The man's face is *unfamiliar* to me.

unfasten un-fas'-ten *unfastens, unfastened, unfastening*. Undo, loosen, as to untie, unlock, unbutton, etc. – Can you *unfasten* this suitcase for me?

unfinished un-fin'-ished. 1. Not all done; not completed.–The story is *unfinished*; you did not read the last page to me.
2. Without paint, varnish, or other finish.– We bought *unfinished* furniture and painted it ourselves.

unfit un-fit'. Not good; not suitable.–The meat is spoilt and is *unfit* to eat.–Your white dress is *unfit* for travelling on the dusty train.

unfold un-fold' *unfolds, unfolded, unfolding*.
1. Open the folds of, spread out, open up.– *Unfold* your handkerchief quickly when you feel you may be going to sneeze.
2. Open. – A bud *unfolds* and becomes a flower as it opens.

unforeseen un-fore-seen'. Not expected, not looked for.–We shall come if nothing *unforeseen* happens.

unfortunate un-for'-tu-nate *unfortunately*. Unlucky, unsuccessful. – The lady is a very *unfortunate* person. She lost her new watch.

unfriendly un-friend'-ly. Not liking other people; not wanting to get to know others. –The boy is so shy that he seems *unfriendly*.

ungrateful un-grate'-ful *ungratefully, ungratefulness*. Not thankful.–The boy is *ungrateful* for the many things you have done for him.

unhappiness un-hap'-pi-ness. Sadness, sorrow. –The boy's selfishness brings *unhappiness* to his parents.

unhappy un-hap'-py *unhappily*. 1. Without cheer, joy, or gladness; sad.–Cinderella was *unhappy* because she couldn't go to the ball.
2. Unlucky, unfortunate. – By an *unhappy* chance, the first day he rode his new bicycle, Jack had a bad fall.

uniform u'-ni-form *uniforms, uniformed, uniformly, uniformity*. 1. Alike in size, shape, speed, or the like.–The telephone poles are *uniform* in size.–The driver drives his car at a *uniform* speed.

2. Clothes that are made to show the wearer's rank or occupation and are exactly like those of other people of the same rank or occupation.–Sailors, soldiers, and nurses wear *uniforms*.

UNIFORMS

Roundhead

Greek

ancient Roman

Horseguard

London policeman

union un'-ion *unions*. 1. A joining together of things into one, or the things that have been joined together.–The United States is a *union* of states.
2. A group of workers who are joined together to bring about better working conditions and better wages.

unit u'-nit *units*. One person or thing or a group of objects or people forming a complete whole.–A division is one *unit* of an army.

unite u-nite' *unites, united, uniting*. To join together as one.–The children *united* in reciting the poem.–The couple were *united* in marriage.

United States U-nit'-ed States. One of the largest countries in the western hemisphere, and the one with the most inhabitants; about 175,000,000 people live in the *United States*. It consists of 50 states and the District of Columbia, in which is located Washington, the capital.

universe u'-ni-verse *universes*. The earth, the sun, and all the stars; everything.

university u-ni-ver'-si-ty *universities*. A place of higher education, often made up of several colleges, which confers degrees on students successful in examinations.–Students learn to be engineers, dentists, teachers, lawyers, and many other things at a *university*.

U
V
W
X
Y
Z

unjust un-just′ *unjustly*. Not fair.—The man was *unjust* to his servant. He dismissed him without letting him explain his absence.

unkind un-kind′ *unkindly, unkindness*. Not gentle or considerate; cruel.—The *unkind* boy abuses his little dog.

unknown un-known′. Not familiar. – The strange woman is *unknown* in the neighbourhood.

unlace un-lace′ *unlaces, unlaced, unlacing*. Take out the strings, loosen the laces of.—Baby likes to *unlace* Mother's shoes.

unless un-less′. If not.—I can't go *unless* you wait for me.

unlike un-like′. Not like; different from.—This fruit is *unlike* any I have ever eaten.

unload un-load′ *unloads, unloaded, unloading*. Remove the load from.—The man *unloaded* his wagon.

unlock un-lock′ *unlocks, unlocked, unlocking*. Unfasten the lock of.—The key would not *unlock* the door.

unlucky un-luck′-y. Unfortunate; having or bringing bad luck.—This is an *unlucky* day for the boy who lost his watch.—He was *unlucky*.

unnecessary un-nec′-es-sar-y *unnecessarily*. Not needed; useless.—The teacher told her pupils that their noise was *unnecessary*.

unpack un-pack′ *unpacks, unpacked, unpacking*. Take out packed contents.—Mary helped Mother *unpack* the suitcase.—We *unpacked* our lunch and had a picnic.

unpleasant un-pleas′-ant. Disagreeable; not pleasant or nice.—When the sun shines, it is a pleasant day. When it rains and is dark, the weather is *unpleasant*.

unpopular un-pop′-u-lar. Not liked or sought after.—A boy who does not tell the truth is *unpopular*.

unprepared un-pre-pared′. Not ready. – The teacher gave us a spelling test, and we were *unprepared* for it.

unreal un-re′-al. Not true; not like actual things.—This is an *unreal* story. Things do not actually happen the way they do in the story.

unreasonable un-rea′-son-a-ble. 1. Foolish; not sensible.—The girl was *unreasonable* about spending her money.—She paid an *unreasonable* price for the dress.
2. Not fair.—The man is *unreasonable* to his workers; he makes them work too hard, and gets angry at them too easily.

unroll un-roll′ *unrolls, unrolled, unrolling*. Roll out or spread out something that has been rolled.—Someone *unrolled* the paper towels. —*Unroll* the ribbon from the spool.

unsafe un-safe′. Dangerous; not safe. – The dirty water is *unsafe* for drinking.

UNITED STATES

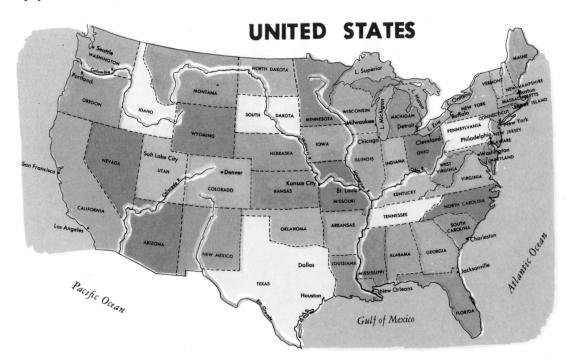

U
V
W
X
Y
Z

unsatisfactory un-sat-is-fac-to-ry. Not good enough; not sufficient; not up to certain standards.–The teacher said Jack's work was *unsatisfactory*.

unseen un-seen'. Not seen; not visible to anyone.–The baby stood behind the chair *unseen*.

unselfish un-self-ish. Thoughtful; considerate of others; generous.–Selfish people think only of themselves. *Unselfish* people are kind and helpful to others.

unsettled un-set'-tled. 1. Upset; not in order. –Father is papering the walls, so our house is *unsettled*.
2. Uncertain; likely to change.–The weather is *unsettled*.

unskilled un-skilled'. Without special ability; not trained.–The man wanted the job but he was *unskilled* in that kind of work.

unsteady un-stead'-y *unsteadily, unsteadiness.* Shaky; not firm or strong.–The sick man's knees were still a little *unsteady*.

untie un-tie' *unties, untied, untying.* Unfasten, undo, loosen the knot of.–It is easier to *untie* one's shoe-laces than it is to tie them.

until un-til'. 1. Up to (a certain time).–Wait here *until* school is ended.
2. Up to (a certain point).–We ate *until* we could eat no more.
3. Till; to.–We had to wait from noon *until* after 4 o'clock for the doctor to come.
4. Before.–Bill won't get here *until* noon.

untrue un-true'. 1. False; not true; not correct; not what really is.–It turned out to be *untrue* that Bill was ill.
2. Not faithful.–The traitor was *untrue* to his country.

unusual un-u'-su-al *unusually.* Different from most; not ordinary; rare or outstanding.–Mary has *unusual* musical talent.–Black flowers are very *unusual*.

unwelcome un-wel'-come. Not wanted.–The visitor felt *unwelcome* among so many strangers.

unwilling un-will'-ing, *unwillingly, unwillingness.* Not willing, not wanting or consenting. –The workman was *unwilling* to work after 6 o'clock in the evening.

unwise un-wise' *unwisely.* Foolish.–It is *unwise* to eat too much.

unworthy un-wor'-thy *unworthily, unworthiness.* 1. Not deserving.–The bad boy is *unworthy* of your kindness.
2. Bad, not deserving praise.–Some of the early American settlers had *unworthy* aims. They wanted to steal Indian land.
3. Not as good as one would expect; not fitting.–The mayor has done nothing *unworthy* of his position.

up. 1. To a higher place.–Bob tried to get his kite farther *up* in the sky.–I was about to go *up* to bed.
2. Upright; straight; on one's feet.–We stand *up* when the headmaster comes in.
3. To or near the top of.–'Jack and Jill went *up* the hill to fetch a pail of water.'
4. Even; along; on a line with.–Baby walks so slowly that she cannot keep *up* with us.
5. To pieces.–Dynamite is used to blow *up* the rocks on the hill.
6. Over; at an end.–Our play time is *up*.
7. Out of bed.–The farmer gets *up* early each morning.
8. Tightly.–Close your pourse *up*.
9. Out of the ground.–The children pulled the weeds *up*.
10. Above the ground.–The spring flowers will soon be *up*.
11. Along.–Our house is just *up* the road from the school.
12. Towards the beginning of (a river).–Henley is farther *up* the River Thames than London.
13. Higher than the horizon.–The sun is *up* in the daytime.

uphold up-hold' *upholds, upheld, upholding.* Agree to; back up with agreement.–The teacher *upheld* Jack's statement. She agreed that he was right.

upholster up-hol'-ster *upholsters, upholstered, upholstering, upholstery, upholsterer.* To make cushions and other padded parts for furniture, and cover them with heavy cloth. –The couches and chairs in the living-room are *upholstered*.

upon up-on'. On; on the top of.–Put the cup *upon* the table.

upper up'-per. Higher; top.–The *upper* part of anything is the higher part.–The *upper* shelves of a cupboard are the ones near the top.

upright up'-right. 1. Straight up and down; standing.–Two of the telegraph poles were blown down in the storm, but the others were *upright*. – Baby can sit *upright* in her cot.

2. Honest.–The mayor is an *upright* man.

uproar up'-roar *uproars*. A loud shouting; a noise or disturbance.–When the goal was disallowed, an *uproar* rose from the crowd.

uproot up-root' *uproots, uprooted, uprooting*. Pull out or tear out by the roots.–A hurricane can *uproot* large trees.

upset up-set' *upsets, upsetting*. 1. Turn over; tip over.–The cat *upset* the tin of fish so that she could eat it.
2. Disturbed; worried.–Father was *upset* when Bob got home late from school.

upside down up'-side down. 1. With the upper part or the top side down.–Turn the clean glasses *upside down* on the shelves.
2. Topsy-turvy. – The boys turned the room *upside down*. They upset everything.

upstairs up'-stairs'. 1. On a floor above the ground floor.–We cook and eat downstairs. We sleep *upstairs*.
2. Up the stairs; up a flight of stairs.–We go *upstairs* to our bedroom.

upstream up'-stream'. From the mouth towards the source of a stream or river.–It is hard to row a boat *upstream*.

up-to-date up'-to-date'. In the latest style or fashion.–Mary's summer dress is *up-to-date*.

upward up'-ward. To a higher place; away from the ground.–The aeroplane shot *upward*. –The smoke floated *upward*.

urchin ur'-chin *urchins*. A mischievous boy.– A little *urchin* ran out and shouted at us as we passed.

urge *urges, urged, urging*. 1. Press someone to do something with entreaty or argument. –Mother urged Bob to go to the doctor.

2. Drive; force.–The angry driver *urged* his horse to go faster by using a whip.

urine u'-rine. A watery fluid given off by the kidneys and stored in the bladder of the body. Later it is released or given out by the bladder.

urn *urns*. A kind of vessel, usually set on a base. – We have an *urn* for flowers.

us. The others and me.–This is our dog. Grandfather gave him to *us*.–Give *us* some books to read.

use (pronounced *uze*) *uses, used, using*. 1. Employ for a purpose.–We *use* a pencil to write with.–We *use* our eyes to see things.
2. Treat.–Jack felt the teacher had *used* him badly.

use (yooss) *uses*. 1. Getting help or work from. –Bob thanked Mary for the *use* of her pen.
2. A need.–We have no *use* for the leaky barrel.
3. A point; a value.–There is no *use* coaxing Father to let you go.
4. A way in which a thing is used. – The teacher asked us to name some of the *uses* of rubber, and Jack mentioned motor-car tyres and heels for shoes.

used (pronounced *yoost*). 1. Accustomed– Grandfather is *used* to getting up early.
2. Was in the habit.–Mary *used* to dance.

useful use'-ful *usefully, usefulness*. 1. Helpful; of value or service.–The child makes himself *useful* around the house.
2. Of some use or help.–A watch is a *useful* gift, one that can be used by its owner.

useless use'-less *uselessly, uselessness*. Worthless, of no use.–This old machine has been *useless* since a large number of the parts were lost.

usher ush'-er *ushers, ushered, ushering*. 1. A person who shows one to a seat in a church, in a theatre, cinema, etc.

2. To lead or bring one to a place. – Mary *ushered* the guests into the living-room and made sure that they were comfortable.

usual u´-su-al *usually*. Ordinary; accustomed; same.–We go to school this year at the *usual* time.–We met at the *usual* place.–It is not *usual* for people to go to work on Sundays.

usually u´-su-al-ly. In the ordinary way.–We do not usually go to bed until 8 o'clock.–Mother *usually* wears her best dress when she gives dinner-parties.

usurp u-surp´ *usurps, usurped, usurping*. Seize or take possession without any right.–Henry Bolingbroke led a rebellion against King Richard II, and *usurped* the throne. He then became King Henry IV.

utensil u-ten´-sil *utensils*. A tool, an instrument, or anything that is used in doing some special kind of work.–Pots and pans, skillets and strainers are kitchen *utensils*. Mops, vacuum cleaners, brushes, and brooms are household *utensils*.

UTENSILS

mop   broom   colander   dustpan   whisk   ladle   frying pan   pancake turner   vacuum cleaner

utter ut´-ter *utters, uttered, uttering*. Speak; say.–No one *uttered* a word.

utter ut´-ter *utterly*. Complete.–The city is in *utter* ruin.

V v

V, v *V's, v's*. The 22nd letter of the alphabet.

vacancy va´-can-cy *vacancies*. 1. An empty space; an empty office, house, apartment.–The sign on the boarding-house said that there were no *vacancies*.
2. An open job; a position waiting to be filled.–When Bob left his job to go to school, he left a *vacancy* to be filled by someone else.

vacant va´-cant. Empty; not occupied.–One house is *vacant*.–The site next door is *vacant*.

vacation va-ca´-tion *vacations*. A period of time away from school, work, or one's usual occupation to do as one chooses, to have fun or rest.–Our summer *vacation* lasts 2 months.

vaccinate vac´-ci-nate *vaccinates, vaccinated, vaccinating*. Inject into the body a certain liquid called vaccine to make one safe from smallpox or another particular disease for a number of years.–Mary was *vaccinated* before she started school.

vaccination vac-ci-na´-tion *vaccinations*. The process of inoculating with vaccine against smallpox.

vacuum vac´-u-um *vacuums*. A space from which all air has been removed.–There is a vacuum inside a radio valve.

vain. 1. Proud.–The girl is *vain* of her looks and the things she can do.
2. *In vain* means without success.–The lifeguard tried to save the drowning boy, but his work was *in vain*.
3. Worthless; useless. – Jack said he would work but his promises were *vain*.

vale *vales*. A valley; low land between hills or mountains.

valentine val´-en-tine *valentines*. A card or other token of love or friendship sent on St Valentine's Day, February 14.

valet val´-et *valets*. A manservant who takes care of his master's clothes and aids him in dressing, and so on.

valiant val´-iant. Brave.–The soldier was *valiant*.

valid va´-lid *validity, validly*. Well-founded, something that cannot be disputed.–When Bob stayed at home because of illness, the teacher said it was a *valid* excuse.

V
W
X
Y
Z

valley val'-ley *valleys*. Low land between 2 hills or mountains.–We went down the hill into the *valley*.

valour val'-our. Great courage.–The sailor received a medal for *valour* for saving his shipmates from drowning.

valuable val'-u-a-ble *valuables*. 1. Worth much money.–A mink coat is *valuable*.
2. Of great worth or necessity.–These papers are *valuable* to the owner, although they are worthless to the man who found them.
3. Things of special worth. – The woman keeps her *valuables* in a safe-deposit box.

valuation val-u-a'-tion. The amount of money a thing is declared to be worth.–The farmer's *valuation* of his farm was £5,000.

value val'-ue *values, valued, valuing*. 1. Worth.–Bob's friendship is of great *value* to Jack.
2. Appreciate; attach worth or *value* to.–Jack *values* Bob's friendship.
3. Worth in money; price.–The *value* of the house is £3,000; but the owners will accept £2,500.

valve *valves*. A device which controls the pressure of flow of air, gas, water, etc. Some *valves* are operated by inner pressure and some by hand.–Water taps are *valves*, and radio *valves* control the flow of electricity.

van *vans*. 1. A covered lorry usually used for carrying furniture.–It took a large *van* to move all the furniture the family had.

2. The leading group of an army or other body that is moving ahead.

vane *vanes*. A device often in the shape of an arrow, which shows the direction the wind is blowing.

vanilla va-nil'-la. A flavouring extract made from the beans of the *vanilla* plant, which grows in warm places. – Mother flavoured the custard with *vanilla*.

vanish van'-ish *vanishes, vanished, vanishing*.
1. Suddenly disappear.–The dog ran past us and *vanished* into the woods.
2. Disappear completely. – After Mary learned to swim, her fear of the water *vanished*.

vapour va'-pour *vapours*. Moisture that can be seen in the air.–Fog, mist, and steam are *vapours*.

varied var'-ied. 1. Bob's collection of shells is *varied*. He has many kinds of shells.
2. One form of the word *vary*. – The sick child's condition hasn't *varied* during the night; his condition has not changed.

variety va-ri'-e-ty *varieties*. 1. A wide selection of many different kinds.–The shop sells a *variety* of sweets.
2. A kind; a type.–The shop now has a new *variety* of cabbage for sale.

various va'-ri-ous. 1. Several different.–Children from *various* countries took part in the programme.
2. Varied; of different kinds.–There were *various* styles of dresses in the window.

varnish var'-nish *varnishes, varnished, varnishing*. 1. A thick, sticky liquid that is put on some furniture, floors, and the like to protect them. *Varnish* makes a hard, glossy finish when it is dry.
2. Cover with *varnish*.–Father *varnished* the new bookcase he made.

vary va'-ry *varies, varied, varying*. 1. Change or make different.–The direction of the wind *varies* often.–The boy tries to *vary* his handwriting so that we will not know whose it is.
2. Be different. – The houses in this street *vary* in size, style, and colour.

vase *vases*. A vessel in which to put flowers, or which is used purely as an ornament.

vast *vastly vastness*. Very large or great, especially covering much space.–A *vast* forest covers the mountains.

V
W
X
Y
Z

vat *vats*. A tub, a barrel, or other large container for holding liquids. – The grocer keeps a *vat* of vinegar in the cellar of his shop.

vault *vaults*. 1. A strong room where things are safe and protected.

2. A small room, usually of stone, for keeping the dead.

veal. Calf meat.–*Veal* is often used for stew.

vegetable veg'-e-ta-ble *vegetables*. A plant that has parts which are used for food. – Spinach is a leafy *vegetable*. We eat the leaves.–Beans and peas are *vegetables*. We eat their pods or seeds.–Carrots and beets are *vegetables*. We eat their roots.

vegetation veg-e-ta'-tion. Plants, trees, and other growing things.–Where the soil is poor, there is little *vegetation*.

vehicle ve'-hi-cle *vehicles*. A car, lorry, bus, wagon, sleigh, or any means used for carrying persons and goods from place to place. *Vehicles* run on wheels or runners.

veil *veils, veiled, veiling*. 1. A piece of very thin or fancy lacy material you can see through. – Many hats have *veils* on them for trimming. –The bride's *veil* was very long and trailing. 2. Cover or hide, or put a *veil* over.–In some countries women *veil* their faces in public.

vein *veins*. 1. One of the blood vessels in the body that carry the blood to the heart.–Look at the under part of your wrist and you can see some of your *veins*. 2. Any line, crack, ridge, or long, thin marking, as the *veins* in marble, in leaves, a *vein* of mineral deposit in a rock, etc.

potatoes spinach corn carrots asparagus yams celery

beetroot cabbage cucumbers **VEGETABLES** radishes pumpkin

onions peppers lettuce tomatoes cauliflower

aubergine beans squashes peas turnips

V
W
X
Y
Z

velocity ve-loc'-i-ty *velocities*. Speed, or how fast a thing travels.–The weather report says that the *velocity* of the wind today is 12 miles per hour.

velvet vel'-vet *velvets*. A very soft cloth of silk, rayon, or cotton, with a thick, short nap.–*Velvet* dresses are beautiful.–Baby's skin is as soft as *velvet*.

velvety vel'-vet-y. As soft as velvet.–Baby has a *velvety* skin.

vendor vend'-or *vendors*. A pedlar; a man who sells things from a cart, wagon, or lorry.–We bought a bag of peanuts from a peanut *vendor*.

veneer ve-neer' *veneers*. 1. A thin layer of good wood laid over a cheaper wood.–This table has a walnut *veneer*.
2. Surface polish.–The boy had only a *veneer* of good manners. The boy behaved well at times, but if he forgot himself he was apt to be rude.

venison ven'-ison. Deer meat. *Venison* tastes much like beefsteak, but it tastes stronger.–Robin Hood and his Merry Men ate *venison*.

ventilate ven'-ti-late *ventilates, ventilated, ventilating*. To change the air in an enclosed place by forcing the old, stale air out and letting fresh air in.–At home we *ventilate* the house by opening windows.–At school the rooms are *ventilated* by air pipes.

ventilation ven-ti-la'-tion. Changing of the air, and bringing in of fresh air.–This room has good *ventilation*. There are 3 windows.

venture ven'-ture *ventures, ventured, venturing*. 1. Dare; take a chance.–Jack *ventured* to say what he thought about the plan.–Mary did not *venture* a second request for spending money after Father said no.
2. Something one sets out to do in which there is a danger of injury or loss.–Father's new business *venture* has been a success.
3. Risk; put in danger.–The fireman *ventured* his life to save Joe from the burning house.

veranda or **verandah** ve-ran'-da *verandas*. A covered space with a roof and pavement, the roof supported by pillars. A *veranda* usually extends along the front or back of a house, and serves as a shelter from the sun or rain.–After dinner we sat on the *veranda* and played cards.

verdict ver'-dict *verdicts*. The decision of a jury after a trial in court.–The *verdict* of the jury in the murder case was: guilty. They decided that the man who was on trial was really the one who had done the killing.

vermin ver'-min. Animals or insects which are harmful or carry disease.–Rats and mice do damage and are *vermin*.

verse *verses*. 1. Each of the numbered sentences in any chapter of the Bible is a verse.
2. A stanza; a group of lines that go together in a poem.–Do you know the second *verse* of 'Annie Laurie'?
3. Poetry. – Robert Louis Stevenson wrote *verse* for children.

vertebra ver'-te-bra *vertebrae*. One of the small bones that make up the spine of all creatures with a backbone.

vertical ver'-ti-cal *vertically*. Standing straight up and down, not leaning.–The flag-pole stands in a *vertical* position.

very ver'-y. 1. Extremely; exceedingly.–Grandmother is *very* kind to us.
2. Same.–The *very* day school started, I went down with the measles.
3. Mere.–The *very* idea of winter makes me shiver.

vessel ves'-sel *vessels*. 1. A pot, bowl, cup, dish, pan, or anything that is hollow and will hold liquids or other substances.
2. A ship or boat; any craft that carries people on the water.
3. One of the tubes that carry the blood through one's body.

vest *vests*. A knitted or woven garment with or without sleeves, worn on the upper part of the body, next to the skin.–In winter I wear a woollen *vest*. In very hot weather I do not wear a *vest* at all.

V
W
X
Y
Z

veteran vet'-er-an *veterans*. 1. A person who has seen long service in the armed services. 2. A person who has worked at the same kind of work for a long time.–The old actor is a *veteran* of the stage.

veterinary vet'-er-i-nar-y. To do with the illnesses and injuries of dogs, cats, cows, horses and many other animals.–An animal doctor is called a *veterinary* surgeon.

vex vexes, vexed, vexing. Make angry; annoy. –The boys' jokes *vexed* the old man.

viaduct vi'-a-duct *viaducts*. A bridge over a road, a part of a city, a low place, etc. A *viaduct* is built to carry trains, lorries, motorcars, etc. *Viaducts* improve safety and speed of transportation.

vibrate vi'-brate *vibrates, vibrated, vibrating*. Shake rapidly; swing or move quickly back and forth.–The strings of musical instruments *vibrate* and give off notes.

vice *vices*. Evil; bad habits.–Laziness and cheating are *vices*.

vice versa vi'-ce ver'-sa. Just the opposite.– Jack likes to play tricks on Mary, and *vice versa*. Mary teases Jack, too.

vicinity vi-cin'-i-ty *vicinities*. A neighbourhood; a section near or around a place.–Mr Jones lives in the *vicinity* of High Street and West Street.

vicious vi'-cious *viciously, viciousness*. Savage; mean; spiteful.–Be careful of the *vicious* dog. He is apt to bite people.

victim vic'-tim *victims*. A person or animal killed or harmed by a happening.–The *victims* of the hotel fire were removed to a hospital.–Many of the *victims* of war were very young children.

victor vic'-tor *victors*. A winner.–We were the *victors* in the football match.–The *victors* in war are the ones who conquer.

victorious vic-to'-ri-ous *victoriously*. Winning; conquering.–Our side was *victorious*. We defeated our enemy.

victory vic'-to-ry *victories*. A success. – Our *victory* in this game made us the champions.

victuals (pronounced *vit'lz*) vict'-uals. Food; things to eat.

view *views, viewed, viewing*. 1. Look at.–We *viewed* the race from the bridge.
2. A scene; that which is seen.–The *view* from the mountain top was beautiful.
3. A thought; an idea; an opinion.–Father spoke his *views* on the election. – Father asked Mother for her *view* on the colour he had chosen to paint the kitchen.
4. Sight.–The aeroplane soon came into *view*.
5. Think about (in some way).–The doctor *viewed* Mary's illness with alarm. He was worried about it.

vigour vig'-our. Strength and great energy.– After eating and resting the man went to work with more *vigour*.

vigorous vig'-or-ous *vigorously*. Strong and energetic.–Rest, exercise, and healthful food kept the boxer *vigorous*.

vile viler, vilest. Bad, very bad, wicked.–What a *vile* smell!–He was a *vile* man; nothing was too evil for him to do.

village vil'-lage *villages*. 1. A place smaller than a town, where a few people live close together.
2. The people in a *village*.–The whole *village* came to put out the fire.

villager vil'-lag-er *villagers*. A person who lives in a village or very small town.

villain vil'-lain *villains*. A wicked person.–Who took the part of the *villain* in the Western film you saw? Who was the criminal?

vim. Energy; strength.–Father has lots of *vim*. He is always ready to work or play.

vine *vines*. A plant that climbs, or crawls on the ground.–Cucumber *vines* crawl. – Morning-glory *vines* climb.

vinegar vin'-e-gar. A sour liquid used in salads, pickles, etc.– Cider that stands a long time turns into *vinegar*.

viola vi-o'-la *violas*. A musical instrument that looks like a large violin, but is somewhat broader. Like a violin, a *viola* is rested under the chin when you play it.

violate vi'-o-late *violates, violated, violating, violation*. Break (rules or laws).–Children who *violate* the rules of the school may be punished.–Citizens who *violate* the laws of the country may get put into prison.

violence vi'-o-lence. Strength, force, roughness.–The storm struck with great *violence*; it hurt many people and did much damage.

violent vi'-o-lent *violently*. Strong; intense; rough.–A *violent* storm lashed the shore and did much damage.–Jack has a *violent* temper when roused.

violet vi'-o-let *violets*. 1. A tiny purple, blue, or white flower strongly scented which blooms in the spring. – We gathered *violets* near the brook.
2. Purplish blue.

violin vi-o-lin' *violins*. A musical instrument with strings.The *violin* is played with a bow, and is held with the large end under the chin.

violinist vi-o-lin'-ist *violinists*. A person who plays the violin.

virgin vir'-gin *virgins*. 1. A maiden; an unmarried girl or woman.–Queen Elizabeth was called the *Virgin* Queen. She never married anyone.
2. (Spelt *Virgin*.) Mary, the Mother of Jesus Christ, the Christian Saviour.

virile vi-rile'. Manly, vigorous.–Courage and love of adventure are *virile* qualities; they are qualities possessed by most men.–This novelist has a *virile* literary style; he writes in a powerful manner.

virtue vir'-tue *virtues, virtuous*. Goodness; a good quality.–Honesty is a *virtue*. It is a quality one must have to be really good.

virtual vir'-tu-al. Being something or someone in effect, though not necessarily named as such.–Alan is now the *virtual* captain of the team, although no captain has been officially appointed or recognized.

virtually vir'-tu-al-ly. Actually, in reality.–In Great Britain, the Prime Minister is *virtually* the man who controls the nation's policies.

viscount (pronounced vi-count) vis'-count *viscounts*. In Great Britain, a nobleman holding a rank between earl and baron. The wife of a *viscount* is *viscountess*.

visible vis'-i-ble. Able to be seen.–The aeroplane flew so high that it was not *visible* from the ground. It could not be seen from the ground.

vision vi'-sion *visions*. 1. The ability to see; eyesight.–The girl's *vision* is poor. She doesn't see well.
2. Anything that is seen in the imagination or in a dream.–The woman had a *vision* of her son, whom she had not seen for many years.

visit vis'-it *visits, visited, visiting*. 1. Go or come to see; be a guest.–Grandma *visited* us. She came to see us and stayed with us a while. She was our guest.
2. A call; a period of staying as a guest.–We made a short *visit* to our great-grandmother's house.

visitor vis'-i-tor *visitors*. A person who comes for a visit; a guest.–Grandmother was a *visitor* at our house.

visor vis'-or *visors*. In olden times, the front part of a helmet, which could be raised and lowered. A *visor* had openings through which a soldier could see and breathe, and it served as a protection for the face.

visual vis'-u-al *visually*. Having to do with seeing or sight.–We learn much through *visual* aids, things that can be seen.

visualize vis'-u-al-ize *visualizes, visualized, visualizing*. Picture in one's mind.–It is hard to *visualize* something that one has never seen.

vital vi'-tal *vitally*. 1. So important that life depends on it.–Food is *vital* to life.
2. Of great importance.

vitamin vi'-ta-min *vitamins*. Any of certain substances found in foods that are needed to make us well and strong. Different kinds of foods have different kinds of *vitamins*. *Vitamins* are named after the letters of the alphabet: *vitamin* A, *vitamin* B, etc.

vivid viv'-id *vividly, vividness*. 1. Bright; clear.–Mary's dress is a *vivid* blue.
2. Clear; plain.–I have a *vivid* picture in my mind of the hat that I want.

V
W
X
Y
Z

vocabulary vo-cab´-u-la-ry *vocabularies.* 1. The words that a person knows and uses in writing and speaking.–Our teacher has a large *vocabulary.* – Using a dictionary will help you to increase the number of words in your *vocabulary.*
2. A list of words and their meanings, alphabetically arranged, or according to the ABC.

vocal vo´-cal *vocally.* Having to do with the voice; expressed with the voice.–*Vocal* organs are the parts of the mouth and throat that we use in talking. Tongue, lips, and *vocal* cords are some of the *vocal* organs.

vocation vo-ca´-tion *vocations.* Trade or work; the kind of work one does for a living.–A doctor's *vocation* is curing or healing sick people. – A mechanic's *vocation* is working with machines.

voice *voices, voiced, voicing.* 1. The sound made by the speech organs (mouth, tongue, throat), as in speaking or singing – The boy's *voice* was loud and clear. He spoke well.
2. Speak; express by saying aloud.–The man *voiced* the reasons he had for voting against the proposal.

volcano vol-ca´-no *volcanoes.* A hill or mountain with a hole called a crater in the top through which melted rock and steam are thrown out.

volume vol´-ume *volumes.* 1. A book.–This bookcase holds many *volumes.*
2. One book in a set of books.–Some books are so long that they are printed in several *volumes.*
3. Amount of space occupied; size in cubic inches, feet, etc.–What is the *volume* of this box? How much room or space does it take up? How much will it hold?

voluntary vol´-un-tar-y *voluntarily.* Done of one's own choice.–The work Mary did was *voluntary.* No one forced her or asked her to do it. She offered to do it.

volunteer vol-un-teer´ *volunteers, volunteered, volunteering.* 1. Offer to do something; offer one's services without being asked or told to do so.–The man *volunteered* to help put out the fire.–Men *volunteer* to serve in the army and navy.
2. A person who *volunteers* for some task or service.–In some small towns the fire brigade is made up of *volunteers.*

vomit vom´-it *vomits, vomited, vomiting.* Throw up, by way of the mouth, food which has been eaten.–Children who eat too much or eat things which they should not eat sometimes become sick and *vomit.*

vote *votes, voted, voting.* 1. Express one's choice by a method decided on beforehand, such as raising the hand or marking on a paper called a ballot what you want or whom you choose for an office.–The children who wanted Jack for their captain *voted* for him by raising their hands.
2. An expression of one's choice by a method decided on beforehand. Each hand raised or each piece of paper showing what or whom you choose is a *vote.*

voter vot´-er- *voters.* A person who votes or has the right by law to vote.–Mother and Father are *voters*; their names are registered on a list of people who have the right to vote.

vow *vows, vowed, vowing.* 1. A promise.–Mary made a *vow* to study more.
2. Make a promise.–Mary *vowed* that she would study more.

vowel vow´-el *vowels.* The letters a, e, i, o, u, and sometimes y are *vowels. Vowels* are spoken with the mouth open.

voyage voy´-age *voyages, voyaged, voyaging.* 1. A trip or journey by sea or over water.–The *voyage* took us across the Atlantic Ocean.
2. Travel over water; make a *voyage.*–We *voyaged* across the Atlantic Ocean.

vulgar vul´-gar *vulgarly.* Coarse; not nice.–The boy's language is *vulgar.*–*Vulgar* language offends or hurts the feelings of people who have tact and good manners.

vulture vul´-ture *vultures.* A large bird that feeds on dead animals.

W w

W, w *W's, w's.* The 23rd letter of the alphabet.

wad *wads, wadded, wadding.* 1. A small amount of any material squeezed together to make a lump or mass, as paper squeezed into a small ball or paper *wad*.
2. Crumple or squeeze into a *wad* or lump.– The boy *wadded* his paper and put it into the waste-paper basket.

waddle wad'-dle *waddles, waddled, waddling.* Walk with short steps and swing from side to side.–Ducks *waddle*.

wade *wades, waded, wading.* 1. Walk along in water.–Children like to *wade* in the sea.
2. Struggle ahead.–We *waded* through the work in spite of many interruptions.
3. Cross; walk through (a body of water).– The horses *waded* the river. They walked through the water from one side to the other.

waffle waf'-fle *waffles.* A cake cooked on a special iron (*waffle iron*) that marks it into small squares. *Waffles* are made of a batter containing mainly eggs, flour, baking powder, and milk.

wag *wags, wagged, wagging.* 1. Move or swing from side to side.– The dog *wags* his tail to show that he is happy or friendly.
2. A swinging motion.–The dog answered Bob's question with a *wag* of his tail.

wage *wages, waged, waging.* 1. Pay; money given for work done, especially if reckoned by the hour.–The boy works for a small *wage*. He works for 10p an hour.
2. Carry on (war). –The people *waged* war against the rats in the town.

wager wa-ger *wagers, wagered, wagering.* 1. A bet.–Many people make *wagers* on horse races. They bet money that a certain horse will win. If the horse they choose wins, they get back more money than they put up. If it does not win, they lose their money.
2. Bet; make a *wager*.–Father *wagered* a small sum on the horse he fancied.

wagon or **waggon** wag'-on *wagons.* 1. A strong 4-wheeled vehicle, often drawn by horses, used to carry heavy loads.–When we were on Grandfather's farm we loved riding on the top of the hay-*wagon*.
2. An open truck or van on the railway, for carrying goods.–We watched the train pulling a long line of coal-*wagons*.

wagtail wag'-tail *wagtails.* A small bird with long wings, so called because of its habit of constantly moving its tail up and down as it runs. One of the best-known varieties in Britain is the pied or water-*wagtail*.

wail *wails, wailed, wailing.* 1. A loud cry of pain or grief.–The dog gave out a *wail* when the car struck him.
2. Cry loudly from pain or grief.–We could hear the woman *wailing* because her child was lost.
3. A mournful sound.–We heard the *wail* of the wind in the night.
4. Make a sad sound.–The cold wind *wailed* in the night.

waist *waists.* 1. The middle part of the body, between the hips and the ribs.–A belt is worn round the *waist*.
2. The part of a garment that goes round the *waist*.–Mother took in the *waist* of her dress.

waistcoat waist'-coat *waistcoats.* A sleeveless garment reaching to the waist and worn by men under a coat or jacket.

wait *waits, waited, waiting.* 1. Stay until some event happens.–You can see Mother if you will *wait* until she arrives.
2. Put off; delay.–Do not *wait* dinner for me. Do not put off dinner until I arrive.
3. *Wait for* means look forward to.–Children *wait for* Christmas. They are ready for it long before it comes.
4. *Wait on* means to serve.–An old lady *waited on* us in the shop. She sold us sweets.
5. The time spent *waiting* for something to happen.–The train was late, so we had a long *wait*.

waiter wait'-er *waiters*. A man who serves food at a table.–The *waiter* at the restaurant served Bob an extra dish of ice-cream.

waitress wait'-ress *waitresses*. A woman who serves food at a table.–The *waitress* at the hotel brought me a clean napkin.

wake *wakes, waked, woke, waking*. 1. Make or become conscious out of sleep; stop sleeping.–I *wake* when the alarm clock rings. The alarm *wakes* me. It makes me stop sleeping.
2. Stir; begin activity.–The flowers and trees *wake* in early spring. They show signs of life and begin to grow.
3. Become alert, show interest.–The girls *woke* up when the comedy picture was shown.

wakeful wake'-ful. Sleepless.–Mother had a *wakeful* night. She could not sleep.

waken wak'-en *wakens, wakened, wakening*.
1. Wake; rouse out of sleep.–I *waken* when the alarm clock rings. The alarm clock *wakens* me.
2. Stir; begin activity.–The flowers *waken* in the spring.

walk *walks, walked, walking*. 1. Go forward on foot, more slowly than in running.–Do not *walk* on the grass. Do not step on it.
2. Take for a *walk*.–Bob *walked* the dog round the streets. He took him slowly round the streets.
3. A trip on foot.–We went for a *walk* in the woods. We didn't ride; we went by foot.

wall *walls*. 1. One of the sides of a room or a building.–Pictures hang on the *walls* of the living-room.–*Walls* separate the rooms in a house.

2. A fence built of solid material, such as stone or brick.–A high stone *wall* was built round the jail to keep the prisoners in.

wallet wal'-let *wallets*. A leather case, which folds shut like a book, for carrying paper money and personal papers.–Father keeps a picture of his family in his *wallet*.

wallop wal'-lop *wallops, walloped, walloping*. Hit hard or beat.–The little boy *walloped* the big boy. He hit him very hard.

wallow wal'-low *wallows, wallowed, wallowing*. Roll or wade in.–Pigs *wallow* in mud and water.

walnut wal'-nut *walnuts*. 1. A large nut, good to eat, with a very rough shell. We ate *walnuts* and raisins after our Christmas dinner.
2. The tree on which *walnuts* grow.
3. The dark wood or timber of the *walnut* tree.–Father's room is furnished in *walnut*.

walrus wal'-rus *walruses*. A large sea animal with tusks. The *walrus* is found in the cold North. Its skin is used for leather.

waltz *waltzes, waltzed, waltzing*. 1. A kind of ballroom dance, in a smooth, regular rhythm.–In the old-fashioned *waltzes* the couples whirled round and round very swiftly.
2. A piece of music written in three-four time, or having 3 beats to the bar.
3. Dance a *waltz*.–Father and Mother like to *waltz*.

wan. Pale, sickly, tired-looking.–Baby looked very *wan* after her long train ride.

wand *wands*. A thin stick to hold in one's hand.–The fairy waved her magic *wand* and the 6 sleek grey rats became 6 fine grey horses.

wander wan'-der *wanders, wandered, wandering*. Roam, ramble, stray.–The children *wandered* through the woods. They went here and there for no special reason.

wanderer wan'-der-er *wanderers*. One who goes here and there for no special reason.

W
X
Y
Z

want *wants, wanted, wanting.* 1. Desire, wish for.–Sally *wants* a doll with red hair.
2. Need of food, money, and other necessary things. – That family has always been in *want*. They have always been poor.–After a war, there is terrible *want* in the world.
3. Needs; things one has to have.–The child's *wants* are few.

war *wars.* 1. Fighting over a period of time between two or more countries, or parts of one country. *War* is carried on with guns, tanks, bomber planes, and other terrible weapons.
2. A planned fight.–Our teacher urged us all to join the *war* on cancer by giving money generously.

warble war'-ble *warbles, warbled, warbling.*
1. Sing a trilling song. – The birds *warble* early in the morning.
2. A trilling song.–We heard the *warble* of the canary.

warbler war'-bler *warblers.* 1. A song-bird.– Our canary is a *warbler.*
2. A singer.–Father calls Mary the *warbler* of the family, because she sings so much.

ward *wards, warded, warding.* 1. A person left in the care of another person, or of a court.– The orphaned boy is the *ward* of his uncle; his uncle acts as his father.
2. A part of a hospital for certain kinds of patients.–People in a hospital who have infectious diseases such as measles, scarlet fever, or smallpox are kept in a special *ward* by themselves.
3. A hospital room with beds for a number of patients.–When Father was in the local hospital, he was in a *ward* until there was a private room for him.
4. One of several parts into which a city is divided.–People living in a certain *ward* vote in that *ward.*
5. Prevent, push (off).–He tried to *ward* off the blow with his arm, but he was too slow. –Grandmother is staying in the mouse today to *ward* off a cold.

warden war'-den *wardens.* An official in certain organizations or institutions.–The heads of certain colleges and schools are called *wardens.*

warder war'-der *warders.* A prison guard.–The *warder* brought the prisoner a meal.

wardrobe ward'-robe *wardrobes.* 1. A piece of furniture with shelves and hooks for holding clothes.

2. All the clothes one has, or a whole outfit for a particular season or time.–Have you bought your winter *wardrobe* yet?–Mary's *wardrobe* is made up of 7 dresses, 4 sweaters, 3 skirts, a hat, 2 pairs of shoes, and other things.

ware *wares.* 1. Goods, things for sale.–Simple Simon asked the Pieman if he might taste his *wares.*
2. Utensils, such as silver*ware*, iron*ware*, hard*ware*, earthen*ware*, etc.

warm *warms, warmed, warming.* 1. Heated, somewhat hot, not cold.–Winter is cold. Summer is *warm.*
2. Heat, make warm.–A fire *warms* the room. It gives off heat that makes the air *warm.*– *Warm* your hands by holding them near the fire.
3. Able to keep or make *warm.*–We wear *warm* clothes in cold weather.
4. Hearty, cordial, glad.–Father received a *warm* welcome when he got home. We showed him that we were happy to see him.
5. Close, nearly right.–Jack hid the thimble on the top of a perfume bottle. When Mary started to look on the dressing-table where the bottle was, she was *warm.*

warmth. Mild heat.–The *warmth* of the sun felt good on my hair.

warn *warns, warned, warning.* Tell ahead of time about some danger or unpleasant happening.–The boy *warned* the signalman of a bridge that had been washed away.–Mother *warned* the children not to play with fire.– A dark cloud *warned* us of a storm.

warning warn'-ing *warnings.* Advance notice of something dangerous or unpleasant. – The policeman gave the reckless man a *warning* not to drive so fast again.–Jack did not pay attention to Mother's *warning* and cut his finger.

warp *warps, warped, warping.* 1. Get dry and become crooked or out of shape.–The top dresser drawer is so *warped* that we cannot push it in.
2. The lengthwise threads in cloth. The threads that go from side to side are called the woof. The *warp* threads are put on the loom and the woof threads are woven in.

W
X
Y
Z

warrant war'-rant *warrants, warranted, warranting.* 1. A written order that gives one the right to do something.–The policeman had a *warrant* to arrest the man on suspicion of murder.
2. Deserve, make just or right.–The punishment the man received was well *warranted.* He deserved it.–Mary often gets more excited than the cause *warrants.*
3. An excuse; a right; a fair cause.–You have no *warrant* to say such a thing.

warrior war'-rior *warriors.* A man who goes to war and fights.–Soldiers are *warriors.*

warship war'-ship *warships.* A ship used for fighting in wartime.

wart *warts.* A lump of hardened skin.–Bob had a *wart* on his thumb.

was. *Was* is used with other words to help tell of something that has already happened. –I *was* sleepy last night, but I am wide awake today.–Jack *was* hungry before he ate; now he is full.–Rain *was* falling when I left for school, but it isn't raining now.

wash *washes, washed, washing.* 1. Clean by the use of water or some other fluid.–We *wash* our hands before we eat.–We *washed* our windows and floors today.
2. Carry, sweep.–The hard rain *washed* away the sand on the side of the hill.
3. A laundry, a pile of things to be *washed.*– Mother had a big *wash* today. There were many clothes to be *washed.*

wash-board wash'-board *wash-boards.* A piece of metal or glass, with ridges on it, in a frame. Clothes being washed are often rubbed on a *wash-board* to get them clean.

washer wash'-er *washers.* 1. A washing machine.–We have a new electric *washer.*
2. A flat piece of metal, rubber, or other material with a hole in it used at the joints of pipes, hoses, etc., to make them tight and prevent leaking. Washers are also used to make nuts and bolts tight.–Father put a *washer* between the hose and the spray to keep the water from spurting out.

washerwoman wash'-er-wom-an *washerwomen.* A woman who makes her living by washing clothes.

washing-day wash'-ing-day *washing-days.* The day on which the household washing is usually done. – Monday is Mother's regular *washing-day.*

wash-out wash'-out *wash-outs.* Disappointing, unsuccessful. – Bob says the new teacher of history is a *wash-out.*–The play was a *wash-out*; we expected it to be much better.

wasn't. Was not.–There *wasn't* an apple left after Jack and Bob found where they were.

wasp *wasps.* A slim-bodied insect, something like a bee, that can sting sharply.–The common *wasp* has yellow and black stripes.– *Wasps* swarm around the kitchen during the summer.

waspish wasp'-ish *waspishly.* Spiteful and ill-tempered.–The assistant in the grocer's shop has a *waspish* nature. She is always finding fault or telling someone off in a sharp manner.

wassail was'-sail. In olden days, a time of feasting and merry-making. – The villagers gathered together on New Year's Eve to make *wassail.*

waste *wastes, wasted, wasting.* 1. Not use, or use badly.–Do not *waste* your paper. Use up all of it, and do not take more than you need. Do not throw away any that can be used.
2. Any material that is left over and cannot be used.–Mother says there is a lot of *waste* on the joint; it has much fat and bone, which cannot be eaten.

3. Useless; of no value; thrown away after being used.–We throw *waste* paper into the *waste*-paper basket.

watch *watches, watched, watching.* 1. A small clock worn on a strap round the wrist, or in the pocket on a chain. We tell time by a *watch.*

pocket watch

wristwatches

2. Look at.–We *watched* the circus parade going by.–Sally likes to *watch* Father shave.
3. Mind, care for.–Mary *watched* Baby all day.–Shepherds *watch* the sheep.
4. Look out (for).–The cat *watched* all day for a chance to steal into the house.
5. Lookout.–Be on the *watch* for Father. Try to see him when he comes.
6. A guard.–The Boy Scouts left a *watch* at the camp. He looked after the camp.
7. A turn to stand guard.–From 8 o'clock until 12 was Bob's *watch.*

watchman watch'-man *watchmen.* A man whose duty it is to watch or guard something.–The *watchman* at the factory gave the alarm, and the police caught the burglars red-handed.

water wa'-ter *waters, watered, watering.* 1. The liquid that fills the oceans, seas, lakes, rivers, etc. Rain is *water.* – We drink pure *water.*–We swim in *water.*–Tears are salty *water.*
2. Put *water* on.–Mary *watered* the flowers so that they would grow.

water-colour wa'-ter-col'-our *water-colours.* 1. Paint made for mixing with water.–We paint some pictures with oil paint, or paint mixed with oil, and some are painted with *water-colours. Water-colours* come out light and thin, and the colour is pure.
2. A picture painted in *water-colours.*–Bob likes to paint *water-colours* of ships at sea.

waterfall wa'-ter-fall *waterfalls.* A stream of water pouring from a high place.–We waded up the brook as far as the *waterfall.*

water-lily wa'-ter-lil'-y *water-lilies.* A plant that grows in water. It has white, yellow, or pink blossoms, and large, flat, green leaves that float on the water.

water-melon wa'-ter-mel-on *water-melons.* A large melon with a green rind, and large, flat, black or white seeds. A *water-melon* is a deep pink or red colour inside. The juice is sweet.

waterproof wa'-ter-proof *waterproofs,* water-*proofed, waterproofing.* 1. Not absorbing water; keeping water out.–Bob's raincoat is *waterproof.*–Galoshes are *waterproof,* too.
2. Treat something so that water will not go through it.–Grandfather put tar on the roof of his barn to *waterproof* it.

water-way wa'-ter-way *water-ways.* A river, canal, lake, etc., on which boats travel.

water-wheel wa'-ter-wheel *water-wheels.* A wheel turned by flowing water to make power to run a machine. – The old mill was run by a *water-wheel.*

wattle wat'-tle *wattles.* The red flesh on the underside of the necks of turkeys, chickens, and some other birds.

wave *waves, waved, waving.* 1. A moving ridge made by the rising and falling of water.–The ocean *waves* washed the boat to shore.

2. To move back and forth in the air.–The flag on the pole *waves* in the wind.–The children *waved* their hands to say good-bye.
3. A ripple.–The hairdresser set the *waves* in Mother's hair.
4. Put *waves* in. – The hairdresser *waved* Mother's hair.

wavy wav'-y *wavier, waviest.* With regular curves or waves. – Mother's hair is *wavy.*– Some lines are *wavy.*

W
X
Y
Z

wax *waxes, waxed, waxing.* 1. A yellowish-white substance used in making honeycombs.–Bees make *wax. Wax* can be moulded when it is warm, and dries solid when it gets cold.–The material that some candles are made of is called *wax.*

2. A polish used on the surface of furniture, floors, motor-cars, etc.

3. Put *wax* on. – Father *waxes* the car to protect the finish from rain, snow, and sun.

way *ways.* 1. A path; a direction.–The cows had trodden a *way* through the pasture.–A large man made his *way* through the crowd.–Show me the *way* to your house.

2. A distance.–It is a long *way* to school.

3. In a certain direction. – The girls went that *way.*

4. A plan, a method, a means.–Bob thought of a *way* to get the rabbit out of the trap.

5. A desire, what one wished.–Mother didn't want us to go, but we got our own *way.* We went in the end.

6. A respect.–Bob's story was the best in several *ways.* It was exciting, the people in it talked like real people, and it was clearly written.–In some *ways* Mary acts younger than Jack.

7. A manner.–Mother has a sweet *way* about her.–People from other lands have different *ways.*

we. You and I; one or more others and myself.–*We* must hurry or we shall be late.–*We* all spelt all the words right today in our class.

weak *weaker, weakest.* 1. Not strong.–Baby was *weak* after her illness.–The footbridge is too *weak* to hold many people.

2. Not easy to believe.–The boy's excuse was *weak.* It didn't sound true.

3. Not very good. – We have a *weak* cricket team.–Jack is a little *weak* in history.–The art teacher said Mary's design was *weak.*

4. Containing very little of the important part.–*Weak* coffee has much water and only little coffee in it.–Adding too much water to soup makes it *weak.*

weaken weak'-en *weakens, weakened, weakening.* To lose strength.–Illness caused the old man to *weaken.*

weakness weak'-ness *weaknesses.* 1. A lack of energy or strength.–After his sickness, the old man's *weakness* forced him to stay in bed.

2. A defect.–There is a serious *weakness* in your argument.

3. Something one cannot resist.–Sweets are Bob's *weakness*; he cannot help eating them.

wealth. 1. Riches.–Ed is a man of great *wealth.* He has much money and property.

2. Much, or a large amount. – Mary has a *wealth* of dark brown hair.

wealthy wealth'-y *wealthier, wealthiest.* Rich.–Some people are *wealthy.* They have much money and property.

weapon weap'-on *weapons.* Anything used in fighting.–Guns, bows and arrows, swords, clubs, etc., are *weapons.*

wear *wears, wore, worn, wearing.* 1. Carry or have on the body, as clothing or an ornament.–People *wear* clothes. They put them on to cover their bodies and keep themselves warm.–Women *wear* earrings on their ears, rings on their fingers, and bracelets on their arms.

2. Clothing.–Men's *wear* is sold in the men's department of the shop.

3. Service; time something can be *worn* or used.–This suit will give you good *wear.* It will last a long time.–Father can get a little more *wear* out of his old shoes.

4. Rub or be rubbed away; make or become smaller, thinner, etc., through use. – The rubber on my pencil is *worn* down close to the pencil.–Mary's shoe *wore* a hole in her stocking.–Running water *wore* away the rock in the river.

weary wea'-ry *wearily, weariness.* Tired; worn out.–Father is *weary* after his day's work.

weasel wea'-sel *weasels.* A quick, small, slender animal that eats birds, mice, and other small animals.

weather weath'-er. The heat, coldness, wetness, or other condition of the air. – In hot *weather* the air is hot or warm. In rainy *weather* the air is wet. In cold *weather* the air is cold.

W
X
Y
Z

weathercock weath'-er-cock *weathercocks.* A device, often cut in the shape of a cock, that turns to show the direction of the wind by facing into it.

weave *weaves, wove, woven, weaving.* 1. Make (cloth or other fabric) by putting threads or strips under and over other threads or strips. –Children *weave* baskets of grass reeds.– Darning socks is a kind of *weaving.*

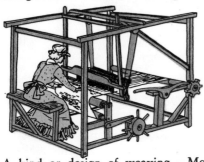

2. A kind or design of weaving. – Mother's skirt has a coarse *weave;* the material is rough.

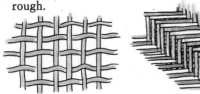

weaver weav'-er *weavers.* A person who makes cloth, rugs, mats, etc., by *weaving.*

web *webs.* 1. A network, as a spider-*web.* The picture shows a spider's *web.* Spiders spin *webs* to catch insects in.
2. The skin that joins the toes of swimming birds.

webbed. Having the toes joined by webs.– Ducks and geese have *webbed* feet. Their toes are joined by skin. *Webbed* feet help them swim.

wed *weds, wedded, wedding.* Marry; become man and wife.–'With this ring I thee *wed,'* said the bridegroom at the wedding.

we'd. 1. We had.–*We'd* better go now.
2. We would.–*We'd* be cold if we had no coats.

wedding wed'-ding *weddings.* A service or ceremony at which a man and a woman are married. – Many *weddings* take place in church.

wedge *wedges, wedged, wedging.* 1. A V-shaped piece of wood or metal used to split wood, keep objects in position, etc. – We put a *wedge* under the door to keep it open.
2. Force; push, crowd in.–A stranger *wedged* himself in front of us.

Wednesday (pronounced *Wensday*) Wednes'-day. The 4th day of the week. – Sunday, Monday, Tuesday, *Wednesday.*

wee. Tiny; very little.–A *wee* boy stopped at the door.

weed *weeds, weeded, weeding.* 1. A plant that is useless or that grows where it is not wanted.–*Weeds* crowd out other plants in the garden.
2. Clear of *weeds.*–Grandfather *weeds* the garden every week. He pulls up the *weeds.*

week *weeks.* 1. The 7 days beginning with Sunday.
2. Seven days one after the other.–Bob has been in the country for a *week.*
3. The 5 or 6 working days of the *week.*–A school *week* has 5 days in it.

week-day week'-day *week-days.* Any day of the week but Sunday; or, sometimes, any day of the week but Saturday and Sunday.

week-end week'-end *week-ends.* The holidays at the end of the week, usually Saturday and Sunday.–We go to school during the week and play during the *week-end.*

weekly week'-ly *weeklies.* 1. Once a week.–We pay for the newspaper *weekly.*
2. A magazine or paper printed each week.– We take two *weeklies.*

weep *weeps, wept, weeping.* Cry.–When Mary broke the dish, she started to *weep.*

weevil wee'-vil *weevils.* A kind of small beetle with a hard-shelled back. – *Weevils* eat grain, and often get into breakfast foods and flour.

weigh *weighs, weighed, weighing.* 1. Find how heavy something is. – Bob *weighed* himself on the tall scales. – The grocer *weighs* the sugar to be sure that he gives you the right amount.
2. Be of a certain weight or heaviness.–Baby *weighed* 6 pounds when she was born.
3. Bend; press. – The trees were *weighed* down with snow. The heavy snow made them bend over.

W
X
Y
Z

weight *weights.* 1. How heavy a thing is; how much a thing weighs on the scales. – Bob weighs 6 stone. His *weight* is 6 stone.
2. A piece of heavy material used to hold something down.–Father has a lead paper-*weight* on his desk.

weird *weirdly, weirdness.* Strange; ghostlike; mysterious.–*Weird* sounds came from the old cabin.

welcome wel'-come *welcomes, welcomed, welcoming.* 1. Permitted.–You are *welcome* to use my racquet I will gladly allow you to use it.
2. Receive gladly. – The people of the city will *welcome* the soldiers home.
3. Gladly received.–We always feel *welcome* at Grandmother's. – Sunday is *welcome* after a hard week's work.–Father said the tie was a most *welcome* present.

weld *welds, welded, welding.* Join pieces of metal by heating them and pressing them together.–Father will *weld* the ends of the wires together. He will join them by heating them till the metal is soft, and then pressing them together.

welfare wel'-fare. Well-being, health.–Grandmother is interested in our *welfare.*

well *wells.* 1. Nicely; in the right or desired way.–Everything went *well* until we came to the river.
2. Thoroughly.–Chew your food *well* before you swallow it.
3. In good health.–Grandfather is *well.* He isn't ill.
4. Right.–It is *well* that you study your spelling words.
5. A hole dug or drilled in the ground to reach gas, oil, or water.

6. Anything like a *well.* – An ink*well* holds ink.

we'll. 1. We will.–*We'll* make it to the top.
2. We shall. – *We'll* be late if you don't hurry.

well-known well'-known'. Known by many people. – George Bernard Shaw, the playwright, was *well-known.* He was known by people everywhere.

welt *welts.* 1. A long swollen place on the skin caused by a whip, rod, etc.
2. Strip of leather sewn round the edges of shoe or boot uppers.

went. One form of the word *go.*–Bob came to school at noon and *went* home at 3 o'clock.

wept. One form of the word *weep.*–The children *wept* when their dog was lost.

were. One form of the word *be.* 1. We *were* sorry you didn't come.
2. You are late today and you *were* late yesterday.
3. If I *were* hungry, I should eat some food; but I am not hungry, so I shall not.

we're. We are.–*We're* ready for school now.

weren't. Were not. – We *weren't* ready for school when Father left.

west. The direction in which the sun sets. – If you stand with your face to the north, *west* is on your left.

west country west coun'-try. The western part of any country.–England, Scotland, etc.; also the south-western counties of England. – Somerset, though not spectacular, is one of the most beautiful counties in the *west country.*

westerly west'-er-ly. Situated in or towards the west.–On the first day of our holiday, we drove 250 miles in a *westerly* direction.

western west'-ern. From, in, or to the west.– Bob lives in the *western* part of the town.

Westminster West'-min-ster. A district in London bordering the River Thames.–There are many important and famous buildings in *Westminster,* including *Westminster* Abbey, *Westminster* Cathedral, and the Houses of Parliament.

westward west'-ward. Towards the west.–The boy turned the corner and went *westward.*

wet *wets, wetted, wetting, wetter, wettest.* 1. Covered or soaked with water or other liquid. –The grass is *wet* with rain.–The towel is *wet.*
2. Rainy.–We had *wet* weather during our holiday.
3. In liquid form; not hardened, not dry.– The paint is still *wet.*
4. Soak, or put a liquid on.–Bob *wets* his hair with water before he combs it.

we've. We have.–*We've* 6 minutes to wait.

whale *whales.* A big sea animal that looks like a fish. The *whale* is the biggest animal on the earth.

wharf *wharfs* or *wharves.* A large dock at which boats can load or unload.

what. 1. A word used to ask questions.–*What* is that noise?–*What* is the name of your teacher?
2. Anything or something that.–Say *what* you want.–The hungry child ate *what* was left over.

whatever *what-ev′-er.* 1. Anything that.–Eat *whatever* you want to eat.
2. No matter what.–Come, *whatever* happens.

what's. What is.–*What's* in the basket?

wheat. An important grain, from which flour, bread, cereals, and other foods are made.–Farmers grow *wheat.*

wheel *wheels.* A round object that turns about its centre.–*Wheels* make machines go.–Cars, wagons, and trains run on *wheels.*

wheelbarrow *wheel′-bar-row* *wheelbarrows.* A little vehicle with 2 legs and one wheel, and pushed by 2 handles. A *wheelbarrow* is used for carrying small loads. – A man can push a *wheelbarrow* filled with sand, stones, or earth.

wheeze *wheezes, wheezed, wheezing.* Breathe heavily with a whistling sound.–When John has a cold, he *wheezes.*

when. 1. At what time.–*When* do you get up?
2. At the time that.–We eat *when* we get hungry.
3. Although.–Bob bought two pencils *when* he needed only one.

whenever *when-ev′-er.* When; any time that. –Some children eat *whenever* they are hungry.–You may go home *whenever* your work is done.

where. 1. In what place.–*Where* did you put your book?
2. At what place.–*Where* did you stop?
3. To what place.–*Where* was the letter sent?
4. From what place.–*Where* did you get that hat?

wherever *wher-ev′-er.* Any place that.–*Wherever* you go, I shall go too.

whether *wheth′-er.* 1. No matter if.–*Whether* it rains or snows, we shall go to the party.–*Whether* you like it or not, I shall do it.
2. If.–Mary didn't know *whether* Bob was home or not.
3. I did not know *whether* to go.

which. 1. What one.–*Which* girl sits here?
2. That.–We play games *which* we like.

while. 1. A time.–Father will be home in a little *while.*
2. During the time that.–*While* we were eating, the doorbell rang.
3. Although.–*While* Mother spoke loudly, I didn't hear her. We were making too much noise.
4. Spend (time).–Bob *whiles* away much of his time reading.

whimper *whim′-per* *whimpers, whimpered, whimpering.* 1. Whine or cry in low, broken sounds.–The dog *whimpers* when he is cold.
2. A sobbing little cry. – We didn't hear a *whimper* from Baby when she fell down.

whine *whines, whined, whining.* 1. To cry in long, low, complaining sounds. – The dog *whines* when he wants to come in.
2. Complain.–The old man always *whines* about his food. He doesn't like it.
3. Cry; beg.–The sick child *whines* for everything he sees.

W
X
Y
Z

whinny whin′-ny *whinnies, whinnied, whinny-ing*. 1. The cry of a horse.–The pony gave a *whinny* when he saw the apple.

2. To give a *whinny*.–Cocks crow. Dogs bark. Horses *whinny*.

whip *whips, whipped, whipping*. 1. Beat; strike. –The man *whipped* the dog for running away.

2. A switch. – The horseman carries a *whip*.

3. Beat with a beater. – Mary *whipped* the cream to make it thick and fluffy.

4. Pull out or away.–Father did not think it funny when Bob *whipped* his chair from under him.

whippet whip′-pet *whippets*. A small kind of dog, somewhat like a greyhound, used chiefly for racing.

whir or **whirr** *whirs, whirred, whirring*. 1. A buzzing sound.–We heard the *whir* of the engines as we passed the factory.

2. Spin or move fast and make a buzzing sound.–The wheels of Grandmother's sewing machine *whir*.–Sally's top *whirs* when she spins it.

whirl *whirls, whirled, whirling*. 1. Turn round and round; spin.–A top *whirls*.–The children *whirled* about the room. – The boy *whirled* the rope about his head.

2. A spinning circle.–My head seems to be in a *whirl*, I am so excited.

whirlpool whirl′-pool *whirlpools*. Water that whirls round and round in a swift circle.– *Whirlpools* often upset boats. – The water ran out of the bath so quickly that it made a little *whirlpool*.

whirlwind whirl′-wind *whirlwinds*. Air or wind blowing round and round, fast and fiercely. A *whirlwind* is a violent wind-storm.

whisk *whisks, whisked, whisking*. 1. Sweep or brush away with a light, easy motion. – Mary *whisked* the scraps of paper from her desk.

2. A sweep or brush.–One *whisk* of the hand and Mary's desk was cleaned.

3. Dash; dart; quickly move.–When the dog chased the cat, she *whisked* up a tree.

whisker whisk′-er *whiskers*. 1. A long, stiff hair that sticks out from the sides of the mouth.– Our white kitten has long black *whiskers*.

2. The beard; stiff hair growing on the cheeks, upper lip, and chin of a man.–Father shaves off his *whiskers* in the morning.

whisky or **whiskey** whis′-ky *whiskies*. A spirit made from wheat or other grains.–*Whisky* is sometimes used as a medicine.

whisper whis′-per *whispers, whispered, whispering*. 1. Speak under the breath with a soft, hissing sound. – When Father is asleep, we *whisper*.

2. A soft, hissing sound, under the breath.– Mother has a cold and can speak only in a *whisper*.

3. Make a low rustling sound. – The wind *whispered* through the leaves on the trees.

4. Tell secretly from one to another.–It was *whispered* about that the teacher wore a wig.

whistle whis′-tle *whistles, whistled, whistling*.

1. A little hollow instrument that makes a shrill note when you put it to your lips and blow through it; any device, big or little, for making such a sound. –The policeman blew a *whistle* to tell the children when to cross the road. – The engine-driver blows the train *whistle*.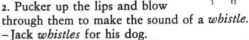

2. Pucker up the lips and blow through them to make the sound of a *whistle*. –Jack *whistles* for his dog.

3. Make a sound like a *whistle*.–The wind *whistles* through the trees.

4. A whistle-like sound.–We heard the *whistle* of the wind in the chimney.

white. The colour of snow. – Mother's hair is coal-black; Grandmother's hair is *white*.– Wild daisies usually have *white* petals.

whiten whit′-en *whitens, whitened, whitening.* Make white; bleach. – Mother hangs the clothes in the sun to *whiten* them.

whither whith′-er. To what or which place; where.–The wolf said, '*Whither* do you go this fine spring morning, Red Riding Hood?'

whittle whit′-tle *whittles, whittled, whittling.* 1. Cut off chips or pieces of wood with a knife. 2. Carve or cut out in a shape.–Bob *whittled* a doll's head for Sally.

whiz or **whizz** *whizzes, whizzed, whizzing.* 1. Fly with a buzzing or humming sound. – Bob bowled the ball so hard that it *whizzed* by the boy who was batting. 2. A humming sound.–The batsman heard the *whiz* of the ball.

who 1. What person; which people. – *Who* would like to go with me? Would you, Mary? –*Who* opened the window? 2. That.–The boy *who* is singing this song is my brother.

whoa. Stop! – The farmer says *whoa* to his horses when he wants them to stand still.

whoever who-ev′-er. Anyone who, any person that.–*Whoever* guesses what I have in my hand may have it.

whole *wholly.* 1. Complete, entire.–We couldn't play chess because we did not have a *whole* set of chessmen. Some were missing.–The fat man ate a *whole* pie. He ate all of it. –The *whole* family came, from Grandfather to Baby. 2. All in one piece.–Do you want to eat the apple *whole,* or would you like it cut up?

wholesome whole′-some *wholesomely, wholesomeness.* Healthful; good for one's health.– Fruits and vegetables are *wholesome* foods.

whom. What person; which people.–To *whom* shall I give the book?–*Whom* do you like better, Bob or Jack?

whoop *whoops, whooped, whooping.* 1. Shout or cry out loudly. 2. A loud shout or cry.–The children gave a *whoop* of joy when they heard the bell.–The Indians gave their war *whoop* and rushed to attack the enemy. 3. The coughing noise made by children who have the whooping-cough.

whooping-cough whoop′-ing-cough. A disease of children.–*Whooping-cough* makes a person cough and whoop. Children catch *whooping-cough* by getting near others who have it.

whose. 1. Which person's.–*Whose* book is this? To whom does it belong? Is it yours, Mary's, or Jack's? 2. The man *whose* hat blew off is Father.– Mary, *whose* cold was worse, did not go out today.

why. For what reason.–*Why* were you late?– I don't see *why* you don't come with us.

wick *wicks.* The soft cord in a candle or the loosely woven tape in an oil lamp that draws up the wax or oil to be burned for light.

wicked wick′-ed *wickedly, wickedness.* Bad or sinful.–The *wicked* king was sorry for his bad deeds when he saw how unhappy he had made the people.

wide *wider, widest.* 1. Broad. – One path was so narrow that only one person could walk along it. The other was *wide* enough for 2 people to walk side by side. 2. As far as it will open.–We open the windows *wide* when we go to bed.

widen wid′-en *widens, widened, widening.* Make or become wide. – The workmen will *widen* the narrow street so that more cars can use it.

widow wid′-ow *widows.* A woman whose husband is dead, and who has not married again.

widower wid′-ow-er *widowers.* A man whose wife is dead and who has not married again.

width *widths.* Distance across or from side to side; how wide a thing is.–The *width* of my desk is 2 feet.–The *width* of the river is 50 feet.

wield *wields, wielded, wielding.* Hold in the hand and use.–Jack is never happier than when he is *wielding* a paint brush.

wife *wives.* A married woman. – Mother is Father's *wife.*–When a man marries, he takes a *wife.*

wig *wigs.* A covering of false hair worn on the head. Some people who have bald heads wear *wigs.* Actors often wear *wigs* to make them look like someone else.

wiggle wig′-gle *wiggles, wiggled, wiggling.* Move uneasily back and forth. – Children sometimes *wiggle* in their seats; they squirm.

wigwam wig'-wam *wigwams*. A tent made of poles covered with skins or bark. Some Indians of America once lived in *wigwams*.

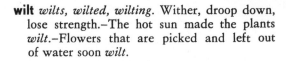

wild *wilder, wildest*. 1. Not tame. – *Wild* animals are those that are not tamed, those which man cannot control. – Lions and tigers are *wild* animals.

2. Not cultivated; not taken care of by people.–*Wild* flowers are flowers that grow of themselves in the fields, woods, and by the roads. Daisies and violets grow *wild*.

wildcat wildcat *wildcats*. A fierce wild animal that looks like a large cat.–*Wildcats* eat the flesh of other animals.

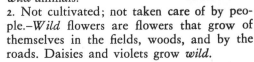

wilderness wil'-der-ness *wildernesses*. A land where no people live.–When Uncle Dick was in Australia, he passed through miles of *wilderness*. There was no sign of any people, and the only growing things grew wild.

will *wills*. 1. Be willing.–Mary can sing well if she *will*.

2. Is or are going to.–Father *will* be home early.–You *will* hear the bells at 6 o'clock if you listen.–It *will* be getting dark earlier now that winter is coming.

3. A paper written according to law which tells what shall be done with a person's belongings after he is dead.–Grandfather has made a *will* leaving his farm to Grandmother.

willing will'-ing. Ready; pleased.–Bob is *willing* to do the work.

willingly will'-ing-ly *willingness*. Gladly. – Mary did the work *willingly*. She didn't mind doing it.

willow wil'-low *willows*. A kind of tree or bush. – Some *willow* trees are called weeping *willows*. Their branches bow down as if they are sad.

wilt *wilts, wilted, wilting*. Wither, droop down, lose strength.–The hot sun made the plants *wilt*.–Flowers that are picked and left out of water soon *wilt*.

wily wi'-ly. Cunning, crafty.–The burglar was *wily*. He climbed through the upstairs window whilst the family was downstairs.

wimple wim'-ple *wimples*. A linen or silk cloth enfolding the head, chin and neck, worn by nuns.

win *wins, won, winning*. We *win* cricket matches by playing better than the other team.–We *win* a spelling contest by spelling better than the other team.–Our armies *won* the victory.–Mary *won* the bet from Bob. She was right.

wince *winces, winced, wincing*. Shrink or draw back quickly.–The horse *winced* when the driver hit him with the whip.

winch *winches*. A mechanical device for lifting or pulling by means of a rope or wire wound around a drum.–The sailors used a *winch* to haul up their fishing-net.

wind (rhymes with *skinned*) *winds, winded, winding*. 1. Air that is moving.–The *wind* blew the apples off the tree.

2. Breath.–The runner was tired and out of *wind* after the race.

3. Make short of breath.–Grandfather was *winded* after climbing the stairs.

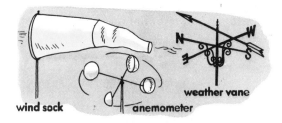

wind sock   anemometer   weather vane

wind (rhymes with *kind*) *winds, wound, winding*. 1. Wrap or twine round; roll up.–The flag *winds* round the flag-pole.–Bob *winds* his kite string into a ball. – Mother *winds* thread on the spool.

2. Turn a part of a machine to tighten a spring, so that the machine will go on working by itself.–Grandfather *winds* his watch every night. He turns the stem round and round so that the watch will go on ticking. –The children's gramophone has to be *wound* by hand.

3. Twist, go this way and that way.–A path *winds* through the woods.

W
X
Y
Z

windmill wind'-mill *windmills*. A mill with machinery worked by the action of the wind on large sails, used for pumping water and for grinding corn.–There are many *windmills* in Holland.

window win'-dow *windows*. An opening in the wall of a building to let in air, light, and sunshine. – We open our *windows* at night for fresh air.

window-pane win'-dow-pane *window-panes*. A piece of glass set in a window to keep out the weather.–The boy tossed a ball through the *window-pane*.

windpipe wind'-pipe *windpipes*. A tube that carries air from the throat to the lungs.

windscreen wind'-screen *windscreens*. A heavy piece of glass in the front of the body of a motor-car to keep out rain, snow, dust, and wind.

windy wind'-y *windier, windiest*. Having a great deal of wind; blowy.–March is a *windy* month. The wind blows hard then.

wine *wines*. A drink made from the fermented juices of fruits or other plants.–*Wine* has some alcohol in it.

wing *wings, winged, winging*. 1. The part of a flying insect, bird, machine, etc., that keeps it up in the air when flying.

2. Anything that sticks out from the side of a body or a main part of a thing.–Mother wants to have another *wing* built on to the house so that Father can have a study.

3. A space off the stage at the right or left.–The children stood in the *wings* until it was time for them to take part in the play.
4. Fly.–The bird *winged* its way south.

wink *winks, winked, winking*. 1. Open and close the eyes quickly.–The sun shining in Baby's eyes made her *wink*.
2. Open one eye and close it as a signal to someone.–Can you *wink*?
3. A minute of sleep–Mother was so tired she said she was going to snatch a few *winks*.
4. Flicker; twinkle.–When Bob opened the door, the candles *winked*.

winner win'-ner *winners*. One that wins or has won.–Our team was the *winner*. It won the game.–Mary's story was the *winner*. It won the prize.

winter win'-ter *winters, wintered, wintering*. 1. The cold season of the year.–Spring, summer, autumn, and *winter* are the 4 seasons.
2. Spend the *winter*.–Our friends *wintered* in the South. They lived there all the *winter*.

wintergreen win'-ter-green. 1. A small plant that has shiny leaves and red berries.
2. A flavouring for sweets, ice-cream, and cakes made from the oil of the leaves of the plant.

wipe *wipes, wiped, wiping*. 1. Make a thing dry or clean by rubbing.–Mary *wiped* the dishes for Mother.–Mother *wiped* the floor with a mop.
2. Rub away.–*Wipe* the jelly from your mouth.

wire *wires, wired, wiring*. 1. A strand or thread of metal.–*Wire* carries electricity for telephones, electric lights, and other things.

2. Put a *wire* round.–Father *wired* the box that he sent to Grandmother.
3. Put electric *wires* in.–We shall *wire* the garage so that we can have a light in it at night.
4. Send a message by telegraph. – When Father was away, he *wired* that he would be home on Sunday.
5. A telegraph message, a telegram.–We received his *wire* on Friday.

wireless wire'-less. 1. A message sent by radio, or without the use of wires.–The ship received a *wireless* from the shore.
2. A *wireless* set, or radio.–We listened to an orchestral concert on the *wireless*.

wire-worm wire'-worm *wire-worms*. A slender worm-like larva which destroys plant roots.

wiry wi'-ry. 1. Resembling wire.–After Ann had been in the rain her hair was *wiry*.
2. Strong, tough.–Jack is not powerfully built but is very *wiry*. That is why he is a good athlete.

wisdom wis'-dom. Good judgement; ability to use one's knowledge to help oneself and others. The professor is well known for his learning and *wisdom*.–You show much *wisdom* in resting before the party.

wise *wiser, wisest, wisely*. Having wisdom.– Father is *wiser* than Jack because he has lived so much longer. He knows more.

wish *wishes, wished, wishing*. 1. Want, desire. –I *wish* we had a dog.–King Midas *wished* for money.
2. An expressed desire.–Bob made a *wish* when he blew out the candles on his birthday cake.
3. Express hope to (a person) for (something pleasant).–I *wish* you a happy birthday.

wisp *wisps*. A small strand or bunch of strands. –The bird carried a *wisp* of grass to its nest and wove it in to line the nest.–Bob dropped a *wisp* of hay when he fed the calf.

wistful wist'-ful *wistfully, wistfulness*. Longing; gently yearning.–Mary looked *wistfully* at the dress. She wished she could buy it, but couldn't afford it.

wit *wits*. 1. The ability to understand quickly and to express thoughts cleverly.
2. Mind, senses. – The Hallowe'en ghost frightened us out of our *wits*.

witch *witches*. An ugly old woman believed to have magic power.–In fairy tales *witches* ride on brooms.

with. *Accompanying, going together.* – Mary said to her friend 'Please come *with* me. Let us go together.'–We eat butter *with* bread.– Here comes Bob *with* his dog.

withdraw with-draw' *withdraws, withdrew, withdrawn, withdrawing*. 1. Draw or pull back.–When the cat scratched Mary's foot, Mary *withdrew* it.

2. Leave, go away.–The firemen had to *withdraw* from the burning building or be injured.

wither with'-er *withers, withered, withering*. Dry up; become lifeless; fade.–Flowers *wither* unless they have water.

within with-in'. 1. Inside.–The boy is hiding *within* the house.
2. Not beyond. – Is the shelf *within* your reach?

without with-out'. 1. Not having; not with.– We went *without* lunch.–We can do *without* many things. We can manage even if we do not have many things.
2. On the outside; outside of.–Those within the house called to those *without*.

witness wit'-ness *witnesses, witnessed, witnessing*. 1. See.–We *witnessed* the fight.
2. A person who knows and can give proof that something happened.
3. Testify to having seen; act as *witness*.– Father *witnessed* Mr Jones's signing of the paper. Father wrote his name on the paper to show that he saw Mr Jones sign the paper.

wives. More than one *wife*.–King Solomon had many *wives*. He married many times.

wizard wiz'-ard *wizards*. A person who is thought to have magic power, or power to do what seems impossible.

wizened wiz'-ened. Shrivelled and dried up. The old woman had a *wizened* face.

wobble wob'-ble *wobbles, wobbled, wobbling, wobbly*. Move shakily; tremble.–The sick boy's legs *wobbled* when he walked.

woe *woes*. Trouble; sorrow.–The old man's heart was heavy with many *woes*.

woke. One form of the word *wake*.–Baby went to sleep but soon *woke*.

wolf *wolves*. A wild animal that looks something like a police dog.–*Wolves* eat other animals.

wolf-hound wolf'-hound *wolf-hounds*. A kind of large dog once used in hunting wolves.

WOOD

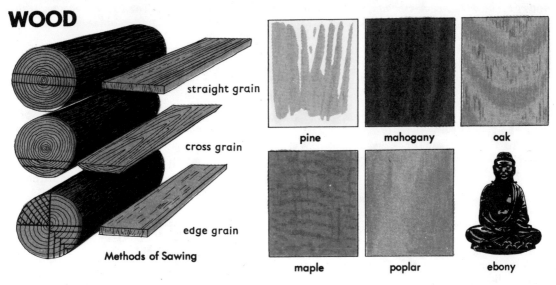

straight grain

cross grain

edge grain

Methods of Sawing

pine   mahogany   oak

maple   poplar   ebony

wolves. More than one wolf.

woman wom′-an *women*. A grown female person.–A girl grows to be a *woman*.–Mother is a *woman*.

women wom′-en. More than one woman. – Mother belongs to a club for *women*.

won. One form of the word *win*. – We *won* the football match. The other team lost.

wonder won′-der *wonders, wondered, wondering*. 1. Want to know.–I *wonder* what Mary has for my birthday present.
2. Be surprised.–I shouldn't *wonder* if it is a new coat.
3. Surprise.–Bob's eyes opened with *wonder* when he saw his new pony.
4. Awe.–We watched the beautiful sunset with *wonder*.
5. Strange, wonderful thing.–Niagara Falls is one of the *wonders* of the world.

wonderful won′-der-ful. 1. Full of surprising or delightful things.–Our trip was *wonderful*. It was full of fun and surprises.
2. Causing one to feel wonder.–Niagara Falls is a *wonderful* sight. It is amazing.

won't. Will not.–I *won't* do such a thing.

woo *woos, wooed, wooing*. Make love to; court.–In the fairy tale the prince *wooed* the beautiful maiden. He made love to her and asked her to marry him.

wood *woods*. 1. The part of a tree under the bark; the inside part of a tree.–We burn *wood* to cook with and to keep us warm. *Wood* is cut into boards and used to build houses, furniture, boxes, and many other things.
2. A place where many trees grow.–The children like to play in the *wood*.

woodchuck wood′-chuck *woodchucks*. An animal of the same family as rabbits and rats. *Woodchucks* sleep all the winter in tunnels which they dig in the ground. They come out for food in the spring. *Woodchucks* are animals of North America.

wood-cutter wood′-cut-ter *wood-cutters*. A man who cuts down trees and chops up wood.

wooded wood′-ed. Covered with many trees. –The hills are *wooded*.

wooden wood′-en. Made of wood.–Some houses are *wooden*; some are made of bricks. – The children marched like *wooden* soldiers.

woodland wood′-land *woodlands*. Land that is covered with many trees. – There is a small stretch of *woodland* near our house.

W
X
Y
Z

woodpecker wood'-peck-er *woodpeckers*. A bird that pecks holes in the bark of trees to catch insects that live under the bark. The feathers in a *woodpecker's* tail are stiff to help him in climbing. His bill is long and sharp. The most common types in Britain are the Green *Woodpecker,* and the Greater and Lesser Spotted *Woodpeckers.*

woodshed wood'-shed *woodsheds*. A shed where firewood can be kept and cut.–We helped Grandfather carry the logs from the *woodshed* into the house.

woodsman woods'-man *woodsmen*. A man who cuts down trees, takes care of a forest, or lives in the forest.

woof. The threads that go from side to side across a piece of cloth. *Woof* threads are also called the weft.

wool. The soft, curly hair of sheep.–A sheep's body is covered with *wool.*–*Wool* is made into yarn, cloth, and clothes.

woollen wool'-len, *woollens*. 1. Made of wool. –*Woollen* clothes are very warm.–*Woollen* blankets keep us warm on cold winter nights. 2. Clothing made of wool.–The shop had a sale of *woollens.*

woolly wool'-ly. Like the wool on a sheep's back.–Mother has a *woolly* blanket.

word *words*. 1. A group of letters that stand for one idea. Several *words* that express one thought make a sentence.–The first *word* that Baby spoke was 'Mamma.' 2. Promise.–I give you my *word* that I will not tell our secret. 3. A message; news.–Father is on a journey, and we have had no *word* from him yet. 4. A short conversation.–Mother had a *word* with Mary's teacher about Mary's work.

wore. One form of the word *wear*.–I wear a clean dress every day. Yesterday I *wore* my best dress.

work *works, worked, working*. 1. Anything we do in an effort to make or get something we want.–Bob did some *work* on his model boat. 2. A trade; a vocation; the thing one does to make a living. Being a doctor, a mechanic, a clerk, a teacher, etc., is *work.*–Mother's *work* is in the home. She washes, cleans the house, cooks, sews, and takes care of the baby. 3. Run; operate.–Our car will not *work.* It needs repairs.

worker work'-er *workers*. 1. A person who works.–Bob is a hard *worker* when he is doing something that interests him. 2. A person who works for wages. – The *workers* in the factory asked for higher wages.

workman work'-man *workmen*. A man who works, especially one who works with his hands.–A gang of *workmen* unloaded the lorry.

workshop work-'shop *workshops*. A shop or room in which work is done.–We do carpentry in our school *workshop.*

world *worlds*. 1. The earth. – The *world* is round.–Ships sail round the *world.* 2. All the people living on earth.–The *world* will soon hear the good news.

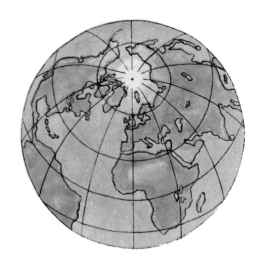

worm *worms, wormed, worming*. 1. A small, slender animal that wriggles along or through the ground.–Robins eat *worms* that live in the ground and are called earth-*worms.*

W
X
Y
Z

2. Wriggle. – The boy *wormed* his way through the crowd so that he could see the parade.

worn. 1. One form of the word *wear.*–I wear this hat every day. I have *worn* it for a year.
2. Tired.–I have worked until I am *worn* out.
3. Damaged by wear or use.–This coat is badly *worn.*

worn-out worn'-out. Made worthless by wear or use.–Mother threw away Mary's *worn-out* shoes. They had been used until they could be worn no longer.

worry wor'-ry *worries, worried, worrying.* 1. Trouble; bother.–Do not *worry* the baby by teasing her.
2. Feel troubled and anxious.–Mother *worries* when we are late from school.
3. An anxious or troubled feeling.–*Worry* over Baby's illness is very tiring to Mother.

worse *bad, worst. Worse* means the opposite of better.–Bad, *worse,* worst; good, better, best.–Father was ill this morning, and to-night he is *worse.*

worship wor'-ship *worships, worshipped, worshipping.* 1. Show deep or loyal respect for.– We go to church to *worship* God. We pay respect to God.
2. Hold dear.–The man *worships* his little daughter.

worst *bad, worse. Worst* means the opposite of best.–Bob is the best boy in school; Bill is the *worst.*–The fire was the *worst* that we ever saw.

worth. 1. Equal to in value.–What is your ball *worth*? How much money would it take to buy it?
2. Have a fortune of.–The king is *worth* millions of pounds.
3. The amount (a sum of money) will buy.– Give me a pound's *worth* of sweets.
4. Good enough for.–Mary's story is *worth* reading. It is good enough to read.

worthless worth'-less. Having no value or worth; not usable.–These worn-out clothes are *worthless.*

worthy wor'-thy. 1. Deserving.–The soldier's bravery is *worthy* of praise.–The Red Cross is *worthy* of our help.
2. Having worth; admirable.–Abraham Lincoln was a *worthy* gentleman. He was an excellent man whom many people liked.

would. 1. Wished to; wanted to; was willing to. –Bob said that he *would* play cricket.
2. *Would* is used to express a condition.–I *would* tell you if I knew. The only reason I don't tell you is that I do not know.
3. Is willing to.–Bob *would* play cricket every day if he had time.
4. *Would* is used to show that something went on regularly for some time.–In summer the children *would* go for long walks in the country.
5. *Would* is used to make a request more polite.–*Would* you close the door for me?
6. Wish.–I *would* that I lived in the country.

wouldn't would'n't. Would not.–I *wouldn't* go if I were you.

wound (rhymes with *crooned*) *wounds, wounded, wounding.* 1. An injury, especially from being shot, cut, bruised, or burned.– The nurse helped to dress the soldier's *wounds.*
2. Hurt, injure.–The soldier was *wounded* in the leg.

wound (rhymes with *sound*). One form of the word *wind.*–Father *wound* the clock last night.

wove. One form of the word *weave.*–Grandmother *wove* a rug out of strips of coloured cloth.

woven wo'-ven. One form of the word *weave.* –Cloth is *woven* from threads.

wrangle wran'-gle *wrangles, wrangled, wrangling.* 1. Quarrel, argue angrily.–Mother told the children not to *wrangle* over their toys.
2. A dispute, a quarrel.–The boys got into a *wrangle* over who was to have the ball first.

wrap *wraps, wrapped, wrapping.* Cover closely with paper or other material; fasten up.– We *wrap* our presents on Christmas Eve.
2. Bundle, dress, clothe. – Mother told the children to *wrap* up well before they went out to play in the snow.
3. An outer garment worn for warmth.–The children took off their wet *wraps* in the hall.

wreath *wreaths.* A ring of leaves or flowers.– Mother hung Christmas *wreaths* in the windows.

wreathe *wreathes, wreathed, wreathing.* Encircle, put a ring or wreath around. – The children *wreathed* their heads with dandelions.

wreck *wrecks, wrecked, wrecking.* 1. What is left of anything after it has been damaged badly by a fire, a storm, or some other accident.–The *wreck* of the ship lay on the beach.

2. Destroy or damage badly.–The driver *wrecked* his motor-car by running it into a furniture van.

3. A person badly affected by illness.–The man looked a complete *wreck* after his long illness.

wreckage *wreck'-age.* 1. What is left after something has been wrecked or badly damaged by fire, storm, or other accident.–We saw the *wreckage* of a boat damaged by a storm.

2. Ruin.–The loss of his money was a *wreckage* of the man's hopes.

wren *wrens.* A small songbird. *Wrens* often build nests in a birdhouse made for them. The nests are dome-shaped with tiny side entrances.

wrench *wrenches, wrenched, wrenching.* 1. A tool for holding and turning nuts or bolts.–Father tightened the nut on the wheel with a *wrench.*

2. Twist or sprain.–You may *wrench* your back if you carry too heavy a load.

wrestle *wres'-tle wrestles, wrestled, wrestling.* Take part in a sport in which each wrestler tries to throw the other to the ground.–These boys are *wrestling.*

wrestler *wres'-tler wrestlers.* A person who wrestles.

wretched *wretch'-ed wretchedly, wretchedness.* 1. Very unhappy.–The lonely old man was *wretched* over the loss of his dog.

2. Poor, miserable, uncomfortable. – The poor family was living in a *wretched* neighbourhood.

wriggle *wrig'-gle wriggles, wriggled, wriggling.* 1. Wiggle, turn and twist.–Do not *wriggle* in your seats.

2. Move by stretching, turning, and twisting. –An earthworm *wriggles* along the ground.

wring *wrings, wrung, wringing.* Twist and squeeze.–Mary *wrings* out the dish-cloth. She twists and squeezes it between her hands to get the water out.

wringer *wring'-er wringers.* A machine with rollers that turn in opposite directions, for squeezing the water out of clothes that have been washed – The *wringer* broke the buttons on Father's shirt.

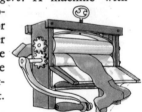

wrinkle *wrin'-kle wrinkles, wrinkled, wrinkling.* 1. A little ridge, fold, or line.–The old woman has many *wrinkles* in her face.– Clothes that have not been ironed often have *wrinkles* in them.

2. Make folds or ridges in.–Do not *wrinkle* your fresh dress before the party.–Mary *wrinkles* her forehead when she does arithmetic.

wrist *wrists.* The joint between the hand and the arm. – You wear a *wrist*-watch or a bracelet on your *wrist.*

write *writes, wrote, written, writing.* 1. Form letters and words.–Mary likes to *write* on the blackboard with chalk. – *Write* your name at the top of the paper.

2. Think up and set down in words.–Jack *wrote* a story called 'The Robber's Revenge.'

3. *Write* a letter.–Father *writes* to Mother every day when he is away.

writer *writ'-er writers.* 1. A person who can write or form letters and words.

2. An author; a person who makes up stories, poems, articles, etc., and has them published. –Who is your favourite *writer*?

writing *writ'-ing writings.* 1. One form of the word *write.*–Mary is *writing* her name on the blackboard.

2. Something written.–My favourite author's *writings* fill 20 books.

written *writ'-ten.* One form of the word *write.* –My letter to Grandmother is all *written* now. I have finished it.

wrong *wrongly.* 1. Not right or good.–It is *wrong* to lie and to steal.

2. Not true or correct.–This answer is *wrong.* It is not the answer to the question.– That is the *wrong* way to play the game. You are not following the rules.

W
X
Y
Z

3. Mistaken; not proper.–It is *wrong* to say 'I seen.' One should say, 'I have seen.'

4. Not meant to be turned upward or seen.–This wall-paper has a right side and a *wrong* side.–Mary put her sock on *wrong* side out.

5. Not as it should be; out of order.–Something is *wrong* with this watch. It won't work. – Is anything *wrong* with you this morning? Don't you feel well?

6. Not the one wanted or meant – You brought me the *wrong* book. I wanted a different one.

wrongful wrong'-ful *wrongfully*. Wrong or unjust.–The man was acquitted after his *wrongful* arrest. He was completely innocent of the offence with which he was charged.

wrote. One form of the word *write*.–I *write* stories in school. Yesterday I *wrote* one about my first piano lesson.

wrought (pronounced *rawt*). 1. An old-fashioned word meaning worked or toiled.–The peasant *wrought* hard in the fields.

2. Brought about. – The man *wrought* great evil in his lifetime.

3. Shaped or fashioned.–The carving was *wrought* from a rough log.–*Wrought* iron is iron worked by hammering.

wrung. One form of the word *wring*.–When I had *wrung* the water out of the dish-cloth, I hung it up.

wry *wryness* wryly. Bent or twisted.–A *wry* look is one that expresses displeasure or disgust.

wryneck wry'-neck *wrynecks*. A bird with a long serpent-like neck.

X x

X, x, *X's, x's*. The 24th letter of the alphabet.

Xmas. A short way of writing the word Christmas.–The seal on the parcel said 'Do not open until *Xmas*.'

X-ray X'-ray *X-rays, X-raying, X-rayed*. 1. A strong ray, something like light, that can go through certain substances, and even through a person's body. *X-rays* are used to see whether bones are broken, roots of teeth diseased, or lungs diseased.

2. A picture taken by an *X-ray*.–I saw the *X-ray* of Jack's broken arm.

3. Take an *X-ray* picture of. – The dentist *X-rayed* Bob's teeth. He examined them by the aid of *X-rays*.

xylophone xy'-lo-phone *xylophones*. A musical instrument on which the keys are bars of wood or metal. A *xylophone* is played by striking the bars with 2 or 4 wooden hammers.

Y y

Y, y *Y's, y's*. The 25th letter of the alphabet.

sailing yacht

motor yacht

yacht (rhymes with *not*) *yachts, yachted, yachting*. 1. A boat used for pleasure or for racing.–We went for a sail in Bob's *yacht*.

2. Sail in a *yacht*.–Bob and I went *yachting*.

yak *yaks*. A long-haired animal of Central Asia, related to the ox. It is used as a beast of burden, especially in Tibet. *Yaks* are also prized for their meat, milk and hides.

yam *yams*. The root of a certain food plant. A *yam* is a kind of sweet potato, and is deep orange in colour. –*Yams* are grown in tropical countries and are widely eaten in America.

Y

Z

yard *yards*. 1. The space or ground around a house, usually paved.–The children play in the *yard*.

2. An area shut in by a fence or a wall, and used for a special purpose.–The prisoners walk every day in the prison *yard*.–We go by the church*yard* on our way home from school. – The cows stood in the farm*yard* waiting for Grandfather to milk them.– Trains go to railway *yards* for repairs.

3. A unit of measure equal to 3 feet or 36 inches. A *yard* is about as long as the distance from a grown person's nose to his fingertips when his arm is held out sideways from the shoulder.–Mother bought a piece of ribbon 1 *yard* long.

yardstick yard'-stick *yardsticks*. A measuring stick 36 inches long.

yarn *yarns*. 1. A thread made by drawing out and twisting wool, flax, cotton, or other fibre. –Stockings, sweaters, and caps are made of *yarn*.

2. A story.–Grandfather tells us long *yarns* about the hardships he had as a boy.

yawn *yawns, yawned, yawning*. 1. Open the mouth and take a long breath.–When Baby is sleepy, she *yawns* and shows her 2 teeth.

2. Opening the mouth and taking a long breath.–Mary was so tired that she could not hide her *yawn*.

year *years*. The time it takes the earth to go around the sun. A *year* has 365 days, 52 weeks, or 12 months in it. Leap *year*, which usually comes every 4 *years*, has 366 days in it.

yearly year'-ly. 1. Once a year.–We pay our rates *yearly*.

2. Each year.–Bob gets £5 *yearly* for pocket money.

yearn *yearns, yearned, yearning*. Long (for), want very much.–The lonely child *yearns* for the love and attention of his friends.

yeast. A substance used in making bread.– *Yeast* causes bubbles, which make bread light. It makes the bread dough rise.

yell *yells, yelling, yelled*. 1. Scream, cry out loudly.–The boys *yelled* when the bear got loose.

2. A scream, an outcry.–We heard the boy's *yell* from the window.

yellow yel'-low *yellows, yellowed, yellowing*. A golden colour like that of butter or the yolk of eggs.

yellow-hammer yel'-low-ham-mer *yellow-hammers*. A bird of the bunting family with a yellow head, neck and breast. Its song has been likened to 'a little bit of bread and no cheese.'

yelp *yelps, yelped, yelping*. 1. Bark sharply.– The dog *yelps* when he is hurt.

2. A sharp cry or bark.–The *yelp* of his dog brought Jack running.

yes. The opposite of no.–We say *yes* when we agree or are willing.–Will you go with me? *Yes,* I would like to go with you.

yesterday yes'-ter-day *yesterdays*. The day before today; the day just past.–Today is Monday; *yesterday* was Sunday.

yet. 1. Up to now; before this time.–The train has not come *yet*. We are waiting for it.

2. Still; even now. – The bells are ringing *yet*. You can still hear them.

3. At some time to come.–I will learn to play the piano *yet*.

4. Still, even.–The wind blew harder *yet* when we turned the corner.

yield *yields, yielded, yielding*. 1. Produce, give forth.–The plum tree *yielded* 4 baskets of fruit.

2. An amount produced.–Four bushels is a large *yield* for a small tree.

3. Give in.–Father *yielded* to Mary's coaxing and let her go to the show.

4. Give up ground; surrender.–The soldiers would not *yield* to the enemy.

Y

Z

yoke *yokes*. 1. The top part of a dress that is cut separately from the dress. – Sally's yellow dress has a white *yoke* with a ruffle around it's edge.

2. A wooden framework placed over the necks of two animals so that they will work together.

yolk *yolks*. The yellow part of an egg.–Mary likes the *yolk* of an egg cooked hard.

yonder yon'-der. Over there, at that place – Look at the sunset *yonder*.

you. The person or persons to whom one is speaking or writing.–*You* may go home now. –*You* are bigger than I am.–All of *you* come with me.

you'd. A short way of writing *you had* or *you would*.–*You'd* see better if you sat nearer to the window.–Before *you'd* walked with us a mile, *you'd* be tired.

you'll. You will.–If you do not hurry, *you'll* be late.

young *younger, youngest*. 1. Not old, not many years old.–Babies are very *young* children.– Boys and girls are *young*.–The apple tree is *young*. It was planted not very long ago. 2. Babies, *young* ones. – A cat carries her *young* by the backs of their necks.–A dog's *young* are her puppies.

youngster young'-ster *youngsters*. A child, a young person.–The *youngsters* at the party played games.

your. Belonging to the person or persons to whom one is speaking or writing.–*Your* nose, *your* toes, *your* hands are all parts of you. *Your* dress belongs to you.

you're. You are.–*You're* taller than I am.

yours. Something that belongs to the person to whom one is speaking or writing.–This hat is *yours*; that one is mine.–My eyes are blue; *yours* are brown.

yourself your-self' *yourselves*. 1. You alone.– If you want your work well done, do it *yourself*. Don't expect somebody else to do it. 2. Your own self. – Dress *yourself* quickly, for breakfast is ready.

yourselves your-selves'. Mother said to us, 'You must play by *yourselves* today, for your friends are gone.'

youth *youths*. 1. Older boys and girls.–The boys' club was built for the *youth* of our town. 2. A young man.–The letter was sent by a *youth* in search of a job.

youthful youth'-ful *youthfully, youthfulness*. Young. – Mother's green dress makes her look *youthful*.–Grandmother is *youthful* in her ideas. She thinks like a young person.

you've. You have.–*You've* written to Grandmother, haven't you?

Yule. An old-fashioned word for Christmas.

Z z

Z, z *Z's, z's*. The 26th and last letter of the alphabet.

zebra ze'-bra *zebras*. An animal that looks something like a horse, but has black and white stripes going round its body.

zephyr zeph'-yr *zephyrs*. A soft, gentle wind that comes from the west; any gentle wind.

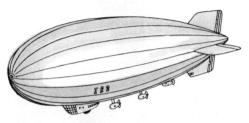

zeppelin zep'-pe-lin *zeppelins*. A kind of balloon that can be steered; a dirigible.–*Zeppelins* were used in World War I.

Z

zero ze'-ro *zeros* or *zeroes*. Nothing; the figure (o) which means none, or nothing.– Mary had every answer wrong in the big arithmetic test; so her mark was *zero*.–When the temperature is *zero* (o°), it is very cold.

zigzag zig'-zag *zigzags, zigzagged, zigzagging.*
1. Having short, sharp turns.– This is a *zigzag* line.
2. Move back and forth, making sharp turns.–The aeroplane *zigzagged* in the sky.

zinc. A soft, bluish-white metal.

zinnia zin'-ni-a *zinnias.* A bright-coloured late summer flower.– *Zinnias* last for a long time.

zone *zones.* 1. An area or place set aside for a special purpose.–We parked our car in the parking-*zone*.
2. One of the great divisions of the earth.– It is very hot in the Torrid *Zone*.–We live in the North Temperate *Zone*.–The Frigid *Zones* are very cold.

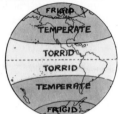

zoo *zoos.* A park where wild animals are kept in fenced areas or in cages, so that people can come and look at them. Most large cities have *zoos*.–Father took the children to the *zoo* to see the baby elephant.

Z

ZOO

Things You Will Want to Know

Days of the Week

Sunday	(Sun.)
Monday	(Mon.)
Tuesday	(Tues.)
Wednesday	(Wed.)
Thursday	(Thurs.)
Friday	(Fri.)
Saturday	(Sat.)

Seasons of the Year

Winter — December 21 to March 20
Spring — March 21 to June 20
Summer — June 21 to September 20
Autumn — September 21 to December 20

Months of the Year

January	(Jan.)
February	(Feb.)
March	(Mar.)
April	(Apr.)
May	
June	(Jun.)
July	(Jul.)
August	(Aug.)
September	(Sept.)
October	(Oct.)
November	(Nov.)
December	(Dec.)

Special Days

New Year's Day	January 1
St Valentine's Day	February 14
St David's Day	March 1
St Patrick's Day	March 17
H.M. Queen Elizabeth II's Birthday	April 21
St George's Day	April 23
H.R.H. Duke of Edinburgh's Birthday	June 10
H.M. Queen Elizabeth II's Official Birthday	June 11
United Nations Day	October 24
H.R.H. Prince of Wales's Birthday	November 14
St Andrew's Day	November 30
Christmas Day	December 25
Boxing Day	December 26

Names of Oceans

Antarctic
Arctic
Atlantic
Indian
Pacific

Names of the Continents

Africa
Antarctica
Asia
Australia
Europe
North America
South America

Abbreviations

Adm. — Admiral	Gen. — General	qt. — quart
A.D — anno Domini	govt. — government	ques. — question
Apr. — April	hr. — hour	Rd. — Road
arith. — arithmetic	i.e. — that is	ret. or retd. — returned
Aug. — August	in. — inch	rgt. — regiment
ave. — avenue	Jan. — January	Ry. — Railway
B.C. — before Christ	Jul. — July	Sat. — Saturday
bldg. — building	Jun. — June	Sept. — September
Capt. — Captain	Lt. — Lieutenant	Sq. — Square
Col. — Colonel	lb. — pound	St. — Street
Co. — Company	Mar. — March	Sun. — Sunday
cwt. — hundredweight	min. — minute	Thurs. or Thur. —
doz. — dozen	Mon. — Monday	Thursday
Dr — Doctor	Mr — Mister	Tues. or Tue. —
e.g. — for example	Mrs — Mistress	Tuesday
etc. — et cetera	Nov. — November	U.N. — United Nations
(and so forth)	Oct. — October	wk. — week
Feb. — February	oz. — ounce	Wed. — Wednesday
Fri. — Friday	P.S. — postscript	Xmas — Christmas
ft. — foot	pkg. — package	yd. — yard
gal. — gallon	P.O. or p. o. — post office	yr. — year
	pt. — pint, part	

60 seconds = 1 minute
60 minutes = 1 hour
24 hours = 1 day
7 days = 1 week
28, 29, 30, or 31 days = 1 calendar month
12 months
(or 365 days) = 1 year
except Leap Year = 366 days

Conversion:
1 kilogramme = 2·2046 pounds

2 pints (pt) = 1 quart (qt)
4 quarts = 1 gallon

10 millilitres (ml) = 1 centilitre (cl)
10 centilitres = 1 decilitre (dl)
10 decilitres = 1 litre (l)

2 halfpennies = 1 penny (p)
2 fifty pence pieces = 1 pound (£)
100 pence = 1 pound

Conversion:
1 litre = 1·7598 pints

16 ounces (oz) = 1 pound (lb)
14 pounds = 1 stone
28 pounds = 1 quarter
4 quarters = 1 hundredweight
(cwt)
20 hundredweight = 1 ton

12 inches (in) = 1 foot (ft)
3 feet = 1 yard (yd)
1,760 yards = 1 mile

100 centimetres (cm) = 1 metre (m)
1,000 metres = 1 kilometre (km)

1,000 grammes (g) = 1 kilogramme (kg)
1,000 kilogrammes = 1 tonne

Conversion:
1 kilometre = 0·6213 mile

Ten Largest Cities in the World

New York, U.S.A.	11,528,649
Tokyo, Japan	11,403,744
Mexico City, Mexico	8,000,000
London, England	7,379,014
Buenos Aires, Argentina	7,200,000
Moscow, U.S.S.R.	7,061,000
Los Angeles, U.S.A.	7,032,075
Chicago, U.S.A.	6,978,947
Shanghai, China	6,900,000
São Paulo, Brazil	5,901,533

Five Longest Rivers in the World

Nile (Africa): about 4,100 miles long
Amazon (South America):
about 4,050 miles long
Mississippi-Missouri (U.S.):
about 3,760 miles long
Yangtse Kiang (China):
about 3,400 miles long
Yenisei (Russia): about 3,300 miles long

Highest Mountain in the World

Mt. Everest, in Tibet—29,028 feet high

Multiplication Table

1	2	3	4	5	6	7	8	9	10	11	12
2	4	6	8	10	12	14	16	18	20	22	24
3	6	9	12	15	18	21	24	27	30	33	36
4	8	12	16	20	24	28	32	36	40	44	48
5	10	15	20	25	30	35	40	45	50	55	60
6	12	18	24	30	36	42	48	54	60	66	72
7	14	21	28	35	42	49	56	63	70	77	84
8	16	24	32	40	48	56	64	72	80	88	96
9	18	27	36	45	54	63	72	81	90	99	108
10	20	30	40	50	60	70	80	90	100	110	120
11	22	33	44	55	66	77	88	99	110	121	132
12	24	36	48	60	72	84	96	108	120	132	144

The Planets

NAME	ORDER IN NEARNESS TO SUN	ORDER IN SIZE
Mercury	1	9
Venus	2	6
Earth	3	5
Mars	4	7
Jupiter	5	1
Saturn	6	2
Uranus	7	3
Neptune	8	4
Pluto	9	8

Rules for the Use of Capital Letters

1. The first word in every sentence should begin with a capital letter.
   We go to school.
   Do you like to read?

2. The first word in every complete line of a poem should usually begin with a capital letter.
   "How do you like to go up in a swing,
   Up in the air so blue?"

3. Use a capital letter for the letter "i" when it stands alone.
   You and I went to a show.

4. The first word and all important words in a title should begin with a capital letter.
   Jack's story is called "The Little Lame Duck on the Pond."

5. The words north, south, east, and west should begin with a capital letter if they refer to a place.
   Eskimos live in the North.

6. Capital letters are used to begin the names of:
   - (a) persons: **John Smith**
   - (b) places: **London, England**
   - (c) months of the year: **May, June**
   - (d) days of the week: **Sunday, Friday**
   - (e) holidays: **Easter, Christmas**
   - (f) organizations: **United Nations, Red Cross**
   - (g) political parties: **Conservative Party, Labour Party**
   - (h) institutions: **Winchester School, Cambridge University**
   - (i) buildings: **St Paul's Cathedral, Corn Exchange**
   - (j) Deity: **God, Christ**
   - (k) titles: **Mr, Mrs, Dr, Rev.**

7. The first word in the salutation of a letter should begin with a capital letter.
   My dear Ruth,

8. The first word of the complimentary closing of a letter should begin with a capital letter.
   Yours sincerely,

RULERS OF GREAT BRITAIN

NAME	REIGN FROM	TO	NAME	REIGN FROM	TO
England			Commonwealth	1649	1653
Ecgbert	828	839	Cromwell—Lord Protector	1653	1658
Aethelwulf	839	856	Charles II	1660	1685
Aethelbald	856	860	James II	1685	1688
Aethelbert	860	866	William III	1688	1702
Aethelred I	866	871	Mary II	1688	1694
Alfred the Great	871	900	Anne	1702	1714
Edward the Elder	900	924	George I	1714	1727
Athelstan	924	940	George II	1727	1760
Edmund I	940	946	George III	1760	1820
Eadred	946	955	George IV	1820	1830
Eadwig	955	959	William IV	1830	1837
Eadgar	959	975	Victoria	1837	1901
Edward the Martyr	975	978	Edward VII	1901	1910
Aethelred II	978	1016	George V	1910	1936
Edmund II (Ironside)	1016		Edward VIII	1936	
Canute	1016	1035	George VI	1936	1952
Harold I	1035	1040	Elizabeth II	1952–	
Harthacanute	1040	1042			
Edward the Confessor	1042	1066	*Wales*		
Harold II	1066		Rhodri Mawr	844	878
William the Conqueror	1066	1087	Anarawd	878	916
William II Rufus	1087	1100	Hywel Dda	916	950
Henry I (Beauclerk)	1100	1135	Iago ap Idwal	950	979
Stephen	1135	1154	Hywel ap Ieuaf	979	985
Henry II Plantagenet	1154	1189	& Cadwallon	985	986
Richard I (Coeur de Lion)	1189	1199	Maredudd ap Owain		
John (Lackland)	1199	1216	ap Hywel Dda	986	999
Henry III	1216	1272	Cynan ap Hywel ap Ieuaf	999	1008
Edward I (Longshanks)	1272	1307	Llywelyn ap Seisyll	1018	1023
Edward II	1307	1327	Iago ap Idwal ap Meurig	1023	1039
Edward III	1327	1377	Gruffydd ap Llywelyn		
Richard II	1377	1399	ap Seisyll	1039	1063
Henry IV (Bolingbroke)	1399	1413	Bleddyn	1063	1075
Henry V	1413	1422	Trahaern	1075	1081
Henry VI	1422	1461	Gruffydd ap Cynan ap Iago	1081	1137
Edward IV	1461	1483	Owain Gwynedd	1137	1170
Edward V	1483		Dafydd ap Owain Gwynedd	1170	1194
Richard III	1483	1485	Llywelyn Fawr (Great)	1194	1240
Henry VII	1485	1509	Dafydd ap Llywelyn	1240	1246
Henry VIII	1509	1547	Llywelyn Yr Ail (Last)	1246	1282
Edward VI	1547	1553	*Scotland*		
Jane (Grey)	1553		Kenneth McAlpine	843	860
Mary I	1553	1558	Donald I	860	864
Elizabeth I	1558	1603	Constantine I	864	877
James I	1603	1625	Aedh	877	878
Charles I	1625	1649	Eocha	878	889

KINGS AND QUEENS OF SCOTLAND

NAME	REIGN		NAME	REIGN	
	FROM	TO		FROM	TO
Donald II	889	900	John Balliol	1292	1296
Constantine II	900	942	Second Interregnum	1296	1306
Malcolm I	942	954	Robert I Bruce	1306	1329
Indulphus	954	962	David II	1329	1371
Duff	962	967	Robert II	1371	1390
Colin	967	971	Robert III	1390	1406
Kenneth II	971	995	James I	1406	1437
Constantine III	995	997	James II	1437	1460
Kenneth III	997	1005	James III	1460	1488
Malcolm II	1005	1034	James IV	1488	1513
Duncan I	1034	1040	James V	1513	1542
Macbeth	1040	1057	Mary Queen of Scots	1542	1567
Malcolm III Ceanmor	1057	1093	James VI (thereafter		
Donald III	1093	1094	James I of England,		
Duncan II	1094		Scotland and Ireland)	1567	1603
Donald III	1094	1097			
Edgar	1097	1107	*Ireland*		
Alexander I	1107	1124	Brian Boru	1001	1014
David I	1124	1153	Interregnum	1014	1064
Malcolm IV	1153	1165	Turlough O'Brien	1064	1086
William the Lion	1165	1214	Murtogh O'Brien &	1086	1119
Alexander II	1214	1249	Domhnall O'Lochlainn	1094	1121
Alexander III	1249	1286	Turlough O'Connor	1121	1156
Margaret	1286	1290	Murtogh O'Lochlainn	1156	1166
First Interregnum	1290	1292	Roderic O'Connor	1166	1198